CONSTITUTIONAL LAW IN IRELAND

By

JAMES CASEY

LL.B. (Q.U.B.), M.A., Ph.D. (Dub.), LL.D. (N.U.I.)

Professor of Law,
University College, Dublin

LONDON
Sweet & Maxwell
1992

Published in 1992 by
Sweet & Maxwell Limited of
South Quay Plaza, 183 Marsh Wall, London E14 9FT.
Computerset by Promenade Graphics Limited, Cheltenham.
Printed and bound in Great Britain by Butler and Tanner
Limited, Frome and London

British Library Cataloguing in Publication Data
A catalogue record for this book
is available from the British Library

ISBN 0–421–440–503

To my Mother
and in memory of my Father

Foreword to the First Edition

The Constitution of Ireland was born 50 years ago on the edge of a Europe which was busily preparing for the most destructive war in history—one in which Ireland did not become a participant. It was a Europe where the concept of human or natural rights counted for little. Large parts of Europe were governed in accordance with Fascist ideology or Marxist ideology, in which human rights counted for little, if anything. In most of the rest of Europe the doctrine or philosophy of legal positivism reigned supreme. That doctrine did not even admit the existence of natural rights. In contrast, in the same epoch, the fundamental rights section of the Constitution of Ireland anticipated both the Universal Declaration of Human Rights and the European Convention for the Protection of Human Rights and Fundamental Freedoms by more than a decade.

By the end of the eighteenth century both the United States of America and France had adopted Constitutions which recognised the doctrine of natural rights. This is the doctrine that man possesses certain rights because he is man and that these rights are not the gift of any positive law or of any state and that they are inalienable rights. These documents, respectively, were clearly influenced by the writings of John Locke and of Rousseau. Neither writer was the discoverer of the original teacher of this doctrine. The sources were to be found in Greek philosophy and later in Roman philosophy. It was adopted and developed by Christian philosophy which came to dominate the thinking on this subject in most of Europe through what became known as Scholastic philosophy. There is evidence that John Locke was acquainted with Scholastic philosophy. No doubt Rousseau was also not unacquainted with it. The Irish Constitution's espousal of the doctrine of natural rights is traceable to the influence of Scholastic philosophy and, in effect, acknowledges natural law as the basis of this philosophy. In the Europe of 50 years ago it was quite startling not only to propound such ideas in a basic law but also to give these moral concepts the force of law by imposing upon the State the obligation to guarantee and to defend these rights. Yet in the decades after the war the notion of natural rights or human rights was to dominate European legal thinking.

In both Irish and American constitutionalism the notion of unenumerated or unspecified natural rights has been accepted. Where these are perceived and acknowledged they are given the full force of the guarantees contained in the respective Constitutions. It is particularly in this respect that the Constitution of Ireland is superior to the European Convention for the Protection of Human Rights and Fundamental Freedoms. That Convention does not seek to confer or bestow any of the rights which it guarantees to protect. But these guarantees apply only to such rights as are specified in the Convention or can be spelled out of those specified rights. Therefore there is no scope for the development of the Irish and American doctrines of unenumerated rights and their protection. Because the Convention is an international treaty it was no doubt felt to be essential that the rights to be protected should be defined as precisely as possible so that the High Contracting Parties would be fully aware of what it was they were guaranteeing by adhering to the Convention. Equally it was understandable that there should also be precision in the statements of the restrictions allowed of these rights. It has been said that because of this the Convention is to be set apart from other systems such as the Constitution of Ireland and the Constitution of the United States. In the field of human rights it reflects much more a lawyer's approach than do the Constitutions of the two countries referred to. It is because of this difference that the interpretation of both the Irish Constitution and the United States Constitution involves much more than simply translating general rules of a document so that they can be applied to specific problems of public policy.

By explaining what the Constitution means in the context of a particular problem the courts shape what the Constitution means in the future and what fundamental values it will enshrine, what aspirations it will encourage and what concrete policies its more political rules will nourish or stifle. The changing nature of the problems facing the modern state require that the courts frequently re-examine their own country's values as well as its traditions. That process produces a dynamism which will endure as long as the Constitution itself endures. Constitutional interpretation is the link between the political and moral concepts upon which the state is founded and which, by being enshrined in the Constitution, give legitimacy to concrete governmental policies and maintain in the citizen's moral rights against the State.

The Constitution represents the social contract existing between the people of the State. It is not simply a composition of exhortations or aspirations which it is hoped will be followed. It is the basic law which distributes powers and imposes obligations and guarantees rights, and which binds the People together with the strongest of moral and legal chains. Constitutionalism is made up not only of the text of the Constitution but also of the constitutional jurisprudence which has been developed by our courts. In this jurisprudence, as well as in the practices and traditional values and glosses that have been developed, is to be found constitutionalism's authority. The Constitution is not simply a combination of laws but is to be read as a whole. A certain skill is required in reading not only the text of the Constitution but also the judicial opinions which have interpreted the Constitution.

Natural rights need no justification. State action which would seek to interfere with them can be sustained only when it can point to some provisions of the Constitution granting the power which the State is asserting. It must always be remembered that the rights guaranteed by the Constitution are not fundamental rights because they find mention in the Constitution but that they find mention there because they are fundamental. Without the Constitution government authority has no rights. While specified rights acquire social acceptance by being incorporated in the Constitution nevertheless the fact that some particular rights are mentioned in the Constitution does not in any way disparage those rights which are not so specified. Where the rights of the individual are concerned the legitimacy of the public policy depends not only on the authenticity of the decision makers' credentials but also the substance of their work. Quite clearly there are fundamental rights which may not be trampled upon even with the active support of the overwhelming majority of people. Thus a law unanimously enacted by the Oireachtas and chosen after a long open public debate in free elections and signed by the President can have no legitimacy if it invades the constitutionally protected rights.

While the Constitution is constantly concerned with the human tendency to act selfishly and to abuse power yet the Constitution is not all about the protection of fundamental rights. In fact only five of the fifty articles are devoted to them. The Constitution provides for very important matters such as the terms under which elections may be held, adult suffrage, parliamentary representation based on approximately equal population, the age at which people may be elected to the Dáil or to the office of President and other such matters. It is because these subjects themselves could be the cause of great tension within the State that they are so clearly spelled out in the Constitution and have rarely required intervention by the courts. But when such matters are brought before the courts the decision must inevitably have a great impact on public policy. In the last analysis it is the Supreme Court, as the head of the judicial branch of government, to which is entrusted the task of reconciling constitutionalism with representative popular democracy.

The Constitution makes the Supreme Court the Court of final appeal. Save for two exceptional jurisdictions, it is constitutionally an appellate court although original jurisdiction may be added by law. The power of the Oireachtas to make exceptions to regulate the appellate jurisdiction of the Supreme Court is a problematic one. If the exercise of that power became so wide and so restrictive as to deprive the Court of its fundamental character as the court of final appeal then a very important constitutional dispute would arise. To some extent the Constitution itself foresaw this danger by prohibiting any legislation which sought to deprive the Supreme Court of its role as the final interpreter of the Constitution itself in that no law may be passed limiting or restricting the appellate powers of the Supreme Court in any case relating to the validity of an Act of the Oireachtas having regard to the provisions of the Constitution.

Every piece of constitutional interpretation has an impact on a wide spectrum of values as well as on people and interests. In the sphere of the penal law it may influence the degree of liberty as well as the internal tranquillity of the entire population. Yet judicial intervention takes effect only in the limited number and kinds of remedies that can be fashioned. Most of these have hitherto tended to be negative rather than positive. For example the courts cannot compel the prosecuting authorities to pursue particular law breakers. They cannot compel the Oireachtas to enact particular laws. To look to the Constitution itself as the source of remedies may produce more positive effects in both procedural and substantive law.

The most marked difference between the courts and the other institutions of the State lies in procedures. In court each side is entitled to be represented by a lawyer. Full evidence and arguments in support of each side's position may be presented. Witnesses may be compelled to testify to what they know. Privilege will be allowed only on the court's authority. It is guaranteed that opposing evidence will be heard and each side will have an opportunity to test the arguments and the evidence of the other. Most importantly, the proceedings take place in public before a judge who must be neutral between the litigants or before a jury whose members are chosen to represent the community by procedures that are designed to ensure impartiality. When the matter is decided the unsuccessful litigant normally has a right of appeal. No other institution of the State operates with such fastidious regard for formal procedures as do the courts.

When a case is decided against the State it may or may not result in striking down some law. But it is not open to complain that the judges are acting undemocratically in overturning the decisions of public representatives or officials. When a policy is set aside or a law is struck down it is because it has gone outside restrictions placed upon the officials or the elected representatives by the Constitution itself. The courts cannot and do not pronounce legislation invalid merely because in their judgment it is unwise or imprudent or even foolish. The courts will not invalidate laws simply because they are either in or out of harmony with some particular school of thought nor would they substitute their judgment for that of the Oireachtas, for example, as to what constitutes the exigencies of the public good justifying the taking of private property unless it is without any reasonable foundation.

Constitutionalism is something to which both the rulers and the ruled are committed. It provides protection for all classes of persons at all times and under all circumstances. Therefore every citizen can go about his business confident in the knowledge that neither the Executive nor the Oireachtas can arbitrarily deprive him of his liberty or interfere with the integrity of his family or invade his privacy save within the limits laid down by the Constitution. Neither can the State be permitted to maintain that certain internal administrative or security matters are too subtle or complex for judicial evaluation. Many of those who seek to have the Constitution replaced are, consciously or unconsciously, seeking to subordinate constitutionalism to representative popular democracy—in other words to give elected representatives a free hand and to be rid of judicial review.

It is often claimed that Eamon de Valera did not relish the process of judicial review. That claim can only be truly evaluated in the light of the fact that he expressly provided for it in the Constitution itself. It is true that in his speeches he did foresee the possibility of conflict between constitutionalism and popular representative democracy in the sense that Parliament might find itself occasionally in some political difficulties because of its failure to observe the Constitution. But when he spoke of the unfettered right of the People to control their own affairs, both domestic and foreign, that was precisely what he meant. In the Constitution, in whose drafting he took a leading role, he quite consciously ensured that elected representatives of the people did not have unfettered power. Whatever occasional political annoyance he may have felt by reason of some interpretation of the Constitution he would have been the first to recognise the importance of maintaining the supremacy of the Constitution. Those who worked with him in purely legal matters can testify that he had the mind of a lawyer. His great capacity to distinguish the particular from the general, which is the stuff in which lawyers deal, was not always welcomed in purely political debates which tended to elevate generalities to the level of received wisdom. His successor as Taoiseach was the late Sean Lemass, a totally different personality. Yet he actually wished that the Supreme Court would be more like the Supreme Court of the United States. The significance of the fact that the experiences of two such great political figures and great parliamentarians should have led them to uphold the primacy of constitutionalism should not be under-estimated. Even elected representatives acknowledge the great pressures that can be brought to bear on them by special interest groups, powerful organis-ations, and the media, to cater for the immediate, and often short-lived, impatient, narrow demands or to react to the last outrage or the last heart-break without due regard to the wider and fundamental issues which may be affected. On such occasions constitutionalism is also the shield of the elected representative. It must however be acknowledged that elected representa-tives may be misled seriously by the effect of the "single opinion" rule enshrined in Articles 26 and 34 of the Constitution where it fosters the illusion that the "single opinion" necessarily represents unanimity. It can conceal fundamental differences of opinion of which the public ought to be aware and which legislators should have available to them in their legislative deliberations. The obligatory concealment of the existence of assenting or dissenting opinions also seriously hampers the development of our consti-tutional jurisprudence, and this effect will get worse as the passage of time removes us further from pre-1937 legislation. The "single opinion" can only be achieved by at least a bare majority of the members of the Supreme Court agreeing not only the result but also the reasons to be stated in support of that result. The German Federal Constitutional Court after several years of being bound by an identical rule was ultimately released from it to the great benefit of German constitutional jurisprudence.

While there may be political advantages to the rule it is in the opinion of many observers and participants too high a price to pay to avoid the shrill rhetoric of the disappointed litigant who endeavours to discredit a "3–2" result by describing it as one carried by "the slenderest of majorities", par-ticularly if such criticism emanates from elected representatives who would, in their own sphere, regard such percentage difference as very substantial. However it is difficult to reconcile the requirement that justice be adminis-tered in public with a requirement that, in some cases, all the judicial opinions in the highest court in the land may not be revealed, particularly in an appeal from the High Court where several opinions may have been pro-nounced. Equally the provison in Article 34 that any law which has been "passed" by the Supreme Court by virtue of Article 26 of the Constitution may never again be questioned in any court, lies uneasily with the view that the Constitution is to be interpreted always as a contemporary law. There may be rare instances where a reference under Article 26 is urgently necess-ary (although public representatives from time to time appear to overlook that this power is the prerogative of the President of Ireland) but it would be wiser to confine the prohibition on further questioning the particular law to a limited number of years. American constitutionalism, to which Irish consti-tutionalism owes so much, has been greatly enriched by the existence of assenting and dissenting opinions in the Supreme Court of the United States. There is a richness in diversity, the learned author's criticism of the diversity of opinions expressed in *G.* v. *An Bord Uchtála* notwithstanding. By a happy coincidence this year marks the 200th anniversary of the Constitution of the United States and the 50th anniversary of the Constitution of Ireland. If we could mark the occasion by removing the "one opinion" rule we would have come several steps closer to fulfilling the wish of Sean Lemass.

In this scholarly and discerning work on the Irish Constitution Professor Casey has added further lustre to Irish legal scholarship. With his customary

clarity of thought and economy of expression, coupled with perceptive comment, he has carefully traced and analysed the growth of Irish constitutionalism. This work will be of enduring value to all who study the subject as well
as those who are privileged to participate in its development. This is the work
of a careful and thorough scholar. I feel greatly honoured to have been
invited by him to contribute a foreword to his excellent study of our Constitution.

Brian Walsh   September 1987
The Supreme Court

Preface

Much has happened in the field of constitutional law since the First Edition of this book was published. I hope the pages which follow adequately chronicle and analyse these developments. I have endeavoured to state the law as it appeared to stand on July 31, 1992.

I acknowledge, with thanks, the assistance given to me by my colleagues in the UCD Law Faculty, particularly Tony Kerr and Noel Travers. James O'Reilly S.C. kindly supplied me both with printed material and stimulating suggestions, and I have derived some valuable insights from conversations with Mr Justice Walsh.

I am very grateful to Cliona Farrell and Mary McCormack for quickly and accurately transforming handwritten drafts into typescript; and to Honóra Ní Chríogáin, who not only helped me in this regard but also provided translations of judgments and other material in Irish.

Once again, however, my greatest debt is to my wife.

James Casey   October 1992
Monkstown
County Dublin

Preface to the First Edition

Though this book is published in the fiftieth anniversary year of Bunreacht na hÉireann, I shall resist the temptation to turn the Preface into an essay on that instrument's merits and defects. But these will surely be much discussed in the near future and I hope that the book may assist readers in making an informed judgment upon them. It is written principally with students in mind, though I trust it will also be of use to judges and practitioners.

Professor Kevin Boyle, on behalf of the publishers, initially offered me the opportunity to write the book. I am grateful to him and them—though sometimes in the travails of composition my prevailing sentiments were far from gratitude! I acknowledge with thanks the assistance of my colleagues Alpha Connelly, Finbarr Murphy and Paul O'Connor, who kindly read parts of the original typescript and gave me the benefit of their expertise in the relevant areas. Two other colleagues, Tony Kerr and Neil McLeod, did a splendid job in keeping me supplied with current Irish material during a sojourn abroad, and I am deeply indebted to both of them.

The galleys were corrected while I was a visiting professor at the University of Granada. Professor José Cazorla and his colleagues of the Departamento de Derecho Politico gave me a most cordial welcome, and I should like to record my appreciation of their kind hospitality. I also wish to thank the Governing Body of University College, Dublin for giving me a year's leave of absence, which enabled me to complete the book earlier than would otherwise have been possible.

In addition to reading the page proofs and writing the Foreword, Mr. Justice Walsh generously supplied me with early copies of significant judgments. For these latest of many kindnesses over the years I am most grateful.

Nuala Clarke and Eileen Dawson, of the Secretary's Office in U.C.D., quickly and accurately converted successive drafts in my idiosyncratic handwriting into typescript. Their efforts are much appreciated.

In the final stages my daughter Elaine gave invaluable help with typing and photocopying. My wife Maisie also relieved me of this (and other) chores, read all the proofs and buttressed my sometimes failing resolve. Though she bears no other responsibility for its contents, without her this book could not have been written.

James Casey   August 1987

Addendum

On August 21, 1992 the Supreme Court delivered judgment in *Att. Gen.* v. *Hamilton*—the Cabinet confidentiality case. The full text of the five separate judgments was printed in *The Irish Times* of August 22. By a 3–2 majority—Finlay C.J., Hederman and O'Flaherty JJ: McCarthy and Egan JJ. dissenting—the court reversed the decision of O'Hanlon J. referred to in Chapter 6 *infra*.

Finlay C.J. held that confidentiality of Government discussions was implicit in Article 28's provisions on collective responsibility. It would be a practical impossibility to carry on the fundamental functions of Government in its absence. Hederman J. concluded that Cabinet confidentiality had been implicitly enshrined in the 1922 Constitution and also in Bunreacht na hÉireann. The very nature of collective responsibility involved the confidentiality of discussions at Government meetings, otherwise its decisions were liable to be fatally weakened by the disclosure of dissenting views. O'Flaherty J. held that observance of confidentiality was a necessary concomitant of the collective responsibility enshrined in Article 28. Constitutionally, the Dáil could not concern itself with the process by which Government decisions were reached; neither could a tribunal of inquiry established by the Oireachtas. McCarthy J., dissenting, was of the opinion that if absolute confidentiality had been intended to attach to Government discussions, the Constitution would have expressly so provided. He declined to imply it. Egan J., also dissenting, held that the tribunal wa entitled to hear evidence concerning Government deliberations, but solely for the purpose of discovering what decision was arrived at.

On a narrow reading the majority decision simply means that tribunals of inquiry may not investigate the decision-making processes of the Government; but it seems to have implications beyond this. The contemporaneous revelation of Cabinet disagreement—whether by leak or otherwise—would seem to be precluded, though this might prove difficult, indeed impracticable, to enforce. If the obligation of confidentiality is both absolute and perpetual, a resigning Minister will presumably be unable to give his/her reasons for departing; while historians, biographers and writers of memoirs may also find themselves inhibited. But nothing in the judgments would prevent a *court* from receiving evidence, in an appropriate case, about discussions at a Government meeting.

Contents

Table of Constitutional Provisions

Table of Cases

Table of Statutes

li

Table of Statutory Instruments

1 Historical and General Introduction

The Treaty of December 6, 1921 was the foundation stone of an independent Ireland. By virtue of that instrument the legislative union which had existed between Ireland and the United Kingdom was dissolved, and the new Irish Free State was to have the status of a self-governing dominion, like Australia, Canada, New Zealand and South Africa. This meant virtually total independence, a great deal more than Britain had ever previously been willing to concede.

The Union of 1800 wrote *finis* to the separate Irish Parliament that had existed since medieval times. Originally this Parliament's legislative power was restricted since, in addition to the royal veto applicable to Irish as to British Bills, the British Privy Council had the right to alter or amend Irish legislative proposals.[1] Moreover the Westminster Parliament claimed power to legislate for Ireland. In 1782–83, however, this situation was modified; the Irish Parliament acquired a greater measure of liberty and Westminster renounced its claim to legislate for Ireland. But "Grattan's Parliament" still had many limitations. The Irish Executive was not responsible to it but to London so that the Lord Lieutenant and other office-holders could not be removed from office by an adverse vote in the Dublin Parliament.[2] In addition the Irish Parliament was quite unrepresentative; its members, like its electorate, were totally Protestant, in a country where over two-thirds of the population was Catholic. Moreover, as Dr. Ó Tuathaigh has observed.[3]

> "Nor indeed was it more than marginally representative of Irish Protestant opinion. Over two-thirds of the 300 MPs sat for 'borough' constituencies, many of which had few or no electors and were simply seats in the gift of a patron. Seats were frequently bought and sold, and the Government's own supply of patronage was bloated with sinecures and pensions."

A variety of reasons—the war with France and the 1798 rebellion among them—inclined the British Government in favour of a union of the parliaments. By the lavish use of patronage a pro-union majority was built up in the Dublin Parliament, and the necessary legislation was passed by May 1800 (the Westminster Parliament also passed legislation in comparable

---

[1] For a fuller treatment see A. G. Donaldson, *Some Comparative Aspects of Irish Law* (Durham, North Carolina 1957), Chap. 2.
[2] See further E. M. Johnston, *Ireland in the Eighteenth Century* (Dublin 1974), Chap. 6; R. B. McDowell, *Ireland in the Age of Imperialism and Revolution 1760–1801* (Oxford 1979), Chap. 6.
[3] Gearoid Ó Tuathaigh, *Ireland before the Famine 1798–1848* (Dublin 1972), p. 9; see also McDowell, *op. cit.*, Chap. 7.

1

terms). The union became operative on January 1, 1801.[4] By its terms Ireland was to be represented in the United Kingdom Parliament by four Church of Ireland bishops and 28 elected peers in the House of Lords, and by 100 members in the House of Commons.[5]

From 1801 until 1921 the whole island of Ireland was governed from London, in the sense that the ultimate policy decisions—legislative, fiscal and administrative—were made there. An Irish Executive, however, was still in existence. Originally this was headed by the Lord Lieutenant in fact as well as in law, though as the 19th century progressed his position tended to become more symbolic, with the Chief Secretary exercising the real authority. The latter was usually a member of the Cabinet and therefore necessarily divided his time between Dublin and London, a factor which, given 19th century communications problems, could operate to leave important decisions to the resident executive in Dublin. This consisted of the Lord Lieutenant, the Lord Chancellor of Ireland, the Attorney General and Solicitor General for Ireland—with, as the 19th century wore on, an increasing role for the civil servants at Dublin Castle, such as the Under-Secretary.[6]

Nineteenth-century developments

A major issue in early 19th century Ireland was the question of Catholic emancipation. In the 18th century Catholics had been subject to many legal disabilities—they could not hold public office, sit in parliament or vote, and their power to acquire land was circumscribed. Towards the end of that century some of these restrictions were relaxed; and the Irish Parliament legislated for, and funded, the establishment of Maynooth as a seminary for training priests.[7] Nonetheless, disabilities still remained and their removal was the object of Daniel O'Connell's campaign, which culminated in the Roman Catholic Relief Act 1829 (10 Geo. IV, c. 7). This permitted Catholics to sit in parliament (both Lords and Commons) and opened up to them all save a few public offices.[8] But an ironic consequence of the Act was a great diminution in the Irish electorate; the franchise qualification was raised to £10 freehold, which reduced the electorate from over 100,000 to around 16,000.[9]

O'Connell's next campaign was for the repeal of the Union. This was in no sense a separatist agitation but rather a claim for a return to the pre-1800 situation. Not finding the support in Britain that Catholic emancipation did, the campaign failed. Pressure for constitutional change continued, however, and in the last quarter of the century this was combined with the land ques-

---

[4] See further Johnston, *op. cit.*, Chap. 7; McDowell, *op. cit.*, Chap. 19.

[5] There were two members for each county, two each for Dublin and Cork, one for Dublin University (Trinity College) and 31 borough members.

[6] See further Ó Tuathaigh, *op. cit.*, Chap. 3; see also R. B. McDowell, *The Irish Administration 1801–1914* (London, 1964). On the law officers see J. P. Casey, *The Office of the Attorney General in Ireland* (Dublin 1980), Chap. 2.

[7] See further McDowell, *Ireland in the Age of Imperialism and Revolution*, Chaps. 3 and 11; Ó Tuathaigh, *op. cit.*, Chap. 2.

[8] The main offices originally excluded were those of Lord Chancellor of Great Britain, Lord Chancellor of Ireland and Lord Lieutenant of Ireland. Following the Office and Oath Act 1867 the disqualification in respect of the Irish Lord Chancellorship was removed, and the Government of Ireland Act 1920 abolished that in regard to the Lord Lieutenancy of Ireland.

[9] Ó Tuathaigh, *op. cit.*, p. 74.

tion to produce a mass movement exhibiting tremendous organisation and discipline. These features were reproduced in Parnell's parliamentary party, whose members were the first to be paid a salary (from party funds). They were also bound by a pledge to sit, act and vote with the party and to resign their seats if a majority of their colleagues resolved that they had not fulfilled this pledge. (The strict party discipline which is so marked a feature of modern Irish politics finds its origins in this period.) An important factor in this regard was the gradual extension of the parliamentary franchise, under which the electorate was increased to 160,000 in 1850, to 230,000 in 1868 and to over 700,000 in 1864 (though this was still only 16 per cent. of the population).[10]

Gladstone's Liberal Government introduced a Home Rule Bill in 1886, under which Ireland was to have a two-chamber legislature with limited powers. An Irish Executive was to be responsible to this body. Irish members would no longer sit in the Westminster Parliament, the ultimate sovereignty of which was specifically preserved by the Bill. But the Prime Minister was unable to carry his entire party with him and the Bill was defeated on its second reading in the House of Commons by 30 votes. The government resigned and the ensuing general election returned the Conservatives— opposed to Home Rule—to power. In 1893 Gladstone, again Prime Minister, introduced a second Home Rule Bill on broadly similar lines to his first[11]; this was rejected by the House of Lords, with its built-in Tory majority.

Twentieth-century developments

By the time another Liberal government came round to Home Rule the House of Lords stumbling-block had been removed. The Parliament Act 1911 clipped the upper House's wings by removing its power to reject Money Bills and substituting for its veto over others a power to delay them for a maximum of two years. This opened the way for the Third Home Rule Bill of 1912, which provided for a legislature consisting of a 40 member senate (whose members were to be nominated by the Crown) and a House of Commons of 164 members (which would have the definitive say in case of conflict). The parliament's powers were restricted, and as in the earlier Bills the ultimate supremacy of Westminster was specifically laid down. The provisions on the Executive were much more detailed so that, for example, the Irish Ministers were both responsible to, and drawn from, the Irish Parliament.[12] This Bill became law as the Government of Ireland Act 1914, but by the time of its passage the First World War was under way and it was specifically provided that the Act should not come into operation until peace was concluded. Additionally, its coming into operation was to be contingent on special amending legislation making provision for Ulster—a reflection of the anti-Home Rule attitude of most of that province.[13]

When the war ended in 1918, however, the question of implementing the

---

[10] See further Joseph Lee, *The Modernisation of Irish Society, 1848–1918* (Dublin 1973), Chaps. 3–5: F. S. L. Lyons, *Ireland Since the Famine* (London 1973), pp. 141–201.
[11] On the Home Rule Bills see Donaldson, *op. cit.*, pp. 61–65.
[12] See further J. H. Morgan, "The Constitution: A Commentary" in J. H. Morgan (ed.), *The New Irish Constitution* (London 1912).
[13] See further Lyons, *op. cit.*, pp. 287–311; Donaldson, *op. cit.*, pp. 68–71.

1914 Act was no longer on the agenda—matters had moved beyond that. Though the rising of Easter 1916 had little popular backing, the execution of its leaders worked a change in public opinion and led to the eclipse of the Irish Parliamentary Party by Sinn Féin. This reconstituted party, which was not prepared to settle for the kind of Home Rule measure acceptable to its predecessors, boosted its popularity by its leading role in the campaign against the British government's decision to impose conscription in Ireland in 1918.[14] In that same year the end of the war brought a general election for the Westminster Parliament. Under the Representation of the People Act 1918 the electorate had been greatly extended, so that it now embraced all males over 21 and, under certain conditions, women over 30. As Professor Murphy has observed[15]:

> "The Irish electorate as a whole jumped from 701,475 to 1,936,673, Dublin City increasing from 35,353 voters to 124,829, Belfast from 57,174 to 170,901, Cork from 12,296 to 45,017, Limerick from 4,875 to 17,121 and Waterford from 2,972 to 12,063. It has been estimated that two-thirds of those on the 1918 Register were about to vote for the first time. Here was an enormous potential for change. Even if revolutionary nationalism had not been in the ascendant, it was very likely that vast masses of new voters, many of them young and poor, would still be ready for political adventure, or at least for some change in the *status quo.*"

The general election of 1918 was a triumph for Sinn Féin, which captured 73 of the 105 Irish seats. The party redeemed its pledge against attendance at Westminster by summoning all Irish M.P.s to meet as Dáil Éireann in January 1919. In the event only its own representatives attended, and since many of those were in prison or in hiding the first Dáil meeting of January 21 found only 28 M.P.s present. Nonetheless the Dáil proceeded to adopt a declaration of independence and several other policy statements and to make arrangements for an attempted takeover of the country's affairs.[16] Simultaneously, and without a Dáil decision, there began an armed campaign against the Crown forces which terminated only with the Truce of July 1921.[17]

To these developments the British coalition government of Lloyd George responded in a variety of ways, including the attempted suppression of Dáil Éireann, the despatch of the "Black and Tans" and another set of proposals for Home Rule. The Bill enshrining these became law as the Government of Ireland Act 1920 (which a signatory of the Treaty scathingly characterised many years later as "a statutory abortion of December 1920, sardonically entitled 'An act to provide for the letter government of Ireland).' "[18] It provided for two Irish parliaments, one for Northern Ireland—*i.e.* the parlia-

---

[14] See further Lee, *op. cit.*, Chap. 6; Lyons, *op. cit.*, pp. 381–438; John A. Murphy, *Ireland in the Twentieth Century* (Dublin 1975), Chap. 1.

[15] Murphy, *op. cit.*, pp. 4–5.

[16] See further Murphy, *op. cit.*, Chap. 1. See also Brian Farrell, *The Founding of Dáil Éireann* (Dublin 1971), Chaps. 5 and 6: the same author's "The Legislation of a 'Revolutionary' Assembly: Dáil Decrees 1919–1922" (1975) X *Irish Jurist* (N.S.) 112; and James Casey "Republican Courts in Ireland 1919–1922" (1970) V *Irish Jurist* (N.S.) 321.

[17] As to which see Lyons, *op. cit.*, pp. 411–427: Murphy, *op. cit.*, Chap. 2; also Charles Townshend, *The British Campaign in Ireland 1919–1921* (Oxford 1975).

[18] Gavan Duffy J. in *Cogan* v. *Minister for Finance* [1941] I.R. 389, 402.

mentary counties of Antrim, Armagh, Down, Fermanagh, Londonderry and Tyrone, and the parliamentary boroughs of Belfast and Londonderry—and another for the rest of the country. Each was to have power "to make laws for the peace, order and good government" of the area within its jurisdiction—a formula taken from the earlier Home Rule Bills and capable of conveying full legislative power. But as with the earlier measures there were restrictions; defence and foreign affairs, for example, were excluded, there were limits on the parliaments' financial powers and the overriding authority of the Westminster Parliament was again specifically affirmed in section 75. To each parliament an executive drawn from its ranks would be responsible. The Lord Lieutenant was to be formal head of both executives, ceremonially summoning and dissolving parliament, assenting to Bills etc.; but he could also "reserve" Bills, a device which could be operated so as to give the London government a veto over Irish measures. Irish representation at Westminster was to continue with diminished numbers. The Act also provided for a Council of Ireland, consisting of parliamentarians from both parts of Ireland elected by their colleagues, to which some modest powers were initially assigned and to which others could be delegated by both parliaments should they so decide. Alternatively both parliaments could establish a parliament for the whole of Ireland, which would replace the Council and both parliaments (s.3).

Professor Lyons has justly described the offer contained in the 1920 Act as "totally divorced . . . from the realities of political life in Ireland . . . "[19] It was not accepted, or acceptable, in the South; but it was accepted in Northern Ireland, an ironic development in that the Ulster Unionists had not sought such home rule and that three counties of historic Ulster were outside their jurisdiction. In May 1921 elections were held for both parliaments and in Northern Ireland the Unionists won 40 of the 52 Commons seats. The new Northern Parliament was opened on June 22, 1921 and the Government of Ireland Act 1920 continued to function as the basic constitutional instrument of Northern Ireland until 1973.[20]

In the South, military operations ceased with the Truce of July 11, 1921. Earlier, in May, elections for the Southern Parliament had been held, for Dáil Éireann, though repudiating the 1920 Act, agreed to use its electoral machinery to renew its mandate. But there was no contest in any of the constituencies, so that the much larger second Dáil contained only Sinn Féin members (124) and (in theory) the four Unionists representing Dublin University. Negotiations—talks about talks—now began between British government and Sinn Féin representatives, and after much difficulty over a suitable formula the Dáil executive accepted an invitation to send delegates to London for a conference "with a view to ascertaining how the association of Ireland with the community of nations known as the British Empire may best be reconciled with Irish national aspirations." The conference began on October 11, 1921 and ended with the signature on December 6 of "Articles of agreement for a treaty between Great Britain and Ireland." This treaty split

---

[19] *Op. cit.*, p. 414.
[20] For a detailed analysis of the 1920 Act see Harry Calvert, *Constitutional Law in Northern Ireland* (Belfast 1968). Political developments in Northern Ireland since 1921 are surveyed in Lyons, *op. cit.*, pp. 695–780; Murphy, *op. cit.*, Chap. 8. Brigid Hadfield, *The Constitution of Northern Ireland* (Belfast 1989) is a comprehensive and up to date account of the subject.

lin cabinet and led to the civil war of 1922–1923; but its terms were
d by the Dáil on January 7, 1922 by 64 votes to 57.[21]

THE TREATY SETTLEMENT

The Treaty provided that Ireland should have the status of a self-governing
dominion—something far beyond the devolution enshrined in the Government of Ireland Act 1920. Article 1 provided that the Irish Free State (as it
was henceforward to be known) should have "the same constitutional status
in the Community of Nations known as the British Empire as the Dominion
of Canada, the Commonwealth of Australia, the Dominion of New Zealand
and the Union of South Africa . . . " Its parliament would have power "to
make laws for the peace, order and good government of Ireland"—a formula
now, of course, no longer hedged about by restrictions; and there was to be
an executive responsible to that parliament. Article 2 provided that the position of the Irish Free State *vis-à-vis* the Westminster Parliament and Government should be that of Canada, and went on to stipulate that the Canadian
analogy should govern the relationship of the Crown (*i.e.* the British Government) and the Westminster Parliament to Ireland. So, too, Article 3 laid it
down that the Crown's representative in Ireland was to be appointed "in like
manner as the Governor-General of Canada and in accordance with the
practice observed in the making of such appointments."

Dr. Kohn summarised what the Treaty offered as follows[22]:

> " . . . full internal self-government, unrestricted financial autonomy, the
> right to maintain an Irish Police Force and an Irish Army subject only
> to the control of the Irish Parliament. In the sphere of external relations
> it involved the concession of the new international status of the British
> Dominions, the right to enter into agreements with Foreign states, free-
> dom from obligations arising from treaties not specifically approved by
> the Irish Parliament, full discretion in the matter of Irish participation
> in British wars, and, lastly, membership of the League of Nations."

Dominion status was, in 1921, far from fully defined. It meant virtually
complete control of domestic affairs, though some relics of colonial subordi-
nation still existed. There was, for example, doubt about the status of the
Governor General—was he in any respect subject to United Kingdom
Government instructions in such matters as assenting to legislation? There
was a right of appeal from the courts of a Dominion to the Judicial Committee of the Privy Council in London (a body usually manned by the Law
Lords). And a Dominion did not have power to legislate with extra-territorial
effect, a matter which could cause practical difficulties.[23] In the field of
foreign affairs the situation was also hazy—the Dominions were just beginning to acquire treaty-making power, and they did not have direct diplomatic relations with foreign states.[24] As the 1920s progressed this situation
changed. New conventions governing Dominion relationships with the

---

[21] The classic account of the Treaty negotiations remains Lord Longford's *Peace by Ordeal* (London 1935).

[22] Leo Kohn, *The Constitution of the Irish Free State* (London 1932), p. 50.

[23] This question is discussed by K. C. Wheare, *The Statute of Westminster and Dominion Status* (5th
ed., Oxford 1953), Chaps. I–IV.

[24] See D. W. Harkness, *The Restless Dominion* (London 1969), pp. 1–13.

United Kingdom emerged and were crystallised in the published *Records of the Imperial Conference*; and the Statute of Westminster 1931 removed the last restrictions from the Dominion Parliaments' legislative power.

The Treaty, however, placed certain special restrictions on the sovereignty of the Irish Free State. Under Article 8 the size of the Irish Defence Forces was to bear the same proportion to Ireland's population as that of Britain's military establishment bore to its population. Article 7 provided for the British retention of certain defence facilities (subsequently known as "the Treaty ports") in time of peace—and for extra facilities in time of war.[25] Paragraph 2 of the Annex also contained defence-related restrictions, among them that submarine cables should not be landed, or wireless stations for communication with places outside Ireland be established, save by agreement with the British Government.

The Treaty made extensive provision (Arts. 11–14) for Northern Ireland. If, within one month of the statutory ratification of the Treaty, its Parliament passed appropriate resolutions, the powers of the Irish Free State Government and Parliament should no longer extend to Northern Ireland, and it would continue to be governed under the 1920 Act. In that event the Council of Ireland would continue in being; and a commission would be established to draw the boundary of Northern Ireland (Art. 12). In the unlikely event of the Northern Ireland Parliament not opting out Articles 14 and 15 made arrangements for the transition.

Finally, the Treaty stipulated that a meeting of the Southern House of Commons elected under the 1920 Act should be summoned forthwith, and the Treaty submitted to it for approval and ratification. (It was likewise to be submitted for approval and ratification by the Westminster Parliament.) A Provisional Government was to be established for the Irish Free State, and the British Government was to transfer to it "the powers and machinery requisite for the discharge of its duties" (Art. 17). This arrangement was not to endure beyond December 16, 1922—by which time, it was anticipated, a new Constitution of the Irish Free State would be in operation.

The British Parliament approved the Treaty on December 16, 1921 and, as already noted, a closely divided Dáil did likewise on January 7, 1922, One week later the formal meeting of the House of Commons of Southern Ireland envisaged in the Treaty took place. This body, which in fact comprised only pro-Treaty TDs and the four Dublin University representatives, approved the Treaty and elected a provisional government.[26] Since that government was not responsible to that parliament, the latter's functions were now at an end; but its virtual *alter ego* the Dáil was still in being. So, too, was the Dáil Ministry, now chaired by Arthur Griffith; thus there were now two executives in being, though their membership overlapped considerably and they met as a single body.[27]

[25] The specific facilities required included the dockyard port at Berehaven, where the British Admiralty was to retain its property and rights. The harbour defences there were to remain in charge of British care and maintenance parties, as were those at Queenstown (Cobh), Lough Swilly and Belfast Lough.

[26] On the status of the Provisional Government and the steps taken to transfer functions to it, see John McColgan, *British Policy and the Irish Administration 1920–22* (London 1983), pp. 90–104.

[27] See further Lyons, *op. cit.*, pp. 439–452: Murphy, *op. cit.*, Chap. 2: J. L. McCracken, *Representative Government in Ireland* (Oxford 1958), Chap. IV; Ronan Fanning, *Independent Ireland* (Dublin 1983), Chap. 1.

On March 31, 1922 the Westminster Parliament passed the Irish Free State (Agreement) Act, which (*inter alia*) gave the Treaty legal force. In Dublin a constitution was being prepared[28] and a draft was taken to London by Griffith in May 1922. There was no legal obligation to consult the British Government in this matter—but since the Constitution had to be confirmed by Westminster legislation, it was prudent to ensure that the British Government accepted it as a proper implementation of the Treaty. In fact that government took objection to many of the provisions as being too republican and alterations had to be undertaken.[29]

On June 16, 1922 there was a general election for the Third Dáil, which was to sit as a constituent assembly to enact the Constitution. Because of the outbreak of civil war the constituent assembly did not meet until September 9. The Constitution Bill was introduced on September 18 and was considered by the constituent assembly on a stage by stage basis, in accordance with what was to become normal legislative procedure. It was finally approved by the constituent assembly on October 25, 1922. On December 5, 1922 the Westminster Parliament enacted the Irish Free State Constitution Act and the Irish Free State (Consequential Provisions) Act, the latter incorporating modifications of the Government of Ireland Act 1920. The need for these was plain by December 7, when the Northern Ireland Parliament exercised its right to opt out of the Free State.[30]

By virtue of its own Article 83, and the Westminster I.F.S. Constitution Act, the Constitution came into operation by royal proclamation on December 6, 1922.

THE 1922 CONSTITUTION

The Constitution was enacted in a curious form. The Constitution of the Irish Free State (Saorstát Éireann) Act 1922 consisted of a preamble, three brief sections and two schedules—the first being the text of the Constitution, the second that of the Treaty. Section 1 of the Act gave the Constitution annexed the force of law. Section 2 declared that the Constitution should be construed with reference to the Treaty, which was likewise given the force of law, and continued:

> " . . . and if any provision of the said Constitution or of any amendment thereof or of any law made thereunder is in any respect repugnant to any of the provisions of the Scheduled Treaty, it shall, to the extent only of such repugnancy, be absolutely void and inoperative. . . . "

Thus the Treaty was locked in as the keystone of the constitutional arch—as the British Government had required. But the preamble did not acknowledge any British authority—proceeding on the view that the power to enact the Constitution came to the constituent assembly from the people, under God. The same theme was taken up in Article 2, which declared that all powers of government and all authority, legislative, executive and judicial in

---

[28] The constitution-making process is discussed by Brian Farrell, "The drafting of the I.F.S. Constitution" (1970) V *Irish Jurist* (N.S.) 115 and 343; (1971) VI *ibid.*, 111 and 345.

[29] See further Thomas Towey, "Hugh Kennedy and the Constitutional Development of the Irish Free State" (1977) XII *Irish Jurist* (N.S.) 355.

[30] The passage of the Constitution, and the U.K. legislation, are fully treated by Kohn, *op. cit.*, Chaps. III and IV.

Ireland were derived from the people. This was entirely at odds with British constitutional theory, under which these powers derived from the monarch. But although that monarch was, by virtue of the Treaty, to make an appearance in the Constitution he was to do so, in Dr. Kohn's words, "as a functionary of the Irish people . . . [31] And throughout the Constitution the symbols of Commonwealth membership necessitated by the Treaty settlement were neutralised by specific dispositions. (Indeed, the Constitution in Art. 1 refers to the "Commonwealth" whereas the Treaty had used the term "Empire.")

The Governor General

Article 12 of the Constitution provided for a legislature, to be known as the Oireachtas, consisting of the king, a popularly elected chamber called Dáil Éireann and a Senate. For this and other purposes within the Irish Free State, the king was to be represented, as in other Dominions, by a Governor General. In theory the British Government was free to appoint to this post whomsoever it wished; but in fact it had undertaken to consult the Dublin Government on the matter. Indeed by 1926 it had become accepted that the choice rested entirely with the Dominion concerned, and that the Governor General acted only on the advice of Dominion Ministers, being in no sense an agent of the London government.[32]

The functions of the Governor General under the Constitution included summoning and dissolving the Dáil, appointing Ministers and assenting to legislation. But these were purely formal acts, involving no power of decision. Thus the Dáil could be dissolved only on the advice of the Executive Council (Art. 28); and the Ministers forming that Council were chosen by its President, who in turn could be appointed only on the nomination of the Dáil (Art. 53). There could therefore be no question of refusing the prime minister a dissolution and choosing a successor (as had happened in Canada in 1926).[33] As for legislation, the assent was to be given automatically. Article 41 contained a provision whereby a Bill could be reserved "for the signification of the King's pleasure" (*i.e.* that of the London government) but this power was to be exercised in accordance with "the law, practice and usage" on the same matter in Canada. Since reservation was a dead letter in Canada well before 1922 the Article 41 power was drained of all vitality.[34]

The Legislature

The Legislature consisted of two Houses, the Dáil and Seanad, the former being popularly elected. It was composed of members representing constituencies fixed by statute. While the total membership was left to be regulated by law, there was to be not less than one deputy per 30,000, nor more than one per 20,000 of the population. Equality of representation as between con-

---

[31] Kohn, *op. cit.*, p. 114.
[32] See Harkness, *op. cit.*, pp. 106–109; also Brendan Sexton, *Ireland and the Crown 1922–1936: The Governor-Generalship of the Irish Free State* (Dublin 1989).
[33] See further Wheare, *op. cit.*, pp. 25, 59–61.
[34] Though the first Governor-General, T. M. Healy, seems to have believed otherwise. Without consulting the Provisional Government, he indicated to the Colonial Secretary—in advance of his formal appointment—that he would keep a watchful eye on Bills, etc. which might in any way conflict with the Treaty. See Sexton, *op. cit.*, p. 85.

stituencies was mandated and they were required to be revised at least once
every 10 years. The electorate embraced all citizens, without distinction of
sex, who had reached 21 (Art. 14); and all such citizens were elegible for
membership (Art. 15). Finally Article 26 decreed an electoral system based
on proportional representation (PR). Unlike Article 16 of the present Constitution it did not specify the precise form of PR to be adopted—but in fact that
chosen was the single transferable vote now enshrined in Article 16. Among
the reasons for specifying PR was a desire to reassure the Southern Unionist
minority.[35]

The Seanad had 60 members. To be eligible one had to have reached 35,
and the electorate originally consisted of all citizens over 30 (Art. 14). A transitional arrangement contained in Article 82, and again designed to reassure
the Southern Unionists, provided that the first Seanad should consist of 30
members elected by the Dáil and 30 others nominated by the President of the
Executive Council. In making his nominations he was to have special regard
to providing representation for groups or parties not adequately represented
in the Dáil.[36] Of the 30 nominees, 15 were to serve for 12 years and 15 for six
years, while of the elected 30, 15 were to have nine year, and 15 three year,
terms. Every three years, therefore, one had an election for a quarter of the
Seanad (Art. 32), the persons then elected serving a full 12 year term. For
such elections the whole State formed one constituency, eligible voters elect-
ing by PR candidates drawn from a panel formed in accordance with Article
33. In fact this system did not work properly, and a constitutional amendment of 1928 made important changes; one-third of the senators would now
retire every three years; the term of office became nine years and the electorate was the Dáil and Seanad—Constitution (Amendment No. 6) Act 1928.

As between the Houses the Dáil was clearly in the dominant position. It
had exclusive power over Money Bills (as defined at length in Art. 35); it
alone was concerned with the estimates (Art. 36) and, of course, the Executive Council was responsible to it alone (Art. 51). The Seanad could amend
non-money Bills and the Dáil had "to consider" any such amendments; but
the Seanad's main power was to delay a Bill for 270 days. Thereafter it was
"deemed to be passed" by both Houses in the form in which it left the Dáil
(Art. 38). Under Article 47 a three-fifths majority of the Seanad could
require a Bill to be submitted to a referendum, but this power was never
exercised and it was abolished in 1928. Though Bills could be initiated in the
Seanad (Art. 39) the government, despite promises, never did this, and the
Seanad was frequently faced with batches of Bills which had to be dealt with
in a very short time. As will be seen, the second chamber came under heavy
fire after Fianna Fáil's advent to power in 1932, but as Professor McCracken
has shown, the Cosgrave Government also viewed it with something less
than rapture.[37]

Under Article 17 every member of the Oireachtas had to take an oath,
swearing true faith and allegiance to the Constitution and fidelity to the

[35] Cornelius O'Leary, *Irish Elections 1918–1977* (Dublin 1979), p. 14.
[36] President Cosgrave's nominations favoured the wealthy and aristocratic segment of the Protestant minority; he included eight peers, four baronets and one knight. See McCracken, *op.
cit.*, p. 138.
[37] McCracken, *op. cit.*, pp. 140–142. See also the account of the Senate by its former Clerk which,
if clearly *parti pris*, may still be read with profit: Donal O'Sullivan, *The Irish Free State and its
Senate* (London 1940).

Monarch. Its wording derived from Article 4 of the Treaty. This was perhaps the single most controversial provision of the Constitution; and their refusal to take the oath kept Mr. de Valera and his followers out of the Dáil until 1927.[38]

Finally it may be noted that Article 49 restricted the power of the executive and asserted the independence of the State by providing that it should not be "committed to active participation in any war without the assent of the Oireachtas."

The Executive

The Constitution provided for an executive drawn from parliament— unsurprisingly, because this was the pattern in other Dominions and, more significantly, was that with which politicians and people were most familiar. Its provisions on the executive again exhibit the pattern of archaic formulae juxtaposed with legal reality. Thus Article 51 declared the executive auth- ority to be vested in the king (though it followed from Art. 2 that its source was the people, not regal prerogative). It was to be exercised by the Gover- nor General in accordance with the Canadian model, and he was to be aided and advised by the Executive Council. This polite formula, decoded, meant that the Governor General's role was purely ceremonial, with the Executive Council wielding the real power.

The composition of the Executive Council was regulated by Articles 51–54. It was headed by a President (*i.e.* prime minister) appointed on the nomination of Dàil Éireann; thus, as a matter of clear constitutional law, the Governor General had no choice as to the appointee. The President's col- leagues—all of whom, like him, had to be members of the Dáil—were chosen by him. Consequently the President had the same freedom in this matter as the British prime minister. The Council consisted of not more than seven, and not less than five, members and it was responsible to the Dáil. This theme was plainly stated in Article 51 and again in Article 53, which pro- vided that the Executive Council should retire from office should it "cease to retain the support of a majority in Dáil Éireann."[39]

The Executive Council, then, was the Cabinet of the Irish Free State—the supreme policy-making body. With a Dáil majority behind it—and the growth of a party system aided this[40]—it was in a powerful position to implement its ideas, as the history of the period 1922–1937 shows.

The Constitution also provided for what come to be known as "Extern Ministers" (Arts. 55–56), though its provisions in this regard were optional, not mandatory. The theory underlying this was that some matters, not essen- tially political in nature, might be better administered by technocrats. A Department of this type could have a Minister who was *individually* respon- sible to the Dáil for its administration and policy. Such Ministers were not required to be deputies (or senators) and they were not members of the Executive Council; thus they would not have a voice in cabinet discussions

---

[38] See further Kohn, *op. cit.*, pp. 215–219.

[39] Nonetheless the Ministers were to continue in office until their successors were appointed. Finding those successors might have taken a long time since the Dáil could not be dissolved on the advice of a defeated Executive Council.

[40] On the growth of parties see Maurice Manning, *Irish Political Parties: An Introduction* (Dublin 1972) and Michael Gallagher, *Political Parties in the Republic of Ireland* (Dublin 1985).

but would also not be bound by collective responsibility. Consequently they would be free to criticise Executive Council policy on any issue. There could be up to seven such Ministers and they were to be chosen by the Dáil, which alone could remove them. In fact, the system never operated in the way envisaged. All the Extern Ministers appointed were active politicians, members of the Dáil and nominees of the Executive Council; and the original design was virtually abolished by constitutional amendment in 1927.[41]

The Judiciary

Articles 64–72 dealt with the courts. They outlined a structure similar to that which operates today—a Supreme Court, a High Court and "courts of local and limited jurisdiction." Judicial independence and security of tenure were provided for, and the details were filled in by the Courts of Justice Act 1924.

The Constitution provided explicitly for judicial review of the validity of legislation, original jurisdiction in such matters being confined (as now) to the High Court. This was a logical consequence of the Constitution's imposing many fetters on the legislative power of the Oireachtas, and was of great potential significance. But, as will appear, judicial review never properly took off under the 1922 Constitution.

The provisions on the courts contained another symbol of Commonwealth membership insisted on by the British Government—the right of appeal to the Judicial Committee of the Privy Council. This was built in to Article 66; but such an appeal required the leave of the Judicial Committee and that body soon indicated that leave would be granted only rarely.[42] Nonetheless the Dublin Government detested the provision and continually, but unsuccessfully, raised the matter at imperial conferences.[43] Eventually the Cosgrave administration decided on unilateral abolition of the appeal, and this was achieved by the de Valera Government in 1933 (see *infra*).

Fundamental rights

The Constitution limited the powers of the Oireachtas in several respects; the British doctrine of the sovereignty of parliament was plainly rejected. Thus Article 43 denied the Oireachtas power to declare acts to be infringements of the law which were not so at the date of their commission. Article 70 guaranteed trial "in due course of law" and, significantly, forbade the creation of "extraordinary courts" and restricted the possible operation of courts-martial. Trial by jury was guaranteed by Article 72 for serious criminal offences.

Articles 6–9 contained a statement of the citizen's fundamental rights. No person could be deprived of liberty except in accordance with law, and *habeas*

---

[41] Constitution (Amendment No. 5) Act 1927. For a fuller discussion of the Extern Ministers idea, see Kohn, *op. cit.*, pp. 271–283; Nicholas Mansergh, *The Irish Free State: Its Government and Politics* (London 1934), pp. 156–171.

[42] See Towey, *op. cit.*, who chronicles the involvement of the Attorney General, Hugh Kennedy, in this issue.

[43] Harkness, *op. cit.*, pp. 112–114, 138–139, 204–207.

corpus was built into the Constitution. Article 7 guaranteed inviolability of the dwelling, which could not be forcibly entered save in accordance with law. Article 8 contained pledges on freedom of conscience and religious belief and practice. Article 9 guaranteed freedom of expression, assembly and association—though statute could "regulate" the latter rights. Finally, Article 10 declared that all citizens had the right to free primary education.

The similar provisions of Bunreacht na hÉireann have given rise to a considerable amount of case law, but no such development occurred under the 1922 Constitution. As already noted, judicial review of the constitutionality of statutes never became established thereunder. In part this was because that Constitution was so easy to amend, in part because the judges—trained under a system where parliament was sovereign—never seemed to attune themselves to this new departure. (Chief Justice Kennedy was, of course, an exception to this.)

Amendment of the Constitution

Article 50 stipulated how, and by what means, the Constitution might be amended. Firstly, only amendments "within the terms of the Scheduled Treaty" were permissible—a logical restriction echoing the terms of section 2 of the constituent Act. As to procedure, it was envisaged that Bills to amend the Constitution would be passed by the Dáil and Seanad and then submitted to a referendum. They would become law only if approved by a majority of voters *on the register*, or by two-thirds of the votes actually cast if less than 51 per cent. of the electorate voted.[44] In such a referendum all citizens having the Dáil franchise could vote (Art. 14).

But Article 50 also provided—fatally—that amendments could be made by ordinary legislation, without a referendum, for eight years after the Constitution came into force—*i.e.* until December 6, 1930. This was much availed of, and generally caused little controversy; but in 1929 an amendment extended the eight year period in Article 50 to 16 years.[45] As will appear, the validity of this was later upheld by the Supreme Court. Thus during its entire period of operation the Constitution could be amended by ordinary legislation. Not all such amendments were specifically so entitled; an Act which conflicted with the Constitution could simply declare that its provisions were to prevail, without specifying which Articles of the Constitution were thereby amended. In *Att. Gen.* v. *McBride* [1928] I.R. 451 Hanna J. criticised such an omnibus drag-net amendment but he was unable to conclude that it was invalid. Indeed in 1924 the Court of Appeal (which continued to function under Article 75 of the Constitution pending the establishment of the courts contemplated therein) found it difficult to see how, during the eight year period, *any* legislation could be challenged as invalid; and it rejected the view that a statute purporting to amend the Constitution must contain a declaration to that effect.[46] In such circumstances judicial review could hardly flourish.

---

[44] This could have caused difficulties if an important but politically uncontroversial amendment failed to bring out a majority of voters, and the referendum provisions of the 1937 Constitution did not follow this precedent.
[45] Constitution (Amendment No. 16) Act 1929.
[46] *R. (Cooney)* v. *Clinton*, reported at [1935] I.R. 245.

The initiative and related devices

Article 48 contemplated a procedure whereby the initiative in regard to legislation, or constitutional amendment, would not be the sole preserve of politicians. The public was to have a role in this regard—provided that the Oireachtas passed the appropriate legislation. But should it fail to do this voluntarily it could be compelled to do so, or to submit the matter to a referendum, by a petition signed by 75,000 registered voters. Legislation governing the initiative was to provide (1) that proposals could be initiated on the petition of 50,000 electors, and (2) that should the Oireachtas reject the proposals they would be submitted to a referendum. This device was fashionable in the new constitutions adopted after World War I, but the government found it unattractive and no steps to implement Article 48 were taken. In 1928 Fianna Fáil, as part of its campaign to abolish the oath, presented a petition signed by 96,000 voters; the government responded by implementing an earlier proposal to abolish the initiative, and this was duly enacted as the Constitution (Amendment No. 10) Act 1928. Cumann na nGaedhael's disenchantment with the device subsequently came to be shared by Fianna Fáil, and the initiative consequently does not feature in the 1937 Constitution.

Article 47 provided for a referendum on ordinary Bills—as distinct from constitutional amendments—in certain circumstances. A Bill passed, or deemed to have been passed, by both Houses could be put in suspension for 90 days on written demand by two-thirds of the Dáil or a majority of the Seanad. This Bill must then be submitted to a referendum if such was demanded by resolution of three-fifths of the Seanad or a petition by one-twentieth of registered voters, and must be approved by a *majority of those voting*. (This did not apply to Money Bills, or Bills declared by both Houses to be "necessary for the immediate preservation of the public peace, health or safety.") This, too, was removed by the Constitution (Amendment No. 10) Act 1928[47]; but unlike the initiative, this idea has left traces in the 1937 Constitution—see Article 27.

The Boundary Commission

Article 12 of the Treaty provided that Northern Ireland (as defined in the Government of Ireland Act 1920) could opt out of the Irish Free State by resolution of its parliament. Should it do so—as it did—a Boundary Commission was to be established to delimit the territorial extent of the two Irish governmental entities. After some difficulties[48] this was duly done; but the Commission's conclusions were such that all three governments agreed to bury its report and preserve the *status quo*, and the agreement in question, which amended the Treaty, was subsequently confirmed by Act of the Oireachtas.[49]

---

[47] For a fuller discussion see Kohn, *op. cit.*, pp. 238–246. Mansergh, *op. cit.*, Ch. VIII is much more critical of the government's approach to these issues.

[48] On the subject of the Boundary Commission see G. J. Hand (ed.), *Report of the Irish Boundary Commission 1925* (Shannon 1970), and Professor Hand's essay "MacNeill and the Boundary Commission" in F. X. Martin and F. J. Byrne (eds.), *The Scholar Revolutionary: Eoin MacNeill 1867–1945* (Shannon 1973).

[49] Treaty (Confirmation of Amending Agreement) Act 1925. See also J. J. Lee, *Ireland 1912–1985: Politics and Society* (Cambridge 1989), pp. 140–150 (this work is henceforward cited as Lee, *Ireland 1912–1985*).

The Constitution in 1932

By 1932 the Constitution had undergone substantial alteration.[50] Sixteen amending Acts had been passed and though some were relatively minor, others were more significant in changing the original design.[51] In particular amendment numbers 6, 7, 8, 9 and 11[52] changed the composition and mode of election of the Seanad, while numbers 12–15 increased its power and status—the period for which it could delay Bills was extended, and one senator could be appointed to the Executive Council.[53] (The individual concerned, however, could not be President, Vice-President or Minister for Finance—compare Article 28.7 of Bunreacht na hÉireann.) The initiative and legislative referendum had been swept away, and Amendment No. 16 of 1929 had extended to 16 years the period during which the Constitution could be amended by ordinary legislation, without a referendum. In addition, the Constitution (Amendment No. 17) Act 1931 had inserted a huge new Article 2A—almost as long as the original text. This was a drastic public safety Act which, when brought into force by executive proclamation (as it could be at any time), purported to abrogate many of the Constitution's guarantees.

Fianna Fáil in power

In the general election of February 1932 Fianna Fáil—the party effectively representing the vanquished of the civil war—became the largest party in the Dáil. Though lacking an overall majority, Eamon de Valera was able to form a government with Labour Party support. He had opposed the Treaty, preferring instead his concept of external association. Under this the Crown would not even have had a symbolic role in Irish internal affairs; thus there would be no oath of allegiance or Governor General. Instead, Ireland would be associated with the Commonwealth/Empire for purposes of foreign affairs and defence, and would recognise the British monarch as head of that association. This was a brilliant anticipation of future developments in Commonwealth relations, but it could not have won acceptance in 1921–22 from a coalition British Government dependent upon Tory votes. When Mr. de Valera came to power, however, his object was so to amend the Treaty settlement as to bring about external association. Though the British Government disliked his approach, developments in Dominion status—and the Statute of Westminster 1931—meant they had little scope for objection on grounds of convention or law.

Mr. de Valera's first efforts were directed at the office of Governor General. He advised the king to dismiss the incumbent, James MacNeill, and

---

[50] No textual alteration had—or could have—established the principle of civilian control of the armed forces, a vital factor in the peaceful political transition of 1932. That principle had been vindicated in the army mutiny of 1924, as to which see the fascinating study by Maryann G. Valiulis, *Almost A Rebellion: The Irish Army Mutiny of 1924* (Cork 1985).

[51] They are conveniently summarised in Kohn, *op. cit.*, pp. 256–257.

[52] Amendment No. 6 was Act No. 13 of 1928; No. 7, Act No. 30 of 1928; No. 8, Act No. 27 of 1978; No. 9, Act No. 28 of 1928 and No. 11, Act No. 34 of 1929.

[53] Amendment No. 12 was Act No. 5 of 1930: No. 13, Act No. 14 of 1928: No. 14, Act No. 8 of 1929 and No. 15, Act No. 9 of 1929.

after some difficulties[54] Domhnall Ó Buachalla was appointed. He did not fulfil the controversial social role of his predecessors, never appeared in public and lived in a modest suburban house rather than in the vice-regal lodge (now Arus an Uachtaráin). His official functions were discharged almost anonymously.[55] Finally, a constitutional amendment of 1936 transferred to the Ceann Comhairle (*i.e.* the chairman of the Dáil) the functions of summoning and dissolving the Dáil and of signing legislation, and abolished the office itself.[56]

The first legislative measure introduced by the new Fianna Fáil Government in March 1932 was the Constitution (Removal of Oath) Bill. This Bill, which as will be seen did more than its title suggests, redeemed an election pledge. The Bill was passed by the Dáil as introduced, but in the Seanad it was subjected to amendments which transformed its character.[57] These were rejected by the Dáil, with the consequence that ordinarily the Bill would have become law only after a 20 month delay; this was the effect of Article 38A inserted by the Constitution (Amendment No. 13) Act 1928.[58] But Article 38A alternatively provided that such a Bill could be deemed to have been passed 60 days after the Dáil reassembled following a general election, and a general election had been held in January 1933. Thus the Constitution (Removal of Oath) Act became law on May 3, 1933.

In November 1933 the Constitution (Amendment No. 22) Act became law. Under this the right of appeal to the Judicial Committee of the Privy Council was terminated. The validity of this was challenged before the Judicial Committee itself in *Moore* v. *Att. Gen. of the I.F.S.* [1935] I.R. 472, the plaintiffs[59] having obtained leave to appeal just before the Act came into force. The Irish Attorney General, it should be noted, did not appear, and was not represented, before the Judicial Committee; but his English *confrère* did appear and argued in support of the Act. The Judicial Committee upheld the Act, and thus dismissed the appeal. Its reasoning may be described as "Westminster-centred" and proceeded thus: the Treaty was given legal force by Westminster's I.F.S. (Agreement) Act 1922: next the I.F.S. Constitution Act 1922 gave the force of law to the I.F.S. Constitution—subject to the Treaty. Article 2 of the Treaty built in the appeal to the Judicial Committee, because such an appeal was part of the law, practice and constitutional usage then governing the relationship of the Crown and British Parliament to Canada. Before the Statute of Westminster 1931 the Irish Free State Parliament could not have abrogated any part of the Treaty—*e.g.* by abolishing the appeal—because the Colonial Laws Validity Act 1865 forbade a Dominion legislature to pass a law repugnant to a Westminster Act. But the Statute of

---

[54] Chronicled by Deirdre McMahon "The Chief Justice and the Governor General Controversy in 1932" (1982) XII *Irish Jurist* (N.S.) 145. See also Sexton, *op. cit.*, pp. 122–141.

[55] See further Sexton, *op. cit.*, pp. 154–158.

[56] Constitution (Amendment No. 27) Act 1936.

[57] See further Kohn, *op. cit.*, pp. 273–386.

[58] The mechanism of Art. 38A was as follows: if the Seanad rejected a Bill, or amended it in ways subsequently rejected by the Dáil, the Bill was effectively in cold storage for 18 months. The Dáil then had one year to send it back; if it did so the Bill could be deemed to have been passed 60 days after the date when it was sent back.

[59] Who had brought proceedings in relation to their claimed rights over a fishery in the river Erne. They won in the High Court ([1929] I.R. 191) but lost in the Supreme Court ([1934] I.R. 44).

Westminster struck off that fetter and there was now no barrier to the Oireachtas doing what it had done. (This conclusion, it may be noted, was in accordance with the legal advice Mr. de Valera had received[60]—but, as will appear, certain problems still existed.)

Fianna Fáil in 1933 lacked a majority in the Seanad, and the system of triennial elections meant that it might take a long time to secure one. The party had committed itself to abolishing the House and the delay in passing the Removal of Oath Bill was hardly calculated to alter this view. A Bill to cut the delaying power to three months was introduced in 1933 (it was also delayed), but this was overtaken by a 1934 Bill to abolish the House. (The Seanad had in the interim delayed *inter alia* a Bill to abolish university representation in the Dáil; another to grant universal suffrage in local government elections; and another to forbid political uniforms (aimed at the Blueshirts.))[61] The abolition Bill was naturally subjected to the Seanad's delaying power, but it became law on May 29, 1936 as the Constitution (Amendment No. 24) Act.

In May 1935 Mr. de Valera indicated to the Dáil that a new constitution was in preparation, and a year later he announced his intention of introducing it before the end of 1936. But the abdication crisis intervened and gave him the opportunity to complete his transformation of the existing one. In all the Dominions legislation was essential to confirm Edward VIII's abdication and regulate the succession. Mr. de Valera's two measures did more. The Constitution (Amendment No. 27) Act 1936 deleted all mention of the king from the Constitution and abolished the office of Governor General. The Executive Authority (External Relations) Act 1936 provided that the diplomatic and consular representatives of the Saorstát should be appointed on the authority of the Executive Council (section 1). It went on to say that every international agreement concluded on behalf of the Saorstát should be concluded by or on the authority of the Executive Council (s.2). Section 3(1) then provided:

> "It is hereby declared and enacted that, so long as Saorstát Éireann is associated with the following nations, that is to say, Australia, Canada, Great Britain, New Zealand and South Africa, and so long as the King recognised by those nations as the symbol of their co-operation continues to act on behalf of each of those nations (on the advice of the several governments thereof) for the purposes of the appointment of diplomatic and consular representatives and the conclusion of international agreements, the King so recognised may, and is hereby authorised to, act on behalf of Saorstát Éireann for the like purposes as and when advised by the Executive Council so to do."[62]

With the passage of that legislation the king was no longer part of the Constitution for internal purposes, and there was no Governor General. Formal functions such as summoning and dissolving the Dáil and assenting to Bills were discharged by others. The king had a purely formal role in foreign rela-

---

[60] See Fanning, *op. cit.*, pp. 110–111.
[61] See further Thomas Garvin, *The Irish Senate* (Dublin 1969), pp. 9–11.
[62] s.3(2) of the Act gave effect to Edward VIII's instrument of abdication and regulated the succession.

tions but since this rested only on statute, changing it would not involve a constitutional amendment. The oath had also gone. Thus by the end of 1936 Mr. de Valera had achieved "external association" and the stage was properly set for the introduction of a new constitution.

In one important respect, however, the Treaty settlement was still not dismantled. The issue of the Treaty ports remained—and this obviously could not be resolved simply by passing a statute. It was a matter both of symbolic and intensely practical significance, for even with a new constitution full sovereignty could hardly be claimed to exist as long as those ports were in British hands. And with war in Europe a possibility the State could hardly appear neutral if one belligerent had bases on its territory. But the Anglo-Irish Agreement of April 25, 1938 provided for the return of the ports to Irish control.[63]

The new Constitution

As already noted, developments by the end of 1936 meant that the 1922 Constitution had been purged of controversial symbols and external association had been realised. Thus the scene was set for Mr. de Valera's promised new constitution. In a sense this might have seemed redundant now, but there were reasons for going ahead. For one thing the Constitution was now a patchwork; the original text had been modified by 27 specific Constitution Amendment Acts, to which one had to add the Constitution (Removal of Oath) Act 1933. It would be open to amendment by way of ordinary legislation at least until December 6, 1938—a period which could, of course, be extended. Consequently it could hardly play that symbolic role as the basic law of the State so clearly attributable to the United States Constitution.

There were, however, also legal reasons, springing from the Supreme Court's decision in *State (Ryan)* v. *Lennon* [1935] I.R. 170. The prosecutors, who were detained in prison pending their trial by the Constitution (Special Powers) Tribunal, sought orders of *habeas corpus* directing their release, and of prohibition restraining the Tribunal from proceeding with their trial. The Tribunal was established under Article 2A of the Constitution, which had been inserted by the Constitution (Amendment No. 17) Act 1931. But, the prosecutors argued, Amendment No. 17 was not a valid amendment of the Constitution—and considered as an ordinary statute it impermissibly conflicted therewith; for it (*inter alia*) authorised the exercise of judicial power by persons who were not judges, contrary to Article 64, and permitted trial without a jury contrary to Article 72. It was not a valid constitutional amendment because it had not been approved in a referendum; and Amendment No. 16—which extended the period during which the Constitution could be amended by ordinary legislation from eight to 16 years—was itself invalid. This argument was rejected by the Supreme Court (Fitzgibbon and Murnaghan JJ.: Kennedy C.J. dissenting), there being nothing in Article 50—the amendment provision—to prevent the extension from eight years to 16 years. But all three judges agreed on the following propositions:

---

[63] The negotiations leading to this agreement are discussed by John Bowman, *De Valera and the Ulster Question 1917–1973* (Oxford 1983), pp. 160–181. See also Robert Fisk, *In Time of War: Ireland, Ulster and the Price of Neutrality 1939–45* (London 1985), pp. 25–44.

4000 8361

(1) the key document was the Constituent Act, passed by the Constituent Assembly
(2) the treaty was built into the constitutional structure by the Constituent Act, section 2—and by the words "within the terms of the Scheduled Treaty" in Article 50
(3) the deletion of the above words from Article 50 would be ineffective because the same restriction appeared in the Constituent Act *and the Oireachtas had no power to amend that.*

The significance of these observations lay in the fact that the Constitution (Removal of Oath) Act 1933 deleted from Article 50 the words "within the terms of the Scheduled Treaty" *and* purported to repeal section 2 of the Constituent Act. And this was the foundation for those subsequent constitutional amendments—such as abolition of the appeal to the Privy Council, the office of Governor General, etc.—which would have conflicted with the Treaty. But the Supreme Court's conclusions obviously placed a large question mark over the validity of those amendments. This was so despite the Judicial Committee's decision in *Moore* v. *Att. Gen.* [1935] I.R. 472—which came after *Ryan's* case—that the Statute of Westminster 1931 removed the fetter imposed by the Treaty on the amendment of the Constitution. For that view—described *supra* as "Westminster-centred"—was based on the premiss that the Constitution's legal roots were in Westminster Acts. The view of the Supreme Court was quite different. Both Kennedy C.J. and Fitzgibbon J. accepted that the Third Dáil enacted the Constitution *of its own supreme authority*, and the same approach seems implicit in the judgment of Murnaghan J. From this it followed that power to amend the Constitution must be found solely in the Constituent Act and the Constitution. It could not be affected by the Statute of Westminster 1931; this merely gave power to pass Acts repugnant to Westminster statutes—but the source of validity of the Constitution was not a Westminster statute.[64]

Mr. de Valera was thus in a kind of legal limbo. He must of necessity have accepted the Supreme Court's view on the Constitution's root of title; anything else would have been a denial of his previous career. Yet that view led on to unacceptable results. On the other hand, the Judicial Committee's conclusion was eminently acceptable—but unfortunately it was based on an inadmissible premiss! This dilemma serves to explain the way the new Constitution was enacted.[65] In the first place Mr. de Valera was emphatic that this was not an amendment of the former instrument; it was an entirely new departure.[66] Secondly, the Constitution was *not* enacted by the now unicameral legislature. The Dáil simply approved the draft, which was then submitted to the people in a plebiscite under legislation passed for that purpose.[67] The people duly approved it and it came into force on December 29, 1937.

The new Constitution was thus plainly rooted in the will of the people and therefore put beyond challenge. Nor could any court entertain a challenge

---

[64] This view was confirmed by the present Supreme Court in *Re Article 26 and the Criminal Law (Jurisdiction) Bill 1975* [1977] I.R. 129, 147, 148.
[65] On the framing of the new Constitution see Dermot Keogh "The Irish Constitutional Revolution: An Analysis of the Making of the Constitution," *Administration*, Vol. 35, no. 4, 4 (1987): also Lee, *Ireland 1912–1985*, pp. 201–209.
[66] See his remarks in the Dáil on May 11, 1937: 67 *Dáil Debs.* cc. 60–75.
[67] Plebiscite (Draft Constitution) Act 1937.

should one be lodged, for all judges were, under Article 58, offered the option of retiring on pension or making a declaration to uphold the Constitution.[68]

Bunreacht na hÉireann—an overview

The new Constitution obviously differs from its predecessor in many respects. That of 1922 opened (Art. 1) with a statement of the Free State's Commonwealth membership; but while the new state (now called Ireland or, in Irish, Éire: Art. 4)[69] was still within the Commonwealth,[70] this fact was not proclaimed in the Constitution. This, of course, was a logical conse-quence of external association, which now rested on the Executive Authority (External Relations) Act 1936. The new Constitution continued that Act in force for so long as the Oireachtas wished. Article 29.4.2° provides:

> "For the purpose of the exercise of any executive function of the State in or in connection with its external relations, the Government may to such extent and subject to such conditions, if any, as may be determined by law, avail of or adopt any organ, instrument or method of procedure used or adopted for the like purpose by the members of any group or league of nations with which the State is or becomes associated for the purpose of international co-operation in matters of common concern."

Thus when the Inter-Party Government of 1948–51 decided to quit the Commonwealth this was effected simply by repealing the 1936 Act.[71]

With equal logic all symbols of Commonwealth membership were purged from the new Constitution. In place of the Governor General a President was to be head of State for internal purposes.[72] His/her powers and functions were meticulously spelt out (see Chap. 3, *infra*), and there was no trace left of the former theory that the head of State is the formal head of the executive; in no sense is the Government today even formally "His/Her Excellency's Government." It was also of symbolic significance, and in keeping with the democratic character of the new Constitution, that provision was made for the election of the President; the Governor General was the choice of the poli-ticians, not the people. This must not be overstressed, however. The new Constitution also provided that if there was only one candidate no election should be necessary (Art. 12.4.5°, and as Chapter 3 *infra* shows, the political parties have often been able to agree on a candidate so that an election con-test has been the exception rather than the rule. Given that the President's functions essentially parallel those of the Governor General, and that all holders of the latter office were Irishmen chosen by Irishmen, one must not make too much of the new dispensation.

The new Constitution differed from its predecessor in many other respects. Its layout was much to be preferred; to take but one example, the fundamen-

---

[68] Art. 58 was one of the transitory provisions which, as authorised by Art. 52, is not printed in texts published after June 25, 1938 (the date the first President took up office). The declar-ation required of judges was that set out in Art. 34.5.

[69] See further pp. 34–35 *infra*.

[70] The British Government, and those of the other Commonwealth nations, did not regard the new Constitution as changing Ireland's Commonwealth status—though London was not enamoured of the document: see Bowman, *op. cit.*, pp. 156–160. It should be noted that Irish Ministers ceased to attend Commonwealth meetings after the change of government in 1932.

[71] Republic of Ireland Act 1948, s.1.

[72] And, after 1948, for external purposes also: Republic of Ireland Act 1948, s.3.

tal rights provisions were so headed and were stated with more emphasis. It contained some entirely new material; thus the 1922 Constitution featured nothing comparable to Article 29 (international relations), Article 41 (the family), Article 42 (education)[73] and Article 43 (property rights). Nor had it any counterpart to Articles 2 and 3 (as to which see Chap. 2, *infra*). The 1937 Constitution was in several places markedly declamatory in its tone, whereas that of 1922 contended itself with a prosaic, not to say pedestrian, statement of legal principles. Bunreacht na hÉireann, while of course stating such principles, also contains aspirations and objectives—witness Article 29.1.2 on international relations, and Article 45's directive principles of social policy. Its tone is also more definitely religious. God is mentioned in the preamble to the Constituent Act of 1922, but the much longer preamble to Bunreacht na hÉireann goes much further with its references to "the Most Holy Trinity" and "our Divine Lord, Jesus Christ." This is echoed in Article 44.1 (religion) which had no counterpart in the 1922 Constitution.[74]

The framers of the new Constitution had in several respects learned from experience. It was decided that amendment of the Constitution should require a referendum—but also that the Oireachtas should have a period of grace during which it could amend the Constitution by ordinary statute. Article 51 made provision accordingly, for a period of three years after the first President's entry on office—which period ended on June 25, 1941. But Article 51 also specifically provided that: (a) Article 46—the referendum requirement—could not be touched; (b) Article 51 itself could not be amended. Thus there was no question of extending the three year period. Nor, after June 25, 1941, could there be any room for an argument that this Constitution was implicitly amended by legislation conflicting with its provisions.[75] The arrangements for coping with emergency situations were quite different in form from those under the earlier Constitution. Its original ban on the creation of "extraordinary courts" (Art. 70) was not repeated; Article 38.3 of Bunreacht na hÉireann specifically authorised the establishment by law of special criminal courts. Thus the expedient adopted in 1931 with the insertion of Article 2A, under which a whole emergency code became part of the Constitution, was not repeated. But the new Constitution gave the Oireachtas large powers to cope with emergencies (Art. 28.3.3°) by virtue of which it could set aside practically all restrictions (see Chap. 7, *infra*).

Notwithstanding this, the degree of continuity between the two documents is very high. Many of Bunreacht na hÉireann's provisions are broadly similar in terms to those of the 1922 Constitution. In many instances the language is identical, and in others there occur only slight verbal changes which do not alter the substance. This holds true, for example, for the provisions on the courts (Arts. 34–36) and on the Dáil (Art. 16). And some of Bunreacht na hÉireann's new material came from pre-existing statutes. Thus it decrees that Dáil deputies shall be elected "on the system of proportional representation by means of the single transferable vote" (Art. 16.2.5°)

[73] Art. 10 of the 1922 Constitution guaranteed all citizens "the right to free elementary education" (compare Art. 42.4) but said no more on the subject.

[74] The extraordinary efforts that went into drafting Article 44—including direct contact with the Vatican—are chronicled in Keogh, *op. cit.*

[75] Art. 15.4 of Bunreacht na hÉireann—which had no counterpart under its predecessor—stipulates that the Oireachtas shall not enact any law repugnant to the Constitution. Should it do so that legislation is void to the extent of such repugnancy.

whereas Article 26 of the 1922 Constitution had referred simply to "principles of proportional representation." But the Electoral Act 1923, which implemented Article 26, provided for the single transferable vote—and its provisions (*inter alia*) on counting the votes are still in force. Again the 1922 Constitution did not specify the declaration to be made by judges, unlike its successor which sets out that declaration in Article 34.5.1°. But that declaration, with minor variations in wording, is that specified under the Courts of Justice Act 1924, s.99. Similarly there was no article of the 1922 Constitution devoted to the office of Attorney General (compare Article 30 of Bunreacht na hÉireann) but that office certainly existed before 1937 and section 6 of the Ministers and Secretaries Act 1924 still applies to it.

The Oireachtas established under the 1937 Constitution is a bicameral legislature, but the balance of power is tipped much more firmly in favour of the Dáil. The new Seanad, however, exhibits certain features of its predecessor—*e.g.* it has 60 members, it contains a nominated element and the electorate is clearly modelled on the amended provisions of the 1922 Constitution (see Chap. 4, *infra*).

Processes of change since 1937[76]

The amendment provisions of Bunreacht na hÉireann—Article 46 and the transitional Article 51—are so worded as to make it clear that the power of amendment is unlimited. Article 46.1 provides:

"Any provision of this Constitution may be amended, whether by way of variation, addition, or repeal . . . "

Thus there was now no scope for an argument based on a narrow interpretation of "amendment," such as was accepted by Kennedy C.J. in his dissenting judgment in *State (Ryan)* v. *Lennon* [1935] I.R. 170.[77]

The amending power has been successfully invoked on 11 occasions to date. The majority of the amendments were effected by the First and Second Amendment of the Constitution Acts, passed in 1939 and 1941 respectively, in the period during which no referendum was required. The first of these extended the scope of the emergency powers provision (Art. 29.3.3°). The second further extended its reach (see Chap. 7, *infra*) but also accomplished much more. In fact the Second Amendment of the Constitution Act made over 20 amendments to the original text, running from Article 11 to Article 47. A few of these were to the Irish text alone, and many of those to both texts were essentially stylistic only. But there were also several amendments of substance. What is now Article 25.4—relating to the Presidential signature of Bills—is an expanded version of the original; Article 24.2 clarifies the situation regarding Bills deemed to have been passed by both Houses; Article 26.3.2° and 27.4.2° are new and designed better to harmonise Article 26 (reference of Bills to the Supreme Court) and 27 (reference of Bills to the people). The major changes, however, affected the courts. Article 26.2.2° and 34.4.5° stipulated that in cases involving the constitutionality of Bills under Article 26, or Acts under Article 34, the Supreme Court must deliver only one opinion; separate concurrences, as well as dissents, were specifically

[76] See also James Casey "Changing the Constitution: Amendment and Judicial Review" in Brian Farrell (ed.), *De Valera's Constitution and Ours* (Dublin 1988), pp. 152–161.
[77] See *Finn* v. *Att. Gen.* [1983] I.R. 154, 163–164 *per* Barrington J.

ruled out. Article 34.3.3° provided that an Act, the Bill for which had been upheld by the Supreme Court on a Presidential reference under Article 26, should thenceforward be immune from challenge. Article 34.3.2° was re-worded to state even more emphatically that only the High Court had orig-inal jurisdiction over actions challenging the validity of statutes in the light of the Constitution. Finally the *habeas corpus* provisions of Article 40.4 were greatly expanded. This was done to ensure that the person having custody of the detainee had an opportunity to justify the detention as lawful; to ensure that if the High Court concluded that a statute authorising the challenged detention was invalid, it should state a case on that issue to the Supreme Court[78] and to empower the High Court to suspend execution of a capital sentence pending a *habeas corpus* application.

It was 31 years before the next amendments were effected.[79] In 1972 the Third Amendment of the Constitution Act amended Article 16.1.2° by lower-ing the voting age to 18. The Fourth Amendment of the Constitution Act 1972 inserted the new Article 29.4.3° to remove any constitutional barriers to the State's joining the European Communities (see Chap. 8, *infra*). The Fifth Amendment of the Constitution Act 1972 altered Article 44.1 by deleting ther-efrom subsections 1 and 2 which dealt with the recognition of certain named churches.[80] In 1979 there were passed the Sixth and Seventh Amendment of the Constitution Acts. The first of these inserted what is now Article 37.2, to protect orders made by An Bord Uchtála (the Adoption Board) against chal-lenges based on separation of powers grounds (see Chap. 9, *infra*). The Seventh Amendment was designed to widen the representation of higher education institutions in the Seanad, and it inserts a new Article 18.4.2° to allow the Oir-eachtas to make provision accordingly (see Chap. 4, *infra*). The Eighth Amendment of the Constitution Act 1983 was the result of a campaign by a private group to have the Constitution amended so as to rule out legislation permitting abortion. The group was able to secure promises to introduce appropriate legislation from the major political parties during a general elec-tion campaign. The 1983 Act introduced a new subsection 3° to Article 40.3:

> "The State acknowledges the right to life of the unborn and, with due regard to the equal right to life of the mother, guarantees in its laws to respect, and, as far as practicable, by its laws to defend and vindicate that right."

The Ninth Amendment of the Constitution Act 1984 amended Article 16.1 by substituting a new subsection 2°. This permits the Oireachtas to confer the right to vote on categories of non-citizens—which has been implemented

---

[78] As the law then stood no appeal lay to the Supreme Court against a *grant* of *habeas corpus*; see Chap. 10 *infra*.

[79] In 1959, and again in 1969, attempts were made to abolish proportional representation, but the Bills were rejected by the people; see further Cornelius O'Leary, *Irish Elections 1918–1977* (Dublin 1979), Chaps. 6 and 7.

[80] They provided: "2° The State recognises the special position of the Holy Catholic Apostolic and Roman Church as the guardian of the Faith professed by the great majority of the citizens.
3· The State also recognises the Church of Ireland, the Presbyterian Church in Ireland, the Methodist Church in Ireland, the Religious Society of Friends in Ireland, as well as the Jew-ish Congregations and the other religious denominations existing in Ireland at the date of the coming into operation of this Constitution."
See further Chap. 19 *infra*.

by the Electoral Act 1985 (see Chap. 4, *infra*).[81] The Tenth Amendment of the Constitution Act 1987, passed in the wake of the Supreme Court's decision in *Crotty* v. *An Taoiseach* [1987] I.L.R.M. 400, permitted the State to ratify the Single European Act (see further Chap. 8 *infra*). At the time of writing,[82] the most recent amendment is the Eleventh Amendment of the Constitution Act 1992, passed to allow the State to ratify the Treaty on European Union—the Maastricht Treaty (see further Chap. 8, *infra*).

The impact of judicial review[83]

The factors which inhibited the development of judicial review under the 1922 Constitution were not present under its successor; but judicial review was nonetheless slow to take off. Only a few cases came before the courts in the first 25 years of Bunreacht na hÉireann's existence— though some of these laid the foundation for future developments and demonstrated that statutes could prove vulnerable to challenge.[84] But it was in the early 1960s that judicial review began to flourish. Its significance lies, not in a head-count of statutes invalidated, but in the creation of a heightened awareness of citizens' rights and of the Constitution's role in diffusing and restricting power. Perhaps the most important development—discussed in Chapter 12, *infra*—has been the judicial recognition that the Constitution protects rights not specifically enumerated therein. That the courts have come to play a vital role in enforcing constitutional mandates is clear, but it is far from easy to encapsulate that role in any short formula. The courts have on several occasions taken a bold initiative to redress grievances that the Oireachtas had, for whatever reason, chosen to ignore. In *de Burca and Anderson* v. *Att. Gen.* [1976] I.R. 38 the Supreme Court struck down as invalid the Juries Act 1927, which excluded non-ratepayers and women from jury service. In that case judgment was delivered on December 12, 1975, and by March 2, 1976 a new Juries Act had been signed into law. Since the Oireachtas does not normally operate with such dispatch and the drafting of a Bill normally takes much longer than the few weeks involved here, it is reasonable to conclude that a draft Bill had in fact existed for some time but had been unable to find a place in the Government's legislative programme. The Supreme Court's decision thus obviously hastened necessary reform.[85] The decision in *McGee* v. *Att. Gen.* [1974] I.R. 284 invalidated a statutory provision denying married persons access to contraceptives, a provision which the Oireachtas could have amended but, despite urgings, seemed unable to bring itself to consider. *Byrne* v. *Ireland* [1972] I.R. 241 established that, contrary to the general

---

[81] A Bill to amend Art. 41 by removing the ban on divorce legislation was rejected in June 1986.

[82] The Government has announced that there will be a further referendum in autumn 1992 on the issues of abortion information and the right to travel abroad for an abortion. For the background see Chap. 12 *infra, s.v.* Abortion.

[83] See Donal Barrington "The Constitution in the Courts," in *Administration*, Vol. 35, no. 4 (1987), pp. 110–127.

[84] Examples are *National Union of Railwaymen* v. *Sullivan* [1947] I.R. 77 (see Chap. 16 *infra*) and *Buckley* v. *Att. Gen.* [1950] I.R. 67 (see Chap. 9 *infra*).

[85] The Committee on Court Practice and Procedure had recommended changes in the law on jury service in March 1965; see its Second Interim Report (Pr. 8328).

assumption, the State *was* liable for the torts of its servants; legislation to make it so liable was promised in 1961 but never enacted.

However, it would be wrong to think that the courts have systematically constituted themselves the State's ultimate policy-makers. Certainly this has occurred in some areas. The Supreme Court's bail decision of 1966 (*People (Att. Gen.)* v. *O'Callaghan* [1966] I.R. 501) has meant that there are limits on the power of the Oireachtas to legislate for pre-trial detention[86]; and it has several times been emphasised that evidence obtained in violation of constitutional rights is inadmissible against an accused person.[87] Nor have the courts been unwilling to strike down legislation as an unjust attack on property rights—something which might seem to be a matter for purely *legislative* judgment.[88] But in a multitude of other instances they have exhibited a marked disinclination to "second-guess" the legislature; thus in *Norris* v. *Att. Gen.* [1984] I.R. 36 the Supreme Court refused to widen the right of privacy so as to invalidate nineteenth-century statutes penalising homosexual conduct between consenting adults in private. By the same token that court refused to hold that legislation treating illegitimate children unfavourably in the matter of intestate succession violated the equality guarantee of Article 40.1, or that the State's failure to give disabled people postal votes when soldiers and policemen had them infringed the same guarantee.[89]

It would equally be wrong to see the judges, on the one side, ranged against the executive and legislature on the other. Clearly, there is and must be some tension between them, since the courts will sometimes be obliged to tell the other branches of government that their chosen solution to a problem is constitutionally deficient. But tension can give place to creative partnership. In 1967, before any formal system of civil legal aid existed, the Attorney General undertook on behalf of the Government to defray the cost of professional representation in *habeas corpus* cases for impecunious applicants, should the courts think such representation necessary. The Supreme Court *per* Walsh J., described this as "a notable contribution to the cause of personal liberty": *Application of Woods* [1970] I.R. 154, 166. And in *State (Healy)* v. *Donoghue* [1976] I.R. 325 the same court built on the legislative provision of criminal legal aid by stressing that District Justices must inform those appearing before them that such aid was available.

Despite the importance of their role under the Constitution, the courts still play a subordinate part in the making of policy for a changing society. There are obvious limits on what they can do in this regard, especially since so many issues of social policy involve questions of priorities in public expenditure. The courts may, by re-interpreting the Constitution, indicate that certain policy choices formerly thought to be precluded are in fact open. But while the courts may invalidate existing legislation, or clear the constitutional path for future legislation, they cannot enact it. It is beyond their

---

[86] The *O'Callaghan* decision was reaffirmed by the Supreme Court in *Ryan* v. *D.P.P.* [1989] I.R. 399. See further Chap. 14 *infra.*, *s.v.* Bail.

[87] *People (Att. Gen.)* v. *O'Brien* [1965] I.R. 142: *People (D.P.P.)* v. *Madden* [1977] I.R. 336; *People (D.P.P.)* v. *O'Loughlin* [1979] I.R. 85; *D.P.P.* v. *Healy* [1990] *People* 2 I.R. 110: *People (D.P.P.)* v. *Kenny* [1990] 2 I.R. 110. See further Chap. 14 *infra*, *s.v. Exclusion* of unconstitutionally obtained evidence.

[88] *Blake* v. *Att. Gen.* [1982] I.R. 117: *Re Article 26 and the Housing (Private Rented Dwellings) Bill 1981* [1983] I.R. 181: *Brennan* v. *Att. Gen.* [1984] I.L.R.M. 355. See Chap. 13 *infra.*

[89] *O'B.* v. *S.* [1984] I.R. 316; *Draper* v. *Att. Gen.* [1984] I.L.R.M. 355. See Chap. 18 *infra.*

power to decree a new social security or health scheme, a revised system of educational provision, a more progressive system of taxation or a new policy for full employment. Such choices remain to be made by the executive and the legislature; nor is there any sign that the courts wish it otherwise.[90]

---

[90] Thus in *Heaney* v. *Minister for Finance* [1986] I.L.R.M. 164, 166 Murphy J. repudiated the idea that Art. 34 of the Constitution vested in judges of the superior courts "vast powers to substitute their view of what is fair and just for that of the Oireachtas which has the right and duty of making the laws in accordance with which justice is to be achieved." And in *O'Reilly* v. *Limerick Corporation* [1989] I.L.R.M. 181, 195 Costello J. said: " . . . I am sure that the concept of justice which is to be found in the Constitution embraces the concept that the nation's wealth should be justly distributed (that is the concept of distributive justice), but I am equally sure that a claim that this has not occurred should, to comply with the Constitution, be advanced in Leinster House rather than in the Four Courts."

2 The People, the Nation and the State

Bunreacht na hÉireann draws a curious distinction between "the people", "the nation" and "the state". "The people", as the Preamble shows, adopted and enacted the Constitution. Article 6 informs us that all powers of government derive from "the people", who have the right to designate the rulers of "the State" and, in final appeal, to decide all questions of national policy. As a logical corollary, Article 46 permits amendment of the Constitution only if a proposal to that effect is approved by the people in a referendum; and Article 27 contemplates the possible submission of legislation to a referendum (see further p. 77 *infra*). By virtue of Article 30.3, all prosecutions on indictment are to be in the name of "the People" (why the word suddenly acquires a capital is unclear).[1] The nation is likewise mentioned in the Preamble. In Article 1 it appears virtually as a synonym for "the people", for the Article refers to its right to choose its own form of government,[2] and to develop its political, economic and cultural life in accordance with its own genius and traditions. The President may address a message to "the Nation" (Art. 13.7.2°) which again suggests an identity between "nation" and "people". However the word seems to be used in a different sense in Article 9.2, where fidelity to the nation is declared to be a fundamental political duty of all citizens.

The terms of Articles 1–3, which form a section headed "The Nation", suggest that the word refers to the people and territory of the entire island—in other words, to the country as a whole. (Unfortunately the Constitution is not at its most systematic in matters of terminology, for the restoration of "the unity of our *country*" is an aspiration of the Preamble). "The Nation" is plainly distinct from "the State"; this appears from (*inter alia*) the fact that Articles 4–11 are headed "the State", while Article 9.2 distinguishes between the fidelity owed to the nation and the loyalty owed to the State.

"The State" would seem to mean the political entity created by the Constitution: thus in *Commissioners of Public Works* v. *Kavanagh* [1962] I.R. 216, 225–226 Ó Dálaigh J. observed that " . . . in 1937 Saorstát Éireann was supplanted by the new State under the Constitution of Ireland." It has rulers and organs of government (Art. 6), owns natural resources (Art. 10) and has revenues (Art. 11). Laws are made for it (Art. 15), it may participate in war (Art. 28) and become party to international agreements (Art. 29). And, as

---

[1] This invocation of the popular will is a common feature of mordern constitutions: compare Art. 20(2) of the West German Basic Law of 1949 and Art. 3 of the French Constitution of 1958.

[2] In Art. 1 the word appears as "Government." Elsewhere in the Constitution, however, "Government" is used to mean "Cabinet": see particularly Art. 28, and contrast Art. 6.

27

Articles 40–44 show, it guarantees certain rights to citizens and other persons. In *Comyn* v. *Att. Gen.* [1950] I.R. 142 these factors led Kingsmill Moore J. to conclude that the State was a juristic person distinct from the citizenry or the Government, just as a company is a legal entity distinct from its shareholders or directors (see especially pp. 158–161 of his judgment). This view was upheld on appeal by the Supreme Court (*ibid.*) and subsequently reaffirmed in *Commissioners of Public Works* v. *Kavanagh* [1962] I.R. 216. The precise juristic nature of the State—whether it is a corporation, an unincorporated association or a legal *persona* of an entirely new type—still awaits judicial resolution.

In *Byrne* v. *Ireland* [1972] I.R. 241 Walsh J. expressed the relationship between "the State" and "the people" thus (at 262):

" . . . the State is the creation of the People and is to be governed in accordance with the provisions of the Constitution which was enacted by the People and which can be amended by the People only . . . in the last analysis the sovereign authority is the People."

But "the State" is not merely an abstract conception. It has a geographical dimension which arguably makes it equivalent in meaning to "country," for the President may not leave "the State" without the Government's consent (Art. 12.9). The same equation appears in Article 8.3 and Article 16. The former allows provision to be made by law for the exclusive use of Irish or English "throughout the State." The latter requires identity in the ratio between Dáil deputies and constituency population "throughout the country" (Art. 16.2.3°) and stipulates that polling at a general election should, as far as practicable, take place on the same day "throughout the country." This equation between "state" and "country" is not accidental.[3] While in popular usage "the State" refers to the 26 counties, this usage is not sanctioned by the Constitution. For though recognising the fact of partition, it purports to be the basic law of a 32 county state.

Article 4 provides that the English-language name of the State is Ireland, Éire being the Irish-language form. (This appears to contradict the Preamble which, in its English version, refers to "the people of Éire.") The expression "Republic of Ireland" finds no place in the Constitution. Its only legal sanction is in the Republic of Ireland Act 1948 (No. 22) which declares it to be "the description of the State." The distinction between a name and a description appears elusive; but the 1948 Act was designed to show that the 26 counties had left the Commonwealth and severed the final link with the British Crown, hence it was appropriate that the word "Republic" be employed. But statute alone cannot rename the State; only an amendment to Article 4—which would necessitate a referendum—can do that. Thus a new "description" was as far as statute could go.[4]

---

[3] Confusingly, the equation is not always found in statutes; thus in the Defamation Act 1961 and the Irish Nationality and Citizenship Act 1986 "the State" is used to mean the 26 counties.

[4] In *Ellis* v. *O'Dea* [1989] I.R. 530 Walsh J. said (at 540): "The name of the State is as provided for in Article 4 of the Constitution. In 1948 the Oireachtas enacted Acht Phoblacht na hÉireann in both the Irish and English languages. In the latter language it is entitled 'the Republic of Ireland Act 1948'. It does not purport to change the name of the State nor could the Oireachtas do so even if it wished. An amendment of the Constitution would be required for a change in name." And McCarthy J. said (at 542): . . . s.2 of the Republic of Ireland Act 1948

In *Ellis* v. *O'Dea* [1989] I.R. 530 the Supreme Court voiced its disapproval of the fact that extradition warrants issuing from United Kingdom courts regularly named the State "Éire". And a majority of the court[5] indicated that such warrants should not be endorsed by the Garda authorities, but should be returned whence they came for rectification. Walsh J. said (at 539–540):

> "In the English language the name of this State is 'Ireland' and is so prescribed by Article 4 of the Constitution. Of course if the courts of the United Kingdom or of other States choose to issue warrants in the Irish language then they are quite at liberty to use the Irish language name of the State as prescribed in the Constitution. However they are not at liberty to attribute to this State a name which is not its correct name. It is quite clear from various warrants which have come before this Court from time to time that this is a conscious and deliberate practice. In effect it is a refusal to recognise a provision of the Constitution of Ireland. Every court in this State, and every member of the Garda Síochána is duty bound to uphold the Constitution and not to condone or acquiesce in any refusal to recognise the Constitution or any part thereof. If the courts of other countries seeking the assistance of the courts of this country are unwilling to give this State its constitutionally correct and internationally recognised name then, in my view, the warrants should be returned to such countries until they have been rectified. Henceforth it should be the care and concern of the requesting prosecuting and judicial authorities of another State not to ignore or brush aside the fundamental law of this State. It should be the concern and care of the Irish authorities not to permit the existence of any such a situation."

This question of nomenclature was discussed by the all-party Committee on the Constitution in its *Report* of December 1967 (Pr. 9817, paras. 15 and 16) as follows:

> "Article 5 states that Ireland is a sovereign, independent, democratic state. It does not, however, proclaim that Ireland is a Republic nor does any other Article of the Constitution, despite the fact that many of its provisions have all the hallmarks one would expect to find in relation to a Republican State. The omission of this proclamation of a Republic in the Constitution of 1937 was deliberate. In dealing with the draft Constitution in the Dáil in 1937, the President of the Executive Council stated that were it not for the Northern problem the Constitution would in all probability contain a flat, downright proclamation of a Republic . . .
>
> The State . . . is a Republic, and internationally recognised as such, but a statement to this effect is not to be found in the Constitution. It is not, of course, essential that the Constitution should specifically deal with our Republican status, and it is worth noting in this connection that there is no provision to this effect in some other republican constitu-

by which it was declared that the description of the State shall be the Republic of Ireland did not, in any fashion, affect the name of the State as prescribed by Article 4 of the Constitution."

[5] Walsh and McCarthy JJ. Finlay C.J. agreed that it was "most undesirable that the name of the State should be incorrectly set out" in such warrants, but reserved his opinion on the consequences that might attach to this (at 545).

tions. Nowadays, however, it is the practice of constitution-makers to adopt an appropriate clause to dispose of this point: see, for example, the Constitutions of Italy, Finland, France and West Germany. In fact, in the French, Italian and West German Constitutions, the Republican status of the State is declared to be unalterable. On balance, therefore, we think it desirable to alter Article 5 of the Constitution so as to provide that the State is a sovereign, independent, democratic Republic."

However, no action has been taken on foot of this recommendation, and the position remains as stated above.

The international stage

It is as "Ireland" that the political entity commonly called "the Republic" is known on the international stage—for example, in the European Communities and at the United Nations. But this issue of nomenclature has given rise to occasional diplomatic difficulties. Normally the letters of credence of an ambassador are addressed to "the President of Ireland"; but it appears that those of United Kingdom ambassadors are addressed to the President *in his/her own name*. The reason for accepting this was explained by the Minister for External Affairs, Mr. Aiken, in Dáil Éireann on February 10, 1954 (144 *Dáil Debs*. c. 40):

> "The credentials presented by the British Ambassador addressed to President Seán T. Ó Ceallaigh were accepted because the Government were convinced that as Britain is keeping Ireland partitioned against the wishes of the majority of the Irish people, it was essential for the peaceful solution of that issue that diplomatic relations should be maintained at the highest level. Such relations are necessary to prevent deterioration of the existing position and to help secure the basis for the friendship which should exist between two close neighbours. I need hardly add that the arrangement made between Ireland and Britain is no precedent for two countries which have no quarrel."

This explanation was given in the context of a dispute as to the accreditation of an Australian Ambassador. It seems that following Ireland's departure from the Commonwealth in 1949, the two Governments were unable to agree on this matter; and the difference of opinion delayed the arrival of an Australian Ambassador in Dublin until 1965 (see *The Irish Times* May 14, 1965). The Irish position was that letters of credence should be addressed to the President of Ireland, and it is implicit in Mr. Aiken's words quoted above that accreditation to the President by name was unacceptable. The Australian view was that accreditation to "the President of Ireland" would imply sovereignty over the whole island and that accordingly the addressee should be "the President of the Republic of Ireland." In his Dáil statement (*loc. cit. supra*) Mr. Aiken made it clear that this was not acceptable to the Irish Government. Eventually a compromise was reached under which the accreditation was from "the Queen of Australia to the President of Ireland." It is not surprising that this formula satisfied the Irish Government; its appeal to the Australian Government presumably reflects the fact that the Australian monarch simultaneously reigns over the United Kingdom of Great Britain

and Northern Ireland, so that in context the words convey a restricted interpretation of "Ireland".[6]

Articles 2 and 3

Article 2 provides that the national territory consists of the whole island of
Ireland, its islands and the territorial seas. This may appear to ignore the
fact of partition, but its existence is recognised by the opening words of
Article 3—"pending the re-integration of the national territory . . . "

Article 3 then goes on to make what may appear to be a claim of jurisdiction over Northern Ireland: it uses the words " . . . without prejudice to the
right of the Parliament and Government established by this Constitution to
exercise jurisdiction over the whole of that (*i.e.* the national) territory . . . "
This has given rise to many objections from Northern Unionists. But is it
mere rhetoric, without legal significance? Mr. Justice Kenny, in a lecture
delivered in Belfast in 1978, seemed to accept that it was.[7] He buttressed this
view by citing a passage from the Supreme Court's judgment in *Re Article 26
and the Criminal Law (Jurisdiction) Bill 1975* [1977] I.R. 129, 147. The court, *per*
O'Higgins C.J., said:

> " . . . the Constitution . . . expresses not only legal norms but basic doc-
> trines of social and political theory . . . the Constitution contains more
> than legal rules: it reflects, in part, aspirations and aims and expresses
> the political theories on which the people acted when they enacted the
> Constitution.
>
> One of the theories held in 1937 by a substantial number of citizens
> was that a nation, as distinct from a State, had rights; than the Irish
> people living in what is now called the Republic of Ireland and in North-
> ern Ireland together formed the Irish Nation; that a nation has a right to
> unity of territory in some form, be it as a unitary or federal state; and
> that the Government of Ireland Act, 1920, though legally binding, was a
> violation of that natural right to unity which was superior to positive
> law.
>
> This national claim to unity exists not in the legal but in the political
> order and is one of the rights which are envisaged in Article 2; it is
> expressly saved by Article 3 which states the area to which the laws
> enacted by the parliament established by the Constitution apply."

These views, however, are no longer authoritative; they were expressly disavowed by Finlay C.J., speaking for the Supreme Court, in *McGimpsey* v. *Ireland* [1990] 1 I.R. 110. The Chief Justice said that Articles 2 and 3 must be
read together with the Preamble, and he was satisfied that the true constitutional position was as follows:

1. The reintegration of the national territory is a constitutional impera-
    tive.[8]

---

[6] In *Ellis* v. *O'Dea* [1989] I.R. 530 Walsh J. said (at 540). "Foreign diplomatic representatives
in this state cannot be accredited to the President of "the Republic of Ireland.""

[7] See (1979) 30 N.I.L.Q. 189. 204–206.

[8] This approach strongly resembles that of the German Constitutional Court to a treaty regulating relations between the two former German states—the *Basic East-West Treaty Case*, 36
BVerfGE 1. An English translation of the judgment appears in Walter Murphy and Joseph
Tanenhaus, *Comparative Constitutional Law: Cases and Commentaries* (New York 1977), pp.
232–239.

2. Article 2 of the Constitution consists of a declaration of the extent of the national territory *as a claim of legal right.*
3. Pending the reintegration of the national territory, Article 3 of the Constitution prohibits the enactment of laws with any greater area or extent of application or extra-territorial effect that the laws of Saorstat Éireann, and this prohibits the enactment of laws applicable in the counties of Northern Ireland.
4. The restriction imposed by Article 3 pending the reintegration of the national territory in no way derogates from the claim as a legal right to the entire national territory.

The words of Article 3's second phrase—"without prejudice to the right of the Parliament and Government established by this Constitution to exercise jurisdiction over the whole of that territory"—were viewed by the Supreme Court as having an effect on the international plane. They are, as Finlay C.J. put it (at 119)

" . . . an express denial and disclaimer made to the community of nations of acquiescence to any claim that pending the reintegration of the national territory the frontier at present existing between the State and Northern Ireland is or can be accepted as conclusive or that there can be any prescriptive title thereby created and an assertion that there can be no estoppel created by the restriction in Article 3 on the application of the laws of the State in Northern Ireland."

The *McGimpsey* case involved a claim that the Anglo-Irish Agreement signed at Hillsborough on November 15, 1985[9] violated Articles 2 and 3 of the Constitution by recognising the legitimacy of the present constitutional arrangements in Northern Ireland. This argument founded in particular on Article 1 of that Agreement, which provides:

"The two Governments
  (a) affirm that any change in the status of Northern Ireland would only come about with the consent of a majority of the people of Northern Ireland;
  (b) recognise that the present wish of a majority of the people of Northern Ireland is for no change in the status of Northern Ireland;
  (c) declare that, if in the future a majority of the people of Northern Ireland clearly wish for and formally consent to the establishment of a united Ireland, they will introduce and support in the respective Parliaments legislation to give effect to that wish."

The Supreme Court was quite clear that there was no conflict between Article 1—or the rest of the Agreement—and the Constitution. Finlay C.J. said (at 120–121):

" . . . the only reasonable interpretation of Article 1, taken in conjunction with the denial of derogation from sovereignty contained in Article 2(b) of the Anglo-Irish Agreement[10] is that it constitutes a recognition of

---

[9] On which see Tom Hadden and Kevin Boyle, *The Anglo-Irish Agreement: Commentary, Text and Official Review* (London 1989).
[10] Art. 2(*b*) closes with the words: "There is no derogation from the sovereignty of either the Irish Government or the United Kingdom Government, and each retains responsibility for the decisions and administration of government within its own jurisdiction."

the *de facto* situation in Northern Ireland but does so expressly without abandoning the claim to the reintegration of the national territory. These are essential ingredients of the constitutional provisions in Articles 2 and 3.

This interpretation is not affected by the provisions of Articles 4(c) or 5(c)[11] nor are either of these two Articles capable of any separate inconsistent interpretation. In so far as they accept the concept of change in the *de facto* status of Northern Ireland as being something that would require the consent of the majority of the people of Northern Ireland these Articles of the Agreement seem to me to be compatible with the obligations undertaken by the State in Article 29.1 and 29.2 of the Constitution, whereby Ireland affirms its devotion to the ideal of peace and friendly co-operation and its adherence to the principles of the pacific settlement of international disputes."

The decision in *McGimpsey's* case thus sets at rest the doubts about the Agreement's compatibility with Articles 2 and 3 of the Constitution voiced in Dáil Éireann in November 1985 by the then leader of the Opposition.[12]

In 1967 the all-party Committee on the Constitution unanimously recommended the replacement of the present Article 3 by the following:

> "1. The Irish nation hereby proclaims its firm will that its territory be re-united in harmony and brotherly affection between all Irishmen.
> 2. The laws enacted by the Parliament established by this Constitution shall, until the achievement of the nation's unity shall otherwise require, have the like area and extent of application as the laws of the parliament which existed prior to the adoption of this Constitution. Provision may be made by law to give extra-territorial effect to such laws."[13]

But this recommendation has not been implemented and Article 3 remains as originally enacted. The divisive and damaging potential of a referendum campaign to effect change explains why successive governments have declined to contemplate this course. But it is now clear that there is considerable parliamentary support for change,[14] and an agreement on future

---

[11] Art. 4(c) of the Agreement provides: "Both Governments recognise that devolution can be achieved only with the co-operation of constitutional representatives within Northern Ireland of both traditions there. The Conference shall be a framework within which the Irish Government may put forward views and proposals on the modalities of bringing about devolution in Northern Ireland, in so far as they relate to the interests of the minority community. Art. 5(c) provides: "If it should prove impossible to achieve and sustain devolution on a basis which secures widespread acceptance in Northern Ireland, the Conference shall be a framework within which the Irish Government may, where the interests of the minority community are significantly or especially affected, put forward views on proposals for major legislation and on major policy issues, which are within the purview of the Northern Ireland Departments and which remain the responsibility of the Secretary of State for Northern Ireland."

[12] See 361 *Dáil Debs.*, cc. 2581 ff (Mr. C. J. Haughey).

[13] *Report* (Pr. 9817), pp. 5–6.

[14] In December 1990 a Workers' Party Bill to amend Articles 2 and 3 was defeated in Dáil Éireann by 74 votes to 66. But the Government's objections to the Bill stressed that it was premature in the light of current regotiations; see the speech of the Taoiseach, Mr. Haughey, at 403 *Dáil Debs.*, cc. 1307–1319. And the Progressive Democrats' leader, Mr. O'Malley (the Minister for Industry and Commerce) supported change, but only in the context of more general constitutional reform; 403 Dáil Debs., cc. 2288–2295.

governmental structures in Northern Ireland—acceptable to both communities there—might well set the scene for it.

Extent of application of laws

Article 3 concludes by providing that laws enacted by the Oireachtas shall have the same area and extent of application—and extra-territorial operation—as the laws of Saorstát Éireann. Hence these laws primarily apply to "the area now known as the Republic of Ireland": *Re Article 26 and the Criminal Law (Jurisdiction) Bill 1975* [1977] I.R. 129, 148. In that case the Supreme Court held that Saorstát Éireann had full power to legislate with extra-territorial effect from its inception. The court pointed out that international law conceded every sovereign state power to legislate with extra-territorial effect, in the sense that it could enact that acts or omissions occurring outside its borders constituted criminal offences which could be prosecuted inside those borders—provided that the offences thus created bore upon the peace, order and good government of the legislating state: the *Lotus* case (1927) P.C.I.J. Ser. A, No. 10.[15]

A recent example of the use of this power is founded in the Dumping at Sea Act 1981, s.2 of which penalises certain conduct outside the State's territorial seas by Irish vessels, aircraft or marine structures. But the principal consequence of the doctrine is that it is competent for the Oireachtas to legislate in respect of matters occurring in Northern Ireland. It has done so by providing that certain acts committed in Northern Ireland constitute criminal offences triable in the Republic: Criminal Law (Jurisdiction) Act 1976.

Although the Supreme Court, in *McGimpsey* v. *Ireland* [1990] 1 I.R. 110, described Article 3 of the Constitution as prohibiting "the enactment of laws applicable in the counties of Northern Ireland" (at 119), this does not cast doubt upon the validity of the 1976 Act. For the court distinguished that prohibition from "the extraterritorial effect of the laws of the State in respect of matters occurring outside the State for which persons are made answerable in the courts of the State" (*ibid.*). Nonetheless, the Supreme Court's observations have clearly opened up the possibility that some statutes may be invalid as being "applicable in the counties of Northern Ireland". It is not easy to identify those provisions which may be vulnerable in this way. Under the present law, for example, graduates of certain universities who are resident in Northern Ireland may vote (by post) in Seanad elections.[16] This would not seem to be tainted by invalidity, for the laws of Saorstát Éireann had a similar application.[17] And the provisions of the nationality law confer-

---

[15] The international law principles of the sovereignty and equality of states would have prevented the Oireachtas established under the 1992 Constitution from legislating for matters within the exclusive jurisdiction of other states. Thus it could not have legislated to establish a statutory corporation in another state and to confer on it powers, duties and functions: *Do negal Fuel & Supply Co. Ltd.* v. *Londonderry Port & Harbour Commrs.* (High Court, Costello J., May 6, 1992.)

[16] See further Chap. 4 *infra S.* v. *Seanad Éireann.*

[17] Under the Electoral Act 1923 citizens who were Dublin University or National University graduates were entitled to be registered in the relevant university constituency (s.1(2)(*c*)), and voting was by post (s.21(2)). Those universities, it may be noted, were then represented in the Dáil.

ring Irish citizenship upon persons resident in Northern Ireland[18] would appear to be proof against challenge for the same reason.[19]

In *State (Devine)* v. *Larkin* [1977] I.R. 24 the prosecutors sought to have quashed certain convictions under the Foyle Fisheries Act 1952 and regulations made thereunder in 1966. Some of these convictions were in respect of acts done in Co. Donegal, others in respect of acts done in Co. Derry. The prosecutors argued that Article 3 limited the power of the Oireachtas to enact laws having extra-territorial effect; its reference to "the laws of Saorstát Éireann" meant laws in force when the 1937 Constitution was enacted. Since there was then no Saorstát Éireann legislation corresponding to the 1952 Act, it was contended, the Oireachtas could not give the 1952 Act an extra-territorial effect. McMahon J. rejected this argument, saying that it would be a strange anomaly if the sovereign independent State constituted in 1937 did not have as ample a power of making law as its predecessor. No reason had been suggested for limiting the State's power by reference to Saorstát Éireann's use of its power to make laws having extra-territorial effect. Mc-Mahon J. concluded that Article 3 meant that laws enacted by the Oireachtas should have the same extra-territorial effect as the laws of Saorstát Éireann were *capable of having*.

It was further argued in *Devine's* case that section 13 of the Foyle Fisheries Act contravened Article 15 of the Constitution, as an invalid delegation of legislative power. Section 13 empowered the Foyle Fisheries Commission (established by the Act) to make regulations applicable to the fisheries of the Foyle area—part of which is in Derry and part in Donegal. Any such regulations required the approval of the Minister for Lands and the Northern Ireland Ministry of Commerce. The contention was that the Oireachtas could not entrust legislative power to a body while submitting the exercise of that power to control by an authority not subject to the laws of the State. Mc-Mahon J. could not accept this ([1977] I.R. 24, 30):

> "If power to make regulations can validly be delegated to one authority, I see no reason why power cannot validly be delegated to another authority, having a legitimate interest in the matter, to disallow regulations of which it does not approve; the question whether the approving authority is or is not subject to our laws seems of no materiality."

However, McMahon J. held certain regulations made in 1966 invalid. These had been made with the approval of the Northern Ireland Ministry of Agriculture, to which the Foyle fishery functions of the Commerce Ministry had been transferred by virtue of a statutory instrument made under a United Kingdom statute. This, McMahon J. held, was insufficient to validate the 1966 regulations. That would require a statutory transfer of the approving power from the Northern Ireland Ministry of Commerce to the

---

[18] The Irish Nationality and Citizenship Act 1956, s.6(1), declares that "every person born in Ireland is an Irish citizen from birth". "Ireland" is defined in s.2 to mean "the national territory as defined in Article 2 of the Constitution."

[19] The Irish Nationality and Citizenship Act 1935 provided, in s.2, that all persons born outside Saorstát Éireann on or after December 6, 1922 whose fathers were Saorstát citizens should be "natural-born citizens of Saorstát Éireann." On one view, Article 3 of the 1922 Constitution made everyone domiciled in Ireland—as a whole—on December 6, 1922 a Saorstát citizen (see the Circuit Court decision in *Re Logue* (1933) 67 I.L.T.R. 253). Thus many people born in Northern Ireland after December 6, 1922 would automatically have qualified for citizenship.

Northern Ireland Ministry of Agriculture by an Act of the Oireachtas. A statutory requirement under the law of the State could not be altered or dispensed with by a law having effect in Northern Ireland only. It could be altered only by legislation having the force of law in the State.[20]

Meaning of "Northern Ireland"

State (*Gilsenan*) v. *McMorrow* [1978] I.R. 360 concerned an application for certiorari to quash a District Court order returning the prosecutor for trial in the Circuit Court. The charges, under section 33(4) of the Larceny Act 1916, involved unlawful possession of a car "knowing the said property to have been stolen in Northern Ireland." It was argued that Northern Ireland was not a geographical area known to the law of the State; the expression could cover some of the northern parts of the area over which the State exercised jurisdiction. The Supreme Court, affirming Gannon J., dismissed this contention. Henchy J. (O'Higgins C.J., Griffin and Parke JJ. concurring) said ([1978] I.R. 300, 370–371):

> "It is true that since 1937 there has been no general statutory interpretation or adaptation of the expression 'Northern Ireland,' but the frequency with which it occurs in our statutes, the unambiguous way in which it has been so used to identify the six counties over which this State does not exercise jurisdiction, and the clear intention of the legislature in such use that the Courts of this State should give judicial recognition to the identity of the territory comprehended by the expression (apart from any other considerations) would make it impossible for our courts to say that 'Northern Ireland' is other than an officially-recognised and clear appellation for the part of this island which has remained within the United Kingdom of Great Britain and Northern Ireland."

Henchy J. went on to point out that the Criminal Law (Jurisdiction) Act 1976—"an Act to extend the criminal law of the State to certain acts done in Northern Ireland"—did not define Northern Ireland. The courts, he said, were bound to take judicial notice of the expression "Northern Ireland" as connoting the part of the island which was outside the functional jurisdiction of the State. Kenny J., who reached a similar conclusion, pointed out that in the Treaty (Confirmation of Amending Agreement) Act 1925 the Oireachtas confirmed an agreement between the Governments which styled themselves as those of Great Britain, the Irish Free State, and Northern Ireland. Clause 1 of that agreement provided that the extent of Northern Ireland for the purposes of the Government of Ireland Act 1920, and of the Anglo-Irish Treaty, should be such as was fixed by section 1(2) of the 1920 Act. This provided that Northern Ireland was to consist of "the parliamentary counties of Antrim, Armagh, Down, Fermanagh, Londonderry and Tyrone and the par-

---

[20] Such legislation was passed in the wake of the *Devine* case: see the Foyle Fisheries (Amendment) Act 1976. This contains an expanded, and adaptable, definition of the appropriate Northern Ireland authority. S.2(2) makes the Act retrospective to March 1, 1962, but a proviso (obviously inspired by Article 15.5 of the Constitution) adds that "nothing in this Act shall have the effect of making or declaring any acts to be unlawful which were not unlawful at the time of their commission."

liamentary boroughs of Belfast and Londonderry." Thus, said Kenny J., the State had recognised the legal existence of Northern Ireland and had fixed its boundaries for the purposes of legislation.

The territorial sea and the continental shelf

Article 2, it will be recalled, provides that the national territory consists of the whole island of Ireland, its islands and the territorial seas. In relation to the latter, one must bear in mind Article 29.3—"Ireland accepts the generally recognised principles of international law as its rule of conduct in its relations with other States." It is those principles of international law that define a State's rights over marine areas.

The Maritime Jurisdiction Acts 1959 to 1988 specify the territorial sea as the portion of the sea 12 nautical miles from the nearest point of "the baseline." The latter is defined as the low-water mark on the coast of the mainland or any island, or on any low-tide elevation not more than 12 nautical miles from the mainland or an island. Section 4(2) of the 1959 Act empowers the Government to make orders prescribing straight baselines in relation to any part of the national territory and the closing line of any bay or mouth of a river. This has duly been done by the Maritime Jurisdiction (Straight Baselines) Order 1959, (S.I. 1959 No. 173). The map annexed to this order shows that full advantage has been taken of the Act's provisions. There are straight baselines, sometimes running from the coast to a low-tide elevation such as a rock, all along the south and west coasts. Thus, for example, a straight line runs across the Shannon Estuary from Loop Head to Kerry Head and, on the south coast, from Ballycotton Island to the Old Head of Kinsale. These straight baselines have the effect that *e.g.* all waters from the Aran Islands to Galway constitute internal waters; so do those of Bantry Bay, Dingle Bay and the Kenmare River—and a considerable stretch of sea beyond them.

These legislative provisions are entirely in accordance with international law, which permits a territorial sea of up to 12 miles, and has rules about baselines which the 1959 Act reproduced.[21]

Under international law states enjoy sovereign rights over their territorial seas, save that foreign ships have a right of "innocent passage" through them. Over internal waters a state's sovereignty is complete. The Maritime Jurisdiction Act 1959, s.5, provides that the State's internal waters extend to all sea areas lying on the landward side of the territorial sea's baseline. The State is declared to have jurisdiction over those areas to the same extent as over its ports and harbours, bays, lakes and rivers. This, however, is stated in the section to be " . . . subject to any right of innocent passage for foreign ships in those sea areas which previously had been considered as part of the territorial seas or of the high seas." This too reproduces the dispositions of international law.[22]

A particular problem arises in regard to the territorial waters around Northern Ireland. These are claimed by the State, on the basis that the Northern Ireland which opted out of the Irish Free State under the Treaty was the Northern Ireland defined in the Government of Ireland Act 1920.

[21] See R. R. Churchill and A. V. Lowe, *The Law of the Sea* (Manchester 1983), Chaps. 2–4.
[22] *Ibid.*, Chap. 3.

That referred to the named counties and county boroughs; but under British and Irish law counties did not include the adjacent territorial sea (this proposition is supported by two Supreme Court decisions—*Smyth* v. *Dun Laoghaire Corporation* (1960) Ir.Jur.Rep. 45 and *Brown* v. *Donegal Co. Council* [1980] I.R. 132). Consequently, it is contended, the Irish Free State retained those waters when Northern Ireland opted out. The Taoiseach, Mr. Lynch, so informed the *Dáil* on February 29, 1972,[23] and this was repeated by the Minister for Foreign Affairs, Mr. Lenihan, on March 3, 1981. The Minister added that Ireland still claimed those waters, though it was aware of a British counter-contention. The question, said the Minister, was not a legal but fundamentally a political one, which required a political solution.[24]

The argument outlined above was considered, but rejected, by the Northern Ireland Court of Appeal in *D.P.P.* v. *McNeill* [1975] N.I. 177. The court—Lowry L.C.J., Curran and Jones L.JJ.—observed that in 1964 the United Kingdom Parliament had passed the Fishery Limits Act in order to give effect to the European Fisheries Convention 1964. Both Ireland and the United Kingdom were parties to this convention, and the court inferred from its terms that there could be no overlapping of states in regard to the waters adjacent to the coasts of Northern Ireland—those coasts being, by the terms of the convention, part of the coasts of the United Kingdom ([1975] N.I. 177, 182, 191.) Moreover, on the proper construction of the Government of Ireland Act 1920 and other relevant enactments, the proposition that the coastal waters of Northern Ireland remained within the jurisdiction of the Irish Free State was unsustainable.

Even if that view is correct,[25] there remains the problem of Carlingford Lough and Lough Foyle, both of which straddle the boundary between Northern Ireland and the Republic. The United Kingdom, it seems, has laid claim to the entire waters of each estuary; when on patrol its naval vessels do not observe a median line between the shores. This claim is not conceded by Ireland, whose vessels began patrolling Carlingford Lough on a similar basis in September 1982: see *The Irish Times*, October 14, 1982.

The Continental Shelf Act 1968 does not incorporate provisions of international law, but it clearly assumes their existence and provides the means of taking advantage of them. The Act, in section 2(1), vests in the Minister for Energy "Any rights of the State outside territorial waters over the sea bed and subsoil for the purpose of exploring such sea bed and subsoil and exploiting their resources . . . " Section 2(3) permits the Government to make orders designating the areas within which these rights are exercisable. Plainly the rights in question are those recognised under international law, which currently admits such rights over an area from the seaward limit of the territorial sea to the point where the depth of the superjacent waters permits the exploitation of natural resources. The latter includes oil, gas and gravel. As the 1968 Act accepts, the rights in question are purely those of exploration and exploitation; the continental shelf does not form part of a coastal state's

---

[23] 259 *Dáil Debs.*, cc. 674–76.

[24] 328 *Dáil Debs.*, c. 475.

[25] For conflicting views on this point, see C. R. Symmons, "Who Owns the Territorial Waters of Northern Ireland?" (1976) 27 N.I.L.Q. 48, who concludes that it is correct, and Thomas Towey 'Who Owns the Territorial Waters of Northern Ireland? The *McNeill* Case: Another View" (1983) 32 I.C.L.Q. 1013, who concludes that it is wrong.

territory.[26] However, the rights recognised are sovereign and exclusive, and it is therefore for Irish law to define the conditions under which exploitation is to be permitted.[27]

Difficulties over the delimitation of the continental shelf between Ireland and the United Kingdom have been resolved, in part, by an agreement of November 7, 1988. This is confined to the continental shelf in the Irish Sea south and south-west of Ireland, and to that in the north-west off the Donegal coast.[28] The agreement, which was approved by Dáil Éireann on November 29, 1988,[29] does *not* deal with Northern Ireland or the maritime zones off its coast.[30] Nor does it apply to the Rockall rock, over which the United Kingdom claims sovereignty and—in addition—a 200 mile exclusive fishery zone measured from that rock. Successive Irish governments have rejected both claims,[31] as they have rejected Danish and Icelandic claims to areas of the Rockall plateau falling within the Irish continental shelf and now undisputed by the United Kingdom.[32]

The exclusive fishery limits of the State exhibit another interaction between international and domestic law. Under the Maritime Jurisdiction Act 1959 these comprised simply the territorial sea, but the 1964 amending Act extended them to 12 miles from the territorial sea baselines. Section 6(2) of the 1964 Act, however, empowered the Government to designate a wider area, and this was done by the Maritime Jurisdiction (Exclusive Fishery Limits) Order 1976 (S.I. 1976 No. 320). This provides that the State's exclusive fishery limits shall include, in addition to the sea areas specified in section 6(1) of the Maritime Jurisdiction Act 1959, "all sea areas between those areas and the line every point of which is at a distance of 200 nautical miles from the nearest point of the baseline." It goes on to make special provision for cases where these limits are inapplicable because of the proximity of the exclusive fishery limits of another state.

These exclusive fishery limits are subject to the Common Fisheries Policy enshrined in European Community law. The Court of Justice has held that the Community controls in principle the questions of access to, and conservation measures in, Community waters.[33] Under the present regime member states are allowed to restrict access to waters in their coastal zones—*i.e.* 12 nautical miles from the relevant baseline. This system will remain in force until December 31, 1992.[34] Conservation measures decreed by the Community include the creation of prohibited or restricted zones, restrictions on

[26] Note, however, that under s.10 of the Customs and Excise (Miscellaneous Provisions) Act 1988, goods grown, produced or manufactured in a continental shelf area are deemed, for customs and excise purposes, to have been grown, produced or manufactured in the State and not to have been imported.
[27] See Churchill and Lowe, *op. cit.*, Chap. 8 and Edward Donelan, *Energy and Mineral Resources in Ireland* (Dublin 1984).
[28] The areas are designated in the Continental Shelf (Designated Areas) Order, 1989 (S.I. No. 141 of 1989).
[29] See 384 *Dáil Debs.*, cc. 2167–2215.
[30] See the statement of the Minister for Foreign Affairs (Mr. Lenihan), 384 *Dáil Debs.*, c. 2177.
[31] See the statement of the Minister for Foreign Affairs (Mr. Lenihan), 384 *Dáil Debs.*, cc. 2174–2175.
[32] 384 *Dáil Debs.*, c. 2211 (Minister of State at the Department of Foreign Affairs, Mr. Calleary).
[33] Case 804/79, *Commission* v. *United Kingdom* [1981] E.C.R. 1045: Case 61/77, *Commission* v. *Ireland* [1978] E.C.R. 417.
[34] EC Regulation 170/83.

the kind of vessels or fishing gear that may be used, and limits on catches.[35] The Community also controls access to Community waters by fishermen from non-member states.[36]

POSITION OF THE STATE IN LAW

Liability in tort

As noted above, the cases of *Comyn* v. *Att. Gen.* [1950] I.R. 142 and *Commissioner of Public Works* v. *Kavanagh* [1962] I.R. 216 establish that the State is a legal person separate and distinct from the citizens—just as a company is a legal entity separate and distinct from its shareholders. So the State can hold property and can sue and be sued. But the full impact of this doctrine was felt only with the Supreme Court's historic decision in *Byrne* v. *Ireland* [1972] I.R. 241. Before this it was commonly believed that the State had inherited the Crown's common law immunity from liability for its employees' torts—so that it was not liable for such torts even where an ordinary employer would be. Indeed the Oireachtas acted on this belief when it made the Minister for Finance legally answerable for the negligent driving of State-owned vehicles; originally Road Traffic Act 1933, s.170, now Civil Liability Act 1961, s.59. This was obviously done on the basis of grafting an exception on to an existing rule.

But *Byrne* v. *Ireland* rejected this thesis. In that case the plaintiff was injured when a public footpath subsided. She claimed that the subsidence was caused by the negligent filling in of a trench by Department of Posts and Telegraphs workmen; that their ultimate employer was the State—"Ireland"—and that it was legally answerable for their fault. Among the arguments put for the defence was that the Constitution, by its declaration in Article 5 that Ireland is a sovereign state, refuted the plaintiff's contention: for a sovereign state could not be subject to the process of its own courts. Stress was laid on the fact that the United States had enjoyed this immunity—despite a written constitution—until it was modified by the Federal Tort Claims Act 1946: and on the fact that in Commonwealth countries such a liability had been imposed by statute.

The Supreme Court held that the State *was* liable for the torts of its employees, and that it could be sued as "Ireland," with the Attorney General joined as the State's legal representative. The declaration as to sovereignty in Article 5, said the court, meant only that the State was not amenable to any external authority for its conduct. The Constitution unmistakably made the people—not the State—the paramount authority, and this was inconsistent with any internal State sovereignty. The court (*per* Walsh J., [1972] I.R. 241, 267–269) also showed, with a wealth of comparative reference, that the immunity claimed was not a necessary attribute of sovereignty, for many unquestionably sovereign states enjoyed no such immunity. Finally, the notion that the State had inherited any common law immunity of the Crown was firmly rejected. The whole tenor of the Constitution negatived any such implication, especially since it had specifically provided for immunity from

---

[35] EC Regulations 170–172/83. [1983] O.J. L24/1, 14, 31.
[36] See further Bryan McMahon and Finbarr Murphy, *European Community Law in Ireland* (Dublin 1989), Chap. 24.

suit for the President (Art. 13.8.1°) and, in a limited sphere, for Oireachtas members (Art. 15.13). Budd J. observed ([1972] I.R. 241, 298):

" . . . one ought to approach the whole question as to the existence in the Constitution of an immunity from suit, be it based upon the sovereignty of the State or otherwise, as if it was something which one should be surprised to find in a modern constitution of a modern State."

While *Byrne's* case establishes the principle that the State may be liable in tort, it necessarily leaves many matters for future resolution.[37] In that instance its liability was vicarious, but presumably in an appropriate case a direct liability could attach so that, for example, the State could be held liable under the rule in *Rylands* v. *Fletcher* (1868) L.R. 3 H.L. 330. It may be anticipated that the State will be liable where a private individual or company would be; but its liability could well extend beyond this. For the State may injure persons in ways not open to private individuals or companies. As Professor Hogg puts it[38]:

"Many of the activities of government which occasionally cause unjustified damage to individuals have no analogy in the private sector; the private citizen does not keep an army, a police force, a post office, courts, gaols or schools: nor does he issue licences, patents and trade marks, or inspect factories, or collect taxes and customs duties—to name just a few of the myriad activities of government."

It may therefore be necessary to go beyond the categories of private law and create a new "public law of torts." The practical implementation of the guarantee in Article 40.3 of the Constitution to vindicate the citizen's personal rights might be thought to require such a development.

The Supreme Court's decision in *Meskell* v. *C.I.E.* [1973] I.R. 121 emphasised that an infringement of a constitutionally guaranteed right could sound in damages even if it did not fit into any of the existing forms of action. The later decision in *Garvey* v. *Ireland* [1981] I.R. 75 shows that there is an implied constitutional right to basic fairness of procedures in decision-making. It would follow that damages may be awarded where a decision is made in violation of such fairness, as was done in *Moran* v. *Att. Gen.* [1976] I.R. 400. This is, of course, a departure from the traditional common law view that a breach of natural justice may result in the annulment of a decision but does not sound in damages, and it illustrates how the imperatives of the Constitution may require reconsideration of existing doctrines. But judicial attachment to such doctrines and unwillingness to see the Constitution as a source of new ones is manifested by the Supreme Court's decision in *Pine Valley Developments Ltd.* v. *Minister for the Environment* [1987] I.R. 23. The case involved lands in Co. Dublin purchased by the plaintiff company in November 1978. These lands—originally agricultural—had the benefit of outline planning permission for industrial buildings granted by the defendant, on appeal from the planning authority's refusal, in March 1977. In February 1982, however, the Supreme Court held that the Minister's decision of March 1977 was *ultra vires* and a nullity: *State (Pine Valley Developments Ltd.)* v. *Dublin Co. Council* [1984] I.R. 407. Thus the plaintiff company found itself owning land which could

---

[37] See W. N. Osborough "The State's Tortious Liability: Further Reflections on *Byrne* v. *Ireland*" (1976) *XI Irish Jurist* (N.S.) 11.
[38] *The Liability of the Crown* (Melbourne 1971), p. 77.

now only be used for agricultural purposes (no further planning application was possible) and would consequently fetch much less than the price paid for it. The plaintiff company sought damages for the loss thus incurred but the Supreme Court held that no liability arose, either at common law or under the Constitution. Finlay C.J. (Griffin and Hederman JJ. agreeing) said that since the Minister had exercised his power in good faith, having obtained and followed the legal advice of the permanent legal advisers attached to his Department, liability could not arise simply because that advice was subsequently shown to be incorrect. Nor was there any unjust attack on property rights so as to ground a claim for damages for breach of constitutional rights. The guarantee of Article 40.3 was a qualified one and the common good could reasonably be regarded as requiring an immunity from liability in situations such as this where a decision had been made *bona fide* and without negligence. Henchy and Lardner JJ. gave judgment to similar effect. (See further Chap. 18, *infra*.)

The *Pine Valley* decision's caution and fidelity to traditional thought patterns is disappointing; for if the law on State liability is to be re-cast this must be done by the courts, the Oireachtas being most unlikely to move in this area. It seems strange that private individuals can sustain loss, *via* State action and through no fault of theirs, but receive no compensation. Courts in other jurisdictions have not been so conservative—the French *Conseil d'Etat* has long recognised State liability in damages for *ultra vires* acts.[39] It is to be hoped that should the Irish courts have a chance to re-think these matters they will have the benefit of the valuable guidance that the French decisions can afford.[40]

Immunity from liability

Byrne v. *Ireland* does not resolve the question whether statute can exempt the State from liability, either generally or in particular circumstances. While there has been no attempt at a statutory reversal of the *Byrne* decision, at least one subsequent provision has conferred a wide-ranging immunity on a State agency. The Postal and Telecommunications Act 1983 provides for the establishment of two companies—An Post and Bord Telecom Éireann—to take over functions previously discharged by the Department of Posts and Telegraphs. Section 64 of the Act provides that An Post (which is granted a statutory monopoly under s.63)

> "shall be immune from all liability in respect of any loss or damage suffered by a person in the use of a postal service by reason of—
> (a) failure or delay in providing, operating or maintaining a postal service,
> (b) failure, interruption, suspension or restriction of a postal service."

By virtue of section 64(2) the company's staff are immune from civil liability

---

[39] See L. Neville Brown and J. F. Garner, *French Administrative Law* (3rd ed., London 1983), pp. 113–125; M. Long, P. Weil and G. Braibant, *Les Grands Arrêts de la Jurisprudence Administrative* (8th ed., Paris 1984) s.v. *Responsabilité*; and Carol Harlow's fine comparative study *Compensation and Government Torts* (London 1982).

[40] See further Bryan McMahon and William Binchy, *The Irish Law of Torts* (2nd ed., Dublin 1990), Chap. 38.

in respect of the same matters, save at the suit of the company. A similar type of immunity is conferred by section 88 on Bord Telecom Éireann and its staff.

The Supreme Court refused to recognise a supposed State immunity from liability in *Ryan* v. *Ireland* [1989] I.R. 177. The plaintiff, an Irish soldier serving with the United Nations contingent in Lebanon, was injured while on sentry duty when hostile forces launched a mortar attack on the camp. He alleged that his superior, an Irish officer, had negligently exposed him to unnecessary risk, and sued the State for damages. Defence counsel, invoking foreign authorities,[41] argued that the State was not liable for injury to Defence Forces personnel caused by negligence during armed conflict or in a theatre of war. The Supreme Court rejected this contention, Finlay C.J., for the court, saying (at 182–183):

> "I . . . conclude that an immunity from suit by, or the negation of any duty of care to, a serving soldier in respect of operations consisting of armed conflict or hostilities has not been established as part of our common law. Even if it had, I conclude that in the blanket form which has been contended for it would be inconsistent with the guarantees by the State to respect, defend and vindicate the rights of the citizens contained in Article 40, s.3, sub-ss. 1 and 2 of the Constitution."

It may be, however, that legislation could be passed to provide for such an immunity "in time of war or armed rebellion", as defined in Article 28.3.3° of the Constitution. For that Article seems to permit the passage of legislation overriding *all* constitutional guarantees.[42]

Treasure trove

One consequence of the decision in *Byrne* v. *Ireland* became manifest in *Webb* v. *Ireland* [1988] I.R. 353. The plaintiffs there were the finders of the celebrated Derrynaflan hoard (a 9th century chalice, paten, strainer and basin) and they sought to recover possession thereof from the State, on whose behalf it was held by the National Museum. The plaintiffs had found the objects, using metal detectors, on land owned by other persons which had been statutorily designated as a national monument. The hoard had been handed over to the National Museum by the plaintiffs pending determination of the legal ownership thereof, and subject to any rights to payment or reward the plaintiffs might have. Eventually the State offered the plaintiffs an award of £10,000, but since the hoard's minimum value was estimated at £2½ million the plaintiffs not surprisingly refused to accept this and sued for the hoard's return. It was argued for the State that the articles were treasure trove and thus State property. Founding on *Byrne* v. *Ireland*, counsel for the plaintiffs contended that treasure trove was not part of Irish law; that the right thereto was part of the Crown's prerogative and was not carried over by the 1922 Constitution. This was accepted by the High Court (Blayney J.) and the Supreme Court on appeal. Finlay C.J. (Henchy and Griffin JJ. concurring) said (at 382):

---

[41] *Dawkins* v. *Lord Paulet* (1869) L.R. 5 Q.B. 94: *Wilson* v. *First Edinburgh City Royal Garrison Artillery Volunteers* (1904) 7 F. 168: *Shaw Savill and Albion Co. Ltd.* v. *Cwth* (1940) 66 C.L.R. 344: *Parker* v. *Cwth* (1965) 112 C.L.R. 295: *Feres* v. *U.S.* (1950) 340 *U.S.* 135. See further Peter Hogg, *The Liability of the Crown* (Melbourne 1971), pp. 78–79, 96–98.

[42] See further Chap. 7 *infra*.

"I agree with the view reached by the learned trial judge in this case that on the authority of *Byrne* v. *Ireland* [1972] I.R. 241 no royal prerogative in existence prior to the enactment of the Constitution of 1922 was by virtue of the provisions of that Constitution vested in the Irish Free State. I agree with the judgment of Walsh J. in *Byrne* v. *Ireland* which was expressly concurred in by a majority of the Court that the provisions of Article 2 of the Constitution of 1922 declaring the Irish Free State to be a sovereign State and the provisions of Article 51 of the same Constitution expressly vesting in the King certain executive functions, being the executive functions of the Irish Free State, are inconsistent with the transference to that State of any royal prerogative. As is also set out in the decision in *Byrne* v. *Ireland*, it must follow from this conclusion that the royal prerogatives were not prerogatives exercisable in Saorstát Éireann immediately before December 11, 1936, and were therefore not captured by Article 49, s.1 of the Constitution.

It was contended on this appeal that it was possible to distinguish between a prerogative of immunity from suit, which was the subject matter of the decision in *Byrne* v. *Ireland* [1972] I.R. 241 and which could be traced to the royal dignity of the King and a prerogative of treasure trove which it was stated could be traced or related not to the dignity of his person but to his position as sovereign or ruler. Such a distinction does not alter the view which I have expressed with regard to the effect of the provisions of the Constitution of 1922, and appears to me to ignore the essential point which is that by virtue of the provisions of the Constitution of 1922 what was being created was a brand new sovereign State and that the function, power or position of the King in that sovereign State was such only as was vested in him by that Constitution and by the State created by it."

Walsh and McCarthy JJ., in their separate judgments, expressly agreed with these conclusions (at 387 and 397–398).

But the Supreme Court, having demolished the State's claim to succeed to a royal prerogative of treasure trove, recognised a republican claim with similar characteristics. Finlay C.J.'s analysis of this matter—which again was accepted by all his colleagues—began by citing the declaration in Article 5 of the Constitution that Ireland is a sovereign state. He continued (p. 383):

"It would, I think, now be universally accepted, certainly by the People of Ireland, and by the people of most modern states, that one of the most important national assets belonging to the people is their heritage and knowledge of its true origins and the buildings and objects which constitute keys to their ancient history. If this be so, then it would appear to me to follow that a necessary ingredient of sovereignty in a modern state and certainly in this State, having regard to the terms of the Constitution, with an emphasis on its historical origins and a constant concern for the common good is and should be an ownership by the State of objects which constitute antiquities of importance which are discovered and which have no known owner. It would appear to me to be inconsistent with the framework of the society sought to be created and sought to be protected by the Constitution that such objects should become the exclusive property of those who by chance may find them.

The existence of such a general ingredient of the sovereignty of the

State, does, however, seem to me to lead to the conclusion that the much more limited right of the prerogative of treasure trove known to the common law should be upheld not as a right derived from the Crown but rather as an inherent attribute of the sovereignty of the State which was recognised and declared by Article 11 of the 1922 Constitution.

For the purpose of determining the issues in this case, therefore, I would conclude that there does exist in the State a right or prerogative of treasure trove, the characteristics of which are the characteristics of the prerogative of treasure trove at common law which I have already outlined in this judgment as they stood in 1922."[43]

At the minimum, then, the State is entitled to the ownership of certain valuable chattels, concealed by someone unknown for their protection and with the intention of subsequently recovering them. This right is superior to that of the relevant landowner, or the finder, and probably[44] does not involve an obligation to pay compensation or any kind of reward. It may be, however, that it extends only to objects made of silver or gold, or a combination thereof, or of the alloy containing a substantial amount of either or both.[45]

Though the Supreme Court disclaimed any competence to frame legislative policy in this area, the *Webb* decision is remarkable for the terms of its invitation to the Oireachtas to regulate this matter by statute. Finlay C.J. said (at 386–387):

"I do not intend to imply by anything contained in this judgment that the right or prerogative of treasure trove which I find to be vested in the State may not be enlarged or varied by legislation.

Indeed, the circumstances of this case may be thought to point to the necessity for such legislation. The right to treasure trove . . . is but an outmoded remnant of the mediaeval prerogatives which were vested at common law in the monarch. As such, its characteristics which restrict the nature of the articles to which it applies; the circumstances to be inferred as to the hiding or concealment of those objects and the vagueness as to the respective rights of the State and the finder may indicate that a variation and extension of the State's rights in regard to ownerless articles of national importance which have been found may be called for.

It may be thought proper, for instance, to provide that all (or specified kinds of) articles or items of archaeological, historical, antiquarian or cultural value or interest should, when apparently ownerless, on being discovered or brought to light be deemed to vest in the State subject to the claim if established of the true owner. Such a provision might

---

[43] Professor J. M. Kelly has doubted the major premiss of the Supreme Court's reasoning—that the Irish Free State, as established in 1922, was sovereign. See his article "Hidden Treasure and the Constitution" (1988) 10 D.U.L.J. 5

[44] The judgment is not entirely clear on this point. Finlay C.J., in considering the characteristics of common law treasure trove, indicated (at 382) that there was no legally enforceable right to a reward. Later, however, he said that it was not necessary to rule on the plaintiff's submission that such a right existed (at 385). This was because the circumstances created in the plaintiffs a legitimate expectation of a reward, which the State could not be permitted to defeat.

[45] Walsh J. took a broader view. He said (at 393): "I see no reason why it should be confined to such items as fall within the definition of treasure trove under the former law. In this country this definition would be of little benefit as so many of our antiquities in chattel form are not

well abolish both any distinction between objects made of different materials and any request for evidence that the objects had been hidden for safe keeping. In ordinary cases it would probably be desirable to have a system of reward so as to encourage finders to deliver up articles or items so found. It may be thought proper that any such system of reward should be counterbalanced by penalties applicable to improper excavation of such articles or to their concealment when found."

Fresh legislation has been promised[46] but none has so far been enacted. However, the National Monuments (Amendment) Act 1987 (passed after the High Court judgment in the *Webb* case) has strengthened the legal protection of heritage material. *Inter alia*, it restricts the use of metal detectors (s.2), protects the sites of historic wrecks (s.3), obliges the finder of an archaeological object to report its finding (s.15) and considerably increases the penalties attached to offences under the National Monuments Act 1930 to 1987.

Liability in contract

The State could not claim an immunity from liability in contract by inheritance from the Crown, for no such immunity existed. Indeed legislation simplified the procedure for suing the State, since a contract made by a Department could be enforced by action against the appropriate Minister; Ministers and Secretaries Act 1924, s.2(1). (The Attorney General's *fiat* was made a condition precedent to any such suit, but this was struck down as unconstitutional in *Macauley* v. *Minister for Posts and Telegraphs* [1966] I.R. 345.)[47]

In *Kenny* v. *Cosgrave* [1926] I.R. 517 the plaintiff, a building contractor, sued the defendant—the President of the Executive Council—in highly unusual circumstances. The plaintiff was engaged on a long-term contract to build houses when, in June 1924, an inter-union dispute arose among his employees and a strike resulted. President Cosgrave told the plaintiff it was vital that there be no compromise with the strikers, and allegedly represented to him that he would be indemnified by the Executive Council for any loss he sustained through resisting the strikers' demands. On the strength of this, the plaintiff claimed, he refused to compromise, with the result that the strike was prolonged until early September 1924 and the plaintiff suffered loss amounting to £15,487. In 1925, however, the Executive Council repudiated the agreement—hence this action.

The Supreme Court, *per* Fitzgibbon J., said that if the object of the action was to make the defendant *personally* liable for a contract entered into in his public capacity, it could not succeed. An "unbroken chain of decisions" showed that this had been "unquestioned law" since 1786. (It would indeed seem that the action was against the defendant personally—otherwise, one assumes, he would have been sued in his official title as had happened in other cases. The Chief State Solicitor, it may be noted, did not act for the

---

made of either gold or silver." Professor Kelly has also suggested that the courts are "entitled to redefine the concept of treasure trove on contemporary criteria of what is valuable." (*op. cit*, at p. 16)

[46] See the remarks of the Taoiseach, Mr. Haughey, in Dáil Éireann on January 27, 1988 (377 *Dáil Debs.*, cc. 2–6).

[47] See further J. P. Casey, *The Office of the Attorney General in Ireland* (Dublin 1980), Chap. 11.

defendant.) Nor could the action succeed if it was one for breach of implied warranty of authority—*i.e.* that Cosgrave had implicitly warranted that he had authority to bind the Executive Council, and could be made personally liable for breach of that warranty. Following *Dunn* v. *MacDonald* [1897] 1 Q.B. 555, the Supreme Court held that Cosgrave could not be made personally liable on such a basis.

Dunn v. *MacDonald*, however, is an unsatisfactory decision, capable of being explained on a narrower basis than the Supreme Court accepted as its *ratio*.[48] It need not be regarded as ruling that a State servant (and even the head of the Government is such in law) can never be liable on an implied warranty of authority. Therefore if a modern Taoiseach acted as Mr. Cosgrave is alleged to have done, it cannot be assumed that he would escape personal liability—*a fortiori* given his dominant role in the public mind and his assumed ability to speak on behalf of the Government. In this regard differences between the respective constitutional positions of the President of the Executive Council and the Taoiseach may be vitally important. Indeed, it is hard to believe that a Taoiseach giving an assurance of the type claimed would find his action subsequently repudiated by the Government.

The Supreme Court gave an additional reason for holding that the defendant could not be liable. To succeed, Kenny would have had to show that Cosgrave had expressly contracted as the agent of the Executive Council *and* that had Cosgrave possessed the authority he claimed, the Executive Council would have been bound. This was on the basis that an agent could not be liable in damages for breach of warranty of authority if the contract would not have been binding on the principal. Here the alleged contract would not have been binding on the Executive Council; it could not promise to pay the plaintiff an indemnity out of public funds without the sanction of the Oireachtas, and no contract to do so would be enforceable against it [1926] I.R. 517, 527). For this proposition the Supreme Court relied upon *Churchward* v. *Reg.* (1865) L.R. 1 Q.B. 173. But the High Court of Australia held in *N.S.W.* v. *Bardolph* (1934) 52 C.L.R. 455 that *Churchward's* case was not authority for the proposition that the State could not enter into a contract involving the payment of public money without (a) statutory authority, or (b) a prior appropriation of money by parliament. The High Court said that parliamentary appropriation was necessary before a *payment* could be made under such a contract—but this did not mean that the contract was not binding before that. Thus the courts could grant a *declaration* as to the true legal position.[49]

It seems unlikely that *Kenny* v. *Cosgrave* would be followed nowadays. The doctrine there propounded is unreal and productive of inconvenience. Unreal, because given modern party discipline a parliamentary refusal to appropriate funds is exceedingly unlikely. It could occur only where the Government so wishes—and then different considerations would apply. Moreover, the 19th century practice in public finance which seems to underlie *Kenny's* case no longer fully obtains. Since 1965 the Minister for Finance has been authorised to issue out of the Central Fund, well in advance of each year's Appropriation Act, four-fifths of the sums appropriated in the preceding year: Central Fund (Permanent Provisions) Act 1965, s.2. The doctrine is

---

[48] See Hogg, *op. cit.*, pp. 140–141.
[49] See further Hogg, *op. cit.*, pp. 120–124: also Colin Turpin, *Government Contracts* (Harmondsworth 1972), pp. 25–27.

also inconvenient because if a State contract only became binding after the enactment of the Appropriation Act, then not only the State but also the other party could resile from it any time beforehand. This could plainly operate against the public interest. The possible injustice to the private contractor should the State take advantage of the supposed rule needs no emphasis; but it seems unlikely that a rule which would permit the State to escape its contractual obligations even where the other party had performed his part could stand with the general guarantee in Article 40.3 of the Constitution.

The Supreme Court in *Kenny's* case also seems to have adopted the much-criticised English High Court decision in *Rederiaktiebolaget Amphitrite* v. *The King* [1921] 3 K.B. 500. There Swedish shipowners sought damages for breach of contract, in that their ship *Amphitrite* was refused a clearance to enable her to leave Britain, despite the fact that they had been promised such a clearance. Rowlatt J. found that the British Government had undertaken that if the ship traded to Britain she would not be subjected to "the delays which were sometimes imposed." But he held that there was no enforceable contract: ([1921] 3 K.B. 500, 503):

> "No doubt the Government can bind itself through its officers by a commercial contract, and if it does so it must perform it like anybody else or pay damages for the breach. But this was not a commercial contract; it was an arrangement whereby the Government purported to give an assurance as to what its executive action would be in the future in relation to a particular ship in the event of her coming to this country. And that is, to my mind, not a contract for the breach of which damages can be sued for in a court of law. It was merely an expression of intention to act in a particular way in a certain event. My main reason for so thinking is that it is not competent for the Government to fetter its future executive action, which must necessarily be determined by the needs of the community when the question arises. It cannot by contract hamper its freedom of action in matters which concern the welfare of the State."

As Professor Hogg has shown[50] this vague doctrine goes too far. No doubt the public interest may sometimes require the State to act contrary to its contractual obligations, but if so it should pay damages for breach of contract. A liability to pay damages would not prevent the taking of such action as the public interest required. While it is true that the grant of an injunction or of specific performance might do so, both these remedies are discretionary and would scarcely be granted if the result might be to jeopardise some public interest. It seems unlikely that an Irish court would nowadays apply the reasoning in the *Amphitrite* case.

A difficulty facing would-be litigants is that an intention to create legal relations is an essential element of a contract. And the Irish courts have shown themselves unwilling to spell a contractual commitment (or an estoppel) out of a course of conduct—see *Leen* v. *President of the Executive Council* [1928] I.R. 408. In *Latchford & Sons Ltd.* v. *Minister for Industry & Commerce* [1950] I.R. 33 the plaintiff company sought certain declarations as to their entitlement to bread subsidy. This subsidy was not provided for in detail by statute, but the expenditure of certain sums on subsidies was authorised, in very general terms, by the annual Appropriation Act. Forms for claiming

---

[50] *Op. cit.*, pp. 130–131.

payment of bread subsidy were issued by the Department, accompanied by "instructions" setting out the terms of the scheme. The plaintiff company's claim for subsidy for a specific period in 1944 was disallowed because during that period it had been convicted of selling bread above the maximum price. The Supreme Court held that the Minister could not lawfully withhold the subsidy on this ground. He had not in his "instructions" reserved power to do this; and although he could change the terms thereof at any time, he could do so only with prospective effect. Until altered or withdrawn the conditions applied, and those who had complied with them were entitled to claim that they had qualified for payment of subsidy. The Supreme Court accordingly granted certain of the declarations sought; but it was emphasised that no contractual relationship existed between the company and the Minister: see [1950] I.R. 33, 40–41.[51]

The declarations granted by the Supreme Court in *Latchford's* case were (a) that the plaintiff company had fulfilled the conditions of entitlement to subsidy (b) that the defendant was not entitled to withhold his recommendation for the payment thereof. The court found it unnecessary to decide whether an order for payment might be made. In *Conroy* v. *Minister for Defence* [1934] I.R. 679 the Supreme Court, having held the plaintiff entitled to a pension under statute, granted a declaration that the defendant was bound to ask the Oireachtas to vote money for payment thereof. Similar relief could presumably be granted in a contract suit against the State, and more direct methods of enforcement may conceivably be available. In *Byrne* v. *Ireland* [1972] I.R. 241 the Supreme Court briefly turned its attention to the question of enforcing a judgment for damages in tort. Walsh J. said that an order for mandamus to compel compliance with the judgment "would be an appropriate step and not without precedent"; [1972] I.R. 241 289. Budd J. declined to worry overmuch on this score ([1972] I.R. 241, 306–307):

> "If the plaintiff is successful, in the ordinary way the damages would be assessed during the course of the trial; there would seem to be no reason to believe that the necessary moneys to meet the decree would not be voted. That would only be what would be normally expected in a State governed according to the rule of law, and there would seem to be no reason to believe that the State would not honour its legal obligations. I would need cogent evidence to be submitted to me before I should be prepared to hold the contrary view . . . It is unnecessary to come to a final decision on the ways and means of enforcing such a decree beyond remarking that *prima facie* the ordinary procedure by way of levy or enforcement by mandamus would both seem to be appropriate."

These considerations would apply equally to a decree for damages for breach of contract.[52]

---

[51] The terms of the present subsidy scheme *are* capable of creating contractual relationships; Costello J. so held in *Kylemore Bakery Ltd.* v. *Minister for Trade, Commerce and Tourism* [1986] I.L.R.M. 529. In *McKerring* v. *Minister for Agriculture* [1989] I.L.R.M. 82 O'Hanlon J. reached a similar conclusion in regard to the Bovine TB and Brucellosis Eradication Schemes instituted in 1976.

[52] The practice in awarding public contracts is set out in *An Outline of Government Contracts Procedures* (1986: Pl. 4120).

Priority of payments

At common law the Crown was entitled to priority of payments for debts owed to it; thus if the debtor's funds were insufficient to meet all claims, other creditors might be squeezed out. Initially it was assumed that the State inherited this right; but additionally section 38(2) of the Finance Act 1924 provided that moneys due or payable to or for the benefit of the Central Fund,[53] should have and be deemed always to have had attached to them "all such rights, privileges, and priorities as have heretofore attached to debts due to the Crown." However, section 38(2) was virtually abrogated by section 99 of the Finance Act 1963, which provided that it should "cease to have effect in so far as it provided that moneys due or payable to or for the benefit of the Central Fund are to be paid in priority to other debts." And its scope had earlier been limited by judicial decisions holding that it applied only to taxes and duties under the care of the Revenue Commissioners: *Re Irish Aero Club* [1939] I.R. 204: *Re P.C., an Arranging Debtor* [1939] I.R. 306: *Re Irish Employers Mutual Insurance Association Ltd.* [1955] I.R. 176 (Supreme Court). Thus, for example, charges for aircraft repairs and aerodrome licence fees, or telephone charges, did not qualify for priority.

Re Irish Employers Mutual Insurance Association Ltd. [1955] I.R. 176 concerned an insurance company which had been wound up by court order. The Commissioners of Public Works had insured with the company but were obliged, in consequence of the winding up, to meet a large number of claims for damages themselves. They now sought payment of the indemnities they would have received but for the winding up, and claimed priority over the other creditors. This claim was founded (a) on section 38(2) of the Finance Act 1924, (b) on the common law prerogative of the king, now existing for the benefit of the State. As to (a), Kingsmill Moore J., and the Supreme Court on appeal, ruled that section 38(2) did not apply to this claim. As to (b), Kingsmill Moore J., after an exhaustive analysis of the authorities, concluded that the origins of this prerogative were feudal and based on the personal pre-eminence of the king and his property. Though in modern Britain it operated to benefit the executive government, traces of its origins remained in the careful preservation of the Exchequer as a royal purse. But the Central Fund of Saorstát Éireann did not possess the characteristics of a royal exchequer, and the prerogative of priority—which depended upon this—no longer existed. On appeal, this conclusion was affirmed by Maguire C.J. and Murnaghan J.: O'Byrne and Lavery JJ. disposed of the case on another ground.[54]

Notwithstanding this, certain sums payable under statutory provisions—including taxes—are still treated as preferential. Thus, under section 81 of the Bankruptcy Act 1988 property or income taxes—not exceeding one year's assessment—owed by the bankrupt are given a certain priority of payment. That is, they appear in a statutory catalogue of preferential payments, which includes wages or salaries, holiday and sick pay, and pensions. These debts rank equally between themselves, and should the bankrupt's property not

---

[53] The Central Fund is now provided for by Art. 11 of the Constitution": "All revenues of the State from whatever source arising shall, subject to such exception as may be provided by law, form one fund . . . "

[54] It was then possible for the Supreme Court to sit with an even number of judges; this is now prohibited by s.7 of the Courts (Supplemental Provisions) Act 1961.

suffice to pay them in full, they abate in equal proportions. Similar priorities exist in the liquidation of companies: see section 285(2) of the Companies Act 1963.[55]

Disclosure of evidential material

A plaintiff who requires documents in the defendant's possession can normally obtain them by a court order for discovery, while other information can be secured in advance of trial by administering interrogatories. At common law, however, the Crown was immune from such process; though it might submit to discovery, this was purely as a matter of grace. After independence the new State did not claim to have inherited these immunities, but instead invoked a broad principle of public policy that if a Minister claimed privilege against disclosure of information on public interest grounds, this was conclusive. In *Leen* v. *President of the Executive Council* [1926] I.R. 456 Meredith J. accepted this view—which meant that the court could not consider the material in order to decide for itself what the public interest required. The practice thus established persisted in the High Court for the next 40 years: see *Smith* v. *Commissioners of Public Works* [1936] Ir.Jur.Rep. 67 and *O'Leary* v. *Minister for Industry & Commerce* [1966] I.R. 676.[56]

It became clear that privilege was being claimed in respect of innocuous documents, where production could not impede or injure the business of government or damage the fabric of the State. Thus in *Murphy* v. *Dublin Corporation and Minister for Local Government* [1972] I.R. 215 the claim related to an inspector's report on a statutory public inquiry into a compulsory purchase order on certain lands. The Supreme Court, in another historic decision, rejected the Minister's claim. The doctrine that such a claim must gain automatic judicial assent was repudiated as inconsistent with the Constitution's provisions on the judicial power (as to which see Chap. 9 *infra*). There was a public interest in the effective administration of justice as well as in the effective functioning of government. Any conflict between those interests must be resolved by the courts themselves; they could not constitutionally delegate this function to others. Thus when an objection to production was made it was appropriate for the court to examine the documents before giving its ruling. Twenty years on, the Supreme Court declined an invitation to overrule or modify the decision in *Murphy's* case, and instead reaffirmed the principles there laid down: *Ambiorix Ltd.* v. *Min. for the Environment* [1992] I.L.R.M. 209.

The *Murphy* and *Ambiorix* cases also gave the quietus to the notion that objection to the production of documents could be based on either of two grounds:

    (a) that disclosure of their *contents* would be against the public interest
    (b) that, irrespective of their contents, they belonged to a *class* of documents in respect of which the public interest required non-production.

Walsh J., with whom the other members of the Court agreed, totally rejected this distinction ([1972] I.R. 215, 235):

    " . . . there can be no documents which may be withheld from production simply because they belong to a particular class of documents. Each

---

[55] See also Michael Forde, *Company Law in Ireland* (Cork 1985), pp. 494 ff.; Ronan Keane, *Company Law in the Republic of Ireland* (London 1985), pp. 319–320.
[56] See Matthew Russell, "A Privilege of the State" (1967) II *Irish Jurist* (N.S.) 88.

document must be decided upon having regard to the considerations which apply to that particular document and its contents. To grant or withhold the production of a document simply by reason of the class to which it belongs would be to regard all documents as being of equal importance notwithstanding that they may not be."

This conclusion was reaffirmed in the *Ambiorix* case, where the Supreme Court rejected an argument that documents prepared by the most senior civil servants and intended to assist the Government in formulating policy should be privileged. Finlay C.J., for the court, said that there could not be a class or category of documents exempted from production by reason of the rank in the public service of the person creating them, or the position of the individual or body intended to use them ([1992] I.L.R.M. 209, 213).

It follows that whether documents such as Cabinet or Cabinet Committee papers are to be disclosed must depend on their *contents* alone. No Irish court has yet had occasion to order production of such material, but the High Court of Australia did so in *Sankey* v. *Whitlam* (1978) 141 C.L.R. 1: see too *Burmah Oil Ltd.* v. *Bank of England* [1980] A.C. 1090.

The Supreme Court in *Murphy's* case further emphasised that once a court was satisfied as to the relevance of the documents, the onus of establishing that they should not be produced is on the person or party who so claims. In the instant case this had not been done. In fact the Minister had simply furnished a certificate, in the customary form, stating his conclusion; he had not given his grounds for fearing injury to the public interest. The Supreme Court found this quite insufficient, and the consequence is that Departments must now identify with some particularity the public interest thought to be in jeopardy and indicate why the danger is believed to exist.

Finally, the Supreme Court ruled that the document in issue in *Murphy's* case could not benefit from what the Court called "executive privilege." This applied only to documents which sprang from the carrying out of the executive functions of the State. However, the inspector's report was not such a document, for in carrying out his appellate functions under the Housing Act 1966—to which the report related—the Minister was not exercising an executive power. He was simply the person designated by the Oireachtas to discharge this appellate function. The Oireachtas was not constitutionally obliged to designate the Minister; it might as easily have selected the chairman of C.I.E. or of the E.S.B. Had it done so, said Walsh J., there would be no question of such persons being granted the executive privilege not to produce the document in question.

The Supreme Court applied the same reasoning in *Geraghty* v. *Minister for Local Government* [1975] I.R. 300. There the plaintiff, who was seeking the annulment of the Minister's decision on a planning appeal, applied for discovery of several documents. The defendant did not resist disclosure of the inspector's report on the public inquiry, but did object to production of 22 other documents. Doubtless as a result of the *Murphy* decision, the certificate adduced specific reasons for resisting production. The Supreme Court, however, found it impossible to distinguish the Minister's appellate functions in planning matters from those in compulsory purchase matters; thus *Murphy's* case applied and no claim of "executive privilege" was possible.[57]

---

[57] The *Murphy* and *Geraghty* cases are discussed in the writer's article "Inadmissibility of evidence on grounds of public interest" (1977) D.U.L.J. 11.

When *Geraghty's* case was in the High Court Kenny J. had excluded one document from production, on the ground that it was written by one civil servant to another and obviously intended to be confidential. The Supreme Court, without discussing the matter, upheld this ruling—which hardly seems compatible with its conclusion that the other documents did not attract executive privilege. It may be noted that in England the confidentiality of a communication will not, without more, protect it from disclosure: see the authorities discussed by Ackner L.J. in *Campbell* v. *Tameside Metropolitan B.C.* [1982] 2 All E.R. 791. But the current Irish position was summarised thus by Costello J. in *Folens* v. *Minister for Education* [1981] I.L.R.M. 21, 22:

> "It seems to me to be established from the cases to which I have referred (*i.e.* the *Murphy* and *Geraghty* decisions) that not all communications which arise in the course of the administration of the Public Services are confidential. The court will examine the documents to see whether a claim to confidentiality can properly exist and if it does it must decide whether the public interest in maintaining confidentiality should not prevail because to do so could result in a denial of justice."[58]

In *Incorporated Law Society* v. *Minister for Justice* [1987] I.L.R.M. 42 Murphy J. ordered the production of certain documents—including correspondence between Ministers—holding that any resulting damage to the efficiency of the public service would be minimal and outweighed by the potential injustice refusal of production would cause to the plaintiffs. Thus the Irish courts now clearly treat departmental claims for privilege with a healthy scepticism.[59] They will be upheld, it appears, only in very special circumstances, such as existed in *O'Mahony* v. *Minister for Defence* (*The Irish Times,* June 28, 1989). There the plaintiff sought damages for personal injuries sustained while on United Nations service with the Defence Forces in Lebanon. The incidents giving rise to these injuries had been the subject of two courts of inquiry, one under Irish, the other under UN auspices. The plaintiff applied for discovery of the two reports. Barrington J. refused the application. In regard to the UN document, he accepted that this had been given to the Irish authorities by an international organisation in circumstances of confidentiality. The government had taken the view that it was under a duty to preserve that confidence. This was a reasonable attitude, and the privilege was properly claimed. In regard to the Irish report, Barrington J. held that, given the nature of the work done by a court of inquiry and the possible security implications, it was not unreasonable that the Minister should provide that the

---

[58] In *Ambiorix Ltd.* v. *Min. for the Environment* [1992] I.L.R.M. 209 it was contended that representations sent to Government Departments by individuals or companies containing sensitive commercial information and intended to be confidential, should be privileged. The Supreme Court ruled against this, saying *per* Finlay C.J. that there was no public interest " . . . in keeping immune from production communications between citizens and departments of the government seeking a particular decision which would favour their interest" (at 215). But the court made it clear that information secured by discovery could be used only for the purpose of the action. To employ it otherwise would be to commit contempt of court. The Supreme Court was also satisfied that it was possible so to regulate the production of the documents as to give the plaintiffs information, while protecting the commercial and financial interests of the defendants.

[59] See also Blayney J's decision in *Private Motorists' Provident Society Ltd.* (*In Liquidation*) v. *P.M.P.A. Insurance plc.* (*Under Administration*) [1990] I.R. 284.

inquiry should be confidential, nor was this beyond the minister's powers. The privilege was thus properly claimed.

It would seem to follow from what was said in *Murphy's* case that State agencies such as C.I.E., the E.S.B. and the I.D.A. cannot claim "executive privilege." (Matters would be otherwise if the ground for such a claim, instead of being performance of an executive function, was simply protection of the public interest.) The Central Bank, however, can resist production of documents. Its officers and employees are subject to a statutory obligation of secrecy under section 16 of the Central Bank Act 1989. In *Cully* v. *Northern Bank Ltd.* [1984] I.L.R.M. 683 O'Hanlon J., speaking of section 16's predecessor, said (at 685–686):

> "It appears to me that the provisions of s.31 of the Central Bank Act 1942 give rise to a claim of privilege on grounds of public policy from disclosure of any information of the type referred to in the oath of secrecy. S.6(1) of the same Act provides that in relation to part, at least, of the functions and duties of the Central Bank 'the constant and predominant aim shall be the welfare of the people as a whole.' This gives some indication of the justification for granting an exceptional degree of protection to the confidentiality of the bank's transactions, as a matter of public interest."

Although section 31 has, as indicated, been repealed and replaced by section 16 of the 1989 Act, O'Hanlon J.'s reasoning would not seem to be affected thereby. The current law is thus presumably as laid down in *Cully's* case.

In the Irish cases the State—represented by a Minister—has normally been a defendant and thus well placed to claim "executive privilege"; but this is not essential. Such claims may be made in proceedings between private parties—as occurred in *Duncan* v. *Cammell Laird Ltd.* [1942] A.C. 624—a suit for damages arising out of the alleged negligent construction of a submarine, where the plaintiff sought production (*inter alia*) of plans and specifications. Presumably the Attorney General could intervene, if necessary, to assert a public interest in non-production: this has occurred in other common law jurisdictions.[60]

The principles set out above are applicable both to civil and criminal cases. As regards the latter, the courts would doubtless be reluctant to accept claims of privilege where to do so would virtually immunise against conviction those who hold or have held high office: see *Sankey* v. *Whitlam* (1978) 142 C.L.R. 1 and *U.S.* v. *Nixon* (1974) 418 U.S. 683. Ordinarily, however, the courts will not order disclosure of the names of those who have given information to the authorities about the commission of offences or the identity of offenders—but they may do so if the interests of justice require it: *Att. Gen.* v. *Simpson* [1959] I.R. 105, at 133 (Davitt P.), 141 (Dixon J., Teevan J. concurring).[61] Communications between one member of the Garda Síochána and another in the course of their duties are not automatically privileged. Whether any such communication is immune from disclosure must depend on its contents, and the possible damage to the public interest must be speci-

---

[60] See Hogg, *op. cit.*, p. 43.
[61] See also *D.* v. *NSPCC* [1977] 1 All E.R. 589, *per* Lord Diplock (at 595) and Lord Simon (at 607).

fied by the person claiming the immunity: *D.P.P. (Hanley)* v. *Holly* [1984] I.L.R.M. 149.[62]

Public interest privilege may also be invoked before a parliamentary committee. This occurred in 1971 during the Dáil Public Accounts Committee's investigation of the expenditure of public funds granted for the relief of distress in Northern Ireland. The committee wished to see a directive issued to the Chief of Staff by the Minister for Defence on February 6, 1970, but General MacEoin replied that the Minister had directed him to claim privilege in regard to it. Subsequently the committee's chairman raised the issue with the Taoiseach, both orally and in writing. Mr. Lynch, however, replied that the issue had been carefully considered by the Government, which had affirmed its earlier decision (*semble* that the Minister's claim was entirely justified): *Committee of Public Accounts: Interim and Final Reports (Order of Dáil of December 1, 1970) Prl. 2574, 1972).*

Limitation of actions

The Statute of Limitations 1957, section 3, lays down a general rule that the Act applies to proceedings by or against "a State authority in like manner as if that State authority were a private individual." "State authority" is defined in section 1 to mean:

(a) a Minister
(b) the Commissioners of Public Works
(c) the Irish Land Commission
(d) the Revenue Commissioners
(e) the Attorney General.

But the Act does not apply to proceedings for the recovery of taxes or duties, or interest thereon—s.3(2)(*a*); and certain other revenue proceedings are also exempted by s.3(2)(*b*) and (*c*).

It follows that the State is subject, just as a citizen would be, to the limitation periods set out in s.11—*e.g.* in contract six years from the date when the cause of action accrued, in negligence or nuisance three years from that date. "State authorities" do, however, enjoy longer limitation periods in regard to actions for the recovery of land—30 years as against 12 for private persons: see s.13. (For actions by a State authority to recover foreshore, the period is 60 years: s.13(1)(*b*).) They are given similarly favourable treatment in respect of actions claiming the sale of land which is subject to a mortgage or a charge—again 30 years as opposed to 12 for private persons: s.32.

The Statute of Limitations does not apply to actions for which periods of limitation are fixed by any other limitation enactment, but it does provide for a State authority to benefit from any such periods as if it were a private individual: s.7. In section 5 the Act preserves "any equitable jurisdiction to refuse relief on the ground of acquiescence or otherwise." One such ground is

---

[62] In *People (D.P.P.)* v. *Eccles* (unreported, 10 February 1986) the Court of Criminal Appeal upheld a claim by a Garda Chief Superintendent in regard to the source of confidential information which he had received. The court concluded that the circumstances were exceptional and justified the chief superintendent in refusing to specify whether the source was inside the Garda Síochána or outside it.

laches.[63] At common law *laches* could not be imputed to the Crown, but it must be doubtful whether the State could now benefit from this doctrine. The trend of the modern Irish cases discussed elsewhere in this chapter suggests otherwise.

Statutes and the State

In *Cork Co. Council* v. *Commissioners of Public Works* [1945] I.R. 561 the former Supreme Court accepted that the State was not bound by statutes unless such statutes were expressly applied to it or it was necessarily implicit in their terms that they bound the State. This view was founded on two alternative grounds: (a) that the State fell heir to a Crown privilege in this regard (b) that this was a general rule in construction of statutes, independent of any royal origins—as was shown by its acceptance in the United States. In *Byrne* v. *Ireland* [1972] I.R. 241 Walsh, J. (Ó Dálaigh C.J. concurring) rejected ground (a) above as erroneous, observing that the basis of the Crown prerogative was that the King personified the State—but Article 2 of the 1922 Constitution repudiated any such idea. Walsh J. indicated that ground (b) may still provide a basis for State exemption from statutory provisions. The following passage from his judgment ([1972] I.R. 241, 278) may however suggest a stricter approach to arguments for exemption:

> "It is . . . apparent from the provisions of s.3 of the Statute of Limitations 1957 . . . that in areas outside the collection of the public revenues and taxes and kindred subjects the public benefit no longer appears to the Oireachtas to require that the State, in its several departments . . . should have exemption from the provisions of the limitation periods laid down in that statute."

Further, the judicial rejection of automatic State privilege in relation to discovery (*Murphy's* case, *supra*) and of the State's supposed immunity in tort (*Byrne's* case, *supra*) may well affect attitudes on this matter—*i.e.* the courts may be readier in future to find a necessary implication that the State is bound. For cogent reasons as to why a stricter approach to exemption is desirable, see Hogg, *op. cit.*, pp. 199–203.

It is commonly supposed that the State is not bound by the provisions of the Local Government (Planning and Development) Acts 1963–1983. The 1963 Act provides (s.84) for a State authority to consult with the planning authority in the case of construction of a new building, and this may well negative any implication that the State is bound by the Act. In a lecture delivered in 1983 Keane J. drew attention to the consequences of such a conclusion[64]:

> "It is remarkable—if it is indeed the case—that of the five great elevations referred to by Dr. Maurice Craig in his definitive architectural history of Dublin (*Dublin 1660–1860: A Social and Architectural History* (Dublin 1949), three could disappear without any element of public inquiry or any control by the planning process. The buildings are the Four Courts,

---

[63] As to which see J. C. Brady and Tony Kerr, *The Limitations of Actions in the Republic of Ireland* (Dublin 1984), Chap. 6.

[64] Ronan Keane, "The 1963 Planning Act—Twenty Years On" (1983) 5 D.U.L.J. (N.S.) 92, 96–97.

the Custom House and the Royal Hospital at Kilmainham, all of which are vested in the Board of Works.[65] It seems clear that the 1963 Act was enacted on the assumption that the State and its agencies were not bound by its provisions; and, for that reason, no express exemption is given to State authorities, although statutory undertakings, such as CIE and the ESB, are given a limited degree of exemption. Obviously, some degree of exemption of the State from planning control is essential; it is clearly necessary for reasons of security that the State should not have to subject plans for prisons and defence installations to public scrutiny. That does not apply, however, to a change of use of premises not coming within those categories or still less to the demolition or irremediable alteration of a building of architectural or historical importance."

Keane J. discusses the authorities mentioned above and concludes that the principle in question is still applicable, and probably proof against constitutional challenge as violating equality before the law.

In conclusion it is relevant to note what may be the beginnings of a new trend. The Landlord and Tenant (Ground Rents) (No. 2) Act 1978 provides, in section 4:

"This Act shall not bind a Minister of the Government, the Commissioners of Public Works in Ireland or the Irish Land Commission."

Section 4 of the Landlord and Tenant (Amendment) Act 1980 similarly restricts the application of that Act to the State; while section 9 of the Dumping at Sea Act 1981 exempts State ships and service aircraft from its provisions.[66] Increasing use of positive exemptions like these may weaken the presumption discussed above.

Remedies against, and in favour of, the State

At common law the Crown was in a favoured position as regards remedies. An order of mandamus would not lie against the Crown, or against any Crown servant to compel him to perform a duty owed by the Crown.[67] It was also doubtful whether an injunction would issue against the Crown.[68]

These restrictions form no part of modern Irish law. It seems that an injunction will not be granted against "Ireland", *eo nomine*,[69] but this should not cause any practical problems since similar relief can be obtained against those—including Ministers—who act on the State's behalf.[70] Thus the

---

[65] It should be stressed that far from demolishing the Royal Hospital, the State has refusbished it at enormous expense and in a way which has earned the praise of Dr. Maurice Craig.

[66] Contrast s.8 of the Air Pollution Act 1989: "This Act shall apply to premises belonging to or in the occupation of the State."

[67] See Hogg, *op. cit.*, Chap. 2.

[68] See Harry Street, *Governmental Liability* (Cambridge 1953), p. 140: Glanville Williams, *Crown Proceedings* (London 1948) p. 136.

[69] In *Pesca Valentia* Ltd. v. *Minister for Fisheries, Ireland and Att. Gen.* [1985] I.R. 193 Finlay C.J., for the Supreme Court, said (at 202): " . . . whilst Ireland may be an appropriate defendant in regard to the claim in the action, it does not appear to be appropriate that any injunction should ever be given against Ireland . . . " No reason was given for this conclusion.

[70] So in the *Pesca Valentia* case, *supra*, an injunction was granted against the Minister for Fisheries and the Attorney General.

Government[71] can be restrained from entering into,[72] or from ratifying,[73] an international agreement alleged to conflict with the Constitution. An injunction has been granted to restrain the responsible Minister from enforcing a statute alternatively claimed to be unconstitutional and to conflict with European Community law.[74] A mandatory injunction may issue to compel a Minister to fulfil a constitutional (or presumably a legal) obligation.[75] An order of mandamus may be granted against a Minister[76] or, if necessary, the Government as a collective entity.[77]

In some Commonwealth jurisdictions interim relief is not available against the Crown.[78] The position in Ireland is different: an interlocutory injunction was granted in *Pesca Valentia Ltd.* v. *Minister for Fisheries* [1985] I.R. 193, and in *Crotty* v. *An Taoiseach* [1987] I.R. 713 Barrington J. granted an interim injunction to restrain the ratification, pending a constitutional challenge, of the Single European Act.[79]

It has sometimes been suggested that at common law the Crown could not be required to give an undertaking as to damages when seeking an injunction. In *Hoffman-La Roche & Co. A.G.* v. *Secretary of State* [1975] A.C. 295 the House of Lords said that this was linked to the Crown's immunity in tort, which had been greatly modified by the Crown Proceedings Act 1947. Consequently the law nowadays was different and it was a matter for the discretion of the court whether an injunction should be granted if an undertaking was refused. Since the Irish State's supposed immunity in tort did not survive *Byrne* v. *Ireland* [1972] I.R. 241, there can be no absolute rule relieving the State from an obligation to give an undertaking. The question is presumably one for the discretion of the court; thus if the State is seeking an injunction to protect or enforce its proprietary or contractual rights, an undertaking might be required. It is unlikely, however, that a court would insist on an undertak-

---

[71] Normally sued by naming as defendants the Taoiseach, the Tánaiste, each Minister and the Attorney General: Anthony Collins and James O'Reilly, *Civil Proceedings and the State: A Practitioner's Guide* (Dublin 1990), p. 121. See further n. 75 *infra*.

[72] *Boland* v. *An Taoiseach* [1974] I.R. 338 (the Sunningdale Agreement of 1973).

[73] *Crotty* v. *An Taoiseach* [1987] I.R. 713 (the Single European Act).

[74] *Pesca Valentia Ltd.* v. *Minister for Fisheries* [1985] I.R. 193. But it is unlikely that an injunction would be granted if the statute was challenged on constitutional grounds alone. See the Supreme Court's decision in *Cooke* v. *Minister for Communitions. The Irish Times, Law Report* February 20, 1989. See also Collins and O'Reilly, *op. cit.*, pp. 140–142, and Chap. 11 *infra.*, *s.v.* Injunctions against statutes.

[75] *Crowley* v. *Ireland and ors.* [1980] I.R. 102. The relief there sought was refused, but neither the High Court nor the Supreme Court suggested that there was no jurisdiction to grant it.

[76] *State (King and Goff)* v. *Minister for Justice* [1984] I.R. 169, where Doyle J. held that any common law rule inhibiting the grant of such relief had not survived the 1922 and 1937 Constitutions.

[77] Costello J. so held in *State (Sheehan)* v. *Government of Ireland* [1987] I.R. 550. Under modern Irish law, he said, such an order was not a prerogative order, nor was the executive established by the Constitution the successor of the Crown. And although Costello J.'s decision on the substantive issue was reversed by the Supreme Court, it was not suggested that his view on the procedural point was wrong. Collins and O'Reilly, *op. cit*, p. 121, n. 47, doubt whether the Government is a legal entity capable of being sued in its own right, and point out that it is not usually sued by name (see n. 68 *supra*). But an entire Article—28—of the Constitution is devoted to "the Government", and the reasoning which has made the State a juristic person may be thought to apply here also. The position in other common law countries is quite different: see M.C. Harris, "The Courts and the Cabinet: Unfastening the Buckle" [1989] *Public Law* 251, particularly pp. 276–279.

[78] See Hogg, *op. cit.*, p. 23.

[79] See further Chap. 8 *infra*.

ing where the State seeks an injunction to restrain a breach of the law harmful to the public. None seems to have been sought, or given, in the recent cases of *Att. Gen. and Minister for Posts and Telegraphs* v. *Paperlink Ltd.* [1984] I.L.R.M. 373 or *Campus Oil Ltd.* v. *Minister for Industry (No. 2)* [1983] I.R. 88; in the latter the defendant was granted a mandatory injunction directing the plaintiffs to comply with the provisions of a statutory order.

State property

Article 10.1 of the Constitution vests all natural resources, including the air and all forms of potential energy and all royalties and franchises, in the State—subject, however, to all estates and interests lawfully vested in any other person or body.[80] Article 10.2 vests in the State all land, mines, minerals and waters previously belonging to Saorstát Éireann. Under Article 10.3, statute may provide for the management of property belonging to the State by virtue of that Article, and for the control of the alienation—temporary or permanent—of the property. Article 10.4 makes identical provision regarding property acquired by the State after the Constitution came into operation. As will be seen, Articles 10.3 and 4 have been implemented, principally by the State Property Act 1954.

The provisions of Article 10, it may be noted, correspond broadly to those of Article 11 of the 1922 Constitution. But there are important differences. Article 11 of the Saorstát Éireann Constitution prohibited the alienation of State property; leases or licences might be granted, but not for a longer term than 99 years and no such lease or licence could contain a provision for renewal. No similar restrictions are to be found in Article 10 of the present Constitution.

The State Property Act 1954, s.5, provides that all State land not vested in another State authority shall be vested in the Minister for Finance. "State land" is defined to include "land which belongs to the State, the Nation, the People or a State authority" (with certain exceptions) and "land" is defined as including *inter alia* land, foreshore, mines and minerals, franchises, easements and profits à prendre. Sections 10 and 11 of the Act permit a State authority (*i.e.* a Minister or the Commissioners of Public Works) to sell, exchange or lease State land vested in it, or grant tenancies or licences therein. The Act does not attempt to control the terms of any such grant, lease, licence, etc.; these are left for the particular State authority to fix. A gratuitous grant of State land for a stated purpose is specifically authorised, as is a lease free of any payment. Under these powers rights over State property could be granted (on payment or otherwise) to a foreign state—*e.g.* for use as an embassy. Such action would not, it seems, be open to constitutional objection: *State (Devine)* v. *Larkin* [1977] I.R. 24, 31.

The 1954 Act also provides, in s.19, for arrangements consequent upon the gift of property (real or personal) to a State authority, or to the State, the Nation or the People. Section 19(6) specifically lays it down that where a gift

---

[80] In *Webb* v. *Ireland* [1988] I.R. 353, 383 Finlay C.J. (Henchy and Griffin JJ. concurring) held that the phrase "all royalties" in Art. 10.1 must be widely construed to embrace the notion of sovereignty. Hence it provided a constitutional foundation for the State's right to treasure trove. Walsh and McCarthy JJ. were unable to accept this view (see Walsh J. at 391–393: McCarthy J. at 398).

of property is subject to conditions, it shall not subsequently be dealt with in a manner inconsistent with those conditions.

Section 73 of the Succession Act 1965—which replaces the common law doctrines of escheat and *bona vacantia*—provides that in default of any person taking the estate of an intestate, the State shall take the estate as ultimate intestate successor. The Minister for Finance is empowered to waive such rights: s.73(2).

At common law the State is owner of the foreshore—the strip between low and high water mark. Members of the public enjoy certain limited rights thereon, including entry upon it for navigation and fishing purposes—but not, without permission or licence of the owner, to take seaweed: *Mahony* v. *Neenan* [1966] I.R. 559, 564–565. The State may grant title to a portion of the foreshore, or it may be acquired by prescription: see *Att. Gen.* v. *McIlwaine* [1939] I.R. 437, 440–441 *per* Johnston J. The Foreshore Act 1933 assumes the existence of this doctrine and makes provision *inter alia* for the granting of leases and licences in respect of the foreshore: ss.2 and 3. Insofar as the powers thus conferred are subject to restrictions (to conform with Art. 11 of the 1922 Constitution) those restrictions are lifted by the State Property Act 1954: see s.3 thereof.

In *Att. Gen.* v. *McIlwaine* [1939] I.R. 437, 447 Gavan Duffy J. was of opinion that the defendant could not have acquired title to the piece of foreshore in question, because the 60 years necessary for this had not elapsed when the 1922 Constitution came into force. By virtue of Article 11 thereof, Gavan Duffy J. held, this land vested in the State from December 6, 1922 and could never thereafter be alienated; and the Nullum Tempus Acts could not "prevail against the emphatic assertion of inalienable State owership contained in Art. 11." In *Linnane* v. *Nestor* [1943] I.R. 208, 213, however, Maguire P. declined to accept Gavan Duffy J.'s conclusion; he thought it not inconsistent with Article 11 to hold that time running in favour of an individual by virtue of pre-1922 acts of ownership was not interrupted by the coming into force of the Saorstát Éireann Constitution.

NATIONALITY AND CITIZENSHIP

These matters are dealt with by the Irish Nationality and Citizenship Acts 1956 and 1986. Under section 6 of the former every person born in Ireland[81] (other than the child of a foreign diplomat) is an Irish citizen from birth. So too is every person, wherever born, whose father or mother was an Irish citizen at the time of that person's birth. However, formalities are required of some. A person, not otherwise an Irish citizen, born in Northern Ireland after December 6, 1922 must declare him-or herself, in the prescribed manner, to be an Irish citizen; if the individual concerned is not of full age his/her parent or guardian may make the declaration (s.7(1)). The 1956 Act also makes special provision for posthumous children (s.29), foundlings (s.10) and adopted children (s.11).

Where a person born outside Ireland claims citizenship through a parent also born outside Ireland, he or she must register under section 27 at a diplomatic mission or consular office or at the Department of Foreign Affairs in

---

[81] A person born on an Irish ship or aircraft, wherever it is, is deemed to have been born in Ireland: s.13(1).

Dublin (s.7(2)). After July 1, 1986 the citizenship of such a person commences only as on and from the date of registration (s.2, 1986 Act).

An alien of either sex who marries an Irish citizen does not acquire citizenship by virtue of such marriage (1986 Act, s.3).[82] But he or she may do so after three years of marriage by lodging a declaration accepting post-nuptial Irish citizenship. The marriage must be subsisting at the date when the declaration is lodged and the parties must be living together as husband and wife (*ibid.*)

An alien may also acquire citizenship by naturalisation. The conditions are set out in section 4 of the 1986 Act and include: good character; at least one year's continuous residence in the State immediately before the application, and four years total residence in the State out of the eight years preceding the application; and an intention to continue to reside in the State after naturalisation. However the Minister for Justice may grant naturalisation certificates, even if the section 4 conditions are not complied with, in certain cases specified in section 5 of the 1986 Act. A naturalisation certificate confers Irish citizenship from the date of issue and for so long as it remains unrevoked (s.18). The procedures for, and grounds of, revocation are set out in section 19; the latter include fraud or misrepresentation regarding the application; failure, shown by overt act, in the duty of fidelity to the nation and loyalty to the State; and the voluntary acquisition, otherwise than by marriage, of another citizenship. (One who marries an alien does not, merely by virtue of the marriage, cease to be an Irish citizen even if he or she acquires the alien's nationality: s.23).

Citizenship may also be renounced—though not during a time of war as defined in Article 28.3.3°, save with the Minister's consent (s.21(2)). The renunciation procedure is set out in section 7 of the 1986 Act.

Aliens

Some—though not all—of the Constitution's fundamental rights provisions apply only to citizens; and *prima facie* it might seem that aliens could not claim the benefit of these. But as shown in Chapter 12 *infra*, matters are not so simple as this. And a combination of constitutional amendment and statutory provision means that certain categories of non-citizens may vote in Dáil elections (see Chap. 4, *infra*). Nonetheless aliens do not have the same rights as citizens; in particular they are not automatically entitled to enter, or to reside in, the State.[83]

The law on aliens is the product of the Aliens Act 1935 and Ministerial

[82] Under s.8 of the 1956 Act the alien wife of an Irish citizen could acquire citizenship by making a declaration accepting it. This could be done at any time after the marriage, or even before it. No similar privilege was extended to alien husbands. This discrimination was the subject of an unsuccessful constitutional challenge in *Somjee* v. *Minister for Justice and Att. Gen.* [1981] I.L.R.M. 324: see Chap. 13 *infra*.

[83] This does not apply to citizens of EC member states, since Title III of the EEC Treaty provides for the free movement of workers and the right of establishment, and the Community legal measures to achieve these goals. See EEC Council Directive 64/221, which *inter alia* permits exclusion or expulsion on grounds of public policy or public security based *exclusively* on the personal conduct of the individual concerned (see Case 41/74, *Van Duyn* v. *Home Office* [1974] E.C.R. 1346; Case 67/74, *Bonsignore* v. *Stadt Köln* [1975] E.C.R. 304). It also stipulates

orders made thereunder. The 1935 Act confers (in s.5) wide powers on the Minister for Justice to make orders regarding aliens in general, or aliens of a particular nationality or other class, or particular aliens. The Minister may *inter alia* prohibit entry or leaving; impose restrictions on landing, entering or leaving; provide for exclusion and/or deportation and make orders for such purposes; restrict residence to particular places or prohibit residence in particular places; require compliance with conditions regarding registration, change of abode, employment, occupation "and other like matters." By virtue of section 6 the contravention of any prohibition of an aliens order, or any order made thereunder, is an offence.

The measures implementing the 1935 Act are the Aliens Order 1946 (S.R. & O. 395 of 1946) and the Aliens (Amendment) Order 1975 (S.I. 1975 No. 128). These provide that "alien" does not include a person born in Great Britain or Northern Ireland (1975 Order, Art. 2(2)).[84] Restrictions on the entry of aliens are imposed in that leave to enter is required. Such leave may be refused on various grounds,[85] including inability to support oneself and any accompanying dependants; suffering from certain diseases or disabilities; previous conviction for certain offences (not necessarily in the State); lack of a valid visa, where required.[86] Conditions on entry may be imposed, such as an obligation to register, and there is a general requirement that *everyone* landing in the State shall be in possession of a valid passport or other document establishing nationality and identity to the satisfaction of an immigration officer. Article 7(3) of the 1946 Order authorises the detention "in such manner as the Minister may direct" of an alien who has landed in contravention of the Order; such detention is to be deemed "to be in legal custody." Article 13 of the same Order deals with deportation, and provides that detention pending deportation is to be deemed lawful custody.[87]

THE IRISH LANGUAGE

Article 8 of Bunreacht na hÉireann provides:

> "1. The Irish language as the national language is the first official language.
> 2. The English language is recognised as a second official language.
> 3. Provision may, however, be made by law for the exclusive use of either of the said languages for any one or more official purposes, either throughout the State or in any part thereof."[88]

The "national" status of Irish is further emphasised by Article 25.5.4° which

---

that previous criminal convictions do not *per se* constitute grounds for such action and imposes a general obligation to give reasons for decisions: see Case 30/77, *R.* v. *Bouchereau* [1977] E.C.R. 2008; Joined Cases 115 and 116/81, *Adoui α Cornuaille* v. *Belguim* [1982] E.C.R. 1665.

[84] A reciprocal measure, in that Irish citizens are not aliens under U.K. law: see E. C. S. Wade and A. W. Bradley, *Constitutional and Administrative Law* (10th ed., London 1985) p. 442.

[85] Set out in Art. 5 of the 1946 Order, as substituted by Art. 3, 1975 Order.

[86] Citizens of a number of states (including EC member states) listed in the 1975 Order do not require a visa.

[87] For the impact of these provisions on family rights under the Constitution see Chap. 17 *infra*.

[88] Art. 8.3 means that either language may be used unless provision has been made by law that one language only is to be used for some official purpose or purposes: *Att. Gen.* v. *Coyne & Wallace* (1967) 101 I.L.T.R. 17, *per* Kingsmill Moore and Walsh JJ.

provides that should a conflict arise between the two texts of the Constitution the one in Irish prevails.[89] But no such rule applies to ordinary legislation. Article 25.4 decrees that the President shall sign a bill in the text in which it was passed by the Oireachtas, and that an official translation shall be issued in the other official language. The text signed by the President is the authoritative version, save where the Act is passed and signed in both languages; in the latter case should a conflict occur between the texts that in Irish prevails. However, the vast majority of statutes are passed in English[90]; thus in legal proceedings, even where conducted in Irish, it is the English text alone that governs.

The Legal Practitioners (Qualification) Act 1929 demands "a competent knowledge" of the Irish language from barristers and solicitors; the Courts of Justice Act 1924, ss.44 and 71, require a degree of fluency in Irish from Circuit Court and District Court judges whose circuits or districts include Gaeltacht areas[91] and a broadly similar requirement applies to the Gardaí (Garda Síochána Act 1924, s.6(2)). Also, under section 2 of the Irish Legal Terms Act 1945 there is established a committee, including judges and practitioners, to settle Irish equivalents of legal terms. Notwithstanding this, it is not generally possible to carry on legal or administrative business in Irish—even in the Gaeltacht—since appropriate forms in the language are not available.[92] The compatibility of this situation with the Constitution has been questioned and it clearly sits uneasily with the judicial exposition of Article 8. In *State (MacFhearraigh)* v. *Gaffney*[93] (High Court, June 1, 1983) O'Hanlon J. said (at p. 5 of his judgment):

> " . . . in the Constitution of Ireland, the Irish language is elevated to a higher status than it had in the first Constitution, since it is described, for the first time, as "the first official language." At the same time, the Parliament is given a wider option to give precedence by law to one language over the other language for official purposes in any corner of the country. Until the Parliament uses this power granted to it . . . it must always be accepted that the Irish language is the first official

---

[89] Such a conflict is not to be assumed: *per* Budd J. in *O'Donovan* v. *Att. Gen.* [1961] I.R. 114, 131. In *Central Dublin Development Association* v. *Att. Gen.* (1975) 109 I.L.T.R. 69, 83 Kenny J. said that the English version of Art. 43.1° and 2° seemed "a most unhappy attempt to reproduce the meaning of that in Irish." Yet the Irish text is well known to be a translation of the English! See generally J. M. Kelly, "The Irish Text of the Constitution" *Justice (Irish Student Law Review)*, Hiliary 1966, p. 8; also Richard F. Humphreys "The Constitution of Ireland: The Forgotten Textual Quagmire" (1987) XXII *Irish Jurist (n.s.)* 169.

[90] Acts amending the Constitution are customarily passed in both languages, as was the Republic of Ireland Act 1948. Normally the only legislation passed in Irish is that affecting the Gaeltacht or the Irish language *e.g.* An tAcht um Bord na Gaeilge 1978— though some such measures are passed in both languages (*e.g.* An tAcht um Údarás na Gaeltachta 1979).

[91] But ss.44 and 71 are heavily qualified; both begin with the words "so far as may be practicable having regard to all relevant circumstances." Both also employ the formula "such a knowledge of the Irish language as would enable him to dispense with the assistance of an interpreter when evidence is given in that language." On the interpretation of s.71 see *Ó Monacháin* v. *An Taoiseach* [1986] I.L.R.M. 660 (the first judgment ever to be reported in Irish).

[92] The situation is documented in the *Report: Irish and the Law (Tuarascail: An Ghaeilge agus an Dlí)* by *Fasach* (a group of Irish-speaking lawyers), published in June 1986.

[93] The judgment—which is in Irish—is entitled *An Stát (Mac Fhearraigh)* v. *Mac Gamhna, Cathaoirleach an Bhinse Achomhairc Fostaíochta.*

language, and that it is the citizen's privilege to demand that it will be used for the administration of official business in the State."

MacFhearraigh's case sprang out of proceedings before the Employment Appeals Tribunal, in which the prosecutor claimed he had been unfairly dismissed. He wished to have the case conducted in Irish as far as possible. It was agreed that some witnesses would give evidence in English and some in Irish, but the prosecutor wanted to have the witnesses for the employers cross-examined through Irish and some of them would not agree to this. The E.A.T. ruled that the cross-examination should be in English since the claimant, his solicitor and counsel understood this as well as they did Irish and it would not be right to spend time on unnecessary translation. The prosecutor sought an order of mandamus requiring the tribunal to permit cross-examination in Irish. O'Hanlon J. granted the order. From the provisions of the Constitution and the authorities thereon he deduced the following principles:

1. When a court or tribunal is seised of a case affecting the personal or property rights of the parties before it, each party has the right to conduct his own side of the case in Irish if he so wishes and to present evidence in Irish; but if the other party's Irish is insufficient an interpreter must be appointed.
2. It is not for the court or tribunal to inquire whether the person wishing to use Irish has a sufficient knowledge of English—he has the right under the Constitution to choose the first official language unless the Oireachtas has provided otherwise. It follows that the person with fluent English has the same right to use Irish as a native of the Gaeltacht with little English. Although this may cause delay, and add to the costs, compliance with the Constitution demands such procedures.
3. Any party wishing to present his own side of the case through the medium of Irish—whether by submission, the giving of evidence, or the questioning or cross-examination of witnesses—has a constitutional right to do so.

But O'Hanlon J. also recognised that it was the duty of courts and tribunals to give fair play to both sides. Thus if one party did not understand the language of the proceedings a translation must be provided—a principle which, in criminal cases, was enshrined in Article 6(3) of the European Convention on Human Rights[94] and had been applied long before it by the High Court in *State (Buchan)* v. *Coyne* (1936) 70 I.L.T.R. 185.[95]

O'Hanlon J. founded upon his own decision in the *MacFhearraigh* case in *Delap* v. *An tAire Dli agus Cirt, Éire agus an tArd Aighne (The Irish Times*

[94] Art. 6(3) provides: "Everyone charged with a criminal offence has the following minimum rights: (a) to be informed promptly, in a language which he understands . . . of the nature and cause of the accusation against him . . . (e) to have the free assistance of an interpreter if he cannot understand or speak the language used in court."
[95] There in District Court criminal proceedings a prosecution witness gave evidence in Irish. Despite a defence request the District Justice refused to permit a translation and went on to give his decision in Irish. The ensuing conviction was quashed, the High Court saying that a fundamental principle of the administration of criminal justice had been disregarded and the decision could not stand.

December 24, 1990).[96] Here he granted the plaintiff, a solicitor practising in Dublin, a declaration that the Minister and the State were constitutionally obliged to provide an official translation into the first official language of the Rules of the Superior Courts (S.I. 1986 No. 15). O'Hanlon J. referred to the citizens' constitutional right of access to the courts, which under the law was conditioned upon observance of the Rules of the Superior Courts. A citizen wishing to use Irish in his/her own side of the case faced a large obstacle if no Irish rules or forms were available. A person so situated was not being accorded treatment equal to that of those satisfied to use only the English version. O'Hanlon J., however, rejected the plaintiff's claim for a declaration that the defendants were constitutionally bound *always* to issue an official translation (in whichever official language) of every Rule of the Superior Courts.

Article 8 of the Constitution was quoted by the European Court of Justice in Case 379/87, *Groener* v. *Minister for Education* [1990] I.L.R.M. 335. This case raised the question whether it was permissible under Community law—specifically Article 48(3), EEC Treaty, and Council Regulation 1612/88 on free movement of workers—to condition appointment to a teaching post in a public educational institution on an adequate knowledge of the Irish language. The plaintiff, a Dutch national, had been turned down for a full-time post as a lecturer in art in the College of Marketing and Design in Dublin on this ground. The evidence established that the teaching of art in this institution was conducted essentially, or indeed exclusively, in English. The Court of Justice, to which the High Court had referred certain questions under Article 177, EEC Treaty,[97] quoted Article 8 of the Constitution and continued ([1990] I.L.R.M. 335, 339–340):

> " . . . although Irish is not spoken by the whole Irish population, the policy followed by Irish governments for many years has been designed not only to maintain but also to promote the use of Irish as a means of expressing national identity and culture. It is for that reason that Irish courses are compulsory for children receiving primary education and optional for those receiving secondary education. The obligation imposed on lecturers in public vocational education schools to have a certain knowledge of the Irish language is one of the measures adopted by the Irish government in furtherance of that policy.
>
> The EEC Treaty does not prohibit the adoption of a policy for the protection and promotion of a language of a member state which is both the national language and the first official language. However, the implementation of such a policy must not encroach upon a fundamental freedom such as that of the free movement of workers. Therefore, the requirements deriving from measures intended to implement such a policy must not in any circumstances be disproportionate in relation to the aim pursued and the manner in which they are applied must not bring about discrimination against nationals of other member states."

Given the importance of education in implementing such a policy, said the

---

[96] The defendants were the Minister for Justice, Ireland and the Attorney General. See too O' Hanlon J's decision in *O Murchú v. Cláraitheoir na gCuideachtaí agus an tAire Tionscáil agus Tráchtála* (High Court, June 20, 1988). The defendants there were the Registrar of Companies and the Minister for Industry and Commerce.

[97] As to which see Chap. 8 *infra*. s.v. Membership of the European Communities.

court, it was not unreasonable to require teachers to have some knowledge of the first national language. But that requirement must be applied in a proportionate and non-discriminatory manner; thus, for example, there could be no requirement that the relevant linguistic knowledge must have been acquired within the national territory.

3   The President and the Council of State

Under Article 12.1 the President takes precedence over all other persons in the State. This, together with the functions performed, shows the holder of the office to be the head of state, though the Constitution does not explicitly so describe the President. Since 1948 he/she has been head of state for external as well as internal purposes: Republic of Ireland Act 1948, s.3. The President is not, however, even formally the head of government, this role being specifically assigned to the Taoiseach (Art. 28.5.1°). The two positions cannot be combined, for the Taoiseach must be a Dáil deputy (Art. 28.7.1°) whereas the President may not be a member of either House of the Oireachtas (Art. 12.6.1°).

The terms of the Constitution show clearly that the President is intended to play a mainly ceremonial role,[1] similar to that of many other heads of state. The decisions involved are, in general, taken "on the advice of the Government"—a polite formula which means that Ministers decide. This general principle is stated clearly and unambiguously in Article 13.9. There are, however, some situations where the President is empowered to make a personal decision: these are examined in detail later.

Election of the President

In contrast with other European constitutions, such as those of Italy or Germany, Bunreacht na hÉireann anticipates the direct election of the President by the people: Art. 12.2.1°. But it also provides that if only one candidate is nominated an election shall not be necessary: Art. 12.4.5°. Should an election prove necessary, it must be held 60 days before the current term expires; or, if the incumbent has been removed, become incapable, resigned or died, within 60 days of the relevant event: Art. 12.3.3°. In an election all citizens eligible to vote in Dáil elections enjoy the franchise: Art. 12.2.2.°.

To be eligible for election, one must be a citizen of at least 35. So says the English version of Article 12.4.1.°; unfortunately the Irish text of the same provision conveys a different message, and by virtue of Article 25.5.4° it is the Irish text which prevails. It requires that a candidate have *completed* his thirty-fifth year—a rather different thing. (This issue also arises under Art.

---

[1] The whole nature of the office suggests that it is non-political, in the sense that its holder, like a judge, is meant to be divorced from party politics. Mr. de Valera, however, is said to have "played a major role in resolving a political crisis within Fianna Fáil when Kevin Boland resigned from the cabinet in protest over the government's policy regarding Northern Ireland": T. Ryle Dwyer, *Eamon de Valera* (Dublin 1980), p. 146.

16, and is more fully considered in Chap. 4 *infra*.) However, this textual conflict has not so far given rise to any difficulty; those persons nominated for election since 1937 were amply qualified even by the more stringent criterion.

A candidate must be nominated by 20 members of the Oreachtas or by four county councils: Art. 12.4.1° and 2°.[2] A former or retiring President may nominate him/herself, as President Hillery did in 1983. The election is to be by secret ballot, and based on proportional representation by the single transferable vote: Art. 12.2.3°. Further details are left to be regulated by law, *i.e.* statute, (Art. 12.5) and such provision is duly made by the Presidential Elections Acts 1937–1973.

Notwithstanding these elaborate provisions, Presidential elections have been the exception rather than the rule. Dr Hyde was unopposed in 1938, as was Mr O'Kelly in 1952, Mr O Dálaigh in 1974 and Dr Hillery in 1976 and 1983. Contested elections have occurred, therefore, only in 1945, 1959, 1966, 1973 and 1990. And only in 1945 and 1990 did proportional representation actually function, for this necessarily requires a minimum of three candidates.[3]

Entry on office, tenure, etc.

The President enters on office by publicly making the declaration set out in Article 12.8 of the Constitution. In practice this is done at a ceremony in Dublin Castle (nowadays televised) attended by, among others, Ministers, Dáil deputies and senators, judges, members of the diplomatic corps and other distinguished figures. The term of office runs for seven years from that date. The office may be held for a maximum of two terms only, whether consecutive or not: Art. 12.3.2°. As noted above, the holder may not simultaneously be a deputy or senator, and a member of the Oireachtas elected to the Presidency is deemed to have vacated his or her seat. (The vacancy would arise automatically, so that a by-election need not await a formal resignation.) Nor may the President hold "any other office or position of emolument": Art. 12.6.3°. This is construed in practice as if it read "any other office of emolument or position of emolument"; hence the President may hold some purely honorary office such as that of Chancellor of the National University of Ireland or patron of some charitable society. The President is provided with an official residence: Art 12.11.1° makes this a constitutional requirement rather than a matter of executive grace (the Irish text, by using the term "státarás" puts this beyond doubt). The emoluments and

---

[2] As Senator Carmencita Hederman discovered in 1990, this makes it impossible for someone to contest the Presidency unless he/she has the support of a political party or a group of parties. In *Lennon* v. *Minister for the Environment* (*The Irish Times*, October 23, 1990) the plaintiff sought an injunction to halt the forthcoming Presidential election because of this. He argued that the provisions of Art. 12.4.2° of the Constitution were contrary to the common good in that they permitted elected politicians unfairly to limit the choice available to the people. Egan J. rejected the application, asking why it had not been made a month earlier. See further Chap. 11 *infra*.

[3] In 1990 the candidates were Mr Austin Currie (F.G.), Mr Brian Lenihan (F.F.) and Mrs Mary Robinson, who was supported by the Labour Party and the Workers' Party. Mrs. Robinson was elected on the second count, following Mr Currie's elimination (*The Irish Times*, November 10, 1990). For the results of earlier elections see *Results of Presidential Elections and Referenda 1937–1979* (Prl. 8624).

allowances are fixed by statute—the Presidential Establishment Acts 1938–1973.[4] By virtue of Article 12.11.3° these may not be diminished during the President's continuance in office, so he/she cannot be nudged into resignation by a legislatively-imposed penury. This guarantee, however, is no more a shield against taxation or inflation than the corresponding one for judges in Article 35.5.

Most of the President's functions are purely formal. Article 13 clearly envisages him or her in the role of ceremonial head of state[5]—summoning and dissolving the Dáil, signing Bills into law, appointing Ministers, the Attorney General (Art. 30.2) the Comptroller and Auditor General (Art. 33.2) and judges (Art. 35.1). In all these matters no question of personal choice arises, the effective decision being made by others. Article 13.9 puts this beyond doubt by laying down that, save where *expressly* provided otherwise, the President's constitutional powers and functions are exercisable only on the advice of the Government. And although additional powers and functions may be conferred on the President by law, these too are subject to the same condition: Art. 13.10 and 11.

Few statutory powers have in fact been conferred upon the President.[6] Under the Republic of Ireland Act 1948, he/she exercises the executive power of the State in foreign affairs, acting on the advice of the Government. This involves the formal accreditation of ambassadors and the reception of foreign envoys accredited to Ireland. In addition, the most formal and significant international agreements may be concluded in the President's name— especially if this practice is followed by the other states parties thereto. Such agreements will, however, be signed on behalf of the State by the Taoiseach or another Minister: see, for example, the Treaty of Accession to the EEC (Prl. 2253, 1972).

A more recent instance is found in the Ombudsman Act 1980, s.2(2). This provides that the Ombudsman shall be appointed by the President on the recommendation of the Dáil and Seanad. It is difficult to square this provision—literally construed—with Article 13.11, which appears to mean that powers conferred by statute on the President are to be exercisable only on the advice of the Government. In practice, of course, the Government will consult the Opposition and an agreed recommendation will emerge; this the Government could then advise the President to accept, so that the Constitution's formal requirements are satisfied. Thus while at first sight the Act apparently conflicts with the letter of the Constitution, *as operated* it may accord with its spirit. Whether this would prove enough to save section 2(2) for judicial condemnation is far from clear.

Like many other heads of state, the President is the titular supreme commander of the Defence Forces (Art. 13.4). But the *actual* command—as is

---

[4] The 1973 Act, in s.2, fixes the President's salary as that of the Chief Justice plus 10 per cent. It also provides for a pension for former Presidents of half the current rate of the Presidential salary (s.3).

[5] For a portrait of Presidential activities see Chap. XII of John N. Young. *Erskine H. Childers, President of Ireland* (Gerrards Cross 1985).

[6] Under the Irish Nationality and Citizenship Act 1956, s.12, the President may grant Irish citizenship to an individual as a token of honour; but it is "the opinion of the Government" which determines whether this shall be done. In addition, the President exercises certain functions under the Institute for Advanced Studies Act 1940, including the appointment of senior professors; s.8. But all those functions are expressed to be exercisable on the advice of the Government.

foreshadowed by Article 13.5.1°—is exercised by the Government, acting through the Minister for Defence (Defence Act 1954, s.17).

Two other provisions serve to emphasise the President's formal, non-executive role. Article 13.7 permits him/her to address a message to the Oireachtas or to "the Nation," but only when its contents have received Government approval. By virtue of Article 12.9 he/she may leave "the State" only with Government consent. Doubtless the rationale of the latter is that a Presidential trip abroad may conceivably have political overtones. Thus in 1981 the Government was reported as having decided that, because of the Northern Ireland situation, it would be inappropriate for President Hillery to attend the wedding of the heir to the British throne (*The Irish Times*, July 8, 1981). It is unclear whether this restriction requires Government clearance for a Presidential journey to Northern Ireland (see further Chap. 2 *supra*).

The prerogative of clemency

In common with several other constitutions, Bunreacht na hÉireann vests the prerogative of clemency in the head of state (Art. 13.6). This power, however, is subject to Article 13.9 and hence exercisable only on the advice of the Government. It has three facets:

(a) the power to pardon
(b) the power to commute (*i.e.* change) punishment
(c) the power to remit any such punishment

It is clear from the terms of Article 13.6 that the power to pardon, and to commute or remit punishment in capital cases, cannot be lodged elsewhere. In contrast, the power of commutation or remission in non-capital cases may be conferred by law on other authorities, and this has duly been done. The Criminal Justice Act 1951, s.23 grants this power to the Government, which is expressly authorised (subs. (3)) to delegate it to the Minister for Justice, and to revoke any such delegation.

It follows that the Government cannot delegate its function of advising the President in regard to pardons, and those granted duly recite the fact that the President has acted on the advice of the Government. This power to pardon has seldom been exercised—indeed there seem to have been three instances only, in 1940, 1943 and 1992.[7]

The Constitution does not descend into detail on the pardoning power, and its incidents thus presumably depend upon the common law. In *Ex p. Garland* (1866) 71 U.S. (4 Wall) 330, 380, Field J., delivering the judgment of the Supreme Court, said:

> "It extends to every offence known to the laws and may be exercised at any time after its commission, either before legal proceedings are taken, or during their pendency, or after conviction and judgment . . . "

He went on to say that a pardon reached both the punishment prescribed for the offence, and the guilt of the offender.[8] In England, the Court of Appeal

---

[7] As regards the 1940 and 1943 cases, see the *Report of the Committee to enquire into Certain Aspects of Criminal Procedure* (March 1990), pp. 16–18. For that of 1992—the Nicky Kelly case—see the text of the Government statement printed in *The Irish Times*, April 29, 1992.

[8] The pardons granted in 1940 and 1943 are in terms which remit the relevant punishment *and* absolve from guilt: *ibid.*

has held, however, that a free pardon does not eliminate a conviction, but only the pains, penalties and punishments that ensue therefrom; thus an appeal against the conviction is still competent—*R*. v. *Foster* [1984] 2 All E.R. 679.

The power to grant a pardon includes power to grant a general amnesty: *U.S.* v. *Klein* (1891) 80 U.S. (13 Wall) 128.[9] It also covers criminal—but not civil—contempt: *Ex p. Grossman* (1925) 267 U.S. 87, 111, where Taft C.J., speaking for the court, stressed that in civil contempts the punishment was remedial and for the benefit of the complainant, and a pardon could not stop it. Irish law, it would seem, is to the same effect: see *State (O)* v. *O'Brien* [1973] I.R. 50, 73 *per* Walsh J.; *Keegan* v. *De Burca* [1973] I.R. 223, 227, *per* Ó Dálaigh C.J.[10]

The Presidential power to commute or remit punishment in capital cases is now inoperative. This is the consequence of the Criminal Justice Act 1990 which provides, in s.1:

"No person shall suffer death for any offence.[11]

The Presidential power would of course revive if the 1990 Act were repealed and capital punishment reinstated. But this seems most unlikely to occur, not least because it would involve a breach of the State's international obligations. For the Sixth Protocol to the European Convention on Human Rights[12]—which Ireland has signed—requires the abolition of the death penalty.

DISCRETIONARY POWERS

As already noted, most of the President's powers are exercisable only on the advice of the Government. In a number of instances, however, he/she is authorised to exercise an independent discretion. These cases are now considered in the specific contexts in which they arise.

---

[9] Under U.S. law the pardoning power embraces the power to commute capital sentences. The Supreme Court has held that this (a) does not require the consent of the person affected: *Biddle* v. *Perovich* (1927) 274 U.S. 480; (b) may be subject to conditions, such as no parole: *Schick* v. *Reed* (1974) 419 U.S. 256. It has also held that the pardoning power flows from the Constitution alone and cannot be modified, abridged or diminished by legislation: *Schick's* case, *supra*. The judicial Committee of the Privy Council has held that a person *prima facie* covered by a valid amnesty, who is later arrested and charged, may plead the pardon in habeas corpus proceedings. He/she is not restricted to invoking the pardon as a plea in bar at the eventual trial: *Philip* v. *D.P.P. of Trinidad & Tobago* [1992] 1 All E.R. 665.

[10] In other states pardons have sometimes been granted before conviction or even the formal institution of proceedings—most notably in the U.S in 1974 when President Ford pardoned Mr. Nixon and in 1986 in Israel when President Herzog pardoned certain members of the security service. Since the power to pardon in Art. 13.9 is not expressed to depend upon conviction, similar action would seem constitutionally permissible in Ireland.

[11] The 1990 Act specifies that a person convicted of treason or murder shall be sentenced to imprisonment for life (s.2). Special provision is made in relation to certain murders and attempts—including the murder or attempted murder of a *Garda* or prison officer acting in the course of his/her duty. Persons convicted of such offences will receive a minimum sentence— 40 years in the case of murder, 20 years in that of attempted murder (s.4). These provisions reflect the previous law and practice, for the Criminal Justice Act 1964 had reduced the categories of capital murder to four. Moreover, the invariable practice had been to commute capital sentences passed under the 1964 Act by substituting a sentence of imprisonment for 40 years.

[12] See further Chap. 8 *infra*.

Summoning and dissolving the Dáil

By virtue of Article 13.2.1° the Dáil is summoned and dissolved by the President on the advice of the Taoiseach. But Article 13.2.2° goes on to provide that the President may 'in his absolute discretion" refuse a dissolution to "a Taoiseach who has ceased to retain the support of a majority in Dáil Éireann." Several points about this require to be noticed.

1. There is no discretion as regards summoning the Dáil—*i.e.* following a general election. The President may act only on the advice of the incumbent Taoiseach—who holds office until the Dáil elects his successor or re-elects him. But this does not mean that a Taoiseach who has lost a general election can defer indefinitely his departure from office. Article 16 lays down an election timetable which avoids this possibility. A general election must take place not later than 30 days after the dissolution of the Dáil (Art. 16.3.2°) and the new Dáil must meet within 30 days of polling day (Art. 16.4.2°).

2. In the circumstances envisaged by Article 13.2.2° an "absolute discretion" is conferred upon the President. Thus while in regard to other discretionary powers the Council of State must be consulted, there is no such obligation in this context.

3. The power to refuse a dissolution has never yet been exercised—though circumstances have certainly arisen when it might have been. In January 1982 the coalition Government led by Dr. FitzGerald was defeated in a Dáil vote on the Budget. The Taoiseach requested a dissolution, and the President agreed. Contemporary reports claimed that the Opposition had urged President Hillery to refuse (*Sunday Tribune*, February 7, 1982). A similar situation arose in November 1982, when the Dáil passed a vote of no confidence in the Fianna Fáil Government of Mr. Haughey. Here again the President acceded to a request for a dissolution.[13]

4. We do not know what factors led President Hillery to decide as he did in these cases. One consequence was three general elections in 18 months—June 1981, February 1982 and November 1982. However, it would be premature to conclude that the power of refusal is now, in practical terms, defunct. The election of June 1981 produced no clear Dáil majority for any party or parties, and the same result—a "hung Dáil—followed that of February 1982. The President might well have reasoned that a fresh appeal to the electorate was the only way to resolve such an *impasse*. His decision might have been different had an alternative government with a clear chance of a reasonable term of office been available.

5. This power to refuse a dissolution is found in other constitutions in the common law world. The view generally held is that a dissolution can be refused only if an alternative government is feasible, can be assured of a working majority and can be expected to carry on for a reasonable period of

---

[13] There was a precedent in 1944. The Fianna Fail minority government—in office since the general election of June 1943—was defeated on a Dáil motion to defer the Transport Bill. Mr. de Valera immediately sought a dissolution and, despite opposition calls for a national government to face the wartime emergency, this was granted by President Hyde. Dr. Gallagher (*op. cit. supra*, p. 85) has noted that " . . . only six of the sixteen [now seventeen] dissolutions since 1937 have taken place on the advice of a Taoiseach who indisputably commanded majority support in the Dáil."

time.[14] Similar considerations must apply to the President's power under Article 13.2.2°; and the difficulty of predicting whether these conditions will be fulfilled need hardly be stressed. Consequently, to allow a dissolution will normally be the wiser and less controversial course.

6. The President must be able to make an informed decision as to whether the conditions mentioned above exist. For this reason there could scarcely be any objection to Opposition leaders communicating to the President their calculations as to the parliamentary arithmetic; the President cannot be assumed to be *au fait* with the position.[15] But any attempt to put pressure on the President would clearly be improper.

7. The most difficult situation would arise if, following a general election, the new Dáil was unable to nominate a Taoiseach—as initially occurred in June/July 1989. If the outgoing Taoiseach then sought a dissolution (assuming this to be constitutionally possible[16]) the President would have a delicate decision to make. No doubt much would depend on the time that had elapsed between the reassembly of the Dáil and the request for a dissolution; an outgoing Taoiseach, defeated for renomination, who *immediately* presented such a request might receive an unsympathetic response.[17] On the other hand, if lengthy negotiations had proved the impossibility of *any* individual securing a Dáil majority the President would have no option but to dissolve.

8. It would seem to follow from the wording of Article 28.10 that a Taoiseach who is refused a dissolution is obliged to resign. It is important to note that the President plays no active role in choosing the new holder of that office. Under Article 13.1.1° the nomination of the new Taoiseach is a matter for the Dáil, and the President is not empowered to entrust anyone with the formation of a new government. In this respect Bunreacht na hÉireann differs from several other European constitutions.[18]

---

[14] See B.S. Markesinis, *The Theory and Practice of Dissolution of Parliament* (Cambridge 1972); Geoffrey Marshall, *Constitutional Conventions* (Oxford 1984) Chap. III; Vernon Bogdamor, "The United Kingdom", in David Butler and D. A. Low (eds.), *Sovereigns and Surrogates* (London 1991), pp. 10–40.

[15] Compare the situation in Tasmania in 1989, where the Governor embarked on a detailed appraisal of the parliamentary situation before commissioning a new premier: see Brian Galligan, "Australia" in Butler and Low, *op. cit.*, at pp. 92–96.

[16] This question is discussed in Chap. 6 *infra*.

[17] This matter gave rise to some controversy in July 1989. Mr C.J. Haughey T.D. failed to secure a majority for his nomination as Taoiseach (as had all others proposed). He formally resigned—though continuing in office, as Art. 28.11.2° requires. In an RTÉ radio interview Mr Haughey affirmed his belief in his authority to seek a dissolution, and said that "the accepted widsom" was that such a request would never be refused. This was severely criticised in Dáil Éireann on July 3, 1989 by the Fine Gael, Labour and Progressive Democrat leaders. Mr. Dukes (F.G.) spoke of an unprecedented attempt to prejudge the President's response to a dissolution request (391 *Dáil Debs.*, c. 66). Mr. Spring (Labour) said that there was no accepted wisdom in this matter; there was only the absolute discretion of the President (*Ibid*, c.68). Mr. O'Malley (P.D.) said that Deputy Haughey had " . . . no right to belittle, prejudge or pre-empt the clear and real role of the President" (*ibid*, c.73). Mr. Haughey replied that he knew the views of a number of Presidents on this matter. There had been nothing sinister in his remarks; it was " . . . simply a question of looking at what the Constitution provides and where the exercise of this or that power might lead us." But he had not discussed this matter with President Hillery, nor had he any intention of doing so (*ibid.*, c. 89).

[18] See further the *Report of the Committee on the Constitution, December 1967* (Pr. 9817), pp. 11–13 and Annex 2; also Vernon Bogdanor, "European Constitutional Monarchies" in Butler and Low, *op. cit.*, pp. 274–297. That some other European Presidents enjoy considerable authority in this regard is shown by Maurice Duverger, *Échec au Roi* (Paris 1978), Chaps. 1–3.

9. As Dr. McDunphy observed, the President is not obliged to state his/her reasons for refusal.[19] Nor is this exercise of discretion subject to judicial review: Article 13.8.1°. It follows that the meaning of the ambiguous phrase on which the power depends—"ceased to retain the support of a majority in Dáil Éireann"—will never be settled by a judicial decision. An allegedly improper refusal of a dissolution could, however, be made the basis for impeachment under Article 12.10.

As noted above, the key phrase "ceased to retain the support of a majority in Dáil Éireann," found in Articles 13.2.2° and 28.10, is ambiguous. It may be expected, however, that the President would interpret it in a way which accords with political practice—as referring to a vote of no confidence or something equivalent thereto, such as a defeat on the Budget. A Government defeated on an issue on which its supporters were given a free vote is not in practice understood to have forfeited the confidence of the Dáil. It may also be expected that the word "in" would be read literally—that is, that the loss of majority support must, and can only, be manifested by a vote on the floor of the Dáil.[20] A harmonious interpretation of the Constitution would seem to demand this; the Taoiseach is put *into* office in this way and it would be strange if he could be put *out* in any other fashion. Furthermore, it has been the experience in other countries—notably in India—that parliamentarians who have allegedly communicated to the head of state their withdrawal of support from a prime minister have subsequently taken a different stance in a parliamentary vote.

Legislation

Under Article 13.3.1° every Bill requires the President's signature for its enactment into law. Article 25 implies that in most cases this is a routine matter, with the President acting on the advice of the Taoiseach. A timetable is fixed by Article 25.1, which envisages the presentation of a Bill to the President for signature as soon as it has been passed. By virtue of Article 25.2.1° the Bill must be signed not earlier than the fifth, and not later than the seventh, day after the date of its presentation to the President. He/she may, however, sign it earlier at the Government's request, provided that the Seanad concurs (Art. 25.2.2°). This provision for an "early signature motion" is an obvious safeguard against a situation where the normal time lag might operate against the public interest. In recent times it has been utilised in regard to the Insurance (No. 2) Act 1983 and the Offences against the State (Amendment) Act 1985—the Bills for which were, by agreement, passed by both Houses in one day. (The first empowered the High Court to appoint an administrator to the ailing P.M.P.A. insurance company; the second established machinery whereby money in a private bank account—thought to belong to an illegal organisation—could be transferred to the control of the High Court.)

Article 13.3.2° obliges the President to promulgate every law made by the

---

[19] *The President of Ireland* (Dublin 1945), p. 52.
[20] As to India, see the cases discussed by J.N. Pandey, *Constitutional Law of India* (20th ed., Allahabad 1989), p. 340–345. In Queensland in 1987 the Governor declined to withdraw the Premier's commission—even though he had demonstrably lost the leadership of his party—

Oireachtas. This is clarified by Article 25.4.2°: promulgation is effected simply by the publication at his/her direction of a notice in *Iris Oifigiúil* (the official gazette) stating that the Bill has become law.

Money Bills

The President's first discretionary power in the legislative sphere arises in regard to Money Bills—a term defined at length in Article 22.1. In regard to such Bills the Seanad's powers are restricted and its time for considering them is much shorter than usual (see Art. 21 and p. 000 *infra*). Should a dispute arise between the two Houses as to whether a Bill is or is not a Money Bill, the Seanad may request the President to refer the issue to a Committee of Privileges (Art. 22.2.2°).

On receipt of such a request the President is obliged to consult the Council of State on the matter (Art. 22.2.3°). As in all such cases, however, the final decision lies with the President. If the request is granted, the President appoints a Committee of Privileges consisting of an equal number of deputies and senators, with a Supreme Court judge as chairman. The size of the committee is not specified. The President must consult the Council of State as to the choice of the individual members. The chairman votes only in the event of a tie.

This power has never been used. Normally the Government will have a majority in the Seanad as well as in the Dáil, and the possibility of conflict between the chambers is therefore remote. A workable constitution must however provided for the abnormal case; and Article 22 envisages a Presidential role in safeguarding the Seanad's position against a Government anxious to hasten the passage of Bills by questionable expedients.

Under the 1922 Constitution one such Committee of Privileges had to be established. Chaired by Kennedy C.J. and constituted at the request of the Dáil, it had to rule on the Land Purchase (Guarantee Fund) Bill 1935. On the chairman's casting vote it was decided that this was a Money Bill.

Article 24

Under Article 24 (which has not so far been invoked) the President again has the task of safeguarding the Seanad's powers and privileges. Article 24 offers the Government a means of curtailing the Seanad's time for considering a Bill. Following the Dáil's passage of the Bill the Taoiseach is permitted to certify it as "urgently and immediately necessary" on certain grounds. This he does by written messages to the President and the chairmen of both Houses. The Dáil may then, by resolution, specify what period the Seanad shall have for considering the Bill. Since Article 24 sets no minimum, that period may be as brief as the Dáil (in reality the Government majority therein) desires.

The effect of Article 24 is temporarily to obliterate the Seanad from the legislative process. For the Seanad is unable to avoid its effect by ignoring the relevant Bill, or rejecting it, or amending it in ways unacceptable to the Dáil.

until he resigned or was defeated in Parliament: see Galligan, *op. cit.*, pp. 85–92. *Contra*, Gallagher, *op. cit.*, who says (at p. 84): " . . . the mere fact that a doomed Taoiseach reaches Arus an Uachtaráin before a vote of censure can be taken should not enhance a request to dissolve." Nonetheless, I still adhere to the opinion expressed above.

Once the specified period has elapsed the Bill is deemed to have been passed by both Houses—Art. 24.2.

For the resolution abridging the Seanad's time for consideration to be effective, however, the President must concur in it. Once again, the Council of State must be consulted—but the President is not bound by its members' views.

The procedure under Article 24 cannot be used in relation to a Bill to amend the Constitution.

Article 26

As noted above, the signature of Bills is normally a routine matter in regard to which the President acts on advice. This does not apply, however, if there is cause to doubt the Bill's constitutionality. In such a case Article 26 empowers the President to refer the Bill—or any specified provision or provisions—to the Supreme Court for a ruling[21] on its validity. Here again the President is obliged to consult the Council of State, though the final decision is his/hers alone.[22]

A President untrained in constitutional law may have difficulty in deciding whether a Bill is of doubtful validity; and currently there are no arrangements for him/her to obtain independent legal advice. One factor that seems to weigh in Presidential decision-making is whether constitutional misgivings have found expression on both sides of the Oireachtas. Thus the Dáil spokesmen of both Government and Opposition effectively invited the President to send the Electoral (Amendment) Bill 1983 to the Supreme Court—as he did. The Article 26 power cannot be used in regard to Money Bills, Constitution amendment Bills or Bills passed under Article 24. Any other Bill will, however, potentially fall within its scope. Article 26 has so far been used eight times, *viz*:

    (a) the Offences against the State (Amendment) Bill 1940 [1940] I.R. 470
    (b) the School Attendance Bill 1942 [1943] I.R. 334
    (c) the Electoral Amendment Bill 1961 [1961] I.R. 169
    (d) the Criminal Law (Jurisdiction) Bill 1975 [1977] I.R. 129
    (e) the Emergency Powers Bill 1976 [1977] I.R. 159
    (f) the Housing (Private Rented Dwellings) Bill 1981 [1983] I.R. 181
    (g) the Electoral (Amendment) Bill 1983 [1984] I.R. 268
    (h) the Adoption (No. 2) Bill 1987 [1989] I.R. 656.

Of these measures (b) (f) and (g) were held unconstitutional. The Council of State was convened to consider four other Bills—the Health Bill 1947, the Income Tax (Consolidation) Bill 1967, the Criminal Justice Bill 1984 and (in October 1991) the Fisheries (Amendment) Bill 1990.

Article 26 imposes tight time-limits. The reference must be made not later

---

[21] Article 26.3 makes it clear that the President is bound by the Supreme Court's decision. If the court finds the Bill repugnant to the Constitution, the President "shall decline" to sign it. If the court finds in favour of the Bill the President "shall sign" it "as soon as may be." Thus the court gives a *ruling*, not an advisory opinion as Kenny J. seems to suggest in *Ryan* v. *Att. Gen.* [1965] I.R. 294, at 311–312.

[22] During the Dáil debate on the Extradition (Amendment) Bill 1987, an amendment was put down specifying that the date for the Act's coming into operation—to be fixed by order— should not be earlier than the date on which judgment had been given by the Supreme Court,

than seven days from the date of the Bill's presentation for signature: Article 26.1.2°. Thus the President has only one week in which to meditate on the Bill, assemble the Council of State and reflect on the views expressed, and make a decision. Article 26.1.3° directs him/her not to sign any Bill referred pending the pronouncement of the Supreme Court's decision.

Should the Supreme Court hold the Bill—or any provision thereof— unconstitutional, the President must decline to sign it: Article 26.3.1°. If the Bill is upheld it is to be signed "as soon as may be" after the date of the Court's decision: Article 26.3.3°.

Article 26 is further considered in Chapter 11 *infra*.

Constitution amendment Bills

Under Articles 46 and 47 the Constitution can be amended only when a Bill for that purpose has been passed by the Oireachtas *and* approved by the electorate in a referendum. Article 46.5 duly provides that the President is to sign such a Bill only on being satisfied that the provisions of that Article have been complied with, and that the Bill has been approved in a referendum.

Article 46.4 specifies that a Constitution amendment Bill "shall not contain any other proposal." This led Barrington J. to conclude that if this provision were infringed the President would be justified in refusing to sign the Bill—on the ground that he/she could not be "satisfied that the provisions of this Article have been complied with" (Art. 46.5): see *Finn* v. *Att. Gen.* [1983] I.R. 154, 162. However, when the case arrived there on appeal, the Supreme Court found it unnecessary to pronounce on this matter: [1983] I.R. 154, 164–65.

Article 27

Article 27, like Article 24, assumes a serious conflict of views between the Dáil and Seanad; and since these have been rare, it too has never yet been utilised. Article 27 presupposes a situation where the Seanad rejects a Bill passed by the Dáil, or passes it only with amendments unacceptable to the Dáil. In the normal course of events the Dáil will have its way: see Article 23. Under Article 27, however, if a majority of senators and not less than one-third of the deputies petition the President not to sign the Bill, he/she may decline to do so until certain specified conditions have been fulfilled. Any such petition must state the grounds on which it is based and must be presented within four days of the date on which the Bill is deemed to have been passed: Art. 27.3. The President is then to consider it "forthwith," consult the Council of State and pronounce a decision within six days: Art. 27.4.1°. This latter time-limit is relaxed somewhat if the Bill has been referred to the Supreme Court under Article 26: see Article 27.4.2°.

The question the petition will raise, and the President must ponder, is— does the Bill contain a proposal of such national importance that the will of the people upon it should be ascertained? (See Art. 27.5.1°.) Should the President conclude that it does, the Taoiseach and the chairmen of both Houses must be informed that he/she will not sign the Bill unless:

following a Presidential reference under Article 26. The amendment was disallowed, the Leas-Cheann Comhairle explaining that this was because it could be prejudicial to the discretion of the President in referring matters (376 *Dáil Debs.* c. 444, December 2, 1987).

    (a) the Bill is approved in a referendum under Article 47.2, or

    (b) is approved by a resolution of the new Dáil, following a general elec-
        tion.

Should the bill be so approved the President is then obliged to sign it: Art.
27.5.2°. The same would, of course, apply if the petition was rejected: Art.
27.6.

Should Article 27 be invoked and a referendum ensue, it would be subject
to Article 47.2. Under this the principle is one of popular *veto*; so even if a
majority should vote against the Bill, it becomes law unless that majority
amounts to one-third of registered voters. Thus, if the total of registered
voters is 1,500,000 and the voting is 400,000 against and 300,000 for, the Bill
in question will become law because the majority against it is not one-third,
i.e. 500,000. This principle is unique to Article 27 cases: it has no application
in a referendum on a Bill to amend the Constitution.

Convening the Oireachtas

The President's final discretionary power is to convene a meeting of either
or both Houses of the Oireachtas: Art. 13.2.3°. He/she is again obliged to
consult the Council of State.

This power has never been exercised,[23] and it is difficult to envisage circumstances in which it would be. Its terms presuppose an unlikely situation—that parliament is in recess, that an emergency arises and yet,
notwithstanding this, the Government declines to recall the chambers. The
Article is, in Professor Chubb's words, "obviously intended to cover an emergency when those whose job it is to call a meeting cannot or will not."[24] But
the President's power does not appear to go beyond formally convening the
meeting. He/she cannot, it seems, address a message to the recalled parliament without Government approval. A general rule requiring such approval
for all Presidential communications (whether with the legislature or the public) is laid down in Article 13.7.3°, and no exception is made for those to a
reconvened Oireachtas. This must rob the reconvening power of real effect,
for it would seem difficult for the President to override Government objections to such a course when he/she has no independent power to explain
what emergency justified so unusual a decision. Moreover it is plain that the
President has no authority to submit to the Oireachtas any personal plans for
meeting the emergency.

THE VALUE OF THE PRESIDENCY

The utility of the office of President has been the subject of frequent discussion. The 1967 *Report* of the Committee on the Constitution[25] devotes
several pages to the office, setting out *inter alia* the arguments for and against

---

[23] The power to address the Dáil and Seanad, following government approval (Art. 13.7.1°) has
been exercised twice—by President de Valera on January 21, 1969 (the 50th anniversary of
the meeting of the first Dáil) and by President Robinson on July 8, 1992. The latter was the
first such address given in Leinster House: see *The Irish Times*, July 9, 1992.

[24] Basil Chubb, *The Constitution and Constitutional Change in Ireland*, p. 27.

[25] This Committee, an all-party body, consisted only of deputies and senators. Its membership
is set out at p. 1 of its *Report* (Pr. 9817).

retaining it, for altering the method of election and for giving the President additional powers. On these issues no consensus was reached. Since then, the value of the office as currently constituted has on occasion been canvassed in the media, but no practical consequences have resulted.[26]

Some commentators seem to envisage an ill-defined leadership role for the President. Whatever the merits of such an idea it is abundantly clear that no such role is conceived of, or can be exercised under, the Constitution as it stands. Making policy is a matter for the Taoiseach and the Government. The structure and terms of the Constitution leave no room for doubt on this point, which is underlined by the Taoiseach's obligation merely to keep the President "generally informed" on matters of domestic and foreign policy: Art. 28.5.2°.

The President is assigned two different roles under the Constitution. The first—and usual—one is as formal head of State, exercising no political power.[27] The second—for special and unusual circumstances—is as a constitutional long stop. It is in this second role that the discretionary powers would come into play. The President's function in such circumstances is to preserve the basic constitutional scheme—for example the position of the Seanad (Art. 22 and 24), or the rights and interests of citizens (Art. 26 and 27).

It is not a sufficient argument against the office that only the Article 26 power has so far been invoked. The political stability which has obviated recourse to the others cannot be assumed to be immutable and, as already mentioned, a workable constitution must be designed for foul as well as fair weather. And if such powers are necessary, the head of State is the logical person to exercise them. In particular, the President's discretionary powers could not properly be entrusted to a judge, because most of them require the exercise of a political—not a legal—judgment.[28]

Other heads of State, though bereft of power in the strict sense, may occasionally exercise influence on a government's policy choices. However, since a condition of such influence is confidentiality about its exercise, the matter is virtually impossible to document.[29] Whether an Irish President can wield such influence is unknown and perhaps unknowable; but it seems unlikely. -

The election in 1990 of the first woman President of Ireland—also the youngest holder of the office so far—may well put the question of enhancing her role firmly on the political agenda. It seems significant that Mrs Robinson has, with Government approval, appointed a special adviser.[30] Possibly,

[26] Possible changes are discussed by Michael Gallagher, *op. cit.*, pp. 89–90.
[27] In 1953 President O'Kelly played a minor role in resolving a dispute between the Government and the Roman Catholic Church over the Health Bill. This included making Arus an Uachtaráin available—presumably as a neutral ground—for consultation between the two sides. See John Whyte, *Church and State in Modern Ireland* (2nd ed., Dublin 1980), pp. 288–290.
[28] This was one of the grounds on which Kennedy C.J. declined to act as Governor General in 1932: see Deirdre McMahon, "The Chief Justice and the Governor General Controversy in 1932" (1982) XVII *Irish Jurist* (N. S.) 145.
[29] See Vernon Bogdanor, "The United Kingdom" and J.R. Mallory, "Canada" in Butler and Low, *op. cit*, at pp. 30–33 and 52 respectively. Since 1978 the President of India has been empowered to ask the Cabinet to reconsider its advice, either generally or otherwise. He/she is, however, bound by advice rendered after such reconsideration: see Pandey, *op. cit*, pp. 270–271.
[30] *The Irish Times*, November 28, 1990.

Presidential state visits abroad may become more frequent, and an increase in the President's powers by statute seems likely to be considered.[31]

Criticism of the President

A crisis arose in 1976 when President Ó Dálaigh resigned, following criticism by the Minister for Defence, Mr. Donegan, of his decision to send the Emergency Powers Bill to the Supreme Court under Article 26. The Minister's language was intemperate and his choice of venue—an army mess-hall—quite inappropriate. Following the President's resignation, the question whether the holder of the office could properly be the subject of criticism was widely discussed. One view was that in exercising any discretionary power the President was making a politically significant—and personal—decision. Consequently he/she must, in the interests of free speech (guaranteed by Art. 40.6.1°i), be as open to criticism as any other person entrusted with such powers. To this it has been objected that it would be improper to criticise the President because he/she cannot answer back.

It is unclear whether the objection implies an inability to reply because it would be incompatible with the dignity of the office, or alternatively because of a constitutional bar to any such reply. As to the latter, the President may address "the Nation" only with Government approval: Art. 13.7. Must he/she then endure criticism in silence if approval is refused for a reply? Perhaps not. The Constitution distinguishes between the Nation, the State and the People. The President could then, arguably, issue without approval a statement in reply to criticism directed to "the People." To do so would not seem to infringe the letter of Article 13.7—whatever *about* its spirit.

If the President's use of discretionary power is open to criticism, as is submitted, such criticism should be reasoned, and temperate in tone. That levelled at President Ó Dálaigh did not satisfy these tests.[32]

No implied powers

On November 17, 1982 the *Irish Times* editorial carried suggestions as to how the President might have spared the country a third general election within 18 months. The writer seemed to believe that if the President thought a given party leader might not, on personality grounds, be able to muster a Dáil majority, he/she could invite another member of that party to form a Government. This is quite inaccurate. The President has no power to ask anyone—be he/she party leader or not—to form a Government. The Constitution does not *explicitly* confer any such authority on the President, and it spells out his/her functions so minutely as to preclude *implying* any such power.[33]

---

[31] On November 27, 1990 the Taoiseach, Mr. Haughey, in reply to a parliamentary question, said there were no current plans for such legislation, nor had he received specific proposals from anyone. But he undertook to keep the matter in mind (403 *Dáil Debs.*, cc. 1–2).

[32] See further Chubb, *op. cit*, pp. 29–30: also David Gwynn Morgan "The Emergency Powers Bill Reference" (1978) XIII *Irish Jurist* (N. s.) 67.

[33] The *Report of the Committee on the Constitution* (December 1967) discusses (pp. 11–13) the question of " . . . an arrangement involving the granting of discretionary powers to the Head of State in this connection." The experienced politicians who composed this committee would hardly have spent time considering this matter had the powers in question already been exercisable.

The same editorial went on to say that if there was any doubt whether the President had such a power, he/she should seek the view of the Supreme Court on the point. It is submitted:

(a) that the President has no power to do this, and
(b) that the Supreme Court has no jurisdiction to entertain any such reference.

As regards (a), the Constitution expressly gives the President power to invoke the Supreme Court's jurisdiction in one situation only—that covered by Article 26. For the reason given above, there can be no room for implying any additional powers. As regards (b), the Supreme Court's role in interpreting the Constitution arises only where the Constitution's conditions are fulfilled. For the court to have jurisdiction it must be presented with a case under Article 26 or, in the ordinary course of litigation, under Article 34. Should the President seek to refer the kind of issue suggested, neither condition would be satisfied and the court, it is submitted, would respectfully but firmly decline jurisdiction.

Non-answerability

As noted earlier, Article 13.8.1° provides that the President is not answerable to the Oireachtas—or to any court—for the exercise or purported exercise of his/her powers and functions. This non-answerability will apply both to the formal and discretionary powers.

In May 1981 a disabled citizen, Mrs Nora Draper, began High Court proceedings for an injunction to restrain the Taoiseach from advising the President to dissolve the Dáil. (The object was to halt the election until postal votes were granted by law to persons in her situation.) Mrs Draper's summons specifically named the President as a defendant, a matter which provoked the wrath of the Supreme Court. Refusing to hear any argument on the point, the Court struck out the President from the proceedings. O'Higgins C.J. observed that this was an open defiance of Article 13.8 and appeared *prima facie* to be an abuse of the process of the courts (*The Irish Times*, May 14, 1982).

In *State (Walshe)* v. *Murphy* [1981] I.R. 275 it was alleged that the respondent District Justice had not been validly appointed because he lacked the requisite statutory qualifications. It was contended, however, that the respondent had been appointed by the President under Article 35.1 and that because of Article 13.8.1° the President's order could not be reviewed by any court. A divisional court of the High Court (Finlay P., Gannon and Hamilton JJ.) rejected this argument. Finlay P., giving the judgment of the court, said ([1981] I.R. 275, 283):

"The consequences of such a doctrine are alarming and appear to me to indicate its unsoundness as a proposition of constitutional law. The President has a very great number of powers and functions which he performs on the advice of the Government, without any discretion on his part. In respect of these matters, apparently, he can not refuse to accede to that advice within the Constitution. Whilst, therefore, such acts require his intervention for their effectiveness in law, in fact they are the decision and act of the Executive. If the submission made on behalf of this respondent were correct, it would mean that the Executive would be in a position to act under the Constitution in respect of a number of matters contrary to the law and even contrary to the Constitution; and that, if such act required for its effectiveness the exercise of a function by the President, such illegal or unconstitutional conduct could not be reviewed by any court.

An extreme example of the consequences of such a doctrine is to be found in the provisions contained in the Constitution for the appointment of a government. Article 13, s.1, subs. 2, provides that the President shall, on the nomination of the Taoiseach and with the previous approval of Dáil Éireann, appoint the other members of the government. Apart from the Taoiseach, the Tánaiste and the Minister for Finance who must be members of Dáil Éireann, the other members of the government must either be members of Dáil Éireann or members of Seanad Éireann: see s.7 of Article 28. If a Taoiseach, with the previous approval of Dáil Éireann, nominated to the President a government consisting of a person who was neither a member of Dáil Éireann nor . . . Seanad Éireann or consisting of more than two persons who were members of Seanad Éireann, and if the President acceded to such nomination and appointed those persons as members of a government, then the illegal and unconstitutional nature of the government so formed could never be reviewed by any court—if the suggested effect of Article 13, s.8, subs.1, of the Constitution were correct."

REMOVAL FROM OFFICE

Permanent incapacity

The Constitution offers two distinct modes of removing the President from office. The first arises under Article 12.3.1° and covers a situation where the President may become "permanently incapacitated." The incapacity must be established to the satisfaction of the Supreme Court, consisting of not less than five judges.

The provision has not yet had to be invoked—which may be fortunate because its laconic terms leave many questions unanswered. It is not clear what procedure is envisaged—trial in open court, a hearing in chambers, or a visit to a hospital by the judges. Equally, there is no guidance as to who may take the initiative in seeking a declaration of incapacity. The Government has the most obvious and direct concern with the President's discharge of his/her duties; and the wording of Article 12.3.1° is probably wide enough to permit the Government to intervene. In addition it seems likely that any person or body with a sufficient interest could take the initiative, for example, a defeated candidate or political party.

Dr. McDunphy suggests[34] that on the court's announcing its view that the President was permanently incapacited, his/her term of office would automatically come to an end. This would appear to be the proper inference from the terms of Article 12.3, considered as a whole, and of Article 14.1 (the Presidential Commission).

---

[34] *Op. cit.*, p. 27.

Impeachment

Bunreacht na hÉireann's provisions on impeachment, though obviously inspired by those in the United States Constitution, are by no means indentical with them. Under Article 12.10.1° the ground is to be "stated misbehaviour"[35]; this would seems to cover anything from a criminal offence to a misuse of the President's discretionary powers. Either House of the Oireachtas may prefer a charge of misbehaviour; but a proposal to do so must be by notice of motion in writing signed by not less than 30 members of that House (Art, 12.10.3°). Further, the adoption of such a proposal requires a resolution supported by not less than two-thirds of the total membership of the relevant House—not, it should be noted, two-thirds of those actually voting: Art. 12.10.4°.

When a charge has been preferred, it is the function of the other House to investigate the charge, or cause it to be investigated—Art. 12.10.5°. It is clear that the investigating House may discharge this function itself, or delegate it to a committee, or a court or tribunal[36]; see Art. 14.8.2°. The President has, under Article 12.10.6°, the right to appear and be represented at the investigation of the charge.

If the charge is sustained, removal may be effected by a resolution supported by not less than two-thirds of the total membership of the investigating House: Art. 12.10.7°. Thus, removal by this process necessitates the concurrence of two-thirds of the total membership of both Houses; and since it is rare for a Government to command two such majorities, cross-party support would be essential.

THE COUNCIL OF STATE

The Council functions solely as an advisory body for the President in the exercise of his/her discretionary powers. The obligation to consult the Council is expressly stated in Articles 22, 24, 26 and 27, and is reinforced by the terms of Article 32. (Note, however, that the power to refuse a dissolution is exempt from any such requirement.)

The membership is regulated by Article 31 and consists of:

(a) the *ex officio* members—*i.e* the Taoiseach, the Tánaiste, the Chief Justice, the President of the High Court, the Chairman of the Dáil, the Cathaoirleach of the Seanad and the Attorney General;

(b) any former President, Taoiseach or Chief Justice able and willing to act as a member;

(c) up to seven other members appointed by the President in his/her absolute discretion. Such members serve only during the term or terms of the President who appoints them (Art. 31.5), and they may be removed for any reason the President deems sufficient (Art. 31.7).

---

[35] The Presidential impeachment provisions of the Indian Constitution (Art. 61) are very similar to those of Bunreacht na hÉireann, though the President of India can be impeached only for "violation of the Constitution."

[36] It is not clear whether delegation of this function to a court or tribunal would require legislation, or whether it might be done simply by resolution. Art. 13.8.2° speaks of a court or tribunal "appointed or designated by either of the Houses of Oireachtas." It may be that the omission from this formula of the words "by law" points to the sufficiency of a resolution for the purpose.

Under Article 31.8 it is for the President to determine the times and places of meetings of the Council of State. Traditionally they are held in Arus an Uachtaráin—the President's official residence.

Perhaps the most unusual feature of the Council's composition is the membership of the Chief Justice and the President of the High Court. Plainly, the holders of those offices might contribute valuably to a discussion on the possible reference of a Bill under Article 26. The difficulty, however, is that either or both may have to sit in the Supreme Court if the Bill is actually referred, and this may inhibit them from expressing any view.

The sole *power* conferred on the Council of State is exercisable only in a very remote contingency. Under Article 14.4, if no President is in office and all potential Presidential Commission members are dead or unable to act, the Council of State must arrange for the functions of the office to be performed.

THE PRESIDENTIAL COMMISSION

Article 14 provides for a Presidential Commission to act in place of the President. This body fills any lacuna occurring, not only through the death, removal from office or resignation[37] of a President but also from his/her absence abroad, temporary or permanent incapacity—or simple failure to perform his/her functions: Arts. 14.1 and 14.5.2°.

The Commission consists of the Chief Justice and the chairmen of the Dáil and Seanad. If the office of Chief Justice is vacant or its holder unable to act, his place is taken by the President of the High Court. The deputy chairmen of the Dáil and Seanad are named as substitutes on a similar basis: Art. 14.2. The Commission may function with two members only: Art. 14.3.

A dissolution of the Dáil does not work a vacancy in the Dáil and Seanad offices mentioned in Article 14. For its purposes, the outgoing chairmen and deputy chairmen remain in the office until their successors are elected: The Supreme Court so held in *Loftus* v. *Att. Gen.* [1979] I.R. 221.

The Presidential Commission has functioned on a number of occasions since 1937, most notably following the death in office of President Childers and the resignation of President Ó Dálaigh.

---

[37] Though clearly contemplating resignation, the Constitution specifies no procedure therefor. In the only case to occur so far President Ó Dálaigh executed an instrument of resignation under his hand and seal, and communicated his decision to the Taoiseach, the Ceann Comhairle and the Cathaoirleach. See also Mc Dunphy, *op. cit.*, Chap. VII.

4   The Composition of the Oireachtas

The Oireachtas is the name given by Article 15.1.1° to the national parliament. It consists of the President, a house of representatives called Dáil Éireann and a Senate called Seanad Éireann: Art. 15.2.1°. The Houses are to sit in or near the city of Dublin, or in such other place as they may from time to time determine: Art. 15.1.3°. In fact both chambers established themselves in Leinster House in 1922 and have never sat elsewhere.

Article 15.2.1° vests "the sole and exclusive power of making laws for the State" in the Oireachtas, and declares that no other legislative authority has power to make laws for the State. This made it clear that the United Kingdom Parliament did not possess any vestigial legislative power over the State. The provision also has important consequences for the separation of powers: see Chapter 9 *infra*.

Should it wish to do so, the Oireachtas has power to devolve law-making powers to subordinate legislatures: Art. 15.2.2°. It would therefore be quite possible, without a constitutional amendment, to devolve power to legislatures established on a provincial basis. Article 15.3 also permits the establishment or recognition of "functional or vocational councils representing branches of the social and economic life of the people." This provision reflects those notions of vocational organisation which were prevalent, particularly in Roman Catholic circles, in the 1930s and 1940s.[1] It has never been utilised and is now probably redundant.

The Oireachtas is forbidden to enact any law which is in any respect repugnant to the Constitution or any provision thereof. Should it do so the law in question is invalid to the extent of any such repugnancy: Art. 15.4. If it stood alone this might constitute no more than an aspiration, but it is complemented and made a reality by the provisions of Article 34 empowering the High Court and Supreme Court to pronounce upon the validity of statutes. As will be seen, the Constitution places numerous restrictions on the legislative power of the Oireachtas, many—though by no means all—springing from the provisions recognising fundamental rights.

One such restriction is imposed by Article 15.5—the Oireachtas is forbidden "to declare acts to be infringements of the law which were not so at the time of their commission." This certainly enshrines the philosophy common to most legal systems and encapsulated in the maxim *nulla poena sine lege*— that a statute declaring conduct to be criminal cannot have retrospective

---

[1] See J. H. Whyte, *Church and State in Modern Ireland* (2nd ed., Dublin 1980), Chap. 4.

effect. But as the Supreme Court made clear in *Magee* v. *Culligan* [1992] I.L.R.M. 186, it goes further. There Finlay C.J., for the court, said (at 190):

" . . . the provisions of Article 15.5 of the Constitution are an expressed and unambiguous prohibition against the enactment of retrospective laws declaring acts to be an infringement of the law, whether of the civil or criminal law. It does not contain any general prohibition on retrospection of legislation, nor can it be by any means interpreted as a general prohibition of that description."[2]

In *Doyle* v. *An Taoiseach* [1986] I.R.L.M. 693 the defence argued that any invalidity affecting a statutory instrument of 1979 which imposed a financial levy had been cured when it was expressly confirmed by the Finance Act 1980, s.79. Henchy J., giving the judgment of the Supreme Court, said this might be so had the levy period postdated the 1980 Act: but in fact that period ran from May to December 1979. Were section 79 held to operate retrospectively the consequence would be that non-payment of the levy in 1979 would be made, *ex post facto*, an infringement of the law. This would make section 79 invalid as repugnant to Article 15.5: thus it must be presumed to have a prospective operation only.

Article 15.6 vests the exclusive right to raise and maintain military or armed forces in the Oireachtas, and forbids the existence of any others. This is built upon by statute: the Offences against the State Act 1939, s.6(1), makes it a felony to form, maintain or be a member of an unauthorised armed or police force. The maximum penalty upon conviction was increased in 1976 to 20 years: Criminal Law Act 1976, s.2.

DÁIL ÉIREANN

Elections to the Dáil are governed principally by Article 16 of the Constitution, as amplified where permissible by statutory provisions. The Supreme Court has called Article 16 "a constitutional code for the holding of an election to Dáil Éireann, subject only to the statutory regulation of such election": *Re Article 26 and the Electoral (Amendment) Bill 1983* [1984] I.R. 268, 275.

The electorate

The basic provision here is Article 16.1.2°, as amended. This posits two categories of persons entitled to vote:

(a) citizens who have reached 18[3]
(b) such other persons who have reached 18 as may be specified by legislation.

The right to vote is, however, subject to two important qualifications stated in Article 16.1.2°. These are that the person is not disqualified by law, and that he or she "complies with the provisions of the law relating to the election of members of Dáil Éireann." In fact, the law nowadays does not impose any disqualification; formerly persons convicted of corrupt or illegal practices were disfranchised, but this was repealed by the Electoral Act 1963.

[2] See too Murphy J.'s decision in *Chestvale Properties Ltd.* v. *Glackin* [1992] I.L.R.M. 221.
[3] The previous age of 21 was reduced to 18 by the Fourth Amendment of the Constitution Act 1972.

The requirement of compliance with the provisions of the electoral law may operate in practice to exclude many persons from voting. By virtue of the Electoral Act 1963, s.26(1), entitlement to vote in a constituency is contingent upon being registered as a Dáil elector in that constituency. Registration in turn is governed by section 5 of the same Act, which requires (*inter alia*) that one be "ordinarily resident in that constituency" on the qualifying date. This has a number of consequences. One is that otherwise eligible citizens who are and always have been resident in Northern Ireland cannot register. Thus they will be unable to vote, not only in Dáil elections, but also in Presidential elections and referenda, since similar registration provisions apply to these: Electoral Act 1963, ss.51 and 70. Citizens over 18 who are resident abroad on the qualifying date will also be unable to register; but this does not apply to someone who, having given up ordinary residence in a constituency, intends to resume it within 18 months: Electoral Act 1963, s.5(4). Nor does it apply to civil servants who are "members of a mission" and who, as a requirement of their duties, are serving outside the State—or to the spouses of such persons: Electoral (Amendment) (No. 2) Act 1986, s.15. Such persons are deemed to be ordinarily resident on the qualifying date in the premises in the State in which, but for the requirements of their duties, they would have been ordinarily resident: s.15(2). They are entitled to postal votes: see section 16 of the 1986 Act.

The electoral register is compiled annually, responsibility therefor being placed on the county councils and corporations: 1963 Act, ss.6 and 7. The qualifying date referred to above is fixed by regulations made by the Minister for the Environment (s.5(6)(*a*)): it is currently September 15. Provision is also made in the 1963 Act for the registration of members of the Defence Forces, hospital patients and prisoners: for a register of postal voters: and for appeals against refusal of registration: see Part II of the Act, *passim*.

The 1963 Act does not further define the key term "ordinarily resident" used in section 5. However, this does not seem to have given rise to any problems; certainly the superior courts have only once had to rule on the interpretation of those words. This occurred in *Quinn* v. *Waterford Corporation* [1990] 2 I.R. 507 where it was held that students could register in both their home and term-time constituencies. McCarthy J., for the court, said that there was a constitutional ban on double voting but none on double registration. And it was quite possible for someone to be "ordinarily resident" in more than one constituency.

Until 1985 only Irish citizens could vote in Dáil elections, Presidential elections and referenda. The Electoral (Amendment) Bill 1983 purported to confer the right to register—and thus to vote—on British citizens ordinarily resident in any constituency on the qualifying date. Deputies on both sides in Dáil Éireann expressed doubts about the constitutionality of this measure, and the President referred the Bill to the Supreme Court under Article 26. The court held the Bill to be repugnant to the Constitution; Article 16 did not contemplate the extension of the franchise to non-citizens: *Re Article 26 and the Electoral (Amendment) Bill 1983* [1984] I.R. 268. In a subsequent referendum the people approved the Ninth Amendment of the Constitution Act 1984, which allows the Oireachtas to confer voting rights on non-citizens. The Electoral (Amendment) Act 1985 accordingly grants such rights—in Dáil elections only—to British citizens of 18 and over resident in the State (the term "British citizens" is defined by reference to the United Kingdom's

British Nationality Act 1981). It also permits the extension of the franchise—by Ministerial order subject to Oireachtas approval—to nationals of other EC member states which grant Irish citizens resident therein the right to vote in parliamentary elections.

The constituencies

Article 16.2.1° provides that the Dáil is to be composed of members "who represent constituencies determined by law." The delimitation of those constituencies is thus primarily for the Oireachtas, but its power in this matter is not unfettered. The minimum number of members for any constituency is three: Art. 16.2.6°; thus a constitutional amendment would be required for the introduction of the United Kingdom single-member constituency. No maximum number of deputies is specified in the Constitution; instead Article 16.2.2° contains a flexible formula for determining the size of the Dáil—there must be not less than one member per 30,000 and not more than one per 20,000 of the population. The Committee on the Constitution noted that "it has always been the practice in dealing with constituency matters by Act of the Oireachtas to adhere as closely as possible to the lower limit of 20,000 persons" (*Report*, p. 19). The Committee accordingly recommended that the Constitution be altered to provide a more realistic tolerance in the range 1: 22,500/17,500 persons. No action has been taken in this regard. Successive redistribution Acts have continued to cleave to the lower figure, despite a widespread feeling that this results in considerable over-representation.

Article 16.2.4° obliges the Oireachtas to revise the constituencies at least once in every 12 years, due regard being had to changes in population distribution. But that must be regarded as an outside limit only. In practice a revision will be required after each census, at least if any substantial changes in population distribution are revealed therein. This is necessitated by Article 16.2.3°, which requires equality of representation, so far as practicable, throughout "the country" (*sic*). Revisions have in fact been carried out much more frequently than every 12 years: see the Electoral (Amendment) Acts 1969, 1974, 1980 and 1983.[4]

There is a strange omission in Article 16.2.3°. It refers to the population of each constituency "as ascertained at the last preceding census," and the operation of its equality principle pivots on this. But Article 16.2.3° fails to specify how frequently the census shall be taken; this is left to be regulated by statute. The machinery is contained in the Statistics Act 1926, ss.2 and 16, and the census is authorised by Ministerial order. The 1926 Act does not fix the intervals but there has usually been a consus every five years. On this basis one should have been taken in 1976, but the Government announced in 1975 that this would not be done. In a period of economic difficulty and financial stringency, it was claimed, the money could be better spent on other things. The sum thus saved was estimated at only £1.7 million and the Opposition complained of a gerrymander: see 285 *Dáil Debs.*, cc. 4–8 (October 22, 1975).

---

[4] In *O'Malley* v. *An Taoiseach* [1990] I.L.R.M. 461 Hamilton P. said (at 464): "The constitutional obligation placed on the Oireachtas is not discharged by revising the constituencies once in every twelve years. They are obliged to revise the constituencies with due regard to

In *O'Malley* v. *An Taoiseach* [1990] I.L.R.M. 461 the plaintiff argued that the current constituencies, fixed by the Electoral (Amendment) Act 1983, were out of line with the Constitution's requirements. The 1986 census returns and the 1988 Dáil Constituency Commission report, he contended, showed that changes in population distribution necessitated a revision—but none had yet been carried out. He consequently sought an injunction restraining the Taoiseach from advising the President to dissolve the Dáil unless and until a revision was carried out. Hamilton P. refused the application, holding that the court had no jurisdiction to place any impediment between the President and his constitutional adviser in this important matter. However, most of Hamilton P.'s judgment consisted of a discussion of the plaintiff's arguments in relation to the constituencies, and he concluded that the Oireachtas was indeed in breach of its constitutional obligation to revise them. This conclusion may perhaps have been *obiter* but it was, on the figures, inevitable.[5]

The *O'Malley* case would not rule an application for a declaration of invalidity *after* a general election had been held; nonetheless it seems unlikely that a court would grant such relief.

To do so would be to create a constitutional *impasse*, for there would be no machinery for resolving the problem. An invalidly elected Dáil cannot, presumably, validly elect a Taoiseach; and the person purporting to be Taoiseach cannot have the authority to advise a dissolution. It seems more probable that in such circumstances the courts would have recourse to "the overriding requirements of an ordered society" invoked by O'Higgins C.J. in an analogous context in *de Burca and Anderson* v. *Att. Gen.* [1976] I.R. 38, 63. It is relevant here to note the former Supreme Court's understanding attitude to a technical breach of Article 16.2.4° in the *Electoral (Amendment) Bill 1961* case (see *infra*).

Article 16.2.3°—judicial exegesis

In *O'Donovan* v. *Att. Gen.* [1961] I.R. 114 Budd J. held the Electoral (Amendment) Act 1959 invalid as an infringement of Article 16.2.3°. He concluded that the dominant principle of Article 16.2.3° was equality of ratio and representation "qualified only by the lesser considerations of practicability" ([1961] I.R. 114, 137). "Practicability" meant difficulties of an administrative or statistical nature so plain that the people must be assumed to have had them in mind when enacting the Constitution. Budd J. firmly rejected the argument that factors like geographical difficulties, sparsely populated areas, travelling and greater demands on deputies' time were relevant to practicability and hence would justify increased representation for western counties. This conclusion was fatal to the validity of the Act in ques-

changes in distribution of the population and when a census return discloses major changes in the distribution of the population there is a constitutional obligation on the Oireachtas to revise the constituencies."
[5] Hamilton P. gave (at 463) examples of the discrepancies in representation between different constituencies. Thus Dublin Central differed from Dublin South West by 39.23 per cent, from Dublin North by 30.29 per cent., from Dublin West by 28.16 per cent. and from Wicklow by 24.81 per cent. Dublin North West differed from Dublin South West by 37.88 per cent., from Dublin West by 26.81 per cent. and from Wicklow by 23.46 per cent.

tion, which contained some significant departures from the national average of one deputy per 20,127 people. Galway South had one deputy per 16,573 people, but Dublin South only one per 23,128 people. Further, the combined population of Donegal, Mayo, Galway and Kerry—532,736—returned 30 deputies; but that of the combined Dublin city constituencies—568,838— returned only 25 deputies.

The Government secured the passage of a new redistribution Bill, which President O'Kelly referred to the Supreme Court: *Re Article 26 and the Electoral (Amendment) Bill* [1961] I.R. 169. The court brushed aside the argument that the Bill was invalid because it had not been passed within the 12 year period stipulated in Article 16.2.4°. Maguire C.J. observed that redistribution Acts had been passed in 1947 and 1959, but the latter had been ruled invalid in *O'Donovan's* case. This was a satisfactory explanation for the delay. The Supreme Court went on to uphold Budd J.'s decision and reasoning in *O'Donovan's* case, and continued ([1961] I.R. 169, 183):

> " . . . exact parity in the ratio between members and the population of each constituency is unlikely to be obtained and is not required. The decision as to what is practicable is within the jurisdiction of the Oireachtas. It may reasonably take into consideration a variety of factors, such as the desirability so far as possible to adhere to well-known boundaries such as those of counties, townlands and electoral divisions. The existence of divisions created by such physical features as rivers, lakes and mountains may also have to be reckoned with. The problem of what is practicable is primarily one for the Oireachtas, whose members have a knowledge of the problems and difficulties to be solved which this Court cannot have. Its decision should not be reviewed by this Court unless there is a manifest infringement of the Article. This Court cannot, as is suggested, lay down a figure above or below which a variation from what is called the national average is not permitted. This, of course, is not to say that a Court . . . may not pronounce on whether there has been such a serious divergence from uniformity as to violate the requirements of the Constitution."

Until 1979 it was the practice for the Government to work out its constituency revision proposals behind closed doors and then present the resultant Bill to the Dáil. This lead to frequent accusations of gerrymandering and in 1979 the decision was taken to establish a non-statutory ad hoc commission to advise and report on constituency formation. This body consisted of a Supreme Court judge, the Secretary of the Department of the Environment and the Clerk of the Dáil. Its report was accepted and implemented without variation, and every revision since then has been based on a Constituency Commission report. Although there is no constitutional or statutory obligation on a Government to establish such a commission or to adopt its report, a convention requiring both seems to be emerging.

This development, however, has not succeeded in eliminating all political controversy from the constituency revision process—for it is the Government which draws up the Commission's terms of reference. And in 1988 it was alleged by Opposition parties that the Government had used this power effectively to compel the Commission to produce a scheme calculated to maximise the possibility of a Fianna Fáil majority in the next Dáil. Lacking a current Dáil majority, and facing an Opposition united against the

Commission's scheme, the Government shelved the report.[6] No such problems arose with the Commission's *Report* of 1990.[7] Though certain of its recommendations were thought bizarre by some,[8] it was accepted that the report must be implemented without demur and this was duly done.[9]

Proportional representation

Article 16.2.5° stipulates proportional representation by the single transferable vote. This system has two main aspects:

(a) the single transferable vote allows the voter to give his preference for the candidates in order—*i.e.* 1, 2, 3, 4, etc.

(b) the vote can be transferred to the next choice when a prior choice has already been elected or eliminated.

The Electoral Acts 1923–1983 lay down the detailed rules which flesh out the constitutional principles. They provide (*inter alia*) for the forms of writs for general and by-elections and of ballot-papers. In regard to the latter, two points may be noted. The names of registered political parties are permitted to appear on ballot papers, and the Electoral Act 1963 sets up a registration system with provision for appeal machinery.[10] The relevant provisions of the Act were unsuccessfully challenged as unconstitutional in *Loftus* v. *Att. Gen.* [1979] L.R. 221. Secondly, the form of ballot paper laid down in Part II of the Second Schedule of the 1963 Act requires that the candidates be listed alphabetically in the order of their surnames. Research suggests that this benefits candidates whose names appear towards the top, and it has been suggested that a random arrangement of names would be preferable. The High Court has held, however, that the Constitution does not require this. In *O'Reilly* v. *Minister for the Environment* [1986] I.R. 143 the plaintiff sought a declaration that the Electoral Act 1963, s.16, was invalid insofar as it imposed this alphabetical requirement. Murphy J. was satisfied, on the evidence, that in Dáil elections over 40 years there had been a significant over-representation of candidates whose surnames began with letters at the commencement of the alphabet. But even if a better system could be devised, it did not follow that the present legislation was invalid. The existing system provided electors with the essential information and gave electors a free choice. If the legislation reflected a certain voter indifference as to outcome there was nothing unreasonble in that. Further, there were practical advantages in alphabetical listing—an established procedure in so many fields.

---

[6] This decision ultimately gave rise to the proceedings in *O'Malley* v. *An Taoiseach* [1990] I.L.R.M. 461.

[7] Pl. 7520. This Commission was slightly larger than its predecessors, having five members. It was chaired by the President of the High Court and its other members were a former Governor of the Central Bank, the Secretary of the Department of the Environment, and the Clerks of the Dáil and Seanad.

[8] Notably the retention of two three-seaters in Mayo, requiring the addition in both cases of parts of Co. Galway, and the creation of a new four-seat constituency of Longford-Roscommon which breached provincial—not mere county—boundaries. See 403 *Dáil Debs.*, cc. 2663–266: 2677–2679: 2681–1686: 1691–1693: 1696–2698 (December 13, 1990): 127 *Seanad Debs.*, cc. 439: 451: 454: 457–459: 471–472: 473–475 (December 19, 1990).

[9] Electoral (Amendment) Act 1990.

[10] The candidates of an unregistered political party cannot now get round this by incorporating the party's name into their own in the nomination papers: see s.17 of the Electoral (Amendment) (No. 2) Act 1986.

The rules governing the count are laid down in the Third Schedule to the Electoral Act 1923. The returning officer is required firstly to ascertain the total number of valid votes. He/she then determines "the quota" which is done by using the formula:

$$\text{quota} = \frac{\text{number of valid votes}}{\text{number of seats} + 1}$$

Where at the end of a count a candidate's votes are equal to or greater than the quota, he/she is deemed to be elected. The surplus votes of that person are then transferred to the continuing candidates according to the preferences they record. If no candidate has now reached the quota, the returning officer excludes the candidate with the lowest number of votes, and transfers these votes in accordance with the next preference specified therein. The process of transfer—either of surpluses or the votes of the eliminated candidates—continues until all the seats are filled. This will occur where the appropriate number of candidates has reached the quota *or* where the number of continuing candidates equals the number of vacancies unfilled.[11]

In 1959, and again in 1969, Fianna Fáil Governments promoted legislation to abolish PR. Their proposals were rejected by the people in referenda, on the second occasion by a larger majority than before.[12]

The secret ballot

Article 16.1.4° provides that no voter may exercise more than one vote at a Dáil election "and the voting shall be by secret ballot." In *McMahon* v. *Att. Gen.* [1972] I.R. 69 the relevant provisions of the Electoral Acts 1923 and 1963 were successfully challenged as violating this requirement. The rules in question—which were directly descended from the Ballot Act 1872—provided that each counterfoil should bear a number, which also appeared on the back of the ballot paper. The presiding officer was instructed to write the elector's number from the electoral register on the counterfoils. Though the law stipulated that only Dáil Éireann or a court could authorise the inspection of ballot papers and counterfoils, it was argued that secrecy was not preserved. Anyone who surreptitiously gained access to these materials could, by checking the electoral register, discover how individual citizens had voted. By a 3–2 majority the Supreme Court held the statutory rules to be constitutionally inadequate. Ó Dálaigh C.J. (Walsh and Budd JJ. concurring) said (at 111):

> "The Constitution does not require the voting citizen to run the risk of disclosure by accident or breach of the law: it entitles him to shut up within the privacy of his own mind all knowledge of the manner in which he has voted, without fear of disclosure. In my opinion a voting system which permits a state official to note the number of the ballot paper of every voter in the State, and which requires this information to be stored for a full year after the poll, of itself offends against the spirit and substance of the declaration that voting shall be by secret ballot.

[11] For a critical survey of PR in Ireland see Cornelius O'Leary, *Irish Elections 1918–1977* (Dublin 1979).
[12] The details may be found in O'Leary, *op. cit.*

Under such a system, the fear of disclosure which secrecy is designed to drive away is ostentatiously retained."

The modifications in the earlier Acts necessary to bring them into line with the Constitution were made by the Electoral (Amendment) Act 1972. However, an unsuccessful prosecution for alleged double voting in 1982[13] showed that further amendment was necessary. The post-*McMahon* unavailability of a ballot paper to establish how an individual had voted had not been adequately catered for. The gap has now been plugged by the short Prevention of Electoral Abuses Act 1983, which redefines the offence of personation. (Note, too, that under section 20 of the Electoral (Amendment) (No. 2) Act 1986 a person who applies for a ballot paper may be required to produce evidence of identity ("a specified document") as a condition of voting.)

Postal voting

Before 1986, postal votes were available to two categories of persons only: members of the Defence Forces (Electoral Act 1923, s.21) and of the Garda Síochána (Electoral Act 1963, s.7(7.4)). All other persons could vote only by going to a polling station and marking a ballot paper there (Electoral Act 1923, Sched. 5, Rule 23). The practical effect of this was to disfranchise many registered voters—disabled persons, merchant seamen, sales representatives, those in hospital on polling day, and others. Those in prison were similarly situated: in *State (Comerford)* v. *Govr., Mountjoy Prison (The Irish Times,* June 1, 1979) the High Court refused an application for an order to the Governor directing him to provide facilities for a remand prisoner to vote in the forthcoming European Assembly elections. Though such elections are not governed by Article 16, it seems probable that the courts would refuse a similar application in regard to a Dáil election.[14] The constitutionality of these restricted postal voting facilities was contested in *Draper* v. *Att. Gen.* [1984] I.R. 277. Mrs. Draper, a registered voter, suffered from advanced multiple sclerosis and could not go to a polling station to vote. She claimed:

(a) that the State was in breach of Article 16.1.2° in failing to provide postal votes for persons like her
(b) that by giving postal votes to some citizens but not to persons like her, the State had violated the equality guarantee of Article 40.1.

The Supreme Court ruled against her claim. The court pointed out that Article 16.7 stipulated that elections were to be regulated by law, and observed that the right to vote was contingent on compliance with the electoral law. The latter specified clearly that the voter must mark the ballot

---

[13] For details see Joe Joyce and Peter Murtagh, *The Boss* (Dublin 1983) Chap. 6.
[14] On the electoral rights of prisoners see further R. Byrne, G. W. Hogan and P. McDermott, *Prisoners' Rights,* (Dublin 1981), pp. 81–85. Note too *Re Att. Gen. of Canada and Gould* (1984) 13 D.L.R. (4th) 485. The respondent, who had been convicted of an offence and was serving a prison sentence, claimed the right to vote in the forthcoming federal general election. The Elections Act 1970 disqualified such prisoners from voting but this, argued the respondent, violated section 3 of the 1982 Charter of Rights and Freedoms and was consequently invalid. The Trial Division of the Federal Court granted him an interlocutory mandatory injunction, but the Court of Apeal (Mahony and Marceau JJ.; Thurlow C.J. dissenting) reversed that decision. The proper purpose of an interlocutory injunction was to preserve or restore the status quo, not to give the plaintiff his remedy, until trial. The Supreme Court of Canada subsequently upheld the Court of Appeal's decision.

paper at the polling station. In making a regulating law, the court said, the State had to strike a balance which would serve the common good. Since postal voting on a wide scale could lead to a high risk of abuse, the court was satisfied that the existing law struck a reasonable balance. The State's failure to provide postal votes for the plaintiff and others similarly situated was not an interference with the exercise of the right to vote under Article 16.1.2°. Nor did it violate the equality guarantee of Article 40.1. Under that provision, the State could validly have made special arrangements in favour of people like the plaintiff—on the ground of their incapacity. But its failure to take such action did not mean that the existing provisions were unreasonable, unjust or arbitrary.

In one respect the court's judgment is somewhat self-contradictory. At one place we are told that while the right to vote is a right to be exercised personally, it is not one of the personal rights of the citizen falling under Article 40. This would mean that the right to vote springs only from Article 16: it is not covered by the more general guarantee of Article 40.3.1°:

> "The State guarantees in its laws to respect, and, as far as practicable, by its laws to defend and vindicate the rights of the citizen."

Later in the judgment, however, the following passage is found ([1984] I.R. 277, 291):

> "The trial judge expressed the view that the right to vote 'is a personal right entitled to the benefit of the guarantee contained in Article 40.3.1°.' The Court reserves its opinion as to whether this view is correct. Even if the right were such a personal right the Court is not satisfied, for the reasons already given, that the State has failed to defend and vindicate this right."

For its finding that extended postal voting entailed a higher risk of abuse the Supreme Court relied on the *Reports* of the Joint Dáil/Seanad Committee on Electoral Law, published in 1962 (thus according them much more weight than they had been given in *McMahon* v. *Att. Gen.* [1972] I.R. 69). It should be noted, however, that the *Report of the Working Party on the Register of Electors* (Pl. 1471)—published in March 1983—proffered a scheme for extended postal voting; its expert authors were satisfied that the risk of abuse would be minimal. Legislation to implement their proposals was promised, but the Electoral (Amendment) (No. 2) Act 1986 extended the system only to certain civil servants working abroad and their spouses. For disabled voters the Act (ss.2–13) introduced a cumbersome system of "special voting," under which such persons may complete their ballot papers at home or in hospital, in the presence of a special presiding officer and a Garda.

Candidature

To be eligible for membership of Dáil Éireann one must be a citizen,[15] have reached 21[16] and not be disqualified by the Constitution or by statute:

[15] A non-citizen obviously cannot sit in Dáil Éireann: whether such a person may be *nominated* (with the object of acquiring citizenship before or after election) is unclear.

[16] A candidate need not be 21 when nominated; it is sufficient if he/she has attained that age by election day. The High Court (Lardner J.) so held in *Hall* v. *Att. Gen.*; see *The Irish Times*, February 5, 1987.

Art. 16.1.1°. The question of whether the second of these conditions is fulfilled involves some difficulties. In the first place, there may well be a conflict between the English and Irish texts of the Constitution. The former says (so far as relevant):

"Every citizen . . . who has reached the age of 21 years . . . ."

The corresponding phrase in the Irish text is:

"Gach saoránach . . . ag a bhfuil bliain agus fiche slán . . . ."

The English text would appear to refer to the attainment of the age of 21: and the common law rule is that this occurs at the first moment of the day preceding the relevant anniversary of one's birth. Thus a person born on January 1, 1964 would attain 21 at the first moment of December 31, 1985. The Irish text, however, suggests that to be eligible a citizen must have *completed* his/her 21st year, so that a person born on January 1, 1964 would become eligible only on January 1, 1986. It should be noted that if a conflict between the two texts does arise here, the Irish text prevails: Art. 25.5.4°.

Secondly, even if the two texts mean the same thing, a further constitutional question arises. Does the Constitution entrench the common law rule referred to above? If so, that rule cannot be modified by statute: a referendum would be necessary to change it—*e.g.* by providing that one should attain a particular age on the commencement of the relevant anniversary of the date of birth.

A number of people are disqualified or incapacitated by the Constitution or by law. The Constitution renders the Comptroller and Auditor General ineligible (Art. 33.3), likewise judges (Art. 35.3). Statute—the Electoral Act 1923, s.51(3)—does the same for full-time members of the Defence Forces, the Garda Síochána, and civil servants (though the terms of employment of the latter may provide otherwise). Section 51(2) of the same Act disqualifies four categories of person:

(a) prisoners[17]
(b) imbeciles and persons of unsound mind
(c) undischarged bankrupts (in 1928 James Larkin, T.D. for Dublin North was found to be disqualified on this ground: see 22 *Dáil Debs.* cc. 1159–1223 (March 14, 1928))
(d) persons convicted of corrupt practices or other election offences.

This last category poses something of a problem. Section 51(2)(*d*) refers to "a person who is by the law for the time being in force . . . in relation to corrupt practices and other offences at elections incapacitated from being a member of the Dáil. . . ."That is, the subsection appears to assume the existence of a body of law on corrupt practices which, *inter alia*, provides the penalty of incapacity upon conviction. But that situation no longer obtains: the Prevention of Electoral Abuses Act 1923, s.6(4), which imposed incapacity on those convicted of corrupt practices, was repealed in 1963 (Electoral Act 1963, First Schedule). This would seem to cut the ground from under the Electoral Act 1923, s.51(2)(*d*).

---

[17] Defined as "persons sentenced to imprisonment with hard labour for any period exceeding 6 months, or to penal servitude for any term." As to the distinction between imprisonment and penal servitude, see E. F. Ryan and P. P. Magee, *The Irish Criminal Process* (Cork 1983) pp. 396–399.

Other persons disqualified by statute are the chairmen and members of various boards, commissions, tribunals, etc. No single statute lists all the posts which entail disqualification: it is necessary to consult each Act establishing a public body to discover the position. The usual legislative technique is to provide that membership of the relevant body ceases upon election or nomination as a deputy or senator and that membership of either House disqualifies one from appointment to the relevant body. Examples are: the Broadcasting Authority Act 1960, s.4(5) and (6): the Air Companies Act 1966, s.14(1): the Local Government (Planning and Development) Act 1983, ss.5(10), 7(7)(*a*) and 7(10)(*c*).

Finally, it may be noted that the President may not be a member of either House—Art. 12.6.1°; nor may any person be a member of both Houses—Art. 15.14.

General Elections

The prelude to a general election is, of course, a dissolution of the Dáil; and this is effected by the President, acting on the advice of the Taoiseach—Art. 13.2.1°. While the Constitution fixes a maximum duration of seven years for the Dáil, it also permits a shorter period to be fixed by statute—Art. 16.5. Taking advantage of this, the Electoral Act 1963, s.10, specifies a maximum life of five years from the date of first meeting. However, neither the Constitution nor statute fixes a *minimum* period, so that the Taoiseach has a very wide margin of discretion as to when a general election shall be held. In practice it is usual for the Taoiseach to consult his Ministerial colleagues about the date, but on a literal reading of Article 13.2.1° he would be acting quite constitutionally if he made his decision on his own.

The dissolution is effected "by proclamation under the Presidential seal, signed by the President and countersigned by the Taoiseach."[18] The general election must, under Article 16.3.2°, take place not more than 30 days after dissolution. Polling "shall as far as practicable take place on the same day throughout the country": Art. 16.4.1°. These words are construed as giving the Oireachtas some leeway to provide otherwise, for the Electoral Act 1963, s.34, permits advance polling on islands. (The effect is to vest a measure of discretion in the returning officer for the relevant constituency.) By virtue of section 24 of the same Act, the date of the poll is fixed by the Minister for the Environment.

Within the framework of the Constitution, the Electoral Acts 1923–1983 establish the detailed machinery for elections, setting out the rules on nominations, voting, counting, etc. They also make provision, as is required by Article 16.6, for the automatic re-election to the Dáil of the outgoing Ceann Comhairle. He is returned for his previous constituency or, if there has been a revision, one akin thereto—which he must specify. The effect is to reduce by one the number of seats to be filled in that constituency. The Constitution does not, of course, guarantee the individual's re-election as Ceann Comhairle, nor is there any practice or usage which does so.

Under Article 16.4.2° the Dáil must meet within 30 days of polling day. The Constitution thus sets out a broad timetable:—dissolution; general election within 30 days; reassembly of Dáil within 30 days of the poll. The five

---

[18] McDunphy, *op. cit.*, p. 51.

year lifespan of the Dáil will start to run from that latter date. One consequence is that a Taoiseach defeated in a general election has no legal means to postpone meeting his fate at the hands of the new Dáil. He cannot alter the reassembly date nor, arguably, can he seek another election. The words "shall meet" in Article 16.4.2 import an automatic obligation to meet following a general election.

By-elections

Article 16.7 anticipates that by-elections—"the filling of casual vacancies"—will be regulated by law, and provision therefor is made by the Electoral Acts 1923–1983. Section 12(2) of the 1963 Act provides for the issue of a writ by the Clerk of the Dáil to the relevant returning officer, directing an election to be held to fill the vacancy. However, the issue of a writ depends on a decision by the Dáil; thus it is that body (in practice prompted by the Government) which decides how long a delay shall elapse between the occurrence of the vacancy and the by-election. This can lead to the under-representation of a constituency for a considerable period.

Political parties

The working of the constitutional machinery, especially as regards elections, presupposes the existence of political parties—but the Constitution studiously ignores their existence. Statute law is not quite so reticent; since 1963 it has been permissible to print party names on ballot papers, and the Electoral Act 1963, s.13, makes elaborate provision in this regard. Otherwise, the law does not regulate the existence, structure or internal affairs of parties. Their methods of selecting candidates and financing their activities are not governed by law, and they are not obliged to publish accounts. Nor are those—whether individuals or companies—who contribute to parties' funds compelled to reveal what they give. Trade unions, however, are subject to legal limitations as regards expenditure on political objects.[19]

SEANAD ÉIREANN

Professor Chubb has well said that the Seanad is "both singular in its composition and circumscribed in its powers."[20] Both factors arise from the difficulty of creating a satisfactory second chamber. The dilemma was classically formulated by the Abbé Sieyès nearly 200 years ago: "when two chambers agree one of them is superfluous, when they disagree one of them is pernicious." Following the abolition of the old Seanad, the Executive Council established a 23 member commission to consider the constitution, powers and functions of a possible second chamber. As Professor McCracken observes[21]:

> "The outcome . . . bore out de Valera's forebodings about the complexity of the problems involved in devising a satisfactory second chamber and illustrated the wide divergence of views held on the sub-

---

[19] See the Trade Union Act 1913, discussed in A. Kerr and G. Whyte, *Irish Trade Union Law* (Abingdon 1985) pp. 89–95.

[20] *The Government and Politics of Ireland*, (2nd ed., London 1982), p. 211.

[21] *Representative Government in Ireland* (Oxford 1958), p. 147.

ject . . . (the commission) produced no fewer than 10 separate reports or reservations: one majority report, three minority reports, and six notes by individual members.''

Mr. de Valera was personally unenthusiastic about a second chamber, but nonetheless took the view that if a substantial segment of public opinion favoured one, the new Constitution should provide accordingly. The provisions, however, leave no room for doubt that the real power lies with the Dáil.

Composition

By virtue of Article 18.1 the Seanad is composed of 60 members, 49 of whom are elected and 11 nominated. To be eligible, one must be eligible to become a member of the Dáil: Art. 18.2.

Elected senators fall into two distinct groups. Six are elected by graduates of higher educational institutions: 43 are elected from a complex system of panels—the electorate not being specified in the Constitution. One rule, however, is common to both groups: the election is to be by proportional representation involving the single transferable vote, and by secret postal ballot (Art. 18.5).

(a) *University Senators*

Originally six senators were to be elected by university graduates, three from the National University and three from Dublin University (Trinity College). (Under the 1922 Constitution each of those institutions had three Dáil seats.) The Seventh Amendment of the Constitution Act 1979 modified this by permitting statute to add other institutions of higher education to this constituency. No such legislation has yet been enacted—notwithstanding the creation of two new universities in 1989[22]—and the system thus remains as it stood in 1979.

Article 18.6 provides that statute shall regulate the election of the Seanad's ''university members.'' The current governing Acts are the Seanad Electoral (University Members) Acts 1937 and 1972. The right to vote is conferred upon every Irish citizen who has received a degree (other than a honorary degree) from one of the two Universities; thus a citizen holding degrees from both acquires two votes. In the Dublin University constituency the holders of certain scholarships are entitled to vote, even as undergraduates, provided they have reached 21 (1937 Act, s.7(2)). The Act also regulates the processes of nomination, voting and counting—the voting being, as Article 18.5 requires, by secret postal ballot.

(b) *Panel Senators*

As already noted, the other 43 senators are elected from a complex series of panels. In regard to this the Constitution merely sets out the general framework, leaving important issues—such as the designation of the electorate—to statute. It follows that, to some degree, reform of the Seanad does not require a constitutional amendment.

Article 18.7.1° requires the formation of five panels of candidates who have knowledge and experience of certain matters:

[22] Dublin City University Act 1989; University of Limerick Act 1989.

"i National Language and Culture, Literature, Art, Education and such professional interests as may be defined by law for the purpose of this panel;
ii Agriculture and allied interests, and Fisheries;
iii Labour, whether organised or unorganised;
iv Industry and Commerce, including banking, finance, accountancy, engineering and architecture;
v Public Administration and social services, including voluntary social activities."

Article 18.7.2° provides that not more than 11, and not less than five, senators shall be elected from any one panel. (This is subject to Article 19, which allows statute to provide for the direct election of senators "by any functional or vocational group or association or council." This again reflects those ideas of vocationalism in vogue in the 1930s and 40s. No such legislation has been passed, and Article 19 is now probably redundant.)

The details of the system thus outlined are filled in by the Seanad Electoral (Panel Members) Acts 1947–72. Section 43 provides that each panel is to be divided into two: the Oireachtas sub-panel—containing the names of candidates nominated by four deputies or senators: and the Nominating Bodies sub-panel—containing the names of candidates nominated by *registered* nominating bodies. (The registration, etc. of nominating bodies is governed by sections 8–20 of the 1947 Act, as amended by sections 3–6 of the 1954 Act.) Under sections 52 of the 1947 Act the number of persons elected from each panel is fixed as follows:

Cultural and Educational panel —	5 members (at least 2 from each sub-panel)
Agricultural panel —	11 members (at least 4 from each sub-panel)
Labour panel —	11 members (at least 4 from each sub-panel)
Industrial and commercial panel —	9 members (at least 3 from each sub-panel
Administrative panel —	7 members (at least 3 from each sub-panel).

The electorate is specified by the Seanad Electoral (Panel Members) Act 1947, s.44, and is:

(a) the members of the new Dáil
(b) the members of the outgoing Seanad
(c) county councillors (including county boroughs such as Dublin, Cork, Dun Laoghaire, etc.).

This produces a total of around 900 persons.

Section 36 of the 1947 Act requires candidates for each panel to satisfy the returning officer (the Clerk of the Seanad: s.4) that they have knowledge and practical experience of the interests and services represented on the panel. The Act provides machinery for judicial determination of such issues.

Although the nominating bodies include institutions such as the Incorporated Law Society, the Bar Council and the Royal Irish Academy (to name but three), in reality the Seanad electoral process is dominated by party poli-

tics. Nowadays even some of the university senators have overt party affilia-
tions. The chances of being elected purely on vocational grounds are virtually nil. It is hard to disagree with Professor Chubb's conclusion: " . . . by
and large, it is merely another selection of a party politicians chosen in an
unnecessarily complicated and not particularly democratic manner."[23]

(c) *Nominated Senators*

Eleven members of the Seanad are nominated by the Taoiseach: Article
18.3. Neither the Constitution nor the law place any restriction on the Taoiseach's choice—save, of course, that his nominees must be eligible for election to the Dáil. In a coalition Government, the smaller party or parties will
expect a share of the nominations; a Taoiseach heading a single-party
Government will have more freedom of choice. Some nominees may be
chosen with an eye to party advantage—for example, an individual who narrowly failed to win a marginal Dáil seat for the party at the last general election. In recent years the practice has grown up of including persons from
Northern Ireland, who will not necessarily share the political outlook of the
Taoiseach.

Normally the Taoiseach makes his nominations only after the other Seanad seats have been filled. There is no constitutional or legal bar to his
appointing someone a senator in order to qualify that person to be a member
of the Government; and in 1982 Dr. FitzGerald as Taoiseach used this device
to appoint Professor James Dooge as Minister for Foreign Affairs.

Timing of Seanad elections

A Seanad general election—for both university and panel seats—takes
place not later than 90 days after the Dáil is dissolved: Art. 18.8. Given the
timetable laid down in Article 16, this means that the new Dáil will have
assembled before the Seanad is elected. As already noted, the Seanad Electoral (Panel Members) Act 1947 builds on this by making the new Dáil part
of the Seanad electorate. That Act also enfranchises the outgoing senators—
which reflects the fact that senators continue to hold office until the day
before polling day in the Seanad general election: Art. 18.9. If a nominated
senator is elected to Dáil Éireann following a dissolution, the Taoiseach is
entitled to nominate a new senator for the short period before polling day in
the Seanad general election. The new senator will then have a vote in that
general election. This power was used by the then Taoiseach, Mr. Liam Cosgrave, in 1977.

As required by Article 18.5, the election is on the basis of proportional representation by the single transferable vote, and by secret postal ballot. The
date for the Seanad's first meeting following the election is fixed by the President on the advice of the Taoiseach.

Casual vacancies

Article 18.10.2° authorises the Taoiseach to fill casual vacancies in the
ranks of nominated senators. There is no restriction on his power to do so,
which may consequently be exercised at any time.

---

[23] *The Government and Politics of Ireland* (2nd ed., London 1982), p. 212.

Article 18.10.3° provides that statute shall regulate the filling of casual vacancies among elected senators. This is done by the 1937 (universities) and 1947 (panel members) Acts already referred to. The only point that requires to be noticed is that in by-elections for panel members, the electorate consists *only* of sitting deputies and senators (1947 Act, s.69).

RELATIONS BETWEEN THE HOUSES

As indicated above, the Constitution makes it clear that the ultimate power lies with the Dáil. Articles 20–24 put this beyond any doubt. They show that the Seanad's only power over legislation is to delay it—and for a relatively brief period only. Moreover, its authority in the financial field is severely restricted.

Financial matters

Article 28.4.3° obliges the Government to prepare estimates of State receipts and expenditure for each financial year, and to present these to Dáil Éireann for consideration. The exclusion of the Seanad from this process could hardly be more pointed.

Article 21 restricts the power of the Seanad over "Money Bills"—a term defined at considerable length in Article 22. Unlike other Bills, these may not be initiated in the Seanad—the Dáil is the only competent forum: Art. 21.1.1°. Nor can they be amended by the Seanad. Its only power is to make "recommendations" concerning them (Art. 21.1.2°)—and these the Dáil is free to reject. Furthermore, the Seanad has only 21 days to deal with a Money Bill. If it has not completed the process by then, the Bill is deemed to have been passed by both Houses at the expiration of the 21 day period: Article 21.2.2°. This also applies if the Bill is returned within the 21 day period, but with recommendations unacceptable to the Dáil. Article 21.2.2° may consequently be regarded as a kind of constitutional guillotine, with the blade automatically falling once the 21 days are up. And it should be noted that it is a self-activating provision—that is, no resolution or other action by the Dáil is required to bring it into play.

While the Seanad's *power* over Money Bills is, therefore, strictly circumscribed, this does not mean that that chamber has no *influence* upon them. Such Bills are, after all, debated—and this affords senators with appropriate expertise an opportunity to give their views. That may have some effect on the Government's thinking. And while the Seanad does not often make a formal recommendation on a Money Bill, the record shows that any recommendation made is likely to be accepted by the Dáil.

The definition of "Money Bill" in Article 22 is plainly of great importance. It antedates Bunreacht na hÉireann, for its terms are identical to those in Article 35 of the 1922 Constitution. In turn, this derived from the Parliament Act 1911, s.1(2), passed to curb the authority of the House of Lords after its rejection of the Finance Bill 1909, which embodied the Budget.

A Money Bill is one "which contains only" provisions dealing with:

(a) the imposition, repeal, remission, alteration or regulation of taxation,
(b) the imposition, for the payment of debt or other financial purposes, of charges on public moneys, or the variation or repeal of any such changes,

(c) supply,
(d) the appropriation, receipt, custody, issue or audit of accounts of public money,
(e) the raising or guarantee of any loan or the repayment thereof,
(f) matters subordinate and incidental to those matters or any of them.

The phrase "which contains only" is particularly significant because many Bills—*e.g.* those establishing new State agencies—will contain incidental financial provisions. These cannot qualify as Money Bills under Article 22, and the Seanad's normal powers over legislation will consequently apply to them.

Article 22 provides the means of resolving disputes over whether a measure is a Money Bill or not. A certificate by the Ceann Comhairle that a Bill is a Money Bill is conclusive, unless a Committee of Privileges— appointed by the President—rules otherwise. A request for reference to such a committee is made by a resolution of the Seanad, passed at a sitting at which not less than half the members are present: Art. 22.2.1°. Should the President refer the question, the committee must report its decision within 21 days from the day the Bill was sent to the Seanad: Art. 22.2.4°. Should it fail to meet this time limit, the Ceann Comhairle's certificate stands confirmed: and this also applies should the President refuse the Seanad's request: Art. 22.2.6°.

The need to utilise this device has not arisen so far. The fact that the Government usually has a majority in the Seanad has avoided any problems in this regard. In 1935 the similar procedure under the 1922 Constitution was invoked in relation to the Land Purchase (Guarantee Fund) Bill. On the casting role of the chairman, Kennedy C.J., the committee decided that the Bill was a Money Bill.

Non-financial legislation

With the exception of Money Bills, and Bills to amend the Constitution (Art. 46.2), any Bill may be initiated in the Seanad. If passed by that body it "shall be introduced" in Dáil Éireann: Art. 20.2.1°. Thus a private member's Bill passed by the Seanad would have to be considered by the Dáil, and cannot simply be ignored. But in practice the overwhelming majority of Bills are Government measures, and Governments only rarely initiate Bills in the Seanad. Among the factors which account for this is that starting in the Seanad might prolong the legislative process. For the Dáil is naturally free to amend the Seanad's Bill; and the Bill, as amended, would have to go back to the Seanad—see Art. 20.1 and 2. (Should the Seanad reject the Dáil's amendments, the time limit provisions of Art. 23 would come into play: Art. 23.2 specifically so provides.)

It should be noted that Article 20.3 permits the adoption of an accelerated procedure for passing Bills—if suitable provision is made in the standing orders of both Houses. That is, a Bill initiated in and passed by the Seanad could be "accepted" by the Dáil (or vice versa), and could thus become law by a procedure simpler than the normal one for passing Bills. A Bill so treated "shall be deemed to have been passed by both Houses." Such a procedure would obviously only be used for simple and non-controversial Bills.

Most Bills are initiated in Dáil Éireann. They *must* be sent to the Seanad where (save for Money Bills) they may be amended: Art. 20.1. However, any such Bill must be disposed of by the Seanad within 90 days, or such longer period as may be agreed by both Houses: Art. 23.1.2°. If, within that period, the Bill is rejected—or not passed—by the Seanad, or is passed with amendments with which the Dáil does not agree, the Dáil can by resolution deem the Bill to have been passed by both Houses. Such a resolution can be passed only within 180 days of the expiry of the Seanad's time for consideration of the Bill (*i.e.* the 90 days or agreed longer period): Art. 23.1.1°. The Bill is deemed to have been passed by both Houses on the day the resolution is passed (*ibid.*).

The same restrictions apply to a Bill initiated in and passed by the Seanad, subsequently amended by the Dáil and then returned to the Seanad: Art. 23.2.1°. In such a situation, time begins to run from the day when the Bill is sent back to the Seanad: Art. 23.2.2°.

It is clear from these provisions that the Dáil can impose its will on the Seanad—as most notably happened with the Third Amendment of the Constitution Bill 1959, rejected by the Seanad. (This Bill, which would *inter alia* have abolished proportional representation, was later rejected in a referendum.) But the Dáil will not always insist on its constitutional prerogatives, and a working arrangement has been devised for resolving conflicts between the Houses, without recourse to formal constitutional powers. This takes the form of a joint conference between representatives of both Houses to resolve differences over Seanad amendments.[24] Such a conference would normally take place against the background of the Dáil's ultimate power to enforce its wishes—but this will not always be the case. If the Dáil has not passed its resolution within the stipulated 180 day period it has lost its right to force the Bill into law against the Seanad's wishes. In such a case the conference discussion would necessarily be on a much more "give and take" basis.

Article 23 affords no clear answer to certain questions. Suppose the Seanad passes a Bill, without amendments, after the 90 day period has expired, and that no Dáil resolution has been passed within the requisite time limits. Does such a Bill die? Or can it be regarded as having been passed by the Dáil and accepted by the Seanad under Article 20.3, so that it is deemed to have been passed by both Houses? If the Bill is amended by the Seanad—its consideration having exceeded the 90 day period—is the Dáil's only recourse to a resolution under Article 23.1.1°? Or may it accept the Seanad's amendments, so that the agreed text of the Bill comes within Article 20.3?

These difficulties arise because it is not entirely clear whether, in the absence of express agreement, the 90 day period can be treated as having been extended. On one view, it is for the Seanad to seek an agreed extension if it fears the period may be exceeded. Another view is that the Dáil's failure to assert its supremacy at the end of the 90 days gives rise to an implicit agreement between the Houses for an undefined extension.[25]

A further problem arises in regard to a Dáil resolution under Article 23.1.1° deeming a Bill to have been passed by both Houses. Which form of the Bill is "deemed to have been passed?" If the Seanad has made amendments to the Bill, the Dáil may not wish to reject them all, even if it finds

---

[24] See Thomas Garvin, *The Irish Senate* (Dublin 1969), p. 42.
[25] See the *Report of the Committee on the Constitution*, December 1967 (Pr. 9817), para. 92.

some unacceptable. Some of the Seanad amendments may have been Government-inspired, and the Government majority in the Dáil will presumably be anxious to retain these. It is not clear, however, that this can be done. The view has been expressed that the Bill is deemed to have been passed *only* in the form in which it left Dáil Éireann.[26] But Article 23.1.1° does not specifically say this—and the historical background may suggest that it was deliberately drafted to allow the Dáil to pick and choose between different Seanad amendments. For the corresponding provision of the 1922 Constitution— Article 38—explicitly used, in its original version, the phrase "deemed to have been passed by both Houses in the form in which it was last passed by Dáil Éireann." Subsequently, the Constitution (Amendment No. 13) Act 1928 inserted a new Article 38A. This allowed the Dáil by resolution (following a prescribed process and after a specified interval) to deem a Bill to have been passed by both Houses in the form in which it left the Dáil with such Seanad amendments as the Dáil agreed to.

In its *Report* of December 1967 the Committee on the Constitution recognised that the true position was doubtful and recommended that Article 23 be expanded to give the Dáil clear authority to pick and choose: see para. 94. But no such amendment has yet been passed.

While they may seem theoretical, the issues raised above would assume importance should a statute be challenged in the courts as not having been passed in conformity with the Constitution's requirements. May the courts entertain a challenge to an Act deemed to have been passed by both Houses, based upon (*e.g.*) discrepancies between its text and that of the Bill when it left the Dáil? This issue is considered in Chapter 11 *infra*.

As noted in Chapter 3 *supra*. Article 24 permits the Seanad's time for considering a Bill to be drastically reduced. This *cannot* be used in regard to Constitution amendment Bills, but it may be used in relation to Money Bills. The Taoiseach must certify that the relevant Bill is "urgent and immediately necessary for the preservation of the public peace and security, or by reason of the existence of a public emergency, whether domestic or international." And the President must concur in the abridgement of the Seanad's time for consideration of the Bill. In any such case, the Bill is automatically deemed to have been passed by both Houses at the close of the Seanad's abridged time for consideration thereof. No Dáil resolution is necessary for this purpose. Any such Act, however, remains in force for only 90 days from the date of its enactment, unless both Houses agree on a longer lifespan and so resolve: Article 24.3.

PROCEDURAL MATTERS

Article 15 sets out certain procedural principles common to both Houses. As with the provisions of Article 16 on Dáil elections, the Constitution does no more than set out general guidelines: thus, for example, the number of readings a Bill receives before passing each House is sensibly left for the standing orders of each House to prescribe.

Article 15.8.1° provides that sittings of each House shall be public. Private sittings may be held "in cases of special emergency," with the assent of two-

---

[26] 27 *Seanad Debs.*, c. 1697: 89 *Dáil Debs.*, c. 843.

thirds of the members present. To date no use has been made of this latter power, which springs from Article 15.8.2°.

Article 15.9.1° obliges each House to elect from among its members a chairman and deputy chairman (in fact the election of a new Ceann Comhairle is the first task of the new Dáil following a general election). The powers and duties of these persons are to be prescibed—presumably (though Art. 15.9 does not say so) by the standing orders of each House. It is clear from Article 15.11 that the chairman or deputy chairman of either House does not ordinarily have a vote. In the case of a tie, however, the person in question has a casting vote—and is *obliged* to exercise it: see Art. 15.11.2°.[27] Here it is appropriate to note the rule laid down in Article 15.11.1°—that all questions in either House shall, unless the Constitution otherwise provides, be decided by a majority of votes of those present and voting. This provision was invoked by the Government in 1980 to explain why a suggestion that the Ombudsman be nominated by a two-thirds majority of both Houses was unacceptable.[28]

Both Houses are *required* to make rules and standing orders: Art. 15.10. As noted above, the Constitution does not attempt to dictate the content of these—save to say that they must prescribe the quorum necessary for the due conduct of business: Article 15.11.3°. In *Re Haughey* [1971] I.R. 217 objection was taken to the fact that in 1938 the Dáil had simply adopted, with certain modifications, the standing orders of the former Dáil under the 1922 Constitution. The Supreme Court held, however, that this action was "susceptible of no other construction than that the new House was 'making' its Standing Orders within the meaning and intention of Article 15" (*per* Ó Dálaigh C.J. [1971] I.R. 217, 258).

Article 15.10 empowers each House to attach penalties for the infringement of its rules and standing orders. It is clear that the only penalties that could constitutionally be enforced—absent legislation—are the suspension or expulsion of a deputy or senator, or the exclusion of a disruptive member of the public. Anything in the nature of a fine or imprisonment would necessitate specific *statutory* provision. And any such statutory provision would have to provide for the trial of the relevant offence in a court of law: it would not be constitutionally possible to give this function to the Houses, or any committee thereof: see *Re Haughey* [1971] I.R. 217.

The standing orders of each House empower the chairman to order members to withdraw, and also provide machinery for suspending members for a specified period. There is no express constitutional warrant for such disci-

---

[27] Certain principles have been established for the exercise of the Ceann Comhairle's casting vote. Professor Hayes ruled in 1923 that a motion calling for expenditure of public funds should command a majority of votes independent of the chairman's (3 *Dáil Debs.*, c. 1331). In 1927 he stated that a motion of no confidence in the Executive Council should be affirmed by a majority of deputies and not merely by the presiding officer's casting vote (20 *Dáil Debs.*, c. 1750). These principles were applied by Dr. O'Connell in June 1982: see 336 *Dáil Debs.*, cc. 1703, 1709, 1723. The first of them was also applied by Mr. Fitzpatrick on November 26, 1986 in a vote on a motion to increase social welfare spending: see 370 *Dáil Debs.*, c. 668. Three weeks later he used his casting vote four times on the committee stage of the Extradition (European Convention on the Suppression of Terrorism) Bill: *The Irish Times*, December 18, 1986. But the most remarkable instance occurred on March 10, 1987 when only the casting vote of Mr. Séan Treacy secured Mr. Haughey's election as Taoiseach: see *The Irish Times*, March 11, 1987.

[28] See 320 *Dáil Debs.*, c. 1177.

plinary measures (contrast the United States Constitution, Art. 1, s.5, cl. 2, which authorises each House to "punish its members for disorderly behaviour"). But such powers have a pedigree antedating both the 1922 and 1937 Constitutions, and experience has shown the need for them. No doubt they are impliedly authorised by the power to make rules and standing orders and to attach penalties for their infringement: Art. 15.10.

The United States Constitution, in Art. 1, s.5, cl. 2, specifically authorises each House of Congress to expel members. A similar power is asserted by the United Kingdom House of Commons, and was most notably exercised in the case of Garry Allighan MP in 1947.[29] While the Constitution does not explicitly grant any such power to the House of the Oireachtas, it is submitted that each could validly expel a member, by majority vote if necessary. Such a power would seem to be necessitated by Article 15.13, which provides that members are not amenable in respect of any utterance in either House 'to any court or any authority other than the House itself." This language obviously predicates a disciplinary function for the Houses. Should a member abuse his/her privilege by making totally unwarranted allegations against a private individual, the appropriate disciplinary sanction might well be expulsion. For the Constitution undertakes to vindicate the good name of every citizen: Art. 40.3.2°. If Article 15.12 bars redress through the courts, it may offer an alternative form of vindication via the expulsion of the offending deputy or senator.

May the validity of disciplinary sanctions imposed on a member of either House be questioned in the courts? Until March 1990 the answer had been assumed to be no. The common law rule that there is no jurisdiction to interfere in the internal affairs of either chamber[30] had been thought to be still applicable. But doubt has been cast on this by a decision of Blayney J. in proceedings brought by Senator David Norris. Senator Norris had been found guilty of a serious breach of privilege by the Seanad's Committee on Procedure and Privileges, and by resolution of the Seanad had been suspended for a week. He applied for leave to challenge this suspension by way of judicial review, alleging that the Committee—which had been chaired by the Cathaoirleach, Senator Doherty—had failed to observe fair procedures.[31] Blayney J. ordered that the suspension be lifted pending the outcome of the proceedings, and granted leave to apply for judicial review (*The Irish Times*, March 17, 1990). But the case proceeded no further. On March 21, 1990 the Seanad rescinded the suspension resolution, confessedly to avoid unnecess-

---

[29] See 443 *H.C. Deb.*, 5 s., cc. 1094 ff.

[30] *Stockdale* v. *Hansard* (1839) 9 A. & E. 1: *Bradlaugh* v. *Gosset* (1884) 12 Q.B.D. 271. See also E.C.S. Wade and A. W. Bradley, *Constitutional and Administrative Law* (10th ed., London 1985), Chap. 12.

[31] The serious breach of privilege of which Senator Norris was acccused lay in making certain unfounded allegations in the chamber against the Cathaoirleach. It later emerged that on March 13, 1990 the Cathaoirleach had been legally advised that, in the circumstances, he should not have chaired the relevant Committee of Procedure and Privileges meeting. The principle of *nemo judex in causa sua* might have been violated, it was suggested, and the case should be re-heard with another person in the chair. This advice was not made known to the Committee when it made its decision on March 14, nor to the Seanad when, on March 15, it voted in support of the recommendation for suspension. Subsequently a motion for Senator Doherty's removal from the office of Cathaoirleach was defeated by 29 votes to 25 (see 124 *Seanad Debs.*, cc. 1039–1145). Senator Doherty later agreed personally to pay the costs of Senator Norris's action (see 125 *Seanad Debs.* c. 382).

ary confrontation with the courts. Both then and subsequently, however, a number of Senators expressed disquiet at the new constitutional vista opened up by the High Court's decision.[32]

The Norris case does not *decide* that the courts can review parliamentary decisions disciplining members. This question would have arisen had the proceedings continued, but in the events which occurred the High Court was deprived of the chance to rule upon it. Nonetheless, the case raises doubts about the validity of the assumption that Leinster House is impregnably fortified against judicial intrusion. It seems probable, however, that judicial intervention—should it occur—will be confined to disciplinary decisions where constitutional rights are alleged to have been infringed. Challenges to procedural rulings of the Ceann Comhairle or Cathaoirleach are unlikely to be entertained by the courts, unless it can be argued that some constitutionally protected interest is at stake and there is no other means of vindicating it.[33] It may be noted that in July 1990 the Opposition parties claimed that a guillotine motion truncating debate on seven Bills violated Dáil standing orders, and had secured legal advice to that effect. But despite threats to do so they did not carry the matter to the High Court, and the dispute was amicably resolved by discussion between the party leaders.[34]

Privileges

Article 15.12 and 15.13 relate to privilege in both Houses, the former dealing with official reports, publications and utterances, the latter with members' immunity from arrest in certain limited circumstances.

The privilege from arrest in Article 15.13 extends to members when going to, returning from or being within the precincts of either House. However, it does not apply to arrest for treason (as defined in Art. 39), felony or breach of the peace.

It had been thought that the privilege applied only to arrests in *civil* cases, thus yielding merely freedom from attachment or committal for contempt, *e.g.* for failure to obey a court order.[35] But uncertainty as to its true scope has been engendered by a controversial case in 1989. There Senator Seán McCarthy had been arrested in Rathmines at 5 a.m. on 23 November and charged with an offence under the Road Traffic Acts. He had spoken in the Seanad the previous evening and subsequently worked late in his office. When arrested, Senator McCarthy invoked Article 15.13 of the Constitution but he was nonetheless brought to a Garda station and charged.[36] However,

---

[32] See 124 *Seanad Debs.*, c. 874 (Senator Manning): 125 *Seanad Debs.*, c. 383 (Senator Manning: cc. 384–385 (Senator Dardis): c. 385 (Senator Upton).

[33] The U.S. Supreme Court has been prepared to review congressional proceedings to see whether constitutionally required procedure has been followed: *U.S.* v. *Ballin* (1892) 144 U.S. 1. And although the Irish courts have held themselves powerless to intervene in the legislative process—see *Wireless Dealers' Association* v. *Fair Trade Commission* (Supreme Court, March 14, 1956)—it was open to the plaintiffs there to question the validity of the challenged measure *after* its passage into law. This would not necessarily be the case with a disputed procedural ruling.

[34] *The Irish Times*, July 3, 1990: 400 *Dáil Debs.*, cc. 1757–1775 (July 3, 1990).

[35] The U.S. Supreme Court has held that Art. 1, s.6 of the U.S. Constitution, which confers a like privilege in precisely similar terms, applies only to arrests in civil cases: *Williamson* v. *U.S.* (1908) 207 U.S. 425. In the U.K. M.P.s and peers have no privilege from *criminal* arrest: see *Stourton* v. *Stourton* [1963] P. 302 and Wade and Bradley, *op. cit.*, pp. 211–212, 228.

[36] See Senator McCarthy's personal statement: 124 *Seanad Debs.*, cc. 1534–1536 (April 5, 1990).

when the case finally came on, it was announced that the D.P.P. was not proceeding further and the charge was accordingly struck out.[37] No reason for this decision was given then or subsequently. Perhaps the view was taken that the constitutional privilege indeed applied, making the arrest and everything consequent thereon invalid. But it is unfortunate that the courts were not given the opportunity to rule on this issue.

In the wake of this affair several senators and deputies expressed concern that privilege should be invoked in such a situation, and deplored the impression given that parliamentarians stood above the law.[38] It now appears that the two Committees on Procedure and Privileges will consider the reach of Article 15.13 and suggest means to ensure that its protection is claimed only sparingly.[39]

By Article 15.13 freedom of speech is guaranteed to parliamentarians, who are not "in respect of any utterance in either House . . . amenable to any court or any authority other than the House itself." This plainly precludes any action for damages for libel or slander founded on a parliamentary speech by a deputy or senator. Were any such proceedings instituted it would presumably be the duty of the relevant court to stop the action (*cf. Dillon* v. *Balfour* (1887) 20 L.R. Ir. 600). The provision is also regarded as covering utterances in official Oireachtas committees, whether established by one House or jointly by both; this is on the basis that any such committee is essentially the *alter ego* of the House which established it and must consequently share the privileges of that House.[40] The position has now been clarified by the Committees of the Houses of the Oireachtas (Privilege and Procedure) Act 1976. This Act applies to committees appointed by either House or jointly by both. It provides that a member of either House shall not, in respect of any utterance in or before a committee, be amenable to any court or authority other than the House or Houses by which the committee was appointed: s.2(1). Moreover, the documents of a committee and "the documents of its members connected with the committee or its functions" wherever published shall be privileged: s.2(2). The same applies to all official reports and publications of a committee, and to the utterances in a committee of the members, advisers, officials and agents of the committee (*ibid.*).

The language of section 2(2) of the 1976 Act is plainly derived from Article 15.12 of the Constitution. This attaches privilege to all official reports and publications of the Oireachtas or of either House thereof. The privilege thus conferred would seem to be *absolute* privilege—that is, no action will lie even should the official report contain false and defamatory statements which could be proved to have been made maliciously.

Article 15.12 also provides that "utterances made in either House wherever published" shall be privileged. This would obviously cover a newspaper report of a Dáil or Seanad speech—and, as has been seen, utterances of deputies or senators in or before an official committee enjoy protection by statute. So, too, do those of the committee's advisers, officials and agents—but the 1976 Act is quite silent on the position of witnesses who do not fall into these categories, and are not members of either House. Though the issue of pro-

---

[37] *The Irish Times*, March 30, 1990.
[38] See *The Irish Times*, March 30, 1990, and 124 *Seanad Debs.*, c. 1218 (Senator Manning): c. 1219 (Senator Murphy): c. 1220 (Senator Upton): (April 3, 1990).
[39] 124 *Seanad Debs.* c. 1221 (April 3, 1990): 404 *Dáil Debs.*, c. 510 (December 19, 1990).
[40] See the *Interim Report of the Public Accounts Committee* (T. 230) December 15, 1970, App. 1.

tecting such witnesses has frequently been raised, no legislation for that purpose has yet been passed. On one view, however, it may not be necessary. Article 15.13 clearly attaches privilege to the utterances of *members* in either House; thus when Article 15.12 privileges the publication of "utterances made in either House," it arguably protects statements by non-members. On the basis that the words "in either House" must receive an extended construction covering official committees, witnesses appearing before such committees would be protected. The fact that statute has not so provided would, on this approach, be beside the point. The 1976 Act covering committee members, advisers, officials and agents may be viewed not as making new law, but as merely declaring the true constitutional position.

In 1975 a tribunal of inquiry was established (under the Tribunals of Inquiry (Evidence) Act 1921) to inquire into the veracity of certain allegations made in Dáil Éireann by two deputies against the then Minister for Local Government. The deputies involved, who later withdrew their allegations and apologised for them, declined to give evidence before the tribunal. Counsel also contended on their behalf that the tribunal could not investigate the allegations in question, as the 1921 Act was never intended to authorise an extra-parliamentary inquiry into allegations made in parliament. The tribunal, which consisted of Henchy, Parke and Conroy JJ., rejected this submission, saying[41]:

> "The establishment of a tribunal under the 1921 Act is in no way inconsistent with the rights of members of parliament. On the contrary, it is an exercise of those rights, for section 1(1) of the Act ensures that a tribunal cannot be set up unless and until both Houses have resolved that 'it is expedient that a tribunal be established for inquiring into a definite matter described in the resolution as of urgent public importance.' The statute does not except from the scope of an inquiry an allegation made in parliament. A tribunal set up under the Act to make an inquiry, so far from representing an intrusion into the affairs of parliament is the instrument chosen by parliament itself to make the inquiry . . . we are satisfied, from a scrutiny of the terms of the 1921 Act, as exemplified by precedent established by both the British and Irish parliaments, that the matters referred to us for inquiry are matters within the contemplation of the statute and that the inquiry does not violate parliamentary privilege . . . ."

In explaining his clients' decision not to attend or give evidence before the tribunal, counsel argued that the deputies' stand was authorised by Article 15.13 of the Constitution. The tribunal found it unnecessary to rule on this matter; it could become a live issue only if the question arose of *compelling* them to give evidence under the provisions of the 1921 Act. In the light of the other evidence available, the tribunal concluded that the deputies' evidence was not essential for a proper investigation. Thus the question remains open. Given the terms of the Tribunals of Inquiry (Evidence) (Amendment) Act 1979, the matter is an important one, for a refusal to attend or give evidence to a tribunal is an offence, punishable on conviction on indictment by a fine not exceeding £10,000 or two years' imprisonment (or both), and on sum-

[41] Prl. 4745, para. 28.

mary conviction by a fine of up to £500 or 12 months' imprisonment (or both).

In *Garda Representative Association* v. *Ireland* [1989] I.R. 193 the plaintiffs asserted a right to be consulted about a proposal affecting certain overtime payments, and relied *inter alia* on a statement by the Minister for Justice in Dáil Éireann.[42] Counsel for the defence argued that Article 15.13 barred such reliance, but Murphy J. held that it did not. He said (at 204–205):

> " . . . the official reports of Parliamentary debates contain a valuable record of the considered views of eminent politicians so that it would be absurd (as well as offensive to the politicians) to proceed on the footing either that the statements were not made or that national organisations and concerned officials do not acquaint themselves with the statements and opinions expressed by politicians and more particularly Ministers in the forum designed for the purpose. In my view the constitutional protection afforded by Article 15 would not in any way prevent the plaintiffs in the present case from adverting to the statement *as some evidence* of the fact that the Minister for Justice shared the views of the plaintiffs that a change with regard to the parading time would entail consultation with the Garda associations." (Italics supplied).

Murphy J. went on to hold that since there was no evidence that the plaintiffs relied upon the Minister's statement, it could not be invoked to support a promissory estoppel. This seems to imply that, had there been such evidence, the statement could have been relied upon for that purpose.

A distinction may obviously be drawn between reliance on a parliamentary statement for evidential purposes, and suing in respect of such a statement. Article 15.13, Murphy J. agreed, would bar the latter. This must presumably apply not only when an individual feels him/herself defamed but also where an attempt is made to found an estoppel *on no other material*. Hence, it is submitted, Murphy J.'s words (italicised above)—"as some evidence." Were a parliamentary statement to be invoked not merely as a link in the chain of proof, but as the sole foundation of the claim, problems might arise. For then, arguably, there would be an attempt to make the Minister" . . . amenable to any court . . . " in a way forbidden by Article 15.13.

The *Garda Representative Association* case would also legitimise the use of parliamentary debates as an aid to the interpretation of statutes. Though infrequently resorted to by the Irish courts these may occasionally be capable of shedding light on difficult issues.[43]

Contempt of parliament

Both Houses of the United Kingdom parliament have long claimed the power to adjudicate upon, and punish people for, "contempt of parliament." What constitutes such a contempt is not entirely clear; no statute regulates the matter, and while precedents clarify the position to some extent, the categories of contempt are said not to be closed. At one time this subject generated a good deal of controversy: the House of Commons was thought by some to be unduly sensitive, and its procedures were regarded as unfair to persons

---

[42] See 372 *Dáil Debs.*, c. 1755 (May 13, 1987).
[43] See further James Casey, "Statutory Interpretation—A New Departure" (1981) 3 D.U.L.J. 110.

haled before it on contempt charges. (The House of Lords, in contrast, led a much quieter life.) In recent times, however, the controversy has abated.[44]

In Ireland contempt of parliament is probably subsumed under Article 15.10 of the Constitution. The power conferred on each House to penalise breaches of its rules or standing orders, to ensure freedom of debate, to protect its official documents and to protect itself and its members against certain kinds of outside interference would seem to cover this ground. The term "contempt," it may be noted, appears in some reports of the Dáil Committee on Procedure and Privileges, where it is treated as a species of breach of privilege. (The Seanad has not had occasion to rule on such issues.)

No Act of the Oireachtas offers a catalogue of breaches of privilege; their scope can be discovered only by examining the precedents. These, however, are relatively few in number, and it is plain that contempt of parliament has never been anything like so controversial an issue here as in the United Kingdom. This may be due in part to the limited powers that the Dáil can exercise in such cases. As noted previously, it would be constitutionally impossible for either House, or any committee, to punish an alleged contemnor by way of fine or imprisonment. (Nor indeed could he/she be punished by the courts, for in the absence of legislation contempt of parliament would not seem to constitute a "criminal charge" under Article 38.1.) Thus a newspaper editor found guilty of falsely imputing dishonourable conduct to members could only be subjected to a formal reprimand. (It is doubtful whether such a person could be brought before parliament unwillingly—by attachment—as in the United Kingdom: this would appear to be a deprivation of liberty not sanctioned by law and thus contrary to Art. 40.4.1°.)

The Dáil Committee on Procedure and Privileges has held the following to be breaches of privilege: a fracas between two deputies in the precincts of Leinster House (*Report* T.119 (1947): T.133 (1952)): the premature publication of a select committee report (T.143 (1953)): a newspaper article "scurrilously abusive of members in the performance of their parliamentary duties" (T.155 (1956)): adverse criticism of the conduct of the Chair, outside the House (T.221 (1970)): unfounded personal allegations by members against other members (T.245 (1975): T.248 (1976)). Breaches of privilege by deputies are normally reported to the House; those by persons outside are usually the subject of no further action.

[44] See the *Report from the Select Committee on Parliamentary Privilege*, H.C. 34 (1967–68).

5   The Functioning of the Oireachtas

Though the Constitution declares, in Article 15.2.1°, that the Oireachtas has the sole and exclusive power of making laws for the State, and goes on to devote seven Articles (20–27) to legislation, it does not undertake to regulate in detail the legislative process. Instead this is left to be dealt with by the standing orders of each House, supplemented by political arrangements.

In the period 1982–1991 the Oireachtas passed 327 measures (323 Acts and four Constitution amendment Bills.[1]) Rounded off, this gives an average of 33 Acts per year—less than in earlier periods[2]—the actual figures being:

1982	29
1983	42 (and a Constitution amendment Bill)
1984	27 (and a Constitution amendment Bill)
1985	24
1986	39 (and a Constitution amendment Bill)
1987	34 (and a Constitution amendment Bill)
1988	35
1989	23
1990	38
1991	32

Virtually all these measures were Government-sponsored. Although ordinary deputies and senators, acting as individuals or on behalf of the Opposition, may introduce Bills the chances of their becoming law are small.[3] If the measure proposed seems a good idea the Government will accept the principle and later introduce its own Bill. Indeed the main object of the exercise may have been to bring about this result. The Westminster practice under which some private members' Bills, on subjects the government approves of but to which it has not given priority in its own programme, become law each year has never taken root in Ireland. Nor has that whereby private members take up issues with a moral dimension—though not in (United Kingdom) party controversy—such as reform of the law on homosexuality or on obscene publications. While 12 private members' Bills

---

[1] One of the Constitution amendment Bills—that to amend Art. 41.3.2° to permit divorce—failed to secure majority support in the subsequent referendum.

[2] McCracken, *op. cit.*, gives the average for the period 1923–1948 as 40.

[3] They will be greater if the Government lacks an overall Dáil majority, as was the case between 1987 and 1989. Thus the Bill which became the Judicial Separation and Family Law Reform Act 1989 began as an Opposition measure.

became law in Ireland in the period 1923–1937,[4] nothing remotely resembling this has occurred in the last 25 years.

The measures passed range so widely in their subject-matter that they cannot be enclosed in any formula. Even in size they vary enormously, from the one page of *e.g.* the Courts (No. 2) Act 1981 to the entire Volume II of 1967 which is the Income Tax Act. Only two recur regularly; each year necessarily sees the passage of a Finance Act (to implement the Budget) and an Appropriation Act (to authorise the spending of money on public services). Apart from these, the decisions as to what Acts shall be passed in a given year are effectively taken by the Government. Since there is always more legislation in the pipeline than there is Oireachtas time available to process it, priorities necessarily have to be established. Thus the fact that a Ministerial Bill is printed and published, though necessarily implying Government approval thereof (see Chap. 6 *infra*), does not guarantee that it will soon (in some cases ever) become law.

The *immediate* sources of legislation are proposals by the relevant Government Departments which, when given Cabinet approval, are put into Bill form by the specialist staff of the Parliamentary Draftsman's office.[5] Their remoter causes may lie *inter alia* in the manifesto of the winning party in the last general election; or the report of a commission or committee[6]; or the requirements of a semi-State body[7]; or the need to amend the law as declared in a judicial decision.[8] Whatever its roots, a Bill will often represent the end of a lengthy preparatory process, involving discussions with other Departments and also with outside interest groups. But the Oireachtas does not really probe this process. Writing in 1974 Professor Chubb rightly said that it was better thought of as a *law-declaring* rather than a *law-making* body; and he continued[9]:

" . . . although the Oireachtas has a comparatively modest role as a policy-maker, it does not perform it well. The Dáil and Seanad are

[4] *Ibid.*, p. 167.
[5] On the drafting of legislation see Gerald McCarthy, "Legislation. Its Preparation and Enactment" in F. C. King, (ed.) *Public Administration in Ireland*, (Dublin 1954), Vol. III, p. 1.
[6] Examples are the Landlord and Tenant (Amendment) Act 1980, implementing recommendations of the Landlord and Tenant Commission; the Sale of Goods and Supply of Services Act 1980, improving consumer protection in ways recommended by the National Consumer Council; and the Family Law Act 1981, the Age of Majority Act 1985 and the Domicile and Recognition of Foreign Divorces Act 1986 implementing (in part) recommendations of the Law Reform Commission. For a (now somewhat out of date) survey of such bodies see Donald Leon, *Advisory Bodies in Irish Government* (Dublin 1963).
[7] Instances are legion. Some examples are the Electricity (Supply) (Amendment) Act 1979, giving the E.S.B. power to engage in the provision of consultancy services abroad and raising the limit on expenditure for capital purposes; the Sea Fisheries (Amendment) Act 1974, increasing Bord Iascaigh Mhara's borrowing powers; and the Industrial Credit (Amendment) Act 1977, doing the same for the Industrial Credit Co.
[8] Examples are the Accidental Fires Act 1943, which reversed *Richardson* v. *Athlone Woollen Mills Co. Ltd.* [1942] I.R. 581 (S.C.); the Foyle Fisheries (Amendment) Act 1976, passed in consequence of *State (Devine)* v. *Larkin* [1977] I.R. 24 (decided by the High Court in November 1975; see Chap. 2 *supra*): the Criminal Justice (Verdicts) Act 1976, passed in consequence of the Court of Criminal Appeal's decision (of November 1975) in *People (D.P.P.)* v. *Rice* [1979] I.R. 15; the Adoption Act 1976, resulting from the Supreme Court's June 1976 decision in *M* v. *An Bord Uchtála* [1977] I.R. 287 (see Chap. 17 *infra*); and the Local Government (Planning and Development) Act 1982, passed in consequence of the Supreme Court's decision in *State (Pine Valley Developments) Ltd.* v. *Dublin Co. Council* [1982] I.L.R.M. 169—see Chap. 2 *supra* and Chap. 18 *infra*.
[9] Basil Chubb, *Cabinet Government in Ireland* (Dublin 1974), p. 65.

neither well organised to perform it, since their procedures are archaic, nor do they have expert staff to conduct the necessary research and pre-pare briefs and other material for use by members. The government, backed by the great resources of manpower and expertise of the civil ser-vice, has almost a monopoly of expert opinion and advice much of which it does not make available to the Oireachtas."

However, since that was written the Houses of the Oireachtas have estab-lished a number of select committees, some composed of deputies *and* sena-tors, which *may* result in a greater parliamentary input into the legislative process.[10]

Procedure on Bills

Public Bills (those sponsored by a Minister or parliamentary group)[11] go through five stages in the House in which they are initiated, four in the other.[12] The first stage—which is purely formal—arises only in the initiating chamber; the Bill goes straight to the second stage in the other House. In both Houses that second stage is a debate on the general principles of the Bill and, if it is opposed, on alternative ideas. The Cabinet Minister, or Minister of State, in charge of the Bill will introduce it, explaining its objectives and its terms, and will close the debate on this stage with a speech replying to the points made by previous speakers. The third stage is a detailed examination, section by section, of the Bill's contents. Its desirability is now established and cannot be reopened at this juncture, and though amendments may be proposed they must respect this principle. (The sponsoring Minister, it should be noted, may well wish to introduce amendments at this stage.) Nor-mally this third stage, like the second, is taken on the floor of the Dáil, but occasionally a Bill is sent instead to a special committee.[13] Such a committee will broadly reproduce the party composition of the Dáil (thus the Govern-ment will have a majority thereon) and will usually consist of deputies with a special knowledge of, or interest in, the Bill's subject-matter. An advantage of this device is that it enables the rest of the Dáil to proceed with other busi-ness, but it is not used as much as it might be.[14] No doubt this is due in part to the fact that such committees get little media publicity (in contrast to the *select* committees considered *infra*).

The fourth (report) stage is usually quite short. The scope for amendment is in practice limited to minor alterations, drafting amendments, etc. (which

[10] See Joseph F. Zimmerman, "An Oireachtas Innovation: Backbench Committees" (1988) 36 *Administration* 265.

[11] Private Bills (which must be distinguished from private members' Bills) are usually promoted by incorporated bodies which wish to have their charters amended. The promoters of such Bills must bear certain expenses.

[12] See generally J. McGowan Smyth, *The Houses of the Oireachtas* (4th ed., Dublin 1979), Chap. 9,; Dáil Éireann, *Standing Orders* 1986, S.O.s 92–121. The shape and form of Bills is governed by the Interpretation Act 1937.

[13] A private Bill would be sent to a *select* committee (consisting of deputies and senators) which would take evidence, hear counsel on behalf of the Bill's promoters—and on behalf of those objecting to it, if any—and make any necessary amendments.

[14] Proposals for Dáil reform announced by the Taoiseach in 1992 suggest greater use of such committees: see *The Irish Times*, May 1, 1992. The 1992 Finance Bill—the longest and most complex so far—went to such a committee.

again may often be sponsored by the relevant Minister). On the fifth stage amendments of a purely verbal nature are alone possible (see the Dáil's Standing Order 107). In fact the fourth and fifth stages often follow immediately upon each other and, depending on the Bill, may take up very little time indeed. Thus the Harbours Bill and Minerals Company Bill both passed the report and final stages on November 12, 1947 (108 *Dáil Debs.*, cc. 1721–1735: c. 1736). So did the Irish Shipping Ltd. Bill on November 20, 1947 (108 *Dáil Debs.*, cc. 2200–2201), while the Poultry Hatcheries Bill went through *all* its stages on the same date (108 *Dáil Debs.*, cc. 2205–2214).

Though, as noted in Chapter 4, there is no constitutional bar to initiating Bills (other than Money Bills) in the Seanad, this is not done as frequently as it might be. It would seem sensible for both chambers to be simultaneously at work on different pieces of legislation, but in practice matters are not usually arranged in this way. Recently, however, a number of Bills—including measures on transport, national monuments and the status of children (illegitimacy)—have first been processed through the Seanad; and in 1986 that House sat on 78 days, the highest figure ever.[15] In fact, this closely approaches the Dáil average of 87 days per year between 1969 and 1978.[16] This surprisingly low figure reflects the facts that the Dáil does not sit on Mondays (or normally on Fridays) and takes lengthy recesses at Christmas, Easter and in the summer.[17]

The committee system

The Dáil and Seanad have a number of committees—some of them joint bodies—which perform a wide range of functions. What might be called housekeeping duties fall to the Joint Library Committee and Joint Restaurant Committee[18]; and reference has already been made to the Dáil's Committee on Procedure and Privileges[19] (see Chap. 4 *supra*). In the 26th Dáil there are two Dáil select committees in operation, *viz.*:

   (a) the Public Accounts Committee
   (b) the Committee on Crime.

Five joint Dáil/Seanad committees have also been functioning, *viz.*:

   (a) on European secondary legislation[20]
   (b) on commercial State-sponsored bodies[21]

[15] Seanad Report, *The Irish Times*, December 20, 1986.
[16] McGowan Smyth, *op. cit.*, p. 50. The 20th Dáil (March 14, 1973—May 25, 1977) sat on 404 days and its successor (July 5, 1977—May 21, 1981) on 328 days; see *Legislative Work of the 20th Dáil* (Stationery Office 1977), p. 3 and *Legislative Work of the 21st Dáil (ibid)*, p. 3.
[17] The Government has submitted proposals for change in this regard to the Committee on Procedure and Privileges. Under these the number of Dáil sitting days per year would increase from 87 to 130: *The Irish Times*, May 1, 1992.
[18] As to these see McGowan Smyth, *op. cit.*, p. 44.
[19] For its composition see *ibid.*, p. 43.
[20] For its terms of reference see 123 *Seanad Debs.* cc. 973–978 (December 6, 1989). These include examining EC regulations, directives, etc., together with regulations made by Irish ministers under the European Communities Acts.
[21] For its terms of reference see 123 *Seanad Debs.*, cc. 987–992 (December 6, 1989).

(c) on women's rights[22]
(d) on employment[23]
(e) on the Irish lanaguage.[24]

In addition, the Government is committed to securing the establishment of a joint committee on foreign affairs which would, *inter alia*, take over the functions of the committee on European secondary legislation.[25]

Most of these bodies have the traditional power "to send for persons, papers and records"—though as noted in Chapter 4 *supra* there is no legislation under which a reluctant witness could be compelled to appear, or be punished for not doing so. But witnesses come voluntarily and the committees do not appear to have had any difficulty in obtaining evidence. They are assisted by a clerk and in addition are empowered to engage the services of experts to aid them in their inquiries[26]—as was done. The work of the committees has received a good deal of sustained media publicity, those on commercial State-sponsored bodies and women's rights being particularly successful in this respect.

It will be clear from the above that these committees are not solely concerned with legislation. The Public Accounts Committee is concerned with finance, and is considered under that heading *infra*. However the remits of several committees specifically involve them with legislation—*e.g.* the Joint Committee on Women's Rights may examine and propose legislative measures, and so too may the Dáil Committee on Crime.

Finance[27]

A number of constitutional provisions, some of which have already been noticed, bear upon the subject of public finance. Article 11, for instance, provides:

> "All revenues of the State from whatever source arising shall, subject to such exception as may be provided by law, form one fund, and shall be appropriated for the purposes and in the manner and subject to the charges and liabilities determined and imposed by law."

This fund is entitled the Central Fund: Constitution (Consequential Provisions) Act 1937, s.6. The banking transactions thereof are effected through the Exchequer Account at the Central Bank (see the Central Bank Act 1971,

---

[22] The terms of reference are set out in 123 *Seanad Debs.*, cc. 977–982. Its task is: (a) to examine or propose legislative measures which would materially affect the interests of women; (b) to consider means by which discrimination against women could be eliminated; (c) to recommend policy and administrative changes to eliminate economic and social disadvantages applying to women in the home.

[23] For its terms of reference see 418 *Dáil Debs.*, cc. 1329–1333 (April 9, 1992).

[24] Its terms of reference are set out in 123 *Seanad Debs.*, cc. 983–987 (December 6, 1989). Its function is to consider the extension of the use of the Irish language in Dáil and Seanad proceedings, and "the promotion of the Irish language in general."

[25] The Minister for Foreign Affairs (Mr. David Andrews T.D.) so informed the Seanad on May 6, 1992: 132 *Seanad Debs.*, c. 813.

[26] This is subject to the consent of the Minister for Finance.

[27] This section draws heavily upon J. B. O'Connell, *The Financial Administration of Ireland* (Dublin 1960) and on *An Outline of Irish Financial Procedures* (Stationery Office).

s.49).[28] Disbursements from this account require the sanction of the Comptroller and Auditor General, whose office is established by Article 33.1 of the Constitution:

> "There shall be a Comptroller and Auditor General to control on behalf of the State all disbursements and to audit all accounts of moneys administered by or under the authority of the Oireachtas."[29]

Money cannot be withdrawn from the Exchequer Account without the Comptroller's sanction, given only where he is satisfied that the requisition is within lawful limits.[30]

Money flows into the Central Fund from a wide variety of sources but it is fed principally by taxation. While the machinery, etc. for collecting taxes is the subject of permanent legislation (*e.g.* the Income Tax Act 1967) the actual rates are fixed by the annual Finance Act. Changes in such rates, in allowances, etc., will already have been announced by the Minister for Finance in his Budget statement in January or February. Following that statement and the Opposition reaction thereto, the financial resolutions are passed (assuming the Government has a reliable majority). These enable any changes in duties (such as those on drink and tobacco) to come into force immediately; for the Provisional Collection of Taxes Act 1927 permits Dáil resolutions approving the Minister's proposals to have legal effect immediately and for four months. By the end of that period the Finance Act will (and must[31]) have been passed,[32] so that the new rates will have legal effect for the whole of the financial year.[33]

The granting of supply

Article 28.4.3° states that:

> "The Government shall prepare Estimates of the Receipts and Estimates of the Expenditure of the State for each financial year, and shall present them to Dáil Éireann for consideration."

This language conceals what may be the difficult process of agreeing on a Budget—a process which begins well before the end of the previous financial year. Ministers must decide how much will be spent on various services such as education, health, social welfare, etc., these decisions necessarily being linked to the amounts the Government thinks it prudent to raise from taxation and/or borrowing. The Department of Finance will earlier have

---

[28] Special temporary arrangements to operate the account through a commercial bank may be made under the State Financial Transactions (Special Provisions) Act 1984.

[29] Art. 33 goes on to provide that the Comptroller and Auditor General shall be appointed by the President on the nomination of the Dáil; that he may not be a deputy or senator or hold any other office or position of emolument; that he has the same security of tenure as a judge; and that he shall report to Dáil Éireann at stated intervals fixed by law.

[30] See further O'Connell, *op. cit.*, Chap. VIII.

[31] Article 17.1.2° lays down the general principle that the legislation required to give effect to the Financial Resolutions of each year shall be enacted within that year.

[32] Thus the Finance Act 1985 became law on May 30, 1985; that of 1984 on May 23, and that of 1983 on June 8.

[33] The financial year is now the calendar year: Exchequer and Local Financial Years Act 1974.

obtained from the other Departments their estimates of proposed expenditure for the forthcoming financial year. In default of agreement between Finance and the spending Departments matters will have to go to the Cabinet.[34] Especially when financial stringency makes cuts inevitable, the difficulty in agreeing spending priorities may be considerable; witness the Labour Ministers' resignation from the Government over this issue on January 20, 1987—which precipitated a general election.

When finally settled the estimates are put before the Dáil—in advance of the Budget—in a bulky volume entitled "Book of Estimates for the Public Service."[35] Each estimate is now described as a Vote and is numbered; and the Vote for a particular Department gives a detailed breakdown of how the money will be spent. It is in three parts, Part I being the *ambit of the Vote* (this alone is placed on the statute book by the annual Appropriation Act). Part II sets out the subheads; though these do not have statutory force they are the basis for accounting by the relevant Department.[36] The non-statutory character of the subheads also enables savings under one to be used to meet excess expenditure on another (this is known as *virement*). *Virement* requires the sanction of the Department of Finance; and it is not possible as between different Votes.[37] Part III of the Vote gives additional details.

While the estimates must be approved by the Dáil in order to give legal authority for the relevant expenditure (known as Supply), they are not in any real sense controlled by that body. (Indeed, so large an assembly could hardly be expected to exercise any real control over a sum like £7,199,991,000—the amount granted by the Appropriation Act 1991). The discussion of the estimates takes the form of a general debate on the policy of the Department whose Vote is under consideration. The debate is ritualistic, with a lengthy speech by the relevant Minister and a reply by the Opposition spokesperson, neither of which may have much to do with the sums of money at issue. In fact the actual figures will be approved "on the nod." This system has been much criticised and reform has been canvassed for some time.

Arrangements to fund public services while the Dáil is discussing the estimates are made by the Central Fund (Permanent Provisions) Act 1965. Section 2 authorises the Minister for Finance to issue out of the Central Fund up to four-fifths of the amount appropriated for each particular service in the preceding financial year. (This is subject to the conditions: (a) that during the year he asks the Dáil to grant Supply for the service in question in respect of that year; (b) that he considers each issue and its application necessary.[38])

---

[34] Thus in 1948–49 the Minister for Health, Dr. Noel Browne, wanted additional staff for his Department. The Department of Finance would sanction only a smaller increase than requested and the Minister brought the issue before the Government. It was referred to the Cabinet's estimates committee, which granted the Minister's request on certain conditions: see Ronan Fanning, *The Irish Department of Finance 1922–1958*, pp. 592–595.

[35] Earlier—usually the weekend before the Budget—there will have appeared the *White Paper on Receipts and Expenditure*.

[36] See further O'Connell, *op. cit.*, Chap. VI and XII.

[37] See further *An Outline of Irish Financial Procedures*, pp. 16–17. As there noted, the Comptroller and Auditor General, and the Dáil's Public Accounts Committee, may question any sanction given.

[38] The role of the Department of Finance is of great significance, for even if the Dáil votes funds for a service they cannot be spent without Finance sanction—which may be subjected to conditions additional to those approved by the Dáil. The statutory basis for this is s.2(4) of the

Section 5, as amended,[39] obliges the Minister to lay before the Dáil each December a statement of the amounts which, from the start of the next financial year, he will be authorised to issue. Under section 3, where the Dáil approves an estimate the amount issuable is automatically increased to the whole figure so approved. Finally the Appropriation Act—which gives statutory effect to the individual estimates—will be passed towards the end of the financial year.[40]

Accounting and audit

By virtue of Article 33.1 of the Constitution it is a function of the Comptroller and Auditor General to "audit all accounts of moneys administered . . . under the authority of the Oireachtas." The Comptroller—an independent constitutional officer—heads a Department whose staff, though appointed by the Minister for Finance, are subject to his regulation and control: Comptroller and Auditor General Act 1923, ss.4 and 6. The Comptroller has the additional duty of reporting to the Dáil "on such matters and at such periods and times as shall from time to time be prescribed by law or required by resolution of Dáil Éireann": *ibid.*, s.7(2). And he inherits all the powers and duties conferred or imposed by pre-Independence statutes.[41]

The Comptroller's audit is concerned with the regularity and accuracy of (principally) the Appropriation Account, which each Department is statutorily[42] obliged to prepare in respect of each Supply grant administered by it.[43] When certified and reported on by the Comptroller the accounts, printed in a single volume, are presented to the Dáil, where they will be examined by the Public Accounts Committee. The Comptroller may qualify the certificate; and the report to the Dáil will draw attention *inter alia* to loss, waste, or uneconomic expenditure, to expenditure in excess of the sum granted or expenditure not supported by Finance authority. Thus, in his report on the 1987 accounts, the Comptroller criticised the practice by Government Departments of deferring payment of matured liabilities to the following year as not being in accordance with prescribed financial procedures. He found that confusion in ACOT over claims for EC funding for training courses had resulted in failure to obtain an additional £485,000 in 1985. He commented adversely on the Justice Department's failure to implement the P.A.Y.E. and P.R.S.I. regulations in respect of certain civilian employees outside Dublin, and on inadequate stocktaking procedures at the Garda depot and in regard to army stores. He was also concerned about two major incidents of disability benefit fraud, and about the circumstances in

---

Ministers and Secretaries Act 1924: "The expenses of each of the Departments of State established under this Act, *to such extent as may be sanctioned by the Minister for Finance*, shall be paid out of moneys provided by the Oireachtas" (italics supplied). For the history of this see Fanning, *op. cit.*, pp. 43–53, 98–105.

[39] By the Exchequer and Local Financial Years Act (Adaptation of Enactments etc.) (No. 2) Order 1974.

[40] Thus the Appropriation Act 1985 became law on December 28, that of 1984 on December 26 and that of 1983 on December 27.

[41] *I.e.* the Exchequer and Audit Departments Acts 1866 and 1921. See further O'Connell, *op. cit.*, Chap. XIII.

[42] By s.22 of the Exchequer and Audit Departments Act 1866.

[43] See further *An Outline of Irish Financial Procedures*, pp. 18–19.

which the Department of Finance had sanctioned a *virement* in moneys voted to the Taoiseach's Department.[44]

The Public Accounts Committee

The Public Accounts Committee is a select committee of the Dáil, appointed under Standing Order 126. Its principal function is to examine and report to the Dáil on the Appropriation Accounts.[45] The committee consists of 12 deputies, none of whom may be a Minister, and its quorum is four. By tradition it is chaired by an Opposition deputy; and the Comptroller and Auditor General is permanently in attendance as a witness. The accounting officer of each Department (usually the Secretary) is questioned by the members. Though the committee has the power to examine Ministers it has done so only in one exceptional case—an affair more fit for a tribunal of inquiry, which it should not have been asked to investigate.[46]

In an article published in 1985 Dr. Eunan O'Halpin examined the working of the Public Accounts committee and found much to criticise.[47] Attendance at, and preparation for, meetings was poor, and the committee's time was not used very effectively. Moreover, the Dáil as a whole had taken little interest in the committee's reports, the first debate on one having occurred only in 1968. Matters appear to have improved somewhat since 1985, though no action has so far been taken or a special report of May 1988 on the future role of the Comptroller and Auditor General and the Public Accounts committee.[48]

Questions, adjournment debates, etc.

Though the Constitution particularly stresses the Dáil's legislative and financial functions, it has never been accepted that it has no others. Like parliamentary bodies elsewhere it is also conceived of as a forum where issues of public—or individual—concern may be raised. Such issues—which need not be connected with finance or involve legislation—may arise out of the policy or administration of a Department. Though Bunreacht na hÉireann is silent on the point, it has always been accepted that a Minister is responsible to the Dáil for the policy and administration of his/her Department. "Responsible" here means "answerable to," in the sense that the Department's actions and decisions may be subjected to question and debate. Though the Minister is, in law, the Department and must answer for the action of every official in it, there is no convention requiring resignation if a mistake of which he/she knew nothing occurs. (Even if some disastrous failure of policy could be laid at the

---

[44] See *Committee of Public Accounts: Interim and Final Reports (Appropriation Accounts 1987)* (Pl. 8439, 1991). The Comptroller had also complained of inadequate staffing levels in his Office. The Public Accounts Committee felt that this matter could be resolved only in the context of its own 1988 special report on that Office, and urged early legislation to implement that report (pp. 90–91).

[45] It also has the function of suggesting alterations and improvements in the form of the estimates presented to the Dáil.

[46] The inquiry into the expenditure of a grant-in-aid of £100,000 for Northern Ireland relief in 1969—most of which was alleged to have gone to the Provisional IRA. The committee's investigation was attended by a multitude of difficulties, legal, political and administrative: see its Interim and Final Reports (of 1970 and 1972) (Prl. 2574).

[47] Eunnan O'Halpin, "The Dáil Committee of Public Accounts" (1985) 32 *Administration* 483.

[48] Pl 5645. See also n. 44 *supra*.

Minister's door, resignation is unlikely unless he/she has forfeited the support of Cabinet colleagues.)[49]

Under the Dáil's Standing Order 32 questions addressed to a Minister must "relate to public affairs connected with his Department, or to matters of administration for which he is officially responsible." If a question submitted does not comply with standing orders it will be refused.[50] No machinery exists for compelling Ministers to answer questions; and although they routinely do so (the answers being prepared by their civil servants) there are some matters, particularly in the security field, on which information is customarily withheld.[51]

Questions are taken for $1\frac{1}{4}$ hours on Tuesdays, Wednesdays and Thursdays (those addressed to the Taoiseach come first but are taken only on Tuesdays and Wednesdays). Under reforms introduced in 1985[52] there is a daily rotation of Ministers[53] and the questions to be taken are selected by lot. A special 15 minute period is set aside during which the main Opposition party or parties may table priority questions.

Though supplementary questions are allowed within limits, there may still be insufficient time for a deputy to ventilate an issue properly. An alternative means of doing so is offered by the daily half-hour adjournment debate. Under S.O. 20(3)(*a*), deputies may notify the Ceann Comhairle of their desire to raise specified matters in this debate. A maximum of three topics will be discussed; if more are notified the Ceann Comhairle will make the selection. A Minister, or Minster of State, will set out in reply the Government's views on the matter raised. The adjournment debate is often used to raise a matter which is of particular concern to a deputy's constituents,[54] but issues of more general relevance may also be raised.[55]

Another form of debate is provided for by the Dáil's Standing Order

---

[49] There is no recorded instance of a resignation in such circumstances. Otherwise the Irish practice is similar to that in the United Kingdom, as to which see Geoffrey Marshall, *Constitutional Conventions*, Chap. IV.

[50] Under S.O. 31 a question must be in writing, and normally several days advance notice is required—though there is provision for "special notice" questions. If a written rather than an oral answer is required the question is distinguished by an asterisk. For the Ceann Comhairle's role in securing compliance with Standing Orders see S.O. 33.

[51] Thus on February 13, 1986 the Minister for Defence, in answering a question about army vehicles, said it was not the practice, in the interests of security, to give details regarding armoured vehicles: 363 *Dáil Debs.*, c. 2682.

[52] And first recommended in 1972: Informal Committee on Reform of Dáil Procedure, *Report* (Prl. 2904) pp. 7–9. Comment on the delay seems superfluous.

[53] Previously questions were taken in the order of Ministerial seniority, which could have the result that some Ministers had the opportunity to answer questions only late in a session, if at all.

[54] Examples are that of November 26, 1947, in relation to Land Commission refusal of permission to sublet a dwelling (109 *Dáil Debs.*, cc. 135–140); of November 18, 1986, about a Co. Limerick farmer's prison hunger strike (369 *Dáil Debs.*, cc. 2695–2704); of November 25, 1986, on the Southern Cross route (a motorway in south Co. Dublin) (370 *Dáil Debs.*, cc. 440–450); and of May 21, 1992, about impending industrial action at a Mullingar primary school (420 *Dáil Debs.*, cc. 160–164).

[55] Examples are the debate of October 22, 1947, alleging corruption in regard to the sale of Locke's distillery, Kilbeggan, Co. Westmeath (108 *Dáil Debs.*, cc. 829–840). (This ultimately led to the establishment of a statutory tribunal of inquiry, which rejected the allegations: Report of the Tribunal appointed by the Taoiseach on November 7, 1947, P. No. 8576.) Also that of November 27, 1986 in regard to a Government invitation to the International Monetary Fund to examine the taxation system (370 *Dáil Debs.*, cc. 830–840); that of December 3,

30^{56}—a $1\frac{1}{2}$ hour debate, displacing the normal order of business, on a "specific and important matter of public interest requiring urgent consideration." This formula replaced an older, narrower one which had become encrusted with so many restrictive precedents that between 1922 and 1972 there had been only 13 such debates, the last occurring in 1947.[57] The result, it was said, was that sudden developments could take place which could be widely discussed by press, television and radio, but which were ignored by the Dáil or discussed only when public interest had evaporated.[58] The new dispensation is designed to permit greater topicality and a number of debates have been allowed under its aegis by the Ceann Comhairle. The advent of live radio and television broadcasting to the Dáil has generated more applications for such debates.

Topical issues of general concern may also be ventilated during Private Members' business (which in practice is controlled by the main Opposition party or parties). This permits a couple of $1\frac{1}{2}$ hour debates each week on Opposition motions—which may involve a Bill on some topic. Non-legislative examples are motions on unemployment and emigration (November 18, 1986),[59] on EC proposals for reforming the Common Agricultural Policy (February 9, 1992),[60] on a light rail transit system for Dublin (May 26, 1992)[61] and on a proposed extension to the British Nuclear Fuels plant at Sellafield in Cumbria (June 30, 1992).[62]

The *sub judice* rule

Discussion of issues in the Oireachtas, whether by way of question or debate, may be inhibited by the *sub judice* rule. This has operated since the foundation of the State and its function is analogous to that of the law on contempt of court—to protect litigants and ensure that actions coming before the courts are not prejudiced by advance discussion. Given the absolute privilege both Houses enjoy (Art. 15.12 and 13) this is understandable, but concern has been expressed that the current practice is unnecessarily restrictive. The matter was extensively canvassed on October 22, 1986 when the Ceann Comhairle ruled out any questions or statements about the removal of Mr. Eddie Collins from his office of Minister of State. (Mr. Collins had instituted libel proceedings against certain publications.) Having explained the purpose of the rule, the Ceann Comhairle[63] warned of the danger that the House might be used as a sort of pre-trial forum or an alternative to court procedures, such as interrogatories or discovery, and of the risk that tribunals, judges and juries might be unfairly influenced. He went on to say that he had carefully considered the questions submitted about the removal of Deputy Collins. A plenary summons for libel had been issued in the High Court and

1987, on Third World Aid (376 *Dáil Debs.*, cc. 875–879); and that of May 21, 1992 in regard to the non-distribution of *The Guardian* newspaper of that date (which contained an advertisement about abortion services in England) (420 *Dáil Debs.*, cc. 157–160).
[56] Similar provision is made by the Seanad S.O. 29.
[57] Informal Committee *Report*, pp. 9–10.
[58] *Ibid.*, p. 10.
[59] 369 *Dáil Debs.*, cc. 1992–2031.
[60] 415 *Dáil Debs.*, cc. 948–980.
[61] 420 *Dáil Debs.*, cc. 451–489.
[62] *The Irish Times*, July 1, 1992.
[63] Mr. Tom Fitzpatrick—a solicitor of long experience.

an appearance had been entered thereto. In the ordinary course the case would come on for hearing before a judge and jury. The Ceann Comhairle was satisfied that the subject-matter of each question would feature in the hearing of the action. Thus the *sub judice* rule applied to these questions. He ended by reminding the House that it had complete control over its own proceedings; thus it could abolish or modify the existing rule, and any changes decided upon could be introduced quite quickly. He would be happy to operate any new procedure, but until one was introduced the existing rule must be applied.[64]

Since that episode the question of modifying the *sub judice* rule has frequently been raised—so far without result. The need for some such rule cannot be gainsaid, but that currently in operation is accepted to be unduly restrictive. Its effect may be to curtail parliamentary debate on matters of public importance, possibly as a result of someone issuing a so-called "gagging writ"—*i.e.* instituting proceedings with no real intention of going to trial but simply to stifle discussion. Indeed the current Dáil practice is now more restrictive than the law of contempt,[65] a fact that has not escaped attention.[66] But although pledges to bring about change featured in the Fianna Fáil—Progressive Democrat Joint Programme for Government of 1989 (and the review of 1991),[67] nothing has yet happened.[68]

The Oireachtas and State-sponsored bodies

The proper oversight of State-sponsored bodies has been a problem felt in many states. They cannot be treated as if they were Government Departments, with the sponsoring Minister answering questions on every aspect of their business; this would be a contradiction of their very establishment. But they are publicly funded; they often have a virtual monopoly on the services provided; and it is important to ensure that they are not run as an annex of the sponsoring Department. To provide parliamentary scrutiny of these bodies is the function of the Joint Committee on State-sponsored Commercial Bodies, first established in 1977. It consists of seven deputies and four senators and has the usual powers, including that to engage expert assistance (subject to Ministerial consent).

Since its original inception the committee has more than once examined the operations of virtually all the bodies within its remit. Most recently it has again concerned itself with Bord na Móna, and has—unsuccessfully—attempted to examine the Irish National Petroleum Corporation Ltd. The nature of its concerns is illustrated by the December 1991 report on Bord na Móna. It recommended that the board's directors—and those of all commercial State-sponsored bodies—should " . . . clearly define in writing their *modus operandi* and terms of reference for nominee directors on subsidiary and

---

[64] 369 *Dáil Debs.*, cc. 13–14.

[65] Especially in the light of O'Hanlon J.'s decision in *Desmond* v. *Glackin* (January 9, 1992), discussed in Chap. 15 *infra*.

[66] In January 1992 the Fine Gael party requested a discussion of the *sub judice* rule at the next meeting of the Committee on Procedure and Privileges, referring to the decision in *Desmond* v. *Glackin*: *The Irish Times*, January 11, 1992.

[67] On April 30, 1992 the Taoiseach, outlining Government proposals for reform of Dáil procedures, anticipated new guidelines to relax the rule for the autumn session: *The Irish Times*, May 1, 1992.

[68] See further *infra, s.v.* The Oireachtas and State-sponsored bodies.

associate companies . . . [including] the circulation of minutes of all subsidiary board meetings to members of the main board . . . " The Committee was also concerned about the company's adverse financial position—a long-running worry—and the wisdom of some of its actions. It accepted the principle of an Exchequer subsidy to the company, and accepted also that a lower than usual rate of return on investment might be justified in its case because of "overriding social issues."[69]

As noted above, in 1990 the committee attempted to examine the Irish National Petroleum Corporation Ltd. (INPC)—established as a private company in 1979 by the then Minister for Industry, Commerce and Energy.[70] Its predecessor had essayed a similar investigation in 1983, but had desisted because of certain legal proceedings. These—reported as *Campus Oil Ltd.* v. *Minister for Industry and Energy* [1983] I.R. 82[71]—had involved a reference to the European Court of Justice under Article 177 of the EEC Treaty,[72] and subsequent High Court proceedings applying the European Court's judgment. In February 1989 the then Minister for Energy declined to allow INPC representatives to appear before the Joint Committee because those proceedings had not been completed. The same happened when the committee was reconstituted following the 1989 general election. The reason then given was that the application of the European Court's ruling was still pending before the Irish courts, even though the plaintiff companies had taken no further steps in the proceedings since July 10, 1984 (the date of the European Court's ruling).[73] On several grounds, however, the committee was " . . . not totally convinced of the cogency of the Minister's arguments . . . " It referred to " . . . the specific and limited nature of the outstanding proceedings (in abeyance) in the High Court"; to the fact that the Minister's invocation of the *sub judice* rule " . . . did not appear to have impeded in any way the planned sale [for which prospectuses had been published and offers invited] of INPC." It suggested that " . . . *sub judice* considerations are being availed of in a somewhat artificial and unreasonable manner by the successive Ministers for Energy to thwart the Joint Committee in examining in a proper mode matters that are already in the public domain and clearly, unambiguously and strictly within the Joint Committee's remit."[74] The committee ended by calling for a clearer delineation of the *sub judice* criteria which would " . . . establish that the arbiter of the *sub judice* practice in the parliamentary process shall be, in cases such as the present, the Joint Committee."

Subordinate legislation

Like other legislatures the Oireachtas necessarily delegates law-making powers to Ministers and other persons and bodies. As is shown in Chapter 9 *infra*, the courts have affirmed the constitutional validity of this practice—within limits. Such delegated or subordinate legislation is subject to a two-

---

[69] Pl. 7381, *Summary of Recommendations*, pp. viii–xi.
[70] As to the power to do this, see *infra* Chap. 9, *s.v.* the Executive Power.
[71] See also *Campus Oil Ltd.* v. *Minister for Industry and Energy* (*No. 2*) [1983] I.R. 88.
[72] Case 72/83, *Campus Oil Ltd.* v. *Minister for Industry and Energy* [1984] E.C.R. 2727.
[73] The correspondence between the committee's chairman and the Minister is printed in the Appendix to its *Report*, pp. 8–12.
[74] Quotations are from the committee's *Report* (Pl. 8491, July 1990).

fold judicial control: it must be both compatible with the Constitution and within the powers conferred by the enabling Act. And the Irish courts apply the *ultra vires* rule with considerable—indeed sometimes excessive—stringency.[75] But additional controls are essential. First, there must be a clear legal obligation to print and publish such material; this is supplied by the Statutory Instruments Act 1947. Secondly, propriety would seem to require that the Oireachtas should supervise the exercise of the powers it has conferred. Thus it is commonly provided in enabling Acts that instruments made thereunder should be laid before the Dáil and Seanad, and may be annulled by resolution passed within specified time-limits.[76] For many years such instruments were regularly examined by an Oireachtas committee,[77] but at present only those made under the European Communities Acts are so scrutinised. This *lacuna* in respect of purely domestic instruments—due to the fact that they do not fall within the remit of any current Oireachtas committee—is regrettable.

The European Communities Acts 1972 and 1973 vest extremely wide regulation-making powers in Ministers and they are extensively availed of. To supervise the exercise of these powers is one of the functions of the Joint Committee on the Secondary Legislation of the European Communities. This body, which consists of 18 deputies and seven senators, is directed to examine regulations under the European Communities Acts and other instruments made under statute and necessitated by the obligations of membership.[78] The committee has found much to criticise and though it has constantly chivvied and harried Departments to wean them away from bad habits, its efforts have not always succeeded. In a report of December 18, 1985 on 33 statutory instruments, the committee complained about the way in which EC directives are sometimes implemented, and—a recurrent theme—about explanatory notes which explain nothing. But the utility of its surveillance is beyond dispute.[79]

---

[75] See *e.g. Minister for Industry and Commerce* v. *Hales* [1967] I.R. 50: *McMeel* v. *Minister for Health* [1985] I.L.R.M. 616.
[76] See further Gerard Hogan and David Morgan, *Administrative Law in Ireland* (2nd ed., London 1991) p. 34.
[77] From 1948 until 1983 by the Seanad Select Committee on Statutory Instruments; from 1983 until 1987 by the Joint Committee on Legislation. See further Hogan and Morgan, *op. cit.*, pp. 35–37.
[78] The committee is also concerned with draft regulations, directives, decisions, recommendations and opinions of the EC Council of Ministers proposed by the Commission; and much effort goes into examining this material. Thus on October 31, 1984 it issued three reports on the application of the milk super-levy, on proposals for a 12th VAT directive and on the implications for the Irish fishing industry of Spanish and Portuguese accession.
[79] For a survey of its work see Mary Robinson, "Irish Parliamentary Scrutiny of European Community Legislation" (1979) 16 C.M.L.R. 9.

6 The Government and the Central Administration

As appears from Article 28, the word "Government" has in Irish constitutional law a precise and technical meaning, equivalent to "Cabinet" in other systems. It is the group of senior Ministers which ultimately decides major questions of policy. The Constitution is quite specific about the size and composition of this body; but as to its powers and functions it is, like the basic laws of many other states, deliberately vague. Thus an impression of the institution derived solely from Bunreacht na hÉireann would be seriously misleading.

Composition

Article 28.1 decrees that the Government shall consist of not less than seven and not more than 15 members. It is headed by the Taoiseach (Art. 28.5.1°) who is elected to that position by the Dáil and formally appointed thereto by the President: Art. 13.1.1°. He then nominates the 14 other members of the Government for formal appointment by the President: Art. 13.1.12°. Theoretically, of course, it is possible for a Taoiseach to opt for a smaller Government, and this sometimes used to happen; the 1944–48 Government had 11 members and that of 1951–54 12. But for many years now the optimum 15 places have been filled, and this pattern is unlikely to be reversed. The increasing concerns of government and the creation of new Departments lead ineluctably to the maximum size. Even so, it is common for members of the Government to head more than one Department—the prime example until 1986 being the Minister for Health and Social Welfare.

In establishing a maximum size for the Government, Bunreacht na hÉireann departs from the British model. There the size of the Cabinet is a matter for the Prime Minister—and it is remarkable how those who, in opposition, favoured a smaller Cabinet find this impossible to achieve on taking power. (If a small Cabinet would mean leaving senior party figures outside, this may be politically impossible.) Bunreacht na hÉireann's limitation of size prevents such a political Parkinson's law from applying: the Taoiseach must cut his Governmental coat according to the constitutional cloth.

When Dr. FitzGerald formed his first coalition administration in 1981, he announced the appointment of Mr. Alexis FitzGerald (who was not a relative) as Special Adviser to the Government. This meant that Mr. FitzGerald would attend Government meetings, having received the papers beforehand, and be at liberty to contribute to discussion. The Opposition leader, Mr.

Haughey, claimed in the Dáil that this was unconstitutional,[1] but the matter was never tested in the courts. (The Taoiseach had earlier informed the Dáil of the Attorney General's view that there was no legal or constitutional bar to the appointment.[2]) It has been said that some members of the Government were unhappy about the innovation, and certainly the experiment has not been repeated.[3]

The Constitution also lays down broad rules as to the composition of the Government. All 15 members must be drawn from the Oireachtas—it is not possible to appoint someone a Government Minister in the expectation that he or she will subsequently acquire a Dáil or Seanad seat. (Contrast section 64 of the Australian Constitution, under which a non-parliamentarian may become a Minister but must, to hold office for longer than three months, acquire a seat in one or other chamber.) Moreover, Article 28.7.1° requires that the Taoiseach, Tánaiste and Minister for Finance be deputies, while no more than two from the total of 15 members may come from the Seanad: Art. 28.7.2°.[4]

Such are the constitutional constraints on the Taoiseach's selection of his Government colleagues. Apart from these, he has—in theory—freedom of choice; but theory and reality differ since there may be some senior party figures whom it would be impolitic to omit. Thus the runners-up in the last party leadership election normally feature prominently in a new Government (a phenomenon discernible not only in Ireland, but also in Australia, Canada and the United Kingdom). In a coalition Government the Taoiseach's freedom to choose will necessarily be more restricted; the minority party will expect a quota of Cabinet posts and its leader will name the persons to hold them. But these political constraints must not be overstated. History shows that a Taoiseach may sometimes spring surprises. A Cabinet post may be given to a newly-elected deputy, as when Mr. Lynch appointed Dr. O'Donoghue Minister for Economic Affairs in 1977, and Dr. FitzGerald assigned Mr. Dukes to Agriculture in 1981. Equally, Mr. Haughey found no place in his short-lived 1982 Government for Mr. Michael O'Kennedy (a former Minister for Finance, and for Foreign Affairs) and preferred Mr. McSharry to more senior party figures for the prestigious Finance position. But a Taoiseach could hardly construct his whole Cabinet on such principles; to attempt this would be likely to create problems within his party. To supplant, in favour of newcomers, those who in opposition were "shadow" Ministers would scarcely cement the loyalty of the latter.

The practical limits on the Taoiseach's freedom of choice cannot be reduced to a series of rules. They depend on too great a range of diverse circumstances for that. But it should be noted that even if his choice of personnel is somewhat restricted, he may enjoy greater liberty in the actual allocation of ministerial responsibilities. In 1973, for example, Mr. Cosgrave appointed Dr. FitzGerald as Minister for Foreign Affairs and Mr. Ritchie

---

[1] 329 *Dáil Debs.*, c. 233 (July 8, 1981).

[2] *Ibid.*, c. 230.

[3] See Ronan Fanning, "Memoir of Alexis FitzGerald" in Patrick Lynch and James Meenan (eds.), *Essays in Memory of Alexis Fitzgerald* (Dublin 1987), pp. 1–17.

[4] In this sphere Bunreacht na hÉireann is remarkably restrictive when compared with other European constitutions. The Spanish Constitution (1978) does not require ministers to be in parliament, and 30% are not: see Antonio Bar, "Spain" in Jean Blondel and Ferdinand Müller-Rommel, *Cabinets in Western Europe* (London 1988), p. 116. The Dutch practice also allows greater flexibility: Rudy Anderweg, "The Netherlands" (*ibid.*).

Ryan as Minister for Finance, even though in opposition their roles had been reversed.

The present constitutional provisions, it may be noted, are sufficiently flexible to accommodate a change in political practice. Should it become the norm for Ministers to be selected by internal vote of the Dáil majority party—as has occurred in Australia—this would not require any constitutional amendment. The Taoiseach would simply submit the names of those selected in this way for appointment in the usual manner. Such a system was, in fact, used by the Labour Party during the first Inter-Party Government (1948–1951), though in more recent coalitions the Labour Party leader has made his own choice of Ministers.

The power to appoint up to two senators as Ministers has been utilised only twice since 1937. Mr. Sean Moylan, who had lost his Dáil seat at the 1957 General Election, was nominated to the Seanad by Mr. de Valera and then appointed as Minister for Agriculture. In 1981 Dr. FitzGerald nominated Professor Dooge (who had never been a deputy) to the Seanad and subsequently assigned Foreign Affairs to him. It seems unlikely that the power will be much used in the future. Senior deputies will hardly view with enthusiasm the assignment of important responsibilities to an "outsider," especially one who has never run for the Dáil. (It may be significant that Dr. FitzGerald appointed no senator to his second Government in 1982.) The use of this device also entails practical problems. Installation as a senator must constitutionally precede appointment as a Minister, but the Seanad elections follow those for the Dáil. Until the person is a senator, all the Taoiseach can do is to announce an intention to appoint him/her as a Minister, and until formal appointment some other Minister will have to stand in. The extra burden of work thus cast on that individual may not make for effective administration.

Role of the Taoiseach

The Taoiseach is head of the Government: Art. 28.5.1°. He is mentioned, of course, in several other Articles of the Constitution, all these references emphasising his status as prime minister. He appoints the other Ministers (Art. 13.1.2°) and may dismiss them "for reasons which seem to him sufficient" (Art. 28.5.2°). It is the Taoiseach who acts as the channel of communication between Government and President—advising on the summoning and dissolution of the Dáil (Art. 13.2.1°), presenting Bills for signature (Art. 25.1) and certifying Bills as urgent under Article 24. The Taoiseach likewise keeps the President "generally informed" on matters of domestic and international policy: Art. 28.5.1°. Finally, his resignation entails that of the entire Government: Art. 28.11.1°.

The Constitution thus assumes that the Taoiseach will be the leading figure in the administration, and modern practice, including media coverage, reinforces this. While he heads a Department, it is not one readily identifiable with any function—unlike Finance, Education or Justice—and his formal legal responsibilities are few.[5] The Department's main function mirrors

[5] There is no constitutional or legal bar to the Taoiseach holding another office; Mr. de Valera used to double as Minister for External Affairs. This is unlikely to happen nowadays. Mr. Haughey took the Gaeltacht portfolio in 1987 and again in 1989, but in recent Governments

that of the Taoiseach himself—co-ordination of policy-making and execution. Thus it operates as the central secretariat of Government—preparing for Government meetings, recording decisions and ensuring that they are implemented. The increase in the Department's size in recent years shows that this is more than a routine function and emphasises how the role and concerns of the Taoiseach have expanded.

In a famous statement Mr. Sean Lemass indicated how he saw the Taoiseach's role[6]:

> "A Minister is supposed to know everything about the affairs of his Department; the Taoiseach is supposed to know something about the affairs of every department. The Taoiseach's primary task, apart from acting as spokesman for the government on major issues of policy, is to ensure that departmental plans are fully co-ordinated; that the inevitable conflicts between departments are resolved, that cabinet decisions are facilitated and that the implications of government policy are fully understood by all cabinet colleagues and influence the shaping of their departmental plans."

But Professor Farrell has shown in his biographical study that this is oversimplified. He refers to Lemass's pre-eminent position and writes that he "saw himself as the man in the driving seat."[7]

The Taoiseach's concerns have expanded since Mr. Lemass' time, one of the factors accounting for this being Irish membership of the EC. Community heads of state and government meet—as the European Council—at least three times a year; and the Taoiseach obviously must be briefed for such encounters. Reflecting this—among other things—the staff of the Taoiseach's Department has increased enormously in recent years, and its structure has altered. Dr. Scott has written[8]:

> "The new structure clearly betokened a more active and interventionist role for the Taoiseach, both in domestic policy co-ordination and in international negotiation. The briefs might continue to come from the line departments, but the scrutiny would be closer and initiatives might flow in the other direction."

Another regular practice emphasising the Taoiseach's central role is that under him there will be a Minister of State who acts (*inter alia*) as Government Chief Whip. It is his function to liaise between the Government and the party in the Dáil, assessing opinion, mustering the vote, etc. Unlike other Ministers of State, he regularly attends Government meetings.

In summary, the office of Taoiseach is what any given holder makes of it— and this depends, not on constitutional or legal rules, but on the currents of politics.

---

that Department has not been the *sole* responsibility of a Cabinet Minister. In addition, a Minister of State (Mr. Denis Gallagher) with specific responsibility for Gaeltacht affairs was appointed.

[6] "Lemass on Government," *Leargas* No. 12, January 1968, p. 3.

[7] Brian Farrell, *Sean Lemass* (Dublin 1983), p. 109: see also the same author's *Chairman or Chief: The Role of the Taoiseach in Irish Government* (Dublin 1971).

[8] See Dermot Scott "EEC Membership and the Irish Administrative System" (1983) 31 *Administration* 147, 173.

The Tánaiste

Under Article 28.6.1° the Taoiseach is *obliged* (the word "shall" is used) to nominate a member of the Government to be Tánaiste. That person is to act in place of the Taoiseach—*e.g.* should the latter be abroad, or ill (Arts. 28.6.2° and 3°). Should the Taoiseach die or become permanently incapacitated, the Tánaiste would stand in until a successor was appointed.

In most recent two-party coalition Governments, the office of Tánaiste has been held by the leader of the smaller party. In single-party Governments the appointment has usually been made on a seniority basis, though that of Mr. McSharry in 1982 departed from this pattern. On the evidence of history the post does not make its holder the heir apparent to the Taoiseach.

Functions of the Government

The text of the Constitution is quite uninformative about the concerns and functioning of the Government. Article 28.2 reveals that the Government exercises the executive power of the State—but this is not very helpful. From Article 29.4.1° it emerges that the executive power has a foreign affairs dimension, but this does not greatly advance matters. Indeed, insofar as it may suggest that the Government exercises *only* the executive power, it is all seriously misleading. In reality it exercises the legislative power of the State as well, given its normally reliable Dáil majority.

The Government's central directing role on policy issues is recognised—if somewhat obliquely—in Article 28.4.3°. Under this, it is to prepare estimates of State receipts and expenditure for each financial year. In modern states, of course, this is far from the mere book-keeping transaction that the Constitution suggests. Equally, Article 28.4.3° speaks of presenting the estimates "to Dáil Éireann for consideration." This language conveys the impression of an advocate presenting an argument to a court—which is quite divorced from reality. The true position is that the Government decides what the expenditure priorities are: fixes the revenue needs—and hence taxation policies—accordingly, and expects the Dáil to agree. In all save the most unusual circumstances, that expectation is fully justified. Another constitutional provision implying executive predominance is Article 17.2, which provides that the Dáil shall not appropriate public money for any purpose unless that purpose has been recommended by the Government. Here is a specific constitutional barrier to the Dáil's adopting a more liberal spending policy than the Government wishes.

The Government, as a collective entity, derives certain powers from the Constitution, while others are conferred upon it by statute. The constitutional powers include nominating judges (Art. 35.1), commuting capital sentences (Art. 13.6) and, in the foreign affairs field, making treaties, establishing diplomatic relations and recognising new states or governments. The statutory powers cover a very wide range of matters—bringing into operation special criminal courts (Offences against the State Act 1939, Part V), making provision in regard to maritime jurisdiction and the continental shelf (Maritime Jurisdiction Acts 1959 and 1964: Continental Shelf Act 1968) and making certain appointments—*e.g.* Prosecution of Offences Act 1974, s.2: Law Reform Commission Act 1975, s.5: Local Government (Planning and Development) Act 1982, s.5 (appointing the chairman of An Bord Pleanála).

Plainly, however, circumstances requiring the exercise of these powers would not arise frequently enough to justify holding two Government meetings a week, as is the norm. It will be the making of policy, rather than the exercise of formal legal powers, which will dominate the agenda. Such policy may relate to legislation, including the priority of Bills in the parliamentary timetable; to revenue and public expenditure[9]; to foreign affairs, including EC matters and the Northern Ireland situation; or to any of the myriad matters that fall within the scope of Government Departments—agriculture, education, defence, health, justice, social welfare, etc.

The *Report of the Public Services Organisation Review Group 1966–1969* ("the Devlin Report") puts the matter thus[10]:

> "In addition to the basic functions of the defence of the nation against outside aggression and the maintenance of law and order, the role of government now embraces the provision of adequate health, education and welfare services. It also embraces the provision of environmental services and assistance of cultural activities. Government must exercise some regulatory function in regard to individual enterprise and ensure that the rights of the individual are exercised with due regard to the general good. It encourages economic activity in the private sector and there are certain activities which it has undertaken itself.
>
> The Government has two main tasks. First, it has to run the country, under the Constitution and in accordance with the rules laid down by the Oireachtas and with the resources granted by and accounted for to the Oireachtas each year. Secondly, it deals in the Oireachtas with changes in legislation affecting the community . . .
>
> Through its legislative programme (including financial measures), the Government exercises its main influence over the future development of the country; thereby, it influences the economy and the structure of society. Acting collectively, the Ministers decide what is needed and how it should be achieved; their decisions depend on the quality of their information and on their assessment of the requirements. They will, of course, become aware of these requirements in several ways— through their political machine, through the press and through the representations of the interests concerned—but, primarily they will need to know the emerging needs of the community through the public service which operates existing programmes."

A former Secretary to the Government has outlined the decision-making procedure as follows[11]:

> "Memoranda on the matters on the Agenda are, normally, submitted, in advance, by the Ministers concerned. Each memorandum sets out the relevant facts and considerations and the decision sought. A procedure has been laid down by the Government which is designed to ensure that every Minister whose Department is particularly affected by a proposal of another Minister will have had an adequate opportunity of considering the matter and of submitting his comments. Acting as the Govern-

---

[9] These matters may at times dominate a succession of meetings: see generally Gemma Hussey, *At The Cutting Edge: Cabinet Diaries 1982–1987* (Dublin 1980).

[10] Paras. 12.1.1–12.1.3.

[11] Muiris Ó Muimhneacháin, *The Functions of the Department of the Taoiseach* (2nd ed., Dublin 1969), p. 17.

ment's secretariat, the Department of the Taoiseach is responsible, under the Taoiseach's directions, for securing compliance with the pre-scribed procedure. The Government's decisions are conveyed, in writ-ing, to the Minister primarily concerned and to any other Ministers affected. The decisions are also recorded in formal Minutes, which are read and signed at the next meeting."

(The minutes referred to may be consulted by researchers in the National Archives after a 30 year delay. They are remarkably uninformative docu-ments, recording only conclusions and giving no indication as to how decisions were reached. Votes are not recorded in them, and it appears that there is no provision for registering dissent.[12])

The procedure described above is applied particularly to legislation. The vast majority of Bills begin as Government measures, the policy they enshrine being initially hammered out by the appropriate Government Department. Standard procedure requires that other Departments be con-sulted, with the Department of Finance being apprised of any financial impli-cations of the proposals. So formalised is the procedure that a Minister proposing legislation must get Government approval firstly for the *heads* of the Bill. Only when this is obtained is the Bill drafted, and it then comes back to the Government for approval in detail. This process can take a long time—especially if the proposals encounter objections from other Departments—and it will often be true that the Dáil and Seanad debates on a Bill are simply the tip of the iceberg. In an emergency, of course, the process may have to be abridged,[13] but these occur infrequently.

Collective responsibility

Article 28.4.1° provides that the Government shall be responsible to Dáil Éireann. This re-emphasises the principle, evident in several other pro-visions, that the Government holds office only so long as it retains the sup-port of a Dáil majority. Indeed Article 28.10 makes this clear beyond dispute.

Article 28.4.2° requires that the Government "meet and act as a collective authority," and goes on to emphasise the Government's collective responsi-bility for the Departments of State administered by its members. It has occasionally been claimed that significant decisions have been taken by a small group of Ministers, including the Taoiseach. Such a practice—a form of prime ministerial government—hardly seems compatible with the Consti-tution. However, there would be no bar to a Cabinet Committee working out proposals for submission to the Government as a whole; and the Constitution does not appear to prohibit a delegation of authority by the Cabinet to a group of Ministers. But it seems that in practice little use is made of such devices, and that most matters are before the Cabinet for *decision*, not merely approval. It has been suggested that there is, in consequence, "a consider-able degree of overload in the Irish Cabinet system."[14]

The notion of collective responsibility is also understood to mean that the Government must present a united front to the public—that all its members must *publicly* support its policies and decisions. A Minister out of sympathy

---

[12] Brian Farrell, "Ireland" in Blondel and Müller-Rommel (*op. cit.*), p. 40.
[13] The procedure for dealing with urgent or confidential matters is described by Farrell, *ibid.*, p. 4.
[14] Farrell, *ibid.*, p. 46.

with Government policy—either generally or on a particular issue—is not entitled to criticise; if impelled to do so he/she must resign to recover his/her freedom of speech. The corollary is sometimes stated to be that a Minister who breaks ranks will be dismissed by the Taoiseach. However, there is nothing automatic about this; a Minister who talks out of turn will not necessarily be sacked—the Taoiseach may judge it opportune to ignore the matter, or merely to issue a private warning. Everything suggests that the action taken depends on the political situation at the time, including the strength of the Taoiseach's own position and the seniority of the alleged delinquent—*e.g.* the case of Mr. Blaney (Minister for Agriculture) in 1969.[15] But that case further suggests that a fundamental divergence of views can be glossed over for a brief period only; matters will come to a head and the result will be a dismissal, as there.[16]

In 1979 Mr. Lynch, as Taoiseach, faced a problem over the Health (Family Planning) Bill—a measure to regulate access to contraception. The Minister for Agriculture, Mr. Gibbons, let it be known that he could not vote for this Bill. Normally this would have been viewed as intolerable, but the matter was regarded as raising issues of conscience and Mr. Gibbons was allowed to abstain.[17] Obviously, such a line of escape would not be available on many Bills.

In a coalition Government the bonds of discipline are looser. Professor Chubb has pointed out that in the period of the two Inter-Party Governments there was collective responsibility on matters which had been agreed as the common programme. On other matters differing views could be—and were—expressed. So long as no Government policy had yet been formulated on such questions, freedom of expression prevailed among Ministers. But once such a policy had been worked out the normal rule applied.[18] A similar practice has obtained in more recent coalition Governments and, as with single-party Governments, when disputes have occurred they have been explained away on the basis that the apparently dissentient Minister was "speaking in a personal capacity." In January 1983, the Minister for Transport and Communications, Mr. Mitchell, was reported as saying that C.I.É. workers might have to take a 10 per cent. wage cut to safeguard jobs. This provoked a union outcry, and it was subsequently stated that the Minister was not enunciating Government policy; no decision on the issue had been taken by the Cabinet.[19] Just after this, the Minister for Finance, Mr. Dukes, was reported to have said that the budget deficit would be around £750 million. This figure involved harsher spending cuts than hitherto anticipated and the Tánaiste and Labour Party leader, Mr. Spring, protested. Subsequently a Government statement was issued which said[20]:

> "The Government has not yet decided on the appropriate level of the current budget deficit . . . There has been concern on the part of the

[15] See Brian Farrell, *Chairman or Chief*, p. 80.

[16] An analogous situation arose in Northern Ireland late in 1968, when there was a marked gap between the statements of Mr. William Craig (Minister of Home Affairs) and those of the embattled Prime Minister, Capt. O'Neill. Eventually Mr. Craig was sacked; see John Harbinson, *The Ulster Unionist Party 1882–1973* (Belfast 1973), pp. 150–151.

[17] See *The Irish Times*, May 5, 1979.

[18] See Basil Chubb, *Cabinet Government in Ireland* (Dublin 1974), Chap. 4.

[19] *The Irish Times*, January 11, 1983.

[20] *The Irish Times*, January 13, 1983.

Taoiseach, the Tánaiste and a number of Ministers of both parties that the figure of £750 million which the Minister for Finance has mentioned as a target to aim at should be taken as reflecting a Government decision on a matter which is still under review."

The same principle of collective responsibility applies in the United Kingdom, not as a rule of law but as a constitutional convention. There it has been applied with an even greater flexibility—most notably in regard to the 1975 referendum on continuing EC membership. Mr. Wilson's Cabinet was deeply divided on this question, 16 members favouring membership and seven withdrawal. Although the Government's formal recommendation to the electorate favoured staying in, the seven dissenters were permitted to advocate withdrawal and they did so vigorously in the referendum campaign. So public a division of Cabinet opinion was unprecedented for a single-party government; but the Prime Minister, when criticised for allowing it, said that so unique was the situation that to create a precedent was entirely justified.[21]

Whether such an expedient could be adopted in appropriate circumstances in Ireland is not clear. The British rule is founded on convention and is not enforceable in the courts: the Irish rule is stated in the constitutional text and would prima facie appear to be cognisable by the courts. Certainly Bunreacht na hÉireann itself does not make the rule judicially unenforceable: contrast the Directive Principles of Social Policy in Article 45, which are specifically ruled out of bounds, or the Presidential immunity provision of Article 13.8.1°. But it seems unlikely that a Taoiseach who adopted such a stratagem would face anything more than parliamentary or public criticism. Proceedings for a declaration that the Constitution was being violated would probably be unsuccessful. It seems likely that the courts would hold that the issue was not justiciable—that of its nature it was inappropriate for judicial resolution and implicitly entrusted to the political, rather than the judicial, forum created by the Constitution.[22]

The demonstrated flexibility and imprecision of the rule reinforces the above conclusion. Much seems to depend upon the felt necessities of the hour, the forbearance of colleagues and a Minister's own judgment of such factors. In the June 1986 divorce referendum campaign the Minister for Education, Mr. Cooney, made his opposition to divorce known, via newspaper reports of speeches, on a number of occasions. Though Fine Gael had allowed a free vote in the Dáil on the relevant Bill, he was alone among his Cabinet colleagues in this view. The Minister was scheduled to appear in a television debate in opposition to the proposed change but he pulled out at a late stage. There were suggestions in the media of a warning that so overt a disavowal of his colleagues would violate collective responsibility. However, the Taoiseach denied that he or the Government had put pressure on Mr. Cooney to withdraw from the programme.[23] The case therefore does not establish that deviation from a common line is permissible via the news-

---

[21] See J. P. Mackintosh, *The British Cabinet* (3rd ed., London 1977), pp. 529–536. The Westland affair in 1986—which brought about the resignation of the Defence and Trade Secretaries (Messrs Heseltine and Brittan)—may not have been unique but it certainly created some precedents. For a survey of the known facts and an analysis of their significance see Geoffrey Marshall "Cabinet Government and the Westland Affair" (1986) *Public Law* 184.

[22] See further Chap. 11, *infra*.

[23] *The Irish Times*, June 21, 1986.

papers but not on television. Such a strange proposition would be difficult to defend.

The rule laid down in Article 28.4.2° formally applies only to members of the Government—"Cabinet Ministers." There can, however, be little doubt that it would also be applied rigorously to the 15 Ministers of State, even though they do not have the same influence over policy as their senior colleagues. The same would doubtless hold for the Attorney General. He is not a member of the Government—Art. 30.4; but he is its adviser on "matters of law and legal opinion": Art. 30.1. Its members would hardly view with equanimity his publicly dissenting from agreed policies.

Cabinet confidentiality

Does the collective responsibility principle set out in Article 28.4.2° involve the confidentiality of Cabinet proceedings, so that Ministers are precluded from revealing what transpired at meetings? In *Att. Gen.* v. *Hamilton* (*The Irish Times,* July 11, 1992) the plaintiff argued that it did. The defendant, Hamilton P., was chairing a statutory tribunal of inquiry into the beef industry and had put a question to a former Minister about a Cabinet meeting on June 8, 1988. Counsel representing the Attorney General at the tribunal objected to this, on the Attorney's express instructions; but Hamilton P. was of opinion that such questions were both permissible and relevant. The matter was carried to the High Court, where O'Hanlon J. ruled in the tribunal's favour. The judge said that if Cabinet meetings were covered by an absolute blanket of confidentiality—as had been argued—then one would expect this to be spelt out in clear terms in the Constitution; but it was not. He held that in relation to any question put to a witness, the chairman of the tribunal was entitled to balance the public interest in the inquiry's subject-matter against the public interest in upholding a claim of confidentiality. The Attorney General's appeal against O'Hanlon J.'s decision was heard by the Supreme Court in July 1992; judgment was reserved (*The Irish Times,* July 25, 1992) and had not been delivered at the time of writing.

In the sense that Ministers have not contemporaneously disclosed in public the arguments advanced, or stances adopted, in arriving at decisions, Cabinet confidentiality has certainly been the general practice of Irish Governments since independence. Whether the pratice derives from a sense of legal or moral obligation, or merely from political prudence, it would be difficult to say. The Taoiseach's power of dismissal (Article 28.9.4°) provides an obvious means of enforcing Cabinet confidentiality on current office-holders, but this would naturally not be available in respect of former Ministers. It is perhaps when such persons wish to publish diaries or memoirs that problems are most likely to arise. There does not appear to be any procedure for vetting such material in advance of publication[24], such as exists in the United Kingdom.[25]

Irish law recognises that, in certain circumstances, a person who receives information in confidence may be restrained from breaching that confidence.

[24] In the preface to her book *At the Cutting Edge: Cabinet Diaries 1982–1987* (Dublin 1990) Mrs. Gemma Hussey states that she omitted only private family material " . . . and paragraphs which my publisher . . . and myself felt were repetitious, libellous, or had security implications . . . "

[25] See Rodney Brazier (ed.), *Constitutional Texts* (Oxford 1990).

If this principle applies to Government business, it would provide a basis for the Attorney General to seek an injunction restraining publication of the kind of material mentioned above.[26] Nothing in O'Hanlon J.'s decision in *Att. Gen.* v. *Hamilton* (*The Irish Times*, July 11, 1992) would preclude such an application. Presumably, however, it would have to be grounded on an allegation that revelation of some specific matter would be contrary to the public interest. It could hardly be founded on a generalised claim that the public interest requires absolute and perpetual confidentiality, lest Ministers be inhibited from expressing themselves freely at Cabinet meetings. For no such application was made in respect of the publication of Mrs. Gemma Hussey's 1982–1987 Cabinet diaries, or of Dr. Garret FitzGerald's autobiography; and it would therefore seem too late to try to establish such a principle.

Resignation of the Taoiseach/Government

Article 28, sections 9–11 of the Constitution deal with the resignation of the Taoiseach/Government. The rules they lay down are clear in some respects, but in others quite uncertain. Two distinct situations appear to be contemplated—firstly, a voluntary resignation; secondly, one that is constitutionally compelled.

Voluntary resignation would arise where the Taoiseach, for personal reasons, is determined to retire from office. This he may effect, under Article 28.9.1°, by placing his resignation in the President's hands. By virtue of Article 28.11.1°, that would entail the resignation of the Government as a whole. The cases of Mr. Lemass (who retired in 1966) and Mr. Lynch (who retired in 1979) show that matters will normally be arranged so as to ensure a smooth transition.[27] A new party leader will be available to succeed the departing Taoiseach and any "interregnum" will be brief. It will also be theoretical, for an outgoing Taoiseach must continue to carry on his duties until his successor has been appointed, and the same applies to the rest of the Government: Article 28.11.1°. Thus, if the person nominated by Dáil Éireann for appointment as the new Taoiseach were to die suddenly *en route* to Arus an Vachtaráin, a power vacuum would not necessarily ensue.

The same rules would apply—and presumably the same procedure would be followed—were the Taoiseach's resignation motivated by political factors, such as an intra-Governmental disagreement so acute as to provoke a crisis. So far, however, no resignation seems to have been prompted by such considerations.[28]

That the Constitution *requires* the Taoiseach to resign in certain circumstances is clear; but those circumstances are not delineated with precision. The difficulty lies in reconciling the provisions of Article 28.10 and 28.11.2°. The former states that:

---

[26] As was done, unsuccessfully, in the United Kingdom in respect of the late Mr. Richard Crossman's 1964–1970 Cabinet diaries; see *Att.-Gen.* v. *Jonathan Cape Ltd.* [1976] Q.B. 752.

[27] Mr. Lemass resigned on November 10, 1966 and Mr. Lynch was appointed on the same day: 225 *Dáil Debs.*, cc. 699–700, 709–710. Mr. Lynch resigned on December 11, 1979, and Mr. Haughey was appointed on the same day: 317 *Dáil Debs.*, cc. 1323–1325, 1428.

[28] It is not impossible that one might be. Professor Chubb records Mr. Lemass as telling an interviewer (after his retirement) that if unable to carry a majority with him on a major point, he would have told ministerial colleagues to accept his view or get another Taoiseach: *The Government and Politics of Ireland* (2nd ed., 1982), p. 203.

"The Taoiseach shall resign from office upon his ceasing to retain the support of a majority in Dáil Éireann unless on his advice the President dissolves Dáil Éireann and on the reassembly of Dáil Éireann after the dissolution the Taoiseach secures the support of a majority in Dáil Éireann."

Article 28.11.2° provides:

"The members of the Government in office at the date of a dissolution of Dáil Éireann shall continue to hold office until their successors shall have been appointed."

If, some time into its period of office, the Government is defeated on an issue of confidence in Dáil Éireann, Article 28.10 would come into play. So if the Taoiseach were refused a dissolution resignation would ensue. That resignation would, however, be essentially theoretical, as Article 28.11.1° would presumably oblige the Taoiseach and Government to "continue to carry out their duties until their successors shall have been appointed." The appointment of those successors would obviously depend upon the parliamentary arithmetic, and might take a considerable time, but a caretaker administration would remain in place and no power vacuum would occur.

The events of June 29, 1989 in Dáil Éireann highlighted the uncertainty surrounding the interplay of Article 28.10 and 28.11.2°. The recent general election had yielded no clear majority for any single party. When the Dáil reassembled a motion that the outgoing Taoiseach, Mr. Haughey, be nominated for appointment was defeated. The others proposed likewise failed to secure nomination. Mr. Haughey then sought an adjournment until July 3 to allow for further consultations, stating that under Article 28.11.2° he and his cabinet colleagues continued in office.[29] But the Labour leader, Mr. Spring, invoked Article 28.10; in his view the Taoiseach *had* failed "to retain the support of a majority in Dáil Éireann" and was obliged to resign unless he sought and was granted a dissolution.[30] Mr. Haughey said that the Attorney General's advice was that Article 28.10 did not require immediate resignation[31]:

"I am . . . advised that it is perfectly in order for me to take a reasonable time to reflect, consider and, if necessary, consult."

But the Opposition leaders demurred to that view and, following a brief adjournment of the house, Mr. Haughey made the following statement[32]:

"It is of critical importance that we not just legally uphold the Constitution, but be seen to do so . . . I would never wish even to appear to do otherwise than adhere strictly to the precepts of the Constitution. Accordingly . . . I now propose to go to the President and to convey my resignation as Taoiseach to him . . . Under Article 28.11 the Government and I will still continue to carry on all duties of Taoiseach and Government until a Taoiseach has been appointed."

The nomination of the Taoiseach did not occur until July 12, 1989,[33] so

[29] 391 *Dáil Debs.*, c. 52 (June 29, 1989).
[30] *Ibid.*, cc. 52–53.
[31] *Ibid.*, c. 54.
[32] *Ibid.*, c. 58.
[33] 391 *Dáil Debs.*, cc. 142–146.

that Article 28.11.2° operated for thirteen days. During that period Mr.
Haughey was referred to by some as "acting Taoiseach"[34] and the Government as a "caretaker administration." Though not sanctioned by the constitutional text, these terms may reflect the political reality of the situation. It
would not seem correct, however, to infer that the Constitution restricts the
powers exerciseable by such an administration. No doubt political wisdom
might suggest restraint in exercising executive power—for example, appointing judges or negotiating treaties. But if the exercise of any such power
became urgently necessary, there would seem to be no *constitutional* impediment thereto. The "continuance in office" provision of Article 28.11 is surely
intended to cover just such situations.

May an "acting Taoiseach" seek a dissolution of the Dáil? The answer is
uncertain. On one view Article 28.10 offers a Taoiseach defeated in the Dáil a
choice—resign, or seek a dissolution. Should the resignation option be
chosen, then the power to seek a dissolution is withdrawn. If correct, this
approach would mean that were the Dáil unable to nominate a successor to
the acting Taoiseach a general election would be possible only via a cum-
brous procedure. The Dáil would have to nominate someone for appointment as Taoiseach on the understanding that he/she would immediately seek
a dissolution. That person would, of course, have to form a Government to
administer the State during the election campaign and pending the assembly
of the new Dáil. The provisions of Article 28 make this quite clear.

The course adopted by Mr. Haughey in June 1989 may well set a precedent for future occasions, *i.e.* that in any similar circumstances the Taoiseach's resignation will be expected. But Mr. Haughey's resignation seems to
have been inspired by considerations of political prudence rather than of constitutional obligation. For he said[35]:

> " . . . I was advised, and I still am advised, that it would be quite
> proper for me to take a reasonable amount of time to consider these
> alternatives [to seek a dissolution, or an adjournment of the Dáil] . . . I
> have been advised that up to a week would be reasonable . . . I wish to
> repeat and to emphasise that I am fully entitled to take until Monday
> [*i.e.* four days later] to reach this decision, but lest there be any misun-
> derstanding or misrepresentation of my position or lest it be misrepre-
> sented in any way, I will, as I have said inform the President of my
> resignation this evening."

However, a former Taoiseach, Dr. FitzGerald, took a different view. His
recollection of the advice given him when a similar situation seemed likely to
arise after the 1987 general election was that he must resign unless he moved
to dissolve the Dáil at once.[36]

On its face the language of Article 28.10 seems peremptory, allowing no
delay in resigning where the alternative of a dissolution has been denied or
ruled out. It is possible, however, that Article 28.10 does not apply to the
situation of June 1989; that it really contemplates a situation where the Taoiseach originally had "the support of a majority in Dáil Éireann" but subsequently lost it. On this basis, the provision relevant to the June 1989

---

[34] *e.g.* by Deputy Spring: 391 *Dáil Debs.*, cc. 67–68.
[35] 391 *Dáil Debs.*, cc. 57–58.
[36] *Ibid.*, c. 55.

situation would instead be Article 28.11.2°—so that a post-election Government is in office by constitutional mandate rather than by Dáil vote. That constitutional mandate would be terminated only when a successor Government is appointed. If the initial vote in the new Dáil failed to produce any such appointment the mandate would continue, and no question of resignation would arise.

This interpretation has the advantage of bringing Article 28.10 and 28.11.2° into harmony with each other, rather than as being in conflict or containing surplusage. Judicial authority can be mustered for this technique of construction.[37] But as against this, it involves giving the words—"ceasing to retain the support of a majority in Dáil Éireann"—something other than their literal meaning. Since several Supreme Court decisions give primacy to the literal meaning of constitutional provisions,[38] it is difficult to know how this issue would be resolved should it arise for judicial decision.

Appointment of Ministers

Members of the Government are formally appointed by the President "on the nomination of the Taoiseach with the previous approval of Dáil Éireann": Article 13.1.2°. The Dáil will thus be invited to approve the Taoiseach's nominees for appointment by the President, and this motion may give rise to a debate. The Taoiseach will usually indicate at this stage the Departments to which the relevant persons will be assigned,[39] though Dáil approval of those assignments is not constitutionally required.[40] The appointment process may, if necessary, be halted by withdrawing the motion.[41]

Tenure of office—a problem situation?

A minister's tenure of office will begin when he/she receives the seal of office from the President, and will normally continue until resignation (or dismissal). But an apparent conflict between two constitutional provisions may create a difficulty where a Minister has lost his/her seat during a general election. Article 28.7.2° stipulates that members of the Government must be deputies or (two only) senators. However, Article 28.11.2° requires outgoing Ministers to carry on until their successors have been appointed. Does this cover a Minister spurned by the electorate?

The 1967 Committee on the Constitution tentatively concluded that it did. Their report, having referred to Article 28.11.2°, continues[42]:

> "Despite the provisions of section 7 of the same Article this seems to enable the old Government to carry on even though some or all of its members might have lost their seats in the general election."

Since the principal concern of Article 28.11 appears to be the avoidance of a

[37] See Chap. 11 *infra.*
[38] *Ibid.*
[39] See the statement of the Taoiseach, Mr. Haughey, on July 12, 1989: 391 *Dáil Debs.*, c. 147.
[40] A point made by the then Taoiseach, Mr. de Valera, on June 9, 1944: see 94 *Dáil Debs.*, c. 43.
[41] As occurred on November 13, 1991 when Deputy McDaid asked that his nomination as Minister for Defence be withdrawn: see 412 *Dáil Debs.*, cc. 1567–68.
[42] Pr. 9817, para. 32.

power vacuum, this view may well be correct. If, therefore, *all* members of the outgoing Government lost their seats they would nonetheless continue in office until replaced. And this would be so even if the reassembled Dáil took some weeks to nominate their successors. During that period Article 28.8 would presumably entitle Ministers to "attend and be heard" in the Dáil, so that they could answer questions and participate in debates. They would not, of course, be entitled to vote.

The electoral holocaust involved in such a scenario is highly unlikely to occur, but individual Ministers have suffered rejection.[43] On the above interpretation this would not affect their legal position. If there were any doubt on the matter—as where a need arose to invoke a statutory power vested in (say) the Minister for Agriculture—the Taoiseach could presumably assign the Department to himself (as has been done when Ministers have been sacked).[44] Alternatively, if a Senator nominated by the Taoiseach could be induced to resign the electorally unfortunate Minister could be nominated to that vacancy. The latter device could not, however, be adopted in the case of the Minister for Finance: Article 28.7.1°.

Ministerial dismissals and resignations

That the Taoiseach has power to dismiss Ministers is clear from Article 28.9.4°. It is a power rarely exercised, not least because the regular Cabinet reshuffles that occur in the United Kingdom have no counterpart in Irish practice. (Dr. FitzGerald's Government changes of February 1986 involved a rearrangement of functions and reassignment of individuals, but no changes in personnel.) So far as Cabinet members are concerned the power has been invoked only on five occasions since 1937. The first two cases both occurred on May 7, 1970 when the appointments of Mr. Blaney (Minister for Agriculture) and Mr. Haughey (Minister for Finance) were terminated.[45] The third instance was in October 1990, when Mr. Haughey sacked the Tánaiste and Minister for Defence, Mr. Lenihan, following the latter's refusal to resign in the wake of a controversy during his campaign for the Presidency.[46] And the fourth and fifth occasions were in November 1991, when Mr. Haughey dismissed Mr. Reynolds (Minister for Finance) and Mr. Flynn (Minister for the Environment) who had supported a challenge to his leadership of Fianna Fail.

Ministerial resignations inspired by distaste for Government policy are rare—and only three clear cases can be identified. These are the resignation of Mr. Patrick Smith (Minister for Agriculture) in 1964; that of Mr. Kevin Boland (Minister for Local Government) in 1970[47]; and that of Mr. Cluskey (Minister for Trade, Commerce and Tourism) in 1983.[48]

---

[43] Most notably, perhaps, Mr. Brian Lenihan (outgoing Minister for Foreign Affairs) who lost his Dáil seat at the 1973 general election.

[44] When Mr. Albert Reynolds was dismissed as Minister for Finance in November 1991, the Taoiseach, Mr. Haughey, temporarily assigned the Department of Finance to himself: see 412 *Dáil Debs.*, c. 853 (November 8, 1991).

[45] For the background see Brian Farrell, *Chairman or Chief*, pp. 78–81.

[46] See further Brian Lenihan, *For The Record* (Dublin 1991), Ch. 10.

[47] See Farrell, *op. cit.*, pp. 65–67, 78–81.

[48] When Dr. O'Donoghue and Mr. O'Malley resigned from Mr. Haughey's government in October 1982 they did so on personality—not policy—grounds. See Joe Joyce and Peter Murtagh, *The Boss* (Dublin 1983), pp. 256–262.

Code of Ministerial conduct

In regard to the business interests of Cabinet Ministers and Ministers of State there has evolved a code of conduct, applied by successive administrations over many years. All Ministers and Ministers of State are made aware of its principles in a document given to them on appointment. It was explained to the Dáil by the Taoiseach, Dr. FitzGerald, in the following terms[49]:

1. No Minister or Minister of State should engage in any activities that could reasonably be regarded as interfering, or being incompatible, with the full and proper discharge of the duties of office.
2. Ministers and Ministers of State should not hold company directorships carrying remuneration. Even if remuneration is not paid it is regarded as undesirable that a Minister or Minister of State should hold a directorship. A resigning director may, however, enter into an agreement with a company under which the company would agree to his reappointment as director on the termination of public office.
3. Ministers and Ministers of State should not carry on a professional practice while holding office but there would be no objection to making arrangements for the maintenance of a practice while holding office and for return to the practice on ceasing to hold office.
4. In cases of doubt the Taoiseach should be consulted.

It will be noted that the Taoiseach's statement made no reference to Ministers' financial interests, such as ownership of shares in companies. Neither they nor other deputies are required to list these in a document available to the public (contrast the register of MPs' interests in the United Kingdom). But the code of conduct provides that when a matter before the Government is one in which a member of the Government or his/her family has a material interest, this should be drawn to the Government's attention before the matter comes up for discussion. Unless the Government decides otherwise, the member concerned should not take part in discussion of the matter or vote on it, or seek to influence the attitude of colleagues.[50]

On October 22, 1986 the Taoiseach, replying to a question, said he had informed members of the Government that they could not belong to organisations with secret membership. He had not, he said, referred to any such organisation by name; but the public were entitled to know if Ministers were members of any organisation whose policy required that participation should not be a matter of public knowledge.[51]

Ministers and Departments

Article 28.12 provides that statute shall regulate the distribution of business among "Departments of State," and shall also deal with the designation of members of the Government to be the Ministers in charge of those Departments. Strictly speaking, it is quite possible for a member of the Government not to be in charge of a Department—to be a Minister without portfolio (see Ministers and Secretaries (Amendment) Act 1939, s.4). This, however, is

---

[49] 369 *Dáil Debs.*, c. 3 (October 22, 1986).
[50] *The Irish Times*, September 25, 1986.
[51] 369 *Dáil Debs.*, cc. 20–22.

unlikely to occur nowadays, the regular practice being for each member of the Government to be the political head of a Department (or Departments: the Taoiseach is authorised to assign more than one Department to a Minister—section 4, Ministers and Secretaries (Amendment) Act 1946.)

The structure of the various Departments, their titles and the distribution of business between them are regulated by the complex Ministers and Secretaries Acts 1924–1980. The 1924 Act lays down the basic pattern, though the names of some of the Departments it refers to have been changed since then (*e.g.* External Affairs to Foreign Affairs: Local Government to Environment) and the functions of several have been altered. Changes of name and redistribution of functions may be effected by a Government order: section 6 of the 1939 Act gives explicit power to this regard. A new Department, however, may be established only by statute—thus the 1966 Act established the Department of Labour and that of 1973 the Department of the Public Service (whose functions were previously discharged by the Department of Finance).

In addition to the Cabinet Minister in overall charge, a Department may also have a Minister of State assigned to it. Originally these junior Ministers were called parliamentary secretaries, and their number was limited to seven. But the Ministers and Secretaries (Amendment) (No. 2) Act 1977 changed their title, and that of 1980 has fixed their number at 15. These Ministers are formally appointed by the Government, but on the nomination of the Taoiseach, so that the effective choice is his.[52] Any person so appointed must be a member of the Oireachtas (1980 Act, s.2), but all those so far appointed have been deputies.

Ministers of State may function as general assistants to the Cabinet Minister heading the Department, performing whatever chores the latter may assign. Or specific areas of authority may be assigned to the Minister of State by Government order: Ministers and Secretaries (Amendment) (No. 2) Act 1977, s.2. This provision is however hedged about with multiple qualifications. Firstly, there must be a specific request from the relevant Cabinet Minister for such an order. Secondly, the delegation lasts only so long as that particular Cabinet Minister and Minister of State are in the relevant Department: should one or the other move elsewhere the delegation automatically ends—s.2(2)(*b*). Thirdly, the delegation of statutory powers and duties does not displace the Cabinet Minister: he or she remains concurrently vested with such powers and capable of exercising them—section 2(2)(*a*). It follows that an independent initiative by a Minister of State is always susceptible of being legally blocked by the Government Minister heading the Department. Finally, the latter remains responsible to the Dáil for the exercise of the relevant powers—section 2(2)(*f*).

A Cabinet Minister has, by virtue of Article 28.8, the right to attend and be heard in each House of the Oireachtas—though he/she may vote only in that to which he/she belongs. Thus a Minister is able to pilot a Bill originating in his/her Department through all its stages in both Houses. The Constitution confers no similar privilege on Ministers of State, and neither does statute. Under section 8 of the Ministers and Secretaries (Amendment) Act 1939 the former parliamentary secretaries has the right to attend and be heard in both Houses, but this was repealed by section 6 of the 1977 (No. 2)

---

[52] 1980 Act, s.2. The removal from office of a Minister of State also requires a Government decision (*ibid.*). This removal power was exercised three times in 1986 and twice in 1991.

Act. The Minister for Finance (Mr. Colley) told the Dáil that section 8 might well be unconstitutional, as infringing the right of each House, under Article 15.10, to make its own rules and standing orders. Hence it was proposed to leave the right of audience and attendance of Ministers of State to be dealt with by the standing orders of each House.[53] This has since been done: see Dáil Éireann Standing Order No. 59 and Seanad Éireann Standing Order No. 50.

The Attorney General

The office of Attorney General[54] is created by Article 30 of the Constitution[55]; which describes the holder as "the adviser of the Government in matters of law and legal opinion." Though not a member of the Government (Article 30.4), the Attorney traditionally attends cabinet meetings. He/she is appointed by the Taoiseach (who may, but is not obliged to, consult colleagues on the selection) and leaves office if the Government changes. The person appointed will thus be someone politically associated with the party (or principal party) in power.[56]

The Attorney General's Office is the principal source of legal advice both for the Government as a whole and for individual Departments. It embraces two other offices, those of the Chief State Solicitor and the Parliamentary Draftsman—the latter being responsible for the drafting of Government sponsored legislation.

Until 1974 the Attorney General was responsible for the prosecution of all serious criminal offences but this function has now, as Article 30.3 permits, been transferred to the Director of Public Prosecutions.[57] The Attorney, however, continues to exercise certain common law functions in civil matters.[58]

The Civil Service

Like political parties, the civil service—another institution vital to the functioning of the State—finds no mention in the Constitution: nonetheless it exists. The permanent staff of each department consists of civil servants of various grades of seniority. At the head of each department is a Secretary, who is appointed by the Government on the recommendation of the relevant Minister (Ministers and Secretaries Act 1924, s.2(2)). Below this official will be a number of Assistant Secretaries, each of whom will be responsible for specific areas of the Department's work. (In some cases a Deputy Secretary

---

[53] 301 *Dáil Debs.*, c. 768 (November 10, 1977).

[54] As to which see generally J. P. Casey, *The Office of the Attorney General in Ireland* (Dublin 1980).

[55] In *S.P.U.C.* v. *Coogan* [19891] I.R. 734 Walsh J. said that Article 30 created a new office and that insofar as Kenny J. in *Macauley* v. *Minister for Posts and Telegraphs* [1966] I.R. 345 seemed to suggest otherwise, his view should not be followed.

[56] That political association is clearly manifested where the Attorney is a Dáil deputy, as a few have been: Casey, *op. cit.*, pp. 64–67.

[57] Prosecution of Offences Act 1974. But under the Fisheries (Amendment) Act 1978 the Attorney General prosecutes in respect of maritime fisheries offences: see Casey, *op. cit.*, pp. 117–118.

[58] Such as representing the public in forensic matters, *e.g.* relator proceedings: see Casey, *op. cit.*, Ch. 10 and Anthony M. Collins and James O'Reilly, *Civil Proceedings and the State: A Practitioner's Guide* (Dublin 1990), Ch. 7. On the Attorney General's role in constitutional litigation see Ch. 11 *infra*.

or Secretaries may be in post immediately under the Secretary.) At lower levels there will be numbers of subordinate officials at varying levels of seniority. The organisation thus staffed has two main roles, described in the *Devlin Report* as follows[59]:

> "The first role of the public service is to serve the Government in a policy—advisory capacity, by sifting and recommending major policy alternatives, by collecting the public input, through appellate, consultative and research systems, and by assisting in the preparation of new legislation and in advice to Ministers.
>
> The second role of the public service is executive. Its task is to assist the Government in the running of the country under the rules laid down by the Oireachtas and to implement its policies . . . "

As the *Devlin Report* shows, the first role is a particular responsibility of senior officials, but it is one they are hampered in discharging by "the press of daily business."[60] The *Report* recommended changes in Departmental structures to remove these barriers, but while some experiments have been carried out, necessary legal changes have not yet been made.[61]

The Minister, as the political head of the Department, is free to reject the advice offered, and to instruct her officials in accordance with his own conclusions. Those instructions will be accepted and implemented, no matter how much they contradict the Departmental advice. At the same time it would be unrealistic not to recognise that senior officials may wield enormous influence; their expertise and experience are unlikely to be matched by the Minister's and he/she may well be wary of going against their advice. The paucity of studies on policy-making in Ireland makes it difficult to document official influence in this sphere.[62]

Section 2(1) of the Ministers and Secretaries Act 1924 states that each Minister, head of a Department, shall be a corporation sole. This has two consequences:

(a) it means that each such Minister is a juristic person, like a company or the State; thus "the Minister for Labour" is a legal entity quite distinct from the individual who holds office at any given time,

(b) the acts of a Department are in law those of the Minister. Thus unless statute specifically provides otherwise, no civil servant can give a decision in his or her own name. Such statutes are rare; Acts, it should be noted, do not confer power on "the Department" but on "the Minister."

There is, and must be, a gap between this legal theory and administrative reality. The difficulty and its solution are thus described in the *Devlin Report*:[63]

---

[59] *Loc. cit.*, paras. 12.2.1, 2.

[60] *Ibid.*, para. 13.1.1.

[61] See Sean Dooney, *The Irish Civil Service* (Dublin 1976), Chap. 9 and Peter Gaffey "The Central Administration" in Frank Litton (ed.) *Unequal Achievement* (Dublin 1982), p. 115 ff.

[62] That of senior figures in a vital Department is illustrated in Ronan Fanning, *The Department of Finance 1922–1958* (Dublin 1978) and Leon O'Broin, *No Man's Man: A Biographical Memoir of Joseph Brennan* (Dublin 1982). See also J. J. Lee, *Ireland 1922–1985: Politics and Society* (Cambridge 1989), *passim*.

[63] *Loc. cit.*, para. 7.1.2.

"With the modern complexity of administration and the mass of detail to be covered, it would be impossible for any Minister to have direct personal knowledge of all the operations of his Department . . . Nonetheless, he is not empowered by statute to delegate his powers to his civil servants. Yet the work has to be done. The modus operandi which has been adopted is to issue letters, minutes and instructions, in the name of the Minister. An official signing the letter expresses himself as having been *"directed* by the Minister to say." The official does not sanction, he conveys the sanction of the Minister. He does not describe himself as authorising, he speaks of the Minister authorising. The personal and final responsibility of the Minister is in every instance stressed. The whole system is extra-statutory but it functions. That it does so is because of the special relationship of trust between the Minister and his officials. The trust is and must be mutual. The official knows that the Minister will stand over his action *vis-à-vis* public and parliament if this action is in conformity with his general views. The Minister knows that the official in taking any action will always be conscious that the Minister may, in relation to the official's action, be challenged: that it is his business to have a convincing answer to such challenge. He knows further that the Minister must be personally consulted and a direction sought from him where the subject matter may have serious public and political implications."

The *Devlin Report* urged that this system be changed, but so far that recommendation has not been implemented. In September 1989, however, the Minister for Finance, Mr. Reynolds, announced that Departments were to be given responsibility for their own budgets, thus ending the system under which authority for expenditure had to be obtained from the Department of Finance. The new arrangements will give Departmental heads fixed allocations for administrative costs, agreed upon two or three years in advance.[64] The Department of Social Welfare became the first to implement the new system,[65] which it was planned to extend to all within two years.

The legal status of civil servants is governed by the Civil Service Regulation Acts 1956 and 1958, which deal *inter alia* with such matters as suspension and discipline in general. Civil servants do not have contracts of employment, but hold office regulated by statute. They are not within the terms of the Unfair Dismissals Act 1977: instead their security of tenure depends on section 5 of the Civil Service Regulation Act 1956, which states:

"Every established civil servant shall hold office at the will and pleasure of the Government."

Several points arise from this. First, the Acts distinguish between established and unestablished civil servants. The latter, who are not numerous, may be dismissed by the Departmental Minister, and their service is not pensionable. The established civil servant, on the other hand, may be dismissed from office only by a collective Government decision. Secondly, the terms of section 5 may mislead: in practice civil servants enjoy great security of tenure, and the power of dismissal has been invoked only rarely. But it has nonetheless been invoked, the most dramatic example being perhaps the dismissal

---

[64] *The Irish Times*, September 8, 1989.
[65] *The Irish Times*, July 5, 1990.

of the Secretary of the Department of Social Welfare in 1951.[66] Finally, section 5 must be read in the light of the Supreme Court's decision in *Garvey* v. *Ireland* [1981] I.R. 75 (as to which see further Chapter 12 *infra*). This means that lawful removal from an established civil service position is contingent upon the holder having been enabled to make a case against such action. The Government will have very wide discretion as to the grounds of removal, save that those grounds must not violate the Constitution. But whatever the grounds, they must be revealed to the individual concerned, who must be given an opportunity to make representations in his/her own defence.[67]

Civil servants are recruited, as to the great majority, by competitions supervised by the independent Civil Service Commission, which is chaired by the Ceann Comhairle. This is a statutory body whose functions and responsibilities are set out in the Civil Service Commissioners Act 1956. Once recruited, civil servants are appointed to Departmental posts—in theory by the Minister, in reality by senior officials. But no Department has a free hand in this matter: both in law and in fact a stringent control is exercised by the Department of Finance. The basis for this is section 2(2) of the Ministers and Secretaries Act 1924, as amended by the Act of 1973.

A distinction exists between the civil service of the Government and that of the State: see *McLoughlin* v. *Minister for Social Welfare* [1959] I.R. 1. The former group comprises the staff of the various Departments, etc.; the latter—much smaller—those of certain other constitutional organs, *e.g.* the President (Presidential Establishment Acts 1938–1973) and the Oireachtas (Staff of the Houses of the Oireachtas Act 1959). In regard to the latter, the Ceann Comhairle and the Cathaoirleach of the Seanad have the appointing and regulatory powers enjoyed by Ministers *quoad* Departments.

Semi-state organisations

As the *Devlin Report* observes, the Ministerial Department seems to have been envisaged in 1924 as the normal vehicle for discharging governmental functions. But as the State's concerns and responsibilities increased, there was a move towards different forms—as with the establishment in 1927 of the E.S.B., the Agricultural Credit Corporation Ltd. and the Dairy Disposal Co. Ltd. The first was a corporation established by statute, the latter two companies incorporated under the Companies Acts—though under specific statutory authority.

The pattern thus established has continued. Where the State has undertaken activities in default of private enterprise—in the fields of transport, power etc.—a semi-State body has been established to run things, under broad Ministerial supervision. In some instances the bodies in question are established by statute—*e.g.* C.I.É. and Bord na Móna, in others the company form is utilised—*e.g.* Aer Lingus. No clear principle governing the precise choice of form can be discerned.

Other bodies carry out functions more closely allied to traditional Departmental responsibilities. Examples are FÁS (the industrial training/job placement body), Bord Fáilte and the Industrial Development Authority (I.D.A.).

---

[66] See the adjournment debate on March 2, 1951: 124 *Dáil Debs.*, cc. 1060–68.
[67] On the dismissal of civil servants serving in a probationary capacity see *State (Daly)* v. *Minister for Agriculture* [1987] I.R. 165.

All these are statutory corporations, but the lack of any clear principle is illustrated by the Shannon Free Airport Development Co. (S.F.A.D.C.O.). Its function includes attraction of industry to the Shannon region, and it is a private company. The I.D.A. plays the same role for the country as a whole, yet it is a statutory corporation. But a more fundamental question arises in regard to all such non-commercial bodies. It was posed by the Devlin Group as follows.[68]

> " . . . the reasons which support the assignment of functions of government to state-sponsored bodies are primarily to be found in those constraints which impede the expeditious discharge of executive functions by the civil service. In the case of the 'commercial' type of body, there is the overriding consideration that the nature of the function is such that it is more suited to operation by the forms and procedures developed in the business sector. For the non-commercial function, every decision to allocate a new function to a state-sponsored body while similar functions are left in the existing civil service structure represents a failure to face the problem of the efficiency of the existing machinery of government, or at least, to think through the roles of the parts of that machinery."

[68] *Loc. cit.*, para. 5.2.28.

7   Emergency Provisions

Many constitutions, especially those of continental Europe, provide for the declaration of a public emergency and a consequent suspension of constitutional rights. Bunreacht na hÉireann adheres to this tradition, which is not surprising in a document prepared and enacted during the 1930s, against a background of domestic political turbulence and grave international tension. Unlike other constitutions, however, Bunreacht na hÉireann does not devote a separate Article to the matter. Its principal provision on the topic is found instead in Article 28, the main subject of which is the Government. This is curious draftsmanship, for the emergency provision—Art. 28.3.3°—does not *directly* invest the Government with extra powers. It does, however, enable the Oireachtas to bestow additional powers upon the executive—even to the extent of overriding constitutional provisions. In *State (Walsh)* v. *Lennon* [1941] I.R. 112, 120 Gavan Duffy J. put it thus:

> "The Constitution here envisages a crisis during which the normal rule of law is, at least to a considerable extent, superseded by the Rule of the Executive in the domain of emergency law . . . subject only to the control of the Legislature."

At this point it will be convenient to set out the text of Article 28.3.3°:

> "Nothing in this Constitution shall be invoked to invalidate any law enacted by the Oireachtas which is expressed to be for the purpose of securing the public safety and the preservation of the State in time of war or armed rebellion, or to nullify any act done or purporting to be done in time of war or armed rebellion in pursuance of any such law. In this sub-section 'time of war' includes a time when there is taking place an armed conflict in which the State is not a participant but in respect of which each of the Houses of the Oireachtas shall have resolved that, arising out of such armed conflict, a national emergency exists affecting the vital interests of the State and 'time of war or armed rebellion' includes such time after the termination of any war, or of any such armed conflict as aforesaid, or of an armed rebellion, as may elapse until each of the Houses of the Oireachtas shall have resolved that the national emergency occasioned by such war, armed conflict, or armed rebellion has ceased to exist."

The text as it now stands is the product of two constitutional amendments passed during the limited period when the Constitution could be amended by ordinary legislation—without recourse to a referendum. The original text consisted of the first sentence, minus the repetition of "in time of war or armed rebellion." The First Amendment of the Constitution Act 1939 inserted the words from "In this sub-section" to "vital interests of the State," while the Second Amendment of the Constitution Act 1941 added the rest, including the repetition of "in time of war or armed rebellion" in the first sentence.

The effect of Article 28.3.3° is to provide a means of freeing the Oireachtas from the limits imposed upon it by the Constitution. When this provision is invoked the Oireachtas becomes free to legislate as it wills, not merely to suspend fundamental rights but any other aspects—such as the separation of powers—of the basic law as well. So long as the statute is expressed to be for the purposes specified, nothing whatever in the Constitution may be invoked to invalidate it. In short, the Oireachtas is given *carte blanche*—such is the effect of the decisions of the former Supreme Court in *Re McGrath and Harte* [1941] I.R. 68 and *State (Walsh)* v. *Lennon* [1942] I.R. 112.

It would be difficult to over-emphasise the plenitude of power thus vested in the Oireachtas. In theory it could, by invoking the Article 28.3.3° formula and keeping the emergency in being, re-write the Constitution—*e.g.* by enlarging the size of the Government, abolishing P.R., extending the life of the Dáil and decreasing the powers of the President.[1] That nothing of this kind has been done shows only that what is constitutionally permissible may not always be viewed as constitutionally proper and may well result more from the fear of electoral reprisals than of judicial intervention.

It might seem that Article 28.3.3° goes further, by specifying that nothing in the Constitution may be invoked "to nullify any act done or purporting to be done in time of war or armed rebellion in pursuance of any such law." This looks very like an attempt to withdraw from the courts their ordinary jurisdiction to pronounce on whether something is *intra vires* or not. Gavan Duffy J. seems to have viewed it in this way: see his remarks in *Re McGrath and Harte* [1941] I.R. 68, 73 and *State (Walsh)* v. *Lennon* [1942] I.R. 112, 120. But this is impossible to square with what was said by the present Supreme Court in *Re Article 26 and the Emergency Powers Bill 1976* [1977] I.R. 159, 173, discussed *infra*.

On September 2, 1939—the day after the German invasion of Poland and the day before the United Kingdom and France declared war on Germany— both Houses of the Oireachtas passed resolutions making Article 28.3.3° operative. The national emergency thus declared remained in force until September 1, 1976, when the 1939 resolutions were abrogated and replaced by new ones referring to a national emergency arising out of the armed conflict taking place in Northern Ireland. It was under cover of the latter resolutions that the Emergency Powers Bill 1976 was passed.

The emergency declared by the 1939 resolutions was invoked to cover the passage under Article 28.3.3° of a series of sweeping Emergency Powers Acts. The 1939 Act, in section 2, allowed the Government to make by order such provisions as were, in their opinion, necessary or expedient for securing the public safety or the preservation of the State, or the maintenance of public

---

[1] Contrast the carefully drawn provisions of the Spanish Constitution of 1978. Art. 55 spells out the *only* rights and liberties that may be suspended when a state of emergency or state of siege (martial law) is proclaimed. Art. 116.2 requires prior parliamentary authority for a proclamation of a state of emergency and limits its duration, whilst Art. 116.4 provides that martial law

order. Originally there was a prohibition on providing for trial by courts-martial of persons not subject to military law, but this was repealed by the Emergency Powers (Amendment) (No. 2) Act 1940. Section 3 of the latter authorised the making of orders to:

" . . . make provision for the trial, in a summary manner, by commissioned officers of the Defence Forces, of any person alleged to have committed any offence specified in such order and, in the case of the conviction of such person of such offence, for the imposition and the carrying out of the sentence of death, and no appeal shall lie in respect of such conviction or sentence."

Order to this effect were duly made, and gave rise to the cases of *Re McGrath and Harte* [1941] I.R. 68 and *State (Walsh)* v. *Lennon* [1942] I.R. 112.

In the first case, McGrath and Harte had been convicted of murder by a military court and sentenced to death. Detained in military custody pending execution of the sentence, they applied for habeas corpus. The High Court and Supreme Court rejected the application, dismissing all the legal arguments put forward by their counsel. He contended that the First Amendment of the Constitution Act 1939 was invalid as not being within the powers of amendment conferred by Article 51 of the Constitution. The Supreme Court said, in rejecting this contention [1941] I.R. 68, 74):

" . . . Art. 51 provides that 'notwithstanding anything contained in Art. 46 hereof any of the provisions of this Constitution, except the provisions of the said Art. 46 and this Article, may, subject as hereinafter provided, be amended by the Oireachtas, whether by way of variation, amendment or repeal, within a period of three years after the date on which the first President shall have entered upon his office.' We are of opinion that the meaning of this Article is too plain to admit of any ambiguity. It expressly authorises the Oireachtas to amend any provision of the Constitution save those contained in Art. 46 and 51."

Less convincingly the Supreme Court rejected a second argument against the 1939 Amendment—that, contrary to Article 25.2.1°, the relevant Bill had been signed by the President earlier than five days after its presentation to him. The Supreme Court said Article 25.2.1° was not intended to apply to Bills to amend the Constitution. However this conclusion is open to challenge.[2] Article 25 certainly excepts from what might be called "the five-day rule" any "Bill containing a proposal for the Amendment of this Constitution." But this plainly looks forward to Article 46—the amendment by referendum Article—which repeatedly uses the words "Bill containing a proposal for the amendment of this Constitution." Such a Bill, when approved in a referendum, must be signed "forthwith": Art. 46.5. The First Amendment of the Constitution Act 1939, however, was passed under the transitional Article 51—to which the referendum requirement, and the whole of Article 46, had no application. Thus although the Bill was a constitutional amendment Bill, there was nothing in the Constitution to exempt it from the "five-

may be proclaimed only by an absolute majority of the Congress of Deputies. Art. 116.5 stipulates that Congress may not be dissolved while a state of emergency or martial law is in operation, and that if the Houses are not in session they must automatically be convened.
[2] As the late Professor John Kelly pointed out: *The Irish Constitution* (2nd ed., Dublin 1984), pp. 135–36.

day rule." Its earlier signature by the President would appear to have necessitated a special request by the Government, with the prior concurrence of the Seanad: Art.25.2.2°. But the Seanad was not asked to concur in any early signature request.

The Supreme Court also held that for the Act to be "expressed for the purpose" mentioned in Article 28.3.3°, it was sufficient that the purpose be stated in the long title. It was not necessary to reiterate that purpose in the enacting portion of the Act: [1941] I.R. 68 at 76. Nor was it necessary for the statute to recite that the Oireachtas had passed the necessary resolutions: proof, or a concession, that they had been passed was enough to bring Article 28.3.3° into play. (Note however that the Emergency Powers Act 1976 did refer to the relevant resolutions, both in its long title and in s.3.) Finally, orders or regulations made under the authority of the relevant statute need not recite the passage of those resolutions: [1941] I.R. 68 at 76.

In *State (Walsh)* v. *Lennon* [1942] I.R. 112, four men—George Plant, Joseph O'Connor, Michael Walsh and Patrick Davern—were about to be tried by a military court on charges of murder. They applied for an order of prohibition to prevent their trial. Since the relevant statutes, and the order made thereunder establishing the military court, had been upheld in *Re McGrath and Harte*, the prosecutors faced grave difficulties. These they attempted to surmount by pointing to special features of their case, the details of which do not emerge fully from the report.[3] Plant and O'Connor were charged before the Special Criminal Court with the murder of Michael Devereux. Michael Walsh and Patrick Davern, alleged accomplices of the two accused, were to be the chief prosecution witnesses against them; but they claimed their statements had been extracted by beating, and refused to testify. The prosecution entered a *nolle prosequi*. By the Emergency Powers Order (No. 41F of 1941) all four were ordered to be tried by a military court. This Order was made on December 31, 1941. The previous day another order, the Emergency Powers (No. 139) Order, 1941, had radically changed the rules of evidence. As Sullivan C.J. put it ([1942] I.R. 112, 130):

> " . . . this Order permits unsworn and unsigned statements of persons not present at the trial to be read as evidence against the accused, and unsworn and unsigned statements made by one accused to be read as evidence against another accused, and to authorise the Court at the trial, if it considers it proper to do so, to disregard any rule of evidence, whether statutory or at common law."

Counsel for the prosecutors argued that this infringed rights guaranteed not only by the Constitution, but by the common law. Such rights were those to personal liberty, to apply for habeas corpus and to be tried in due course of law. The High Court rejected this argument. The rights in question were expressed clearly in Articles 38 and 40 of the Constitution, and had no existence independent of it (see Maguire P. at 117, Gavan Duffy.J. at 122 and Martin Maguire J. at 123–4). In regard to Order No. 41F of 1941 the Supreme Court, *per* Sullivan C.J. said ([1942] I.R. 112, 129–130):

> "In determining the validity of the Order, this Court must give effect to the provisions of Art. 28, s.3, of the Constitution, which makes it imposs-

---

[3] The above is based in part upon J. Bowyer Bell, *The Secret Army* (paperback ed., London 1972).

ible to invoke any other Article of the Constitution to invalidate this or any other Order made in pursuance of an Act passed by the Oireachtas and expressed to be for any of the purposes mentioned in the said Article. See the judgment of this Court in the case of *McGrath and Harte*. In view of the extremely wide provisions of s.2, subs. 1, of the Emergency Powers Act, 1939, and of the provisions of s.3 of the Emergency Powers (Amendment) (No. 2) Act, 1940, this Court is of opinion that the Order in question comes within the powers conferred upon the Government by the said sections and cannot be impugned."

The Supreme Court also rejected arguments based on the entry of a *nolle prosequi* in the Special Criminal Court, and the subsequent changes in the rules of evidence in advance of a new trial. The entry of a *nolle* was no bar to a fresh prosecution, and the change in the rules of evidence was authorised by the relevant statutes. Arguments that this change was oppressive and unjust to the accused were the concern of the Oireachtas, not the courts (see [1942] I.R. 112, 130–131).

Of the four accused, three—Plant, Davern and Walsh—were convicted and sentenced to death; but Plant alone was executed, by firing squad. The previous death sentences on McGrath and Harte had also been carried out.[4]

As already noted, the 1939 resolutions bringing Article 28.3.3° into force were annulled in 1976 and replaced by new ones referring to a national emergency arising out of the armed conflict in Northern Ireland. These resolutions, which are still in force, were the vehicle for the passage of the Emergency Powers Bill 1976—which President Ó Dálaigh referred to the Supreme Court under Article 26 of the Constitution. The kernel of the Bill was in section 2, which provided for the arrest and detention of persons for a maximum of seven days. It should be noted that the Attorney General asked the Supreme Court to deal with the case on the basis that section 2 would have been invalid unless saved by Article 28.3.3°. Consequently the court heard no argument on this matter, and expressed no opinion on whether section 2 *would* have been unconstitutional without the protection of Article 28.3.3°: *Re Article 26 and the Emergency Powers Bill 1976* [1977] I.R. 159, 172.

This was the first occasion on which a measure purportedly covered by Article 28.3.3° had been the subject of a Presidential reference under Article 26. The Supreme Court held that a Bill passed under such circumstances could properly be the subject of such a reference. But the court's jurisdiction was circumscribed:

"When a bill is validly referred to the Court under Article 26, the test of its repugnancy or invalidity is what its force and effect will be if and when it becomes law. Thus, in regard to a bill which is to take effect as law under Article 28, s.3, subs. 3, if it is shown to the Court that the preliminary and procedural requirements for the passing of the bill by both Houses of the Oireachtas have been complied with, it is *ipso facto*, because of the exemption granted by Article 28, s.3, subs. 3, incapable of being struck down on the ground of repugnancy to the Constitution or to any provision thereof." ([1977] I.R. 159, 174).

Having found that these preliminary and procedural requirements were satisfied, the court upheld the Bill.

[4] See Bell, *op cit.*, pp. 224, 250.

The *Emergency Powers Bill* case settled several additional points. One was that Article 28.3.3° contemplates two types of legislation—that designed for a time of war or armed rebellion, and that meant to cope with an emergency occasioned by an external armed conflict. Legislation of the first type, it was held, required no resolutions; it could be enacted if war or armed conflict were imminent, and would come into operation if the relevant event occurred. Legislation of the second type *does* require resolutions. And it was held that if legislation is passed under cover of resolutions referring to an armed conflict, this restricts its sphere of operation. It would not then be applicable to a time of war or armed rebellion because not expressed to be for that purpose: [1977] I.R. 159, 174–175.

It was further held that when the Oireachtas resolutions recite the existence of a state of affairs necessary to bring Article 28.3.3° into operation, there is a presumption that the facts so stated are correct; and this presumption is to be acted upon until displaced: [1977] I.R. 159, 175. Though the court did not say so, the burden of displacing that presumption would obviously be a very heavy one. As to whether the courts could review the contents of the resolutions—to determine whether they had any factual foundation—the Supreme Court reserved its opinion: [1977] I.R. 159, 176.

No less significant was what the court said in regard to section 2 ([1977] I.R. 159, 173):

> " . . . it is important to point out that when a law is saved from invalidity by Article 28, s.3, subs. 3, the prohibition against invoking the Constitution in reference to it is for the purpose of invalidating it. For every other purpose the Constitution may be invoked. Thus, a person detained under s.2 of the bill may not only question the legality of his detention if there has been non-compliance with the express requirements of s.2, but may also rely on provisions of the Constitution for the purpose of construing that section and of testing the legality of what has been done in purported operation of it. A statutory provision of this nature which makes such inroads upon the liberty of the person must be strictly construed. Any arrest sought to be justified by the section must be in strict conformity with it. No such arrest may be justified by importing into the sections incidents or characteristics of an arrest which are not expressly or by necessary implication authorised by the section.
>
> . . . the section is not to be read as an abrogation of the arrested person's rights (constitutional or otherwise) in respect of matters such as the rights of communication, the right to have legal and medical assistance, and the right of access to the Courts. If the section were used in breach of such rights the High Court might grant an order for release under the provisions for habeas corpus contained in the Constitution."

This approach could hardly contrast more strongly with the laissez-faire attitude of the former Supreme Court in the 1940s cases. It was subsequently applied in the High Court by Finlay P. to hold that a second detention, arising from suspicion of involvement in the same offence, was not justified by section 2 and was therefore unlawful. He accordingly granted the prosecutor an order of habeas corpus: *State (Hoey)* v. *Garvey* [1978] I.R. 1. As to the right to legal advice, see *State (Harrington)* v. *Commissioner, Garda Síochána* (High Court, December 14, 1976).

It remains to note that the Emergency Powers Act 1976 has for some time been in abeyance; but it can be brought into operation again at any time by Government order: s.1(2)(c). Such an order does not require Oireachtas approval but it may be annulled by resolution of either House: s.1(3). If the Emergency Powers Act 1976 is brought into force, it brings in its train section 15 of the Criminal Law Act 1976—which confers powers of arrest and search on members of the Defence Forces in certain circumstances: see s.15(8) of the latter Act.

Views of the Committee on the Constitution

Article 28.3.3° was discussed by the Committee on the Constitution, which reported in December 1967.[5] The Committee referred to the provision's background and to its effect, using the curious formula that it gave "the Government power to suspend certain provisions of the Constitution in peace time" (para. 103). Explaining the continuance in force of the 1939 resolutions, the Committee said international conditions had influenced successive Governments. In the absence of peace treaties between the contestants involved in the war, it had always been deemed prudent to maintain a state of readiness for emergency conditions in the country. Moreover, the annulment of the resolutions "might possibly, also have given rise to some political misunderstandings in relation to some of the belligerent countries . . . " (para. 104). The caution thus exhibited seems remarkable.
The Committee went on to consider how Article 28.3.3° might be amended. It recommended that a clause be added to provide that resolutions declaring an emergency should have effect only for three years unless renewed—with special provision for a situation where the Oireachtas was unable to meet. (Unfortunately, the Committee does not seem to have considered more recent constitutions; but the emergency provisions of the West German (Art. 80a and Chap. Xa) and Spanish Constitutions (Arts. 55 and 116) would repay study.) The Committee also took the view that the Government's power, under Article 28.3.2°, to take necessary steps for the preservation of the State in the case of actual invasion required amendment. Developments in long-range warfare, including missiles, made the words "actual invasion" no longer appropriate. But this, like the Committee's other recommendations, has not been implemented.

Article 40.4.6°

The Constitution's other emergency provision is found in Article 40.4.6°. This provides that nothing in the habeas corpus provision—Article 40.4— may be invoked to prohibit, control or interfere with any act of the Defence Forces during the existence of a state of war or armed rebellion. It must be read in conjunction with Article 38.4.1°, which appears to authorise the establishment—purely by executive decree—of military tribunals to deal with a state of war or armed rebellion. In making habeas corpus unavailable to challenge the activities of such bodies, Article 40.4.6° would seem to reproduce the common law position: see *R. v. Allen* [1921] 2 I.R. 241: *R. (Ronayne*

---

[5] *Report of the Committee on the Constitution* (Pre. 9817), paras. 102–106.

& Mulcahy) v. *Strickland* [1921] 2 I.R. 333: *R.* (*Childers*) v. *Adj. General, Provisional Forces* [1923] 1 I.R. 14.

Persons detained pending trial by such tribunals would thus have difficulty in challenging such detention by habeas corpus. Presumably, however, it would be for the courts to say whether a state of war or armed rebellion actually existed: such was the common law position—*R.* (*Garde*) v. *Strickland* [1921] 2 I.R. 317, and see the United States Supreme Court's decision in *Ex p. Milligan* (1866) 71 U.S. (4 Wall.) 2. And although Article 40.4.6° impedes the grant of habeas corpus, other remedies such as the injunction or declaration may be available. Possibly certiorai or prohibition may also lie: the House of Lords decision in *Re Clifford and O'Sullivan* [1921] 2 A.C. 570 may not be an accurate guide to modern Irish law on the scope of these remedies.[6]

Finally, it should be noted that Article 40.4.6° does not purport to offer any protection against suit once the state of war or armed rebellion is over. Individual members of the Defence Forces (or the State) might consequently be sued—*e.g.* for assault or false imprisonment—though the Oireachtas would no doubt pass an Act of indemnity, as it did to cover acts done during the civil war (Indemnity Act 1923) and War of Independence (Indemnity Act 1924).

---

[6] See Law Reform Commission Working Paper No. 8, *Judicial Review of Administrative Action: the Problem of Remedies* (1979): Anthony M. Collins and James O'Reilly, *Civil Proceedings and the State in Ireland: A Practitioners' Guide* (Dublin 1990), Chap. 4.

8 International Relations

The whole of Article 29 is devoted to international relations. Its provisions might be thought to combine aspirations and concrete legal principles; the first two sections use language reminiscent of the Preamble and express ideas realisable only by action in concert with other states.[1] The goal of the United Nations organisation is obviously, in the language of Article 29.1, "peace and friendly co-operation amongst nations founded on international justice and morality"[2] and Ireland has contributed towards that goal by its membership of that body since 1955. It has twice served on the Security Council, and an Irish diplomat, Mr. F. H. Boland, was president of the General Assembly in 1960. On several occasions Ireland has made troops available for service with UN peacekeeping forces, most notably in the Congo and in Lebanon.[3] Statutory cover for this latter development was provided by the Defence (Amendment) (No. 2) Act 1960.

In Article 29.2 the State "affirms its adherence to the principle of the pacific settlement of international disputes by international arbitration or judicial determination." It might have been assumed that, in pursuance of this goal, the State would have made a declaration under Article 36(2) of the Statute of the International Court of Justice, accepting as compulsory in relation to any other state accepting the same obligation, the court's jurisdiction over certain kinds of legal disputes. The more so since the Irish Free State had in 1929 signed the similar "optional clause" of the Statute of the Permanent Court of International Justice—with a good deal of fanfare. But the political reasons, connected with Commonwealth membership, for the 1929 decision no longer obtain, and this may explain why no similar obligation has been accepted since.[4]

---

[1] But note that in *McGimpsey* v. *Ireland* [1990] 1 I.R. 110 Finlay C.J., for the Supreme Court, spoke of " . . . *the obligations undertaken by the State* in Art. 29, ss.1 and 2 of the Constitution, whereby Ireland affirms its devotion to the ideal of peace and friendly co-operation and its adherence to the principles of the pacific settlement of international disputes." (Italics supplied.) The Supreme Court there invoked Art. 29.1 and 2 in support of the conclusion that the Anglo-Irish Agreement of 1985 was compatible with the Constitution.

[2] Art. 1 of the UN Charter, which states its purposes, refers *inter alia* to maintaining international peace and security, developing friendly relations among nations and achieving international cooperation in solving international problems.

[3] For further details see John P. Duggan, *A History of the Irish Army* (Dublin 1991), Chap. 8.

[4] For the 1929 action and its background, see David Harkness, *The Restless Dominion* (London 1969), pp. 141–144. On the International Court of Justice, see Ian Brownlie, *Principles of Public International Law* (3rd ed., Oxford 1979), Chap. XXXI.

Article 29.3

Article 29.3 declares that the State "accepts the generally recognised principles of international law as its rule of conduct in its relations with other States." This is more than an aspiration; the former Supreme Court treated it as importing such generally recognised principles into Irish domestic law. In *Saorstát and Continental Steamship Co.* v. *De Las Morenas* [1945] I.R. 291, 298 O'Byrne J. said:

> "The immunity of sovereign states and their rulers from the jurisdiction of the courts of other States has long been recognised as a principle of international law, and must now be accepted as a part of our municipal law by reason of Article 29, para. 3, of our Constitution. . . . "[5]

But it may not have been necessary to read Article 29.3 in this way. There is ample authority for the proposition that customary international law was part of the common law—see *The Paquete Habana* (1900) 175 U.S. 677; *West Rand Central Gold Mining Co. Ltd.* v. *The King* [1905] 2 K.B. 391.

The "generally recognised principles of international law" do not constitute an immutable code; they are capable of change in accordance with modifications in the practice of states.[6] And what Article 29.3 imports into Irish domestic law is the relevant principles in their *current* formulation, *not* as they may have existed in 1937. This is clear from the Supreme Court's decision in *Government of Canada* v. *Employment Appeals Tribunal* [1992] I.L.R.M. 325. Here a chauffeur employed at the Canadian Embassy in Dublin had been dismissed. Claiming that his dismissal was unfair, he proceeded against the Canadian government before the Employment Appeals Tribunal. The defendant government argued that the tribunal lacked jurisdiction, since Canada enjoyed sovereign immunity and this had not been waived. The tribunal, however, rejected this submission and, following the defendant government's withdrawal from the proceedings, found in the chauffeur's favour. This decision was upheld by the High Court in certiorari proceedings, but the Supreme Court unanimously reversed this ruling. The court held, in essence, that even if the doctrine of sovereign immunity had narrowed in its scope,[7] it would still apply to the instant claim.[8]

Four of the five Supreme Court judges[9] stated clearly that "the generally recognised principles of international law" are susceptible of change, reflecting the practice of states. McCarthy J. said (at 327–328):

> "It is a generally recognised principle of international law that foreign States and their agents at one time enjoyed sovereign immunity from

---

[5] Recognition of states and governments is discussed in Chap. 9, *infra*.

[6] As to how these principles are to be discovered, see D. P. O'Connell, *International Law* (2nd ed., London 1970). Chap. 1. Note the range of sources consulted by Hanna J. in *Zarine* v. *Owners of S.S. Ramava* [1942] I.R. 148, which included not only English and U.S. authorities but also textbooks and articles in legal periodicals.

[7] It no longer protects commercial or trading transactions by a state: see *I Congreso del Partido* [1983] A.C. 244.

[8] On the basis that the trust and confidentiality reposed in the driver of an embassy car creates a bond with the employers which has the effect of involving him/her in the employing government's public business organisation.

[9] Hederman J. did not find it necessary to consider whether the classical doctrine of sovereign immunity had been modified.

being impleaded before any court or administrative tribunal[10] in the domestic arena. The history of that immunity is detailed in the judgment . . . by O'Flaherty J. I accept his conclusion that it is now clear that the general principles of international law have so developed as to depart radically from the absolute state immunity doctrine to a much more restrictive view of sovereign immunity. It is, still, immunity but its application is restricted."

And O'Flaherty J. (Finlay C.J. and Egan J. concurring) said (at 333):

"Ireland's obligation is to accept the generally recognised principles of international law as its rule of conduct in its relations with other states (Art. 29.3). The "generally recognised principles" of international law change from time to time, as the debate and research in this case has demonstrated. The Oireachtas is, of course, entitled to enact any legislation it pleases in accordance with the Article but the courts, also, must make the appropriate declaration when called upon from time to time . . . it is now clear that the general principles of international law have so developed as to depart radically from the absolute state immunity doctrine to a much more restrictive view of sovereign immunity."

It is still unclear whether the generally recognised principle of international law are imported into the legal system at the constitutional—or a lower level. If they have constitutional status they could not be abrogated by statute; thus if it was desired to uproot completely the principle of restricted sovereign immunity, a constitutional amendment would be required. The issue—on which the Supreme Court has yet to rule—is the subject of conflicting opinions. In *State (Sumers Jennings)* v. *Furlong* [1966] I.R. 183 Henchy J.— then a High Court judge—said (at 190):

" . . . section 3 of Article 29 of the Constitution was not enacted, and is not to be interpreted in these Courts, as a statement of the absolute restriction of the legislative powers of the State by the generally recognised principles of international law. As the Irish version makes clear, the section merely provides that Ireland accepts the generally recognised principles of international law as a guide (*ina dtreoir*) in its relations with other states . . . Having regard to the statement in Article 6 of the Constitution that the legislative powers of the State derive, under God, from the people and the wording of section 3 of Article 29, I would respectfully adopt the *dictum* of Davitt P. in the Ó Laighléis case (at page 103): "Where there is an irreconcilable conflict between a domestic statute and the principles of international law or the provisions of an international convention, the Courts administering the domestic law must give effect to the statute."[11]

---

[10] The *Government of Canada* case establishes, for the first time in Irish law, that sovereign immunity applies to proceedings before an administrative tribunal, at least where the tribunal's powers are akin to those of the Employment Appeal Tribunal.

[11] It is not clear whether these observations were cited to O'Hanlon J. in *Murphy* v. *Asahi Synthetic Fibres Ltd.* [1985] I.R. 509. There, s.361(1) of the Income Tax Act 1967 provided for agreements with other states on double taxation, and for Government orders to give effect thereto. When such orders were made the arrangements were to have the force of law, notwithstanding anything in any enactment. O'Hanlon J. said, *obiter*, that by virtue of Article 29 provisions of such an agreement would prevail over subsequent inconsistent legislative provisions. On

But three of the Irish members of the Law Enforcement Commission which reported in 1974[12]—Walsh J., Mr. T. A. Doyle (as Doyle J. then was) and Mr. Declan Quigley—took a different view. Having referred to Article 29.3, they wrote[13]:

> "The constitutional provision is in terms an express commitment on the part of the State. The Courts can intervene to set aside any executive or legislative act which contravenes this or any other constitutional provision . . .
>
> These members cannot advise that the Government of Ireland could legally enter into any agreement *or that the legislature could validly enact any legislation* affecting its relations with other states which would be in breach of the generally recognised principles of international law." (Italics supplied.)

The provisions of Article 29.4 and 5 are considered in the following chapter. They permit the executive to commit the State to international obligations—*i.e.* to assume burdens that would be enforced by an international court or tribunal, even if not by an Irish court. But such executive action cannot of itself result in a change in the domestic law.[14] Article 29.6 makes it clear that an international agreement can be incorporated into the domestic law of the State *only* by decision of the Oireachtas. This is normally done by legislation, though since Article 29.6 merely says "determined by the Oireachtas" it could conceivably be done by simple resolution. Statutes implementing international agreements usually schedule the agreement's text, even if its provisions are reproduced in the body of the Act: see *e.g.* the Air Navigation and Transport Act 1975. This, of course, is particularly desirable where the Act specifically incorporates the agreement into the domestic law of the State, as do *e.g.* the Diplomatic Relations and Immunities Act 1967, s.5 (the 1961 Vienna Convention on Diplomatic Relations) and the Genocide Act 1973, s.2 (the UN Convention on the Prevention and Punishment of the Crime of Genocide).

The European Convention on Human Rights

Although the State is a party to the European Convention on Human Rights, that instrument has not been made part of the domestic law of the

this view, Art. 29 operates to preclude the Oireachtas from enacting legislation inconsistent with the State's obligations under an international agreement. (This matter is not touched upon in the Supreme Court's decision on appeal in *Murphy's* case—[1986] I.R. 777.)

[12] The Commission, consisting of eight members jointly appointed by the British and Irish governments, was established to consider " . . . how most effectively, from a legal point of view, to bring to trial persons alleged to have committed crimes of violence, however motivated, in any part of Ireland irrespective of the part of Ireland in which they were located": *Report* (Prl. 3832), para. 1.

[13] Paras. 63 and 66. Note also that those members did not accept that there was any conflict between the English and Irish texts of Art. 29.3. They pointed out, *inter alia*, that in the official Irish-language text of the EC Treaties *treoir* is the term for "directive."

[14] In certain circumstances it may, however, have an indirect effect. Thus in *Fakih* v. *Minister for Justice* (High Court, O'Hanlon J., March 6, 1992) three aliens had been refused leave to land by the defendant. They sought refugee status and claimed to be entitled to have their applications considered in accordance with the UN Convention on the Status of Refugees, 1951 as amended by the Protocol on the Status of Refugees, 1967. The State had adopted these as part of its international obligations, but they did not form part of the domestic law of the State.

State.[15] Hence its provisions cannot be relied upon in an Irish court to challenge legislation inconsistent with them. In *Re Ó Laighléis* [1960] I.R. 93, the applicant argued that the Offences against the State (Amendment) Act 1940, under which he had been interned, was inconsistent with the Convention and could therefore no longer be operated. (He could not attack the validity of the Act because the relevant Bill had been upheld by the Supreme Court on a reference under Article 26, and Article 34.4.3° bars any further challenge in such circumstances.) The Supreme Court rejected this contention, saying *per* Maguire C.J. (at 124–25):

> "The insuperable obstacle to importing the provisions of the Convention . . . into the domestic law of Ireland—if they be at variance with that law—is, however, the terms of the Constitution of Ireland. By Article 15.2.1° of the Constitution it is provided that "the sole and exclusive power of making laws for the State is hereby vested in the Oireachtas: no other legislative authority has power to make laws for the State." Moreover, Article 29 . . . provides at section 6 that 'no international agreement shall be part of the domestic law of the State save as may be determined by the Oireachtas.'
>
> The Oireachtas has not determined that the Convention . . . is part of the domestic law of the State, and accordingly this Court cannot give effect to the Convention if it be contrary to domestic law or purports to grant rights or impose obligations additional to those of domestic law.
>
> No argument can prevail against the express command of section 6 of Article 29 of the Constitution before judges whose declared duty it is to uphold the Constitution and the laws.
>
> The Court accordingly cannot accept the idea that the primacy of domestic legislation is displaced by the State becoming a party to the Convention. . . . "

This decision was specifically approved and followed by the present Supreme Court in *Application of Woods* [1970] I.R. 154, where reliance on the UN Universal Declaration of Human Rights was ruled out on similar grounds.[16]

In *Norris v. Att. Gen.* [1984] I.R. 36 the plaintiff challenged certain pre-Constitution statutory provisions which criminalised homosexual activities, even when engaged in by consenting adults in private. One of his arguments was based on the fact that the European Court of Human Rights had held the similar Northern Ireland legislation inconsistent with the Convention in *Dudgeon v. U.K.* (1981) 4 E.H.R.R. 149. There was a presumption, it was

---

However a letter written to the United Nations High Commisioner for Refugees on behalf of the Minister for Justice in December 1985 had stated that asylum applications would be processed in accordance with the Convention and Protocol. O'Hanlon J. held that the applicants consequently had a legitimate expectation that their claims would be determined in this way.

[15] Incorporation would not seem to pose any great technical difficulties; see Joseph Jaconelli, "The European Convention on Human Rights as Irish Municipal Law" (1987) XXII *Irish Jurist* (n.s.) 13. But Walsh J. has suggested that if incorporated as a *law*, it would be subordinate to the Constitution (and thus of limited utility); and if incorporated at constitutional level it might conflict with some existing provisions. See Brian Walsh, "Reflections on the Effects of Membership of the European Communities in Irish Law" in F. Capotorti *et al.* (eds.), *Du Droit International au Droit de L'integration: Liber Amicorum Pierre Pescatore* (Baden-Baden 1987), p. 805.

[16] That declaration, it should be noted, was proclaimed by the UN General Assembly and is not an "international agreement" within the meaning of Article 29.6—though this does not affect the validity of the Supreme Court's conclusion.

contended, that the Constitution was compatible with the Convention; thus in determining the consistency of legislation with the Constitution under Article 50, one should examine the legislation for consistency with the Convention. Four of the five Supreme Court judges expressly rejected this argument (McCarthy J. found it unnecessary to consider the point). O'Higgins C.J., for himself, Finlay P. and Griffin J. said (at 66):

> " . . . acceptance of (counsel's) submission would be contrary to the provisions of the Constitution itself and would accord to the Government the power, by an executive act, to change both the Constitution and the law. The Convention is an international agreement to which Ireland is a subscribing party. As such, however, it does not and cannot form part of our domestic law, nor affect in any way questions which arise thereunder. This is made quite clear by Article 29.6 of the Constitution. . . . "

O'Higgins C.J. went on to quote Maguire C.J.'s observations in *Re Ó Laighléis* [1960] I.R. 93—reproduced above—and expressed his agreement with them.

Henchy J. said (at 68–69):

> " . . . the constitutional question that calls for resolution is unaffected by the fact that the precise statutory provisions in question in this case were held by the European Court of Human Rights in *Dudgeon* v. *United Kingdom* to be in breach of Article 8 of the European Convention for the Protection of Human Rights and Fundamental Freedoms. That Convention, as has been held by this Court, although it has by its terms a binding force on the Government of this State as one of its signatories, forms no part of the domestic law of this State."

Again, in *O'B.* v. *S.* [1984] I.R. 316 the issue posed was—did the intestate succession provisions of the Succession Act 1965 exclude illegitimate children—and if so, was this repugnant to the Constitution? During the argument reference was made to the decision of the European Court of Human Rights in *Marckx* v. *Belgium* (1979–80) 2 E.H.R.R. 330. Giving the judgment of the Supreme Court, Walsh J. dealt with this matter thus (at 338):

> "That decision was relied upon by the defendant in the present case, although admittedly as being more in the nature of an indication of how the Court ought to decide this case if it was free to follow that case. The *Marckx Case* can have no bearing on the question of whether any provision of the Act of 1965 is invalid having regard to the provisions of the Constitution. In so far as that case may be in conflict with the Act of 1965, this Court is obliged to follow the provisions of the Act of 1965: see Article 29, s.6, of the Constitution."

In *E.* v. *E.* [1982] I.L.R.M. 497 the High Court rejected an attempt, based on somewhat different grounds, to invoke a judgment of the European Court of Human Rights for domestic purposes. The defendant in this case was involved in complex family law proceedings. He needed legal representation and applied for this to the Legal Aid Board, which refused his application. An appeal against this decision was pending. In the meantime, the defendant served notice on the Attorney General that, at the resumed family law proceedings, he would apply for a High Court order directing payment by the

State of his costs. In support of the argument that the State could be made liable in this way, counsel for the defendant strongly relied on the judgment in *Airey* v. *Ireland* (1979) 2 E.H.R.R. 305. The European Court of Human Rights had there effectively held Ireland's failure to provide free civil legal aid a violation of Articles 6 and 8 of the Convention. Counsel argued that a judgment of that court, in proceedings to which the State was a party, bound the State for the future and could be given effect to in subsequent proceedings against the State in the domestic courts. But O'Hanlon J. was unable to accept this, saying (at 499):

> "It appears to me that the defendant in the present proceedings is claiming that the State in setting up the Scheme of Civil Legal Aid and Advice did not go far enough in complying with the requirements of the European Convention, as interpreted by the Court of Human Rights in the *Airey* case, and that as a result the defendant . . . , is in danger of finding himself without any legal representation in continuing proceedings of a nature and complexity comparable to those which obtained in the *Airey* case. As this contention is strongly disputed by the Attorney General, it appears to me to be a dispute which should properly be determined by the procedure provided for in the European Convention, involving a reference of the matter to the European Commission initially, with the possibility of a later determination by the Court of Human Rights.
>
> In so far as the present application before the High Court is concerned, I am satisfied that the defendant cannot establish that any existing right he enjoys under Irish law has been infringed, and I have to determine the case on this basis."[17]

It may be, however, that the Convention, and judgments of the Court based thereon, can be used in the domestic courts for limited purposes[18]— such as deciding whether an alleged rule forms part of the common law or not. And in an appropriate case a court might prefer an interpretation of a statute which was consistent with the Convention to one—equally open on the wording—which was not. See the brief remarks of Henchy J. in *State (D.P.P.)* v. *Walsh* [1981] I.R. 412, 440 and in *Ó Domhnaill* v. *Merrick* [1984] I.R. 151, 159.

Invoking the European Convention externally

The above cases show that the European Convention cannot be enforced through the domestic courts; but this certainly does not mean that it is devoid of practical effect. The State has long recognised the competence of the European Commission on Human Rights to receive individual petitions claiming violation of the Convention. Indeed, the first case ever dealt with by the Commission was that of *Ó Laighléis* in 1957. A note on these proceedings appears at [1960] I.R. 134–5.

Should the Commission find the petition admissible (as to which see Convention, Art. 27), it examines the issue and, if necessary, conducts an investi-

---

[17] See G. F. Whyte, "The Application of the European Convention on Human Rights Before The Irish Courts" (1982) 31 I.C.L.Q. 856.

[18] It may be used as evidence in support of a conclusion that a claimed constitutional right, implicitly guaranteed by the Constitution, exists—see *O'Leary* v. *Att. Gen.* [1991] I.L.R.M. 454 and *State (Healy)* v. *Donoghue* [1976] I.R. 325, 351, *per* O'Higgins C.J.

gation. The Commission then places itself at the disposal of the parties with a view to securing a friendly settlement (Art. 28). Should this be achieved, the Commission will then draw up a report which is sent to the state(s) concerned, the Committee of Ministers and the Secretary General of the Council of Europe for publication. Failing a solution the Commission draws up a report stating its findings of fact, and whether those facts disclose a breach by the relevant state of its Convention obligations. This is transmitted to the Committee of Ministers and the state(s) concerned. The case may then be referred to the Court of Human Rights under Article 48 by *inter alios* the Commission or the defendant state; no individual or group, it should be noted, may invoke the court's jurisdiction (see Art. 44). Alternatively, if the matter is not referred to the court within three months of the report's transmission to the Committee of Ministers, the latter body decides whether the Convention has been violated and, if so, what must be done to rectify the situation. Such a decision is binding: see Convention, Art. 34.4.

Though the court cannot annul a national statute and has no formal power to enforce its decisions, these are in both legal and practical terms binding upon the defendant state: see Article 53 of the Convention. The state will, if necessary, be obliged to amend its law to accord with the court's ruling. Thus in Ireland the Scheme of Civil Legal Aid and Advice (which is set out in a White Paper: Prl. 8543) owes its origins to the court's decision in *Airey* v. *Ireland* (1979) 2 E.H.R.R. 305, referred to above.

The institutions discussed, it should be noted, have nothing to do with the European Communities (EEC, etc.). They operate under the aegis of the Council of Europe—a body with a much wider membership (including, *e.g.* the Scandinavian countries) than the Communities.

Membership of the European Communities

By signing the Treaty of Accession in 1972 Ireland undertook to become a member of the European Communities—*i.e.* the Coal and Steel Community, the Economic Community, and the Atomic Energy Community. Because of the legal structure of these entities this was more than the signing of an international agreement; it had the character of subscribing to an external constitution,[19] almost as if the State was joining a federation. Consequently it entailed not merely changes in domestic law but in the Constitution itself—hence the new Article 29.4.3°, inserted, following a referendum, by the Third Amendment of the Constitution Act 1972.

The new sub-section began by providing that the State could become a member of the Communities, which were specified by name. But this, as will appear, would have been insufficient. Thus it went on to state that:

> "No provision of this Constitution invalidates laws enacted, acts done or measures adopted by the State necessitated by the obligations of membership of the Communities or prevents laws enacted, acts done or

---

[19] The constitution of the Communities is to be found in a series of treaties. The foundation documents are the 1951 European Coal and Steel Community Treaty and the 1957 European Economic Community and European Atomic Energy Community Treaties. Those have subsequently been amended, most notably by the Merger Treaty of 1985 (creating common institutions for the three Communities) and the Single European Act of 1986. In February 1992

measures adopted by the Communities, or institutions thereof, from having the force of law in the State."

The need for so comprehensive an amendment lies in the nature of the Communities (which are governed by a single Council of Ministers, Commission, Parliament and Court).[20] The Council of Ministers and Commission have power, in accordance with the Treaties' provisions, *inter alia* to make regulations. A regulation is "binding in its entirety and directly applicable in all member States" (Art. 189, EEC Treaty). Thus a regulation promulgated in Brussels immediately becomes part of Irish domestic law, and may be relied upon in any relevant proceedings before an Irish court. This would have been quite incompatible with Article 15's vesting of the sole and exclusive power of making laws for the State in the Oireachtas, and its trenchant declaration that no other legislative authority has such power. But Article 29.4.3° was effective to remove any difficulty on that score.

It was equally effective to remove a difficulty which would have arisen in regard to the European Court of Justice.[21] Article 177, EEC Treaty grants that court jurisdiction to give "preliminary rulings" *inter alia* on the interpretation of the Treaties and the validity and interpretation of acts of Community institutions—such as regulations or directives issued by the Council or Commission. It goes on to empower a national court[22] before which such a question is raised to request a preliminary ruling from the European Court.[23] Finally, Article 177 *obliges* a court before which such a matter is raised to bring it before the European Court, if that national court is one "against whose decisions there is no judicial remedy under national law." One effect of this is to oblige the Supreme Court to send questions of EC law to the Luxembourg court: though the obligation is not quite absolute—see the European Court's judgment in Case 283/81, *CILFIT* v. *Ministry of Health* [1982] E.C.R. 3415. Such an obligation might well have run counter to Article 34 of the Constitution, especially—though not exclusively—the declaration that "the decision of the Supreme Court shall in all cases be final and conclusive" (Art. 34.4.6°). In passing, it may be noted that the Article 177 obligation is by no means confined to the Supreme Court: it would also apply to the High Court, and the Circuit Court, when hearing certain appeals.

Similarly, the Constitution's international relations provisions might have

another amending instrument—the European Union Treaty—was signed in Maastricht. Like the earlier amendments it will come into force "after being ratified by all the Member States in accordance with their respective constitutional requirements": Art. 236, EEC Treaty.

[20] On these institutions see Bryan McMahon and Finbarr Murphy, *European Community Law in Ireland* (Dublin 1989), Chap. 4; T. C. Hartley, *The Foundations of European Community Law* (2nd ed., Oxford 1988), Chaps. 1 and 2; D. Lasok and J. W. Bridge, *Law and Institutions of the European Communities* (5th ed., London 1991), Chaps. 5–9.

[21] The European Court of Justice is properly regarded as having a constitutional jurisdiction analogous to that of the High Court and Supreme Court: see Ole Due, "A Constitutional Court for the European Communities" in Deirdre Curtin and David O'Keeffe (eds.), *Constitutional Adjudication in European Community Law and National Law: Essays for the Hon. Mr. Justice T. F. O'Higgins* (Dublin 1992), p. 3; F. G. Jacobs, "Is the Court of Justice of the European Communities a Constitutional Court?" in *ibid.*, p. 25; Donal Barrington, "The Emergence of a Constitutional Court" in James O'Reilly (ed.), *Human Rights and Constitutional Law: Essays in Honour of Brian Walsh* (Dublin 1992), p. 251.

[22] Or a tribunal such as the Labour Court or Employment Appeals Tribunal.

[23] Whether such a request is made is a matter for the national court's discretion; the parties to the action are not entitled to *demand* that it be made.

presented an obstacle. The Communities can in certain fields enter into treaty obligations which bind the member States (see Art. 228, EEC Treaty). This might not have been compatible with Article 29.4.1°, which vests the executive power of the State in regard to foreign relations in the Government though perhaps Article 29.4.2°, designed to cover continuing Commonwealth membership, might have been prayed in aid.

Constitutional barriers having been removed by Article 29.4.3°, the Oireachtas passed the European Communities Act 1972. The key provision is section 3:

> "From the 1st day of January, 1973, the treaties governing the European Communities and the existing and future acts adopted by the institutions of those Communities shall be binding on the State and shall be part of the domestic law thereof under the conditions laid down in those treaties."

This is plainly effective to incorporate into Irish domestic law not only the Treaties but all existing and future regulations, directives, etc., as well as judgments of the Court of Justice.[24] It follows that a litigant before an Irish court may invoke appropriate provisions of the Treaties—*e.g.* to challenge the validity of legislative measures not in conformity therewith—a consequence which the European Court had in any event held to flow from the nature of the Communities: Case 26/62 *Van Gend en Loos* v. *Netherlands Fiscal Administration* [1963] E.C.R. 1. An accidental result is to extend the jurisdiction of the District and Circuit Courts. By virtue of Article 34.3.1° of the Constitution, those courts may not rule on the constitutionality of post-1937 statutes—but they are now entitled to hold statutes of any vintage inconsistent with European law. This follows from the European Court's decision in Case 106/77, *Amministrazione delle Finanze dello Stato* v. *Simmenthal* [1978] E.C.R. 629.

In addition to the power to make regulations, the Treaties give the Council of Ministers and Commission power to issue directives (Art. 189, EEC Treaty). These are binding, as to the result to be achieved, on each member State, but the means of achieving that result are left to the choice of the national authorities. Thus each government may decide for itself whether to implement a directive by statute or secondary legislation.[25] The European Communities Acts 1972 and 1973 provide one mechanism for implementing directives by empowering any Minister to make regulations for that purpose. It should be noted that the Court of Justice has held that directives may, if certain conditions are satisfied, have direct effect in the legal systems of the member States—*i.e.* may shape the relations between member States and

---

[24] On the impact of European Community law in the domestic legal order, see McMahon and Murphy, *op. cit.*, *passim*; Madeleine Reid, *The Impact of Community Law on the Irish Constitution* (Dublin 1990); Anthony M. Collins and James O'Reilly, "The Application of Community Law in Ireland 1973–1989" (1990) 27 C.M.L.R. 315.

[25] Administrative action—such as issuing a circular—will not do; the directive must be implemented by transposing its terms into national law as binding provisions: Case 102/79, *Commission* v. *Belgium* [1980] E.C.R. 1473 and Case 145/82, *Commission* v. *Italy* [1983] E.C.R. 711. See also *Browne* v. *An Bord Pleanála* [1989] I.L.R.M. 865, where Barron J. held that a directive on environmental matters had not been properly implemented by a circular sent by the Department of the Environment to the planning authorities. See further G. W. Hogan, "Legal Status of Administrative Rules and Circulars" (1987) XXII *Irish Jurist* (n.s.) 194.

individuals and be capable of being invoked before national courts: Case 41/ 74, *Van Duyn* v. *Home Office* [1974] E.C.R. 1337.[26]

Although the Treaties do not contain fundamental rights provisions akin to those of Bunreacht na hÉireann, the European Court has often said that such fundamental rights are part of the Communities' law. Those rights, the court has indicated, may be drawn from two sources—the constitutional traditions of the member States, and the European Convention on Human Rights.[27] This has an interesting consequence, described thus by Dr. Temple Lang:

> " . . . the result of its (the European Court's) case law is that, *at least in the sphere of directly applicable Community law, the provisions of the Convention are, in effect, now a part of Irish law.* The European Convention can now be relied on in Irish courts, in the Community sphere, almost as if it had been enacted into Irish law."[28]

The European Parliament is basically a consultative rather than a legislative assembly. The Council of Ministers is not collectively responsible to it— though it has power to sack the Commission. However, the Parliament's role in the Community law-making process was enhanced by the Single European Act of 1986, and will be further expanded when the Maastricht Treaty comes into force. Originally nominated, its members are now directly elected. Ireland has 15 seats which are allocated among constituencies specified by statute. The rules governing elections are broadly similar to those for Dáil elections, though in Assembly elections both Irish citizens and nationals of any other member state may vote.[29]

---

[26] National courts must not allow member states to take advantage of their own failure to implement directives by pleading such an omission in a defence to a claim. Instead they must "disapply" any conflicting provisions of national law—provided that the conditions for direct effect are satisfied: Case 148/78, *Pubblico Ministero* v. *Ratti* [1979] E.C.R. 1629: Case 286/85, *McDermott and Cotter* v. *Minister for Social Welfare* [1987] E.C.R. 1453. Moreover, the European Court of Justice has held that national courts may hold member states liable in damages for non-implementation of directives—*whether they have direct effect or not*—at the instance of persons suffering loss through such inaction: Joined Cases C–6/90 and C–9/90, *Francovich and Bonifaci* v. *Italy* (November 19, 1991). See Deirdre Curtin, "State Liability under Community Law: A New Remedy for Private Parties" (1992) *Industrial Law Journal* 74. Note too that when the Maastricht Treaty enters into force the European Court of Justice, at the instance of the Commission, will be able to impose a "lump sum or penalty payment" on a member state found not to have fulfilled an obligation under the Treaties—such as implementing a directive: Art. 171, as substituted.

[27] Note the brief reference to the European Convention on Human Rights in the preamble to the Single European Act; also Title I, Art. F(2) of the 1992 Maastricht Treaty: "The Union shall respect fundamental rights, as guaranteed by the European Convention for the Protection of Human Rights and Fundamental Freedoms signed in Rome on 4 November 1950 and as they result from the constitutional traditions common to the Member States, as general principles of Community law."

[28] John Temple Lang, "European Community Law, Irish Law and the Irish Legal Profession" (1983) 5 D.U.L.J. (n.s.) 1, 3 (italics in original). See also his essay "The Widening Scope of Constitutional Law" in Curtin and O'Keeffe, *op. cit.* n.19 *supra*, p. 229.

[29] See the European Assembly Elections Acts 1977–1984. Note that Art. 88(2) of the Maastricht Treaty provides that " . . . every citizen of the Union [*i.e.* everyone who is a national of a member state] residing in a Member State of which he is not a national shall have the right to vote and to stand as a candidate in elections to the European Parliament in the Member State in which he resides, under the same conditions as nationals of that State." There is, however, provision for derogations where warranted by problems specific to a member state.

Article 29.4.3°—6°

As originally enacted,[30] Article 29.4.3° did three things. Firstly, it permitted the State to join the European Communities. This "licence to join," as it
has been called,[31] did not merely sanction adherence to the Communities as
they existed in 1973. It authorised the State—without further constitutional
amendment—to join in amendments of the founding treaties so long as these
did not alter the essential scope or objectives of the Communities. The
Supreme Court so held in *Crotty* v. *An Taoiseach* [1987] I.R. 713, where Finlay
C.J., giving the judgment of the court, said (at 767):

> "To hold that the first sentence of Article 29, s.4, subs. 3 does not auth-
> orise any form of amendment to the Treaties after 1973 without a further
> amendment of the Constitution would be too narrow a construction; to
> construe it as an open-ended authority to agree, without further amend-
> ment of the Constitution, to any amendment of the Treaties would be
> too broad."

The court concluded that the amendments effected by the Single European
Act—and incorporated into the domestic law by the European Communities
(Amendment) Act 1986—were within the scope of the authorisation given by
Article 29.4.3°. It is clear, however, that fundamental changes in the Com-
munities' objectives,[32] or decision-making processes,[33] would require a fresh

---

[30] Following the Eleventh Amendment of the Constitution Act 1992 the original Article 29.4.3°
was amended, and three new subsections were added to Article 29.4. Thus the text now reads:
> "3° The State may become a member of the European Coal and Steel Community
> (established by Treaty signed at Paris on the 18th day of April, 1951), the Euro-
> pean Economic Community (established by Treaty signed at Rome on the 25th
> day of March, 1957) and the European Atomic Energy Community (established
> by Treaty signed at Rome on the 25th day of March, 1957). The State may ratify
> the Single European Act (signed on behalf of the Member States of the Communi-
> ties at Luxembourg on the 17th day of February, 1986, and at The Hague on the
> 28th day of February, 1986).
> 4° The State may ratify the Treaty on European Union signed at Maastricht on the
> 7th day of February, 1992, and may become a member of that Union.
> 5° No provision of this Constitution invalidates laws enacted, acts done or measures
> adopted by the State which are necessitated by the obligations of membership of
> the European Union or of the Communities, or prevents laws enacted, acts done or
> measures adopted by the European Union or by the Communities or by institu-
> tions thereof, or by bodies competent under the Treaties establishing the Commu-
> nities from having the force of the law in the State.
> 6° The State may ratify the Agreement relating to Community Patents drawn up
> between the Member States of the Communities and done at Luxembourg on the
> 15th day of December, 1989."
[31] By Barrington J. in *Crotty* v. *An Taoiseach* [1987] I.R. 713, at 756.
[32] Finlay C.J., delivering the Supreme Court's judgment in *Crotty* v. *An Taoiseach* [1987] I.R. 713,
said (at 767): "It is the opinion of the Court that the first sentence in Article 29, s.4, subs. 3 of
the Constitution must be construed as an authorisation given to the State not only to join the
Communities as they stood in 1973, but also to join in amendments of the Treaties *so long as
such amendments do not alter the essential scope or objectives of the Communities.*" (Italics supplied).
Finlay C.J., speaking for himself, also stated (at 771) that if the Communities developed from
an economic into a political union, Irish adherence thereto would require a constitutional
amendment. This view was shared by Walsh J. (at 776) and Griffin J. (at 789).
[33] As regards the Council of Ministers' decision-making process, the SEA substituted voting by
qualified majority for the previous unanimity requirement in some instances. In *Crotty* v. *An
Taoiseach* [1987] I.R. 713 the Supreme Court, *per* Finlay C.J., said of this (at 770): " . . . it is
the opinion of the Court that neither the proposed changes from unanimity to qualified

constitutional amendment, and it was accepted from an early stage that this would apply to the Maastricht Treaty. This is hardly surprising, since that treaty contemplates *inter alia* " . . . monetary union, ultimately including a single currency . . . " and " . . . the implementation of a common foreign and security policy including the eventual framing of a common defence policy, which might in time lead to a common defence."[34] Aspirational though some of this language may sound, the Supreme Court's decision in *Crotty* v. *An Taoiseach* [1987] I.R. 713 on Title III of the Single European Act (see *infra*) could admit of no doubt that a constitutional amendment was necessary to permit Irish ratification of a treaty containing it.

The second effect of the original Article 29.4.3° was to remove any constitutional barrier which might prevent " . . . laws enacted, acts done or measures adopted by the Communities, or institutions thereof, from having the force of law in the State." As already noted, this cleared the constitutional path for the direct applicability of Community regulations, and for the incorporation into domestic law of directives, decisions and rulings of the European Court of Justice. It follows that these "laws enacted, acts done or measures adopted" by Community institutions cannot be made the subject of a constitutional challenge in the Irish courts—provided that they are validly enacted, done or adopted. But even if their validity is impugned—*i.e.* it is argued that they are *ultra vires* the treaties—Irish courts may not *finally* rule on this issue. For such matters fall exclusively within the jurisdiction of the European Court of Justice in Luxembourg,[35] as that court itself made abundantly clear in Case 314/85, *Foto-Frost* v. *Hauptzollamt Lübeck-Ost* [1987] E.C.R. 4199.[36] This was accepted by Murphy J. in the High Court in *Lawlor* v. *Minister for Agriculture* [1990] 1 I.R. 356—a case involving both EC and national regulations—where he said (at 378):

> " . . . it is no part of the function of this court to determine whether or not any part of the EEC regulations is invalid . . . "

Any challenge to those regulations in the instant proceedings, Murphy J. recognised, would require a reference to the Luxembourg court under Article 177 of the EEC Treaty.

The third effect of the original Article 29.4.3° was to relax any constitutional restrictions that might invalidate " . . . laws enacted, acts done or measures adopted by the State necessitated by the obligations of membership of the Communities . . . " The crucial word here is, obviously, "necessit-

---

majority . . . bring these proposed amendments outside the scope of authorisation contained in Article 29, s.4, subs. 3 of the Constitution. *As far as Ireland is concerned, it does not follow that all other decisions of the Council which now require unanimity could, without a further amendment of the Constitution, be changed to decisions requiring less than unanimity.*" (Italics supplied). It would follow that any proposal to move from unanimity to qualified majority for admission of new member states would require a constitutional amendment. (The Maastricht Treaty proposes no change in this regard: see Title VII Article O.)

[34] Title I, Art. B.

[35] Article 173, EEC Treaty provides: "The Court of Justice shall review the legality of acts of the Council and Commission other than recommendations or opinions . . . " Art. 177 provides: "The Court of Justice shall have jurisdiction to give preliminary rulings concerning: . . . (b) the validity . . . of acts of the institutions of the Community."

[36] The court stressed that the unity of the Community's legal order would be jeopardised by divergent views in the courts of the member states on the validity of Community Acts.

ated." In its overall context—especially the phrase "obligations of membership"—this conveys the idea of something imperatively required, or made
mandatory, by such membership. It would not appear sufficient that Community membership makes what has been done "convenient" or "desirable."[37] Walsh J., writing extra-curially in 1987, said[38]:

> "What are the acts or measures "necessitated by the obligations of
> membership of the Communities" or "laws enacted, acts done or
> measures adopted by the Communities or institutions thereof"? Surely
> only matters which can be made the subject of a regulation or a direct-
> ive, apart from the express provisions of the Treaties, can be regarded as
> laws, acts or measures necessitated by membership of the Communities.
> Indeed this view was confirmed during a Judicial Conference by mem-
> bers of the Court of Justice when they visited Ireland in June 1978 to
> confer with the judges of the Supreme Court and the High Court."

But Murphy J. adopted a broader interpretation of "necessitated" in *Lawlor* v. *Minister for Agriculture* [1990] 1 I.R. 356, where he said (at 377):

> " . . . the word "necessitated" [in the original Article 29.4.3°] could not
> be limited in its construction to laws, acts or measures all of which
> required in all of their parts to be enacted, done or adopted by the obli-
> gations of membership of the Community . . . the word 'necessitated' in
> this context must extend to and include acts or measures which are con-
> sequent upon membership of the Community and in general fulfilment
> of the obligations of such membership, and even where there may be a
> choice or degree of discretion vested in the State as to the particular
> manner in which it would meet the general spirit of its obligations of
> membership."

This highlights the difficulty that a directive, though binding as to the result
to be achieved, may sometimes concede member states a considerable
measure of discretion as to attaining the desired end. Nonetheless, as Gerard
Hogan has observed, Murphy J.'s broad interpretation of "necessitated" flies
in the face of the parliamentary history of what became the original Article
29.4.3°.[39]

In *Greene* v. *Minister for Agriculture* [1990] 2 I.R. 17 Murphy J. repeated his
observations in *Lawlor's* case, and continued (at 25):

> "I have no doubt but that laws enacted, acts done and measures
> adopted by the State are necessitated within the meaning of the Third
> Amendment [the original Article 29.4.3°] even where the particular

---

[37] Thus if the regulation-making powers conferred on Ministers by the European Communities
Acts 1972 and 1973 violate the non-delegation of legislative power doctrine, they would not be
saved by Article 29.4.3°. See further Gerard Hogan and David Morgan, *Administrative Law in
Ireland* (2nd ed., London 1991), pp. 16–19: Anthony Whelan, "Article 29.4.3° and the meaning of 'Necessity' " (1992) 2 *Irish Student Law Review* 60.

[38] Brian Walsh, "Reflections on the Effects of Membership of the European Communities in
Irish Law" in F. Capotorti *et al.* (eds.) *Du Droit International au Droit de L'integration: Liber Amicorum Pierre Pescatore (Baden-Baden 1987)*, p. 805.

[39] G. W. Hogan, "The Supreme Court and the Single European Act" (1987) XXII *Irish Jurist*
(n.s.) 55, 59–62.

actions of the State involve a measure of choice, selection or discretion. If there were no such flexibility it would hardly be necessary to say that the particular actions were adopted by the State at all. Presumably they would have operated as a Community regulation rather than as a direct-ive by it."

Perhaps the true situation is that where the State implements a directive which permits a choice between methods A, B and C, the method *actually chosen* is immune from constitutional challenge. But matters would be differ-ent if the terms of the directive conferred a much wider discretion. This seems to be accepted by Murphy J. in *Greene's* case when he says (at 25):

" . . . there must be a point at which the discretion exercised by the State or the national authority is so far-reaching or so detached from the result to be achieved by the directive that it cannot be said to have been "necessitated" by it . . . It does seem to me that the word 'necessitated' as used in Article 29, s.4, subs. 3 involves questions of degrees of necess-ity or at least limits to discretion."

Greene v. *Minister for Agriculture* [1990] 2 I.R. 17 concerned schemes made by the Minister in pursuance of Council Directive 75/268/EEC, which dealt with mountain and hill farming. It authorised member states to introduce the special system of aids provided for in its Article 4. These were annual headage payments, to be fixed by member states subject to minimum and maximum amounts stipulated in the directive. Article 6.2 provided:

"Member States may lay down additional or restrictive conditions for granting the compensatory allowance."

The Ministerial schemes took advantage of this by inserting a means test; they would benefit only farmers whose off-farm income combined with that of their spouses did not exceed a specified amount. This was impugned by the plaintiffs, *inter alia* on the ground that it treated married couples less favourably than unmarried couples living together, thus violating the State's constitutional pledge to " . . . guard with special care the institution of Mar-riage, on which the Family is founded, and to protect it against attack" (Article 41.3.1°).[40] Murphy J. held that these provisions of the schemes were not protected by Article 29.4.3°; hence they were open to constitutional chal-lenge, to which they proved vulnerable.

The final question relating to what is now Article 29.4.5° is—who has authority to interpret it? Judicial *dicta* are quite clear that the answer is: only the Irish courts. In *S.P.U.C. (Ireland) Ltd.* v. *Grogan* [1989] I.R. 753 Walsh J. (Hederman J. concurring) said (at 768–769):

"In the last analysis only this Court can decide finally what are the effects of the interaction of the 8th Amendment of the Constitution [Article 40.3.3°[41]] and the 3rd Amendment of the Constitution [the orig-inal Article 29.4.3°]."

---

[40] See further Chap. 17 *infra*.
[41] Which provides: "The State acknowledges the right to life of the unborn and, with due regard to the equal right to life of the mother, guarantees in its laws to respect, and, as far as practi-cable, by its laws to defend and vindicate that right."

And McCarthy J. said (at 770):

> "The sole authority for the construction of the Constitution lies in the Irish courts, the final authority being this Court."[42]

But these statements were made in the context of a possible conflict between Community law and the Constitution on the subject of abortion, the question being one of a possible collision between the original Article 29.4.3° and the "pro-life" guarantee of the subsequently-enacted Article 40.3.3°. In certain other situations the construction of what is now Article 29.4.5° by the Supreme Court might well require a reference to the Luxembourg court under Article 177. For the question whether a domestic measure is necessitated by the obligations of Community membership could well involve difficult questions of interpreting the Treaties, and/or other Community legal measures. Article 177 makes it clear that such matters fall within the jurisdiction of the European Court of Justice, and that a court such as the Supreme Court[43] is obliged to refer such matters to it. Thus while the Supreme Court would have the last word it would not seem able to "go it alone".

Crotty v. *An Taoiseach*: The Decision

The second sentence of the present Article 29.4.3°—added by the Tenth Amendment of the Constitution Act 1987—reads as follows:

> "The State may ratify the Single European Act (signed on behalf of the Member States of the Communities at Luxembourg on the 17th day of February, 1986, and at the Hague on the 28th day of February, 1986.)"

The necessity for this amendment sprang from the majority decision of the Supreme Court in *Crotty* v. *An Taoiseach* [1987] I.R. 713, arguably the most significant, and certainly one of the most controversial, of its decisions.

In that case the plaintiff argued that, absent a fresh constitutional amendment, the State lacked power to ratify the Single European Act (SEA). This measure—an amendment of the EC treaties—consisted of a preamble and four Titles, of which the most important were Titles II and III. The former amended the existing EC Treaties in a number of ways[44]; the latter introduced a new system of European co-operation in the field of foreign policy.

---

[42] This view also has the extra-curial support of O'Higgins J.: "Should a question arise as to whether a particular measure is . . . 'necessitated' it would seem to me to be one exclusively for the High Court under the provisions of Article 34.3.2° of the Constitution. I cannot see on what basis jurisdiction to decide what is, essentially, a question as to the validity of a law having regard to the Constitution, can be conferred on or exercised by any other court." See T. F. O'Higgins, "The Constitution and the Communities—Scope for Stress?" in James O'Reilly (ed.), *Human Rights and Constitutional Law: Essays in Honour of Brian Walsh* (Dublin 1992), p. 229.

[43] The relevant portions of Art. 177 provide: "The Court of Justice shall have jurisdiction to give preliminary rulings concerning:
  (a) the interpretation of this Treaty;
  (b) the validity and interpretation of acts of the institutions of the Community . . .
Where any such question is raised in a case pending before a court or tribunal of a Member State, against whose decisions there is no judicial remedy under national law, that court or tribunal shall bring the matter before the Court of Justice."

[44] *E.g.* by providing that the Council of Ministers could, at the request of the Court of Justice, create a new Court of First Instance with limited jurisdiction (Title II, Chap. I): by changing, in six instances, the decision-making process of the Council of Ministers by substituting a qualified majority for the previous unanimity requirement (*ibid.*, Chap. II): and by inserting

On December 10, 1986 Dáil Éireann approved the SEA, pursuant to
Article 29.5.2° of the Constitution.[45] Shortly thereafter the Oireachtas
enacted the European Communities (Amendment) Act 1986, to make the
SEA—though *not* Title III thereof—part of the domestic law of the State.[46]
In the Government's view these measures set the stage for Irish ratification of
the SEA, which under its Article 33.1 was to be done by depositing an instrument of ratification with the Italian government. The requisite instrument
had been sealed by the President and was ready for deposit, when such
action was restrained by an interlocutory injunction granted by Barrington J.
on Christmas Eve 1986.[47]

The plaintiff's claim for a permanent injunction came on before a divisional court—Hamilton P., Barrington and Carroll JJ.—in mid-January
1987. The court, in a lengthy judgment *per* Barrington J., dismissed the claim
and discharged the interlocutory injunction. The plaintiff immediately
appealed to the Supreme Court, which continued the injunction pending a
final hearing.[48]

As indicated above, the Supreme Court, in a single judgment,[49] rejected
the plaintiff's claim insofar as it asserted the constitutional invalidity of the
European Communities (Amendment) Act 1986. But by a 3:2 majority—
Walsh, Henchy and Hederman JJ.; Finlay C.J. and Griffin J. dissenting—the
court upheld his claim that Title III of the SEA could not be ratified without
a new constitutional amendment.

Title III of the SEA[50] provided that EC member states should " . . .
endeavour jointly to formulate and implement a European foreign policy"
(Article 30.1). It called for information and consultation on foreign policy
matters of general interest, and for due consideration of the desirability of
adopting and implementing common European positions. To increase their
capacity for joint action in the foreign policy field, the member states were to
" . . . ensure that common principles and objectives are gradually developed
and defined" (Article 30.2(*c*)), and the determination of such common positions was to " . . . constitute a point of reference . . . " for their policies

---

new provisions giving the Community competence in the fields, *inter alia*, of social policy,
research and technological development, and the environment (*ibid.*, subsections III, V and
VI).

[45] Which provides: "The State shall not be bound by any international agreement involving a
charge upon public funds unless the terms of the agreement shall have been approved by Dáil
Éireann." Two points of interest arise in this connection. Firstly, the Government had been
advised by the Attorney General that Dáil approval of the entire Single European Act was
constitutionally necessary. The correctness of this view is attested to in *Crotty v. An Taoiseach*
[1987] I.R. 713, *per* Walsh J. (at 780) and Griffin J. (at 790). Secondly, the Opposition moved
to attach to the Dáil's approval a declaration on Irish neutrality. The Attorney General
advised the Government (a) that such a qualified approval might raise constitutional problems under Article 29.5.2° (b) that, in addition, it might create legal confusion in relation to
the status of the Irish ratification (see 370 *Dáil Debs.*, cc. 2356–2357, December 10, 1986, *per*
the Minister for Foreign Affairs, Mr. Peter Barry T.D.).

[46] In particular by amending the key phrase in the European Communities Acts 1972–1985—
"treaties governing the European Communities"—to include the relevant provisions of the
SEA.

[47] Following a 2-day hearing at the judge's home: see [1987] I.R. 713, 718–735.

[48] [1987] I.R. 713, 761–763.

[49] Since the European Communities (Amendment) Act 1986 was a post-constitution Act, the
"one-opinion rule" of Article 34.4.5° applied.

[50] Which will be repealed when the Maastricht Treaty enters into force, and replaced by that
instrument's Title V: Provisions on a Common Foreign and Security Policy.

(*ibid.*). Title III also established the political and administrative arrangements for this "European Political Cooperation," with a secretariat based in
Brussels.

The view of the Supreme Court majority was, as indicated, that Title III
could not be ratified by the State in the absence of a constitutional amendment.[51] Walsh, Henchy and Hederman JJ. concluded that the Constitution,
especially in Articles 1 and 5,[52] enshrined *full* sovereignty in foreign affairs—
a sovereignty which the Government, in conducting those affairs, was bound
to respect. Under Article 28.2 its power to conduct those affairs was ". . .
subject to the provisions of this Constitution . . . "; thus the Government
lacked authority to qualify or restrict that sovereignty in the manner envisaged by Title III. Nor could Title III be saved by arguing that it did little
more than formalise existing practices and procedures. It was a binding
international treaty which was not static in its terms, and which went beyond
existing arrangements.[53] And in response to the contention that the courts
could not interfere with the exercise of the Government's treaty-making
power, the Supreme Court majority stated that intervention *was* permissible
here, given the courts' function of upholding the primacy of the Constitution.[54]

Crotty v. *An Taoiseach*: The Aftermath

One result of *Crotty's* case was to embarrass two administrations of differing political complexions—the Fine Gael/Labour coalition which signed the
SEA and its Fianna Fáil successor. For the case had a twofold consequence:
(a) the State could not ratify the SEA without a new constitutional amendment (b) the necessary delay in holding a referendum delayed the coming
into operation of the SEA throughout the European Community.[55]

---

[51] All five judges seem to have agreed that adherence to the SEA could not be an obligation
necessitated by membership of the European Communities, so as to attract the protection of
the original Art. 29.4.3° of the Constitution. Finlay C.J. (at 771), Walsh J. (at 780) and
Henchy J. (at 784) stated this explicitly, and Griffin and Hederman JJ. must be taken as having accepted it implicitly.

[52] Art. 1 provides: "The Irish nation hereby affirms its inalienable, indefeasible, and sovereign
right to choose its own form of Government, to determine its relations with other nations, and
to develop its life, political, economic and cultural in accordance with its own genius and traditions." Art. 5 provides: "Ireland is a sovereign, independent, democratic state."

[53] Finlay C.J. and Griffin J., dissenting, denied that Title III obliged the State to cede any sovereignty or national interest in the foreign policy sphere, or give other EC member states a veto
on Irish foreign policy decisions. (Griffin J. laid particular emphasis on the repeated use in
Title III of the word "endeavour.") Nothing in the Constitution ruled out arrangements for
consultation and discussion of foreign policy issues.

[54] Distinguishing *Boland* v. *An Taoiseach* [1974] I.R. 338, where the Supreme Court had refused
to grant an injunction restraining the executive from implementing the Sunningdale Agreement of 1974, which the plaintiff had alleged to be in contravention of Arts. 2 and 3 of the
Constitution. The *ratio* of that decision, as Walsh J. pointed out in *Crotty's* case (at 779–780)
seems to have been that the Sunningdale Agreement was not an agreement or treaty, but
merely a declaration of policy and hence not restrainable.

[55] In consequence of Art. 236, EEC Treaty, which provides that amendments to the foundation
treaties come into force only " . . . after being ratified by all the Member States in accordance
with their respective constitutional requirements." See further John Temple Lang, "The
Irish Court Case which delayed the Single European Act" (1987) 24 *C.M.L.R.* 709: Kieran
Bradley, "The Referendum on the Single European Act" (1987) 12 *Eur. Law Rev.* 301. It is
not clear, however, why an international agreement finalised in February 1986 was not
brought before the Dáil until December 10 of that year.

The shock apparently generated by the *Crotty* decision is evidenced in the Dáil debates on the Tenth Amendment of the Constitution Bill 1987.[56] It was suggested that the line between executive and judicial power had been blurred, with the result that no one could be certain about the constitutional limits on the Government's power to conduct international relations. These criticisms, though inflated by a certain amount of rhetoric, nonetheless contained a kernel of truth. For the decision could raise questions about the validity of the State's adherence to the United Nations Charter[57] and, perhaps, its acceptance of the European Convention on Human Rights.[58]

The plaintiffs in *McGimpsey* v. *Ireland* [1990] 1 I.R. 110 founded principally upon *Crotty's* case in their assault on the Anglo-Irish Agreement of 1985. That instrument, they contended, was invalid in that it flouted Articles 2 and 3 of Bunreacht na hÉireann, and that it unconstitutionally fettered the executive in its conduct of international relations under Articles 28 and 29 of the Constitution. The Supreme Court unanimously repelled these objections, holding that though Articles 2 and 3 made re-integration of the national territory a constitutional imperative, the Anglo-Irish Agreement did not run afoul of this.[59] Nor had the executive unconstitutionally fettered its power to conduct the State's international relations; the analogy sought to be drawn between the Anglo-Irish Agreement and the Single European Act was misconceived.[60]

Neutrality

Ireland, as is well known, did not participate militarily in the Second World War—though as that conflict progressed its neutrality became definitely more *nuancé*.[61] Since that time the State has professed itself neutral—a notion that at times savours of the theological *mysterium tremendens*. In contrast with Austrian, Swedish or Swiss neutrality, Irish neutrality is not enshrined

---

[56] See 371 *Dáil Debs.*, c. 2195 (April 22, 1987) where the Taoiseach, Mr. Haughey, said; " . . . the judgments in so far as they affect the boundaries between executive and judicial areas of responsibility have caused widespread surprise"; c. 2216, where Mr. Peter Barry T.D. quoted these words and added: "Certainly that is true . . . "; c. 2240, where Mr. Dick Spring T.D. said: " . . . the judgments of the majority of the Supreme Court in the Crotty case have exploded our traditional understanding [of Article 29.4.1°]." Mr. Spring also observed (at c. 2248): " . . . that decision establishes a new summit in the range of judicial activism . . . This majority decision was surprising because of its novelty. The traditional view of the Constitution whereby external relations were a matter for the Government subject to the supervision of the Dáil can no longer pass muster." See, too, the comments of the then Attorney General—Peter Sutherland S.C., "Twin Perspectives: an Attorney General views Political and European Dimensions" in Brian Farrell, *De Valera's Constitution and Ours* (Dublin 1988), p. 185.

[57] See G. W. Hogan, "The Supreme Court and the Single European Act" (1987) XXII *Irish Jurist* (*n.s.*) 55, at 69.

[58] Under this the State has pledged itself to safeguard a series of rights the content of which is ultimately determined by the European Court of Human Rights. *Quaere* whether this might imply an illegitimate surrender of sovereignty?

[59] See further Chap. 2 *supra*.

[60] On the ground that that the SEA—unlike the Agreement—could oblige the Government in conducting foreign policy to subordinate the State's national interests to those of other member states: [1990] 1 I.R. 110, 122.

[61] On Irish cooperation with the Allied powers see Ronan Fanning, *Independent Ireland* (Dublin 1983), pp. 123–125.

in the Constitution, in the law or in a international agreement.[62] And the definition of the concept by the larger political parties seems to depend upon whether they are in government or in opposition—so much so that Professor Chubb has written of " . . . the shibboleths associated with the concept of neutrality Irish-style . . ."[63]

It seems clear that there is no constitutional barrier to the State's joining a military alliance. But implementing the terms of a particular alliance might well raise difficulties. As Michael McDowell S.C. has pointed out, Article 15.6.2° would appear to prohibit the maintenance of foreign forces or bases in the State.[64] And Article 28.3.1°,[65] when read in the light of *Crotty* v. *An Taoiseach* [1987] I.R. 713—he thought—would seem to underline:

" . . . the fact that the State cannot bind itself to become party to an armed conflict or war by way of a formal military alliance. Any international agreement which purported to bind Ireland to participate in a war, be it offensive or defensive in any prescribed circumstances in advance, would amount to an unlawful usurpation of a right vested in Dáil Éireann, a right which cannot be pledged away in advance."[66]

It is certainly possible to find treaties of military alliance which might commit the State in the way envisaged; the NATO treaty is an example. But it may be argued that unless any such treaty clearly and unmistakeably pledged the State to take *immediate* offensive action, its constitutionality, if challenged, would be upheld. For the presumption of constitutionality would surely apply,[67] with the consequent judicial assumption that the executive would necessarily observe the restrictions imposed on it by Bunreacht na hÉireann.

It is relevant to note also the possibility that the implementation of any

---

[62] See Patrick Keatinge, *A Singular Stance: Irish Neutrality in the 1980s* (Dublin 1984).
[63] Basil Chubb, *The Politics of the Constitution* (Dublin 1991), p. 114. Fanning, *op. cit.*, pp. 176–177 demonstrates how pragmatic, rather than principled, was Ireland's initial attitude to NATO membership.
[64] 371 *Dáil Debs.*, c. 2316 (April 22, 1987). Art. 15.6.2° provides: "No military or armed force, other than a military or armed force raised and maintained by the Oireachtas, shall be raised or maintained for any purpose whatever."
[65] Which provides: "War shall not be declared and the State shall not participate in any war save with the assent of Dáil Éireann." This provision was the subject of lively controversy during the 1991 Gulf War, when the question of granting U.S. forces involved in that conflict refuelling and transit facilities at Shannon seemed likely to arise. But the Taoiseach, Mr. Haughey, pointed out that no such requests had been received. If they were, and if they were granted, this—he said—would not breach Art. 28.3.1°. "[I]t would place an extraordinary strain on ordinary language if the mere granting of peripheral facilities could be interpreted as making Ireland a participant in the war"; 404 *Dáil Debs.*, c. 645 (January 18, 1991). In addition, the U.N. Security Council had authorised the use of military force against Iraq (Resolution 678 of November 29, 1990), and had requested all states to provide appropriate support. He concluded, therefore, that a decision to grant such facilities, if requested, would be a policy decision in the field of external relations, which Article 29.4.1° authorised the Government to make and which did not require Dáil assent: *ibid.*, c. 646. The Minister for Foreign Affairs, Mr. Collins, had earlier stated that the Attorney General had so advised: *The Irish Times*, January 16, 1991.
[66] 371 *Dáil Debs.*, c. 2316 (April 22, 1987). Note that defence treaties pose constitutional problems—still unresolved—as to the spheres of Presidential and Congressional authority under the U.S. constitution: see Laurence H. Tribe, *American Constitutional Law* (2nd ed., Mineola, N.Y. 1988), p. 233 ff.
[67] See further Chap. 11 *infra*.

treaty of military alliance might have to run another constitutional gauntlet—that of Article 29.1 and 2. For a state which

> " . . . affirms its devotion to the ideal of peace and friendly cooperation
> amongst nations founded on international justice and morality" (Article
> 29.1)

and

> . . . affirms its adherence to the principle of the pacific settlement of
> international disputes by international arbitration or judicial determi-
> nation" (Article 29.2)

could scarcely embark upon military adventures without satisfying itself that
all other avenues were closed.

9 The Separation of Powers

Article 6 of the Constitution speaks, in classical terms, of the "powers of government, legislative, executive and judicial." Were that its sole reference to the matter there might be no practical consequences; the separation of powers would be a philosophical concept only, its actual content subject to variation by statute. Later provisions, however, make the separation doctrine a real limitation on legislative power. Article 15.2.1° vests the law-making power in the Oireachtas. Articles 28.2 and 29.4.1° lodge the executive power—including that in regard to foreign relations—in the Government, and Articles 34.1. and 37 the judicial power in the courts.

This is not to say that the Constititution accepts the separation doctrine in anything like its purest form. In contrast with the United States Constitution, which separates the personnel of executive and legislature, Bunreacht na hÉireann insists that the former must be drawn from the latter. And though judges may not sit in parliament, they can play a role in the legislative proccess—*e.g.* by chairing commissions or committees on various issues. Further, the Constitution may be said to give the courts a legislative role, if only in a negative sense, by entrusting to them the power to declare legislation unconstitutional. Nonetheless, it remains true that in Ireland the separation of powers is more than a mere rule of political wisdom which must give way when expedience ("sound public policy") requires.[1]

THE LEGISLATIVE POWER

The Constitution vests the sole and exclusive power of making laws for the State in the Oireachtas: Article 15.2.1°. This clearly means that the Irish executive cannot, unlike its counterparts in some other states, claim any *inherent* law-making power.[2] Thus the United Kingdom concept of the prerogative Order in Council—which regulates *inter alia* the civil service[3]— would seeem to have no application in Ireland. To be valid, any instrument issued by the executive which purported to have legal effect would require to be founded in statute.

---

[1] Cp. the Report of the Committee on Ministers' Powers (1932), Cmnd. 4060, p. 95.

[2] Contrast the position in France where, long before Art. 37 of the 1958 Constitution, the executive was recognised as having an autonomous *pouvoir réglementaire*. See the decisions in *Heyries*, CE 28 juin 1918, Rec. 651 and *Labonne*, CE 8 août 1919, Rec. 737. On the position in Spain see Javier Perez Royo, *Las Fuentes del Derecho* (2nd ed., Madrid 1985), pp. 123–127.

[3] See *Council of Civil Service Unions* v. *Minister for the Civil Service* [1984] 3 All E.R. 935.

It is also clear from Article 15.2.1° that the executive cannot by *ipse dixit* suspend the operation of a statute. One had thought this proposition needed no authority[4] but the High Court found occasion to emphasise it in *Duggan* v. *An Taoiseach* [1989] I.L.R.M. 710. There the Farm Tax Act 1985 had established a special system of farmer taxation and a number of civil servants were temporarily promoted—potentially for a five year period—to carry out functions associated therewith. However, in his 1987 budget statement the Minister for Finance announced a policy change. Henceforward, he said, farmers would be made liable for income tax, the collection of farm tax would be halted and the 1985 Act would be repealed. Shortly thereafter all work in connection with farm tax ceased, and the appointments of the temporary staff were terminated with effect from December 31, 1987. But the 1985 Act still stood unrepealed. The plaintiffs (the temporary staff) sought, *inter alia*, a declaration that the decision to cease collecting the farm tax was invalid.

Hamilton P. held that it was. Citing Articles 15.2.1° and 28.2 of the Constitution, he concluded that it was exclusively for the Oireachtas to *make* laws and that the Government's task, as the executive, was to *enforce* them. He continued by observing that the key sections of the Act were mandatory—*e.g.* section 9:

> "There shall be charged, levied and paid for each year . . . a tax to be called farm tax."

And the 1985 Act still remained in effect. Hamilton P. went on ([1989] I.L.R.M. 710, 730):

> "Having reached the decision to cease levying the farm tax . . . it was perfectly open to the respondents as the Government of the State to introduce and to seek to have enacted legislation repealing the provisions of the Farm Tax Act 1985. This has not been done. Consequently, I am satisfied that the direction given by . . . the Government . . . was unlawful."[5]

It would seem to follow from the above that any decision by the Garda Síochána or the prosecuting authorities to cease enforcing a particular penal provision would be invalid. For statutes characteristically create criminal offences in mandatory terms ("It shall be an offence . . . "). This analysis finds support in a *dictum* of McCarthy J. in *Norris* v. *Att. Gen.* [1984] I.R. 36, at 81:

> " . . . the sections impugned are, subject to the constitutional considerations, prima facie part of the law of the State. If there were a positive decision made by the Gardaí or the Director of Public Prosecutions never to prosecute in any such case, in my view it would be unlawful as a positive decision not to enforce the law."

---

[4] Though authority was to be found in a New Zealand case whose title evokes the Irish diaspora—*Fitzgerald* v. *Muldoon* [1976] 2 N.Z.L.R. 615.

[5] In a later case also involving the Farm Tax Act 1985—*Purcell* v. *Att. Gen.* [1990] 2 I.R. 405—Barron J. said that legislation was enforced because it was the will of the Oireachtas. If it were interfered with unlawfully then what remained could not be the will of the Oireachtas. In that event, it ceased to be enforceable not only for the future but for the past also. Consequently the applicant was not liable to pay farm tax for the year 1986.

Constitutional Limits on the Delegation of Legislative Power

As currently construed, Article 15.2.1° goes beyond what is stated above, by limiting the power of the Oireachtas to delegate law-making functions to Ministers or other bodies. In *City View Press Ltd.* v. *AnCO* [1980] I.R. 381 the Supreme Court recognised that the delegation of legislative power to Ministers and others was a long-standing phenomenon, and in the complex, intricate and ever-changing situations which confront the modern state, an understandable one. But the courts nonetheless had the task of ensuring that constitutional limits were not transgressed. The judgment continues:

> "In discharging that responsibility, the Courts will have regard to where and by what authority the law in question purports to have been made . . . the test is whether that which is challenged as an unauthorised delegation of parliamentary power is more than a mere giving effect to principles and polices which are contained in the statute itself. If it be, then it is not authorised; for such would constitute a purported exercise of legislative power by an authority which is not permitted to do so under the Constitution. On the other hand, if it be within the permitted limits—if the law is laid down in the statute and details only are filled in or completed by the designated Minister or subordinate body—there is no unauthorised delegation of legislative power." ([1980] I.R. 381, 399).

The statutory provision impugned in the *City View Press* case[6] allowed AnCO (the industrial training authority) to impose levies on firms for the purpose of financing its training activities. It refrained from specifying how these levies were to be calculated and imposed no ceiling upon them; but despite this the Supreme Court upheld its constitutionality. If provisions of such vagueness can pass muster it is not easy to imagine what would not. It seems significant that to date only one statutory provision has been condemned as an unconstitutional delegation of legislative power—and that on rather special grounds.[7]

The issue has arisen in three subsequent Supreme Court cases—*Cooke* v. *Walsh* [1984] I.R. 710, *Harvey* v. *Minister for Social Welfare* [1990] 2 I.R. 232 and *McDaid* v. *Sheehy* [1991] 1 I.R. 1. In all three, however, the court declined to entertain the constitutional questions raised. The *Cooke* and *Harvey* decisions founded in part on the presumption of constitutionality,[8] by means of which the parent Acts were given a restrictive interpretation so that the relevant Ministerial orders were held *ultra vires*. In part, too, those decisions invoked the doctrine "reach constitutional issues last"[9]—which specifically underpins *McDaid* v. *Sheehy*, a case which requires fuller treatment.

McDaid v. *Sheehy* [1991] 1 I.R. 1 involved a revenue offence, with a statutory background of appropriate Byzantine complexity. An essential ingredient in that offence was supplied by an order made in 1975 under the Imposition of Duties Act 1957.[10] The key portions of section 1 of that Act provided:

---

[6] s. 21 of the Industrial Training Act 1967.
[7] See *East Donegal Co-op. Ltd.* v. *Att. Gen.* [1970] I.R. 317, discussed *infra* pp. 184–185.
[8] As to which *infra*.
[9] As to which *infra*.
[10] See the perceptive note on the Act by G. W. Hogan ((1985) 7 D.U.L.J. 134), arguing that it could not withstand constitutional challenge.

"The Government may by order:

(a) impose . . . as from any specified day, a customs duty of such amount as they think proper on any particular description of goods imported into the State . . .
(b) impose . . . an excise duty on any particular matter or thing as from any specified day . . . "

Section 2 provided that every such order should have statutory effect immediately upon being made, but would lapse unless confirmed by statute passed before the end of the year following that in which it was made. The applicant had been convicted of the relevant offence in 1986. He sought to have his conviction quashed, arguing *inter alia* that section 1 of the 1957 Act was an unconstitutional delegation of legislative power.

Blayney J. in the High Court held that section 1 was invalid. Having quoted the test laid down in the *City View Press* case, he continued ([1991] 1 I.R. 1, 9):

"In my opinion the power given to the Government here is a power to legislate. It is left to the Government to determine what imported goods are to have customs and excise duty imposed on them and to determine the amount of such duty. And the Government is left totally free in exercising this power. It is far from a case of the Government filling in only the details . . . . I am satisfied . . . that the provisions of the Act of 1957 . . . are invalid having regard to the provisions of the Constitution."

But the 1975 Order had been confirmed by section 46 of the Finance Act 1976 and Blayney J. found that this rendered it valid. Thus there was no constitutional or legal defect in the offence of which he had been convicted in 1986, and an order quashing that conviction was refused. On appeal, the Supreme Court, fastening on this point, refused to rule on the constitutionality of the 1957 Act. Whatever its prior status, the order made thereunder was legally valid after the passage of the 1976 Finance Act. And given that the applicant had been convicted in 1986, resolution of the constitutional issue could not assist him; his conviction would stand in any event. Consequently, as Finlay C.J., speaking for the majority,[11] put it ([1991] 1 I.R. 1, 20):

" . . . I am satisfied that this Court should treat the decision of the learned trial judge on the question of the constitutional validity of s.1 of the 1957 Act as being technically *obiter dictum*, and as such, not justifying the declaration of constitutional invalidity contained in his order. That portion of the order should accordingly be set aside . . . "

The Supreme Court's ruling in *McDaid's* case gives the 1957 Act only a stay of execution. For Blayney J.'s reasoning on the constitutional question seems unimpeachable, and the 1957 Act is beyond salvation—unless the *City View Press* case is overruled, and there is at present no evidence that this will happen.

The cases surveyed above show that this facet of the separation of powers has teeth. The Oireachtas, it seems, may delegate a power to put flesh on the

[11] Finlay C.J., Griffin, Hederman and O'Flaherty JJ.; McCarthy J. dissenting.

bones of an Act; but anything going beyond this will be constitutionally suspect. Many statutory provisions necessarily now have a shadow cast upon
them. A *fortiori*, an Act which is essentially a vehicle for the making of regulations must be in peril: an example would be the Tobacco Products (Control
of Advertising, Sponsorship and Sales Promotion) Act 1978. And even if the
statute or section is upheld, this may be at the price of a narrow interpretation which invalidates regulations made under it.

Orders Bringing Acts Into Force

Many statutes defer the date of their coming into operation by giving a
Minister power to make an order bringing them into effect. The reasons for
this are perfectly understandable; for example, the operation of the Act may
require new administrative arrangements and time may be needed to establish these. But what is the position if, years after the passage of the Act, no
such order has been made? This has in fact happened with the Health (Mental Services) Act 1981, s.2 of which makes typical provision in this regard:

> "This Act shall come into operation on such day or days as many be
> fixed therefor by order or orders of the Minister either generally or with
> reference to any particular purpose or provision and different days may
> be so fixed for different purposes and different provisions of this Act."

In *State (Sheehan)* v. *Govt. of Ireland* [1987] I.R. 550 Henchy J. said that if on
its true reading such a statutory provision *obliged* the executive to bring an
Act into operation, it would be " . . . unconstitutional for the government to
achieve by their prolonged inactivity the virtual repeal of the section" (at
561). But there the Supreme Court (McCarthy J. dissenting) held that no
such obligation was contained in section 60(7) of the Civil Liability Act 1961.
It provided:

> "This section shall come into operation on such day, not earlier than the
> 1st day of April, 1967, as may be fixed therefor by order made by the
> Government.".

Despite (or perhaps because of) the fact that section 60 embodied an important law reform,[12] no such order had ever been made.

Since the language of section 60(7) is that normally utilised in such provisions, situations where an obligation to act can be implied will plainly be
rare. And if, as in *Sheehan's* case, the implementation of the relevant provision
requires what Henchy J. called " . . . the necessary deployment of financial
or other resources . . . ", the courts will be especially reluctant to find any
such obligation. An additional difficulty arises from that case, for both Finlay
C.J. (at 559–60) and Griffin J. (at 562) expressly reserved their opinions on
whether the courts could direct the making of any such order by the executive.[13]

[12] Before the enactment of section 60, road authorities were liable for *misfeasance* in regard to
public roads and footpaths—*i.e.* for positive acts of negligence in the construction or maintenance thereof. But they were not liable for *non-feasance*—*i.e.* a total failure to maintain a road or
footpath so that it fell into disrepair. Section 60 imposed liability for non-feasance.
[13] For an incisive critique of *Sheehan's* case see G. W. Hogan, (1987) 9 D.U.L.J. 91.

Parliamentary Control

In the *City View Press* case the Supreme Court referred to the fact that the subordinate legislation involved there was subject to annulment by resolution of either House of the Oireachtas. This, said the court, retained a measure of control in the two Houses and was therefore a safeguard. In *Burke v. Minister for Labour* [1979] I.R. 354 the Supreme Court seemed to view with disfavour the absence of similar controls in the minimum wage provisions of the Industrial Relations Act 1946—though the judgement was not rested on this ground. In fact, most enabling Acts contain some provision for parliamentary control, either by providing for annulment of regulations or—more rarely—by requiring parliamentary approval before they come into force. Whether, on the basis of the above authorities, failure to provide for such control would *per se* be a ground for constitutional challenge, is unclear.

Many such control provisions permit the annulment of orders or regulations by resolution of *either* House of the Oireachtas. The constitutionality of this practice has never been tested in Ireland, but similar provisions were held invalid by the United States Supreme Court in *Immigration and Naturalisation Service* v. *Chadha* (1983) 462 U.S. 919. The court said that under the Constitution bicameral action was the rule; when one House was permitted to act alone the text made this clear. Similar considerations might be thought to apply under Bunreacht na hÉireann, since the Dáil alone is mentioned in Articles 17, 28.3, 28.4 and 29.5. As against this, the United States Constitution has features unknown to Bunreacht na hÉireann, such as the Presidential veto on legislation and the "states' house" composition of the Senate. Since *some* reliance was placed on these features in *Chadha's* case, an Irish court might find its conclusions inapplicable here.

The *East Donegal Co-op.* Case

Only one statutory provision has fallen foul of the Consitution on the ground of excessive delegation and the case in question ante-dates *City View Press*. *East Donegal Co-op Ltd.* v. *Att. Gen.* [1970] I.R. 317 concerned the Livestock Marts Act 1967, which set up a licensing scheme for such marts. The Act allowed the Minister for Agriculture to grant or refuse licences, to attach to a licence such conditions as he thought proper, and to revoke licences in certain situations. Section 4 authorised the Minister to exempt from the Act's provisions "any particular business or business of any particular class or kind." The Supreme Court, *per* Walsh J. held that in the context "any particular business" must mean some individual enterprise—a business identified by reference to its proprietor or conductor. This was a far reaching power to dispense individuals from the application of statutory provisions. Noting that Article 40.1 guaranteed the equality of all citizens before the law, Walsh J. continued ([1970] I.R. 317, 350):

> "The constitutional right of the Oireachtas in its legislation to take account of diffence of social function and difference of capacity, physical and moral, does not extend to delegating that power to members of the Executive, to the exclusion of the Oireachtas, in order to decide as between individuals (all of whom are, by the terms of an Act, bound by it) which of them shall be exempted from the application of the Act—

unless such exemption were necessary to avoid an infringement of the constitutional rights of such individuals which infringement, because of circumstances peculiar to them, would necessarily result from the application of the statutory provision without such exemption. No such justification appears in the provision under consideration. In the view of this Court the provision purporting to grant power to the Minister to exempt 'any particular business' is invalid . . . "

The doctrine espoused by the Supreme Court in the *City View Press* case is well known in the United States. In two celebrated decisions earlier in this century it was invoked to invalidate statutory delegations of power: *Panama Refining Co.* v. *Ryan* (1935) 293 U.S. 388 and *Schechter Poultry Corpn.* v. *United States* (1935) 295 U.S. 495. In the last 50 years, however, no statute has been struck down on this ground. The courts have always found the terms of any challenged delegation sufficiently precise to be valid, sometimes displaying remarkable inventiveness in the process; see particularly *Amalgamated Meat Cutters* v. *Connally* (1971) 337 F.Supp. 737. Many American commentators, therefore, view the non-delegation doctrine as a dead-letter, and it seems curious that a doctrine which now lacks practical significance in the land of its origin should be imported into Ireland in the 1980s. The High Court of Australia has refused to apply the separation of powers idea in this way, despite constitutional provisions akin to those in Ireland. See *Victoria Stevedoring Co.* v. *Dignan* (1931) 46 C.L.R. 73, especially the judgments of Dixon and Evatt JJ.[14]

No Judicial Legislation

That the courts have an important role in making law—indeed a duty to do so—is now clearly accepted. And the judicial exposition of Bunreacht na Éireann is testimony as to the way this role has been discharged. By identifying unenumerated rights, re-examining common law doctrines in the light of the Constitution and "unmaking" laws by striking down statutory provisions as unconstitutional, the courts have transformed our understanding of the basic law. It is also recognised, however, that this law-creating process has its limits, though since these are vague and imprecise, judicial opinions as to their location may well differ sharply. This occurred in *F. (Orse. C.)* v. *C.* [1991] I.L.R.M. 65, where the applicant sought the annulment of her marriage on the ground that prior thereto her husband had (unknown to her) been a practising homosexual. By reason of this, it was contended, he lacked the capacity to form or maintain a normal marital relationship. This ground of nullity had been accepted in a number of High Court decisions, but in the instant case Keane J. declined to follow them. He observed that the law on nullity was founded upon section 13 of the Matrimonial Causes and Marriage Law (Ireland) Act 1870, which required the High Court to:

" . . . proceed and act and give relief on principles and rules which, in the opinion of the said Court, shall be as nearly as may be conformable

---

[14] But Professor Leslie Zines thought that the statute there in issue *should* have been held invalid; the power it conferred—which ran to modifying earlier statutes—had been used for diametrically opposed purposes for successive governments. See *The High Court and the Constitution* (Sydney 1981), p. 134.

to the principles and rules on which the ecclesiastical courts of Ireland
have heretofore acted and given relief . . . "

Keane J. accepted that this did not fossilise the law in its 1870 state; existing
grounds of nullity must be understood in the light of developments in scientific knowledge. But the courts could not add new grounds which the legislature had failed to create, and the ground invoked here fell into that
category.[15] To formulate such new grounds, Keane J. said, constituted " . . .
an impermissible assumption of the legislative function which Article 15.2.1°
of the Constitution vests exclusively in the Oireachtas." ([1991] I.L.R.M. 65,
83).

On appeal, however, the Supreme Court took a different view. Finlay C.J.
observed that the general ground here invoked had been developed by analogy with the pre-existing ground of impotence.[16] To apply it to a case where
one party to a marriage had, unknown to the other, an inherent and unalterable homosexual orientation was " . . . a necessary and permissible development of the law of nullity." ([1991] I.L.R.M. 65, 93).

If in the above case the High Court appears to have taken a conservative,
and the Supreme Court a more radical, stance, the opposite was true in *L*. v.
L. [1989] I.L.R.M. 528: [1992] I.L.R.M. 115. Barr J. had there invoked
Article 41.2 of the Constitution to hold that a woman who opted for the full-
time role of wife and mother was entitled, on the breakdown of the marriage,
to a beneficial interest of up to 50 per cent. in the family home and its contents. But a unanimous Supreme Court reversed this decision. Finlay C.J.
concluded that this was not a case of developing an existing common law
principle, but of identifying a brand new right. Unless this was clearly warranted by the Constitution or was essential to protect a right guaranteed
thereunder, it was a usurpation of the legislative function.

The Supreme Court's approach in *L*. v. *L*. may have been influenced by
the fact that legislation for joint ownership of the matrimonial home had
been promised by the 1983–87 coalition Government, though never enacted.
The fact that the Judicial Separation and Family Law Reform Act 1989 gave
the courts wide-ranging powers to make property adjustment orders[17] may
also have had an influence. That is, the Oireachtas had recently occupied
itself with matrimonial property matters, but had refrained from taking the
step involved in the High Court judgment. But one cannot conclude that the
action, or inaction, of the Oireachtas will determine the judicial development
of the law. For in *F*. (*Orse. C.*) v. *C*. [1991] I.L.R.M. 65 the Supreme Court—
unlike the High Court—was quite unmoved by the fact that the Oireachtas
had, despite frequent prompting, refrained from adding to the established
grounds of nullity.

Where statute law is involved, the courts are particularly zealous not to
trespass upon the domain of the Oireachtas. In *State* (*Murphy*) v. *Johnson*
[1983] I.R. 235 the Supreme Court declined to correct by interpretation "an

---

[15] Keane J. pointed out that the Law Reform Commission's 1984 report on nullity of marriage—
which has not been implemented—had specifically recommended the introduction of a new
ground based on homosexual orientation. See *Report on Nullity of Marriage*—LRC 9–1984, pp.
105 *et seq.*

[16] Citing Barrington J.'s decision in *R.S.J.* v. *J.S.J.* [1982] I.L.R.M. 263 and Costello J.'s
decision in *D*. v. *C*. [1984] I.L.R.M. 173.

[17] See ss.15–22 of the Act; also William Duncan and Paula Scully, *Marriage Breakdown in Ireland*:
Law and Practice (Dublin 1990), Chap. 13.

obvious and palpable error" in section 23 of the Road Traffic (Amendment) Act 1978. To do this, it was held, would be tantamount to amending the provision, which was not within the competence of the courts. Equally, in *Maher* v. *Att. Gen.* [1973] I.R. 140 the Supreme Court had found constitutional fault with section 44(2) of the Road Traffic Act 1968, which made a certain document "conclusive evidence" in criminal proceedings.[18] The vice lay solely in the word "conclusive"; had it been omitted the sub section would have survived scrutiny. The Supreme Court was therefore pressed to apply the doctrine of severance, striking down only the offending word and leaving the remainder of the sub section as a live, operable provision. But after an exhaustive analysis of the Act and its legislative history, the court decided that it could not do this. To do so would produce a result entirely at variance with the clear intention of the Oireachtas, and would mean that the court was exceeding its functions.

A similar caution is evident from *McGrath* v. *McDermott* [1988] I.R. 258. In that case a taxpayer had entered into a series of transactions solely for the purpose of creating entirely artificial capital losses, which would then be set off against actually realised capital gains. Thus the amount of capital gains tax payable would be reduced. The scheme was in technical compliance with the relevant provisions of the Capital Gains Tax Act 1975, and the question the courts had to answer was—could the real, as opposed to the artificial, nature of the transactions be considered, so as to conclude that they had failed to achieve their objective? The unanimous answer of the Supreme Court was—No. Finlay C.J. said ([1988] I.R. 258, 276):

> "The function of the courts in interpreting a statute of the Oireachtas is . . . strictly confined to ascertaining the true meaning of each statutory provision . . . . The courts have not got a function to add to or delete from express statutory provisions so as to achieve objectives which to the courts appear desirable. In rare and limited circumstances words or phrases may be implied into statutory provisions solely for the purpose of making them effective to achieve their expressly avowed objective . . .
> . . . for this Court to avoid the application of the provisions of the Act of 1975 to these transactions could only constitute the invasion by the judiciary of the powers and functions of the legislature, in plain breach of the constitutional separation of powers."

THE EXECUTIVE POWER

Article 28.2 informs us that the executive power of the State is to be exercised by or on the authority of the Government. From Article 29.4.1° we learn that the executive power has a foreign affairs dimension, but otherwise the Constitution is silent as to what it involves. Other constitutions are equally laconic in this regard, and it has been suggested that so indefinite is the notion of executive power that it amounts to what is left when the legislative and judicial powers are subtracted.

Constitutions which provide for an executive in parliament are rarely troubled about executive power. For the executive, having by definition a majority in parliament, can normally equip itself by statute with any new powers it

[18] See further *infra*.

may consider necessary; and it is mainly from statute that the executive derives the extensive powers it nowadays wields. However, it has been laid down that the executive power of the State, in the sense used in the Constitution, is distinct from any power the executive may possess under statute: *State (C)* v. *Minister for Justice* [1967] I.R. 106, 118: *Murphy* v. *Dublin Corporation* [1972] I.R. 215, 238. Thus an important question arises—does the constitutional grant of the executive power *ipso facto* create power? In other words—may the Government exercise power without statutory authority?

(a) *Foreign affairs*

In foreign affairs it may, and does: few statutory provisions intrude into this area. The Government concludes international agreements by virtue of its executive power. It is obliged to lay such agreements before the Dáil (Art. 29.5.1°) but they are binding without either advance or subsequent Dáil approval. If, however, the agreement involves a charge on public funds, its terms must be approved by the Dáil (Art. 29.5.2°). Article 29.5.3° provides:

> "This section (*i.e.* Article 29.5) shall not apply to agreements or conventions of a technical and administrative character."

In *State (Gilliland)* v. *Governor, Mountjoy Prison* [1987] I.R. 201 the Supreme Court interpreted this to mean that:

(a) an international agreement of a technical and administrative character need not be laid before the Dáil;

(b) if such an agreement involves a charge on public funds, Dáil approval is *not* required.

The meaning of the phrase "technical and administrative character" has not been canvassed in the courts—though in *Gilliland's* case Barrington J. accepted the concession by both counsel that an extradition treaty did not fall into this category. It seems likely that in practice disputes on this point would essentially arise between government departments (*e.g.* Foreign Affairs and Finance) and would be settled by rulings of the Attorney General. Some agreements which might seem to fall into this category have in fact been approved by, and scheduled to, statutes: *e.g.* Bretton Woods Agreements (Amendment) Act 1977: International Common Fund for Commodities Act 1982.[19] In 1985 the State entered into agreements with the People's Republic of China in regard to an exhibition of a celebrated collection of terracotta figures at the Royal Hospital, Kilmainham. Though under the agreements the State was liable for certain costs, including compensation for any damage, it might have been thought that they were "of a technical and administrative character." However, they were approved by the Dáil on October 31, 1985: see 361 *Dáil Debs.*, cc. 877–81.

In *State (Gilliland)* v. *Governor, Mountjoy Prison* [1987] I.R. 201 the prosecutor claimed that an extradition agreement between Ireland and the United States was not binding on the State because, though involving a charge on public funds, it had not been approved by Dáil Éireann. Article XVII of the

[19] It may be that "agreements or conventions of a technical and administrative character" relates principally to those produced under the aegis of bodies such as the Universal Postal Union, the International Telecommunications Union and the Intergovernmental Maritime Consultative Organisation (as to which see D. W. Bowett, *The Law of International Institutions* (London 1963) pp. 98–100).

treaty provided that the requested state should, subject to specified exceptions, bear all expenses arising out of the extradition request and proceedings. And the Attorney General was to provide the representation of the interests of the United States in any relevant proceedings in Ireland. It was common case that the treaty was laid before the Dáil under Article 29.5.1°— but equally that Dáil approval of its terms was not sought. Counsel for the defendant conceded that he could not rely here on the Extradition Act 1965, s.5—which provides that the expenses incurred by the Minister for Justice in administering the Act shall be paid out of moneys provided by the Oireachtas—because expenses incurred under this treaty would, in part, be expenses of the Attorney General. But he argued that the Attorney's expenses were covered by the vote each year for his Office in the annual Appropriation Act. Barrington J. held that the term "charge on public funds" in Article 29.5.2° could not refer to a permanent charge authorised by a permanent Act of parliament, or to an annual charge authorised by parliament for one year. It must refer to commitments to meet costs or expenses which parliament had not yet authorised. It was aimed at precisely the kind of permanent commitment to defray unspecified future or contingent expenses contained in this treaty. Barrington J. characterised Article 29.5.2° as asserting the Dáil's power over the Executive in the sphere of foreign relations in the event of the Executive entering into an international agreement involving a charge on public funds. This treaty purported to impose a charge on public funds—a permanent international financial commitment which would not exist but for it; and not having been approved by the Dáil, that treaty could not be binding on the State. It followed that the Extradition Act 1965 (Part II) (No. 20) Order 1984 (S.I. 1984 No. 300) which, consequent upon the treaty, purported to make Part II of the Act operative as regards the United States, was invalid.

Subsequently, the Supreme Court affirmed Barrington J.'s conclusion. Finlay C.J., for the court, said that the crucial question in deciding whether an international agreement involved a charge on public funds was whether the terms of the agreement itself created such a charge. An international agreement (outside the "technical and administrative" category) which involved purely incidental and consequential expenses would have to be laid before the Dáil, but would not require its approval. But Article XVII of this treaty, by its own terms, created a charge on public funds and since it had not been approved by the Dáil it could not bind the State. The 1984 order based on that treaty was consequently invalid.[20]

Gilliland's case raised another constitutional point, but since Barrington J. decided it adversely to the prosecutor he did not refer it to the Supreme Court. It concerned the Extradition Act 1965, s.8(5):

> "Every extradition agreement and every order applying this Part otherwise than in pursuance of an extradition agreement shall, subject to the provisions of this Part, have the force of law in accordance with its terms."

Counsel for the prosecutor submitted that this meant an extradition agree-

---

[20] This decision clearly came as a surprise to the Government, and the Taoiseach was reported as saying that all existing treaties would now have to be examined to see if they were affected by it: see *The Irish Times*, July 26, 1986.

ment, once executed and ratified, had the force of law within the State. Section 8(5) was thus an unconstitutional delegation of legislative power. Barrington J. could not agree. Having referred to *City View Press* v. *AnCo* [19801] I.R. 381 he said that in the Extradition Act 1965 the Oireachtas had laid down principles and policies, and established machinery and procedures, concerning extradition. But it had left to the Government the question whether an extradition treaty should be entered into. It was not necessary that the Oireachtas should enact a specific statute in regard to each extradition treaty that was to be enforced in the domestic law of the State. Moreover, every extradition treaty would have to be laid before the Dáil, and if it involved a charge on public funds, approved by that body. Barrington J. also concluded that, read in its context, section 8(5) did not have the meaning contended for. Despite difficulties in the wording, the phrase "subject to the provisions of this Part" must be construed as a reference back to section 8(1); thus an extradition treaty did not become part of the domestic law unless the Government made an order under section 8(1). And by virtue of section 4, every such order was subject to Oireachtas control.

These considerations would seem to validate statutory provisions such as the Protection of Employment Act 1977, s.3(2). This Act relates to collective redundancies and imposes certain obligations on employers. Section 3(2) provides that the Minister for Labour may by order amend any provision of the Act so as to comply with any international obligations on collective redundancies that the State has decided to assume. Any such order must be approved in draft by both Houses: section 4(2). If the international agreement is scheduled to the draft order, then Oireachtas approval of both may be secured and the Constitution's requirements presumably satisfied. The Oireachtas is determining that the international agreement shall be part of the law of the State (satisfying Art. 29.6) and is giving sanction to whatever new principles and policies the order contains (thus complying with *City View Press* v. *AnCo*). A more difficult problem is posed by provisions such as the Maritime Jurisdiction Act 1959, s.7(1). This permits the Government, having regard to any international agreement to which the State is a party, to make orders prescribing fish conservation measures applicable outside exclusive fishery limits. Under section 7(2) contravention of such an order is an offence punishable with heavy penalties. The order must be laid before the Dáil and Seanad and may be annulled by either House. No doubt if the order schedules the agreement the latter will then effectively be laid before the Dáil, thus satisfying Article 29.5.1° But the agreement is nonetheless essentially made part of the domestic law by executive order, and it is difficult to see how Article 29.6 is satisfied. And if section 7 represents, in the language of Article 29.6, a determination by the Oireachtas that *any* international agreement on the matter shall by executive order become part of the domestic law, this hardly seems consonant with *City View Press* v. *AnCo*.

The recognition of foreign states or governments is an established executive function. Should the question whether a state or government is recognised arise in legal proceedings, the court will make inquiry of the Department of Foreign Affairs, and will treat its answer as conclusive: *Zarine* v. *Owners of S.S. Ramava* [1942] I.R. 148.

Although the Ministers and Secretaries Act 1924 vests in the Department of Foreign Affairs the function of granting passports (s.1(xi)), neither that

Act, nor any other, requires a citizen wishing to travel abroad to obtain a passport. In practice, however, admission to a foreign country is contingent upon the production of such a document. The High Court has held that a citizen has a right to travel outside the State—and thus a right to a passport—springing from the general guarantee of Article 40.3: *State (M)* v. *Att. Gen.* [1979] I.R. 73. The right in question is not absolute, and may have to yield to considerations of public order and the common good. It would seem to follow that the denial or revocation of a passport may be challenged in the courts. However, if the decision is based on national security or broad foreign policy grounds, recent United States authority suggests the courts will defer to it: *Haig* v. *Agee* (1981) 453 U.S. 280: *Regan* v. *Wald* (1984) 468 U.S. 222.[21]

The extradition of persons wanted for prosecution or punishment in another country is governed by the Extradition Acts 1965 to 1992. This provides for the procedure governing requests for extradition, for arrest and detention (under the order of a court) and for the surrender of the person sought. Extradition may not be granted in respect of certain offences, among them revenue offences, political offences and offences connected with a political offence,[22] or where there is a real danger that a person extradited would be ill-treated in breach of his/her constitutional rights.[23]

The 1965 Act must be regarded as the sole and exclusive source of the power to extradite: surrender may take place only in accordance with its terms. Apart from those places to which Part III of the Act applies (Northern Ireland, England and Wales, Scotland, the Isle of Man and the Channel Islands) there must be a statutory order bringing Part II into operation in regard to a specific country. A pre-condition of the making of any such order is an extradition agreement providing for reciprocal surrender, or assurances acceptable to the Government that reciprocal facilities will be afforded: section 8.

It is probably open to the Government to request the surrender of a wanted person from a foreign country to which Part II has not been applied. The making of such a request would seem to be an act of international intercourse, and hence within the constitutional grant of the executive power, requiring no statutory authority: see *Barton* v. *Commonwealth* (1974) 131 C.L.R. 477—a decision of the High Court of Australia. For the reasons given above, however, such a request could not properly contain an assurance of reciprocity.

(b) *Domestic affairs*

In certain circumstances the constitutional grant of the executive power may enable the Government to act without statutory authority in domestic affairs. It seems clear, however, that it could not, without statutory warrant,

---

[21] See the discussion of the right to travel in Chap. 12 *infra*.

[22] The Supreme Court's approach to the political offence exemption has fluctuated somewhat. Contrast *McGlinchey* v. *Wren* [1982] I.R. 154 and *Quinn* v. *Wren* [1985] I.R. 322 with *Finucane* v. *McMahon* [1990] 1 I.R. 165 and *Carron* v. *McMahon* [1990] 1 I.R. 239. See further Alpha Connelly, "Non-Extradition for Political Offences" (1982) XVII *Irish Jurist* (N.S.) 59, and "Ireland and the Political Offence Exception to Extradition" (1985) 12 *Journal of Law and Society* 153: Colin Campbell, "Extradition to Northern Ireland: Prospects and Probabilities" (1989) 52 M.L.R. 585: Gerard Hogan and Clive Walker, *Political Violence and the Law in Ireland* (Manchester 1989), Chap. 14.

[23] *Clarke* v. *McMahon* [1990] 1 I.R. 228: *Finucane* v. *McMahon* [1990] 1 I.R. 165.

take action imposing obligations or burdens on any citizen. The absence of any Irish judicial authority on this point doubtless reflects consistent legal advice to Governments that statutory authority is essential for such action. Foreign decisions confirm this. In *Youngstown Sheet and Tube Co.* v. *Sawyer* (1952) 343 U.S. 579 the Supreme Court had to consider the validity of President Truman's order to the defendant (the Secretary of Commerce) to seize the country's steel mills and keep them in operation. A steel strike was threatened which would have halted almost all production—a matter with obvious defence implications at a time when United States forces were engaged in Korea. It was admitted that no statute authorised such action, but the defendant contended that the constitutional grant of the executive power to the President was sufficient. The Supreme Court rejected this argument and held the seizure unlawful. The Supreme Court of India applied the same principle in *State of Madhya Pradesh* v. *Singh* [1967] All I.R. (S.C.) 1170. Here the defendant had been ordered by the state government to reside only in a specified place. The statute under which this order was issued had been ruled unconstitutional, but counsel for the state government argued that the order was supportable under the constitutional grant of the executive power. The Supreme Court rejected this contention, holding that where the citizen's rights were prejudicially affected, executive action must be supported by the authority of law.

In other contexts, however, statutory authority would not seem to be necessary. Schemes to give benefits of various kinds—grants, subsidies, etc.—do not have to be enshrined in statute, though statutory authority to spend the relevant sum will be required. The scheme for compensating physically injured victims of violent crime rests solely on a White Paper issued by the Department of Justice in 1974 (Prl. 3658), and statutory authority to disburse the relevant sums is granted annually in the Appropriation Act. Precisely the same applies to the Scheme of Civil Legal Aid and Advice, the details of which appear only in a Justice Department White Paper (Prl. 8543) of 1979.[24]

It is presumably under its executive power that the Government establishes commissions and committees to inquire into some subject (*e.g.* industrial relations, itinerancy, taxation) and report thereon. Such bodies, of course, function on the basis of evidence voluntarily tendered: and it would not be possible to clothe them with authority to compel the attendance of witnesses or the production of documents. An inquiry necessitating such powers could be established only under statute—the Tribunals of Inquiry (Evidence) Acts 1921 and 1979.

The executive may also, without statutory authority, make contracts, and acquire and dispose of property. (See the decision of the High Court of Australia in *Johnson* v. *Kent* (1974) 132 C.L.R. 164.) It may also engage in economic activity, *e.g.* by forming a company for some purpose. Specific statutory authority would not seem to be necessary here; the executive is presumably as much entitled as any other body of persons to use the machinery of the Companies Acts. In some instances it has done so under specific statutory mandate, but in other cases—*e.g.* the *Dairy Disposal Co. Ltd., Irish Steel Hold-*

---

[24] Though the Legal Aid Board has urged that the scheme be put on a statutory footing, since its present basis has caused operational difficulties—especially in staffing matters: see its 1983/ 84 *Report* pp. 2, 7, 8.

ings Ltd., Irish Shipping Ltd. and the original *Coras Trachtála Teo.*—there was no such authorisation.[25]

No Irish court has had to pronounce on the validity of such exercises,[26] but they find support in a decision of the Supreme Court of India—*Ram Jawaya Kapur* v. *State of Punjab* [1955] All I.R. (S.C.) 549. The plaintiff claimed that the state could not carry on a business solely on the foundation of the constitutionally-granted executive power; statutory authority was essential. The Supreme Court rejected this argument, giving reasons which are precisely applicable to the constitutional structure in Ireland. Stressing the fact that the Indian Constitution provided for a parliamentary executive, the court observed that this involved a Cabinet enjoying a majority in the legislature, and deciding important questions of policy. Should it decide to carry on a business then normal procedure would be followed—the estimated expenditure would be shown in the annual financial statement and approved in the Appropriation Act. So long, therefore, as the business was carried out in pursuance of the Cabinet's policy, and with the tacit approval of the parliamentary majority, it was in accordance with constitutional principles.

At common law the Crown had power to grant a charter conferring corporate personality on a number of persons seeking this privilege and could grant a new charter amending an earlier one (for an Irish example, see *Gray and Cathcart* v. *Provost, Fellows and Scholars of Trinity College Dublin* [1910] 1 I.R. 370). It may well be that the Government now enjoys this power, as one of the prerogatives continued by Article 49 of the Constitution. But the power is not exercised, and an authoritative source has written[27]:

> " . . . no single instance of the grant of a charter can be found since 1922 and I think the prevailing feeling is that this method is inappropriate in the modern democratic state where the same end may be attained through the Oireachtas in the form of a private or a public Bill."

The private Act has become the normal mode of amendment; thus the charter of the Institute of Civil Engineers of Ireland has been amended by private Acts of 1960 and 1968, and that of the Royal College of Surgeons in Ireland by a private Act of 1965.

Devolving Executive Power

The National Treasury Management Agency Act 1990 provides for the establishment of this body to borrow money for the Exchequer and manage the national debt. The Act provides that the Agency performs its functions "on the authority of the Government" (section 3) and "subject to the control and general superintendence of the Minister [for Finance]." Those functions—which are performed on behalf of the Minister—are delegated to the Agency by Government order (section 5). But they remain vested in the Minister, concurrently with the Agency, and the Minister continues to be

[25] See J. B. O'Connell, *The Financial Administration of Ireland* (Dublin 1960), Chap. XV.
[26] In *McKerring* v. *Minister for Agriculture* [1989] I.L.R.M. 82 O'Hanlon J. observed that the Bovine Brucellosis and TB Eradication schemes had no statutory basis. Their conditions, and any changes therein, were notified to the farming community by newspaper advertisement. O'Hanlon J. commented: "It all seems a remarkably informal way to spell out and organise a scheme on which, apparently, hundreds of millions of pounds have already been spent." ([1989] I.L.R.M. 82, 84).
[27] Philip O'Donoghue S.C. in *Public Administration in Ireland* (Dublin 1949), Vol. II, p. 120.

responsible to Dáil Éireann for their performance. The Agency is constituted a body corporate by section 3.

When the Bill for this Act was before the Dáil questions were raised as to its constitutionality. It was suggested[28] that Government functions could be devolved only to Departments of State, on the basis of Article 28.12:

> "The following matters shall be regulated in accordance with law, namely, the organisation of, and distribution of business amongst, Departments of State . . . "

But the Minister for Finance, Mr. Reynolds, was satisfied that the arrangements proposed were constitutionally sound. He stressed the Minister's continuing responsibility, and went on[29]:

> "I would refer to Article 28.2 of the Constitution which states:
>> 'The executive power of the State shall, subject to the provisions of this Constitution, be exercised by or on the authority of the Government.'
>
> The Government have exercised their authority to delegate the authority to the National Debt Management Agency. The Central Bank is another example of an agency dealing with the central financial affairs of the State, such as monetary policy."

The Minister stressed that the Attorney General had thoroughly examined the whole area and had also sought the best outside advice available.[30] He (the Minister) was consequently happy "that the whole exercise is valid and entirely within the Constitution."[31]

The device utilised in the 1990 Act assumes—surely correctly—that Article 28 of the Constitution is not intended to fossilise the administration of the State in the mould of 1937. Indeed both the constitutional text and contemporaneous practice suggest otherwise. Article 30.3 specifically permits the transfer of the prosecuting function[32] from the Attorney General to another person. And although Article 28.4.2° might appear to imply that each member of the Government *must* administer a Department of State, it has not been so interpreted. Witness section 4(1) of the Ministers and Secretaries Amendment Act 1939:

> "Nothing in the Ministers and Secretaries Acts, 1924 and 1928, or this Act shall render it obligatory for every member of the Government to be a Minister having charge of a Department of State."

THE JUDICIAL POWER

The constitutional provisions which govern this matter are Articles 34.1 and 37.1. The former lays down the general principle that administering justice is a function solely reserved to courts established, and judges appointed, under the Constitution. The latter adds a significant qualification: statute may authorise the exercise of "limited functions and powers of a judicial nature"

---

[28] By Deputy Mervyn Taylor: 401 *Dáil Debs.*, cc. 645–48 (July 6, 1990).
[29] 401 *Dáil Debs.*, c. 655.
[30] *Ibid.*
[31] 401 *Dáil Debs.*, c. 664.
[32] In *Morrison* v. *Olson* (1988) 487 U.S. 654, 706 Scalia J. spoke of prosecuting crimes as "a quintessentially executive function."

by persons who are not judges or bodies which are not courts—but not in "criminal matters." The principles flowing from these provisions may be stated as follows:

   (a) the administration of justice in criminal matters is an exclusive function of the courts erected, and judges appointed, under the Constitution (this is, however, subject to the provisions of Art. 38 on special criminal courts, as to which see Chap. 10 *infra*)

   (b) in civil matters, *limited* judicial functions and powers may be conferred on persons who are not judges or bodies which are not courts

   (c) subject to (b), the administration of justice in civil matters is a function reserved to the courts.

Criminal Matters

The expression "criminal matters" in Article 37.1 is not defined, but its meaning has been clarified by judicial exegesis. In *Goodman International* v. *Hamilton* [1992] I.L.R.M. 145 the Supreme Court approved Finlay P.'s statement, on behalf of a divisional court, in *State (Murray)* v. *McRann* [1979] I.R. 133, 135:

> "A criminal matter within the meaning of Article 37 can be construed as a procedure associated with the prosecution of a person for a crime. It may be the preliminary investigation of such a charge, it may be the trial itself, it could be an appeal from the trial, or, presumably, an application for bail pending trial or appeal. The essential ingredient of a criminal matter must be its association with the determination of the question as to whether a crime against the State or against the public has been committed."

Since the principal characteristic of a crime is that it carries a punitive sanction, as distinct from mere fiscal reparation,[33] it would follow that any conduct attracting a possible fine and/or imprisonment would give rise to a "criminal matter" in terms of Article 37.1. And, subject to Article 38's provisions on special criminal courts, only judges may impose sanctions in respect of such conduct. Consequently, the Oireachtas—unlike some other legislatures[34]—may not try, convict or sentence persons for contempt. That is clear from the Supreme Court's decision in *Re Haughey* [1971] I.R. 217.

This aspect of the separation of powers doctrine does not prevent a tribunal of inquiry established under statute[35] from investigating allegations of criminal conduct and reporting thereon to the Oireachtas. For such a body has no power to inflict any penalty or punishment, nor can its findings of fact be used in any subsequent proceedings. The Supreme Court so ruled in *Goodman International* v. *Hamilton* [1992] I.L.R.M. 145.

In *Re Haughey* [1971] I.R. 217 Ó Dálaigh C.J. summarised the position as follows (at 249–50):

> "The Constitution vests the judicial power of government solely in the Courts and reserves exclusively to the Courts the power to try persons

---

[33] See the judgment of Kingsmill Moore J. in *Melling* v. *Ó Mathghamhna* [1962] I.R. 1, at 24–33.

[34] Such as the Australian federal parliament: *R.* v. *Richards, ex p. Fitzpatrick* (1955) 92 C.L.R. 157.

[35] As, for example, under the Tribunals of Inquiry (Evidence) Acts 1921 and 1979.

on criminal charges. Trial, conviction and sentence are indivisible parts of the exercise of this power . . . "

Thus a statutory provision enabling the Revenue Commissioners to choose the penalty in a customs case (a fine of £100 or three times the value of the goods) was unconstitutional: *Dealton* v. *Att. Gen.* [1963] I.R. 170.[36] So was section 7 of the Prevention of Crime Act 1908 which, as adapted by later statutes, allowed the Minister for Justice to transfer incorrigible Borstal detainees to prison with or without hard labour. The Supreme Court found the power to impose hard labour—as an extra punishment not sanctioned by the sentencing court—invalid: *State (Sheerin)* v. *Kennedy* [1966] I.R. 379.

The cases do not deny the Oireachtas power to fix mandatory sentences. They do, however, establish that where the precise sentence is a matter of discretion, only a judge may make the choice: see Walsh J. in *State (O)* v. *O'Brien* [1973] I.R. 50, 67. And the executive may quite constitutionally be given a statutory power to transfer prisoners from one type of detention to another—provided the conditions of detention are the same. In *State (Boyle)* v. *Governor, Military Detention Barracks* (judgment delivered March 3, 1981) the Supreme Court considered the constitutionality of the Prisons Act 1972. This allowed the Minister for Justice to direct the transfer of individuals from prison to military custody. Under section 2(9) the Minister was obliged to make regulations governing such military custody, and those regulations had, in effect, to be the same as for prisons. It was argued that the power to transfer could result in a punishment different from that originally imposed—a punishment selected by the Minister. Thus it was in effect a power to vary sentences and, consequently, inconsistent with the judicial power. The Supreme Court declined to accept this analysis. This transfer power, said the court, was not a judicial, but an administrative, power, exercisable only when the Act's conditions were satisfied. And it must be assumed that the Minister's regulations corresponded with what the Act demanded—that conditions of detention in military custody corresponded with those in prison. Thus the Act authorised only punishment in accordance with the sentence of the relevant court.

Powers of Peace Commissioners

Peace commissioners—who are certainly not judges—are appointed by the Minister for Justice under section 88 of the Courts of Justice Act 1924. They discharge functions which, prior to independence, fell to justices of the peace, such as signing summonses and warrants.[37] Several statutes of more recent vintage—such as the Misuse of Drugs Acts 1977–1984—have conferred similar functions upon them.

In *Byrne* v. *Grey* [1988] I.R. 31 the High Court sustained the constitutionality of those provisions of the Misuse of Drugs Acts 1977–1984[38] which authorised peace commissioners to issue search warrants. The power to do this was conditioned upon the peace commissioner's being satisfied by infor-

---

[36] Likewise statutory provisions authorising the Revenue Commissioners to order the release of a person convicted of certain offences before the expiry of the sentence imposed by a court: *Murphy* v. *Wallace* (High Court, Barron J., July 17, 1990).

[37] s.88(3), Courts of Justice Act 1924.

[38] s. 26(1), Misuse of Drugs Act 1977, as amended by s.13, Misuse of Drugs Act 1984.

mation on oath of a Garda Síochána member that there was reasonable ground for suspecting certain matters. Hamilton P. concluded that the peace commissioner must *personally* be satisfied that there was reasonable ground for suspicion. He/she was not entitled to rely on the mere averment of the Garda Síochána member.[39] Thus, in reaching a decision the peace commissioner was "obliged to act judicially." However, this did not mean that the peace commissioner was administering justice in a criminal matter. Hamilton P. quoted and applied the words of Barr J. in *Ryan* v. *O'Callaghan* (High Court, July 22, 1987):

> "The search of premises by the police under the authority of a search warrant is no more than part of the investigative process which may or may not lead to the arrest and charging of a person in connection with the crime under investigation or any other crime. In my view, the prosecution of an offence commences when a decision is made to issue a summons or prefer a charge against the person in respect of the particular crime alleged. It follows, therefore, that the issue of a search warrant prior to a commencement of a prosecution is part of the process of criminal investigation and is executive rather than judicial in nature."

And in *Berkeley* v. *Edwards* [1988] I.R. 217 Hamilton P. upheld, for the same reasons, the validity of the provisions of the Larceny Act 1916[40] empowering peace commissioners to issue search warrants.

It remains unclear whether issuing a summons, or a search warrant, is an exercise of judicial power and thus constitutionally incapable of bestowal on persons who are not judges. Two Supreme Court cases touch upon—but do not appear to *decide*—the point. In *State (Clarke)* v. *Roche* [1986] I.R. 619 it was held that the issuing, under section 10 of the Petty Sessions (Ireland) Act 1851, of a summons to initiate summary criminal proceedings in the District Court was "a judicial as distinct from an administrative act" ([1986] I.R. 619, 641). But the court, *per* Finlay C.J., also said (*ibid.*):

> "No argument in this case was submitted to the Court with regard to the consequences from the point of view of constitutional validity of a conclusion that the powers given to the Peace Commissioner and District Court clerk to receive a complaint and issue a summons constituted the carrying out of a judicial act in a criminal matter. I, therefore, express no view upon it . . . "

In *Rainey* v. *Delap* [1988] I.R. 470 the Supreme Court held rules 29 and 30 of the District Court Rules 1948[41] *ultra vires* insofar as they purported to authorise a District Court clerk to receive a complaint and issue a summons. Finlay C.J., again speaking for the court, said (at 480):

> " . . . it is not necessary for me to decide whether these rules are also invalid in that they could be taken to purport to vest in a person who is not a judge a limited function of a judicial nature in a criminal case in breach of Article 37 of the Constitution."

These reservations might suggest a serious doubt as to the constitutional

---

[39] This view was endorsed by the Court of Criminal Appeal and the Supreme Court in *People (D.P.P.)* v. *Kenny* [1990] 2 I.R. 110.
[40] Larceny Act 1916, s.42(1) as applied by the Courts of Justice Act 1924, s.88(3).
[41] S.I. 1948 No. 199.

propriety of giving such functions to persons other than judges. But it is to be noted that in *Clarke's* case Finlay C.J. (his colleagues concurring) indicated that there would be no constitutional problem in repealing section 10 of the Petty Sessions (Ireland) Act 1851, and replacing it with a provision more suitable for the modern District Court. He said ([1986] I.R. 619, 641):

> "Consideration . . . should be given to replacing s.10 and s.11 of the Act of 1851 with statutory provisions more suitable to the modern District Court which could include the procedure for the issuing of summonses, in criminal cases at least, *as being an administrative procedure only* and which could then, without any question of constitutional challenge, provide that the complaint should be made to the District Court and that the summons should be issued by the officers of that court upon the making of the complaint." (Italics supplied.)

That suggestion has been implemented by the Courts (No. 3) Act 1986, section 1(1) of which provides:

> "Proceedings in the District Court in respect of an offence may be commenced by the issuing, *as a matter of administrative procedure*, of a document (referred to subsequently in this section as "a summons") by the appropriate office of the District Court." (Italics supplied).

The 1986 Act, however, does not repeal that of 1851. Instead, as the Supreme Court held in *D.P.P.* v. *Nolan* [1990] 2 I.R. 526, 545, " . . . the procedures provided for in the Act of 1986 must be considered as parallel to those provided for in the Act of 1851."

Given that the 1986 Act is manifestly inspired—even as to its language— by the Supreme Court's observations in *Clarke's* case, a challenge to its validity would seem futile. There remains, however, the problem of the parallel procedure created by the 1851 Act which, as adapted, permits the issuing of summonses by District Court clerks or peace commissioners. Clearly, if this is a judicial function in the sense of Article 37.1, it could not validly be entrusted to such persons. But *Clarke's* case is hardly an authority for the proposition that issuing summonses is a constitutionally protected judicial function, for if it were the Supreme Court could not have made the recommendations that led to the 1986 Act.

The constitutionality of statutory provisions authorising peace commissioners to issue arrest warrants also still awaits resolution. The matter was raised in *Farrell* v. *Farrelly* [1988] I.R. 201, but O'Hanlon J. found it unnecessary to rule thereon.[42] The argument seems to have been that if the issue of a summons was a judicial act—as *State (Clarke)* v. *Roche* [1986] I.R. 619 held—then so too was the issue of an arrest warrant. The object of each document was to procure the attendance in court of the person named therein. The decision to issue an arrest warrant, it was urged, was a more weighty one since it permitted a deprivation of liberty; for even if the person arrested obtained bail, he/she would be deprived of liberty between the time of arrest and that of the grant of bail.

The argument advanced in *Farrell's* case is not necessarily invalidated by what appears an erroneous submission as to the *ratio* of *Clarke's* case. For

---

[42] *Inter alia* on the ground that the arrests in the instant case were valid at common law, so that whether the warrants were valid or invalid they were superfluous: [1988] I.R. 201, 204.

even if the issue of a summons is *not* a constitutionally protected judicial function, it does not follow that the issue of an arrest warrant falls into the same category. In regard to arrest warrants, different considerations—such as the deprivation of liberty—apply. But there are countervailing considerations. On the authorities, the judicial power in criminal matters is concerned with trial, conviction and sentence. It does not embrace the initiation of proceedings, for the Constitution itself provides for such initiation by a non-judicial person—the Attorney General.[43] Moreover, both the common law[44] and a host of statutory provisions[45]; permit arrest without warrant. If, in many situations, an individual may be deprived of liberty by simple decision of a police officer, it would seem difficult to contend that to issue a document authorising such deprivation is a judicial act.

In *O'Mahony* v. *Melia* [1989] I.R. 335 Keane J. held unconstitutional provisions empowering peace commissioners to remand persons arrested in custody, or to grant them bail, pending their appearance before the District Court. Fortified by an *obiter dictum* of Walsh J.,[46] Keane J. concluded that in making such a decision a peace commissioner was administering justice or, in other words, exercising the judicial power of the State.[47] He said ([1989] I.R. 335, 341):

> "Before deciding whether the person concerned should be admitted to bail or remanded in custody, the commissioner must hear the contentions of both parties and any evidence that is put before him. He must take into account the various considerations which should be present to the mind of a judge in hearing such an application. He must then come to a determination as to whether the person concerned should be detained in custody for a period of up to eight days or released on bail. The decision taken by the peace commissioner and the process by which it is arrived at appear clearly to have the characteristics of a judicial rather than an administrative act."

This reasoning, it may be noted, lends no support to the view that issuing an arrest warrant is a judicial function. For such warrants are normally issued on an *ex parte* Garda application, and the question of hearing both parties' contentions does not arise.

Duration of Sentences: Judicial vs. Executive Power

State (O) v. *O'Brien* [1973] I.R. 50 raised the question of the precise dividing line between judicial power and executive power. The applicant had been convicted of murder in 1956, when he was 16 years old. At the time the sentence for murder was death; but in the case of a "young person" under the

---

[43] Or "some other person authorised in accordance with law to act for that purpose": Article 30.3. *Cf.* Costello J. in *Wheeler* v. *Culligan* [1989] I.R. 344, at 348–49: " . . . the Attorney General is not administering justice when he weighs up evidence before deciding whether to prosecute or not in cases in which he is a prosecuting authority . . . "

[44] See Chap. 14 *infra*.

[45] For a list see E. F. Ryan and P. P. Magee, *The Irish Criminal Process* (Cork 1983), App. G.

[46] In *State (Lynch)* v. *Ballagh* [1986] I.R. 203, 210. That *dictum* seems to have been approved by the Supreme Court in *State (Clarke)* v. *Roche* [1986] I.R. 619, 641.

[47] The expression "administering justice" derives from Art. 34.1 of the Constitution, while "exercising the judicial power" derives from Art. 37.1. The Supreme Court has held that they mean the same thing: *Goodman International Ltd.* v. *Hamilton* [1992] I.L.R.M. 145.

Children Act 1908—a category into which O fell—there was substituted instead by section 103 a sentence of detention during His Majesty's pleasure. When passing sentence on O, Teevan J. said that he should be "detained until the pleasure of the Government be made known concerning him." This was done on the basis that all powers exercisable by the monarch were necessarily executive powers, and hence had been inherited by the Government. But on O's application for habeas corpus the majority of the Supreme Court (Ó Dálaigh C.J., Walsh, Budd and FitzGerald JJ.: McLoughlin J. dissenting) rejected this view. The flexibility of the British constitution, it was pointed out, meant that judicial power could be conferred upon the monarch, even though he was in theory the head of the executive. It could not therefore be said that the Irish Government had *necessarily* inherited all powers vested in the monarch; whether or not it had inherited any given power must depend upon an examination of the true nature of the power in question. That conferred by the Act of 1908 was a judicial power and was now vested in the courts, not in the Government. It must now be understood as giving the trial court power to order detention for an indefinite period, a sentence which could at any time be terminated by the court, or which could be remitted by virtue of Article 13.6.

The decision in *O.'s* case generated doubts about section 2 of the Trial of Lunatics Act 1883, which deals with "guilty but insane" verdicts. Section 2 empowers a jury to bring in a special verdict to that effect, and continues:

> "Where such special verdict is found, the Court shall order the accused to be kept in custody as a criminal lunatic, in such place and in such manner as the Court shall direct *till the pleasure of the Lord Lieutenant shall be known* . . . " (Italics supplied.)

Shortly after *O.'s* case the practice developed of making an order that the defendant be detained in the Central Mental Hospital until further order. In *Application of Gallagher* [1991 1 I.R. 31 Johnson J. had initially made such an order in regard to the applicant, who had been found "guilty but insane" by a Central Criminal Court jury in July 1989. Just over six months later Gallagher applied for his release, on the basis of expert testimony that he was now sane. Johnson J. then amended his original order and directed that the applicant be detained in the Central Mental Hospital until the pleasure of the Government concerning him was known.[48] On appeal the Supreme Court upheld the correctness of the amended order.[49] It rejected an argument that the words italicised above in section 2 were constitutionally infirm as authorising the executive to exercise a judicial power. McCarthy J., in a judgment concurred in by his colleagues, said ([1991] 1 I.R. 31, 37):

> "The overriding circumstance is that the special verdict is a verdict of acquittal; the trial is concluded; the court does not pronounce a sentence; the role of the court is to order the detention of the person, the for-

---

[48] This on the basis that the Government, as the executive, had inherited the Lord Lieutenant's powers under the 1883 Act. See s.11 of the Adaptation of Enactments Act 1922 and s.4(1) of the Constitution (Consequential Provisions) Act 1937.

[49] This matter had been the subject of differing views amongst the judges of the High Court. In *Application of Ellis* [1990] 2 I.R. 291 O'Hanlon J. had made an order in the form subsequently approved in *Gallagher's* case, and Johnson J. had followed this precedent. But in *Application of Neilan* [1990] 2 I.R. 267 Keane J. had concluded that the 1883 Act was invalid as conferring judicial power on the executive.

mer accused, until the executive, armed with both the knowledge and resources to deal with the problem, decides on the future disposition of the person."

Consequently it was for the Government, or the Minister for Justice, to determine if and when the detained person was to be released. Shortly thereafter it was announced that the Minister for Justice had established a small expert committee to advise him on applications for release.[50]

The location of the dividing line between judicial and executive power in regard to sentences has also generated controversy in connection with certain types of suspended sentence.[51] In *State (Woods) v. Att.Gen.* [1969] I.R. 385 Butler J. had sentenced Woods to seven years penal servitude, with a proviso that when he had completed three years the rest of the sentence would be suspended, provided he had obeyed prison discipline. It was argued that this sentence was unconstitutional because the question whether or not Woods had obeyed prison discipline would naturally be decided by the governor. Thus, it was contended, the precise length of Woods' term in prison would be determined by someone who was not a judge. But the Supreme Court was satisfied that in pronouncing sentence Butler J. had reserved to himself the determination of the question whether Woods had obeyed prison discipline. Accordingly, it was held that the sentence contained no constitutional flaw.[52]

A different ground of challenge was invoked against a similar sentence by the same judge in *People (D.P.P.) v. Aylmer* (Supreme Court, December 18, 1986). There Butler J., when sentencing the applicant to ten years imprisonment, had directed that he be brought back before the court after he had served three years. If in the meantime he had conformed with normal prison discipline and had endeavoured to learn a skill, the court would consider suspending the balance of the sentence. It was argued that this sentence was unconstitutional as an interference with the executive power vested in the Government—i.e. the power to commute the sentence under Article 13.6 of the Constitution. Henchy, Griffin and Hederman JJ. held that in the circumstances of the case it was unnecessary to rule on the validity of the sentence, and they offered no views on the matter. Walsh and McCarthy JJ., however, concluded that no invalidity attached to the sentence. Walsh J. said (pp. 8 and 9 of his judgment):

> "Mr. Justice Butler had the undoubted power to impose a sentence of ten years imprisonment for the offence. He also had power to suspend the sentence in whole or in part upon such conditions as he might fix. The power of the executive . . . is a power to commute sentences not to suspend them . . . Mr. Justice Butler's order . . . could [not] be construed as a direction expressed or implied to the executive not to exercise the powers of commuting the sentence. The sentence imposed by Mr.

---

[50] The committee's terms of reference are " . . . to advise the Minister . . . as to whether the applicant is suffering from any mental disorder warranting his continued detention in the public and private interests (including the question of whether he would be a potential danger to any member of the public if released) . . . ": *The Irish Times*, November 22, 1991.

[51] The practice of suspending sentences has no statutory basis. For its origins see W. N. Osborough, "A Damocles Sword Guaranteed Irish: the Suspended Sentence in the Republic of Ireland" (1982) XVII *Irish Jurist* (n.s.) 221.

[52] In *People (D.P.P.) v. Cahill* [1980] I.R. 8 the Court of Criminal Appeal (Henchy, D'Arcy and Keane JJ.) held that this form of reviewable sentence was undesirable.

Justice Butler in no way involved an encroachment by the judicial arm of government upon the executive power. The sole power to impose a sentence is vested in the judicial arm of government and the sole arm to attach conditions to it is the judicial arm. The executive cannot impose a sentence of any description nor can it attach conditions to a sentence. Its power in respect of sentences is one of commuting or remitting sentences imposed by a court exercising criminal jurisdiction."[53]

No Executive/Legislative Intervention

Re Haughey [1971] I.R. 217 established that the administration of justice in criminal matters embraced trial, conviction and sentence. Save for the entry of a *nolle prosequi*,[54] no executive intervention in this process, once begun, is permissible. In *State (C.)* v. *Minister for Justice* [1967] I.R. 106 the provision impuned as invalid was the Lunatic Asylum (Ireland) Act 1875, s.13. This (as adapted and amended) empowered the Minister for Justice to direct that where a prisoner on remand was certified to be of unsound mind, he should be confined in a mental hospital until such time as he was certified to have recovered. The Minister could then direct that he be once again brought before the court which had remanded him. The Supreme Court found this power inconsistent with the Constitution. Ó Dálaigh C.J. observed that in 1875 an omnipotent parliament could enact this provision, with no problems about the separation of powers. But it was otherwise now. Section 13 would permit the court's remand to be set at naught and could be operated so as to effect an adjournment *sine die* of the preliminary investigation. This was " . . . about as large an intrusion upon a court proceeding as one could imagine" (at 116). The court found it possible to cut away the offending words, so that section 13 remains in force. Thus the Minister may still issue his directive, but when the original remand period ends the accused must be brought back before the District Court for trial, preliminary examination or further remand, as the court may direct.

A much more remarkable intervention was authorised by section 62 of the Courts of Justice Act 1936. This permitted the Director of Public Prosecutions, on a District Justice's refusing to send an accused forward for trial on indictment, himself to direct a return for trial. Section 62 was challenged—but upheld by the Supreme Court—in *State (Shanahan)* v. *Att. Gen.* [1964] I.R. 239. More recently, however, *Shanahan's* case has been overruled, and section 62 struck down, in *Costello* v. *D.P.P.* [1984] I.R. 436. In conducting the preliminary examination of an indictable offence, the Supreme Court held, a District Justice was exercising the judicial power of the State. When, in the exercise of such judicial power, there was a determination of the relevant justiciable issues, that determination could not be set aside or reversed by any other authority. The giving of a direction under section 62 was an interfer-

---

[53] Given the executive power stemming from Article 13.6, there can scarcely be any constitutional question-mark over ss.1 and 2 of the Prisons (Ireland) Act 1907 which authorise the remission of sentences for good behaviour.

[54] The sole source of power to enter a *nolle prosequi* is now s.12 of the Criminal Justice (Administration) Act 1924: Finlay P. so held in *State (O'Callaghan)* v. *Ó hUadaigh* [1977] I.R. 42. The power is exercisable by the D.P.P., or by the Attorney General in those cases where he is still a prosecuting authority. Its exercise may be open to judicial review: *State (McCormack)* v. *Curran* [1987] I.L.R.M. 225.

ence by the executive in the judicial domain, and any statutory provision purporting to authorise such interference was *ipso facto* repugnant to the Constitution.

Costello's case was distinguished in *O'Shea* v. *D.P.P.* [1989] I.L.R.M. 309. There the District Court had sent the appellant forward for trial on a charge of receiving. The indictment actually preferred against him, however, contained two counts—a modified one of receiving and another of burglary. These counts were inserted by the D.P.P. in exercise of the power contained in section 18 of the Criminal Procedure Act 1967,[55] and it was agreed that they were founded on the documents and exhibits considered by the District Court. Founding on *Costello's* case, the appellant contended that section 18 was unconstitutional as permitting an executive intrusion into the judicial domain in a criminal matter. The Supreme Court ruled otherwise. Finlay C.J. distinguished *Costello's* case on the ground that there section 62 of the 1936 Act permitted the D.P.P. to make an order which directly conflicted with the District Court's order of discharge. Section 18 of the 1967 Act did not do this. The fundamental decision of the District Court was that the accused should be sent forward for trial. Only when such a decision was made did the power to substitute or add counts arise. Finlay C.J. continued ([1989] I.L.R.M. 309, 322):

> "Having regard to the provisions of the Prosecution of Offences Act 1974, the Director of Public Prosecutions in commencing and conducting criminal prosecutions discharges a statutory function in the name of the People permitted by Article 30.3 of the Constitution. It is and must be an inherent part of the function of a prosecutor of a criminal offence triable on indictment to frame the precise form of the indictment and thereby to ensure that the true issue between the People and the accused is properly and fairly put before the court. To do so is an administrative or executive and certainly is not a judicial function. By substituting or adding a count the Director of Public Prosecutions is not purporting to determine any issue between the People and the accused, but is merely providing the vehicle for the determination of such issues by the court and the jury."[56]

Article 1, section 9 of the U.S. Constitution forbids Congress to pass any "Bill of Attainder." In *Cummings* v. *Missouri* (1866) 71 U.S. (4 Wall.) 277 the Supreme Court, *per* Field J., defined this term as follows (at 323):

> "A bill of attainder is a legislative act, which inflicts punishment without a judicial trial . . . . In these cases the legislative body in addition to its legitimate functions, exercises the powers and office of a judge, it assumes, in the language of the text books, judicial magistracy; it pronounces upon the guilt of the party without any of the forms or safe-

---

[55] s.18 provides: "where a person has been sent forward for trial under this Part the indictment against him may include, either in substitution for or in addition to counts charging the offence for which he has been sent forward, any counts founded on any of the documents (including any depositions and any statement taken under s.7) and exhibits considered by the justice at the preliminary examination, being counts which may lawfully be joined in the same indictment."

[56] In *Walsh* v. *President of the Circuit Court* [1989] I.L.R.M. 325 the Supreme Court reaffirmed *O'Shea* v. *D.P.P.* and reversed Murphy J.'s decision that s.18 was unconstitutional.

guards of a trial; it determines the sufficiency of the proofs produced, whether conformable to the rules of evidence or otherwise; and it fixes the degree of punishment in accordance with its own notions of the enormity of the offense."[57]

The text of Bunreacht na hÉireann contains no similar prohibition, but there can be no doubt that any legislation of this kind would violate its separation of powers provisions. Quite apart from the authorities already discussed, *Buckley* v. *Att. Gen.* [1950] I.R. 67[58] shows that the Oireachtas may not determine the outcome of *civil* proceedings. *A fortiori*, given Article 37.1, it could not attempt to administer justice in a criminal matter.

In *Maher* v. *Att. Gen.* [1973] I.R. 140 a much less dramatic legislative intervention was condemned as unconstitutional. This was section 44(2) of the Road Traffic Act 1968, which provided that in prosecutions for "driving under the influence" an analyst's certificate as to the concentration of alcohol in a blood or urine sample should be "conclusive evidence" as to the concentration of alcohol in the body of the person from whom the sample was taken. The sub-section was assailed as an invalid legislative infringement upon the judicial power, and the Supreme Court agreed that it was. In entrusting the administration of criminal justice exclusively to the courts, it was held, the Constitution necessarily reserved to them the power to determine whether all the essential ingredients of an offence had been proved against an accused person. Since it made the analyst's certificate *conclusive* evidence, section 44(2) purported to remove the determination of an essential ingredient from the courts. Hence it was invalid.

Criminal Offences and Disciplinary Proceedings

Where certain conduct is simultaneously a criminal offence and an offence against prison discipline, statute may validly assign the determination of the latter issue to the prison authorities. In *State (Murray)* v. *McRann* [1979] I.R. 33, the prosecutrix, a prisoner in Limerick prison, was adjudged by the respondent Governor to have committed a breach of discipline—common assault. In accordance with the statutory rules governing prisons, he imposed a penalty on her which included loss of privileges. She sought to have the decision quashed, arguing that since common assault was a criminal, as well as a disciplinary, offence this was an unconstitutional exercise of judicial power in a criminal matter. But a divisional court of the High Court (Finlay P., Murnaghan and Gannon JJ.) disagreed with this analysis. "Criminal matter" in Article 37.1 meant a procedure associated with the prosecution of someone for a crime—an offence against the state or public. The Governor, however, was not concerned with any such issue. His sole concern was with whether a breach of prison discipline had occurred and, if so, which of the permitted penalties should be imposed. The fact that certain

---

[57] A more recent example is *U.S.* v. *Lovett* (1946) 328 U.S. 303, where the House Un-American Activities Committee had made charges against three government employees. After investigation, the House Appropriations Committee had found that the three had engaged in "subversive activity." Congress then enacted legislation prohibiting the use of funds to pay them. The Supreme Court held this legislation an unconstitutional bill of attainder.

[58] Considered *infra*.

conduct might at one and the same time be a breach of discipline and a criminal offence did not make its investigation the investigation of a criminal offence.

This reasoning was applied by the Supreme Court in *Keady* v. *Commissioner, Garda Síochána* [1992] I.L.R.M. 312. In 1983 the plaintiff, then a member of the Garda Síochána, was charged with certain criminal offences. When his trial came on a *nolle prosequi* was entered on all charges. Thereafter disciplinary proceedings were instituted against him,[59] arising out of the same facts which had led to the criminal charges. Following a formal inquiry[60] he was found guilty and dismissed from the force. His contention that the inquiry had unconstitutionally adjudicated upon criminal matters was rejected. O'Flaherty J., whose colleagues concurred, said ([1992] I.L.R.M. 312, 321):

> "The reference in Article 37 of the Constitution excepting "criminal matters" must mean that there can be no trial of a person on a criminal charge save as provided for in Article 38. This cannot be held to exclude allegations of criminal conduct in other circumstances. Clearly many cases taken in the courts on the civil side may involve allegations of criminality: allegations of dangerous driving, fraud and perjury are random examples. There is no constitutional basis for saying that such allegations cannot be aired before administrative tribunals or before inquiries which have a statutory basis or at other domestic tribunals or inquiries."

Internment

It remains to note that the internment provisions of the Offences against the State Act 1939 were held invalid by Gavan Duffy J. on the ground that they amounted to an executive administration of criminal justice: *State (Burke)* v. *Lennon* [1940] I.R. 136. The power to intern depended upon a Minister's being "satisfied" as to certain matters, and Gavan Duffy J. concluded that the Minister's decision to order internment was "equivalent to a judgment pronounced against the internee for his dangerous activities" (at 152). Thus it was an invasion of the judicial power and hence repugnant to the Constitution. The Government, after an unsuccessful attempt to appeal this decision, responded by securing the passage of a Bill which re-enacted, with some amendments, the condemned provisions. The major change was that the power to intern was now conditioned upon a Minister's being "of opinion" as to the relevant matters. President Hyde referred the Bill to the Supreme Court under Article 26 of the Constitution. The Supreme Court found the argument that under this Bill the Minister was administering justice "wholly unsustainable": In *Re Article 26 and the Offences against the State (Amendment) Bill 1940* [1940] I.R. 470, 479.

---

[59] Under the Garda Síochána (Discipline) Regulations 1971 (S.I. No. 316 of 1971), made under s.14(1) of the Police Forces Amalgamation Act 1925. These have since been replaced by the Garda Síochána (Discipline) Regulations (S.I. No. 94 of 1989), made under the same statutory authority.

[60] Provided for by the same 1971 Regulations. The Supreme Court has held that courts should be slow to interfere with Garda disciplinary decisions: *Stroker* v. *Doherty* [1991] 1 I.R. 23, and this was reiterated in *Keady's* case.

Civil Matters

Article 37.1 gives the Oireachtas more leeway in civil than in criminal matters. "Limited functions and powers of a judicial nature" may be given to bodies which are not courts or persons who are not judges. Gavan Duffy J. once called this "a necessary, precautionary declaration": *O'Doherty* v. *Att. Gen. and O'Donnell* [1941] I.R. 569, 581—and its necessity arises from the terms of Article 34.1. Grave difficulties could have arisen had no exception been created to the principle there laid down, that justice must be administered by judges. No such exception had been made under the corresponding provisions of the 1922 Constitution, and this had given rise to doubts over the powers of the Master of the High Court: see *Roe* v. *McMullen* [1929] I.R. 9. Article 37.1 at least sets these doubts to rest.

Article 37.1 is obviously the constitutional foundation for the many statutes devolving judicial powers, such as those establishing the Censorship of Publications Board, the social welfare appeals system, the Employment Appeals Tribunal and others. It would presumably also validate the statutory provisions allowing the Board of Charitable Donations and Bequests to vary the terms of certain charitable trusts. But it does not permit legislative or executive intervention in pending proceedings. In *Buckley* v. *Att. Gen.* [1950] I.R. 67, an action was pending to determine the ownership of the funds of the old Sinn Féin organisation. The pleadings were closed and the case was ready for hearing as soon as a judge was available. The Oireachtas then passed the Sinn Féin Funds Act 1947, section 10 of which provided: (a) that all further proceedings in the action should be stayed; (b) that on an application by the Attorney General, the High Court should dismiss the action. Gavan Duffy P. denounced this measure as unconstitutional, and on appeal his view was affirmed by the Supreme Court. O'Byrne J. said (at 84):

> "In bringing these proceedings the plaintiffs were exercising a constitutional right and they were and are entitled to have the matter in dispute determined by the judicial organ of the State. The substantial effect of the Act is that the dispute is determined by the Oireachtas . . . this is clearly repugnant to the Constitution."

The prosecutor in *State (Divito)* v. *Arklow U.D.C.* [1986] I.L.R.M. 123 sought to shelter under the *Buckley* principle, in rather different circumstances. The facts were that in April 1982 Part III of the Gaming and Lotteries Act 1956 was in force in Arklow. Under it, the District Court granted the prosecutor a gaming licence. In June 1982 the Council's appeal to the Circuit Court was allowed. Divito then modified his premises in order to make a fresh application to the District Court. In January 1983 he published in the newspapers a statutory notice of intention to apply in March 1983 to the District Court for a licence. However, in February 1983 the Council rescinded its adoption of Part III; consequently, when in March Divito's application came on, it was adjourned and still stood adjourned. It was argued that the council's conduct amounted to an unconstitutional intrusion upon the judicial power. The decision to rescind frustrated Divito's application to the District Court and was analogous to the legislation condemned in *Buckley's* case.

The Supreme Court rejected this argument. The District Court was not seised of any pending proceeding. In February 1983, when the Council rescinded its earlier decision, the District Court had not acquired jurisdiction to make any order. It could not have such jurisdiction until Divito's application was moved, and by then the 1956 Act was not applicable in Arklow. This was not an unconstitutional invasion of the judicial process.[61]

To decide whether Article 37.1 validates a given statute one must determine

    (a) whether the power conferred is "judicial" (or, which comes to the same thing, involves the administration of justice)[62]
    (b) if so, whether it is "limited."

Nature of judicial power: introduction

The presence of Article 37.1 in the Constitution obviously springs from a desire to avoid the rigidities of its predecessor.[63] Its underlying philosophy is surely that the legal system was not to be frozen in the mould of 1937; that within limits, the Oireachtas could hive off existing jurisdictions from the courts and transfer them to other bodies, and create new justiciable controversies to be decided by bodies other than the courts. In other words, the conception appears to have been that the courts would, and must, continue to exercise certain "core functions" (such as adjudicating in criminal matters) while others could be devolved.

As Dr. Marshall has written[64]:

"Belief in the importance of protecting the judicial power from encroachment by the legislature or executive must at least invoke the idea that there is an appropriate area for its operation."

Article 37.1 would appear to enshrine that belief, and to give the courts the task of defining the "appropriate area for its operation." This would suggest a purposive approach, the question being—what characteristics and qualifications do judges possess which would make them the only proper arbiters of such disputes? But the courts—doubtless inhibited by judicial modesty[65]— have in general[66] abstained from adopting this approach. Instead they have preferred to use analogy and history as guides, looking at what courts characteristically do and have done, and deriving a number of tests from this. In

---

[61] See, too, the Supreme Court's subsequent decision in *Application of Camillo* [1988] I.R. 104.

[62] In *Goodman International* v. *Hamilton* [1992] I.L.R.M. 145 the Supreme Court held that these concepts are indistinguishable.

[63] In *Madden* v. *Ireland & Att. Gen.* (unreported, No. 1977/2407P, May 22, 1980) McMahon J. said (pp. 8–9 of his judgment): "Experience has shown that modern government can not be carried on without many regulatory bodies and those bodies can not function effectively under a rigid separation of powers. Art. 37 had no counterpart in the Constitution of Saorstát Éireann and in my view introduction of it to the Constitution is to be attributed to a realisation of the needs of modern government."

[64] Geoffrey Marshall, *Constitutional Theory* (Oxford 1971), p. 120.

[65] A virtue invoked by Kingsmill Moore J., speaking for the Supreme Court, in *Att. Gen.* v. *Ryan's Car Hire Ltd.* [1965] I.R. 642, 653: "If it could safely be assumed that all members of a Supreme Court were perfectly endowed with wisdom and completely familiar with all branches of law, to treat their judgments as infallible would need but little justification. Judicial modesty has refrained from putting forward such a claim . . ."

[66] A possible exception is the decision of the former Supreme Court in *Re Solicitors Act 1954* [1960] I.R. 239, considered *infra*.

consequence, the line between the constitutionally permissible and the constitutionally prohibited is blurred.[67]

The Oireachtas has made little use of the freedom conferred by Article
37.1. Disputes arising out of the social welfare system are adjudicated upon
by specialised tribunals outside the court structure.[68] The Employment
Appeals Tribunal[69] has jurisdiction over a number of job-related issues, most
notably unfair dismissals.[70] The Labour Court (which is *not* composed of
judges) adjudicates on equal pay[71] and other equal treatment disputes.[72]
(These, it should be noted, may involve complex issues of fact and law—
including EC law.[73]) None of these developments has so far been the subject
of constitutional challenge.

The uncertain state of the law in this area is demonstrated by the decision
to add a new section to Article 37. What is now Article 37.2 was inserted by
the Sixth Amendment of the Constitution Act 1979, designed specifically and
solely to preserve adoption orders made by An Bord Uchtála from constitutional challenge. That Board—established by the Adoption Act 1952—is
the only body empowered to make adoption orders; no court has authority to
do so. While it has usually been chaired by a judge, the Board is not a court,
and its membership includes a majority of persons who are not judges. In *M.
v. An Bord Uchtála* [1977] I.R. 287 the plaintiffs contended that the 1952 Act
invalidly conferred a non-limited judicial power on the Board. In a judgment
which unfortunately has not been reported, Butler J. rejected this argument,
holding that the Board's functions were purely administrative. The Supreme
Court found it possible to decide the case on other grounds, and consequently declined to pronounce on the constitutional question. Subsequently,
in *G. v. An Bord Uchtála* [1980] I.R. 32, Walsh J. took the view that the Board
was exercising an administrative, not a judicial function (see [1980] I.R.
71–72). But the other four members of the Supreme Court said this issue had
not been argued, and declined to express any views on the matter. To quiet
any lurking doubts on this very important issue a constitutional amendment
was felt desirable: hence Article 37.2.[74]

Finally, it is important to note that no tribunal or other body established
under the shelter of Article 37.1 can be placed beyond the supervisory juris-

---

[67] See further James Casey, "The Judicial Power under Irish Constitutional Law" (1975) 24
I.C.L.Q. 305.
[68] See Pt. VIII of the Social Welfare (Consolidation) Act 1981, as amended by Pt. V of the
Social Welfare Act 1990.
[69] Which normally sits in divisions of three, consisting of a barrister or solicitor plus a representative of employers and one of workers.
[70] A jurisdiction created by the Unfair Dismissals Act 1977.
[71] Under the Anti-Discrimination (Equal Pay) Act 1974.
[72] Under the Employment Equality Act 1977.
[73] See *e.g. Murphy* v. *Bord Telecom Éireann* [1988] I.L.R.M. 53: *Aer Lingus Teo.* v. *Labour Court*
[1990] I.L.R.M. 485.
[74] In *The Irish Constitution* (2nd ed., Dublin 1984) the late Professor John Kelly queried whether
such an ad hoc amendment was desirable. He suggested that it might subsequently be held to
involve the proposition that An Bord Uchtála was exercising non-limited judicial power, and
that this might mean the invalidation of statutes conferring analogous powers on other non-
judicial bodies. This could be a danger: but it is plain from the historical background that
Art. 37.2 was enacted *ex abundanti cautela*. The Supreme Court has on three occasions referred
to the history behind a constitutional amendment—*State (Sheerin)* v. *Kennedy* [1966] I.R. 379,
387: *State (Browne)* v. *Feran* [1967] I.R. 147, 168: *Re Article 26 and the Emergency Powers Bill 1976*
[1977] I.R. 159, 171. Presumably, then, the courts may look behind Article 37.2, and if this is
done the danger feared should not arise.

diction of the High Court.[75] Thus an allegedly invalid decision would be open to challenge even if the relevant statute neglected to provide for an appeal to the High Court.

The decisions

In *McDonald* v. *Bord na gCon* (*No.* 2) [1965] I.R. 217 Kenny J. formulated five criteria for deciding whether a power is judicial in nature. These criteria have been applied in a number of subsequent cases,[76] and they won clear approval from the Supreme Court in *Goodman International* v. *Hamilton* [1992] I.L.R.M. 145. It would seem—though the question is still unsettled[77]—that all five criteria must be satisfied if the power in question is to qualify as judicial.

These five criteria are ([1965] I.R. 217, 231):

"1. [A] dispute or controversy as to the existence of legal rights or a violation of the law;
2. The determination or ascertainment of the rights of parties or the imposition of liabilities or the infliction of a penalty;
3. The final determination (subject to appeal) of legal rights or liabilities or the imposition of penalties;
4. The enforcement of those rights or liabilities or the imposition of a penalty by the Court or by the executive power of the State which is called in by the Court to enforce its judgment;
5. The making of an order by the Court which as a matter of history is an order characteristic of Courts in this country."

In *Kennedy* v. *Hearne* [1988] I.R. 481 the plaintiff challenged the constitutionality of section 7 of the Finance Act 1968. This established a procedure for dealing with employers who had failed to pay the monthly instalments of tax deducted from employees' wages. The Revenue Commissioners were authorised to issue an estimate of the sum due which, if the employer took no action within a stated period,[78] could be enforced.[79] It was argued that the Revenue Commissioners were here administering justice, because they were deciding whether a person was in default in payment of taxes. Dismissing this contention, the Supreme Court held that the first of Kenny J.'s criteria was not satisfied, since no justiciable controversy existed here. A usual feature of such a controversy, said the court, was that two parties were contesting some matter, whether of fact or law, with conflicting or contradictory assertions concerning it. But here the Revenue Commissioners did not decide in favour of one contender against another. Nor was Kenny J.'s second criterion satisfied, for the Revenue Commissioners' determination that the tax had not been paid did not impose a liability on the taxpayer or

---

[75] See Chap. 10 *infra*, S.v. Supervisory Jurisdiction.
[76] *e.g. Application of Neilan* [1990] 2 I.R. 267: *Wheeler* v. *Culligan* [1989] I.R. 344.
[77] The Supreme Court's decision in *Keady* v. *Commr., Garda Síochána* [1992] I.L.R.M. 312 seems to leave the matter open.
[78] By giving notice to the Revenue Commissioners within fourteen days from the service of the notice on him/her, requiring the claim to be referred for decision to the Appeal Commissioners: Finance Act 1968, s.7(2)(*a*).
[79] Under s.485 of the Income Tax Act 1967, by the issuing of a certificate to the country registrar or sheriff, who was then empowered to levy execution on the goods and chattels of the defaulter.

affect any of his rights. What was capable of imposing a liability or affecting rights was the fact of default in payments. If, through a mistake, that fact was absent—as had happened here—anything occurring subsequently was a nullity.

Finally, in what seems to be an application of Kenny J.'s fifth criterion the Supreme Court, *per* Finlay C.J., said ([1988] I.R. 481, 489):

> "A further test which can be applied to the question whether this section allows the exercise of a judicial function is whether it has the effect of invading or ousting any of the functions vested in the judges by Article 34 of the Constitution. The Court is satisfied that it has not."

The reason was that where, as here, the enforcement procedure had been set in train erroneously—no default in payment having occurred—the courts could intervene. They were empowered to resolve the issue between the taxpayer and the Revenue Commissioners, halt the enforcement process and compensate the taxpayer in respect of any loss already incurred. The section did not, therefore oust the jurisdiction of the courts.[80]

In *Wheeler* v. *Culligan* [1989] I.R. 344 the plaintiff attacked as unconstitutional section 2 of the Extradition (Amendment) Act 1987, which gave the Attorney General an entirely new function of vetting certain extradition applications. He was empowered to direct that a foreign arrest warrant be not endorsed for execution by the Garda Síochána; and he was *obliged* to give such a direction

> " . . . unless the Attorney General, having considered such information as he deems appropriate, is of opinion that
> (a) there is a clear intention to prosecute or, as the case may be, to continue the prosecution of the person named or described in the warrant concerned for the offence specified therein . . . and
> (b) such intention is founded on the existence of sufficient evidence."[81]

It was claimed that in reaching an opinion on the matters referred to and deciding whether to issue a direction, the Attorney General was administering justice. But Costello J. could not accept this. Having referred to Kenny J.'s five criteria, Costello J. continued ([1989] I.R. 344, 348):

> "As to number (1), in examining the information referred to in the section and arriving at the opinions he is required to arrive at under the section, he is not, in my view, considering as a judge does a dispute or controversy as to the existence of a legal right. As to (2), he is not making any determination of rights. As to (3), he is not making any final determination of any legal rights. As to (4), he is not enforcing any rights or liabilities, and as to (5), he is certainly not making any order which is characteristic of a court of this country."

Costello J. also drew an analogy between these functions of the Attorney General and those of the Garda Commissioner in endorsing extradition warrants for execution in the State. In regard to the latter the Supreme Court had ruled that they did not unconstitutionally involve the Commissioner in administering justice: *Shannon* v. *Fanning* [1984] I.R. 548. The Com-

---

[80] In *Deighan* v. *Hearne* [1990] 1 I.R. 499 the Supreme Court, following *Kennedy* v. *Hearne*, rejected challenges to the validity of ss.184(2) and 485 of the Income Tax Act 1967.

[81] Extradition Act 1965, s.44B, inserted by s.2(1)(*a*), Extradition (Amendment) Act 1987.

missioner's endorsement did not in itself lead to extradition, which could occur only on foot of a District Court order. Thus, the Commissioner's function was merely procedural, not judicial. This, said Costello J., was true also of the Attorney General's new functions. These involved him in taking a procedural decision necessary to be taken before justice was subsequently administered in the courts.

In *Goodman International* v. *Hamilton* [1992] I.L.R.M. 145 it was argued that a tribunal of inquiry into the beef industry, established under statute,[82] was unconstitutionally administering justice, as its remit covered matters which were the subject of current civil proceedings. The Supreme Court rejected this contention. Invoking Kenny J.'s five criteria, Finlay C.J. said that the tribunal's activities fulfilled none of them—with the possible exception of the first. The fifth criterion in particular was not satisfied, for it had never been a judicial function to make a finding of fact *in vacuo* and to report on this to the legislature. Even in ordinary litigation the courts did not make findings of fact which did not have an effect on the determination of a right.[83]

The five criteria formulated by Kenny J. in *McDonald's* case have thus clearly provided a useful test for deciding whether a power is judicial. But the fifth of them—" . . . the making of an order . . . which as a matter of history is . . . characteristic of courts in this country"—may be somewhat misleading. (The same applies to the Supreme Court's reformulation of that fifth criterion in *Kennedy* v. *Hearne*, which involves asking whether the challenged provisions have " . . . the effect of invading or ousting any of the functions vested in the judges by Article 34 . . . ") For some orders traditionally made by Irish courts do not result from the exercise of judicial power in the sense intended by the Constitution.[84] The test of history would also exclude from the ambit of the judicial power new justiciable controversies created by statute leading to a novel kind of order.[85] The Constitution can hardly have been intended to produce the latter result, or to freeze what may be mere historical accident into constitutional dogma.

The meaning of "limited"

Only if the power devolved by statute is truly of a judicial nature does the question whether it is "limited" arise. For subject to other constitutional con-

---

[82] Tribunals of Inquiry (Evidence) Acts 1921 and 1979.

[83] Finlay C.J. also rejected the plaintiffs' argument that the tribunal could usurp the courts' functions in respect of existing or future civil proceedings. Its findings of fact could not be used in any existing or potential litigation.

[84] Cp. Keane J. in *Application of Neilan* [1990] 2 I.R. 267, 278: " . . . a wide variety of powers which might, on one view, be regarded as executive are at present vested in the judiciary, such as the wardship jurisdiction of the High Court and the various jurisdictions vested in the High Court under the Companies Acts, 1963 to 1986."

[85] That a power may be in essence judicial even if it has never been vested in the courts was suggested in the *Report of the Committee on the Price of Building Land* (Pr. 3632). The majority of that committee, including Kenny J., recommended that a new jurisdiction should be conferred on the High Court, under which it could declare certain lands to be "designated areas." These would be lands which, in the court's opinion, would be used for future development *and* whose market value had been increased by works carried out by a local authority. Once lands were designated in this way the local authority would have power to acquire them compulsorily at existing use value plus 25 per cent. The majority believed the courts would

straints—such as the fundamental rights provisions—the Oireachtas may confer *unlimited* powers of a non-judicial nature on any person or body.

The former Supreme Court's decision in *Re Solicitors Act 1954* [1960] I.R. 239 is the principal authority on the meaning of "limited." The court had concluded that the powers given by that Act to the Disciplinary Committee of the Incorporated Law Society were judicial in nature. But they were not limited so as to be saved by Article 37.1. The limitation posited by that provision did not relate to the number of persons affected, nor to the number of powers conferred nor to their subject-matter.[86] The court, *per* Kingsmill Moore J., said ([1960] I.R. 239, 263–264):

> " . . . it is the powers and functions which are in their own nature to be limited. A tribunal having but a few powers and functions but those of far-reaching effect and importance could not properly be regarded as exercising "limited" powers and functions . . . The test as to whether a power is or is not 'limited' . . . lies in the effect of the assigned powers when exercised. If the exercise of the assigned powers and functions is calculated to affect in the most profound and far-reaching way the lives, liberties, fortunes or reputations of those against whom they are exercised they cannot properly be described as 'limited.' "[87]

The *Solicitors Act* case and professional discipline

In *Re Solicitors Act* 1954 [1960] I.R. 239 the Disciplinary Committee of the Incorporated Law Society had found two solicitors guilty of professional misconduct and ordered that their names be struck off the roll of solicitors. The Committee was acting under the 1954 Solicitors Act, which had transferred the power to strike off from the Chief Justice to the Committee, and also empowered it to order the making of restitution or satisfaction to any aggrieved party. An appeal from the Committee's decisions lay to the Chief Justice. The two solicitors argued that the 1954 Act unconstitutionally conferred a non-limited judicial power on the Disciplinary Committee. The Supreme Court, reversing the High Court,[88] accepted this argument.

In concluding that the powers conferred on the Disciplinary Committee were judicial in nature, the Supreme Court used analogy and history as guidelines. Kingsmill Moore J., speaking for the court, referred to the power to strike a solicitor off the roll as a sanction whose consequences could be

---

hold that a decision whether lands should be included in a designated area was an administration of justice, and that authority to make such decisions could be entrusted only to the courts.

[86] The Supreme Court's reasoning on this point is not beyond criticism: see the author's article "The Judicial Power Under Irish Constitutional Law" (1975) 24 *I.C.L.Q.* 305, 321–22.

[87] In *State (Calcul Ltd.)* v. *Appeal Commissioners* (1984 No. 640 S.S., December 18, 1986) Barron J. applied these tests to the statutory functions of the Appeal Commissioners under the Income Tax Acts. He concluded that, given the nature of the orders they were empowered to make, the Commissioners were not exercising judicial functions; or, alternatively, that their powers and functions were "limited" within the meaning of Art. 37.1.

[88] As the 1954 Act envisaged, the proceedings—in form an appeal against the Disciplinary Committee's decision—came on before Maguire C.J. He ruled that in hearing the appeal he was acting as a judge of the High Court: [1960] I.R. 239, 242. (This would engage the appellate jurisdiction of the Supreme Court); see Art. 34.4.3° and Chap. 10 *infra*, *S.* v. *Appellate* jurisdiction (a) from the High Court.

more severe than a term of imprisonment. He continued ([1960] I.R. 239, 274–75):

> "The imposition of a penalty, which has such consequences, would seem to demand from those who impose it the qualities of impartiality, independence and experience which are required for the holder of a judicial office, who, under the criminal law, imposes a fine or short sentence of imprisonment."

A further analogy was found in the power to order the making of restitution or satisfaction. This could presumably only be exercised in cases of misconduct; but misconduct would include fraud and negligence—matters in respect of which courts could award damages. The power given to the Committee could not be distinguished from that possessed by the courts.

> "The questions which can arise before the Committee are as contentious, as difficult, and as important as the questions which would arise before a Court trying a common law action for negligence or fraud. In the opinion of the Court a tribunal which may make such an order is properly described as administering justice and such a tribunal unless composed of judges is unconstitutional." (At 274.)

A combination of history and necessity was also invoked.

> "Historically the act of striking solicitors off the roll has always been reserved to judges. It is necessary for the proper administration of justice that the Courts should be served by legal practitioners of high integrity and professional competence and that the judges should have the power not only of removing those who in their opinion fail to meet the requirements of the office but of retaining those who do." (At 275.)

Thus the powers conferred on the Disciplinary Committee were judicial.

For the reasons already given, the Supreme Court further concluded that the judicial powers thus conferred were not "limited" in the sense of Article 37.1. The disciplinary provisions of the 1954 Act were therefore unconstitutional. And the argument that the provision of an appeal to the Chief Justice made all well was specifically rejected. The existence of an appeal to the courts could not restore constitutionality to a tribunal whose decisions, if unappealed, amounted to an administration of justice.

The *Solicitors Act* case obviously raises questions as to the validity of the statutes governing discipline in other professions. The relevant bodies may lack power to order restitution, and the disciplinary powers they exercise may never have been lodged with the courts; but they have power to deprive individuals of the right to practise their professions. Is this enough to make their function judicial (and, presumably, not "limited")? The recent Supreme Court decision in *Keady* v. *Commr., Garda Síochána* [1992] I.L.R.M. 312 suggests that the answer is—No. The court there rejected the plaintiff's attempt to apply the *Solicitors Act* reasoning to Garda disciplinary procedures. O'Flaherty J., his colleagues concurring, said that the situation relating to solicitors must be regarded as exceptional, even anomalous, and owed a great deal to the fact that, historically, judges had always been responsible for the decision to strike solicitors off the roll. On this basis, the true *ratio* of the *Solicitors Act* case would depend upon the historical factors there invoked.

As a consequence, the statutes governing discipline in other professions should be constitutionally safe—at least so far as the separation of powers is concerned.

Years before *Keady's* case was decided statutes had altered the disciplinary procedures in certain professions, and judicial decisions had upheld the new systems. In *M. v. Medical Council and Att. Gen.*[1984] I.R. 485, the plaintiff sought a declaration that certain disciplinary provisions of the Medical Practitioners Act 1978 were repugnant to the Constitution. Under the Act a Fitness to Practise Committee (composed of members of the Medical Council) was to inquire into allegations of (*inter alia*) professional misconduct. The Committee reported to the Council, which could decide that the practitioner's name should be erased from the register. The practitioner was entitled to apply to the High Court within 21 days to cancel the decision. If no such application was made, the Council could apply to the High Court for confirmation of the decision, and the High Court was to confirm it unless it saw good reason to the contrary. Finlay P. distinguished the *Solicitors Act* case, saying ([1984] I.R. 485, 497–98):

> "There is a very striking difference between the extent and nature of the powers there conferred on the disciplinary committee and the powers conferred by the Act of 1978 on the Fitness to Practise Committee and/or the Council.
>
> Neither the Committee nor the Council has any power to erase the name of a practitioner from the Register; to suspend him from practice; to make him pay compensation or to award costs against him. The only power vested in them in regard to any of these matters (other than the payment of compensation which is not provided for in the Act at all) is to initiate proceedings in The High Court which may lead to an order by The High Court in respect of any of those matters. Not only is this difference between the provisions contained in the two statutes striking, but it seems to me to go to the root of the decision of the Supreme Court in the *Solicitors Act 1954* case."

No doubt in the expectation that the Supreme Court would accept Finlay P.'s reasoning in the *M.* case, the statutes governing discipline in the dental and nursing professions were re-cast on the pattern of the Medical Practitioners Act 1978.[89] Though the matter has not arisen directly before that court, this expectation seems justified. In *K. v. An Bord Altranais* [1990] 2 I.R. 396 the Supreme Court had to consider the construction—as distinct from the validity—of the Nurses Act 1985. In the course of his judgment, with which Griffin and McCarthy JJ. agreed, Finlay C.J. said (at 403):

> "The essence of the procedure contained in this Act for the regulation of the registration and disciplining of members of the nursing profession is that it is in the court, namely, the High Court, that the decision effective to lead to an erasure or suspension of the operation of registration must be made. The necessity for that procedure to vest that power unequivocally in the court, in my view, arises from the constitutional frailty that would attach to the delegation of any such power to a body which was not a court established under the Constitution, having regard to the

---

[89] Dentists Act 1985, ss.39(3) and (4): Nurses Act 1985, ss.39(3) and (4).

decision of the former Supreme Court in *In re The Solicitors Act* [1960] I.R. 239."

Disciplinary provisions of this type would thus seem to be challenge-proof.

Unresolved questions

Possible constitutional difficulties appear to have influenced the form of the Unfair Dismissals Act 1977. This Act created a new jurisdiction over unfair dismissals disputes, and vested it in the Employment Appeals Tribunal. That body—which is not composed of judges—has the power to determine claims of unfair dismissal (as very broadly defined in the Act). Should it find in favour of the employee, the Tribunal may determine that the employer should reinstate—or alternatively re-engage—the employee, or pay compensation not exceeding 104 weeks remuneration. It would appear that the power conferred upon the Tribunal is a judicial one; it is plainly analogous to the courts' traditional jurisdiction over contracts. Whether it is "limited" may be open to question. The Tribunal can (and has) assessed compensation in sums larger than the Circuit Court may award in damages. And a determination in favour of reinstatement is analogous to the award of a decree of specific performance—which the courts have always declined to grant in respect of contracts of employment. However, the Act consistently refers to the "determinations" (not "decisions" or "awards") of the Tribunal. And Section 10 contains machinery for the enforcement of Tribunal determinations, under which the Minister for Labour may, if an employer has not complied with a determination, institute proceedings in the Circuit Court against that employer "for redress under this Act." The Circuit Court is authorised to *order* the employer to make "the appropriate redress," should it find the employee entitled thereto. In no sense is the Circuit Court bound by the Tribunal's determination, either as to the entitlement to redress, or the form it should take.

The restricted authority of the Tribunal may be compared with that of the Labour Court in sex discrimination cases under the Employment Equality Act 1977. Section 24 of that Act empowers the court (which is *not* composed of judges) to make *orders* directing implementation of an earlier determination. Failure to carry out such an order (which may be one for payment of up to 104 weeks remuneration) is a criminal offence, punishable on summary conviction by a fine. (For the reasons given earlier in this chapter, this offence is triable only in the regular courts.) Whether this withholding from the Employment Appeals Tribunal of the power to make binding orders makes it proof against constitutional challenge still awaits decision.

Mandatory Orders

In *State (O'Rourke)* v. *Kelly* [1983] I.R. 38, section 62(3) of the Housing Act 1966 was challenged as an unconstitutional invasion of the judicial power. Section 62 provides a mechanism whereby a housing authority (in this case Dublin Corporation) may recover possession of a dwelling provided by it. An application is made to the District Court for a warrant authorising recovery. Section 62(3) then provides:

" . . . the justice shall, in case he is satisfied that the demand mentioned in the said subsection (1) has been duly made, issue the warrant."

This, it was argued, deprived the District Justice of any real discretion in the matter and was thus an invalid intrusion into the judicial domain. The Supreme Court rejected this contention. O'Higgins C.J., delivering the judgment of the court, said ([1983] I.R. 38, 61):

> "It will be seen that it is only when the provisions of sub-s. 1 of s.62 have been complied with and the demand duly made to the satisfaction of the District Justice that he must issue the warrant. In other words, it is only following the establishment of specified matters that the sub-section operates. This is no different to many of the statutory provisions which, on proof of certain matters, make it mandatory on a court to make a specified order. Such legislative provisions are within the competence of the Oireachtas."

The report (though not the judgment) shows that in 1968 the High Court had held that section 62(1) imposed a condition precedent to the issue of a warrant under subsection (3). This was proof of the following matters:

(a) that the dwelling was provided by a local authority under the Housing Act 1966
(b) that there was no tenancy in the dwelling
(c) that possession had been duly demanded
(d) that the occupier failed to give possession
(e) that the demand stated the authority's intention, in the event of non-compliance, to apply for a warrant.

Presumably this is what the Supreme Court meant by "the establishment of specified matters." On that basis it is clear that section 62(3) did not attempt to convert the District Justice into a mere rubber-stamp; he/she would make a judicial determination as to whether the statutory preconditions existed.

O'Rourke's case was distinguished in *State (McEldowney)* v. *Kelleher* [1983] I.R. 289. At issue here was a provision of the Street and House to House Collections Act 1962, which regulates the collection of money from the public. It is an offence to hold such a collection without a permit, an application for which is made to the local Garda Chief Superintendent. He is directed to refuse an application if (*inter alia*) he is of opinion that the proceeds, or part thereof, would be used for an unlawful object or for the benefit of an unlawful organisation (section 9). Section 13 provides for an appeal to the District Court against refusal of a permit; but sub-section (4) provided that an appeal must be disallowed if, on the hearing thereof, a member of the Garda Síochána not below the rank of Inspector stated on oath that he had reasonable grounds for believing that the proceeds would be used for an unlawful object or for the benefit of an unlawful organisation.

The prosecutor McEldowney had been refused a permit and his appeal to the District Court had been disallowed, the District Justice holding that section 13(4) gave him no alternative. In certiorari proceedings McEldowney then challenged the validity of section 13(4). Costello J. rejected the challenge, holding that the Oireachtas was free to decide whether, and on what conditions, an appeal should lie to the District Court in such a matter. Having opted to give that court an appellate jurisdiction, the Oireachtas was at liberty to decide that certain issues should not be justiciable by the court. By so deciding, it was not infringing the judicial power; it was merely delimiting the jurisdiction conferred on that court. Moreover, *State (O'Rourke)* v. *Kelly*

[1983] I.R. 58 showed that the fact that a District Justice was required by law to make a mandatory order was not *per se* unconstitutional. On appeal the Supreme Court reversed this decision and held section 13(4) unconstitutional. Had the Oireachtas wished to treat cases covered by the subsection as matters in which no jurisdiction existed, it would have said so clearly. The true effect of the subsection was that, if evidence of a certain type was given, the District Justice was obliged to disallow the appeal; all discretion to do otherwise was removed. The court referred to *Buckley* v. *Att. Gen.* [1950] I.R. 67, *Maher* v. *Att. Gen.* [1973] I.R. 140 and *State (C.)* v. *Minister for Justice* [1967] I.R. 106. The judgment (*per* Walsh J.) then continues ([1983] I.R. 289, 306):

> "In the opinion of the court the present case falls squarely within the principles enunciated in those decisions. The statute creates a judicial controversy and then purports to compel the court to decide it in a particular way upon a particular statement of opinion being given upon oath as to whether or not a statutory reason for refusing the permit exists, whatever opinion the court may have formed on the issue in question or might have formed if it had heard any evidence upon it."

Moreover, *O'Rourke's* case was distinguishable:

> "It is not . . . an authority for the proposition that the District Court in the exercise of its judicial functions must adjudicate in a particular way upon the issues in dispute irrespective of the opinion, if any, which has been formed by the District Justice upon the issues before him." ([1983] I.R. 289, 307).

McEldowney's case does not decide that the Oireachtas must provide an appeal against such administrative decisions; nor that, should it do so, the appeal must lie to the courts. If statute grants such an appeal to the courts, it may by using appropriate language withhold certain matters from that appellate jurisdiction. What the Oireachtas may not do is to grant an appeal to the courts and then attempt, in one or more areas, to dictate the outcome.[90]

The decision in *McEldowney's* case raises a doubt as to the correctness of part of the High Court's conclusions in *O'Reilly & Judge* v. *D.P.P. & Att. Gen.*[1984] I.L.R.M. 224. There an attack had been launched against the validity of section 48, Offences against the State Act 1939. This provides that where a person's trial is pending before the Circuit Court or Central Crimi-

---

[90] *McEldowney's* case seems to have been given an extended application in *Cashman* v. *Clifford* [1989] I.R. 121. There the applicant asserted that part of the Betting Act 1931, dealing with the registration of bookmaker' premises, was unconstitutional. A Cork bookmaker had applied, in accordance with the Act, to the local Garda Superintendent for a certificate of suitability for new premises. The applicant had objected, as he was entitled to do, and the Garda Superintendent had refused the certificate. The bookmaker exercised his statutory right of appeal to the District Court—at which point the applicant found himself shut out, for section 13(5)(*a*) provided that only the Garda Superintendent and the Revenue Commissioners were entitled to be heard and adduce evidence in opposition to the bookmaker's appeal. Founding on *McEldowney's* case Barron J. held section 13(5)(*a*) unconstitutional. That decision, he said, disposed of the arguments that the Oireachtas was merely limiting the right of appeal, and that there was no *lis* before the District Court. And the impugned provision, though not seeking to impose a particular decision on the District Court, was nonetheless an interference with the judicial process. It impermissibly restricted the District Court by limiting the persons who might be heard or adduce evidence before it.

nal Court, the D.P.P. may apply to the High Court for the transfer of the trial
to a special criminal court. Such application is grounded upon the D.P.P.'s
certificate that the ordinary courts are, in his opinion, inadequate to secure
the effective administration of justice and the preservation of public peace
and order in relation to the trial of that person on that charge. On the hearing of the application "the High Court shall make the order applied for. . . .
" This, it was contended, was an unconstitutional intrusion upon the judicial
power.

Carroll J. declined to accept the argument. In her view the constitutional
jurisdiction of the High Court was limited by Article 38.3 (which authorises
the establishment of special criminal courts). Thus the provision for a
mandatory order transferring the trial did not constitute an unwarranted
intrusion on the High Court's powers.

The conclusion that Article 38.3 operates to limit the High Court's jurisdiction seems questionable. It may limit that court's criminal jurisdiction, in
the sense that it loses authority to try cases properly transferred to a special
criminal court. However, it does not clearly indicate an intention to deprive
the High Court of its normal judicial discretion. The effect of the Offences
against the State Act 1939, s.48, is to require the High Court to rubber-stamp
the conclusions of the D.P.P. Unlike the provision at issue in *O'Rourke's* case
(*supra*), the section does not require the High Court to be satisfied as to the
matters in the certificate. Consequently the court is bereft of all discretion
over the important question—should the accused be tried with or without a
jury?

It cannot be denied, however, that the Constitution foresaw the need for
special criminal courts, and gave the Oireachtas great latitude in deciding
how their jurisdiction is to be invoked. The terms of Article 38.3 make this
plain. And invoking that jurisdiction *via* the D.P.P.'s certificate has several
times been judicially approved (see *Re the Criminal Law (Jurisdiction) Bill 1976*
[1977] I.R. 129, 151). Practical difficulties would attend any statutory
requirement that the High Court be satisfied as to the matters certified. This
would involve the disclosure in open court of the material on which the
D.P.P. based his opinion. Finlay P., in a slightly different context, once described such disclosures as "a security impossibility": *Savage* v. *D.P.P. & Att.
Gen.* [1982] I.L.R.M. 385, 389.

It must therefore be doubtful whether the Supreme Court would invalidate
section 48—*McEldowney's* case notwithstanding. In matters involving security, a pattern (similar to that in other countries) of judicial deference to legis-
lative/executive judgment is plain: see the Supreme Court's judgment in *State
(Lynch)* v. *Cooney* [1982] I.R. 337.

The *Abbey Films* Case

Abbey Films v. *Att. Gen.* [1981] I.R. 158 raised an unusual aspect of the separation of powers. For the claim was not that the relevant statute deprived
the High Court of power but rather that it was accorded too much. The case
arose from an investigation into film distribution by the Examiner of Restrictive Practices, under the Restrictive Practices Act 1972.

Section 15 of that Act provides that an officer authorised by the Examiner
may enter business premises and require the production of documents relating to the business. Section 15(4) states that failure to comply with such a

requirement is an offence. Section 15(3) provides that where a person refuses to comply with such a request, he shall within seven days apply to the High Court for a declaration "that the exigencies of the common good do not warrant the exercise by the Examiner of the powers conferred on him by this section." If such a declaration is granted, the Examiner must withdraw the requirement.

An authorised officer called at the plaintiff company's business premises in November 1976 and required to see records relating to the distribution of certain films. This was refused. The plaintiff company applied to the High Court for a declaration under section 15(3), arguing also that section 15 was invalid. McWilliam J. rejected the latter claim and the plaintiff appealed to the Supreme Court. It was contended that section 15 violated the separation of powers because:

(a) it empowered the High Court to decide upon the exigencies of the common good; and this was a purely *legislative* function,

(b) it usurped the legislative function by empowering the High Court to create offences.

Both contentions were dismissed. As to the first the Supreme Court, *per* Kenny J., noted that the framers of the Constitution had not adopted a rigid separation between the legislative, executive and judicial powers. The judgment continues ([1981] I.R. 158, 171):

"The promotion of the common good is one of the aims (as stated in the preamble) which the people wished to achieve by adopting a Constitution. While this promotion is primarily the function of the legislature, the Courts are invested with the jurisdiction to determine whether what is purported to be done in the interests of the common good is or is not repugnant to the Constitution. Furthermore, there is nothing to prevent the legislature from investing the Courts with the sole jurisdiction to determine whether a particular act is or is not required by the exigencies of the common good. That is what is being done by section 15. We reject the submission that it is repugnant to the Constitution."

The plaintiff company's second argument was disposed of as follows (*loc. cit. supra*):

"What the High Court has to decide under that sub-section is whether, in a particular case, the exercise of the powers of the examiner was or was not warranted by the exigencies of the common good. This is not the creation of a new offence: it is the application of the concept of the common good to the facts of the particular case. The offence is created by the legislature: the question whether it has been committed is to be decided by the Courts, and this involves no more than a determination whether the exercise of the powers of the Examiner was or was not warranted by the exigencies of the common good."

Matters excepted

It remains to note two matters which are unaffected by the concept of the judicial power. Firstly, this doctrine has no application to bodies which derive their jurisdiction from contract—such as disciplinary committees of clubs, trade unions or sporting organisations. This was made clear in the

Solicitors Act case: see the judgment of Kingsmill Moore J.—[1960] I.R. 239, 264. The same would apply to any tribunal established—whether for disciplinary or other purposes—by any church: *State (Colquhoun)* v. *D'Arcy* [1936] I.R. 641.

Secondly, a statutory body may come under a "duty to act judicially"—in the sense of being obliged to observe basic fairness of procedure in making the decisions entrusted to it. But this does not mean that the body in question is then exercising the judicial power of the State. Thus the Land Commission has been held to be under a duty to act judicially: *State (Crowley)* v. *Irish Land Commission* [1951] I.R. 250: *Foley* v. *Irish Land Commission* [1952] I.R. 118. Nonetheless, its powers have always been classified as administrative, not judicial: *Lynham* v. *Butler (No. 2)* [1933] I.R. 74: *Fisher* v. *Irish Land Commission* [1948] I.R. 3. The same distinction has repeatedly been drawn by the Supreme Court.[91]

Judges, courts and non-judicial powers

Subject to the Article 37.1 exception, the Constitution decrees that only courts and judges may exercise judicial power. This plainly acts as a barrier, keeping other bodies and persons out of that field; but the question also arises whether it confines courts and judges therein. May courts and judges exercise *only* judicial power? For example, the Supreme Court held in *Application of Gallagher* [1991] 1 I.R. 31 that statute had correctly lodged with the Government the power to decide when persons found "guilty but insane" should be released, since this was an executive power. Could amending legislation then constitutionally transfer it to the courts?

In other countries with broadly similar constitutional provisions this question has received a somewhat *nuancé* answer. The United States Supreme Court has held that Congress may delegate certain non-judicial functions to courts, provided that these do not trench upon the prerogatives of executive or legislature and that they are appropriate to the central mission of the judiciary. Thus it could delegate to the Supreme Court authority to establish rules for the conduct of its own business, to prescribe rules of procedure for lower federal courts in civil and criminal cases, and to revise the federal rules of evidence: *Mistretta* v. *U.S.* (1989) 488 U.S. 361. In addition, as Blackmun J., for the court, said in that case (at 388–89):

> " . . . by established practice we have recognized Congress' power to create the Judicial Conference of the United States, and the Rules Advisory Committee that it oversees, and the Administrative Office of the United States Courts whose myriad responsibilities include the administration of the entire probation service. These entities, some of which are comprised of judges, others of judges and nonjudges, still others of non-judges only, do not exercise judicial power in the constitutional sense of deciding cases and controversies, but they share the common purpose of providing for the fair and efficient fulfillment of responsibilities that are properly the province of the Judiciary."

Furthermore, the United States Constitution does not prevent individual

---

[91] See *McDonald* v. *Bord na gCon (No. 2)* [1965] I.R. 217: *State (Grahame)* v. *The Racing Board* (May 29, 1981): *O'Brien* v. *Bord na Móna* [1983] I.R. 255.

judges from *voluntarily* undertaking extrajudicial activity (it would appear that they cannot be compelled to do such work). The Supreme Court so ruled in *Mistretta* v. *U.S.* (1989) 488 U.S. 361, founding confessedly on historical practice.[92]

The position in Australia is broadly similar. In *Hilton* v. *Wells* (1985) 157 C.L.R. 57, 67 Gibbs C.J., speaking for the majority of the High Court,[93] accepted the proposition

" . . . that it is not permissible, under the Constitution, for the Parliament to confer any non-judicial power on any court established under Ch. III of the Constitution unless the power conferred is merely ancillary or incidental to the exercise of judicial power."

But, he added, there was no constitutional impediment preventing Parliament from conferring non-judicial power on a particular individual who happened to be a member of a court. Thus in *Hilton's* case the majority upheld a federal statute authorising judges to issue warrants for the interception of communications passing over telecommunications systems. It was accepted that under the Australian Constitution this was not a judicial power, nor was it ancillary or incidental to any judicial function. But, in the view of the majority, the statute conferred this power on the judges as individuals, as designated persons.[94] In Australia also, as in the United States, serving judges may voluntarily undertake extrajudicial activity.[95] The practice in Ireland certainly sanctions the voluntary discharge by judges of extrajudicial duties. Judges have chaired commissions and committees[96] and served on statutory tribunals of inquiry.[97] The constitutionality of this practice has never been tested, perhaps because a challenge to it seems unlikely to succeed. For one may perhaps derive from several provisions of the Constitution sanction for the judicial undertaking of non-judicial work. Thus, under

---

[92] Blackmun J. cites a multitude of examples, including John Jay's simultaneous service as (first) Chief Justice and Ambassador to England, Oliver Ellsworth's doubling as Chief Justice and Ambassador to France and John Marshall's briefly overlapping roles as Secretary of State and Chief Justice. He mentions, too, that five Supreme Court justices served on the Electoral Commission which decided the outcome of the disputed 1876 Hayes/Tilden Presidential Election; that Roberts J. was a member of the Commission which investigated the attack on Pearl Harbor; that Jackson J. was one of the prosecutors at Nuremberg; and that Warren C.J. chaired the Commission investigating the assassination of President Kennedy. Blackmun J. is undoubtedly right to add (at 400–01): " . . . these extrajudicial activities spawned spirited discussion and frequent criticism, and . . . some of the judges who undertook these duties . . . may have looked back on their service with regret . . . "

[93] Gibbs C.J., Wilson and Dawson JJ: Mason and Deane JJ. dissenting.

[94] Mason and Deane JJ. dissented on this point. They concluded that the function of issuing warrants was imposed on the judges of the Federal Court as a function to be performed by them as judges of that court in their capacity as such.

[95] Professor Zines has written: "The classical examples are the appointment of Sir John Latham and Sir Owen Dixon [both Chief Justices of Australia] to diplomatic positions. Federal judges and judges of State courts exercising federal jurisdiction have from time to time engaged in government enquiries and been members of quasi-judicial tribunals such as the Trade Practices Tribunal and the Administrative Appeals Tribunal." Leslie Zines, *The High Court and the Constitution* (Sydney 1981), p. 175.

[96] Most notably, perhaps, Walsh J. and Keane J. have successively presided over the Law Reform Commission since its establishment in October 1975.

[97] To take only the four most recent, the tribunal of inquiry into the beef industry was chaired by Hamilton P.; that on the "Kerry Babies" case (Pl. 3514: 1985) by Lynch J.; that on the fire at the Stardust, Artane (Pr. 853; 1980) by Keane J.; and that into the Whiddy Island disaster (Prl. 8911: 1980) by Costello J.

Article 12.3.1°, the judges of the Supreme Court decide upon Presidential incapacity; under Article 22.2.3°, a Supreme Court judge would preside over the Committee of Privileges there envisaged; and under Article 14.2 the Chief Justice (or the President of the High Court) is designated as a member of the Presidential Commission. One may note also that, by Article 31.2.i, the Chief Justice and the President of the High Court are both *ex officio* members of the Council of State—which certainly does not exercise judicial functions.

If the Constitution implicitly accepts that judges may undertake non-judicial work, this would not of itself authorise the statutory conferment of non-judicial functions on a court. In *McDonald* v. *Bord na gCon* (*No.* 2) [1965] I.R. 217, however, Kenny J. indicated that there was no constitutional objection to this.[98] He said (at 230):

> " . . . new powers and functions may be conferred on Courts and judges although the exercise of these powers and functions is not an administration of justice. Article 26 of the Constitution, dealing with the reference of Bills to the Supreme Court, is an example of this, for if the President refers a Bill to the Supreme Court for a decision as to whether it or any part of it is repugnant to the Constitution, it seems to me that the Supreme Court when deciding the matter is not administering justice but is giving an advisory opinion."[99]

This, however, is not entirely convincing, for arguably the Constitution may lay down rules which the Oireachtas could not enact. The fact that by express constitutional provision the Chief Justice and the President of the High Court are members of the Council of State would hardly warrant a statute making them members of a council to advise the Attorney General. Perhaps the most that can be said is that non-judicial functions may validly be conferred on courts, provided that they are analogous to functions that are truly judicial and that their exercise would not interfere with, or compromise, judicial independence.

---

[98] In *Application of Neilan* [1990] 2 I.R. 267 Keane J., having quoted Kenny J.'s observations, said that this could not be regarded as settled law. But Keane J. described the topic as "one of no little difficulty" (at 278), and since it was not necessary to do so, expressed no opinion on it.

[99] Since Art. 26.3 makes it clear that the Supreme Court's decision on the Bill—whether in favour or against—is *binding* on the President, it is difficult to see how it can be described as an "advisory opinion."

10 The Courts

The basic constitutional provisions relating to the courts are Articles 34–36 and 38. These trace the broad outline of the judicial system, and the structure and jurisdiction of the several courts. The appointment and tenure of judges is regulated, trial by jury provided for, and wide powers conferred on the Oireachtas to establish special (*i.e.* non-jury) criminal courts.

Article 34 sketches the grand design of the courts system (the details, under Article 36, being regulated by statute). It lays down the general principle that justice is to be administered in public, and provides for courts of first instance, and a court of final appeal—the latter being the Supreme Court: Article 34.4.1°. The courts of first instance fall into two categories:

(a) the High Court—referred to by name in Article 34.3.1°, and invested by it with the amplest jurisdiction possible
(b) the "courts of local and limited jurisdiction" referred to in Article 34.4.4°.

It should be noted that the courts discussed below—with the exception of the special criminal courts—were established only in 1961: Courts (Establishment and Constitution) Act 1961. Before that Act came into force, the similar system established by the Courts of Justice Act 1924 was in place. This was specifically foreseen and authorised by Article 58 of Bunreacht na hÉireann—one of the transitory provisions not now printed in copies of the Constitution. That situation was, under Article 58, to continue "until otherwise determined by law." In *State (Killian)* v. *Minister for Justice* [1954] I.R. 207 the former Supreme Court held that Article 34 contemplated a fresh establishment of courts by statute, and that the courts then existing functioned under Article 58. Subsequently the Courts (Establishment and Constitution) Act 1961 disestablished the former courts, and established the new ones (with continuity of personnel), while the Courts (Supplemental Provisions) Act 1961 regulated their several jurisdictions.

Administration of Justice in Public

Article 34.1 provides:

"Justice . . . save in such special and limited cases as may be prescribed by law, shall be administered in public."

This obviously states a general principle—applicable both to civil and criminal cases—and simultaneously allows exceptions to be made to it. Several statutory provisions prescribe such exceptions, chiefly in relation to family law proceedings and certain commercial cases. *Prima facie* these provisions would seem to answer the constitutional description "special and limited cases."

In *Re R. Ltd.* [1989] I.R. 126 the Supreme Court considered the application of one such provision, section 205(7) of the Companies Act 1963. This provides as follows:

> "If, in the opinion of the court, the hearing of proceedings under this section would involve the disclosure of information the publication of which would be seriously prejudicial to the legitimate interests of the company, the court may order that the hearing of the proceedings or any part thereof shall be in camera."

In these proceedings, which alleged oppression of the company's minority shareholders, the High Court had ordered that the entire case be heard in camera. The Supreme Court (Walsh, Griffin and Hederman JJ.; Finlay C.J. and Hamilton P. dissenting) allowed an appeal against this order. In the view of the majority, section 205(7) conferred a discretion on the High Court and created a condition precedent to its exercise—serious prejudice to the company's legitimate interests. But that was *not* the sole relevant consideration. Walsh J. said (at 137):

> "In seeking to avail of the protection apparently offered by the subsection the party seeking it must be able to satisfy the court that not only would the disclosure of information be seriously prejudicial to the legitimate interests of the company, but it must also be shown that a public hearing of the whole or of that part of the proceedings which it is sought to have heard other than in a public court would fall short of the doing of justice."

Some statutory provisions enacted under cover of Article 34.1 lay down a mandatory rule[1]; others confer a discretionary power on the court.[2] Insofar as the latter do not already contain one, the decision in *Re R. Ltd.* adds a new condition precedent—that the doing of justice requires an order for privacy. Indeed, this is recognised by section 31 of the Companies (Amendment) Act 1990, which provides:

> "The whole or part of any proceedings under this Act may be heard otherwise than in public if the court, in the interests of justice, considers that the interests of the company concerned or of its creditors as a whole so require."

No doubt this will become the standard statutory formula in future.

So far as mandatory provisions are concerned, the position is unclear.

---

[1] *e.g.* the Succession Act 1965, ss.56(11), 119, 122; the Family Law (Maintenance of Spouses and Children) Act 1976, ss.25(1) and (2), 28(1)(*d*); the Family Law (Protection of Spouses and Children) Act 1981, s.14(1).

[2] *e.g.* the Courts (Supplemental Provisions) Act 1961, s.45 (which allows for privacy of proceedings in (a) urgent applications for habeas corpus, bail, prohibition or injunction; (b) matrimonial causes and matters; (c) lunacy and minor matters; and (d) "proceedings involving the disclosure of a secret manufacturing process"); the Marriage Act 1972, ss.1(3)(*c*) and 7(3)(*c*); and—curiously—the Family Law (Protection of Spouses and Children) Act 1981, s.14(2).

These appear to be confined to the family law area[3] though, curiously, the High Court has a discretion in regard to applications under the Marriage Act 1972.[4] A typical provision is section 34 of the Judicial Separation and Family Law Reform Act 1989:

"Proceedings under this Act shall be heard otherwise than in public."

Though the peremptory language of such provisions may seem to preclude implying any conditions precedent, the presumption of constitutionality may perhaps require this. Alternatively, they might be regarded as creating an irrebutable presumption in favour of privacy, justified by the State's duty under Article 41 to protect the institutions of marriage and the family, and, under Article 40.3, to defend as far as practicable the unenumerated right of access to the courts.

Re R. Ltd. establishes another important point. The majority judgment states that Article 34.1 removed any *general* judicial discretion to have proceedings heard in camera. Such power will exist only where expressly conferred by a statute enacted, re-enacted or applied by a statute passed after the coming into force of the Constitution. And the philosophy underlying that constitutional provision was thus expounded by Walsh J. ([1989] I.R. 126, 134):

"The actual presence of the public is never necessary but the administration of justice in public does require that the doors of the courts must be open so that members of the general public may come and see for themselves that justice is done. It is in no way necessary that the members of the public to whom the courts are open should themselves have any particular interest in the cases or that they should have had any business in the courts. Justice is administered in public on behalf of all the inhabitants of the State."

COURTS OF LOCAL AND LIMITED JURISDICTION

The Oireachtas is *obliged* to create such courts, the language of Article 34.3.4° being mandatory ("The Courts of First Instance shall . . . include courts of local and limited jurisdiction . . . ").[5] Statute—the Courts (Establishment and Constitution) Act 1961—has created "the District Court" and "the Circuit Court"; thus each is a single unified court covering the entire State. Each of these courts has a limited jurisdiction: but Article 34.3.4° requires jurisdiction to be *local* as well as limited. For a court to have "local" jurisdiction its authority must presumably be confined to a clearly defined geographical area. In *State (Hunt)* v. *O'Donovan* [1975] I.R. 39 counsel for the respondent argued before the Supreme Court that the Circuit Court did not fall within

---

[3] See the provisions mentioned in n. 1 *supra* and the Judicial Separation and Family Law Reform Act 1989, s.34.

[4] These "may be heard and determined in private": ss.1(3)(*c*) and 7(3)(*c*). As Walsh J. observed in *Re R. Ltd.* [1989] I.R. 126, at 136, the various statutory provisions in this field, whether mandatory or discretionary, " . . . display a varied and unexplained choice of words to describe hearings other than in public, such words as "in camera," "in private" and "in chambers." "

[5] In *Tormey* v. *Att. Gen.* [1985] I.R. 289 Henchy J., giving the judgment of the Supreme Court, referred to Art. 34.3.4° as " . . . the . . . mandatory provision, which requires Parliament to establish courts of local and limited jurisdiction, with a right of appeal as determined by law . . . "

Article 34.3.4°; it was a national, not a local, court. Unfortunately, the Supreme Court did not rule on the correctness or otherwise of this submission. In a five line statement by FitzGerald C.J. the court announced its decision—that the appellant had not shown section 13(2) of the Criminal Procedure Act 1967 to be unconstitutional. The *reasons* which led to this conclusion were not given.

The District and Circuit Courts are the only courts in our system capable of qualifying as local and limited. If they do not so qualify, it does not follow that they are not lawfully established. The Supreme Court has held that the Oireachtas is not confined to the structure outlined in Article 34—it may validly create other courts also: *People (Att. Gen.)* v. *Conmey* [1975] I.R. 341, 349; *State (Boyle)* v. *Judge Neylon* [1986] I.R. 551. If, however, the District and Circuit Courts do not come under Article 34, it would seem to follow that the Oireachtas has neglected its constitutional duty to create courts of local and limited jurisdiction.

Both the District and the Circuit Courts are local *in their actual operation.* Each District or Circuit Court judge[6] has jurisdiction to hear only cases brought against defendants living in, or which arise from events occurring or properly situated in, the relevant District or Circuit. The former Supreme Court held that this was sufficient to satisfy the "local and limited" provisions of the 1922 Constitution (Article 64): *Grimes* v. *Owners of S.S. Bangor Bay* [1948] I.R. 350, 357–8. The same view prevails today: in *State (Hunt)* v. *O'Donovan* [1975] I.R. 39 Finlay J. appears to have regarded the Circuit Court as falling within Article 34.3.4°.[7]

At present, the jurisdiction of the District and Circuit Courts is limited in a variety of ways. In the criminal sphere, the District Court's jurisdiction is exclusively a summary one, over minor offences. The Circuit Court has a very extensive jurisdiction over indictable offences, a limited range of the gravest offences, however, being reserved purely for the Central Criminal Court (*i.e.* the High Court).[8] On the civil side, neither has so comprehensive a jurisdiction as the High Court; and in those matters over which they are given authority, a financial ceiling is generally imposed. Is the latter essential, or may statute give one of the lower courts a jurisdiction equivalent to that of the High Court in a given range of matters (*e.g.* matrimonial causes)?

A decision of the former Supreme Court—*Grimes* v. *Owners of S.S. Bangor Bay* [1948] I.R. 350—indicates that the answer is "No." There O'Byrne J.

---

[6] s.21 of the Courts Act 1991 alters the title of members of the District Court from "Justice" to "Judge."

[7] See further J. P. Casey "The Constitution and the Legal System" (1979) XIV *Irish Jurist* (N.S.) 14. In *State (Boyle)* v. *Judge Neylon* [1986] I.R. 551 the Supreme Court was invited by counsel to *assume* that the Circuit Court fell under Article 34.3.4°, and that invitation seems to have been accepted (at 555). At p. 558 of the report, however, is found the statement that " . . . the constitutional provisions relating to Courts of local and limited jurisdiction were fulfilled by the establishment of the Circuit Court, exercising its jurisdiction on a local basis . . . "

[8] s.25 of the Courts (Supplemental Provisions) Act gives the Central Criminal Court exclusive jurisdiction over treason, murder, attempt to murder, conspiracy to murder and piracy. Section 10 of the Criminal Law (Rape) (Amendment) Act 1990 adds to this list rape, aggravated sexual assault and offences (*e.g.* attempt, conspiracy) connected therewith. S.10 implements a Law Reform Commission recommendation (*Report on Rape and Allied Offences*, LRC 24–1988, pp. 19–20). The Commission said that the High Court should have " . . . a realistic and comprehensive criminal jurisdiction" and emphasised that its call for the transfer of rape and aggravated assault to the High Court " . . . should be seen as part of a larger process." The

(with whom Maguire C.J., Murnaghan and Geoghegan JJ. agreed) said (at 358):

"... counsel for the defendants was forced to contend, and did contend, that the jurisdiction of the Circuit Court in Admiralty proceedings was unlimited. This contention seems to me to be quite untenable. If a statute purported to confer upon any Court of first instance, other than the High Court, such unlimited jurisdiction, it would, in my opinion, contravene the clear intendment of the Constitution and would, for that reason, be outside the powers conferred upon the Oireachtas and invalid."

Though this case has not been overruled, it is doubtful whether so strict a veiw would find favour nowadays. Article 34 seems to contemplate two classes of "Courts of First Instance"—(a) the High Court "invested with full original jurisdiction in and power to determine all matters and questions whether of law or fact, civil or criminal": and (b) the courts of "local and limited jurisdiction." Thus, seen in its overall context, the word "limited" may imply only that the relevant courts may not be erected into a localised replica of the High Court. Short of that, the extent and amplitude of jurisdiction conferred on the lower courts would seem to be a matter within the discretion of the Oireachtas. The Constitution, as the framework for government in a changing society, must surely be interpreted to afford the flexibility which social and economic developments may require. Restrictions on the jurisdiction of (say) the Circuit Court thought appropriate 20 years ago may no longer be suitable; and in so far as they depend on the absence of appropriate machinery in that court, the remedy is plainly in the hands of Government and Oireachtas. On this view, then, there is no constitutional barrier to the Oireachtas giving the Circuit Court *in certain fields* a concurrent jurisdiction with the High Court. Indeed, this has been done by the Courts Act 1981, as interpreted by Gannon J. in *R.* v. *R.* [1984] I.R. 296.

Section 31, Courts Act 1981

An apparent exception to the localised nature of the Circuit Court's jurisdiction arises under section 31 of the Courts Act 1981. This provides for the transfer of criminal trials from the Circuit Court sitting outside the Dublin Circuit to the Dublin Circuit Court.[9] Section 31 may therefore involve the Dublin Circuit Court in hearing cases originating in any part of the State; and at first sight it is not easily reconcilable with the "local jurisdiction" requirement of Article 34.3.4°.

The validity of section 31 was impugned in *State (Boyle)* v. *Judge Neylon* [1986] I.R. 551. There the prosecutor's case had been transferred, at the D.P.P.'s request, from the Wicklow Circuit Court to that in Dublin. He

Commission suggested that kidnapping, fraud, crimes involving the use of firearms and explosives and major drugs offences be considered for transfer to the Central Criminal Court's exclusive jurisdiction.

[9] It replaces s.6 of the Courts Act 1964, under which such cases were transferred to the Central Criminal Court, *i.e.* the High Court. Under s.11 of the Courts (Supplemental Provisions) Act 1961 the High Court, when exercising its criminal jurisdiction, "... shall be known ... " as the Central Criminal Court. In *People (Att. Gen.)* v. *Bell* [1969] I.R. 24, at 48, the Supreme Court said it was extremely doubtful if statute could alter or modify the name of the High Court, whatever jurisdiction it might be exercising.

argued that section 31 was invalid because its transfer provisions meant that the Dublin Circuit Court was now no longer a court of "local jurisdiction."

The Supreme Court affirmed, on somewhat different grounds, Gannon J.'s conclusion[10] that section 31 was valid. The court, *per* Walsh J., said that Article 34.3.4° must be construed in the light of its purpose, which was to provide local—and thus cheaper and more convenient—venues for litigants. The statutory dispositions relating to the Circuit Court fufilled this objective. The ability to transfer a case from one locality to another did not alter the essentially local exercise of the Circuit Court's jurisdiction. "Local jurisdiction" in Article 34.3.4° did not necessarily require a connection with the place of residence of one party or the other, and the Oireachtas had power in the interests of justice to provide for transfers. This reasoning, however, seems to read Article 34.3.4° as if it read *"mainly* local"—which it does not. Nor does it explain how the Dublin Circuit Court, now falling heir to a jurisdiction formerly exercised by the High Court, remains a court of local and limited jurisdiction.

Appeals

Article 34.3.4° refers to "Courts of local and limited jurisdiction *with a right of appeal as determined by law.*" The question has arisen whether the italicised words guarantee a right of appeal in all circumstances. If this is the case, no decision of the Circuit Court could be made final—which would place a number of statutory provisions in jeopardy. However, in *State (Hunt)* v. *O'Donovan* [1975] I.R. 39, Finlay J. refused so to construe Article 34.3.4°. He had no difficulty in interpreting sub-article 4° as prohibiting the creation of a court of local and limited jurisdiction from which there was no appeal at all. But there was, said Finlay J. (at 48):

" . . . a very large gap between that interpretation and one which excludes the right of the law (*i.e.* statute) to determine from which precise decision an appeal will lie."

Thus the Oireachtas has a very wide discretion in the matter of providing appeals from the lower courts. What proportion of their decisions might constitutionally be made final it is impossible to say.

THE HIGH COURT

The constitutional foundation of the High Court's jurisdiction lies in Article 34.3.1°, which provides that it shall have "full original jurisdiction in and power to determine all matters and questions, whether of law or fact, civil or criminal." Gavan Duffy P. once described this as investing the High Court with "an impressive and comprehensive jurisdiction which it is our duty to maintain": *Att. Gen.* v. *Connolly* [1947] I.R. 213, 223. It is a provision which has several important effects.

Criminal jurisdiction

Although Article 34.3.1° provides that the High Court shall have full original jurisdiction in criminal matters, the court's actual criminal work is now-

[10] Gannon J.'s judgment is reported in [1986] I.L.R.M. 337.

adays only a fraction of its civil business. Most criminal cases are tried in the District and Circuit Courts. While the High Court does enjoy an exclusive jurisdiction to try criminal cases on indictment, this is not very extensive in its reach: though since it embraces the most serious offences it is both symbolically and practically important.[11]

Under present arrangements, the High Court exercises summary jurisdiction only over criminal contempts: for the rest it tries cases solely with a jury. In *Re Haughey* [1971] I.R. 217, the Supreme Court, *per* Ó Dálaigh C.J., said (at 253–4):

> "By the provisions of Article 38, s.2 of the Constitution the trial of minor offences without a jury is restricted to courts of summary jurisdiction. It is true that the High Court possesses a universal jurisdiction in matters civil and criminal but that does not make it a court of summary jurisdiction within the provisions of s.2 of Article 38. A court of summary jurisdiction within the meaning of that section is one whose criminal jurisdiction to try and to convict is restricted to the trial of minor offences. The term 'court of summary jurisdiction' was well known prior to the enactment of the Constitution; the expression appeared in almost identical words in the Constitution of Saorstát Éireann and, prior to that, in s.13 of the Interpretation Act, 1889. Under our law that jurisdiction is exercised only by the District Court. In accordance with the provisions of s.5 of Article 38, the jurisdiction of the High Court to try criminal offences is a jurisdiction to try them only with a jury."

In *Tormey* v. *Att. Gen.* [1985] I.R. 289 the plaintiff invoked Article 34.3.1° in his attack upon the validity of section 32(1) of the Courts Act 1981, which repealed section 6 of the Courts Act 1964. The plaintiff had been charged with fraudulent conversion, and returned for trial in the Dublin Circuit Court. For unexplained reasons he wished to be tried in the High Court, or alternatively in the Circuit Court sitting outside Dublin. However, no machinery exists for a transfer to the Central Criminal Court; such had existed under section 6 of the Courts Act 1964, but that had been repealed. Its replacement—section 31 of the Courts Act 1981—provides *only* for transfers from the Circuit Court sitting in the provinces to the Dublin Circuit Court. The plaintiff contended that section 32 invalidly cut down the jurisdiction conferred on the High Court by Article 34.3.1°. His argument ran thus—Article 34.3.1° gives the High Court full original criminal jurisdiction. So long as section 6 of the 1964 Act was in force this principle was respected, for any indictable offence triable in the Circuit Court could be transferred to the Central Criminal Court. But with the repeal of section 6 only a small range of cases was now triable in the Central Criminal Court. This, it was urged, was an invalid attempt to cut down the plenitude of jurisdiction conferred by the Constitution.

The Supreme Court, *per* Henchy J., rejected this argument. Article 34.3.1°, it was held, must not be read literally or in isolation; rather, it must be read, and construed in harmony, with the other provisions of Article 34. Those, and other provisions such as Article 38, conferred jurisdiction to try offences on other courts. This must entail the exclusion of the High Court from those areas, otherwise the allocation of jurisdiction would be overlapping and

---

[11] See n. 10 *supra*.

unworkable. In essence, therefore, the Supreme Court held that under Article 34.3.4°, the Oireachtas could give exclusive jurisdiction over certain criminal matters to the courts of local and limited jurisdiction (the District and Circuit Courts). The High Court's full original jurisdiction would still exist and be exercisable to ensure that justice was done in those local courts. That is, the High Court would have jurisdiction to *review* the proceedings in the lower court—by certiorari, prohibition or mandamus. (And it would follow that the Oireachtas could not close off that avenue to the High Court.)[12]

Civil jurisdiction

The "full original jurisdiction" conferred upon the High Court by Article 34.3.1° extends to civil, as well as criminal, matters. But this does not mean that the High Court is *obliged* to exercise this jurisdiction by taking cases that fall within the statutory limits of the lower courts. In *Ward* v. *Kinehan Electrical Ltd.* [1984] I.R. 292 the defendant applied to have an action remitted to the Circuit Court on the ground that any damages recoverable by the plaintiff could not exceed the jurisdictional limits of that court. The plaintiff, resisting this application, submitted that the statutory provisions allowing remittal were invalid because Article 34.3.1° gave every citizen a right to have his case—however trivial—determined by the High Court. This contention was rejected by McMahon J., who said ([1984] I.R. 292, 295):

> "In my opinion, Article 34, s.3 can not be construed as conferring a universal right of recourse to the High Court for the determination of all justiciable disputes. The High Court is the only court of first instance expressly referred to in the Constitution but, having regard to the fact that Article 34, s.3, subs. 4, provides for the establishment of other courts of first instance (which, unlike the High Court, would have local and limited jurisdiction), the provisions of s.3 which invest the High Court with full original jurisdiction can only be understood as referring to the extent of the jurisdiction which the High Court is capable of exercising. It can not be construed as creating a right of access to the High Court for the determination of all matters and questions because Article 36 enables laws to be made for the distribution of jurisdiction and business among all the Courts which may be established under the Constitution, including Courts of first instance other than the High Court. It follows, therefore, that business which falls within the full original jurisdiction of the High Court may be assigned, within the limits expressed and implied in the Constitution, to some other court."

Thus McMahon J. held the remittal provisions—Courts of Justice Act 1924, s.25, as amended by Courts of Justice Act 1936, s.11—compatible with the Constitution.[13]

Those statutory provisions are predicated on the assumption that the High Court *may*—but need not—exercise jurisdiction in cases assigned to the lower

[12] See further G. W. Hogan "Reflections on the Supreme Court's decision in *Tormey* v. *Attorney General*" (1986) 8 *D.U.L.J.* 31.
[13] But as Hogan, *op. cit.*, points out (p. 34) it is not entirely clear that the decision in *Ward's* case can stand with the subsequent Supreme Court decision in *Tormey* v. *Att. Gen.. Tormey's* case, however, does not explicitly overrule *Ward's* case—which was cited to the court: see [1989] I.R. 289, at 292.

courts. Statutes assigning *exclusive* jurisdiction over some issues to the lower courts would be a different matter—and it has been doubted whether this may validly be done.[14] That such doubts are well founded is suggested by Gannon J.'s judgment in *R.* v. *R.* [1984] I.R. 296. In that case the plaintiff was seeking various orders against her husband. For reasons which do not appear, she wished to bring her proceedings in the High Court. What she sought was:

    (a) custody of, and maintenance for, the children—under the Guardianship of Infants Act 1964, as amended by the Courts Act 1981;

    (b) maintenance for herself—under the Family Law (Maintenance, etc.) Act 1976, as amended by the Courts Act 1981;

    (c) an order barring her husband from the matrimonial home—under the Family Law (Protection of Spouses and Children) Act 1981.

The lower courts clearly had jurisdiction over these claims. The Family Law (Protection, etc.) Act 1981 referred only to these courts. The original section 23 of the Family Law (Maintenance, etc.) Act 1976 said jurisdiction thereunder was exercisable by the District, Circuit and High Courts. But the Courts Act 1981 had inserted a new section 23, which referred only to the District and Circuit Courts. And it had performed a similar kind of surgery on the Guardianship of Infants Act 1964. Did this mean that the High Court was excluded—and if so, was this constitutionally permissible?

Gannon J. pointed out that these statutes fell to be construed in accordance with the presumption of constitutionality. They could be declared invalid only if they were incapable of interpretation and effective implementation consistent with the Constitution. But such was not the case. These statutes contained nothing restricting or removing any jurisdiction from the High Court. By the operation of Article 34.3.1° the High Court therefore retained jurisdiction over claims such as the plaintiff's. However, it was open to the High Court to decline to entertain any such proceedings, on the ground that relief was available in the lower courts.[15]

In the course of his judgment Gannon J. said ([1984] I.R. 296, 308–09):

> "From the amplitude of jurisdiction with which the High Court is invested by Article 34 of the Constitution, it follows that the Oireachtas does not add to or increase the jurisdiction of the High Court by legislation. It follows also that the Oireachtas cannot create validly, in accordance with the Constitution, a new juridical jurisdiction, and withhold it from the High Court; nor can it reduce, restrict or terminate any jurisdiction of the High Court.
>
> If I am correct in understanding the effect of Article 34, s.3, subs. 1, the jurisdiction, authority and powers with which the High Court is invested by that Article of the Constitution include all such functions, authorities, duties and powers as are incident to any and every part of the jurisdiction without any necessary intervention of the legislature. It follows that all such matters come within the ambit of the phrase ' . . .

[14] For details see J. P. Casey "The Constitution and the Legal System" (1979) XIV *Irish Jurist* (N.S.) 14, 22–3.

[15] See the Practice Direction issued following this judgment: [1984] I.L.R.M. 148. In *O'R.* v. *O'R.* [1985] I.R. 367 Murphy J. held that the High Court should decline jurisdiction unless satisfied that in the circumstances of a particular case a failure to exercise jurisdiction might result in a denial of justice.

foregoing provisions of this Constitution relating to the Courts' in the introductory part of Article 36, and that 'the said Courts' mentioned in paragraph (iii) of that Article are those courts only which are referred to in paragraph (ii) of the Article as 'all other courts.' For these reasons I would reject, as wrong in law, the contentions (advanced on behalf of the Attorney General) that under Article 36 of the Constitution the Oireachtas may confer upon and withdraw from the High Court, or confer upon other courts to the exclusion of the High Court, jurisdiction in the matters of family law, custody of children and maintenance which are under consideration in these proceedings."

If this is correct, it would appear that Article 34.3.1° confers on the High Court jurisdiction over *all* justiciable issues. If jurisdiction over some such issue is not assigned by statute to another court, the High Court will be the appropriate forum—no statutory provision being necessary to achieve this result.[16] Further, the various jurisdictions conferred on the lower courts would properly be regarded as concurrent with that of the High Court, which would however normally remit appropriate cases to those lower courts. Finally, statute could not validly confer exclusive jurisdiction on those lower courts; thus the Malicious Injuries, and Landlord and Tenant, Acts which appear to give exclusive jurisdiction to the Circuit Court, would to that extent be constitutionally suspect.

Some of these propositions, however, like the decision in *R.* v. *R.* itself, may be open to question. It has been suggested that they cannot stand with the later Supreme Court decision in *Tormey* v. *Att. Gen.* [1985] I.R. 289.[17] One commentator, indeed, has said that " . . . the decision in *R.* v. *R.* was authoritatively reversed by the Supreme Court in *Tormey.*"[18] But the reversal—if such it be—is implicit only, for neither *R.* v. *R.* nor any other decision is cited in the judgment in *Tormey's* case. It would flow, in part, from the statement that Article 34.3.1° cannot be read literally; in part also from the way in which the central question in the case is posed,[19] and from the following passage of Henchy J.'s judgment ([1989] I.R. 289, 296):

> "If, in exercise of its powers under Article 34, s.3, subs. 4, Parliament commits certain matters or questions to the jurisdiction of the District Court or of the Circuit Court, the function of hearing and determining those matters may, expressly or by necessary implication, be given exclusively to those courts."

As against the conclusion that *R.* v. *R.* is implicitly overruled by *Tormey's* case, it may be argued that the former concerned civil—not criminal—proceedings. And although there are constitutional provisions affecting criminal jurisdiction which require to be harmonised with Article 34.3.4°—such as Article 38.2 on the trial of minor offences by courts of summary jurisdiction,

[16] This proposition is supported by the Supreme Court decision in *Tormey* v. *Att. Gen.* [1985] I.R. 289, at 296.

[17] Hogan, *op. cit. supra*, pp. 33–36.

[18] David Gwynn Morgan "Constitutional Interpretation" (1988) 10 *D.U.L.J.* 24, 41.

[19] "The central question in this case is whether [Art. 34.3.4°] means that the jurisdiction thus created is to be exercised concurrently with the original jurisdiction conferred on the High Court by Art. 34, s.3, subs. 1 or whether it means that there may be instituted a local and limited jurisdiction which may be exercised to that extent to the exclusion of the High Court": *per* Henchy J. [1985] I.R. 289, at 294.

and Article 38.3 on trial by special criminal courts—these have no counterpart in respect of civil jurisdiction. It would thus be possible to uphold the result in *Tormey's* case, while not accepting all of the reasoning. But uncertainty will persist until the opportunity for a definitive Supreme Court pronouncement arises.

In its *Eleventh Interim Report* (Prl. 1835) the Committee on Court Practice and Procedure suggested that the original jurisdiction of the Supreme Court be increased by empowering it to try, on consent of the parties, net issues of law of importance initiated in the High Court. This was to be possible only in cases whose resolution required no decision on any disputed point of fact. Though the matter is not mentioned in the *Report*, this was presumably thought to be compatible with Article 34.3.1°. To be so, however, the question of transfer, notwithstanding the parties' wishes, would surely have to remain at the discretion of the High Court. A provision for automatic transfer, upon consent, would hardly square with Article 34.3.1°; it would amount to the effective withdrawal of certain justiciable issues from the High Court.

Statute—it would seem—may not fetter the powers of the High Court in relation to matters before it. In *Re McAllister* [1973] I.R. 238, the High Court had to consider the Irish Bankrupt and Insolvent Act 1857, s.385. This provided (*inter alia*) that if a person should not fully answer any lawful question to the satisfaction of the court, it should be lawful for the court to commit him to prison "there to remain without bail . . . " Kenny J. referred to Article 34.3.1° and continued:

> "I do not think that the National Parliament has power to pass legislation that the High Court shall not give bail to an accused person and so the words 'without bail' are repugnant to the Constitution and did not become part of the law of Saorstát Éireann or of the State."

This observation is best regarded as applicable only to the special case of bail. Article 34.3.1° preserves the High Court's jurisdiction, but not necessarily all the traditional incidents of that jurisdiction. It hardly constitutes a bar to the statutory substitution of one kind of relief for another (*e.g.* damages in lieu of an injunction) or to some statutory regulation of the procedure for obtaining relief (*e.g.* special rules in regard to injunctions in labour disputes).[20]

Supervisory jurisdiction

A traditional—and hallowed—function of the High Court is to ensure that inferior tribunals and administrative bodies stay within the jurisdiction conferred on them by law. Gavan Duffy J. viewed Article 34.3.1° as confirming and entrenching that jurisdiction, and he believed that statutory provisions purporting to exclude it were invalid. In *Murren* v. *Brennan* [1942] I.R. 466 he said, *obiter*, that a statutory provision making a Minister's decision on a legal matter "final" could not "exclude the constitutional jurisdiction of the High Court in a case deemed by the High Court to call for interference" (at 476). He used similar language in *O'Doherty* v. *Att. Gen. & O'Donnell* [1941] I.R.

---

[20] The Industrial Relations Act 1990, s.19 restricts the power of the courts—including the High Court—to grant injunctions in labour disputes.

569, 580–1, while in *Re Loftus Bryan's Estate* [1942] I.R. 185, he held section
48(1) of the Land Law (Ireland) Act 1881—which provided that the Land
Commission should not be restrained in the exercise of its powers by the
order of any court—inconsistent with the Constitution.

Though Gavan Duffy J.'s views have not been expressly approved by the
Supreme Court, it nonetheless seems to be generally accepted that Article
34.3.1° bars any legislative attempt to oust the High Court's jurisdiction over
justiciable issues. That supervisory jurisdiction is treated as axiomatic by the
Supreme Court in *Loftus* v. *Att. Gen.* [1979] I.R. 221 and *Irish Family Planning
Association* v. *Ryan* [1979] I.R. 295: and the matter seems to have been put
beyond doubt by *Tormey* v. *Att. Gen.* [1985] I.R. 289. Those responsible for
framing legislation take the same view, for there appears to be no modern
statutory provision purporting to exclude such supervision. One may,
however, find provisions imposing a very brief time limit on bringing
proceedings.

THE SUPREME COURT

Article 34.2 refers to "a Court of Final Appeal," and Article 34.4.1° provides
that it shall be called the Supreme Court. In *State (Browne)* v. *Feran* [1967]
I.R. 147, 157, Walsh J. (with whom the other members of the Supreme Court
agreed) said Article 34.4.1 did not mean that the Supreme Court should be
only a court of final appeal. The Constitution itself, in Article 12.3.1° and 26,
had expressly provided otherwise.

Original jurisdiction

The Constitution directly endows the Supreme Court with original jurisdiction in two matters. The first, under Article 12.3.1°, is that of determining,
should the situation arise, the permanent incapacity of the President of Ireland. The second arises under Article 26, which as already noted, allows the
President to refer certain Bills to the Supreme Court for a ruling on their constitutionality—a power exercised on eight occasions to date.

In *State (Browne)* v. *Feran* [1967] I.R. 147 it was held that statute could confer further original jurisdiction upon the Supreme Court. As noted *supra*, the
Committee on Court Practice and Procedure suggested that this power might
be used to provide for the possible transfer of certain constitutional questions
from the High Court to the Supreme Court. This recommendation has not
been implemented, and the Supreme Court's original jurisdiction remains
that conferred by the Constitution.

Appellate jurisdiction (a) from the High Court

Article 34.4.3° provides that the Supreme Court shall, with such exceptions and subject to such regulations as may be prescribed by law, have
appellate jurisdiction from all decisions of the High Court. But the Oireachtas is barred from excepting cases involving the constitutionality of statutes:
Article 34.4.4°.

Article 34.4.3° thus lays down an important general principle—all High
Court decisions may be appealed to the Supreme Court unless statute provides otherwise. Such an appeal lies automatically, without any need to seek

leave. With one exception, the Supreme Court has interpreted the words "all decisions" literally. Thus in *State (Browne)* v. *Feran* [1967] I.R. 147 it held, overruling the former Supreme Court's decision in *State (Burke)* v. *Lennon* [1940] I.R. 136, that an appeal lay against the grant—as well as the refusal—of an order of habeas corpus. Equally, an appeal will lie against a discretionary order for costs, in civil or criminal matters: *Vella* v. *Morelli* [1968] I.R. 11: *People (Att. Gen.)* v. *Bell* [1969] I.R. 24. Indeed, where the Supreme Court is as fully informed as the trial judge in respect of all the relevant material—as where there was no oral testimony—it has power to substitute its own view in regard to *any* exercise of discretion. It is not confined to interfering only where there is error in principle: see *Jack O'Toole Ltd.* v. *Maceoin Kelly Associates* [1987] I.L.R.M. 269.

The exception to this pattern occurred in *Campus Oil Ltd.* v. *Minister for Industry* [1983] I.R. 82. Here Murphy J. in the High Court had made an order referring certain questions arising in the action to the Court of Justice of the European Communities under Article 177 of the Treaty of Rome. The defendants sought to appeal against this order, but the Supreme Court held that no appeal lay. Walsh J. (O'Higgins C.J. and Hederman J. concurring) said that an order of reference such as this was not a "decision" within Article 34.4.3°. But even if it were, Article 177 of the Treaty of Rome must, by virtue of (the original) Article 29.4.3° of the Constitution, be treated as qualifying Article 34.4.3°.

The *Campus Oil* case is a curious one. To hold that an order of reference to the EC Court is not a "decision" within Article 34.4.3° because it has no legal effect on the parties to the litigation seems a very narrow view. The reference will involve delay and extra costs—matters which will certainly affect the parties. Moreover, it would follow from this conclusion that a decision *not* to refer is not subject to appeal—a result which may be disadvantageous. Also, it has been pointed out that the Supreme Court has become *plus catholique que le pape*—for the European Court of Justice does not object to the existence of appeals against orders of reference.[21] This matter may have to be reconsidered at some future date.

In the sphere of criminal appeals Article 34.4.3° has been interpreted quite literally; this has produced surprising, and to some people alarming, results. In *People (Att. Gen.)* v. *Conmey* [1975] I.R. 341 a majority of the Supreme Court held that an appeal would lie to that court against a conviction in the Central Criminal Court. This appeal was an alternative to the statutory avenue of appeal to the Court of Criminal Appeal.[22] In subsequent cases that conclusion was challenged—and then reaffirmed—by differently constituted courts: *People (D.P.P.)* v. *Shaw* [1982] I.R. 1: *People (D.P.P.)* v. *Lynch* [1982] I.R. 64.[23] Most recently it has been reiterated by a majority of the Supreme Court in *People (D.P.P.)* v. *O'Shea* [1982] I.R. 384. In that case a majority also held that an appeal would lie against a Central Criminal Court *acquittal*.[24] As a result of *O'Shea's* case the position in regard to criminal appeals is as follows:

---

[21] See the valuable notes of David O'Keeffe (1983) 5 D.U.L.J. 286 and Finbarr Murphy (1984) 21 C.M.L. Rev. 28.

[22] *Conmey's* case is discussed by the author at (1975) X *Irish Jurist* (N.S.) 300.

[23] See the author's note on these cases at (1981) XIV *Irish Jurist* (N.S.) 271.

[24] For a fuller discussion of *O'Shea's* case see G. W. Hogan (1983) 5 D.U.L.J. 254.

(a) a person convicted in the Central Criminal Court may appeal either
    to the Court of Criminal Appeal (C.C.A.) or to the Supreme Court
(b) a person convicted in the Circuit Court or Special Criminal Court is
    confined to appealing to the C.C.A.
(c) the prosecution may appeal to the Supreme Court against a Central
    Criminal Court acquittal (or perhaps against sentence alone)[25]
(d) the prosecution cannot appeal against Circuit Court or Special Crimi-
    nal Court acquittals: the statutory provisions on the C.C.A. do not
    permit this.

The new jurisdiction over appeals against Central Criminal Court acquittals
must apply to *all* such acquittals; the fact that in *O'Shea's* case the acquittal
had been directed by the trial judge cannot limit the scope of the Supreme
Court's decision. However, O'Higgins C.J. (Walsh and Hederman JJ. concurring) indicated that acquittals duly recorded by a jury on consideration of
the evidence would not be disturbed. In practical terms, appeals would be
brought only where a ruling or direction by the trial judge was claimed to be
in error. Whether, if such an appeal were allowed, a new trial could be
ordered, remains unsettled.[26] But there could be no question of the Supreme
Court entering a guilty verdict. As McCarthy J. pointed out in *People
(D.P.P.)* v. *Quilligan (No. 2)* [1989] I.R. 46, at 60, " . . . this would deprive an
accused of the constitutionally guaranteed right to trial by jury in other than
minor offences."

The complex position outlined above is difficult to justify. If appeals
against acquittals are desirable, this must be so for all—not just those
recorded in the Central Criminal Court. And the literal reading of Article
34.4.3° produces a clear inequality of treatment as between acquitted persons—an inequality which may flow from the Constitution's terms, but nonetheless hardly seems defensible. The remedy lies within the power of the
Government and Oireachtas. Should they feel that appeals against acquittal
are undesirable, legislation can be enacted to reverse the *O'Shea* decision—*i.e.*
in the language of Article 34.4.3°, "excepting" such appeals from the
Supreme Court's appellate jurisdiction. Alternatively, if it is believed that
appeals against acquittal are desirable, legislation could provide for such to
lie from *all* trial courts. Finally, if the view is taken that appeals—of whatever
nature—should lie only to the Court of Criminal Appeal, statute could bring
about this result—subject to the provisions of Article 34.4.4°.

Article 34.4.3°

As already indicated, Article 34.4.3° permits the Oireachtas to make
"exceptions" to the general principle it states, and also to "regulate" the
right of appeal from High Court decisions. To date there have been few

---

[25] In *People (D.P.P.)* v. *Conroy (No. 2)* [1989] I.R. 160 the appellant, who had pleaded guilty to
    manslaughter in the Central Criminal Court, appealed to the Supreme Court against the
    severity of his sentence. The court substituted a sentence of 17 years penal servitude for that
    of penal servitude for life originally imposed. Presumably the D.P.P. could invoke this juris-
    diction to entertain appeals against Central Criminal Court sentences.
[26] The issue arose—but was not resolved—in *People (D.P.P.)* v. *Quilligan (No. 2)* [1989] I.R. 46.
    Walsh and McCarthy JJ. held that a new trial *could* be ordered, Henchy and Griffin JJ. that it
    could not. Hederman J. reserved his position on the jurisdictional question, holding that the
    order here sought should not be made.

exceptions—among them are High Court decisions on appeals from the Circuit Court.[27] An instance of the regulation of the right of appeal is section 52 of the Courts (Supplemental Provisions) Act 1961, under which the High Court's determination on a case stated by the District Court may be appealed only with the leave of the High Court.[28] Cases involving the validity of post-Constitution Acts may not be excepted from the Supreme Court's appellate jurisdiction: Article 34.4.4°. This would not seem to prevent the Oireachtas from *regulating* appeals in such cases, *e.g.* by stipulating that leave to appeal be obtained. And it does not protect the Supreme Court's appellate jurisdiction over cases involving pre-Constitution Acts.

The power to prescribe exceptions and regulations conferred by Article 34.4.3° seems certain to be utilised on an extensive scale when the projected Court of Civil Appeal is established. A Courts and Court Officers Bill for this purpose is promised in the revised Programme for Government published in October 1991.[29] The intention is to lighten the workload of the Supreme Court, which has increased markedly in recent years, giving rise to serious delays.[30] The proposed court would not, of course, be able to entertain cases involving the validity of post-Constitution statutes: Article 34.3.2°. These would continue to go directly from the High Court to the Supreme Court, as presumably would applications under Article 40.4.2° (the habeas corpus provision).

A statute excepting cases from the Supreme Court's appellate jurisdiction must be clearly referable to the present Supreme Court as established in 1961: *Dillon-Leetch* v. *Calleary* (Supreme Court, July 25, 1973). And the subtraction from the appellate jurisdiction must be clear and express. Thus in *People (Att. Gen.)* v. *Conmey* [1975] I.R. 341 the majority refused to treat the statutory provisions establishing the Court of Criminal Appeal as excepting Central Criminal Court convictions from the Supreme Court's appellate jurisdiction. So too in *People (D.P.P.)* v. *O'Shea* [1982] I.R. 384 a majority rejected the contention that the Criminal Procedure Act 1967, s.34, operated to foreclose appeals against acquittals. That section permits the prosecution to appeal to the Supreme Court—without prejudice to the acquittal—where a trial judge has, on a question of law, directed a jury to return a verdict in favour of an accused. O'Higgins C.J. (with whose judgment Walsh and Hederman JJ. agreed) said ([1982] I.R. 384, 404):

> "The section relied on neither purports to be a regulation as envisaged by Article 34.4.3°, nor does it refer to the appellate jurisdiction which it is supposed to curtail. I regard it as a section of general application conferring on the Supreme Court an additional consultative jurisdiction in relation to questions of law arising on directions given by trial judges in both the Central Criminal Court and the Circuit Court. It is in no way

---

[27] Courts of Justice Act 1936, s.39, re-enacted by the Courts (Supplemental Provisions) Act 1961, s.48: see *Eamonn Andrews Productions Ltd.* v. *Gaiety Theatre Enterprises Ltd.* [1973] I.R. 295.

[28] In *Minister for Justice* v. *Wang Zhu Jie* [1991] I.L.R.M. 823 the Supreme Court held that s.52 regulated the right of appeal from the High Court in accordance with Art. 34.4.3°, and that no appeal lay from a High Court judge's refusal of leave.

[29] See *The Irish Times*, October 19, 1991.

[30] See Gerard Hogan "The Supreme Court: Too Much Work, Too Few Resources" in William Duncan (ed.), *Some Current Problems in Irish Law* (Dublin 1987), pp. 75–85.

inconsistent with the continuation of the Supreme Court's full appellate jurisdiction under Article 34.4.4° of the Constitution."

A similar approach may be seen in the civil case of *Holohan* v. *Donohoe* [1986] I.R. 45. The question raised here was—had the Supreme Court power, when it found a High Court jury's award of damages excessive, to re-assess the damages itself? Or was it obliged to order a new trial, particularly if that was the plaintiff's wish? By a 4–1 majority (Finlay C.J., Henchy, Griffin and Hederman JJ.: McCarthy J. dissenting) it was held that the court *had* power, in an appropriate case, to substitute its own assessment of damages for that of the jury. In the opinion of the majority, the court's jurisdiction to hear such appeals sprang from Article 34.4.3° of the Constitution. And the authorities showed that only clear and unambiguous statutory language could regulate, or create exceptions to, the jurisdiction thus conferred. The question then was—did section 96 of the Courts of Justice Act 1924 (re-enacted by section 48 of the Courts (Supplemental Provisions) Act 1961) have this effect? Section 96, so far as material, provides as follows:

> "Every appeal from a judgment of the High Court or the Circuit Court in an action tried by a judge and jury or from any other judgment of the High Court or Circuit Court, founded on the verdict of a jury in a civil case shall be made by way of motion before the appellate tribunal for a new trial . . . In any appeal to which this section applies, the appellate tribunal may, in lieu of ordering a new trial, set aside the verdict, findings and judgment appealed against and enter such judgment as the Court considers proper."

The majority view was that section 96 did not modify the Supreme Court's powers on such an appeal. As Henchy J. put it ([1986] I.R. 45, 57–58):

> "It is plain that section 96 does not create any exception from the right of appeal from the High Court to the Supreme Court. As to effecting a regulation of the right of appeal, s.96 plainly does so in that it provides that an appeal in a civil jury trial shall be initiated by a motion for a new trial. But, beyond providing further that the Supreme Court may, on hearing such an appeal, in lieu of ordering a new trial, set aside the verdict, findings and judgment appealed against and enter such judgment as the Court considers proper, the section is silent as to the scope of the Court's jurisdiction. Neither the restriction of the form of the appeal nor the provision enabling the Court to enter such judgment as it thinks proper when the verdict, findings and judgment appealed against are set aside could be said to deprive the Court of jurisdiction to assess damages in lieu of ordering them to be re-assessed in the High Court . . . s. 96 could not, by any stretch of interpretation, be said to be so clear and unambiguous in its scope as to deprive this Court of jurisdiction to make such order as it deems necessary for the purpose of doing justice in the disposition of the appeal, and in particular, to assess damages rather than order a new trial on the issue of damages."

Thus it is now established that the Supreme Court has power to re-assess damages itself. Whether it will do so depends on a number of factors, of which the plaintiff's wishes are but one; and the court will choose the course—re-assessment or an order for a new trial—that will best serve the interests of justice.

Appellate jurisdiction (b) from other courts

Article 34.4.3° provides that the Supreme Court shall have "appellate jurisdiction from such other courts as may be prescribed by law." Such jurisdiction is thus entirely statutory in origin: Walsh J., speaking for the Supreme Court, said in *State (Browne)* v. *Feran* [1967] I.R. 147, 156:

> " . . . before this Court can exercise appellate jurisdiction from decisions of courts other than the High Court that appellate jurisdiction must first have been bestowed affirmatively by Act of the Oireachtas."

And presumably the Oireachtas is as free to withdraw jurisdiction as to bestow it: the above-quoted words of Article 34.4.3° do not permit of any other construction.

The two main statutory provisions conferring additional appellate jurisdiction on the Supreme Court are the Courts of Justice Act 1924, s.29 (as re-enacted in the 1961 courts legislation) and the Courts of Justice Act 1947, s.16. The former provides for appeals, in limited circumstances, from decisions of the Court of Criminal Appeal. The latter permits a Circuit Court judge to state a case on a question of law, arising in a matter pending before him or her, for the opinion of the Supreme Court.

Section 29 of the 1924 Act requires that, for an appeal to go to the Supreme Court, a certificate must state that a point of law of exceptional public importance is involved, and that it is desirable in the public interest that an appeal should be taken. Such a certificate may be granted by: (a) the Court of Criminal Appeal; (b) the Attorney General; or (c) the Director of Public Prosecutions (Prosecution of Offences Act 1974, s.3(4)). Should all these refuse, no appeal can be brought; there is no machinery for seeking a certificate from the Supreme Court itself, and no appeal appears to lie to it from a refusal to certify. In a case where the Court of Criminal Appeal has quashed a conviction, the prosecution cannot avail of section 29: the former Supreme Court so ruled in *People (Att. Gen.)* v. *Kennedy* [1946] I.R. 517.

Although the granting of a section 29 certificate gives the right of appeal, the certificate does not limit the scope of the appeal—which is not confined to the point of law stated therein: *People (Att. Gen.)* v. *Giles* [1974] I.R. 422 and *People (D.P.P.)* v. *Shaw* [1982] I.R. 1. On such an appeal the Supreme Court has all the powers exercisable by the Court of Criminal Appeal—including power to affirm or quash a conviction, or to order a retrial: Courts of Justice Act 1928, s.5 (re-enacted by the Courts (Supplemental Provisions) Act 1961, s.48).[31]

The Courts of Justice Act 1947, s.16, as noted, permits a Circuit Court judge to state a case on a question of law arising in a matter pending before him or her, for the determination of the Supreme Court. There must be an application in that behalf, and the judge is empowered to adjourn the pronouncement of the judgment or order pending the Supreme Court's ruling. Section 16 was upheld as constitutionally valid in *People (Att. Gen.)* v. *McGlynn* [1967] I.R. 332, where the Supreme Court also held that the power thus conferred cannot be exercised in the course of a criminal trial with a

---

[31] In *People (D.P.P.)* v. *Egan* [1990] I.L.R.M. 780 the Supreme Court held that the Court of Criminal Appeal was not empowered to substitute its own subjective view for the verdict of the jury, *i.e.* it could not interfere with that verdict on the basis of a "lurking doubt" or "the feel of the case." Presumably the Supreme Court is similarly fettered.

jury. Essentially, then, section 16 is primarily relevant to civil proceedings; it may be used at whatever stage the trial judge thinks appropriate: *Doyle* v. *Hearne* [1987] I.R. 601.

Consultative jurisdiction: Article 40.4.3°

When the High Court is hearing a habeas corpus application under Article 40.4 of the Constitution, it normally has full jurisdiction to rule on any legal or constitutional issues raised. But Article 40.4.3° creates an exception to this. Should the High Court form the view that a person is detained under a statute which is constitutionally invalid, it *must* state a case on the matter for the Supreme Court's determination. This provision was not part of Bunreacht na hÉireann as originally enacted: it was inserted by statute during the period when the Constitution could be amended without referendum. And it was adopted as a consequence of *State (Burke)* v. *Lennon* [1940] I.R. 136. There Gavan Duffy J. found the internment provisions of the Offences against the State Act 1939 invalid, and granted habeas corpus to several persons detained thereunder. Since the former Supreme Court held it had no jurisdiction to hear an appeal from this decision, there was no means of testing the correctness of the High Court's conclusion. Article 40.4.3° ensured that this would not occur again.

Since the Supreme Court's decision in *State (Browne)* v. *Feran* [1967] I.R. 147, an appeal now lies against the grant of habeas corpus. Thus the problem Article 40.4.3° was designed to cope with has now disappeared: and the provision could, without loss, be repealed. It applies only to legislation passed since the Constitution came into force. In *State (Sheerin)* v. *Kennedy* [1966] I.R. 379, Kenny J. stated a case under Article 40.4.3° in regard to the Prevention of Crime Act 1908, s.2, as amended. The Supreme Court declined to entertain the question, holding that it was not one as to the "validity" of a law under Article 40.4.3°, but one as to the inconsistency of a pre-Constitution Act with the Constitution under Article 50. The latter kind of question could not come before the Supreme Court in a case stated. It follows that habeas corpus challenges to pre-Constitution Acts must now follow the ordinary pattern with the High Court ruling on all questions raised. Such decisions may be appealed to the Supreme Court in the usual way. In challenges to post-Constitution Acts otherwise than by habeas corpus—*e.g.* proceedings for a declaration, certiorari or prohibition—the same applies.

But Article 40.4.3° will apply at least to some delegated legislation made under the authority of post-Constitution statutes. This is one effect of *State (Gilliland)* v. *Governor, Mountjoy Prison* [1987] I.R. 201. There the prosecutor was detained, pending his extradition to the United States, on foot of a District Court order made under the Extradition Act 1965. That Act had been made applicable to the United States by the Extradition Act 1965 (Part II) (No. 20) Order 1984 (S.I. 1984 No. 300), which in turn was based on a treaty between Ireland and the United States. In his habeas corpus application the prosecutor claimed that the 1984 Order was invalid because the treaty it was based upon, though involving expenditure by the State, had not been approved by the Dáil—contrary to Article 29.5.2°. In the High Court Barrington J. concluded that the 1984 order was indeed invalid and he stated a case under Article 40.4.3°. The Supreme Court (Finlay C.J., Henchy and Griffin JJ.: Hederman and McCarthy JJ. dissenting) held that the 1984

Order was a "law" within the meaning of Article 40.4.3°; thus that court had jurisdiction to answer the question raised. Finlay C.J. (Henchy and Griffin JJ. concurring) thought the intention underlying Article 40.4.3° was that a discharge from custody authorised by legislative provisions should await a Supreme Court decision on their validity. It was therefore logical that Article 40.4.3° should apply not only to the Extradition Act 1965 itself, but also to the machinery established thereunder for applying it by Government Order. (The dissenters felt that "law" in Article 40.4.3° referred only to Acts.) On a narrow reading only statutory instruments closely akin to the 1984 order will attract Article 40.4.3°—*i.e.* it will capture only those on which a statute's operation pivots.

Finality of Supreme Court decisions

Article 34.4.6° provides that the decision of the Supreme Court "shall in all cases be final and conclusive." Since Irish entry into the European Communities, however, this statement must be understood in a special sense. Article 177 of the Treaty of Rome—which now forms part of Irish law—operates to deprive the Supreme Court of power to rule finally on questions of EC law. If in proceedings before the Supreme Court a question is raised as to:

(a) the interpretation of the EC Treaties, or
(b) the validity and interpretation of acts of Community institutions (*e.g.* regulations or directives issued by the Commission or Council), or
(c) the interpretation of the statutes of bodies established by an act of the Council

then, theoretically, the Supreme Court *must* bring that matter before the European Court of Justice. For the Supreme Court is plainly "a court . . . against whose decisions there is no judicial remedy under national law," in terms of the third paragraph of Article 177. The obligation, however, is not as absolute as might appear; in Case 283/81, *CILFIT* v. *Ministry of Health* [1982] E.C.R. 3415 the Court of Justice accepted that it would not arise where the Community provision in question had already been interpreted by that court, or where the correct application of Community law was so obvious as to leave no scope for any reasonable doubt.[32]

In *Kerry Cooperative Creameries Ltd.* v. *An Bord Bainne* [1991] I.L.R.M. 851 Finlay C.J., speaking for the Supreme Court, said (at 854–55):

> "In any case where the judge of first instance has, as he is clearly entitled to do, reached a decision on one or more questions of European Community law, coming within the categories mentioned in Article 177 of the Treaty, this Court as a final court of appeal cannot affirm, vary or reverse such a decision, but must, if the resolution of such questions is necessary to enable it to give its judgment, refer those questions for a preliminary ruling to the Court of Justice of the European Communities pursuant to Article 177. If, of course, this Court decides that the resolution of such questions is not necessary to enable it to give judgment in the case, then no reference is made. In either event it is not appropriate

---

[32] Though the court emphasised the need for caution in reaching any such conclusion, given *inter alia* the different languages in which Community law is drafted and the fact that it has its own peculiar terminology.

for this Court to express any view on issues of European Community law arising in this manner, except for the particular instance where it may conclude that what was alleged to be an issue of EC law is in fact incapable of any but one resolution, and has so clearly been determined."

Composition

The Constitution does not fix the size of the Supreme Court for all purposes. It merely stipulates that the court must not consist of less than five judges when exercising its functions under Articles 12 or 26. In regard to the much more significant appellate jurisdiction—including appeals involving the constitutionality of statutes—no minimum or maximum number of judges is prescribed. This *lacuna* is filled by statute: the Courts (Supplemental Provisions) Act 1961, s.7, provides that in cases involving the validity of a statute the court must consist of five judges. (The same section empowers the Chief Justice, or in his absence the senior ordinary judge of the Supreme Court, to determine that other cases should be heard by a three-judge court; and it decrees that the court may *not* consist of four judges.)

By section 1(2) of the Courts (Establishment and Constitution) Act 1961 the Supreme Court was constituted of the Chief Justice, and such number of ordinary judges of that court as might from time to time be fixed by Act of the Oireachtas. Section 4(1) of the Courts (Supplemental Provisions) Act 1961 fixed that number at four. However, the President of the High Court is, *ex officio*, an additional judge of the Supreme Court: Courts (Establishment and Constitution) Act 1961, s.1(3). Further, if an ordinary judge of the Supreme Court is appointed to the Law Reform Commission, an extra judge may validly be appointed: Law Reform Commission Act 1975, s.14(1). This would apply even if the Commissioner-judge is available to sit on occasion in the Supreme Court. Consequently the Chief Justice may at times have available to sit with him five Supreme Court judges plus the President of the High Court. But even this margin sometimes fails to produce a five-judge court, and it is necessary to request a High Court judge to sit. This is authorised by the Courts (Establishment and Constitution) Act 1961, s.2(5).

Doubts have been expressed about the validity of bringing High Court judges in to sit in the Supreme Court. These are based upon the fact that a judge of the High Court is appointed specifically to *that* court, as is shown by the declaration required to be made under Article 34.5.1°, to execute the office of judge of the High Court. From this is derived the implication that the person concerned cannot act as a Supreme Court judge. Further evidence is found in Article 34.4.5°, which requires the decision of the Supreme Court to be "pronounced by such one of the judges of that court as that court shall direct."[33] But the statutory provisions sanctioning this practice benefit from the presumption of constitutionality, and it is difficult to accept that the factors outlined above are sufficient to rebut that presumption. Moreover, Article 36, iii, provides that statute shall regulate the "constitution and organisation" of the courts. A divisional court held in *State (Walshe)* v. *Murphy* [1981] I.R. 275, 287 that "constitution" here involves the concept of appointment, formation or making-up.

---

[33] See the Eleventh Interim Report of the Committee on Court Practice and Procedure (Prl. 1835), para. 5.

Doubt has also been expressed as to whether the Supreme Court could properly sit in two divisions or chambers—*e.g.* to clear a back-log of non-constitutional cases. A former Minister for Justice (Mr. Desmond O'Malley) informed a Dáil committee that he and his officials had once considered this possibility in order to clear arrears of business; and he thought it was not pre-cluded (*semble*, by the Constitution). But the then Attorney General (Mr. Declan Costello) remarked that there was some controversy on this point.[34]

The foundation for these doubts is not clear. The Constitution certainly refers throughout to "the Supreme Court," but this can scarcely imply that the court must always sit as a single entity. Some weight must be given to the already-noted fact that Article 36, iii allows "the constitution and organis-ation of the said courts" to be regulated by statute.

The fact that the Constitution does not fix the size of the Supreme Court theoretically leaves open the possibility of "court-packing." That is, a Government annoyed by a decision or decisions of the Supreme Court could increase its size, and then hope to influence the outcome of future cases by appointing its supporters to the new positions. The United States Constitu-tion similarly fails to fix the Supreme Court's size, and charges of "court-packing" have certainly been levelled there.[35] But an Irish Government deciding on such a course would first have to promote legislation to authorise the increase in size. The political controversy which would certainly arise might daunt the boldest heart. Even should the executive get its way it would still have to find "reliable" appointees. But it cannot be guaranteed that an individual's view on some question, formed *ex parte*, will remain unchanged after the matter has been thrashed out in forensic argument. In Ireland, Maguire C.J. admitted that he had reversed his view on the validity of taxing judges' salaries following such argument: *O'Byrne* v. *Minister for Finance* [1959] I.R. 1, 37. In the United States, Chase C.J. held unconstitutional a statute which he had earlier sponsored as Secretary of the Treasury: *Hepburn* v. *Griswold* (1870) 8 Wall. 603, 625. As Chief Justice Hughes wrote[36]:

> "If conscientious, able and independent men are put on the bench, you cannot predict their course as judges by reference either to partisan motives or to personal or party loyalties." (*op. cit.* p. 49).

"Court-packing" in Ireland may be regarded as more a theoretical danger than a real possibility.

APPOINTMENT OF JUDGES

By virtue of Article 35.1 all judges (save those of special criminal courts) are appointed by the President. However, as noted earlier, the President here acts on the advice of the Government: thus it is the executive which makes the effective choice. With occasional exceptions Governments tend to favour their own supporters, but it would be quite inaccurate to assume that the calibre of appointees (at least in the higher courts) is lowered thereby. Indeed, current judicial salaries compare so unfavourably with potential earnings at the bar as to make judicial appointments relatively unattractive.

[34] Law Reform Commission Bill 1975, Special Committee, D 18, No. 3, p. 47.
[35] Charles Evans Hughes, *The Supreme Court of the United States*, (New York 1928), pp. 51–53.
[36] *Ibid.*, p. 49.

Whereas it was once possible to appoint people at around the age of 40, more recent appointees have generally been in the mid-fifties or older.[37]

The Constitution does not lay down any qualifications for judicial appointment, the matter being left for regulation by statute. In *State (Walshe)* v. *Murphy* [1981] I.R. 275, the contrary was argued. Statute, it was contended, could deal only with the matters mentioned in Article 36. These included the number of judges, their remuneration, retirement, pensions, and terms of appointment—and this last phrase did not include qualifications for appointment. A divisional court accepted this argument only in part. "Terms of appointment" in Article 36, ii, did not cover qualifications for appointment, but this did not mean that the Oireachtas lacked power to prescribe such qualifications. Under Article 36, iii, it was authorised to regulate the constitution and organisation of the courts. And "constitution," with its connotations of appointment or formation, was wide enough to encompass prescribing qualifications. (As noted *supra*, the court also held that Article 13.8.1° did not preclude judicial review of the legality of appointments.)

For appointment to the Supreme Court or High Court, the only qualification prescribed is that one be a practising barrister of not less than 12 years' standing (Courts (Supplemental Provisions) Act 1961, s.5). To qualify for appointment as a Circuit Court judge it is necessary to be a practising barrister of not less than 10 years' standing (*ibid.* s.17). District Court judges may be appointed from amongst barristers and solicitors of not less than 10 years' standing (*ibid.* s.29(2)). It is curious that solicitors are eligible only for appointment to the District Court, especially as they have enjoyed the right of audience in *all* courts since 1971 (Courts Act 1971, s.17).

In *State (Walshe)* v. *Murphy* [1981] I.R. 275 the respondent had been appointed as a temporary District Justice under the Courts of Justice Act 1936, s.51(1) (as applied and amended by the Courts (Supplemental Provisions) Act 1961, s.48). This empowered the Government to appoint "persons who are practising barristers or solicitors of 10 years' standing at least at the date of appointment . . . " The respondent was appointed on April 22, 1981. He had practised at the bar from November 1962 until February 1971, when he became a legal assistant in the Attorney General's Office. In May 1973 he became examiner of titles in the Land Commission, from which post he resigned on April 16, 1981. On April 17, 1981 he attended a consultation and gave advice for which he received a fee. It was contended that this career pattern did not qualify the respondent for appointment. Properly construed, the statute required a period of actual practice at the bar of not less than 10 years. Counsel for the respondent argued *contra* that the Act referred to the period since call to the bar. The respondent's call preceded his appointment by more than 18 years, so he fulfilled the statutory requirement.

A divisional court (Finlay P., Gannon and Hamilton JJ.) accepted the prosecutor's argument. In enacting the relevant provision the legislature intended to prescribe a minimum degree of competence and skill for appointment as a District Justice. To interpret "10 years' standing at least" as referring only to the date of call to the bar would frustrate that intention. Finlay P. (Gannon and Hamilton JJ. concurring) said ([1981] I.R. 278, 289):

---

[37] For an interesting—if somewhat outdated—survey of Irish courts and judges see Paul C. Bartholomew, *The Irish Judiciary* (Dublin 1971).

"Therefore I conclude that in the context of these statutes the words 'practising barristers or solicitors of 10 years standing at least' . . . must be construed as indicating . . . a person who is a practising barrister at the time of his appointment and whose aggregated practice as a barrister at that time is not less than 10 years. There is, of course, no warrant for implying from the words contained in the subsection any requirement that these 10 years must have immediately preceded the date of the appointment or that there must have been a continuous period of 10 years." ([1981] I.R. 278, 289).

The respondent, it was held, met neither qualification. He had not practised as a barrister for a full 10 years. His period in the public service could not be counted for this purpose, since he had not then been on hazard and offering himself as a barrister to the public at large during that time. Nor was he a practising barrister at the time of his appointment. He had just resigned after 10 years as a lawyer in the public service, and was shortly to take up appointment as a District Justice. A single instance of legal advice being given during that period was insufficient to constitute him a practising barrister within the meaning of section 51 of the 1936 Act.

It is not uncommon for a Government to nominate the Attorney General for appointment as a judge of the superior courts. It has also been known for a Government to insist that the Attorney should not engage in private practice while holding office. But an Attorney who has served on such terms may not now be qualified for *immediate* appointment. Even if he has practised for 15 years, he may not be a *practising barrister at the time of appointment* under the doctrine in *Walshe's* case.

Every person appointed a judge under the Constitution must make and subscribe the declaration set out in Article 34.5.1.°. The Chief Justice is required to do so in the presence of the President of Ireland, other judges must do so in open court in the presence of the Chief Justice or senior available judge of the Supreme Court (Article 34.5.2°). The declaration must be made and subscribed before entering upon judicial duties—and not later than 10 days after the date of appointment, or such later date as the President determines (Art. 34.5.3°). A failure to comply with this requirement means that the judge is deemed to have vacated office (Art. 34.5.4°).[38]

Judicial Independence

Article 35.2 states that all judges "shall be independent in the exercise of their judicial functions and subject only to the Constitution and the law." And this is reinforced by making judges ineligible for membership of the Oireachtas. Article 35.3, which so provides, also forbids judges "to hold any other office or position of emolument." This is understood to mean that a judge can be appointed to another office, while remaining a judge, so long as no extra remuneration is involved. Hence the Law Reform Commission Act 1975 contemplates the appointment of a judge to the Commission; and

[38] The declaration—to uphold the Constitution and the laws—has more than symbolic significance. In *State (Byrne)* v. *Frawley* [1978] I.R. 326 Henchy J. (Griffin and Parke JJ. concurring) said it would impose a duty on a judge to terminate any proceedings before him if it was "shown to him that they have been authoritatively declared to rest on an unconstitutional statute" (at 344).

Walsh J. served as its first President. Similar provisions may be found in the
Adoption Act 1952, s.8(4), and in the (now repealed) Local Government
(Planning and Development) Act, 1976, s.4. Moreover, it is the established
practice to call upon judges to chair commissions, as well as statutory tribunals of inquiry.

The independence guaranteed by Article 35.2[39] may serve as one of the
constitutional underpinnings[40] of the common law rule that judges are
immune from liability for acts done in the performance of their judicial
duties. This protects them from liability, not only in defamation,[41] but more
generally. In *Coyle* v. *Roe* (*The Irish Times*, June 26, 1984) Hamilton J. struck
out as an abuse of process the plaintiff's claim for damages for, *inter alia*, conspiracy against the defendant Circuit Court judge. Hamilton J. said that a
judge acting in the exercise of his functions was protected, and described this
rule as "absolute and universal." An allied protection exists for Circuit and
District Court judges in regard to judicial review proceedings challenging
their decisions. In *McIlwraith* v. *Judge Fawsitt* [1990] 1 I.R. 343 Finlay C.J.,
for the Supreme Court, put it thus (at 346):

> " . . . under no circumstances should the High Court upon application
> for judicial review with regard to either a decision of a District Justice or
> of a Circuit Court judge award costs to a successful applicant in a case
> where there is no question of impropriety or *mala fides* on the part of the
> judge concerned and where he has not sought to defend an order which
> apparently is invalid."[42]

And the Chief Justice hinted that even if costs were properly awarded against
the judge, he/she might not necessarily suffer financially. He said (at 347):

> "Considerations of the obligation owed by the executive under the Con-
> stitution to support the judiciary in the carrying out of its separate
> duties under the Constitution may well lead in appropriate cases to an
> obligation which the courts could enforce against the executive to
> indemnify members of the judiciary in regard to costs which are prop-
> erly awarded against them, but no question of that description has been

---

[39] Which was notably asserted by O'Hanlon J. in April 1992 when, as newly appointed President of the Law Reform Commission, he was reported as having made certain controversial
statements on abortion (see n. 61 *infra*). Subsequently a report in *The Irish Times* of April 8,
1992 said that the judge had been "summoned" to attend a meeting with the Taoiseach (Mr.
Reynolds) and the Attorney General (Mr. Whelehan) in order to explain his position. On
April 9, 1992 *The Irish Times* printed a statement by O'Hanlon J. in which he referred to that
report, and continued: "I think it is important to point out, in the interest of preserving the
status and independence of the Judiciary in the exercise of its functions under the Constitution, that there is no power whatever conferred on the Executive to "summon" a Judge of the
High Court to attend a meeting with the Taoiseach, or to require him to "explain his position" about anything.
If any such decision was reached by the Cabinet in the terms referred to in the public press,
then I would have to seek to have it revoked before I would be prepared to respond to an invitation by the Taoiseach to attend a meeting for the purpose of discussing any matters that
may be of concern to him and to the Government."
[40] Others may exist: see W. N. Osborough "The State's Tortious Liability: Further Reflections
on *Byrne* v. *Ireland*—II" (1976) XI *Irish Jurist* (N.S.) 279, 288–89.
[41] *Macaulay & Co. Ltd.* v. *Wyse-Power* (1943) 77 I.L.T.R. 61.
[42] The Supreme Court said that the other contesting party should be added as a further respondent in judicial review proceedings.

debated before this Court on this appeal and it is not necessary for me to express any opinion upon it."

In *Maharaj* v. *Att. Gen. of Trinidad (No. 2)* [1978] 2 All E.R. 670 a judge had committed the appellant, a barrister, to a short sentence of imprisonment for contempt of court. In so doing he had, as the Privy Council held in earlier proceedings,[43] violated natural justice. The present claim was *inter alia* for damages for wrongful detention and false imprisonment. In constitutional terms, he claimed that his constitutional right not to be deprived of liberty without due process of law[44] had been violated, and that section 6 of the Constitution[45] gave the High Court jurisdiction to award him damages. By a 4–1 majority[46] the Judicial Committee found in his favour. Lord Diplock said that the judge's order had contravened the appellant's constitutional right. And following his release, the only practicable form of redress was monetary compensation. To hold the state liable for this was within the High Court's constitutional jurisdiction, and did not subvert the rule that a judge could not be made personally liable for what he/she had done when acting or purporting to act in a judicial capacity. Lord Diplock said ([1978] 2 All E.R. 670, 679):

> "The claim for redress under s.6(1) for what has been done by a judge is a claim against the state for what has been done in the exercise of the judicial power of the state. This is not vicarious liability: it is a liability of the state itself. It is not a liability in tort at all: it is a liability in the public law of the state, not of the judge himself, which has been newly created by s.6(1) and (2) of the Constitution."

In Ireland the only form of State liability so far recognised is vicarious liability. If the common law rule on judicial immunity has been constitutionalised then, as Professor Osborough has suggested,[47] the State would not be answerable in respect of any act to which judicial immunity attached. This difficulty could be outflanked: a broad view of the State's obligations under Article 40.3 could found an independent State liability on the basis of the *Maharaj* reasoning. But the current tendency is to emphasise that Article 40.3 imposes no *general* obligation to defend and. vindicate the personal rights of the citizen. It is to defend and vindicate them "by its laws," and this phrase is not construed to cover the common (or judge-made) law: *Crowley* v. *Ireland* [1980] I.R. 102 and *Igoe* v. *Ireland* [1989] I.R. 386, 393, *per* Blayney J.[48]

In *Valente* v. *The Queen* (1985) 24 D.L.R. (4th) 161 the Canadian Supreme Court considered the concept of judicial independence under the Charter of Rights (s.11(d)). In an unanimous and exhaustive judgment, *per* Le Dain J.,

---

[43] *Maharaj* v. *Att. Gen. of Trinidad* [1977] 1 All E.R. 411.

[44] Guaranteed by section 1 of the Trinidadian Constitution.

[45] s.6 provided that a person alleging a violation of constitutional rights could "apply for redress." S.6(2) empowered the court, upon such application, to make such orders as it considered appropriate for enforcing the protection of the relevant constitutional right.

[46] Lords Diplock, Salmon, Russell and Keith: Lord Hailsham dissenting.

[47] *Op. cit. supra*, p. 289.

[48] What Kenny J. said on this matter in *Crowley's* case would seem to be part of the Supreme Court's *ratio decidendi*, and would thus have bound Blayney J. in *Igoe's* case. But it directly contradicts what Kenny J., in his separate judgment, said about Article 40.3 in *People (D.P.P.)* v. *Shaw* [1982] I.R. 1, 62: "The obligation to implement this guarantee is imposed not on the Oireachtas only but on each branch of the State which exercises the powers of legislating,

it was held that its ingredients were: security of tenure (removal only for cause); security of remuneration (no arbitrary interference therewith by the executive); and independence in administrative matters bearing directly on the judicial function (the assignment of judges, arrangement of court sittings, lists, etc.). Bunreacht na hÉireann plainly guarantees the first two of these; tradition and practice ensure the third, and a purposive interpretation of "independent" in Article 35.2 would invalidate any statute giving the executive power to manipulate cause lists.

The judgment in *Valente's* case notes (at 188–190) a widely held view that the courts should have financial independence—*i.e.* prepare their own budgetary estimates, the responsible Minister presenting these to parliament as a conduit; that expenditure of the budget, once approved, should be a judicial responsibility; likewise all aspects of administration, including recruitment, etc. of court staff. The United States Supreme Court has long enjoyed such powers, which are also possessed by the German Constitutional Court.[49] Whether such matters come within the concept of independence under Article 35.2 has not yet been decided. Were they held to do so it would doubtless be beneficial. Recurrent problems over staffing and accommodation might not occur if presiding judges could deal directly with the Government on such matters, instead of funnelling requests through the bureaucracy.

Judicial Remuneration

Article 35.5 declares that the remuneration of a judge shall not be reduced during his/her continuance in office. By virtue of Article 36.ii and iii the levels of judicial remuneration are plainly a matter for the Oireachtas, so Article 35.5 merely guarantees the judge the salary level prevailing at the date of appointment. Like any other, a judicial salary may be eroded by inflation but Article 35.5 is not to be construed as a shield against this: the judges have no constitutional claim to index-linking. So much is clear from *O'Byrne* v. *Minister for Finance* [1959] I.R. 1. The plaintiff was the widow and executrix of the late Mr. Justice O'Byrne, a judge of the High Court 1926–40, and of the Supreme Court 1940–54. During his entire tenure of office his salary was paid after deduction of tax. His widow claimed that this was unconstitutional and she sought repayment of the sums involved. Her claim was based on Article 68 of the 1922 Constitution, it being common case that under the transitory provisions of the 1937 Constitution, this still governed the position of High Court and Supreme Court judges. The relevant portion of Article 68 provided that the judges' remuneration should not be "diminished" during their continuance in office. By a 3–2 majority the Supreme Court held against the plaintiff. Maguire C.J. (Haugh J. concurring) concluded as follows ([1959] I.R. 1, 38):

> "The prohibition in the Article must be read in the context of the Article as a whole. The purpose of the Article is to safeguard the independence of judges. To require a judge to pay taxes on his income on the same

executing and giving judgment on those laws: Article 6. The word 'laws' in Article 40, s.3 is not confined to laws enacted by the Oireachtas but comprehends the laws made by judges and by ministers . . . when they make statutory instruments or regulations."

[49] See Donald Kommers, *Judicial Politics in West Germany* (Beverly Hills, 1976), p. 91.

basis as other citizens and thus to contribute to the expenses of government cannot be said to be an attack upon his independence."

Kingsmill Moore J., in a separate judgment, reached a similar conclusion.

Article 35 of Bunreacht na hÉireann differs somewhat in arrangement from Article 68 of the former Constitution, and with regard to remuneration the word "reduced" has been substituted for "diminished." But these factors are not sufficient to distinguish *O'Byrne's* case, which may safely be taken as still authoritative. And if Article 35.5 does not protect judges from a tax liability shared with other citizens, it can hardly protect them from inflation, whose ravages are felt by all.[50]

Judicial numbers, remuneration, retirement etc.

By virtue of Article 36 several matters affecting the courts are left to be regulated by statute. Among those are the number of judges of the various courts, a matter already considered in regard to the Supreme Court. The size of the High Court is currently fixed at 17 (the President of that court and 16 ordinary judges).[51] However, where a High Court judge is appointed to the Law Reform Commission, the Government is empowered to appoint an additional judge.[52] The Circuit Court's composition is currently regulated by the Courts Act 1991, s.18, the court consisting of the President and 17 ordinary judges. The size of the District Court is fixed by the Courts Act 1991, s.19 as the President and 45 ordinary judges.

For the reason given *infra*, the Oireachtas has power to legislate for the appointment of temporary judges to the lower courts. Advantage has been taken of this to allow the Government to appoint temporary Circuit Court—Courts of Justice Act 1936, s.14—and District Court judges—s.51 *ibid*. Both these provisions are continued in force by the Courts (Supplemental Provisions) Act 1961, s.48. As a consequence, the number of judges functioning at any given time in these courts may be greater than the apparent statutory maximum. A judge appointed on such a basis is usually named to fill the next permanent vacancy in the appropriate court.

Remuneration levels are similarly regulated by Act of the Oireachtas—the cumbrously titled Oireachtas (Allowances to Members) and Ministerial, Parliamentary and Judicial Offices (Amendment) Act 1983. This reflects the practice of recent years whereby parliamentary, ministerial, judicial and civil service salaries are related to one another and increases decided upon by the Government at the same time. The Government also has power to increase judicial salaries by order. Any such order must be laid before both Houses of the Oireachtas, but only the Dáil seems to have power to annul it. It is a measure of the law's complexity in this area that this power to make orders is conferred by the Courts (Supplemental Provisions) Act 1961, s.46(9). This was inserted by the Courts (Supplemental Provisions) (No. 2) Act 1968, s.1(3)(*b*)—which has been amended by the Oireachtas (Allowance to Mem-

---

[50] This conclusion seems implicit in *U.S.* v. *Will* (1980) 449 U.S. 200 where it was held that the Compensation Clause of the Constitution did not prevent Congress from abrogating planned, but not yet effective, cost of living increases for judges.

[51] Courts Act 1991, s.17.

[52] Law Reform Commission Act 1975, s.14(1)(*b*), as amended by s.17 of the Courts Act 1991.

bers) etc. Act 1977, s.11, and by section 8(*b*) of the similarly titled Act of 1983!

Under the Courts (Supplemental Provisions) Act 1961, s.46(4), judicial salaries are charged on the Central Fund. Thus expenditure on them does not require to be authorised by the annual Appropriation Act.[53]

The age of retirement is also fixed by statute. For judges of the Supreme Court and High Court it is 72 years[54]; for Circuit Court judges 70 years[55] and for District Court judges 65 years.[56] However, a District Court judge may thereafter be continued in office until he or she reaches the age of 70.[57] For this purpose a committee consisting of the Chief Justice, the President of the High Court and the Attorney General must be satisfied that the judge is not suffering from any disability which would render him or her unfit to continue to discharge effectively the duties of the office.[58]

JUDICIAL TENURE

The Constitution protects only the security of tenure of Supreme Court and High Court judges (Art. 35.4.1°). Judges of the other courts depend upon statute for their guarantee. This is the result of Article 36.ii which leaves the "terms of appointment" of such judges to be "regulated in accordance with law." Because of this, legislation can and does permit the appointment of temporary Circuit Court and District Court judges. It would not be possible, in view of the terms of Articles 34 and 35, to have such an arrangement in regard to the superior courts.

In *Magee* v. *Culligan* [1992] I.L.R.M. 186 the Applicant's extradition had been ordered by a District Court judge who, at that time, held a temporary appointment. Seeking to have the order quashed, the applicant argued that the legislation authorising such temporary appointments[59] was unconstitutional. This contention was rejected by the Supreme Court; the appointment of District Court judges for fixed short periods was not inconsistent with any constitutional provision. The court emphasised, however, that during the fixed period of office such a judge would benefit from the constitutional guarantees of independence in the exercise of judicial functions and against reduction in remumeration.

Article 35.4.1° provides that a judge of the Supreme Court or High Court "shall not be removed from office except for stated misbehaviour or incapacity." Removal would be effected by the President "by an order under his hand and seal" (Art. 35.4.3°) upon his being notified by the Taoiseach that the Dáil and Seanad had passed resolutions for such removal. To that notification must be annexed copies of the resolutions, certified by the Chairman

---

[53] In the *Valente* case discussed *supra*, the Canadian Supreme Court thought this desirable, but not an essential component of the concept of judicial independence.

[54] Courts of Justice Act 1924, s.12 and Courts (Supplemental Provisions) Act 1961, s.12.

[55] Courts (Supplemental Provisions) Act 1961, s.18(1).

[56] *Ibid.*, s.30(1).

[57] Courts of Justice (District Court) Act 1949, s.2.

[58] See, too, the Courts (No. 2) Act 1988, passed to enable this committee to make, with retrospective effect, warrants covering a year or years when one was not issued through error or oversight. There is a saver for constitutional rights—s.1(3). See further Chap. 14 *infra*, *s.v.* Trial in Due Course of Law.

[59] s.5(1), Courts of Justice Act 1936, as applied by s.48 of the Courts (Supplemental Provisions) Act 1961.

of each House (Art. 35.4.1°, 2°). Even though the Constitution does not require it, statute demands the same procedure for the removal of Circuit Court and District Court judges (respectively Courts of Justice Act 1924, s.24, Courts of Justice (District Court) Act 1946, s.20).

Several points arise in regard to this removal procedure (which has never yet been invoked). Firstly, the Dáil and Seanad resolutions may be passed by a simple majority of those present and voting. This follows from the general principle laid down in Article 15.11.1°, reinforced by the Presidential removal provisions of Article 12, which specifically require resolutions supported by not less than two-thirds of the total membership of both Houses. Secondly, "stated misbehaviour" suggests that the removal resolutions must find as a fact that this misbehaviour has occurred—and also implies that the judge must be notified in advance of the charges and must be allowed an opportunity to rebut them. This latter implication is strengthened by the Supreme Court's decision in *Garvey* v. *Ireland* [1981] I.R. 75—that anyone threatened with removal from a whole-time pensionable office must be accorded basic fairness of procedure. In the circumstances this would probably require: (a) advance notice of the charges; (b) a trial-type hearing (perhaps by a parliamentary committee); (c) a full opportunity for the judge to make his/her case and to rebut the charges, including the opportunity to be legally represented, if desired: see *In re Haughey* [1971] I.R. 217, 263–64 *per* Ó Dálaigh C.J.

The third and final issue that arises is the meaning of the word "misbehaviour." Recently the question has been extensively canvassed in Australia, where section 72 of the Constitution permits removal of High Court Justices only "on the ground of proved misbehaviour or incapacity." In February 1984 the Commonwealth Solicitor-General was asked to give a written opinion on the meaning of "misbehaviour." His opinion was tabled in Parliament and released to the press. The Solicitor-General's view was that misbehaviour under section 72 was limited to matters pertaining to: (a) judicial office, including non-attendance, neglect of or refusal to perform duties; (b) the commission of an offence against the general law of such a quality that the incumbent was unfit to exercise the office. This opinion was contested by others, including a former Commonwealth Attorney-General, who took the view that certain kinds of non-criminal, non-judicial conduct could afford grounds for removal.[60]

It may be that "misbehaviour" under Article 35.4.1° has the wider meaning, embracing conduct not only on, but off, the bench—with the latter not being confined to criminal conduct. What might be forgiven in the ordinary citizen may not necessarily be pardoned in the judge.[61] If, for example, it was

---

[60] See (1984) 58 *Australian Law Journal* 309–312.

[61] This may be thought to be illustrated by the events of April 1992, when O'Hanlon J.'s appointment as President of the Law Reform Commission was terminated by the Government. Following upon the Supreme Court's decision in *Att. Gen.* v. *X.* (as to which see Chap. 12 *infra, s.v.* Abortion), in which the court had held abortion constitutionally permissible in limited circumstances, O'Hanlon J. had given interviews to the media in which he had suggested a constitutional amendment to rule out abortion. He was also quoted as saying that he would favour abandoning membership of the European Communities if it meant the introduction of abortion into Ireland (*The Sunday Tribune*, April 5, 1992). On April 8, 1992 the judge met the Taoiseach and the Attorney General. On April 9, the Taoiseach (Mr. Reynolds) wrote to him, objecting to his expressing publicly views on a " . . . a subject of imminent decision by the Government and of great public controversy . . . " and which tended

proved that a judge had given advice, on a matter of political controversy, to one of the parties contesting a general election, might this not constitute misbehaviour? Such conduct would not be criminal and would not relate directly to the judge's performance of his/her duties; but it would surely weaken public confidence in judicial impartiality and independence. Perhaps one may say, adapting the words of Lord MacMillan in *Donoghue* v. *Stevenson* [1932] A.C. 562, 619:

> "The categories of misbehaviour are never closed."

There are some "disciplinary" provisions which apply only to judges of the District Court. (It seems strange that they alone should be singled out in this way.) Under section 10(4) of the Courts (Supplemental Provisions) Act 1961 where the Chief Justice forms the opinion that a District Court judge's conduct is "such as to bring the administration of justice into disrepute," he "may interview the [judge] privately and inform him of such opinion." No sanction is provided to compel the judge to mend his/her ways. Section 36(2) of the same Act provides another control mechanism. When it appears to the President of the District Court that the conduct of a colleague is prejudicial to the prompt and efficient discharge of the business of the court, the President may investigate the matter, and may report the result to the Minister for Justice. The President must consult the judge concerned. If an unfavourable report were received, the Minister might well invoke the powers conferred by the Courts of Justice (District Court) Act 1946, s.21. By virtue of this the Minister may request the Chief Justice to appoint a Supreme Court or High Court judge to hold an inquiry—which may be into a District Court judge's mental or physical health, or his/her conduct "either generally or on a particular occasion." The judge appointed may conduct the inquiry as he/she thinks proper, and may conduct it in private or in public. On completion thereof a report is sent to the Minister for Justice who would then presumably have to consider initiating the procedure for the judge's removal by resolutions of the Dáil and Seanad. (This inquiry procedure has been used only once—in 1957; the judge concerned resigned.)

TRIAL OF OFFENCES

Article 38 of the Constitution sets down the basic procedural and jurisdictional rules governing the trial of offences. Article 38.1 declares that "no person shall be tried on any criminal charge save in due course of law." The expression "criminal charge" is not defined—though it occurs again in Article 38.5, which establishes the general principle that no person may be tried on a criminal charge without a jury. This latter principle is, however, subject to the exceptions stated in Article 38 itself. Military tribunals are one such exception (s.4), another is special criminal courts (s.3), while section 2 permits "minor offences" to be tried by "courts of summary jurisdiction."

Article 38 gives rise to a multitude of questions. What is a "criminal

" . . . to suggest to the Government how the policy of the State should be formulated or in what sense it should be directed." Noting that O'Hanlon J. had declined to resign from his office as President of the Law Reform Commission, the Taoiseach stated that the Government had decided " . . . to terminate forthwith your appointment . . . " O'Hanlon J. replied that he would withdraw from the office of President of the Commission, though he felt under no legeal obligation to do so (*The Irish Times*, April 13, 1992).

charge" or "due course of law?" How may one distinguish a "minor offence" (triable summarily) from a non-minor one (triable only with a jury)? What, indeed, does the word "jury" connote? All these matters have troubled the courts,[62] as have questions involving the special criminal courts foreseen and provided for by Article 38.3.

"Criminal charge"

The former Supreme Court, in *Melling* v. *Ó Mathghamhna* [1962] I.R. 1, discussed the *indicia* of a criminal offence. The question there at issue was whether the District Court proceedings envisaged by the Customs Consolidation Act 1876, s.186, involved criminal charges (and, if so, were these "minor offences" under Article 38.2). Kingsmill Moore J. said these proceedings had several features which were regarded as *indicia* of crimes:

(1) they were offences against the community at large and not against an individual

(2) the section was punitive and not merely a matter of fiscal reparation for the penalty was £100 or three times the value of the goods: and failure to pay, even where the offender lacked the means, involved imprisonment

(3) they required *mens rea*, for the act had to be done "knowingly" and "with intent to evade the prohibition or restriction." Though *mens rea* was not an invariable ingredient of an offence, where it was an element this was generally an indication of criminality.

Ó Dálaigh J. said that one of the chief characteristics of civil liability was the obligation to make reparation, and not to have to suffer imprisonment if unable to do so. But it was *not* a feature of civil proceedings that (as under s.186) the plaintiff could have the defendant detained in jail and keep him there unless he could obtain bail. Nor could he obtain a warrant for search, entry and seizure (as under s.205 of the 1876 Act). Nor, in civil proceedings, could the plaintiff put the defendant in jail because he could not pay the damages awarded. The factors mentioned by Ó Dálaigh J. were also stressed by Lavery J. in whose judgment Maguire C.J. and Maguire J. concurred.

A similar question arose in the more recent case of *McLoughlin* v. *Tuite and others* [1989] I.R. 82. Here the plaintiff had failed to deliver income tax returns demanded from him under the Income Tax Act 1967, s.172. The defendant inspector of taxes accordingly instituted civil proceedings against him, under section 500 of the 1967 Act, claiming £5500 in aggregated penalties for this failure. The plaintiff argued that the penalties imposed under section 500 were punitive in nature and thus involved "criminal charges" under Article 38; they were not civil penalties recoverable as a liquidated sum in the civil courts. Dismissing this claim, the Supreme Court stressed that section 500 must be viewed in the overall context of the taxation code. This contained many provisions designed to ensure that each taxpayer paid a fair proportion of the taxes levied, having regard to his/her income or wealth, and also to ensure that such payments were made with a promptitude which

---

[62] "Troubled" seems the *mot juste*. Cp. Kingsmill Moore J. in *Melling* v. *Ó Mathghamhna* [1962] I.R. 1, 21: "Two questions, which at first sight would appear to be simple, thus arise for decision. Are the charges criminal? If so, are they minor? The argument of these deceptive simplicities occupied over three weeks."

would avoid the need for short-term Exchequer borrowing. The means chosen to achieve this end was a series of incentives and deterrents, such as penal rates of interest on delayed payments; and the provision for a penalty for failure to make a return fell into that same category. Against this background Finlay C.J., giving the judgment of the court, analysed section 500 in the light of *Melling's* case. He concluded as follows ([1989] I.R. 82, 90):

> " . . . the only feature which could be said to be common between the provisions of s.500 . . . and the ordinary constituents of a criminal offence is that the payment of a sum of money is provided for which is an involuntary payment and which is not related to any form of compensation or reparation necessary to the state but is rather a deterrent or sanction. The Court is not satisfied that the provision for a penalty in that fashion in a code of taxation law, with the general features which have been shortly outlined in this judgment, clearly establishes the provisions of the section as creating a criminal offence."

"Due course of law"

Article 38.1, as already noted, stipulates that no person shall be tried on any criminal charge "save in due course of law." The meaning of this phrase is more fully considered in Chapter 14 *infra*: but it is appropriate to notice here the High Court decision in *Curtis* v. *Att. Gen.* [1986] I.L.R.M. 428. The plaintiff had been charged with customs offences under the Customs Consolidation Act 1876, s.186, (as amended). The total estimated value of the allegedly smuggled goods was £31,352. If convicted, the plaintiff faced a fine of £94,056—*i.e.* three times the estimated value of the goods, as provided by section 186. Section 34(4)(*d*)(i) and (iv) of the Finance Act 1963 provided that if the estimated value was challenged the District Justice should determine the value before proceeding with the hearing. The value so determined was "final and not appealable"; and at the trial, whether on indictment or summarily, that value was to be take conclusively as being the value of the goods, without any further evidence of that value.

It was claimed that these portions of section 34(4) were repugnant to Article 38, and Carroll J. so held. The authorities established that in a criminal case all relevant issues of fact should be left to a jury to decide. Here the value of the goods fell into this category; a jury would be entitled to take the value into account into account in deciding whether the necessary *mens rea* existed. This statutory exclusion of a material fact from the jury was repugnant to Article 38, ss. 1 and 5. Additionally, to empower a court (the District Court) which did not have jurisdiction to try an offence[63]:

(a) to decide a material issue without appeal
(b) effectively, to decide the punishment if the accused was found guilty

was repugnant to Article 38, sections 1 and 2. And finally the relevant provisions of section 34(4) were invalid because they produced the unjust result that, on appeal, the Court of Criminal Appeal could not consider the finding as to value. It would be unjust if the Court of Criminal Appeal was precluded from reducing a fine because the District Court's finding on value was unap-

---

[63] Many charges brought under s.186 would not be triable in the District Court because the potential fines would take the offences out of the "minor" category. See *infra*.

pealable, where the Court of Criminal Appeal would otherwise have held that valuation excessive.

Minor and non-minor offences

Article 38.2 permits "minor offences" to be tried by "courts of summary jurisdiction." Delivering the Supreme Court's judgment in *Re Haughey* [1971] I.R. 217, 254, Ó Dálaigh C.J. made it clear that the latter phrase referred only to the District Court.

Read together, Article 38, ss. 2 and 5, yield two broad principles:

    (a) minor offences may be tried in the District Court
    (b) "non-minor" offences *must* be tried elsewhere—with a jury.[64]

The importance, for an accused person, of the distinction between these types of offence will be plain.

Since Article 38 offers no tests for distinguishing between minor and "non-minor" offences, it has fallen to the courts to devise them. The authorities establish that the primary test is the severity of punishment authorised by law to be imposed: *Melling* v. *Ó Mathghamna* [1962] I.R. 1: *Conroy* v. *Att. Gen.* [1965] I.R. 411. Secondary considerations are the moral quality of the acts necessary to constitute the offence; the state of the law when the Constitution was enacted, and public opinion at the time of that enactment: *Conroy's* case *supra.* The Supreme Court added the rider that some offences—such as murder, manslaughter or rape, as currently defined by law—were of such grave moral guilt that they could not be minor offences under Article 38 even if the punishment prescribed by law was minimal: *per* Walsh J. [1965] I.R. 411, 436.

Also in *Conroy's* case Walsh J., speaking for the Supreme Court, elaborated on the meaning of "punishment" in this connection ([1965] I.R. 411, 441):

> " . . . the punishment which must be examined for the purpose of gauging the seriousness of an offence is what may be referred to as 'primary punishment.' That is the type of punishment which is regarded as punishment in the ordinary sense and, where crime is concerned, is either the loss of liberty or the intentional penal deprivation of property whether by means of fine or other direct method of deprivation."

The offence in issue in that case was drunken driving, constituted by the Road Traffic Act 1961, s.49. The penalty authorised to be imposed on summary conviction was imprisonment for up to six months plus a fine of £100. However under section 26 of the Act the court was obliged to impose a disqualification from holding a driving licence. The Supreme Court held that such disqualification, though possibly having severe consequences for the individual, could not be taken into account in applying the "severity of punishment" test. It was essentially a finding that the person concerned was unfit to hold a driving licence. Applying this reasoning, Carroll J. held in *State (Pheasantry Ltd.)* v. *Donnelly* [1982] I.L.R.M. 512, that the automatic forfeiture of a liquor licence under the Intoxicating Liquor Act 1927, s.28—fol-

---

[64] Subject, of course, to Art. 38.3's provisions on special criminal courts, as to which see *infra*.

lowing a third summary conviction—was similarly not "primary punishment."

McWilliam J. reached the opposite conclusion in *Kostan* v. *Ireland and Att. Gen.* [1978] I.L.R.M. 12. This concerned an offence, triable only summarily, under the Fisheries (Consolidation) Act 1959, s.221. The penalty specified was a maximum fine of £100 plus the mandatory forfeiture of the catch and the fishing gear—here valued at £102,040. McWilliam J. rejected the defendants' argument that the forfeiture was analogous to the disqualification in *Conroy's* case; this forfeiture was primary punishment, not a more remote consequence of conviction. The judge consequently granted a declaration that section 221 was repugnant to the Constitution. His decision is not cited by Murphy J. in *Cartmill* v. *Ireland* [1987] I.R. 192—with the consequence that the cases are difficult to reconcile. The question in *Cartmill's* case was whether offences under the Gaming and Lotteries Act 1956, s.4(1)(c) were minor or not. Such offences were, again, triable only summarily. Under section 44 of the Act a District Court judge could, on conviction, impose a fine of up to £100 and/or three months' imprisonment; but he/she also had power, under section 47, to order the forfeiture of the machines. The plaintiff claimed that his machines were worth about £120,000 and that the power to deprive him of property of such value took the offence out of the minor category. Murphy J., however, held that the possible forfeiture of the machines did not constitute primary punishment; it was analogous to the driving disqualification in *Conroy's* case. It is true that the forfeiture in *Kostan's* case was mandatory whereas that in *Cartmill's* case was discretionary, but this can scarcely found a distinction between them. It may be, however, that a distinction is to be drawn between forfeiture of property—lawful in itself—used in committing an offence (*Kostan's* case), and forfeiture of property which is inherently designed for the commission of offences (*Cartmill's* case).

In *Cullen* v. *Att. Gen.* [1979] I.R. 394 the plaintiff sought a declaration that the Road Traffic Act 1961, s.57 was invalid. Section 56(1) of that Act made it an offence to use a vehicle in a public place without an approved policy of insurance. On summary conviction the maximum penalty was imprisonment for six months and a fine not exceeding £100. However, under section 57 the District Court could, in certain circumstances, go further. If the court was satisfied that the negligent use of the vehicle had caused injury to someone then present and represented, who would be entitled to recover damages in civil proceedings against the convicted person, it could impose an additional fine equal to the damages recoverable. The actual operative words of the section were:

> "The court may, if it thinks fit and the person present or represented consents, inflict on the convicted person, in addition to any other punishment, a fine not exceeding the damages which, in the opinion of the court, the person present or represented would be entitled to recover against the convicted person."

Section 57(2) directed payment of this additional amount to the injured party. It was argued that section 57 was invalid because it provided for the summary trial of a "non-minor" offence—the District Court could, in addition to the normal fine and/or imprisonment, award unlimited damages. Hamilton J. accepted the contention and granted a declaration that section

57(1) and (2) were invalid. These provisions purported to increase the penalty to such an extent as to take the section 56 offence out of the minor category.

The report informs us that an appeal against this decision was lodged, but subsequently withdrawn. This is regrettable since it is not clear that the judgment can stand with *Conroy's* case. The order to pay damages would not appear to be "an intentional penal deprivation of property"; the object is not to punish the offender but to compensate the victim. The fact that section 57 used the words " . . . in addition to any other punishment . . . " and referred to the damages as "a fine" is not conclusive. Section 27(1)(*a*) of the same Act expressly characterised a disqualification order as a punishment, but in *Conroy's* case the Supreme Court refused to accept it as such. Walsh J. said ([1965] I.R. 411, 439) that the statutory description was not conclusive: the court itself must determine the nature of the relevant order from an examination of its essential qualities.[65]

It would be unfortunate if every provision on the lines of section 57 offended against the Constitution, because it represents a useful device. The underlying idea is that it is sometimes convenient to apply civil and criminal sanctions in the same proceedings (the intervention of a *partie civile* is familiar in French criminal law). In avoiding unnecessary litigation, and consequently saving expense, the idea seems a beneficial one, and it would be regrettable if the Constitution barred the Oireachtas from adopting it.[66]

Despite a considerable volume of case-law, the precise dividing line between "minor" and "non-minor" offences remains unclear. *Conroy's* case [1965] I.R. 411 upheld a statutory provision for a maximum punishment on summary conviction of six months' imprisonment and a fine of £100. By contrast, in *State (Sheerin)* v. *Kennedy* [1966] I.R. 379 it was held that a provision permitting imprisonment for up to three years following summary conviction did not create a minor offence.[67] However, it is still uncertain what maximum period of imprisonment—over six months and less than three years—will keep an offence within the minor category. Also unclear is the precise combination of imprisonment and monetary penalty that will tilt the balance.

[65] See further J. P. Casey (1976) XI *Irish Jurist* (N.S.) 326.
[66] The Law Reform Commission has expressed its agreement with this view: see its *Report on Malicious Damage* (LRC 26–1988), p. 37.
[67] In *J.* v. *District Justice Delap* [1989] I.R. 167 the applicant had been charged in the District Court with an offence of malicious damage. The respondent concluded that the offence was minor in nature and fit to be tried summarily on a guilty plea. Upon convicting the applicant, he directed that he be detained in Trinity House School, Lusk, Co. Dublin until he attained the age of 19. This amounted to a period of detention of about three years and four months, and it was authorised by ss.57(1) and 65 of the Children Act 1908, as amended. The applicant argued that an offence attracting such a period of detention could not qualify as minor.

Barr. J. rejected this contention, pointing out that in *Sheerin's* case the Supreme Court had distinguished between detention in prisons and kindred institutions and detention in training and instructional institutions. The school in question here was managed by the Department of Education, was staffed by teachers and had no connection with the Department of Justice or the prison service. It was not intended to be a place of punishment but of education and training, and the obligation to remain there should not be regarded as a period of imprisonment in the penal sense of that term. Though such detention had in it an element of punishment, its primary purpose was educational. Barr J. contrasted this period of detention with a sentence of imprisonment. The former related to the school's function as a place of instruction and correction; the latter to the gravity of the offence and the character of the convicted person.

Recent cases give some limited guidance as to the maximum fine that will keep an offence in the minor category (where statute provides *only* for a monetary penalty on summary conviction). As already noted, McWilliam J. in *Kostan* v. *Ireland, supra,* ruled that an offence carrying a financial penalty of over £102,000 could not be tried summarily. In *O'Sullivan* v. *Hartnett and Att. Gen.* [1983] I.L.R.M. 79 the plaintiff faced charges in the District Court under the Fisheries (Consolidation) Act 1959, s.182(2)(*a*)—which forbids (*inter alia*) the unlawful capture of salmon. Section 182 contemplates summary trial only; and, the penalty specified is a fine not exceeding £25, with an additional £2 for each unlawfully captured fish. Section 182(5) further provides for the mandatory forfeiture of the fish. The plaintiff stood charged in respect of 900 salmon, and thus faced a possible financial penalty of nearly £10,000 (including the value of the fish). The Supreme Court held that this could not constitute a minor offence and that the District Court summonses must be struck out in that court for want of jurisdiction.

In reaching this conclusion the Supreme Court upheld the High Court decision of McWilliam J. but varied the High Court order because this did not properly reflect what McWilliam J. had decided. The order indicated that the judge had declared offences under section 182(2)(*a*) not to be minor offences, *i.e.* that the subsection was invalid. The Supreme Court took the view that McWilliam J. had held only that the particular offence charged against the plaintiff was not a minor offence.[68]

The Supreme Court's decision in *O'Sullivan's* case presumably means that an offence carrying a possible financial penalty of nearly £10,000 cannot rank as minor. What lesser figure represents the borderline is as yet undecided. In that same case in the High Court McWilliam J. was of opinion that a possible fine of £1825 was above the limit. The judge discussed that figure (made up of £25 + £2 × 900) because, in his view, the value of the forfeited fish was not to be taken into account. A person who was unlawfully in possession of property could not be said to be penalised if it was taken from him in the course of enforcing the law. One assumes that this matter was not argued before the Supreme Court, for it is not mentioned in the judgment. This also refers to the plaintiff facing forfeiture of the salmon (worth several thousand pounds) *and* a fine of up to £10,000. The mysterious mathematics of this explains why the opening sentence of this paragraph is so tentative.

In *State (Rollinson)* v. *Kelly* [1984] I.R. 248, Griffin J. suggested (at 263) that a fine "fairly considerably in excess" of £500 would not take an offence out of the minor category. The other members of the Supreme Court did not comment on this *dictum*; but Henchy and Hederman JJ.—like Griffin J.— referred to the issue of inflation. In *Melling* v. *Ó Mathghamna* [1962] I.R. 1, it was observed, a fine of £100 was held not to take an offence out of the minor category, and £100 then was equivalent to £900 in 1984. The *ratio* in *Rollin-*

---

[68] Since the relevant section provided only for summary trial, the fact that this offence was not minor meant that no machinery existed for trying the plaintiff in respect thereof. It is possible, however, that retrospective legislation could validly be enacted to cope with such cases—by providing that "non-minor" s.182 offences could be tried on indictment. Such legislation, being purely procedural, would not amount to declaring criminal acts which were not so at the time of their commission: thus it would not violate Art. 15.5. Nor would it, in cases like *O'Sullivan's,* run counter to the rule against double jeopardy—assuming that that rule has constitutional status. For it has application only where an individual has already been in danger of conviction by a court of competent jurisdiction: see the discussion in *People (D.P.P.)* v. *O'Shea* [1982] I.R. 384.

son's case is that an offence carrying in 1984 a possible fine of £500 was still a minor offence. But it seems safe to conclude that a maximum penalty of £1000 would not violate the limit.

Rollinson's case, as noted, settles an important point—for "severity of punishment" test purposes, the relevant date is the date when the fine is imposed, not the date when the statute was passed. Thus, if in 1992 a person is convicted and given the maximum fine under a 1926 Act creating an offence and attaching a penalty on summary conviction of up to £500, that fine is to be considered by reference to the value of £500 in 1992, not 1926 (when, of course, it would have been much greater.) On another point there was no definite ruling. What is the position where an individual faces, or has been convicted upon, multiple charges—each involving a minor offence—so that the total financial penalty runs to thousands of pounds? Henchy J. expressed no view on this because no argument had been addressed to the court on this point; [1984] I.R. 248, 261. But Hederman J.; thought it made no difference (at 267):

> "In the present case there were several convictions each of which being, in my opinion, a conviction of a minor offence. The fact that when all these offences are added together the total amount of the penalties is a considerable amount of money which, if it were the penalty imposed for one of those convictions, would be sufficient to carry it out of the minor category does not in my view change the essential character of each of the offences whose combined penalties reach such a sum. Each offence must be regarded as a separate offence. They might well have been tried on different days or even different months. The fact that they were all tried on the same day does not alter their essential character."

A similar conclusion had been reached by Murphy J. in the earlier High Court case of *Charlton* v. *Ireland* [1984] I.L.R.M. 39; and Hederman J's. reasoning was applied by Carroll J. in *State (Wilson)* v. *District Justice Neylon* [1987] I.L.R.M. 118.

Finally, *Rollinson's* case showed a difference of opinion as to the proper test in such cases. O'Higgins C.J. and Hederman J., following earlier Supreme Court decisions such as *In re Haughey* [1971] I.R. 217, affirmed the traditional view—the test is the maximum penalty the offence might attract to the accused in the court of trial. Henchy and Griffin JJ. indicated a wish to reconsider this matter, suggesting that the determining factor should be the penalty *actually* imposed. The fifth member of the court, McCarthy J. did not refer to this matter.

Summary disposal of indictable offences

The distinction between minor offences (triable summarily) and "non-minor" offences (triable only with a jury) is crucially important in operating the statutory provisions which allow indictable offences to be dealt with summarily. If there is to be a trial, the relevant provisions are the Criminal Justice Act 1951, s.2 as amended by the Criminal Procedure Act 1967, s.19. The conditions for their applicability are:

(a) The offence charged must be one which comes within Schedule 1 of the 1951 Act, as amended by the 1967 Act. This lists a range of offences, including perjury, assault, indecent assault, offences under the Larceny Act 1916 and obtaining by false pretences.[69]

(b) The District Court judge must be of opinion that the facts proved or alleged constitute a minor offence fit to be tried summarily.

(c) The accused must be told he/she has the right to be tried with a jury; and having been told, must indicate that he/she does not object to a summary trial.

The Criminal Justice Act 1951, s.4 (as amended) limits the sentencing power of the District Court in regard to the scheduled offences; the maximum penalty that may be imposed is 12 months in prison and a fine of £1000.[70] In considering (b) above the District Court judge must necessarily bear in mind the decisions previously mentioned, and his/her restricted sentencing powers (see *State (O'Hagan)* v. *Delap* [1983] I.L.R.M. 241). If the judge concludes that the case should not be tried summarily there is power to send the accused forward for trial on indictment: Criminal Justice Act 1951, s.2(3). Should the District Court judge form the *initial* view that the facts alleged constitute a minor offence, but later conclude that the facts *proved* contradict this opinion, the summary trial must be discontinued and the procedure for the preliminary examination of an indictable offence initiated: *Feeney* v. *District Justice Clifford* [1989] I.R. 668.

The Criminal Procedure Act 1967, s.13, allows the District Court to dispose of a much wider range of indictable offences where the accused pleads guilty. Here the sentencing power is again confined to 12 months' imprisonment and a fine of £1000.[71] The consent of the D.P.P. is a prerequisite.[72] The discretion conferred on the District Court judge would seem to involve consideration of the gravity of the offences alleged, and the adequacy of the sentencing powers to reflect this. The District Court judge, it may be noted, is authorised to send the accused foward for sentence to a higher court.[73]

In *Feeney* v. *District Justice Clifford* [1989] I.R. 668 the applicant had appeared in the Cork District Court charged with four offences, all scheduled under the Criminal Justice Act 1951. On the facts being outlined the respondent concluded that the offences were minor and fit to be tried summarily. The applicant did not object, and went on to plead guilty. The court was then informed that the applicant was currently serving a sentence which made it impossible to impose the custodial sentence of two years the judge had intended. He consequently concluded that the offences were *not* fit to be tried summarily and initiated the procedure for sending the applicant forward for trial to the Circuit Court. The applicant moved to quash this decision and the Supreme Court granted him the order sought. McCarthy J. (Finlay C.J. and Hederman J. concurring) sympathised with the judge's dilemma. He was well entitled to conclude that the maximum penalty he could lawfully impose fell short of what was appropriate in the circumstances. But what had been done was not possible. McCarthy J. summed up thus ([1989] I.R. 668, 678):

---

[69] In regard to some of these scheduled offences, the D.P.P.'s consent to a summary trial is essential: 1967 Act, s.19(1).

[70] The figure of £1000 is substituted for £100 by the Criminal Justice Act 1984, s.17.

[71] Criminal Procedure Act 1967, s.13(3)(*a*), as amended by the Criminal Justice Act 1984, s.17.

[72] Criminal Procedure Act 1967, s.13(2)(*a*).

[73] *Ibid.*, s.13(2)(*b*).

"If on the facts alleged, a district justice concludes that an offence is a minor offence fit to be tried summarily and the person accused pleads guilty, whether or not the district justice expressly records a conviction, orally or in writing, once he embarks upon an inquiry as to the penalty appropriate to the offence, in my judgment he is precluded from changing his mind. There is, in law, no such thing as a provisional conviction."[74]

THE JURY IN CRIMINAL CASES

There is no constitutional right to *civil* jury trial. This nowadays exists only in the High Court, having been abolished in the Circuit Court by the Courts Act 1971, s.6. The continuance, or otherwise, of such mode of trial rests in the hands of the legislature.[75]

By virtue of Article 38.5, it is otherwise in criminal matters. Save for the cases specified in that Article "no person shall be tried on any criminal charge without a jury." This formula has been treated by the courts as guaranteeing a right to jury trial for "non-minor" offences: *Re Haughey* [1971] I.R. 217, 248. But Ó Dálaigh C.J., speaking for the Supreme Court, also said in that case (at 252):

"Trial by jury of non-minor offences is mandatory, it is not simply a right to be adopted or waived at the option of the accused."

Article 38.5 gives no indication what precisely is meant by the word "jury." However, some judicial guidance appears from *de Burca & Anderson* v. *Att. Gen.* [1976] I.R. 38. Henchy J. (at 74) focussed on purpose:

"There is no doubt that the primary aim of s.5 of Article 38 in mandating trial by jury for criminal offences other than minor ones . . . is to ensure that every person charged with such an offence will be assured of a trial in due course of law by a group of laymen who, chosen at random from a reasonably diverse panel of jurors from the community, will produce a verdict of guilty or not guilty free from the risks inherent in a trial conducted by a judge or judges only, and which will therefore carry with it the assurance of both correctness and public acceptability that may be expected from the group verdict of such a representative cross-section of the community."

Griffin J. took a similar view (at 82).

In the *de Burca & Anderson* case the Supreme Court held the Juries Act 1927 unconstitutional in so far as it: (i) required a property qualification; (ii) operated effectively to exclude women from jury service. The Oireachtas quickly passed the Juries Act 1976, which cured these defects and extended liability for jury service to virtually all citizens between 18 and 70 (s.6). This Act provides for the drawing of jury panels from the electoral register by "random or other non-discriminatory selection" (s.11). It also requires the selection of the jury from this panel by balloting in open court (s.15). This process *could* conceivably produce a jury which was not a reasonable cross-section of the

---

[74] The Supreme Court suggested that the law should be changed to give the prosecution an absolute right—identical to that of the accused—to object to a summary trial.

[75] The Courts Act 1988 abolished jury trial in High Court actions for personal injuries or fatal accidents.

community, but this could not be a ground for constitutional complaint: see
de Burca & Anderson v. *Att. Gen.* [1976] I.R. 38, *per* O'Higgins C.J. (at 61) and
Griffin J. (at 84).[76]

When the Constitution was enacted trial with a jury involved (*inter alia*):
(a) a jury of 12; (b) a unanimous verdict. The size is still fixed at 12 but the
Criminal Justice Act 1984, s.25 now provides for majority verdicts: subsection (1) runs:

> "The verdict of a jury in criminal proceedings need not be unanimous in
> a case where there are not fewer than 11 jurors if 10 of them agree on the
> verdict."

In *O'Callaghan* v. *Att. Gen. & D.P.P.* (High Court, Blayney, J., May 22, 1992)
the plaintiff, who had been convicted on larceny and robbery charges by a
majority jury verdict in the Circuit Court, impugned the constitutionality of
this provision. His principal argument was that "jury" in Article 38.5 must
be regarded as involving the essential features of jury trial as understood in
1937. Unanimity was one such essential feature, and hence constitutionally
protected. Blayney J., in rejecting this contention, founded upon *dicta* in the
de Burca & Anderson case, among them Walsh J.'s observation that Article
38.5 did not imply unanimous verdicts ([1976] I.R. 38, 67) and the statements by Henchy and Griffin JJ. on the aim behind jury trial ([1976] I.R. 38,
74, 82). He noted also that the United States Supreme Court had ruled that
unanimity was not a constitutionally required feature of criminal juries:
Apodaca v. *Oregon* (1972) 406 U.S. 404: *Duncan* v. *Louisiana* (1968) 391 U.S.
145: *Williams* v. *Florida* (1970) 399 U.S. 78.[77] Blayney J. expressed his conclusion as follows (pp. 9–10 of his judgment):

> " . . . the essence of trial by jury is that the decision as to the guilt or
> innocence of the accused is made by a group of his fellow citizens and
> not by a Judge or a number of Judges. If that is so, is a trial any less a
> trial by jury because the decision of the accused's fellow citizens, instead
> of being unanimous, is taken by a substantial majority? In my opinion it
> is not. The guilt or innocence of the accused is still being decided by the
> jury."

History lends some support to the argument that Article 38.5 does not
require unanimity. Article 72 of the 1922 Constitution used words identical
to those in Article 38.5—"no person shall be tried on a criminal charge without a jury." Yet this did not inhibit the Oireachtas from providing for majority verdicts in the Juries (Protection) Act 1929, s.5(1). This suggests that the
term "jury" *simpliciter* would not automatically have implied unanimity to
the People when in 1937 they enacted the Constitution.

In the *de Burca & Anderson* case Walsh J. further indicated that Article 38.5

[76] In its Consultation Paper on Rape (October 1987) the Law Reform Commission considered—but rejected—a suggestion in favour of compulsory equal representation of men and
women on juries in all rape and sexual assault cases (see pp. 78–81 of the paper). Though the
Commission did not refer to the matter, it must be doubtful whether any such arrangement
would be compatible with the Constitution.

[77] The U.S. decisions, however, present a slight difficulty, for the state statutes there in issue
were—and could only be—tested against the due process guarantee of the 14th Amendment.
The word "jury" does not appear in that provision; but it *does* appear in the 6th Amendment
(which binds only the Federal authorities), and a majority of the Supreme Court in *Apodaca* v.
Oregon (1972) 406 U.S. 404 held that the 6th Amendment's guarantee *did* require unanimity.

did not require a jury of 12 persons ([1976] I.R. 38, 67). This view is supported by a decision of the United States Supreme Court—*Williams* v. *Florida* (1970) 399 U.S. 78. White J., giving the opinion of the court, said that the performance of the jury's essential role was not a function of the number making it up. The number of 12—sanctified by the common law—was a historical accident wholly without significance. In subsequent cases the United States Supreme Court declined to accept a five person jury—*Ballew* v. *Georgia* (1978) 435 U.S. 223, and held that trial by a non-unanimous jury of six violated the relevant constitutional guarantees—*Burch* v. *Louisiana* (1974) 441 U.S. 130.

The Juries Act 1976, s.5, constitutes each administrative county a jury district and provides that every issue triable with a jury must be tried with a jury from the jury district in which the court is sitting. The designation of counties for this purpose doubtless proceeds in part from convenience; but Article 38 has been construed as requiring some such limitation on jury districts. In *State (Byrne)* v. *Frawley* [1978] I.R. 326, Henchy J. (Griffin and Kenny JJ. concurring) said (at 347):

> "For the formation of a constitutional jury, there must be a valid nexus between juror and jury district. This is needed to ensure that the jury's verdict will have the quality of a community decision; for a jury so constituted will reach its verdict in the knowledge that, in a real and special sense, its members will have to live with that verdict."

SPECIAL CRIMINAL COURTS

Article 38.3.1° permits the Oireachtas to legislate for the establishment of special criminal courts to try offences "in cases where it may be determined in accordance with such law that the ordinary courts are inadequate to secure the effective administration of justice, and the preservation of public peace and order." By virtue of Article 38.3.2° it is for statute to prescribe the constitution, powers, jurisdiction and procedure of such special courts. Furthermore, the provisions of Articles 34 and 35 do not apply to them: Article 38.6. Thus the members of such courts are not constitutionally required to make the declaration in Article 34.5.1°: they need not be appointed by the President under Article 35.1: nor do they necessarily have the guarantees of independence and security of tenure contained in Article 35.2 and 4.

The main legislation governing such special courts is Part V of the Offences against the State Act 1939. And it will be seen that in enacting this, the Oireachtas has taken full advantage of the elbow-room offered by the Constitution. Part V comes into force whenever the Government make a proclamation to that effect; and this the Government may do if satisfied "that the ordinary courts are inadequate to secure the effective administration of justice and the preservation of public peace and order": section 35(2). Such a proclamation may be annulled by a resolution of the Dáil (s.35(5)) but it does not require any form of approval by the Dáil. In *Re Mac Curtain* [1941] I.R. 83 it was contended that section 35(2) was unconstitutional, because the Oireachtas ought to decide the issue itself. Instead it had invalidly conferred a legislative power on the Government. The former Supreme Court rejected this argument as incompatible with the clear terms of Article 38.3.1°. This, said, Sullivan C.J., expressly provided that the inadequacy of the ordinary

courts was to be determined in the manner provided by the Act establishing
special courts. It was left to the legislature to choose the particular method
by which the question should be determined, and any provision so made was
in accordance with the Constitution.[78]

The composition of such courts is regulated by section 39. Each must consist of an uneven number of members, not being less than three—section
39(1). All members are appointed—and removable at will—by the Government: section 39(2). And while judges—including retired judges—may be
(and since 1972 exclusively have been) appointed as members, so may barristers and solicitors of not less than seven years standing—or Defence Forces
officers not below the rank of commandant (s.39(3)). In the years 1939–46
and 1961–62 the special courts which then sat were composed solely of
Defence Forces officers. In *Re Mac Curtain* [1941] I.R. 83 it was argued that a
court so composed was really a military tribunal under Article 38.4, not a
special court under Article 38.3. Giving the judgment of the former Supreme
Court, Sullivan C.J. said (at 90):

> "Reliance was placed on the facts that the Court was composed of mili-
> tary officers and sat in a Military Barracks, and that the accused was in
> military custody. [Article 38.3.2°] empowers the legislature to prescribe
> the constitution, powers, jurisdiction and procedure of the Special
> Courts. The legislature has prescribed the constitution of Special Courts
> in s.39 of the Act. Subs. 3 of that section provides that no person shall be
> appointed to be a member of a Special Criminal Court unless he is a
> Judge of the High Court or the Circuit Court, or a Justice of the District
> Court, or a barrister . . . or a solicitor of not less than seven years stand-
> ing, or an officer of the Defence Forces not below the rank of comman-
> dant. It has not been suggested that any member of the Court by which
> the appellant was tried was not duly qualified under that section. The
> Special Criminal Court in this case, although it was constituted entirely
> of officers of the Defence Forces, was, in our opinion, a tribunal quite
> distinct from the Military Tribunal contemplated by [Art. 38.4]."

The principal question in *McGlinchey* v. *Govr., Portlaoise Prison* [1988] I.R.
671 was—could persons who, on appointment to the Special Criminal Court,
were serving judges but had since retired, lawfully continue to sit on that
court? The Supreme Court, affirming the decision of the High Court,
answered that they could. Finlay C.J. said ([1988] I.R. 671, 703–04):

> "The evidence before the High Court, which is quite clearly correct, is
> that at the time of the appointment of two of the members of the Special
> Criminal Court concerned, they were, respectively, judges of the High
> Court and the Circuit Court. At the time of the appointment of the third
> member . . . he was a solicitor of not less than seven years standing. At
> the time of the trial, each of the persons concerned was qualified within
> s.39, subs. 3, that is to say that two members who had formerly been
> judges of the High Court and Circuit Court remained, as they had been,

[78] In *McGlinchey* v. *Govr., Portlaoise Prison* [1988] I.R. 671 it was claimed that there was a fatal
lacuna in the 1939 Act. Though Part V conferred several powers on the Government, including power to establish *additional* courts, it was submitted that by an oversight no power to
establish the *initial* court had been bestowed. A divisional court of the High Court (Gannon,
Carroll and Lynch JJ.) held that such a power arose by necessary implication, and this was
affirmed by the Supreme Court on appeal.

barristers of not less than seven years standing, and the solicitor was still a solicitor of not less than seven years standing. I . . . am quite satisfied that there is no substance in this point . . . "

In *Eccles & others* v. *Ireland* [1985] I.R. 545 the validity of section 39(2) and (4) of the 1939 Act was impugned. (S. 39(2) provides that special criminal court members are removable at will by the Government, while section 39(4) allows the Minister for Finance to fix the remuneration and allowances of members.) The plaintiffs had all been convicted of capital murder, and sentenced to death,[79] by a special criminal court consisting of Hamilton J., Judge Desmond and Mr. Cathal OFlóinn, former President of the District Court. Though the independence and integrity of the court which tried the plaintiffs was not questioned, it was argued that under section 39(2) and (4) special criminal courts did not enjoy real judicial independence, and that consequently the plaintiffs had not been tried in due course of law as guaranteed by Article 38.1.

Delivering the judgment of the Supreme Court, Finaly C.J. said the contention was that section 39(2) gave the Government an unfettered power to remove members of a special criminal court if their decisions did not favour the executive's interests; and that section 39(4) gave a similar unfettered power to influence decisions to the Minister for Finance. These submissions, however, were incorrect in law. The powers granted must be exercised in accordance with the principles stated in *East Donegal Co-op. Ltd.* v. *Att. Gen.* [1970] I.R. 317. The judgment continues ([1985] I.R. 545, 549):

> "If either [the Government or the Minister] were to seek to exercise its power in a manner capable of interfering with the judicial independence of the Court in the trial of persons charged before it it would be attempting to frustrate the constitutional right of persons accused before that Court to a trial in due course of law. Any such attempt would be prevented and corrected by the courts established under the Constitution. Whilst, therefore, the Special Criminal Court does not attract the express guarantees of judicial independence contained in Article 35 of the Constitution, it does have, derived from the Constitution, a guarantee of judicial independence in the exercise of its functions."[80]

The Offences against the State Act 1939, s.43, invests a special criminal court with jurisdiction to try and to acquit or convict "any person lawfully brought before that Court for trial under this Act." It also confers ancillary jurisdictions, such as the power to sentence convicted persons "to suffer the punishment provided by law in respect of such offence": section 43(1)(a). The ancillary jurisdictions also include power to admit to bail, to administer oaths, and to punish persons for contempt of the court, whether committed in its presence or not. However, it may be noted that for the contempt offence of "scandalising" a special criminal court, the normal practice has been to invoke the jurisdiction of the High Court: *Att. Gen.* v. *Connolly* [1947] I.R. 213: *In re Hibernia National Review Ltd.* [1976] I.R. 389: *State (D.P.P.)* v. *Walsh* [1981] I.R. 412.

---

[79] The death sentences were subsequently commuted, in accordance with the normal practice: see Chap. 3 *supra*.

[80] Several months after this case the Government had to fill vacancies in the special criminal court membership. It is interesting to note that all the new appointees were *serving* judges (see *The Irish Times*, Spetember 6, 1986).

The jurisdiction of special criminal courts extends both to "scheduled" and non-scheduled offences. Section 36 of the 1939 Act sets up machinery whereby the Government may, by order, schedule "offences of any particular class or kind under any particular enactment." Offences (whether summary or indictable) so scheduled are triable in a special criminal court, and must, if the D.P.P. so requests, be directed there by a District Court judge. But non-scheduled offences may also be sent to a special court, under machinery in section 46, when the D.P.P. certifies his opinion that the ordinary courts are inadequate to secure the effective administration of justice and the preservation of public peace and order in relation to the trial of the accused on the relevant charge. In *Mac Curtain's* case [1941] I.R. 83 the former Supreme Court rejected the argument that this provision (s.46(2)) was an unconstitutional conferment of judicial power on a member of the Executive, and this was confirmed in *Re Article 26 and the Criminal Law (Jurisdiction) Bill, 1975* [1977] I.R. 129, 151.

Section 47 of the Act enables an accused to be brought *directly* before a special court to be charged—whether with a scheduled or non-scheduled offence. And section 48 provides a means whereby a trial scheduled for the Circuit Court or Central Criminal Court may be transferred to a special criminal court. The D.P.P. gives a certificate in the form mentioned *supra* and makes an application to the High Court grounded upon that certificate. Thereupon, under section 48(*a*), "The High Court shall make the order applied for . . . " In *O'Reilly & Judge* v. *D.P.P. and Att. Gen.* [1984] I.L.R.M. 224, the constitutionality of this provision was unsuccessfully challenged on separation of powers grounds.[81]

By virtue of section 44, every special criminal court conviction or sentence is appealable to the Court of Criminal Appeal. The convicted person must obtain a certificate from the special court that the case is a fit one for appeal—or leave to appeal from the Court of Criminal Appeal itself. (The same conditions apply to appeals from the regular courts.) There is no provision for an appeal against an acquittal.[82]

MILITARY TRIBUNALS

Article 38.4.1° permits the establishment of military tribunals to try offences against military law by persons subject thereto. The Defence Act 1954 makes provision accordingly, defining those subject to military law (ss.118–119), offences against military law (ss.124–169) and dealing with the composition and functioning of courts-martial (ss.185–226). Under the Courts-Martial Appeals Act 1983, a person convicted by a court-martial may appeal to the Courts-Martial Appeal Court. This body, as is apparent from section 9, is essentially the Court of Criminal Appeal under another name. It has similar powers, including the power to order a retrial (s.18). An appeal lies to the Supreme Court only if the Courts-Martial Appeal Court—or the Attorney General—certifies that the decision involves a point of law of exceptional public importance and that an appeal is desirable in the public interest.

Article 38.4.1° also appears to envisage the establishment of military tribunals—without statutory basis—"to deal with a state of war or armed rebellion." This is considered in Chapter 7 *supra*.

[81] See Chap. 9 *supra*.
[82] For a detailed study of the functioning of special criminal courts, see Mary Robinson, *The Special Criminal Court* (Dublin 1974).

11   Constitutional Issues in the Courts

The Constitution posits two separate and distinct methods by which the validity of legislative measures may be tested in the courts. The first arises under Article 26, with its provision for the Presidential reference of a Bill to the Supreme Court. As noted in Chapter 3 *supra*, this has been used eight times so far. The second—infinitely more common—method is by ordinary legal proceedings in which the validity of an Act is put in issue.

Article 26

The Article 26 procedure had no counterpart under the 1922 Constitution, and nothing comparable exists in the United States. Constitutions of more recent vintage, however, have broadly analogous mechanisms—*e.g.* section 76 of the German Federal Constitutional Court Act and Article 61 of the French Constitution of 1958.[1] And Canada has long had a comparable procedure at both federal and provincial level, under which a great number of constitutional issues have been determined.[2]

The relatively infrequent use of Article 26 may be due to the disadvantages associated with it. First among these is the necessarily abstract character of the proceedings. The Supreme Court, of course, hears arguments pro and contra the Bill's validity, put by the Attorney General (or counsel on his behalf) and by counsel assigned by the court: see Art. 26.2.1°. But the court has before it no concrete dispute between parties, and can obviously have no evidence as to how the Bill will operate in practice. While in some situations this may pose no problems, in others it may considerably hamper the court. In *Re Article 26 and the Housing (Private Rented Dwellings) Bill 1981* [1983] I.R. 181, the Supreme Court itself voiced doubts about the appropriateness of the Article 26 machinery for certain types of Bill. The measure there under review had been passed by the Oireachtas to replace the Rent Restrictions Acts, which the Supreme Court had ruled invalid in *Blake* v. *Att. Gen.* [1982] I.R. 177. This Bill too was struck down—the first time this had happened to

---

[1] Note also Art. 161.1(*a*) of the Spanish Constitution of 1978 and the *Ley Orgánica del Tribunal Constitucional* (L.O.T.C.) (Arts. 31–34), which allow 50 deputies or 50 senators to challenge the validity of a law immediately upon its publication. Up to 1984 those persons could mount a similar constitutional attack upon a Bill, but the L.O.T.C.'s provisions permitting this have been repealed.

[2] See Joseph Jaconelli, "Reference of Bills to the Supreme Court—A Comparative Perspective" (1983) XVIII *Irish Jurist* (N.S.) 322.

a measure designed to replace a judicially condemned statute. The Supreme
Court's judgment was curious in its form, almost one-third of its length being
devoted to a general consideration of the Article 26 procedure; and it seems
to contain an implicit request to the President that no similar Bills should be
sent to the court in future. Delivering the court's judgment O'Higgins C.J.
said ([1983] I.R. 181, 186–187):

> "Article 26, s.2, subs. 1 says that the Court's decision is to be reached
> after hearing arguments by, or on behalf of, the Attorney General and
> by Counsel assigned by the Court. That article makes no reference to
> the hearing of evidence. In fact, in none of the references that have come
> to the Court so far has evidence been heard. The difficulties that could
> confront a court of at least five judges in reaching a unitary decision on
> the basis of conflicting evidence is too obvious to need elaboration. It is
> not necessary in this case to decide whether evidence may, or should be,
> heard when considering a reference under Article 26. In this, as in all
> earlier references, the matters argued have had, in the absence of evi-
> dence, to be dealt with as abstract problems, to the extent that, unlike
> practically all other cases that come before the Court, there is an
> absence or shortage of concrete facts proven, admitted, or projected as a
> matter of probability. The Court, therefore, in a case such as this, has to
> act on abstract materials in order to cope with the social, economic, fis-
> cal and other features that may be crucial to an understanding of the
> working and the consequences of a referred bill. Whether the constitu-
> tionality of a legislative measure of that nature . . . is better determined
> within a fixed and immutable period of time by means of a reference
> under Article 26 (in which case, if no repugnancy is found, the decision
> may never be questioned again in any court), rather than by means of
> an action in which specific imputations of unconstitutionality would fall
> to be determined primarily on proven or admitted facts, is a question on
> which we refrain from expressing an opinion.
> *Ryan* v. *Attorney General* ([1965] I.R. 294) is a good illustration of the pro-
> cedural difficulties and differences already mentioned. In this case the
> plaintiff questioned the validity of an Act of the Oireachtas. The result
> depended on findings of fact based on lengthy oral evidence which was
> largely scientific in nature and complex in character. This Court upheld
> the High Court decision (that the Act was not invalid) on the basis of
> that court's findings of fact; but the Court made it clear that, if in the
> future the scientific evidence available should be such as to warrant a
> different conclusion on the facts, the question of the validity of the Act
> could be reopened. If the bill for that Act had been referred to the Court
> under Article 26 of the Constitution, the case for invalidity would have
> been broadly the same, yet it is doubtful in the extreme if it would have
> been possible for the Court, not later than 60 days after such reference,
> to have heard and determined all the matters which necessarily fell to be
> determined in that case. Furthermore, the Court's decision on such a
> reference would have been subject to the provisions of Article 34, s.3,
> subs. 3 of the Constitution."

In the above case, it will be noted, the Supreme Court left open the question
whether evidence could be "heard" in an Article 26 case. For the reasons
given by the court, evidence in the form of conflicting oral testimony would

present practical problems. But if evidence is admissible in such cases, it could possibly be presented in documentary form such as the well-known "Brandeis brief" in the United States.[3] Canadian courts dealing with abstract constitutional references have held such material admissible and found it useful; witness the Supreme Court's decision in *Reference re Anti-inflation Act* (1976) 68 D.L.R. (3d) 452. The tight time-limits of Article 26 might, however, pose difficulties in the compilation of such material.

Another disadvantage is that should the Supreme Court decide that even a minor provision of a Bill is invalid, the entire measure falls and the President must refuse to sign it. Such is the effect of Article 26.3.1°. The Supreme Court stressed this point in the *Housing (Private Rented Dwellings) Bill* case ([1983] I.R. 181, 186);

> " . . . the Court's function under Article 26 is to ascertain and declare repugnancy (if such there be) to the Constitution in a referred bill or in the specified provision or provisions thereof. It is not the function of the Court to impress any part of a referred bill with a stamp of constitutionality. If the Court finds that any provision of a referred bill or of the referred provisions is repugnant, then the whole bill fails . . . thus there may be areas of a referred bill or of referred provisions of a bill which may be left untouched by the Court's decision. The authors of a bill may therefore find the Court's decision less illuminating than they would wish it to be."

This point, however, should not be overstressed. The difficulty envisaged has not yet arisen, and the judgments delivered in Article 26 cases have focussed on the key provisions of the relevant bills.

Perhaps the major disadvantage lies in Article 34.3.3°, which has the effect that a Bill upheld under Article 26 is thereafter totally immune from challenge in any legal proceedings. This provision formed no part of the original Constitution; it was inserted by ordinary legislation during the three year period when amendment without a referendum was permissible. Article 34.3.3° compounds the difficulty created by the abstract nature of the proceedings. The court can only guess how the Bill may work in practice. If, later on, unanticipated situations arise which show the measure in a different light and give grounds for doubting its validity, nothing can then be done.

Article 34.3.3° was discussed by the Committee on the Constitution, but that body was unable to reach an agreed conclusion on the matter: *Report*, paras. 98–99. One view was that the provision should be deleted, so that the constitutionality of any enactment could be challenged at any time. This was especially appropriate given the Supreme Court's abandonment of the strict doctrine of precedent. If that court could at any time reconsider previous decisions in ordinary constitutional cases, it was argued, it should have a similar freedom under Article 26. Here it may be noted that since 1967 the Supreme Court has on a number of occasions overruled its previous decisions, most notably perhaps in *Costello* v. *Att. Gen. and D.P.P.* (see Chap. 9, *supra*). This may seem to lend extra weight to the argument mentioned above; but in fact the argument seems to be based on a misconception.

---

[3] As to which see Paul Brest, *Processes of Constitutional Decisionmaking* (Boston 1975) Chap. 8.

Article 34.3.3° does not give the Supreme Court's decision an absolutely binding status; its effect is purely to immunise the law upheld in the relevant case. If, in ordinary constitutional proceedings, the Supreme Court wishes to reconsider its reasoning in a previous Article 26 case it would seem perfectly free to do so; and in *State (Lynch)* v. *Cooney* [1982] I.R. 337, the court repudiated part of the reasoning in the *Offences against the State (Amendment) Bill* case [1940] I.R. 470. Of course, if the Supreme Court should entirely disavow its reasoning in an Article 26 case, the position of the relevant Act—assuming it was still in force—would then be quite anomalous. Upheld on the basis of reasoning now found unacceptable, it would nonetheless be impervious to forensic challenge under Article 34.3.3°. Were such a situation to arise the pressure for the repeal of the Act would obviously be considerable.

The opposing argument was that the total deletion of Article 34.3.3° would defeat the whole object of the Article 26 procedure. This was to get an early and definite ruling on a measure whose validity was in doubt, an exercise which would be pointless if the question could be reopened shortly thereafter. A compromise was therefore suggested—to amend Article 34.3.3° so that the validity of the relevant measure could be challenged after the lapse of seven years. Paragraph 99 continues:

> "This would provide some answer to the criticism that the existing arrangements have the effect of calcifying the law for all time, and it would be in harmony with the abandonment of *stare decisis* for ordinary proceedings. The waiting period would have the advantage of enabling the courts to have a further look at provisions approved under Article 26 after they have been in actual operation for a period of time; under these conditions the decision of the courts would be more realistic than the decision *in vacuo* which must be taken under Article 26."

This seems a sensible and workable compromise, but it has not been adopted and Article 34.3.3° remains in its original form.

The function of Article 26 is to provide a speedy decision on the validity of a legislative measure. It is of course true that should the relevant Bill be simply signed into law, its validity may then be questioned in ordinary legal proceedings. But there may be a considerable delay before an individual with the requisite *locus standi*, and the ability to finance proceedings, appears. Further, if a statute is invalidated years after its enactment, there may be difficulties in unscrambling what has been done under it. The Article 26 procedure perhaps works best in cases which raise a pure question of constitutional interpretation—a prime example being the decision on the Electoral (Amendment) Bill 1983. Had that measure been struck down after becoming law, and following a general election in which unqualified persons had voted, the consequences might have been far-reaching.

Finally, the limited use so far made of Article 26 must be viewed in proper perspective. To contrast the number of measures ruled invalid under this procedure with the far greater number struck down in ordinary proceedings is quite misleading. Many of the statutes invalidated in such ordinary proceedings simply could not have been referred under Article 26, since they antedated the Constitution. Nor is it legitimate to point to post-Constitution measures like the Rent Acts, and ask why these were not referred under Article 26 in the 40s or early 60s. The answer must be that in the then state of our constitutional case-law, it would not have occurred to anyone that they were challengeable—whether in Article 26 or in ordinary proceedings.

Article 34

The Irish Constitution expressly grants the courts power to pronounce on the constitutionality of statutes; the matter is not left to be inferred, as in Australia or the United States (see *Marbury* v. *Madison* (1803) 5 U.S. (1 Cranch) 137). Article 34.3.2° provides that the High Court's jurisdiction "shall extend to the validity of any law having regard to the provisions of this Constitution," while the appellate jurisdiction of the Supreme Court in such cases is guaranteed by Article 34.4.4°.

In *State Sheerin* v. *Kennedy* [1966] I.R. 379 the Supreme Court construed the words "validity of any law having regard to the provisions of this Constitution" as referring only to statutes passed after Bunreacht na hÉireann came into force. On this basis, Article 34.3.2° and 34.4.4°guarantee the jurisdiction of the High Court and Supreme Court to pronounce on the validity of such statutes. They have nothing to do with pre-Constitution Acts, which are technically tested for "inconsistency" with the Constitution, under Article 50. Presumably the High Court's jurisdiction to pronounce on such inconsistency derives from the omnibus jurisdiction-conferring provisions of Article 34.3.1°. But this analysis gives rise to a difficulty; there would seem to be nothing to prevent the Oireachtas from legislating to stop appeals to the Supreme Court in cases involving inconsistency under Article 50. The Oireachtas, as has been noted, is empowered to create exceptions to the general principle that all High Court decisions are appealable (Art. 34.4.3°). It may not except cases which involve "the validity of any law having regard to the provisions of this Constitution"; but, as we have seen, this relates only to post-Constitution Acts.

Article 34.3.2° also prohibits other courts from involving themselves with issues as to the validity of post-Constitution Acts. Not only may these courts not pronounce on such matters, but they may not even allow any such question to be raised "whether by pleading, argument or otherwise." This prohibition binds not only the District and Circuit Courts, but also the Court of Criminal Appeal, the Courts-Martial Appeal Court and the special criminal courts established under Article 38.[4] However, the interpretation in *Sheerin's* case of the key phrase "validity of any laws" means that this prohibition does not apply to pre-Constitution statutes—whether of the United Kingdom Par-

---

[4] In *Minister for Labour* v. *Costello* [1988] I.R. 235 the defendant had argued in the District Court that, in the circumstances of the case, the offence charged under the Industrial Relations Act 1946, s.45 fell outside the minor category, and thus outside the District Court's jurisdiction. A case was stated to the High Court, where O'Hanlon J. held that it was not open to the defendant to rely on this plea in the District Court, given Article 34.3.2°. He continued ([1988] I.R. 235, 241):

"Furthermore, I am of opinion that it is not permissible to raise the issue of constitutionality by way of case stated from the District Court having regard to the decision of the former Supreme Court in *Foyle Fisheries Commission* v. *Gallen* [1960] Ir.Jur.Rep. 35. The District Justice must proceed on the assumption that powers conferred on him by Act of the Oireachtas, enacted subsequent to the enactment of the Constitution of 1937, may lawfully be exercised by him unless and until the statute has been successfully impugned in proceedings appropriate for that purpose."

liament or the Oireachtas of Saorstát Éireann. But it does not appear that the power thus revealed has ever been exercised.[5]

Common law rules

What has been said so far relates to the validity of statutes. But the category of constitutional cases embraces more than this, for there may be issues arising under the Constitution which do not involve any such questions. Examples which are discussed more fully elsewhere in this book are: *Boland* v. *An Taoiseach* [1974] I.R. 338: *Crowley* v. *Ireland* [1980] I.R. 241: *Meskell* v. *C.I.E.* [1973] I.R. 121 and the cases involving Article 40.3.3° (the "pro-life" provision).[6] Several cases have involved the question whether supposed rules of the common law had survived the coming into force of Bunreacht na hÉireann.[7]

Grounds of review

In many instances the plaintiff's claim will be that statute has invalidly infringed on rights guaranteed by the Constitution, whether expressly or by implication. But this does not exhaust the possibilities; anyone who can demonstrate injury traceable to an arguable violation of the Constitution may carry a complaint before the courts. In that sense one has a right to the due observance of the Constitution's commands—*e.g.* as to trial by jury or the separation of powers. On this basis, one could presumably challenge the validity of a statute by undertaking to show that its enactment did not conform to the Constitution's provisions on the legislative process. Thus if a Bill deemed to have been passed by both Houses under Article 21 arguably was not a Money Bill, the ensuing Act could in appropriate circumstances be the subject of forensic challenge. So, too, in regard to a Bill, deemed by resolution of the Dáil to have been passed by both Houses under Article 23.1, which contains certain Seanad amendments. A litigant affected by the resultant "Act" may ask a court whether, in the light of discrepancies between the texts of the measure as it left the Dáil and that purported to have been enacted, the statute is valid. The same would hold if it could be shown that the President had inadvertently signed a Bill earlier than the fifth day after its presentation to her, without prior Seanad concurrence in a Government request to do so (Art. 25.2.1°).

Two decisions of Johnston J. might seem to cast doubt on the above propositions. In *O'Crowley* v. *Minister for Finance* [1935] I.R. 536 the plaintiff

---

[5] Note, however, that in *People (D.P.P.)* v. *T.* (Court of Criminal Appeal, Rec. No. 106/88, July 27, 1988) that court was prepared to hold that any provision of the Criminal Justice (Evidence) Act 1924 which resulted in a wife not being a competent witness against her husband in a prosecution for incest did not survive the coming into operation of the Constitution.

[6] *Att. Gen. (S.P.U.C. (Ireland) Ltd.)* v. *Open Door Counselling Ltd.* [1988] I.R. 593: *S.P.U.C. (Ireland) Ltd.* v. *Coogan* [1989] I.R. 734: *S.P.U.C. (Ireland) Ltd.* v. *Grogan* [1989] I.R. 753: *Att. Gen.* v. *X.* (*The Irish Times*, February 18, 1992).

[7] *e.g.* Re *Tilson* [1951] I.R. 1 (father's right to control education of children): *Byrne* v. *Ireland* [1971] I.R. 241 (State's immunity from tort liability): *State (D.P.P.)* v. *Walsh* [1981] I.R. 412 (common law defence of marital coercion available to wife): *S.* v. *S.* [1983] I.R. 68 (rule that a wife could not give evidence that her husband was not the father of her child): *People (D.P.P.)* v. *T.* (Court of Criminal Appeal, July 27, 1988) (common law rule that one spouse not competent witness against the other): *C.M.* v. *T.M. (No. 2)* [1990] 2 I.R. 52 (common law rule of wife's dependent domicile).

attempted to query an Act which had been certified as a Money Bill under Article 35 of the 1922 Constitution. Johnston J. thought this impossible (at 549):

> "In the present case the Bill was certified by the Chairman of the Dáil as a 'Money Bill' and the Senate acquiesced in that view and did not exercise its right to have the matter referred to the Committee of Privileges mentioned in Article 35. I must therefore receive, apply and construe the Act . . . in exactly the same way as I would any Act which did not originate as a Money Bill, and I have no authority to inquire how or by what process as a Public Act it reached the statute book . . . "

In *Halpin* v. *Att. Gen.* [1936] I.R. 226 it was argued that the Land Act 1933 was invalid because it did not contain a proper enacting clause ("Be it enacted by the Oireachtas . . . "). The plaintiff exhibited a copy of the Bill which omitted this formula; but the Act as published included it, as did the copy deposited with the Supreme Court under Article 42 of the 1922 Constitution. Johnston J. accepted the latter copy as conclusive, in accordance with Article 42. The case, therefore, does not establish what would be the position had the enacting clause been omitted. (If it was clear that the measure represented the will of both Houses, it might be thought pedantic to deny it legal force because of the omission of an incantatory formula not required by the Constitution). However, the deposited copy did not include an indorsement by the Clerk of the Dáil of the date of the Act's passage—as required by section 8(2) of the Interpretation Act 1923. Johnston J. held that this could not affect the validity or efficacy of the legislation ([1936] I.R. 226, 244). He then quoted with approval the observations of Audette J. in *Rex* v. *Irwin* [1926] Exch. Canada 126:

> " . . . when a statute appears on its face to have been duly passed by a competent legislature, the Courts must assume that all things have been rightly done in respect of its passage through the Legislature and cannot entertain any argument that there is a defect of parliamentary procedure lying behind the Act as a matter of fact."

Those views, however, fail to take account of the fact that in certain respects Irish legislative procedure is regulated, not by mere parliamentary standing orders, but by the Constitution. And the courts have the function of deciding whether the Constitution's prescriptions have been fulfilled. It is significant that in *Re McGrath and Harte* [1941] I.R. 68, the Supreme Court entertained—even if it dismissed—an argument that the First Amendment of the Constitution Act was invalid because it had been signed by the President earlier than specified in Article 25.2.1°. This can only have been done on the basis that the courts are empowered to examine the constitutional legitimacy of the process whereby a particular Bill is said to have become law. Their jurisdiction to do so finds impressive support from two decisions of the High Court of Australia—*Cormack* v. *Cope* (1974) 131 C.L.R. 432 and *Victoria* v. *Commonwealth* ("the PMA Case") (1975) 134 C.L.R. 81. Both cases involved section 57 of the Australian Constitution, which establishes a special procedure under which legislation may be passed at a joint sitting of both Houses. In each of the cases, a majority of the judges held that failure to comply with section 57's provisions would mean that the resulting measures were invalid: see (1974) 131 C.L.R. at 452 (Barwick C.J.), 464 (Menzies J.), 466

(Gibbs J.), 472 (Stephen J.), and 474 (Mason J.): and (1975) 134 C.L.R. at 118–20 (Barwick C.J.), 164 (Gibbs J.), 177–78 (Stephen J.) and 181–82 (Mason J.).

The conclusions of Johnston J. mentioned above may have been unduly influenced by United Kingdom practice, under which the courts cannot look behind a statute. But this rule plainly does not hold good everywhere; thus in *U.S.* v. *Ballin* (1892) 144 U.S. 1 the Supreme Court was prepared to examine congressional proceedings to see whether constitutionally required procedure had been followed. The approach of the British courts is unacceptable under Bunreacht na hÉireann, for reasons identical to those stated by Gibbs J. in *Victoria* v. *Commonwealth* (1975) 134 C.L.R. 81, 163:

> "In the United Kingdom, if a statute has been passed by Parliament, the Courts will not entertain a suggestion that there has been irregularity or impropriety in the course of its passage. The decisions which have expounded and applied this principle are, however, no authority for holding that a court has no jurisdiction to go behind a statute which has not been passed by Parliament as ordinarily constituted, but has been enacted by a different method which the Constitution permits to be used only if certain conditions are satisfied. A law so enacted will be valid only if the conditions are satisfied, and the courts have jurisdiction to declare the invalidity of any such law if there has been a failure to satisfy those conditions. The principle that the courts may not examine the way in which the law-making process has been performed has no application where a legislature is established under or governed by an instrument which prescribes that laws of a certain kind may only be passed if the legislature is constituted or exercises its functions in a particular manner, *e.g.* by the members of both Houses sitting together (as was required by the South Africa Act: *Harris* v. *Minister of the Interior* (1952) (2) S.A.L.R. 428); *sub. nom. Harris* v. *Donges* ([1952] 1 T.L.R. 1245) or by a two-thirds majority (which was rendered necessary by the Ceylon (Constitution) Order in Council considered in *Bribery Commissioner* v. *Ranasinghe* [1965] A.C. 172). These cases decide that when the law requires a legislature to enact legislation in a particular manner, the courts may investigate whether the legislature has exercised its powers in the manner required; this is recognised also in *McCawley* v. *The King* ([1920] A.C. 691) and *McDonald* v. *Cain* ([1963] V.L.R. 411)."

A hierarchy of norms?

The Supreme Court has accepted that the Constitution recognises a hierarchy of rights. Thus the right to life has been held superior to other constitutional rights, such as those to personal liberty[8] or to disseminate or receive information.[9] But what, beyond this, is entailed in the concept has yet to be worked out.

In *People (D.P.P.)* v. *Shaw* [1982] I.R. 1 Kenny J. expressed his view on the matter as follows (at 63):

> "There is a hierarchy of constitutional rights and, when a conflict arises

[8] *People (D.P.P.)* v. *Shaw* [1982] I.R. 1.
[9] *Att. Gen. (S.P.U.C. (Ireland) Ltd.)* v. *Open Door Counselling Ltd.* [1988] I.R. 593.

between them, that which ranks higher must prevail . . . the decision on the priority of constitutional rights is to be made by the High Court and, on appeal, by this Court. When a conflict of constitutional rights arises, it must be resolved by having regard to (a) the terms of the Constitution, (b) the ethical values which all Christians living in the State acknowledge and accept and (c) the main tenets of our system of constitutional parliamentary democracy."

These tests, however, may not prove easy to apply in concrete cases. In particular, there may be difficulty in identifying the ethical values to which Kenny J. referred. Indeed, this was recognised by the Supreme Court in *State (Keegan)* v. *Stardust Compensation Tribunal* [1986] I.R. 642, in rejecting the suggestion that the alleged unreasonableness of an administrative decision should be tested by the extent to which it failed to meet accepted moral standards. Henchy J., his colleagues concurring, said on this point (at 658):

"The concept of 'accepted moral standards' represents a vague, elusive and changing body of standards which in a pluralist society is sometimes difficult to ascertain . . ."

McCarthy J., in his judgment in *Murray* v. *Ireland* [1991] I.L.R.M. 465, uses the expression "hierarchy of constitutional norms" (at 476, 477). The word "norms" is capable of embracing more than "rights," but it is not clear whether an extension of the existing doctrine was intended. If it were, Irish law may be poised to develop on the lines of its German counterpart, of which Professor Kommers has written[10]:

" . . . the Court has postulated the existence of constitutional principles so fundamental to the political order that even the various provisions of the basic law are subordinate to them. Thus, even a constitutional amendment is subject theoretically to review on constitutional grounds if it offends or abrogates one of these principles, giving rise to the possibility of an 'unconstitutional constitutional norm.' "

It seems clear that Irish law could not fully accommodate the German doctrine thus outlined. The notion of an unconstitutional amendment is, on several grounds, alien to Bunreacht na hÉireann. The language of Article 46.1, permitting amendment "whether by way of variation, addition or repeal" could hardly be wider. In addition, the process of amendment requires a referendum and hence approval by the people (Article 46). Since the latter have, under Article 6, the right "in final appeal, to decide all questions of national policy, according to the requirements of the common good," they may presumably amend the Constitution in any way they choose.[11] But the question might arise whether some provisions of the Constitution may be more fundamental than others. Such an argument was advanced in *Lennon* v. *Minister for the Environment (The Irish Times*, October 23, 1990), where the

[10] Donald P. Kommers, *Judicial Politics in West Germany: A Study of the Federal Constitutional Court* (Beverly Hills/London 1976), p. 210.
[11] In *Finn* v. *Att. Gen.* [1983] I.R. 154 Barrington J. concluded that by Art. 46.1 "the people intended to give themselves full power to amend any provision of the Constitution . . ." (at 164–64). And in *Slattery* v. *An Taoiseach* (Supreme Court, June 19, 1992) Hederman J. said: "A proposal to amend the Constitution cannot per se be unconstitutional . . . " (p. 17 of his judgment).

plaintiff sought an injunction to halt the Presidential election scheduled for November 7. His claim was that the election would be undemocratic, since the range of candidates was arbitrarily restricted by the nomination provisions of Article 12.4.2° of the Constitution. Those provisions, he submitted, were contrary to the common good and unconstitutional. Egan J. rejected the plaintiff's application on the ground of his delay, but expressed no opinion on his constitutional submission.

Procedure

Save for Article 26, and the habeas corpus provisions of Article 40.4, no specific procedure is established for raising constitutional complaints. A constitutional issue, in the sense used above, may arise in any form of proceedings, be it a claim for a mandatory injunction as in *Crowley* v. *Ireland* [1980] I.R. 102, or for damages for breach of constitutional rights as in *Meskell* v. *C.I.E.* [1973] I.R. 121. A challenge to the validity of a statute may be mounted in habeas corpus proceedings, though by far the most usual form is a simple action for a declaration. In such actions it is common to name the Attorney General as defendant, an especially appropriate procedure given the role assigned to the Attorney under Article 30 of the Constitution. The 1986 Rules of the Superior Courts cater for a situation where the constitutionality of a statute is raised in other proceedings, by requiring the service of notice on the Attorney that a constitutional issue has been raised. Order 60, rule 1 demands this, and rule 3 stipulates that the Attorney General shall thereupon be entitled to appear in the action and to become a party to the proceedings as regards the question of the validity of the law.[12] (Note also Order 60, rule 2, which requires notice to the Attorney General if a question of the *interpretation* of the Constitution—*i.e.* not involving the validity of a law—arises in any action or matter.)[13]

Before 1982 the view seems to have been held in some quarters that the constitutionality of a statute could not be raised in certiorari proceedings. This doubt, which does not appear to have found reported judicial expression, was difficult to understand; the supposed problem had not occurred to the High Court or Supreme Court when they successively considered the validity of the Adoption Act 1952 in such proceedings—*State (Nicolaou)* v. *An Bord Uchtála* [1966] I.R. 567. That challenges in such a form were quite permissible was put beyond doubt by *State (Lynch)* v. *Cooney* [1982]

---

[12] The Attorney General may, as a notice party, independently appeal to the Supreme Court, as occurred in *Murphy* v. *Roche and Ors* [1987] I.R. 106.

[13] In *State (D.)* v. *Groarke* [1988] I.R. 187 it was submitted that Ord. 60, r. 1 did not apply to pre-Constitution statutes, in the light of the Supreme Court's decision in *State (Sheerin)* v. *Kennedy* [1966] I.R. 379. But Carroll J. held that *Sheerin's* case did not decide this particular point, and continued (at 190):

> "In my opinion the purpose of Ord. 60 is to enable the Attorney General to argue for the constitutionality not only of post-Constitution statutes but of pre-Constitution ones as well. A large body of our statute law dates from before the Constitution. I cannot accept that O.60 should be interpreted so that it would be possible for a pre-Constitution statute to be declared unconstitutional in an action between two private individuals without the knowledge of the Attorney General."

This ruling was accepted by the applicant, and consequently the issue did not arise before the Supreme Court on appeal: [1990] 1 I.R. 305, 312.

I.R. 337; and it is now quite common for them to be mounted in applications for judicial review.[14]

Limitations on jurisdiction

While it is a function of the courts to police the Constitution, they do not have a roving commission to discover and set right wrongs. They can act only within the jurisdiction conferred upon them by the Constitution, and in properly structured proceedings. The judges are keenly aware of the difficulty and delicacy of the power entrusted to them to review the constitutionality of statutes, and they have developed a number of rules to guide them in this task. Thus in *Tormey* v. *Att. Gen.* [1985] I.L.R.M. 375 the Supreme Court emphasised that the courts' jurisdiction extended only to *justiciable* issues. In the nature of things, remarked Henchy J., there were matters and questions which were not amenable to determination in any court; they were not justiciable. Neither in that, nor in any other judgment, has the Supreme Court attempted to list non-justiciable questions, and no test for identifying them has been laid down.

In *Baker* v. *Carr* (1962) 369 U.S. 186 the United States Supreme Court, *per* Brennan J., proferred the following tests of non-justiciability:

> " . . . a textually demonstrable constitutional commitment of the issue to a co-ordinate political department; or a lack of judicially discoverable and manageable standards for resolving it; or the impossibility of deciding without an initial policy determination of a kind clearly for non-judicial discretion; or the impossibility of a court's undertaking independent resolution without expressing lack of the respect due to co-ordinate branches of government; or an unusual need for unquestioning obedience to a political decision already made; or the potentiality of embarrassment from multifarious pronouncements by various departments on one question."

See also *Powell* v. *McCormack* (1969) 395 U.S. 486 and *Goldwater* v. *Carter* (1979) 444 U.S. 996.

The House of Lords has said that justiciability relates to whether a particular matter is appropriate for resolution by the judicial process: *Council of Civil Service Unions* v. *Minister for the Civil Service* [1984] 3 All E.R. 935. What national security required was there held to be a non-justiciable question; Lord Diplock said that the judicial process was "totally inept to deal with the sort of problems which it involves (at 952: see also Lords Fraser (at 944), Scarman (at 947–48) and Roskill (at 958)). The Canadian Supreme Court also stressed the appropriateness factor in *Operation Dismantle* v. *The Queen* (1985) 18 D.L.R. (4th) 481; see Wilson J.'s extended discussion at 498–505. But it would seem that justiciability is to be considered on a case-by-case basis, and the Canadian Supreme Court was averse to erecting broad categories of non-justiciable issues. Thus Dickson C.J. had no doubt that disputes of a political or foreign policy nature might properly be cognisable by the courts (at 494).

While the approaches described above have not been explicitly adopted by

---

[14] *e.g. O'Shea* v. *D.P.P.* [1988] I.R. 655: *Hyland* v. *Minister for Social Welfare* [1989] I.R. 624: *Harvey* v. *Minister for Social Welfare* [1990] 2 I.R. 232: *McDaid* v. *Sheehy* [1991] 1 I.R. 1.

any Irish court, the philosophy behind them seems to have inspired some of the Irish decisions such as *Boland* v. *An Taoiseach, infra.* In *Macken* v. *An Taoiseach* (*The Irish Times*, May 26, 1984) the plaintiff sought an injunction to restrain the government from allowing President Reagan to bring into the State any equipment necessary to launch nuclear missiles. He claimed that to allow in such equipment would necessarily threaten his life and that of his family and other citizens, contrary to the Constitution and natural law. Lynch J. refused the application, holding that the defence of the State and of the people was a matter for the Government. It was open to the Government to decide what weapons they would employ for that purpose, or what weapons they would not, and if the Government decided that they wished to have or store or keep nuclear weapons in the State, that was a matter for them. External relations were also a matter for the Government to deal with. The Government decided on behalf of the people of Ireland its relations with other people and states, and it was a matter for the Government, acting on behalf of the people, whom they would invite as visitors and on what terms. In inviting the President of the United States the Government did so as representatives of the people of Ireland, elected in free elections by secret ballot, and it was for them to decide the conditions on which the visit of the President of the United States should be made.

Lynch J.'s decision was, therefore, based essentially on separation of powers grounds. In the broadly analogous case of *Operation Dismantle* v. *The Queen* (1985) 18 D.L.R. (4th) 481, the Canadian Supreme Court took a different line. The plaintiff organisations and unions sought an injunction to restrain the Canadian government from permitting, by agreement with the United States, the testing of cruise missiles in Canada. Their claim was that this decision infringed the rights to life and security of the person guaranteed by the Charter of Rights and Freedoms. But the court held that the causal link between the government's actions and the alleged violation of Charter rights was too uncertain, speculative and hypothetical to sustain a cause of action.

Inappropriateness for resolution by the judicial process may be said to underlie Costello J.'s decision in *McKenna* v. *An Taoiseach* (High Court, June 8, 1992). The background to this case was a referendum, fixed for June 18, on the Eleventh Amendment of the Constitution Bill—designed to permit the State to ratify the Treaty on European Union (the Maastricht Treaty). The plaintiff's principal argument was that the Government was using public funds to finance a partisan campaign in favour of a "Yes" vote, and that this violated the Constitution. She sought injunctions, alternatively (a) restraining the Government from advocating an affirmative vote without setting out impartially the arguments on both sides, or (b) requiring the Government to make available proportionate funding to those parties and groups opposing ratification. Costello J. refused the relief sought. He understood that the plaintiff might feel aggrieved, but continued (pp. 5–6 of his judgment):

> " . . . not every grievance can be remedied by the courts. And judges must not allow themselves to be led, or indeed voluntarily wander, into areas calling for adjudication on political and non-justiciable issues. They are charged by the Constitution with exercising the judicial power of government and it would both weaken their important constitutional role as well as amount to an unconstitutional act for judges to adjudicate

on such issues . . . Should the Government decide that the national interest required that an advertising campaign be mounted which was confined to extolling forcibly the benefit of an affirmative vote, it would be improper for the courts to express any view on such a decision. The object of such a campaign would, of course, be to influence voters' attitudes. But to adjudicate on a claim that the use of public funds to finance such a campaign was unfair because it distorted public attitudes would involve an assessment of the effect of such a campaign on public attitudes, the strength of the opposing campaign of those propounding a "no" vote, and the forces influencing the voters' ultimate decision. Such an assessment is not just one of establishing facts but calls for a careful analysis and a balancing of complex political and social factors. It is one for political analysts to make, not for judges."

The separation of powers doctrine underlies the decisions in the two cases involving the proposed Eighth Amendment of the Constitution ("the pro-life Amendment"). Both actions had the same objective—to stop the referendum taking place. In *Roche* v. *Ireland* (High Court: Carroll J., June 17, 1983) the plaintiff claimed the proposed amendment was so vaguely worded that he could not know how he should vote and would have to abstain; thus he would be deprived of his constitutional right to vote in the referendum. Carroll J. did not accept this submission, but in any event went on to observe that a constitutional amendment involved "a particularly solemn legislative process"; not only the Oireachtas but also the people took part. With this process the courts had no jurisdiction to interfere; the separation of powers under the Constitution would preclude that. Carroll J. founded on an unreported Supreme Court decision of 1956—*Wireless Dealers' Association* v. *Fair Trade Commission* (March 14, 1956). There the Dáil had passed a certain Bill and the appropriate Minister was about to introduce it into the Seanad. The plaintiff association believed the Bill to be constitutionally invalid and sought an injunction to prevent its being proceeded with. The Supreme Court refused the application, emphasising that the sole jurisdiction in regard to the constitutionality of Bills was that arising under Article 26. Carroll J. said this case showed that the courts could not intervene in the normal legislative process; *a fortiori*, she observed, they could not do so in the more solemn legislative process of a constitutional amendment.

In the second case—*Finn* v. *Att. Gen.* [1983] I.R. 154—Barrington J. in the High Court accepted this view.[15] On appeal the Supreme Court was even more emphatic. Legislation, it was held, could be reviewed for constitutionality in two situations only;

(a) Bills referred under Article 26
(b) Acts challenged in ordinary proceedings.

Save in these excepted cases, said the court, there was no jurisdiction to construe or review the constitutionality of a Bill, whatever its nature. The courts

---

[15] In *Mhic Mhathuna* v. *Ireland and Att. Gen.* (*The Irish Times,* June 10, 1986) Hamilton P., following these decisions, refused an injunction to restrain the holding of the 1986 divorce referendum.

had no power to interfere with the legislative process.[16] This was reiterated in *Slattery* v. *An Taoiseach* (Supreme Court, June 18, 1992), where the court rejected an application to restrain the holding of the referendum on the Eleventh Amendment of the Constitution Bill. It was claimed that the Government had not sufficiently informed the electorate about the implications of the Maastricht Treaty. Hederman J. cited the *Wireless Dealers' Association* case and said (p. 13 of his judgment):

> "The real point in this case is to ask this Court to prevent the operation of legislative and constitutional procedures which are in train. This is something the Court has no jurisdiction to do. What the Government is doing is implementing the decision of the Dail and the Seanad."

McCarthy J. said (p. 2 of his judgment):

> "It may be that circumstances could arise in which the judicial organ of government would properly intervene in this process; such is not the case here. In my judgment, the application made by the Plaintiffs has no foundation whatever; to grant an order such as sought would be a wholly unwarranted and unwarrantable intervention by the judiciary in what is clearly a legislative and popular domain. See *Finn* v. *Attorney General and others* [1983] I.R. 154."

And Egan J. said that the appellants were seeking the aid of the courts to interfere in a legislative process. In his opinion, it would be totally wrong if the courts were to intervene in a process authorised by the Constitution.

The Supreme Court had reasoned similarly in the earlier case of *Boland* v. *An Taoiseach* [1974] I.R. 338. There the plaintiff sought an injunction to restrain the Government from signing the Sunningdale Agreement, on the ground that this would be incompatible with Articles 2 and 3 of the Constitution. The Supreme Court rejected the claim, principally on the ground that there was no jurisdiction to intervene at this stage. Formulating foreign policy was a function of the executive, not of the courts.[17] The question of judicial review could arise here only if the agreement were translated into statute. On the basis of these decisions it may confidently be predicted that should the President attempt to refer to the Supreme Court some issue other than the validity of a Bill, the court would decline to entertain it.

Over the last 20 years many Irish interest groups, aggrieved by some item of legislation but unable to secure its amendment through the political process, have turned to the courts. Their aim is to have the legislation condemned as unconstitutional, in the hope that the resulting vacuum will spur executive and legislature into action. The success of several such efforts has emboldened others to try, with the consequence that the courts are occasionally invited to assume an unfamiliar and unwelcome role. In *O'Reilly* v. *Limerick Corporation* [1989] I.L.R.M. 181 the plaintiffs were members of the traveller community living in caravans on unofficial sites in Limerick. They

---

[16] In *Crotty* v. *Ireland* (*The Irish Times*, December 2, 1986) Carroll J., presumably with these decisions in mind, refused an application for liberty to serve short notice of motion for an injunction to restrain discussion in Dáil Éireann of the Bill implementing the Single European Act (see Chap. 8 *supra*).

[17] *Boland's* case was distinguished by the majority of the Supreme Court in *Crotty* v. *An Taoiseach* [1987] I.R. 713 (see Chap. 8 *supra*).

were without running water, or toilet facilities, or a refuse collection service and were living in what Costello J. described as "conditions of great poverty and deprivation." They claimed, *inter alia*, damages against the State, arguing that their constitutional rights had been infringed. These rights, it was contended, embraced a right to be provided with a minimum standard of basic material conditions, springing from Article 40.3 and/or Article 41.2. Costello J. held that he lacked jurisdiction to award the damages sought. The claim, he concluded, involved the proposition that there had been "a failure to distribute adequately in the plaintiffs' favour a portion of the community's wealth" (at 194). To admit it would therefore be to involve the courts in supervising the allocation of resources. Costello J. continued ([1989] I.L.R.M. 181, 195):

> "The courts' constitutional function is to administer justice but I do not think that by exercising the suggested supervisory role it could be said that a court was administering justice as contemplated in the Constitution. What could be involved in the exercise of the suggested jurisdiction would be the imposition by the court of its view that there had been an unfair distribution of national resources. To arrive at such a conclusion it would have to make an assessment of the validity of the many competing claims on those resources, the correct priority to be given to them and the financial implications of the plaintiffs' claim . . . In exercising this function the court would not be administering justice as it does when determining an issue relating to commutative justice but it would be engaged in an entirely different exercise, namely, an adjudication on the fairness or otherwise of the manner in which other organs of State had administered public resources. Apart from the fact that members of the judiciary have no special qualification to undertake such a function, the manner in which justice is administered in the courts, that is on a case-by-case basis, make them a wholly inappropriate institution for the fulfilment of the suggested role. I cannot construe the Constitution as conferring it on them . . . I am sure that the concept of justice which is to be found in the Constitution embraces the concept that the nation's wealth should be justly distributed (that is the concept of distributive justice), but I am equally sure that a claim that this has not occurred should, to comply with the Constitution, be advanced in Leinster House rather than in the Four Courts."[18]

Injunctions against statutes

It was noted above that in *Wireless Dealers' Association* v. *Fair Trade Commission* (March 14, 1956), the Supreme Court refused to enjoin the introduction into the Seanad of an allegedly unconstitutional Bill. One ground of decision was that the ensuing Act would be open to challenge in the ordinary way.[19] But this does not mean that an injunction may not be granted to restrain the enforcement of an allegedly unconstitutional Act. The Supreme Court upheld the grant of such an injunction in *Pesca Valentia Ltd.* v. *Minister for Fisheries* [1985] I.R. 193. Here the plaintiff company owned three fishing

---

[18] See also Carroll J.'s decision in *Mhic Mhahtuna* v. *Att. Gen.* [1989] I.R. 504.
[19] See the similar approach of the High Court of Australia in *Cormack* v. *Cope* (1974) 131 C.L.R. 432.

vessels, formerly registered in Spain but since May 1981 registered in Ireland. The defendant Minister had issued a licence in respect of each vessel,
acting under section 2 of the Fisheries (Amendment) Act 1983. Each licence
contained a condition that the vessel should not be used for sea fishing,
within the State's exclusive fishery limits or otherwise, unless 75 per cent. or
more of the crew were Irish citizens or citizens of another EC member state.
In September 1984 one of the plaintiff's vessels was arrested, and the master
was charged with fishing otherwise than in accordance with the licence. His
trial was pending in the Cork Circuit Court. The plaintiff company had commenced proceedings for a declaration that the relevant parts of the Fisheries
(Amendment) Act 1983 were repugnant to the Constitution[20] and to EC law;
and pending the trial of that action it now sought an interlocutory injunction
to restrain the defendants from enforcing, or attempting to enforce, the condition in the licences.

The plaintiff argued: (a) that compliance with the condition was impossible; Irish fishermen would not accept the long voyages and hard work
involved in fishing for hake[21]; (b) if the three boats were prevented from fishing pending trial of the action, the company would be put out of business.
The defendants contested these conclusions of fact and contended that to
permit the boats to fish pending trial of the action would damage Irish
fishery interests and the employment of Irish fishermen. They also argued
that the normal principles governing applications for interlocutory injunctions did not apply to cases such as this. The 1983 Act was presumed to be
constitutional and, it was contended, the courts should never grant an
injunction which prohibited—even for a temporary period—the exercise of a
power contained in a post-Constitution statute. Alternatively, an injunction
should be granted only in the most exceptional circumstances, such as the
imposition of a drastic penalty or the establishing by the plaintiff that a statutory provision was clearly unconstitutional. This did not apply here. The
plaintiff company submitted that this application was governed by the ordinary principles—was there a fair question to be tried, and where did the
balance of convenience lie? On both counts, it was entitled to an injunction.

The Supreme Court, *per* Finlay C.J., held that it would be inconsistent
with the courts' duty to protect persons against invasion of their constitutional rights if no power existed in an appropriate case to enjoin action
based on a statute which might eventually be held unconstitutional. In particular this power must exist in an appropriate case where the action authorised was under a penal section, involving conviction of and punishment for a
criminal offence. The presumption of constitutionality was material to the
issue whether the plaintiff had established a fair question to be tried. The
impeding of executive action consequent upon granting an injunction was

---

[20] This constitutional challenge was subsequently abandoned: *Pesca Valentia Ltd.* v. *Minister for
Fisheries (No. 2)* [1990] 2 I.R. 305, 313. Keane J., finding that a preliminary ruling on certain
EC law issues was required, made an order referring them to the European Court of Justice:
[1990] 2 I.R. 305, 318. That court answered those questions in the defendant's favour: Case
223/86, *Pesca Valentia Ltd.* v. *Minister for Fisheries* [1988] E.C.R. 83, and Keane J. subsequently
dissolved the injunction.

[21] In subsequent proceedings Keane J. found that the evidence " . . . establishes overwhelm-
ingly that Irish fishermen are not prepared to crew on vessels which are more than a day or
two out of port and, since the large deep sea fishing vessels employed by the plaintiff are
usually at sea for 12 days or more, efforts to recruit predominantly Irish crews were wholly
unsuccessful": *Pesca Valentia Ltd.* v. *Minister for Fisheries (No. 2)* 2 I.R. 305, 313.

likewise a matter for consideration on the balance of convenience. Here, however, the plaintiff had established a fair question to be tried, and the balance of convenience lay with it.[22]

The Supreme Court went on to point out that the High Court had granted the injunction against all three defendants—the Minister, Ireland and the Attorney General. But the court observed that while Ireland might be an appropriate defendant in the action, it did not seem appropriate that any injunction should ever be granted against Ireland. Thus the order was altered by making the injunction only against the Minister and the Attorney General. The order was further varied to permit the Minister to ascertain, by any lawful means short of arresting the plaintiff's employees or vessels, whether breaches of the licences were occurring.

In some situations an invasion of constitutional rights under a statute subsequently invalidated could not be adequately compensated for by damages—assuming such can be awarded. It is therefore important that the courts be prepared to contemplate restraining the enforcement of a challenged statute pending trial of an action to determine its validity, and the *Pesca Valentia* case is valuable in its recognition of this. But while the case establishes that no special principles apply to such proceedings, it unfortunately gives little guidance as to the factors which should govern the exercise of judicial discretion; and it sits uneasily with earlier decisions on similar issues.[23] In addition, a subsequent decision has further muddied the waters. In *Cooke* v. *Minister for Communications* (*The Irish Times*, February 20, 1989) the Supreme Court declined to grant the plaintiff an interlocutory injunction restraining the defendant from exercising his statutory power[24] to order disconnection of the plaintiff's telephone and electricity supply. The plaintiff was broadcasting without a licence, in breach of the Broadcasting and Wireless Telegraphy Act 1988. He had instituted proceedings impugning its validity. In an *ex-tempore* judgment Walsh J. (Griffin and Hederman JJ. concurring) said that the law as it stood rendered unlicensed broadcasting illegal. The court, being bound to uphold the law, could not restrain the Minister from exercising his statutory powers where this injunction would have the effect of permitting illegal activity.

The Supreme Court in *Cooke's* case presumably felt that the *Pesca Valentia* case (which is not cited in the judgment) was distinguishable, but it did not

---

[22] In *Beara Fisheries Ltd.* v. *Minister for the Marine* [1987] I.R. 413 Carroll J. granted a similar injunction to the plaintiff company pending a ruling by the European Court of Justice on the questions referred by the High Court.

[23] See J. P. Casey "Enjoining the Enforcement of Statutes" (1985) 7 *D.U.L.J.* 123. A further problem is identified by Keane J. in *Pesca Valentia Ltd.* v. *Minister for Fisheries (No. 2)* [1990] 2 I.R. 305, 324–25—the question of enforcing the undertaking as to damages required of those seeking interlocutory injunctions. Counsel for the defendants submitted that the damages could be quantified (a) by reference to the profits made by the plaintiff during the period when the injunction was in force, or (b) by reference to the fines that would have been imposed, and the catches confiscated, had the prosecutions restrained by the injunction proceeded. Keane J. rejected both possibilities. As to (a), the fish caught by the plaintiff were not the defendants' property. As to (b), to proceed on this basis would be wholly wrong in principle. It would be imposing a penalty on the plaintiff rather than compensating the defendants; and given that the plaintiff had never been tried by judge and jury on the relevant charges " . . . such a procedure would seem to be constitutionally suspect in the highest degree" ([1990] 2 I.R. 305, 324).

[24] Under the Broadcasting and Wireless Telegraphy Act 1988, s.7.

explain why.[25] Perhaps the distinction lies in the fact that the latter case
involved pending criminal proceedings, whereas the former did not. Another
factor is that *Pesca Valentia* involved, as *Cooke's* case did not, issues of EC
law.[26] In a decision subsequent to *Pesca Valentia*, the European Court of Justice has emphasised that national courts must be able to grant interim relief
temporarily setting aside national legislative provisions which might prevent
Community law rules from having full force and effect: Case C–213/89, *Fac-
tortame Ltd.* v. *Secretary of State for Transport* [1991] 1 All E.R. 70.

Reach constitutional issues last

The Supreme Court has repeatedly emphasised that the validity or otherwise of a statute will be pronounced upon only if this is essential for the disposition of the instant case.[27] This is a familiar principle in United States
constitutional law under the shorthand description "Reach constitutional
issues last." It requires that if the case can be decided on a non-constitutional
ground this course should be taken.

The same order of ideas lies behind the Supreme Court's acceptance, in
Condon v. *Minister for Labour* [1981] I.R. 62, of the American notion of "mootness." In that case the plaintiff bank officials challenged the validity of the
Regulations of Banks (Remuneration and Conditions of Employment) (Temporary Provisions) Act 1975. Under this the Minister for Labour had made
an order preventing the implementation of a new pay agreement between the
Irish Bank Officials Association and the Associated Banks. The Act came
into operation on December 15, 1975 and expired on June 29, 1976; thus
although it was in force when the plaintiffs commenced their proceedings
(December 23, 1975) it had expired when the case came before the High
Court (July 23, 1976). The defendants consequently argued that there was
now no subject matter in respect of which the relief claimed could operate.
The plaintiffs pointed out that an identical Act had been passed in 1973, and
was in operation from July to December of that year. The Supreme Court
upheld McWilliam J.'s rejection of the defence submission. Kenny J. (with
whom O'Higgins C.J. and Parke J. agreed) said ([1981] I.R. 62, 70–71):

> "As a general rule, the Court does not determine constitutional issues
> when some non-constitutional point makes it possible to dispose of the
> case; nor does the Court do so when its decision would be an academic
> exercise only or, to use the language of judges in the United States of
> America, when the case is moot.

[25] In *Grange Developments Ltd.* v. *Dublin Co. Council (No. 4)* [1989] I.R. 377 Murphy J. noted the
"apparent discrepancy" between the two cases, though he had no doubt they could be distinguished on their facts. In the instant case Murphy J. refused to grant an injunction
restraining the plaintiffs from enforcing an award in their favour on the ground that the
award was based on unconstitutional legislation (the defendants having instituted proceedings to challenge it).
[26] On that basis, injunctions would rarely be granted. Cp. Anthony M. Collins and James
O'Reilly, *Civil Proceedings and the State in Ireland: A Practitioner's Guide* (Dublin 1990), p. 141: "It
may be questioned whether a statable case can ever be so strong as to require a court to in
effect find that a statutory provision is inconsistent with the Constitution by granting a plaintiff interlocutory relief which amounts to a vindication of the argument asserted thereby."
[27] See *M.* v. *An Bord Uchtála* [1977] I.R. 287, 293: *Roche* v. *Minister for Industry and Commerce* [1978]
I.R. 149, 152: *O'B.* v. *S.* [1984] I.R. 316, 328: *Cooke* v. *Walsh* [1984] I.R. 710, 728: *Brady* v.
Donegal Co. Council [1989] I.L.R.M. 282, 292–93: *McDaid* v. *Sheehy* [1991] 1 I.R. 1, 17.

When money has been paid or contracts entered into under the Act impugned, the Court must decide the case. When neither of these has happened the Court, in my opinion, should determine the issue when similar legislation is likely to be enacted by the Oireachtas in the future. In most cases there is an interval of at least six months between the day when an Act is signed by the President and the day on which a case challenging its validity is heard. If similar legislation were to be introduced again, it would have a period of six months at least during which it would be presumed to be valid: if the case which challenges the legislation were to be heard even though the relevant Act was not then in force, the Government and the members of Dáil and Seanad Éireann would know whether such an Act was valid. Moreover, the refusal of the Court to decide a case because an Act impugned has been repealed, or has lapsed or has ceased to be in operation by reason of a ministerial order, would give the Oireachtas a most convenient way of avoiding the judicial review by the Court of the constitutional validity of the Act. If a Bill is introduced which contains a provision that the Act shall cease to be in operation when a Minister makes an order having that effect the Oireachtas, by inserting such a section in any Bill, could remove short-term legislation from effective judicial review. But judicial review was intended by those who enacted the Constitution to extend to all legislation whether it be long- or short-term.

These principles, derived from the very nature of judicial review have been adopted by the Federal Supreme Court in the United States of America and, in my view, they should be the rules by which the judges of the High Court determine whether they will decide constitutional issues when the Act whose validity is in question is spent, or has been repealed, or is no longer in operation because of a governmental or ministerial order."[28]

The "rules" to which Kenny J. refers are presumably rules to guide the exercise of the courts' discretion in this matter. That such a discretion exists—even where there is no continuing live controversy—is emphasised by the decision of the Supreme Court of Canada in *Borowski* v. *Canada (Att. Gen.)* (1989) 57 D.L.R. (4th) 231. Among the guidelines for the exercise of that discretion formulated by Sopinka J. for the court were: was there still a proper adversarial context? Did the case raise an issue of public importance, resolution of which was in the public interest? (*I.e.* the court must consider the social cost of leaving the matter undecided.) Would pronouncing a judgment in the absence of a dispute affecting the parties' rights be viewed as intruding into the role of the legislative branch?[29] Subsequently, in *Tremblay* v. *Daigle*

---

[28] Kenny J. cited, and founded upon, a number of United States Supreme Court decisions, including *Southern Pacific Terminal Co.* v. *Interstate Commerce Commission* (191) 219 U.S. 498 and *Moore* v. *Ogilvie* (1969) 349 U.S. 418.

[29] On this ground the court declined to adjudicate on the plantiff's claim—that the therapeutic abortion provisions of the Canadian Criminal Code infringed the constitutionally guaranteed right to life of the foetus. Those provisions had already been ruled unconstitutional—as infringing the rights of women—by the Supreme Court in *Morgentaler* v. *The Queen (No. 2)* (1988) 44 D.L.R. (4th) 385. Sopinka J. said that there was no longer a live controversy or concrete dispute as the substratum of the appeal had disappeared. He continued (at 249): "The appellant is requesting a legal opinion on the interpretation of the *Canadian Charter of Rights and Freedoms* in the absence of legislation or other governmental action which would otherwise

(1989) 62 D.L.R. (4th) 634 the court exercised its discretion to waive the mootness rule. In that case the plaintiff sought an injunction to prevent the defendant, his former girlfriend, from having an abortion. An injunction was granted by the Quebec Superior Court and this decision was affirmed by the Quebec Court of Appeal. The defendant appealed to the Supreme Court of Canada, but while the case was at hearing she had the abortion. The Supreme Court nonetheless decided, after hearing argument on the matter, that the appeal should continue. As the judgment[30] expresses it (at 664):

> " . . . the court decided in its discretion to continue the hearing of this appeal although it was moot, in order to resolve the important legal issue raised [whether the foetus had a right to life under the Quebec Charter of Human Rights and Freedoms[31] or the Civil Code of Lower Canada[32]] so that the situation of women in the position in which Ms. Daigle found herself could be clarified."[33]

Locus standi

The issues considered so far relate to the timing of judicial review. The matter of *locus standi* deals with the question—who may complain that a statute is invalid? This topic had received no extended discussion until the Supreme Court decision in *Cahill* v. *Sutton* [1980] I.R. 269. There the plaintiff instituted proceedings for breach of contract against the defendant, a consultant gynaecologist, in respect of alleged negligent treatment. She became aware of the breach of contract in 1968 but did not commence proceedings until 1972, four years after the cause of action accrued. The defence accordingly pleaded that the claim was barred by section 11(2)(*b*) of the Statute of Limitations 1957, and the High Court accepted this submission. Subsequently the plaintiff raised in the High Court an issue as to the constitutionality of section 11(2)(*b*). It was argued that the limitation period therein contained—three years from the date when the cause of action accrued—was capable of violating constitutional rights. It was liable to defeat a right of action before the relevant individual was aware of its existence, and consequently ran counter to the guarantees of Article 40.3. To be compatible with the latter, it was argued, section 11(2)(*b*) should have a saving clause to

bring the Charter into play . . . This is not a request to decide a moot question but to decide a different, abstract question. To accede to this request would intrude on the right of the executive to order a reference and pre-empt a possible decision of Parliament by dictating the form of legislation it should enact. To do so would be a marked departure from the traditional role of the court."

[30] Which—unusually—bears the name of no individual judge but instead is "By the Court."

[31] In particular, s.1, which provides: "Every human being has a right to life . . . "

[32] In particular Art. 18, which provides: "Every human being possesses juridicial personality."

[33] Cp. *M.F.* v. *Supt., Ballymun Garda Station* [1991] 1 I.R. 189. There four children had been taken into care at the instance of the Eastern Health Board. In habeas corpus proceedings the High Court found the procedure followed unlawful and ordered their return to their mother. The Board appealed, but did not seek an order returning the children to its custody. In his judgment, with which his colleagues concurred, O'Flaherty J. said (at 200): "In a ruling at the commencement of the hearing the Court reaffirmed the strictness of the rule against giving a decision on a moot point but recognised that cases concerning the care and custody of children and the protection of their rights are in a special and, possibly, unique category . . . In these circumstances . . . it is proper that this Court should give a decision which will be as helpful as possible to all those concerned with the welfare of children, including parents, social workers, gardaí, other members of the judiciary and the legal profession in general."

cover cases where the relevant facts were unknown to the plaintiff during the three year period.

The Supreme Court held that the plaintiff lacked the necessary standing to challenge section 11(2)(*b*). It was pointed out that even if the provision were qualified by a saving clause of the kind suggested this would avail the plaintiff nothing, because she was at all times aware of the facts necessary to found her claim. Henchy J. (O'Higgins C.J., Griffin, Kenny and Parke JJ. concurring) said ([1980] I.R. 269, 280);

> "That being the legal predicament in which the plaintiff finds herself, the argument formulated on her behalf is not that she is unjustly debarred from suing because of the alleged statutory defect but that a person to whom the suggested saving provision would apply if it had been enacted could claim successfully in the High Court a declaration that s.11, subs. 2(*b*) is unconstitutional because the suggested saving provision is not attached to it. Therefore, the plaintiff is seeking to be allowed to conjure up, invoke and champion the putative constitutional rights of a hypothetical third party, so that the provisions of s.11, subs. 2(*b*) may be declared unconstitutional on the basis of that constitutional *jus tertii*—thus allowing the plaintiff to march through the resulting gap in the statute. The question which the Court has to consider is whether such an indirect and hypothetical assertion of constitutional rights gives the plaintiff the standing necessary for the successful invocation of the judicial power to strike down a statutory provision on the ground of unconstitutionality."

Ruling that it did not, the court stressed the disadvantages that would result from permitting unrestricted liberty to challenge statutes. Unless there existed concrete personal circumstances pointing to a wrong suffered or threatened, cases would tend to lack reality. There was also a risk of abuse, with the courts becoming "the happy hunting ground of the busybody and the crank" (*per* O'Higgins C.J. at 278). Consequently there must be some limitation, and this was found in a general rule that, as Henchy J. put it (at 282), "the challenger must adduce circumstances showing that the impugned provision is operating, or is poised to operate, in such a way as to deprive him personally of the benefit of a particular constitutional right."

The general rule is formulated in three different ways in the judgment. The first one is in the terms already quoted. The second, at 284, refers to a plaintiff being required

> " . . . to show that the impact of the impugned law on his personal situation discloses an injury or prejudice which he has either suffered or is in imminent danger of suffering."

Later at 286, is found this passage:

> "The primary rule as to standing in constitutional matters is that the person challenging the constitutionality of the statute, or some other person for whom he is deemed by the court to be entitled to speak, must be able to assert that, because of the alleged unconstitutionality, his or that other person's interests have been adversely affected, or stand in real or imminent danger of being adversely affected, by the operation of the statute."

It seems clear that these three formulations are in descending order of stringency, the first being more restrictive than the third, and are capable of giving rise to different results. But the dangers that might otherwise arise from this are minimised by the Supreme Court's recognition that the rule—however formulated—is merely a rule of practice and thus, as Henchy J. put it (at 285) "must, like all such rules, be subject to expansion, exception or qualification when the justice of the case so requires."

Henchy J. went on to say that in some instances the plaintiff's want of the normal *locus standi* would be overlooked. Such a situation might arise where those prejudicially affected by the impugned statute were not in a position to assert adequately, or in time, their constitutional rights. Or the plaintiff's lack of a prejudice or injury peculiar to himself might be disregarded if the impugned provision was directed at or operable against a grouping which included the challenger, or with whom the challenger might be said to have a common interest.[34] These examples, however, were mere illustrations, said Henchy J., and he continued (at 285):

" . . . the stated rule of personal standing may be waived or relaxed if, in the particular circumstances of a case, the court finds that there are weighty countervailing considerations justifying a departure from the rule."

Thus *Cahill* v. *Sutton*, while holding that a prospective challenger must ordinarily show that the statute has some impact on his/her interests, lays down no inflexible rule. The courts have a wide discretion to entertain constitutional challenges by plaintiffs who cannot meet this requirement. Experience suggests the wisdom of this. The plaintiff in *O'Donovan* v. *Att. Gen.* could hardly have shown that the statutory redistribution of Dáil seats he complained of affected him more than any other Dublin resident. The plaintiff in *McMahon* v. *Att. Gen.*, who challenged certain provisions of the Electoral Acts as violating the secrecy of the ballot, was, though a citizen, not on the register of Dáil electors. And his case, it will be recalled, was not that a violation of secrecy had ever occurred but that the legislation created circumstances—however unlikely—in which it *could* occur. Plainly, therefore, he could not possibly prove any injury or prejudice to himself. *Cahill* v. *Sutton* does not mean that such plaintiffs must now be turned away. In a case like *O'Donovan's* the High Court would be entitled to conclude that seeking a plaintiff with a clearer individual stake is seeking the impossible. In a case like *McMahon's*, to turn away the plaintiff may be simply to postpone—unnecessarily—the resolution of a constitutional question affecting the public at large. This would hardly accord with the public interest, which the primary rule of *locus standi* is intended to serve.[35]

---

[34] One wonders whether this could cover cases such as *Educational Co. Ltd.* v. *Fitzpatrick* (No. 2) [1961] I.R. 330 and *Murtagh Properties Ltd.* v. *Cleary* [1972] I.R. 330. In both, employers sought to enjoin picketing which was *prima facie* protected by statute, arguing that the picketing infringed the constitutional rights of their employees.

[35] Cp. *Re Annemans' Application* [1990] 3 C.M.L.R. 341, where a group of citizens impugned the constitutionality of the Belgian legislation on European Parliament elections. (It was alleged that the constitution's equality guarantee had been violated in that the votes of Dutch and French speakers would not carry equal weight.) The *Cour d'Arbitrage* held that an *actio popularis* was inadmissible; only a person whose legal situation could be directly affected by the contested measure had the requisite interest. However, since the Act in question here concerned

Subsequent cases have—happily—confirmed that *Cahill* v. *Sutton* posed no threat to the *O'Donovan/McMahon*—style plaintiff—the "private attorney-general," in the language of United States law. In *Crotty* v. *An Taoiseach* [1987] I.R. 713 the plaintiff, who queried the validity of ratifying the Single European Act without amending the Constitution, was suing simply as a citizen. He was patently unable to show any injury peculiar to himself from such ratification, and counsel for the State argued that he consequently lacked the *locus standi* requisite to challenge it. But the Supreme Court rejected this contention, Finlay C.J. saying (at 766):

> "The Court is satisfied, in accordance with the principles laid down in *Cahill* v. *Sutton* [1980] I.R. 269, that in the particular circumstances of this case where the impugned legislation . . . will if made operative affect every citizen, the plaintiff has a *locus standi* to challenge the Act notwithstanding his failure to prove the threat of any special injury or prejudice to him, as distinct from any other citizen, arising from the Act."

Passages in the individual judgments in *Crotty's* case seem to accept the proposition that the Government is under a duty to observe the commands of the Constitution.[36] This duty is presumably owed to the people at large, with the consequence that any citizen has the right—and hence the *locus standi*—to enforce its due performance. Thus, though the dictum of Walsh J. in *S.P.U.C. (Ireland) Ltd.* v. *Coogan* [1989] I.R. 734, 743 that:

> " . . . every member of the public has an interest in ensuring that the fundamental law of the State is not defeated"

was not specifically assented to by his colleagues, it nonetheless appears to represent the law. In this respect Irish law is in marked contrast with that of the United States, as witness the statement of Rehnquist J., for the majority, in the *Valley Forge Christian College* case[37]:

> "This Court repeatedly has rejected claims of standing predicated on 'the right, possessed by every citizen, to require that the Government be administered according to law' . . . "[38]

Though issues of *locus standi* have been raised much more frequently by the defence in constitutional cases since *Cahill* v. *Sutton*, any fears that the gates of the courts were being shut have so far proved without foundation. No one has been turned away on this ground—though some plaintiffs have had subsidiary arguments dismissed. Thus in *Norris* v. *Att. Gen.* the plaintiff was challenging certain 19th century statutes which penalised homosexual conduct between consenting male adults in private. He contended (*inter alia*) that aspects of these Acts also struck at certain conduct by

---

the right to vote—"the fundamental political right of representative democracy"—every elector or candidate had the requisite interest to challenge provisions thereof likely to affect his/her vote or candidature adversely.

[36] See Walsh J. at [1987] I.R. 713, at 779: Henchy J. at 786–87: Griffin J. at 793.

[37] *Valley Forge Christian College* v. *Americans United for Separation of Church and State, Inc.* (1982) 454 U.S. 464, 482–83. For a severe criticism of this decision see Laurence Tribe, *Constitutional Choices* (Cambridge, Mass., 1985), Chap. 8.

[38] See further James Casey, "*Crotty* v. *An Taoiseach*: A Comparative Perspective" in James O'Reilly (ed.), *Human Rights and Constitutional Law: Essays in Honour of Brian Walsh* (Dublin 1992), p. 189.

married persons, and thus unconstitutionally invaded marital privacy. But the Supreme Court refused to consider this matter since the plaintiff was not married and had indicated that he never would be. Equally, in *Madigan* v. *Att. Gen.* [1986] I.L.R.M. 136 the plaintiffs claimed that Part VI of the Finance Act 1983, which introduced a residential property tax, was invalid. In the High Court the plaintiffs advanced arguments based not only on their own factual circumstances but also on other hypothetical situations. O'Hanlon J. refused to consider the latter contentions and on appeal the Supreme Court upheld this conclusion. Thus, for example, an argument based on the impact of this tax on persons who lived abroad but retained an Irish domicile could not be considered.[39] In *Madigan's* case counsel for the plaintiffs had founded on an observation by Ó Dálaigh C.J. in *O'Brien* v. *Keogh* ([1972] I.R. 144, 157):

> " . . . where a question of the constitutionality of a statutory provision is raised before the Court, the Court's duty in testing the provision is to examine it in as wide a manner as if the provision had been the subject of a reference under Article 26 of the Constitution; that is to say, the Court must advert as best it can to the full scope of the provision away and beyond the problem presented by the circumstances of the particular case then before the Court."

But O'Hanlon J. held that this dictum was inconsistent with the later decisions in the *Cahill* and *King* cases. On appeal the Supreme Court did not specifically refer to this matter; however its approval of O'Hanlon J.'s conclusions on *locus standi* can only mean that Ó Dálaigh C.J.'s observation is no longer good law.

The presumption of constitutionality

The presumption of constitutionality has two facets, the first relating to the onus of proof in constitutional cases, the second to the interpretation of challenged statutes. To date the latter has been much the more significant.

The first aspect of the presumption was thus explained by the Supreme Court, *per* Ó Dálaigh C.J., in *Ryan* v. *Att. Gen.* [1965] I.R. 294, 353:

> "There is a presumption that a statute is constitutional and the onus of showing that it is unconstitutional rests on the plaintiff who attacks it. Where on the face of the statute nothing unconstitutional appears and the attack is based on its alleged effect, and the conclusion as to the effect has to be based on evidence of a disputed character, a plaintiff must fully satisfy the Court that its effect is such as he contends."

This aspect of the presumption applies also to Bills referred to the Supreme Court by the President under Article 26,[40] and to resolutions of both Houses of the Oireachtas (*e.g.* to establish a tribunal of inquiry under the Tribunals of Inquiry (Evidence) Acts 1921 and 1979.)[41]

---

[39] See also *King* v. *Att. Gen.* [1981] I.R. 233, 250, 258, 263.
[40] *Re Art. 26 and the Criminal Law (Jurisdiction) Bill 1975* [1977] I.R. 129, 144: *Re Article 26 and the Adoption (No. 2) Bill 1987* [1989] I.R. 656, 660.
[41] *Goodman International* v. *Hamilton* [1992] I.L.R.M. 145 where Finlay C.J. said (at 165): "It seems to me inescapable that having regard to the fact that the presumption of constitutional validity which attaches to both statutes and bills derives, as the authorities clearly establish, from the respect shown by our organ of State to another, and by the necessary comity between

In many constitutional cases the effect of a challenged statute is easily proved, or indeed may be admitted; and the outcome turns on a pure question of constitutional interpretation—does the provision invoked have the meaning, or reach, contended for by the plaintiff? (See *Ryan* v. *Att. Gen.* [1965] I.R. 294, at 343.) In such situations the presumption scarcely matters. But *Ryan's* case illustrates those situations where it does come into play.[42] The challenge there was to legislation providing for the compulsory fluoridation of public water supplies. This, contended the plaintiff, violated her constitutional rights and those of her family. In essence, the plaintiff's main argument was that fluoridation was dangerous to health, and thus compulsory fluoridation must violate the implicit constitutional right to bodily integrity. The case was before the High Court for 65 days, most of that time being taken up with highly technical scientific evidence as to the benefits, or dangers, of fluoridation. Kenny J. found that the evidence led by the plaintiff had failed to show that the statutory level of fluoridation was harmful to health. On appeal the Supreme Court held that these findings were correct and unimpeachable on the evidence given.

In recent times evidence has been a vital factor in cases involving the Constitution's property rights guarantees. This is particularly true of *Blake* v. *Att. Gen.* and *Brennan* v. *Att. Gen.* (as to which see Chap. 18 *infra*). As the High Court judgment of Barrington J. in the latter case ([1984] I.L.R.M. 449) shows, evidence—some of a highly technical character—was given by soil scientists and statisticians. Economists and auctioneers also testified, and in addition there was a large volume of documentary evidence. In that case, as also in *Blake* v. *Att. Gen.*, the plaintiffs succeeded in rebutting the presumption and the legislation impugned was held to be invalid.

Where the challenged legislation is, on its face, clearly in violation of some constitutional provision the presumption is inapplicable—*M* v. *An Bord Uchtála* [1975] I.R. 81, 86–87 *per* Pringle J. Nor does it apply to legislation antedating the Constitution, whether passed by the Westminster Parliament or by the Oireachtas under the 1922 Constitution: see the Supreme Court's decisions in *State (Quinn)* v. *Ryan* [1965] I.R. 70, 125: *State (Sheerin)* v. *Kennedy* [1966] I.R. 379, 386 and *McMahon* v. *Att. Gen.* [1972] I.R. 69, 101. If, however, a provision in a pre-Constitution statute is extended and expanded by a post-Constitution amendment, the entire provision will benefit from the presumption: *E.S.B.* v. *Gormley* [1985] I.L.R.M. 494, 498. But it should not be assumed from this that pre-Constitution Acts are more vulnerable to challenge than later measures. In practice a plaintiff challenging a pre-Constitu-

the different organs of State, then it must apply in precisely the same way to a resolution of both Houses of the Oireachtas, even though it does not constitute legislation."

In *McGimpsey* v. *Ireland* [1988] I.R. 567 Barrington J. took the view that, given its basis in the respect owed by one organ of State to another, the presumption should also apply to a treaty. He said (at 582): " . . . unless the treaty expressly contradicts some provision of the Constitution the onus is on the plaintiff clearly to establish that the Government has violated the Constitution in entering into the treaty. This onus must necessarily be a heavy one. The conduct of the foreign policy of the State is not a matter which easily lends itself to judicial review and if there is any area in which judicial restraint is appropriate, that is it." On appeal the Supreme Court made no reference to this issue: [1990] 1 I.R. 110.

[42] If a lower court, about to hear a case involving a challenged post-Constitution statute, is asked for an adjournment pending resolution of that challenge, the presumption will be an important factor in the exercise of discretion: see *State (Llewellyn)* v. *Ó Donnchadha* [1973] I.R. 151.

tion statute—of whatever vintage—may face as heavy a burden as if he/she were impugning a more recent Act. In *Norris* v. *Att. Gen.* [1984] I.R. 36, O'Higgins C.J. (Finlay P. and Griffin J. concurring) noted that pre-Constitution statutes, under Article 50.1, continued to be of full force and effect "subject to this Constitution and to the extent to which they are not inconsistent therewith." This meant, said the Chief Justice, that the laws in question operated unless inconsistency was established; and the onus of establishing such inconsistency was placed on the person who challenged their continued validity. He added that this was not to say that such laws enjoyed a presumption of constitutionality; they did not. Nonetheless, the effect of this decision and that in *Garvey's* case *infra* is to blur the distinction between pre- and post-Constitution Acts.

The general rule in legal proceedings is that the person who asserts must prove: thus it is not easy to see what the onus of proof aspect of the presumption adds. (In the *Paperlink* and *Cafolla* cases—discussed in Chapter 12 *infra*—Costello J. rejected attempts to place on the State the onus of proving a statute valid.) The interpretation aspect, however, is a different matter. Here the *locus classicus* is the Supreme Court's judgment in *East Donegal Co-op Ltd.* v. *Att. Gen.* [1970] I.R. 317, where it was laid down that if a statutory provision is open to differing constructions, one constitutional, the other not, the court must opt for the former. This may mean choosing the narrower of the possible meanings, and the result may be to cut down considerably the scope of the relevant provision.[43] It follows that this facet of the presumption may operate—though at a cost—to save a provision from condemnation. In *Re Haughey* [1971] I.R. 217 a portion of the challenged statute provided that if a witness before the Dáil's Public Accounts Committee refused to answer a lawful question, he should be guilty of an offence. Section 3(4) then said that the committee's chairman could " . . . certify the offence of that person . . . to the High Court . . . ," which could then punish him as if he had been guilty of contempt of the High Court. Counsel for the plaintiff argued that the words quoted meant that the committee was empowered to try and to convict the witness, and to send him on to the High Court only for sentence. The Supreme Court, *per* Ó Dálaigh C.J., noted that this was the committee's interpretation; and if one applied the ordinary canons of construction to section 3(4) that view had much to commend it. But that would mean an invalid bestowal of judicial power on persons who were not judges, so that section 3(4) would be unconstitutional. Therefore it was the court's duty to apply different canons of construction, to preserve if possible the validity of section 3(4). It did so by holding the certificate equivalent to a summons or indictment—*i.e.* trial, conviction and sentence were exclusively for the High Court, the certificate being merely the machinery for getting the case before that court. (This saved the Act only temporarily, for it fell on another ground examined later in the judgment.)

It was emphasised in the *East Donegal* case that this benevolent technique has its limits. If the challenged provision is clear and unambiguous—and invalid on that basis—it may not be saved by giving it a construction which

---

[43] In *McGimpsey* v. *Ireland* [1988] I.R. 567 Barrington J. held that this would have no application to the interpretation of treaties: "An international treaty has only one meaning and that is its meaning in international law" (at 582). However, the German Constitutional Court held the presumption of constitutionality applicable to the interpretation of a treaty between the

does violence to its language. The constitutional construction which the courts are obliged to prefer must be one that is fairly and reasonably open given the language used. It is not for the courts to indulge in legislating, under the guise of interpreting.

Since, as explained above, pre-Constitution Acts do not benefit from the presumption of constitutionality, it should logically follow that this beneficial rule of construction does not apply to them. However, the Supreme Court held in *Garvey* v. *Ireland* [1981] I.R. 75 that section 6(2) of the Police Forces Amalgamation Act 1925 had to be operated and applied in a constitutional manner. The court did not say that the provision attracted the presumption in its interpretative aspect, but its conclusion is not far distant from this.

The *East Donegal Co-op.* doctrine also involves the proposition that all powers conferred by the relevant Act are to be exercised conformably with the Constitution.[44] Thus in *Harvey* v. *Minister for Social Welfare* [1990] 2 I.R. 232 it was claimed that section 75 of the Social Welfare Act 1952 invalidly delegated legislative power to the Minister. Finlay C.J., for the Supreme Court, having referred to the *East Donegal Co-op.* case, continued ([1991] 2 I.R. 232, 241):

> "The Court is satisfied that the terms of s.75 of the Act of 1952 do not make it necessary or inevitable that a Minister for Social Welfare making regulations pursuant to the power therein created must invade the function of the Oireachtas in a manner which would constitute a breach of the provisions of Article 15, s.2 of the Constitution. The wide scope and unfettered discretion contained in the section can clearly be exercised by a Minister making regulations so as to ensure that what is done is truly regulatory or administrative only and does not constitute the making, repealing or amending of law in a manner which would be invalid having regard to the provisions of the Constitution."[45]

Severance

In some instances a court will find that part only of a statutory provision is infected with unconstitutionality; the vice may lie in a phrase or a single word. In such cases the court may find it possible to invalidate that phrase or word alone, so that the rest of the provision remains in effect and capable of being operated. But this possibility will not always be open, as *Maher* v. *Att. Gen.* shows. There it was laid down that the invalid portion may be severed only if: (a) the rest can survive independently and be

former Federal and Democratic Republics: *Basic East–West Treaty Case* (1973), translated in Walter Murphy and Joseph Tanenhaus, *Comparative Constitutional Law: Cases and Commentaries* (New York, 1977), pp. 232–239.

[44] And that " . . . the Oireachtas intended that proceedings, procedures, discretions, and adjudications which are permitted, provided for or prescribed by an Act . . . are to be conducted in accordance with the principles of constitutional justice": *per* Walsh J. [1970] I.R. 317, 341. In *Goodman International* v. *Hamilton* [1992] I.L.R.M. 145 this was held applicable to a tribunal of inquiry established by Oireachtas resolutions under the Tribunals of Inquiry (Evidence) Acts 1921 and 1979.

[45] The court went on to hold that portion of the regulations there impugned (the Social Welfare (Overlapping Benefits) (Amendment) Regulations 1979, S.I. No. 118 of 1979) were in direct contradiction to the provisions of the Social Welfare Act 1979, s.7. This was an unconstitutional use of the power vested in the Minister, and the relevant portion of the regulations was *ultra vires*.

capable of being operated independently; (b) that in its truncated form the provision is compatible with the legislative intent and policy.[46]

In *King* v. *Att. Gen.* [1981] I.R. 233, 251, O'Higgins C.J. suggested that while legislative intent was relevant to severance issues affecting post-Constitution Acts, it had none where pre-Constitution statutes were concerned. But the majority of the Supreme Court disagreed. Henchy J. (Griffin and Parke JJ. concurring) said (at 260):

> " . . . Article 50, s.1 cannot be held to give the Courts power to declare that a truncated or residual part of a statutory provision has constitutional validity as a law, unless the relevant court first finds that such part had the force of law in Saorstát Éireann immediately prior to the coming into operation of the present Constitution. This necessarily involves a finding that, in that form and to that extent, it was expressly or impliedly enacted as a law by the legislative authority or authorities from which it emanated."[47]

In the *King* case this produced an odd result. It was held that certain portions of section 4 of the Vagrancy Act 1824 were inconsistent with the Constitution, and had ceased to have any force or effect. But the tainted portions, the majority held, could not be severed. Nor could the whole of section 4 be condemned, because the plaintiff lacked *locus standi* to raise that more general challenge. "Limbo" is presumably the appropriate term for the curious constitutional half-world to which section 4 has now been consigned!

The case of *T. O'G.* v. *Att. Gen.* [1985] I.L.R.M. 61 seems to represent a gloss on the principles stated above. There the plaintiff and his wife—a childless couple—were in process of adopting a child, who had been in their custody for six months. Before the adoption order could be made the plaintiff's wife was killed in a road accident, and because of this he found that the adoption could not now take place. This consequence flowed from the Adoption Act 1974, s.5(1) which provided that, in circumstances such as these, a widower could adopt only if he had another child in his custody. The plaintiff did not satisfy this condition, and he brought proceedings for a declaration that section 5(1) was invalid. McMahon J. held that it did indeed violate the equality guarantee of Article 40.1. The severance issue arose because if all of section 5(1) fell, the plaintiff's victory would have been a Pyrrhic one; no widower would have been eligible to adopt a child. Consequently it was argued that invalidity attached only to the proviso—*i.e.* the requirement that an eligible widower must have another child in his custody. McMahon J. concluded that the proviso was severable; the section, in his view, would have been enacted without the proviso had it been realised that it was repugnant to the Constitution.

> "The purpose of the section is to avoid disrupting the child/parent relationship on the death of the wife. If the Legislature had appreciated that the guarantee of human equality in the Constitution required that the widower should be entitled to obtain an adoption order where he did not have another child in his custody the section would have been enacted without the proviso." ([1985] I.L.R.M. 61 65–66)

---

[46] The United States Supreme Court applies similar tests: see *Alaska Airlines, Inc.* v. *Brock* (1987) 480 U.S. 678.

[47] Finlay P. had anticipated this reasoning in *State (Att. Gen.)* v. *Shaw* [1979] I.R. 136.

Everyone will appreciate the humanity and sympathy of the result thus achieved; but whether it is consistent with the principles set out earlier is doubtful. To ask whether the Oireachtas would have done something had it suspected it might be invalid is wholly speculative. Where this the true test then surely *Maher's* case would have had a different outcome on the severance question, with amending legislation being unnecessary. In the adoption sphere, the pattern since the original Act of 1952 shows a gradual and cautious widening of the categories of persons eligible to adopt. It is difficult to be certain that, had the Oireachtas realised its 1974 extension might be partly invalid, it might not have preferred the status quo.

Effect of a ruling of invalidity

The precise effect of a ruling that a statute—or a provision thereof—is invalid or inconsistent is an issue that has arisen only in recent years. The problem may be stated thus: if in 1992 a court holds a 1952 statute unconstitutional this clearly means that, in technical terms, the Act is invalid under Article 15.4. But from when? The date of its enactment—*i.e.* its signature by the President in 1952? The date when the court gives judgment in 1992—or some other date? And are matters different where the condemned measure is a pre-Constitution Act held inconsistent under Article 50?

In *Murphy* v. *Att. Gen.* [1982] I.R. 241 the plaintiffs attacked the provisions of the Income Tax Act 1967 dealing with the taxation of working married couples. It was contended that, whatever the position in 1967, changes in tax rates, and the effect of inflation, meant that such couples were now treated less favourably than people who simply chose to live together. This could not be squared with the guarantee of equality before the law (Art. 40.1) or the guarantees regarding the family based on marriage (Art. 41). The Supreme Court found for the plaintiffs on the latter ground. As the report shows, the court was subsequently asked to clarify its judgment by specifying the date from which the relevant provisions were invalid. This, of course, was a vital issue from the State's point of view. If the relevant provisions had always been invalid, the bill for overpaid tax— for all such couples—might be enormous. The Supreme Court held that this matter was not covered by the "one opinion rule" of Article 34.4.5°, and so separate judgments were delivered: see O'Higgins C.J. [1982] I.R. 241, 293. By a 4–1 majority it was held that the relevant provisions were invalid from the date of enactment: see Henchy J. (Parke J. concurring) at 308–313: Griffin J. (Parke J. concurring) at 328–331: and Kenny J. at 333. In particular, it was held that the terms of the Constitution ruled out any possibility that the courts could hold legislation invalid prospectively only, or with limited retrospectivity.[48]

Where a pre-Constitution Act is held inconsistent under Article 50, it must apparently be deemed to have bitten the dust in 1937. As Henchy J. graphically put in *Murphy's* case ([1982] I.R. 241, 307):

"Such a declaration under Article 50, s.1 amounts to a judicial death

---

[48] Matters are different where the issue is the alleged retrospectivity of a judicial decision. It has been sought to give retrospective effect to the Supreme Court's decision in *State (Clarke)* v. *Roche* [1986] I.R. 619, so as to invalidate summonses, and District Court convictions founded

certificate, with the date of death stated as the date when the Constitution came into operation."

But the Constitution (here exhibiting a Transylvanian or Caribbean influence) nonetheless recognises the statutory undead, or zombie Act. So although the relevant provisions of the Income Tax Act, 1967 were invalid from the date when the President signed the Bill, this did not mean they were totally without effect. The Supreme Court, while cleaving to the principle of invalidity *ab initio*, was able to avoid its consequences by deploying the equitable notions of laches (delay) and waiver. In *Murphy's* case, therefore, the plaintiffs could obtain tax refunds only from the tax year 1978–79, the year in which they had begun their proceedings. Other couples would be able to recoup only from the tax year 1980–81 (the Supreme Court's judgment having been given on January 25, 1980)—or an earlier year if they had commenced proceedings therein. Henchy J. put the matter thus ([1982] I.R. 241, 318):

> " . . . the plaintiffs' right to recover the sums by which they claim the State was unjustly enriched, by the collection of the taxes that have now been held to have been unconstitutionally imposed, begins for the year 1978–79, that is, the first year for which they effectively objected to the flow of those taxes into the central fund. Up to that year the State was entitled, in the absence of any claim of unconstitutionality, to act on the assumption that the taxes in question were validly imposed, that they were properly transmissible to the central fund, and that from there they were liable to be expended, according to the will of Parliament, for the multiplicity of purposes for which drawings are made on the central fund of the State. Equally, every taxpayer whose income tax was deducted from his earnings throughout a particular tax year . . . could not avoid having imputed to him the knowledge that the tax he was paying was liable to be immediately spent by the State. As time went by, his right to complain of the State's unjust enrichment ran the risk of being extinguished by laches on his part."

Analogous reasoning—this time based on the notion of waiver—had been employed in *State (Byrne)* v. *Frawley* [1978] I.R. 326. The prosecutor there had been convicted by a jury in the Circuit Court. That jury had been empanelled under the Juries Act 1927, which on December 12, 1975 the Supreme Court held inconsistent with the Constitution: *de Burca and Anderson* v. *Att. Gen.* [1976] I.R. 38. The prosecutor's trial began before, and was concluded after, December 12. He now sought habeas corpus on the ground that he was not being detained in accordance with law, the jury which convicted him having been chosen unconstitutionally. A divisional court of the High Court (Finlay P., Murnaghan and McMahon JJ.) rejected this claim, as did the Supreme Court on appeal. While the decision was unanimous the Supreme Court was divided as to the reasons, Henchy, Griffin and Parke JJ. taking a different view from O'Higgins C.J. and Kenny J. The majority founded on the facts that the prosecutor had had an opportunity, in the middle of his trial, to object to the jury's composition; this he had not taken. And although

---

thereon, which had been issued before that ruling. But in *White* v. *Hussey* [1989] I.L.R.M. 109 Barr. J. was of opinion that had the Supreme Court intended its decision to have retrospective effect, it would specifically have said so. See also *Connors* v. *Delap* [1989] I.L.R.M. 93.

he had appealed to the Court of Criminal Appeal, his grounds of appeal did not refer to the composition of the jury. It was not until some five months after his trial that he first complained of this matter. Now it was too late for him to raise the issue. Henchy J. concluded thus ([1978] I.R. 326, 350):

> "The constitutional right to a jury drawn from a representative pool existed for his benefit. Having knowingly elected not to claim that right, it would be contrary to the due administration of justice under the Constitution if he were to raise the claim in the present proceedings when, by deliberate choice, it was left unasserted at the trial and subsequently in the Court of Criminal Appeal. What has been lost in the process of events is not the right guaranteed by the Constitution but the prisoner's competence to lay claim to it in the circumstances of this case."

In *Reid* v. *Limerick Corporation* [1985] I.L.R.M. 366 the defendants had compulsorily acquired, under the Housing Act 1966, certain property owned by the plaintiff. An arbitration was held, under the Acquisition of Land (Assessment of Compensation) Act 1919, to determine the compensation payable. For the purposes of this arbitration the valuation date was, by virtue of the 1966 Act, March 11, 1977—the date of the service of the notice to treat. And the applicable rule, under the 1919 Act, was that the value was open market value. On March 11, 1977 the plaintiffs' premises were let on tenancies controlled by the Rent Restrictions Acts 1960 and 1967. The arbitration, however, took place on March 9, 1982—and by that date the Supreme Court had given judgment in *Blake* v. *Att. Gen.* [1982] I.R. 117, holding the key provisions of the Rent Restrictions Act 1960 invalid. The arbitrator stated a case for the High Court under the 1919 Act. He wished to know if he was to value the premises on the basis that the Rent Acts were in force on March 11, 1977—in which case the total value would be £7250·00: or on the basis that those Acts were not applicable (because void *ab initio*)—in which case the total value would be £17,500.

Finlay P. referred to the Supreme Court majority's conclusion in *Murphy* v. *Att. Gen.*—that the courts may have to accept and recognise things done under an invalid statute. Here, if the court held that the arbitrator was to value these premises on the basis that the Rent Restriction Acts did not apply to them in March 1977, it would be saying he should find as a fact something that was palpably untrue. Consequently the arbitrator must value the premises on the basis that on the valuation date the Rent Restrictions Acts were valid measures.

Counsel for the plaintiff had referred to Article 40.3, under which the State guarantees (*inter alia*) to protect property rights against unjust attack, and to vindicate those rights if injustice was done. This obligation, it was contended, fell on the courts as much as on the other branches of government, and it would entitle the court in this case to hold that the valuation should ignore the Rent Restrictions Acts. But the form of the proceedings, said Finlay P., militated against this conclusion. The claimant was seeking to operate a statutory machinery for assessing the value of her property at a particular time and in a particular manner. That task was allotted to the arbitrator and to him alone. Since he was not a High Court judge it would not be open to him to award the plaintiff any form of damages or compensation for the consequences of the enactment of the Rent Restrictions Acts. Nor would it be appropriate for the High Court to answer the question of law raised under

298 *Constitutional Issues in the Courts*

the statutes which bound his arbitration in a fashion that would give such relief. (Finlay P.'s decision was affirmed on appeal by the Supreme Court: [1987] I.L.R.M. 83).

No such procedural problem would arise if a plaintiff in a similar case sought damages from the State for failure to protect her constitutional rights. This matter is further considered at Chapter 18 *infra*.

The doctrine that an Act held unconstitutional is void *ab initio* gives rise to questions as yet unanswered. One is illustrated by the Road Traffic (Amendment) Act 1973, s.7. This amended section 44(2) of the 1968 Act, which had been held invalid in *Maher* v. *Att. Gen.* (see p. 000 *supra*); and it did so by substituting for "conclusive evidence" the words "be sufficient evidence until the contrary is shown." But was there anything to amend? The Supreme Court had held the entire subsection invalid; and the decision in *Murphy* v. *Att. Gen.* [1982] I.R. 241 means that it was without legal effect from the time of passage—see the *Housing (Private Rented Dwellings) Bill* case [1983] I.R. 181 at 186. Thus the method of amendment chosen might not seem open to the Oireachtas. Section 7, however, declares that section 44 is to "have effect as set out in the Table to this section," and that Table sets out the entire text of section 44 as amended. Perhaps, then, this may be taken as a re-enactment of section 44.

The majority conclusion in the *Murphy* case bears upon a problem which still awaits resolution—if the Supreme Court overrules one of its earlier decisions holding a statute invalid, is the effect to revive the statute? Or must the Oireachtas, the way now having been cleared, re-enact the measure? In the United States re-enactment is not required: see *Chicot County Drainage District* v. *Baxter State Bank* (1940) 308 U.S. 371, 374. But in Ireland re-enactment *may* be necessary. In *Murphy's* case it was pointed out that whereas judicial review of statutes arises only by implication under the United States Constitution, Bunreacht na hÉireann specifically provides therefor; and there are other differences between the two which were held to make some American options unavailable to the courts here. It should be noted, however, that the question posed above was not specifically referred to in the *Murphy* judgments.

As Professor McMahon has suggested, it is possible to provide an analysis which would obviate the need for any re-enactment.[49] To be law, a measure must fulfil two conditions—(a) pass through the legislative process; (b) conform to the Constitution. If an Act is held invalid, condition (b) is not satisfied; but if the decision as to invalidity is later overruled, then both conditions would seem to be fulfilled. The invalidity flows from the earlier decision, and if that is overruled the invalidity arguably no longer exists. On this basis, the *Chicot County* doctrine could be accepted in Ireland. It would fit in with the observable fact that a judicial finding of unconstitutionality does not *repeal* a statutory provision.

Precedent in constitutional cases

The Supreme Court indicated, in *State (Quinn)* v. *Ryan* [1965] I.R. 70, that it would hold itself free to depart, where necessary, from its own earlier decisions in constitutional cases. *A fortiori* the same freedom applied in regard

[49] See (1981) XVI *Irish Jurist* (n.s.) at 200.

to decisions of the former (pre-1961) Supreme Court. This gave the court the same liberty as was enjoyed by its United States and Australian counterparts. This freedom has since been used; in *Blake* v. *Att. Gen.* [1982] I.R. 117 the court overruled an earlier decision in *Att. Gen.* v. *Southern Industrial Trust* (1957) 94 I.L.T.R. 161. And as noted *supra*, *Costello* v. *D.P.P. and Att. Gen.* [1984] I.R. 436 overruled *State (Shanahan)* v. *Att. Gen.* [1964] I.R. 239.[50]

Even now, many issues coming before the Supreme Court are there for the first time. Consequently the power to depart from earlier decisions has seldom had to be invoked. With the passage of time and the accretion of decisions, however, it will inevitably become more important. And as it does, so the disadvantages of Articles 26.2.2° and 34.4.5° will become more apparent. Both provisions impose on the judges of the Supreme Court a "one opinion rule"—the former in Article 26, and the latter in ordinary, cases. The result is that the court may produce only one judgment; dissents, or concurrences with reasoning different from the main judgment, are alike forbidden. Even their existence may not be disclosed. This restriction does not apply to pre-Constitution Acts—or to constitutional questions other than the validity of a post-Constitution statute; and the many cases involving such matters show plainly and unmistakeably that the judges are not always of one mind. There is no reason to suppose that a similar divergence of opinion may not occur in a case involving a post-Constitution Act—but here an artificial unanimity is imposed upon the court. This is unfortunate, because one factor that may lead to the re-examination of an earlier decision is the existence of a cogent dissent, as a wealth of United States experience testifies.

The "one opinion rule" of Articles 26 and 34 formed no part of Bunreacht na hÉireann as originally enacted by the people; it was inserted by statute in 1941, during the period when the Oireachtas could amend the Constitution without a referendum. (Thus in *Re Article 26 and the Offences against the State (Amendment) Bill 1940* Sullivan C.J. said that the decision now announced was "the decision of the majority of the Judges": [1940] I.R. 470, 475.) The judges are, to say the least, not enamoured of the rule, and have successfully striven to limit its operation.[51] In 1970 the Committee on Court Practice and Procedure suggested that the rule should be abolished, stigmatising it as "undesirable and injurious" and inhibiting the development of constitutional case law. The committee also pointed to the anomaly that if the case on appeal had been heard by a divisional court of the High Court, several

---

[50] In *McGimpsey* v. *Ireland* [1990] 1 I.R. 110 the court disavowed the statements about Arts. 2 and 3 in its judgment in *Re Article 26 and the Criminal Law (Jurisdiction) Bill 1975* [1977] I.R. 129.

[51] This was true until *State (Gilliland)* v. *Governor, Mountjoy Prison* [1987] I.L.R.M. 278 where the Supreme Court held, by a 3–2 majority, that a 1984 statutory instrument made under the Extradition Act 1965 and applying that Act to the United States was a "law" for the purposes of Art. 40.4.3°. With unimpeachable logic the majority, noting that the words "validity of such law" were common to Arts. 40.4.3° and 34.4.5°, held that the latter's "one opinion rule" must apply to the judgment on the substantive issue. Hederman J., who dissented, concluded that Art. 40 used "law" in different ways. In Art. 40.4.1° and 2° it clearly meant the whole body of the law; but in Art. 40.3.2° it meant an Act of the Oireachtas, and this interpretation was reinforced by a consideration of Art. 15 McCarthy J., also dissenting, agreed with this reasoning and also pointed out that the majority's conclusion meant that the 1984 statutory instrument was being accorded a cachet denied to pre-Constitution statutes. He also noted that in *Quinn's Supermarket Ltd.* v. *Att. Gen.* [1972] I.R. 1, the Supreme Court, though holding a 1948 statutory instrument constitutionally invalid, did not apply the "one opinion rule."

opinions might have been pronounced publicly in that court, as in *State (Nicolaou)* v. *An Bord Uchtála* [1966] I.R. 567.[52] That no action has been taken on this recommendation, despite several intervening referenda, may owe something to the fact that the Committee on the Constitution took a different view in its *Report* of December 1967.[53] That body concluded that it was the majority opinion which really mattered "and any publication of other opinions would only tend to create uncertainty in the minds of the people on matters of constitutional importance." But a great deal has happened in our constitutional law since that was written, and the somewhat paternalistic view there expressed now needs reconsideration.[54]

The one opinion rule has another disadvantage. If a majority of Supreme Court judges agree as to the disposition of a case but cannot reach agreement as to the reasons therefor, the only recourse is to announce the outcome—*i.e.* whether the appellant has succeeded or not. This would seem to have occurred in *State (Hunt)* v. *O'Donovan* [1975] I.R. 39.

Decisions of constitutional courts in other jurisdictions are frequently cited to, and mentioned by, Irish courts. This is particularly true of United States Supreme Court decisions, much less so of those from the High Court of Australia— which reflects the fact that many Irish constitutional cases involve fundamental rights issues on which the Australian Constitution has little to say. For similar reasons Canadian precedents have seldom been invoked, though this will presumably change with the spate of cases generated by the new Canadian Charter of Rights and Freedoms. (It is less easy to say why Indian precedents—potentially so instructive—have been overlooked.) But all such foreign decisions have persuasive authority only; and the Supreme Court has emphasised that, given the difference in some constitutional provisions between the two states, United States Supreme Court decisions must be used with care. See particularly *O'B.* v. *S.* [1984] I.R. 316.

CONSTITUTIONAL INTERPRETATION[55]

Some provisions of the Constitution are quite clear in their meaning—an example would be Article 12.6.1° ("The President shall not be a member of either House of the Oireachtas.") But many others are susceptible of differing interpretations. Article 7 provides that "the national flag is the tricolour of green, white and orange." If a future Government changed the design from vertical to horizontal bands would it be violating the Constitution? Does "tricolour" necessarily import vertical bands? Is the fact that vertical bands were in use when Bunreacht na hÉireann was enacted conclusive?

In several places Bunreacht na hÉireann poses similar problems of construction. As with other constitutions, the principles it lays down are very broadly expressed and the courts have a difficult task in giving them more precise definition. A number of interpretative techniques are available to

---

[52] See the Committee's Eleventh Interim Report (Prl. 1835), para. 24.

[53] Prl. 9817, para. 100.

[54] Though the case of *G.* v. *An Bord Uchtála* [1980] I.R. 32—discussed in Chap. 17 *infra*—might furnish support for an argument that the "one opinion rule" should be extended rather than abolished.

[55] See Gerard Hogan "Constitutional Interpretation" in Frank Litton (ed.), *The Constitution of Ireland 1937–1987* (Dublin 1988), pp. 173–191: David Gwynn Morgan "Constitutional Interpretation: Three Cautionary Tales" (1988) 10 *D.U.L.J.* 24.

them to carry out this function. These resemble the approaches to statutory interpretation, though the Supreme Court has denied that the "canons of construction" appropriate for statutes are applicable to constitutional interpretation: *State (Browne)* v. *Feran* [1967] I.R. 147, 159. The court also said in that case that the Constitution was the basic and fundamental law of the State and must be construed as such. Unfortunately, the import of this is not entirely clear—especially in view of the Supreme Court's later reminder that the Constitution is a political as well as a legal document: *Re Article 26 and the Criminal Law (Jurisdiction) Bill* [1977] I.R. 129, 147. Costello J. may have harmonised these observations in the *Paperlink* case [1984] I.L.R.M. 373, 385 when he said:

> "The Constitution is a political instrument as well as a legal document and in its interpretation the courts should not place the same significance on differences of language used in two succeeding sub-paragraphs as would, for example, be placed on differently drafted sub-sections of a Finance Act. A purposive, rather than a strictly literal, approach to the interpretation of the sub-paragraphs is appropriate."

It will be clear from what follows that the Supreme Court has applied different interpretative approaches to different constitutional provisions. Nor is it helpful to speak of preferring a broad and generous to a narrow and pedantic construction. As the Judicial Committee observed in *James* v. *Commonwealth of Australia* [1936] A.C. 578, this may not be of assistance where what has to be interpreted is a constitutional guarantee of rights.

Literal interpretation

In some situations the Supreme Court has given constitutional provisions an absolutely literal interpretation. This is most notably true of Article 34.4.3°, which lays down the general principle that the Supreme Court has appellate jurisdiction from all decisions of the High Court. Thus it has been held that an appeal lies against a Central Criminal Court conviction or acquittal (see Chap. 10, *supra*).[56]

People (D.P.P.) v. *O'Shea* [1982] I.R. 384 shows a marked difference of judicial opinion on the true construction of Article 34.4.3°. The majority— O'Higgins C.J., Walsh and Hederman JJ.—preferred to interpret "all decisions" literally. While accepting that a literal construction might be outweighed by countervailing considerations, they were unable to conclude that those canvassed here were sufficient to tilt the scales. In particular, the majority could not accept that Article 38.5's jury trial guarantee meant that there could be no appeal against an acquittal by a jury. The argument to this effect relied on the principle that at common law such verdicts were unappealable; but to interpret Article 34.4.3° by reference to such matters was, as O'Higgins C.J. put it, to rely on what was formerly the law and say that the Constitution could not achieve what it expressly provided for (at 403). The decision in *State (Browne)* v. *Feran* [1967] I.R. 147 rejected any such approach.

---

[56] Not all the provisions of Art. 34 have been given a literal interpretation. One would scarcely so describe the construction of "courts of local and limited jurisdiction" (Art. 34.3.4°) in *State (Boyle)* v. *Judge Neylon* [1986] I.R. 551, discussed in Chap. 10 *supra*.

O'Higgins C.J. summarised the majority's approach as follows ([1982] I.R. 384, 397–98):

"The Constitution, as the fundamental law of the State, must be accepted, interpreted and construed according to the words which are used; and those words, where the meaning is plain and unambiguous, must be given their literal meaning. Of course, the Constitution must be looked at as a whole and not merely in parts and, where doubt or ambiguity exists, regard may be had to other provisions of the Constitution and to the situation which obtained and the laws which were in force when it was enacted. Plain words must, however, be given their plain meaning unless qualified or restricted by the Constitution itself."

In some respects this passage is not a very helpful guide. The Chief Justice seems to indicate that recourse is to be had to the Constitution as a whole only where the immediately relevant provision is ambiguous. The difficulty is that sometimes a provision will seem perfectly plain when viewed in isolation; only when it is read in the wider context may an ambiguity emerge. It is noteworthy that in *East Donegal Co-Op. Ltd.* v. *Att. Gen.* [1970] I.R. 317 the Supreme Court rejected any such approach to the interpretation of *statutes*. There Walsh J., speaking for the court, said (at 341):

"The long title and the general scope of the Act . . . constitute the background of the context in which it must be examined. The whole or any part of the Act may be referred to and relied upon in seeking to construe any particular part of it, and the construction of any particular phrase requires that it is to be viewed in connection with the whole Act and not that it should be viewed detached from it. The words of the Act, and in particular the general words, cannot be read in isolation and their content is to be derived from their context. Therefore, words or phrases which at first sight might appear to be wide and general may be cut down in their construction when examined against the objects of the Act which are to be derived from a study of the Act as a whole including the long title. Until each part of the Act is examined in relation to the whole it would not be possible to say that any particular part of the Act was either clear or unambiguous."

It might be thought that the approach thus outlined would have equal validity when interpretation of the Constitution is in issue (see the remarks of Henchy J. in *Tormey* v. *Ireland* [1985] I.R. 289, 295–96 quoted *infra*.

A further problem arises with the rule that plain words are to be given their plain meaning; for the meaning that to one judge is plain may seem to another perverse and unreal. This is shown by *O'Byrne* v. *Minister for Finance* [1959] I.R. 1. Put in abstract terms the question there was—when Article 68 of the 1922 Constitution (and Art. 35.5 of Bunreacht na hÉireann) said that a judge's remuneration should not be diminished during his continuance in office, did this preclude the deduction of tax from his salary? In the High Court Dixon J. was of opinion that "the plain, ordinary meaning of the words" did not prevent such deduction ([1959] I.R. 1, 21)—a conclusion he fortified by reference to Article 68's broad historical background. His decision was approved by a 3–2 majority in the Supreme Court. There Kingsmill Moore J. did not accept that the words of Article 68, in their plain meaning, precluded taxation. But Lavery J. reached the opposite conclusion. For him, the words used plainly forbade deduction of tax; any other conclusion could rest only on unproved and unprovable assumptions as to what those who framed the Constitution intended.

Harmonious construction

To consider a specific statutory provision divorced from its overall context may mislead as to its meaning, and the same applies to constitutional provisions. The outstanding example is *Quinn's Supermarket Ltd.* v. *Att. Gen.*, but the point has arisen in other cases also. There is, however, an obvious limitation here. No doubt the Constitution should be so construed as to make it a harmonious whole; but it clearly does not follow that every provision thereof is capable of shedding light on the construction of another. The provisions on the Presidency are unlikely to assist in determining whether something is a minor offence under Article 38, or those on Seanad Éireann in deciding what is an "unjust attack" on property rights under Article 40.3.

In *Dreher* v. *Irish Land Commission* [1984] I.L.R.M. 94 the plaintiff's claim was that the statutory system under which compulsory acquisitions of land by the defendants were paid for in Land Bonds, not cash, was an unjust attack on his property rights, contrary to Article 40.3. The system, he argued, did not provide for fair compensation. The Supreme Court noted that the Land Purchase Acts had previously been upheld as conforming with Article 43 of the Constitution, and this had not been challenged in the instant case. But, said the court, any State action authorised by Article 43 and conforming to it could not by definition be unjust for the purpose of Article 40.3.2°. Similar reasoning is found in *O'B* v. *S.* [1984] I.R. 316, which concerned the intestate provisions of the Succession Act 1965. These, as the Supreme Court held, excluded illegitimate children from succeeding upon intestacy, so it was necessary to consider their compatibility with the Constitution. The respondent argued that such discrimination violated the equality guarantee of Article 40.1. The Supreme Court rejected this argument, founding upon Article 41 under which the State undertakes to protect the family based on marriage. To violate the equality guarantee, it was held, a discrimination must be unjust, unreasonable or arbitrary. But if that discrimination could be justified under some other provision of the Constitution, it could not fall foul of Article 40.1. And having regard to the constitutional guarantees relating to the family (Art. 41), the court was unable to find that the differences created by the Succession Act were necessarily unreasonable, unjust or arbitrary.

Where harmonious and literal interpretation lead to different conclusions the courts should prefer the former. The reasons underlying this choice were expressed by Henchy J., giving the judgment if the Supreme Court, in *Tormey* v. *Att. Gen.* [1985] I.R. 289, 295–96:

> "The rule of literal interpretation, which is generally applied in the absence of ambiguity or absurdity in the text, must here give way to the more fundamental rule of constitutional interpretation that the Constitution must be read as a whole and that its several provisions must not be looked at in isolation, but be treated as interlocking parts of the general constitutional scheme. This means that where two constructions

of a provision are open in the light of the Constitution as a whole, despite the apparent unambiguity of the provision itself, the Court should adopt the construction which will achieve the smooth and harmonious operation of the Constitution. A judicial attitude of strict construction should be avoided when it would allow the imperfection or inadequacy of the words used to defeat or pervert any of the fundamental purposes of the Constitution. It follows from such global approach that, save where the Constitution itself otherwise provides, all its provisions should be given due weight and effect and not be subordinated one to the other. Thus, where there are two provisions in apparent conflict with one another, there should be adopted, if possible, an interpretation which will give due and harmonious effect to both provisions. The true purpose and range of a Constitution would not be achieved if it were treated as no more than the sum of its parts."

Historical interpretation

The courts have often recognised that the history behind Bunreacht na hÉireann may be useful in construing its provisions. That Constitution, after all, was not written on a *tabula rasa*: many of its provisions are copied verbatim from the 1922 Constitution, while others have an even longer pedigree. One must note, however, that the Dáil debates on the draft Constitution have never been cited in judgments nor, it seems, referred to in argument before the courts. This contrasts with the position in the United States, where counsel and the courts often make use of corresponding (though much older) material—see, *e.g. Brown* v. *Board of Education* (1959) 347 U.S. 483: *Powell* v. *McCormack* (1969) 395 U.S. 486. The Irish practice, however, corresponds to that relating to the federal constitution in Australia. There the record of debates at the 1898 Constitutional Convention are not used by the courts as an aid to interpretation. One of the reasons for this rule is equally applicable in Ireland—that the delegates at that convention were merely producing a draft for submission to the people in a referendum.[57]

Many instances exist of the Irish courts invoking the aid of history in construing the Constitution. In *Re Article 26 and the Offences against the State (Amendment) Bill 1940* [1940] I.R. 470 the Supreme Court had to consider a measure which permitted internment by Ministerial warrant without trial. The court, *per* Sullivan C.J., noted that prior to the enactment of the Constitution, the Irish Free State Oireachtas had passed several Acts permitting executive detention. The framers of the Constitution must have known of the existence and effect of these Acts; yet the Constitution contained no express provision against such legislation. This was a matter to which the court must attach considerable weight, since many Articles of the Constitution prohibited in plain terms the passage of specified legislation. Much later, in *Conroy* v. *Att. Gen.* [1965] I.R. 411, the Supreme Court resolved that in determining whether an offence was minor under Article 38.2, secondary considerations were the state of the law when the Constitution was enacted, and public opinion at that time. (The court did not explain how the latter was to be discovered.) The court also observed that in 1937 the people gave themselves

---

[57] See Sir Richard Eggleston in *Labor and the Constitution 1972–1975* (Gareth Evans, ed., Melbourne 1977), p. 297.

the present Constitution with full knowledge of the existing structure of the courts and the modes of trial. A similar approach was adopted in *Re Haughey* [1971] I.R. 217, 254 in construing the words "courts of summary jurisdiction" in Article 38.2.

But historical considerations are not always treated as conclusive. In 1937 no appeal lay against an acquittal on indictment, yet this did not deter the Supreme Court from holding in *O'Shea's* case (*supra*) that such an appeal now lies under Article 34.4.3°. Similarly the voting system used in 1937 provided for qualified—not absolute—secrecy; nonetheless the Supreme Court ruled in *McMahon* v. *Att. Gen.* [1972] I.R. 69 that Article 16.1.4° required the latter. In both of these cases it might be said that the Supreme Court majority found that other considerations favoured a literal interpretation of the relevant constitutional provisions. The same cannot be said of *McGee* v. *Att. Gen.* [1974] I.R. 284. There it was claimed that part of section 17 of the Criminal Law (Amendment) Act 1935 was inconsistent with the Constitution, in that its practical effect was to forbid the use of contraceptives even to married persons. This, asserted the plaintiff, violated the personal rights and/or family guarantees of the Constitution (Arts. 40 and 41), which must be understood as guaranteeing marital privacy. Thus the plaintiff was not relying on a literal interpretation of the Constitution; on the contrary, she was arguing for an extended interpretation based on the implication of rights not specifically stated in the text.

O'Keeffe P. in the High Court rejected this argument. In his view, one had to assess the state of public opinion at the time the Constitution was enacted, to see whether it had the effect alleged. The 1935 Act was barely two years old when the Constitution was adopted, and section 17, though technically opposed, was adopted without a division. O'Keeffe P. could not accept that this reflected a public opinion in favour of such a right of privacy as the plaintiff alleged was guaranteed under the Constitution. However, by a 4–1 majority the Supreme Court reversed this decision. The court identified an implied constitutional right of privacy in the conduct of marital relations, following from Article 41 (Walsh J.) or Article 40.3 (Budd, Henchy and Griffin JJ.). And the impugned portion of section 17 invalidly intruded on this. The point taken by O'Keeffe P. was not referred to, nor did the court explain fully whence this constitutional right of marital privacy originated.

In the *McGee* case Walsh J. stressed a factor militating against a purely historical interpretation of the Constitution—its character as the fundamental law. This point was reiterated by O'Higgins C.J. in *State (Healy)* v. *Donoghue* [1976] I.R. 325, 347:

> "The preamble to the Constitution records that the people 'seeking to promote the common good, with due observance of prudence, justice and charity, so that the dignity and freedom of the individual may be assured, true social order attained, the unity of our country restored, and concord established with other nations, do hereby adopt, enact and give to ourselves this Constitution.' In my view, this preamble makes it clear that rights given by the Constitution must be considered in accordance with concepts of prudence, justice and charity which may gradually change or develop as society changes and develops, and which fall to be interpreted from time to time in accordance with prevailing ideas. The preamble envisages a Constitution which can absorb or be adapted

to such changes. In other words, the Constitution did not seek to impose for all time the ideas prevalent or accepted with regard to these virtues at the time of its enactment."

McCarthy J., in *Norris* v. *Att. Gen.* [1984] I.R. 36, also stressed the need to treat the Constitution as a living document. But he was alive to a difficulty this involves—how can the courts discover what ideas of prudence, justice and charity prevailed in 1937? McCarthy J. referred to the impossibility of identifying the "standards and mores" of the Irish people in 1937—and added that it was no easy task to do so today ([1984] I.R. 36, 96).[58] Yet the notion of the Constitution as a living document plainly requires the courts to discharge the latter task—though we still lack an authoritative statement as to precisely how they are to do this.

Similar questions, it should be noted, have arisen elsewhere. In *Edwards* v. *Att. Gen. for Canada* [1930] A.C. 124 the issue was whether the word "persons" in section 24 of the British North America Act 1867 (the Canadian constitution) included women. Section 24 dealt with the composition of the Canadian Senate. Reversing the decision of the Canadian Supreme Court, the Judicial Committee held that "persons" did include women. It was irrelevant that in 1867 women did not have the vote, and could not hold public office, in the United Kingdom. As Lord Sankey L.C. put it, the "appeal to history" was not conclusive; rather it had to be recognised that the British North America Act had "planted in Canada a living tree capable of growth and expansion . . . "

Purposive interpretation

On occasion the Supreme Court has eschewed a literal interpretation of a constitutional provision in favour of one based upon its purpose. The pre-eminent example is *Quinn's Supermarket* v. *Att. Gen.* [1972] I.R. 1, which involved the construction of Article 44.2. This provision's guarantee of the free profession and practice of religion is peculiarly liable to conflict with its prohibition of discrimination (for or against) on the ground of religious belief. If observant Sikhs, obliged by their faith to wear turbans, cannot consequently wear safety helmets at work, may the law exempt them from an obligation imposed on all other persons? In the *Quinn's Supermarket* case the Supreme Court held that the primary aim and object of Article 44.2 was to guarantee the free practice and profession of religion. Consequently, a legislative discrimination in favour of a group, which was necessitated by that primary aim and object, would not offend against Article 44.2.3°. It would be completely contrary to the spirit and intendment of Article 44 to permit its non-discrimination provision to become the means of restricting or preventing the free profession or practice of religion.

In that case the dominant purpose of the relevant Article was discernible on its face. It would be an infinitely more difficult exercise to discover the purpose of certain other constitutional provisions, and any conclusion on the

---

[58] A view which seems to be confirmed by the subsequent Supreme Court decision in a non-constitutional case—*State (Keegan)* v. *Stardust Compensation Tribunal* [1986] I.R. 642—where it was held that administrative decisions could not be tested for unreasonableness by reference to "accepted moral standards," on the basis that this represented "a vague, elusive and changing body of standards which in a pluralist society is sometimes difficult to ascertain": *per* Henchy J. at 658.

point might risk being stigmatised as purely speculative. Here, however, history may assist, as is again evident from *O'Byrne* v. *Minister for Finance, supra.* There the majority of judges held that the purpose of guaranteeing judges' salaries against reduction was to preserve their independence. So much was clear from constitutional history, not only in Ireland but in other common law countries. But in 1922, when the Irish Free State Constitution was being drafted, judges' salaries had long been subject to tax without any suggestion that their independence was compromised thereby.

O'Byrne's case, it should be noted, is unusual in that all possible approaches to interpretation suggested the same answer—that there was (and is) nothing unconstitutional in taxing judge's salaries. Article 35.5 of the present Constitution, literally construed, does not forbid this, and history lends no support to the contrary view. Sections 2, 3 and 4 of that Article show plainly that its dominant theme is protection of judicial independence; thus the literal construction of section 5 accords with the Article's basic purpose and is in harmony with its other provisions.

A new approach?

None of the techniques outlined above can be said to be the dominant—much less the "correct"—approach. Constitutional interpretation is not, and cannot be, a mechanical process leading to a pre-ordained conclusion. No matter how inevitable a given judgment makes a particular conclusion seem, that conclusion results from a creative choice, and there will inevitably be room for differences of view as to its "correctness." It is important also to note that although the courts have the last word on constitutional interpretation, they are not the only branch of government to be concerned with this matter. Both executive and legislature may have to undertake this task,[59] in which they will necessarily be guided by the approaches of the courts.

In a perceptive essay Gerard Hogan[60] has analysed the existing approaches and found them wanting. The historical approach, he suggests, can offer little guidance on the constitutional problems of today.[61] (This, with respect, is too strong.) The doctrine of harmonious interpretation permits extra-constitutional principles to be smuggled in and also lends itself to subjective interpretation. What is required instead is an "approach that seeks to construe the Constitution from within its corners and upholds only those guarantees protected either expressly or by necessary implication."[62] But this valiant attempt to produce certainty seems destined to fail of its purpose. Within its corners the Constitution contains many vague phrases—such as the reiterated term "the common good," or the preamble's invocation of "Prudence, Justice and Charity." And one person's "necessary implication" may seem quite unnecessary—perhaps even fanciful—to another.

[59] *e.g.* Art. 15.10 (discussed in the debate on the Ministers and Secretaries (No. 2) Bill 1977: 301 *Dáil Debs.*, c. 768): Art. 15.11.1° (discussed in that on the Ombudsman Bill 1980: 320 *Dáil Debs.*, c. 1177: Art. 28 (discussed in the debate on the nomination of the Taoiseach in 1989: 391 *Dáil Debs.*, cc. 51–62, and in that on the National Treasury Management Agency Bill 1990: 401 *Dáil Debs.*, cc. 646–66).
[60] "Constitutional Interpretation" in *The Constitution of Ireland 1937–1987* (Frank Litton, ed., Dublin 1988), p. 173.
[61] p. 176.
[62] p. 188.

The late Professor John Kelly[63] offered the fruitful suggestion that a balance could be found between the historical approach and that which takes the constitution, in Walsh J.'s words, to be "speaking always in the present tense." Professor Kelly's view was that both had a part to play in constitutional interpretation—but in different areas. He wrote[64]:

> "1. The 'present-tense' approach is appropriate to *standards* and *values*. Thus elements like 'personal rights,' 'common good,' 'social justice,' 'equality,' and so on, can (indeed can only) be interpreted according to the lights of today as the judges perceive and share them. The same would go, as Walsh J. says in the context of the private property guarantees of Articles 40.3 and 43, for concepts like 'injustice.'
>
> 2. The historical approach, on the other hand, is appropriate where some law-based *system* is in issue, like jury trial, county councils and the census. These the Dáil and people built into the base of the state; if their removal or transformation is needed, it must be authorised by the people in a referendum; they cannot be whittled away by ordinary legislation subject only to 'present-tense' constitutional scrutiny.
>
> 3. This need not mean that the shape of such systems is in every respect fixed in the permafrost of 1937. The courts ought to have some leeway for considering which dimensions of a system are secondary, and which are so material to traditional constitutional values that a willingness to see them diluted or substantially abolished without a referendum could not be imputed to the enacting electorate."

As their author clearly recognised—he called them "rough rules"—these guidelines are far from being a sort of judicial computer programme. For example, it may not always be easy to discern what dimensions of a system are secondary; does the fact that in 1937 a jury decision had to be unanimous mean that the unanimity rule can be altered only by constitutional amendment?[65] But Professor Kelly has supplied a valuable insight into this difficult area, and its adoption by the courts would certainly assist in clarifying matters.

---

[63] Who was critical of the Supreme Court's "over-literal interpretation of a document not originally intended to be so minutely parsed and scrutinised": "Fundamental Rights and the Constitution," in *De Valera's Constitution and Ours* (Brian Farrell, ed., Dublin 1988), p. 170.

[64] "The Constitution: Law and Manifesto," in Litton, *op. cit.*, n. 60 *supra*, p. 215.

[65] See further Chap. 10 *supra*, *s.v.* The Jury in Criminal Cases.

12   Personal Rights and the Constitution

Articles 40–44 of the Constitution—which are headed "Fundamental Rights"—recognise and guarantee certain personal rights regarded as classical in liberal democracies. These include inviolability of the dwelling, freedom of association, expression and assembly, property rights and freedom of religion. But these Articles are emphatically not the only source of constitutionally-protected rights; other provisions play a role here too. Article 38.1's declaration that "No person shall be tried on any criminal charge save in due course of law" is a fount of rights in the sphere of criminal procedure,[1] while a series of rights in the electoral field flow from Article 16.[2] More generally, constitutional provisions imposing restrictions on the State or its institutions, which do not employ the language of rights, are nevertheless capable of generating them. Thus a person specially affected (at least[3]) may invoke the separation of powers provisions[4] or the non-retroactivity prohibition of Article 15.5.[5]

In addition to this, the Supreme Court accepted in the seminal case of *Ryan* v. *Att. Gen.* [1965] I.R. 294 that Article 40.3 of the Constitution guarantees rights not expressly enumerated elsewhere—a view which has never since been questioned. It would be difficult to exaggerate the importance of this doctrine of "unenumerated rights," the content of which is examined *infra*.

Self-executing rights

Most constitutional rights, whether enumerated or unenumerated, vest directly in their beneficiaries; they are "self-executing" and do not require any legislative action.[6] As Ó Dálaigh C.J. expressed it in *State (Meads)* v. *Govr., Portlaoise Prison* (Supreme Court, July 26, 1972):

> "The High Court is the appropriate forum for the declaration of human rights. Constitutional rights, for enforcement, do not require statutory vesture unless the Constitution itself were to express such a limitation."

---

[1] See further Chap. 14 *infra*, *s.v.* Trial in due course of law.
[2] See further Chap. 4 *supra*.
[3] See Chap. 11 *supra*, *s.v. locus standi*.
[4] See Chap. 9 *supra*.
[5] See *supra*.
[6] Cp. Henchy J. in *Re J., an infant* [1966] I.R. 295, 307: "I am satisfied that s.1 of the Legitimacy Act, 1931, operated to endow the child in this case with membership of a family founded on the institution of marriage. It is an example of the way in which certain constitutional rights—for example, citizenship and rights founded on citizenship—may be conferred by the operation of an Act of Parliament."

And in *Att. Gen. (S.P.U.C. (Ireland) Ltd.)* v. *Open Door Counselling Ltd.* [1988] I.R. 593, Finlay C.J. said (at 624–625):

> "The function of the courts . . . is not dependent on the existence of legislation, when their jurisdiction to defend and vindicate a constitutionally guaranteed right has been invoked . . . "

Thus the right of dissociation vests directly in individuals, who can enforce it against those who would deny it to them,[7] and the right to life of the unborn has likewise been treated as self-executing.[8]

Limiting rights

In *Murray* v. *Ireland* [1991] I.L.R.M. 465 McCarthy J. said (at 477):

> "It is difficult to identify a constitutional right that is unqualified, the right to life itself is not absolute (see Art. 13.6)."

The rights enumerated in Article 40 are all either expressly or implicitly subject to qualification. Freedom of expression, assembly and association are all "subject to public order and morality" (Art. 40.6.1°) and to specific individual qualification also. The rights to personal liberty and to inviolability of the dwelling are both subject to regulation "in accordance with law," a phrase which, while not giving the legislature *carte blanche*, clearly affords it some leeway. And the unenumerated rights, as is evident from their textual base in Article 40.3, are guaranteed "as far as practicable," and the State's obligation is to protect them "as best it may from unjust attack." This point was emphasised in *Moynihan* v. *Greensmith* [1977] I.R. 55, where O'Higgins C.J., for the court, said (at 71):

> " . . . the guarantee of protection given by Article 40, s.3, subs. 2, is qualified by the words 'as best it may.' This implies circumstances in which the State may have to balance its protection of the right as against other obligations arising from regard for the common good."

May one conclude from these textual differences that some constitutional rights have more protection against legislative interference than others? Costello J. has suggested that such an approach would be wrong. In *Murray* v. *Ireland* [1985] I.R. 532 he said (at 538–39):

> "The rights expressly referred to in the section of the Constitution headed 'Fundamental rights' are variously described and the language used to protect them is quite remarkably different. Thus the Family's rights are described in Article 41 as being 'alienable and imprescriptible' and as being 'antecedent and superior to all positive law,' whilst the right of parents to educate their children is described in Article 42 as being 'inalienable' but not as being 'imprescriptible.' Neither of these adjectives are used in Article 40, s.4, subs. 1 to describe the right to liberty or the personal rights, including the right to bodily integrity, referred to in Article 40, s.3, subsection 1. It is abundantly clear that too literal a construction of the Constitution could lead to absurdities. It is now well established that the Constitution does not *confer* on citizens of

---

[7] *Meskell* v. *C.I.E.* [1973] I.R. 121.
[8] *Att. Gen. (S.P.U.C. (Ireland) Ltd.)* v. *Open Door Counselling Ltd.* [1988] I.R. 593: *Att. Gen.* v. *X.* (*The Irish Times*, March 6, 1992).

the State fundamental human rights but *recognises* their existence as being antecedent and superior to positive law and protects them accordingly (see *McGee* v. *The Attorney General* [1974] I.R. 284) but the rights so recognised are not only those limited few which are so expressly described in the Constitution. Similarly, the power of the State, to delimit the exercise of constitutionally protected rights, is expressly given in some Articles and not referred to at all in others, but this cannot mean that, where absent, the power does not exist. For example, no reference is made in Article 41 to any restrictive power but it is clear that the exercise by the Family, of its imprescriptible and inalienable right to integrity as a unit group, can be severely and validly restricted by the State when, for example, its laws permit a father to be banned from a family home or allows for the imprisonment of both parents of young children. As I suggested in *The Attorney General* v. *Paperlink Ltd.* [1984] I.L.R.M. 373 at p. 385, in construing the Constitution, the courts should bear in mind that the document is a political one as well as a legal one and whilst not ignoring the express text of the Constitution, a purposive approach to interpretation which would look at the whole text of the Constitution and identify its purpose and objectives in protecting human rights, is frequently a desirable one. This view seems to be in accord with that recently expressed in the Supreme Court in *Tormey* v. *Ireland* [1985] I.R. 289 by Mr. Justice Henchy who referred to the need to adopt a construction of the constitutional provisions which would 'achieve the smooth and harmonious operation of the Constitution' and to avoid a strict construction which 'would allow the imperfection or inadequacy of the words used to defeat or pervert any of the fundamental purposes of the Constitution.'

It does not follow, therefore, that because the Constitution ascribes to only some human rights, characteristics of inalienability and imprescriptibility, the Constitution should be construed as implying that other fundamental human rights lack these qualities, or that only those rights are superior to positive law which are so expressly described in the Constitution. The right to life, for example, is one of the personal rights expressly referred to in Article 40, s.3, subs. 2 and the right not to be tortured is one of the personal rights protected but not expressly enumerated in Article 40, s.3, subsection 1. Both these rights must surely be reckoned as amongst the most important basic human rights and the Constitution should be interpreted to give effect to this view, even though neither is expressly described as being inalienable and imprescriptible or as being superior to positive law. So, if the court is required to make a valuation between two constitutionally protected human rights, (as it was required to do in *People* v. *Shaw* [1982] I.R. 1), it should have particular regard to the intrinsic nature of the rights concerned, a view consistent with the views of Mr. Justice Griffin at p. 56 and Mr. Justice Kenny at p. 63 of that report.''

In an extra-curial development of these views,[9] Costello J. has called attention to the fact that the preamble shows one of the constitution's pur-

---

[9] Declan Costello, "Limiting Rights Constitutionally" in *Human Rights and Constitutional Law: Essays in Honour of Brian Walsh* (James O'Reilly, ed., Dublin 1992), p. 177.

poses as being " . . . to promote the common good . . . so that the dignity and freedom of the individual may be assured . . . " He continues[10]:

"When therefore the exigencies of the commmon good are called in aid to justify restrictions on the exercise of basic rights it has to be borne in mind that the protection of basic rights is one of the objects which the common good is intended to assure."

Costello J. goes on to say[11]:

" . . . obviously laws may interfere with the enjoyment of personal rights (as when, for example, powers of search trench on the right to privacy) and questions arise as to the constitutional validity of such laws. Here again the concept of the common good is a relevant consideration for unless the personal right involved is an absolute one whose exercise can in no circumstances be restricted then there has been no unconstitutional failure on the part of the State to respect, defend or vindicate the right in suit if the impugned restriction is one reasonably necessary in order to promote the common good."

It would follow from the above that one should not lay undue emphasis on differences in the language used in the Constitution to permit limitations on fundamental rights. For whether the restriction is expressed to be permissible "in the public interest" (as with Article 40.6.1° iii), or is merely capable of being imposed "in accordance with law" (as with Article 40.4 and 5), the concept of the common good lies behind the words used. Thus if the exigencies of the common good[12] do not justify the limitation imposed it will be repugnant to the Constitution.

These views still await explicit endorsement by the Supreme Court, though acceptance of them seems implicit in some of its decisions. This is particularly true of *Cox* v. *Ireland*[13] (July 11, 1991) where a legislative intrusion on personal rights, *via* criminal penalties, was found—effectively— to be disproportionate to the objective sought to be attained. Finlay C.J., delivering the single judgment, said that to protect public peace and order and maintain its own authority, the State was entitled to impose onerous penalties to deter the commission of crimes. But in pursuing these objectives it must in its laws, as far as practicable, continue to protect the constitutional rights of citizens. Here the impugned provision constituted " . . . a failure of such protection not warranted by the objectives which it is sought to secure" (p. 21).

It would thus appear that the courts are now prepared to test the validity of statutes restricting constitutional rights by reference to a principle of proportionality[14] similar to that applied by the European Court of Human Rights.[15] It is a principle also applied—against a markedly different textual background—by the Supreme Court of Canada. The Canadian Charter of

---

[10] At p. 178.

[11] At p. 179.

[12] For a discussion of this concept see John Finnis, *Natural Law and Natural Rights* (Oxford 1980), *passim*.

[13] See further Richard F. Humphreys, "Constitutional Law—Techniques of Analysis: Blacklists and Short-Cuts" (1991) 13 *D.U.L.J.* (N.S.) 118.

[14] See also *Hand* v. *Dublin Corporation* [1991] 1 I.R. 409.

[15] As, *e.g.* in *Dudgeon* v. *U.K.* (1981) 4 E.H.R.R. 149.

Rights and Freedoms, in section 2, appears to guarantee certain rights in absolute terms[16]; but section 1 establishes that these guarantees are

" . . . subject only to such reasonable limits prescribed by law as can be demonstrably justified in a free and democratic society."

In *R.* v. *Edwards Books and Art Ltd.* (1986) 35 D.L.R. (4th) 1 Dickson C.J. explained how section 1 is applied (at 41):

"Two requirements must be satisfied to establish that a limit is reasonable and demonstrably justified in a free and democratic society. First, the legislative objective which the limitation is designed to promote must be of sufficient importance to warrant overriding a constitutional right. It must bear on a 'pressing and substantial concern.' Secondly, the means chosen to attain those objectives must be proportional or appropriate to the ends. The proportionality requirement, in turn, normally has three aspects: the limiting measures must be carefully designed, or rationally connected, to the objective; they must impair the right as little as possible; and their effects must not so severely trench on individual or group rights that the legislative objective, albeit important, is, nevertheless, outweighed by the abridgement of rights."

Whether the Irish courts will go quite this far remains to be seen.

In *Aughey* v. *Att. Gen.* [1989] I.L.R.M. 87 Walsh J., delivering the Supreme Court's judgment, said (at 90):

"Only post-Constitution legislation can give effect to a permitted statutory qualification upon any right guaranteed or granted by the Constitution."

It would follow that any pre-Constitution statutes qualifying those rights would fail the test of consistency with the Constitution under Article 50. It seems unlikely, however, that many such legislative provisions survive to run this constitutional gauntlet.

Balancing constitutional rights

On occasion one person's exercise of his/her constitutional rights will collide heavily with those of others. A vigorous invocation of the right to express one's convictions and opinions may trench heavily upon another's right to reputation. In exercising their right to strike, primary teachers may defeat a child's right to free primary education.[17] And the right to life of the unborn, guaranteed by Article 40.3.3°, is capable of conflicting with that of the mother, equally guaranteed therein.[18]

In resolving such conflicts the courts will obviously have to weigh carefully the constitutional rights involved and endeavour to achieve an accommo-

---

[16] s.2 provides: "Everyone has the following fundamental freedoms: (a) freedom of conscience and religion; (b) freedom of thought, belief, opinion and expression, including freedom of the press and other media of communication; (c) freedom of peaceful assembly; and (d) freedom of association."

[17] *Crowley* v. *Ireland* [1980] I.R. 102.

[18] *Att. Gen.* v. *X.* (*The Irish Times*, March 6, 1992).

dation between them.[19] This may involve ranking rights in a hierarchy, perhaps deploying a purposive interpretation of the Constitution to this end.[20] But as Costello J. warned in *Murray* v. *Ireland* [1985] I.R. 532, to speak of balancing rights may sometimes mislead. There the court was invited to balance the right to procreate children claimed by the plaintiffs, a husband and wife both serving prison sentences, against the "right" of the State to imprison them. Costello J. thought this approach conceptually incorrect, saying (at 540):

> " . . . the indiscriminate ascriptions of 'rights' to the State can lead to confusion and is not appropriate when what is in issue is the exercise by one of the organs of government of a *power* conferred by law. This is the position in the present case. The Governor of Limerick prison is detaining the plaintiffs in custody, by virtue of a warrant issued by a court of law, after a finding of guilt in a criminal trial. The State, through the governor, is thus exercising a legal *power* to deprive the plaintiffs of their constitutional *right* to liberty. The court is, therefore, being asked to adjudicate on the validity of the exercise of a legal power and not on a conflict between the exercise of two competing rights. This distinction, between the exercise of a power and the exercise of a right, (a point emphasised by some legal theorists), is a useful one to bear in mind in the context of constitutional disputes. The Constitution, in protecting and guaranteeing the citizens' rights, has imposed very clear and specific correlative duties on the State to protect and vindicate them, but it has also designated the State the guardian of the common good and has empowered it to restrict those rights in certain circumstances. So, this is not a case in which the court should balance the so-called "right" of the State to imprison wrongdoers against the plaintiffs' right to beget children. The issue is, whether the restrictions on the plaintiffs' rights, caused by the exercise of the State's power to imprison the plaintiffs, are constitutionally permissible."

UNENUMERATED RIGHTS

The doctrine of unenumerated rights springs from the wording of Article 40.3. Its first subsection contains a general guarantee of the personal rights of the citizen; its second pledges protection "in particular" for "the life, person, good name, and property rights of every citizen." Since the other provisions of Article 40 do not specifically protect the citizen's right to life or a good name, the inference has been drawn that those provisions are not an exhaustive enumeration of the rights guaranteed. Ultimately, it falls to the courts to determine which unenumerated rights the Constitution implicitly guarantees. In discharging this function they have drawn upon a wide variety of sources. They have, in some instances, invoked other provisions of the Constitution, such as the Directive Principles of Social Policy in Article 45. In

---

[19] This is not to imply that only the courts have a role in attempting to reconcile conflicting constitutional rights. The Oireachtas plainly has a function here too, though it cannot be said to have discharged it very assiduously. See further James Casey, "Government and Politics in the Irish Republic: Judicial Activism and Executive Inertia," in *Northern Ireland: Politics and the Constitution* (Brigid Hadfield, ed., Buckingham 1992), p. 165.

[20] Perhaps the best example is *Quinn's Supermarket Ltd.* v. *Att. Gen.* [1972] I.R. 1.

other situations they have given constitutional status to rights recognised at common law, and there has also been recourse to notions of rights inherent in the human personality or springing from the democratic nature of the State. The rights that have been recognised so far may be listed as follows:

(a) the right to strike
(b) the right of dissociation[21]
(c) the right to privacy
(d) the right to earn one's living
(e) the right to communicate
(f) the right of access to the courts
(g) the right to legal representation on criminal charges[21a]
(h) the right to protection of one's health
(i) the right to travel
(j) the right to marry and found a family
(k) the right to fair procedures in decision making.

Sources

As noted above, some of these rights have been derived by implication from specific constitutional provisions. Thus the right to refuse to join a union was derived from the freedom of association guarantee of Article 40.6.1° iii, on the basis that freedom of association necessarily implied freedom to dissociate—*Educational Co. Ltd.* v. *Fitzpatrick (No. 2)* [1961] I.R. 345. The right of access to the courts is founded, at least in part, on Article 34.3.1°'s declaration on the jurisdiction of the High Court: see *Macauley* v. *Minister for Posts and Telegraphs* [1966] I.R. 345, 358. Likewise, the right to legal representation on criminal charges derives from Article 38.1's declaration that "no person shall be tried on any criminal charge save in due course of law": see *State (Healy)* v. *Donoghue* [1976] I.R. 325.

A more unlikely source, at first glance, are the Directive Principles of Social Policy contained in Article 45. These are prefaced by a declaration that the application of the principles in the making of laws "shall be the care of the Oireachtas exclusively, and shall not be cognisable by any court under any of the provisions of this Constitution." Nonetheless, the High Court has several times held that Article 45 may be prayed in aid to illuminate other constitutional provisions. In *Murtagh Properties* v. *Cleary* [1972] I.R. 330 Kenny J. took the view that he could have regard to Article 45 in considering whether a claimed personal right (of equal access to employment) arose under Article 40.3. Finlay J. sought guidance from it in *Landers* v. *Att. Gen.* (1973) 109 I.L.T.R. 1, in attempting to clarify the expression "exigencies of the common good" in Article 43. In *Att. Gen.* v. *Paperlink Ltd.* [1984] I.L.R.M. 373, Costello J. likewise held that he was entitled to look to Article 45 to ascertain what personal rights were included in Article 40.3.1°, and what limitations the State could impose on such rights in the interests of the common good.

However, the guidance available from other provisions of the Constitution

---

[21] On the right to strike and the right of dissociation, see Chap. 16 *infra*.
[21a] As to this, see Chap. 14, *infra*.

is limited, and the courts have had to derive unenumerated rights from less concrete sources. So the right to travel abroad—and thus to obtain a passport—was held by Finlay P. to flow from the Christian and democratic nature of the State: *State (M)* v. *Minister for Foreign Affairs* [1979] I.R. 73. In *McGee* v. *Att. Gen.* [1974] I.R. 284 a majority of the Supreme Court concluded that Article 40.3.1° embraced a right of marital privacy. Henchy J. approached the matter as follows ([1974] I.R. 284, 325):

> " . . . the unspecified personal rights guaranteed by subs. 1 of s.3 of Article 40 are not confined to those specified in subs. 2 of that section. It is for the Courts to decide in a particular case whether the right relied on comes within the constitutional guarantee. To do so, it must be shown that it is a right that inheres in the citizen in question by virtue of his human personality. The lack of precision in this test is reduced when subs. 1 of s.3 of Article 40 is read (as it must be) in the light of the Constitution as a whole and, in particular, in the light of what the Constitution, expressly or by necessary implication, deems to be fundamental to the personal standing of the individual in question in the context of the social order envisaged by the Constitution."

It is, however, obvious that although this method of approach may reduce the imprecision in question, it is far from completely eliminated. Judges may well form different views on "the social order envisaged by the Constitution" and on what it implicitly deems "fundamental to the personal standing" of individuals. Indeed, the division of opinion in the Supreme Court in *Norris* v. *Att. Gen.* [1984] I.R. 36 (discussed *infra*) shows this clearly.[22]

May international legal instruments to which the State is a party—such as the European Convention on Human Rights—be used as a guide in this area? It would seem that they may, but only to confirm the existence of an unenumerated right, such as one recognised at common law.[23] Where the constitutional text, or the implications to be drawn from it, resist recognition of the right claimed, its protection by an international instrument cannot overcome this.[24]

Finally, it must be stressed that the Constitution's unenumerated rights are no more absolute than those actually specified. These rights derive their protection from Article 40.3, which contains phrases such as "as far as practicable" and "as best it may."

---

[22] Similar issues have arisen in the U.S., where the Supreme Court has identified several rights not mentioned in the constitutional text—such as the right to privacy and the rights to travel and to marry—and characterised these as fundamental. There is great controversy over the source of such rights, and a degree of doctrinal confusion over whether they are protected against the states by the Due Process or Equal Protection clauses of the 14th Amendment. This has generated a vast literature. See further Polyvios G. Polyviou, *The Equal Protection of the Laws* (London 1980) Chap. 5: William B. Lockhart, Yale Kamisar and Jesse H. Choper, *Constitutional Rights and Liberties: Cases and Materials* (5th ed., St. Paul, Minn. 1981), pp. 129–215: Jerome A. Barron and C. Thomas Dienes, *Constitutional Law: Principles and Policy* (2nd ed., Charlottesville, Va. 1982), Chap. 8: Gerald Gunther, *Individual Rights in Constitutional Law: Cases and Materials* (3rd ed., Mineola, N.Y. 1981), pp. 190–266.

[23] See particularly *O'Leary* v. *Att. Gen.* [1991] I.L.R.M. 454, where Costello J. concluded that the Constitution guaranteed the presumption of innocence in criminal trials. He noted its universal recognition, as evidenced by international instruments, but also emphasised that in 1937 it " . . . had long been an integral part of the common law tradition . . . " (at 459).

[24] See *Norris* v. *Att. Gen.* [1984] I.R. 36, discussed *infra*.

The right to privacy

In *McGee* v. *Att. Gen.* [1974] I.R. 284 a majority of the Supreme Court identified an unemunerated right of marital privacy. The plaintiff there was a married woman with four children, who had been advised against a further pregnancy by her doctor. She attempted to import spermicidal jelly but it was seized by customs officers, acting under section 42 of the Customs Consolidation Act 1876, as amended by the Criminal Law Amendment Act 1935, s.17(3).[25] The plaintiff sought a declaration that section 17 of the 1935 Act was inconsistent with the Constitution. Unsuccessful in the High Court, she appealed to the Supreme Court which, by a 4–1 majority,[26] held that section 17(3)[27] did not survive the enactment of the Constitution. Article 40.3.1° guaranteed a right of privacy in marital relations, including a right to decide to use contraceptives, and section 17(3) violated this guarantee.[28]

The plaintiff in *Norris* v. *Att. Gen.* [1984] I.R. 36 sought to build on the *McGee* decision to establish that certain 19th century statutes penalising homosexual conduct between consenting male adults in private were unconstitutional. His argument was that the Constitution guaranteed a right of privacy (of which marital privacy was but one aspect), and that this meant there was a limit on the State's power to control personal conduct where neither the common good nor the protection of public order or morality necessitated such control. The Supreme Court seems to have accepted that such a right of privacy *is* guaranteed; certainly the majority judgment (by O'-Higgins C.J.) does not deny the existence of this wider right, and it is specifically accepted by Henchy and McCarthy JJ. in their dissents. The essential disagreement between majority and minority was as to whether the right invalidated the provisions impugned.[29] For the majority which held that it did not, O'Higgins C.J. said that the preamble to the Constitution indicated an acceptance of Christian values. This militated against any conclusion that in adopting the Constitution "the people rendered inoperative laws which had existed for hundreds of years prohibiting unnatural sexual conduct which Christian teaching held to be gravely sinful" (at 64). Moreover, the State was entitled to discourage conduct which was "morally wrong and

---

[25] s.17(3) provided that contraceptives should be included among the table of prohibited goods in s.42 of the 1876 Act.

[26] Walsh, Budd, Henchy and Griffin JJ.; FitzGerald C.J. dissenting.

[27] The plaintiff had impugned the whole of s.17, but the court found it unnecessary, in the circumstances, to rule on this. S.17(1), it may be noted, made it unlawful to sell, or expose, offer, advertise or keep for sale, or to import or attempt to import, any contraceptive. Nothing in the 1935 Act made their *manufacture* in Ireland illegal, but it seems that they were not produced within the State. Nor did the Act explicitly make their *use* unlawful, but that was its practical effect.

[28] As a consequence of the *McGee* decision, it became lawful for anyone to import contraceptives—though it would still have been unlawful to *sell* them. A Government-sponsored Bill to reform the law failed in 1974 when the Taoiseach, Mr. Cosgrave, and other deputies on the Government side, voted against it. (The Government parties had allowed a free vote, but the Opposition whip was on.) The Health (Family Planning) Act 1979, s.4, forbade the sale of contraceptives save by chemists and to purchasers with a doctor's prescription. This restriction was relaxed somewhat by the Health (Family Planning) (Amendment) Act 1985, which also made it clear that it was now lawful to sell contraceptives to single persons over 18. This age has been lowered to 17 by the similarly titled Act of 1992.

[29] Offences against the Person Act 1861, ss.61 and 62, and Criminal Law Amendment Act 1885, s.11.

harmful to a way of life and to values which the State wishes to protect"
(*ibid.*). Male homosexuality increased the incidence of venereal disease and
was injurious to the institution of marriage which the Constitution pledged
the State to protect (Art. 41.3.1°).

In dissent Henchy and McCarthy JJ. held that the onus lay on the State to
show that the maintenance of public order and morality outweighed the
plaintiff's claim to privacy. This onus had not been discharged; the consensus of the evidence given in the High Court was that the beneficial effects of
relaxing the impugned provisions would outweigh any possible ill-effects on
society as a whole.[30] (Henchy J., it may be noted, described the relevant provisions as "doomed" and referred to the judgment of the European Court of
Human Rights in *Dudgeon* v. *U.K.* (1981) 4 E.H.R.R. 149.[31])

O'Higgins C.J. stressed that a right of privacy could never be absolute.
Many acts done in private were condemned by the law—he instanced incest,
suicide attempts, suicide pacts and mercy killing. The dissenters accepted
this proposition—Henchy J. said it would not be constitutional to decrimina-
lise all homosexual acts. Factors such as the protection of the young, the
maintenance of the family, the upholding of marriage and other aspects of
the common good required that homosexual acts be made criminal in many
circumstances ([1984] I.R. 36, 78–79) and McCarthy J. agreed with this (at
104).[32]

The result of the *Norris* case would appear to be that the Constitution may
acknowledge a zone of autonomy, within which an individual *must* have freedom to act without legal hindrance. Just how wide that zone may be is
unclear. Many restrictions on individual freedom of action are arguably
imposed for the benefit of others, or of society as a whole. Legislation on the
wearing of safety helmets by motor cyclists or certain workers is an example.
Nor should the difficulty of adjudicating in this area be underestimated. It
would be all too easy for the courts to appear to be constituting themselves
super-legislatures, determining issues of public policy under the guise of constitutional adjudication.[33]

The privacy recognised by the Constitution may well extend beyond
autonomy. Arguably it also embraces the "right to be let alone"—to be free

---

[30] For a critical examination of the *Norris* decision see Conor Gearty (1983) 5 *D.U.L.J.* 264.

[31] Where that court held the same statutory provisions—then still in force in Northern Ireland,
though not in the rest of the United Kingdom—violative of the European Convention. It subsequently reached the same conclusion *vis à vis* the Republic in *Norris* v. *Ireland* (1989) 13
E.H.R.R. 186.

[32] It has occasionally been suggested that one effect of the Supreme Court's decision in the *Norris*
case is that legislation decriminalising sexual activity between consenting male adults in private would be constitutionally invalid. The Law Reform Commission has conclusively
answered this. "The case, of course, decided nothing of the sort: the only issue before the
Court was whether the existing law rendering all homosexual behaviour between males at
any age criminal was inconsistent with the Constitution. Any remarks in the judgment of O'-
Higgins C.J. which might suggest that he viewed legislation which decriminalised homosexual actions between consenting adults as constitutionally suspect—and it is by no means clear
that this is what he intended to convey—were accordingly not necessary for the purpose of
that decision and *obiter*": *Report on Child Sexual Abuse* (LRC–32: 1990), p. 47.

[33] Courts in the U.S. have reached opposite conclusions on whether legislation requiring motor
cyclists to wear crash helmets is an impermissible invasion of liberty. In *State of Oregon* v. *Fet-
terly* (1969) 254 Or. 47, 456 P. 2d 996 the Supreme Court of Oregon held it was not; but in
American Motorcycle Association v. *Davids* (1968) 11 Mich. App. 351, 158 NW 2d 72 the Michi-
gan Court of Appeals held that it was.

from certain kinds of intrusion by public or private bodies. In the *Norris* case McCarthy J. observed that the Constitution, in various places, recognised this aspect of privacy. He pointed out that Article 16.1.4° guaranteed secrecy in voting; that Article 34 gave a limited right of privacy to certain litigants; and that Article 40.5 guaranteed the inviolability of the dwelling. It would not, therefore, be difficult for the Irish courts to recognise a tort of invasion of privacy committed by the unjustified publication of discreditable (but true and thus not defamatory) statements about an individual. Some state courts in the United States have done this, the classic example being *Melvin* v. *Reid* (1931) 112 Cal. App. 285, 297 P. 91. There Gabrielle Darley, a prostitute, was charged with murder. After a sensational trial she was acquitted. She left her profession, married one Melvin and made a new life for herself among friends who knew nothing of her past life. Seven years after the trial, a film entitled "The Red Kimono" told the story of the trial. It used the name Gabrielle Darley, and revealed her past to her new friends. The Californian courts held this an invasion of privacy and awarded Mrs Melvin damages.[34]

In *Kennedy* v. *Ireland* [1987] I.R. 587 the first two plaintiffs were journalists, whose telephones had been tapped on foot of a warrant issued by the Minister for Justice. Conversations had been recorded and transcripts of them made. It was admitted that there was no justification for this. The plaintiffs claimed damages for breach of their constitutional rights. Hamilton P. accepted that the Constitution guaranteed an unenumerated right to privacy; it was one of the fundamental personal rights of the citizen which flowed from the Christian and democratic nature of the State. Hamilton P. continued (at 593):

> "The nature of the right to privacy must be such as to ensure the dignity and freedom of an individual in the type of society envisaged by the Constitution, namely, a sovereign, independent and democratic society. The dignity and freedom of an individual in a democratic society cannot be ensured if his communications of a private nature, be they written or telephonic, are deliberately, consciously and unjustifiably intruded upon and interfered with. I emphasise the words 'deliberately, consciously and unjustifiably' because an individual must accept the risk of accidental interference with his communications and the fact that in certain circumstances the exigencies of the common good may require and justify such intrusion and interference. No such circumstances exist in this case."

Since it was admitted that there had been a deliberate, conscious and unjustifiable interference by the State with the plaintiffs' telephonic communications, their constitutional right to privacy had been invaded and the State was liable in damages for this. The first two plaintiffs were awarded £20,000 each.

Hamilton P. made it clear that the right to privacy was not unqualified. Its exercise could be restricted by reference to the constitutional rights of others,

---

[34] See further William Cohen and John Kaplan, *Constitutional Law: Civil Liberty and Individual Rights* (2nd ed. Mineola N.Y. 1982) pp. 181–193. The French courts also recognised such a right on a pure judge-made law basis: see the decision of the Cour d'Appel of Paris, D.1970, 466; also D.1977.83 (*note* Lindon).

or the requirements of the common good or of public order and morality. The interception of communications—oral or written—is therefore not unconstitutional *per se*, and it is authorised by statute. As the law stands at present, opening or generally tampering with a postal packet is a criminal offence: Postal and Telecommunications Services Act 1983, s.84. So, too, is the interception of telecommunications messages: *ibid.*, s.98. In both instances, however, no offence is committed by a person acting in pursuance of a direction issued by the Minister for Communications under section 110 of the Act: see sections 84(2)(*b*) and 98(2)(*a*)(ii). Section 110(1)(*b*) enables the Minister to issue directions in writing to An Post or An Bord Telecom "to do (or refrain from doing) anything which he may specify from time to time as necessary in the national interest. . . . " Under the practice currently obtaining—though not mentioned in the 1983 Act—a warrant from the Minister for Justice would precede any direction from the Minister for Communications.

The relevant provisions of the 1983 Act might be vulnerable to constitutional challenge in that they contain no external safeguards, such as a requirement that any interception be pursuant to a court's authorisation. Nor is there any procedure for administrative or judicial review of Ministerial warrants. In *Malone* v. *U.K.* (1984) 7 E.H.R.R. 14 the absence of adequare safeguards and review procedures in the comparable British arrangements led the European Court of Human Rights to condemn them as violating the Convention. The Government has accepted that current Irish arrangements are likewise incompatible with Convention standards, and legislation has been introduced to rectify this.[35]

In the United States the constitutional right of privacy was first recognised in *Griswold* v. *Connecticut* (1965) 381 U.S. 479, where the Supreme Court held a state statute denying married persons access to contraceptives invalid. This was subsequently broadened in *Roe* v. *Wade* (1973) 410 U.S. 113 to invalidate many statutory restrictions on abortion. Some professed to fear a similar development in Ireland following on the decision in *McGee* v. *Att. Gen.* [1974] I.R. 284. The right of privacy there recognised, it was suggested, might be so developed as to invalidate sections 58 and 59 of the Offences against the Person Act 1861, which forbid abortion.[36] Any such possibility—which is thought to have been very remote—was precluded by the Eighth Amendment of the Constitution Act 1983. This amends Article 40 by adding a new subsection to section 3 as follows:

> "3° The State acknowledges the right to life of the unborn and, with due regard for the equal right to life of the mother, guarantees in its laws to respect, and, as far as practicable, by its laws to defend and vindicate that right."

This provision is considered further *infra, s.v.* Abortion.

---

[35] The Interception of Postal Packets and Telecommunications Messages (Regulation) Bill 1992 passed its second stage in Seanad Éireann on May 6, 1992: see *The Irish Times*, May 7, 1992, p. 5.

[36] s.58 makes it an offence for a woman to procure her own miscarriage by *unlawfully* administering to herself "any poison or other noxious thing" or by *unlawfully* using "any instrument or other means whatsoever." It is also an offence for any other person to attempt to procure a woman's miscarriage by these means. The maximum sentence on conviction for any of these offences is penal servitude for life.

The right to earn a living

This right was first recognised by Kenny J. in the High Court in *Murtagh Properties* v. *Cleary* [1972] I.R. 330. The publican plaintiffs sought injunctions to restrain picketing at their premises. The picketing was organised and carried on by a union representing those employed in the licensed trade, and was designed to compel the plaintiffs to cease employing part-time bar waitresses. This, the union claimed, was in breach of agreements made between it and the relevant employers' association. The plaintiffs argued that the picketing was not protected by the Trade Disputes Act 1906, because it was designed to compel them to infringe the bar waitresses' constitutional right to earn a livelihood. The defendants denied that any such constitutional right existed.

Kenny J. referred to *Ryan* v. *Att. Gen.* [1965] I.R. 294 as having established that the Constitution protected rights not specifically enumerated therein. The right relied on here derived from Article 45.2.i:

> "The State shall, in particular direct its policy towards securing
>   i. That the citizens (all of whom, men and women equally, have the right to an adequate means of livelihood) may through their occupation find the means of making provision for their domestic needs."

The defendants argued that the courts could not have regard to Article 45, which is expressed to be for the guidance of the Oireachtas only and which states that the application of its social policy principles in the making of laws "shall not be cognisable by any Court under any of the provisions of this Constitution." But Kenny J. held that this did not mean that the courts could not have regard to the terms of the Article. They had no jurisdiction to consider the application of its principles in the making of laws, but this did not mean they could not take it into consideration in deciding whether a claimed constitutional right existed. Kenny J. concluded that Article 45.2.i logically involved that each citizen, male or female, had the right to earn a livelihood. It followed that a policy or general rule under which anyone sought to prevent an employer from employing men or women on the ground of sex alone was prohibited by the Constitution. Here the purpose of the picketing was to compel employers to breach the bar waitresses' constitutional rights, and by analogy with *Educational Co. Ltd.* v. *Fitzpatrick (No. 2)* [1961] I.R. 345 (discussed in Chap. 16 *infra*) it must be enjoined. Kenny J. also concluded that the right to earn a living was not enforceable against the State ([1972] I.R. 330, 336). The reasons for this view are not clear; it cannot be founded on a general doctrine that unenumerated rights are unavailable against the State for no such general doctrine exists. Perhaps it was felt to flow from the unusual source—Article 45—of this particular right, though it is not easy to see why this should affect matters. At any rate Kenny J.'s conclusion placed the State under no constitutional obligation to enact legislation on unfair dismissal or equal pay; and the statutes on these matters[37] are in fact the consequence of European Community membership.

A facet of this general right was discussed by Finlay J. in *Landers* v. *Att.*

---

[37] Anti-Discrimination (Pay) Act 1974 and Employment Equality Act 1977.

Gen. (1973) 109 I.L.T.R. 1. The plaintiff's eight year old son had considerable musical talent and had become a successful singer. However, the plaintiff and the boy's manager were convicted of contravening sections 2(*b*) and
(*c*) of the Prevention of Cruelty to Children Act 1904, which limited the
extent to which young children could take part in public entertainment. The
plaintiff contended that these provisions were unconstitutional on various
counts. Finlay J. dismissed all the plaintiff's arguments. While he accepted
that there existed an unenumerated right "to prepare for and follow a chosen
career," he concluded that the impugned provisions did not impermissibly
infringe this right.

The implications of the right identified in the *Landers* case remain to be
worked out. It clearly opens the way to challenging unreasonable restrictions
on entry to a trade or profession, whether imposed by statute or by private
arrangements; but no such challenges have as yet occurred. The same
applies to the more general "right to work" recognised by the Supreme Court
in *Murphy* v. *Stewart* [1973] I.R. 97. There Walsh J. speaking for the court,
indicated that if a union was abusing its monopoly of certain jobs so as to
prevent the exercise of the constitutional right to work, the question of compelling the union to accept people into membership—or of breaking the
monopoly—might arise.

The question of a statutory monopoly and its impact on the right to earn a
livelihood were canvassed in *Att. Gen. and Minister for Posts and Telegraphs* v.
Paperlink Ltd. [1984] I.L.R.M. 373. In 1981 the defendant company had
begun to operate a courier service in and around Dublin. This involved, as
Costello J. found, delivering letters in breach of the statutory monopoly conferred on the Minister by the Post Office Act 1908, s.34(2); and the plaintiffs
were seeking to restrain this. The defendants pleaded that section 34(2) was
unconstitutional as an invalid restriction on their freedom to earn a livelihood. The State monopoly thereby established, it was contended, was an
unjust attack on their right to earn a livelihood, in violation of Article
40.3.2°—the notion of justice in this context being illuminated by the provisions of Article 45.3.1°:

> "The State shall favour and, where necessary, supplement private
> initiative in industry and commerce."

This meant, said the defendants, that the onus was on the State to justify any
interference with private initiative in matters of commerce.

Costello J. rejected the defendants' arguments. He agreed that the State
had a duty, derived from Article 40.3, by its laws to protect as best it might
from unjust attack the personal right to earn a livelihood. And he accepted
that the courts could consider Article 45 for the limited purposes of ascertaining what personal rights were included under Article 40.3.1°, and what legitimate limitations in the interests of the common good the State might impose
on such rights. But Article 45.3.1° must not be pushed too far. It demonstrated a view that the social order should not be based on a system in which
all the means of production were owned by the State, and a preference for
one in which industry and commerce were mainly carried on by private citizens rather than State agencies. However, it did not follow that the Oireachtas could not legislate to establish State trading corporations or public
utilities, nor was it legitimate to infer that the State was called upon in legal
proceedings to justify a State monopoly.

The defendants further argued that the monopoly was inefficiently administered, and that it was possible to organise one less restrictive of their
rights. Thus, they said, the "attack" on those rights was "unjust." To under-
pin this argument they wished to call two economists and two accountants to
give expert evidence. But Costello J. ruled that the proposed evidence would
be inadmissible. While it would not be in the public interest that a statutory
monopoly was inefficiently administered, this—if it were the fact—could not
make the relevant Act unconstitutional. Inefficiency in administration would
not of itself mean that anyone's constitutional rights were being infringed.
Equally, evidence as to alternative ways of organising the postal service
could not be admitted. This would involve the court in an unconstitutional
departure from its role as laid down in the Constitution. Costello J. continued ([1984] I.L.R.M. 373, 388–389):

> "(The defendants) seek to adduce expert evidence for the purpose of
> establishing (presumably contrary to the views of any expert evidence
> which the plaintiffs might call in rebuttal) that the national postal ser-
> vice could be so organised as to provide the benefits of the present
> national system whilst at the same time permitting the defendants to
> operate in Dublin their courier service. They then submit that in the
> light of the evidence I should hold that the 1908 Act is unconstitutional
> because by changing the law or amending the statute in the way sug-
> gested the restriction on the defendants' right to earn a livelihood could
> be raised. But this court is not the forum in which to decide whether a
> postal service organised on lines advocated by the defendants' experts is
> one which meets the requirements of the common good. These are
> matters for the Oireachtas to determine. I must, of course, defend the
> citizen's rights against any unjust attack, and hold, if necessary, that an
> existing law has placed an excessive limit on the citizen's right to earn a
> livelihood. But to carry out the inquiry which the defendants ask me to
> perform and, thereafter, make a determination on an alternative to the
> existing postal service, would amount to an unwarranted and unconsti-
> tutional interference with the powers of government exclusively con-
> ferred on the executive and the Oireachtas, a point strikingly illustrated
> by the fact that as this case was at hearing the Dáil was itself considering
> a Bill to establish a different method of organising the postal system to
> that contained in the 1908 Act. Just as the courts must not permit the
> legislature to interfere with the judicial function, so too they must be
> astute to see that they do not themselves depart from their constitution-
> ally defined role."

It is interesting to note that the statutory monopoly is now contained in the
Postal and Telecommunications Services Act 1983, s.63. This confers on An
Post "the exclusive privilege" of conveying postal packets within, to and
from the State. Section 63(2) recites the grounds on which this privilege is
granted, referring to:

(a) An Post's primary purpose of providing a national postal service and
    the general duty imposed on it by section 13 of the Act
(b) the fact that a privilege of this kind "is appropriate having regard to
    the area and population of the State and the present state of develop-
    ment of postal technology"

(c) the fact that "a viable national postal system involves subsidisation of some loss-making services by profit-making services."

Such recitals are unusual in Acts of the Oireachtas; the considerations motivating the legislature's action must normally be gleaned from the overall text of the Act or from the parliamentary debates.[38] In the United States, however, such recitals—or "findings"—frequently appear in measures passed by the Federal Congress. While not conclusive as to constitutionality[39] they may play a useful role where the test of validity is reasonableness ("rationality")[40] and may also assist in the statute's interpretation.[41]

The right to earn a livelihood was also invoked, in rather different circumstances, in *Cafolla* v. *O'Malley and Att. Gen.* [1985] I.R. 486. The plaintiff sought a declaration that the Gaming and Lotteries Act 1956, s.14(*b*) and (*d*) was repugnant to the Constitution. He was the proprietor of an "amusement hall" in Dublin in which he operated gaming machines as defined in the 1956 Act. Section 14(*b*) and (*d*) limited the stake and the prize in each game to $2\frac{1}{2}$p and 50p respectively. Essentially, his claim was that while these provisions might have been valid when enacted, because of events occurring since then they now operated to infringe his constitutional right to earn a livelihood. He pointed out that since 1963, when he started his business, the excise duty payable in respect of each slot-machine had increased from £50 to £300, while that on the licence for the premises had increased from £40 to £300. Additionally, between 1956 and 1984 the Consumer Price Index had gone up by 950 per cent., while the cost of wages, rates and other charges had also risen—in some instances beyond 950 per cent.

Costello J. accepted that the restrictions imposed on the plaintiff's means of livelihood by the 1956 Act were now more onerous that when he commenced business. But the fact that the number of licences in force had increased from 82 in 1956 to 394 in 1982 gave rise to the inference that these factors did not render such business unprofitable. The judge agreed that a statute which was initially valid might be rendered constitutionally infirm by subsequent events, citing *Brennan* v. *Att. Gen.* [1984] I.L.R.M. 355 (as to which see Chap. 18 *infra*). So the issue here was—did this legislation *now* invalidly restrict the constitutional right to earn a livelihood, and thus contravene Article 40.3? Costello J. went on to say ([1985] I.R. 486, 494):

> " . . . what is here to be considered is a claim that the Act is now unjust because of its damaging effect on the profitability of the plaintiff's business. But laws having such an effect do not necessarily conflict with the Constitution. Laws may, for example, with constitutional propriety pro-

---

[38] Occasionally the long title of an Act will refer to the constitutional provisions believed to authorise its passage; see, *e.g.* Offences against the State Act 1939; Emergency Powers Act 1976. A particularly noteworthy example is the Rent Restrictions (Temporary Provisions) Act 1981, passed to close the gap created by the Supreme Court's decision in *Blake* v. *Att. Gen.* [1982] I.R. 117.

[39] See *Carter* v. *Carter Coal Co.* (1936) 298 U.S. 238. Also *Australian Communist Party* v. *Commonwealth* (1951) 83 C.L.R. 1.

[40] See *Hodel* v. *Virginia Surface Mining & Reclamation Assn.* (1981) 452 U.S. 264: *F.E.R.C.* v. *Mississippi* (1982) 456 U.S. 742.

[41] Costello J. has suggested that the process of constitutional adjudication could be assisted if greater use was made of such recitals. They " . . . would help not only in ascertaining the intention of parliament but also the reasons for its decisions and the aims the legislation was designed to achieve": Declan Costello, *op. cit.* n. 9 *supra*, p. 186.

hibit fishermen from fishing at certain times and limit the nature and size of their catches, restrict the hours of trading in licensed premises, fix the price at which goods can be sold or services remunerated, all of which adversely affect the livelihood of those engaged in the activity concerned. Laws may even prohibit an existing business activity, as was shown in *PMPS and Moore* v. *Att. Gen.* [1984] I.L.R.M. 88."

Costello J. held that the onus was on the plaintiff to establish that the restrictions he complained of were not reasonably required by the exigencies of the common good. If he could not do this then no injustice had been established, because no injustice arose from a restriction so required. The fact that the Act's limits now operated more restrictively than in 1956 could not justify an assumption that this restriction was not required by the common good. Nor was it for the courts to decide what levels of restrictions were reasonably necessary to curb gaming in licensed amusement halls; those were matters peculiarly within the jurisdiction and competence of the Oireachtas. The courts could, however, consider whether such restrictions were capable of being justified by reference to the common good. Costello J. tested this by considering whether the Oireachtas could now constitutionally re-enact section 14. The plaintiff, said the judge, had not shown that it would be unreasonable for the Oireachtas to conclude that present day social conditions required the maintenance of the 1956 limits, notwithstanding the decline in the value of money since then. Nor had he shown that there would be any disproportion between the aims of the 1956 Act and the imposition of controls operating more restrictively than they did in 1963. It followed that if the impugned provisions could validly be re-enacted now, they could not be said to be constitutionally invalid.

The Supreme Court accepted Costello J.'s conclusions and his reasoning. The Court, *per* Finlay C.J., emphasised that even if the impugned legislation had now made this sort of business totally unprofitable, it would have been beyond challenge. It is clear, then, from these cases that one who seeks to upset an alleged statutory restriction on his/her right to earn a livelihood faces an uphill struggle.

In *Hand* v. *Dublin Corporation* [1991] 1 I.R. 409 the plaintiffs were street traders in Dublin who, by the terms of the Casual Trading Act 1980, required licences to operate as such. But they had contravened the Act's provisions and had been convicted at least twice of doing so. When they applied for licences for the year beginning December 1, 1985 their applications were refused pursuant to section 4(6) of the Act. This prohibited (though not permanently) the grant of such licences to persons convicted of two or more offences under the Act within a specified period of time. The plaintiffs claimed that section 4(6) was an unjust attack on their constitutional right to earn a livelihood, because the disqualification it imposed was out of proportion to the nature of the offences committed by them. The Supreme Court rejected this claim. Griffin J., delivering the judgment of the court, pointed out that the right to earn a livelihood was not unqualified; thus it could be subjected to legitimate legal restraints. In enacting the impugned legislation the Oireachtas had to strike a balance between the legitimate rights and interests of those affected by it. These included members of the public using the streets, those lawfully engaged in casual trading and those carrying on business in premises in the neighbourhood of the casual trading area. The

statutory disqualification imposed by section 4(6) was not unjust or
unreasonable, and consequently did not violate the rights protected by
Article 40.3.2° of the Constitution.[42]

The right to earn a livelihood is protected not only against action by the
State or its agents but also against action by private parties. In *Parsons* v.
Kavanagh [1990] I.L.R.M. 560 the plaintiff operated a passenger bus service
between Dublin and Clonmel on foot of a licence granted under the Road
Traffic Acts. Towards the end of 1986 the defendants began to provide a
competing service at lower prices, but they had no licence to do so. The
plaintiff sought an injunction to stop this. O'Hanlon J. concluded that, at
common law, she would not have been entitled to enforce the Road Traffic
Acts against the defendants. But the constitutional right to earn one's living
altered matters. O'Hanlon J. said (at 566):

> "I take the view . . . that the constitutional right to earn one's livelihood
> by any lawful means carries with it the entitlement to be protected
> against any unlawful activity on the part of another person or persons
> which materially impairs or infringes that right."

Accordingly, the injunction sought was granted.

An unlawful interference with this constitutional right could, of course,
also sound in damages. But it has been held that mere proof of pecuniary loss
is insufficient to show that the right has been infringed: *Moyne* v. *Londonderry
Harbour Commissioners* [1986] I.R. 299. Nor, it seems, does an otherwise lawful
act which causes such loss invade that right so as to create liability in
damages: *ibid*.

The right to communicate

In the *Paperlink* case it was argued that one of the unenumerated rights
flowing from Article 40.3 was a right of citizens freely to communicate with
each other. Costello J. accepted that Article 40.3 embraced a right to communicate; the act of communication was the exercise of such a basic human
faculty that a right to communicate must inhere in the citizen by virtue of his
human personality and must be guaranteed by the Constitution. But, said
the judge, this right was obviously not an absolute one. Laws could restrict
the nature of the matter communicated (*e.g.* by prohibiting the communication of confidential information, or treasonable, blasphemous, obscene or
defamatory matter). And they could also restrict the mode of communication
(*e.g.* by prohibiting communication by advertisement contrary to the planning code or by radio contrary to wireless telegraphy regulations). Thus it
would be incorrect, and seriously misleading, to refer to a "right to communicate freely."

The right to communicate is distinct from the right to express one's convictions and opinions. The latter derives from Article 40.6.1°i; the former is protected by Article 40.3 and would refer to communication not involving
convictions and opinions. In the *Paperlink* case Costello J. rejected the argu-

---

[42] It was contended—apparently somewhat diffidently—that the right to earn a livelihood was a
property right. The Supreme Court assumed, without deciding, that it might so qualify. In
the result this made no difference, nor is it easy to see how it could have.

ment that the statutory monopoly on delivery of letters infringed the right to communicate; indeed by making available a nation-wide delivery service for letters it facilitated the exercise of that right.

In *Kearney* v. *Minister for Justice* [1986] I.R. 116 Costello J. had to consider whether the right to communicate was infringed by a prison rule for providing the reading, and possible censorship, of a prisoner's correspondence. Rule 63 of the Rules for the Government of Prisons 1947 (S.I. 1947 No. 320) provides as follows:

> "Every letter to or from a prisoner shall be read by the Governor or other responsible officer deputed by the Governor, and initialled by him and if the contents are objectionable it shall not be forwarded, or the objectionable part shall be erased, according to discretion. The Governor shall use his discretion in communicating or withholding from a prisoner at any time the contents of any letter addressed to the prisoner, but shall note in his journal every case in which he thinks it proper to withhold a letter, which according to the rules, might be communicated to or written by a prisoner."

The plaintiff argued that this was an unjustifiable restriction on his right to communicate. The only justifiable restriction, it was argued, would be one based on prison security considerations, and then only if suitable procedural safeguards existed. Since Rule 63 applied to *all* letters and contained no procedural safeguards, it was invalid.

Costello J. reaffirmed his earlier view that Article 40.3.1° guaranteed a right to communicate, but that it was not absolute and could be regulated by law. When the State lawfully exercised its power to imprison a citizen, one consequence was deprivation of the right to exercise many other constitutionally protected rights. The citizen could, however, still exercise those rights which did not depend on continuance of personal liberty and did not impose unreasonable demands on the place of imprisonment. Here the uncontradicted evidence showed it was necessary, in the interests of prison security, to read all letters—even those to solicitors, since there was actual experience of abuse by a solicitor of the confidential solicitor-client relationship. Thus the evidence showed that the restriction imposed by Rule 63 was justifiable and hence not unconstitutional.

The judge noted that the wide term "objectionable" in Rule 63 was restrictively interpreted in practice. So far as incoming mail was concerned, only matter which could endanger security was regarded as subject to the rule. Matter in outgoing mail was treated as "objectionable" only if it could endanger security or could properly be regarded as infringing other prisoners' rights to privacy. Thus the power of censorship conferred by the rule was within the reasonable requirements of the public service. As to procedural protection, though Rule 63 itself offered no protection against abuse, the Prison Rules made provision elsewhere for the hearing of prisoners' complaints and the redress of grievances (Rule 114), which would cover complaints of improper use of Rule 63.

It might have been thought that Rule 63, on its face, was too sweeping to be a reasonable restriction on the right to communicate: see the United States Supreme Court's decision in *Procunier* v. *Martinez* (1974) 416 U.S. 396, referred to by Costello J. But whatever its potential reach, its application had been narrowed in practice; and the result of *Kearney's* case would appear to be that the narrower interpretation is now authoritative—*i.e.* that prison governors may not now assert a wider power to intervene.

The plaintiff Kearney had also complained that, as a result of unauthorised action by prison officers, letters passed for delivery to him had not been received. Costello J. found that this had happened, and that the the plaintiff's constitutional right to communicate had thus been breached. This was a wrong committed by a servant of the State, and Ireland could be liable therefor. Even though the acts were unauthorised, they were connected with the functions for which the officers were employed, and the judge declined to hold that those acts were outside the scope of the officers' employment.[42] Since the plaintiff had sustained no loss, nominal damages of £25 only were awarded, Costello J. holding that there was insufficient evidence of oppression or vindictiveness to justify an award of exemplary damages. (The plaintiff was the only person affected; and effective steps had been taken to ensure against repetition of such acts.)

The recognition of a right to communicate would seem relevant to the issue of interception of letters and phone calls discussed *supra*. The question whether existing or proposed legislation on this matter fulfils the State's duty under Article 40.3 to protect this right may fall to be considered by the courts.

The right of access to the courts

This right was first recognised by Kenny J. in the High Court in *Macauley* v. *Minister for Posts and Telegraphs* [1966] I.R. 345. The plaintiff there sought a declaration that the Ministers and Secretaries Act 1924, s.2(1) was unconstitutional in that before one could sue a Minister one had to obtain the Attorney General's fiat. Kenny J. held that one of the rights included under Article 40.3 was a right to have recourse to the High Court to defend and vindicate a legal right. This was a necessary inference from the breadth of jurisdiction conferred on the High Court by Article 34.3.1°, and such a right of recourse existed also at common law. The statutory requirement of the fiat—which could be refused for any reason—was a failure by the State to defend and vindicate the citizen's personal rights in terms of Article 40.3, and section 2(1) was invalid insofar as it imposed that requirement.

In later cases the description of the right has been broadened; in *O'Brien* v. *Manufacturing Engineering Co. Ltd.* [1973] I.R. 334, the Supreme Court, *per* Walsh J., referred to "the right to litigate claims which are justiciable in law." This plainly includes a right to sue for damages in contract, tort, etc., but it would seem also to cover a claim for relief in respect of an allegedly invalid administrative decision, *e.g.* for a declaration, certiorari, mandamus or prohibition. Such a formulation of the right would mean it was available in respect of *all* courts. Costello J. appears to have accepted this in *State* (*McEldowney*) v. *Kelleher* [1983] I.R. 289, 287 where he referred to a right to have recourse in appropriate cases to the District Court to defend or vindicate a legal right.

Experience has shown that statutory limitation periods may sometimes be

---

[42] This approach seems remarkably similar to the notion of *cumul des responsabilités* in French administrative law, as to which see M. Long, P. Weil and G. Braibant, *Les Grands Arrêts de la Jurisprudence Administrative* (8th ed., Paris 1984), pp. 329–333.

vulnerable to challenge as infringing this right. In *O'Brien* v. *Keogh* [1972] I.R. 144 the Supreme Court held that section 49(2)(*a*)(ii) of the Statute of Limitations 1957 was invalid on this ground. The effect of that provision was to establish two different limitation periods for infants suing for damages for personal injuries: (1) three years (the period applicable to adults) for infants in the custody of a parent when the cause of action accrued; (2) six years for other infants. Ó Dálaigh C.J., giving the judgment of the court, held that this failed to match up to the guarantee of Article 40.3. It provided inadequate safeguards for the rights of infants where—as here—a defendant parent could raise the statute against proceedings taken outside the three year period.

The result of *O'Brien* v. *Keogh* was that the limitation period in respect of infants became the period expiring three years after the date when he/she attained full age. If the previous law was capable of working injustice to plaintiffs, this new situation seemed to pose similar dangers for defendants. Perhaps for this reason the Supreme Court held, in *Ó Domhnaill* v. *Merrick* [1984] I.R. 151, that even if a claim was made within that extended limitation period, it could nonetheless be struck out if there had been inordinate and inexcusable delay in prosecuting it. Earlier, in *Moynihan* v. *Greensmyth* [1977] I.R. 55 the same court hinted that *O'Brien* v. *Keogh* might require re-examination. O'Higgins C.J., for the court, said (at 71):

" . . . the Court reserves for a case in which the point has been duly raised and argued the question whether it was correctly decided in *O'Brien* v. *Keogh* that s.49, subs. 2(*a*)(ii) of the Statute of Limitations, 1957, is repugnant to the Constitution."

That case, however, has not yet arisen. In the meantime the Law Reform Commission has concluded that the *O'Brien* v. *Keogh* approach should be maintained, and the Oireachtas has implemented this recommendation.[43]

Fixing limitation periods obviously involves balancing the interests of prospective plaintiffs and those of prospective defendants, and is *prima facie* a matter for the Oireachtas. So long as the period fixed provides an adequate opportunity to ascertain whether one has a right of action and to institute proceedings, it will be valid: *O'Brien* v. *Manufacturing Engineering Co. Ltd.* [1973] I.R. 334.[44]

Section 11 of the Statute of Limitations 1957 established the limitation periods for certain kinds of actions by stipulating that the relevant time began to run " . . . from the date on which the cause of action accrued." In *Cahill* v. *Sutton* [1980] I.R. 269 the plaintiff argued that section 11(2)(*b*)— which decreed a three year period from that date in personal injuries claims—was repugnant to the Constitution. She wished to argue that if the cause of action accrued when the alleged breach of duty occurred—rather than when its consequences manifested themselves—then the subsection could operate to shut out someone's claim before he or she knew it existed, and thus violate constitutional rights. Holding that she lacked *locus standi* to raise this point, the Supreme Court declined to rule on it. Nonetheless, the court exhorted the Oireachtas to amend section 11(2)(*b*) by allowing an

---

[43] See *Report on the Statute of Limitations: Claims in Respect of Latent Personal Injuries* (LRC 21–1987) pp. 51–52: Statute of Limitations (Amendment) Act 1991, s.5.
[44] See also *Moynihan* v. *Greensmyth* [1977] I.R. 55.

extension of time in cases where the plaintiff could not have known of the cause of action within the three year period.

In *Morgan v. Park Developments Ltd.* [1983] I.L.R.M. 156 section 11(2)(*a*) of the 1957 Act was in issue. This provided for a six year limitation period for certain tort actions " . . . from the date on which the cause of action accrued." Carroll J. held that the date of accrual of a cause of action for negligence in the building of a house was the date of discoverability—*i.e.* the date when the defects were discovered or could reasonably have been discovered. She said that the 1957 Act must be presumed to be constitutional and interpreted accordingly. A construction which would deprive the plaintiff of his right of action before he knew he had one would be " . . . indefensible in the light of the Constitution" (at 160). But this was overruled by the Supreme Court in *Hegarty* v. *O'Loughran* [1990] 1 I.R. 148. The words " . . . from the date on which the cause of action accrued"—used throughout section 11— were capable of only one meaning, and to interpret them as referring to the date of discoverability would be to legislate.

The Statute of Limitations (Amendment) Act 1991—implementing recommendations of the Law Reform Commission[45]—now clearly lays down a discoverability test for personal injuries actions.[46] But proceedings such as those in *Morgan* v. *Park Developments Ltd.* would not be affected, and the limitation period remains six years from the date when the cause of action accrued. In accordance with *Hegarty* v. *O'Loughran* [1990] 1 I.R. 148, this means that the time limit begins when provable injury, capable of attracting monetary compensation, occurred. This is not necessarily the date of the occurrence of the alleged wrongful act; nonetheless the plaintiff in any such proceedings will not have the leeway a discoverability test would afford. Section 11(2)(*a*) may therefore have to face a future constitutional challenge—as it did *not* in *Hegarty* v. *O'Loughran* [1990] 1 I.R. 148. In this connection it may be noted that in 1982 the Law Reform Commission proposed the introduction of a discoverability test for defective premises claims—*e.g.* negligence in the building of a house as in *Morgan* v. *Park Developments Ltd.*[47] But this recommendation has not been implemented.

Some enactments impose time limits much shorter than those of the Statute of Limitations. A notable example is section 82(3A) of the Local Government (Planning and Development) Act 1963[48]:

> "A person shall not by prohibition, certiorari or in any other legal proceedings whatsoever question the validity of
> (a) a decision of a planning authority on an application for a permission or approval under Part IV of the Principal Act,
> (b) a decision of the Board on any appeal or on any reference
> (c) a decision of the Minister on any appeal,
> unless the proceedings are instituted within the period of two months commencing on the date on which the decision is given."

---

[45] See the *Report* cited in n. 43 *supra*.
[46] See ss.2 and 3.
[47] *Report on Defective Premises* (LRC 3–1982), pp. 8–10, 37–39.
[48] See also s.78(2) of the Housing Act 1966, which provides that a person aggrieved by the confirmation of a compulsory purchase order may question its validity by an application to the High Court—but the application must be brought within three weeks of the publication of the notice of confirmation. S.78(4) makes it clear that this application is the sole and exclusive

In *Brady* v. *Donegal Co. Council* [1989] I.L.R.M. 282 the plaintiffs wished to challenge a planning decision of the defendant council, but through no fault of theirs found their path blocked by section 82(3A).[49] They accordingly impugned its constitutionality, arguing that the right to challenge the Council's decision was a property right, and that the subsection was an unjust attack thereon. Costello J. observed that (at 287)

> " . . . the Oireachtas was balancing on the one hand the public interest in the application of certain aspects of the planning code and on the other the interests of those members of the public who were the holders of a constitutionally protected right to apply to the court to challenge the decisions of planning authorities."

Costello J. went on to say that a judicial discretion to raise the bar imposed by section 82(3A) would cause only a slight loss to the public interest, whereas the gain in the protection of constitutional rights would be very considerable. He concluded that, unmodified, the subsection was unreasonable and hence unconstitutional. On appeal, however, the Supreme Court held that no proper factual basis had been laid in the High Court for deciding this issue. Consequently, it set aside Costello J.'s judgment and order and remitted the action for retrial by the High Court. Notwithstanding this, however, a constitutional sword of Damocles seems to be suspended over section 82(3A) and similar provisions.

For some plaintiffs the constitutional right of access to the courts may, on grounds of expense, prove theoretical only; the cost of litigation may bar the way as effectively as any statutory limitation period. Though a scheme of civil legal aid has existed since 1986, it has never been capable of meeting all the demands made upon it. Even if the would-be plaintiff manages to secure legal assistance (perhaps on a "no foal, no fee" basis), or decides to appear in person, court fees may pose a problem. This issue has been canvassed in the High Court, though not yet in circumstances affording a proper occasion for resolving it.[50] In *MacGairbhith* v. *Att. Gen.* (High Court, November 13, 1991) O'Hanlon J. declined to do so, holding that more detailed evidence was required and that the plaintiff's *locus standi* was in doubt.[51] Nonetheless, he said (p. 2 of the judgment):

> "The levies payable to the State by litigants in the form of stamp duty on legal documents and other charges have risen in our own time to levels which would have been unthinkable in former times. On top of these standard charges of which the plaintiff complains, the imposition of VAT on solicitors' and barristers' fees (initially at 25 per cent) must have had a calamitous effect on litigants who had no possibility of setting it off against VAT credits to which they might have been entitled.

---

route to the High Court by decreeing that otherwise a confirmed compulsory purchase order may not be questioned by prohibition or certiorari " . . . or in any legal proceeding whatsoever."

[49] s.82(3A) was inserted by s.42 of the Local Government (Planning and Development) Act 1976.

[50] See also *Application of J.C.* (High Court, Barrington J., July 25, 1985).

[51] Because the plaintiff had clearly exercised his right of access to the courts on a number of previous occasions, and there was no evidence that he had sustained undue hardship by having to pay the levies of which he complained.

These charges levied by the State are the price the citizen has to pay for access to the Courts where his rights under the Constitution and the ordinary law are to be protected, and disputes are to be resolved between parties in an orderly and acceptable manner. I have no doubt that the frightening cost of litigation, made up in part of these heavy charges levied by the State, are a major deterrent to people who wish to have access to the Courts established under the Constitution and may in many cases actually prevent parties from availing of rights nominally guaranteed to them under the Constitution."[52]

Similar issues have arisen in the United States, and the Supreme Court there has invalidated state legislation requiring plaintiffs to pay court fees and costs (averaging $60) in order to sue for divorce. In *Boddie* v. *Connecticut* (1971) 401 U.S. 371, the court, *per* Harlan J., said that the Constitution's due process guarantee prohibited states from denying, solely on grounds of inability to pay, access to the courts to individuals seeking judicial dissolution of their marriages. Any other conclusion would mean that individuals would be faced with exclusion from the only forum empowered to settle their disputes. But in *U.S.* v. *Kras* (1973) 409 U.S. 434, a 5–4 majority concluded that due process was not violated when the Federal Bankruptcy Act conditioned the right to discharge on payment of $50 fees. The court, *per* Blackmun J., distinguished *Boddie's* case on the ground that the emphasis there on the exclusive nature of the judicial remedy had no counterpart in the bankruptcy situation. A debtor could, in theory and in practice, adjust his debts by appropriate agreement with his creditors. The same majority upheld, in *Ortwein* v. *Schwab* (1973) 410 U.S. 656, an Oregon statute exacting a $25 filing fee for judicial review of administrative decisions on welfare benefits.

In *M.C.* v. *Legal Aid Board and ors.* [1991] 2 I.R. 43 the applicant was a separated wife who had custody of the only child of the marriage, and was living on social welfare. Her husband had initiated nullity proceedings against her and she had applied for legal aid to defend them, but consideration of her application was deferred because of a backlog of work. It was admitted that she was eligible for such aid, on the criteria prescribed, but no decision on her application had yet been made. In addition to an order of mandamus directing the Board to consider her application, she sought declarations against the Minister for Justice and the Attorney General that her constitutional rights to equality and of access to the courts had been infringed. Gannon J. refused the relief sought.[53] By instituting the nullity proceedings, he said, the husband had invoked the jurisdiction of the courts to determine a private civil dispute. But the existence of that dispute did not confer any duty

---

[52] The plaintiff further complained that his constitutional rights had been infringed in that the State had failed to provide a law library in which persons like him could study the law of the country. O'Hanlon J. held that no such obligation could be derived from the unspecified rights guaranteed by the Constitution. (In earlier proceedings the same plaintiff had claimed access to the judges' library in the Four Courts, maintaining that it was a public law library. Costello J. dismissed his claim, holding that the library in question was not a public library. It was as private as any library in any Department of State or in any university: *The Irish Times*, May 16, 1990.)

[53] Gannon J. did, however, grant a declaration that the Legal Aid Board had a duty to consider the application within a reasonable time and that it had failed to do so; and a declaration that the Board's refusal to process and consider the application constituted an unlawful fettering of the discretion vested in it.

on the State or any of the respondents to either of the parties to it, either under the Constitution or at law. Gannon J. continued [1991] 2 I.R. 43, 55:

> "The duty of administering justice and adjudicating by due process does not create any obligation on the State to intervene in any private civil litigation so as to ensure that one party is as well equipped for their dispute as is the other. The fact that the existence of fundamental personal rights is expressly recognised by the Constitution does not impose on the State any duty to intervene in aid of a party involved in any private civil dispute in relation to any such personal rights . . .
>
> I am not convinced that there is any provision in the Constitution which imposes a duty on the State to provide any form of support for civil litigation among citizens. In the absence of such duty I can find no express or implied right in any citizen to require the State to provide financial support for, or to afford free facilities for, civil litigation of a dispute with another citizen."[54]

The constitutional right of access to the courts does not preclude an order requiring the would-be plaintiff to give security for costs[55]: *Salih* v. *General Accident Fire and Life Assurance Corpn. Ltd.* [1987] I.R. 628, 631, *per* O'Hanlon J. But it is a factor to be considered in determining the amount of such security; so said McCarthy J. in *Fallon* v. *An Bord Pleanála* [1991] I.L.R.M. 799, at 811 (see too Hederman J. at 808).

Bula Ltd. v. *Tara Mines Ltd.* [1987] I.R. 85 was a dispute between two mining companies, in which the plaintiffs were alleging unlawful abstraction by the defendants of the plaintiffs' ore. The plaintiffs sought an order for inspection of the defendants' mining activities, an application resisted by the defendants on a variety of grounds, *inter alia* that the plaintiffs had not made out a *prima facie* case. Murphy J. did not accept this argument, saying (at 92–93):

> " . . . the rights of litigants to seek and the power of the courts to grant relief or assistance of a procedural nature must be viewed in the context of litigation and the administration of justice as a whole. It is the right of citizens under the Constitution to have access to the courts for the resolution of justiciable controversies. Apart from particular provisions which enable the courts to stay or dismiss proceedings which are vexatious or an abuse of the process of the court, there is not in general any obligation imposed on a litigant to verify his cause of action or produce evidence in support thereof as a condition of instituting proceedings. Undoubtedly this valuable right of access to the courts may impose serious burdens on the chosen defendant. Inevitably the litigation will involve the defendant in costs which he may or may not recover from the plaintiff, and depending on the nature of the proceedings the very fact of the litigation may be a cause of considerable embarrassment to the alleged wrongdoer. In a proper case, however, this embarrassment should be short lived . . .

---

[54] A person who incurs expense in being legally represented before a statutory inquiry has no constitutional right to be reimbursed by the State, even if his/her conduct was part of the inquiry's subject-matter: *K. Security Ltd.* v. *Ireland and Att. Gen.* (High Court, Gannon J., July 15, 1977): *Condon* v. *C.I.É. and ors.* (High Court, Barrington J., November 16, 1984).

[55] As to which see Ord. 29, r. 6 of the Rules of the Superior Courts 1986 (S.I. No. 15 of 1986).

If, then, a citizen is free to institute proceedings he must be at least equally free to invoke the procedures of the court to present his case properly. In my view the right of a party to seek and obtain an order for inspection (or indeed an order for discovery which may be equally burdensome) is in no way dependent upon the court being satisfied as to the strength of the plaintiff's case."

This judgment must be understood as invoking the right of access to the courts in support of current court procedures—not as freezing those procedures for all time. Murphy J. recognised that the institution of proceedings may be burdensome for the defendant; and while this has to be accepted, legislative action may be necessary to curb the possibility of abuse in some instances. Thus journalists claim that the threatened (or actual) issue of a writ for libel is used by individuals solely as a means of gagging the press; that is, that there is no real intention of going to trial and that the object is to halt the publication of material of public interest, from fear of injunctions and/or contempt proceedings (see further Chap. 15, *infra*). If this is so, there would not seem to be any constitutional bar to the enactment of appropriate legislation. The right of access to the courts is not an unqualified right, and it is plainly the function of parliament to strike a just balance between the rights of prospective plaintiffs and defendants.[56]

The right to the protection of one's health

In *Ryan* v. *Att. Gen.* [1965] I.R. 294 the Supreme Court upheld Kenny J.'s conclusion that one of the unenumerated rights protected by Article 40.3 was the right to bodily integrity. The court found it unnecessary to define the term, and declined to pronounce on Kenny J.'s definition. He had said ([1965] I.R. 294, 313–14):

> "I understand the right to bodily integrity to mean that no mutilation of the body or any of its members may be carried out on any citizen under the authority of the law except for the good of the whole body and that no process which is or may, as a matter of probability, be dangerous or harmful to the life or health of the citizen or any of them may be imposed (in the sense of being made compulsory) by an Act of the Oireachtas."

However, the Supreme Court went on to say (at 348) that the State had "the duty of protecting the citizens from dangers to health in a manner not incompatible or inconsistent with the rights of those citizens as human persons." (See too Walsh J. in *McGee* v. *Att. Gen.* [1974] I.R. 284, 315.) Presumably,

---

[56] The right of access to the courts was invoked in unusual circumstances in *Mapp* v. *Gilhooley* [1991] I.L.R.M. 695. In his claim for damages for personal injuries against the defendants, the plaintiff, a minor, had been allowed to give unsworn oral evidence because he did not understand the nature of an oath. The defendants argued on appeal that it was a fundamental rule of the common law that oral evidence must be given on oath or affirmation. The plaintiff contended that any such rule could not have survived the enactment of the Constitution, as it would represent an unjust and invidious discrimination against a person such as the plaintiff. Alternatively, it was claimed, it would be an impermissible restriction on his right of access to the courts. The Supreme Court found for the defendant. Finlay C.J. (O'Flaherty J. concurring) said the broad purpose of the common law rule was to ensure as far as possible that such *viva voce* evidence should be true, by providing a moral or religious and legal sanction against

then, neither the State nor anyone else may insist upon a person undergoing medical treatment that he/she wishes to decline—even if death may result. To do so would surely trench impermissibly upon the right of privacy.[57]

The State's duty to protect individuals' health is primarily discharged by appropriate legislative and administrative action; but the duty would also fall on the courts in certain cases. The traditional *parens patriae* jurisdiction (the foundation of wardship proceedings) might be invoked should parents, on religious grounds, refuse to sanction a blood transfusion necessary to save a child's life. Though such issues have not arisen before the Irish courts, they have been much canvassed elsewhere. The relevant authorities are surveyed by the Supreme Court of Canada in *Re Eve* (1986) 31 D.L.R. (4th) 1. There it was held that the courts could not consent, on behalf of a mentally retarded woman also suffering from extreme difficulty in communicating with others, to her sterilisation in order to save her from a possible pregnancy, and from parental obligations she was allegedly incapable of fulfilling. La Forest J., giving the judgment of the court, said (at 34):

> "The importance of maintaining the physical integrity of a human being ranks high in our scale of values, particularly as it affects the privilege of giving life. I cannot agree that a court can deprive a woman of that privilege for purely social or non-therapeutic purposes without her consent. The fact that others may suffer inconvenience or hardship from failure to do so cannot be taken into account. The . . . *parens patriae* jurisdiction exists for the benefit of those who cannot help themselves, not to relieve those who may have the burden of caring for them."

It can hardly be doubted that, were a similar case to come before them, the Irish courts would endorse these views.[58] Whether the Oireachtas could grant jurisdiction to authorise such intervention is unclear. In *Re Eve supra* La Forest J. noted that any Canadian legislation to this end would raise an issue under the Charter of Rights; but he understandably did not indicate how that issue might be resolved.

State (C.) v. *Frawley* [1976] I.R. 365 was, to say the least, an unusual case. It was an application by the prosecutor for habeas corpus. He was in prison serving sentences imposed by the Circuit Court but his challenge was not to the validity of his conviction or the warrant issued pursuant thereto. Instead, his complaint was about the conditions of his detention; these were such as to make that detention not "in accordance with law" under Article 40.4.2° of the Constitution. The prosecutor had been diagnosed as suffering from a sociopathic personality disturbance so acute that for periods he was temporarily of unsound mind. He was physically strong, with an aggressive and continuous hostility towards authority, in pursuit of which he exhibited physical courage tantamount to recklessness. He had made repeated attempts to

---

deliberate untruth. Such a rule could not be inconsistent with the Constitution, either as discriminatory or as an impermissible restriction on the right of access to the courts. The Law Reform Commission has recommended the abolition of the oath and the substitution of an affirmation therefor: *Report on Oaths and Affirmations* (LRC 34–1990).

[57] See further Declan Costello, "The Terminally Ill: The Law's Concerns" (1986) XXI *Irish Jurist* (N.S.) 35.

[58] On the remarkable facts of *Re B (a minor)* [1987] 2 All E.R. 206 the House of Lords held that sterilisation had been shown to be for the welfare and in the best interests *of the ward herself*, and that leave to perform it had rightly been granted. See further T. A. M. Cooney, "Sterilisation and the Mentally Handicapped" (1989) 11 *D.U.L.J.* (N.S.) 56.

escape, involving dangerous feats of climbing, and had a record of swallow-ing metal objects which had to be removed from his stomach by surgery. Further abdominal surgery now constituted a risk to his health. On several occasions he had been certified as insane and transferred to the Central Mental Hospital for short periods of a month or less. For most of the time in prison he had been kept in solitary confinement, and when not so confined he was usually kept handcuffed for some period. To prevent him escaping, or injuring himself, he was deprived of some of the ordinary equipment of a prisoner such as cutlery, a bed with springs and a transistor radio. During his periods in the Central Mental Hospital his treatment consisted only of sedation and custodial care, his behaviour having prevented any effective therapy.

The expert evidence showed that the only long term psychiatric treatment which would have a reasonable chance of success in C.'s case would be his detention in a very specialised unit. No such institution or facilities existed in Ireland and the number of persons who would need similar treatment was very small. And even if finance was available, it would be several years before such a unit could be operative.

Counsel argued that the prosecutor's right to bodily integrity obliged the State to protect the prosecutor's health as far as reasonably possible in the circumstances. But his present detention failed to secure him that consti-tutional right and was thus unlawful. Furthermore, freedom from torture or inhuman or degrading treatment was also an unenumerated constitutional right—which the prosecutor's present detention violated. Finlay P. held that the principle of the right to bodily integrity did not apply only to legislation (as in *Ryan* v. *Att. Gen.* ([1965] I.R. 294)) but would also operate to prevent an act or omission of the executive which, without justification, would expose the health of a person to risk or danger. This applied to persons in prison. But the vital question here was whether the executive had failed in its duty. The restrictions the prosecutor complained of were imposed to prevent him from injuring himself. Nor could the executive's failure to provide him with treatment of a very special kind in an institution not existing in the State con-stitute a breach of its duty, which was not an absolute one.

Finlay P. went on to refer to Kenny J.'s observation in *Ryan's* case that the citizen had personal rights flowing from the Christian and democratic nature of the State. This being so, said the President, it was beyond argument that they included freedom from torture and from inhuman and degrading treat-ment and punishment. Such a conclusion appeared to him inescapable even if there had never been a European Convention on Human Rights or if Ire-land had never been a party to it.[59] But the prosecutor's conditions of deten-tion did not constitute a failure to protect him from those things. The restrictions imposed on him were not punitive or malicious; they were intended to prevent him from escaping or injuring himself. Finlay P. added ([1976] I.R. 365, 374);

> "I must construe the entire concept of torture, inhuman or degrading treatment and punishment as being not only evil in its consequences but evil in its purpose as well. It is most commonly inspired by revenge,

---

[59] Art. 3 of the Convention forbids torture or inhuman or degrading treatment or punishment. The European Court of Human Rights found that the U.K. had violated this provision in its treatment of certain internees in Northern Ireland—*Ireland* v. *U.K.* (1978) 2 E.H.R.R. 25.

retaliation, the creation of fear or improper interrogation. It is to me inconceivable to associate it with the necessary discharge of a duty to prevent self-injury or self-destruction."

The application for habeas corpus was accordingly refused.

In his judgment in *People (Att. Gen.)* v. *O'Brien* [1965] I.R. 142, 150, Kingsmill Moore J. (Lavery and Budd JJ. concurring) said *obiter* that to countenance the use of evidence extracted or discovered by gross personal violence would "involve the State in moral defilement." It seems plain therefore that the State cannot countenance such treatment for any purpose, however laudable it may seem, including the gathering of evidence or intelligence. Evidence obtained by such means would clearly be held inadmissible, but such conduct could also presumably be restrained by injunction and penalised by damages.

Should conditions in a prison or other place of detention pose a health hazard for prisoners, the High Court may order their improvement: *State (Richardson)* v. *Governor, Mountjoy Prison* [1980] I.L.R.M. 82, as explained in *State (Comerford)* v. *Governor, Mountjoy Prison* [1981] I.L.R.M. 86, 90.

The right to travel

In *Ryan* v. *Att. Gen.* [1965] I.R. 294, 313 Kenny J. instanced as a personal right of the citizen the right to free movement *within* the State. This was further developed in *State (M)* v. *Att. Gen.* [1979] I.R. 73, where Finlay P. identified a broader right to travel—and to obtain a passport for this purpose. The President was careful to point out that without making arrangements with other sovereign states, the State could not by law or executive act guarantee citizens free movement outside the State. The Constitution could not, and should not, be construed as imposing on the State an obligation to make such agreements in any event or upon any terms. (Presumably the President wished to avoid any interpretation of the Constitution which might impede the executive in formulating and implementing foreign policy—a function committed to it by Article 29.4.) However, where such arrangements already existed a citizen had an unenumerated constitutional right to a passport permitting him or her to avail of facilities under them. To this right, however, there were "obvious and justified restrictions"—for example, an undischarged obligation to the State by the person seeking a passport or seeking to use one, as where a person had entered into a recognisance to appear before a criminal court for the trial of an offence.

The conditions for the issue of a passport are not specified in statute or in regulations (see Chap. 9 *supra*). Thus the matter remains one for executive discretion. The above case indicates that the discretion is not unfettered and that its exercise may be subjected to judicial review. Nonetheless the discretion is plainly an extensive one. Executive decisions preventing travel to certain states on foreign policy grounds are unlikely to be quashed by the courts. In *State (M)* v. *Att. Gen.* Finlay P. referred to the United States Supreme Court's recognition of a constitutional right to travel in *Kent* v. *Dulles* (1958) 357 U.S. 116. That court reaffirmed this in *Aptheker* v. *Secretary of State* (1964) 378 U.S. 500, striking down a statute which denied passports to members of an organisation "with knowledge or notice" that it was required to register as "a Communist organisation." However, in *Zemel* v.

Rusk (1965) 381 U.S. 1, the Court upheld the executive's refusal to issue passports for travel to Cuba; such a restriction was justified by "the weightiest considerations of national security." Similarly in *Haig* v. *Agee* (1981) 453 U.S. 280, a 7–2 majority upheld the revocation of the respondent's passport on the ground of his activities in exposing undercover C.I.A. agents. The freedom to travel abroad, said Burger C.J., was subordinate to national security and foreign policy considerations, and was subject to reasonable regulation.

Even if one has a passport the right to travel may be impeded by restrictions on taking money abroad—whether to one state or generally. The Irish courts have not had occasion to consider whether such restrictions (for which provision is made by the Exchange Control Acts 1954–1982) would be valid. In *Regan* v. *Wald* (1984) 468 U.S. 222 the United States Supreme Court upheld 1982 Treasury regulations banning tourist and business travel to Cuba, founding on *Zemel* v. *Rusk*. Rehnquist J., giving the majority judgment, said that the restrictions here were justified by weighty concerns of foreign policy, and referred to the Court's "classical deference to the political branches in matters of foreign affairs." Irish decisions in other areas touching upon security, such as *State (Lynch)* v. *Cooney* [1982] I.R. 337 and *Savage* v. *D.P.P. & Att. Gen.* [1982] I.L.R.M. 385, would suggest that the *Regan* case might be followed here.

State (M) v. *Att. Gen.* [1979] I.R. 73 concerned a baby girl born to an Irish woman and a Nigerian man. The parents were not married, and did not intend to marry, and they had decided that the child should go to Nigeria and be brought up there. The mother accordingly applied for a passport. However, the Department of Foreign Affairs rejected the application; to issue a passport, it was felt, would be to aid and abet a breach of the Adoption Act 1952. Section 40(1) forbade the removal from the State of any child under seven years of age who was an Irish citizen. Under subsection (2) this ban did not apply to the removal of an illegitimate child under one year of age, with the mother's approval, for the purpose of residing with a relative outside the State—but the father's parents did not count as relatives for this purpose. Subsection (3) provided:

> "Subsection (1) shall not apply to the removal of a child (*not being an illegitimate child under one year of age*) by or with the approval of a parent, guardian or relative of the child."

Finlay P. held that in circumstances such as these, a child had a constitutional right to travel outside the State at the choice of its mother or legal guardian, subject to the power of the courts to intervene to ensure the child's welfare. Since section 40 made no provision for exceptional cases (*e.g.* by vesting a discretion in the courts) it failed to defend and vindicate that right. But the whole section need not fall; it was necessary only to declare unconstitutional section 40(2) and the italicised words in subsection (3).

The constitutional right to travel abroad was one of the matters which led O'Hanlon J. to refuse an interlocutory injunction in *Lennon* v. *Ganly* [1981] I.L.R.M. 84. There the plaintiff sought to restrain the Irish Rugby Football Union (I.R.F.U.), which had organised a tour of South Africa, from using the word "Irish" to describe the party and from associating with it such symbols as the shamrock, the tricolour and the national anthem. O'Hanlon J. declined to grant the relief sought. The defendants, and the players participating in the tour, had a prima facie right to travel abroad for the purpose of taking part in sporting fixtures if they so wished. They could be restrained from exercising that right only if it was in some way unlawful for them to act in the manner proposed. While there had been widespread international condemnation of apartheid, there was no rule of international law which compelled one state to refuse to have anything to do with another state where apartheid was practised. The I.R.F.U., by maintaining sporting links with South Africa, was no more in breach of international law than were the Government and the State in permitting the continuance of trading relations with that country. In addition, the plaintiff had not shown that any rights of his would be infringed by the proposed tour, nor had he satisfactorily explained his delay in bringing the proceedings.

In *Att. Gen.* v. *X.* (*The Irish Times*, March 6, 1982) three members of the Supreme Court held, *obiter*, that the right to life of the unborn was superior in constitutional ranking to the right to travel. Thus, absent a threat to her life, the mother could be enjoined from travelling outside the jurisdiction to have an abortion. See further *infra, s.v.* Abortion.

The right to marry and found a family

In his seminal judgment in *Ryan* v. *Att. Gen.* [1965] I.R. 294, Kenny J. suggested that the right to marry was one of the citizen's personal rights. This was founded on by the plaintiffs in *Murray* v. *Att. Gen.* [1985] I.R. 532—a husband and wife each of whom had been convicted of capital murder and sentenced to life imprisonment. While the prison authorities allowed them to meet regularly, those visits were strictly supervised and intimate marital relations were not permitted to them. The plaintiffs had no children but they wished to start a family, and by the time they were released it would be biologically impossible for them to do so. Consequently they claimed that they had a constitutionally protected right to beget children, and that this right was being unconstitutionally infringed; and they sought declarations that they were entitled to be provided with facilities enabling them to exercise this right.

Costello J. held that the right to beget children was a personal right protected by Article 40.3.1°. The issue here was, therefore, whether the restrictions on the right caused by the exercise of the State's power to imprison the plaintiffs was constitutionally permissible. The judge concluded that no claim by the plaintiffs to be allowed to leave prison on bail, from time to time, to exercise the right here in issue could be sustained, as it was incompatible with the constitutionally permitted restriction on their liberty. Citing the United States Supreme Court's decision in *Wolff* v. *McDonnell* (1974) 418 U.S. 539, Costello J. said that a prisoner could exercise such rights as did not place unreasonable demands on the place where he was imprisoned. Observing that the right claimed by the plaintiffs must extend to *all* married prisoners, even those with children, the judge held that it would place unreasonable demands on the prison service to require prison authorities to make facilities available within the confines of the prison to enable all such persons to exercise the right to beget children. And if this was so, prisoners in that category, including the plaintiffs, could not validly complain that the exercise of their rights had been unconstitutionally restricted. On appeal the Supreme Court upheld Costello J.'s decision: [1991] I.L.R.M. 465.

The right to beget children is thus not an absolute one, and the same must hold for the right to marry. The law may therefore place restrictions on the right to marry, as it does by specifying age limits and prohibiting marriage with certain relatives. And if the State decided to follow United States practice in requiring a blood test as a precondition of marriage, a statute so ordaining would doubtless pass constitutional muster. But any such restriction must be reasonable. So, for example, a statute setting a minimum age for marriage higher than the voting age of 18 would be open to challenge on this basis. So too might be some of the law's current prohibitions on marriage between relatives—*e.g.* those between first cousins or between certain persons related by affinity rather than by consanguinity.[60]

In *Zablocki* v. *Redhail* (1978) 434 U.S. 374 the United States Supreme Court had to consider a Wisconsin statute which forbade marriage by any state resident with minor children not in his custody whom he was obliged by a court order to support, unless he could show compliance with that order and the children were not then, and were not likely to become, public charges. The court held that the statute violated the equal protection guarantee of the 14th Amendment because it unreasonably interfered with the exercise of a fundamental right. There were other effective means open to the state to compel compliance with court orders for maintenance—such as contempt proceedings, criminal penalties and attachment of earnings orders. And since the statute did not prevent the father from taking on any and every new financial commitment, it could not be argued that it protected his ability to meet his maintenance obligations. Should the Oireachtas adopt such a policy, the resulting statute would plainly be challengeable as an invalid restriction on the right to marry. But whether the Irish courts would uphold such a challenge is another issue. They have traditionally been somewhat more deferential to legislative judgment than their United States counterparts, and they might well prefer the approach of Rehnquist J. in his dissenting judgment. He stressed that because of the limited amount of funds available for the support of needy children, the state had an exceptionally strong interest in securing as much support as their parents were able to pay. Thus in his view the statute was sufficiently rational to satisfy the 14th Amendment.

The right to marry normally entails a right to the society of one's spouse; but this, of course, is no more absolute than the former right. A person deprived of that society by State action—as where a husband or wife is imprisoned or, if in the Defence Forces, is sent to serve abroad—cannot claim that this is unconstitutional. Nor can an Irish citizen whose alien spouse is required to leave the State: *Pok Sun Shum* v. *Ireland* [1986] I.L.R.M. 593: *Osheku* v. *Ireland* [1987] I.L.R.M. 330.

Though the right to marry, as a fundamental personal right, qualifies for protection under Article 40.3, other rights flowing from it may not so qualify. In *Abdelkefi* v. *Minister for Justice* [1984] I.L.R.M. 138 the second plaintiff, an Irish citizen, was married to an alien who had been refused permission to live in Ireland; and it seemed doubtful if he would be permitted to re-enter the

---

[60] The present law on prohibited degrees of relationship is set out in the Law Reform Commission's *Report on Nullity of Marriage* (I.R.C. 9–1984), pp. 45–48. The Commission recommended that marriages between first cousins should be permitted, and that all prohibitions based on affinity should be abolished—pp. 135–42.

State. The second plaintiff said that she wished to visit her relations in Ireland from time to time, and claimed that she had an unenumerated right to do so in the company of her husband. Barron J. held, however, that the fulfilment of her desire to visit her immediate family in her husband's company was not a right of such a fundamental nature as to be guaranteed under Article 40.3.

The right to fair procedures in decision-making

The common law concept of natural justice guaranteed a right to fairness of procedure in decision-making. At a minimum, this meant that a person affected by a decision had a right to a fair hearing by an unbiased body.[61] Now that common law doctrine has been elevated to constitutional status. In *Garvey* v. *Ireland* [1980] I.R. 75 the Supreme Court held the doctrine applicable to section 6(2) of the Police Forces Amalgamation Act 1925, under which the Government was empowered at any time to remove the Garda Commissioner from office. O'Higgins C.J. (Parke J. concurring) said ([1980] I.R. 75, 97):

" . . . by Article 40, s.3, there is guaranteed to every citizen whose rights may be affected by decisions taken by others the right to fair and just procedures. This means that under the Constitution powers cannot be exercised unjustly or unfairly."

Henchy J. said (at 100):

" . . . the statements in certain decisions of this Court to the effect that the Constitution impliedly assures to the citizen basic fairness of procedure mean that, where the occasion so requires, in order to effectuate the guarantees he will be held entitled to natural justice—a concept which is not confined to the two main principles of *nemo judex in causa sua* and *audi alteram partem*. It should be noted that those guarantees are protective against an unjust attack as well as vindicative in the event of an unjust attack."

Griffin J. said (at 108):

"Article 40, s.3 of the Constitution . . . has been held by this Court to be a guarantee of fair procedures, and statutes which permit decisions to be taken which may affect the rights or fortunes of individual citizens should be construed as providing for fair procedures. The rules of natural justice are only the rules of fair play and fair procedures put into practice."

One consequence of this elevation would plainly be that a statute, or statutory regulations, requiring decisions to be made following unfair procedures would be presumptively invalid. But such a situation is unlikely to occur, since it will usually be possible to read an obligation to follow fair procedures into the relevant provisions. The true importance of constitutionalising the right to a fair hearing seems to lie elsewhere—*e.g.* in emphasising the need for its recognition and application by the courts so that it does not suffer the tem-

---

[61] See, *e.g. Maunsell* v. *Minister for Education* [1940] I.R. 213: *State (Horgan)* v. *Exported Live Stock Insurance Board* [1943] I.R. 581: *Foley* v. *Irish Land Commission* [1952] I.R. 118: *Re Estate of Roscrea Meat Products Ltd.* [1958] I.R. 47.

porary eclipse natural justice underwent in Britain before *Ridge* v. *Baldwin*
[1964] A.C. 60; in broadening the scope of the principle so as to embrace
more than the two classical maxims *nemo judex in causa sua* and *audi alteram partem*; and in creating an Irish analogue of the fertile Due Process clauses of the
United States Constitution.[62] Finally, this new development paves the way
for recognising damages as a remedy for violation of fair procedures, since
there is an unenumerated right to such procedures and it is already established law that the violation of constitutional rights may sound in damages
even if no common law head of liability exists: *Meskell* v. *C.I.E.* [1973] I.R.
121.

The right to fair procedures is, of course, no more absolute than any other
constitutional right and may have to yield to countervailing considerations.
Thus, on grounds *inter alia* of practicability, it does not apply to a legislative
process, as where a Minister makes regulations under statutory authority—
Cassidy v. *Minister for Industry and Commerce* [1978] I.R. 297, 304 *per* McMahon
J. (see too *Bi-Metallic Investment Co.* v. *Colorado* (1915) 239 U.S. 441). Nor does
it apply to emergency situations—*e.g.* where swift action is necessary to protect the interests of the public: *O'Callaghan* v. *Commissioners of Public Works*
[1985] I.L.R.M. 364—or of the State: *State (Lynch)* v. *Cooney* [1982] I.R.
337.[63] The United States Supreme Court has recognised this also: *North
American Cold Storage Co.* v. *Chicago* (1908) 211 U.S. 306 (summary seizure of
contaminated food): *Fahey* v. *Mallonee* (1947) 332 U.S. 245 (emergency action
to prevent further mismanagement of a bank): *Hodel* v. *Virginia Surface Mining
Association* (1981) 452 U.S. 264 (summary orders to cease mining operations
on health, safety or environmental grounds). ·

What fair procedure requires depends on the context, statutory and otherwise: see *Doupe* v. *Limerick Co. Council* [1981] I.L.R.M. 456. The basic principle is that the person affected must be given notice of what is proposed, and
a proper opportunity to make his or her case—which normally involves the
disclosure of all relevant information in the possession of the decision-making
body; *Nolan* v. *Irish Land Commission* [1981] I.R. 23: *State (Williams)* v. *Army
Pensions Board* [1983] I.R. 308. Reasons for decisions are not generally
required—*State (Cole)* v. *Labour Court* (High Court, Barron J., July 24, 1983):
State (Kenny and Hussey) v. *An Bord Pleanála* (Supreme Court December 20,
1984).[64] The United States Supreme Court, by contrast, treats the need for
reasoned decisions as axiomatic; *Goldberg* v. *Kelly* (1970) 397 U.S. 254.

Fair procedures may in some instances require that a person affected by a
decision be allowed legal representation. In *Re Haughey* [1971] I.R. 217 Ó
Dálaigh C.J. (Walsh and Budd JJ. concurring) said (at 264):

> " . . . in proceedings before any tribunal where a party is on risk of hav-
> ing his good name, or his person or property, or any of his personal
> rights jeopardised, the proceedings may be correctly classified as pro-
> ceedings which may affect his rights, and in compliance with the Consti-

---

[62] One could wish that the citation of U.S. authority, so common in Irish courts when the validity of statutes is in issue, were extended to this sphere also.

[63] See, too, *State (Jordan)* v. *Commissioner, Garda Síochána* [1987] I.L.R.M. 107, and *Clancy* v. *Ireland* [1988] I.R. 326.

[64] See, however, *International Fishing Vessels Ltd.* v. *Minister for the Marine* [1989] I.R. 149, where
Blayney J. found the Minister's failure to give reasons, when asked for them, a violation of fair
procedure. The judge stressed how disadvantageous this was for the applicants, in terms of
deciding upon a possible forensic challenge.

tution the State, either by its enactments or through the Courts, must outlaw any procedures which will restrict or prevent the party concerned from vindicating those rights.''

This was said in the context of a statutory inquiry where the procedures adopted allowed witnesses to be accompanied by lawyers for purposes of consultation, but not to examine other witnesses or address the committee. But the Supreme Court held that the applicant here was not a mere witness, since his conduct was the very subject-matter of the inquiry. Thus to deny him the right to legal representation was to violate fair procedures.

Should fair procedure involve legal representation it would be representation at the affected person's expense. There is no obligation on the deciding body—or the State—to fund such representation: *Condon* v. *C.I.E. and others* (High Court, Barrington J., November 16, 1984). The United States Supreme Court has gone further than this, holding that due process may require provision of legal representation at public expense in some cases—*Lassiter* v. *Dept. of Social Services* (1981) 452 U.S. 18. So too it has held that in paternity claims where a state is heavily involved the state must pay for blood-grouping tests for an impecunious defendant—*Little* v. *Streater* (1981) 452 U.S. 1.

In *S.* v. *S.* [1983] I.R. 68 O'Hanlon J., founding on the rights of access to the courts and to fair procedures, held that the supposed rule whereby a woman was barred from giving evidence that a man other than her husband had fathered her child was not part of modern Irish law.[65] Thus the notion of basic fairness of procedures would seem to have an evidential dimension—as is true of due process in the United States. In *Santosky* v. *Kramer* (1982) 455 U.S. 745, for example, a New York statute provided that the Family Court could terminate parents' rights over a child where the child was permanently neglected. A finding to this effect had to be supported by a "fair preponderance of the evidence." The Supreme Court, by a 5–4 majority, held this invalid; due process required a standard of "clear and convincing evidence."

The second facet of classical natural justice is enshrined in the maxim *nemo judex in causa sua*. This means, as Griffin J. put it in *Corrigan* v. *Irish Land Commission* [1977] I.R. 317, 327, that "a person in a judicial or quasi-judicial capacity in a matter which is otherwise within his jurisdiction may be disqualified from hearing that matter by reason of actual or presumed bias on his part." Clearly this too now has constitutional status; but, as United States experience shows, it is easier to persuade a court that a given decision is invalid than it is to obtain a ruling that a statute setting up a decision-making process has established an invalid system.

In *O'Brien* v. *Bord na Móna* [1983] I.R. 255 the plaintiff invoked the maxim *nemo judex in causa sua* in his challenge to the validity of part of the Turf Development Act 1946. This Act established the defendant board to develop the country's peat resources and equipped it with extensive powers of compulsory purchase. The board sought to acquire bogland belonging to the plaintiff. He contended that the Act failed to honour the constitutional guarantee of fair procedures deriving from Article 40.3. It was, he said, defective in that:

[65] s.46(1) of the Status of Children Act 1987 now provides: "The evidence of a husband or wife shall be admissible in any proceedings to prove that marital intercourse did or did not take place between them during any period."

(a) it failed to require that notice of intention to make a compulsory purchase order be given to a person affected

(b) it failed to provide for any inquiry or for an opportunity for representations or objections

(c) the absence of any procedure for confirmation or appeal made the
board judge in its own cause.

Keane J. rejected arguments (a) and (b). The 1946 Act attracted the presumption of constitutionality, and this required that the powers thereby conferred be exercised in accordance with fair procedures. The fact that the
board's power was not expressly circumscribed by any rules of procedure did
not relieve it of the obligation to act in accordance "with constitutional justice": [1983] I.R. 255, 268.[66] But Keane J. accepted argument (c). While the
maxim *nemo judex in causa sua* applied to judicial, and not administrative, functions that of the board in issue here was judicial. Its decision, however, could
not be impartial or disinterested, for it necessarily had an interest in achieving the objectives for which it was created. The judge then went on to point
out that the constitutional guarantee of fair procedures was not absolute; it
was qualified by the words "as far as practicable" and "as best it may" in
Article 40.3. Nonetheless, he concluded that it would have been practicable
for the Oireachtas to honour that guarantee by an alternative form of procedure, involving confirmation by another body (see [1983] I.R. 255,
268–274). The plaintiff was consequently granted a declaration that sections
29 and 30 of the Act were invalid.

On appeal the Supreme Court reversed this decision. It concluded that
although Bord na Móna was obliged to act judicially when making a compulsory purchase order, this did not mean that its function here could be classified as judicial. On analysis of the 1946 Act the Supreme Court was satisfied
that an order for compulsory acquisition thereunder was essentially an
administrative act. It would be reviewable by the courts should the board act
"from an indirect or improper motive or without due fairness of procedure or
without proper consideration for the rights of others"—[1983] I.R. 255, 283.
But the absence of a right of appeal or provision for external confirmation did
not constitute a breach of the plaintiff's constitutional rights.[67]

The Supreme Court's approach to this matter is similar to that of its
United States counterpart. In *Withrow* v. *Larkin* (1975) 421 U.S. 35 there was
a challenge to a Wisconsin statute which created an examining board to
license physicians. The board was entitled *inter alia* to institute criminal proceedings, or action to revoke a licence, in certain circumstances. It was
argued that for the board both to investigate and adjudicate was a violation
of due process, but the Supreme Court rejected this contention. White J., for
the court, said that the argument that the combination of investigative and
adjudicative functions necessarily created an unconstitutional risk of bias
had a difficult burden of persuasion to carry. It had to overcome a presumption of honesty and integrity in those serving as adjudicators. And it had to
convince that, under a realistic appraisal of psychological tendencies and
human weakness, conferring investigative and adjudicative powers on the
same individuals posed such a risk of actual bias or prejudgment that the

---

[66] On appeal, the Supreme Court affirmed these conclusions—[1983] I.R. 255, 281.

[67] The board's decision was annulled by the Supreme Court on a different procedural ground—
see [1983] I.R. 255, 287–288.

practice must be forbidden if the guarantee of due process was to be adequately implemented.[68]

ABORTION

Long before the enactment of the Constitution the law prohibited abortion, whether self-induced or performed by another: s.58, Offences against the Person Act 1861.[69] The prohibition, however, was not total, since the word "unlawfully" recurs throughout the section; and in the United Kingdom, where the same Act applied, medical opinion came to accept abortion as lawful in situations threatening the mother's mental or physical health, as well as her life.[70] It seems most unlikely that Irish practice went so far, though the factors governing this were probably moral and religious rather than legal. There does not appear to have been a prosecution under the 1861 Act since independence.[71]

The court's recognition of an unenumerated constitutional right of privacy led some to fear an Irish parallel to developments in the United States, where a similar right had successfully been invoked to invalidate statutes criminalising abortion: *Roe* v. *Wade* (1973) 410 U.S. 113. A campaign was therefore launched to secure a constitutional amendment to protect unborn life,[72] and this culminated in the passage of the Eighth Amendment of the Constitution Act 1983. This inserted a new Article 40.3.3°, which provides as follows:

> "The State acknowledges the right to life of the unborn and, with due regard for the equal right to life of the mother, guarantees in its laws to respect, and, as far as practicable, by its laws to defend and vindicate that right."

This provision has given rise to considerable litigation, both within Ireland and in European fora.

The first case was *Att. Gen. (S.P.U.C. (Ireland) Ltd.)* v. *Open Door Counselling Ltd.* [1988] I.R. 593. The plaintiffs sought an injunction restraining the defendants from counselling or assisting pregnant women within the jurisdiction to obtain an abortion or to obtain advice thereon. The High Court granted the order and the defendants appealed. The Supreme Court held that Article 40.3.3° was self-executing, and imposed an obligation not only on

---

[68] See further Bernard Schwartz, *Administrative Law: A Casebook* (2nd ed., Boston 1983), pp. 483–514.

[69] s.58 provides: "Every woman, being with child, who, with intent to procure her own miscarriage, shall unlawfully administer to herself any poison or other noxious thing, or shall unlawfully use any instrument or other means whatsoever with the like intent, and whosoever, with intent to procure the miscarriage of any woman, whether she be or be not with child, shall unlawfully administer to her or cause to be taken by her any poison or other noxious thing, or shall unlawfully use any instrument or other means whatsoever with the like intent, shall be guilty of felony, and being convicted thereof shall be liable, at the discretion of the court, to be kept in penal servitude for life, or for any term not less than three years,—or to be imprisoned for any term not exceeding two years, with or without hard labour, and with or without solitary confinement." Note also s.59, which makes it an offence knowingly to supply any poison, instrument, etc. for use in procuring a miscarriage.

[70] See John Keown, *Abortion, Doctors and the Law* (Cambridge 1988), Chap. 3.

[71] Charges of murder have, however, been brought where women have died as a consequence of an abortion: see *People (Att. Gen.)* v. *Cadden* (1956) 91 I.L.T.R. 97, and the 1940 case of *Daly* there referred to.

[72] See further Tom Hesketh, *The Second Partitioning of Ireland?* (Dun Laoghaire 1990), Chap. 1.

the Oireachtas but also on the courts. Finlay C.J., his colleagues concurring, said (at 623):

> "If it is established to the satisfaction of the Court that the admitted activities of the defendants constitute an assistance to pregnant women within the jurisdiction to go out of the jurisdiction for the purpose of having an abortion, then that is an activity which directly threatens the right to life of the unborn, not only in a single case but in all cases of women who are assisted by those activities to have an abortion.
>
> If, therefore, the jurisdiction of the courts is invoked by a party who has a *bona fide* concern and interest for the protection of the constitutionally guaranteed right to life of the unborn, the courts, as the judicial organ of government of the State, would be failing in their duty as far as practicable to vindicate and defend that right if they were to refuse relief upon the grounds that no particular pregnant woman who might be affected by the making of an order was represented before the court."

The defendants argued, *inter alia*, that one of the unenumerated constitutional rights was a right to receive and impart information; that this included a right in pregnant women to receive information about the availability of abortion outside the jurisdiction; and that the courts could not make an order impeding the exercise of that right. The Supreme Court rejected this argument, Finlay C.J. saying (at 625):

> "The performing of an abortion on a pregnant woman terminates the unborn life which she is carrying. Within the terms of Article 40, s.3, subs. 3 it is a direct destruction of the constitutionally guaranteed right to life of that unborn child.
>
> It must follow from this that there could not be an implied and unenumerated constitutional right to information about the availability of a service of abortion outside the State which, if availed of, would have the direct consequence of destroying the expressly guaranteed constitutional right to life of the unborn . . . no right could constitutionally arise to obtain information the purpose of the obtaining of which was to defeat the constitutional right to life of the unborn child."

The court also rejected the defendants' argument that the case involved questions of EC law, necessitating a reference to the European Court of Justice under Article 177, EEC Treaty.[73] It therefore affirmed the High Court decision, though varying the terms of the order.[74] Subsequently the defendants claimed that their rights under the European Convention of Human Rights had been infringed, and the Commission ruled in their favour. The case was referred to the European Court of Human Rights, which has heard it, but no judgment has yet been delivered.

---

[73] Finlay C.J., for the court, said on this point ([1988] I.R. 593, 626): " . . . what is here sought to be restrained is assistance to a pregnant woman to travel abroad and obtain the service of abortion. Since no claim is made on behalf of the defendants that that is a corollary right to whatever rights such woman may have under the Treaty, it follows that no question of the interpretation of the Treaty falls to be decided in this case for the purpose of determining the issue between the parties."

[74] The injunction, as granted by the Supreme Court, was worded as follows ([1988] I.R. 593, 627): "And it is ordered that the defendants and each of them, their servants or agents, be perpetually restrained from assisting pregnant women within the jurisdiction to travel abroad

The next two cases to come before the courts also involved the provision of information on the availability of abortion outside the jurisdiction. In *S.P.U.C. (Ireland) Ltd.* v. *Coogan* [1989] I.R. 734 the plaintiff organisation sought an injunction restraining members of the students' union at University College Dublin from publishing the "Welfare Guide UCD 88/89," which contained information about abortion clinics in England, including addresses. Carroll J. declined to grant the order, holding that the Attorney General was the proper party to move in such a case.[75] The Supreme Court held, by a 4–1 majority,[76] that the plaintiff organisation had *locus standi* to seek the order. It was a person with a *bona fide* interest and concern in the subject-matter of the proceedings. Upon discovering that various student bodies proposed to publish similar guides in the 1989/90 academic year, the plaintiff organisation again moved to restrain them, issuing a plenary summons, and seeking an interlocutory injunction pending trial. Carroll J. decided that an issue of EC law arose[77] and sought a preliminary ruling thereon from the European Court of Justice. She did not grant the interlocutory injunction sought. The plaintiff appealed to the Supreme Court which unanimously held that it should be granted.[78] The decision to seek a preliminary ruling under Article 177, EEC Treaty, did not automatically postpone a ruling on the application for an interlocutory injunction. Finlay C.J. (Walsh, Griffin and Hederman JJ. concurring) said that the *Open Door Counselling* case clearly established that the activities of the defendants in these proceedings were unlawful. The fact that the mode of communication was different here did not alter matters; the illegality lay in the fact that the information on abortion was conveyed to pregnant women. On the balance of convenience question Finlay C.J. said (at 765):

" . . . where an injunction is sought to protect a constitutional right, the only matter which could properly be capable of being weighed in a balance against the granting of such protection would be another competing constitutional right. I am quite satisfied that in the instant case where the right sought to be protected is that of a life, there can be no question of a possible or putative right which might exist in European law as a corollary of a right to travel so as to avail of services, counterbalancing as a matter of convenience the necessity for an interlocutory injunction."

It appears from the judgment of McCarthy J. that no argument based on

---

to obtain abortions by referral to a clinic, by the making for them of travel arrangements, or by informing them of the identity and location of and method of communication with a specified clinic or clinics or otherwise."

[75] In the *Open Door Counselling* case the plaintiff organisation—the Society for the Protection of Unborn Children (Ireland) Ltd.—had originally instituted the proceedings in its own name. On its *locus standi* to do this being challenged, the Attorney General gave leave for his name to be used in relator proceedings, and the action continued with the Attorney as nominal plaintiff: [1988] I.R. 593 at 619. On relator proceedings see J. P. Casey, *The Office of the Attorney General in Ireland* (Dublin 1980), pp. 148–157.

[76] Finlay C.J., Walsh, Griffin and Hederman JJ.: McCarthy J. dissenting.

[77] As to whether there was a right to receive, and to give, information about abortion under Community law.

[78] The court held that an appeal would lie notwithstanding the absence of a formal order declining to grant the injunction sought. The High Court had made a determination affecting one of the parties, and this was a decision appealable to the Supreme Court under Article 34.4.3° of the Constitution.

the Constitution's freedom of expression guarantee and its relation to Article 40.3.3° was addressed to the Supreme Court. In theory, therefore, this question remains open; but it can hardly be doubted that the Supreme Court would treat any relevant exercise of this right as subordinate to the right to life of the unborn.[79] The *Open Door Counselling, Coogan* and *Grogan* cases indicate that, absent a threat to the life of the mother, no other constitutional right could prevail against that. And *dicta* in the latest Supreme Court decision—*Att. Gen.* v. *X.* (*The Irish Times*, March 6, 1992)—confirm this conclusion.

Att. Gen. v. *X.* involved an application to enjoin a 14½ year old girl, pregnant as a result of rape, from travelling to England for an abortion.[80] There was evidence from an experienced clinical psychologist of a real and substantial risk that the girl would take her own life. Costello J. granted the order sought, holding that the risk to the life of the girl was of a different order of magnitude than the certainty that the life of the unborn would be terminated if the order was not made. On appeal[81] the Supreme Court reversed this decision, holding—by a majority[82]—that there was a real and substantial threat to the life of the girl, and that in such circumstances the termination of the pregnancy was constitutionally permissible.

The *X.* case was the first in which the Supreme Court had to consider a conflict between the right to life of the foetus and that of the mother. The court concluded that Article 40.3.3.° permitted abortion, within or without the jurisdiction, in situations where there was a real and substantial risk to the life of the mother which could be avoided only by the termination of her pregnancy. But a risk to mental or physical health will not suffice; the reference to the mother's equal right to "life" in Article 40.3.3.° is not, it seems, to be construed to cover these matters. Moreover, a majority of the court was clearly of opinion (a) that absent a risk to the mother's life, her constitutional right to travel abroad would be subordinate to the right to life of the unborn; (b) that in such situations the court could grant injunctions restraining a pregnant woman from travelling abroad to have an abortion.

Though its outcome was welcomed, the reasoning in the *X.* case caused consternation in different quarters. "Pro-life" campaigners were appalled that the decision had authorised abortion within the jurisdiction; this, they claimed, contravened the will of the people as expressed in the 1983 referendum.[83] Others were aghast at the prospect of women being restrained from travelling abroad to have an abortion. As McCarthy J. pointed out in his judgment, this relief would be available against any pregnant woman, even if

---

[79] The High Court and Supreme Court decisions are severely criticised on free speech grounds by James Friedman, "On the Dangers of Moral Certainty and Sacred Trusts" (1988) 10 *D.U.L.J.* (N.S.) 71.

[80] The girl's parents, who had informed the Gardaí that a crime had been committed, subsequently told them of a family decision to go to England to have the pregnancy terminated. They inquired whether, if certain scientific tests were carried out on the foetus with a view to DNA identification of the father, such evidence would be admissible in court. The Gardaí consulted the Director of Public Prosecutions, who communicated the information thus received to the Attorney General.

[81] The Government had made it clear that the appellants' costs would be met out of public funds.

[82] Finlay C.J., McCarthy, O'Flaherty and Egan JJ.: Hederman J. dissenting.

[83] Given that in 1983 the people had voted for a text clearly recognising the potential for conflict between the rights to life of the mother and the foetus, this is not easy to understand.

she was merely on holiday in the State and irrespective of her nationality or of the place of conception. It would also follow from the earlier Supreme Court rulings on Article 40.3.3° that such relief could be sought by the Attorney General,[84] or by an organisation like S.P.U.C. (Ireland) Ltd., or by the father of the unborn child.[85]

Perhaps because of its special facts, the *X.* case indicates a less absolutist approach to Article 40.3.3.°'s guarantee of unborn life than the prior Supreme Court decisions. And in the light of that case the decisions on abortion information now appear somewhat anomalous. For if a woman may lawfully seek an abortion abroad—even if only in limited circumstances—it would be curious if she could not obtain information enabling her to seek one.

It is a regrettable fact that since 1983 no legislation whatever has been passed on foot of Article 40.3.3°, despite its terms. The task of working out its implications has been left entirely to the courts. This display of political pusillanimity—remarkable even by the usual standards—was severely castigated by McCarthy J. in the *X.* case. It cannot continue, for given that limited abortion is now clearly lawful within the jurisdiction, it will be necessary to spell out in detail the circumstances in, and the conditions upon, which such operations may be performed.

The European law dimension

As noted *supra*, the defendants in the *Open Door Counselling* case invoked the European Convention on Human Rights, claiming that the injunction granted against them violated their rights thereunder. The Commission found in their favour and the case went on to the Court, where judgment has been reserved. It should be noted, however, that even if the Court upholds their claim they will not automatically be entitled to resume their activities. As explained in Chapter 8, the European Convention on Human Rights is not part of the domestic law; and though rulings of the Court of Human Rights clearly bind the State on the international plane, they do *not* override conflicting decisions of the Irish courts. The State would, of course, be under an international obligation to bring its law into line with the decision of the Strasbourg court, but it is not clear that this could be done merely by statute. Given that the Supreme Court's ruling in the *Open Door Counselling* case was based squarely on the terms of Article 40.3.3°, a constitutional amendment may first be required.

The abortion controversy also involves issue of European Community law. Some of these were canvassed, but not resolved, in the *Open Door Counselling* case[86]; however, as already noted, Carroll J. in the *Grogan* case referred certain questions to the European Court of Justice for a preliminary ruling under Article 177. The judgment of that court—*S.P.U.C. (Ireland) Ltd.* v. *Grogan* [1991] 3 C.M.L.R. 849—held that medical termination of pregnancy, performed in accordance with the law of the state in which it was carried out,

---

[84] The Attorney General's decisions in matters such as this are taken independently of the Government. In the *X.* case Finlay C.J. and Hederman J. stated clearly that the Attorney had been not merely entitled, but bound, to institute the relevant proceedings.

[85] As occurred in the Canadian case of *Tremblay* v. *Daigle* (1989) 62 D.L.R. (4th) 634.

[86] See n. 73 *supra*.

constituted a service within the meaning of Article 60 of the Treaty.[87] But the court rejected the defendants' claim that they had a right under Community law to disseminate information about such services, saying ([1991] C.M.L.R. 849, 891):

> "As regards . . . the provisions of Article 59 of the Treaty,[88] which prohibit any restriction on the freedom to supply services, it is apparent from the facts of the case that the link between the activity of the student associations . . . and medical terminations of pregnancies carried out in clinics in another Member State is too tenuous for the prohibition on the distribution of information to be capable of being regarded as a restriction within the meaning of Article 59 of the Treaty."

The court further said (at 891):

> "The information to which the national court's questions refer is not distributed on behalf of an economic operator established in another Member State."

Two things might seem to follow from these statements. Firstly, that had the students' unions been receiving fees from the foreign clinics for distributing the information, their activity in doing so would be protected by Community law. And by virtue of what is now Article 29.4.5°, nothing in Article 40.3.3° could be invoked to restrict that activity.[89] Secondly, the abortion clinics themselves could not be prevented from advertising within Ireland the service they offered. However, Article 66 of the Treaty states that the provisions of Articles 55–58 apply to the freedom to provide services; and Article 56 permits member states to limit that freedom *vis à vis* foreign nationals *inter alia* "on grounds of public policy." In Case 30/77, *R.* v. *Bouchereau* [1977] E.C.R. 1999, 2014 the European Court of Justice said that to justify a derogation on this ground there must exist

> " . . . a genuine and sufficiently serious threat to the requirements of public policy affecting one of the fundamental interests of society."

As Costello J. pointed out in *Att. Gen.* v. *X.* (*The Irish Times*, February 18, 1992) Article 40.3.3° is a statement of Irish public policy on the right to life of the unborn. And it may certainly be argued that protecting that right engages interests fundamental to Irish society, so that the *Bouchereau* conditions for derogating from Articles 59 and 60 of the EEC Treaty are satisfied. But matters are complicated by the European Court's decision in Case

---

[87] Art. 60—so far as relevant—provides: "Services shall be considered to be 'services' within the meaning of this Treaty where they are normally provided for remuneration . . . 'services' shall in particular include: (a) activities of an industrial character; (b) activities of a commercial character; (c) activities of craftsmen; (d) activities of the professions . . . "

[88] Art. 59—so far as relevant—provides: "Within the framework of the provisions set out below, restrictions on freedom to provide services within the Community shall be progressively abolished during the transitional period in respect of nationals of Member States who are established in a State of the Community other than that of the person for whom the services are intended . . . "

[89] The European Court of Justice has held that the first paragraph of Art. 59—quoted *supra*—is directly applicable and creates individual rights which national courts must protect: Case 33/74, *van Binsbergen* [1974] E.C.R. 1299: Joined Cases 110 and 111/78, *Ministère Public* v. *van Waesemael* [1979] E.C.R. 35. This would engage that portion of Article 29.4.5° which provides: "No provision of this Constitution . . . prevents laws enacted, acts done or measures adopted by the Communities or institutions thereof from having the force of law in the State."

C260/89, *Elliniki Radiophonia Tileorassi—AE* v. *Dimotiki Etairia Pliroforissis* (June 18, 1991). There the court held that where a member state invokes Articles 56 and 66 to justify legislation restricting the freedom to provide services, that legislation must be compatible with *all* the principles of Community law and in particular with those protecting fundamental rights. Thus the relevant national court and, where required, the European Court of Justice, would have to assess any national ban on access to abortion information by reference *inter alia* to Article 10 of the European Convention on Human Rights. That provision protects the right to freedom of expression, defined to include " . . . freedom . . . to receive and impart information . . . without interference by public authority and regardless of frontiers." A signatory state may, however, restrict the exercise of this freedom, provided that the restriction is " . . . prescribed by law and . . . necessary in a democratic society . . . for the protection of health or morals, [or] for the protection of the . . . rights of others." It is well established that these words give signatory states a "margin of appreciation," though this is far from unlimited.[90]

As noted above, the European Court of Human Rights is currently seised, in the *Open Door Counselling* case, of the question whether Article 10 of the Convention permits the ban on abortion information which the Supreme Court has derived from Article 40.3.3° of the Constitution. Should it hold that restriction incompatible with Article 10, the European Court of Justice will presumably do the same if an appropriate case comes before it. For it would surely be bizarre if the Luxembourg court took a view of Article 10 different from that of the Strasbourg court, whose very *raison d'être* is to interpret the Convention.

Community law on freedom to provide services also impinges on abortion in another way, for that law clearly recognises a right to travel to receive services—including medical services—in another member state: Joined Cases 286/82 and 26/83, *Luisi and Carbone* v. *Ministero del Tesoro* [1984] E.C.R. 377.[91] Moreover, Council Directive 73/148/EEC requires member states to abolish restrictions on the movement of nationals wishing to go to another member state as recipients of services (Article 1). Specifically, they must grant to such persons the right to leave their territory. By virtue of Article 8, the member states may derogate from the provisions of this directive only " . . . on grounds of public policy, public security or public health." In *Att. Gen.* v. *X.* (*The Irish Times*, February 18, 1992) Costello J. was of opinion that Article 40.4.3° represented a valid derogation from the directive's provisions, so that there was no Community law barrier to enjoining the defendant from travelling abroad for an abortion. On appeal, the Supreme Court expressed no view on this matter, holding that since the case could be decided under Irish law alone, that course should be adopted.

---

[90] The European Court of Human Rights seemed prepared to allow a wider margin of appreciation in the obscene publications case of *Handyside* v. *U.K.* (1976) 1 E.H.R.R. 737 than in the homosexuality case of *Dudgeon* v. *U.K.* (1981) 4 E.H.R.R. 149. In the latter case the court said that both the object of the restriction and the nature of the activities involved would affect the margin of appreciation. It went on to say (paras. 52/53 of the judgment) that the *Dudgeon* case concerned " . . . a most intimate aspect of private life." Thus, under Art. 8(2) " . . . particularly serious reasons . . . " must exist before interference on the part of the public authorities could be legitimate. Further, in Art. 8 the notion of "necessity" was linked to the concept of a "democratic society," and two hallmarks of the latter were tolerance and broadmindedness. Consequently, any restriction must be " . . . proportionate to the legitimate aim pursued."

[91] See too Case 186/87, *Cowan* v. *Trésor Public* [1989] E.C.R. 195.

The Fourth Protocol to the European Convention on Human Rights guarantees freedom to leave one's own country (Article 2.2). This may be subjected only to restrictions which " . . . are in accordance with law and are necessary in a democratic society . . . for the maintenance of *"ordre public"* . . . [or] for the protection of the rights and freedoms of others." It seems likely that the validity of a derogation from Directive 73/148/EEC falls to be judged in the light of this provision, on the basis of the European Court of Justice's decision in Case C260/89, *Elliniki Radiophona Tileorassi—AE* v. *Dimotiki Etairia Pliroforissis* (June 18, 1991). In *Att. Gen.* v. *X.* Costello J. thought that restrictions on the right to travel abroad flowing from Article 40.3.3° were compatible with European Convention guarantees. The European Court of Human Rights, he said,

> " . . . has allowed, when considering limitations imposed by national laws on the Convention's guaranteed rights, national authorities a margin of appreciation in relation to laws dealing with moral issues." (*The Irish Times*, February 18, 1992, p. 6.)

For the reason already given, the Supreme Court did not discuss this issue on appeal. Since it has not been the subject of a ruling by the European Court of Justice either, it is not yet possible to say how it will be resolved.

As if all this were not enough, there are two further complications. The first arose in the wake of the European Court of Justice's decision in Case C159/80, *S.P.U.C. (Ireland) Ltd.* v. *Grogan* [1991] 3 C.M.L.R. 849. At that time the Maastricht Treaty was in the final stages of negotiation, and the Irish Government secured the insertion of a protocol (No. 17) in the following terms:

> "Nothing in the Treaty on European Union, or in the Treaties establishing the European Communities, or in the Treaties or Acts modifying or supplementing those Treaties, shall affect the application in Ireland of Article 40.3.3 of the Constitution of Ireland."

The original purpose behind this seems to have been to ensure that within the State Article 40.3.3°, as interpreted by the Irish courts, should continue to be of full force and effect. On this basis the existing rulings barring access to abortion information would effectively be confirmed, and immunised against challenge under Community law. So too would restrictions on travelling abroad for an abortion, such as the Supreme Court subsequently held in *Att. Gen.* v. *X.* (*The Irish Times*, March 6, 1992) to be authorised by Article 40.3.3°.

In the aftermath of the *X.* case the Government sought to have this protocol amended to ensure the right to travel. (Had any such change occurred, of course, it would not have affected the content of Article 40.3.3° itself; nor would it automatically have reversed the Supreme Court's majority view on the travel issue.) But the text of the treaty was now finalised, and signed, and a majority of member states declined to reopen *any* issue. However, it was agreed to append to the text a solemn declaration, giving a "legal interpretation" of Protocol No. 17:

> " . . . that it was and is their intention that the protocol shall not limit freedom either to travel between Member States or, in accordance with conditions which may be laid down, in conformity with Community

law, by Irish legislation, to obtain or make available in Ireland, information relating to services lawfully available in Member States.

At the same time the High Contracting Parties solemnly declare that, in the event of a future constitutional amendment in Ireland which concerns the subject-matter of Article 40.3.3 of the Constitution of Ireland and which does not conflict with the intention of the High Contracting Parties hereinbefore expressed, they will, following the entry into force of the Treaty on European Union, be favourably disposed to amending the said protocol so as to extend its application to such constitutional amendment if Ireland so requests."

At the time of writing, Protocol No. 17 is not in force; like the rest of the Maastricht Treaty, it will enter into force only when the entire document has been ratified by *all* member states in accordance with their respective constitutional requirements (Article 236, EEC Treaty). A complicating factor—to say the least—is that on June 2, 1992 the Danish electorate, in a referendum, rejected ratification of the Treaty. If this position is maintained[92] then the Treaty cannot enter into force as a Community legal instrument—though the ratifying states could presumably enter into some arrangement putting it into effect as between themselves.

Should the Treaty enter into force as originally intended, then Protocol No. 17 will fall to be interpreted. The "solemn declaration" will be a guide to its construction[93]—even though its terms appear to be at variance with the original purpose behind the protocol's insertion. Thus it would be open to the European Court of Justice to hold that the protocol does not limit the right to travel to obtain, or wholly restrict the right to information about, abortion services lawfully available in another member state.

The protocol and "solemn declaration," however, do not operate to amend Article 40.3.3° as interpreted by the Supreme Court. To guarantee the right to travel and to receive information a constitutional amendment will be required; it is by no means clear that, absent a ruling of the European Court of Justice, the protocol and "solemn declaration" would influence the Supreme Court's construction of Article 40.3.3°.[94] At the time of writing the Government has stated that a referendum on these issues will be held in

---

[92] There is no time limit for ratifying the Treaty. Art. R.2 of its Title VII provides: "This Treaty shall enter into force on 1 January 1993, provided that all the instruments of ratification have been deposited [with the government of the Italian Republic], or, failing that, on the first day of the month following the deposit of the instrument of ratification by the last signatory State to take this step."

[93] Art. 31(3) of the Vienna Convention on the Law of Treaties (1969) provides that in interpreting any treaty there must be taken into account any later agreement between the parties concerning the interpretation of the treaty or the application of its provisions.

[94] It is interesting to note that on April 28, 1992 the Taoiseach, Mr. Reynolds, told the Dáil that if ratification of the Maastricht Treaty was approved in a referendum, the Attorney General would not seek any injunction against a woman travelling abroad for an abortion. This was on the basis that: "Once the people have endorsed a Treaty, to which is annexed Protocol No. 17, and with which is associated the Solemn Declaration, to which, of course, Ireland is a party, it will then be demonstrably clear that public policy as expressed by the people in the referendum does not contemplate interference, consequent on Art. 40.3.3°, with rights to travel" (418 *Dáil Debs.*, c. 1564). At a press conference on April 23 the Taoiseach said that private persons would not be similarly inhibited, but he suggested that should they apply the courts would take the outcome of the Maastricht Treaty vote into account: *The Irish Times*, April 24, 1992.

November 1992.[95] One may perhaps infer from the terms of the "solemn declaration" that the amendment proposed will guarantee the right to travel—and not merely to other Community states—in absolute terms, whereas the right to information[96] will be subject to qualification by law. And if any such amendment is carried, the other Community member states will view sympathetically an Irish request to alter Protocol No. 17 so as to protect that amended text. If, therefore, the amendment additionally ruled out the performance of abortions within Ireland, this ban could be protected against Community law influence arising from the freedom to provide services in another member State.

CITIZENS AND NON-CITIZENS

Many of the rights conferred or recognised by Bunreacht na hÉireann apply to "citizens" only. This is true of the equal protection guarantee (Art. 40.1); the rights specified in Article 40, such as freedom of association, of expression and certain others; and the unenumerated rights deriving from Article 40.3. Other provisions, however, have a broader reach. The guarantees to the family given in Article 41 are not qualified by citizenship, nor—in the main—are those on education, religion and property in Articles 42–44. But even within this broad classification there are differences. Article 44.2.1° guarantees freedom of religion to "every citizen"; but Article 44.2.3° forbids the State to discriminate on the ground of religious profession, belief or status—a guarantee which could presumably be availed of where necessary by a non-citizen. Equally, Article 40.4.1° provides that "no citizen" shall be

---

[95] The Government decided that the referendum necessary to permit ratification of the Maastricht Treaty should be held first (on June 18, 1992). The Taoiseach, Mr. Reynolds, informed the Dáil on April 28, 1992 that there would be no advantage in holding a referendum on travel, information and other matters before this, since the protocol related only to Art. 40.3.3° as it stood when the Treaty was signed (*i.e.* February 7, 1992). Other member states, it was clear, would agree to a change in its terms only when the ratification process was complete (418 *Dáil Debs.*, c. 1562).

[96] The issue of abortion information was highlighted on May 20, 1992 when it was stated on the 9 p.m. RTÉ television news that the *Guardian* of May 21 would carry a full-page advertisement relating to English abortion clinics. On learning of this, the distributors collected the copies at Dublin Airport and withheld them from circulation in the Republic: *The Irish Times*, May 22, 1992. They did not consult with, or inform, the Gardaí: *ibid.* On May 21 the Taoiseach stated in the Dáil that the Government had had no prior knowledge of, or involvement in, the matter: 420 *Dáil Debs.*, c. 5.

The distributors' action was, it seems, based on legal advice which founded upon the Supreme Court's decisions. Note also s.16(1) of the Censorship of Publications Act 1929 (as amended by s.12 of the Health (Family Planning) Act 1979) which provides: "It shall not be lawful for any person, otherwise than under and in accordance with a permit in writing granted to him under this section—

    (a) to print or publish or cause or procure to be printed or published, or
    (b) to sell or expose, offer, or keep for sale, or
    (c) to distribute, offer or keep for distribution,

any book or periodical publication (whether appearing on the register of prohibited publications or not) which advocates or which might reasonably be supposed to advocate the procurement of abortion or miscarriage or any method, treatment or appliance to be used for the purpose of such procurement." The Censorship of Publications Board is empowered to ban periodical publications which have " . . . advocated the procurement of abortion or miscarriage or the use of any method, treatment or appliance for the purpose of such procurement . . . "

deprived of his personal liberty save in accordance with law. But the immediately following habeas corpus provisions refer to the unlawful detention of "any person" and provide for an obligatory High Court inquiry into any such complaint. Thus the procedure may be operated by an alien; *State (Kugan)* v. *Station Sergeant, Fitzgibbon Street Garda Station* [1986] I.L.R.M. 95.

In *State (Nicolaou)* v. *An Bord Uchtála* [1966] I.R. 567 the prosecutor challenged the validity of the Adoption Act 1952. Though he was not a citizen of Ireland his arguments invoked Article 40.1 and 40.3.1° as well as Articles 41 and 42. Counsel for the Attorney General told the courts that he was instructed, as a matter of policy, not to submit that the prosecutor's rights were any less than those of a citizen. Counsel for the prosecutor argued that the word "citizen" was used in different senses in different parts of the Constitution, and that under the fundamental rights provisions the prosecutor could qualify as a citizen. In the High Court Murnaghan and Teevan JJ. declined to express any concluded view on this point. Teevan J., however, said he did not think the courts were obliged to deny "the constitutional protection of those natural rights enshrined in the Constitution" to every non-citizen merely on the ground of his non-citizenship. Where there was no conflict between the common good and the right sought to be asserted by a non-citizen, the courts should not feel obliged to refuse to hear the non-citizen's plaint where his own personal rights were involved. Teevan J.'s view was that the matter was one for discernment according to the particular circumstances. In some situations "it would be no more than impertinent" for a non-citizen to attack the constitutionality of a statute; or it might be "necessary or prudent" to take the non-citizenship point ([1966] I.R. 567, 599–600). Henchy J. could find nothing to support the prosecutor's contention that "citizens" was equivalent to "persons" in Articles 40.1 and 40.3. The citizens referred to in Article 40.1 were the same as those in Article 40.2—*i.e.* citizens as defined in Article 9. The purpose of Article 40.3 was to state a constitutional right which attached to citizenship and fell as a duty on the State. It was only a citizen who could claim that right, and he was entitled to it as a constitutional incident of his citizenship ([1966] I.R. 567, 616–617).

The Supreme Court, for its part, considered all the prosecutor's constitutional arguments. Noting that the High Court judgments partly rested on the appellant's non-citizenship, the court, *per* Walsh J., continued ([1966] I.R. 567, 645):

> "This Court expressly reserves for another and more appropriate case consideration of the effect of non-citizenship upon the interpretation of the Articles in question and also the right of a non-citizen to challenge the validity of an Act of the Oireachtas having regard to the provisions of the Constitution."

Two separate issues are involved here—the right of a non-citizen to challenge the validity of a statute, and the question whether such a person may invoke certain rights recognised by the Constitution. As regards the first, there can hardly be any absolute bar to such a challenge. A non-citizen would seem perfectly entitled to challenge a statute providing for the summary trial of a non-minor offence. The prohibition on this springs from Article 38, which is not confined by reference to citizenship; and such a challenge was successfully mounted by an alien in *Kostan* v. *Att. Gen.* [1978] I.L.R.M. 12. The same must surely apply to any of the Constitution's other restrictions on legislative power which do not invoke citizenship—*e.g.* the ban on retrospective legislation in Article 15.5, or the various provisions underpinning the separation of powers (see Chap. 9 *supra*). Similarly, a non-citizen would seem perfectly entitled to challenge a statute dealing with the courts which is claimed to be contrary to Article 34. Finally, since the rights recognised in Articles 41–44 are not confined to citizens, these provisions may be invoked by aliens—either to challenge statutes or administrative action.

In *Northampton Co. Council* v. *A.B.F. and M.B.F.* [1982] I.L.R.M. 164 the plaintiff authority was seeking the return of an infant child whose father had unlawfully removed her from the jurisdiction of the English courts. If returned, it was proposed to have the child adopted, a course to which her mother consented though her father was totally opposed to it. (Under Irish law, no adoption would be possible in such circumstances.) The defendant father sought to invoke the family guarantees in Article 41 but counsel for the applicant authority argued that only citizens were entitled to the protection of this Article. In refusing to make the order sought at this interlocutory stage, Hamilton J. rejected this latter contention. Non-citizenship could have no effect on the interpretation of Article 41 or to entitlement to the protection it afforded. The judge continued ([1982] I.L.R.M. 164, 166):

> "What Article 41 does is to recognise the Family as the natural primary and fundamental unit group of society and as a moral institution possessing inalienable and imprescriptible rights antecedent and superior to all positive law, which rights the State cannot control. In the words of Walsh J. already quoted, 'these rights are part of what is generally called the natural law' and as such are antecedent and superior to all positive law.
>
> The natural law is of universal application and applies to all human persons, be they citizens of this State or not, and in my opinion it would be inconceivable that the father of the infant child would not be entitled to rely on the recognition of the Family contained in Article 41 for the purpose of enforcing his rights as the lawful father of the infant. . . . "

A similar view of the scope of Article 41 was taken by Barrington J. in *State (Bouzagou)* v. *Station Sergeant, Fitzgibbon Street Garda Station* [1985] I.R. 426.

In *State (McFadden)* v. *Governor, Mountjoy Prison* [1981] I.L.R.M. 113 the prosecutor, a British subject, was resisting extradition; and he claimed that the procedures prior to the making of the extradition order violated the Constitution. Article 40.3 was a guarantee of basic fairness of procedures—which he had not been accorded. On this point Barrington J. said (at 117):

> "The prosecutor is not an Irish citizen, but (counsel for the respondent) has taken no point on this. It appears to me that he was right not to do so. The substantive rights and liabilities of an alien may be different to those of a citizen. The alien, for instance, may not have the right to vote or may be liable for deportation. But when the Constitution prescribes basic fairness of procedures in the administration of the law it does so, not only because citizens have rights, but also because the courts in the administration of justice are expected to observe certain forms of due process enshrined in the Constitution. Once the courts have seisin of of a dispute, it is difficult to see how the standards they should apply in

investigating it should, in fairness, be any different in the case of an alien than those to be applied in the case of a citizen."

This reasoning would avoid several difficulties. If "citizen" in Article 40 cannot be treated as equivalent to "person," certain curious results would seem to follow. Evidence obtained in breach of constitutional rights, inadmissible in criminal proceedings against a citizen, might be held admissible against an alien. An example would be statements obtained during the course of detention which, in the case of a citizen, would violate Article 40.4.1°; or real evidence obtained by a search which would, in case of a citizen, violate the guarantee of Article 40.5. Any such developments, however logical, would leave the State in breach of its obligations under the European Convention on Human Rights, which protects "persons." But since Article 38.1 guarantees that "no person" shall be tried on any criminal charge "save in due course of law" the way is open to avoid any such result by reading "due course of law" in the light of those guarantees. Support for an extended interpretation of Article 38.1 may be found in the Supreme Court's decisions in *State (Healy)* v. *Donoghue* [1976] I.R. 325, and *King* v. *Att. Gen.* [1981] I.R. 233.

In *State (Trimbole)* v. *Governor, Mountjoy Prison* [1985] I.R. 550 the applicant, who was not an Irish citizen, sought his release from detention pending his extradition to Australia. His case was that the extradition proceedings were tainted by illegality because of his original detention under section 30 of the Offences against the State Act 1939. This, he contended, was a gross misuse of the Act; there was no genuine suspicion that he had committed a scheduled offence under the 1939 Act, as section 30 requires, and the real object was to ensure that he would be available for arrest and detention when the Extradition Act was made applicable to Australia, as it subsequently was. Egan J. found that such was the purpose of that detention, and referred to "a gross misuse of section 30 which amounted to a conscious and deliberate violation of constitutional rights" ([1985] I.R. 550, 556). Citing *McFadden's* case (*supra*) Egan J. said that Trimbole's non-citizenship did not deprive him of the right to basic fairness of procedure. The Supreme Court, which upheld Egan J.'s order for release, also referred to the applicant's "constitutional rights"—see Finlay C.J. at [1985] I.R. 550, 575, 577.

It would thus appear that, for many purposes, the supposed distinction between "citizens" and "persons" has no practical consequences. A rationale for this was offered by Barrington J. in *Finn* v. *Att. Gen.* [1983] I.R. 154, 159–160:

" . . . Articles 40 to 44 (inclusive) are in a section of the Constitution which is headed "Fundamental Rights." Article 40 is headed "Personal Rights." It is arguable that those rights derive not from a man's citizenship but from his nature as a human being. The State does not create these rights, it recognises them, and promises to protect them . . . Articles 41, 42 and 43 recognise that man has certain rights which are antecedent and superior to positive law. By doing so, the Constitution accepts that those rights derive not from the law but from the nature of man and of society, and guarantees to protect them accordingly . . . The fact that the wording of Article 40, s.3, commits the State to protect and vindicate the life of 'every citizen' does not justify the inference that it relieves the State of the obligation to defend and vindicate the lives of persons who are not citizens. This is because the whole scheme of moral and political values which are clearly accepted by the Constitution indicates otherwise."

In summary, then, it would seem that non-nationals will in practice be able to invoke the Constitution for most purposes[97]—including, in some instances, to challenge the validity of statutes. But whether a non-national could invoke the equality guarantee of Article 40.1—or the general guarantees of Article 40.3—for the latter purpose is as yet unclear.

May legal—as distinct from human—persons invoke guarantees of constitutional rights? In *Quinn's Supermarket* v. *Att. Gen.* [1972] I.R. 1 the Supreme Court held that corporate bodies could not rely on Article 40.1—which is by its own terms confined to human persons; but the plaintiff company was permitted to invoke Article 44.2.3° (forbidding religious discrimination), which does not use the terms "person" or "citizen." Presumably, therefore, a corporate body could claim the protection of other constitutional provisions with similar neutral phrasing—*e.g.* the ban on retrospective legislation in Article 15.5.[98] A more difficult question arises in regard to those provisions referring to "citizens." That word carries overtones of human rather than legal personality, as is shown by Article 9.2's demanding, as "fundamental political duties of all citizens", fidelity to the nation and loyalty to the State. It would seem impossible to require such pledges from artificial persons.

In *P.M.P.S. Ltd. and Moore* v. *Att. Gen.* [1983] I.R. 339 the plaintiff society was a body corporate registered under the Industrial and Provident Societies Act 1893. It sought to challenge certain legislation as violative of the property guarantees of Article 40.3 and 43. But Carroll J. held that the society as such could have no rights under these provisions. The terms of Article 43.1.1° showed that the rights protected were those of a human person, and this was also true for Article 40.3. However, a shareholder in the society could claim that his or her constitutional rights had been invaded. On appeal the Supreme Court accepted the latter proposition, concluded that it was unnecessary to decide the question of the society's rights and therefore expressed no opinion on this matter.

This acceptance of a shareholder suing in effect on a company's behalf should avoid most problems. In some circumstances, however, it may be essential that the chosen shareholder is an Irish citizen. In *Chestvale Properties Ltd.* v. *Glackin and ors.* [1992] I.L.R.M. 221 the plaintiff company wished to challenge the validity of Part II of the Companies Act 1990, on the ground that it failed to protect and vindicate the company's property rights guaranteed under Article 40.3 of the Constitution. Murphy J. said that " . . . in the particular circumstances of this case . . . " the absence of an individual Irish citizen asserting his/her own constitutional rights ruled out this constitutional argument.[99]

---

[97] In the telephone-tapping case of *Kennedy & Ors.* v. *Ireland* [1987] I.R. 587, Hamilton P. noted that the first plaintiff was not a citizen, but said he was entitled to the same personal rights as if he were (at 593).

[98] This proposition seems to have been accepted by Murphy J. in the *Chestvale Properties* case, *supra*, at 229.

[99] At [1992] I.L.R.M. 221, 229 Murphy J. remarks that counsel for the applicants had consciously rejected the shareholder plaintiff solution.

13   Equality

Article 40.1 of the Constitution provides:

"All citizens shall, as human persons, be held equal before the law.

This shall not be held to mean that the State shall not in its enactments have due regard to differences of capacity, physical and moral, and of social function."[1]

(In *O.B.* v. *S.* [1984] I.R. 316 the Supreme Court referred to the second paragraph above as "the proviso" and that term is used in what follows.)

Article 40.1 fulfils a special function in the Constitution. Whereas other provisions protect substantive rights, this does not; instead it forbids the State, in legislating or administering the law, from discriminating between citizens in ways which are unjust, unreasonable or arbitrary.[2] Thus there may not be a constitutional right to (say) civil legal aid, but if the State opts to provide it this must be done in a way which does not arbitrarily discriminate between similarly circumstanced individuals. Likewise, there may be no constitutional bar to imposing certain burdens on the citizen (*e.g.* compulsory military service) but again Article 40.1 would require even-handedness in this regard.

The equality guarantee has counterparts in many other constitutions[3]—

[1] Ideas of equality also underlie other provisions, *e.g.* there must be no sex discrimination in nationality or citizenship laws (Art. 9.1.3°), or in regard to voting rights (Art. 16.1.2°) or eligibility for election to the Dáil or Seanad (Arts. 16.1.1° and 18.2). Likewise, under Art. 16.2.3° the dominant principle in fixing Dáil constituency boundaries is equality of parliamentary representation of the population: *per* Budd J. in *O'Donovan* v. *Att. Gen.* [1961] I.R. 114 at 138. Note too Art. 40.6.2°, forbidding political, religious or class discrimination in laws regulating freedom of association or assembly.

[2] It will not, it seems, apply to the operation of an international agreement. In *McGimpsey* v. *Ireland* [1990] 1 I.R. 110 it was argued that insofar as the Anglo-Irish Agreement (in Arts. 4 and 5) cast the Irish Government in the roll of protector of the Northern Ireland minority community's interests, it violated Art. 40.1 of the Constitution. This was rejected by the Supreme Court, Finlay C.J. (at 122) saying: "The Anglo-Irish Agreement is not a 'law' within the meaning of that term contained in Art. 40, s.1 of the Constitution. A provision for the capacity of the Irish Government in regard to possible devolution in Northern Ireland to put forward views and proposals as to the modalities of bringing that about could not be the holding of any person equal or unequal before the 'law'." This appears to involve the (logical) conclusion that "law" in Art. 40.1 means statute, regulation or common law rule. *Quaere* the case of a purely administrative scheme, such as was involved in *Greene* v. *Minister for Agriculture* [1990] 2 I.R. 17. Perhaps it would be captured if it enshrined policies that could equally well have been implemented by statute or (as there) regulations made under the European Communities Acts.

[3] Examples are Art. 3 of the West German Basic law of 1949: Art. 14 of the Spanish Constitution of 1978: s.15 of the Canadian Charter of Rights and Freedoms of 1981.

most notably the equal protection clause of the United States Constitution's
14th Amendment. That clause has spawned an enormous and complex
volume of case-law, which in turn has generated a vast literature.[4] Its application by the Warren Court often produced dramatic results and it became
the most dynamic of the United States Constitution's provisions.[5] This has
not happened in Ireland with Article 40.1, despite its relatively frequent
invocation in constitutional cases and counsel's citation of relevant United
States authorities. Only a single statutory provision has so far been invalidated purely by reliance on Article 40.1[6]; though many alleged to violate it
have in fact been struck down, this has been done on other grounds. Indeed,
as will appear, the Irish courts show a marked reluctance to apply Article
40.1. They have given it a restricted ambit; they prefer to decide cases on
other grounds; and they have often justified statutory discriminations by
reasoning that does not probe very deeply.

The contrast with United States judicial attitudes could hardly be more
marked. But it should be noted that many United States equal protection
decisions essentially protect fundamental rights not expressed in the constitutional text—for example, rights in regard to marriage and procreation,[7]
voting[8] and criminal justice.[9] The Irish courts have no need to utilise Article
40.1 for such purposes, since they can instead invoke the unenumerated
rights doctrine under Article 40.3—and this has occurred.[10] However this
does not wholly explain the contrast in attitudes, which may also stem from
other causes. Chief among these may be that equal protection adjudication,
involving as it may a decision that a statute is arbitrary or unreasonable, can
all too readily give the impression that courts are acting as "super-legislatures"—imposing their own policy preferences on the public. This may, of
course, happen in other spheres of constitutional decision-making, but there
at least the constitutional text normally provides a clearer foundation for the
conclusion reached.[11]

[4] References will be found in Polyvios G. Polyviou, *The Equal Protection of the Laws* (London
1980): Francis X. Beytagh, "Equality under the Irish and American Constitutions: A Comparative Analysis" (1983) *XVIII Irish Jurist* (n.s.) 56 and 219: M. Forde, "Equality and the
Constitution" (1982) *XVIII Irish Jurist* (n.s.) 295.
[5] Thus Professor Gunther writes of equal protection having "burgeoned into a major interven-
tionist tool during the Warren era, especially in the 1960s" and being "a prolific source of
modern constitutional litigation": *Individual Rights in Constitutional Law: Cases and Materials*
(3rd ed., Mineola N.Y. 1981) pp. 291 and 294.
[6] *T. O'G.* v. *Att. Gen.* [1985] I.L.R.M. 61—considered *infra*.
[7] *e.g. Skinner* v. *Oklahoma* (1942) 316 U.S. 535 (invalidating a statute providing for compulsory
sterilisation after a third conviction for certain crimes): *Zablocki* v. *Redhail* (1978) 434 U.S. 374
(statute forbidding certain persons to marry without court approval).
[8] *e.g. Gray* v. *Sanders* (1963) 372 U.S. 368: *Reynolds* v. *Sims* (1964) 377 U.S. 533 (asserting a basic
standard of equality among voters in apportioning state legislative seats): *White* v. *Weiser*
(1973) 412 U.S. 783 (same in regard to federal congress).
[9] *e.g. Douglas* v. *California* (1963) 372 U.S. 353 (requiring state provision of counsel in criminal
appeals for those unable to pay fees): *Roberts* v. *La Vallee* (1967) 389 U.S. 40 (poor persons
entitled to free transcript of preliminary ruling for use at trial).
[10] Similar developments have taken place in the U.S. *via* the due process clauses. The principle
by which decisions are based on these rather than equal protection is not easy to discern: see,
e.g. Boddie v. *Connecticut* (1971) 401 U.S. 371: *Little* v. *Streater* (1981) 452 U.S. 1 (access to *civil*
justice).
[11] *e.g.* the cases on property rights—see Chap. 18 *infra*. The unenumerated rights doctrine under
Art. 40.3 is a notable exception: see Chap. 12 *supra*.

The basis of review

The object of Article 40.1, read as a whole, is to forbid arbitrary, unreasonable or unjust ("invidious") discrimination: *O'B.* v. *S.* [1984] I.R. 316, 335. It does not guarantee absolute equality for all citizens in all circumstances; discrimination based on a recognition of differences in relevant circumstances is legitimate. Walsh J. summarised the authorities thus in *de Búrca and Anderson* v. *Att. Gen.* [1976] I.R. 38, 68:

> " . . . Article 40 does not require identical treatment of all persons without recognition of differences in relevant circumstances but it forbids arbitrary discrimination. It imports the Aristotelian concept that justice demands that we treat equals equally and unequals unequally."

That the keynote is reasonableness or rationality appears from the Supreme Court's decision in *Dillane* v. *Att. Gen.* [1980] I.L.R.M. 167,[12] where Henchy J. for the court, said (at 169):

> "When the State, whether directly by statute or mediately through the exercise of a delegated power of subordinate legislation, makes a discrimination in favour of, or against, a person or a category of persons, on the express or implied ground of a difference of social function, the courts will not condemn such discrimination as being in breach of Article 40.1 if it is not arbitrary, or capricious, or otherwise not reasonably capable, when objectively viewed in the light of the social function involved, of supporting the selection or classification complained of."

And the test was further amplified by Walsh J., giving the Supreme Court's judgment in *O'B.* v. *S.* [1984] I.R. 316, 335;

> " . . . the object and the nature of the legislation concerned must be taken into account, and . . . the distinctions or discriminations which the legislation creates must not be unjust, unreasonable or arbitrary and must, of course, be relevant to the legislation in question."

However simple its formulation may seem this test is notoriously difficult to apply to concrete situations. Thus in *Norris* v. *Att. Gen.* [1984] I.R. 36 at 49, McWilliam J. in the High Court said he had some difficulty in ascertaining the limits to be placed on the right to equal treatment and the stage at which discrimination became "invidious" or "arbitrary." Clearly those terms are not synonymous with "unwise" or "unfair." In *Dillane's* case (*supra*) Henchy J. said that whether the court approved of the legislative distinction was irrelevant; what mattered was whether it could reasonably have been arrived at as a matter of policy by those in whom law-making power was vested.

That applying Article 40.1 may involve the courts in scrutinising the balance of costs and advantages struck by the legislature is shown by *O'Brien* v. *Manufacturing Engineering Co. Ltd.* [1973] I.R. 334. The plaintiff there had

---

[12] There a prosecution for road traffic offences brought by a Garda against the plaintiff had been withdrawn. The District Justice wished to award the plaintiff costs but could not do so; for though Rule 67 of the District Court Rules 1948 authorised the award of costs it stipulated that this did not apply to, among others, a Garda acting in discharge of his duties as a police officer. The plaintiff claimed that this was a breach of Art. 40.1, but the Supreme Court said it was a discrimination which "could reasonably be thought a justifiable concomitant of the social functions of the members of the Garda Síochána when carrying out their duties as police officers" (at 169).

been injured at work in circumstances covered by the Workmen's Compensation Acts, and had accepted payments from his employer thereunder. In such circumstances the injured worker could also sue the employer for damages at common law, but the proceedings had to be instituted within 24 months of the date of the accident. The plaintiff's proceedings were commenced 26 months after that date and were thus barred by section 6(1) of the Workmen's Compensation (Amendment) Act 1953. He claimed this provision was invalid, since under the Statute of Limitations 1957 an action similar to his was barred only after three years. The Supreme Court ruled against this. The Oireachtas had given persons like the plaintiff the advantage, not enjoyed by all, of immediate payments under the Workmen's Compensation Acts. The *quid pro quo* of a shorter limitation period for a common law action was valid so long as that shorter period was reasonable; and the court found that the 24 months period here was not unreasonably short.

Irish and United States law contrasted

The basis of review emerging from the Irish decisions mentioned resembles the "rationality test" traditionally used by the United States Supreme Court in matters of economic and social regulation. It was formulated by Pitney J., for the court, in *Royster Guano Co.* v. *Virginia* (1920) 253 U.S. 412 at 415 as follows:

"(T)he classification must be reasonable, not arbitrary, and must rest upon some ground of difference having a fair and substantial relation to the object of the legislation, so that all persons similarly circumstanced shall be treated alike."[13]

For many years the application of this test by that court resulted in "an extreme deference to legislative classifications and a virtually automatic validation of challenged statutes."[14] This was due in part to the rule that if any state of facts could reasonably be conceived that would uphold the statute, the existence of that state of facts at the time the law was enacted must be assumed.[15] In other words, the courts could uphold a statute on grounds that might never have occurred to the legislators. Subsequently the United States Supreme Court developed a "strict scrutiny" test—applicable where statutes employed "suspect classifications" such as race, or those involving "fundamental rights" such as voting. This, in contrast with the rationality test, was usually fatal to the statute under examination. Later again, an intermediate standard evolved. The position was summarised in Brennan J.'s opinion for the court in *Plyler* v. *Doe* (1982) 457 U.S. 202, 216–217:

"(In) applying the Equal Protection Clause to most forms of state action, we . . . seek only the assurance that the classification at issue bears some fair relationship to a legitimate public purpose. But we would not be faithful to our obligations . . . if we applied so deferential a standard to every classification. The Equal Protection Clause was intended as a restriction on state legislative action inconsistent with ele-

[13] This passage was cited and applied by O'Hanlon J. in the High Court in *Madigan* v. *Att. Gen.* [1986] I.L.R.M. 136.
[14] Gunther, *op. cit.*, p. 293.
[15] *Lindsley* v. *Natural Carbonic Gas Co.* (1911) 220 U.S. 61.

mental constitutional premises. Thus we have treated as presumptively invidious those classifications that disadvantage a "suspect class," or that impinge upon the exercise of a "fundamental right." With respect to such classifications, it is appropriate to enforce the mandate of equal protection by requiring the state to demonstrate that its classification has been precisely tailored to serve a compelling governmental interest. In addition, we have recognised that certain forms of legislative classification, while not facially invidious, nonetheless give rise to recurring constitutional difficulties; in these limited circumstances we have sought the assurance that the classification reflects a reasoned judgment consistent with the idea of equal protection by inquiring whether it may fairly be viewed as furthering a substantial interest of the state."

These developments have not won universal applause; Marshall J. for example, has frequently deplored the court's approach[16] while commentators have also been critical.[17] The confusion is hardly eased by decisions which apply the traditional rationality test in a much tougher way than before.[18]

Against this background the Irish law is (deceptively) simple. It has not been suggested that there is more than one test applicable. And though *some* classifications in *some* contexts may engender greater judicial suspicion than others, it can hardly be said that a "suspect classifications" category exists. But in contrast with their United States counterparts the Irish courts have almost invariably shown great deference to legislative judgment. In *Murphy* v. *Att. Gen.* [1982] I.R. 241, Kenny J., for the Supreme Court, said that an inequality would not be set aside as repugnant to the Constitution "if any state of facts exists which may reasonably justify it" (at 284). This is very close to the United States position that, in some situations, any justification that the courts, aided by the ingenuity of counsel, can conjure up will suffice; and many of the Irish decisions seem to proceed on this basis. The problem with such reasoning is that it may ascribe to legislation a rationality it does not really possess. The artificiality of this process is exacerbated if the hypothetical justification then receives a very benevolent scrutiny.

The restricted scope of Article 40.1

It was suggested above that the Irish courts show a marked reluctance to apply Article 40.1 and prefer to invoke substantive constitutional rights against a challenged statute. There is abundant evidence for these assertions. In *Murphy* v. *Att. Gen.* [1982] I.R. 241 a married couple, both in outside employment, challenged provisions of the Income Tax Act 1967 claiming that they were taxed more heavily than would have been the case had they simply lived together. This, they asserted, was a breach of Article 40.1 and Article 41. Their claim succeeded on the Article 41 ground. The Supreme Court's judgment, *per* Kenny J., is a very curious production, which devotes more space to the failed Article 40.1 arguments than to the successful contentions based on Article 41. Moreover, it contains a proposition that is plainly

---

[16] See his opinion in *Massachusetts Board of Retirement* v. *Murgia* (1976) 427 U.S. 307, reiterating earlier views; also that of Stevens J. in *Craig* v. *Boren* (1976) 429 U.S. 190.

[17] See Beytagh, *op. cit.*, pp. 247, 251, 254.

[18] See, *e.g. Reed* v. *Reed* (1971) 404 U.S. 71.

untenable—that this unfavourable tax treatment of married couples may be balanced against other discriminations worked by the law in favour of married couples. On this basis the State could no doubt balance refusing university places to blind people against favourable discriminations in other areas (special welfare allowances, exemption from jury service, help with voting, etc.) It seems significant that no such notion appears in the Supreme Court's later judgment in *O'B*. v. *S*. [1984] I.R. 316.

The *Murphy* case represents the low-water mark of the equality guarantee. But earlier and later judgments, while not going so far, still exhibit the same reserve about Article 40.1. It has been held that legislation differentiating citizens or discriminating between them does not need to be justified under the proviso if justification can be found for it under other constitutional provisions.[19] Thus in *O'B*. v. *S*. [1984] I.R. 316 the Supreme Court found, as a matter of interpretation, that the intestate succession provisions of the Succession Act 1965 discriminated against illegitimate children. But having regard to the constitutional guarantees relating to the family, the court was unable to hold that the differences thus created were necessarily unreasonable, unjust or arbitrary. A law aimed at implementing those guarantees (which the court saw as the purpose of the impugned provisions) did not require to come within the proviso to be valid.[20] Similar reasoning is found in *Dennehy* v. *Minister for Social Welfare* (High Court, July 26, 1984). There the plaintiff, a married man with two children, had been deserted by his wife. He applied for benefit as a "deserted spouse" under the Social Welfare (Consolidation) Act 1981 but his claim was refused because the relevant sections (100 and 195) applied only to *wives*. It was admitted that had the plaintiff been a woman he would have qualified under section 100. He therefore contended that section 100 was unconstitutional *inter alia* as violating Article 40.1 Barron J., having referred to a number of Irish and United States authorities,[21] concluded against the plaintiff. Having regard to Article 41.2, he did not think it unreasonable, unjust or arbitrary for the Oireachtas financially to protect deserted wives who were mothers having dependent children residing with them, or to recognise that mothers who had had to care for children would have lost out in the labour market and so were likely to need similar protection if deserted.[22]

---

[19] Conversely, the Supreme Court held in *Dillane* v. *Att. Gen.* [1980] I.L.R.M. 167 that a distinction permitted by Art. 40.1 could not constitute an "unjust attack" on property rights for the purposes of Art. 40.3.2.°.

[20] Though the court did not expressly so hold, it may be that the legislation in question could not have come within the proviso, for it was observed that no question there arose of any difference of physical or moral capacity. And the court scouted any notion that illegitimacy could attribute any social function to a person (at 333).

[21] Barron J. said it was inviting to seek to decide the case on the basis of the principles established in the U.S. cases. But "they were decided upon a different Constitution and on the basis of a different constitutional jurisprudence." For similar reasons the Supreme Court in *O.'B.* v. *S.* [1984] I.R. 316, though discussing the relevant U.S. authorites, held them inapplicable (at 336–338).

[22] Counsel had argued that there were other provisions of the social welfare code which the plaintiff could have availed of and which granted similar amounts. But Barron J. did not accept this, saying: "It is no answer to a charge of discrimination that the person claiming to be discriminated against is treated equally as well or even better under a different section in the same code. The question is whether persons in the same position are treated alike in the same circumstances" (pp. 9–10 of the judgment). This, though inconsistent with *Murphy* v. *Att. Gen. (supra)*, is surely correct.

The courts have also held that Article 40.1 does not apply to *legal* persons: *Quinn's Supermarket Ltd.* v. *Att. Gen.* [1971] I.R. 1. Thus in contrast to the equal protection guarantee in the United States, it cannot be invoked by a company. Any other conclusion would, of course, be difficult to reconcile with the wording (" . . . citizens, as human persons . . . "). More seriously, the scope of Article 40.1 has been cut down by what seems an undue emphasis on the words "as human persons." In *Quinn's Supermarket Ltd.* v. *Att. Gen.* (*supra*) the Supreme Court held that the guarantee "refers to human persons for what they are in themselves rather than to any lawful activities, trades or pursuits which they may engage in or follow" (at 14). Subsequently, in *Murtagh Properties* v. *Cleary* [1972] I.R. 330, Kenny J. said the guarantee had nothing to do with the conditions on which people were employed.[23] In *Condon* v. *Minister for Labour* (High Court, June 11, 1980) McWilliam J. held that legislation preventing bank clerks from receiving pay increases at levels above those in national wages agreements did not violate Article 40.1; the discrimination in question did not relate to any facet of human personality. The Supreme Court has extended this to revenue-raising measures such as rating or taxing Acts. In *Brennan* v. *Att. Gen.* [1984] I.L.R.M. 355 it was held that a complaint about the arbitrary nature of the farm-rating system was not cognisable under Article 40.1. This was repeated in the context of the residential property tax, introduced by Part VI of the Finance Act 1983: *Madigan* v. *Att. Gen.* [1986] I.L.R.M. 136.[24] There O'Higgins C.J., delivering the judgment of the court, said (at 161):

> "This tax is correctly described as a tax on owners who occupy and enjoy their residential property. It does not relate to the treatment of citizens as human persons and is not cognisable under Article 40.1."

So marked in this narrowing of the guarantee's scope that in *O'Reilly* v. *Minister for the Environment* [1986] I.R. 143 counsel for the plaintiff, who was challenging the alphabetical listing of candidates' names on Dáil ballot papers, conceded that he could not invoke Article 40.1.[25] The late Professor Kelly justifiably described this as an "exceedingly narrow view of the equality guarantee—almost suggesting that human personality could exist in

---

[23] Note however that Art. 119 of the EEC Treaty lays down the principle of equal pay for equal work. This is implemented by E.C. Council Directive 75/117. For the European Court's interpretation of these provisions see *Macarthys Ltd.* v. *Smith*, Case 129/79 [1980] E.C.R. 1275 and *Garland* v. *British Rail Engineering Ltd.*, Case 12/81 [1982] E.C.R. 359. Other aspects of equal treatment are likewise dealt with in directives—which may be invoked before national courts. Thus E.C. Council Directive 76/207 governs equality of access to jobs and of working conditions, etc.; for its interpretation see *Johnston* v. *Chief Constable, R.U.C.*, Case 222/84 [1986] 3 All E.R. 135. E.C. Council Directive 79/7 covers equal treatment in matters of social security: for its interpretation see *Drake* v. *Chief Adjudication Officer*, Case 150/85 [1986] 3 All E.R. 65.

[24] In the *Brennan* case the relevant legislation was held to be an unjust attack on property rights contrary to Art. 40.3. This was also invoked in the *Madigan* case but to no avail. See Chap. 18 *infra*.

[25] Counsel reserved the right to plead Art. 40.1 before the Supreme Court and to invite reconsideration of the restrictive interpretation hitherto given it. In *Greene* v. *Minister for Agriculture* [1990] 2 I.R. 17 similar problems arose in a challenge to an EC-inspired headage scheme allegedly discriminating on income grounds—though the claim succeeded on a different constitutional basis (see Chap. 17 *infra*). To date the Supreme Court has not been vouchsafed an opportunity to reconsider this line of authority—though given cases like *Doyle* v. *Hearne* (*No. 2*) [1988] I.R. 317 the auguries are not promising.

a void . . . "[26] Its effect must necessarily be to cut down severely the range of matters regarding which Article 40.1 may be invoked. For some plaintiffs this will pose no great problem in that their claims can be framed under some other constitutional provision—*e.g.* a failure to defend and vindicate an unenumerated right. But that will plainly not be true for all.

The reluctance to invoke Article 40.1

The Supreme Court's decision in *O'Brien* v. *Keogh* [1972] I.R. 144 exemplifies the judicial reluctance to found decisions on Article 40.1 and the preference for invoking substantive constitutional rights. The challenge there was to section 49(2)(a)(ii) of the Statute of Limitations 1957, which had the effect that infants in the custody of a parent were subject to a limitation period of three years from accrual of the cause of action, whereas those not in such custody could sue at any time within three years of attaining majority. A contention that this violated the equality guarantee failed, the Supreme Court holding that (as Ó Dálaigh C.J. put it at 156):

> "Far from effecting inequality, the purpose of the provision would appear to attempt to establish equality between the two groups . . . Article 40 does not require identical treatment of all persons without recognition of differences in relevant circumstances. It only forbids invidious discrimination."

However the court went on to hold the provision invalid as infringing Article 40.3. The right to litigate claims was a property right which the State was obliged to defend and vindicate, and it was concluded that section 49(2)(a)(ii) did not do so; in effect its division of infants into two categories was too broad to give their rights reasonable protection. But as has been pointed out by Dr. Forde,[27] the same result could easily have been reached on the basis of Article 40.1. The Act recognised that some infants needed lengthy limitation periods, but the blanket distinction it made failed to follow through the logic of this perception.[28]

A similar reluctance is manifest in *de Búrca and Anderson* v. *Att. Gen.* [1976] I.R. 38, in which the validity of the Juries Act 1927 was assailed by two women who were facing trial on indictment. It was argued that since the Act expressly confined jury service to rate-payers (and thus property-owners) and, in practice, excluded women, the plaintiffs—women of no property—coyld not obtain a fair trial. Though the Supreme Court found for the plaintiffs (unanimously on the property qualification ground: by a 4–1 majority on the sex discrimination ground) the bases for decision were not uniform. Henchy and Griffin JJ. chose to decide on the basis of Article 38.5's jury trial guarantee, a course which, though plainly legitimate in the circumstances of

---

[26] "Equality before the Law in Three European Jurisdictions" (1983) *XVIII Irish Jurist* (n.s.) 259, 265.

[27] *Op. cit.*, p. 331. Note too his comment that the judgment "demonstrates some discomfort with the equality norm . . . " (*ibid.*).

[28] Few Supreme Court decisions have come under so much fire as *O'Brien* v. *Keogh*. In *Moynihan* v. *Greensmyth* [1977] I.R. 55 the Supreme Court queried its correctness on the substantive issue, while following *Cahill* v. *Sutton* [1980] I.R. 269 it is doubtful whether the plaintiff in *O'Brien* had *locus standi*. And the *O'Brien* conclusion—that a non-arbitrary discrimination could nonetheless be an unjust attack under Art. 40.3—is directly contradicted by the later decision in *Dillane's* case; see n. 18 *supra*.

the case, is nonetheless significant. Budd J. found for the plaintiffs on both grounds but his brief judgment does not state whether his decision was based on Article 38.5 or 40.1 Only O'Higgins C.J. and Walsh J. clearly founded their conclusions on Article 40.1. Both agreed that the property qualification was invalid; it had nothing to do with honesty, intelligence, impartiality or any other quality desirable in a juror.[29] But they disagreed as to the sex discrimination argument. O'Higgins C.J. was of opinion that the provision whereby women were exempt from jury service unless they applied for inclusion did not violate the Constitution. Reading Article 40.1 in the light of the Constitution as a whole—and especially Article 41.2—special provision for women was not invidious, unjust or unfair.[30] Walsh J., however, held that the Act swept too broadly in this regard[31]:

> "The statutory provision does not seek to make any distinction between the different functions that women may fulfil and it does not seek to justify the discrimination on the basis of any social function. It simply lumps together half of the members of the adult population, most of whom have only one thing in common, namely, their sex. In my view, it is not open to the State to discriminate in its enactments between the persons who are subject to its laws solely upon the ground of the sex of those persons. If a reference is to be made to the sex of a person, then the purpose of the law that makes such a discrimination should be to deal with some physical or moral capacity or social function that is related exclusively or very largely to that sex only."

Classification

The legislature may—in some cases must—classify people for the purpose of according them different treatment. The Constitution itself does this in places—for example, by age in regard to voting in Dáil elections, in eligibility for election to the Dáil or the Presidency. Many statutory provisions employ a similar age discrimination—this is true in regard to driving licences, gun licences, jury service and other things.[32] It may be objected that these sweep too widely—that, for example, many persons over 70 could make a valuable contribution to a jury's work. But such line-drawing is generally considered to be legitimate, partly on grounds of practicability. How long would it take, and how much would it cost, to segregate those who could usefully serve from those who could not?[33]

---

[29] [1967] I.R. 38 at 61–62, 68–69. Neither supported Pringle J.'s conclusion in the High Court that a right to serve on a jury was not an essential attribute of human personality but something analogous to trading activities and thus not touched by Art. 40.1

[30] *Ibid.*, at 58–60.

[31] *Ibid.*, at 71.

[32] In *Landers* v. *Att. Gen.* (1973) 109 I.L.T.R. 1 one line of attack on s.2 of the Prevention of Cruelty to Children Act 1904 was that a law barring every child under 10 from singing professionally in public failed to take account of special talents and thus was unfairly discriminatory in breach of Art. 40.1. But Finlay J. (as he then was) could not be persuaded that preventing a child from doing this until the age of 10, or from singing in a pub between 9 pm and 6 am under the age of 14, was an invidious discrimination.

[33] The U.S. Supreme Court has rejected equal protection challenges to compulsory retirement laws, holding that the drawing of lines in this area is peculiarly a legislative task, and that perfection in making the necessary classifications is neither possible nor necessary. See *Massachusetts Board of Retirement* v. *Murgia* (1976) 427 U.S. 307: *Vance* v. *Bradley* (1979) 440 U.S. 93.

The Juries Act 1976 furnishes several interesting examples of legislative classification. Having laid down in section 6 the basic principle that all citizens between 18 and 70 on the Dáil electoral register are qualified and eligible, the Act proceeds to graft exceptions thereon. Thus certain categories of people are ineligible (s.7 and Sched. 1, Part 1); these include the D.P.P. and his staff. In the context of criminal juries this exclusion is perfectly rational; a jury would hardly be thought impartial if it contained a representative of the public prosecutor. A different reason would support the similar exclusion of solicitors' apprentices, solicitors' clerks and others doing legal work in solicitors' offices; the danger feared here is doubtless that such a person might dominate the jury. But university law students are not excluded, yet the danger envisaged might spring as readily from a student of mature years. Might the failure to cover such persons invalidate this exclusion, or is it sufficient that the legislature aims simply at the most likely target? Again, all members of the Garda Síochána and the permanent Defence Forces are ineligible. Is it rational to treat these two groups similarly? So far as criminal juries are concerned, the reasons given above in regard to the D.P.P. would apply to the Gardaí, given their role in the investigation of crime. But the Defence Forces have no such role, and the effect is to exclude members from civil as well as criminal juries.

The Act goes on to provide that eligible persons may be excused from jury duty on showing good reason (s.9(2)). Certain categories of persons are, however, excusable as of right and these include practising doctors, nurses, veterinary surgeons, etc. Such persons plainly fulfil a definite social function and there is authority for drawing distinctions in regard to them.[34] What is not clear is whether the discrimination—prima facie valid under Article 40.1—is challengeable because it goes too far. Arguably while such persons may need to be excused at certain times, an automatic right thereto sweeps too widely.[35]

Over-inclusive classifications

A classification is over-inclusive when it is too widely drawn, covering persons who ought reasonably to be excluded. Into this category would fall the discrimination alleged in *Finnegan* v. *An Bord Pleanála* [1979] I.L.R.M. 134 which was that section 15 of the Local Government (Planning and Development) Act 1976, in requiring of every appellant to An Bord Pleanála a deposit of £10, impermissibly discriminated on grounds of wealth. The Supreme Court had little difficulty in disposing of this argument. The purpose of the section, said the court, was to prevent appeals which lacked reality or substance. The amount of the deposit was not so high as to prevent genuine appeals being brought, and it was returnable—whatever the out-

---

[34] See *de Búrca and Anderson* v. *Att. Gen.* [1976] I.R. 38 at 72, *per* Walsh J.: "To be an architect or a doctor . . . is to have a social function . . . "

[35] In many instances the U.S. Supreme Court has held that legislative classifications need not be perfect; see n. 33 *supra* and *Dandridge* v. *Williams* (1970) 397 U.S. 471: *New York City Transit Authority* v. *Beazer* (1979) 440 U.S. 568. In others it has insisted on a closer fit between the ends sought and the means adopted to achieve them; *e.g. Craig* v. *Boren* (1976) 429 U.S. 190: *Orr* v. *Orr* (1979) 440 U.S. 268.

come—when the appeal was determined or withdrawn. There was no unconstitutional discrimination here.[36]

The sex discrimination challenged in the *de Búrca and Anderson* case was, on Walsh J.'s reasoning, invalid because over-inclusive. This is clear from his statement at [1976] I.R. 38, 71:

" . . . the Oireachtas could validly enact statutory provisions which could have due regard . . . to differences of capacity both physical and moral and of social function in so far as jury service is concerned. For example, it could provide that all mothers with young children could be exempt from jury service. On virtually the same considerations, it could provide that all widowers, husbands with invalid wives, and husbands deserted by their wives would be entitled to a similar exemption if they were looking after their young children. It might also provide exemptions for the proprietors of one-man businesses who have no assistance, whether the proprietors be men or women. It could provide that certain occupations such as a general practitioner in the medical profession (whether man or woman) be exempt because of the importance of the social function fulfilled by persons of such occupation."

The one case so far in which judgment against a statutory provision was founded on Article 40.1 also falls into the over-inclusive category. This was *T. O'G* v. *Att. Gen.* [1985] I.L.R.M. 61, in which the plaintiff challenged the proviso to section 5(1) of the Adoption Act 1974. He and his wife had planned to adopt a child but his wife was killed in an accident before an adoption order could be made. At this time the child had been in their custody for six months. The plaintiff wished to adopt the boy, but the proviso to section 5(1) prevented this by prescribing that only a widower with another child in his custody could apply for an order. It was argued that this discrimination was unreasonable and arbitrary, and McMahon J. agreed. He said ([1985] I.L.R.M. 61, 64, 65):

"Widowers as a class are not less competent than widows to provide for the material needs of children and their exclusion as a class must be based on a belief that a woman by virtue of her sex has an innate capacity for parenthood which is denied to a man and the lack of which renders a man unsuitable as an adopter. This view is not supported by any medical evidence adduced before me and the fact that s.5 permits a widower who has already custody of a child to adopt another appears to be an admission that a man may acquire skills and capacities necessary to be an adopter . . . I am satisfied that the proviso to s.5 is founded on an idea of difference in capacity between men and women which has no foundation in fact and the proviso is therefore an unwarranted denial of human equality and repugnant to Article 40.1."

In enacting the condemned provisions of the Juries Act 1927 and the Adoption Act 1974 the Oireachtas seems to have unquestioningly accepted doubtful ideas about social roles—"a woman's place is rarely in the jury-box": "men can't raise children." It seems to have done something similar in part of the Adoption Act 1952, but here the judicial disposal of the consti-

[36] The court noted that deposits are required of candidates for the Dáil. These however are larger (£100) and are forfeited unless the candidate obtains ⅓ of the quota. Presumably the *Finnegan dictum* does not preclude a challenge to this.

tutional challenge was disappointingly different. In *State (Nicolaou)* v. *An Bord Uchtala* [1966] I.R. 567, the prosecutor, an unmarried father, questioned the validity of his child's adoption, which had occurred without his consent. Under section 14(1) of the 1952 Act consent to an adoption was required of: (a) the mother; (b) the guardian; (c) any person having charge of or control over the child. The prosecutor here did not fall into categories (b) and (c). The child, born on February 23, 1960, had lived with him and her mother in London up to June 16, 1960 when the mother took her to Ireland. The adoption order was made on September 13, 1961. Between June 16, 1960 and September 13, 1961 the prosecutor therefore did not have charge of or control over the child. He argued that section 14(1) violated Article 40.1. The Supreme Court disagreed. It was pointed out that section 14(1) did not discriminate against natural fathers *as such* (*i.e.* a natural father might in appropriate circumstances fall within category (c) above). Nor was there any unfair discrimination in the fact that section 14(1) gave rights to some persons but not others. The court admitted that some natural fathers took an interest in their offspring but did not consider that the failure to accord them rights on a more generous scale invalidated section 14(1). A different result was reached by the United States Supreme Court in *Caban* v. *Mohammed* (1974) 441 U.S. 380—an attack on a New York statute giving the mother (but not the father) of an illegitimate child the power to veto adoption by refusing consent thereto. By a 5–4 majority the court held this insufficiently refined to be valid. It arbitrarily classified unmarried fathers as invariably less qualified and entitled than mothers to exercise a concerned judgment as to the fate of their children. This approach seems more in harmony with the Constitution than than in *Nicolaou's* case.

Under-inclusive classifications

Such a classification is one which is essentially too narrow—where the class benefited or burdened is unreasonably small. The claim in *Dennehy* v. *Minister for Social Welfare*—discussed *supra*—was of this nature, the plaintiff's case being that to confine welfare benefits to deserted *wives* alone violated Article 40.1. Such claims often involve a special difficulty; should the plaintiff succeed he/she will obtain a declaration that the relevant statutory provisions are unconstitutional. But how will the plaintiff benefit thereby? Had Mr. Dennehy succeeded *he* would not thereby have obtained any welfare benefits; initially at least he would simply have prevented *anyone* from getting them. This point is taken up again *infra*, but it may be noted at this juncture that such will not always be the case. An individual convicted under a statute found to be impermissibly narrow would plainly gain from a declaration to that effect.

In *Loftus* v. *Att. Gen* [1979] I.R. 221 the plaintiffs were members of a political party which had been refused registration under the Electoral Act 1963 and thus could not have its name on ballot papers. They challenged provisions of the Act on various grounds, arguing in particular that section 13—which provided for automatic registration of existing parties then represented in the Dáil—violated Article 40.1. The Supreme Court rejected this contention saying, *per* O'Higgins C.J. (at 242–243):

" . . . it was proper for the Oireachtas to have regard to the existing distinction between political parties who were then represented in the Dáil and those who were not. The very fact of being represented in the Dáil satisfied in respect of each such party the statutory requirements that the party be genuinely political and . . . organised to contest elections. To require existing parties, not then represented, or newly formed parties, to . . . satisfy those requirements, in the manner laid down . . . is a treatment of such parties in a manner necessarily different but not invidious or unfair.''

The late Professor Kelly suggested that the Supreme Court here did not give sufficient attention to the *result* of this legislative distinction. Its sole consequence was to give some groups an automatic right to put their names on ballot papers, whereas others had to satisfy specified criteria to gain this end. Such a distinction he describes as "merely officious, the work of a legislative busybody, and not directed to serving any serious constitutional value or public interest."[37] This seems true; the classification looks like a legislative sledge-hammer to crack a minuscule nut. (Contrast the legislative distinctions between trade unions as regards negotiating licences, and the formation of new unions, which were enacted for serious public policy reasons.)[38]

A similar under-inclusiveness point formed part of the plaintiff's contentions in *Norris* v. *Att. Gen.* [1984] I.R. 36 where the challenge was to 19th century statutes penalising homosexual behaviour. It was argued that the Criminal Law Amendment Act 1885, s.11—which struck solely at acts of gross indecency between males—discriminated on grounds of sex contrary to Article 40.1. A majority of the Supreme Court rejected this, saying *per* O'Higgins C.J. (at 59):

"The legislature would be perfectly entitled to have regard to the difference between the sexes and to treat sexual conduct or gross indecency between males as requiring prohibition because of the social problem which it creates, while at the same time looking at sexual conduct between females as being not only different but as posing no such social problem."[39]

Here again the court is constructing a hypothesis on which the legislature *could* rationally have acted—thus the standard of review is a very deferential one. Whether, in the particular context, this is appropriate seems questionable. It is established that 19th century statutes do not benefit from any presumption of constitutionality (see Chap. 11 *supra*). The proviso to Article 40.1 uses the words " . . . the State . . . in its enactments . . . "; only by a legal fiction is the Criminal Law Amendment Act 1885 regarded as one of "the State's enactments." Given that before 1937 it could never have had to run the gauntlet of an equal protection challenge, it may not be outlandish to suggest that in such instances the presumption should be reversed—*i.e.* that

---

[37] *Op. cit.*, p. 286.

[38] See A. Kerr and G. Whyte, *Irish Trade Union Law* (Abingdon 1985), Chap. 2.

[39] Henchy J., who dissented on other grounds, concurred with the majority on this point. He said (at 70–71): "The sexual acts left unaffected are for physiological, social and other reasons capable of being differentiated as to their nature, their context, the range of their possible consequences and the desirability of seeking to enforce their proscription as crimes . . . it was and is a matter of legislative policy to decide whether a compulsion of the common good is capable of justifying the distinction drawn. I would hold that the proviso . . . makes constitutionally acceptable . . . the line of demarcation between the acts made criminal by the impugned sections and those which the plaintiff complains are left unproscribed by the criminal law."

the burden of proving genuine (not hypothetical) rationality should lie on the State.

Lack of success also attended the plaintiff's efforts in *Draper* v. *Att. Gen.* [1984] I.R. 277 to persuade the Supreme Court that Article 40.1 had been violated. The essence of Mrs. Draper's case was that the Oireachtas, in giving postal votes to Gardaí and Defence Forces members but not to disabled voters like her, had discriminated in an arbitrary way. But the Supreme Court could discern no breach of Article 40.1. While under it the State could validly make special provision for disabled people, the fact that it had not done so did not make the provisions assailed unreasonable, unjust or arbitrary. The State, said the court, might well regard the cost and risk involved in providing special facilities for particular groups as not justified, having regard to the numbers involved, their widespread dispersal throughout the country and the risk of electoral abuses. This seems another example of extraordinary deference to legislative judgment. The Constitution establishes a democratic state (Art. 5), stresses the principle of voter choice via Dáil and Presidential elections and referenda, and is at pains to secure equal weighting of votes in Dáil elections (Art. 16.2). Arguably, in such a context, the ability to vote should be maximised, and since a satisfactory scheme of postal voting had been worked out by departmental experts[40] it seems that only legislative inertia prevented progress. In other contexts the Supreme Court has found it possible to galvanise the Oireachtas into activity[41] and it is regrettable that it did not do so here.[42]

In *Somjee* v. *Minister for Justice* [1981] I.L.R.M. 324 the plaintiffs were a married couple, the wife being an Irish citizen and the husband an alien. He applied for naturalisation but his application was deferred pending his completion of two years residence in Ireland (a statutorily-authorised concession by the Minister). Under section 8 of the Irish Nationality and Citizenship Act 1956, an alien woman who married a citizen could obtain citizenship almost immediately. The plaintiffs complained that the Act's discrimination between alien men and women was a breach of Article 40.1. Keane J. disagreed. He observed that the Act did not discriminate between male and female applicants for citizenship. Only where aliens married Irish citizens was a distinction drawn and this was " . . . more properly regarded as conferring a form of privilege on female aliens rather than . . . being invidiously discriminatory against male aliens."[43] The judge continued (at 326):

> "I am entitled to presume that, in conferring this privilege, which does not necessarily involve any invidious discrimination, the legislature was having regard to the social, economic and political conditions which might prevail in the various jurisdictions from which alien aspirants for citizenship might come. It was open to the legislature to take the view that, in some at least of these jurisdictions, the likelihood of females

---

[40] See the *Report* of the Working Party on the Register of Electors (March 1983).

[41] See the concluding section of Chap. 1, *supra*.

[42] Contrast the British Columbia Court of Appeal's decision in *Re Hoogbruin el al. and Att. Gen. of British Columbia* (1985) 24 D.L.R. (4th) 718. The Electoral (Amendment) (No. 2) Act 1986 now gives special (non-postal) voting facilities to disabled persons: see Chap. 4, *supra*.

[43] At 326. This conclusion seems doubtful. It is established that benign as well as adverse discrimination is covered by Art. 44.2.3° (see Chap. 18 *infra*) and the same seems true of Art. 40.1. Thus in the *de Búrca and Anderson* case O'Higgins C.J. and Walsh J. indicated that it did not matter whether exemption from jury service was regarded as a privilege or a burden.

being engaged in any of the activities which might be relevant in considering an application for citizenship[44] was sufficiently remote to justify the automatic granting of citizenship to female aliens upon their marriage to Irish citizens. It follows that . . . the provisions of the sections in question do no more than provide a diversity of arrangements which is not prohibited by Article 40.1."

Here again the court ascribes a rational purpose to the legislature without inquiring whether there is any real foundation for this. It may well be that in 1956 the Oireachtas simply acted reflexively, following traditional and stereotyped thought patterns (a similar distinction between husbands and wives existed in pre-independence British nationality law[45]). Indeed the impugned section has now been replaced by a sex-neutral provision: see the Irish Nationality and Citizenship Act 1986, s.3, discussed in Chapter 12 *supra*.

Reference was made above to a problem peculiar to under-inclusiveness claims—how will the plaintiff benefit? This seems to have made its first appearance in the *Somjee* case where Keane J. pointed out that were the impugned provisions invalidated, the plaintiffs would not benefit thereby. A declaration to that effect "would not redress any injustice to which either of them was subjected or in any sense known to the law vindicate their personal rights" (at 327). The Supreme Court took up this theme in *Norris* v. *Att. Gen.* [1984] I.R. 36, O'Higgins C.J. saying (at 59–60):

" . . . in alleging discrimination because the prohibition on the conduct which he claims he is entitled to engage in is not extended to similar conduct by females, the plaintiff is complaining of a situation which, if it did not exist or were remedied, would confer on him no benefit or vindicate no right of his which he claims to be breached."[46]

And in the later case of *O'B.* v. *S.* [1984] I.R. 316 that court pointed out that if the existing rules on intestate succession were held unconstitutional this would avail the plaintiff nothing, since the resultant absence of any rules would leave her without any claimable share.

It is noteworthy that this issue has been canvassed only in situations where the court has already decided adversely to the plaintiff. One may feel that it would present little difficulty in a different situation. Plainly, as Keane J. noted in the *Somjee* case, the courts have no mandate to substitute repaired legislative measures for any struck down. But if invalidating provisions means leaving a legislative vacuum a court should not necessarily be inhibited by this. The assumption must be that the Oireachtas will choose to enact more extensive provisions or to remove the impugned discrimination in some other way. In a not dissimilar context such an assumption has the *imprimatur* of the Supreme Court, as may be seen from the final part of its judgment in *Blake* v. *Att. Gen.* [1984] I.R. 117, 141–142.

---

[44] It is not clear what Keane J. had in mind in referring to "activities which might be relevant in considering an application for citizenship." These factors appear to be set out in s.15 of the 1956 Act, which *inter alia* imposed certain durational requirements and the making of a declaration. S.15(*b*) demanded that the applicant be "of good character" but this can hardly depend on one's country of origin.

[45] British Nationality and Status of Aliens Act 1914, s.10.

[46] It should be noted that Mr. Norris had never been prosecuted—let alone convicted—under the provisions he challenged.

Justifying discrimination

In *State (Hartley)* v. *Governor, Mountjoy Prison* (Supreme Court, December 21, 1967) the prosecutor, who was facing extradition to Britain, argued that Part III of the Extradition Act 1965 was contrary to Article 40.1. Under that Act extradition to most jurisdictions was governed by Part II, while that to Britain, Northern Ireland, the Isle of Man and the Channel Islands was regulated by Part III. This latter contained less extensive privileges and safeguards than Part II; hence the claim that the equality guarantee had been breached. The Supreme Court dismissed the claim, pointing out that Ireland was a party to the European Convention on Extradition whereas the United Kingdom was not. That Convention, however, permitted signatory states to regulate their extradition arrangements with non-signatory states on a different basis; hence the difference between Part II (which enacted the Convention) and Part III (which did not—though influenced by its terms.[47]) The judgment, *per* Ó Dálaigh C.J., continued:

> "Article 40 . . . does not require the State to make the same extradition arrangements with all States. This would obviously be impossible, as is demonstrated by the fact that Great Britain (*sic*) is not a party to the European Convention. A diversity of arrangements does not effect discrimination between citizens in their legal rights. Their legal rights are the same in the same circumstances. This in fact is equality before the law and not inequality. . . . "

The final three sentences above have often been cited in later judgments, though this practice has recently become less noticeable. Perhaps this is because they are apt to mislead. Thus in *O'Brien* v. *Manufacturing Engineering Co. Ltd.* [1973] I.R. 334, Pringle J. quoted them in support of his statement that there was no unfair discrimination provided that every person in the same class was treated in the same way. While this is true it presupposes that the class has not been arbitrarily selected in the first place.[48] A statute prescribing mandatory capital punishment for litter offences only would treat all persons in the class equally; but it may confidently be assumed that no court would now end its Article 40.1 inquiries at that point. It is arguable, however, that in *Hartley's* case the inquiry was terminated prematurely. The legislation there created two classes—those extradited to the United Kingdom and those extradited elsewhere—and gave them different legal rights. But logically there would seem to be only one class—persons whose extradition is sought—and prima facie they should all receive equal treatment. Nor is the justification offered for the Act's distinction convincing. While the European Convention on Extradition permits different arrangements with non-signatory states it does not require them—and Part II of the 1965 Act has been made applicable to non-signatory states such as the United States and Australia.

[47] For the background to the Act and an analysis of its terms see Paul O'Higgins, "The Irish Extradition Act 1965" (1966) 15 *I.C.L.Q.* 369.

[48] A point forcefully made by McIntyre J. of the Supreme Court of Canada in *Andrews* v. *Law Society of British Columbia* (1989) 56 D.L.R. (4th) 1. Referring to the "similarly situated test"—the doctrine that equality requires similar treatment of persons similarly situated—he said (at 11–12): "The test as stated . . . is seriously deficient in that it excludes any consideration of the nature of the law. If it were to be applied literally, it could be used to justify the Nuremberg laws of Adolf Hitler. Similar treatment was contemplated for all Jews."

In *State (H)* v. *Daly* [1977] I.R. 90 the prosecutor, who had been imprisoned for (civil) contempt of court, had been found to be of unsound mind and transferred to the Central Mental Hospital. The statute authorising this also provided that the person in question should be detained there until recovery. In habeas corpus proceedings the prosecutor contended that he was entitled to be released, on the ground *inter alia* that the relevant statutory provisions violated Article 40.1. It was pointed out that under the Mental Treatment Act 1945 the Minister for Health was empowered to send an inspector to examine any person in any mental institution. But whereas any such inspector was obliged to report on the legality of the detention as regards those detained in district mental hospitals, this did not apply to detentions in the Central Mental Hospital. Finlay P. could not accept that this "distinction in detail" breached Article 40.1. He pointed out that the prosecutor was entitled to question the legality of his detention under Article 40.4 of the Constitution; and that the President of the High Court was empowered, by the Mental Treatment Act 1945, to send an inspector to report on any matter concerning a detainee in *any* mental hospital. Finlay P.'s conclusion would seem to be that there was here no arbitrary discrimination because the distinction affected nothing of substance.

A different justification was offered for upholding the challenged discrimination in *State (Hunt)* v. *O'Donovan* [1975] I.R. 39. The prosecutor there had pleaded guilty in the District Court to certain indictable offences and had been sent forward for sentence to the Circuit Court, under section 13(2) of the Criminal Procedure Act 1967. The Circuit Court sentenced him to two years imprisonment. He subsequently lodged an appeal but this was struck out by the Court of Criminal Appeal for want of jurisdiction, since that court was empowered only to hear appeals in "cases tried on indictment" (Courts of Justice Act 1924, s.63) and the prosecutor had not been so tried. In these habeas corpus proceedings he argued *inter alia* that the interaction of these statutory provisions worked an invalid discrimination contrary to Article 40.1. That is, whereas he was deprived of an appeal, another person convicted after trial on similar charges would not be. Finlay J. (as he then was) dismissed this contention. A person could not be dealt with under section 13 of the 1967 Act unless he so wished. There was no legal or moral duty to plead guilty in the District Court, and even if this were done that plea could still be withdrawn in the Circuit Court—indeed the judge was obliged to ask if the accused wished to do this. The choice given was not illusory, and practitioners were well accustomed to using an early admission of guilt to urge leniency in sentence, often with success. Moreover, the procedure under section 13(2) had a brevity and speed which might constitute an advantage to an accused. Thus there was here no invidious discrimination.[49]

It is noticeable that an appeal has now been provided for in such circum-

---

[49] In *Doyle* v. *Hearne* (No. 2) [1988] I.R. 317 it was argued that the Supreme Court should not construe s.20 of the Intoxicating Liquor Act 1962 in such a way as would give some, but not all, licence holders a right automatically to block the grant of licences to others in certain cases. To do so, it was urged, would be to create an invidious discrimination contrary to Article 40.1. But the Supreme Court held that no other construction was open, given the plain and unambiguous meaning of the words used. It also held that the resulting discrimination was not invidious, Finlay C.J. saying (at 325): "There could be no question of any licensed trader having a constitutional right to block the granting of a licence to an applicant." But, with respect, it is difficult to see how this is relevant. The result of the court's decision is that the *legal* rights of some differ from those of others similarly situated.

stances: Criminal Procedure (Amendment) Act 1973, s.1—passed shortly
after the Supreme Court had dismissed Hunt's appeal.[50] This strongly suggests that the unequal situation complained of was the result of a legislative
oversight; and if that be so it seems strange that the courts should hypothe-
sise rational justifications for it. But this tendency is noticeable in other cases
also.

Equality in the administration of the law

Two Supreme Court decisions establish that Article 40.1 forbids unreasonable or unjust discrimination in the application or administration of the law,
and is not confined to its enactment. The first is *East Donegal Co-op Ltd.* v. *Att.
Gen.* [1970] I.R. 317. In the High Court O'Keeffe P. had struck down as
invalid the Livestock Marts Act 1967, under which such marts could be carried on only with a licence from the Minister for Agriculture. The statute
gave the Minister wide discretionary powers in granting and revoking
licences and in attaching conditions thereto, and O'Keeffe P. had concluded
that in certain respects the Act could be operated within its limits so as to
differentiate between citizens in an arbitrary manner, with no possibility of
judicial review. The Supreme Court reversed this decision and upheld the
Act, stating that the Ministerial discretion must be exercised in the light of
constitutional guarantees and solely to further the objects of the Act. Any
alleged departure from these principles could be reviewed by the courts. It
would follow from this that if different conditions were attached to two
licences in a given district the Minister would have to be able to show
rational justification for so acting. And there seems little doubt that a case
like *Yick Wo* v. *Hopkins* (1886) 118 U.S. 356 would be decided in the same way
by the Irish courts. There a San Francisco ordinance prohibited operating a
laundry, without the consent of the Board of Supervisors, except in a brick or
stone building. The Board granted permits to operate laundries in wooden
buildings to all but one of the non-Chinese applicants but none to around 200
Chinese applicants. The Supreme Court concluded from this evidence that
the equal protection clause had been breached, saying (*per* Matthews J. at
373–374):

> "Though the law itself be fair on its face and impartial in appearance,
> yet, if it is applied and administered by public authority with an evil eye
> and an unequal hand, so as . . . to make unjust and illegal discrimi-
> nations between persons in similar circumstances, material to their
> rights, the denial of equal justice is still within the prohibition of the
> Constitution."

Thus a pattern of administrative discrimination based on considerations of,
e.g. sex, race, nationality or political allegiance would violate Article 40.1.[51]

[50] Without giving any reasons: see [1975] I.R. at 53. Presumably in this "one opinion rule" case
a majority of the court agreed on the result but not on the supporting grounds.
[51] It seems unlikely that an Irish court would produce a result like that in *Kotch* v. *Board of River
Pilot Commissioners* (1947) 330 U.S. 552. Under Louisiana law all ships approaching New
Orleans had to be guided by a state pilot. Such pilots were appointed on the nomination of a
board composed of pilots which, it was claimed, nominated only relatives and friends of
incumbent pilots. By a 5–4 majority the U.S. Supreme Court rejected an equal protection
challenge. Black J., for the majority, said the objectives of the whole system were safety and
efficiency, and it could not be said that the method adopted was unrelated to those objectives.
Family and neighbourly tradition might benefit morale and *esprit de corps*.

This conclusion is reinforced by the second case—*McMahon* v. *Leahy* [1984] I.R. 525—where the plaintiff was resisting an application for his extradition to Northern Ireland. He was one of a group of five prisoners who on March 10, 1975 had escaped from lawful custody in Northern Ireland and sought refuge in the Republic. Extradition proceedings had been instituted against the four others in 1975 but the High Court had directed the release of all four on the basis of the then understanding of the "political offence" exception. The Supreme Court held that McMahon could not now be extradited on the relevant charge. O'Higgins C.J. said that if this application succeeded four citizens who had been involved in the same escape as a fifth person would have been held by the courts to be exempt, while the fifth person, in respect of whom no different considerations applied, would have been held not to be exempt. It was the courts' clear duty to see that the obligation under Article 40.1's guarantee of equal treatment was discharged; thus the State could not be allowed to contest McMahon's claim that his offence was political. Henchy J. elaborated on the Article 40.1 aspect (at 541):

> " . . . if the order of extradition sought against the plaintiff were to be made, it would patently result in unequal treatment, at the hands of the Courts, of citizens who, as human beings, are in equal condition in the context of the law involved . . . I am unable to see how such inequality of treatment could be said to be in conformity with the implicit guarantee in Article 40, s.1, that like persons must be treated alike by the laws . . . the presumption of constitutionality extends to both the substance and the operation of a statute. . . . "

In the *East Donegal* case the Supreme Court held unconstitutional part of a minor provision of the Livestock Marts Act 1967—s.4(1)—under which the Minister for Agriculture could grant exemption from the Act's provisions to "any particular business." This, said the court, could only mean in its context granting exemption to specific firms; it was thus a far-reaching power to dispense individuals from the application of statutory provisions. This could not be done, as Walsh J., delivering the judgment of the court, explained ([1970] I.R. 317, 350):

> "The constitutional right of the Oireachtas in its legislation to take account of difference of social function and difference of capacity, physical and moral, does not extend to delegating that power to members of the Executive, to the exclusion of the Oireachtas, in order to decide as between individuals (all of whom are, by the terms of an Act, bound by it) which of them shall be exempted from the application of the Act— unless such exemption were necessary to avoid an infringement of the constitutional rights of such individuals which infringement, because of circumstances peculiar to them, would necessarily result from the application of the statutory provision without such exemption. No such justification appears in the provision under consideration. In the view of this Court the provision purporting to grant power to the Minister to exempt "any particular business" is invalid having regard to the provisions of the Constitution."

This conclusion might seem to produce administrative difficulties but presumably any such could be overcome by providing for Oireachtas approval of Ministerial orders exempting individuals.

Common law rules

That common law rules are subject to the equality guarantee is shown by
State (D.P.P.) v. Walsh [1981] I.R. 412 where Henchy J. (Griffin and Kenny
JJ. concurring) held that the common law defence of marital coercion available to a wife in certain circumstances did not survive the enactment of the
Constitution. It presupposed a disparity in status between husband and wife
which ran counter to the normal relations between a married couple in
modern times. The judge continued:

> "A legal rule that presumes, even on a prima facie and rebuttable basis,
> that a wife had been coerced by the physical presence of the husband
> into committing an act prohibited by the criminal law, particularly
> when a similar presumption does not operate in favour of a husband for
> acts committed in the presence of his wife, is repugnant to the concept of
> equality before the law guaranteed by the first sentence of Article 40, s.1,
> and could not, under the second sentence of that Article, be justified as a
> discrimination based on any difference of capacity or of social function
> as between husband and wife."

Article 40.1 has also contributed to the demise of the common law doctrine
that a wife's domicile depended upon that of her husband. Walsh J. in *Gaffney v. Gaffney* [1975] I.R. 133, 152 and McCarthy J. in *K.D. v. M.C.* [1985]
I.R. 697, 705 had both suggested, *obiter*, that this did not survive the enactment of the Constitution. The doctrine received its *coup de grace* from Barr J.
in *C.M. v. T.M.* [1991] I.L.R.M. 268, where he said (at 271):

> "In my view the old doctrine of dependent domicile of a wife, which in
> given circumstances may have particularly unjust consequences for her,
> also offends the principle enshrined in Article 40.1 of the Constitution
> that all citizens shall be equal before the law."[52]

Some other common law rules may be similarly open to question. One
such is the rule that only a wife can obtain alimony in divorce *a mensa et thoro*
proceedings (or in nullity proceedings *pendente lite*.)[53] In the context of
"gender-neutral" maintenance provisions such as the Family Law (Maintenance, etc.) Act 1976, these rules seem to be based on the stereotyped thinking
about the status of women condemned in the *Walsh* case. It is noteworthy
that in *Orr v. Orr* (1979) 440 U.S. 268 the United States Supreme Court
found Alabama alimony statutes making a husband alone liable therefor a
violation of equal protection. By the same token the common law rule
whereby a wife (only) may pledge her husband's credit for necessaries[54]
would appear to be under-inclusive.

---

[52] Barr J. also founded on Art. 41 and Art. 40.3.1°, saying in regard to the latter ([1991]
I.L.R.M. 268, 271–72): "The old doctrine of dependent domicile clearly militated against a
married woman by depriving her of domiciliary rights which she enjoyed as a single woman
by obliging her to acquire and retain the domicile of her husband in all circumstances while
the marriage subsisted. In my view, a married woman's right to an independent domicile,
now specifically recognised by statute, is a fundamental personal right within the ambit of
Art. 40.3.1° which the State has an obligation by its laws to respect, defend and vindicate."
See further Chap. 17 *infra*.

[53] For references see the Law Reform Commission *Reports* on Divorce a Mensa et Thoro (L.R.C.
8–1983), p. 24 and on Nullity of Marriage (L.R.C. 9–1984), p. 74.

[54] *Chappell v. Nunn* (1879) 4 L.R. Ir. 316; *Moylan v. Nolan* (1866) 17 I.C.L.R. 427: *Devine v. Mona-
han* (1933) 67 I.L.T.R. 44.

The most recent decision in this area—*McKinley* v. *Ireland* (*The Irish Times*, July 28, 1992)—is also the most notable, as the first where a sexually discriminatory common law privilege has been extended rather than uprooted. There the Supreme Court, founding on Article 40, held that a wife could claim damages for loss of her husband's consortium. Previously the common law had recognised such a right in a husband; however, though there was no Irish decision directly in point, *dicta* in two Supreme Court decisions indicated that the action was an anomaly which ought not to be extended.[55] In *McKinley's* case, however, the Supreme Court was not deterred by this consideration. McCarthy J. said that the solution was not to deny the husband's right, but under Article 40 of the Constitution, to enforce the wife's right to equality:

> "The simpler solution is to make the common law conform to the Constitution by declaring that the established right of the husband still exists and to deny such a right to the wife would be infringing Article 40."

Hederman J. spoke to similar effect, as did O'Flaherty J., who also invoked Article 41's protection of marriage.

Private action

A point still unresolved is whether Article 40.1 applies only to the State (in its executive, legislative and judicial organs) or whether it may also affect actions by private persons or bodies. The words "equal *before the law*" and the reference to "the State . . . in its enactments" might suggest the former conclusion. However in *Meskell* v. *C.I.E.* [1973] I.R. 121 the Supreme Court found Article 40.6.1° iii directly applicable to private action, in the particular instance dismissal of an employee for not being a union member. This may be a precedent for a similar application of Article 40.1. It may be objected that Article 40.6.i° iii refers to a *right* whereas Article 40.1 does not. But it would seem just as legitimate to read Article 40.1 as implying a broad right to equal treatment as to read Article 40.6.1° iii as implying a "right of dissociation."

The late Professor Kelly noted the predominant German view that the equality clause of the *Grundgesetz* does not apply generally to private law relationships because this would mean an excessive encroachment on individual freedom.[56] And he suggested that the Irish courts would share this view. This may well be true; Article 40.1 may be found not to be a "self-executing" provision. But it could provide constitutional underpinning for legislation— such as a race relations Act—designed to achieve an equality goal and yet arguably interfering with constitutional rights (*e.g.* freedom to hire and fire, or to refuse to let property, etc.) And it seems clear from *McMahon* v. *Leahy* (*supra*) that the courts could not lend their aid, if called on to do so, to private arrangements which worked an arbitrary discrimination—just as the United States courts could not enforce a racially motivated restrictive covenant: *Shelley* v. *Kraemer* (1948) 334 U.S. 1.

---

[55] *Spaight* v. *Dundon* [1961] I.R. 201: *O'Haran* v. *Divine* (1964) 100 I.L.T.R. 53. See further Law Reform Commission Working Paper No. 7—1979: *The Law Relating to Loss of Consortium and Loss of Services of a Child*, Chap. 1.

[56] *Op. cit.*, pp. 266–267.

14   Personal Liberty

Article 40.4 of the Constitution opens with a declaration as follows:

"1° No citizen shall be deprived of his personal liberty save in accordance with law."

On its face this provision might seem to give the Oireachtas *carte blanche* to enact anything it wished, so that personal liberty would be at the mercy of a bare parliamentary majority. But it is now clear that the phrase "in accordance with law" means something more than "as statute shall ordain"— though how much more is uncertain as the matter has not been put to the proof. The courts have, however, read the Constitution as reinforcing the common law's traditional presumption in favour of liberty. Thus in *People (Att. Gen.)* v. *O'Callaghan* [1966] I.R. 501 the Supreme Court held that a person awaiting trial could be refused bail only in narrowly-defined circumstances, which could not include Garda fears that he or she might commit further offences if allowed bail. Ó Dálaigh C.J. said (at 509) that deprivation of liberty must be considered a punishment and punishment began *after* conviction. Walsh J. (Budd J. concurring) said (at 516–517):

" . . . it would be quite contrary to the concept of personal liberty enshrined in the Constitution that any person should be punished in respect of any matter upon which he has not been convicted or that in any circumstances he should be deprived of his liberty only upon the belief that he will commit offences if left at liberty, save in the most extraordinary circumstances carefully spelled out by the Oireachtas and then only to secure the preservation of public peace or order or the public safety and the preservation of the State in a time of national emergency or in some situation akin to that."

The Supreme Court there repudiated the notion that, emergency situations apart, the Constitution gave any countenance to preventive detention. It would seem to follow that witnesses to a crime cannot be detained against their will even if the police reasonably believe that this is necessary to ensure their safety. Such a form of detention was ruled out by the Irish Court of Appeal in *Connors* v. *Pearson* [1921] 2 I.R. 51 and it may be assumed that it would also be ruled out today.[1]

---

[1] In *Re Morrissey* (*The Irish Times*, December 2, 1976) McMahon J. refused bail to an accused charged with murder, accepting Garda evidence that the accused might not be available to stand trial because of threats of violence against him. The judge also noted the Garda belief

The principles laid down in *O'Callaghan's* case have since been re-affirmed by the full Supreme Court in *Ryan* v. *D.P.P.* [1989] I.R. 399. In that case the court also rejected a novel argument—that the accused's constitutional right to liberty should be balanced against possible injury to the constitutional rights of others. Finlay C.J., for the court, stressed the problems this suggested approach would entail—*e.g.* how would an intention to commit further offences while on bail be proved, and what standards of proof would apply? If, as suggested, the courts had power to act on the basis of a suspected intention, he could not understand why this should be confined to cases where someone was applying for bail. The Chief Justice concluded as follows ([1989] I.R. 399, 407):

> "The criminalising of mere intention has been usually a badge of an oppressive or unjust legal system. The proper methods of preventing crime are the long-established combination of police surveillance, speedy trial and deterrent sentences."

And McCarthy J., concurring separately, summarised the objections thus ([1989] I.R. 399, 410):

> "The pointing finger of accusation, not of crime done, but of crime feared, would become the test. Such appears to me to be far from a balancing of constitutional rights; it is a recalibration of the scales of justice."

ARTICLE 40.4.2°–5°

The classical common law machinery for challenging the legality of a detention is habeas corpus; and Article 40.4.2°–5° makes this procedure part of the Constitution.[2] It envisages a complaint alleging unlawful detention "by on or behalf of any person to the High Court or any judge thereof . . . " When such a complaint is lodged there must be an inquiry *forthwith* into the legality of the detention and the High Court must, if satisfied that the detention is not lawful, order the release of the detainee. Several aspects of Article 40.4.2° call for comment.

A. The complaint and complainant

As noted above Article 40.4.2° speaks of a complaint[3] "by or on behalf" of any person. These clearly cover a complaint by a detainee or by counsel on his/her behalf; but the Supreme Court has made it clear that a complaint

that the accused might interfere with a witness. The latter ground is a recognised reason for refusing bail (see *infra*); whether the former ground *alone* would justify a refusal seems doubtful on the authorities.
[2] See Anthony M. Collins and James O'Reilly, *Civil Proceedings and the State in Ireland: A Practitioner's Guide* (Dublin 1990), Chap. 3
[3] Which may be an informal document such as a letter to the court: see Michael Kenny "Informality in Modern Irish Habeas Corpus Practice" (1974) IX *Irish Jurist* (N.S.) 67. A similar informality exists in relation to prisoners' applications for judicial review: see *Ryan* v. *Govr., Limerick Prison* (High Court, November 18, 1988) where Murphy J. said:
> "This is one of the many applications for Judicial Review made by persons in custody and forwarded . . . to the Central Office of the High Court for consideration by a Judge . . . This procedure is informal—perhaps excessively so—but it does undoubtedly have the merit that it is both inexpensive and expeditious."

may be lodged by an individual on behalf of someone else. In *Application of Woods* [1970] I.R. 154, 157 Ó Dálaigh C.J., speaking for the full court, said:

> " . . . it is not questioned that under Article 40, s.4, subs. 2, a person has the right to complain to the High Court on behalf of another person that that person is being unlawfully detained. This right includes a right to state the grounds which are put forward for alleging that such other person is being unlawfully detained."

It does not, however, include a right to be heard in argument in the course of proceedings arising out of the complaint: *ibid.*[4]

In such a situation the court will carefully consider whether there is an arguable case for relief, and whether it would be proper to assign counsel and a solicitor to act on the person's behalf if he/she is unable, for financial reasons, to secure such assistance personally. Should the court make such an assignment the costs will be borne out of public funds: this was announced by counsel for the Attorney General in *Application of Woods* [1970] I.R. 154, 158.

B. The forum

The complaint is made to "the High Court or any judge thereof" and the judge to whom it is made "shall forthwith enquire into the said complaint." Should the judge who hears the complaint take the view that there is nothing to inquire into—*i.e.* refuse to grant a conditional order—it appears that a fresh application may be made to another judge. But this would not be so if a conditional order had been granted and the first judge had subsequently refused to make it absolute, for then the High Court in the person of that judge would have inquired into the detention and pronounced it lawful; see the former Supreme Court's decision in *State (Dowling)* v. *Kingston (No. 2)* [1937] I.R. 699.[5] The only recourse then available is an appeal to the Supreme Court. But a fresh application to a different judge *on different grounds* appears competent: see *Application of Woods* [1970] I.R. 154, discussed *infra*.

The complaint may be made outside High Court sitting hours and, if necessary, to a judge at his or her residence. It then becomes the duty of the judge to inquire "forthwith" into the complaint. The urgency with which such applications are treated, and considerations of personal convenience set aside, is illustrated in *State (Trimbole)* v. *Governor, Mountjoy Prison* [1985] I.R. 550. There a complaint was made to Egan J. at 3 p.m. on October 26, 1984. The judge granted a conditional order and held the inquiry under Article 40.4 between 7 and 10 p.m. that same evening.

The meaning of "forthwith" in Article 40.4.2° was discussed in *State (Whelan)* v. *Governor, Mountjoy Prison* [1983] I.L.R.M. 52. There the prosecutor had been granted a preliminary order for an inquiry under Article 40 and the proceedings came on for hearing on January 11, 1979. The prosecutor was relying on a High Court decision then under appeal and the judge was informed of this. By consent the proceedings were adjourned, the prosecutor

---

[4] The Supreme Court reiterated this in *Application of McAliskey* (*The Irish Times*, July 28, 1987). It did, however, treat the documentation supplied by the applicant as having been supplied by the prisoner (Dominic McGlinchey) himself.

[5] See also *McGlinchey* v. *Ireland* [1990] 2 I.R. 215.

being admitted to bail. Subsequently the Supreme Court overruled the High Court decision relied on by the prosecutor, and the adjourned Article 40 application came on before Barrington J. It was argued that the procedure adopted on January 11, was unconstitutional; there could be no adjournment under Article 40 save in the specific circumstances contemplated by Article 40.4.3°. Barrington J. rejected this argument. On an application under Article 40, he said, the High Court's duty was forthwith to inquire into the legality of the detention but once the inquiry was entered on, and provided the urgency and importance of the proceedings were kept in mind, the court was entitled to conduct the inquiry in the manner it thought best calculated to resolve the issues of law and fact raised, and to achieve the interests of justice. Should the application raise difficult issues of fact or law the court might have to consider whether the applicant should be admitted to bail until those issues were resolved. Barrington J. continued ([1983] I.L.R.M. 52, 55):

> "The duty of the High Court 'forthwith' to enquire into the legality of the prosecutor's detention stresses the importance and urgency of habeas corpus proceedings. But it does not mean that the High Court should skimp its enquiry or proceed on an inadequate understanding of the law or the facts. When, as in the present case, the enquiry proceeds upon a basis which appears to have been humane and sensible and which was in fact agreed to by counsel representing the prosecutor at the relevant time . . . it will be extremely difficult to challenge the proceedings later.
>
> While I would not like in any way to detract from the urgency of habeas corpus proceedings the word 'forthwith' used in Art. 40.4.2° appears to govern the proceedings in the preliminary order. The words the court 'shall forthwith' enquire into the said complaint and 'may' order the person in whose custody the prisoner is being detained to produce the body and certify in writing the grounds of his detention on 'a named day' seems to illustrate this. Presumably the court could on the application for the preliminary order be satisfied that the complaint was groundless and could dismiss the application without calling on the governor to produce the body or certify the grounds of the detention. But if the court does call on the governor to justify the imprisonment and adjourn the enquiry to a 'named day' there is nothing in the Constitution to say that the enquiry must be completed on that day."

Presumably, then, the fact that the prosecutor Whelan consented to the adjournment made little difference; that is, he could not have *insisted* on the proceedings being completed on January 11.

It appears that a High Court judge continues to be bound by Article 40.4 even if he/she is, under statute, discharging some other whole-time function such as chairing a board or commission[6]; also that an application thereunder may competently be made to the President of the Circuit Court, who has, by virtue of office, the status of a High Court judge.[7]

---

[6] This view was expressed by the Attorney General, Mr. Declan Costello, in the Special Committee proceedings on the Law Reform Commission Bill 1975: see the *Report*, D 18, No. 2, p. 22.

[7] Courts (Establishment and Constitution) Act 1961, s.2(4). An example of such an application is *State (Woods)* v. *Governor, Portlaoise Prison* (1974) 108 I.L.T.R. 54.

C. The procedure

The procedure outlined in Article 40.4.2° involves an immediate inquiry into the complaint, with if necessary an order for the subsequent production of the prisoner and a statement of the grounds on which he/she is detained. Then when the person is produced, and the custodian given an opportunity of justifying the detention, the court "shall" make an order for the release unless satisfied that the detention is in accordance with law. This procedure is often described using the language traditional in State-side applications— conditional order, cause shown, order made absolute or discharged; however order 84, Rule 1(3) of the Rules of the Superior Courts 1986 stipulates that the habeas corpus procedure there specified does not apply to an order under Article 40.4.[8] Only if the custodian has waived the right to argue in justification of the detention may an absolute order be made in the first instance: see the Supreme Court's decisions in *State (Rogers)* v. *Galvin* [1983] I.R. 249 and *Application of Zwann* [1981] I.R. 395.

The references in Article 40.4.2° to an order for the production of the body of the detainee do not require that such an order be made. The power is an enabling one and the High Court has jurisdiction to proceed in the applicant's absence: The Supreme Court so held in *State (M. Woods)* v. *Kelly* [1969] I.R. 269.

An appeal lies to the Supreme Court in any Article 40.4 matter, whether against a refusal of a conditional order, or a refusal—or grant[9]—of an order absolute. On an appeal from a refusal of a conditional order the Supreme Court may either require the respondent to justify the detention before it or remit the matter to the High Court: *State (Williams)* v. *Kelly* [1970] I.R. 259. Ó Dálaigh C.J. there said (at 262) that in cases of urgency and cases where no issues of fact arose for determination the court's practice had favoured retention.[10] That case also decides that an applicant has no right to have the case determined by a full Supreme Court of five judges, since by statute it is for the Chief Justice, or in his absence the senior ordinary judge, to decide whether the court should consist of three or five judges.[11]

Should the Supreme Court remit the matter to the High Court, identifying a specific point as arguable, the applicant will not necessarily be confined to that point in the High Court proceedings: see *McGlinchey* v. *Govr., Portlaoise Prison* [1988] I.R. 671. There Gannon J., on behalf of a divisional court, said (at 688):

[8] It is expressed to apply to applications under the Irish Habeas Corpus Act 1782 (*recte* 1781). Whether this Act (21 and 22 Geo. III, c. 11) is still in force was left open by the Supreme Court in *Zwann's* case [1981] I.R. 395, though Griffin J. (at 404) said it must be a matter of considerable doubt whether the right to habeas corpus existed apart from Art. 40.2.2°. See Kevin Costello, "A Consitutional Antiquity?—The Habeas Corpus (Ireland) Act 1782 Revisited" (1988) XXVIII *Irish Jurist* (N.S.) 240.

[9] The existence of an appeal against a *grant* of habeas corpus was recognised by the Supreme Court in *State (Browne)* v. *Feran* [1967] I.R. 147: see Chap. 10 *supra*.

[10] In *Application of McAliskey* (*The Irish Times*, July 28, 1987) the Supreme Court said that in an appeal against refusal of a conditional order its function was confined to considering whether any arguable issue had been raised; and if one had been, to remit the matter to the High Court, without forming or expressing any view on its merits. (The relevant passage appears at [1988] I.R. 671, 700–701.)

[11] Courts (Supplemental Provisions) Act 1961, s.7(4).

" . . . it is open to the court to ascertain if there may be, on the evidence presented to it, any other ground in law, as well as that identified by the Supreme Court, for dissatisfaction with the detention."

And the applicant there was permitted to raise several points above and beyond that identified by the Supreme Court.

In *Application of Woods* [1970] I.R. 154 the prosecutor had made an earlier application under Article 40.4 which had ultimately been dismissed by the Supreme Court. Subsequently he applied again, but the High Court rejected his application on the basis that the Supreme Court had ruled his detention on the challenged warrant valid and that to entertain this application would amount to hearing an appeal from that decision. But the Supreme Court held that this went too far. Ó Dálaigh C.J., speaking for the full court, said (at 162–163):

" . . . neither the High Court nor the Supreme Court warrants, by its decision in an application for *habeas corpus*, that every possible ground of complaint has been considered and ruled. This would cast on the court an impossible burden. Such matters as are considered by the Supreme Court in its judgment are finally decided for the High Court. But this will not preclude an applicant from later raising a new ground even though that ground might have been, but was not, put forward on the first application.

The principles which apply in litigation *inter partes* are not applicable in habeas corpus. The duty which the court has under the Constitution of ordering the release of a person, unless satisfied that he is lawfully detained, requires that the court should entertain a complaint which bears on the question of the legality of the detention—even though in earlier proceedings the applicant might have raised the matter but did not do so. The duty of the courts, to see that no one is deprived of his personal liberty save in accordance with law, overrides considerations which are valid in litigation *inter partes*. If, therefore, the applicant raised matters before the President on this application which had not been ruled on a previous application—and it is not clear from the documents before us whether such was the case or not—the duty of the High Court under the Constitution was to examine such grounds and say whether or not it was satisfied that the applicant was being detained in accordance with law."

The Supreme Court also stated in the *Woods* case that on an Article 40.4 application the court was not confined to examining the illegality complained of by the applicant. It must also be alert for other grounds which might render the detention unlawful. An instance where this occurred is *State (Holmes) v. Furlong* [1967] I.R. 210, where the issue which proved decisive in favour of granting habeas corpus was raised by the Supreme Court itself: see p. 217 of the report.

It has several times been emphasised that the object of an Article 40.4 application is to inquire into the legality of the prosecutor's detention. Such proceedings "are not suitable for the judicial investigation of complaints as to conviction, sentence or conditions of detention which fall short of that requirement": the Supreme Court so stated, *per* O'Higgins C.J., in *State (McDonagh) v. Frawley* [1978] I.R. 131, 137. Such complaints fall to be investigated in other forms of proceedings. Finlay P. elaborated on this in *Cahill* v. *Governor, Military Detention Barracks, Curragh Camp* [1980] I.L.R.M. 191, 210:

> "The application to the High Court under Article 40 of the Constitution for an enquiry as to the legality of the detention of any citizen is a peculiar and unique procedure. It can be made in the most informal way either by the applicant himself or by any other person . . . *bona fide* interested on his behalf. It can be made, as no other application can be made, to a chosen judge of the High Court and must if practicable and possible be discharged by him. Procedures concerning it are freed from many of the rules of procedure and restrictions applicable to any other form of application to the High Court, and the relief claimed and granted in appropriate cases, namely that of release from custody or detention, is immediate and in a sense dramatic.
>
> *Prima facie*, such procedure must not . . . be debased and certainly should not . . . become a vehicle by way of special, informal and expeditious procedure for the pursuit of other remedies. It cannot, therefore, as a matter of practice or a matter of course be a procedure initiated in the hope or expectation that some relief such as *mandamus* will be achieved instead."[12]

Nonetheless, it seems that an order of mandamus may be granted, where appropriate, in proceedings begun under Article 40.4: *State (Richardson)* v. *Governor, Mountjoy Prison* [1980] I.L.R.M. 82, as explained in *State (Comerford)* v. *same* [1981] I.L.R.M. 86, 90.

Should the court conclude that the detention complained of is unlawful it must immediately order the release of the prisoner. There can be no question of a stay of execution pending an appeal: the Supreme Court's ruling to this effect in *State (Browne)* v. *Feran* [1967] I.R. 147 at 169 was re-affirmed in *Trimbole's* case [1985] I.R. 550 at 567.

In *State (McDonagh)* v. *Frawley* [1978] I.R. 131, 137 the Supreme Court, *per* O'Higgins C.J., said that if the court was not satisfied that the detention was in accordance with law it must make an order for release

> " . . . and notwithstanding judicial *dicta* to the contrary, the order for release may not be coupled with an order of rearrest. The protection of personal liberty, which Article 40, s.4 is intended to ensure, would be hollow and ineffectual if the order for release was not unqualified and unconditional."

But the judgment in *McDonagh's* case does not specify where these earlier dicta are to be found, and what was said there can hardly be regarded as overruling a constant practice evident in a number of Supreme Court decisions from 1963 to 1970. If it is established that a prisoner is being held

---

[12] Cp. the observations of Finlay C.J., giving the judgment of the Supreme Court, in *McGlinchey* v. *Govr., Portlaoise Prison* [1988] I.R. 671, 701: "The enquiry under Article 40 of the Constitution is one of the most fundamentally important procedures created by the Constitution. It is an enquiry which permits a citizen or indeed some other person on his behalf in limited circumstances to apply to a judge of the High Court and to appeal to this Court for an enquiry as to the legality of detention. It is not subject to any special procedures; it is not subject to any special rules, and deals only with the question of the legality of the detention of the person who applies. It is given such a simple and uncomplicated procedure because it deals with an essential and vital matter, the liberty of the individual. It is therefore important that it should not be debased by being used for purposes for which it was not intended."

on a defective warrant the court cannot, consistently with Article 40.4.2°, ignore that defect. But if the person was properly convicted, or the detention is otherwise lawful, he or she can hardly be set at liberty. As the Supreme Court, *per* Ó Dálaigh C.J., said in *State (Dillon)* v. *Kelly* [1970] I.R. 175, 178–179:

> "It has repeatedly been stated in this Court that, when a prisoner is lawfully undergoing a sentence of imprisonment but his detention has been temporarily rendered illegal by his being detained in a prison not authorised by law, it is the duty of the court which orders his release from such unlawful detention to ensure that the prisoner is immediately rearrested and lodged in a lawful place of detention to serve out the unexpired portion of his sentence."

In that case the applicant had been transferred from Mountjoy Prison to Portlaoise Prison under an order of the Minister for Justice. The High Court found the Minister's order invalid, and the detention consequently unlawful, and granted an absolute order under Article 40.4. The Supreme Court issued a warrant for the applicant's apprehension and detention in Mountjoy Prison in accordance with the terms of the sentence.[13]

DETENTION IN ACCORDANCE WITH LAW

Several kinds of detention are authorised by law and it is now necessary to consider them *seriatim*.

A. Imprisonment following on conviction

A person detained following on conviction and sentence is *prima facie* detained in accordance with law: *State (McDonagh)* v. *Frawley* [1978] I.R. 131, 136. A divisional court (Maguire P., O'Byrne and Gavan Duffy JJ.) said in *State (Cannon)* v. *Kavanagh* [1937] I.R. 428, 435 that "it would require most exceptional circumstances for this Court to grant even a conditional order of habeas corpus to a prisoner so convicted." The reasoning behind this is that the legal system provides convicted persons with rights of appeal, and an appeal is the proper course in such cases. In *Application of Lucey* [1972] I.R. 347, the Supreme Court said that a person undergoing a lawful sentence could not be released on habeas corpus unless there had been something such as a fundamental failure of natural justice in the course of the trial. This was re-stated and amplified in *State (McDonagh)* v. *Frawley* [1978] I.R. 131, 136–137, *per* O'Higgins C.J.:

> "The stipulation in Article 40, s.4, subs. 1 of the Constitution that a citizen may not be deprived of his liberty save 'in accordance with law' does not mean that a convicted person must be released on habeas corpus merely because some defect or illegality attaches to his detention. The phrase means that there must be such a default of fundamental requirements that the detention may be said to be wanting in due process of law. For habeas corpus purposes, therefore, it is insufficient for the prisoner to show that there has been a legal error or impropriety, or even

---

[13] A similar course had been adopted in *State (Brien)* v. *Kelly* [1970] I.R. 69 and *Tynan* v. *Governor, Portlaoise Prison* (Supreme Court, December 12, 1963).

that jurisdiction has been inadvertently exceeded. For example, if the judge at a murder trial in which the accused was convicted were to impose a sentence of imprisonment for life, instead of penal servitude for life as required by the statute, the resulting detention would be imposed technically without jurisdiction. But the prisoner would not be released under Article 40, s.4, for it could not be said that the detention was not 'in accordance with the law' in the sense indicated. In such a case the court would leave the matter of sentence to be rectified by the Court of Criminal Appeal; or it could remit the case to the Court of trial for the imposition of the correct sentence. . . . "[14]

It would follow from this that to overturn a conviction on habeas corpus it would be necessary to show that the trial had not been in due course of law as required by Article 38.1. This might apply if an individual had been convicted under an unconstitutionally vague statute, or on the basis of evidence obtained by a conscious and deliberate violation of his/her constitutional rights (as to these see *infra*). Anything falling short of this would presumably be a matter to be raised on appeal.

It is also clear that a complaint about conditions of detention will not suffice. In *State (Smith and Fox)* v. *Governor, Curragh Military Detention Barracks* [1980] I.L.R.M. 208 Barrington J. found on the medical evidence that the prosecutor Fox was suffering from reactive depression, and that by his nature he found it difficult to endure prison conditions. Thus he had suffered more deeply from his confinement that prisoners normally did or than a court would normally contemplate in imposing a term of imprisonment. Nonetheless Barrington J. held that these facts alone could not make illegal a detention which was otherwise legal. The matters urged were matters which the Minister for Justice might take into account in deciding whether to remit portion of the prosecutor's sentence or release him on parole.

B. Imprisonment for contempt of court

What was said about imprisonment following on conviction applies also to imprisonment for contempt of court. Such imprisonment may be for civil or criminal contempt, and there are important differences between the two. The Supreme Court pointed out in *Keegan* v. *de Búrca* [1973] I.R. 223 that criminal contempt consists in behaviour calculated to prejudice the due course of justice, such as contempt in the face of the court, words written or spoken or acts calculated to prejudice the due course of justice, or disobedience to an order of habeas corpus by the person to whom it is directed—to give but some examples. Thus scandalous and unfounded abuse of a judge or a court will constitute a criminal contempt[15]; so too will publication of material from a case heard *in camera*[16] or publication of material calculated to prejudice a fair trial.[17]

It is, for several reasons, unlikely that imprisonment for criminal contempt would give rise to habeas corpus proceedings. In the first place such

---

[14] This passage was quoted and applied by Finlay C.J., giving the judgment of the Supreme Court, in *McGlinchey* v. *Govr., Portlaoise Prison* [1988] I.R. 671, at 702.

[15] See, *e.g. State (D.P.P.)* v. *Walsh* [1981] I.R. 412 and Chap. 15 *infra*.

[16] *Re Kennedy and McCann* [1976] I.R. 382.

[17] See *Cullen* v. *Toibín* [1984] I.L.R.M. 577 and *State (D.P.P.)* v. *Independent Newspapers Ltd.* [1985] I.L.R.M. 183, discussed in Chap. 15 *infra*.

imprisonment—though undoubtedly available—is rare in practice. In the reported cases the most common form of criminal contempt is "scandalising the court" (on which see further Chap. 15 *infra*) and the usual penalty imposed has been a fine[18] or binding over.[19] Secondly, the sentence of imprisonment, if imposed, would normally be imposed by the High Court— and an appeal would lie to the Supreme Court. Thus in *Keegan* v. *de Búrca* [1973] I.R. 223 the defendant had been committed for contempt by the President of the High Court for refusing to answer a relevant question put by him. His order provided that she should be imprisoned until she purged her contempt. On appeal the Supreme Court held that this was contempt in the face of the court. It thus constituted a common-law misdemeanour punishable by imprisonment and fine without limit. However, the object of such punishment was punitive, not coercive, and only a determinate penalty could be imposed.

An inferior court—into which category fall the Circuit and District Courts—has jurisdiction only to deal with contempt exhibited in the face of the court. Any other form of contempt falls to be dealt with by the High Court: see the divisional court decisions in *Att. Gen.* v. *O'Ryan and Boyd* [1947] I.R. 70 (scandalising a Circuit Court Judge) and *Att. Gen.* v. *Connolly* [1948] I.R. 213 (scandalising a special criminal court).[20] Thus an appeal to the Supreme Court will be available: see Article 34.4.3° of the Constitution, discussed in Chapter 10 *supra*.

Notwithstanding the above an application under Article 40.4 might be appropriate if an inferior court attempted to imprison someone for an offence committed outside the precincts, or for refusing to answer an *irrelevant* question, or imposed an indeterminate sentence for contempt in the face of the court.

So far as civil contempt is concerned imprisonment here is coercive, the object being to compel compliance with a court order such as an injunction. The imprisonment is therefore necessarily of indefinite duration, terminable where the court is satisfied that its order will be obeyed or when the person seeking the order waives his/her rights; see *Keegan* v. *de Búrca supra*: *State* (*Commins*) v. *McRann* [1977] I.R. 78. In the case of imprisonment for civil contempt of the High Court, there is a remedy by way of appeal to the Supreme Court. Imprisonment for civil contempt by the Circuit Court may not be questioned in Article 40 proceedings; so said Finlay P. in *State* (*H.*) v. *Daly* [1977] I.R. 90 at 93.[21]

C. Detention following arrest

(a) *At common law*

An arrest is "the actual or notional seizure of a person for the purpose of imprisonment"—*per* O'Higgins C.J. in *People* (*D.P.P.*) v. *Walsh* [1980] I.R.

---

[18] This was done in *Att. Gen.* v. *O'Kelly* [1928] I.R. 308: *Att. Gen.* v. *O'Ryan and Boyd* [1946] I.R. 70 and in *Re Kennedy and McCann supra*.

[19] This was done in *Att. Gen.* v. *Connolly* [1948] I.R. 213. In *State* (*D.P.P.*) v. *Walsh* (Finlay P., October 21, 1981) a suspended sentence of 18 months imprisonment was imposed.

[20] A Special Criminal Court has power, under s.44(1)(e) of the Offences Against the State Act 1939, to punish for contempt, whether committed in its presence or otherwise. But it does not appear that this has been invoked.

[21] A criminal contempt may sometimes necessitate jury trial—*State* (*D.P.P.*) v. *Walsh* [1981] I.R. 412, but civil contempt does not: *State* (*H.*) v. *Daly* [1977] I.R. 90.

294 at 306.[22] It may be with or without a warrant, the latter being by far the more common. A warrant represents judicial authority given pursuant to statute for the arrest; but the common law confers ample authority to arrest without a warrant. A Garda has a general power to arrest on reasonable suspicion of felony, whether or not a felony has been committed; and the fact that the arresting officer is acting as the agent of colleagues—*i.e.* that they, not he or she, have the reasonable suspicion—is immaterial: *People (D.P.P.)* v. *Walsh* [1980] I.R. 294, 300. In addition many statutory provisions authorise arrest without warrant; these are conveniently listed in Appendix G. of Ryan and Magee's *The Irish Criminal Process.*

Save under special statutory provisions, such as are found in the Offences against the State Acts or the Criminal Justice Act 1984, an arrest is for a strictly limited purpose. The courts have frequently stressed that a lawful arrest is simply a process to compel the attendance before a court of a person charged with an offence. The arresting officer is therefore obliged to bring the accused person before a District Justice or peace commissioner as soon as reasonably possible for the purpose of being charged.[23] If this is not done the detention of the accused becomes unlawful from the time when he or she could first have been brought before a District Judge or peace commissioner. From this two consequences flow. Firstly an application for an order under Article 40.4 would be competent. Secondly, evidence obtained from the accused during an unlawful detention will normally be inadmissible at the trial.[24]

In *Re Ó Laighléis* [1970] I.R. 93, 129 the former Supreme Court said, *per* Maguire C.J.:

> "We accept it as settled law that in the case of an arrest without the production of a warrant the arrest will not be lawful unless the person being arrested is told why he is being arrested or unless he otherwise knows: see *Christie* v. *Leachinsky* [1947] A.C. 537, 587. The reason for the rule is not far to seek. Arrest must be for a lawful purpose; and since no one is obliged to submit to an unlawful arrest the citizen has a right before acquiescing in his arrest to know why he is being arrested."

This rule was reaffirmed by the present Supreme Court in *People (D.P.P.)* v. *Walsh* [1980] I.R. 294. It is not necessary that precise or technical language be used; but the arrested person must be informed in substance why this restraint on his/her liberty is being imposed: *Christie* v. *Leachinsky* [1947] A.C. 573, 587 *per* Viscount Simon. Failure to observe this rule may make the arresting officer liable for false imprisonment—and may make the ensuing detention unlawful. But this will depend on the circumstances of the particular case: see *People (D.P.P.)* v. *Walsh* [1980] I.R. 294.

The rule that an arrested person must be brought before a District Justice or peace commissioner as soon as possible is reinforced by the Criminal Justice Act 1951, s.15 (as substituted by the Criminal Justice Act 1984 s.26). This requires that a person arrested pursuant to a warrant be brought before

---

[22] See the extended treatment of this topic in E. F. Ryan and P. P. Magee, *The Irish Criminal Process* (Cork 1983), Chap. 5.

[23] *People (D.P.P.)* v. *O'Loughlin* [1979] I.R. 85: *People (D.P.P.)* v. *Walsh* [1980] I.R. 294: *People (D.P.P.)* v. *Higgins* (Supreme Court, November 22, 1985).

[24] *People (D.P.P.)* v. *Shaw* [1982] I.R. 1: *O'Loughlin's* case *supra*: *People (D.P.P.)* v. *Lynch* [1982] I.R. 64: *Higgins'* case *supra*. See further *infra* under "Trial in Due Course of Law."

a judge of the District Court "as soon as practicable" (s.15(1)). Equally, a person arrested without warrant must, on being charged, be brought before a judge of the District Court "as soon as practicable" (s.15(2)). This phrase is further elucidated by sub-section 3 which provides that where a person is arrested (with or without a warrant) after 10 p.m. on any evening and the appropriate judge of the District Court is due to sit not later than noon on the following day, it shall be sufficient if the arrested person is brought before the court at the commencement of the sitting. This reproduces the common law position as expounded in *People (D.P.P.)* v. *Walsh* [1980] I.R. 294, and *People (D.P.P.)* v. *Shaw* [1982] I.R. 1. 35, 52, 63.

No detention for questioning. Apart from special statutory provisions considered *infra*, there is no power to arrest or detain someone for questioning or for the purpose of obtaining evidence against him/her.[25] This is clearly established by *People (D.P.P.)* v. *Higgins* (Supreme Court, November 22, 1985). There Finlay C.J., speaking for the full court, reaffirmed the principles laid down in *Dunne* v. *Clinton* [1930] I.R. 366 (High Court): Supreme Court February 12, 1931[26] and *People (D.P.P.)* v. *O'Loughlin* [1979] I.R. 85. The judgment continues (pp. 11–12):

> "This matter was also dealt with by this Court in *The People* v. *Walsh* [1980] I.R. 294, where at page 299, O'Higgins C.J. stated as follows:
> > "It has been stated many times in our Courts that there is no such procedure permitted by the law as 'holding for questioning' or detaining on any pretext, except pursuant to a court order or for the purpose of charging and bringing the person detained before a court.' "

In the instant case the appellant Higgins had been arrested on February 7, 1982 on suspicion of having committed the offence of dangerous driving under section 53 of the Road Traffic Act 1961. He was brought to Kells Garda Station about 8 p.m. No steps were taken to hold a special court or to grant the appellant bail. Instead the arresting officer contacted Gardaí at other stations in the county to say that the appellant was in his custody, in case they wished to interview him about other offences. Around 11 p.m. Gardaí from Navan station arrived and questioned the appellant. At about 11.20 p.m. he made admissions in regard to the offences of which he was subsequently convicted. The Supreme Court held that at the time when he was alleged to have made these admissions, he was not being detained for the purpose of being charged or brought before a court but rather for the purpose of being interrogated. His detention was therefore unlawful to the knowledge of the Gardaí concerned and was a conscious and deliberate violation of his constitutional rights. Hence the statements he was alleged to have made were inadmissible in evidence against him.

Though the Gardaí have no common law power to arrest or detain people for questioning, they are at liberty to question anyone, whether suspected or not, from whom they think useful information regarding an offence may be

---

[25] But see J. Paul McCutcheon, "Arrest, Investigation and Section 30" (1987) 9 *D.U.L.J.* 46, who argues that the distinction between common law arrest and detention for questioning under s.30 of the Offences against the State Act 1939 is more apparent than real.

[26] Printed in *Judgments of the Court of Criminal Appeal 1924–1978* (Gerard Frewen, ed., Dublin n.d.), pp. 564–567.

obtained. (Subject to certain statutory exceptions there is no obligation to answer such questions.) To facilitate such questioning a practice has grown up of inviting suspects to come to a Garda station "to assist with inquiries." The person concerned will then be questioned intensively, with a view to eliciting a confession. Only when such a statement is made and recorded will the person be formally charged. The theory behind all this is that the suspect is voluntarily in the Garda station, so that he or she has not been arrested or detained for questioning. The courts have not specifically disapproved of this practice, but they will not always accept the supposed voluntary nature of the suspect's presence in the Garda station. If at the trial an issue is raised as to whether the accused was in custody at the time an alleged statement was made, the onus of proof is on the State to establish either that the accused was not in custody or that the custody was lawful: *People (D.P.P.)* v. *Conroy* [1986] I.R. 460.[27]

Bail. Though it is lawful for the Gardaí to detain a person arrested after 10 p.m. until a sitting of the District Court next morning, this will not necessarily happen. For the officer in charge of the relevant Garda station has a general power to release the person concerned on bail if he/she considers it prudent to do so and no warrant directing detention is in force. This power is conferred by section 31(1) of the Criminal Procedure Act 1967. Should the decision be in favour of bail the Garda officer may take from the person concerned "a recognisance, with or without sureties, for his due appearance before the District Court at the appropriate time and place."[28]

In *State (D.P.P.)* v. *District Justice Ruane* (High Court, February 6, 1987) it was argued that the new section 15(2) of the Criminal Justice Act 1951 (inserted by the Criminal Justice Act 1984, s.26) impliedly repealed the station bail provisions of the Criminal Procedure Act 1967. Since section 15(2) required a person arrested without warrant to be brought before a District Justice or peace commissioner as soon as practicable, it was contended, the power to grant station bail could not now be exercised. But Blayney J. declined to accept this, holding that section 15(2) applied only where the person arrested was kept in custody by reason of station bail not being granted. In such circumstances, the provision must be strictly complied with. But if the arrested person *was* granted station bail then he/she ceased to be in custody, and section 15(2) did not require to be complied with. Blayney J. continued (p.8 of his judgment):

> "This construction fully protects the rights of the accused. He is either set at liberty by being granted station bail, or he is brought with all

---

[27] Issues of fact and law relating to the question whether an accused was lawfully in custody at the time an alleged statement was made are to be tried by the judge in the jury's absence: so held in *Conroy's* case *supra*, overruling in this respect *People (D.P.P.)* v. *Lynch* [1982] I.R. 64.

[28] Rule 39(1) of the District Court Rules 1948 (as substituted by the District Court (Criminal Procedure Act 1967) Rules 1985 (S.I. 1985 No. 23)) provided that the recognisance might be a condition for the accused's appearance at the next District Court sitting 'or at any subsequent sitting thereof to be held not later than 30 days after such sitting." In *State (Lynch)* v. *District Justice Ballagh* [1986] I.R. 203 the Supreme Court held that this rule was *ultra vires* the District Court Rules Committee, since it did not relate to the practice and procedure of that court as required by the Courts of Justice Act 1924, s.91 and the Courts (Supplemental Provisions) Act 1961, ss.34 and 48. And it was stated that a court sitting several days after the arrest, on a date convenient to the Gardaí, was not "the appropriate time and place" within the meaning of s.31 of the Criminal Procedure Act 1967.

reasonable speed before a District Justice or a Peace Commissioner. And it enables full effect to be given to both of the provisions. And finally, because it fully protects the rights of the accused, it is in my opinion eminently reasonable."

The provisions of the Criminal Justice Act 1951 authorising peace commissioners to grant bail or remand in custody were held unconstitutional by Keane J. in *O'Mahony* v. *Melia* [1989] I.R. 335. Consequently persons refused Garda bail will not be able to secure it unless a judge of the District Court is available. But this will not warrant prolonged detention in custody, for "the obligation remains on the gardaí to bring arrested persons before a court with reasonable expedition": *per* Keane J. in *O'Mahony's* case, at 342.[29] If, on appearing before the District Court, the accused is remanded on bail, and then and there finds it, the remit is to the next sitting of the District Court. In any other event it is to a sitting of that court within eight days of the arrest. These provisions are contained in section 15(4–6) of the Criminal Justice Act 1951 (as substituted by the Criminal Justice Act 1984, s.26). Under Part III of the Criminal Procedure Act 1967, the District Court has a general power to remand an accused from time to time as occasion requires. Such remand may be in custody or on bail. Section 28 obliges a District Court judge to grant bail "if it appears to him to be a case in which bail ought to be allowed." An appeal against refusal of bail lies to the High Court: s.28(3).[30] Section 29 lists several offences in respect of which the High Court alone may grant bail; these include certain offences under the Offences against the State Act 1939 and the Official Secrets Act 1963, together with murder, attempted murder and conspiracy to murder. But it is important to note that there is no offence for which bail may not be granted; the concept of a non-bailable offence has no place in Irish law.[31]

The bail provisions of Part III must be read in the light of the Supreme Court's decisions in *People (Att. Gen.)* v. *O'Callaghan* [1966] I.R. 501 and *Ryan* v. *D.P.P.* [1989] I.R. 399. Their effect is to create a strong presumption in favour of bail, emphasising the principle that innocence is presumed until conviction. In particular the court has rejected the suggestion that a person could be denied bail on the ground that he or she might commit further offences while at liberty. The test to be applied in all bail applications is the probability of the applicant evading justice if bail were granted. Among the factors to be considered in this regard are the seriousness of the charge, the nature of the evidence, the likely sentence if the applicant should be found guilty and the fact (if such exists) that he/she had failed to answer to bail on an earlier occasion. Also relevant are the possibility of the accused's disposing of stolen property, destroying evidence or interfering with prospective witnesses or jurors. There must, however, be a reasonable probability that such things will occur, and an objection to bail by the prosecution on such grounds must be supported by evidence sufficient to enable a court to arrive at its own conclusions on probability. A court may not act simply on the

---

[29] See, too, s.15 of the Criminal Justice Act 1951, discussed at *supra*.

[30] Note however that the High Court's jurisdiction to grant bail does not depend on this provision. It springs from the original jurisdiction conferred on that court by Art. 34.3.1°: see Walsh J. in *O'Callaghan's* case [1966] I.R. 501, 511.

[31] In *People (Att. Gen.)* v. *Gilliland* [1985] I.R. 643 the Supreme Court held that the test for granting bail in extradition cases was the same as that for bail in ordinary criminal cases.

basis of someone else's belief; it must itself be satisfied that the objection made is sufficient to enable the court to arrive at the necessary conclusion of probability.

A court granting bail may require the applicant to produce independent sureties to help guarantee the accused's compliance with the bail conditions. Section 27 of the Criminal Procedure Act 1967 directs that in such circumstances the court shall satisfy itself as to the sufficiency of the persons proposed. In *O'Callaghan's* case it was emphasised that there was no rule of law that sureties must be householders, or own their own houses—though ownership of a house was relevant in considering a person's financial ability to meet the demands of the bail. As to the amount required, the Supreme Court said this "must be just and reasonable in all the circumstances having regard to the condition and ability of the accused, bearing in mind all the time the overriding test of the probability of the accused failing to appear for trial" ([1966] I.R. 501, 518–519). The figure must not be so large as to deny bail and lead to inevitable imprisonment.[32]

The *O'Callaghan* decision has been criticised as leading in practice to a situation where persons accused of serious offences—and thus facing long sentences—who are granted bail have an incentive to commit further offences while on bail. Whether or not this is true, the Criminal Justice Act 1984, s.11 provides that any sentence passed for an offence committed while on bail shall be *consecutive* on any existing sentence, or any sentence simultaneously imposed for the original offence.[33] Under section 13 of the Act, failure to surrender to bail is an offence punishable on summary conviction by a fine of up to £1000 and/or 12 months imprisonment. Section 13(3) stipulates that any such offence shall be treated as an offence committed while on bail for the consecutive sentence purposes of section 11.

(b) *Under the Criminal Justice Act 1984*

In the late 1970s much public disquiet was engendered by a perceived rise in criminal offences—particularly in thefts, house-breaking and burglary. There were calls for increased police powers to cope with this, since many Garda representatives indicated that the current law unduly hampered their investigations. The Garda Commissioner particularly complained of the lack of power to detain suspects for questioning—the only practicable method, he claimed, of obtaining evidence in most cases.[34] Successive governments undertook to consider necessary changes in the law. This proved to be an uncommonly lengthy process but it eventually culminated in the Criminal Justice Act 1984.

The 1984 Act effectively empowers the Gardaí to detain certain persons for questioning. The provisions in this regard did not come into immediate operation; section 1(2) made their implementation contingent on: (a) the creation

---

[32] See further Ryan and Magee, *op. cit.*, Chap. 7.

[33] Though in the case of the District Court this is subject to an aggregate sentencing limit of two years.

[34] Patrick McLaughlin, "Legal Constraints in Criminal Investigation" (1981) *XVI Irish Jurist* (N.S.) 217: See also Raymond Byrne, Thomas Cooney, Paul Mc Cutcheon and Paul O'Connor, *Innocent until Proven Guilty?*, I.C.C.L. Report No. 7 (Dublin 1983); Dermot P. J. Walsh, "The Impact of the Antisubversive Laws on Police Powers and Practices in Ireland: The Silent Erosion of Individual Freedom" (1989) 62 *Temple Law Review* 1099.

by statute of independent machinery for adjudicating on complaints against the Gardaí, and; (b) the making of regulations under section 7. The first condition was fulfilled by the passage of the Garda Síochána (Complaints) Act 1986,[35] and the second by regulations made in 1987 for the treatment of persons in custody in Garda stations.[36] The latter provide, as section 7 requires, for assigning to a specific officer responsibility for overseeing the application of the regulations at a particular station. Failure by a Garda to observe these regulations does not *of itself* make him/her liable to civil[37] or criminal proceedings; nor does it *of itself* affect the lawfulness of the custody of the detained person or the admissibility in evidence of any statement made by that person (s.7(2)). But such a failure *will* make the Garda liable to disciplinary proceedings (s.7(4)). The detention for questioning provisions (ss.4–6), it should be noted, have effect only for four years from the date they come into operation, unless each House of the Oireachtas resolves that they should continue.

Section 4 of the Act applies to any offence for which a person of full age and capacity and not previously convicted may be punishment by imprisonment for five years or more, and to an attempt to commit any such offence. "Imprisonment" is defined to include penal servitude and detention in St. Patrick's Institution (s.3(1)). This covers a very wide range of offences; they include (this list is not comprehensive) many kinds of assaults and larcenies, burglary, certain offences involving drugs and firearms, several sexual offences, murder and manslaughter. Section 4 provides that where a Garda arrests someone suspected, with reasonable cause, of having committed such an offence the person may be detained in a Garda station if the officer in charge of the station has reasonable grounds for believing "that his detention is necessary for the proper investigation of the offence" (s.4(2)). In no case may such detention be for longer than 12 hours (s.4(a)) and the second six hour period (if there is to be one) must be authorised by an officer not below the rank of superintendent (s.4(3)).[38] Time between midnight and 8 a.m.

---

[35] This Act applies in relation to all members of the force save the Commissioner and a Deputy Commissioner when standing in for him (and the Criminal Justice Act 1984, s.1(2) under which the complaints machinery would apply only to persons below chief superintendent rank, is amended by s.16). The Act provides for complaints by members of the public in regard to Garda conduct, for their investigation by designated Garda officers and for a report to the Garda Síochána Complaints Board established thereunder. The Board may appoint a three person tribunal consisting of two Board Members and a senior Garda officer (see the second Sched.) to consider disciplinary action—including dismissal—against a Garda member. A tribunal decision may be appealed to the Appeal Board. Under s.13 the Complaints Board is to produce an annual report—and others—each of which must be laid before the Dáil and Seanad.

[36] The Criminal Justice Act 1984 (Treatment of Persons in Custody in Garda Stations) Regulations 1987 (S.I. No. 119 of 1987). These require that records be kept of the arrest and detention (Reg. 7): and that persons be informed about the offence triggering the arrest and of the right to consult a solicitor (Reg. 8). Reg. 12 covers questioning ("interviews"). These are to be conducted in a fair and humane manner (and note the general obligation under Reg. 3 to act with due respect for the personal rights of individuals in custody and their dignity as human persons). The names and ranks of the questioning officers must be given; no more than two officers may question a person at any given time (two others may be present); and no questioning session may last more than four hours. Reg. 20 forbids ill-treatment or threats thereof.

[37] The State may be liable in negligence towards a person injured while in custody: see *McKevitt v. Ireland* [1987] I.L.R.M. 541.

[38] If given orally, such a direction is to be recorded in writing as soon as practicable.

allowed for rest, or for medical attention outside the station, does not count (s.4(6) and (8)).[39]

Section 4(6)(a) makes it clear—if somewhat obliquely—that the purpose of detention[40] is to permit questioning of the suspect, and this also appears from the regulations made under section 7. The Act does not impose an obligation to answer any such questions; but failure to explain certain matters may lead to adverse inferences being drawn from that silence at any trial (see ss.18–19, considered *infra*.) In addition, section 6 permits other investigative techniques. A Garda may demand of the detainee his name and address; cause him to be searched, photographed and fingerprinted; subject him to firearms or explosive tests by taking swabs from his skin or samples of his hair; and seize and retain for testing anything he has in his possession. However, a decision to photograph or fingerprint a detainee requires the authority of a superintendent (s.5(2)). The power to search does not authorise a Garda to require a person to remove his underclothing, save where there is reasonable cause to suspect that the detainee has concealed on his person a controlled drug or explosive substance; again, the authority of a superintendent is required for such a search.

Several provisions of the Act impose obligations on the Gardaí.[41] Where there are no longer reasonable grounds for suspecting the person detained he must be released from custody "forthwith," unless his detention is authorised apart from the Act (s.4(4)). Further, when there is sufficient evidence to charge a detainee this must be done, unless the person concerned is suspected of another serious offence within the Act and the officer in charge of the station has reasonable grounds to believe his continued detention necessary for the proper investigation of that offence (s.4(5)). Section 5(1) requires that the detainee be informed "without delay" that he is entitled to consult a solicitor, and to have the fact and the place of his detention notified to "one other person reasonably named by him"; and should the detainee so wish, the solicitor and named person must be notified accordingly "as soon as practicable."[42]

Section 10 of the 1984 Act places limits on the power to rearrest a released detainee. Where no charge has been made against such a person he shall not be arrested again for the same offence, or for any other offence of which, at the time of the first arrest, he was suspected or ought reasonably to have been suspected by the arresting officer—except under a warrant of the District Court.[43] The District Court judge must be satisfied on information sworn by a superintendent (at least) that the Gardaí now have further information as to the released person's participation in the crime. Should the warrant issue,

---

[39] s.4(6) does not give a detainee a *right* to a rest period, but in appropriate circumstances a court might well hold that uninterrupted questioning between midnight and 8 a.m. was unjust and oppressive and any statement resulting therefrom inadmissible: see *Lynch's* case [1982] I.R. 64.

[40] s.4 authorises detention, not arrest; the justification for the latter must rest on reasonable suspicion of a serious offence covered by the section. Thus it would seem that an arresting Garda must specify the offence concerned; a reference to s.4 would be inadequate.

[41] s.8 of the Act makes detailed provision regarding the destruction of photographs and fingerprints.

[42] s.5(2) makes special provision for persons under 17.

[43] But a released detainee may be arrested for any offence "for the purpose of charging him with that offence forthwith"—s.10(2).

the person arrested under it again becomes subject to section 4—*i.e.* he may again be detained for questioning for a maximum 12 hours (s.10(1)). This does not apply to a person arrested under the Offences against the State Act 1939, s.30 who is released without charge. Such a person *cannot* be detained under section 4 in connection with the offence in respect of which he was arrested, or any other offence of which he was or ought reasonably to have been suspected at that time; and there is no provision for obtaining a warrant for such arrest (s.10(3)). But section 4(10) preserves the operation of section 30 of the 1939 Act, and there would not appear to be any bar to a rearrest under section 30.

The constitutionality of the 1984 Act's detention for questioning provisions has not yet been tested.[44] They clearly depart from the common law position but it would be difficult to show that the Constitution will not tolerate this. A challenge to the 48 hours detention provided for by the Offences Against the State Act 1939, s.30 has been repelled (*D.P.P.* v. *Quilligan*, Supreme Court, July 14, 1992), and it seems unlikely that the courts would invalidate the shorter periods envisaged by the 1984 Act. However, they will obviously insist on scrupulous observance of the safeguards built into the Act: see *Quilligan's* case, discussed *infra*. Thus it may be anticipated that failure to comply with section 5—*i.e.* to inform a detainee of his right to consult a solicitor,[45] or notify a solicitor on request—will render any statement given inadmissible in evidence.

(c) *Under section 30 of the Offences against the State Act 1939*

Section 30 of the Offences against the State Act 1939, it should be noted, is part of the *permanent* legislation of the State—unlike Part V, dealing with special criminal courts, which requires a proclamation to bring it into force. Section 30(1) confers on every Garda a wide power, exerciseable without warrant, to stop, search, interrogate and arrest any person suspected[46] of any offence under the Act—or of a scheduled offence—or of having any information about any such offence. Moreover, a person arrested thereunder may be detained in a Garda station, a prison "or some other convenient place" for 24 hours initially and, if an officer of at least chief superintendent rank

---

[44] In *Keating* v. *Govr., Mountjoy Prison* [1991] 1 I.R. 61 the applicant had argued in the District Court that his detention under s.4 had been unlawful, and had sought his release. The judge refused his application and remanded him in custody. The applicant then sought an order under Art. 40.4.2°. This was refused successively by the High Court and Supreme Court. The case sheds no light on s.4, but it is clearly laid down that the District Court has no function of inquiring into the legality of a person's detention in such circumstances. To do this would be " . . . an unwarrantable and unlawful usurpation of the constitutional role of the High Court . . . ": *per* McCarthy J. at 65. Any such matter would be relevant only to the admissibility of evidence obtained during the allegedly unlawful detention.

[45] This statutory obligation, it may be noted, goes further than the Constitution—influenced common law. Though a person in custody has a constitutional right of reasonable access to a solicitor—*People (D.P.P.)* v. *Healy* [1990] 2 I.R. 73—it has not yet been held that the Gardaí are obliged to inform him/her of that right.

[46] In *People (D.P.P.)* v. *Quilligan* [1986] I.R. 495 Walsh J., with whose judgment Hederman and McCarthy JJ. agreed, said that if the arresting Garda did not have the required suspicion—which was a question of fact—any action taken under s.30 would be illegal. The suspicion must be bona fida held and not unreasonable. That this matter was not beyond judicial review was established, he said, by the court's decision in *State (Trimbole)* v. *Governor, Mountjoy Prison* [1985] I.R. 550. This view has since been confirmed: see *D.P.P.* v. *Quilligan* (Supreme Court, July 14, 1992).

directs, for another 24 hours (s.30(3)).[47] The person detained may be searched, fingerprinted and photographed, and subjected to firearms and explosives tests; and anything in his/her possession may be seized and retained for testing (Criminal Law Act 1976, s.7).

The offences created by the 1939 Act are, as its name suggests, offences against the State; they include obstruction of government (s.7),[48] organising secret societies in the Defence Forces or Garda (s.16) and membership of an unlawful organisation (s.21). Offences are "scheduled" under section 36 by a Government order—which does not require Oireachtas approval.[49] Any offence whatever may be scheduled, so long as the Government is satisfied that it should be triable in a special criminal court; thus Part V of the Act, which deals with such courts, must be in force. In fact the number of such offences is small—included are offences under the Malicious Damage Act 1861, the Explosive Substances Acts and the Firearms Acts.[50]

As noted above, the constitutionality of section 30 was impugned in *D.P.P.* v. *Quilligan* (Supreme Court, July 14, 1992). The principal ground of challenge[51] was that it insufficiently respected the right of personal liberty guaranteed by the Constitution. In rejecting this argument, the Supreme Court held that persons arrested under section 30 were protected in a number of ways, as outlined by Walsh J. in *People (D.P.P.)* v. *Quilligan* [1986] I.R. 495. Thus the person detained had, *inter alia*, a right to legal and medical assistance, a right of access to the courts, a right to remain silent and the associated right to be told of that right. Any of these protections could be made effective either by ordering release of the person detained under Article 40, or by excluding evidence obtained in violation of the rules governing a section

---

[47] s.30 does not require that such a direction be given in, or reduced to, writing, but it is the practice to record a direction in writing. In *People (D.P.P.)* v. *Nicholas Kehoe* [1985] I.R. 444, the Court of Criminal Appeal said that such a record should not state the exact time of commencement and termination of the extension period, lest some bona fide error occur. It should simply state that the arrested person was to be detained for a further 24 hour period commencing upon the expiry of the 24 hour period from the time of arrest.

Should the validity of the extension be challenged it will be necessary to prove that the senior Garda officer who authorised it entertained the same suspicion as the arresting officer: *People (D.P.P.)* v. *Byrne* [1989] I.L.R.M. 613.

[48] The reach of s.7 is illustrated by *People (D.P.P.)* v. *Patrick Kehoe* [1983] I.L.R.M. 237 (C.C.A.).

[49] Though under the Statutory Instruments Act 1947 they must be published, etc.

[50] Offences against the State (Scheduled Offences) Orders 1972, S.I. 1972 No. 142 and 282. The Law Reform Commission has recommended that, because of the unnecessary confusion and expense caused thereby " . . . malicious or criminal damage offences should not be scheduled under the 1939 Act": *Report on Malicious Damage* (LRC 26–1988), pp. 33–34. The Commission noted that the scheduling of such offences, by enabling the Gardaí to hold people in custody for up to 48 hours, had resulted in the bringing to justice of murderers and other serious offenders who might otherwise have escaped prosecution. But the Commission said (p. 34): "The argument that it is necessary to have malicious damage offences scheduled in order properly to investigate other offences has no validity. It would seem to us more convincing to argue for longer periods of detention for such other offences." Since that was written the Oireachtas has passed the Criminal Damage Act 1991, which implements the Law Reform Commission's principal recommendations. This repeals most of the Malicious Damage Act 1861, and in particular those provisions scheduled under the 1939 Act. At the time of writing no order scheduling the replacement offences created by the 1991 Act has been made.

[51] Two other arguments were advanced. The first was based on a claimed constitutional privilege against self-incrimination (as to which see *infra*). The second, founded upon Article 40's equality guarantee, was that the disparty of rights between persons arrested at common law and those arrested under section 30 was an invidious discrimination prohibited by that provision. The Supreme Court held that no such invidious discrimination had been established.

30 detention. In addition, the purposes of section 30 were limited, as Walsh
J. (Hederman and McCarthy JJ. concurring) had pointed out in *People
(D.P.P.)* v. *Quilligan* [1986] I.R. 495, at 509:

> "The object of the powers given by s.30 is not to permit the arrest of
> people simply for the purpose of subjecting them to questioning. Rather
> is it for the purpose of investigating the commission or suspected com-
> mission of a crime by the person already arrested and to enable that
> investigation to be carried on without the possibility of obstruction or
> other interference which might occur if the suspected person were not
> under arrest. Section 30 is part of the statute law of the State perma-
> nently in force and it does not permit of any departure from normal
> police procedure save as to the obligation to bring the arrested person
> before a court as soon as reasonably possible."

Accordingly the Supreme Court was not satisfied that section 30 constituted
a failure by the State as far as practicable by its laws to defend the citizen's
personal right of immediate liberty.

In *D.P.P.* v. *Quilligan* (July 14, 1992) Finlay C.J., delivering the single
judgment of the Supreme Court, said (p. 18):

> "At the time of the arrest the suspect must be informed, if he does not
> already know, of the offence pursuant to the Act of 1939 or scheduled for
> its purposes, of which he is suspected, otherwise his arrest will be unlaw-
> ful . . ."

The court did not say, however, that this unlawful arrest would infect any
ensuing detention; and it does not seem possible to infer any such proposition. For in the next succeeding paragraph the court explicitly refers to the
possibility that refusal to grant a reasonable request for legal assistance may
render a detention unlawful. The position thus seems to be as stated by the
Court of Criminal Appeal in *People (D.P.P.)* v. *Campbell* (February 7, 1983),[52]
that an invalid arrest under section 30 will not necessarily invalidate detention consequent thereon. That court, it may be noted, has also held that the
suspicion grounding a section 30 arrest need not be personal to the arresting
Garda, but may be that of a superior who has directed the arrest: *People
(D.P.P.)* v. *McCaffrey* [1986] I.L.R.M. 687.

There is nothing to prevent a section 30 arrest after a common law arrest:
People (D.P.P.) v. *Nicholas Kehoe* [1985] I.R. 444 (C.C.A.). Nor is there anything to prevent the Gardaí from moving an arrested person from one permitted place (*e.g.* a Garda station) to another: *People (D.P.P.)* v. *Kelly (No. 2)*
[1983] I.R. 1, 21. But in that case the Supreme Court emphasised that if this
was done in bad faith or to harrass the detainee, or to isolate the detainee
from assistance or access to which he was entitled, the detention would
become unlawful.

Persons arrested under section 30 on suspicion of a scheduled offence may,
under section 52, be required while in custody to give a full account of their

---

[52] This judgment is printed in *Judgments of the Court of Criminal Appeal* 1979–1983 (Gerard
Frewen, ed., Dublin 1984), pp. 131–152. This is henceforward cited as 2 Frewen.
  The constitutional validity of s.52 does not seem to have been impugned to date. In *D.P.P.* v.
Quilligan (Supreme Court, July 14, 1992) Finlay C.J., for the court, said (p. 11): "The pro-
visions contained in section 52 were not invoked at any stage in the instant case before this
Court and no challenge or query to the constitutional validity of that section has been made."

movements and actions during a specified period, and to give all information in their possession in regard to the commission or intended commission by another person of any offence under the 1939 Act or any scheduled offence. A refusal to give such an account or information, or the giving of false or misleading information, is an offence punishable by up to six months imprisonment (s.52(2)). But the questioning of a person detained under section 30 is not confined to such matters. In *People (D.P.P.)* v. *Kelly (No. 2)* [1983] I.R. 1 it was argued that persons arrested under section 30 could be interrogated only *before* arrest, and thereafter persons could be asked only for an account of their movements, etc. under section 52. This proposition was rejected both by the Court of Criminal Appeal and the Supreme Court. In *Quilligan's* case (July 14, 1992) the Supreme Court re-affirmed this rejection, adding that the detainee was not obliged to answer any such additional questions and he/she should be told this.

It is not the law that a person arrested under section 30 on suspicion of a scheduled offence may be questioned about that offence *only*. This is clear from *People (D.P.P.)* v. *Patrick Walsh* [1986] I.R. 722. The appellant had been convicted of murder in the Central Criminal Court. He claimed that his detention under section 30 was unlawful and that statements he made while detained—the key prosecution evidence against him—were inadmissible. The facts were that on July 2, 1983 an elderly woman was found dead in her house in Listowel, having received multiple injuries and a very severe head wound. A pane of glass in a door was broken, and so was a heavy metal pot, probably the murder weapon. On July 5, Walsh was arrested under section 30 on suspicion of having committed a scheduled offence—malicious damage to the pane and the metal pot. It was admitted that while the Gardaí arrested Walsh on that suspicion, they also wanted to question him about the killing. Walsh was detained for over 24 hours, a valid extension order having been made, during which time he was fingerprinted and questioned and made the statements led in evidence at his trial. The Court of Criminal Appeal rejected the argument that it was unlawful to question Walsh about the murder. Finlay C.J., for the court, said that at least in a case such as this, where the scheduled offence and the murder formed part of the same transaction, there were no grounds for inhibiting Garda interrogation in regard to the entire transaction. This view of the law is clearly confirmed by the Supreme Court's decision on appeal in that case and in *People (D.P.P.)* v. *Quilligan* [1986] I.R. 495. It was further contended on Walsh's behalf that section 30 should be interpreted by reference to the long title and the rest of the Act, so that the power to arrest thereunder arose only if the person arrested was suspected of having committed a scheduled offence for subversive or terrorist motives. The Court of Criminal Appeal rejected this submission, a decision confirmed on appeal by the Supreme Court for the reasons given in *People (D.P.P.)* v. *Quilligan* [1986] I.R. 495.

It was also argued on Walsh's behalf that the use of section 30 here, given the relatively trivial malicious damage caused—less than £50—was merely a colourable device to permit interrogation on a murder charge. Finlay C.J., for the Court of Criminal Appeal, referred to two earlier cases in which this point was raised. The first was *State (Bowes)* v. *Fitzpatrick* [1978] I.L.R.M. 195, a habeas corpus application challenging the validity of the prosecutor's detention under section 30. There too Bowes' arrest was on suspicion of a malicious damage offence, it being admitted that he was suspected of involvement in a murder carried out with a knife which had been damaged during the killing. Finlay P. ordered Bowes' release, being satisfied on the evidence that the arrest was merely a pretext to enable his detention for questioning for murder. The second case was *People (D.P.P.)* v. *Towson* [1978] I.L.R.M. 122. There the arrest under section 30 was on suspicion of being in possession of firearms with intent to endanger life. The Gardaí were investigating a murder by shooting. The Court of Criminal Appeal held the arrest valid; the suspicion of the accused's involvement in the murder inevitably involved a suspicion of a scheduled firearms offence. Accordingly, said the court, there was "no spurious invention of some imagined offence." It was a correctly held suspicion of an offence arising out of the matter being investigated. The decisions in the *Bowes* and *Towson* cases thus represent opposite ends of a spectrum, and in the instant case of *Walsh* the Court of Criminal Appeal held that this was at the *Towson* end. The court upheld the view of the trial judge, O'Hanlon J., that the malicious damage offence here was "a real offence and was necessarily involved as part of the same incident or transaction as the murder and that, accordingly, the arrest was justified." On appeal the Supreme Court agreed with this conclusion, Walsh J. saying for the court [1986] I.L.R.M. 722, 731:

> "The fact that there was a great disproportion between the nature of the offences in question and that the greater concentration of police effort was on the investigation into the more serious of them namely, the murder charge, is not in itself sufficient to establish as a reasonable probability that the arrest in respect of the malicious damage charge was simply a colourable device to hold the accused in custody for an ulterior purpose on an alleged offence in which the guards had no real interest."

Section 30 clearly vests wide—though not unlimited—powers in the Gardaí, which are capable of being abused. It is widely believed that they have been so abused—*e.g.* by using alleged suspicion of a scheduled offence as a holding charge to permit interrogation about a more serious one—and there is evidence that this has occurred, though the frequency of such abuse is not known.[53] But the *Bowes* case *supra* shows that Article 40.4 is available to test the legality of a section 30 detention, and its effectiveness in this regard is also demonstrated by *State (Trimbole)* v. *Governor, Mountjoy Prison* [1985] I.R. 550.[54] There the applicant had been arrested under section 30 on October 25, 1984 and was informed on the following day that his detention for a further 24 hours had been directed. That same day an application for habeas corpus was made to Egan J. The Garda evidence was that the applicant was suspected of being in possession of a gun on October 24, but Egan J. was satisfied that no genuine suspicion to that effect could have been entertained and that the detention of the applicant was illegal. Accordingly, his release

---

[53] On February 26, 1985 the Minister for Justice, Mr. Michael Norman T.D., provided the following statistics for persons arrested and charged under the Act between 1980 and 1984 (356 *Dáil Debs.*, c. 741):

	No. arrested	No. charged
1980	1874	168
1981	2303	323
1982	2308	256
1983	2334	363
1984	2216	374

[54] Also reported *sub. nom. Trimbole* v. *Governor, Mountjoy Prison* [1985] I.L.R.M. 465.

was ordered. Shortly thereafter the applicant was rearrested outside the Four Courts on foot of a warrant under the Extradition Act 1965, with a view to his extradition on serious criminal charges to Australia. Reciprocal extradition arrangements between Ireland and Australia, necessary for the 1965 Act to operate, came into force only on October 26. In subsequent proceedings Egan J. held that Trimbole's detention under the 1965 Extradition Act was tainted by the illegality of his original arrest and that his release therefrom must be ordered. On appeal, the Supreme Court agreed, Finlay C.J. saying that Trimbole's purported arrest under section 30 was a flagrant misuse of that provision, and a deliberate and conscious violation of his constitutional rights which infected the otherwise lawful later detention under the Extradition Act warrant.

The decisions surveyed above thus make it clear that the courts will, in an appropriate case, hold a section 30 arrest invalid so as to taint with illegality any subsequent detention. This will be so where the court is satisfied that the alleged suspicion is not genuine, as in *Trimbole's* case; or is a mere device to hold someone for interrogation about a quite different and unrelated offence, as in *Bowes'* case; or is "a spurious invention of some imagined offence." The legality of the detention, however, does not depend upon the existence of a link between the scheduled offence and the graver charge under investigation; the Supreme Court so held in *People (D.P.P.) v. Howley* [1989] I.L.R.M. 629. Nor is there any requirement that investigation of the scheduled offence be the dominant motive of the detention: *ibid.*[55]

As noted above, the Supreme Court has recently stressed in *D.P.P. v. Quilligan* (July 14, 1992) that a person detained under section 30 benefits from a number of constitutional and legal safe-guards. The court emphasised that such a person retains all his/her constitutional rights. In addition, the Judges' Rules—as to which see *infra*—apply to any questioning when in detention. Moreover, the court affirmed the conclusion reached by Walsh J. in *People (D.P.P.) v. Quilligan* [1986] I.R. 495, at 508:

> "During his detention . . . he must not be subject to any form of questioning which the courts would regard as unfair or oppressive either by reason of its nature, the manner in which it is conducted, its duration or the time of day, or its persistence into the point of harrassment where it is not shown that the arrested person has indicated clearly that he is willing to continue to be further questioned. *A fortiori* this applies to cases where the initial period of twenty-four hours is extended to forty-eight hours by virtue of the provisions of s. 30, subs. 3 of the Act of 1939 . . ."

(d) *Detention under emergency provisions*

The Emergency Powers Act 1976 (on which see Chap. 7 *supra*) authorises the Gardaí to stop, search, question and arrest without warrant persons reasonably suspected of offences under the Offences against the State Act 1939, or of a scheduled offence under that Act, or of having documents, articles, or other things, or information, relating to the commission or intended commission of such an offence: s.2(1). The arrested person may be detained in a Garda station, prison "or other convenient place" for 48 hours

---

[55] For a critical analysis of *Howley's* case, see J. Paul McCutcheon, "Criminal Law—Section 30 Yet Again" (1980) 10 *D.U.L.J.* 158.

from the time of arrest, and this period may be extended for a further five days by direction of an officer not below the rank of chief superintendent: s.2(3). The total permissible period of detention is thus seven days—and the 48 hours allowable under the Offences against the State Act 1939 may *not* be added to this, for the powers conferred by section 30 of that Act are not exercisable while section 2 is in force: s.2(5). The language of section 2 is borrowed from section 30, thus the person detained may clearly be questioned as he/she could be under that provision; and the arrest is not merely for the purpose of charge—see s.2(4).

Section 2 is not currently in force, but it may be brought into operation at any time by Government order. Should this happen, it would remain in force for 12 months from the commencement of the relevant order (s.1(2)(c))—though the order may specify a shorter period. The Government is also empowered to make an order extending the initial period of operation for a further 12 months (s.1(2)(a)), and successive orders of this kind are permitted. Every order made under section 1 must be laid before each House of the Oireachtas. The order is valid and effective as soon as the Government makes it but either House may annul it within 21 days of its laying: s.1(3). The Act would automatically expire should the Oireachtas revoke its emergency resolutions of September 1, 1976: s.3.

If the Emergency Powers Act 1976 comes into force it brings in its train section 15 of the Criminal Law Act 1976. This permits a Garda officer of chief superintendent rank or above to request that members of the Defence Forces be made available for police duties. Thereupon the relevant members of the Defence Forces acquire extensive powers to stop and search vehicles, and persons therein, and to arrest people without warrant. A person so arrested is to be delivered into Garda custody "as soon as may be" or released—but may be held for up to six hours after the arrest. The extensive grounds for such an arrest are set out in section 8; they include offences under the Offences against the State Act 1939, those scheduled under that Act, murder, manslaughter, Firearms Acts offences and those under the Criminal Law Act 1976 itself. As to the rights of a person detained under section 2, see Chapter 7, *supra*.

The other form of emergency detention known to Irish law is internment without trial under the Offences against the State (Amendment) Act 1940. As already noted the Bill for this Act was referred by President Hyde to the Supreme Court under Article 26 and was upheld as valid. Thus the Act is now immune from constitutional challenge, by virtue of Article 34.3.3°— assuming that that provision's reference to "the Supreme Court" encompasses the Supreme Court as established in 1924 and continued by Bunreacht na hÉireann pending the establishment of a new one, which is a point as yet unresolved.[56]

The core of the 1940 Act is in Part II, which may be brought into operation at any time by Government proclamation: s.3. No Oireachtas approval of such a proclamation is required—though the Dáil (alone) may by resolu-

---

[56] In *State (Lynch)* v. *Cooney* [1982] I.R. 337 at 376 Henchy J. said: " . . . the Supreme Court which gave that judgment was the Supreme Court which was empowered to function as such under the transitory provisions of the Constitution . . . and was not the Supreme Court which was required by Art. 34, s.1, of the Constitution to be established by law and which was eventually so established by the Courts (Establishment and Constitution) Act 1961."

tion subsequently annul it: s.3(4). Section 4(1) allows a "Minister of State" (which must now be understood to mean a Cabinet Minister[57]) to issue a warrant ordering the arrest and detention of some person, where he is of opinion that that person is engaged in activities which, in the Minister's opinion, are "prejudicial to the preservation of public peace and order or to the security of the State." The person named in such a warrant may be arrested by any member of the Garda Síochána and, following arrest, is to be detained in a prison or other prescribed place until release or until Part II ceases to be in force. After arrival at the place of detention the detainee must be furnished with a copy of the ministerial warrant and of section 8 of the Act (see *infra*). Any Garda member may demand a detainee's name and address, and cause him/her to be searched, photographed or fingerprinted: s.5.

Section 8 of the Act requires the establishment of a commission to which a detainee may apply in writing to consider the continuation of the detention. Its three members are appointed by the Goverment. One must be a Defence Forces officer with not less than seven years service, while the other two must be barristers or solicitors of not less than seven years standing, or be or have been judges of the regular courts: s.8(2)(*b*). The commission's function is to inquire into the grounds of the applicant's detention, and it must be furnished with all such relevant Government information, and documents in Government possession "or procurement," as it shall call for: s.8(3)(*c*). Should the commission report that no reasonable grounds exist for the continued detention of the applicant he/she is to be released "with all convenient speed": s.8(3)(*d*).

These internment provisions have been utilised twice—during the wartime emergency, and from 1957–1961—on both occasions principally against the IRA. That they have not been invoked during the 1970s and 1980s, despite Provisional IRA activity on both sides of the border, may owe something to the politically disastrous use of the same weapon in Northern Ireland in the early 1970s.[58] On the second occasion of their use they faced a novel legal challenge—for incompatibility with the 1950 European Convention on Human Rights, to which Ireland is a party. Such administrative detention is not compatible with Article 5 of the Convention, but the Irish Government argued that Article 15 applied. This permits a State to derogate from its Convention obligations in time of a public emergency threatening the life of the nation, provided that the measures taken are "strictly required by the exigencies of the situation." (The Secretary General of the Council of Europe must be kept fully informed of the measures taken and the reasons therefor.) The European Court of Human Rights, on examining the facts, held that internment, despite its gravity, was a measure required by the circumstances: *Lawless* case, Publications of the Court, Series A, p. 36.

The same plaintiff had earlier questioned the legality of his detention in the Irish courts: *Re Ó Laighléis* [1960] I.R. 93. That the 1940 Act was beyond

---

[57] A warrant issued under the 1940 Act is an "instrument" under the Interpretation Act 1937, s.2 and in respect of any such instrument made after the Ministers and Secretaries (Amendment) (No. 2) Act 1977, the Schedule to the Interpretation Act is amended by substituting "Minister of the Govenment" (defined as "a member of the Government having charge of a Department of State")—see s.4 of the 1977 Act.

[58] See *Ulster*, by *The Sunday Times* Insight Team (Harmondsworth 1972) Chaps. 15–17.

constitutional challenge was accepted by counsel and the court. An attempt to rely on the European Convention on Human Rights was ruled out (see Chap. 9 *supra*) and the applicant's other arguments also met with no success. Thus the contention that the 1940 Act was defective in its form and could not be brought into operation because no express power to make the necessary proclamation was conferred on the Government, was dismissed as wholly unsustainable. When a statute provided that certain consequences followed if and when an act was done, power to do that act was given. The court pointed out that Article 28.3.3° did not confer express power to pass emergency resolutions; it merely stated what consequences should follow if this were done. But the power of the Houses to pass such resolutions could not be doubted. The court went on to hold that a person arrested under a Ministerial warrant must be told of the warrant's existence and that he was being arrested thereunder. But even if the applicant could show his arrest was unlawful, said the court, this would not render unlawful his subsequent detention under the Ministerial warrant. At most it might give the applicant "other rights" (presumably to sue for damages for false imprisonment) in respect of the period until the warrant was shown to him (at 129).

The former Supreme Court also repeated what had been said in the Article 26 reference case ([1940] I.R. 470, 479) that the validity of the Ministerial opinion grounding the exercise of the power to detain could not be questioned in any court. These dicta were subsequently disavowed by the present Supreme Court in *State (Lynch)* v. *Cooney* [1982] I.R. 337, 359–361; thus it may now be open to the courts to review such Ministerial decisions to ensure that they are taken in good faith, are factually sustainable and not unreasonable. But attention must be drawn to Henchy J.'s caveat that there might be cases where, because the prescribed opinion was necessarily subjective, it would be "difficult, if not impossible, to subject to scrutiny the reasoning or the thought processes of the person or body exercising the power" ([1982] I.R. 337, 381). The security considerations that have led High Court judges to hold certain decisions of the D.P.P. unreviewable[59] might be thought to apply *a fortiori* to the 1940 Act.

In *Re Ó Laighléis* the former Supreme Court also considered the functions and procedure of the Commission established under section 8 of the 1940 Act. The applicant had sought review of his case by that body, which had sat for the purpose on September 17, 1957. At that hearing the applicant was represented by solicitor and counsel, as was the Attorney General. The commission concluded that it had power to sit in public or *in camera* but doubted if it had power to administer an oath. It was also announced that the commission had been furnished by the Department of Justice with a file marked "Secret and Confidential," containing *inter alia* an unsigned Special Branch report. This, the commission ruled, it could consider without necessarily making full disclosure thereof to the applicant. Subsequently the commission adjourned to await the outcome of the instant proceedings. The Supreme Court stressed that the commission was not a court, and its only duty was to inquire into the grounds of detention. The Act did not require the commission to disclose information it received to an applicant. Section 8, said the court, contemplated "an inquiry which is entirely of an administrative

---

[59] See *Savage* v. *D.P.P.* [1982] I.L.R.M. 385: *O'Reilly & Judge* v. *D.P.P.* [1984] I.L.R.M. 224.

character" and the applicant's complaints about its procedures were founded on the incorrect assumption that the commission was a court. In any event, it was held, legal flaws in the commission's procedures would not make the applicant's detention unlawful, since they could not affect the validity of the Ministerial warrant—the legal basis for that detention.

The conclusion that flaws in the commission's procedures cannot affect the validity of the detention is unimpeachably correct; yet the unresolved question of procedure is plainly important. While the former Supreme Court did not explicitly say so, its judgment seems to mean that the commission had no common law duty of disclosure to an applicant. Whether that view is tenable nowadays is open to doubt. In applying the notion of basic fairness of procedures (as to which see Chap. 12 *supra*) the Supreme Court has insisted that decision-making bodies must disclose to an affected person all relevant information they possess— see, *e.g. Nolan* v. *Irish Land Commission* [1981] I.R. 23: *State (Williams)* v. *Army Pensions Board* [1983] I.R. 308. In the latter case, however, Henchy J. suggested *obiter* that State security or other public policy considerations might relieve from this general obligation; and in *Doupe* v. *Limerick Co. Council* [1981] I.L.R.M. 456, 463 Costello J. thought the duty to disclose was not absolute. It seems likely that if this matter is tested in the future the courts will hold that the commission is obliged only to let the applicant know the gist of the case againt him/her.

It is unusual in a democratic society to keep a statute authorising internment permanently on the statute book. In other jurisdictions where this has been done, such as Northern Ireland and India, the power has been abused by the executive; and while there may be no ground for fearing such occurrences in the Republic the constant availability of such power is undesirable. It is quite clear that the Oireachtas can speedily clothe the executive with such power by statute should an emergency arise, and it would be preferable from the standpoint of respect for civil liberties if this were done.

(e) *Detention under the Mental Treatment Acts, etc.*

In Ireland, as in other states, persons innocent of crime may lose their liberty by virtue of detention in mental hospitals. Under the Mental Treatment Act 1945, s.163 (as amended by s. 7 of the 1961 Act) an application for recommendation for reception into a mental hospital may be made by *inter alios* a husband, wife, or other relative to a doctor. The doctor may refuse the recommendation; but should he/she decide to make it there must be an examination of the individual concerned. The recommendation must also certify that the person is of unsound mind and is a proper person "to be taken charge of and detained under care and treatment" (s.163(2)), and is unlikely to recover within six months. Section 165—see *infra*—authorises intervention by a Garda officer in certain circumstances. Section 166 authorises the commitment of persons of unsound mind who are "not under proper care or control." By virtue of section 167 the recommendation authorises the conveyance of the persons named to the district mental hospital. Detention there depends on an examination by the chief medical officer, and his/her being satisfied that the patient should be received. A number of other safeguards are provided for, including (s.199) a requirement that a copy of every reception order must be sent to the Minister for Health. And not later than 21 days after reception, the chief medical officer of the district mental hospital must send the Minister a report on the mental and bodily health of the patient: s.201. Nonetheless, it may be questioned whether in all respects the safeguards satisfy the Constitution, or beyond it the European Convention on Human Rights.

The only provision of the 1945 Act whose constitutionality has been tested is section 165. This permits a Garda to detain a person believed to be of unsound mind, where the Garda is of opinion that it is necessary for the public safety or that of the person concerned that he/she be placed forthwith under care and control. The Garda must immediately apply to a doctor for an order for the reception and detention of that person in the district mental hospital. In the relevant case—*Re Philip Clarke* [1950] I.R. 253—the prosecutor had been detained under such a reception order (following an examination by two doctors) and he sought habeas corpus. The principal argument advanced on his behalf was that no judicial determination was interposed between his arrest and his subsequent detention in the mental hospital. The impugned legislation, said the court, was "of a paternal character, clearly intended for the care and custody of persons suspected to be suffering from mental infirmity and for the safety and well-being of the public generally" (at 247). The judgment, *per* O'Byrne J., continues (at 248):

> "That section is carefully drafted so as to ensure that the person, alleged to be of unsound mind, shall be brought before, and examined by, responsible medical officers with the least possible delay. This seems to us to satisfy every reasonable requirement, and we have not been satisfied, and do not consider that the Constitution requires, that there should be a judicial inquiry or determination before such a person can be placed and detained in a mental hospital.
>
> The section cannot, in our opinion, be construed as an attack upon the personal rights of the citizen. On the contrary it seems to be designed for the protection of the citizen and for the promotion of the common good."

The certainties implicit in the 1949 judgment are not universally felt nowadays. Factors such as changing patterns of behaviour, disputes among experts as to what mental illness is, and abuses of psychiatric treatment in some countries have engendered caution—and this has been reflected in judicial decisions elsewhere. The present Supreme Court is free to reconsider the *Clarke* decision and there seem to be several reasons why it should do so. When Article 40.4 declares that no citizen shall be deprived of his/her personal liberty save in accordance with law, it implicitly requires certain safeguards—one example being a trial "in due course of law" under Article 38.1. But the adequacy of the law's safeguards for civil—as opposed to criminal—commitment seems doubtful. This is particularly true of section 166 which, as noted *supra*, authorises the commitment of persons who are "not under proper care or control." This certainly is a provision "of a paternal character," reflecting an attitude which may not find support today. In *O'Connor* v. *Donaldson* (1975) 422 U.S. 563 the United States Supreme Court unanimously held that a finding of mental illness *alone* could not justify locking up persons against their will and keeping them indefinitely in simple custodial confinement. There was no constitutional basis for confining such persons involuntarily "if they are dangerous to no one and can live safely in freedom" (at 575). Nor could a State incarcerate people simply to ensure them better standards of living than they enjoyed outside. This heightened concern for individual liberty seems more in harmony with recent Irish decisions than the approach in *Philip Clarke's* case.[60]

The United States Supreme Court has also held that since civil commitment for any purpose constitutes a significant deprivation of liberty, and involves a stigma for the individual committed, due process protection applies. This *seems* to require a judicial determination[61]; and the detention must be justified by proof more substantial than proof on a preponderance of the evidence. Proof beyond a reasonable doubt, however, was held inappropriate in the context of psychiatric diagnosis. So a middle level of burden of proof was required that struck a fair balance between the rights of the individual and the legitimate concerns of the state: *Addington* v. *Texas* (1979) 441 U.S. 418. This approach contrasts markedly with that in *Philip Clarke's* case, and it is to be hoped that the Irish courts may have an opportunity to re-examine this whole issue.

Even if the constitutional adequacy of the 1945 Act is reaffirmed, certain facets thereof may not survive scrutiny by the organs of the European Convention on Human Rights. In *Winterwerp* v. *Netherlands* (1979) 2 E.H.R.R. 387 the Court of Human Rights elucidated the requirements of Article 5(1)(*e*) of the Convention, which provides:

> "1. Everyone has the right to liberty and security of person. No one shall be deprived of his liberty save in the following cases and in accordance with a procedure prescribed by law:
> (e) the lawful detention . . . of persons of unsound mind . . . "

This, said the court, meant that, save in emergency cases, an individual must not be deprived of liberty unless he/she was reliably shown to be of unsound mind. There must be mental disorder—objectively determined—of a kind or degree warranting compulsory confinement; and the validity of continuing confinement depended on the persistence of such disorder. In the later case of *X.* v. *U.K.* (1981) 4 E.H.R.R. 181 the court held that a person of unsound mind compulsorily detained in a psychiatric institution for an indefinite or lengthy period was entitled, under Article 5(4),[62] to take proceedings at reasonable intervals before a court[63] to put in issue the lawfulness under the

---

[60] In *Winterwerp* v. *Netherlands* (1979) 2 E.H.R.R. 387, 401 the European Court of Human Rights stressed that persons could not be detained as mentally ill simply because their views or behaviour deviated from the norms prevalent in a particular society. This parallels Stewart J.'s statement in *O'Connor* v. *Donaldson supra* that mere public intolerance or animosity could not justify the deprivation of physical liberty.

[61] In the later case of *Parham* v. *J.R.* (1979) 442 U.S. 584, the court considered the constitutional requirements of the procedure for confining children in mental hospitals at their parents' instance. It was held that th risk of error in the parental decision meant that there must be another decision by "a neutral factfinder" who could refuse admission. But it was not necessary that that person should be a judge: a staff physician in the relevant hospital was acceptable. So too were informal interview, etc., techniques rather than a formal or quasi-formal hearing. Since the court there laid heavy emphasis on the significance of *family* decisions it may be that due process requires more in non-family situations. It is noteworthy that in *Addington's* case *infra* there had been a trial with a jury to determine whether the petitioner was mentally ill.

[62] "Everyone who is deprived of his liberty by arrest or detention shall be entitled to take proceedings by which the lawfulness of his detention shall be decided speedily by a court and his release ordered if the detention is not lawful."

[63] This, it was held, did not necessarily require a court of the classical kind—*i.e.* part of the state's standard judicial machinery. Thus a tribunal akin to the E.A.T. (see Chap. 9 *supra*) would presumably suffice.

Convention of his/her continued detention—whether that detention was ordered by a civil or criminal court or some other authority. This was not satisfied by the person's ability to apply for (English) habeas corpus because the scope of judicial review thereunder was too limited. But it would be satisfied by "automatic periodic review of a judicial character" (at 207).

Under the Irish Mental Treatment Acts a person detained in a mental hospital is entitled to have a letter, unopened, forwarded to *inter alios* the President of the High Court or the Inspector of Mental Hospitals.[64] The President of the High Court may require the Inspector to visit any person detained as of unsound mind and report to him. The Acts also provide that a patient who has recovered must be discharged; and a patient could obviously apply for an order under Article 40.4 of the Constitution. An Article 40.4 inquiry *may* probe more deeply than does the English habeas corpus procedure—but it is not clear that all this is sufficient to satisfy Article 5(4) of the Convention. It does not amount to a regular scrutiny of the continued lawfulness of the individual's detention.

The Health (Mental Services) Act 1981 contains provision for psychiatric review boards for each health board area. However, it has not been—and will not now be—brought into force. Instead the Government has pledged itself to secure the enactment of fresh legislation, and in June 1992 it published a *Green Paper on Mental Health* (pl. 8918) to stimulate discussion of the matter. This accepts that current Irish law (including the 1981 Act) is " . . . not entirely in accordance with the State's international obligations" (para. 17.7), and contemplates review of decisions to detain by an independent review body which is not a court in the strict sense. Other changes in existing law—such as in the criteria for involuntary admission and the duration of detention—are likewise foreshadowed.[65]

Section 38 of the Health Act 1947 authorises the compulsory detention and isolation of persons diagnosed as having certain kinds of infectious diseases whose isolation is necessary to avoid the spread of infection. If isolation in the person's home is not possible, the director of community care (a doctor) may order his/her detention in "a specified hospital or other place." Under the amending section 35 of the 1953 Act a second medical opinion is required. The infected individual is detained until it is certified that he or she is no longer a probable source of infection. A copy of every such order must be sent to the Minister, to whom the detained person may also appeal in writing for release. If the Minister has made no determination within 21 days of receipt of the appeal, release is mandatory.

This power of detention has, it seems, been very little used,[66] and its constitutional validity has not been tested. On the basis of the *Philip Clarke* approach—which may still be appropriate in this *physical* illness context—it would pass constitutional muster. The European Convention on Human Rights specifically permits detention in such circumstances—see Article

---

[64] A doctor, whose appointment by the Minister of Health is required under s.12 of the 1945 Act. The Inspector is obliged to make regular inspection visits to mental hospitals and to consider, on application, the continued propriety of a patient's detention. He/she must furnish an annual report to the Minister, which must be laid before the Oireachtas and a copy thereof sent to the President of the High Court: s.201.

[65] Part Two of the *Green Paper* is devoted to mental health legislation. It summarises the current law (Chap. 16), and international law and principles in relation to mental disorder (Chap. 17, and Appendix.)

[66] See Brendan Hensey, *The Health Services of Ireland* (3rd ed., Dublin 1979), p. 193, n. 15.

5(1)(*e*). A person alleging an invalid detention under section 38 could seek an inquiry under Article 40.4 of the Constitution. Given the context of (presumably) short-term detention, this may well be enough to satisfy the requirements of Article 5.4 of the European Convention on Human Rights.

Damages for unlawful detention

Article 5(5) of the European Convention on Human Rights requires that everyone who has been the victim of arrest or detention in contravention of Article 5 shall have an enforceable right to compensation. In Ireland a person who can establish that his/her detention was not in accordance with law may recover damages for false imprisonment and/or violation of constitutional rights. Success will, of course, depend on convincing a court that the factual or legal basis for detention was lacking.[67] A person who claims that his/her detention *following trial* was unlawful may face difficult problems in this regard: see *Kelly* v. *Ireland and Att. Gen.* [1986] I.L.R.M. 318 *Breatnach* v. *Ireland* [1989] I.R. 489.

Surveillance

The lawfulness or otherwise of police surveillance of persons or premises had not been considered by the Irish courts until the remarkable case of *Kane* v. *Govr., Mountjoy Prison* [1988] I.R. 757. The applicant there had been detained for 48 hours under section 30 of the Offences against the State Act 1939. Just before his release the Gardaí learned that an application for his extradition was in the pipeline, but there was evidence of a prior decision to place him under surveillance. He was, as a result, under intense surveillance for some seven hours, being followed wherever he went by Gardaí in cars or on foot. Eventually, following a car chase and a confrontation with a Garda, the applicant was arrested on charges of breach of the peace and malicious damage. Admitted to bail on these charges, he was promptly re-arrested *on foot* of an extradition warrant. In the High Court it was contended that the case was on all fours with *State (Trimbole)* v. *Govr., Mountjoy Prison* [1985] I.R. 550—*i.e.* that the surveillance, and the arrest that followed, were a mere device to keep the applicant available for the purpose of executing the extradition warrant when issued. Egan J. found as a fact that this was not so, and held the surveillance justified in the circumstances. On appeal the Supreme Court affirmed this conclusion, though its members differed somewhat on the lawfulness of surveillance where extradition is involved. Finlay C.J. (Henchy and Griffin J. concurring) was prepared to assume, without deciding, that a right of privacy may exist in an individual, even while travelling in the public streets and roads.[68] Overt surveillance of the kind proved here would, unless

---

[67] An example is *Smith* v. *Ireland, The Irish Times,* July 26, 1986 where a High Court jury awarded the plaintiff £28,000 damages for an unjustified arrest under the Offences against the State Act 1939, s.30

[68] Finlay C.J. had earlier rejected the applicant's claim that, in the circumstances, he continued in Garda detention from the time of his release until that of his subsequent arrest. He said (at 768): "The essential feature of detention in this legal context is that the detainee is effectively prevented from going or being where he wants to go or be and instead is forced to remain or go where his jailer wishes him to remain or go. When the applicant left Granard Garda station, the evidence clearly establishes that what he wanted to do was to go Cavan. He was free to do so and he achieved his purpose."

capable of justification, be objectionable and unlawful. The Chief Justice continued (at 769):

> "Such surveillance is capable of gravely affecting the peace of mind and public reputation of any individual and the courts could not, in my view, accept any general application of such a procedure by the police, but should require where it is put into operation and challenged a specific adequate justification for it."

Here justification was afforded by the duty to execute an extradition warrant.

It was on this point that McCarthy J. (Hederman J. concurring) partially dissented. He was clear that the Gardaí could lawfully "stake-out" premises they believed would be burgled; and they could also lawfully "overtly or otherwise" follow a suspect with a view to investigating or detecting crime. But they could not ordinarily embark on overt surveillance of a person for the purpose of executing an anticipated extradition warrant. To do so would be to interfere with his/her privacy and freedom of movement for a circumstance that might never arise. However, the situation here was different; the extradition process had not only been commenced but was reaching finality. Hence the Garda action was not excessive, and thus not unlawful.[69]

Overt surveillance of the type involved in *Kane's* case seems to be rare in practice, and hence unlikely to trouble the courts again. But it is now established as lawful, provided that its form is proportionate to a lawful end sought to be attained. It would seem probable, also, that covert surveillance—such as a "stake-out" on a suspected drug-dealer's house—is valid, provided that it is for the purpose of investigating or detecting crime, and that no disproportionate invasion of privacy is involved. *Kane's* case is, however, no authority for covert surveillance involving the interception of telephonic or other communications; in that area different considerations may apply.[70]

TRIAL IN DUE COURSE OF LAW

Article 38.1 of Bunreacht na hÉireann states that "no person shall be tried on any criminal charge save in due course of law." The courts have breathed life into the concluding words by reading them as broadly analogous to the due process guarantees of the United States Constitution and requiring "fundamental fairness in criminal trials."[71] The doctrinal foundation for this was explained as follows by O'Higgins C.J. in *State (Healy)* v. *Donoghue* [1976] I.R. 325, 348–349:

> " . . . the concept of justice, which is specifically referred to in the preamble in relation to the freedom and dignity of the individual, appears again in the provisions of Article 34 which deal with the Courts. It is justice which is to be administered in the Courts and this concept of justice must import not only fairness, and fair procedures, but also

[69] For a critical analysis of the case see Richard Humphreys, "Surveillance and Subversion: A Tangled Judicial Maze" (1989) 11 *D.U.L.J.* 138.
[70] See further Chap. 12 *supra. s.v.* The Right of Privacy.
[71] *Per* Griffin J. in *Healy's* case *supra* at 357. Presumably this would preclude future recourse to the technique adopted in *State (Walsh)* v. *Lennon* [1942] I.R. 112 (discussed in Chap. 7 *supra*)—*i.e.* aborting criminal proceedings by the entry of a *nolle prosequi*, changing the rules of evidence and then launching a fresh prosecution.

regard to the dignity of the individual. No court under the Constitution has jurisdiction to act contrary to justice . . . (Article 38.1) must be considered in conjunction with Article 34; with Article 40, s.3, subs. 1, under which the State guarantees in its laws to respect, and, as far as practicable, by its laws to defend and vindicate the personal rights of the citizen"; and with subs. 2 of the same section under which "the State shall, in particular, by its laws protect as best it may from unjust attack and, in the case of injustice done, vindicate the life, person, good name and property rights of every citizen." Being so considered, it is clear that the words "due course of law" in Article 38 make it mandatory that every criminal trial shall be conducted in accordance with concepts of justice, that the procedures applied shall be fair, and that the person accused will be afforded every opportunity to defend himself. If this were not so, the dignity of the individual would be ignored and the State would have failed to vindicate his personal rights."

The United States Supreme Court has held that 14th Amendment due process guarantees a defendant against conviction under vague and indefinite laws[72]; and the rights to a speedy trial,[73] to legal representation,[74] to exclude illegally obtained evidence[75] and to be free from compelled self-incrimination[76] and double jeopardy.[77] As will subsequently appear, the Irish courts have subsumed some—but not all—of these rights under the "due course of law" rubric.

The presumption of innocence

At common law an individual was presumed innocent until found guilty, and as a corollary the prosecution had to prove that person's guilt beyond a reasonable doubt: *Woolmington* v. *D.P.P.* [1935] A.C. 462. This principle has found expression in international instruments[78] and constitutional documents,[79] and the United States Supreme Court has held it implicit in the 14th Amendment's due process guarantee: see *e.g. Re Winship* (1970) 397 U.S. 358. The importance of the principle was explained thus by Dickson C.J. in the Canadian Supreme Court in *Reg.* v. *Oakes* (1986) 26 D.L.R. (4th) 200, 212–213:

"The presumption of innocence protects the fundamental liberty and human dignity of any and every person accused by the State of criminal conduct. An individual charged with a criminal offence faces grave social and personal consequences, including potential loss of physical liberty, subjection to social stigma and ostracism from the community, as well as other social, psychological and economic harms. In light of the

[72] *Papachristiou* v. *City of Jacksonville* (1971) 405 U.S. 156.
[73] *Klopfer* v. *North Carolina* (1967) 386 U.S. 213.
[74] *Gideon* v. *Wainwright* (1963) 372 U.S. 335.
[75] *Mapp* v. *Ohio* (1961) 367 U.S. 543.
[76] *Malloy* v. *Hogan* (1964) 378 U.S. 1.
[77] *Benton* v. *Maryland* (1969) 395 U.S. 784.
[78] *e.g.* Art. 11(1) of the Universal Declaration of Human Rights (1948): Art. 14(2) of the International Covenant on Civil and Political Rights (1966).
[79] *e.g.* The Canadian Charter of Rights and Freedoms, s.11(*d*). Many of the post-independence constitutions of British Commonwealth countries provide similarly: see, *e.g.* s.20(2)(*a*) of the Gambia Constitution of 1970, discussed in *Att. Gen. of the Gambia* v. *Jobe* [1984] 1 A.C. 689.

gravity of these consequences, the presumption of innocence is crucial. It ensures that until the State proves an accused's guilt beyond all reasonable doubt, he or she is innocent. This is essential in a society committed to fairness and social justice. The presumption of innocence confirms our faith in human-kind; it reflects our belief that individuals are decent and law-abiding members of the community until proven otherwise."

Though the presumption has always been part of Irish law[80] and the State is under an international obligation to respect it,[81] it was not until *O'Leary* v. *Att. Gen.* [1991] I.L.R.M. 454 that it clearly achieved constitutional status. Costello J. there said (at 458):

"I have little difficulty . . . in construing the Constitution as conferring on every accused in every criminal trial a constitutionally protected right to the presumption of innocence."

Costello J. based this conclusion on two grounds. Firstly, the Constitution was to be construed in the light of contemporary concepts of fundamental rights, and as international human rights instruments showed, the right to the presumption of innocence now enjoyed universal recognition.[82] Secondly, the presumption had for so long been a fundamental postulate in Irish criminal trials that a trial held otherwise than in accordance with it would *prima facie* be one not held in due course of law.

But Costello J. was of opinion that the right in question was not an absolute right whose enjoyment could never be abridged. The Oireachtas could in certain circumstances restrict the exercise of the right[83]; in particular it could shift the *evidential* burden of proof. If, however, statute shifted the *legal* burden of proof—as where its effect would be that the court *must* convict the accused should he/she fail to adduce exculpatory evidence—then the Constitution might be infringed. But all would depend on the way in which the statute was drafted. A provision requiring an inference to be drawn once certain facts were established would therefore not necessarily be unconstitutional.

In *O'Leary's* case the plaintiff had been convicted in the Special Criminal Court of two offences—(a) membership of an unlawful organisation, contrary to section 21 of the Offences against the State Act 1939 (as amended); (b) possession of incriminating documents, contrary to section 12 of the same Act. In regard to (a), a Garda Chief Superintendent gave evidence that he believed that on April 18, 1987 the plaintiff was an IRA member. This evidence was authorised by section 3(2) of the Offences against the State (Amendment) Act 1972:

[80] In *People (Att. Gen.)* v. *O'Callaghan* [1966] I.R. 501 Ó Dálaigh C.J. referred to "the requirement that a man shall be considered innocent until he is found guilty" and "the principle . . . that every man is deemed to be innocent until tried and duly found guilty" (at 508, 509). See, too, the Court of Criminal Appeal's decisions in *McMahon* [1946] I.R. 267: *Oglesby* [1966] I.R. 152: *Byrne* [1974] I.R. 1 and the Supreme Court's decision in *Quinn* [1965] I.R. 366.
[81] By virtue of Art. 6(2) of the European Convention on Human Rights, as to which see the *Pfunders* case (*Austria* v. *Italy*) (1963) VI Yearbook E.C.H.R. 740.
[82] Costello J. cited, *inter alia*, Art. 11 of the United Nations Universal Declaration of Human Rights and Art. 6(2) of the European Convention on Human Rights.
[83] Costello J. refers to the European Human Rights Commission's decision in *X.* v. *U.K.*, Application No. 5124/71, *Collection of Decisions ECHR* 135. See also the decision of the European Court of Human Rights in *Salabiaku* v. *France* (1991) 13 E.H.R.R. 379.

"Where an officer of the Garda Síochána, not below the rank of Chief Superintendent, in giving evidence in proceedings relating to an offence under the said section 21, states that he believes that the accused was at a material time a member of an unlawful organisation, the statement shall be evidence that he was then such a member."

In regard to (b), the prosecution adduced evidence that the plaintiff had been found in possession of 37 copies of a poster showing a man in paramilitary uniform brandishing a rifle, and displaying the words "IRA calls the shots." (These qualified as incriminating documents under the 1939 Act.)[84] Section 24 of that Act provides that:

"On the trial of a person charged with the offence of being a member of an unlawful organisation, proof to the satisfaction of the court that an incriminating document relating to the said organisation was found on such person or in his possession or on lands or in premises owned or occupied by him or under his control shall, without more, be evidence until the contrary is proved that such person was a member of the said organisation at the time alleged in the said charge."

The plaintiff claimed that section 3(2) of the 1972 Act and section 24 of the 1939 Act were an unconstitutional infringement of the presumption of innocence.

Costello J. was unable to see how section 3(2) of the 1972 Act impinged upon the presumption of innocence.[85] All it did was to make admissible as evidence certain statements which would otherwise be inadmissible. It could not be construed as meaning that the accused *must* be convicted absent exculpatory evidence.

As regards section 24, Costello J. concluded that it too did not infringe the presumption of innocence. It did not oblige an accused to give evidence, but merely shifted an evidential burden on to an accused to whom it was applied. Costello J. said ([1991] I.L.R.M. 454, 463):

"If it was intended that the court could not evaluate the evidence and that it *must* convict in the absence of exculpatory evidence I think the section would have been differently worded. As actually drafted it seems to me that the court may evaluate and assess the significance of the evidence of possession and if it has a reasonable doubt as to the accused's guilt of membership of an unlawful organisation it must dismiss the charge, even in the absence of exculpatory evidence. If this is so then the section does not infringe an accused's right to the presumption of innocence."

Constitutionalising the presumption of innocence will therefore not have the effect of invalidating *all* reverse-onus provisions. Much will depend on

---

[84] s.2 of the Act provides that: "the expression 'incriminating document' means a document of whatsoever date, or bearing no date, issued by or emanating from an unlawful organisation or appearing to be so issued or so to emanate or purporting or appearing to aid or abet any such organisation or calculated to promote the formation of an unlawful organisation."

[85] Note, however, that in *People (D.P.P.)* v. *Cull* (1980) 2 Frewen 36 the Court of Criminal Appeal, *per* Gannon J., described s.3 of the 1972 Act as " . . . not consistent with the presumption of innocence nor with the burden of proof otherwise imposed upon the prosecution in criminal trials." Because of this it had to be strictly construed. (By virtue of Art. 34.3.2° the question of its validity was not—and could not have been—raised before that court.)

how the particular provision is drafted; if it merely gives legal effect to an inference which could reasonably be drawn from the facts established by the prosecution, it will pass muster. In addition, the right to be presumed innocent is not absolute. Its source is Article 38.1's phrase "in due course of law",[86] and the Supreme Court has held that that phrase requires " . . . a fair and just balance between the exercise of individual freedoms and the requirements of an ordered society": *Re Article 26 and the Criminal Law (Jurisdiction) Bill 1975* [1977] I.R. 129, 152. Reverse-onus provisions may sometimes be necessary to strike the balance; thus the European Commission on Human Rights has upheld such a provision in United Kingdom legislation on living on the earnings of prostitution—*X.* v. *U.K.* Application No. 5124/71, *Collection of Decisions E.C.H.R.* 135. The Commission decided that such a provision was reasonable in the interest of an efficient maintenance of the legal order, and observed that to oblige the prosecution to obtain direct evidence of living on immoral earnings would in most cases make its task impossible.

Vague and indefinite laws

The Supreme Court's decision in *King* v. *Att. Gen.* [1981] I.R. 233 establishes that statutory provisions creating criminal offences in vague and indefinite terms are invalid. There parts of section 4 of the Vagrancy Act 1824—which created the offence of "loitering with intent"—were struck down. The section applied to every "suspected person or reputed thief" proved to have been frequenting, or loitering in, various public places "with intent to commit a felony." But to prove that intent no overt act was necessary; instead that intent could be inferred from the circumstances and the accused's previous convictions. The court unanimously held that this could not stand. Henchy J. (Griffin and Parke JJ. concurring) said (at 257):

" . . . the ingredients of the offence and the mode by which its commission may be proved are so arbitrary, so vague, so difficult to rebut, so related to rumour or ill-repute or past conduct, so ambiguous in failing to distinguish between apparent and real behaviour of a criminal nature . . . so out of keeping with the basic concept inherent in our legal system that a man may walk abroad in the secure knowledge that he will not be singled out from his fellow-citizens and branded and punished as a criminal unless it has been established beyond reasonable doubt that he has deviated from a clearly prescribed standard of conduct, and generally so singularly at variance with both the explicit and implicit characteristics and limitations of the criminal law as to the onus of proof and mode of proof, that it is not so much a question of ruling unconstitutional the type of offence we are now considering as identifying the particular constitutional provisions with which such an offence is at variance."

He went on to say that the offence, both in its essential ingredients and the mode of proof of its commission, violated Article 38.1 and Article 40.4.1°—the latter because the guarantee that no citizen should be deprived of personal liberty save in accordance with law meant "without stooping to

---

[86] Costello J. so held in *O'Leary's* case, [1991] I.L.R.M. 454, 461.

methods which ignore the fundamental norms of the legal order postulated by the Constitution." Kenny J., in his separate concurring judgment, said that both the section's governing phrases "suspected person" and "reputed thief" were so uncertain that they could not form the foundation for a criminal offence. He referred to Article 38.1, saying that if the ingredients of an offence were vague and uncertain the trial of an alleged offence based on those ingredients was not in due course of law.[87]

This vagueness doctrine is not confined to legislation; Kenny J. in *King's* case noted that it could apply to common law offences also.[88] The occasion for so applying it has not yet arisen.

The right to a speedy trial

In *State (O'Connell)* v. *Judge Fawsitt* [1986] I.L.R.M. 639 the High Court and Supreme Court successively held that the Constitution guarantees that a trial will occur with reasonable expedition. In that case the prosecutor had been charged in Cork with certain offences on January 25, 1981. Following a series of remands on bail he was returned for trial on July 8, 1982, but no trial was fixed until July 12, 1984. By then the prosecutor was working in England. He returned for each session but his case was not taken and a series of adjournments—all resisted by him—ensued. (There was much pressure of criminal business in Cork city and county and only one judge available for both civil and criminal business. A second judge had since been appointed.) This continued throughout 1984 and into 1985. The prosecutor's return trips were costing him a week's wages each time, and to some extent imperilling his job. On February 5, 1985 the case was called but two defence witnesses, previously available, were not available then. The case was adjourned to February 7, by which time one of those witnesses was available, though the other was not. At the prosecutor's instance the case was then adjourned to April 30. His application for prohibition to halt any further proceedings was refused by Murphy J., who thought it preferable that the Circuit Court judge in Cork should deal with the question of continuing or dismissing the proceedings. The Supreme Court reversed Murphy J. on this point. Finlay C.J., for the court, said that if a person's trial had been so excessively delayed as to prejudice his chance of a fair trial the appropriate remedy for defending and protecting his constitutional rights was an order of prohibition. An application to dismiss might be an alternative remedy in summary cases, but in trials on indictment it was otherwise. A person charged with an indictable offence whose chances of a fair trial had been prejudiced by excessive delay should not be put to the risk of being arraigned and pleading before a jury.

---

[87] In its *Report on Malicious Damage* (LRC 23–1987) the Law Reform Commission rightly observed that *King's* case could not "be regarded as authority for a general proposition that any law permitting the introduction of evidence of an accused's previous convictions . . . offended the constitutional guarantees of trial in due course of law and of fair procedures in such trials." It was also pointed out that the section impugned in *King* made the previous convictions one of the ingredients of the offence. The Commission considered that s.43(1) of the Larceny Act 1916, which permitted evidence of previous convictions to be given, was not necessarily invalidated by the *King* decision (see p. 40). However, the Commission noted that s.43(1) was rarely relied on by the prosecution, and it recommended that it be repealed. This has been done by s.5 of the Larceny Act 1990.

[88] Citing *dicta* of O'Byrne J. in *Att. Gen.* v. *Cunningham* [1932] I.R. 28, 32 and in *People (Att. Gen.)* v. *Edge* [1943] I.R. 115, 142.

Here a material witness for the defence was not, and could not now be made, available; thus the delay was both excessive and prejudicial and the prosecutor was entitled to prohibition.

What is reasonable expedition must depend on the circumstances. In the High Court Murphy J. drew on decisions from the United States, Jamaica and Canada[89] for guidance as to the relevant factors. A balance must be struck between the fundamental right to a fair trial within a reasonable time and the public interest in the attainment of justice in the context of the prevailing system of legal administration. The factors to be assessed in striking the balance were:

    (a) the length of the delay. Here the simplicity or complexity of the charges would be relevant.

    (b) the prosecution's reasons justifying the delay. A deliberate attempt to hamper the defence would weigh more heavily than overcrowded courts—but the latter must be considered since it was ultimately the State's, rather than the defendant's, responsibility.

    (c) the responsibility of the defendant for asserting his rights.

    (d) prejudice to the defendant. Relevant here would be whether the defendant was in custody or on bail, and impairment of the defence because witnesses were no longer available.[90]

Hannigan v. *Clifford* [1990] I.L.R.M. 65 raised a kindred question—of delay in charging, rather than delay in trial. The applicants had been arrested on September 3, 1986 under section 30 of the Offences against the State Act 1939, but were later released without charge. Subsequently, on February 9, 1988, they were charged before the District Court with offences alleged to have been committed on August 17, 1986. They argued, in effect, that the delay in charging them prejudiced their right to a fair trial. The Supreme Court rejected this claim in the circumstances, but accepted that an avoidable delay in charging which could hamper the conduct of an accused's defence and thus prejudice a fair trial, would fall under the *O'Connell* principle.

A properly constituted court

The constitutional guarantee of trial in due course of law requires that the court of trial be properly constituted. This was established by the Supreme Court's decision in *Shelly* v. *District Justice Mahon* [1990] 1 I.R. 36. On May 28, 1987 the respondent had convicted the applicant of a road traffic offence. Before that date the respondent had attained the age of 65—the statutory retirement age for District Justices. He could have been continued in office on a year to year basis but, because of an oversight, the conditions governing this had not been fulfilled. Following the discovery of this omission, the Courts (No. 2) Act 1988 was enacted to allow the retrospective extension of such terms of office. A saver (section 1(3)) provided, in effect, that any such retroactive validation should be limited so as not to conflict with a consti-

---

[89] *Klopfer* v. *North Carolina* (1967) 386 U.S. 514: *Bell* v. *D.P.P. of Jamaica* [1985] 2 All E.R. 585 (P.C.): *R.* v. *Cameron* (1982) 6 W.W.R. 270.

[90] See too *State (O'Keeffe)* v. *McMenamin* [1986] I.L.R.M. 653; *N.C.* v. *D.P.P.* [1991] 1 I.R. 471. A delay which, in itself, may not be excessive may, in conjunction with other circumstances, produce unfairness justifying an injunction to prevent a prosecution: *O'Connor* v. *D.P.P.* [1987] I.L.R.M. 723.

tutional right of any person. In the High Court Blayney J. had no doubt that the general validation must necessarily be limited so as not to apply to criminal convictions. On appeal, the Supreme Court, in a majority decision,[91] agreed. Walsh J put the matter thus (at 42):

" . . . the applicant, like all persons accused of criminal offences, had a constitutional right to have his case decided in a court set up under the Constitution and presided over by a judge appointed in accordance with the Constitution. He was not afforded that right. His case was not heard by a judge appointed under the Constitution."[92]

The same error, in regard to the same District Justice, gave rise to a more difficult question in *Glavin* v. *Govr., Training Unit, Mountjoy Prison* [1991] I.L.R.M. 478. Here the applicant had been returned for trial on indictment by District Justice Mahon, again on a date subsequent to the justice's 65th birthday. In the Circuit Court he pleaded guilty to the charge and was sentenced to a term of imprisonment. He now sought *habeas corpus*, claiming that his return for trial was invalid and that in consequence the Circuit Court lacked jurisdiction to convict and sentence him. The Supreme Court unanimously accepted this argument. As O'Flaherty J. expressed it ([1991] I.L.R.M. 478, 492):

"The single question for resolution is whether the entitlement to a proper, valid preliminary examination is so inexorably bound up with the trial that it should be held that a failure to hold a proper preliminary examination means that there has been a failure to afford the due process that is required by Article 38.1 of the Constitution. I believe that the two are so connected . . . The argument put by the appellants is that the entitlement to a preliminary examination is a legal right and that no constitutional right has been infringed. That would appear to be superficially correct but once it is realised that the holding of the preliminary examination and the trial are inextricably bound together then it must follow that if there has been a failure to hold a proper preliminary examination the trial or anything that happens after a purported return for trial is not in accordance with the Constitution; there is a failure of due process."

The same constitutional principle would obviously apply to the Special Criminal Court, but thus far the attempts so to apply it have been unsuccessful.[93]

The right to cross-examine and confront witnesses

The constitutional right to a trial in due course of law clearly embraces the right to cross-examine and confront witnesses. This is established by the Supreme Court's decision in *Rt Haughey* [1971] I.R. 217. There Ó Dálaigh C.J. (Walsh and Budd JJ. concurring) said (at 261):

[91] Walsh, Griffin, Hederman and McCarthy JJ: Costello J. dissenting.

[92] Walsh J. (with whom Hederman J. agreed) did not identify the precise source of the constitutional right. Griffin J. derived it from Article 34.1 and Article 38.1 (at 45). McCarthy J. based himself on Article 34.1 and found it unnecessary to decide whether Article 38.1 had been breached (at 50–51).

[93] See the cases of *Eccles* v. *Ireland* [1985] I.R. 545 and *McGlinchey* v. *Govr., Portlaoise Prison* [1988] I.R. 671, discussed in Chap. 10 *supra, s.v.* Special Criminal Courts.

" . . . an accused person has a right to cross-examine every witness for the prosecution, subject, in respect of any question asked, to the court's power of disallowance on the ground of irrelevancy. An accused, in advance of cross-examination, cannot be required to state what his purpose in cross-examining is."

The Chief Justice clearly regarded this right—long recognised at common law—as being implicit in, and reinforced by, Article 38.1 (at 264). The later decision in *State (Healy)* v. *Donoghue* [1976] I.R. 325 confirms this: see O'Higgins C.J. at 349–350.

Is the right to cross-examine an absolute one, guaranteeing in every case direct and uninhibited questioning of prosecution witnesses by defence counsel? The Law Reform Commission thinks not,[94] pointing out that it cannot take that form where a witness does not speak English, or is non-speaking or has a speech defect. The Commission has recommended that in child sexual abuse cases, where the interests of justice so require, cross-examination should be conducted *indirectly* through a special child examiner appointed by the court.[95] If, as is arguably the case, the concept of "trial in due course of law" is not totally fixed and immutable, but involves a balance between the rights of the victim and of the accused, to adopt this proposal would not offend against the Constitution.

The Sixth Amendment of the United States Constitution provides:

"In all criminal prosecutions, the accused shall enjoy the right . . . to be confronted with the witnesses against him . . . "

Does Article 38.1 enshrine a similar right of face-to-face confrontation? If it does, then even in child sexual abuse cases statute could not allow the giving of evidence from behind a screen or by means of closed-circuit television. The Law Reform Commission, however, has concluded that the Constitution is not so restrictive. It says[96]:

"There is . . . no authority for the proposition that a constitutional right of physical confrontation, as distinct from a right to cross-examination, can be derived from the guarantee of fair procedures. A right to cross-examine, or indeed to be present when evidence is given during or before a trial, does not *ipso facto* include a right to physical confrontation.
 . . . while we are sure that the Irish courts would hold that the guarantee of fair procedures under the Constitution would entail the right to cross-examine State witnesses, we do not agree that the courts would refuse to contemplate any further exceptions to the rule against the admission of out of court statements."

Consequently, the Commission has recommended that in prosecutions for alleged child sexual abuse:

" . . . that use of closed circuit television (or, if unavailable, a screen) should be the rule where a witness in these cases is under 17 years of age unless the court, for special reasons, decides otherwise."[97]

[94] *Report on Child Sexual Abuse* (LRC 32–1990), p. 77.
[95] *Ibid.*, p. 78.
[96] *Consultation Paper on Child Sexual Abuse* (August 1989), p. 139.
[97] *Report on Child Sexual Abuse*, p. 72.

The Government-sponsored Criminal Evidence Bill 1992 will, if enacted, give effect to this recommendation.

Legal representation

The Criminal Justice (Legal Aid) Act 1962 was the first systematic approach to the problem of impecunious defendants. The Act provides for free legal aid in summary trials, trials on indictment, appeals and cases stated. Entitlement to legal aid is conditioned upon it appearing to the relevant court that the accused's means are insufficient and that the gravity of the charge or "exceptional circumstances" make legal aid essential in the interests of justice. Application must be made for such aid, which always involves representation by a solicitor but by counsel only in certain cases.[98]

In *State (Healy)* v. *Donoghue* [1976] I.R. 325 the prosecutor, then 18, was charged on June 12, 1974 with breaking and entering. He pleaded guilty and was later sentenced to three months. He was not told of his right to apply for legal aid and was not legally represented. Subsequently Healy and a 16-year-old co-accused, Foran, were charged with other offences. Their application for legal aid was granted. Several adjournments then ensued because, by reason of a dispute over the scheme's operation, no solicitor appeared to represent them. On June 29, 1985, despite a defence application for a further adjournment, they were convicted and sentenced to six months. The Supreme Court unanimously held that the convictions could not stand and granted certiorari to quash them. The *ratio decidendi* would appear to be that Articles 38.1, 40.3 and 4 provide constitutional safeguards for impecunious persons charged with criminal offences. The 1962 Act implements this, and the courts must give it full effect. Thus a person facing a possible prison sentence who has no lawyer and cannot provide himself with one must be informed of his right to legal aid. In the instant case, therefore, Healy's 1974 conviction must be quashed because he was not so informed. So too must the January 1975 convictions, because legal aid for the accused having been found esential in the interests of justice, it was a violation of their constitutional rights to convict them in its absence.

This constitutional right to criminal legal aid arises only, it seems, where a defendant is at risk of losing his/her liberty.[99] But this does not simply depend upon the gravity of the charge. The 1962 Act refers to "exceptional circumstances" and in *Healy's* case Henchy J. (at 354) explained what this phrase would cover:

> "A person who has been convicted and deprived of his liberty as a result of a prosecution which, because of his poverty, he has had to bear without legal aid has reason to complain that he has been meted out less than his constitutional due. This is particularly true if the absence of legal aid is compounded by factors such as a grave or complex charge; or ignorance, illiteracy, immaturity or other conditions rendering the

---

[98] See further Ryan and Magee, *op. cit*, Chap. 8.

[99] It is not a right to have legal assistance of one's choice; the practitioners concerned must have declared themselves willing to provide legal aid by going on the panels, and even then the District Court enjoys a certain discretion. As to how this is to be exercised, see *State (Freeman)* v. *Connellan* [1986] I.R. 433.

accused incompetent to cope properly with the prosecution; or an inability, because of detentional restraint, to find and produce witnesses; or simply the fumbling incompetence that may occur when an accused is precipitated into the public glare and alien complexity of courtroom procedures, and is confronted with the might of a prosecution backed by the State. As the law stands, a legal-aid certificate is the shield provided against such an unjust attack."

In *State (O.)* v. *Daly* [1977] I.R. 312 O'Higgins C.J., for the Supreme Court, said that *Healy's* case applied only "to the trial of persons charged with criminal offences and not to the earlier or ancillary stages of criminal proceedings" (at 315). Thus it had no application in the instant case where a patient in a district mental hospital was charged with an indictable offence, and a District Justice was sitting under section 207 of the Mental Treatment Act 1945 to determine whether there was a prima facie case and whether the accused would be unfit to plead. Should the District Justice find the accused unfit to plead he was to certify that the accused was suitable for transfer to the Central Mental Hospital. The Supreme Court described the procedure under section 207 as ancillary and preparatory. No trial could take place and no punishment could be imposed. The District Justice had no power to order the transfer; this could be done only by the Minister for Health on a psychiatric report from the Inspector of mental hospitals.

A person in Garda (or presumably other) custody has a constitutional right of reasonable access to a lawyer and refusal to permit such access will render the detention illegal—*People (D.P.P.)* v. *Healy* [1990] 2 I.R. 73. But the Court of Criminal Appeal has held that the Gardaí are not obliged to inform him/her about that right or to proffer the assistance of a lawyer without request—*People (D.P.P.)* v. *Madden* [1977] I.R. 336; *ibid.* v. *Farrell* [1978] I.R. 13. Thus there is no Irish equivalent of that element in the United States "Miranda warnings"[1] whereby a person in custody must be told, prior to questioning, that he/she has the right to legal advice. Nor under Irish law has a person in custody the right to the presence of a lawyer while being questioned: *People (D.P.P.)* v. *Pringle* (1981) 2 Frewen 57. These *lacunae* have been cogently criticised for failing to recognise the importance of the pre-trial stage of criminal procedure.[2]

O'Higgins C.J. said in *Healy's* case that there was no compulsion to accept legal aid; a person could waive his rght thereto and defend himself. Griffin J. in the same case spoke (at 361) of a defendant "intelligently and understandingly" waiving his right to legal aid. Such a waiver may be express or, as in *State (Sharkey)* v. *District Justice McArdle* (Supreme Court, June 4, 1981), implied. There the prosecutor, when charged in court on June 3, 1980, was asked if he wanted legal aid. When he replied that he did he was remanded on bail, but when the case came up one week later he had taken no steps about getting it. Though he knew he had to complete an application form he did not do so—apparently in the belief that someone had to supply him with one. Consequently, on June 10, 1980 he was not legally represented; but he

---

[1] So named after the U.S. Supreme Court's celebrated decision in *Miranda* v. *Arizona* (1966) 384 U.S. 436.

[2] See Ryan and Magee, *op. cit.*, pp. 221–224: Paul O'Connor and Thomas Cooney, "Criminal Due Process, the Pre-Trial Stage and Self-Incrimination" (1980) XV *Irish Jurist* (N.S.) 219.

did not protest about this and he gave evidence on oath in mitigation. He now sought certiorari to quash this conviction, founding on *Healy's* case. The Supreme Court held that in these circumstances the District Justice could not but have concluded that the prosecutor had elected to dispense with legal aid. Henchy J., for the court, said (p. 6 of the judgment):

"The decision in *The State (Healy)* v. *Donoghue* [1976] I.R. 325 is . . . of no help to him, for it is clear from the judgments in that case that even if the defendant in this case could bring himself within the same entitlement as the convicted youths in that case were found to have had, his responsible and necessarily implied renunciation of legal aid deprived him of the standing to complain that the sentence was wrongly imposed for want of recognition of his right to be tried with legal aid."

Exclusion of unconstitutionally obtained evidence[3]

Several decisions of the Court of Criminal Appeal and the Supreme Court have established the principle that evidence obtained by a deliberate and conscious violation of constitutional rights by the State or its agents must be excluded absent "extraordinary excusing circumstances."[4] No question of judicial discretion arises; the court has a duty to exclude evidence thus obtained, and the accused may therefore be said to have a correlative constitutional right to have it excluded. In *People (D.P.P.)* v. *Kenny* [1990] 2 I.R. 110 the Supreme Court majority made it clear that this exclusionary rule differs markedly from its U.S. counterpart. The latter—which is subject to a range of exceptions—is founded on a desire to deter unlawful police conduct; see *U.S.* v. *Leon* (1983) 468 U.S. 897. But the Irish rule instead embodies what Finlay C.J. in *Kenny's* case called "the absolute protection test."

Despite a suggestion to the contrary,[5] it is now clear that the principle stated above applies to statements, and is *not* confined to physical evidence such as drugs or stolen property: *People (D.P.P.)* v. *Higgins* (Supreme Court, November 22, 1985). And it is also clear that for a violation of constitutional rights to be "conscious and deliberate," it is *not* necessary that those who perpetrated it should have acted wilfuly or *mala fide*: *People (D.P.P.)* v. *Kenny*

---

[3] Though primarily relevant in criminal cases, the principle that unconstitutionally obtained evidence must be excluded is not confined to these. In the civil case of *O.C.* v. *T.C.* (High Court, December 9, 1981) McMahon J. ruled inadmissible evidence—photographs and letters—obtained by the wife "in flagrant violation of the husband's constitutional right to the inviolability of his home."

[4] *People (Att. Gen.)* v. *O'Brien* [1965] I.R. 142 (S.C.): *People (D.P.P.)* v. *Madden* [1977] I.R. 336 (C.C.A.): *ibid.* v. *Farrell* [1978] I.R. 13 (C.C.A.): *ibid.* v. *O'Loughlin* [1979] I.R. 85 (C.C.A.): *ibid.* v. *Shaw* [1982] I.R. 1 (S.C.): *ibid.* v. *Higgins* (Sup.Ct., November 22, 1985): *ibid.* v. *Healy* [1990] 2 I.R. 73: *ibid.* v. *Kenny* [1990] 2 I.R. 110. The pre-*Higgins* decisions are the subject of a detailed critical analysis by Paul O'Connor "The Admissibility of Unconstitutionally Obtained Evidence in Irish Law" (1982) XVII *Irish Jurist* (N.S.) 257, to which I am greatly indebted.

[5] In *People (D.P.P.)* v. *Shaw* [1982] I.R. 1. Ths view—which seems to have been *obiter*—was based on the fact that the foundation case of *People (Att. Gen.)* v. *O'Brien* [1965] I.R. 142 concerned *real* evidence (stolen goods found in the accused's residence under a defective search warrant). Though supported by a 4-1 majority of the Supreme Court, it can no longer be regarded as authoritative, since it is plainly inconsistent with the subsequent Supreme Court decisions in *Higgins* (November 22, 1985) and *Healy* [1990] 2 I.R. 73.

[1990] 2 I.R. 110.[6] As McCarthy J. put it in *People (D.P.P.)* v. *Healy* [1990] 2 I.R. 73, 88–89:

" . . . the only test is whether or not the act or omission that constituted such violation was itself a conscious and deliberate act; the fact that the violator did not realise he was in breach of a constitutional right is irrelevant."

For, as McCarthy J. went on to observe, if it were otherwise there would be a premium upon ignorance.

In strictly limited circumstances the breach of constitutional rights may be excused and the evidence admitted. Thus in the *O'Brien* case [1965] I.R. 142, the evidence—stolen goods—was found in the accused's dwelling. The search warrant was incorrectly made out in respect of 118 *Cashel* Road, Crumlin, instead of 118 *Captain's* Road, Crumlin but the Gardaí were unaware of this and the error was inadvertent. The Supreme Court held that the evidence should not be excluded. Apart from such inadvertent mistakes, there appear to be two other excusable categories—(a) evidence obtained by a search warrant incidental to and contemporaneous with a lawful arrest though made without a warrant: (b) "extraordinary excusing circumstances"—such as the imminent destruction of vital evidence or the need to rescue a victim in peril. Walsh J. in *O'Brien's* case said (at 170) that a suspect had no constitutional right to destroy or dispose of evidence or imperil the victim.

Category (a) above seems to cover a wide range of matters. It must be read in the light of the later Supreme Court decision in *Jennings* v. *Quinn* [1968] I.R. 305 where O'Keeffe J. (Ó Dálaigh CJ. and Walsh J. concurring) stated the law on police powers as follows (at 309):

" . . . the public interest requires that the police when effecting a lawful arrest, may seize, without a search warrant, property in the possession or custody of the person arrested when they believe it necessary to do so to avoid the abstraction or destruction of that property and when that property is:
(a) evidence in support of the criminal charge upon which the arrest is made, or
(b) evidence in support of any other criminal charge against the person then in contemplation, or
(c) reasonably believed to be stolen property or to be property unlawfully in the possession of that person;

and that they may retain such property for use at the trial of the person arrested, or of any other person or persons, on any criminal charge in which the property is to be used in support of the charge or charges . . . "

Though the *Jennings* case did not involve any question of the admissibility of evidence so seized, it would seem logical to assume that it is admissible.[7]

---

[6] The need for an element of *mala fides* or wilfulness was likewise suggested by the majority in *Shaw's* case. But that case is plainly overruled in *Kenny*: see Finlay C.J. (Walsh and Hederman JJ. concurring), [1990] 2 I.R. 110, 134.

[7] The *Jennings* case must now be considered in the light of s.9 of the Criminal Law Act 1976: see further Ryan and Magee, *op. cit.*, pp. 142–176.

Category (b)—"extraordinary excusing circumstances"—was considered by the Supreme Court in *People (D.P.P.)* v. *Shaw* [1982] I.R. 1. There the accused was arrested with another person in Co. Galway late on September 26, 1976. About one hour later he was informed of the grounds of arrest—possession of a stolen car—and it was accepted that he was in lawful custody from then until 10.30 a.m. on September 27, when the District Court sat. But the accused was not brought before the court; his first court appearance was on the evening of September 29. Prime facie therefore his detention was unlawful between 10.30 a.m. on September 27 and the evening of September 29. The reason why the Gardaí continued to detain the appellant was that they suspected the appellant and his companion of involvement in the abduction and possible murder of two young women—Elizabeth and Mary—and they wished to question him about this. Moreover they believed it possible that Mary, at least, might still be alive and might be found. At around 6.50 p.m. on September 28 the accused completed a statement admitting to the rape and murder of Mary. Subsequently the appellant volunteered to accompany Gardaí to locations in Connemara to indicate where the body had been disposed of and certain items concealed ("the Connemara episode"). The appellant was subsequently convicted of rape and murder. On appeal it was argued that neither his statements of September 28 nor the evidence obtained during the Connemara episode should have been admitted because the appellant was at both times in unlawful custody, and there had been a deliberate and conscious breach of his constitutional right to liberty.

The Supreme Court unanimously held that the challenged evidence was admissible, but differing reasons were given for this conclusion. Griffin J. (Henchy, Kenny and Parke JJ. concurring) took the view that the appellant's constitutional right to liberty had to be subordinated to the obligation to vindicate Mary's constitutional right to life. Thus the appellant's continued detention was lawful.[8] The judgment is, however, internally inconsistent for Griffin J. in a subsequent passage[9] said that the Garda concern for Mary's right to life was "an extraordinary excusing circumstance for keeping the appellant in custody for what would otherwise have been an impermissibly long period." But if the detention was lawful, the question of extraordinary excusing circumstances can hardly arise: the word "excusing" suggests that an illegality has occurred but may be overlooked, not that the illegal quality has been expunged.

The analysis of Walsh J. was quite different. He did not regard the Garda concern for Mary's right to life as *justifying* the illegal detention. Rather, it furnished extraordinary excusing circumstances for admitting the appellant's *statements*.[10] As regards the evidence resulting from the Connemara episode, Walsh J. held that this was admissible because, although the appellant's detention continued to be unlawful, he voluntarily went to Connemara; thus he consented to a condition of imprisonment during that period.[11] Had his detention during that episode been unlawful there could not have been extraordinary excusing circumstances, in Walsh J.'s view, because the Gardaí

---

[8] See [1982] I.R. 1, at 55. Kenny J., in his separate concurring judgment, also said the appellant's continued detention was unlawful—at 63.

[9] At 56.

[10] [1982] I.R. 1, 42–43. This distinction is important, for the potential right to a remedy in damages remains if the State action—however well-intentioned—remains illegal.

[11] [1982] I.R. 1, 40.

could not—given the appellant's confession—reasonably have believed Mary was still alive.[12] The conflict between these approaches still awaits resolution.[13]

Illegally obtained evidence

The principle discussed above refers to evidence obtained in breach of *constitutional* rights; and the authorities indicate that absent inadvertence or extraordinary excusing circumstances it is automatically inadmissible. Evidence obtained in breach of *legal* rights is treated differently. In *D.P.P.* v. *McMahon and ors.* [1986] I.R. 393 the Supreme Court unanimously held that, as Finlay C.J. put it (at 399):

> " . . . evidence obtained by illegal means, not involving conscious and deliberate violation of constitutional rights, shall be admissible unless the court in its discretion excludes it."

And the Supreme Court affirmed the judgment of Kingsmill Moore J. in *O'Brien's* case [1965] I.R. 142, 160–161 in which certain factors governing the exercise of discretion were canvassed. Thus the presiding judge must balance the public interest in the detection and punishment of crime against the public interest in the repression of illegal investigative methods, and the balance struck must depend on a consideration of all the circumstances of a given case.

McMahon's case was a prosecution of three publicans for alleged violation of the gaming legislation. The principal prosecution evidence was that of Gardaí who had entered the relevant premises for the express purpose of getting such evidence. They did not identify themselves or state their purpose, and they had no search warrants or statutory authority to enter. Thus the Supreme Court held that they were in law trespassers and the evidence they obtained was obtained by unlawful means—though not by any infringement of constitutional rights. The court, having held that the evidence was admissible, subject to the trial judge's discretion, said that in striking the required balance particular importance might attach to the fact that the Gardaí were merely trespassers, not involved in any criminal or opprobrious conduct; and that the offence of permitting gaming on licensed premises could be considered as one with grave social consequences. In his separate concurrence McCarthy J., taking up a point made by Kingsmill Moore J. in *O'Brien's* case, said that should further evidence disclose a policy of such warrantless searches the discretion must be exercised so as to exclude the relevant evidence ([1986] I.R. 393, 401–402).

It is significant that the Supreme Court in *McMahon's* case discerned no violation of constitutional rights. The Constitution's only *explicit* provision agaist such unlawful searches is in Article 40.5:

> "The dwelling of every citizen is inviolable and shall not be forcibly entered save in accordance with law."

---

[12] At 39. The majority view, *per* Griffin J., was that the Gardaí could not risk accepting the accuracy of the accused's statements.

[13] For detailed critical analyses of the *Shaw* decision see O'Connor, *op. cit.*; also F. McAuley and P. McCutcheon, "*The People* v. *Shaw*: An Analysis" (1981) *D.U.L.J.* 63, and "*Shaw* and the Admissibility of Unconstitutionally Obtained Statements" (1982) *D.U.L.J.* 86.

Since the "searches" in *McMahon's* case were not of the appellant's dwelling, that provision could have no relevance. It would, of course, be possible to construct an unenumerated right—deriving from Article 40.3—to be free from unreasonable searches and seizures, analogous to the United States Constitution's 4th Amendment[14]; but the Supreme Court was plainly not minded to engage in this.

The guarantee of Article 40.5, it should be noted, is *not* against forcible entry only. It means that the dwelling of every citizen (here doubtless synonymous with "person") is inviolable save where entry is permitted by law and that, if necessary, such law may permit forcible entry. So said Walsh J. (Ó Dálaigh C.J. concurring) in *O'Brien's* case ([1965] I.R. 142, 169), and in *D.P.P.* v. *Gaffney* (1987] I.R. 173 McCarthy J. expressed his agreement with this view (at 184). Thus absent a warrant, or specific statutory authority, Garda officers or other State agents may enter a dwelling only by invitation or permission. Such invitation or permission may be express—or it may be inferred from the circumstances; thus a failure expressly to refuse entry *might* be construed as an implied permission to enter. But everything depends on the circumstances of the particular case. If the Garda entry is not authorised by law, and is thus in breach of Article 40.5, an arrest consequent thereon will be illegal: see *D.P.P.* v. *Gaffney* [1987] I.R. 173.

It is not clear whether a driveway in the immediate vicinity of a dwelling and forming part of its curtilage attracts the protection of Article 40.5. The point was raised, but not resolved, in *D.P.P.* v. *McCreesh* (Supreme Court, March 7, 1991), since it was possible to decide the case on a non-constitutional ground.[15] Even if it is, statute could, presumably, authorise entry thereon by agents of the State—at least in specified and limited circumstances.

In *People (D.P.P.)* v. *Lawless* (C.C.A., November 28, 1985) the appellant had been convicted of possession of heroin for purposes of supply, contrary to the Misuse of Drugs Act 1977. On foot of a technically defective search warrant the Gardaí entered premises on which the appellant was found and there obtained evidence—packets of heroin which had been flushed down a toilet—against him. It was argued that the trial judge should have excluded this evidence. For the Court of Criminal Appeal McCarthy J. observed that since the warrant was defective the search was unlawful; but this did not breach any constitutional right of the appellant, who neither owned nor rented the flat in question. Moreover, the Garda action was not a deliberate and conscious violation of any rights. There was no evidence of deliberate deceit or illegality, nor of any policy to conduct searches without a warrant. And had there been a violation of constitutional rights there would have existed extraordinary excusing circumstances—the need to prevent the imminent destruction of vital evidence.

Assuming no breach of constitutional rights has occurred, an accused's statements to police are admissible in evidence provided that they are volun-

---

[14] "The right of the people to be secure in their persons, houses, papers, and effects, against unreasonable searches and seizures, shall not be violated, and no Warrants shall issue, but upon probable cause, supported by Oath or affirmation, and particularly describing the place to be searched, and the persons or things to be seized."

[15] The Gardaí who had arrested the defendant in his driveway were held to have been trespassing, with the result that the arrest was unlawful.

tary. But even here the trial judge has a discretion to exclude them—particularly, though not exclusively, if a breach of the Judge's Rules[16] has occurred. Those rules are not rules of law—they originated as judicial *guidance* to the police— and a breach of them does not *per se* make a statement inadmissible: *McCarrick* v. *Leavy* [1964] I.R. 225. Nonetheless the Court of Criminal Appeal, *per* O'Higgins C.J., warned in *People (D.P.P.)* v. *Farrell* [1978] I.R. 13, that they would "be departed from at peril."[17]

A statement not answering the legal description "voluntary" is inadmissible; no question of judicial discretion arises here—*McCarrick* v. *Leavy supra*: *People (Att. Gen.)* v. *Cummins* [1972] I.R. 312. Factors negating voluntariness include oppressive questioning—that which by its nature and duration or other surrounding circumstances so affects the individual that his will crumbles: see *People (D.P.P.)* v. *Pringle* ((1981) 2 Frewen 57). Though frequently invoked as a ground for excluding statements this has seldom succeeded; but it did in *People (D.P.P.)* v. *Lynch* [1982] I.R. 64, where the appellant had been questioned for almost 22 hours without rest or sleep.

Finally, it should be noted that objections to the admissibility of evidence—whether on constitutional grounds or otherwise—must be made in the court of trial (or on appeal therefrom). Rulings upon such issues cannot be sought in advance from the High Court, whether in judicial review proceedings or otherwise. In *Ryan* v. *D.P.P.* [1988] I.R. 232, 234 Barron J. said: "Such rulings form no part of the supervisory jurisdiction of this court."

The privilege against self-incrimination

The United States Constitution, in its 5th Amendment, contains a specific privilege against self-incrimination,[18] which has been held binding on the states *via* the due process clause of the 14th Amendment: *Malloy* v. *Hogan* (1964) 378 U.S. 1. There Brennan J. referred to the privilege as "the right of a person to remain silent unless he chooses to speak in the unfettered exercise of his own will, and to suffer no penalty." Thus a statute compelling someone to give answers to police questions would be unconstitutional unless it gave immunity from prosecution to that person: *Counselman* v. *Hitchcock* (1892) 142 U.S. 547. The privilege does not rule out compulsory taking of blood samples from a suspected drunken driver: *Schmerber* v. *California* (1966) 387 U.S. 757; or a statutory obligation on a driver involved in an accident to stop and give his/her name to the other driver: *California* v. *Byers* (1971) 402 U.S. 424. But comment by the prosecution—or the judge—on an accused person's failure to testify has been held to violate this guarantee: *Griffin* v. *Illinois* (1965) 380 U.S. 609.

If Bunreacht na hÉireann makes the presumption of innocence and proof beyond a reasonable doubt basic—and irreducible—elements in the law of criminal procedure, a logical case can be made that this must hold also for the privilege against self-incrimination.[19] Certainly the pre-Constitution law

---

[16] The Judges' Rules are printed as an appendix to this Chapter.

[17] On the whole subject of statements see the excellent treatment in Ryan and Magee, *op. cit.*, pp. 113 ff.

[18] "No person . . . shall be compelled in any criminal case to be a witness against himself."

[19] And it has been: see Paul O'Connor and Thomas Cooney, "Criminal Due Process, The Pre-Trial Stage and Self-Incrimination" (1980) *XV Irish Jurist* (N.S.) 219.

recognised such a privilege. Thus a person was not obliged to answer police questions, and had to be cautioned to this effect. This is clear from the former Supreme Court's decision in *State (McCarthy)* v. *Lennon* [1936] I.R. 485. The prosecutor there had been convicted of certain offences by the Constitution (Special Powers) Tribunal established under Article 2A of the 1922 Constitution (as to which see Chap. 1 *supra*). He sought certiorari to quash this conviction, arguing that evidence—in the form of statements he made in Garda custody—should not have been admitted against him, on the basis that he was compelled by section 15 of Article 2A to answer Garda questions. Though holding by a majority (Fitzgibbon and Murnaghan JJ.: Kennedy C.J. dissenting) that these statements were *now* admissible, the court was unanimously of the view that they would not have been admissible before Article 2A was inserted in 1931. Kennedy C.J. and Fitzgibbon J. referred to the long-standing acceptance of the maximum *nemo tenetur seipsum accusare*[20] while Murnaghan J. said (at 504–505):

> "Under the law in force in Ireland during several centuries before the adoption, in the year 1922, of the Constitution, it was an established maxim that no man is bound to incriminate himself . . . it is not disputed that until Article 2A was inserted in the Constitution the statements in question must have been rejected."

At one stage Fitzgibbon J. suggested (at 499) that Article 73 of the Constitution enshrined this principle; but it is not clear that he intended this to mean it was beyond the power of the Oireachtas to modify it. And Kennedy C.J. specifically contemplated parliamentary modification of the principle (at 496).

The Criminal Justice (Evidence) Act 1924 reinforced this right to silence by providing that the prosecution could not compel a defendant to testify, nor comment on the defendant's failure to do so of his own accord (s.1(*b*)). Nor could it comment on the fact that the accused, when charged, remained silent. But no such restriction was imposed on the trial judge, who could comment on the accused's silence when charged, or his failure to testify at the trial.[21] The 1924 Act also provided that should an accused choose to testify he could be asked any question "notwithstanding that it would tend to criminate him as to the offence charged"—section 1(*e*)—and he had no privilege to refuse to answer.

As the law stood in 1937, therefore, the privilege against self-incrimination was recognised in Irish law—subject to Article 2A. Bunreacht na hÉireann did not specifically incorporate the privilege, so that if it has achieved constitutional status this must be by implication from Article 38.1 and Article 40.3 and 4. In the bankruptcy case of *Re McAllister* [1973] I.R. 238 Kenny J. declined to decide whether the Constitution conferred a right against self-incrimination. Nonetheless he held that a bankrupt could decline to answer any question which might incriminate him or disclose that he had committed a criminal offence. It was, said Kenny J., the practice of the judges who had exercised the bankruptcy jurisdiction during the previous 20 years to warn witnesses that they were not obliged to answer questions if their replies

---

[20] At 495 (Kennedy C.J.): 499 (Fitzgibbon J.).
[21] See *Att. Gen.* v. *Fleming* [1934] I.R. 166 (C.C.A.); but note *Att. Gen.* v. *Durnan (No. 2)* [1934] I.R. 540 (C.C.A.)

would show they had committed a criminal offence. (This must have been a judicial gloss on the statutory provisions. In England it had been held that although other witnesses were entitled to the privilege, the *bankrupt* could not refuse to answer questions on this ground—*R.* v. *Scott* (1856) 7 Cox C.C. 164: *R.* v. *Erdheim* [1896] 2 Q.B. 260.[22])

The question whether, and to what extent, the Constitution may recognise such a privilege has not so far arisen squarely for decision. The matter was raised, but not resolved, in *D.P.P.* v. *Quilligan* (Supreme Court, July 14, 1992). Their one argument against the validity of section 30 of the Offences against the State Act 1939 was that a person detained thereunder could be subjected to protracted interrogation by the Gardaí. This impermissibly conflicted with what was claimed to be an unenumerated constitutional right of silence or protection against self-incrimination. But Finlay C.J., delivering the single judgment of the court, said (pp. 21–22):

> " . . . no detailed submission of any description was put before the Court as to the reasons why the Court should conclude that a right of silence or a right to be protected against self-incrimination was an unenumerated personal right deriving protection from Article 40 of the Constitution. No decision of the High Court or of this Court was referred to by Counsel on behalf of the Appellants indicating the existence of such a right as a constitutional right, unenumerated or not specified. . . . The Court does not find it necessary, therefore, to express any view on the question as to whether or in what circumstances or subject to what qualifications, if any, a right of silence or protection against self-incrimination is an unenumerated right pursuant to the Constitution."

The Court of Criminal Appeal has noted that the Constitution does not expressly refer to this privilege and has declined to follow United States decisions—such as *Miranda* v. *Arizona* (1966) 384 U.S. 436—which apply it to the pre-trial stage: *People (D.P.P.)* v. *Pringle* ((1982) 2 Frewen 57). Thus a person being questioned by Gardaí has no constitutional right to have a lawyer present—*People (D.P.P.)* v. *Farrell* [1978] I.R. 13: *Pringle's* case *supra*. Nor would it be a ground for excluding statements made by an accused that he/she was compelled to answer them on pain of penalty under the Offences against the State Act 1939, s.52: the Court of Criminal Appeal so held, *obiter*, in *People (D.P.P.)* v. *McGowan* [1979] I.R. 45.

If the Constitution implicitly enshrines a privilege against self-incrimination on United States lines, then section 52 of the 1939 Act would be of doubtful validity. Also open to challenge would be certain provisions of the Criminal Justice Act 1984 which are on similar lines to section 52—*e.g.* sections 15 and 16, which create offences of withholding information regarding firearms or ammunition, and stolen property, respectively. Sections 18 and 19 of the same Act in effect allow a court to draw inferences from an accused's failure to account for specified matters; such inferences may be treated as corroborating other evidence but are not *alone* sufficient for a con-

---

[22] Kenny J.'s view that the bankrupt could refuse to answer questions finds no support in the Bankruptcy Law Committee Report (Prl. 2714). (The committee was chaired by Budd J.).

viction. And in both instances the accused must have been told in advance in ordinary language what the effect of failure might be.[23]

It seems unlikely that the courts will invalidate such provisions. In no decision so far has it been suggested that section 52 of the Offences against the State Act 1939 is of doubtful validity. As for the inferences open under section 18 and 19 of the Criminal Justice Act 1984, the judicial attitude seems likely to be that a person convicted on the basis of those provisions has been tried in due course of law. Although the notion of "due course of law" has affinities with the United States due process guarantees, it can hardly be contended that Irish courts are bound by United States decisions as to what due process requires. The more so since views on that subject have changed. In *Griffin* v. *Illinois* (1965) 380 U.S. 609 the Supreme Court held that a judge may not comment on an accused's failure to testify or invite the jury to draw inferences therefrom. But this was on the basis—established in *Malloy* v. *Hogan* (1964) 378 U.S. 1—that the due process clause of the 14th Amendment incorporates *vis-à-vis* the states the 5th Amendment's prohibition against self-incrimination. Such reasoning is obviously not *per se* applicable under Bunreacht na hÉireann. And it is notable that in the earlier case of *Adamson* v. *California* (1947) 332 U.S. 46 a majority of the Supreme Court did not think such a judicial comment or invitation violated the due process guarantee of the 14th Amendment. The Irish courts seem likely to accept the *Adamson*, rather than the later *Griffin*, approach.

Section 20 of the Criminal Justice Act 1984 requires an accused to give advance notice if he intends to rely on an alibi defence. The United States Supreme Court has held that such a rule does not breach the privilege against self-incrimination: *Williams* v. *Florida* (1970) 399 U.S. 78. It is not likely that section 20, if weighed in the constitutional balance, will be found wanting.

Double jeopardy

As with the privilege against self-incrimination, so the common law recognised a right against double jeopardy. Thus in bar of a trial on indictment one could plead in appropriate circumstances *autrefois acquit* or *autrefois convict*—a prior acquittal, or conviction, of the offence charged; and a similar rule applied in regard to summary prosecutions.[24] This common law rule was enshrined in the 5th Amendment of the United States Constitution[25] and it has, like the privilege against self-incrimination, been held binding on the states *via* the 14th Amendment's due process clause: *Benton* v. *Maryland* (1969) 395 U.S. 784. No doubt Article 38.1's guarantee of trial in due course of law incorporates a similar idea; but the Irish concept of double jeopardy is not identical to that of the United States. There the 5th Amendment has been held to bar appeals against acquittals in federal cases, even where

---

[23] In *Connolly* v. *Salinger* [1982] I.L.R.M. 482 the Supreme Court declined to hold that a Garda officer was obliged, when requiring a blood or urine sample from a person arrested for drunken driving, to caution the person that he was not obliged to furnish a sample and that the result of any analysis might be to incriminate him. No such caution was "proper or necessary."

[24] See generally Ryan and Magee, *op. cit.*, pp. 271–279.

[25] " . . . nor shall any person be subjected for the same offence to be twice put in jeopardy of life or limb." The relevant authorities on double jeopardy are surveyed by Blackmun J. in his judgment for the court in *U.S.* v. *Di Francesco* (1980) 449 U.S. 117.

directed by the trial judge—*Fong Foo* v. *U.S.* (1962) 369 U.S. 141; and this applies also to the states via the 14th Amendment: *Benton's* case *supra*. But *Palko* v. *Connecticut* (1937) 302 U.S. 319—which *Benton* overruled—saw no violation of due process in statutory provision for an appeal against acquittal; and an Irish court might prefer the *Palko* approach. Indeed in *People (D.P.P.)* v. *O'Shea* [1982] I.R. 384 a 3–2 majority in the Supreme Court held that an appeal lay to that court against a Central Criminal Court acquittal (see further Chap. 10 *supra*), and arguments based on double jeopardy were rejected.[26] Presumably if an acquittal in a trial held to have been flawed[27] is set aside on appeal a retrial may be ordered.[28] Presumably also the Oireachtas could legislate to provide for such appeals from courts other than the Central Criminal Court.

The United States doctrine holds that a defendant has been in jeopardy even if the indictment is defective or the jury unlawfully selected: *Benton's case supra*. This is not accepted in Ireland; if the court lacked jurisdiction for whatever reason, the accused was not in jeopardy and may be re-tried. This is so whether the trial was a summary one or with a jury.[29] But both systems agree that any sentence imposed upon a person convicted on a retrial must give credit for any period in custody on foot of the invalid first conviction; *North Carolina* v. *Pearce* (1969) 395 U.S. 711: *State (Tynan)* v. *Keane* [1968] I.R. 348. In both systems, too, a person whose conviction is set aside on an appeal *by him/her* may be re-tried. *North Carolina* v. *Pearce supra* shows that there is no constitutional bar to this in the United States. The point has never been tested in Ireland, though the Court of Criminal Appeal has since 1928 had power to order a retrial[30] and this has often been exercised. The power may not be used where the prosecution has a failed to adduce an essential proof: *People (Att. Gen.)* v. *Griffin* [1974] I.R. 416.[31] But there is no bar to ordering successive retrials if necessary: *People (Att. Gen.)* v. *Kelly (No. 2)* [1938] I.R. 109. It seems safe to assume that section 5(1)(*b*) is proof against constitutional challenge.

It is not the law in Ireland that an acquittal on a criminal charge, irrespective of the reason therefor, precludes a disciplinary investigation arising out of the same facts: *McGrath* v. *Commr., Garda Síochána* [1991] 1 I.R. 69, *per* Finlay C.J. (Griffin J. concurring) (at 71) and McCarthy J. (at 75). But the disciplinary investigation may be prohibited by the courts if, in the particular circumstances, it would amount to an unfair procedure: *ibid*.

Sentences

Until recently it appeared that the Constitution had little relevance to sentences. The familiar pattern is that the legislative prescribes a maximum sentence for an offence, while within the range so established a court fixes the

---

[26] *Per* O'Higgins C.J. at 406–407: Walsh J. at 416–419. For the contrary view see Henchy J. at 437–439.

[27] *e.g.* by misdirection of the judge, the admission of inadmissible evidence, etc.

[28] This point was raised—but not resolved— in *People (D.P.P.)* v. *Quilligan (No. 2)* [1989] I.R. 46; see Chap. 10 *supra.*, *s.v.* The Supreme Court.

[29] *Conlin* v. *Patterson* [1915] 2 I.R. 169: *State (Tynan)* v. *Keane* [1968] I.R. 348 (S.C.): *State (de Búrca)* v. *Barry* (High Court, Barrington J., July 17, 1980).

[30] s.5(1)(*b*), Courts of Justice Act 1928.

[31] The same holds true in the U.S.: see *Burks* v. *U.S.* (1978) 437 U.S. 1 and *Greene* v. *Massey* (1978) 437 U.S. 19.

precise penalty in a concrete case.[32] Mandatory sentences—though constitutional[33]— are rare; the principal example appears to be mandatory life sentence for murder or treason under the Criminal Justice Act 1990.[34]

Now, however, it is clear that while the Oireachtas enjoys a large margin of appreciation in prescribing sentences, its power is subject to certain broad limits. The Supreme Court's decision in *Cox* v. *Ireland and Att. Gen.* (No. 361/ 90, July 11, 1991) means that the Constitution requires some proportionality between the gravity of the offence and the punishment prescribed therefor. In that case the plaintiff, a community school teacher, had in February 1988 been convicted by the Special Criminal Court of a scheduled offence under the Offences against the State Act 1939. He was sentenced to two years' imprisonment which, with remission, he duly served. The school board was prepared to re-employ him from September 1989 but was informed that section 34 of the 1939 Act prevented this. This provision applied only to persons convicted in the Special Criminal Court of scheduled offences under the 1939 Act and stipulated that, in addition to any punishment imposed by that court, they should suffer certain forfeitures and disqualifications. Thus they would immediately forfeit any post remunerated from public funds and any pension payable out of such funds. They would also be disqualified for seven years from holding any post remunerated out of public funds, and—in perpetuity—from receiving any pension or gratuity payable therefrom. The Supreme Court held section 34 unconstitutional. To protect public peace and order and maintain its own authority, said the court, the State was entitled to impose onerous penalties as a deterrent to the commission of crimes. But in pursuing these objectives it must, as far as practicable, continue to protect citizens' constitutional rights. On analysis, section 34 constituted a failure of such protection not warranted by the objectives sought to be achieved.[35]

It seems unlikely that many statutory provisions will fall victim to the proportionality principle implicit in *Cox's* case. But the recognition of that principle may provide constitutional security against the legislature's being stampeded by public opinion into prescribing absurdly tough penalties for relatively innocuous offences.

---

[32] A table of the penalties prescribed in respect of indictable offences appears in Appendix H of Edward F. Ryan and Philip P. Magee, *The Irish Criminal Process* (Dublin 1983).

[33] Certainly they do not offend against the separation of powers provisions: see *State (O.)* v. *O'Brien* [1973] I.R. 50, 67 *per* Walsh J.

[34] s.2. This life sentence replaces the death penalty: see Chap. 3 *supra, s.v.* The Prerogative of Clemency.

[35] The court reached this conclusion on a combination of grounds: (a) that s. 34 *prima facie* constituted an attack on the constitutional right to earn a livelihood, and on constitutionally protected property rights such as those to a pension, gratuity, etc. already earned: (b) it applied only to scheduled offences—but these varied in seriousness, some carrying only a maximum fine of £IR 25: (c) the mandatory nature of its forfeiture provisions took no account of individual motive: (d) they applied *only* to a conviction in the Special Criminal Court, and whether or not the accused appeared in that court depended upon an executive decision by the D.P.P.

APPENDIX TO CHAPTER 14

The Judges' Rules[36]

1. When a police officer is endeavouring to discover the author of a crime there is no objection to his putting questions in respect thereof to any person or persons, whether suspected or not, from whom he thinks that useful information may be obtained.

2. Whenever a police officer has made up his mind to charge a person with a crime, he should first caution such person before asking him any questions, or any further questions as the case may be.

3. Persons in custody should not be questioned without the usual caution being first administered.

4. If the prisoner wishes to volunteer any statement, the usual caution should be administered. It is desirable that the last two words of such caution should be omitted, and that the caution should end with the words "be given in evidence."

5. The caution to be administered to a prisoner when he is formally charged should therefore be in the following words: "Do you wish to say anything in answer to the charge? You are not obliged to say anything unless you wish to do so, but whatever you say will be taken down in writing and may be given in evidence." Care should be taken to avoid the suggestion that his answers can only be used in evidence against him, as this may prevent an innocent person making a statement which might assist to clear him of the charge.

6. A statement made by a prisoner before there is time to caution him is not rendered inadmissible in evidence merely because no caution has been given, but in such a case he should be cautioned as soon as possible.

7. A prisoner making a voluntary statement must not be cross-examined and no questions should be put to him about it except for the purpose of removing ambiguity in what he has actually said. For instance, if he has mentioned an hour without saying whether it was morning or evening, or has given a day of the week and day of the month which do not agree, or has not made it clear to what individual or what place he intended to refer in some part of his statement, he may be questioned sufficiently to clear up the point.

8. When two or more persons are charged with the same offence and their statements are taken separately, the police should not read these statements to the other persons charged, but each of such persons should be given by the police a copy of such statements and nothing should be said or done by the police to invite a reply. If the person charged desires to make a statement in reply the usual caution should be administered.

9. Any statement made in accordance with the above rules should, whenever possible, be taken down in writing and signed by the person making it after it has been read to him and he has been invited to make any corrections he may wish.

---

[36] Printed as App. D of the *Report* of the Committee to Recommend Certain Safeguards for Persons in Custody (Prl. 7158).

15 Freedom of Expression and Assembly

FREEDOM OF EXPRESSION

Article 40.6.1°i of the Constitution provides as follows:

> "The State guarantees liberty for the exercise of the following rights,
> subject to public order and morality:
> i. the right of the citizens to express freely their convictions and
> opinions.
>
> > The education of public opinion being, however, a matter of such
> > grave import to the common good, the State shall endeavour to
> > ensure that organs of public opinion, such as the radio, the press,
> > the cinema, while preserving their rightful liberty of expression,
> > including criticism of Government policy, shall not be used to
> > undermine public order or morality or the authority of the State.
> >
> > The publication or utterance of blasphemous, seditious or
> > indecent matter is an offence which shall be punishable in accord-
> > ance with law."

It will be clear from this that the guarantee of freedom of expression is a
much qualified one. Not only is the citizen's right subject to legislative
restriction in the name of public order or morality, but the "organs of public
opinion" may be subjected to control on the same grounds, as well as of "the
authority of the State." And—unusually—blasphemy is made an offence by
the Constitution itself, so that the Oireachtas has no choice in this matter.

The freedom of expression guarantee has received little attention from the
courts, which may reflect a low level of public concern on this issue.[1] Certainly there has been nothing remotely resembling the volume of litigation
over the First Amendment in the United States.[2] But it would be wrong to
conclude that speech is not comparatively free in Ireland. Article 40.6.1°i
plainly protects the right of the media to criticise Government policy—a
right exercised daily—and there has never been any question of excluding
Opposition parties from the publicly-owned broadcasting facilities, as has
happened in France.[3] Indeed statute lays on the R.T.É. Authority an obli-

---

[1] Though it should be noted that the Law Reform Commission has recently published consultation papers, and reports, on contempt of court, the crime of libel and the civil law of defamation.

[2] As to which see Eric Barendt, *Fredom of Speech* (Oxford 1987)—a comparative analysis of the
subject in English, German, US and European Human Rights Convention law.

[3] See J. E. S. Hayward, *Governing France: the One and Indivisible Republic* (2nd ed., London 1983),
pp. 159–171.

gation of impartiality and objectivity in regard to matters of public controversy or political debate: Broadcasting Authority Act 1960, s.18 (as amended
by section 8 of the 1976 Act).[4] Further, although the common law on contempt of court may restrict freedom of expression, in practice this branch of
the law has not generated in Ireland anything like the controversy it has in
England. Though all the elements of the Irish media have had brushes with
the law of contempt, there has not been any campaign for its reform and
newspaper editors seem more worried about libel.[5] Nor are there any Irish
equivalents of the controversial decisions in *Att. Gen.* v. *Times Newspapers Ltd.*
[1974] A.C. 273 (see *infra*) or *Home Office* v. *Harman* [1983] 1 A.C. 280[6]—both
of which gave rise to further proceedings under the European Convention on
Human Rights.[7]

   In Ireland both common and statute law impose restrictions on freedom of
expression. Some of these are traditional in the common law world and are
imposed in the interests of the administration of justice or of protecting individual reputations. Others are clearly referable to public morality, *e.g.* controls on obscene material, or of the authority of the State, *e.g.* the
Broadcasting Authority Act 1960, s.31.

Article 40.6.1°i: scope

   The fact that Article 40.6.1°i refers to " . . . convictions and opinions . . . "
has provoked discussion about its scope[8]; are assertions of fact not covered?
If not, this would not mean that they were bereft of constitutional protection,
for they could presumably shelter under the unenumerated right to communicate guaranteed by Article 40.3.[9] But as Mr. Nial Fennelly S.C. has
pointed out,[10] this would create anomalies and difficulties. For example, it
would entail the conclusion that a publication consisting of mixed facts and
opinions would be covered by two differently worded guarantees. The better
approach would seem to be to read Article 40.6.1°i broadly, rather than to
focus too closely on the possible imperfections of its wording. Thus its purpose should be seen as guaranteeing liberty of expression—the phrase
actually used in its second paragraph. There are no indications that the

---

[4] See also ss.9 and 18 of the Radio and Television Act 1988, which impose similar obligations
   on independent radio and TV companies.
[5] See the results of interviews recorded by Kieran Woodman, *Media Control in Ireland 1923–1983*
   (Galway 1985), pp. 199–204.
[6] Where it was held that a solicitor who allowed a journalist post-trial access to documents
   obtained by discovery (the contents of which had been read out in court) was guilty of contempt. Note the observations of Finlay C.J. (Hederman, O'Flaherty and Egan JJ. concurring)
   in *Ambiorix Ltd.* v. *Minister for the Environment* [1992] I.L.R.M. 209, 215: "As a matter of
   general principle . . . a party obtaining the production of documents by a discovery in an
   action is prohibited by law from making any use of any description of such documents or the
   information contained in them otherwise than for the purpose of the action. To go outside
   that prohibition is to commit contempt of court."
[7] See *Sunday Times* v. *U.K.* (1979) 2 E.H.R.R. 245, discussed *infra*. In the *Harman* case a friendly
   settlement—involving an undertaking to change the law as laid down by the House of
   Lords—was arrived at: see 100 *H.C. Debs* (6s), c. 17 (June 23, 1986).
[8] See Appendix A of the Law Reform Commission's *Report on the Civil Law of Defamation* (1991).
[9] As to which see Chap. 12 *supra, s.v.* the right to communicate.
[10] Nial Fennelly, "The Irish Constitution and Freedom of Expression" in Deirdre Curtin and
   David O'Keeffe (eds.), *Constitutional Adjudication in European Community and National Law* (Dublin 1992), p. 183. He also points out that the reference in the third paragraph to " . . . blasphemous, seditious or indecent matter . . . " must apply to factual material.

courts would read it narrowly, and there is good reason why they should not. Article 40.6.1°i is the constitutional counterpart of Article 10 of the European Convention on Human Rights. This guarantees " . . . freedom of expression . . . ," defined to include " . . . freedom to hold opinions and to receive and impart information and ideas . . . " The judgment of O'Hanlon J. in *Desmond* v. *Glackin* (High Court, January 9, 1992)—considered *infra*— would suggest that Article 10 should inform the construction of Article 40.6.1°i.

The "organs of public opinion" are specifically mentioned in the second paragraph of Article 40.6.1°i. Does this give the media a greater measure of freedom than individual citizens? After a careful analysis[11] the Law Reform Commission concluded that, in the sphere of defamation at least, it did not. This view would seem to be correct. On its face, the language of the second paragraph does not suggest a privileged position for the media. Indeed, the specific reference to "the authority of the State," in addition to "public order and morality," could on a literal interpretation be taken to contemplate more, rather than less, legal restriction of the media. Moreover, as Professor Barendt has shown, there are problems of principle in recognising a right of media freedom distinct from freedom of expression—for example, would the former right inhere in the owner, the editor or the journalists?[12] It is noteworthy that in the United States—even with a specific textual reference to the press[13] and a Supreme Court solicitous for its liberty[14]—no such right has been recognised.[15]

Contempt of court[16]

In *Att. Gen.* v. *Times Newspapers Ltd.* [1974] A.C. 273 Lord Simon of Glaisdale said (at 315–316):

> "The law of contempt . . . is the means by which the law vindicates the public interest in due administration of justice—that is, in the resolution of disputes . . . by independent adjudication in courts of law according to an objective code."

He went on to observe that in contempt cases, two public interests were liable to conflict with each other—that in freedom of discussion and that in the unimpeded settlement of disputes according to law, and it was the task of the courts to strike a balance between these two interests. Broadly similar views were expressed by the other law lords, and an injunction was granted prohibiting publication in *The Sunday Times* of an article on the marketing of the drug thalidomide in Britain by Distillers Company (Biochemicals) Ltd. This was on the basis that its publication would prejudge issues in pending

[11] *Report on the Civil Law of Defamation* (1991), pp. 118–120.

[12] *Op. cit*, n. 2 *supra*, pp. 68–72.

[13] The First Amendment reads, so far as relevant: "Congress shall make no law . . . abridging the freedom of speech, or of the press . . . "

[14] As a long line of cases from *Near* v. *Minnesota* (1931) 283 U.S. 597 onwards—including *New York Times Co.* v. *Sullivan* (1964) 376 U.S. 254, discussed *infra*—testifies.

[15] The Supreme Court has refused to recognise a journalistic privilege to keep sources confidential: *Branzburg* v. *Hayes* (1972) 408 U.S. 665, or a right of media access to prisons: *Pell* v. *Procunier* (1974) 417 U.S. 817.

[16] For a thorough survey of this topic (which of course goes well beyond free expression issues) see the Law Reform Commission's *Consultation Paper on Contempt of Court* (July 1991).

litigation against Distillers. Subsequently, however, the European Court of Human Rights concluded (by a bare majority of 11–9) that the injunction could not be justified under Article 10(2) of the European Convention on Human Rights. The restraint in question, said the court, was not "proportionate to the legitimate aim pursued; it was not necessary in a democratic society for maintaining the authority of the judiciary": *Sunday Times* v. *U.K.* (1979) 2 E.H.R.R. 245, 282. The court accepted that the law of contempt was not *per se* an infringement of the Convention, but it gave freedom of expression—"one of the essential foundations of a democratic society"— much greater weight than the House of Lords had done, saying ((1979) 2 E.H.R.R. 245, 280):

> " . . . the courts cannot operate in a vacuum. Whilst they are the forum for the settlement of disputes, this does not mean that there can be no prior discussion of disputes elsewhere, be it in specialised journals, in the general press or amongst the public at large. Furthermore, whilst the mass media must not overstep the bounds imposed in the interests of the proper administration of justice, it is incumbent on them to impart information and ideas concerning matters that come before the courts just as in other areas of public interest. Not only do the media have the task of imparting such information and ideas: the public also has a right to receive them."

The European Convention on Human Rights, of course, is not part of the domestic law of the State. None the less, it is capable of influencing the content, and the administration, of the law on contempt of court. In *Desmond* v. *Glackin* (High Court, January 9, 1992) O'Hanlon J. explained why (p. 33 of his judgment):

> "As Ireland has ratified the Convention and is a party to it, and as the law on contempt of court is based . . . on public policy I think it is legitimate to assume that our public policy is in accord with the Convention or at least that the provisions of the Convention can be considered when determining issues of public policy. The Convention itself is not a code of legal principles which are enforceable in the domestic courts, as was made clear in *In re Ó Laighléis* [1960] I.R. 93, but this does not prevent the judgment of the European Court [in the *Sunday Times* case] from having a persuasive effect when considering the common law regarding contempt of court in the light of the constitutional guarantees of freedom of expression contained in our Constitution of 1937. Henchy J. expressed the view in *The State (D.P.P.)* v. *Walsh* [1981] I.R. 412, at p. 440, that there was a presumption that our law on contempt is in conformity with the Convention, particularly Articles 5 and 10(2)."

(a) *Restrictions relating to criminal proceedings*[17]

It is a contempt of court—and restrainable by injunction, or punishable by fine and/or imprisonment—to make comments on, or statements about, pending criminal proceedings calculated or intended to interfere with the pending decision. In *Att. Gen.* v. *Cooke* (1924) 58 I.L.T.R. 157 the applicants were defendants in District Court proceedings which arose out of their picketing certain premises in Dublin. The day following their arrest, and

---

[17] See further the Law Reform Commission's *Consultation Paper on Contempt of Court*, pp. 74–101.

while the proceedings were pending, the *Evening Mail* published a leading article in which the scenes outside the premises in question were described as "a disgrace to the city and a menace to its peace." It further stated that no trade dispute existed and that intimidatory methods had been adopted, and urged the Government to protect the public from such treatment. It was alleged that this was calculated to prevent a fair trial. In the High Court Sullivan P. (O'Shaughnessy and Murnaghan JJ. concurring) said that the court must be careful, on the one hand, not to permit any comments to be made in a newspaper on pending proceedings which were calculated or intended to interfere with the pending decision; and, on the other hand, not to interfere with the right and freedom of the press to comment on matters of public interest and concern. Here the court concluded that the article was neither calculated (*i.e.* likely) nor intended to interfere with the District Justice's decision. A factor which weighed with the court here—and many years later with the Supreme Court in *Cullen* v. *Toibín* (discussed *infra*)—was that the case would be heard by a professional judge[18] rather than a lay tribunal. Statements or comments about a criminal case pending before a jury may be viewed less benevolently.[19]

The impugned statement or comment will constitute contempt only if a court has seisin of the case in respect of which contempt is alleged. In *State (D.P.P.)* v. *Independent Newspapers Ltd.* [1985] I.L.R.M. 183 the D.P.P. sought a conditional order of attachment in respect of material published in the *Evening Herald* on March 30, 1984. This stated that the D.P.P. intended to bring indecency charges against a local authority councillor. Neither the councillor nor the local authority was named, though his political party was identified; nor, at the time of publication, had any charge been brought. However, the grounding affidavit linked the publication with a charge brought against a named accused on April 1, 1984. O'Hanlon J. rejected the application, saying that it was very unusual for such an application to be brought in respect of material published before anyone had been charged in respect of a particular offence. He declined to follow *dicta* in certain English cases[20] indicating that this was competent. The judgment continues ([1985] I.L.R.M. 183, 184–185):

> " . . . I have not been referred to any decided case in this jurisdiction or in the other common law jurisdictions where attachment for contempt of

---

[18] This factor was also present in the leading U.S. case on contempt by publication—*Bridges* v. *California* (1941) 314 U.S. 252. A majority of the Supreme Court there held that statements relating to pending decisions, by judge alone, could be punished only if the threat to fair administration of justice was "extremely serious" and "the degree of imminence extremely high." It has been suggested that this test, as there applied, means "that almost nothing said outside the courtroom is punishable as contempt": Laurence Tribe, *American Constitutional Law* (Mineola, N.Y. 1978), p. 624. Though the U.S. Supreme Court has not had occasion to rule on statements alleged to cause possible prejudice in a jury trial, Professor Tribe thinks that the logic of *Nebraska Press Association* v. *Stuart* (1976) 427 U.S. 539 is that such statements cannot be punished as contempt. The philosophy underlying these decisions is clearly not accepted in other common law jurisdictions.

[19] The fear is usually that a jury may be prejudiced *against* the accused; but a comment or statement calculated or intended to generate prejudice in his/her favour is also a contempt. See *Att. Gen.* v. *Hibernia National Review Ltd.* (High Court, Pringle J., May 16, 1972), discussed in the Law Reform Commission's *Consultation Paper on Contempt of Court*, pp. 76–79.

[20] *R.* v. *Parke* [1903] 2 K.B. 432; *R.* v. *Daily Mirror* [1927] 1 K.B. 845; *R.* v. *Savundranayagan* [1968] 3 All E.R. 439.

court has been grounded upon material published when no court has actually had seisin of the case in respect of which contempt is alleged. As the courts must always have regard to the countervailing importance of preserving the freedom of the press, I do not consider that the facts disclosed in the affidavit grounding the present application are of such a character as would justify me in extending the law as to contempt of court in the manner now sought by the Director of Public Prosecutions."

It would thus appear that in Irish, as in Australian,[21] law there cannot be a contempt unless proceedings are pending at the time of the publication complained of. This condition will be satisfied if a person has been arrested and charged—*R.* v. *Clarke, ex p. Crippen* (1910) 103 L.T. 636—but, as the *Independent Newspapers* case shows, it is not enough that proceedings are "imminent."[22]

In the remarkable case of *Re MacArthur* [1983] I.L.R.M. 355 the applicant, then facing trial on murder charges, claimed that six contempt offences had been committed by the press and others. He had been arrested in the flat of the then Attorney General (Mr. Patrick Connolly), who shortly thereafter went abroad for a prearranged holiday. The intense media coverage of the affair brought about a change of plan and the Attorney General returned to Dublin. His subsequent offer to resign was accepted by the Taoiseach (Mr. Haughey), who held a press conference in which he praised the Gardaí for their investigation and said they had found "the right man."[23] This statement, claimed the applicant, was a contempt. Refusing the application, Costello J. noted that the Government Information Service had asked journalists not to report this remark, and that the remark was a slip of the tongue. He continued:

> "It is true that the test which the court is to apply in an application of this sort is whether the words complained of are calculated to prejudice the due course of justice (see *Keegan* v. *de Búrca* [1973] I.R. 223 at 227) and that the test is an objective test. (See *R.* v. *Evening Standard Co.* [1954] 1 Q.B. 578.) But if, as here, it is established that the words were spoken inadvertently in the course of a long press conference in which it was necessary to answer many questions, some of which touched on a pending criminal trial, and if it is shown, as it is shown here, that immediate steps were taken to avoid any possible prejudice . . . and . . . that any possible prejudice can be obviated by the direction which the trial judge can give to the jury, then it seems to me highly unlikely that the court would exercise its extraordinary punitive powers and punish such a person for contempt in the circumstances which I have outlined."

It was also alleged that the Taoiseach was in contempt in authorising publication of part of a letter written to him by the applicant. But Costello J. did not think it a contempt to publicise the applicant's statement to the Taoiseach that the former Attorney General was unaware that he (MacArthur)

---

[21] *James* v. *Robinson* (1963) 109 C.L.R. 593.

[22] The Law Reform Commission has recommended that, in certain limited circumstances, the law of contempt should extend to cover situations where criminal—or civil—proceedings are imminent: *Consultation Paper on Contempt of Court* (1991), pp. 320–321.

[23] These facts, not set out in the report, are taken from Joe Joyce and Peter Murtagh, *The Boss* (Dublin 1983), Chap. 11.

was under suspicion by the Gardaí. It was argued that part of this material was prejudicial to the accused but Costello J. observed that since contempt was a criminal offence it must be proved beyond a reasonable doubt. He was not satisfied that the applicant had established a prima facie case that a court would hold the words complained of capable of the meaning he alleged.

Costello J. found that some of the other allegations did not constitute contempt—*e.g.* to describe a dead person as murdered when someone stood charged with his murder. But the *Sunday World's* publication of a photograph of the applicant—given that visual identification of the accused might be an issue at the trial—was a prima facie contempt, notwithstanding that the possible prejudice might be obviated by the trial judge's direction to the jury. However, he declined to make a conditional order for attachment as matters then stood, saying ([1983] I.L.R.M. 355, 358):

> "Heretofore, in this country and in England applications in relation to criminal contempt in connection with pending criminal trials have been made by one or other of the law officers and presently the matter is being considered by the Director of Public Prosecutions. I think it is undesirable when the Director of Public Prosecutions is investigating possible contempts of court for an *ex parte* application to be brought by an accused himself pending the outcome of the Director's investigations. I will not refuse this application therefore, but adjourn it with liberty to re-enter it either before me or another judge of the High Court when the Director has indicated what steps he proposes to take in the light of the investigations which he has caused to be carried out. If the Director decides to make no application to the court then the question can then be considered whether the court has jurisdiction to make an order on the application of an accused person."

Costello J.'s implicit doubt regarding an accused person's standing to apply personally for attachment has not subsequently come up for resolution. *Cullen* v. *Toibín* [1984] I.L.R.M. 577 (discussed *infra*) assumes such power but is perhaps an authority *sub silentio*. But a rule under which only the D.P.P. could apply would be one of doubtful wisdom; to leave room, in the exceptional case, for an application by the accused would provide a fail-safe device against a possible error of judgment by the Director.[24] A practice under which such applications were permissible but, because lacking the D.P.P.'s sponsorship, were regarded sceptically by the court might strike the proper balance.

Some statutory provisions give courts a discretion to exclude the public from criminal trials in specified circumstances, but they add that this does not include bona fide representatives of the press.[25] An exception is section 5 of the Punishment of Incest Act 1908, by virtue of which all proceedings under that Act must be held *in camera*. This provision may well be open to constitutional challenge. Canadian courts have struck down similar sweep-

---

[24] Such is the position in England: see J. Ll. J. Edwards, *The Attorney General, Politics and the Public Interest* (London 1984), pp. 161–168. Note that this was one of the grounds on which the Supreme Court upheld a private individual's right to initiate a prosecution in *State (Ennis)* v. *District Justice Farrell* [1966] I.R. 107.

[25] Children Act 1908, ss.114 and 131, as amended by Children Act 1941, s.29: Criminal Justice Act 1951, s.20(3): Criminal Procedure Act 1967, s.16(2).

ing provisions in the juvenile justice field—*Re Southam Inc. and the Queen* (*No. 1*) (1983) 146 D.L.R. (3d) 408. But provisions vesting a discretion in the trial court to exclude the press if specified criteria are satisfied have been upheld: *Re Southam Inc. and the Queen* (*No. 2*) (1984) 14 D.L.R. (4th) 683.[26] Such provisions seem better calculated to strike the appropriate balance between the competing interests involved—freedom of the press on the one hand and protection from damaging publicity on the other. It is the policy adopted in the Criminal Law (Rape) Act 1981, s.6.[27]

Under section 17(1) of the Criminal Procedure Act 1967 no information in regard to a preliminary examination may be published, save the accused's name, the charge and the decision thereon (however, the District Justice may, at the accused's request, permit the publication of additional material: s.17(3)). A contravention of this provision is punishable by the High Court as if it were contempt of that court (*i.e.* imprisonment and/or fine, without limit)—s.17(2).[28] The object of this provision is clearly to ensure that if the accused is returned for trial, the jury will decide solely on the basis of the evidence then adduced. Its constitutionality has not yet been tested but it seems unlikely that any challenge to it would succeed. No doubt the virtual "no prior restraint" doctrine of United States constitutional law would be fatal to such a provision—see *Nebraska Press Association* v. *Stuart* (1976) 427 U.S. 539—but that doctrine is unlikely to win acceptance in Ireland. Among the substitutes for pre-trial publicity bans canvassed by the United States Supreme Court is "searching questioning of prospective jurors, to screen out those with fixed opinions as to guilt or innocence." This process can, of course, make the task of empanelling a jury almost interminable, and it would seem to be ruled out by the Court of Criminal Appeal's decision in *People* (*Att. Gen.*) v. *Lehman* (*No. 2*) [1947] I.R. 137. An Irish court is likely to prefer the reasoning upholding broadly similar provisions in *Re Southam Inc. and the Queen* (*No. 2*) *supra.*

Section 17 would not, of course, prevent the publication of a background article, or the broadcasting of a similar radio or television programme, while a trial was pending; but such action could constitute contempt, or be

---

[26] The Ontario High Court's decision in this case was confirmed by the Court of Appeal, and the Supreme Court of Canada refused leave to appeal: (1968) 26 D.L.R. (4th) 479.

[27] As inserted by the Criminal Law (Rape) (Amendment) Act 1990, s.11. This provides that in proceedings for rape and sexual assault offences the judge shall exclude from the court all persons save (*inter alios*) bona fide representatives of the press and such other persons as the judge may in his/her discretion permit to remain. Under s.6(2), however, only court officers and persons directly concerned in the proceedings may be present when an application for leave to adduce evidence, or ask questions, about the complainant's previous sexual experience is being heard.

[28] The constitutionality of this provision may be doubtful in the light of *Re Haughey* [1971] I.R. 217, where a similar formula in the Committee of Public Accounts (Privilege and Procedure) Act 1970, s.3(4) was condemned as invalid. This was because it created a non-minor offence (the possible punishment being imprisonment and/or fine without limit), yet provided only for summary trial thereof in the High Court. In addition, the High Court's jurisdiction to try criminal offences was a jurisdiction to try them only with a jury. The sole exception was the power to try contempt charges summarily—an exception based on the High Court's inherent jurisdiction under Article 34 to ensure the administration without obstruction. This was applied in *Desmond and Dedeir* v. *Glackin* (High Court, O'Hanlon J., February 25, 1992: Supreme Court, July 29, 1992) to invalidate the comparable phrase in s.10(5) of the Companies Act 1990. Clearly, however, s.17(2) of the 1967 Act is much more closely connected with the administration of justice than the provisions thus struck down.

restrainable by injunction, if calculated to prejudice a fair trial.[29] In *Cullen* v. *Toibín* [1984] I.L.R.M. 577 a person convicted of murder in the Central Criminal Court sought an injunction to restrain publication of an article about him in *Magill* magazine while his appeal to the Court of Criminal Appeal was pending. He claimed that publication would be prejudicial to the conduct of his appeal. The Supreme Court, reversing Barrington J., refused to grant the injunction. O'Higgins C.J. observed that the Court of Criminal Appeal would be asked to consider pure questions of law relative to the appeal. Publication of this article could not affect the objective consideration of legal arguments.[30] Moreover, the freedom of the press and of communication guaranteed by the Constitution could not be lightly curtailed. The courts could restrict it in the manner suggested here only where such action was necessary for the administration of justice. It must be noted, however, that the Supreme Court, differing from Barrington J., thought it "highly improbable" that the Court of Criminal Appeal would order a retrial. This suggests that had such a retrial been a possibility the result of the case might have been different.

The Criminal Law (Rape) Acts 1981 and 1990 forbid the publication or broadcasting, after a person has been charged with "a sexual assault offence"[31] of matter likely to identify the complainant (s.7(1)) or the accused (s.8(1)). However a court may relax these restrictions on various stated grounds. Contravention of these prohibitions is an offence punishable, on conviction on indictment, with a fine of up to £10,000 and/or imprisonment for up to three years (s.11) or, on summary conviction, with a fine not exceeding £1,000 and/or up to 12 months' imprisonment (s.12). It should also be noted that section 4 of the Offences against the State (Amendment) Act 1972—discussed *infra*—applies to criminal, as well as to civil, proceedings.

(b) *Restrictions relating to civil proceedings*[32]

The publication, or broadcasting, of material calculated or intended to prejudice the fair trial of a civil action constitutes contempt, and is punishable or restrainable by injunction. In *Lovell and Christmas* v. *O'Shaughnessy* (1934) 69 I.L.T.R. 33 the defendants in a civil action tried with a jury were erroneously described by counsel as *chartered* accountants (they were in fact *incorporated* accountants). The secretary of the Institute of Chartered Accountants wrote to the newspapers to correct this misdescription and his letter was published in the *Evening Herald*. Hanna J. said it was a contempt to publish during the hearing and pendency of an action comments on any of

---

[29] In May 1985, two Donegal-based itinerants sought an injunction to prevent R.T.É. from screening a programme about attacks on elderly people in the West of Ireland. The plaintiffs faced charges in relation to violent crimes and claimed that their trial in the Circuit Court in Donegal would be prejudiced were the programme shown. Hamilton P., who viewed the programme, allowed it to be broadcast, save for an interview lasting about three minutes: *The Irish Times*, May 31, 1985.

[30] In England a divisional court took a similar approach in *R.* v. *Duffy, ex p. Nash* [1960] 2 Q.B. 188. But *Cullen's* case is criticised in the Law Reform Commission's *Consultation Paper on Contempt of Court* as taking too extreme a line on judicial objectivity: see pp. 97–99.

[31] Defined in s.1 to include, *inter alia*, rape, attempted rape, burglary with intent to commit rape, aggravated sexual assault, attempted aggravated sexual assault, sexual assault and attempted sexual assault.

[32] See the Law Reform Commission's *Consultation Paper on Contempt of Court*, pp. 101–116.

the parties calculated to affect the free course of justice. This letter, he held, was calculated to give the impression that the defendants were in some way disparaged by not being chartered accountants, and it could have affected the minds of some jurors. Accordingly it was a contempt. Here, as in the criminal sphere, the concern is with a fair trial and with shielding jurors from possibly prejudicial material. Since trial by judge alone is now the norm, the danger of such prejudice is diminished.

In *State (Butterly)* v. *Moore and others (The Irish Times,* August 10, 1985) Murphy J. held that a song or ballad could constitute contempt just as much as a leading article in a newspaper. In this case the complaint was about a widely-distributed record featuring a song about the Stardust fire tragedy of February 1981. It was claimed by the applicants (the owners of the premises) that some of the lyrics prejudiced the fair trial of personal injury actions, shortly to be heard, in which they were defendants. Murphy J. agreed that this was so; statements in the lyrics went further than anything said by other commentators, and constituted a real and serious threat to a fair trial of the civil proceedings.

Statements or comments on pending civil proceedings may constitute contempt, apart from any threat to a fair trial, if they expose a party to public obloquy for bringing or defending the proceedings. The rationale underlying this is that the individual concerned is exercising his/her constitutional right of access to the courts, and must not be unlawfully obstructed in doing so. In *Desmond* v. *Glackin and ors.* (High Court, January 9, 1992) the applicant sought to have the second-named defendant, the Minister for Industry and Commerce (Mr. Desmond O'Malley, T.D.) attached for contempt in respect of remarks made during a radio interview. The Minister had appointed Mr. Glackin to conduct an inquiry under section 14 of the Companies Act 1990 into the control of certain companies involved in the purchase of a site in Dublin and its subsequent sale to the State-owned Telecom Éireann. This transaction had generated great public controversy, not least because the property had been sold for £4 million in 1989, whereas it had cost TÉ £9.4 million in 1990. The applicant, Mr. Desmond, who had been interviewed on several occasions by Mr. Glackin, decided to challenge the validity of Mr. Glackin's appointment, and of certain of his actions. He obtained both the High Court's leave to apply for judicial review and also certain reliefs pending the hearing of the judicial review application. On the following day the Minister gave a radio interview in which he reflected adversely on Mr. Desmond's attitude to the inquiry and his institution of the judicial review proceedings.[33] O'Hanlon J. said that the Minister's comments must be considered against the whole background of the "Telecom affair." In his affidavit in the judicial review proceedings Mr. Desmond had made serious allegations against the defendants, and these had been given widespread publicity. Having listed these, O'Hanlon J. continued (at p. 39 of his judgment):

"These are all serious allegations made against the Minister and the Inspector [Mr. Glackin], not merely of mistakes of law in the manner in

---

[33] It was also claimed that the Minister had been guilty of "scandalising the court," in that *inter alia* he had said that " . . . the High Court certainly facilitated Mr. Desmond in blocking the inquiry." But O'Hanlon J. held that, unfortunate as the Minister's choice of words was, this offence had not been established by the evidence.

which they are interpreting their powers, but of *mala fides* and improper motives in the manner in which Mr. Desmond is being treated and the statutory powers are being utilised. It is perfectly permissible to make such allegations and to seek to substantiate them in the course of the judicial review proceedings, but it seems to conflict with some of the basic principles of fair play if all these heavy blows can be delivered in open court on an *ex parte* application, and can be duly reported on a nationwide basis accompanied by a commentary from Mr. Desmond's public relations advisers, while denying the right to the Minister and the Inspector to reply immediately in equally forthright terms in defence of their own good name and reputation."

Though the Minister was ill-advised to give a live interview, said O'Hanlon J., the matter was an ongoing one which had occupied the public mind for months. In this situation, and in the context of the Minister's statements as a response to well-publicised allegations against him, the law struck the balance in favour of freedom of discussion. Moreover, where the court was in doubt whether the conduct complained of amounted to contempt, the complaint must fail.

Also relevant here is section 4 of the Offences against the State (Amendment) Act 1972, which provides as follows:

"(1)(*a*) Any public statement made orally, in writing or otherwise, or any meeting, procession or demonstration in public, that constitutes an interference with the course of justice shall be unlawful.

(*b*) A statement, meeting, procession or demonstration shall be deemed to constitute an interference with the course of justice if it is intended, or is of such a character as to be likely, directly or indirectly, to influence any court, person or authority concerned with the institution, conduct or defence of any civil or criminal proceedings (including a party or witness) as to whether or how the proceedings should be instituted, conducted, continued, or defended, or as to what should be their outcome."

One who makes a statement of the kind described is guilty of an offence and liable, on summary conviction, to a fine of up to £200 and/or 12 months' imprisonment or, on conviction on indictment, to a fine not exceeding £1,000 and/or up to five years' imprisonment. And section 4(3) provides:

"Nothing in this section shall affect the law as to contempt of court."

It does not appear that section 4 has ever been invoked, and there is certainly no judicial authority as to its interpretation. It would seem desirable that it should be applied in such a way as not to imperil legitimate freedom of expression, and to accord with the European Convention on Human Rights as expounded in the *Sunday Times* case.

Statute, in the form of the Censorship of Publications Act 1929, forbids the publication of certain material arising out of judicial proceedings. It is unlawful to print:

(a) any indecent matter the publication of which would be calculated to injure public morals, or

(b) any indecent medical, surgical or physiological details the publication of which would be calculated to injure public morals (s.14(1)).

Section 14(2) makes it unlawful to publish evidence given in proceedings for
divorce, nullity of marriage, judicial separation or restitution of conjugal
rights (though the names of the parties, the charges, defences and the court's
decision, *inter alia*, may be printed).[34] Under section 15 contravention of
these prohibitions is an offence punishable on summary conviction by a fine
of up to £500 and/or six months' imprisonment.

Section 14(2) is virtually identical to section 30(1) of the Alberta Judica-
ture Act, the validity of which was challenged before the Canadian Supreme
Court in *Edmonton Journal* v. *Att. Gen. for Alberta* (1989) 64 D.L.R. (4th) 577.
That court, by a 4–3 majority,[35] held that section 30(1) impermissibly
restricted the freedom of expression guaranteed by the Charter of Rights and
Freedoms. Cory J. (Dickson C.J. and Lamer J. concurring) stressed the
importance of the courts' role in society and said that this required that they
be open to public scrutiny and public criticism. This in turn depended on the
public's receipt of information *via* the newspapers or other media. Section
30(1) inhibited publication of important aspects of court proceedings, and
although it pursued a legitimate objective—protection of individual privacy—there was a lack of proportion between that objective and the means
chosen to attain it. Privacy could be protected by less sweeping measures, as
by giving the trial judge a discretion to prohibit publication or to hold *in
camera* hearings where necessary. Wilson J. agreed with this analysis.

Whether the Irish courts would reach the same conclusion about section
14(2) is a nice question. The importance of the courts' role in Irish society
cannot be gainsaid; and the administration of justice in public is a value
recognised in the Constitution, and emphasised by the Supreme Court in *Re
R. Ltd.* [1989] I.R. 126.[36] But the Constitution also protects individual privacy; thus section 14(2) represents a potential conflict of constitutional values
similar to that in the *Edmonton Journal* case.[37] Since the Irish Supreme Court
has accepted a proportionality principle,[38] the Canadian Supreme Court's
reasoning could be applied to section 14(2). However, such provisions are
capable of being justified as facilitating access to the courts, in that people
might be discouraged from seeking relief in matrimonial matters by fear of
undue publicity. In the *Edmonton Journal* case the majority could not accept
this justification, since the statistical evidence available did not support it;
Cory J. pointed out that in 1984 the divorce rate was some 20 times higher
than in 1935 and some 40 times higher than in 1920. It is clear that in Ireland
litigation of family law issues has considerably increased in recent years, but
this can hardly prove that to modify section 14(2) would not have a deterrent
effect.

[34] This was inspired by the U.K.'s Judicial Proceedings (Regulation of Reports) Act 1926—see
Michael Adams, *Censorship: The Irish Experience* (Alabama 1968), pp. 21–22, 40. Proceedings
for restitution of conjugal rights have been abolished by s.1 of the Family Law Act 1988.
[35] Dickson C.J., Lamer, Cory and Wilson JJ.: La Forest, L'Heureux-Dubé and Sopinka JJ. dissenting.
[36] See further Chap. 10 *supra*, *s.v.* Administration of Justice in Public.
[37] Where Wilson J. said (at 593): "In this case the values in conflict are the right of the public to
an open court process, which includes the right of the press to publish what goes on in the
courtroom, and the right of litigants to the protection of their privacy in matrimonial disputes. It is clear that both values cannot be fully respected given the context in which they
come into conflict in this case."
[38] See further Chap. 12 *supra*, *s.v.* Limiting Rights.

Perhaps some indication of the courts' likely approach to this matter may be found in the events preceding the Supreme Court hearing of the appeal in *Att. Gen.* v. *X.*—the controversial abortion case—in February 1992. The case had been listed for hearing *in camera*, and before it opened solicitors acting for *The Irish Times*, the *Irish Press* and the *Sunday Tribune* applied to the Registrar for leave to report on the proceedings on the ground of their unprecedented public interest and public and private importance. They undertook not to identify or approach the defendants, and to obey all directions of the court. This application was refused by the Registrar on behalf of the Chief Justice. When the court sat, counsel applied on behalf of RTÉ for the case to be heard in public because of the public interest therein. The court refused the application.[39]

(c) *Other restrictions*

Publication of the details of a case which has been heard *in camera*[40] will constitute contempt: *Re Kennedy and McCann* [1976] I.R. 382. So too will "wild and baseless allegations of corruption or malpractice"[41] made against a court or a judge. This latter form of contempt has the archaic description "scandalising the court." In *State (D.P.P.)* v. *Walsh* [1981] I.R. 412, 421 O'Higgins C.J. explained its ambit thus:

> "This form of contempt is committed where what is said or done is of such a nature as to be calculated to endanger public confidence in the court which is attacked and, thereby, to obstruct and interfere with the administration of justice. It is not committed by mere criticism of judges as judges, or by the expression of disagreement—even emphatic disagreement—with what has been decided by a court. The right of the citizens to express freely, subject to public order, convictions and opinions is wide enough to comprehend such criticism or expressed disagreement."

In an earlier case—*Re Hibernia National Review Ltd.* [1976] I.R. 388—Kenny J., speaking for the Supreme Court, had quoted (at 391) Lord Atkin's observations in *Ambard* v. *Att. Gen. for Trinidad and Tobago* [1936] A.C. 322, 335:

> " . . . no wrong is committed by any member of the public who exercises the ordinary right of criticising, in good faith, in private or public, the public act done in the seat of justice. The path of criticism is a public way: the wrong-headed are permitted to err therein: provided that members of the public abstain from imputing improper motives to those taking part in the administration of justice, and are genuinely exercising a right of criticism, and not acting in malice or attempting to impair the

---

[39] *The Irish Times*, February 25, 1992.
[40] The English Court of Appeal has held that there is an inherent jurisdiction in the High Court to impose restrictions on publication for the protection of children, *e.g.* in wardship cases: *Re M. and anor. (minors)* [1990] 1 All E.R. 205. But it is a delicate jurisdiction, involving a balancing exercise, in which the court must weigh the need to protect the ward from harm against the right of the press (or other outside bodies) to publish or to comment: *Re W. (a minor)* [1992] 1 All E.R. 794, where the Court of Appeal said that account must be taken of Art. 10 of the European Convention on Human Rights.
[41] *Per* O'Higgins C.J. in *State (D.P.P.)* v. *Walsh* [1981] I.R. 412, 421.

administration of justice, they are immune. Justice is not a cloistered virtue: she must be allowed to suffer the scrutiny and respectful, even though outspoken, comments of ordinary men."[42]

The *Walsh* and *Hibernia* cases both arose out of a trial for capital murder in the Special Criminal Court. A statement by Walsh (published *inter alia* in *The Irish Times*) had described that court as having so abused the rules of evidence as to make the court akin to a sentencing tribunal. But the Court of Criminal Appeal had found that the trial in question had been conducted with absolute fairness and could not be criticised; and the alleged contemnors had not tried to rebut this conclusion. The Supreme Court held that this statement was a major criminal contempt.[43] In the earlier *Hibernia* case the review of that name had published letters about the same trial which implied that it had been a travesty. The Supreme Court held that this was capable of amounting to contempt; but the court, having quoted the above words of Lord Atkin, was careful to add (*per* Kenny J. [1976] I.R. 388, 391):

> "The Court wishes to emphasise that criticism of the retention of the death penalty, of the Offences against the State Acts or any of their provisions, and of the establishment of the Special Criminal Court are not a contempt of court. These are matters which may validly be debated in public even if the comments made are expressed in strong language or are uninformed or foolish."

It would thus appear that "scandalising the court" has a restricted compass and that, in particular, it does not strike at criticism of judicial decisions, even where couched in intemperate terms. Nor should it inhibit discussion of alleged judicial malpractice, for it seems clear from the *Walsh* case that it is a defence to such a contempt charge to show that the allegations are true.

This aspect of contempt applies only to courts properly so called and to the judges of such courts. It has no relation to a judge acting in some extra-judicial capacity, such as chairing a commission or committee. The Judicial Committee so held in *Badry* v. *D.P.P. of Mauritius* [1982] 3 All E.R. 973.

Where a tribunal of inquiry has been established under the Tribunals of Inquiry (Evidence) Acts 1921 and 1979, statements or comments on the matters to be investigated which would, if the tribunal had been the High Court, have been contempt of that court constitute an offence. The penalty on conviction on indictment is a fine of up to £10,000 and/or imprisonment for up to two years; on summary conviction it is a fine of up to £500 and/or 12 months' imprisonment: 1979 Act, s.3.[44]

---

[42] See too the judgment of Carroll J. in *Weeland* v. *R.T.É.* [1987] I.R. 662.

[43] The court also held, by a majority, that where a major charge of criminal contempt (such as scandalising the court) involves live issues of fact (as where the accused denies the charge) the accused is entitled to have the issues of fact determined by a jury. But the question whether the facts so found amount to contempt is a question of law for the judge.

[44] The Law Reform Commission has recommended that such "deemed contempt" provisions (of which there are many) should be repealed: *Consultation Paper on Contempt of Court*, pp. 421–423. It suggests that: "The generic criminalisation of conduct in relation to tribunals by reference to contempt of the High Court must surely be unconstitutional in view of the arbitrary imposition of criminal responsibility which it necessarily involves" (p. 422). It suggests instead the creation of *specific* offences penalising conduct which would improperly impinge on the work of tribunals: pp. 427–431.

Public order and the authority of the State

Article 40.6.1°i declares, in its final paragraph, that is an offence to publish or utter seditious matter. Thus the common law on sedition is clearly continued in force. The scope of this offence—which in the 18th and 19th centuries was used oppressively against those who questioned the established order—is not precisely defined, but its gist appears to be an intention to incite people to violence.[45] No one seems to have been charged with sedition since the foundation of the State, doubtless because alternative charges are available under modern statutes—principally the Offences against the State Acts 1939–1972. These create a battery of offences restricting freedom of expression—advocating the usurpation or unlawful exercise of government functions (1939 Act, s.6), or the obstruction of government functions, legislative, executive or judicial (1939 Act, s.8). Section 9 of the 1939 Act makes it an offence to incite or encourage any State employee to refuse, neglect or omit to perform his duty, or to be negligent or insubordinate in its performance; likewise to advocate or encourage the doing of any such thing.[46]

The 1939 Act also strikes at "incriminating," "treasonable" and "seditious" documents.[47] An incriminating document is one issued by or emanating from an unlawful organisation, or calculated to promote the formation of such an organisation. "Treasonable document" includes a document relating directly or indirectly to the commission of treason. "Seditious document" covers *inter alia* documents "containing matter calculated or tending to undermine the public order or the authority of the State" or those "in which words, abbreviations or symbols referable to a military body are used in referring to an unlawful organisation." Under section 10 of the 1939 Act it is an offence to print, publish, distribute or offer for sale any incriminating, treasonable or seditious document. (Their possession is also unlawful: s.12.)

Section 10(2) is particularly sweeping in its scope. Under this provision it would be an offence for a newspaper or periodical to publish "any letter, article or communication" sent or contributed by or on behalf of an unlawful organisation, or a statement emanating from an unlawful organisation. In practice, however, newspapers have for years reported IRA and INLA statements claiming, or denying, responsibility for some murder or bombing, and no prosecutions have been launched. Clearly, though, section 10(2) captures a wide range of material, going well beyond the Act's own definitions of treasonable or seditious documents, and including communications on social or economic issues not obviously calculated to further the aims of the relevant unlawful organisation. In the United States a statute which swept so widely would be held unconstitutional—see, *e.g. Gooding* v. *Wilson* (1972) 405 U.S.

---

[45] See *R.* v. *Burns* (1886) 16 Cox C.C. 355; *R.* v. *Aldred* (1909) 22 Cox C.C. 1: also David Williams, *Keeping the Peace* (London 1967), pp. 197–204. The Law Reform Commission has doubted whether advocacy of violence is part of the definition of seditious matter in Irish law: *Consultation Paper on the Crime of Libel* (1991), pp. 59–61. Nonetheless, the Commission recommended the abolition, without replacement, of the common law offence of seditious libel; its essence was punishable under statutory provisions, and its unsettled ambit made it constitutionally doubtful: Chap. 7.

[46] A separate offence of causing, or attempting to cause, disaffection in the Garda Síochána is created by the Garda Síochána Act 1924, s.14, as extended by the Police Forces Amalgamation Act 1925, s.19.

[47] The 1972 Act, in s.5, expands the definition of "document" to include *inter alia* photographs, discs, tapes and films.

518: *Ernoznik* v. *Jacksonville* (1975) 422 U.S. 205. But although this "overbreadth" doctrine has won acceptance in the Irish Supreme Court,[48] the decision in *State (Lynch)* v. *Cooney* [1982] I.R. 337 (see *infra*) does not suggest that it would be applied in the freedom of expression context.

Sections 13 and 14 of the 1939 Act are concerned with the provenance of documents printed for reward. Under the former the printer must record on a copy of the relevant document the name and address of the person for whom it was printed; keep this copy for six months; and produce it for police inspection if required. Section 14 requires the printer of any document intended to be sold or distributed, or to be publicly or privately displayed, to print his name and business address on such document. Both sections, as noted above, apply only to documents *printed for reward*; thus they have no application where an organisation or body produces its own material.[49]

Save to the extent mentioned, the Offences against the State Acts do not restrict the freedom of the press; they contain no machinery for censorship[50] and there are no legal means by which the press may be told what should or should not be printed.[51] With the broadcasting media it is otherwise. The R.T.É. Authority, constituted under the Broadcasting Authority Acts 1960 and 1976, is subject to directives from the Minister for Communications issued under section 31(1) which, as substituted by section 16 of the 1976 Act, provides:

> "Where the Minister is of the opinion that the broadcasting of a particular matter or any matter of a particular class would be likely to promote, or incite to, crime or would tend to undermine the authority of the State, he may by order direct the Authority to refrain from broadcasting the matter or any matter of the particular class, and the Authority shall comply with the order."

Any such order is to remain in force for a maximum 12 months, but it may be extended for further periods, each of a maximum of 12 months: s.31(1A). Every order—including an extension order—must be laid before both Houses and may be annulled by resolution of either: s.31(B). By virtue of section 12 of the Radio and Television Act 1988, all such orders are binding on independent radio and television companies.

The principal order made under section 31(1) is now the Broadcasting Authority Act 1960 (s.31) Order 1983 (S.I. 1983 No. 17). This has been renewed annually by subsequent orders (and was preceded by others to similar effect). It directs the Authority to refrain from broadcasting "any matter which is an interview, or report of an interview" with a spokesman for various organisations—the IRA, Sinn Féin, the INLA, the UDA and "any organisation which in Northern Ireland is a proscribed organisation" under

---

[48] See the judgment of Henchy J. (Griffin and Parke JJ. concurring) in *King* v. *Att. Gen.* [1981] I.R. 233, 257.

[49] In *Talley* v. *California* (1960) 362 U.S. 60 the U.S. Supreme Court held unconstitutional a Los Angeles ordinance that penalised the distribution of handbills not bearing the names and addresses of those who prepared, distributed or sponsored them. The court, *per* Black J., said such an identification requirement restricted freedom to distribute information and thus freedom of expression. Identification and fear of reprisal might deter perfectly peaceful discussions of public matters of importance.

[50] Such machinery existed, and gave rise to much controversy, under the Emergency Powers Acts of the wartime period: see Robert Fisk, *op. cit.*, 162–171 and Appendix 1.

[51] See Woodman, *op. cit.*, p. 201. Self-censorship does of course exist: *ibid.*, pp. 202–203.

section 28 of the U.K.'s Northern Ireland (Emergency Provisions) Act 1973. R.T.É. has also produced guidelines for staff regarding compliance with this order.[52]

Two matters in relation to this order call for comment. One is that Sinn Féin—though well known as the political wing of the IRA—is not itself an unlawful organisation; no suppression order under the Offences against the State Act 1939, s.19 has been made against it. Nonetheless the order prohibits interviews with party spokesmen on any topic whatsoever. It is not clear that section 31, construed in the light of Article 40.6.1°i, authorises the making of so sweeping an order. The second is the extension of the ban to organisations proscribed under Northern Ireland law. This too is of questionable validity. In effect the Minister, the delegate of the Oireachtas, has sub-delegated his power to the Secretary of State for Northern Ireland—the latter is empowered to decide who may be interviewed on R.T.É. programmes. This sits uneasily with Article 15.2.1° of the Constitution. It *may* be that the Oireachtas itself could make such provision by statute,[53] but it is doubtful that it can be made by Ministerial order. Moreover there is a general principle that a legislative power must be exercised by the person to whom it is given, unless statute expressly or impliedly provides for sub-delegation.[54] Section 31(1) does not appear to do this.

Another order under section 31(1) was made on February 9, 1982.[55] A general election was then in progress and the R.T.É. Authority had allocated television and radio time to the various parties, including Sinn Féin which had seven candidates in the field. Sinn Féin was given five two-minute programmes which were to be broadcast on February 10 and 11. The order prohibited the transmission of:

"(a) a broadcast, whether purporting to be a political party broadcast or not, made by, or on behalf of, or advocating, offering or inviting support for the organisation styling itself Provisional Sinn Féin

(b) a broadcast by any person or persons representing, or purporting to represent, the said organisation."

(The substance of this order is now contained in that of 1983 referred to above.)

In *State (Lynch)* v. *Cooney* [1982] I.R. 337 the person selected by Sinn Féin to make its broadcasts challenged the validity of the Minister's order, contending *inter alia* that section 31(1) was unconstitutional. In the High Court O'Hanlon J. concluded that section 31(1) vested in the Minister an absolute discretion not amenable to judicial review. This went further than was constitutionally permissible, given the guarantee of Article 40.6.1°i. On appeal, the Supreme Court overruled the *dicta* in its earlier decisions which had led O'Hanlon J. to hold the Minister's decision unreviewable. Section 31(1) had

---

[52] These are printed by Woodman, *op. cit.*, pp. 236–239, who also discusses the directive's impact within R.T.É.—pp. 189–196.

[53] See *State (Devine)* v. *Larkin* [1977] I.R. 24, discussed in Chap. 2 *supra*. But that case concerned a fishery which straddled the border and had to be regulated by agreement between the two states.

[54] See H. W. R. Wade, *Administrative Law* (6th ed., Oxford 1988) Chap. 11: S. A. de Smith, *Judicial Review of Administrative Action* (4th ed., London 1980) pp. 300–309: Paul Craig, *Administrative Law* (London 1983) pp. 372–373.

[55] The Broadcasting Authority Act 1960 (s.31) (No. 2) Order 1982 (S.I. 1982 No. 21).

to be construed in accordance with the Constitution; so construed it did not exclude review by the courts, and any opinion formed thereunder by the Minister must be factually sustainable and not unreasonable. The Supreme Court went on to consider the arguments that the Minister's order was *ultra vires* section 31(1), all of which it rejected. In particular the court dismissed the contention that the actual broadcasts contained no material deserving condemnation. Whatever their contents, it was held, they were intended to seek support for Sinn Féin; and on the uncontroverted evidence the Minister had reasonable grounds for believing that Sinn Féin aimed at undermining the authority of the State.[56]

In *O'Toole* v. *R.T.É.* *(The Irish Times,* August 1, 1992) the defendant body's interpretation of the Ministerial order under section 31 was successfully challenged. The plaintiff, a member of Sinn Féin, had been elected chairman of the strike committee during a protracted dispute at a Dublin bakery. In that capacity he was interviewed six times by R.T.É., but only one interview was broadcast; when R.T.É. discovered that he was a Sinn Féin member they declined to transmit any others. This was apparently on the basis that under the section 31 order, R.T.É. was precluded from broadcasting interviews with Sinn Féin members. O'Hanlon J. ruled that this was incorrect and granted declarations accordingly. The judge said that no member of the public had an automatic right to be heard on radio or television. The broadcasting authority must have a general power to regulate programmes and determine their contents. But this power was circumscribed by the Broadcasting Authority Acts and the Constitution. O'Hanlon J. pointed out that there was no evidence that the plaintiff had, in any of the interviews, identified himself as a Sinn Féin spokesman, or mentioned Sinn Féin in any way. Under section 18 of the Broadcasting Authority Act 1960 R.T.É. had an obligation of impartiality and objectivity in regard to matters of public controversy or political debate. This obligation, said O'Hanlon J., was infringed when R.T.É. refused on arbitrary grounds to allow the views of workers involved in a major industrial dispute to be put forward by their elected spokesman. The Ministerial order did not prohibit all access to the airwaves by Sinn Féin members (had it done so, the judge indicated, its compatibility with section 31 would have been open to considerable doubt). Hence the obligation imposed by section 18 had not been qualified in the way suggested by R.T.É. And just as that obligation would be breached if R.T.É., on its own authority, denied access to the airwaves on criteria of race, colour or creed, the same would hold if it did so on the basis of membership of non-proscribed organisations such an Sinn Féin.

Section 31(1) is, of course, directed only at radio and television. But the terms of Article 40.6.1°i are broad enough to permit similar legislation applicable to the press—for this is one of the "organs of public opinion" referred to therein. No such legislation has, however, been enacted.

Under section 4(1) of the Prohibition of Forcible Entry and Occupation

---

[56] The European Commission on Human Rights subsequently upheld the orders made under s.31 against challenge under Article 10 of the Convention. Though constituting an interference with freedom to receive and impart information and ideas, such orders had the legitimate aim of protecting national security and preventing disorder and crime. Since they also qualified as "necessary in a democratic society," they were justified under Art. 10(2): *The Irish Times,* June 11, 1991.

Act 1971 it is an offence to encourage or advocate the commission of the offence of forcible entry of land or a vehicle.[57] The penalties are set out in section 7. A much wider prohibition is contained in section 5 of the Misuse of Drugs Act 1984, which prohibits *inter alia* the publication, sale or distribution of books, periodicals or other publications which advocate or encourage the use of any controlled drug[58] (otherwise than in treatment by a doctor). The prohibition extends to any publication containing advertisements advertising "any use of a pipe, utensil or other thing" in connection with a controlled drug.

Finally, the Prohibition of Incitement to Hatred Act 1989 makes it an offence—in specified circumstances—to publish, distribute or display written material, or to use words, or to distribute, show or play a recording of visual images or sounds. The written material, words, etc. must, however, be "threatening, abusive or insulting" *and* intended or likely, having regard to all the circumstances, to stir up hatred (s.2). This key term is defined in section 1 to mean "hatred against a group of persons in the State or elsewhere on account of their race, colour, nationality, religion, ethnic or national origins, membership of the travelling community or sexual orientation." The broadcasting of threatening, abusive or insulting visual images or sounds intended or likely to stir up hatred is likewise an offence (s.3(1)). So, too, is the preparation or possession likely to stir up hatred (s.4(1)). The Act sets out certain defences, and as an additional safeguard proceedings under sections 2, 3 and 4 may be taken only by, or with the consent of, the Director of Public Prosecutions: section 8. Persons found guilty of offences under those sections are liable, on summary conviction, to a fine not exceeding £1,000 and/or a maximum six months' imprisonment; on conviction on indictment, to a fine not exceeding £10,000 and/or imprisonment for up to two years.

Access to official information

In *Cullen* v. *Toibín* [1984] I.L.R.M. 577, 581 McCarthy J. spoke of the citizen's " . . . right to be informed." The source, and scope, of this right was not identified, but it might well derive by implication from Article 40.6.1°i or, alternatively, from the unenumerated right to communicate invoked by Costello J. in *Att. Gen. & Minister for Posts & Telegraphs* v. *Paperlink Ltd.* [1984] I.L.R.M. 373. Whatever its source, this right is clearly no more absolute than

---

[57] s.4(2) goes on to provide that where a statement in contravention of subs. (1) is made by or on behalf of a group of persons, every person who is a member of the group and who consented to the making of the statement shall be guilty of an offence under that subsection. By virtue of s.4(3), in a prosecution of a group member for a s.4(1) offence, the court, having regard to all the circumstances, " . . . may regard proof of the defendant's membership of the group and of the making of the statement by or on behalf of the group as proof of consent on the part of the defendant in the absence of any adequate explanation by him." In *Dooley* v. *Att. Gen.* [1977] I.R. 205 several provisions of the 1971 Act—including s.4(3)—were assailed as invalid. The report states (at 207) that on July 14, 1975 " . . . the Chief Justice stated that the Supreme Court would not express at that stage any opinion on the constitutionality of s.4, subs. 3, of the Act of 1971." Griffin J. then delivered the court's single judgment on the other impugned provisions, ss.1, 2 and 3, which had been attacked as violating Article 40's pledge of equality, the argument being essentially that it penalised conduct by certain individuals which, if engaged in by other persons similarly circumstanced, was not so affected. The court found itself able to interpret those provisions so as to avoid this conclusion.

[58] As defined in the Misuse of Drugs Act 1977, s.2.

any other; it may have to cede priority to competing constitutional values. The citizen presumably cannot claim an untrammelled right of access to official information, even for the purpose of communicating it. And the existing law strives officiously to make this clear. Only to a limited extent does the law recognise a right of access to official information, whether for the purpose of communicating it or otherwise. Under the National Archives Act 1986 there is a general right to inspect Departmental records[59] over 30 years old (s.10(1)); but this does not apply where an authorised officer certifies under section 8(4) that to make specified material available for public inspection would be "contrary to the public interest" (a term not further defined).[60] It is lawful for a Government Minister to grant access to Departmental records less than 30 years old (s.10(6)), but this is a matter of executive grace and favour.[61] Given that Ministers have occasionally refused information even to members of the Oireachtas, it is unlikely that this power to grant access will be much used.

Professor Chubb has noted that the Irish administrative tradition is "one of considerable reticence, even secrecy."[62] This may originate in the similar tradition in Britain, and it is noteworthy that the Irish legislation on official secrets finds its roots in that of the United Kingdom. But it has been invoked relatively infrequently and has generated nothing like the controversies of its United Kingdom counterpart.[63] The legislation—the Official Secrets Act 1963—deals in Part III with spying ("prejudice to the safety or preservation of the State"); but there appears to have been only one prosecution under that Part.[64] Part II ranges much more widely, and the Act is thus open to Professor Mathews' objection of "conflat(ing) and confus(ing) acts of spying with the simple disclosure of official information."[65]

The kernel of the Act lies in sections 4 and 6. Section 4(1) provides that a person shall not communicate any official information to any other person unless he is duly authorised to do so, or he does so in the course of duty as holder of a public office, or it is "his duty in the interest of the State" to communicate it. "Official information" covers any information "which is secret or confidential or expressed to be either." This obviously leaves the issue of classifying information wholly to executive discretion (in contrast with U.S. law)[66] so that everything not expressly exempted could be categorised as secret or confidential. "Duly authorised" means authorised by a Minister or

---

[59] Widely defined in the Act to include Cabinet records, those of individual Departments and of many other bodies (*e.g.* the Revenue Commissioners, the Garda Síochána and the D.P.P.): see s.1(2), s.2, and the Schedule.

[60] s.8(4) also covers (*inter alia*) material containing information supplied in confidence, or which would or might cause distress or danger to living persons, or would or might be likely to lead to defamation proceedings.

[61] In the preface to his book *The Vatican, the Bishops and Irish Politics 1919–39* (Cambridge 1986) Dermot Keogh states that in 1977 he was granted access to Department of Foreign Affairs archives by the then Minister, Dr. Garret FitzGerald; but he had not, by 1985, succeeded in having the decision acted upon by the Department!

[62] *The Government and Politics of Ireland*, p. 326.

[63] As to which see Anthony Mathews, *The Darker Reaches of Government* (Cape Town 1978) Chap. VI: James Michael, *The Politics of Secrecy* (Harmondsworth 1982), Chap. 3.

[64] *People (Att. Gen.)* v. *Crinnion and Wyman* [1976] I.R. 29. Note that proceedings under this Act may be partly *in camera;* s.12.

[65] *Op. cit.*, p. 102.

[66] As to which see Mathews, *op. cit.* pp. 56–61: Stephen Breyer and Richard Stewart, *Administrative Law and Regulatory Policy* (2nd ed., Boston 1985), pp. 1231–32.

State authority[67] or by some person authorised in that behalf by a Minister or State authority (*e.g.* a senior public servant). As to "duty in the interest of the State," this presumably covers a situation where a public servant discloses confidential information in order to reveal alleged Ministerial or official wrongdoing. (This seems to have occurred when the Opposition leader was informed about the events leading to the "Arms Crisis" of May 1970, and when the story of irregular telephone tapping broke in 1982.)

Section 4(3) makes it unlawful for a person to obtain official information where he is aware, or has reasonable grounds for believing, that its communication would contravene section 4(1). Under section 6 a person shall not retain any official document, or anything constituting or containing official information, when he has no right to retain it. This does not apply to a former Minister or Minister of State, who does not therefore commit an offence should he or she take away original documents on quitting office: section 6(3).[68] Restrictions are also placed by section 5 on disclosure by contractors or their employees of confidential information in State contracts. The penalties are stipulated in section 13. Prosecution on indictment is applicable only where there is prejudice to the safety or preservation of the State; otherwise offences are triable only summarily, with a penalty on conviction of a fine not exceeding £100 and/or six months' imprisonment (s.13(2)). Proceedings under the Act require the Attorney General's consent (s.14(1)): thus the normal rule under which an individual, a Garda or a Minister could prosecute summarily as a common informer is here set aside,[69] and this affords some safeguard.

Although, as noted above, the Act has seldom been invoked, it has not remained a dead letter.[70] In 1976 *The Irish Times* was threatened with prosecution when it was about to publish details of a proposed deal between the State and Bula Mining Ltd., but no proceedings ensued. On February 3, 1984 the *Irish Independent's* editor was convicted of violating the Act by publishing two photo-fit pictures circulated in a Garda internal bulletin. The following day *The Irish Times* criticised the affair in an editorial, claiming that the bulletin was far from being a confidential document, and that the information it contained was invariably "low-grade stuff." The Act, said the editorial, was "breached hundreds of times each day, by reporters, researchers, social workers, members of the general public—anyone who seeks information through anything other than strictly laid-down and usually slow and unsatisfactory channels." The Act, it was claimed, was outdated and ought to be refined.

While some official information clearly needs the kind of protection given by the 1963 Act, this cannot be true of it all. The matter needs re-examin-

---

[67] Defined in s.2 to mean the Attorney General, the Comptroller and Auditor General, the Revenue Commissioners, the Commissioners of Public Works or the Irish Land Commission.

[68] The Taoiseach may direct such a person to return the original documents (presumably he or she may keep copies) "and any such person shall comply with all such directions": s.6(3). No sanction is provided for in the event of non-compliance.

[69] As to this see J. P. Casey, *The Office of the Attorney General in Ireland* (Dublin 1980), Chap. 6. The Attorney's role under s.14(1) is not affected by the Prosecution of Offences Act 1974 (which established the D.P.P.)—see s.3(5) of that Act.

[70] In the period May 30, 1972–August 31, 1974 10 persons were convicted in the Special Criminal Court of offences under the Act: see Mary Robinson, *The Special Criminal Court* (Dublin 1974), p. 47.

ation, especially in the light of the freedom of information legislation now in force in many common law countries.[71]

Public morals

The final paragraph of Article 40.6.1°i states that the "publication or utterance of . . . indecent matter is an offence which shall be punishable in accordance with law." The Oireachtas thus has no discretion as to penalising such conduct—though it would appear to have some leeway in giving content to the vague term "indecent," as it has done. But the word's presence in the Constitution would seem to preclude any challenge to a statute which employs it, based on the contention that it is too vague to be a valid regulation of free expression.[72]

At common law the publication of obscene material was an indictable offence: *R.* v. *Hicklin* (1868) L.R. 3 Q.B. 360.[73] After independence, however, it was decided that an alternative mode of control was required and legislation providing for a form of censorship was enacted.[74] This system is still in place, its statutory basis being the Censorship of Publications Act 1946 and 1967. Unlike the wartime censorship of newspapers it is not a system of prior examination; rather, it takes effect only following publication. The Censorship of Publications Board—which consists of five persons appointd by the Minister for Justice—is empowered to make prohibition orders in respect of books and periodical publications. The statutes specifically empower customs officials to detain books on importation, for the purpose of forwarding them to the Board for examination (1946 Act, s.5). The Board may also receive complaints about books from members of the public, and additionally act on their own initiative (s.6 *ibid.*). Section 14 then provides that it is an offence, save in accordance with a permit,[75] to "sell, or expose, offer, advertise or keep for sale" or "distribute, or offer or keep for distribution" any prohibited book or periodical publication. Such an offence is triable only summarily, the penalty being a fine of up to £50 and/or six months' imprisonment—and the forfeiture of the material (1946 Act, s.14(2)).

Section 6(2) of the 1946 Act directs the Board to have regard to certain matters, including the literary, artistic, scientific or historic merit or importance of the book, and the nature and extent of its likely circulation. Under section 6(3) the Board "may" communicate with the author, editor or publisher and take into account any representation made by him. In *Irish Family Planning Association Ltd.* v. *Ryan* [1979] I.R. 295 the Supreme Court held that the Board had a discretion in this matter, which must be exercised in a just

[71] Accounts of such legislation may be found in Mathews, *op. cit.* and Michael, *op. cit.*
[72] See, for example, *Re Luscher and Deputy Minister, Revenue Canada* (1985) 17 D.L.R. (4th) 503, where a statutory provision forbidding the importation of material " . . . of an immoral or indecent character" was held unconstitutional because too vague. The court said that the words "immoral" and "indecent" (which were not further defined) were highly subjective and emotional in their content, and the subject of widely differing opinions honestly held by reasonable people.
[73] The ingredients of the offence of obscene libel are analysed in the Law Reform Commission's *Consultation Paper on the Crime of Libel* (1991), Chap. 5. In Chap. 9 the Commission notes that there is a substantial number of legislative provisions for the regulation of obscene matter, and it consequently recommended the abolition of the common law offence.
[74] For the background see the previously cited works of Adams and Woodman.
[75] Granted at his/her discretion by the Minister for Justice—s.19, 1946 Act. It would follow from *East Donegal Co-Op Ltd.* v. *Att. Gen.* [1970] I.R. 317 that this discretion is not unfettered.

and fair manner. They could not adopt a general policy of never communicating with the persons mentioned.

Where the Board, having examined a book, are of opinion that

(a) it is "indecent or obscene," or
(b) it "advocates the procurement of abortion or miscarriage or the use of any method, treatment or appliance for the purpose of such prevention or procurement"[76]

they may by order prohibit its sale and distribution (s.7). "Indecent" is defined in section 1 as including "suggestive of, or inciting to, sexual immorality or unnatural vice or likely in any other similar way to corrupt or deprave." The word "obscene" is not defined in the legislation, but at common law the test of obscenity was "whether the tendency of the matter charged as obscene was to deprave and corrupt those whose minds are open to such immoral influences and into whose hands a publication of this sort may fall"—*R.* v. *Hicklin* (1868) L.R. 3 Q.B. 360, 371. There would thus appear to be a degree of overlap between "indecent" (as defined) and "obscene." The latter term, however, is not confined to sexual corruption or depravity: in *John Calder (Publications) Ltd.* v. *Powell* [1965] 1 Q.B. 509 it was held that advocacy of drug-taking constituted obscenity.

In *Irish Family Planning Association Ltd.* v. *Ryan* [1979] I.R. 295 Kenny J. said (at 319):

> "The words 'indecent or obscene' in the Act of 1946 mean that the book is, in its general tendency, indecent or obscene. They do not mean that there are indecent or obscene passages in the book: if they did, a prohibition order could be made in respect of Shakespeare's plays for they (*e.g.* 'Timon of Athens') contain indecent or obscene passages. But this is absurd and leads me to the conviction that 'indecent or obscene' in the Act of 1946 means 'in its general tendency indecent or obscene.' These latter words were used in the Censorship of Publications Act, 1929 but, for some reason, were omitted from the Act of 1946. Their omission, in my opinion, makes no difference to the meaning of the words 'indecent or obscene.' "

The other members of the Court did not refer to this matter but, given section 6(2), Kenny J.'s conclusion seems unimpeachable.

So far as periodical publications (defined in s.1) are concerned, the Board must, upon complaint, examine "the issues recently theretofore published." They may make a prohibition order if of opinion that the said issues "have usually or frequently" been indecent or obscene; or have advocated the procurement of abortion; or "have devoted an unduly large proportion of space to the publication of matter relating to crime"[77]—section 9. There is nothing corresponding to section 6(2), nor any reference to communicating with the editor or publisher; but in some situations at least for the Board to act with-

---

[76] Originally books advocating "the unnatural prevention of conception" were also included, but the words quoted were deleted from s.7 by s.12(3) of the Health (Family Planning) Act 1979.

[77] This latter provision does not appear to have been invoked for many years. If it were it would surely be vulnerable to constitutional challenge for intolerable vagueness. Many reputable newspapers—not least in Ireland—could fall foul of this by simply publishing bona fide news reports and articles. And while the indecency ground can claim constitutional sanction, as can that re abortion (see Art. 40.3.3°), this cannot.

out doing so might be held to violate the constitutional guarantee of fair procedures (see Chap. 12 *supra*).

Where a prohibition order has been made in regard to a book or publication,[78] an appeal lies to the Appeal Board (see ss.8 and 10). This body comprises five persons appointed by the Minister for Justice, the chairman being a qualified lawyer (s.3). An appeal may be lodged, in the case of a book, by the author, editor or publisher, or by any five deputies or senators (s.8(1)): in the case of a periodical publication, by the publisher or any five deputies or senators (s.10(1)).

It should be noted that the Acts do not make the private possession of indecent or obscene material an offence. Any legislation which attempted this might be constitutionally vulnerable as an unwarranted intrusion on individual privacy.[79] But the customs authorities have a general power to seize indecent or obscene material under the Customs Consolidation Act 1876, s.42. These powers are declared not to be affected by the censorship of publications legislation (s.5(4), 1946 Act); however, it appears that customs officials in practice confine themselves to using their powers under that legislation to refer material to the Censorship Board (and to detaining material prohibited by it).[80]

At one time the Board's operations caused much controversy; some of the works banned were of unquestionable literary merit and could not reasonably be regarded as indecent or obscene.[81] Nowadays, however, it impinges very little on the public consciousness.[82] The possibility of a constitutional challenge to its existence thus seems remote[83]—though grounds for such a challenge may exist. In *Irish Family Planning Association Ltd.* v. *Ryan* [1979] I.R. 295 all members of the Supreme Court said that the making of a prohibition order carried the implication that those responsible for the publication were guilty of a criminal offence. This consorts oddly with the Constitution's requirement that criminal justice be administered only by courts and judges—see Chapter 9 *supra*. Admittedly the Board does not try, convict or sentence people; but a prohibition order made by it may ground criminal proceedings. The Board may not be administering criminal justice but it is

---

[78] Under s.13 every prohibition order must be published in *Iris Oifigiúil*; and s.16 obliges the Board to maintain a register of prohibited publications, which is open to public inspection (s.16(7)).

[79] The U.S. Supreme Court so held in *Stanley* v. *Georgia* (1969) 394 U.S. 557.

[80] See Adams, *op. cit.*, pp. 171–175. In September 1985 it was reported that customs officials had stopped a consignment of "Breaking the Silence—Lesbian Nuns on Convent Sexuality," with a view to referring the book to the Board. But a senior official overruled this decision (*The Irish Times*, September 3, 1985). It should be noted that customs officials may not detain, for the purpose of reference to the Board, a book carried by or forming part of the personal luggage of an incoming traveller: s.5(3), 1946 Act.

[81] See Adams, *op. cit.*, p. 192: pp. 247–249 list some books banned in the period 1946–1966. They include, *e.g.* Kingsley Amis' *Lucky Jim*: Aldous Huxley's *The Devils of Loudun* and Ernest Hemingway's *Fiesta*.

[82] Note, however, that the Law Reform Commission has suggested " . . . that an examination of (a) legislation on obscene and indecent matter and (b) the various schemes of censorship is necessary if we are to attach due weight to the Irish Constitutional guarantee of free speech": *Consultation Paper on the Crime of Libel* (1991), p. 156.

[83] In the *Irish Family Planning Association* case the relief sought included declarations that ss.6 and 7 of the 1946 Act were unconstitutional (see [1979] I.R. 295 at 297). However, since the Board's order was held *ultra vires* the court found it unnecessary to rule on the constitutional question raised.

exercising a judicial power[84] and it is questionable whether that power is "limited" in terms of Article 37.1.

Censorship of films is regulated by the Censorship of Films Act 1923–1970. These make provision for the office of Official Censor and stipulate (1923 Act, s.5) that it is an offence to show a film *in public* unless the Official Censor has certified that it is fit for public exhibition. The censor may grant a limited certificate laying down specific conditions (*e.g.* as to the classes of persons who may see the film): section 6(1), 1923 Act. He/she may refuse a certificate if of opinion that a film, or part thereof, is "indecent, obscene or blasphemous" or because its public exhibition "would tend to inculcate principles contrary to public morality or would be otherwise subversive of public morality"—section 7(2), 1923 Act (though a restricted certificate may still be granted: s.7(3) *ibid.*). From that decision an appeal lies to an Appeal Board consisting of nine members appointed by the Minister for Justice; the quorum is three—1923 Act, s.3, as amended by 1925 Act, s.6.[85]

As Dr. Woodman observes,[86] censorship of films never generated the same controversy as censorship of books. This may have been in part because film societies could show uncertified films to their members. No doubt too the censor nowadays applies the very vague language[87] of the legislation in a commonsense way, aware that television has ruled out Grundyism in this field.

The Official Censor is given a new, analogous, role under the Video Recordings Act 1989. He/she is empowered to grant "supply certificates" in respect of video works, declaring them to be fit for viewing (s.3(1)), and is required to classify them by reference to the age of those who may view them (s.4(1)). It is an offence to supply or offer to supply an uncertificated video work (s.5(1)); to have such an article in one's possession for purposes of supply (s.6(1)); or to exhibit it elsewhere than in a private dwelling (s.11(1)). Where the Official Censor is of opinion that the work is unfit for viewing he/she is to make a prohibition order in respect of it (s.3(3)). It is an offence to possess for purposes of supply a recording of a prohibited work (s.8(1)); to supply or offer to supply such a recording (s.9(1)); to exhibit it elsewhere than in a private dwelling (s.11(1)); or to import it into the State without a permit (s.16(1)).

The grounds upon which the Censor may find the video work unfit for viewing (and so refuse a supply certificate and make a prohibition order) are wider than those under the Censorship of Films Acts. They are stated thus in section 3(1)[88]:

" . . . that the work is unfit for viewing because—

---

[84] Kenny J. so held in the *Irish Family Planning Association* case (see p. 319 of the report).

[85] The 1925 Act extended the Censor's powers to cover pictorial advertisements for films, and the 1930 Act to sound-tracks.

[86] *Op. cit.*, p. 124.

[87] That they would not survive constitutional scrutiny in the U.S. is shown by *Interstate Circuit Inc.* v. *Dallas* (1968) 390 U.S. 676, where a much more detailed film censorship ordinance was held too vague. Perhaps an Irish court would prefer the view of Harlan J., the sole dissenter, who said (at 709): " . . . the Court has demanded greater precision of language from the City of Dallas than the Court can itself give, or even than can sensibly be expected in this area of the law."

[88] The Censor may not refuse a supply certificate in respect of a video work which enjoys a certificate under the Censorship of Films Acts: s.3(2). But he/she is empowered to make a prohibition order in respect of such a work, in which case the supply certificate would lapse: s.7(2).

(*a*) the viewing of it—
   (i) would be likely to cause persons to commit crimes, whether by inciting or encouraging them to do so or by indicating or suggesting ways of doing so or of avoiding detection, or
   (ii) would be likely to stir up hatred against a group of persons in the State or elsewhere on account of their race, colour, nationality, religion, ethnic or national origins, membership of the travelling community or sexual orientation, or
   (iii) would tend, by reason of the inclusion in it of obscene or indecent matter, to deprave or corrupt persons who might view it,
   or
(*b*) it depicts acts of gross violence or cruelty (including mutilation or torture) towards humans or animals.''

An appeal against a prohibition order, or a classification decision, lies to the Censorship of Films Appeal Board: section 10. Orders of the Board revoking a prohibition order must be published in *Íris Oifigiúil* (s.10(5)), as must all prohibition orders (s.7(3)). The Censor is also obliged to maintain a Register of Certificated Video Works (s.14(1)) and one of Prohibited Video Works (s.15(1)); both may be inspected by members of the public free of charge at all reasonable times.[89]

At least one film—the Monty Python *Life of Brian*—appears to have been refused a certificate as blasphemous, but otherwise this ancient offence has had no impact in modern Irish legal practice. Nonetheless the Constitution itself declares that the publication or utterance of blasphemous material is an offence punishable in accordance with law: Article 40.6.1°i. Spoken blasphemy is a common law misdemeanour punishable by fine and/or imprisonment. Written blasphemy is covered by the Defamation Act 1961, s.13(1) which provides that every person who composes, prints or publishes any blasphemous libel shall, on conviction on indictment, be liable to a fine not exceeding £500 or imprisonment for up to two years, or both, or to penal servitude for up to seven years. Section 13(2) makes provision for the seizure and disposal, following conviction, of the blasphemous matter.

In England it has been held that the essence of blasphemous libel is an indecent and offensive attack on Christianity or the scriptures, or on sacred persons or objects, calculated to outrage the feelings of the general body of the community: see the Court of Appeal decision in *R.* v. *Lemon* [1978] 3 All E.R. 175. It is not necessary to prove an intention to blaspheme: *R.* v. *Lemon* [1979] 1 All E.R. 895 (H.L.). Moderate and reasoned comment on such matters, even if it be hostile, does not attract liability. It seems safe to conclude that Irish law is to the same effect[90]—though no prosecution for blas-

---

[89] According to a report in *The Irish Times*, March 26, 1992, the total number of works banned by then had reached 54.

[90] The present Irish law of blasphemous libel is analysed in the Law Reform Commission's *Consultation Paper on the Crime of Libel* (1991), Chap. 4. In Chap. 8 the Commission states: "We are of the view that there is no place for the offence of blasphemous libel in a society which respects freedom of speech. The strongest arguments in its favour are (i) that it causes injury to feelings, which is a rather tenuous basis on which to restrict speech, and (ii) that freedom to insult religion would threaten the stability of society by impairing the harmony between its groups, a matter which is open to question in the absence of prosecution. Indeed we consider the absence of prosecution to indicate that the publication of blasphemous matter is no longer a social problem" (p. 172). The Commission noted that incitement to hatred on religious grounds is now penalised by the Prohibition of Incitement to Hatred Act 1989, and suggests

phemy has been brought since the foundation of the State. The fears of a broad interpretation of the offence which would penalise the non-believer, voiced by Professor O'Higgins in 1960,[91] have not been borne out, and it seems unlikely that they will be.[92]

In *O'Mahony* v. *R.T.É.* (*The Irish Times*, September 14, 1985) a Dublin solicitor sought an injunction to prevent R.T.É. screening an interview with two lesbian ex-nuns. The basis of the application appears to have been that this would violate Article 40.6.1°i, in that it would undermine public morality, and that it was contrary to the Christian ethical values of the Constitution. Barr J. refused to grant an order because: (a) it was not clear that the interview would be screened (though in fact it was broadcast); (b) the application, made on the day of transmission, was too late—given that the applicant knew of the possibility of this broadcast several days earlier. It is not entirely clear, therefore, whether an injunction might have been issued had the application been made earlier. But Article 40.6.1°i hardly seems to prevent discussion of subjects, not *per se* indecent, seditious or blasphemous, that some would prefer to see avoided. And the admitted Christian ethos of the Constitution seems a slender foundation on which to build—without benefit of statute—a novel and potentially wide-ranging inhibition of free expression.

Defamation

Article 40.6.1°i does not expressly subject freedom of expression to restriction in the interests of individual reputation—the objective of the law of defamation. But given that Article 40.3.2° specifically refers to the citizen's good name, it would seem that such restriction is constitutionally permissible and that "public order" must be understood to comprehend this.

(a) *The civil law*
The civil law on defamation[93] is a blend of common law and statute—principally the Defamation Act 1961. The gist of the tort was explained thus by

that that Act's provisions may adequately cover any problems existing in this area. The Commission would wish to see the offences of blasphemy and blasphemous libel abolished without replacement but recognises that this is not constitutionally permissible at present (p. 172). Accordingly, it recommends that blasphemous libel be replaced by a statutory offence of publication of blasphemous matter. The gist of this would be publication of matter " . . . the sole effect of which is likely to cause outrage to a substantial number of adherents to any religion by virtue of its insulting content concerning a matter or matters held sacred by that religion . . . " (pp. 173–178).

[91] "Blasphemy in Irish Law" (1960) 23 M.L.R. 151.

[92] In *R.* v. *Chief Metropolitan Magistrate, ex p. Choudhury* [1991] 1 All E.R. 306—a case concerning Salman Rushdie's *The Satanic Verses*—the Divisional Court held that the common law of blasphemy protected only the Christian religion. The court could not, and should not if it could, extend the law to cover other religions. "It would be virtually impossible by judicial decision to set sufficiently clear limits to the offence, and other problems involved are formidable": *per* Watkins L.J. at 318. The House of Lords refused leave to appeal: *ibid.*, at 323. The position in Ireland is unclear. Article 44's guarantees of religious freedom and of non-discrimination might argue for extended coverage (though an Irish court asked to make that extension would surely have to face the difficulties canvassed in *Choudhury's* case). On the other hand the preamble is strongly redolent of Christianity. See the careful analysis in the Law Reform Commission's *Consultation Paper on the Crime of Libel* (1991), pp. 81–83, which suggests that the law may protect only religious beliefs in the Judaeo-Christian tradition.

[93] As to this see the Law Reform Commission's *Consultation Paper on the Civil Law of Defamation* (1991) and its *Report on the Civil Law of Defamation* (December 1991).

the Supreme Court, *per* Walsh J., in *Quigley* v. *Creation Ltd.* [1971] I.R. 269, at 272:

" . . . words are defamatory if they impute conduct which would tend to lower that person in the eyes of a considerable and respectable class of the community, though not in the eyes of the community as a whole. The test is whether it will lower him in the eyes of the average right-thinking man. If it will, then it is defamatory if untrue."

It follows from this that truth (justification) is a defence in a defamation action. Another is privilege—which may be absolute (that conferred by Article 15.12 of the Constitution on utterances in the Dáil or Seanad seems to be of this kind) or qualified (a complete defence provided the defendant was not actuated by malice).

In *Macaulay & Co. Ltd.* v. *Wyse-Power* (1943) 77 I.L.T.R. 61 the plaintiffs sought damages for slander from the defendant Circuit Court judge in respect of a statement made by him in the course of civil proceedings. Martin Maguire J. held that the matter complained of arose while the judge was exercising his judicial functions. A long line of authority established that no action would lie in such circumstances against a judge of a court of record.[94] Thus the action was not maintainable and must be dismissed. Since the privilege in question (which is absolute) is based on the public interest in the effective administration of justice, it can hardly be doubted that it still forms part of the law. Parties, counsel, witnesses and jurors are similarly protected.[95]

In the interests of free speech the courts will not restrain the publication of material, even if defamatory, where the defendant intends to plead the defences of justification or fair comment on a matter of public interest—*Bonnard* v. *Perryman* [1891] 2 Ch. 269: *Frazer* v. *Evans* [1969] 1 Q.B. 349. In *Sinclair* v. *Gogarty* [1937] I.R. 377 (where neither defence was pleaded) the Supreme Court described the jurisdiction to grant such an injunction as being of a delicate nature, and said it should be granted only where any jury would say that the matter was libellous and where, if the jury did not so find, the court would set aside the verdict as unreasonable.

The United States Supreme Court has held that the common law of libel must, in certain respects, yield to free speech considerations. Thus in *New York Times* v. *Sullivan* (1964) 376 U.S. 254 it concluded that a public official could recover damages for defamatory statements about his official conduct only if he could show that the statement was made with knowledge that it was false or with reckless disregard of whether it was false or not. Subsequently, in *Gertz* v. *Robert Welch Inc.* (1974) 418 U.S. 323, the court ruled that plaintiffs in defamation suits could recover only such damages as would compensate for *actual* injury; thus *punitive* damages could no longer be awarded.[96] These conclusions were based upon various considerations, including the inhibiting effect of the pre-existing law on freedom of expression, due to fear of the expense and uncertainty of legal actions; and

---

[94] Citing *e.g.*, *Tughan* v. *Craig* [1918] 1 I.R. 245.
[95] *Kennedy* v. *Hilliard* (1859) 10 I.C.L.R. 195: *McLaughlin* v. *Doey* (1893) 32 L.R. Ir. 518.
[96] Some aspects of traditional defamation law that worried the U.S. Supreme Court in the above cases were dealt with by the Defamation Act 1961—*e.g.* unintentional defamation (see s.21) and the broadening of the justification and fair comment defences by ss.22 and 23.

the fact that public figures have easier access to the media, and hence more opportunity to rebut false statements, than private persons.

It follows that United States defamation law, as shaped by constitutional considerations, offers less protection to public figures than others. It is doubtful whether the Irish courts could (or should) develop the law along such lines. The practical effect of doing so might well be to make it impossible for a public figure to vindicate his/her right to a good name, thus raising problems under Article 40.3.1° of the Constitution. In addition, the equality guarantee of Article 40.1 would seem to militate against differential treatment of one group of citizens.[97] Nor is there any sign that the courts would be prepared to consider any such development. In *Hynes-O'Sullivan* v. *O'Driscoll* [1988] I.R. 436 the Supreme Court refused to extend the defence of qualified privilege beyond existing limits. This defence applies where the person communicating the defamatory statement has a duty or interest to make it, and the person to whom it is made has a corresponding duty or interest to receive it. It was suggested that the privilege should obtain where the maker of the statement honestly—though mistakenly—believed that the recipient had a duty or interest in receiving it. Henchy J. (Hederman J. concurring) ruled out any such extension on constitutional grounds,[98] saying (at 499):

> "I cannot believe that the guarantee in Article 40, s.1, sub-s. 3 of the Constitution that the State will protect, and, as far as practicable, by its laws defend and vindicate the personal rights of the citizen, would be effectuated if a right to defame with impunity is recognised on such a purely subjective basis. An occasion of qualified privilege is to be given recognition only to the extent that it is necessary under Article 40, s.6, sub-s. 1 to recognise, on an objective basis, the right to express freely convictions and opinions. The constitutional priorities would be ignored if the law considered an occasion of qualified privilege to depend only on the honest opinion of the communicator as to the existence of a right or duty in the other person to receive the communication. The constitutional right to one's reputation would be of little value if a person defamed were to be deprived of redress because the defamer honestly but unjustifiably believed that the person to whom the words were published had a right to receive the communication."

And McCarthy J. spoke to similar effect (at 454).

In the *Hynes-O'Sullivan* case Henchy J. said that the law on qualified privilege must reflect " . . . a due balancing of the constitutional right to freedom of expression and the constitutional protection of every citizen's good name" (at 450). This must hold true for the law of defamation in general, but it is doubtful whether the current law achieves the proper equilibrium. As Dr. Woodman shows, the possibility of libel actions causes the Irish media more concern than any of the other restraints on freedom of speech, and the self-censorship factor that worried the United States Supreme Court plainly obtains in Ireland.[99] Public figures have a right to their good names, but they

---

[97] Conceivably, however, the Oireachtas could validly legislate for such differential treatment. For the proviso to Art. 40.1 entitles the State " . . . in its *enactments* . . . " to have due regard to differences of social function. A public figure, such as a politician, would seem to have a social function different from that of a private citizen.

[98] In terms of *judicial* development of the law only, for he clearly contemplates possible legislative change.

[99] *Op. cit.*, pp. 196–204.

are not entitled to undeserved reputations that fear-induced media caution may secure to them.

In a lengthy consultation paper, and a subsequent report, issued in 1991 the Law Reform Commission gave careful consideration to the tort of defamation, with particular reference to the Constitution and the European Convention on Human Rights. The Commission concluded—surely correctly—that the Constitution left the Oireachtas a wide measure of discretion in reconciling the competing rights of the citizen to a good name and to freedom of expression.[1] It found that the existing law did not strike the proper balance, and recommended the repeal of the Defamation Act 1961 and its replacement by a new statute. The latter should, *inter alia*, define defamation[2]; list the factors to be taken into account in awarding damages[3]; and provide that damages in defamation actions should be assessed by the judge rather than the jury.[4]

Three of the Commission's recommendations are particularly noteworthy. The first is to cope with the problem of "gagging writs," of which the media frequently complain. These are proceedings designed to prevent publication of further material on the same topic—such as further articles in a series—with no intention of pursuing the matter to trial. The Commission recommends that the court should have power, on application by the defendant, to dismiss the proceedings for want of prosecution if the plaintiff has taken no step in the proceedings within one year of their initiation.[5] The second is for the introduction of a new—and accelerated—procedure for obtaining a declaratory judgment. This would bar any subsequent claim for damages arising out of the same publication. The third is for a new defence of reasonable care, applicable to claims for general damages.[6] Thus if it were established that the defendant exercised reasonable care prior to publication in trying to ascertain the truth of the defamatory allegation, the plaintiff could not be awarded general damages (which, of their nature, are not capable of precise calculation).[7] He/she would, however, be able to secure a declaratory order or correction order,[8] as well as damages for any financial loss sustained.

---

[1] *Report on the Civil Law of Defamation* (1991), Appendix A, "The Constitution and the Law of Defamation."

[2] *Ibid.*, p. 96. The suggested definition would emphasise that defamatory matter is (a) untrue, and (b) tends to injure the plaintiff's reputation in the eyes of reasonable members of the community.

[3] *Ibid.*, pp. 103–104.

[4] *Ibid.*, p. 106. The Commission recommended that jury trial of defamation actions be restored in the Circuit Court, subject to the same limitation: p. 77. Since it thought the jury's role essential, but felt jury trial was not feasible in the District Court, it recommended that defamation actions should remain outside that court's jurisdiction.

[5] *Ibid.*, pp. 92–93.

[6] *Ibid.*, pp. 49–55. The Commission considered the U.S. public figure/public official doctrine, but concluded that it should not be adopted here. It would not serve the public interest, in that it would protect negligent false factual assertions. Moreover, " . . . it would appear not to preserve the balance required by the Constitution between the competing rights of reputation and freedom of expression": pp. 49–50.

[7] In its *Consultation Paper* the Commission noted a general feeling among the media and booksellers that the current level of damages was unwarrantedly high. The Commission pointed out that though awards seemed to be on the increase, they had not reached anything like the levels in some English cases. Moreover, the criticism voiced against some English awards—that they were grossly out of proportion to damages for personal injuries awarded by judges—did not apply in Ireland: pp. 348–349. Nonetheless, the Commission agreed that some changes in the law were necessary to ensure proportionality between the injury suffered and the damages awarded.

[8] This declaratory order is distinct from the declaratory judgment referred to above: see *Report*, p. 70. The proposed correction order would authorise the courts to direct publication of a statement that the original matter was false and defamatory.

The Commission's proposals have been widely welcomed. There can be little doubt that if enacted they will provide a much more sensitive and delicate adjustment of the conflicting constitutional interests involved than does the current law.

(b) *The criminal law*[9]

At common law defamatory libel is a criminal offence (slander, the other form of defamation, is not). The gist of the offence lies in publishing *written* material; radio and TV broadcasts, which in civil law are treated as libel, rather than slander, are—anomalously—not covered.[10] The distinction between civil libel and its criminal counterpart is vague and elusive; it seems to rest solely in that the criminal libel must be grave, not trivial, so serious that it is proper for the criminal law to be invoked.[11] Where the alleged defamatory libel is contained in a newspaper, leave to commence a prosecution must be obtained from a High Court judge sitting *in camera*: section 8, Defamation Act 1961. The factors governing the exercise of judicial discretion here were considered by Gannon J. in *Hilliard* v. *Penfield Enterprises Ltd.* [1990] 1 I.R. 138—a case which suggests that leave will not readily be granted. And it is the fact that prosecutions for defamatory libel are extremely rare in modern Ireland.

The Law Reform Commission has examined this offence in a consultation paper and a subsequent report.[12] It found the existing law anomalous and objectionable in several respects, among them the fact that truth is a defence only if it is also shown that publication of the matter was for the public benefit: section 6, Defamation Act 1961. The Commission thought it objectionable in principle that a person could be punished for publishing a true statement; and it regarded the criterion of public benefit as too vague a test for criminal law purposes. The vagueness of the "seriousness" ingredient similarly perturbed the Commission, as did the fact that statute gave some special protections to newspapers but not to other defendants.[13] This inequality of treatment, it was observed, might well fall foul of Article 40.1 of the Constitution. The Commission concluded thus[14]:

> "We are of the view that the defects in the law regarding the offence of defamatory libel render the offence in its present condition highly unacceptable. We are strongly opposed to the retention of the offence of defamatory libel in its present form. It runs contrary to many modern principles of criminal liability and fair trial, and threatens freedom of speech to a high degree, in theory if not in practice, so long as it continues to exist in its present state."

[9] See the Law Reform Commission's *Consultation Paper on the Crime of Libel* (August 1991), Chaps. 2 and 6.

[10] The reason lies in s.15 of the Defamation Act 1961, which treats such broadcasts as publication in permanent form, and thus as libels; but it applies to *civil* proceedings only.

[11] It is *not* necessary to prove that the alleged libel has a tendency to provoke a breach of the peace: *Hilliard* v. *Penfield Enterprises Ltd.* [1990] 1 I.R. 138.

[12] The *Report on the Crime of Libel* was published in May 1992.

[13] *Consultation Paper* pp. 129, 132.

[14] *Ibid.*, p. 134.

However, the Commission was of opinion that to abolish the offence entirely would deprive the criminal law of a valuable—even if rarely used—weapon.[15] Accordingly it recommended that it be retained, but in a confined and modernised form.[16] That recommendation, if implemented, would remove the threats to freedom of expression posed by the current law.

Breach of confidence

In *House of Spring Gardens Ltd.* v. *Point Blank Ltd.* [1984] I.R. 611 the Supreme Court accepted that Irish law protects one who imparts information to another in confidence against the use of that information to his/her detriment. This jurisdiction was invoked, in unusual circumstances, in *Att.-Gen. for England and Wales* v. *Brandon Book Publishers Ltd.* [1986] I.R. 597. The plaintiff there sought to restrain publication by an Irish firm of a book written by a deceased member of the British secret service—Joan Miller's *One Girl's War*. It was claimed that publication would be in breach of the duty of confidence owed by Joan Miller to the Crown. Carroll J. refused to grant an interlocutory injunction. Under Article 40.6.1°i, she held, there was a *prima facie* constitutional right to publish information, and the onus was on the plaintiff to establish that the defendant should not exercise that right. In the *House of Spring Gardens* case what was in issue were the principles to be applied between private individuals in a commercial context. But the present case involved information shared between a government and a private individual; and the law was that confidentiality would only be protected in this context where disclosure would be likely to injure the public interest.[17] However, no public interest of the Irish State was affected here. Carroll J. ended her judgment by saying ([1986] I.R. 597, 602):

> "In these circumstances I have no doubt that the balance of convenience must lie with the right of the defendant to exercise its constitutional right to publish. The existence of a constitutional right cannot be measured in terms of money: what is at stake is the very important constitutional right to communicate *now* and not in a year or more when the case has worked its way through the courts."

It is obvious that different considerations would apply had the book in that case been written by an Irish civil servant.[18] The public interest would then enter the equation, and if disclosure of the relevant information would be likely to injure that interest the courts could restrain it. For, as Carroll J. recognised, the constitutional right to publish is by no means absolute; by the terms of Article 40.6.1° it is " . . . subject to public order . . . " But a court asked to enjoin publication in the circumstances envisaged would plainly have to balance the public interest in freedom of expression against whatever public interest would allegedly be injured by disclosure of the information. This was the approach adopted by the English courts in the celebrated *Spy-*

---

[15] P. 146.

[16] Pp. 135–160.

[17] Applying *Commonwealth* v. *John Fairfax and Sons Ltd.* (1980) 147 C.L.R. 39.

[18] In *Att. Gen.* v. *Guardian Newspapers Ltd.* (*No.* 2) [1988] 3 All E.R. 545 the House of Lords held that a former member of the security service was under a lifelong duty of confidence—independent of official secrets legislation—towards the Crown. No doubt the Irish courts would adopt a similar approach. Whether such a duty would bind other civil servants is unclear.

catcher litigation,[19] when the Attorney-General sought to have certain newspapers restrained from revealing the contents of a book written by a former MI5 member. The divergence of views among the judges who heard these cases[20] show how difficult the balancing exercise may be.

Breach of confidence was one of the grounds for restraining publication in the remarkable case of *A.C.C. Ltd.* v. *Irish Business* in 1985. The defendant magazine proposed to publish certain articles about the affairs of the State-backed Agricultural Credit Corporation. The A.C.C. sought and obtained an interim injunction restraining the publication of one article on the ground that it was defamatory. The order was granted following an *ex parte* application to O'Hanlon J. at his home. Apparently the media were then informed that they could not publicise the fact that an order had been made or why, though it was not clear that the judge had so ruled.[21] This misunderstanding was later clarified. A few days later, when the interlocutory proceedings came on before Lardner J., *Irish Business* gave an undertaking not to publish the original article; but they wished to substitute another for it. This too the A.C.C. sought to restrain on the ground that it was based on documents which belonged to them, and that their publication would be a breach of confidence and/or copyright. *Irish Business* admitted the A.C.C.'s property in the documents and Lardner J. concluded that the journal had probably been given copies by an A.C.C. employee. This would be a breach of that employee's duty, and the A.C.C. was entitled to an injunction to restrain such a breach of confidence. Lardner J. was not satisfied that publication of the article would be in the public interest; it could shake the confidence of depositors, and the public, in the A.C.C. and gravely damage the corporation. In addition, the judge accepted that publication would be a breach of the A.C.C.'s copyright in the documents.[22]

Disclosure of journalists' sources

Though it is the practice of journalists not to reveal the sources of information given to them in confidence, the law does not accord them any testimonial privilege in this matter. In *Re Kevin O'Kelly* (1974) 108 I.L.T.R. 97 the Court of Criminal Appeal said that journalists had no greater legal or

[19] *Att. Gen.* v. *Guardian Newspapers Ltd.* [1987] 3 All E.R. 316 (application for interlocutory injunctions): *Att. Gen.* v. *Guardian Newspapers Ltd.* (*No. 2*) [1988] 3 All E.R. 545 (application for permanent injunctions). The interlocutory injunctions were granted by a 3–2 majority in the House of Lords—Lords Brandon, Ackner and Templeman: Lords Bridge and Oliver dissenting. This despite the fact that the book—Peter Wright's *Spycatcher*—had been published in the U.S. in July 1987, and the U.K. government had decided not to attempt to prevent copies being imported. In a remarkably trenchant dissent Lord Bridge said: "If the government are determined to fight to maintain the ban to the end, they will face inevitable condemnation and humiliation before the European Court of Human Rights in Strasbourg": [1987] 3 All E.R. 316, 347. This prophecy proved accurate; the Strasbourg court held that the injunctions were an unjustified interference with the freedom of expression guaranteed by Art. 10 of the Convention: *Sunday Times* v. *U.K., Observer and Guardian* v. *U.K., The Times,* November 27, 1991.

[20] See Eric Barendt, "Spycatcher and Freedom of Speech" [1989] *Public Law* 204.

[21] Nor that such a ruling would be competent, for s.45 of the Courts (Supplemental Provisions) Act 1961—which governed the application—has never been understood to prevent reporting of *ex parte* applications, *e.g.* for injunctions in labour disputes. Its terms ensure privacy of proceedings, in the sense that the public is not admitted; they do not refer at all to questions of media coverage—contrast the Criminal Procedure Act 1967, s.17, discussed *supra.*

[22] *The Irish Times,* August 8, 1985. See also the articles by Adrian Hardiman in *The Irish Times,* September 10 and 11, 1985, and Gene Kerrigan in *Magill* magazine, September 1985.

constitutional immunity than other citizens; and the fact that information was given in confidence did not create a privilege against disclosure. This was, of course, a criminal case but it seems unlikely that there is a different rule for civil proceedings. And although the Court of Criminal Appeal's observations were technically *obiter*[23] they represent the settled common law position.[24]

In its Consultation Paper on Contempt of Court the Law Reform Commission accepted that the law on journalistic privilege was as stated above.[25] The Commission took the view, however, that the rule denying such privilege was not rooted in the Constitution, so that it would be open to the Oireachtas to abrogate or modify it.[26] Nonetheless, the Commission recommended that the law should not be altered, fearful of the risk to the public interest that change might entail.[27]

In March 1992 two *Sunday Business Post* journalists, Mr. Damien Kiberd and Mr. Brian Carey, were ordered by Hamilton P.—then chairing a tribunal of inquiry—to appear before him to answer questions about the sources on which two articles were based. The articles were apparently not based on evidence so far given before the tribunal, and there was concern that they derived from material served on certain persons prior to their giving evidence. A judicial review application by the two journalists, claiming that Hamilton P.'s order was *ultra vires* section 4 of the Tribunals of Inquiry (Evidence) (Amendment) Act 1979,[28] was dismissed by Blayney J. He held that the order was necessary, lest people be deterred from proffering evidence to the tribunal by fear that it might previously appear in the press: *The Irish Times*, March 21, 1992. Subsequently the two journalists declined to reveal their sources to the tribunal and Hamilton P. directed that the papers be sent to the Director of Public Prosecutions: *The Irish Times*, March 26, 1992.

The Broadcasting Complaints Commission

Though Ireland has no equivalent of the United Kingdom Press Complaints Commission it does have a broadly similar body to investigate certain types of complaints about radio and television broadcasts.[29] The Broadcasting Complaints Commission is established under section 18A–C of the Broadcasting Authority Act 1960 (inserted by s.4 of the 1976 Act). It consists

---

[23] In that Mr. O'Kelly, who had been gaoled for contempt for refusing to answer questions in a Special Criminal Court trial, was appealing only against sentence, not against conviction.

[24] See *O'Brennan* v. *Tully* (1935) I.L.T.R. 115: *Att. Gen.* v. *Mulholland* [1963] 2 Q.B. 477: *McGuinness* v. *Att. Gen. of Victoria* (1940) 63 C.L.R. 73.

[25] Pp. 14–20.

[26] Pp. 245–247. The Commission was careful to add, however, that the Constitution does not give the Oireachtas *carte blanche* in prescribing the rules of evidence. It said (at p. 245): "We consider that the Constitution permits a legislative exclusion of this nature, provided that it serves a rational goal, which can be justified on the basis of factors to which the Constitution attaches importance, and which do not infringe against the requirements of constitutional justice."

[27] P. 247.

[28] Which provides: "A tribunal may make such orders as it considers necessary for the purposes of its functions, and it shall have, in relation to their making, all such powers, rights and privileges as are vested in the High Court or a judge of that Court in respect of the making of orders."

[29] s.11(3) of the Radio and Television Act 1988 empowers the Minister for Communications to make regulations extending the Commission's jurisdiction to cover complaints against broadcasts by independent companies.

of a chairman and at least two other members, who are appointed by the Government for renewable five year terms. During their terms of office members can be removed only for "stated reasons" and provided both Houses so resolve.

The Commission's function is to adjudicate on complaints that broadcasts have infringed specified guidelines in the Acts. Complaints may relate to:

(1) a failure to maintain objectivity and impartiality in news broadcasts and current affairs programmes
(2) the inclusion in broadcasts of "anything which may reasonably be regarded as being likely to promote, or incite to, crime or as tending to undermine the authority of the State"
(3) failure to comply with an order made under section 31
(4) unreasonable encroachment on individual privacy[30]
(5) complaints about violation of the relevant advertising standards code.[31]

Any person may lodge a complaint in writing. The broadcasting body must be given an opportunity to comment on it and the Commission may extend such an opportunity to an employee of the broadcasting body. The complaint is considered in private. The decision must be notified to the complainant and the broadcasting body, and the latter must inform the Commission within 14 days whether or not it accepts the decision. Should it not do so this must be noted in the annual report which the Commission is obliged to furnish to the Minister for Communications, and which is laid before both Houses.

The fact that the Commission has no power to award costs, and no jurisdiction over complaints of alleged defamation, clearly shows it is not envisaged as a substitute for the courts. Nor does the Act purport to take away any legal remedy a complainant may have.

Freedom not to express opinions

In the United States it has been held that legislation may not compel individuals to express or subscribe to opinions they do not hold. Thus New Hampshire could not, under pain of criminal sanctions, compel car-owners to display the state's motto "Live Free or Die" on their licence-plates: *Wooley v. Maynard* (1977) 430 U.S. 705.[32] Such issues have not yet arisen in Ireland; should they do so it seems likely that the United States approach will be followed. From the provisions of Article 40.6.1°iii (the right of association) the courts have inferred a right to dissociate and it would clearly be possible to carry out a similar operation under Article 40.6.1°i. Recognition of such a right would imply that, absent an emergency, the law could not dictate what newspapers must print. In *Miami Herald Publishing Co.* v. *Tornillo* (1974) 418

---

[30] The Commission upheld a complaint on this ground in October 1986, finding that an R.T.É. programme on child sexual abuse should not have identified the victims by name, even with parental consent: *The Irish Times*, October 10, 1986.
[31] s.4 of the Broadcasting Act 1990 authorises the Minister for Communications to draw up such codes, after consultation with the R.T.É. Authority and the Independent Radio and Television Commission.
[32] Nor could school pupils, under threat of penalties, be compelled by law to salute and pledge allegiance to the national flag: *West Virginia State Board of Education* v. *Barnette* (1943) 319 U.S. 624.

U.S. 241 a unanimous Supreme Court invalidated a Florida statute granting a political candidate a right to equal space in reply to a newspaper's attacks on his record. Such a legislative intrusion on editorial control and judgment was incompatible with the First Amendment.[33] But a city ordinance forbidding newspapers to carry job advertisements in sex-designated columns was upheld (by a 5–4 majority) in *Pittsburgh Press Co.* v. *Pittsburgh Commission on Human Relations* (1973) 413 U.S. 376. (S.8(1) of the Employment Equality Act 1977, prohibiting discriminatory advertising, seems to apply to the advertising medium as well as to the advertiser.)

FREEDOM OF ASSEMBLY

Article 40.6.1°ii guarantees the right of citizens to assemble peaceably and without arms. As with the other matters embraced by Article 40.6, the exercise of this right is subject to public order and morality. However, in addition, it is stipulated that provision may be made by law to prevent or control meetings "which are determined in accordance with law to be calculated to cause a breach of the peace or to be a danger or nuisance to the general public." Furthermore, legal provision may be made for the prevention or control of meetings in the vicinity of either House of the Oireachtas.

The right of assembly recognised in Article 40.6.1°ii has not received much judicial consideration. It would appear to be regulated partly by the common law and partly by statute—*e.g.* the Offences against the State Act 1939. But there is no *general* statutory provision for prevention or control of certain meetings comparable to the United Kingdom's Public Order Act 1986, s.13. (The Criminal Justice Bill 1967, Part VI was designed to make such provision but the Government, following much protest, decided to drop the measure.)

Article 40.6.1°ii gives no guidance as to *where* the recognised right of assembly is to be exercised. Obviously it may be exercised in private premises (*e.g.* by renting a hotel function room to hold a meeting) but only with the owner's consent; the Constitution's property rights guarantees would surely preclude any other conclusion. The position in regard to publicly-owned premises (such as town halls) is unclear. There appears to be no statutory obligation to rent suitable premises on a non-discriminatory basis to organisations desiring to use them for meetings; the matter would seem to be left to the unfettered discretion of those in whom title to the property is vested.[34] An exception to this is in section 30(3) of the Electoral Act 1923, under which a candidate at any election is entitled to the use at reasonable times of a room in "any public elementary school" in the constituency for the purpose of holding a public meeting. (The school authorities may charge for "any actual and necessary expenses" they incur in this connection.)

So far as highways are concerned, in *Ferguson* v. *O'Gorman* [1937] I.R. 620 the former Supreme Court—founding on earlier authorities[35]—held that the

---

[33] In a brief concurrence Brennan and Rehnquist JJ. noted that the decision implied no view on the constitutionality of statutes giving persons able to prove defamatory falsehoods a statutory action to require publication of a retraction.

[34] Or others: in September 1986 it was reported that the Minister for the Gaeltacht had refused to allow community halls in Gaeltacht areas, built with State aid, to be rented to Sinn Féin (*The Irish Times*, September 22, 1986). This action was apparently taken under a clause in the relevant agreements.

[35] *Harrison* v. *Duke of Rutland* [1893] 1 Q.B. 142: *Hickman* v. *Maisey* [1900] 1 Q.B. 752.

principal right of the public was that of passage, but that other reasonable and usual modes of use were also covered. The court did not refer to the question of holding meetings, but it may be thought that Article 40.6.1°ii has at least the effect of recognising exercise of the right of assembly as a reasonable mode of using the highway and other public places. This, if accepted, would immunise those assembling from liability in trespass towards the owners of the subsoil, and in nuisance towards occupants of adjoining property. Criminal liability for obstructing the highway[36] might still arise but this would seem to depend on the reasonableness of the use.

At common law a more favourable view was taken of processions on the highway than of stationary meetings. In *Lowdens* v. *Keaveney* [1903] 2 I.R. 82 a band playing party tunes in the streets of Belfast was followed by a large crowd. A police constable cautioned the band from going down a particular street, as an obstruction would be caused. They nonetheless persisted, the crowd followed and the free passage of pedestrians and vehicles was temporarily interrupted. The divisional court quashed convictions for obstruction on the ground that the magistrates had neglected to consider whether this user of the street was reasonable in the circumstances. Lord O'Brien C.J. said that there might be considerable, even complete, obstruction and yet the use of the street might be quite reasonable. There must, he added, be give and take and regard be had to the incidents of everyday life. Gibson J. suggested that reasonableness involved having regard to such factors as the occasion, the duration of the user, the place and the hour; the whole matter, in his view, was one of degree. The *Lowdens* decision was approved and applied by the English Court of Criminal Appeal in *R.* v. *Clarke* (*No.* 2) [1964] 2 Q.B. 315. (See too the Supreme Court's decision in the non-public order case of *Wall* v. *Morrissey* [1969] I.R. 10.)

Professor Williams has pointed out[37] that this more favourable approach to processions seems curious today, when some at least could prove more disruptive than stationary meetings on the highway. As he says, the standard of reasonableness ought to be the same in each case and the courts ought to treat all alleged obstructions alike "without having recourse to theoretical questions as to what is or what is not linked to the common-law right of passage."

Statutory control

As noted above, there is no *general* statutory provision for prevention or control of certain meetings. But section 27(1) of the Offences against the State Act 1939 declares it unlawful to hold a public meeting[38] "which is held or purports to be held by or on behalf of or by arrangement or in concert with an unlawful organisation or which is held or purports to be held for the purpose of supporting, aiding, abetting, or encouraging an unlawful organisation or of advocating the support of an unlawful organisation." Under section 27(2) a Garda officer of at least chief superintendent rank who is of opinion that a proposed meeting would fall within this comprehensive category may prohibit it; thereupon the holding of such meeting becomes

---

[36] This is an offence at common law, triable on indictment or (more usually) summarily under the Summary Jurisdiction (Ireland) Act 1851, s.13. See too the Road Traffic Act 1961, s.98.
[37] *Keeping the Peace*, p. 216.
[38] Defined in s.27(5) so as to include processions and meetings in the open or in buildings.

unlawful. Organisers and participants then become liable, on conviction, to a fine of up to £500 and/or 12 months' imprisonment (s.27(4), as amended by s.2(7) of the Criminal Law Act 1976).

Section 4 of the Offences against the State (Amendment) Act 1972—discussed earlier—strikes at meetings, processions or demonstrations which constitute an interference with the course of justice (as there defined). But the section does not create machinery for *prohibiting* such gatherings; it provides solely for prosecution after the event. Section 28 of the Offences against the State Act 1939 provides for the banning of meetings in the vicinity of the Oireachtas. This, however, is not automatic; it depends on action by the Gardaí. The section covers meetings or processions in streets or open spaces within half a mile of the Houses of the Oireachtas, on a day on which either the Dáil or the Seanad is sitting. A Garda officer of at least chief superintendent rank may prohibit the assembly in advance; should it be in progress any Garda member may require the participants to disperse. The penalty, on summary conviction, for contravening section 28 is a fine of up to £50 and/or three months' imprisonment.

A notable difference between sections 27 and 28 of the 1939 Act is that the former provides for possible High Court review of a prohibition (s.27(3)), whereas the latter does not. In theory it might be possible to challenge a section 28 prohibition by an application for judicial review, but it is difficult to see what the grounds for such an application might be. The section is not confined—*e.g.* by reference to meetings calculated to influence parliamentary deliberations—and appears to vest an unfettered discretion in the Gardaí. Perhaps if it could be shown that some meetings were allowed and others forbidden a court might intervene, but this is not clear. In the United States section 28 (which seems never to be invoked nowadays) would not survive constitutional scrutiny. The reason was thus stated by the Supreme Court, *per* Goldberg J., in *Cox* v. *Louisiana* (1965) 379 U.S. 536, 557–8:

> "(It) is clearly unconstitutional to enable a public official to determine which expressions of view will be permitted and which will not or to engage in invidious discrimination among persons or groups either by use of a statute providing a system of broad discretionary licensing power or, as in this case, the equivalent of such a system by selective enforcement of an extremely broad prohibitory statute."

Article 40.6.1°ii, of course, specifically permits provision to be made "by law" to prevent or control meetings in the vicinity of the Oireachtas; but in so far as section 28 answers Goldberg J.'s description it may not necessarily qualify as "law" in the contemplation of the Constitution.[39] The section should be repealed, and if a replacement is thought necessary it should take the form of a total ban on such meetings (as was proposed in the Criminal Justice Bill 1967).

Police control

Since Article 40.6.1°ii recognises only the right of *peaceful* assembly, meetings which are not peaceable may involve the common law offences of riot or unlawful assembly. The elements of the former are uncertain. In the English

---

[39] In *Melbourne Corporation* v. *Barry* (1922) 31 C.L.R. 174 the High Court of Australia invalidated a by-law requiring the City Council's permission for all save military or funeral processions.

case of *R.* v. *Cunninghame Graham and Burns* (1888) 16 Cox C.C. 420, Charles J. said (at 427):

" . . . a riot is a disturbance of the peace by three persons at the least who, with an intention to help one another against any person who opposes them in the execution of some enterprise or other, actually execute that enterprise in a violent or turbulent manner to the alarm of the people. Whether such enterprise be a lawful or unlawful one does not matter . . ."[40]

But in *R.* v. *Latchford* (1888) Crimes Act Cases 282 the Irish Exchequer Division, *per* Palles C.B., said there could not be a riot unless parties were assembled together for an illegal purpose. However, since prosecutions for riot rarely occur nowadays (which does not mean that the offence is obsolete) the occasion for an authoritative statement of modern Irish law has not arisen.

The hallowed phrase "reading the Riot Act" refers to the proclamation set out in section 2 of the (Irish) Riot Act 1787 (27 Geo. III, c. 15). But it is in no sense essential to the commission of the offence that the proclamation should have been read, and in the circumstances of modern Ireland its references to "our sovereign lord the king" may not be calculated to induce tranquillity.

Charges of unlawful assembly are still brought—Mr. Peter Robinson M.P. was charged with this (*inter alia*) in September 1986 in respect of incidents in Co. Monaghan earlier in that year. In *Barrett* v. *Tipperary* (*N.R.*) *Co. Council* [1964] I.R. 22 McLoughlin J. said that an unlawful assembly at common law was an assembly of three or more persons: (a) for purposes forbidden by law, such as that of committing a crime by open force; or; (b) with intent to carry out any common purpose, lawful or unlawful, in such a manner as to endanger the public peace, or to give firm and courageous persons in the neighbourhood of such assembly reasonable grounds to apprehend a breach of the peace in consequence of it. The judge added (at 28):

" . . . I have never come across a case in which unlawful assembly was held to exist where there was not some evidence of force or violence in the commission of an offence or of some show of force or violence or of some breach of the peace or of some conduct tending to excite alarm in the mind of a person of firm and reasonable courage."

In the English case of *Kamara* v. *D.P.P.* [1973] 2 All E.R. 1242 the House of Lords held that the appellants, nine Sierra Leone students who had forcibly occupied Sierra Leone government premises in London, were rightly convicted of unlawful assembly (*inter alia*). An unlawful assembly need not be in a public place and it was not necessary to show that fear was engendered in persons beyond the bounds of the building. The threat to the public peace could take the form of danger to the security of innocent third parties, members of the public not participating in the illegal activities in question.

Those participating in an unlawful assembly are of course open to prosecution; but in addition the police have power to disperse the assembly. This is evident from a line of 19th century Irish cases, probably still good law, which emphasise the policeman's duty to preserve the peace and grant a wide discretion over the means to achieve that end. In *Humphries* v. *Connor* (1864) 17 I.C.L.R. 1 the plaintiff had chosen to walk through the streets of Swanlinbar wearing an orange lily. This caused a hostile crowd to gather and threaten

---

[40] See too *R.* v. *Birt* (1831) 5 C. & P. 154: *Field* v. *Receiver of Metropolitan Police* [1907] 2 K.B. 853.

the plaintiff with violence. The defendant, an R.I.C. inspector, asked the plaintiff to remove the lily and on her refusing to do so he removed it himself. The plaintiff sued for damages for assault. The court (O'Brien, Hayes and Fitzgerald JJ.) stressed the defendant's duty to preserve the peace and prevent any breach thereof, and held that any act necessary to that end was lawful. In *O'Kelly* v. *Harvey* (1883) 14 L.R. Ir. 105 a Land League meeting at which Parnell was to speak had been announced for Brookeborough, Co. Fermanagh. Placards then appeared calling on Orangemen to assemble on the occasion and "give Parnell and his associates a warm welcome." When the Land League met, the defendant, a justice of the peace, called on them to disperse and when they refused he put his hand on the plaintiff in an attempt to disperse the meeting. The plaintiff's action for assault was dismissed, the Court of Appeal holding that the defendant was justified in dispersing the meeting if he reasonably believed that by no other means could he discharge his duty of preserving the peace. Finally, in *Coyne* v. *Tweedy* [1898] 2 I.R. 167 the plaintiff was in dispute with another cleric as to which of them was parish priest of Killannin. The plaintiff and a number of his supporters had taken possession of the parish church, and his rival, with another body of supporters, attempted to gain entry. An angry altercation took place between the reverend contenders, the plaintiff pushed his rival back and the latter's supporters made a rush at the plaintiff. The defendant, an R.I.C. inspector, then removed the plaintiff from the premises. Again the plaintiff's action for assault failed, the Court of Appeal upholding the jury's verdict that the defendant's action was reasonable and necessary to prevent a breach of the peace and thus a lawful execution of his duty.

As to the degree of force which may be used to disperse a riot or unlawful assembly, the authorities establish that this must be moderate and proportioned to the circumstances of the case and to the end to be attained. The use of firearms is permissible only in extreme cases; in *Lynch* v. *Fitzgerald* [1938] I.R. 382, Hanna J., having examined the authorities, said that the armed forces (including armed Gardaí) could fire on an unlawful or riotous assembly only where such a course was necessary as a last resort to preserve life. In the instant case, this requirement had not been met and the defendants, who had shot and killed the plaintiff's son, were held liable in damages. (Hanna J. also directed that the papers be sent to the Attorney General, stating his opinion that the facts disclosed a prima facie case of manslaughter and that the criminal liability of the defendants should be investigated by a jury. However no prosecution ensued.)

The *Humphries, O'Kelly* and *Coyne* cases mentioned above have the effect of vesting a considerable discretion in the police. They also mean that persons may be restrained from pursuing a lawful course of conduct because of threatened or actual violence by others. However it cannot be gainsaid that the very object of some meetings or processions may be to provoke violence by others; the right of assembly is not always invoked for laudable motives. The cases cited enable the police to cope with such "bad faith" assemblies. Of course they also produce a risk of abuse—that the police may interfere with bona fide meetings because this is easier than affording proper protection. It therefore behoves the courts to be vigilant to ensure that this does not happen and that the police genuinely had reasonable grounds for acting as they did. Nonetheless it would be preferable if this matter was regulated by statute, as the Criminal Justice Bill 1967, ss.30 and 31, proposed. The system

envisaged required advance notice to the Gardaí of meetings and processions, with a power to impose conditions on, or prohibit, the proposed
assembly on stated grounds. It would have spelt out the factors to be taken
into account, forbidden discrimination between different groups and provided for High Court review of an order imposing conditions on, or prohibiting, a meeting. The enactment of such provisions would do much to clarify
the law and be more in accordance with the spirit of Article 40.6.1°ii than the
common law rules outlined above.

Binding over

At common law magistrates were recognised as having a jurisdiction to
bind persons over to keep the peace and be of good behaviour, and to furnish
securities for this purpose; in default the persons concerned could be committed to prison. This jurisdiction was exercised in many 19th century Irish
public order cases. Though certainly exercisable following conviction for an
offence, the jurisdiction to bind over did not depend upon such a conviction.
In *R. (Orr)* v. *Londonderry JJ.* (1891) 28 L.R. Ir. 440 Holmes J. explained it
thus (at 462–463):

> " . . . the object of requiring sureties of the peace or for good behaviour
> is not to punish past crime, but to guard against future lawlessness. In
> most of the cases in which such sureties are required, the person ordered
> to give them has done nothing for which he could be made responsible in
> a criminal or civil Court; and I am quite prepared to hold that an
> unnecessary and unreasonable persistence in language or conduct calcu-
> lated to provoke violence or tumult may afford good grounds for the
> exercise of this jurisdiction against a person who is himself free from any
> criminal or evil motive."

In that case it seems to have been accepted that persons organising a lawful
and peaceful procession might be bound over if there was a threat of a breach
of the peace by others. The earlier English case of *Beatty* v. *Gillbanks* (1882) 9
Q.B.D. 308 had rejected any such idea, but in *Wise* v. *Dunning* [1902] 1 K.B.
167 a later divisional court indicated that, in so far as there was any conflict
between the *Orr* and *Beatty* cases, the former was to be preferred.

The preventive jurisdiction represented by binding over might still perhaps be exercised following a conviction for unlawful assembly or some other
public order offence, such as committing a breach of the peace.[41] But it must
be very doubtful whether it could be exercised in the absence of a conviction.
Any such decision would seem to represent that form of preventive justice
condemned by the Supreme Court in the bail case of *People (Att. Gen.)* v.
O'Callaghan [1966] I.R. 501, and to be contrary to the philosophy underlying
Articles 38.1 and 40.4.1° of the Constitution.

Other offences

Under section 38 of the Offences against the Person Act 1861 it is an
offence wilfully to "obstruct any peace officer in the due execution of his

---

[41] In *Att. Gen.* v. *Cunningham* [1932] I.R. 28 the accused had been convicted in the Circuit Court
on an indictment containing four counts. The Court of Criminal Appeal quashed the conviction on count four because it did not contain a sufficient statement of the offence. But the

duty." The penalty on conviction on indictment is imprisonment for up to
two years; on summary conviction, a fine of up to £1,000 and/or 12 months'
imprisonment.[42] In the English case of *Duncan* v. *Jones* [1936] 1 K.B. 218 it
was held that where a policeman reasonably apprehended that a breach of
the peace would result from the holding of a public meeting, it was his duty
to prevent this, and if he was deliberately obstructed in doing so this
amounted to wilful obstruction in the execution of his duty. The effect again
was to vest a considerable discretion in the police, extending to prohibiting
the holding of a meeting, *e.g.* if a hostile element in the audience was anticipated.

It is not clear whether *Duncan's* case represents modern Irish law. The
principles on which it is based—the duty of the police to prevent breaches of
the peace and to take any reasonably necessary steps towards that end—
underlie the *Humphries—O'Kelly—Coyne* cases discussed earlier; but no post-
independence court has had occasion to consider their applicability. An
obvious danger lies in the wide discretion given to the police, which is
capable of abuse especially if the courts decline to examine closely the justification for preventive action. *Duncan's* case has been criticised on this latter
ground,[43] and if it does represent modern Irish law it is to be hoped that the
courts will recognise the need for vigilant scrutiny, as the United States
Supreme Court did in *Feiner* v. *New York* (1951) 340 U.S. 315.

Section 2 of the Prohibition of Incitement to Hatred Act 1989 has the effect
of penalising things said at a public meeting[44] which are (a) threatening,
abusive or insulting[45] *and* (b) are intended, or likely, to stir up hatred against
a group of persons on the grounds of their race, colour, nationality, religion,
ethnic or national origins, membership of the travelling community or sexual
orientation. A Garda member who reasonably suspects that someone has
committed such an offence may arrest him/her without warrant: section
10(1).[46]

Some protection for a lawful meeting is afforded by the Public Meeting Act
1908, s.1. This provides that any person who at a lawful public meeting acts
in a disorderly manner for the purpose of preventing the transaction of the
business for which the meeting was called together, or who incites others to
do so, shall be guilty of an offence. The maximum penalty is a fine of £5 or
one month's imprisonment. Nowadays it is held in some circles that there
can be no free speech for certain viewpoints, and it is thought proper to take
concerted action to disrupt relevant meetings. The 1908 Act's penalties may
be inadequate to cope with this, and it is noteworthy that in 1985 the Law
Reform Commission proposed that they be increased to a fine of £100 and/or
one month's imprisonment. In appropriate circumstances persons acting
thus could be prosecuted on indictment for creating a breach of the peace.

court also held that on a properly framed charge of breach of the peace a jury must have
found the appellant guilty; consequently he was bound over to keep the peace for three years
and in default to be imprisoned for six months.

[42] Criminal Justice Act 1951, s.4, as amended by s.17, Criminal Justice Act 1984. (Offences
under s.38 of the 1861 Act are scheduled offences under the 1951 Act.)

[43] See Williams, *op. cit.*, pp. 119–125.

[44] Defined in s.2(3) as "a meeting at which the public are entitled to be present, on payment or
otherwise and as of right or by virtue of an express or implied permission."

[45] In *Brutus* v. *Cozzens* [1973] A.C. 854 the House of Lords held that similar words in s.5 of the
Public Order Act 1936 must be given their ordinary English meaning.

[46] As to the penalties upon conviction, see *supra.*

This is recognised as a common law offence in Ireland—*Att. Gen.* v. *Cunningham* [1932] I.R. 28, where the Court of Criminal Appeal held that the gist of the offence was an act of a nature to cause reasonable alarm and apprehension to members of the public.

In *Thomas* v. *Sawkins* [1935] 2 K.B. 249 the appellant was one of the organisers of a meeting, held in private premises, to which the public had been invited. The respondent, a police sergeant, and an inspector insisted on attending, despite repeated requests from Thomas to leave. Thomas then attempted to eject the inspector but was restrained by Sawkins. Subsequently Thomas prosecuted Sawkins for assault, and when the magistrates dismissed the charge he appealed to the divisional court. The court (Lord Hewart C.J., Avory and Lawrence JJ.) dismissed the appeal, but the scope of the decision has never been clear. The court seems to have proceeded on the basis that the police had reasonable grounds for anticipating seditious speeches and/or a breach of the peace. Lord Hewart C.J. concluded that the police had a right of entry if they reasonably believed *any* offence was imminent or likely to be committed. Avory J. seemed to hold that the right of entry arose from a reasonably anticipated breach of the peace. Lawrence J., with *Humphries* v. *Connor* (1864) 17 I.C.L.R. 1 obviously in mind, said that if a policeman was entitled to commit an assault to preserve the peace he was equally entitled to commit a trespass.[47]

There is no Irish decision equivalent to *Thomas* v. *Sawkins*—though once again its conclusion may follow on logically from the 19th century Irish trilogy of *Humphries/O'Kelly/Coyne*. But it seems a moot point whether a modern Irish court would go so far.

Picketing

The Irish courts have proceeded on the basis that picketing is unlawful unless covered by the Industrial Relations Act 1990, s.14.[48] That is, the picketing—unless so covered—constitutes the tort of nuisance and is in addition an offence ("watching and besetting") under the Conspiracy and Protection of Property Act 1875, s.7.[49] There are good grounds for believing that this view is incorrect.[50] Its consequences are that, absent a trade dispute, picketers protesting about a publican's prices, a supermarket's standards or an unauthorised development are in breach of the law. Such a result—assuming peaceful picketing—would consort oddly with the proclaimed right of assembly; and to protect trade union pickets—but not others—from liability would hardly be congruent with equality before the law.[51]

---

[47] For a critical analysis of the case see Williams, *op. cit.*, pp. 144–149.
[48] s.14 replaces s.2 of the Trade Disputes Act 1906.
[49] See especially *Educational Co.* v. *Fitzpatrick* [1961] I.R. 345.
[50] An admirable analysis is to be found in Tony Kerr and Gerry Whyte, *Irish Trade Union Law* (Abingdon 1985), Chap. 10.
[51] See *Police Dept. of Chicago* v. *Mosley* (1972) 408 U.S. 92.

16　Freedom of Association

Article 40.6 of Bunreacht na hÉireann protects freedom of association in the following terms:

> "1° The State guarantees liberty for the exercise of the following rights, subject to public order and morality:
> (iii) The right of the citizens to form associations and unions.
> Laws, however, may be enacted for the regulation and control in the public interest of the exercise of the foregoing right.
> 2° Laws regulating the manner in which the right of forming associations and unions . . . may be exercised shall contain no political religious or class discrimination."

It will be clear from this that the guarantee is a qualified one, with the Oireachtas empowered to intervene in the name of public order, public morality, or more generally, "the public interest." But in fact there are few restrictions on freedom of association. In general, clubs, societies and other organisations may be formed and dissolved at will, and no prior judicial or administrative sanction, such as exists in other states, is required.[1] However, the full benefits of association may be subject to compliance with legal requirements; thus while any group of persons is at liberty to carry on a business, if its members seek the privilege of limited liability they must comply with the provisions of the Companies Acts.

POLITICAL PARTIES

There are no restrictions on the formation of political parties, but for the party's name to appear on ballot papers registration is essential. This is governed by the Electoral Act 1963, s.13. Application is made to the Registrar of Political Parties (who is the Clerk of the Dáil), and he is obliged to register it if, in his opinion, it is "a genuine political party" and "is organised to contest a Dáil election or a local election" (s.13(2)(b)). He must refuse registration if the name of the applicant party is identical with that of any party already registered, or so nearly resembles such name as to be calculated to mislead, confuse or deceive; or if the name, in his opinion, is unnecessarily long; or, if

---

[1] See the decision of the French *Conseil Constitutionnel* of July 16, 1971, D.S. 1972. 685.

the party operates only in relation to a particular part of the State, its name does not indicate this (s.13(5)). An appeal from the Registrar's decision lies to an appeal board consisting of a High Court judge, the Ceann Comhairle (or Leas Ceann Comhairle) of the Dáil and the Cathaoirleach (or Leas Cathaoirleach) of the Seanad—section 13(8).

In *Loftus* v. *Att. Gen.* [1979] I.R. 221 the Supreme Court laid it down that the words "genuine political party" in section 13(2)(*b*) did not refer to the extent to which the group in question had established itself in the public consciousness, or to the range or effectiveness of its organisation. A group would be "a genuine political party" if it was bound together by the cohesion of common political beliefs or aims, and by being organised for electoral purposes into an entity to such an extent and with such distinctiveness as to justify its claim to be a truly political party in its own right. The court also held that the words "organised to contest a Dáil election" did not relate to the degree or perfection of the organisation, but to the fact of being organised for that object and purpose. Finally, the court ruled that parties with nationwide ambitions, whose actual current strength restricted their activity to a particular area, did not fall within section 13(5)(*c*). They were not the local parties envisaged by that provision, but small national parties.

UNLAWFUL ORGANISATIONS

Part III of the Offences against the State Act 1939 contains extensive provisions in regard to unlawful organisations. By virtue of Section 18, such an organisation is one which

"(a) engages in, promotes, encourages, or advocates the commission of treason or any activity of a treasonable nature[2] or

(b) advocates, encourages or attempts the procuring by force, violence or other unconstitutional means of an alteration of the Constitution, or

(c) raises or maintains or attempts to raise or maintain a military or armed force in contravention of the Constitution or without constitutional authority, or

(d) engages in, promotes, encourages or advocates the commission of any criminal offence or the obstruction of or interference with the administration of justice or the enforcement of the law, or

(e) engages in, promotes, encourages, or advocates the attainment of any particular object, lawful or unlawful, by violent, criminal, or other unlawful means, or

(f) promotes, encourages or advocates the non-payment of moneys payable to the Central Fund or any other public fund or the non-payment of local taxation . . . "

---

[2] This must be read subject to Art. 39: "Treason shall consist only in levying war against the State, or assisting any State or person or inciting or conspiring with any person to levy war against the State, or attempting by force of arms or other violent means to overthrow the organs of government established by this Constitution, or taking part or being concerned in or inciting or conspiring with any person to make or take part or be concerned in any such attempt."

Section 19 empowers the Government to make suppression orders in regard to unlawful organisations. Any such order must be published in *Iris Oifigiúil* (the government gazette): s.19(3). Save in regard to an application for a declaration of legality, a suppression order is conclusive evidence for all purposes that the organisation in question is an unlawful organisation within the meaning of the Act: s.19(4). One consequence of a suppression order is that all the organisation's property becomes forfeit to and vested in the Minister for Justice: s.22(*a*).

Section 20 provides that any person claiming to be a member of an organisation subject to a suppression order may, within 30 days of the order's publication, apply summarily to the High Court for a declaration that the organisation is not an unlawful one. Such a declaration, if granted, annuls the suppression order: s.20(4). An appeal lies to the Supreme Court from the High Court's decision, at the instance either of the applicant or the Attorney General: s.20(4) and (5). Should the application fail, and the applicant subsequently be prosecuted for membership of an unlawful organisation, evidence given by him or on his behalf in the application is inadmissible in the prosecution: s.20(6). As to the consequences of a declaration of legality, see s.23.

By virtue of section 21 membership of an unlawful organisation is a criminal offence, punishable on summary conviction by a fine not exceeding £50 and/or three months imprisonment; or, on conviction on indictment, to imprisonment for a term not exceeding seven years (s.21(2)(6), as amended by the Criminal Law Act 1976 s.2(6)). It is a good defence for the person charged to show that he did not know the organisation was an unlawful organisation; or that as soon as reasonably possible after he became aware of its real nature, or after its suppression by order, he ceased to be a member and dissociated himself therefrom—s.21(3). On a charge of membership of an unlawful organisation, proof that an incriminating document relating thereto was found on the person charged, or in his possession or on lands or premises owned, occupied or controlled by him is evidence of such membership until the contrary is proved: s.24. Further, under section 3(1) of the Offences against the State (Amendment) Act 1972, any statement, oral or written, by an accused implying or leading to a reasonable inference that he was a member of an unlawful organisation is evidence of such membership. "Conduct" here includes an omission by the accused to deny published reports that he was a member of an unlawful organisation (though the fact of such denial is not by itself conclusive). By virtue of section 3(2) of the 1972 Act, a statement by a Garda officer not below the rank of Chief Superintendent that he believes that the accused was at a material time a member of an unlawful organisation is admissible in evidence—*before a special criminal court only*. (Such a statement is not of course, conclusive and may be rebutted by the accused's sworn denial.)

It is likewise an offence to recruit for an unlawful organisation, or to incite or invite other persons to join, take part in, support or assist its activities: Criminal Law Act 1976, s.3. The punishment on conviction on indictment is imprisonment for a term not exceeding 10 years.

Power to close buildings used for the purposes of an unlawful organisation is conferred on senior Garda officers by section 25 of the 1939 Act (as amended by Section 4, Criminal Law Act 1976). An application may be made to the High Court for the quashing of any such order on the ground of unreasonableness: s.25(3).[3] No such order may be in force for more than three years: s.25(6), inserted by Criminal Law Act 1976, s.4.

TRADE UNIONS

Trade unions are regulated by the Trade Union Acts 1871–1990. It has long been an object of legislative policy to reduce their number, not least because different unions recruit the same kinds of workers, and competition between them has given rise to prolonged industrial disputes. This policy has been implemented in two distinct ways, firstly by restricting negotiating rights, and secondly by facilitating the voluntary amalgamation of unions. Thus the Trade Union Act 1941, s.6, provides that it is an offence for any group of persons to carry on negotiations for the fixing of wages or other conditions of employment, unless such body is the holder of a negotiation licence or is an excepted body. This Act, as amended, sets out the conditions for the grant of a negotiating licence, and defines the term "excepted body."[4] The Trade Union Act 1975 simplified the procedure for voluntary amalgamations[5] and provided for State grants towards expenses incurred thereby.[6]

Part III of the 1941 Act established a Trade Union Tribunal which had power, on the application of any union claiming to have organised a majority of workers of a particular class, to grant a determination that such union alone should have the right to organise members of that particular class. Under section 34(3), following such a determination, no other trade union could thereafter lawfully accept as a new member any workers of that class. In *N.U.R.* v. *Sullivan* [1947] I.R. 77 the plaintiffs sought a declaration that

---

[3] The first—and it seems so far the only—such application was *Ó Brádaigh* v. *Fleming* (*The Irish Times*, November 20, 1972). The order there was made in relation to part of certain premises in Dublin allegedly used by Sinn Féin. Kenny J. held that an order under s.25 would be set aside if the relevant Garda officer could not, on the evidence available to him, be reasonably satisfied that the building was being used for the purposes of an unlawful organisation. But it was sufficient if there was evidence on which a reasonable person could so conclude. In the instant case there was *inter alia* evidence of resort to the building by persons convicted under the Offences against the State Act of membership of an unlawful organisation, and it was a legitimate inference that they were there for the purposes of such organisation. The application was dismissed.

[4] On these matters see A. Kerr and G. Whyte, *Irish Trade Union Law* (Abingdon 1985), Ch. 2: Michael Forde, *Industrial Relations Law* (Dublin 1991), Ch. 2.

[5] In *N.U.J.* v. *Sisk* [1992] I.L.R.M. 96, the High Court had held that the Trade Union Act 1975 did not contemplate a merger between an Irish union and another which, though carrying on activities in Ireland, was not registered here. The Supreme Court reversed this decision. Finlay C.J. (Hederman, O'Flaherty and Egan JJ. concurring) said (at 111):

> "The right of members of a trade union to vote in favour of a transfer of engagements by that trade union to another, whether one registered within the state or not, would appear to me to be a necessary and valuable expansion of the general right to form trade unions and belong to them. If ss.2, 3 and 4 of the Act of 1975 were to be construed as prohibiting members of a trade union within the State from voting by an appropriate majority to transfer the engagements of that trade union to another trade union operating within the State but not registered under the Acts, this would necessarily be a regulation and control of the exercise of that right and would fall to be justified in the public interest.
>
> It does not seem to me, therefore, appropriate that the legislature should be interpreted as having by some form of implication, as distinct from a very express provision, regulated, controlled or restricted this particular right."

[6] See Kerr and Whyte, *op. cit.*, p. 77. S.22 of the Industrial Relations Act 1990 further relaxes the conditions for such grants: see Forde *op. cit.*, pp. 267–272.

Part III was unconstitutional. They argued that under it those who wished for an effective service would be compelled to join a privileged union, exercising a monopoly in organising workers of that grade, instead of being free to join any union they liked. In terms of Article 40.6.1°iii, they contended, this was not a "regulation" of the right to form unions, but a total prohibition thereof.

In the High Court Gavan Duffy J., in a judgment emphasising the constitutional power of the Oireachtas, upheld the validity of Part III. Citing United States authority, he concluded that the phrase "regulation and control" was broad enough to include prohibition; and he found that the text of the Constitution supported this view ([1947] I.R. 77, 88):

> "Side by side with the right to form unions, subject to laws for regulation and control in the public interest, the text places the right of free assembly, subject to laws for the prevention or control of certain troublesome sorts of meetings. It is insisted that the word 'prevent' is used in the one case and not in the other, but the more significant fact seems to me to be that the next subsection (Art. 40, clause 6, par. 2) goes on to group the restrictive laws for both rights as regulating laws, so that prevention and control must have been regarded as being only species of regulation . . . "

On appeal the Supreme Court, *per* Murnaghan J., reversed this decision and declared Part III unconstitutional. Article 40.6.1°iii, it was held, meant that each citizen was free to associate with others of his choice for any object agreed on by him and them—though the Oireachtas could regulate and control this process. Part III of the 1941 Act limited the citizens' right to one of joining one or more prescribed associations. The judgment continues ([1947] I.R. 77, 192):

> "Both logically and practically, to deprive a person of the choice of the persons with whom he will associate, is not a control of the exercise of the right of association, but a denial of the right altogether. It was stressed, in argument, that control, in the public interest, was given to the Oireachtas and that such control might extend to depriving the citizen of all freedom of choice of his associates, provided he could join a prescribed association for the particular object. The Constitution states the right of the citizens to form associations and unions in an emphatic way, and it seems impossible to harmonise this language with a law which prohibits the forming of associations and unions, and allows the citizens only to join prescribed associations and unions."

The Supreme Court's conclusions seem open to question, and there are grounds for doubting whether they would be accepted nowadays.[7] No attention was given to Gavan Duffy J.'s view—surely vital—that the constitutional text itself indicated that "regulation" could include prevention. Nor was sufficient attention directed to the Constitution's qualification on the

---

[7] In *Aughey* v. *Att. Gen.* [1989] I.L.R.M. 87 the Supreme Court was invited to reconsider *N.U.R.* v. *Sullivan* and to hold that "regulation" in Article 40.6.1°iii could include prohibiton. But given its interpretation of the statutory provision there impugned, the court found it unnecessary to embark on any such review.

freedom of association guarantee. The Supreme Court questionably described the Constitution as stating the right to form associations and unions "in an emphatic way." But that right is given no more emphasis than any other guaranteed by Article 40, and it is difficult to see how a guarantee can be described as "emphatic" when the right guaranteed is immediately subjected to regulation and control by law. However, the Supreme Court seemed unprepared to allow the proviso much scope.

A quite different attitude was manifest in the much later case of *P.M.P.S. Ltd. and Moore* v. *Att. Gen.* [1983] I.R. 339. The plaintiff society, an industrial and provident society, and Mr. Moore, a shareholder, impugned the validity of the Industrial and Provident Societies (Amendment) Act 1978, which (*inter alia*) forbade the Society to accept or hold deposits. This, Mr. Moore claimed, was a violation of his right of association. The society was formed for the purpose of taking deposits, and to prohibit it by law from doing what he and his associates joined together to achieve was to frustrate the right of association. The Supreme Court found this contention unsustainable. In an earlier part of its judgment the court had characterised the 1978 Act as a reasonable regulation and control of the range of business the society might transact. The judgment, *per* O'Higgins C.J., continues ([1983] I.R. 339, 361–62):

> "Mr. Moore's right to associate with others has not been interfered with. The exercise of such a right is not prevented by a law limiting and controlling in the public interest what such an association may do. In this instance, the law which is impugned does no more than to regulate what the society or association may do and this is not an infringement of Article 40, s.6, subs. 1(iii) of the Constitution."

While the issue dealt with in the above case is not identical with that in *N.U.R.* v. *Sullivan* the observations quoted indicate a much greater deference to legislative judgment than in the earlier case. Thus legislation of the kind condemned in *N.U.R.* v. *Sullivan* might nowadays stand a better chance of surviving judicial scrutiny.

As the law stands today, an individual is free to join any union—or none. For practical reasons there is an advantage in joining an established union with a negotiating licence, but the law does not compel one to do this. New unions may be formed and may qualify for negotiating licences if they fulfil the statutory requirements. Thus, for most workers, restrictions on this aspect of freedom of association hardly exist. But some are in a special situation: as in most states, public employees such as members of the Garda Síochána, the Defence Forces or the Civil Service are restricted in their freedom of association. The validity of one such restriction was recently tested in *Aughey* v. *Ireland* [1989] I.L.R.M. 87. The plaintiffs, who were members of the Garda Síochána sought a declaration that section 13 of the Garda Síochána Act 1924 (inserted by section 1 of the Garda Síochána Act 1977) was unconstitutional. Section 13 provided for the formation of independent representative associations, unconnected with any outside person or body, and continued:

> "(3) It shall not be lawful for a member of the Garda Síochána to be or become a member of any trade union or of any association other than an association established under this section of which the objects or one of

the objects are or is to control or influence the pay, pensions or conditions of service of any police force."[8]

This, argued the plaintiffs, denied them freedom of association; they were subjected to the kind of compulsion condemned in *N.U.R.* v. *Sullivan* [1947] I.R. 77.

In the High Court Barrington J. rejected this contention, holding that the public order qualification in Article 40.6.1°iii justified this statutory restriction ([1986] I.L.R.M. 206). The Supreme Court affirmed his ruling, though on somewhat different grounds. Walsh J., giving the judgment, said that section 13 imposed no prohibition on members of the Garda Síochána forming or joining trade unions or other associations, provided that their objects did not include controlling or influencing the pay, pensions or conditions of service of any police force. Hence the issue was whether section 13 was valid as a "regulation and control in the public interest" of the plaintiffs' right of association. Walsh J. concluded that it was ([1989] I.L.R.M. 87, 92–93):

> "The plaintiffs have the undoubted right to form associations and unions and that right is guaranteed by the Constitution. But because they are police officers the law has provided that there shall be excluded from the objects of such associations or unions the objects of seeking to influence or to control the 'pay, pensions or conditions of service of any police force.' The members of the Garda Síochána may pursue these objects only through associations based on rank and formed pursuant to s.13(1). Such exclusions are captured by the expressions 'regulation or control'. While these are important exclusions they do not affect the many other objectives that can legitimately be those of a trade union or an association. The statute concentrated on areas of particular sensitivity in a police force. If these areas became the subject of multi-union or multi-association agitation or industrial action by members of the Garda Síochána, it would be a matter of grave public concern and public interest particularly because of the fact that the Garda Síochána is a unitary national police force. In the light of these considerations it cannot be said that s.1 of the Garda Síochána Act 1977 amending by substitution s.13 of the Garda Síochána Act 1924, is an unreasonable or disproportionate regulation of the exercise of the right guaranteed by the Constitution, nor can it be said to strike at the roots of that constitutionally guaranteed right, namely the right to form associations and unions."

"Freedom of dissociation"

Two Supreme Court decisions make it clear that there is a constitutional right not to be compelled to be a member of a union—*Educational Co. Ltd.* v. *Fitzpatrick (No. 2)* [1961] I.R. 345 and *Meskell* v. *C.I.É.* [1973] I.R. 121. In the former case certain of the defendants, members of the Irish Union of Distributive Workers and Clerks, were employed by the plaintiff company.

[8] Broadly similar provisions are contained in the Defence (Amendment) Act 1990, which provides for the establishment of representative associations in the Defence Forces. The matters these associations may raise include remuneration but exclude "matters relating to any operation and the raising, maintenance, command, constitution, organisation and discipline of the Defence Forces."

Though most of the company's workers belonged to the union, there were nine who did not, and the union's efforts to persuade them to join were unavailing. When asked to make union membership obligatory, on pain of dismissal, the company refused. The union then called a strike and placed a picket on the company's premises. When the company sought an injunction to restrain the picketing, the defendants argued that the picketing was protected by the Trade Disputes Act 1906, s.2. To this the plaintiff company replied that insofar as section 2 authorised picketing to secure compulsory union membership, it was repugnant to Article 40.6.1°iii of the Constitution. The Supreme Court accepted this latter contention by a 3–2 majority— Kingsmill Moore, Ó Dálaigh and Haugh JJ.: Maguire C.J. and Lavery J. dissenting.

The majority decision in the *Educational Co.* case is based on two separate and distinct lines of reasoning, Kingsmill Moore J. (Ó Dálaigh J. concurring) held that Article 40.6.1°iii carried an implied guarantee that citizens should not be compelled to join associations against their will; he referred to " . . . the right of free . . . dissociation guaranteed by the Constitution": ([1961] I.R. 345, 397, 398). Picketing with such an aim was coercion, and statute could not legalise it. Haugh J. concluded that the nine non-union employees had exercised their right of association—by forming a temporary combination the object of which was to stay out of the union. The defendants' conduct interfered with the exercise of this right and could not be protected by section 2 of the 1906 Act.

In *Meskell* v. *C.I.É.* [1973] I.R. 121 the plaintiff had been employed as a bus conductor by the defendant company for 15 years. At all times he had been a union member though under no contractual obligation in that regard. In 1958 the company made membership of the appropriate trade union a condition of employment for new workers, but difficulties later arose in regard to persons who were falling into arrears with union dues. Eventually the company and the unions agreed upon a plan whereby all the company's workers would be dismissed and simultaneously offered new contracts of employment. These were on the same terms as before—but with the addition that each worker would now accept an obligation to be at all times a member of a representative union. The plaintiff refused to accept the new terms and his dismissal accordingly took effect. He sued for damages, claiming that his dismissal resulted from a conspiracy between the defendant company and the unions and was a violation of his constitutional rights. In the High Court Teevan J. dismissed the suit but his decision was reversed by the Supreme Court (Ó Dálaigh C.J. Walsh and Budd JJ.). The judgment of Walsh J. (Ó Dálaigh C.J. and Budd J. concurring) reaffirms the existence of an implied constitutional right of dissociation. One who had suffered damage by virtue of a breach, or infringement, of a constitutional right was entitled to redress against those infringing that right. Here the plaintiff was entitled to a declaration that his dismissal was a denial and violation of his constitutional rights, and that the agreement between the unions and C.I.É. to procure or cause that dismissal was an actionable conspiracy because the means employed constituted a breach of the plaintiff's constitutional rights. Additionally, he was entitled to such damages as might, upon inquiry, be proved to have been sustained by him.

Walsh J. made it clear that an employer's powers of dismissal must now be understood as having been qualified by the Constitution. To dismiss, or threaten to dismiss, a worker for exercising the constitutional right of association would give rise to liability in damages. The same applied where the worker insisted on his/her right to dissociate.

Dismissal on grounds of union membership is now covered by the Unfair Dismissals Act 1977, s.6(2). This provides that a dismissal shall be deemed unfair if it results wholly or mainly from

> "(a) the employee's membership or proposal that he or another person become a member of, or his engaging in activities on behalf of, a trade union or excepted body under the Trade Union Acts, 1941 and 1971, where the times at which he engages in such activities are outside his hours of work or are at times during his hours of work in which he is permitted pursuant to the contract of employment between him and his employer so to engage."[9]

Section 6(2)(*a*) does not protect union members against discriminatory action falling short of dismissal. Nor does it assist someone refused employment because of his/her union membership. Most notably, it offers no protection to those who exercise their constitutional right of dissociation. Of course, it does not follow that such persons are without legal remedy. Following *Meskell* v. *C.I.É.* an individual dismissed for refusing to join a union may bring an action in the courts. There will certainly be a remedy in damages; whether an order for reinstatement in one's job could be obtained is unclear, the point being left open in *Meskell's* case (see [1973] I.R. 121, 135). Equally unresolved is the question whether a refusal of employment motivated by union membership (or the lack thereof) may involve liability: in *Meskell's* case Walsh J. specifically declined to express any view on this point (see [1973] I.R. 121, 136). In *Educational Co. Ltd.* v. *Fitzpatrick (No. 2)* [1961] I.R. 345, 396 Kingsmill Moore J., *obiter*, indicated that the law could not intervene here, but this view is open to question.[10] As to disciplinary action falling short of dismissal, it is possible that this may give rise to liability if motivated by union membership or non-membership. In *Meskell's* case Walsh J. spoke of a person being "penalised" for exercising his/her constitutional rights ([1973] I.R. 121, 135) and such treatment would seem to answer this description.

The closed shop

It will be clear from the cases examined above that the Constitution is a barrier to the operation of a closed shop—*i.e.* a system under which one's continued employment depends on remaining a member of a union. *Meskell's* case means that enforcing such a system by dismissal, or the threat thereof, may be legally precarious. Union attempts to *secure* such a system may also run foul of the law; the *Educational Co.* case shows that picketing to compel union membership is restrainable by injunction. Other forms of action are likewise doubtful, even though the judgments in the *Educational Co.* case are carefully limited. A union which calls a strike to enforce a closed shop may incur liability in tort—*e.g.* for inducing breaches of employment contracts or for conspiracy. Such statutory protection against liability as normally exists

---

[9] For a discussion of this provision see Kerr and Whyte, *op. cit.*, pp. 33–37: Forde, *op. cit.*, pp. 63–64.
[10] See J. P. Casey (1972) 21 I.C.L.Q. 699, 717.

here under the Industrial Relations Act 1990 is probably inapplicable, since there is necessarily involved an attempt to deprive individuals of their right to dissociate.

The decisions in *N.U.R.* v. *Sullivan, Educational Co.* v. *Fitzpatrick* and *Meskell* v. *C.I.É.* would likewise pose barriers to any *legislative* attempt to create, or aid the operation of, a closed shop. In any event the European Convention on Human Rights would inhibit any such action: see the judgment of the Court of Human Rights in *Young, James, and Webster* v. *U.K.* (1981) 4 E.H.R.R. 38.

In *Becton Dickinson Ltd.* v. *Lee* [1973] I.R. 1 Henchy J.—the only member of the Supreme Court to refer to the matter—suggested that there was no constitutional impediment to providing by contract that membership of a particular union should be a prerequisite for a particular employment (at 48). If this is so, then an employer could make union membership a condition of a job offer. Henchy J., however, expressed no view on whether a condition requiring indefinite union membership would be compatible with the Constitution. This must limit the utility of the device—which, in any event, given the facts in *Meskell's* case, would seem to apply only where a totally new workforce is being recruited.

Workers who choose not to join a union may nonetheless benefit from improved terms and conditions negotiated by that union—which may well be resented by unionised colleagues whose membership contributions help to fund the negotiators' salaries. But if the non-unionists are legally entitled to the improvements[11] the employer cannot withhold them; and even if no legal entitlement exists, to withhold them may be impracticable. Whether, if it were practicable, such a discrimination would be invalid as pressurising the non-unionists to forgo their right of dissociation is not clear.[12] An alternative would be an arrangement under which non-members contribute to union funds at the same level as their colleagues. This device—known as "the Rand formula"—is familiar in Canada, where the Supreme Court has rejected a claim that it infringed the freedom of association guaranteed by the Charter of Rights and Freedoms: *Lavigne* v. *Ontario Public Service Employees' Union* (1991) 81 D.L.R. (4th) 545. Three members of the court—La Forest, Sopinka and Gonthier JJ.—held that freedom of association embraced freedom from compelled association.[13] Nonetheless, the Rand formula was validated by section 1 of the Charter[14] as a justifiable limitation on that freedom.[15] Its objectives, of encouraging union democracy and permitting unions to be players in the broader political, economic and social debates in

---

[11] As would be the case where the terms of a collective agreement are incorporated into individual contracts of employment: see further Kerr and Whyte, *op. cit.*, pp. 159–165: Forde, *op. cit.*, pp. 99–100.

[12] The Belgian Conseil d'État concluded that such a differentiation is valid, but the German Federal Labour Court took the opposite view: see Casey, *op. cit.* n. 4 *supra*, pp. 708–709.

[13] Wilson, L'Heureux-Dubé and Cory JJ. held that freedom of association did *not* include freedom not to associate. McLachlin J. held that *if* freedom of associaton embraced freedom not to associate it was as a guarantee against "coerced ideological conformity".

[14] s.1 provides: "The Canadian Charter of Rights and Freedoms guarantees the rights and freedoms set out in it subject only to such reasonable limits prescribed by law as can be demonstrably justified in a free and democratic society."

[15] The appellant Lavigne also founded on the fact that there were no legal restraints on the uses to which his payments could be put. And the union had given financial support to several causes of which he disapproved. This, he claimed, violated his right to freedom of expression under s.2(b) of the Charter. The Supreme Court also rejected this argument: see further Ch. 15 *supra*.

society, were important; and the means chosen to advance them were proportional to those ends.[16]

The textual differences between the Canadian Charter and Bunreacht na hÉireann offer an obvious means of distinguishing the *Lavigne* case; consequently one cannot be certain that an Irish version of the Rand formula would survive constitutional scrutiny. It must be borne in mind, however, that the right of dissociation under Bunreacht na hÉireann is not absolute. If it derives its protection from Article 40.6.1°iii, then it is subject to regulation and control in the public interest. Alternatively, if it gains its constitutional shelter from Article 40.3—as an unenumerated right—it is protected "as far as practicable." Whether either of these qualifications would permit limitations similar to those allowable under section 1 of the Canadian Charter still awaits resolution.

No constitutional right to join a union

Article 40.6.1°iii refers to a right to "form" associations and unions; and it has been held that, subject to one possible exception, the Constitution confers no right to join a union. This is a matter for the rules, and the members, and an individual refused admission can get no help from the Constitution—*Tierney* v. *Amalgamated Society of Woodworkers* [1959] I.R. 254: *Murphy* v. *Stewart* [1973] I.R. 97. In the latter case, however, Walsh J. (with whom the other members of the Supreme Court agreed) said ([1973] I.R. 97, 117):

> " . . . in ordinary circumstances before a person can join an existing union or association he must be entitled to do so either by law, or by the rules of that association or union, or by the consent of its members. This is, broadly, speaking, the effect of the decision in *Tierney* v. *Amalgamated Society of Woodworkers*; but it is not a completely unqualified statement of the constitutional position. It has been submitted in this Court on behalf of the plaintiff . . . that among the unspecified personal rights guaranteed by the Constitution is the right to work. I accept that proposition. The question of whether that right is being infringed or not must depend upon the particular circumstances of any given case; if the right to work was reserved exclusively to members of a trade union which held a monopoly in this field and the trade union was abusing the monopoly in such a way as to effectively prevent the exercise of a person's constitutional right to work, the question of compelling that union to accept the person concerned into membership (or, indeed, of breaking the monopoly) would fall to be considered for the purpose of vindicating the right to work."

An obligation to admit to membership someone whom existing members declined to be associated with might seem to run counter to *their* constitutional right of dissociation. But if the obligation is imposed in the interests of a person's constitutional right to work, different considerations may arise.

An individual whose wish to transfer from one union to another is frustrated by the first union's refusal to consent thereto cannot claim an infringement of his/her constitutional rights: *Murphy* v. *Stewart* [1973] I.R. 97.

---

[16] Wilson J. (L'Heureux-Dubé and Cory JJ. concurring) said that if she was wrong in holding that the constitutional right of association did not involve a right not to associate, she would hold that the Rand formula was justified under s.1 of the Charter.

The Constitution and the rights of union members

Union members' rights depend initially on the relevant rule book. But its contents are subject to constitutional constraints; thus any provisions on the disciplining of members would fall to be assessed in the light of the constitutional guarantee of fair procedures.[17] However there is more. In *Doyle* v. *Croke* (High Court, No. 1126P, May 6, 1988) Costello J. so held, following a decision of Finlay P. in *Rodgers* v. *I.T.G.W.U.* [1978] I.L.R.M. 51. Costello J. said (pp. 15–16 of his judgment):

> "That decision established that a member of a trade union has a right to require that in the conduct of the affairs of the trade union fair procedures will be adopted, and that in certain circumstances the failure to give notice of a proposed resolution could amount to a breach of fair procedures and be a ground for invalidating it . . . if the constitutional right of citizens to form associations and unions is to be effective the Article in which it is to be found should not be construed restrictively as the right would be of limited value if it did not protect individual members against procedures which might be unfair to them."[18]

Arrangements for a meeting to discuss some pertinent issue—such as the terms for settling a dispute[19]—must comport with these principles, otherwise any resolution passed may be open to challenge.

COLLECTIVE ACTION AND THE CONSTITUTION

No right to recognition

Trade unions plainly exist to represent their members, either on the industrial or political fronts. For this they need to secure recognition from employers as the negotiating bodies on behalf of their members. But a trade union, even one which holds a negotiating licence, cannot claim a constitutional right to be recognised for negotiating purposes, nor will its members have a right of action if it is not recognised. McWilliam J. so held in *Abbott and Whelan* v. *I.T.G.W.U. and Southern Health Board* (High Court, December 2, 1980). The plaintiffs there were non-nursing staff employed by the Southern Health Board. Like the plaintiffs, the majority of such staff were members of the Irish Transport and General Workers' Union (I.T.G.W.U.), and the Board recognised that union as the negotiating agent for such staff. Subsequently the plaintiffs and other left I.T.G.W.U. and joined the Amalgamated Transport and General Workers' Union (A.T.G.W.U.). These transfers were not consented to by I.T.G.W.U., which carried the matter to the Irish Congress of Trade Unions (I.C.T.U.), of which both unions were members. I.C.T.U. found that A.T.G.W.U. was in breach of the rules, that it should not attempt to organise these workers and should encourage them to rejoin I.T.G.W.U. In the meantime, a dispute had arisen with the Southern Health Board which concerned an A.T.G.W.U. member; but the Board refused to negotiate with A.T.G.W.U. on the matter, as it feared that to do so

---

[17] See further Kerr and Whyte, *op. cit.*, Ch. 5: Forde, *op. cit.*, pp. 259–265.
[18] This broad reading of Article 40.6.1°iii led Costello J. to reject the criticism of *Rodgers* v. *I.T.G.W.U.* in Kerr and Whyte, *op. cit.*, pp. 24–26.
[19] As in *Doyle* v. *Croke* itself.

might result in industrial action by I.T.G.W.U. The plaintiffs then instituted proceedings claiming, *inter alia*, an order restraining the defendants from interfering with the plaintiffs' constitutional right to join the union of their choice and to be represented by it in negotiations with their employers.

McWilliam J. referred to *N.U.R.* v. *Sullivan* [1947] I.R. 77, *Educational Co.* v. *Fitzpatrick (No. 2)* [1961] I.R. 345, and *Meskell* v. *C.I.É.* [1973] I.R. 121. In these cases, said the judge, active steps were taken to compel citizens to forgo their constitutional rights; but here no such situation arose. The plaintiffs were contending that the Board, which did not wish to negotiate with the A.T.G.W.U., must nonetheless do so, so that the plaintiffs could obtain certain advantages from the exercise of their constitutional rights. This was a great extension of the principle that a citizen must not be coerced into joining a union against his will, and there was no authority for extending it thus far. The Board's refusal to negotiate with A.T.G.W.U. was not coercion within the principles established by the authorities. McWilliam J.'s conclusion that there was no constitutional right to recognition or to negotiate was accepted by Murphy J. in *Inspector of Taxes Association* v. *Minister for the Public Service* (March 24, 1983).[20] It would also derive implicit support from the Supreme Court decision in *P.M.P.S. and Moore* v. *Att. Gen.* [1983] I.R. 339. And courts in other countries have reached similar conclusions: see the Indian Supreme Court's decision in *All India Bank Employees Association* v. *National Industrial Tribunal* A.I.R. (1962) Sup.Ct. 171: that of the Judicial Committee in *Collymore* v. *Att.-Gen. of Trinidad & Tobago* [1970] A.C. 538; and that of the Canadian Supreme Court in *Professional Institute of the Public Service of Canada* v. *Commr. of the Northwest Territories* (1990) 72 D.L.R. (4th) 1.

There is no general *statutory* obligation on employers to recognise or negotiate with unions. However, a dispute over such matters is a "trade dispute" within the Industrial Relations Act 1990, so a union may take industrial action to secure recognition, without incurring legal liability. Or it may seek a Labour Court recommendation on the matter (as the term implies, there is no legal obligation on the employer to accept this).[21]

The right to strike

The Constitution does not specifically recognise a right to strike but in the *Educational Co.* case Kingsmill Moore J. took the view that it did so by implication. He said ([1961] I.R. 345, 397):

"The right to dispose of one's labour and to withdraw it seem to me a fundamental personal right which, though not specifically mentioned in the Constitution as being guaranteed, is a right of a nature which I cannot conceive to have been adversely affected by anything within the intendment of the Constitution."

But this implicit constitutional right to strike is far from being an absolute one. As an implied—or "unenumerated"—right, it would derive its protection from Article 40.3, and would consequently have to yield to the considerations of practicability and justice mentioned therein. It is therefore probable

---

[20] The Supreme Court's judgment on appeal in this case—reported at [1986] I.L.R.M. 296—does not refer to this matter.
[21] See further Kerr and Whyte, *op. cit.*, pp. 19–23: Tony Kerr, "Irish Industrial Relations Legislation: Consensus not Compulsion" (1991) 20 *Industrial Law Journal* 240.

that some legislative restrictions on the right to strike would be upheld—*e.g.* a prohibition on strikes by public servants (including the Garda Síochána and the Defence Forces), or, perhaps, a temporary general prohibition to enforce a statutory incomes policy. The Canadian Supreme Court has rejected a challenge, on freedom of association grounds, to a statute restricting public servants' right to strike: *Reference re Public Service Employee Relations Act (Alberta)* (1989) 38 D.L.R. (4th) 161.

The right to strike may not be exercised so as to violate the constitutional rights of others. In *Crowley* v. *Ireland* [1980] I.R. 102 the Irish National Teachers Organisation was in dispute with the board of management of the Drimoleague national schools in West Cork, over the appointment of a principal teacher. A strike ensued at three of the seven schools and the I.N.T.O. issued a circular to teachers in neighbouring schools, instructing them not to enrol Drimoleague pupils. The plaintiffs claimed damages, on the basis that the I.N.T.O. directive was an unlawful interference with their constitutional right to free primary education, which sprang from Article 42.4—"The State shall provide for free primary education . . . "

McMahon J. held that the State's constitutional duty to provide for free primary education created a corresponding right to receive such education. If I.N.T.O. members' refusal to enrol Drimoleague children was a partial withdrawal of labour, and thus the exercise of a constitutional right, it was nonetheless actionable. The exercise of a constitutional right for the purpose of infringing the constitutional rights of others was an abuse of that right. The teachers who refused to enrol the Drimoleague children in adjoining schools, said McMahon J., did not act primarily for the purpose of exercising a right to work or not to work, or to choose the conditions under which they would work. Their purpose was rather to deprive the children of primary education in order to exert pressure on the management.[22]

---

[22] No appeal was brought to the Supreme Court against this aspect of McMahon J.'s judgment: see [1980] I.R. 102, 120. Subsequently, in *Hayes* v. *Ireland & Ors.* [1987] I.L.R.M. 651 Carroll J. awarded one of the affected children damages against (*inter alios*) the I.N.T.O. She concluded that an entitlement to damages arose as a result of the unlawful interference by the defendants with a constitutional right. And since this was not a tort action—but rather a *Meskell*-type claim for damages for interference with a constitutional right—s.4 of the Trade Disputes Act 1906 (which protected unions against tort liability) did not apply. (Section 4 has now been repealed, but it is re-enacted in substance by section 13 of the Industrial Relations Act 1990.) In *Conway* v. *I.N.T.O.* [1990] I.L.R.M. 497 the Supreme Court held that the High Court had correctly awarded exemplary, as well as compensatory, damages to the children affected.

17   The Family and Education

Articles 41 and 42 of the Constitution are devoted to the topics of the family and education. There is a degree of overlap in the subject-matter and the philosophical basis of the two Articles, and it is appropriate to treat them together.

The Constitution treats the family as a vital social institution, describing it as "the natural primary and fundamental unit group of Society" (Art. 41.1.1°). The State, therefore, guarantees to protect the family in its constitution and authority "as the necessary basis of social order and as indispensable to the welfare of the Nation and the State" (Art. 41.1.2°). The family is further acknowledged as "the primary and natural educator of the child" (Art. 42.1).

Professor Whyte has emphasised the influence of Catholic teaching on Articles 41 and 42.[1] This is perhaps most immediately noticeable in the bar on introducing divorce legislation (Art. 41.3.2°), but it would also explain the natural law philosophy which imbues both Articles. In Article 41.1.1°, for example, the family is recognised as "a moral institution possessing inalienable and imprescriptible rights, antecedent and superior to all positive law." Likewise, Article 42.1 refers to the "inalienable right and duty" of parents in the matter of education, and Article 42.5 to the "natural and imprescriptible rights of the child." In *Ryan* v. *Att. Gen.* [1965] I.R. 294, 308 Kenny J. said that "inalienable" meant "that which cannot be transferred or given away," while "imprescriptible" meant "that which cannot be lost by the passage of time or abandoned by non-exercise." This would indeed appear to be the usual meaning of these words; but the Supreme Court has yet to pronounce on this matter, and in *G.* v. *An Bord Uchtála* [1980] I.R. 32, 79 Walsh J. spoke of some inalienable rights being "absolutely inalienable" while others were "relatively inalienable."

Though the term "family" is not defined in the Constitution the Supreme Court has held that it means the family based on marriage—*State (Nicolaou)* v. *An Bord Uchtála* [1966] I.R. 567: *G.* v. *An Bord Uchtála* [1980] I.R. 32.[2] This includes both married couples with children and those without: *Murray* v. *Att.*

---

[1] *Church and State in Modern Ireland* (2nd ed., Dublin 1980), pp. 52 and 377; see also W. R. Duncan, "Supporting the Institution of Marriage in Ireland" (1978) XIII *Irish Jurist* (N.S.) 215.

[2] This approach has been criticised as too narrow: see the *Final Report* of the Task Force on Child Care Services, pp. 214–215, and also Michael Staines "The Concept of 'The Family' under the Irish Constitution" (1976) *XI Irish Jurist* (N.S.) 223.

Gen. [1984] I.L.R.M. 542.[3] The guarantees of Articles 41 and 42 are therefore confined to such families,[4] but this does not mean the law is obliged to refuse all consideration to other "families." In *Nicolaou's* case the Supreme Court did not appear to see any constitutional difficulty in a particular statute treating an unmarried couple and their children as a family for specific purposes.[5] Few statutes, however, seem to do this. In particular, the legislation on maintenance and family protection clearly presumes marriage: see the Family Law (Maintenance, etc.) Act 1976 and the Family Law (Protection of Spouses and Children) Act 1981. Thus the barring order provisions of the 1981 Act would not be available to a person living in a *"de facto* relationship."

In Article 41.3, of course, the State pledges itself "to guard with special care the institution of Marriage . . . and to protect it against attack." In *Murphy* v. *Att. Gen.* [1982] I.R. 241 Kenny J., speaking for the Supreme Court, said that this was a guarantee that this institution in all its constitutional connotations would be given special protection so that it would continue to fulfil its function as the basis of the family and as a permanent, indissoluble union of man and woman. The court there held that to tax a working married couple more heavily than if the partners were single infringed this guarantee. Subsequent decisions have made it clear that the true *ratio* of *Murphy's* case is that the State may not penalise marriage,[6] whether through the taxation system or otherwise. Thus in *Hyland* v. *Minister for Social Welfare* [1990] I.L.R.M. 213 the Supreme Court invalidated section 12(4) of the Social Welfare (No. 2) Act 1985,[7] under which a married couple received less in certain social welfare payments than a couple simply living together.[8] It rejected the contention that the difference in objectives between taxation statutes and social welfare statutes made *Murphy's* case distinguishable. In *Greene* v. *Minister for Agriculture* [1990] 2 I.R. 17 a subsidy scheme for farmers in disadvantaged areas contained a means test under which the off-farm incomes of married couples—but not of persons choosing to live together—were aggregated. Murphy J. said (at 26).

> " . . . The imposition of a scheme by the State or any of its agents on married couples living together which is substantially different from one placed on unmarried couples living together is in breach of the pledge by the State to guard with special care the institution of marriage and to protect it against attack."[9]

[3] But not an unmarried mother and her child: *G* v. *An Bord Uchtála* (*supra*). See further *infra*. Nor, since marriage means a valid subsisting marriage under the law of the State, does it include parents married in accordance with the rites of the Roman Catholic church subsequent to a church (but without a civil law) annulment of a previous marriage.
[4] Note, however, that in *L.* v. *L.* [1992] I.L.R.M. 115 McCarthy J. said (at 123): " . . . I am not to be taken as holding that these guarantees [of Article 41.2] are restricted to mothers of families based upon the institution of marriage."
[5] In *Jordan* v. *O'Brien* [1960] I.R. 363 the former Supreme Court held that there could be no presumption that the word "family" in a statute meant "family" under Art. 41.
[6] See *Muckley* v. *Ireland* [1985] I.R. 472 and *Hyland's* case *supra*.
[7] Which was enacted to implement Council Directive 79/7/EEC on the elimination of sex discrimination in social security matters.
[8] But the Hylands' victory proved a Pyrrhic one, for instead of increasing the payments to married couples the Government and Oireachtas opted to cut the entitlements of cohabiting couples. See the Social Welfare (No. 2) Act 1989.
[9] See also *H.* v. *Eastern Health Board* [1988] I.R. 747.

Article 41.3 is not understood to mean that the State must close its eyes to social facts. Thus the Social Welfare (Consolidation) Act 1981 provides for maternity allowances and maternity grants for all mothers, married or single (ss.24–28, 104–106) and single mothers are specifically declared eligible for social assistance allowances, and given equality of treatment with deserted wives, prisoner's wives and widows (s.195–197). Nor is the payment of children's allowances conditioned upon marriage (see s.224). It does not appear that there is anything unconstitutional in this.[10]

Articles 41 and 42 clearly impose obligations on the State. In appropriate cases these may be discharged by the courts as the judicial arm of the State,[11] but the primary duty of fulfilling those obligations must obviously lie on the Oireachtas. Should it be thought to have failed in this regard it seems very unlikely that the courts could provide a remedy. Under Article 41.2.2° the State must "endeavour to ensure that mothers shall not be obliged by economic necessity to engage in labour to the neglect of their duties in the home." It would surely be difficult for a court to prescribe measures for the fulfilment of this obligation, since this would involve questions of public expenditure priorities and value judgments.[12] Such matters do not appear to present a justiciable issue.[13]

Among the measures enacted to fulfil the State's constitutional obligations is the Family Home Protection Act 1976—designed to limit the power of a spouse to alienate the family home without the prior written consent of the other spouse. In *Hamilton* v. *Hamilton* [1982] I.R. 466, 484 Henchy J. said that the Act effected "a novel and profound change in substantive land law and, consequently, in the law of conveyancing." He went on to add that this had been done "presumably as an implementation of the constitutional duty that falls on the State to protect the family and to guard with special care the institution of marriage" (at 485). Equally, in *W.* v. *Somers* [1983] I.R. 122, 126 McCarthy J., speaking for the Supreme Court, referred to:

> " . . . the concern of the legislature, in enacting the Act of 1976, to fulfil the function of the legislative branch of the State as set out in Article 41, section 1, of the Constitution . . . In my view, the Act of 1976 must be used primarily to secure the protection of the family in the family home, and all other claims to the premises that constitute such home must remain secondary to it. The judicial branch of government of the State must also recognise its duty under Article 41 and seek to achieve the objectives as set out in that Article."

In the *Hamilton* case the Supreme Court held that the 1976 Act was not

---

[10] In *MacMathuna* v. *Att. Gen.* [1989] I.R. 504 Carroll J. rejected the plaintiffs' contention that the benefits given to unmarried mothers infringed Art. 41.3.1°. The extra support given to single parents (including unmarried mothers) was child-centred and could not be characterised as an attack on the institution of marriage.

[11] This was clearly accepted by the Supreme Court in *L.* v. *L.* [1992] I.L.R.M. 115: see Finlay C.J. (Hederman J. concurring) at 121, and Egan J. at 126.

[12] See O'Flaherty J. in *L.* v. *L.* [1992] I.L.R.M. 115, 124: "If a mother in dire economic straits were to invoke this section it would be no answer for the State to say that it did not have to make any effort in her regard at all, though it would be open for it to say that it was doing its best having regard to the State's overall budgetary situation."

[13] In *State of Himachal Pradesh* v. *Student's Parent* [1986] L.R.C. (Const.) 208 the Indian Supreme Court ruled that courts could not oblige the executive to initiate legislation. This was not a matter within the judicial sphere and functions.

intended to have retrospective effect; thus a contract of sale already entered into was not affected by its subsequent enactment. O'Higgins C.J. was of opinion that had the Act been intended to frustrate pre-existing contractual rights it would have been unconstitutional as an unjust attack on property rights ([1983] I.R. 466, 477). But Henchy J., though expressing no conclusion on this point, noted that the State's constitutional duties in regard to property rights would have to be balanced against other such duties, such as the protection of marriage and the family. This question would assume great importance if legislation providing for joint ownership of the matrimonial home, and clearly intended to have retrospective effect, should be enacted.

The provisions of Article 41 have no *direct* impact upon matrimonial property law; though they might support legislation to recast that law, they provide no basis for judicial remoulding thereof. The Supreme Court made this clear in *L. v. L.* [1992] I.L.R.M. 115, rejecting the argument that Article 41 could authorise the award of a share in the matrimonial home to a deserted wife and mother who did not otherwise qualify for such.[13a] Though sympathetic to the objective in view the court held that its attainment was beyond judicial competence. As McCarthy J. put it (at 124):

> "It would be making a quantum leap in constitutional law to hold that by her life within the home the mother acquires a beneficial interest in it."

However, as is pointed out in Chap. 18 *infra*,[14] the decision in *L. v. L.* seems implicitly to affirm the constitutionality of the radical property adjustment provisions of the Judicial Separation and Family Law Reform Act 1989. Additionally, it seems to clear the path for legislation on joint ownership of the family home.

Notwithstanding the language of Article 41, the rights of the family are not absolute. As Costello J. said in *Murray* v. *Ireland* [1985] I.L.R.M. 542, 548:

> " . . . it is clear that the exercise by the family of its imprescriptible and inalienable right to integrity as a unit group can be severely and validly restricted by the State when, for example, its laws permit a father to be banned from a family home or allow for the imprisonment of both parents of young children."

It follows that certain of the marital rights protected by the Constitution[15] may validly be suspended during a period of imprisonment. In *Murray* v. *Ireland* [1991] I.L.R.M. 465 Finlay C.J. (Hamilton P., O'Flaherty and Keane JJ. concurring) said (at 472):

> " . . . only a right of communication, and that without privacy, and a right by communication to take some part in the education of the chil-

---

[13a] *Via* the constructive or resulting trust device; see James C. Brady, "Trusts, Law Reform and the Emancipation of Women" (1984) 6 *D.U.L.J.* (N.S.) 1, and the Supreme Court decisions in *McC.* v. *McC.* [1986] I.L.R.M. 1 and *N.* v. *N.* [1992] I.L.R.M. 127.

[14] *S.v.* Property Rights and Family Reponsibilities.

[15] See Finlay C.J. (Hamilton P., O'Flaherty and Keane JJ. concurring) in *Murray* v. *Ireland* [1991] I.L.R.M. 465, at 472: " . . . the fact that the Constitution so clearly protects the institution of marriage necessarily involves a constitutional protection of certain material rights. They include the right of cohabitation; the right to take responsibility for and actively participate in the education of any children born of the marriage; the right to beget children or further children of the marriage; and the right to privacy within the marriage: privacy of communication and of association."

dren of the marriage would ordinarily survive a sentence of imprisonment as a convicted prisoner."

Nor does Article 41 guarantee an alien spouse or parent a right to enter or reside in the State,[16] or immunise him/her from deportation.[17] But the power to deport an alien[18] has constitutionally—imposed limits, as is shown by *Fajujonu v. Minister for Justice* [1990] 2 I.R. 151. In this case the first two plaintiffs were a Nigerian citizen and a Moroccan citizen who had come to Ireland in 1981. By virtue of the Aliens Act 1935 and regulations made thereunder, they required—but did not have—the leave of the Minister for Justice to remain in the State. The third plaintiff, their daughter, was an Irish citizen, having been born in Ireland in 1983 (and they had two more children, also born in Ireland, after the institution of these proceedings). In 1984 the first plaintiff was offered a job, and his prospective employer sought a work permit from the Department of Labour. Officials from that Department contacted their colleagues in Justice, who in turn interviewed the plaintiffs. The outcome was a request to the first plaintiff to make arrangements to leave the State—though no deportation order was made against him. Among the reasons for refusing him permission to remain was that he was unable to support his family without assistance from the State. The plaintiffs challenged the Minister's decision, invoking Article 41.

The Supreme Court held that the Minister must reconsider his decision in the light of the important constitutional rights involved. Finlay C.J. stated those rights as follows (at 162):

" . . . where, as occurs in this case, an alien has in fact resided for an appreciable time in the State and has become a member of a family unit within the State containing children who are citizens, . . . there can be no question but that those children, as citizens, have got a constitutional right to the company, care and parentage of their parents within a family unit. I am also satisfied that *prima facie* and subject to the exigencies of the common good that that is a right which these citizens would be entitled to exercise within the State."

And Walsh J. said (at 164):

" . . . the first two plaintiffs and their three children constitute a family within the meaning of the Constitution and the three children are entitled to the care, protection and the society of their parents in this family group which is resident within the State."

The court also made it clear that while parents in this position *could* be deported, weighty grounds would be required to legitimise such action. Thus Finlay C.J. said (at 162):

" . . . the question then must arise as to whether the State, acting through the Minister for Justice . . . can under any circumstances force the family so constituted . . . to leave the State. I am satisfied that he can, but only if, after due and proper consideration, he is satisfied that the interests of the common good and the protection of the State and its

[16] *Abdelkefi v. Minister for Justice* [1984] I.L.R.M. 138.
[17] *Pok Sun Shum v. Ireland* [1986] I.L.R.M. 593: *Osheku v. Ireland* [1986] I.R. 733.
[18] As to which see Kevin Costello, "The Irish Deportation Power" (1990) 12 *D.U.L.J.* (N.S.) 81.

society justifies an interference with what is clearly a constitutional right.

> ... the reason ... which would justify the removal of this family as it now stands, consisting of five persons three of whom are citizens of Ireland, against the apparent will of the entire family, outside the State has to be a grave and substantial reason associated with the common good."

Walsh J. said (at 166):

> "[The Minister] would have to be satisfied, for stated reasons, that the interests of the common good of the people of Ireland and of the protection of the State and its society are so predominant and so overwhelming in the circumstances of the case, that an action which can have the effect of breaking up this family is not so disproportionate to the aim sought to be achieved as to be unsustainable."

In *P.H.* v. *John Murphy and Sons Ltd.* [1987] I.R. 621 Costello J. declined to construe Article 41 as creating a remedy in damages for loss of non-pecuniary benefits sustained by children through injury negligently inflicted on their father. The father of the five plaintiffs had sustained appalling injuries while working for the defendants, resulting in irreversible brain damage and permanent hospitalisation. A claim for damages on his behalf was settled for £420,000—a sum which, of course, would have reflected the five plaintiffs' economic dependence upon him. In these proceedings, those plaintiffs claimed damages on their own behalf on the basis, *inter alia*, that the defendants' negligence had infringed the rights each one derived from Articles 41 and 42 of the Constitution. Each plaintiff, it was argued, was a member of a family of which Mr. H. was the father, and was entitled to the benefits flowing from the love and affection, the guidance and example which the father of a family bestows upon his children.

Costello J. found that the common law did not permit an award of damages under such circumstances, and turned to consider the plaintiffs' constitutional argument. He concluded that the basis of the claim must be found in Article 41.1.1°,[19] rather than Article 41.1.2°,[20] since the latter referred to *the State's* obligations towards the family. However, the undefined rights guaranteed by Article 41.1.1° must be the same as those protected under Article 41.1.2°. It would be unreasonable to construe the Constitution so that the rights protected by the State's "recognition" in Article 41.1.1° were wider or narrower than those the State "guarantees to protect" in Article 41.1.2°.[21] Consequently, said Costello J., one should look at the duties imposed under Article 41.1.2° and derive from these the correlative rights protected under both sub-sections of Article 41.

Costello J. was of opinion that Article 41.1.2° protected the family against *legislation* impairing "its constitution and authority", or *deliberate* acts of State officials having the same effect. But it did not provide a guarantee against

---

[19] Which reads: "The State recognises the Family as the natural primary and fundamental unit group of Society, and as a moral institution possessing inalienable and imprescriptible rights, antecedent and superior to all positive law."

[20] Which reads: "The State, therefore, guarantees to protect the Family in its constitution and authority, as the necessary basis of social order and as indispensable to the welfare of the Nation and the State."

[21] Costello J. agreed with what Kenny J. had said on this point in *Ryan* v. *Att. Gen.* [1965] I.R. 294, at 309.

negligent acts of State officials, even though such acts could destroy the "constitution and authority" of the family unit—as where the parents of a family were killed by the negligent driving of a State-owned vehicle and the children were dispersed into different foster homes. He said (at 626–627):

> "It must be remembered that the court is construing a constitutional document whose primary purpose in the field of fundamental rights is to protect them from unjust laws enacted by the legislature and from arbitrary acts committed by State officials. It would require very clear words to construe the State's constitutional obligations (as distinct from its common law obligations) as including a duty to ensure that its officials would not drive carelessly. I do not think that the words employed in Article 41 are apt to do so, and the State's guarantee of protection does not, in my judgment, include a guarantee that its officials will drive State vehicles without negligence."

On this basis Costello J. concluded that Article 41 did not offer protection against negligent acts by private persons.[22]

It is not clear why Costello J. thought Article 41's guarantee confined to protection against legislation or deliberate action by officials. The text does not appear to demand such a conclusion, and the State's guarantee "to protect the Family in its constitution and authority" is presumably to be effectuated by the judicial branch of government[23] as well as by the others. But the courts, though accepting that the Constitution creates rights of action against private persons for breach of constitutionally protected rights,[24] have generally been reluctant to move beyond the established categories of the law of torts.[25]

In *People (D.P.P.) v. T.* (July 27, 1988)[26] the Court of Criminal Appeal considered Article 41 in the context of a case where a father had been convicted of sexual offences against his daughter. The accused's wife had given evidence as a witness for the prosecution—invalidly, as he claimed on appeal, founding on the common law rule that one spouse was not a competent witness against the other. This rule, it was contended, was reinforced by the Constitution, since to allow a spouse to give evidence in such circum-

---

[22] Costello J. reached a similar conclusion on the plaintiffs' Art. 42 argument. Though the father's injuries disabled him from exercising his constitutional right to educate his children—and their rights to be educated by him—Art. 42 did not create an ancillary right not to be injured by negligence impairing the exercise of those rights.

[23] Art. 41 was invoked by Carroll J. in *E.R.* v. *J.R.* [1981] I.L.R.M. 125, in considering whether a priest could claim privilege in respect of communications made to him as a marriage counsellor. Carroll J. said that the provision of confidential marriage counselling which could help a couple over a difficulty in their marriage was protection of the most practical kind for the family and should be fostered. A guarantee of confidentiality, which would not be breached by giving evidence in court, was essential for this, and the communications must therefore be regarded as privileged. The privilege, however, was that of the people consulting, not the counsellor, and it could be waived by them. Carroll J. went on to reserve the question whether such a privilege could arise if the counsellor were not a minister of religion. It is difficult to see why it should not, since the confidentiality would seem to arise from the counselling function, not the profession of the counsellor.

[24] See *Meskell* v. *C.I.É.* [1973] I.R. 121.

[25] See further William Binchy, "Constitutional Remedies and the Law of Torts" in James O'Reilly (ed.), *Human Rights and Constitutional Law: Essaus in Honour of Brian Walsh* (Dublin 1992), p. 201.

[26] For analysis of, and comment upon, this case see Claire Jackson, "Evidence—Competence and Compellability of Spouses as Prosecution Witnesses" (1989) 11 *D.U.L.J.* (N.S.) 149.

stances would be a violation of the protection of the family guaranteed by Article 41. The Court of Criminal Appeal rejected this argument. While Article 41 established that the family as a unit had its own special rights, other provisions make it clear that each member of that unit had his/her own constitutionally-guaranteed personal rights. The judgment, *per* Walsh J., continues (pp. 43–44):

> "In the form of a common law rule the law has recognised a rule to the effect that one spouse may not give evidence against the other in a criminal prosecution. Insofar as that may be based upon a view that it would tend to rupture family relationships it must be set against the public interest in the vindication of the innocent who have been subjected to injustice. As both may be said to fall within the provisions of Art. 41 of the Constitution it is the view of the Court that the interest of the child must prevail because what is alleged against the applicant is an attack of a particularly unpleasant kind upon his own child and therefore an attack upon the very fabric of the family itself and the bodily integrity of a member of that family."

It follows from this that the common law rule can have no application in cases where one member of a family is alleged to have committed an offence against another. The position may be different where the alleged offences do not cause injury to the family as a unit.

The bar on divorce

Article 41.3.2° declares that "no law shall be enacted providing for the grant of a dissolution of marriage." This obviously prevents the Oireachtas from legislating to confer a divorce jurisdiction on the courts[27]—but it might also prohibit the introduction of nullity legislation so widely framed that it could be characterised as "back-door divorce."

The historical background of Article 41.3.2° requires some explanation. Before independence the Irish courts had no jurisdiction to dissolve marriages. The Matrimonial Causes Act 1857 which gave the English courts jurisdiction in divorce matters did not apply to Ireland, where a dissolution continued to be available only by private Act of Parliament. As the 1922 Constitution had no provision analogous to Article 41.3.2°, it raised no barrier to legislation conferring divorce jurisdiction on the courts, but none such was ever passed. However, when in 1925 an attempt was made to introduce private divorce Bills, the President of the Executive Council persuaded the Oireachtas to prohibit such a course.[28] Thus Article 41.3.2° gave constitutional expression to a determination already evident.

The High Court has, however, jurisdiction to declare a marriage null and void. This it received, via Article 34.3.1°, by inheritance from its predecessors—a jurisdiction traceable ultimately to the Matrimonial Causes and

---

[27] An amendment intended to delete this provision and to replace it with one permitting limited divorce was defeated in a referendum in 1986. The turnout was 62.7%, and the proposal was rejected by 63.1% to 36.3%. See Brian Girvin, "The Divorce Referendum in the Republic; June 1986" (1987) 2 *Irish Political Studies* 93 and John Coakley," Moral Consensus in a Secularising Society: The Irish Divorce Referendum of 1986" (1987) 10 *West Eur. Politics* 291.

[28] For the background, see Ronan Fanning, *Independent Ireland* (Dublin 1983), pp. 54–57.

Marriage Law (Ireland) Amendment Act 1870. For many decades there were very few such suits but in recent years the jurisdiction has been invoked with increasing frequency, and the courts have developed and expanded the grounds for relief.[29] Thus the Supreme Court has held that the concept of duress in nullity is not limited to threats of physical injury or other harmful consequences; the vital issue is whether the consent to marriage was a fully free exercise of the independent will of the parties—*N. (orse. K.)* v. *K.* [1986] I.L.R.M. 75. Finlay C.J., Griffin and McCarthy JJ. there emphasised that the indissolubility of marriage under the Constitution necessitated that the contract be entered into only with full and free consent.

The jurisdiction to annul is quite distinct from a jurisdiction to dissolve. An annulment proceeds upon the basis that the marriage in question was legally invalid from its commencement; a decree of divorce relates to circumstances (*e.g.* irretrievable breakdown of the relationship) arising after the commencement of the marriage. But nullity legislation too widely drawn could obviously obscure that distinction. Thus although the Law Reform Commission recommended changes in the law it suggested that wilful refusal to consummate a marriage should not become a ground for nullity, *inter alia* because this "might well raise difficulties under Article 41 of the Constitution."[30]

In *Dalton* v. *Dalton* [1982] I.L.R.M. 418 the parties had entered into a separation agreement, and now applied to have the agreement made a rule of court, under the Family Law (Maintenance of Spouses and Children) Act 1976, s.8. O'Hanlon J. observed that save for clause 11, the agreement met the requirements of section 8. But clause 11 provided that the parties agreed to obtain a decree of divorce *a vinculo*, and that the husband agreed not to contest any divorce proceedings instituted by the wife. The agreement showed a County Dublin address for each of the parties, and there was no indication that either was domiciled outside Ireland or intended to acquire a non-Irish domicile in the future. O'Hanlon J. said that if the court made this agreement a rule of court it would be lending its support to a course of conduct which was contrary to public policy within the jurisdiction; consequently the application must be refused.[31]

Recognition of foreign divorces

While the Irish courts cannot grant a dissolution of a marriage, they may, in appropriate circumstances, recognise decrees of foreign courts as valid and effective under Irish law. Such an issue may arise in a wide variety of situations, and may have to be resolved by bodies other than the courts, as the following examples show. A person seeking to marry in Ireland will have to demonstrate that he or she is legally free to do so. If a prior marriage was dissolved by decree of a foreign court, the registrar of marriages will have to

---

[29] See Paul O'Connor, *Key Issues in Irish Family Law* (Dublin 1988), Part 1.

[30] L.R.C. 9—1984: *Report on Nullity of Marriage*, p. 146.

[31] In *Robert Draper* v. *Att. Gen.* (*The Irish Times*, November 25, 1986) the plaintiff claimed that the New Testament and the Mosaic law provided for divorce for the Christian. The State must consequently recognise his right as a Christian to divorce and make provision "for the public order of same." On an application by the defendant, O'Hanlon J. struck out the action; the pleadings failed to disclose a reasonable cause of action with some prospect of success.

determine whether that decree qualifies for recognition under Irish law. A similar issue could confront the Adoption Board (An Bord Uchtála) in resolving whether prospective adopters qualify as "a married couple" under the Adoption Act 1952, s.11(1)(*a*). The Department of Social Welfare may have to consider the effect of a foreign divorce decree in ruling on a claim for deserted wife's benefit under the Social Welfare (Consolidation) Act 1981, ss.100–103 and 195. Finally, the courts may be concerned with the matter, in cases involving legislation conferring rights on a "spouse." Such cases might arise under the Family Law (Maintenance, etc.) Act 1976—as in *T.* v. *T.* [1983] I.R. 29; or the Family Law (Protection of Spouses and Children) Act 1981; or the Succession Act 1965, which gives a surviving spouse a specified share in a deceased's estate (see s.67 (intestacy) and 111). It was the latter Act that gave rise to the cases of *Bank of Ireland* v. *Caffin* [1971] I.R. 123 and *Gaffney* v. *Gaffney* [1975] I.R. 133.

At first sight, Article 41.3.3° might appear to rule out the recognition of foreign divorce decrees. It provides:

> "No person whose marriage has been dissolved under the civil law of any other state but is a subsisting valid marriage under the law for the time being in force within the jurisdiction of the Government and Parliament established by this Constitution shall be capable of contracting a valid marriage within that jurisdiction during the lifetime of the other party to the marriage so dissolved."

But in *Mayo-Perrott* v. *Mayo-Perrott* [1958] I.R. 336 a majority of the Supreme Court held that this did not forbid the recognition of foreign divorce decrees. Kingsmill Moore J.'s view in that case, which has since become canonical, was that when the Constitution was enacted "a divorce effected by a foreign court of persons domiciled within its jurisdiction was regarded as valid in our jurisdiction" ([1958] I.R. 336, 346). The Oireachtas could change this rule but unless and until it did so, the rule remained in force. This conclusion was accepted by Kenny J. in the High Court in *Bank of Ireland* v. *Caffin* [1971] I.R. 123, and by O'Higgins C.J. and Walsh J. in *Gaffney* v. *Gaffney* [1975] I.R. 133. The Supreme Court's decision in *T.* v. *T* [1983] I.R. 29 accords with this; so as the law then stood a divorce decree pronounced by a competent court in a jurisdiction in which both parties were then domiciled would be recognised under Irish law.

The Domicile and Recognition of Foreign Divorces Act 1986, s.5(1), substitutes a new rule for that stated above. Under this, a divorce will be recognised if granted in a jurisdiction where *either* spouse was domiciled at the date of the institution of the divorce proceedings. But under section 5(5) this applies only to a divorce granted after the commencement of the Act—*i.e.* three months after July 2, 1986 (s.6(2)). Thus the recognition of divorces granted before then still depends on the previous law.

It should be emphasised, however, that by no means every foreign divorce will qualify for recognition. Mere production of the foreign decree is not conclusive, for an Irish court may go behind it if, for example, it is claimed that the defendant spouse was not given adequate notice of the divorce proceedings. Or there may have been such collusion between the parties as to amount to a fraud upon the foreign court; in which case an Irish court may refuse recognition even if the matter could not now be reopened in the foreign court: *B.(L)* v. *B.(H)* [1980] I.L.R.M. 257. Such grounds for refusal of recognition are not affected by the Domicile and Recognition of Foreign Divorces Act 1986—see s.5(6).

For the purpose of recognition it is the Irish rules on domicile, not those of the decree-granting jurisdiction, which must be satisfied. It follows that if in state X domicile may be acquired by two weeks' residence, a divorce obtained on this basis will not be recognised under Irish law. This still cleaves to the traditional rule that one is domiciled in the jurisdiction where one intends to reside permanently or indefinitely: see *Re Joyce* [1946] I.R. 227, 301 *per* Black J. (Sullivan C.J. and Murnaghan J. concurring): *Re Sillar* [1956] I.R. 344: *Re Adams* [1967] I.R. 424. *A fortiori*, if the foreign court's jurisdiction to grant the decree is based solely on the *residence* of the parties (or of one party) that decree will not be recognised in Ireland: see *C.* v. *C.* (High Court, Kenny J., July 27, 1973) and *K.D.* v. *M.C.* [1985] I.R. 697. (This is slightly modified by s.5(4) of the Domicile and Recognition of Foreign Divorces Act 1986—which applies only where *neither* spouse is domiciled in the State. Its effect is that a divorce will be recognised if, though not *granted* in the jurisdiction where either spouse is domiciled, it is *recognised* in that jurisdiction, or both those jurisdictions. Thus if the former spouses, domiciled respectively in states A and B, obtain in state C a divorce which will be recognised under both A's and B's law, it will be recognised in Ireland—provided it was granted after the commencement of the Act).

Section 5(3)(c) of the 1986 Act resolves, for the future, a point hitherto unsettled—whether a Northern Ireland divorce will be recognised in the Republic. It provides for the recognition of such a divorce where *either* spouse is domiciled in Northern Ireland at the date of the institution of the divorce proceedings. This clearly assumes that Article 41.3.3°'s reference to "the jurisdiction of the Government and Parliament established by this Constitution" relates only to the Republic—*i.e.* the area over which jurisdiction is actually exercised or, in the language of Article 3, the "area and extent of application" of the laws.

At common law a woman's domicile became, on marriage, that of her husband and remained so until the marriage was terminated by death or divorce. This meant that her domicile changed with her husband's, even if she never visited the relevant place. So a woman domiciled in Ireland who married a man domiciled in Spain acquired a Spanish domicile; if her husband moved to Peru and became domiciled there so, too, would she—and all this without necessarily leaving Ireland! It would follow that if the husband obtained a divorce in Peru (being domiciled there), that divorce would qualify for recognition under Irish law because *both* parties would, on the above basis, be domiciled in that jurisdiction.

The Domicile and Recognition of Foreign Divorces Act 1986, s.1(1) abolishes the common law rule and provides that a married woman has an independent domicile, determinable on the same basis as that of any other person. But section 2 provides that the domicile that a person had at any time before the commencement of the Act is to be determined as if that Act had not been passed. However, this does not necessarily involve applying the common law rule of the wife's dependent domicile, for there are grave doubts as to whether that rule survived the enactment of the Constitution. In *C.M.* v. *T.M.* (*No.* 2) [1990] 2 I.R. 52 Barr J. was prepared to hold that it had not, a view supported *obiter* by Walsh J. in *Gaffney* v. *Gaffney* [1975] I.R. 133, 152 and McCarthy J. in *K.D.* v. *M.C.* [1985] I.R. 697, 705.

Court orders consequent on divorce—enforcement

In *Mayo-Perrott* v. *Mayo-Perrott* [1958] I.R. 336 the former Supreme Court
held that the Irish courts could not entertain actions to enforce an award of
costs in foreign divorce proceedings. To do so would be contrary to public
policy as reflected in Article 41.3.2° of the Constitution. But it does not follow
that every order consequent on divorce is unenforceable in Ireland. In *Sachs*
v. *Standard Chartered Bank (Ireland) Ltd.* [1987] I.L.R.M. 297 the wife had
obtained an absolute decree of divorce from an English court on October 5,
1984. An order of January 3, 1985 ancillary to that decree directed the husband to pay the wife a lump sum of £35,000 sterling. The present proceedings
were for the enforcement of the latter order against an account containing
£75,000 sterling which the husband had with the defendant bank. For the
husband, it was argued that this was an order ancillary to divorce proceedings analogous to the order for costs in the *Mayo-Perrott* case, and that to
enforce it would be contrary to public policy under Article 41.3.2°. Counsel
for the wife contended that the *Mayo-Perrott* decision related only to costs and
had no application to an order making financial provision for one of the parties to the dissolved marriage. Such an order did not necessarily arise from
the divorce decree but from the breakdown of the marriage, and could
equally, under English law, have been made in proceedings for judicial separation.

Barrington J. held that the wife *could* enforce her claim. Should a marriage
break down, said the judge, then whether the parties sought a judicial separation or a divorce, problems could arise concerning the custody and maintenance of children or the maintenance of one of the parties to the dissolved
marriage. These were universal problems arising not from divorce proceedings as such, but from the breakdown of the marriage. The judgment continues (p. 9):

> "In *Mayo-Perrott* v. *Mayo-Perrott* the issue was whether an Order for the
> payment of the costs of the divorce proceedings themselves was enforce-
> able in Ireland. Costs are the sinews of litigation and it is not surprising
> that the Supreme Court held that the part of the Order of the English
> Court awarding costs could not be severed from the part granting a dis-
> solution of marriage. But, in the present case . . . there are two separate
> Orders, the first granting the divorce and the second dealing with finan-
> cial matters consequent upon the dissolution of the marriage. There is
> no evidence that the problems of the Court making the second kind of
> Order are in any significant way different from the problem which
> would face a Court in Ireland attempting to make proper financial pro-
> vision for a wife or children consequent upon the granting of a decree of
> judicial separation."

Barrington J. went on to observe that the divorce decree here would appear
to qualify for recognition under Irish law. In his view it would be strange if
the Irish courts, while recognising the validity of the divorce itself, refused to
enforce the property provisions consequent thereon although similar financial provisions could be made in Ireland following on the breakdown of a
marriage. The judge referred to the Maintenance Orders Act 1974, which
provides machinery for the enforcement in Ireland of United Kingdom maintenance orders. Section 9 of the Act contemplated refusal of such enforce-

ment in certain limited circumstances, including where "recognition or enforcement would be contrary to public policy." But section 3, in defining "maintenance orders," provided in sub-section (2) that it included an order "incidental to a decision as to the status of natural persons." Since a maintenance order consequent upon a dissolution of marriage answered this description, it seemed to Barrington J. that the Oireachtas contemplated that the enforcement of such an order would not necessarily be contrary to public policy.

On appeal the Supreme Court upheld Barrington J.'s view. Finlay C.J., for the court, referred to the cases establishing that foreign divorce decrees could be recognised under Irish law. It would be strange, he continued, if public policy allowed this yet forbade the execution of a final judgment for maintenance.

The *Sachs* case goes beyond previous decisions, which had held only that a foreign maintenance order could be enforced by an Irish court if, on the facts, it could be regarded as separate from the divorce decree—*M. v. M.* (High Court, Hamilton J. July 11, 1978): *G. v. G.* [1984] I.R. 368. A maintenance order contemporaneous with, and inextricable from, a divorce decree would not have answered this description, and thus might have been regarded as analogous to the unenforceable order for costs in *Mayo-Perrott* v. *Mayo-Perrott*. But the *Sachs* case resolves any doubts in this regard. Happily so, since otherwise the enforcement of maintenance obligations could depend on accidents of timing or the peculiarities of a given jurisdiction's procedures; the resultant discrimination between people with the same financial needs would be hard to justify.

GUARDIANSHIP, CUSTODY AND ADOPTION

Articles 41 and (particularly) 42 of the Constitution have a considerable impact on the issues of guardianship, custody and adoption, since they lay down principles within which the Oireachtas must operate when legislating on these matters. Article 42.1 recognises the family as the child's primary and natural educator, and states that the parents have the "inalienable" right and duty to provide for the "religious and moral, intellectual, physical and social education" of their children. Should the parents fail in this, the State[32] may act—but only within the restrictive terms of Article 42.5:

> "In exceptional cases, where the parents for physical or moral reasons fail in their duty towards their children, the State as guardian of the common good, by appropriate means shall endeavour to supply the place of the parents, but always with due regard for the natural and imprescriptible rights of the child."

Guardianship

This is regulated by the Guardianship of Infants Act 1964 which provides that the father and mother of an infant[33] are his or her joint guardians

---

[32] Which covers not only the Oireachtas, but also the courts "functioning as the State in its judicial aspect": *per* Henchy J. in *Re J. an infant* [1966] I.R. 295, 307.

[33] Defined in s.2 as a person under 21; but see now the Age of Majority Act 1985 which reduces the age to 18 (s.2(1)). Note the special provision regarding maintenance or support in s.2(4)(viii).

(s.6(1)).[34] In *B.* v. *B.* [1975] I.R. 54 the Supreme Court described this as a statutory expression of the rights already guaranteed by the Constitution. While the Act empowers a court to appoint guardians in certain specified situations this, as Walsh J. noted in *B.* v. *B.* (*supra*, at 61) does not include power to displace "either one or both of the parents from the position of guardian or guardians." Thus if a child is in the custody of persons other than the parents the latter nonetheless remain guardians; and no court has power to appoint the actual custodians as guardians, either with, or to the exclusion of, the parents. It follows that in such a case the parents must be consulted on all matters affecting the child's welfare.

Guardians are prima facie entitled to custody of the child: s.10(2). This again reflects the constitutional position, as Henchy J. noted in *G.* v. *An Bord Uchtála* [1980] I.R. 32, 85[35]:

> "The Constitution does not pronounce specifically on rights of custody, but it is necessarily inherent in the provisions I have cited (Articles 41.1, 42.1, 42.5) that, in the case of children whose parents were or have become married, the primary right to custody is vested in the parents, for custody will normally be necessary for the effectuation of the parents' constitutional right and duty to provide . . . for the religious and moral, intellectual, physical and social education of their children."

A court may, however, order custody to be given to (or retained by) non-guardians; this is clear from section 11 of the Guardianship of Infants Act 1964, considered *infra*.

Any guardian (whether having custody of the child or not) may apply to a court for its directions on any question affecting the child's welfare and the court may make such order as it thinks proper (s.11(1)). In particular, under section 11(2)(*a*), the court may give such directions as it thinks proper regarding the child's custody "and the right of access to the infant of his father or mother." Thus if a child is in the custody of persons other than the parents, the latter are as guardians entitled to apply under section 11—even if they are not seeking custody—should they be dissatisfied with, *e.g.* the arrangements made for the child's education.

In *any* proceedings regarding custody or upbringing—under section 11 or otherwise—the court is to regard the child's welfare as the first and paramount consideration—section 3. This provision is further considered *infra*.

Custody

As already noted, the parents of a child are prima facie entitled to custody (whether this is simply a rule of prudence or the expression of a *right* is unclear).[36] But in any event it is not beyond control. In *Re Frost, Infants* [1947] I.R. 3, 28 the Supreme Court, *per* Sullivan C.J., declined to accept the proposition

> " . . . that the rights of the parents, or of the surviving parent, are absol-

---

[34] Under s.6(4) of the mother of an illegitimate child is his/her guardian.

[35] See also Kenny J. at 97.

[36] Henchy J.'s language in *G.* v. *An Bord Uchtála*, cited above, suggests a right, and Kenny J. in the same case (at 97) speaks of a constitutional right of parents to custody. But in *J.* v. *D.* (Supreme Court, June 22, 1977) Kenny J. denied that there was any right: there was merely a rule of prudence that in most cases the best place for a child was with the parents.

ute rights, the exercise of which cannot in any circumstances be controlled by the Court. That a child has natural and imprescriptible rights is recognised by the Constitution (Art. 42, 5) and if Mr. Ryan's . . . proposition were accepted, it would follow that the Court would be powerless to protect those rights should they be ignored by the parents. I am satisfied that the Court has jurisdiction to control the exercise of parental rights, but in exercising that jurisdiction it must not act upon any principle which is repugnant to the Constitution."

Custody of a child may pass from the parents to others by voluntary arrangement or by order of a court committing him or her to the care of the relevant health board.[37] In any such case it would be open to the parents to apply under the Guardianship of Infants Act to recover custody of the child. And, as already noted, section 3 of that Act is crucial:

"Where in any proceedings before any court the custody, guardianship or upbringing of an infant . . . is in question, the court in deciding that question, shall regard the welfare of the infant as the first and paramount consideration."[38]

"Welfare" is defined in section 2 to comprise "the religious and moral, intellectual, physical and social welfare of the infant."[39] Section 16 permits a court to refuse custody to parents who have abandoned or deserted a child or in other specified ways have been unmindful of their parental duties; indeed in any such case there seems to be an onus on the parents to prove that they are fit persons to have custody.

Plainly, there may be some tension between those provisions and those of Articles 41 and 42. Thus in *Re O'Brien* [1954] I.R. 1 the father had placed his daughter in the care of her maternal grandmother when his first wife died. He remarried in 1949 and now wanted his child back, as did his second wife. The grandmother asserted that the child's welfare required that she remain with her, invoking section 3 of the Custody of Children Act 1891 (which was similar in terms to s.16 of the 1964 Act). The Supreme Court concluded that, in the circumstances, section 3 did not apply; the father had not been unmindful of his parental duties. Not did the child's welfare require that she stay where she was. The court assumed, without deciding, that section 3 was consistent with the Constitution and thus carried over by Article 50. The judgment, *per* O'Byrne J., went on to quote Article 42.1 and continued (at 10):

"This seems to contemplate and require that the children should be members of the family and attached to the parental home. The sanctity of the family and the enduring existence of parental authority seems to me to be guaranteed by these provisions . . . the framers of the Constitu-

---

[37] See the Child Care Act 1991, s.13.

[38] See also s.24 of the Child Care Act 1991: "In any proceedings before a court under this Act in relation to the care and protection of a child, the court, having regard to the rights and duties of parents, whether under the Constitution or otherwise, shall—(a) regard the welfare of the child as the first and paramount consideration, and (b) in so far as is practicable, give due consideration, having regard to his age and understanding, to the wishes of the child."

[39] It has been noted that this wording derives from Art. 42.1. See Walsh J. in *B.* v. *B.* [1975] I.R. 54, 61: Finlay C.J. in *K.C. and A.C.* v. *An Bord Uchtàla* [1985] I.L.R.M. 302, 317.

tion considered, and enacted, that the best interests and happiness of the
child would be served by its being a member of the parental household."

The judge referred to Article 42.5 and held that it had not been shown that
the father had failed in his duty thereunder. The court offered no interpretation of Article 42.5 but indicated that in any conflict between it and section
3 of the 1891 Act the latter must give way.

It is difficult to envisage a case where a court would find that parents, having been unmindful of their duties, were not fit persons under section 16 of
the 1964 Act and yet had *not* failed in their duties under Article 42.5. But the
child's welfare criterion of section 3 is clearly apt to clash with the parent's
constitutional rights. In *Re J. an infant* [1966] I.R. 295 the child was born outside wedlock in November 1964. One month later she was placed for adoption and eventually an order was made; but this was later quashed as
defective by the High Court. Meanwhile the child's parents had married in
August 1965, with the result that the child was now legitimated,[40] and as the
law then stood she could not now be adopted.[41] The parents sought to
recover custody from the would-be adopters, who invoked section 3 and
claimed that the child's welfare required that she stay with them. A divisional court (Murnaghan, Teevan and Henchy JJ.) held that the child—
who was now 18 months old—must be restored to her parents. The judges
did not believe that this would imperil her welfare,[42] but Teevan and Henchy
JJ. observed that if section 3 purported to diminish or curtail the rights of
parents to control of their children, a question of its constitutionality would
arise. From this decision one must infer that even if the evidence clearly
showed that the child's welfare required that she remain with the would-be
adopters, the parents must nonetheless be given custody—assuming, as was
held to be the situation here, this was not an "exceptional case" under
Article 42.5.

A somewhat more flexible approach seems to emerge in the recent
Supreme Court decision in *Re J.H. (an infant)* [1985] I.R. 375.[43] There an
unmarried mother had consented to her child being placed for adoption and
the child had duly been placed with prospective adopters. Subsequently the
mother refused her consent to the adoption, and shortly thereafter she married the child's father. The child was therefore now legitimated, though the
birth had not yet been re-registered (the High Court having enjoined this
pending resolution of these proceedings). There then ensued litigation in
which the adopting couple sought an order under section 3 of the Adoption
Act 1974 dispensing with the parents' consent to the adoption, while the
parents asked for custody of the child. Lynch J. pointed out that section 3

---

[40] This is the effect of the Legitimacy Act 1931, s.1. Henchy J. said (at 307) that s.1 operated to
endow the child with membership of a family founded on the institution of marriage. It was
an example of the way in which certain constitutional rights—*e.g.* citizenship and rights
founded thereon—could be conferred by the operation of a statute.

[41] Subsequently the Adoption Act 1964, s.2, permitted the adoption of a legitimated child where
the child's birth had not been re-registered and the father consented or his consent was dispensed with.

[42] Murnaghan J. (at 301) pointed to the parents' right and duty to provide for the child's education (under Art. 42.1). Should they seek to exercise this while the child was in the would-be
adopters custody, this would create difficulties that would not be consistent with the child's
welfare.

[43] For an illuminating discussion of this case see Paul A. O'Connor, *Key Issues in Irish Family Law*
(Dublin 1988), pp. 97–103.

could only apply if the father had expressly or impliedly agreed to the placing of the child for adoption; but this was not the case here. The judge thus refused the adopting couple the order they sought but he granted them custody of the child, with rights of access by the natural parents. On appeal the Supreme Court had to decide only the question of custody.

Finlay C.J. (with whose judgment the other members of the court agreed) stated the legal principles applicable as follows:

1. This child, being the child of married parents, and now legitimated, had rights under the Constitution as a member of a family. These were:
   (a) to belong to a unit group possessing inalienable and imprescriptible rights antecedent and superior to all positive law (Art. 41.1)
   (b) to protection by the State of the family to which it belonged (Art. 41.2)
   (c) to be educated by the family and to be provided by its parents with religious, moral, intellectual, physical and social education (Art. 42.1).
2. The State could supplant the role of the parents in providing for the child's educational rights under Article 42 only in exceptional circumstances (Art. 42.5).
3. The 1964 Act must, if possible, be interpreted consistently with the Constitution.

Finlay C.J. went on to say that in a case such as this, where there was a custody conflict between the "constitutional family" and others, the balance of welfare could not be the sole criterion. He continued ([1985] I.R. 375, 395):

" . . . s.3 of the Act of 1964 must be construed as involving a constitutional presumption that the welfare of the child, which is defined in s.2 of the Act in terms identical to those contained in Article 42.1, is to be found within the family unless the Court is satisfied on the evidence that there are compelling reasons why this cannot be achieved, or unless the Court is satisfied that the evidence establishes an exceptional case where the parents have failed to provide education for the child and continue to fail to provide education for the child for moral or physical reasons."

It will be noted that the court grafts two exceptions on to the parental custody principle—(1) an "exceptional case" under Article 42.5 (2) "compelling reasons" why the child's welfare cannot be achieved in parental custody.[44] The court did not specify the constitutional basis for exception (2). Presumably it springs from an acceptance that a child has constitutional rights just as parents do (which was recognised in the *Frost* case *supra*) and that in case of conflict there is no rule giving parental rights primacy. There is some authority for this latter proposition; see Walsh J. in *G.* v. *An Bord Uchtála* [1980] I.R. 32, 78 and Ellis J. in *P.W.* v. *A.W. and others* (High Court, April 21,

---

[44] In *J.* v. *D.* (Supreme Court, June 22, 1977) a father's attempt to recover custody of his children from their maternal grand-aunts failed, on the ground that the children's welfare ordained that they stay put. In the *J.H.* case Finlay C.J., having referred to this, said: "Insofar as that judgment may be construed as clearly indicating that in the case of legitimate children, paramount consideration of their welfare as defined in the Act of 1964 can be applied as the sole test without regard to the provisions of Art. 41 and 42 of the Constitution, I must, respectfully, refuse to follow it."

1980). But it is not as clear as might be wished that a "child-centred" approach to such questions of custody is compatible with the Constitution. Indeed doubts on this score are reinforced by the final stage of the *J.H.* case. The Supreme Court had referred the matter back to Lynch J. to reconsider the custody issue in the light of the principles it had laid down. Lynch J. found that to return the child (who had now been in the adopters' custody for two and a half years) to the parents would involve "a very considerable short term upset for the child," and he remained "uncertain and apprehensive regarding the medium and long term effects of a transfer of custody now" ([1985] I.R. 375, 398, 399). But he was satisfied that the parents could and would provide a good home for the child; and he did not think "that such adverse effects as may result from such transfer have been sufficiently established to such a degree as to rebut the constitutional presumption that the welfare of the child is to be found within its constitutional family or amount to compelling reasons why this cannot be achieved" (at 400). Lynch J. therefore awarded custody to the parents.

The contrast between Lynch J.'s first and second judgments is very marked. At the earlier stage the judge had examined the custody issue from the child's point of view. The risk of long term psychological harm and of unhappiness led him to believe she should stay where she was. Now, applying the law laid down by the Supreme Court, he reached the opposite conclusion. The inference would seem to be that this latter conclusion does not completely accord with the child's welfare.

Article 42.5

Article 42.5, it will be recalled, provides as follows:

> "In exceptional cases, where the parents for physical or moral reasons fail in their duty towards their children, the State as guardian of the common good, by appropriate means shall endeavour to supply the place of the parents, but always with due regard for the natural and imprescriptible rights of the child."

Though the subject-matter of Article 42 is education, Article 42.5 extends beyond this. It would authorise State action to protect the child's personal rights generally: *Re Article* 26 *and the Adoption* (*No. 2*) *Bill 1987* [1989] I.R. 656, 663. But it does not mean that the children whose parents have failed in their duty to them become the children of the State or that they are to be disposed of as such: *ibid.*

In that same case the Supreme Court, *per* Finlay C.J. said (at 663):

> "The State would, in any event, by virtue of Article 40, s.3 of the Constitution be obliged, as far as practicable, to vindicate the personal rights of the child whose parents have failed in their duty to it.
>
> The Court rejects the submission that the nature of the family as a unit group possessing inalienable and imprescriptible rights, makes it constitutionally impermissible for a statute to restore to any member of an individual family constitutional rights of which he has been deprived by a method which disturbs or alters the constitution of that family if that method is necessary to achieve that purpose. The guarantees afforded to the institution of the family by the Constitution, with their consequent benefit to the children of a family, should not be construed

so that upon the failure of that benefit it cannot be replaced where the circumstances demand it, by incorporation of the child into an alternative family."

The Court went on to say, in effect, that Articles 40.3 and 42.5 must be read together. Consequently, action by the State pursuant to Article 40.3, designed to vindicate the child's personal rights, must have due regard to his/her natural and imprescriptible rights. These are, presumably, the rights referred to in *Re J.H. (an infant)* [1985] I.R. 375—*i.e.* to belong to a constitutionally protected family and to be educated by it. Thus, it seems, legislation must strike a proper balance between the personal, and the natural and imprescriptible, rights of the child. As a result, action removing the child from his/her family would appear to require a conclusion that nothing less would protect his/her constitutional rights.

These principles would seem to have influenced the drafting of the Child Care Act 1991,[45] which gives each health board the function of promoting the welfare of children in its area who are not receiving adequate care and protection: section 3(1). Section 3(2) provides that in performing this function each board shall:

"(b) having regard to the rights and duties of parents, whether under the Constitution or otherwise—
  (i) regard the welfare of the child as the first and paramount consideration, and
  (ii) in so far as is practicable, give due consideration, having regard to his age and understanding, to the wishes of the child; and
(c) have regard to the principle that it is generally in the best interests of a child to be brought up in his own family."

Section 24 enjoins any court hearing proceedings under the Act to have regard to the matters mentioned in (b) *supra*.[46] The court is *not* directed to consider the principle stated in section 3(2)(*c*); but it would seem to follow from *Re J.H. (an infant)* [1985] I.R. 375 that it must.

The *J.H.* and *Adoption (No. 2) Bill* cases confirm that the constitutional rights of the family do not vest exclusively in—so that they may be asserted only by—the parents. They would seem also to confirm the approach of Ellis J. in the complex custody case of *P.W.* v. *A.W., M.M. and Att. Gen.* (High Court, April 21, 1980.) The plaintiff and the first defendant were the parents of four children, of whom the youngest was Annette. In consequence of strained relations between the parents, and the mother's psychiatric illness, arrangements were made to have the children looked after by relatives. In

[45] It replaces the relevant provisions of the Children Act 1908, discussed by the Supreme Court in *M.F.* v. *Supt., Ballymun Garda Station* [1991] 1 I.R. 189, where O'Flaherty J. (at 201) described the 1908 Act as " . . . now showing its age . . . " and Finlay C.J. said that there was an urgent necessity for a modern Act making a more efficient and simpler procedure for the protection of children available to the courts (at 197).

[46] In *M.F.* v. *Supt., Ballymun Garda Station* [1991] 1 I.R. 189 Finlay C.J. referred (at 197) to " . . . the continued absence in our jurisprudence of separate representation for children." O'Flaherty J. noted (at 200) that child care proceedings " . . . are possibly unique in that the fundamental rights of persons are in issue in litigation in which they are not represented." S.25 of the 1991 Act now empowers the relevant court to order that the child be joined as a party, or have such rights of a party as may be specified. This may include legal representation, in which case any costs or expenses incurred are to be paid by the health board concerned.

the case of Annette this task was undertaken by the second defendant (the father's sister) and her husband, Annette going to live with them. Following the breakdown of the marriage the mother obtained custody of the three other children—though the father was contesting this. The High Court had, however, given custody of Annette to M.M. The mother now sought to have this order varied in her favour. Ellis J. accepted that, other things being equal, the mother should have custody of a very young child. This, however, was but a rule of prudence and there could be circumstances—not necessarily involving intentional misconduct or misbehaviour—where the interests of the child would require giving custody to the contending parent, or a stranger. Section 3 of the Guardianship of Infants Act 1964 made the child's welfare the first and paramount consideration; and Ellis J. refused to grant custody to the mother because this would not conduce to Annette's welfare. In *J.* v. *D.* (Supreme Court, June 22, 1977) it had been held that section 3 empowered the court to grant custody to a stranger as against a parent, and Ellis J. concluded that Annette's welfare required that she remained in the custody of M.M.

Counsel for the mother had argued that if section 3 of the 1964 Act permitted a parent's rights to be taken away and conferred on a stranger, it was repugnant to Articles 41 and 42 of the Constitution. Nor did Article 42.5 apply here, for the mother had not failed in her duty towards Annette for physical or moral reasons and thus had not forfeited her constitutional right to custody. However Ellis J. saw the essence of the case as being the protection of *the child's* constitutional rights. In finding that this could best be achieved in M.M.'s custody, he did not think he was trespassing on the constitutional rights of A.W. or of the W. family. Nothing in the Constitution indicated that in cases of apparent conflict a parent's rights always had primacy; and in any event the mother here would retain her rights as guardian.

Ellis J. went on to say (at pp. 71–72 of his judgment):

> "If, however, there is a conflict between the constitutional rights of a legitimate child and the prima facie constitutional right of its mother to its custody, I am of opinion that the infants' rights, which are to be determined by regard to what is required for its welfare, should prevail, even if its welfare is to be found in the custody of a 'stranger,' if for good and justifiable reason . . . valid objection can be taken to the mother's inability to provide for her child's welfare, either emanating from the mother herself or for reasons connected with the child's welfare, and not necessarily confined to failure by the parents (here A.W.) of their duty towards their children for physical and moral reasons, whereby the parents', or as here the mother's, custody would or could not vindicate, protect or be compatible with the child's constitutional rights including its welfare."

Were it necessary, the judge continued, he would find that this was an "exceptional case" in terms of Article 42.5. He also held that the mother had failed in her duty towards the child "for physical reasons" under that provision. "Physical" in Article 42.5 would include reasons of health—here the illness which had disabled the mother from carrying out her duties towards Annette.

Finally Ellis J. said (at pp. 73–74):

> " . . . it was held in *Re Frost Infants* [1947] I.R. 3 that the rights of

parents are not absolute rights and that a child also had natural and imprescriptible rights of its own, and further that to afford protection to the rights of the child the Court regarded itself as having jurisdiction to control the exercise of parental rights. In my opinion, the inalienable and imprescriptible rights of the family under Article 41 of the Constitution attach to each member of the family including the children. Therefore in my view the only way the 'inalienable and imprescriptible' and 'natural and imprescriptible' rights of the child can be protected is by the Courts treating the welfare of the child as the paramount consideration in all disputes as to its custody, including disputes between a parent and a stranger. I take the view also that the child has the personal right to have its welfare regarded as the paramount consideration in any such dispute as to its custody under Article 40.3 and that this right of the infant can additionally arise from 'the Christian and democratic nature of the State.' "

The *P.W.* case shows that a "child-centred" approach can be reconciled with the Constitution. But it must obviously be taken as having been modified—in part at least—by the later Supreme Court decision in *Re J.H. (an infant)* [1985] I.R. 375. Moreover the father P.W. seems to have supported his sister M.M.'s continuing custody of Annette; a case where *both* parents opposed the custody of a stranger would plainly involve different considerations.

The decision in *Re Article 26 and the Adoption (No. 2) Bill 1987* [1989] I.R. 656 raises a question as to the present status of an earlier Supreme Court decision—*Re Doyle (an infant)* [1989] I.L.R.M. 277. The case—decided in December 1955—involved a challenge to the validity of section 10 of the Children Act 1941. This allowed a District Justice to send to an industrial school a child under 15 who was not an orphan and whose parents were unable to support him/her. The consent of the parents was required; alternatively the consent of one parent would suffice if the court was satisfied that the consent of the other parent could be dispensed with (*i.e.* if he/she was in desertion, in prison or mentally incapable). In this case the prosecutor (whose wife had deserted him) had availed of section 10 to have his daughter sent to an industrial school. Later, when he found himself able to support his child he applied for her discharge, but this was refused. (Section 10 *required* discharge in such circumstances if application was made by the parents, the surviving parent or, in the case of an illegitimate child, the mother; but it gave no such right to the father here). The High Court refused the prosecutor an order of mandamus directing the Minister to return the child, on the ground that no valid application had been made.[47] The prosecutor then sought habeas corpus, claiming that his daughter's detention was illegal and that section 10 was repugnant to Article 41 and 42 of the Constitution. The High Court held that it was and stated a case for the Supreme Court under

---

[47] *Re Doyle, an infant* [1956] I.R. 217. Curiously, no reference was made to s.69 of the Children Act 1908, under which the Minister could discharge a child irrespective of any application by the parents. The Supreme Court said in the later proceedings that s.69 conferred a discretionary power on the Minister. But given the family's constitutional rights, one would have thought that this discretion could only be exercised so as to vindicate those rights. This would certainly be the law today as a result of decisions such as *East Donegal Co-op. Ltd.* v. *Att. Gen.* [1970] I.R. 317; *Irish Family Planning Association* v. *Ryan* [1979] I.R. 295; *Garvey* v. *Ireland* [1981] I.R. 75: *State (Lynch)* v. *Cooney* [1982] I.R. 337.

Article 40.4.3°. That court agreed that section 10 was invalid. Article 42, it was held, enshrined the common law principle that parents had a right to control the education of their children which they could not surrender. Thus that principle was now beyond the reach of ordinary legislation. Moreover, Article 42.2 and 3 expressly secured to parents the continuing right to choose the nature of their children's education. Parents must be entitled to change and substitute schools as they thought proper, and to hold that a choice once made was binding for the period of a child's education would be to deny that right. Therefore section 10, insofar as it allowed a parent to deprive himself/herself of control of a child, was repugnant to the Constitution.[48]

Counsel for the Attorney General sought to justify section 10 under the "exceptional case" provisions of Article 42.5. The court said it might well be that Article 42.5 protected section 10 insofar as the latter permitted the State to supply the place of the parents because of lack of means. But Article 42.5 would not validate a permanent surrender of the parents' rights and duties; it envisaged only a temporary surrender, for the period during which the parents were unable to provide for the children's education. It was also argued that once the child went to the industrial school, extended detention there might be essential to enable her to be properly educated. But the Supreme Court rejected this, holding that Article 42.5 did not enable the legislature to take away the right of a parent, who was in a position to do so, to control the child's education where there was nothing culpable on the part of parent or child.

The report of the *Doyle* case makes clear the Minster's concern that the child's welfare might be prejudiced by discharging her—that the father's arrangements for having her looked after were not satisfactory. But even had this been demonstrably the case it seems clear from the Supreme Court's judgment that it could not be a factor in deciding custody. Thus considerations of the child's welfare would be subordinated to the vindication of the parents' constitutional rights. However, though the *Doyle* case has not been explicitly overruled, it must be doubtful whether the Supreme Court would now give such apparent primacy to parental rights. The State's obligation to protect and vindicate a child's personal rights under Article 40.3 would seem to require more of a balancing exercise than was there contemplated.

In *State (D.C.)* v. *Midland Health Board* (High Court, July 31, 1986) Keane J. held that while Article 42.5 would validate statutory dispositions for taking children at risk into care, a statutory scheme which did not keep to a minimum the interval of time between the child's removal and the determination of its future custody by a court would constitute an impermissible violation of the parents' constitutional rights. But he also concluded that section 24 of the Children Act 1908, and its associated procedural rules, was not such a scheme. The replacement provisions of the Child Care Act 1991[49] seem to be equally free of any such vice.

---

[48] It was subsequently replaced by the Children Act 1957, s.5.

[49] s.13(7)(a)(i) of the Act permits a District Court judge, when making an emergency care order, to direct that the address or location of the place where the child is being kept be withheld from the parents. In *State (D. and D.)* v. *G. and Midland Health Board (No. 2)* [1990] I.L.R.M. 130 the Supreme Court accepted the validity of such a procedure. But Finlay C.J., for the court, said (at 139): "Such an exclusion of knowledge should not . . . be lightly undertaken, having particular regard for the fact that questions of proper access and communication between such parents and the child may in some instances still be a very necessary ingredient in the welfare of the child."

Adoption

Disputes arising out of adoption, and related issues of custody, have generated a good deal of constitutional litigation. Until 1952 legal adoption did not exist in Ireland, but it was introduced by the Adoption Act of that year.[50] Though that Act has several times been amended, the basic features have been maintained and two in particular call for mention. One is that adoption orders can be made only by the Adoption Board (An Bord Uchtála); no court is invested with jurisdiction in this regard.[51] The second is that the statutory consequences of the making of an adoption order are far-reaching. The mother or guardian loses all parental or guardianship rights and is freed from all parental or guardianship duties. Further, the legal status of the child is altered, since he or she now stands in relation to the adopters as a child born to them in lawful wedlock.

Adoption of non-marital children

A child whose parents have not married—or who is an orphan—may be adopted: Adoption Act 1952, s.10(*c*). Subject to the Adoption Act 1974 (considered *infra*) the making of an adoption order requires "the consent of every person being the child's mother or guardian or having charge of or control over the child"; 1952 Act, section 14(1). Thus the consent of the natural *father* is not a prerequisite,[52] and this was upheld as constitutionally valid by the Supreme Court in *State (Nicolaou)* v. *An Board Uchtála* [1966] I.R. 567. It did not, said the court, violate the equality guarantee of Article 40.1, nor did it violate the unenumerated rights guarantee of Article 40.3. Those rights were "the natural personal rights"; and the court was not satisfied that the father of a non-marital child had any natural right to the custody or society of that child.[53]

The validity of the 1952 Act's provisions for the adoption of non-marital children was affirmed in *Nicolaou's* case. Walsh J., delivering the judgment of the Supreme Court, said (at 644):

> " . . . the mother of an illegitimate child does not come within the ambit of Articles 41 and 42 of the Constitution. Her natural right to the custody and care of her child, and such other natural personal rights as she may have . . . fall to be protected under Article 40, section 3, and are

---

[50] The background to this Act—including the campaign for such legislation—is set out in Whyte, *op. cit.*, pp. 183–193, 274–277.

[51] The 1984 *Report* of the Review Committee on Adoption Services recommended that An Bord Uchtála should be replaced by a specialist Adoption Court, chaired by a High Court judge: see Chap. 9 thereof. This has not been implemented.

[52] Note, however, that s.12 of the Status of Children Act 1987 amends the Guardianship of Infants Act 1964 by permitting an unmarried father to be appointed by a court as a guardian of his child.

[53] Under s.16 of the 1952 Act the natural father does not have a statutory right to be heard before an adoption order is made; but An Bord Uchtála has a discretion to hear persons other than those listed (s.16(1)(i)). In *Nicolaou's* case Walsh J. said (at 639) that a refusal to hear a natural father based on a general policy not to do so would be unlawful. Given developments since 1966 in the constitutional concept of basic fairness of procedures (as to which see Chap. 12 *supra*) a failure to hear a natural father in an appropriate case might be a ground for quashing the adoption order. As a matter of practice, however, An Bord Uchtála will grant a natural father's request to be heard: *Report of the Review Committee on Adoption Services*, May 1984 (Pl. 2467), para. 5.35.

not affected by Article 41 or 42 of the Constitution. There is no provision in Article 40 which prohibits or restricts the surrender, abdication or transfer of any of the rights guaranteed in that Article by the person entitled to them. The Court therefore rejects the submission that the Adoption Act, 1952, is invalid in as much as it permits the mother of an illegitimate child to consent to the legal adoption of her child, and lose, under the provisions of s.24(b) of the Act, all parental rights and be freed from all parental duties in respect of the child."

Though possibly *obiter*, these views were confirmed by the majority of the Supreme Court in *G.* v. *An Bord Uchtála* [1980] I.R. 32 (see O'Higgins C.J. at 55: Walsh J. at 66–67 and Parke J. at 99). Thus the natural mother of a non-marital child must be regarded as having an unenumerated right, protected by Article 40.3, to the custody of that child.[54] Because it is not inalienable, however, this right can be surrendered or abandoned; thus there is no consti-tutional bar to the mother's consenting to the child's adoption. The *G.* case also establishes that the child has unenumerated rights protected by Article 40.3—to be protected, reared and educated in a proper way.

Under Irish law adoption is a consensual process, in two stages: (1) the mother must consent to the placement of the child for adoption; (2) she must later consent to the making of an adoption order.[55] However, under the Adoption Act 1974 this second consent may be dispensed with. Section 3 of that Act provides:

"(1) In any case where a person has applied for an adoption order relat-ing to a child and any person whose consent to the making of an adop-tion order relating to the child is necessary and who has agreed to the placing of the child for adoption either—
(a) fails, neglects or refuses to give his consent, or
(b) withdraws a consent already given,
the applicant for the adoption order may apply to the High Court for an order under this section.
(2) The High Court, if it is satisfied that it is in the best interests of the child so to do, may make an order under this section
(a) giving custody of the child to the applicant for such period as the Court may determine, and
(b) authorising the Board to dispense with the consent of the other per-son referred to in subsection (1) of this section to the making of an adoption order in favour of the applicant during the period afore-said."

Section 3 was discussed by the Supreme Court in *G.* v. *An Bord Uchtála* [1980] I.R. 32. This unsatisfactory decision would furnish evidence for the extension of the "one-opinion rule" discussed in Chapter 11 *supra*. From the five separate judgments only a few propositions emerge which command the assent of a majority of the court. In the High Court Finlay P. had held that the natural mother and the child both had constitutional rights, and that sec-tion 3 must be construed in accordance with those constitutional rights. Thus

---

[54] Finlay P. expressly so held in *S.* v. *Eastern Health Board* (High Court, February 28, 1979).
[55] For a fuller discussion of this matter see Chaps. 5 and 6 of the *Report* of the Review Committee on Adoption Services; also Paul A. O'Connor, *Key Issues in Irish Family Law* (Dublin 1988), Part 2.

the court should grant an order only if the mother had capriciously or irresponsibly refused or withdrawn her consent, or had abandoned or deserted the child; or unless she had failed to satisfy the court that she was a fit and proper person to have custody of the child; or unless the overwhelming interests of the child's welfare required that it should not be restored to the mother's custody. On appeal, all members of the Supreme Court *appear* to have concluded that Finlay P. had applied the wrong test, and that no question of striking a balance between the mother's and the child's constitutional rights arose. Nonetheless a majority—Walsh, Henchy and Kenny JJ.—held that Finlay P. had reached the correct conclusion in the case. Henchy and Kenny JJ. however, took the view that the mother's right to custody was *legal*, not constitutional—a proposition rejected by Walsh J. O'Higgins C.J. and Parke J. agreed with Walsh J. that the natural mother's right was on the constitutional plane, but they also concluded that by placing the child for adoption she had surrendered this right. Walsh J. did not accept that such was the effect of her actions.

In *S.* v. *Eastern Health Board* (High Court, February 28, 1979) Finlay P. concluded from the *G.* case that an unmarried mother's right to custody was constitutional in origin. To create a valid alienation of that right, he said, the agreement to place for adoption must have been made freely, with full knowledge of its consequences and under circumstances where neither the advice of persons engaged in the transaction nor the surrounding circumstances deprived the mother of the capacity to make a fully informed free decision. This requirement of a fully informed and free consent has been reiterated by the Supreme Court in *Re D.G., an infant* [1991] 1 I.R. 491.[56] There Finlay C.J. (McCarthy and O'Flaherty JJ. concurring) added (at 515):

> " . . . a mother agreeing to place her child for adoption could not be said to reach a fully informed decision so to agree, unless at the time she made the agreement she was aware that the right which she undoubtedly has to withdraw that consent or to refuse further to consent to adoption, is subject to the possibility that, upon application by the prospective adopting parents, the court could conclude that it was in the best interests of the child to dispense with the mother's consent, and if following upon such a decision the board decided that it was appropriate to order the adoption of the child, she (the mother) could lose, forever, the custody of the child."[57]

If the consent to placement was valid then the test applicable in proceedings under section 3 of the Adoption Act 1974 is that of the child's best interests.[58] The picture is not clouded by any question of the mother's constitutional rights since these are treated as having been waived. But if the consent was defective no such waiver has occurred; thus in a custody suit between the mother and the would-be adopters the court may have to balance the mother's constitutional rights against those of the child. Since

---

[56] See also *V.C.* v. *J.M. and G.M.* [1987] I.R. 510.

[57] Factors other than this—such as fear, stress or anxiety—may negative the existence of a fully informed and free consent: see further O'Connor, *op. cit.*

[58] It seems curious that this should be so. One would have thought that the consent to placement would merely put the mother's rights "in temporary abeyance," as Henchy J. put it in *G.* v. *An Bord Uchtála* [1980] I.R. 32, 89. For an analysis of this matter see O'Connor, *op. cit.*, pp. 77–82.

the mother's rights are protected by Article 40.3, which does not offer an absolute guarantee, it seems constitutionally legitimate that the child's welfare should be the first and paramount consideration—as it is under section 3 of the Guardianship of Infants Act 1964. There is no presumption that that welfare is prima facie to be found by a return to the custody of the mother.

It cannot be too strongly emphasised that an order under section 3 of the Adoption Act 1974 merely authorises An Bord Uchtála to dispense with the mother's consent to the making of an adoption order. It does not follow that an adoption order *will* be made, for An Bord Uchtála will have to consider several other issues. Should it decline to make an adoption order the mother may seek to recover custody of the child. Any such proceedings would be governed by the provisions of the Guardianship of Infants Act 1964.[59]

Adoption and marital children

Until 1988 children born to married parents were eligible for adoption only in strictly limited circumstances. These arose purely under the Adoption Act 1964, section 2, and related to children born before the marriage of their parents.[60] If the birth had not been re-registered, *and* the parents consented,[61] such a child could be adopted.

However, the category of marital children eligible for adoption has been broadened by the Adoption Act 1988. This implemented a recommendation of the Review Committee on Adoption Services, which observed that current restrictions were depriving many children in care of the right to grow up in a stable home environment with legal security.[62] The committee recognised, however, that to legislate for the adoption of marital children might pose constitutional problems; thus they recommended that any doubts should be resolved in advance, either by an appropriate constitutional amendment or by securing the reference of the relevant bill to the Supreme Court under Article 26. The second course was chosen; following the passage of the Adoption (No. 2) Bill 1987, President Hillery referred it to the Supreme Court. The court ruled that the bill was not repugnant to the Constitution, or to any provision thereof: *Re Article 26 and the Adoption (No. 2) Bill 1987* [1989] I.R. 656.[63]

[59] In *S.* v. *Eastern Health Board* (High Court, February 28, 1979) Finlay P., though granting orders under the 1974 Adoption Act, s.3 also granted the mother a declaration that if An Bord Uchtála did not make an adoption order in favour of the applicants within six months, then absent any change in her circumstances there were no grounds for refusing to return the child to her. (See too his decision in *State (P.M.)* v. *G.M.* (November 27, 1984)). But the longer the child has been in the prospective adopters' custody the less likely is an order in the mother's favour. See Barron J. in *V.C.* v. *J.M. and G.M.* [1987] I.R. 510, at 521–522.

[60] By virtue of the Legitimacy Act 1931, s.1, the subsequent marriage rendered the child legitimate from the date thereof. Originally this applied only where " . . . the father and mother . . . could have been lawfully married to one another at the time of birth . . . " (s.1(2)); thus it would have had no application if at the time the child was born either parent was married to someone else. S.1(2), however, has now been repealed by s.7 of the Status of Children Act 1987.

[61] Or their consent was dispensed with under s.3 of the Adoption Act 1974. This could not be done if the father had not consented to the child's placement for adoption: see *Re J.H. (an infant)* [1985] I.R. 375, 384–385 *per* Lynch J.

[62] *Report of the Review Committee on Adoption Services* (Pl. 2467, May 1984), p. 11.

[63] Though bearing the date 1987, the bill was passed only on June 15, 1988. The President referred it on June 23, the Supreme Court delivered judgment on July 26 and the bill was signed into law on that date.

The 1988 Act was very carefully framed, and the Supreme Court's decision on the bill showed how necessary this was. Both the long title and the body of the Act invoke Article 42.5 of the Constitution by implication,[64] and stringent conditions are imposed on the making of adoption orders. They can be made only where the High Court authorises An Bord Uchtála so to do, and that court must be satisfied as to the several matters set out in section 3(1). These are:

"(I) that—
(A) for a continuous period of not less than 12 months immediately preceding the time of the making of the application, the parents of the child to whom the declaration under *section 2(1)* relates, for physical or moral reasons, have failed in their duty towards the child,
(B) it is likely that such failure will continue without interruption until the child attains the age of 18 years,
(C) such failure constitutes an abandonment on the part of the parents of all parental rights, whether under the Constitution or otherwise, with respect to the child, and
(D) by reason of such failure, the State, as guardian of the common good, should supply the place of the parents,
(II) that the child—
(A) at the time of the making of the application, is in the custody of and has a home with the applicants, and
(B) for a continuous period of not less than 12 months immediately preceding that time, has been in the custody of and has had a home with the applicants,
and
(III) that the adoption of the child by the applicants is an appropriate means by which to supply the place of the parents . . . "

But even to establish all these matters will not suffice, given the concluding words of section 3(1):

" . . . the Court may, if it so thinks fit and is satisfied, having had due regard for the rights, whether under the Constitution or otherwise, of the persons concerned (including the natural and imprescriptible rights of the child), that it would be in the best interests of the child to do so, make an order authorising the Board to make an adoption order in relation to the child in favour of the applicants."

The constitutional doubts as to the validity of such legislation sprang, of course, from the provisions of Articles 41 and 42. The position occupied by, and the rights secured to, the family by these Articles might seem to preclude any transfer of parental rights and duties, even if the parents agreed or if such rights had been abused or duties neglected. As against this, the "exceptional case" provision of Article 42.5 might be prayed in aid, though on one view these would warrant only measures for temporary care of the child.[65]

In *Re Article* 26 *and the Adoption (No. 2) Bill 1987* [1989] I.R. 656 the Supreme Court declined to read Article 42.5 so narrowly. The court noted

---

[64] The long title recites that it is "An Act to provide, in exceptional cases, where the parents for physical or moral reasons have failed in their duty towards their children, for the supplying, by the adoption of the children, of the place of the parents . . . "
[65] See the discussion in the report cited in n. 59 *supra*, pp. 13–14.

that Article 40.3 would oblige the State, as far as practicable, to vindicate the rights of a child whose parents had failed in their duty to him or her. Finlay C.J., delivering the judgment, went on to say (at 663):

> "The Court rejects the submission that the nature of the family as a unit group possessing inalienable and imprescriptible rights, makes it constitutionally impermissible for a statute to restore to any member of an individual family constitutional rights of which he has been deprived by a method which disturbs or alters the constitution of that family if that method is necessary to achieve that purpose. The guarantees afforded to the institution of the family by the Constitution, with their consequent benefit to the children of a family, should not be construed so that upon the failure of that benefit it cannot be replaced where the circumstances demand it, by incorporation of the child into an alternative family."

The court ruled that Article 40.3 and 42.5 should be read together, so that action by the State pursuant to the former in an endeavour to vindicate the child's personal rights must have due regard to his/her natural and imprescriptible rights. The latter would seem to be those identified in *Re J.H. (an infant)* [1985] I.R. 375—to belong to a constitutionally protected family and to be educated by it. The inference would appear to be that the bill would be valid only if a proper balance was achieved between these potentially conflicting sets of rights.

The court laid stress on a number of the bill's features, in a way which suggests that nothing less would pass constitutional muster. Thus it was noted that the matters set out in section 3(1) were not merely matters to be taken into consideration in exercising a general discretion but were essential proofs requiring separately to be established. Failure in any one of them prohibited the making of an authorising order, no matter how desirable this might be in the child's interests. Referring to the requirement of parental failure in duties towards the child, the court said (at 664):

> " . . . the failure must be construed as being total in character. No mere inadequacy of standard in the discharge of the parental duty would, in the opinion of the Court, suffice to establish this proof. Furthermore, the failure must arise for physical or moral reasons. This does not mean that the failure must necessarily in every case be blameworthy, but it does mean that a failure due to externally originating circumstances such as poverty would not constitute a failure within the meaning of the subclause."

In regard to what is now section 3(1)(I)(*c*) the court held (at 664):

> "The concept of abandonment of parental rights falls to be considered after it has been established that a failure of parental duty for physical or moral reasons has continued for more than twelve months and is likely to continue until the child attains eighteen years of age. The sub-clause clearly envisages that there might be cases where such a failure was established but an abandonment of rights was not proved. An abandonment could be established by evidence of the conduct of the parent or parents concerned which would in certain cases include statements made by them and/or the nature and type of the failure in duty which had been established. A mere statement by a parent or parents that they

wished to abandon a child would not necessarily constitute proof in any particular case of the fact of abandonment but may do so. Failure of parental duty established under sub-clause (I)(A) and (B) is not of itself evidence of abandonment. The necessity for the proof of abandonment indicates a special regard for the constitutionally protected parental rights."

Finally, the court noted that the Act gives the High Court " . . . a final and residual discretion . . . " to refuse to make the order if it is satisfied that it would be " . . . in the best interests of the child to do so" (at 666–667). The " . . . best interests of the child . . . ", consequently, did not imply " . . . some simple material test . . . " but would " . . . necessarily be adjudged against the background of its constitutional rights." It would therefore involve, in the words of Finlay C.J. (at 665):

> " . . . proper consideration of all the consequences, from the point of view of the child, of bringing it by adoption out of the family into which it was born and into an alternative family."

Religious upbringing of children

Disputes over the religious upbringing of children have often provoked controversy in Ireland.[66] It has been the constant policy of the Roman Catholic church to seek assurances that the children of a religiously mixed marriage are brought up as Catholics. To this end the non-Catholic partner has been required, as a condition of a church marriage, to give undertakings on this matter. At common law such ante-nuptial agreements or undertakings were not legally enforceable; the father was regarded as having complete control over the children in this, as in other, matters. But in *Re Tilson* [1951] I.R. 1 the Supreme Court held that this rule had not survived the enactment of the Constitution. Article 42.1 meant that where the mother and father were alive they had a joint right and duty to provide for the religious education of their children. Murnaghan J. (Maguire C.J., O'Byrne and Lavery JJ. concurring) said (at 34):

> " . . . the true principle under our Constitution is this. The parents— father and mother—have a joint power and duty in respect of the religious education of their children. If they together make a decision and put it into practice it is not in the power of the father—nor is it in the power of the mother—to revoke such decision against the will of the other party. Such an exercise of their power may be made after marriage when the occasion arises; but an agreement made before marriage dealing with matters which will arise during the marriage and put into force after the marriage is equally effective and of as binding force in law."

If there is no express ante-nuptial agreement one may be implied from the conduct of the parties, as in *Re May* [1959] I.R. 74. There the parents had been married in a Roman Catholic church and their five children has been baptised as Catholics. Later, however, the father had become a Jehovah's Witness and he now wished his children to follow his example. The mother did not. She applied for the children to be made wards of court, and sought

---

[66] See further Whyte, *op. cit.*, pp. 169–171, 322–325.

guardianship and custody of the children and directions as to their upbringing. Davitt P. held that, in all the circumstances, an agreement between the parents must be implied; no other inference could reasonably be drawn. It followed that neither parent had the right to depart in any way from this agreement. So long as the wife objected, the husband had no right to interfere with the children's religious beliefs.[67]

In *Re Blake* [1955] I.R. 89 a testator had bequeathed property to trustees on trust to apply the income for the maintenance and education of his daughter's children, and on majority or marriage to apportion the capital in equal shares between them. This, however, was subject to their being brought up in the Roman Catholic faith. The daughter had become a member of the Church of Ireland and her three sons had been brought up in that church. In the High Court Dixon J. had to consider whether the condition was void as contrary to public policy. Following Gavan Duffy P.'s decision in *Burke and O'Reilly* v. *Burke and Quail* [1951] I.R. 216, Dixon J. held that it was. Article 42 of the Constitution stated public policy on such questions by declaring and guaranteeing the parental right and duty of education. Any attempt to restrict or fetter that right could not be aided by the courts; consequently this condition was void and of no effect. (Unfortunately for the children, this meant that the bequest failed).

The position of mothers

In Article 41.2.1° the State recognises that "by her life within the home, woman gives to the State a support without which the common good cannot be achieved." Consequently "the State shall . . . endeavour to ensure that mothers shall not be obliged by economic necessity to engage in labour to the neglect of their duties in the home" (Art. 41.2.2°). These provisions obviously reflect role assumptions which are no longer valid, but they clearly do not bind the State to a philosophy that woman's place is in the home. Nor would they provide any foundation for legislative restrictions on married women entering the labour market. Any such restriction would prima facie violate the equality guarantee of Article 40.1 and would hardly be capable of being justified under Article 41.2. Indeed the only legal effect of the latter would seem to be to oblige the State to ensure that mothers do not *have* to work outside the home. If they *choose* to do so, that is plainly their right.

EDUCATION

As noted *supra*, Article 42.1 declares the family to be the primary and natural educator of the child; and the State guarantees to respect parental rights and duties in this regard. The remainder of Article 42 emphasises freedom of parental choice in educational matters, and effectively guarantees variety in educational provision. Thus parents are free to provide this education in their homes, or private schools, or in schools "recognised or established" by the State (Art. 42.2). But the State may not oblige parents "in violation of their conscience and lawful preference" to send their children to State-established

---

[67] These principles apply to the exercise of jurisdiction under the Guardianship of Infants Act 1964—*i.e.* the resolution of any dispute between the parents (who are joint guardians) as to the religious upbringing of their children: see *H.* v. *H.* (High Court, Parke J., February 4, 1976).

schools, or to any particular type of school designated by the State (Art. 42.3.1°).

It will thus be apparent that the State's *powers* are limited (though for financial reasons its *role* is not). But some powers it does have. It may, as noted, establish schools; and, more importantly, it has a constitutional obligation to fix minimum educational standards. For Article 42.3.2° provides:

"The State shall . . . as guardian of the common good, require in view of actual conditions that the children receive a certain minimum education, moral, intellectual and social."

Article 42.4 imposes another obligation on the State—to "provide *for* free primary education." The same provision permits the State to provide "other educational facilities and institutions"—due regard being had to the rights of parents. Finally Article 42.4 envisages State funding for non-State run schools ("private and corporate educational initiative").

Meaning of "education"

One of the arguments advanced against the fluoridation legislation in *Ryan* v. *Att. Gen.* [1965] I.R. 294 was that it violated parental rights in education, contrary to Article 42.1. "Education," it was contended, included the whole process of rearing and nurturing. Kenny J., however, was of opinion that while the word undoubtedly had this wide meaning at one time, such usage had become obsolete by 1937. He continued (at 310):

" . . . it seems to me that the terms of the Article show that the word 'education' was not used in this wide sense in the Constitution. Section 1 of the Article recognises the 'right and duty of the parents to provide, according to their means, for the religious and moral, intellectual, physical and social education of their children,' but in section 2 it is provided that the parents are free to provide *this* education in their homes or in schools recognised or established by the State. The education referred to in section 1 must, therefore, be one that can be provided in schools and must, therefore, be one of a scholastic nature."

On appeal, the Supreme Court, *per* Ó Dálaigh C.J., likewise dismissed this argument, albeit in slightly different terms (at 350):

"Education essentially is the teaching and training of a child to make the best possible use of his inherent and potential capacities, physical, mental and moral. To teach a child to minimise the dangers of dental caries by adequate brushing of his teeth is physical education for it induces him to use his own resources. To give him water of a nature calculated to minimise the danger of dental caries is in no way to educate him, physically or otherwise, for it does not develop his resources."

In *Landers* v. *Att. Gen.* (1975) 109 I.L.T.R. 1, Finlay J. thought there was no inconsistency between these definitions. Applying Kenny J.'s "scholastic" test, he dismissed a claim that legislation which prevented children under 16 from following a professional singing career violated Article 42. Whatever else it included, said Finlay J. "education" under Article 42 did not include

"the public singing career of a child between the age of seven and ten years."
It might be otherwise if the legislation in any way inhibited the child's training or practice in his musical accomplishment.

Primary education

Article 40.4 obliges the State to "provide *for* free primary education." The
preposition "for" is significant, since behind it lies the whole history of such
education in Ireland. The Supreme Court recognised this in *Crowley* v. *Ireland*
[1980] I.R. 102. As Kenny J. put it (at 126):

> " . . . the State is under no obligation to educate. The history of Ireland
> in the 19th Century shows how tenaciously the people resisted the idea
> of State schools. The Constitution must not be interpreted without refer-
> ence to our history and to the conditions and intellectual climate of 1937
> when almost all schools were under the control of a manager or of
> trustees who were not nominees of the State. That historical experience
> was one of the State providing financial assistance and prescribing
> courses to be followed at the schools; but the teachers, though paid by
> the State, were not employed by and could not be removed by it; this
> was the function of the manager of the school who was almost always a
> clergyman. So s.4 of Article 42 prescribes that the State shall provide *for*
> free primary education. The effect of this is that the State is to provide
> the buildings, to pay the teachers who are under no contractual duty to
> it but to the manager or trustees, to provide means of transport to the
> schools if this is necessary to avoid hardship, and to prescribe minimum
> standards."

See, too, O'Higgins C.J. at 122–123.

It has been estimated that more than 95 per cent. of primary education in
Ireland is State-aided. This education is provided in "national schools"; but
despite their name these are not owned, run or fully-financed by the State.
Most of them are denominational in character and traditionally their
managers were clergymen. Nowadays boards of management exist, but while
the boards have (*inter alia*) the power to appoint teachers, an appointment
requires the prior approval of the patron (in Roman Catholic schools the
local bishop).

As regards finance, the local community (acting in practice through the
churches) provides the site for a national school. It also pays about 15 per
cent. of the capital costs of building and furnishing the school—the State
meeting the 85 per cent. balance. The State pays in addition around 80 per
cent. of the running costs of each school—and the full salary of the teachers.
It also provides a free school transport system.[68]

The system thus outlined may be open to objection from a philosophical
standpoint,[69] but *Crowley's* case has confirmed its constitutional validity. It

---

[68] The above account draws heavily on John Coolahan, *Irish Education: Its History and Structure*
(Dublin 1981), Chap. 10. This deals with the post-1960 period, the earlier history being
treated in Chap. 1.

[69] See Desmond M. Clarke, *Church and State: Essays in Political Philosophy* (Cork 1984), Chap. 8,
and Chap. 19 *infra*.

should, however, be noted that the State cannot *insist* on denominational schools. If a group of parents wishes, and is able to, arrange for a non-denominational national school the State could not constitutionally refuse it aid. Nor has it attempted to do so.[70]

In the *Crowley* case the precise nature of the State's obligation regarding primary education was examined. There a dispute over a teaching appointment had led to the closure of three national schools in Drimoleague parish, Co. Cork. All the teachers, save one, had withdrawn their labour as from April 1, 1976. Nearly 200 children were affected by this. Initially, on union instructions, their enrolment at neighbouring schools was refused but this ban was later lifted. In effect, all organised schooling in the parish was at an end, and matters remained thus until January 1978, when the Department of Education arranged to transport the affected children to other schools in adjoining parishes. This was *not* the result of Departmental initiative but the consequence of a mandatory injunction granted by the High Court.

In the subsequent proceedings the six infant plaintiffs claimed a violation of their constitutional rights in that since January 1978 they were not receiving free primary education in accordance with Article 42.4. This was because their education was not provided within Drimoleague parish, was not reasonably accessible and was defective in other ways. In the High Court McMahon J. was unable to accept these arguments. Article 42.4 did not require that the primary education stipulated should be given in the parish where the pupils lived. Any other conclusion would make it constitutionally impossible to amalgamate schools in several parishes. On the facts, McMahon J. found that the system of buses now provided a reasonably accessible primary education for the Drimoleague children. As to the defects complained of, the two major ones were the lack of remedial treatment to compensate for the loss of schooling already suffered, and the fact that unfavourable staff/student ratios in the neighbouring schools meant a loss of individual attention. McMahon J. accepted that these complaints might be well-founded; but he nonetheless held that the State was now discharging its constitutional obligation towards those children. (It seems that no appeal was brought against this part of the judgment: see Kenny J. [1980] I.R. 102 at 129).

In respect of the pre-bussing period, however, McMahon J. took a different view (rather oddly, because he says (at 112) that no claim was based on this). The State's constitutional duty to provide for free primary education created a corresponding right to receive primary education in those for whom it was designed. And when that obligation was not being discharged the onus was on the State to show that the absence of free primary education was not due to a breach of obligation on the State's part. The situation in the Drimoleague schools between March 1976 and December 1977 was prima facie evidence of a breach of obligation by the State. The Minister had failed to displace that prima facie inference that the State had defaulted on its constitutional obligation.

By a 3–2 majority the Supreme Court (Kenny, Henchy and Griffin JJ.; O'Higgins C.J. and Parke J. dissenting) reversed this decision. Kenny J. said

---

[70] See Whyte, *op. cit.* pp. 394–395. As there noted, some Ministers seem to find the attendant administrative problems more difficult than do others; see a letter of complaint from Sligo parents in *The Irish Times*, July 22, 1986.

the totality of the evidence did not show that the State had been in breach of its obligation. The majority saw the claim as based on Article 40—*i.e.* that the children's right to free primary education had to be defended and vindicated under Article 40.3.1°. But the obligation under Article 40, said Kenny J., was not a *general* obligation to defend and vindicate the personal rights of the citizen. It was a duty to do so *by its laws*, and no indication had been given of the kind of legislation that could have been passed to provide free primary education for the plaintiffs.[71] The State could not by law compel teachers to teach when they did not wish to do so.

This is a most unsatisfactory decision. Its result is to validate total Ministerial inactivity in such circumstances. The State is not obliged to provide substitute teachers or to pay any recruited by the parents; nor is it required to take any subsequent steps to minimise the educational disadvantages suffered by the children. Indeed, as Professor Osborough has pointed out, even the provision of transport to neighbouring schools was not seen as constitutionally required.[72] Nor is it clear why Article 40.3 was invoked. The constitutional right to free primary education could have been treated as springing directly from Article 42.4—*i.e.* as a right correlative to the duty imposed by that provision. Such an analysis would have avoided the unreal question posed by the Supreme Court as to what legislation might have been enacted to cure the Drimoleague problems—an especially unreal question given the dearth of legislation on primary education in Ireland. Moreover, to concentrate attention on Article 42.4 is advantageous in emphasising the State's constitutional obligation here. For, as the judgments in *Byrne* v. *Ireland* [1972] I.R. 241 show, failing action by other organs of State it falls to the courts to secure the performance of such obligations.

Compulsory attendance

This matter is regulated by the School Attendance Act 1926. The Act applies to children between six and 15 (the latter age fixed by a Ministerial order of 1972 made under power conferred by section 24). Section 17 provides that if, without reasonable excuse, a parent fails or neglects to cause a child to attend school, the enforcing authority shall serve on the parent a warning in the prescribed form. Failure to comply with such a warning is an offence. Obviously, this Act must not be applied in such a way as to conflict with constitutional rights; so parents must be at liberty to educate their children at home, if they so wish and if this can be done without adverse effect on the children. Judge Esmonde so ruled in a Circuit Court case in Mayo: see *The Irish Times*, February 22, 1986.

The School Attendance Bill 1942 was designed to amend and supplement the 1926 Act. Professor Osborough has shown that its aims and provisions were a matter of considerable controversy,[73] which no doubt explains why

---

[71] This approach to Art. 40.3 does not seem to be consistent with what Kenny J. said in *People (D.P.P.)* v. *Shaw* [1982] I.R. 1, at 62: "The word 'laws' in Article 40, s.3 is not confined to laws which have been enacted by the Oireachtas but comprehends the laws made by judges and by Ministers of State when they make statutory instruments or regulations."

[72] W. N. Osborough, "Education in the Irish Law and Constitution" (1978) XIII *Irish Jurist* (N.S.) 145.

[73] Osborough, *op. cit.*, pp. 172–180.

President Hyde referred the Bill to the Supreme Court for a ruling as to whether section 4 was repugnant to the Constitution. Section 3(1) of the Bill obliged parents to send their children to "a national school, a suitable school or a recognised school." Section 3(2) listed reasonable excuses for failure to comply with this obligation. Section 4(1) then provided:

"A child shall not be deemed for the purposes of this Act to be receiving suitable education in a manner other than by attending a national school, a suitable school or a recognised school unless such education and the manner in which such child is receiving it have been certified under this section by the Minister to be suitable."

The Supreme Court found section 4 repugnant to the Constitution: *Re Article 26 and the School Attendance Bill 1942* [1943] I.R. 334. The Constitution, it was held, contemplated that normally the right and duty of educating children was vested in parents. The State could interfere only to the limited extent mentioned in Article 42—*i.e.* to require that children receive "a certain minimum education" (Art. 42.3.2°). That phrase could be defined by statute, but only so as to effectuate the general provisions of Article 42.3.2° without contravening other constitutional provisions. The expression, in the court's view, indicated "a minimum standard of elementary education of general application" ([1943] I.R. 334, 345). Under section 4, however, the Minister might prescribe a higher standard than could qualify as a minimum standard under Article 42.3.2°. Moreover, the standard contemplated by section 4 might vary from child to child and was, accordingly, not a standard of general application such as the Constitution envisaged. The section was therefore beyond the constitutional pale. Additionally, it offended because the Minister was required to certify not only the education but the *manner* in which the child was receiving it. On this the court, *per* Sullivan C.J., said ([1943] I.R. 334, 346):

"We do not consider that this is warranted by the Constitution. The State is entitled to require that children shall receive a certain minimum education. So long as parents supply this general standard of education we are of opinion that the manner in which it is being given and received is entirely a matter for the parents and is not a matter in respect of which the State under the Constitution is entitled to interfere."

From both a legal and educational viewpoint this decision now has a very old-fashioned air. The Supreme Court's fears that a Minister, reasonably exercising his powers under the Bill, might prescribe a standard higher than the constitutional one, would not be felt today. The presumption of constitutionality, as expounded by the Supreme Court in *East Donegal Co-op Ltd.* v. *Att. Gen.* [1970] I.R. 317, would cover this point. As for the minimum standard, the court seems to have viewed this as something static—yet few would disagree that the minimum standard thought appropriate for the 1940s might be altogether inappropriate for the 1990s. Nor would it be accepted nowadays that educational content and teaching methods are separable in the way the Supreme Court seemed to think.

The *School Attendance Bill* case may have had little long-term effect on Irish educational provision; after all, the whole system has been transformed since then. One unfortunate consequence may however remain. The dearth of legislation on primary and secondary education in Ireland has often been commented upon.[74] Costello J. drew attention to it in *O'Callaghan* v. *Meath Vocational Education Committee* (High Court, November 20, 1990):

> "It is a remarkable feature of the Irish system of education that the administration by the Department of Education is largely uncontrolled by statute or statutory instruments and that many hundreds, perhaps thousands, of rules and regulations, memoranda, circulars and decisions are issued and made by the Department and the Minister (dealing sometimes with the most important aspects of educational policy) not under any statutory power but merely as administrative measures. These measures are not, of course, illegal. But they have no statutory force, and the sanction which ensures compliance with them is not a legal one but the undeclared understanding that the Department will withhold financial assistance in the event of non-compliance."

Professor Osborough has noted that this framework virtually withdraws primary education from parliamentary control. The absence of legislation, he has suggested, may be due to a fear of a repetition of the judicial reverse suffered in 1943.[75]

Second level education

Second level education is again mainly denominational. Most secondary schools are owned by Roman Catholic religious orders, while there are also some Protestant schools and a few which cater for other denominations. These schools are grant-aided by the State, which also effectively pays the teachers' salaries.[76] The constitutional authority for this lies in that portion of Article 42.4 which provides that the State "shall endeavour to supplement and give reasonable aid to private and corporate educational initiative."

The demoninational nature of the system is highlighted by the case of *Flynn* v. *Sister Power and Sisters of the Holy Faith* [1985] I.L.R.M. 336. This was a claim under the Unfair Dismissals Act 1977. The plaintiff had been employed as a teacher in a convent secondary school run by the respondents in New Ross. Her claim that she had been unfairly dismissed was rejected by the Employment Appeals Tribunal and, on appeal, by the Circuit Court. The plaintiff then appealed to the High Court. Costello J. said that the school principal had received formal complaints from parents that an association had developed between Ms Flynn and a local man whose wife had left him. At an interview with the principal, the plaintiff said she regarded this as her own business and of no concern to the school authorities or parents. Subsequently the plaintiff went to live with the man and his children and she became pregnant by him. After several interviews, and the birth of her baby, the plaintiff was dismissed.

Costello J. observed that the key question, under section 6(1) of the 1977 Act, was whether "having regard to all the circumstances there were substantial grounds justifying the dismissal." The evidence showed that the main complaint against the plaintiff was that she openly rejected the norms of behaviour and the ideals which the school existed to promote. The judge stressed that the school was a religious, not a lay, one and such a school had

---

[74] Coolahan, *op. cit.* p. 159.
[75] Osborough, *op. cit.* p. 174.
[76] For fuller details see Coolahan, *op. cit.*, Chap. 12.

long established and well-known aims. In assessing the effect of the plaintiff's conduct on the school, the respondents were entitled to conclude that her conduct was capable of damaging their efforts to foster in their pupils norms of behaviour and religious tenets which the school had been established to promote. Thus they had substantial grounds for dismissing her.

There does not appear to have been any discussion of constitutional rights in this case. It might be argued that Ms. Flynn had an unenumerated constitutional right of privacy, guaranteeing her choice of lifestyle and that her dismissal violated that right. But this argument could be met with the reply that Ms. Flynn had waived her right by accepting employment in a school whose character she knew. A court might well treat this as a waiver—see *McGrath and Ó Ruairc* v. *Trustees of Maynooth College* [1979] I.L.R.M. 166, discussed in Chapter 19 *infra*. Indeed in the *Flynn* case Costello J. observed that the plaintiff "knew from her own upbringing and previous experience as a teacher the sort of school in which she sought employment, and should have been aware of the obligations she would undertake by joining its staff" ([1985] I.L.R.M. 336, 343).

18 Property Rights

The Constitution contains two references to property rights. They are mentioned in Article 40.3.2° where the State pledges itself "as best it may" to protect property rights from unjust attack and, if injustice is done, to "vindicate" those rights. Later in the text appears the cross-heading "Private Property" and below it the terms of Article 43;

> "1.1° The State acknowledges that man, in virtue of his rational being, has the natural right, antecedent to positive law, to the private ownership of external goods.
>
> 2° The State accordingly guarantees to pass no law attempting to abolish the right of private ownership or the general right to transfer, bequeath, and inherit property.
>
> 2.1° The State recognises, however, that the exercise of the rights mentioned in the foregoing provisions of this Article ought, in civil society, to be regulated by the principles of social justice.
>
> 2° The State, accordingly, may as occasion requires delimit by law the exercise of the said rights with a view to reconciling their exercise with the exigencies of the common good."

The precise relationship between Article 40.3.2° and Article 43 is still unclear; indeed in hardly any branch of constitutional law has judicial opinion shown so much fluctuation. But the conclusions of Kenny J. in the High Court in *Central Dublin Development Association* v. *Att. Gen.* (1975) 109 I.L.T.R. 69, 86 still appear to summarise the position accurately:

(1) The right of private property is a personal right;
(2) In virtue of his rational being, man has a natural right to individual or private ownership of worldly wealth;
(3) This constitutional right consists of a bundle of rights most of which are founded in contract;
(4) The State cannot pass any law which abolishes all the bundle of rights called ownership or the general right to transfer, bequeath and inherit property;
(5) The exercise of these rights ought to be regulated by the principles of social justice and the State accordingly may by law restrict their exercise with a view to reconciling this with the exigencies of the common good;
(6) The courts have jurisdiction to inquire whether the restriction is in accordance with the principles of social justice and whether the

legislation is necessary to reconcile this exercise with the demands of the common good;

(7) If any of the rights which together constitute the conception of ownership are abolished or restricted (as distinct from the abolition of all the rights), the absence of compensation for this restriction or abolition will make the Act which does this invalid if it is an unjust attack on property rights.

The application of these broad principles to concrete cases is difficult, since the judicial perception of what principles of social justice and the demands of the common good require may differ considerably from those of the executive and legislature. But any post-1937 Act restricting property rights will benefit from the presumption of constitutionality; and the pattern of decisions shows a general judicial deference to the political branches' judgment. Indeed the judicial approach to such matters seems to remain that suggested by Kenny J. in the celebrated water fluoridation case of *Ryan* v. *Att. Gen.* [1965] I.R. 294, 312–313:

"None of the personal rights of the citizen are unlimited: their exercise may be regulated by the Oireachtas when the common good requires this. When dealing with controversial social, economic and medical matters on which it is notorious views change from generation to generation, the Oireachtas has to reconcile the exercise of personal rights with the claims of the common good and its decision on the reconciliation should prevail unless it was oppressive to all or some of the citizens or unless there is no reasonable proportion between the benefit which the legislation will confer on the citizens or a substantial body or them and the interference with the personal rights of the citizen. Moreover, the presumption that every Act of the Oireachtas is constitutional until the contrary is clearly established applies with particular force to this type of legislation."

The early cases

Fisher v. *Irish Land Commission* [1948] I.R. 3 was a challenge, on separation of powers grounds, to section 39 of the Land Act 1939. It is significant for the plaintiff's concession that the Constitution did not prevent the legislature expropriating owners so as to make land available for public purposes (in this instance redistribution of farmland). It is clear that the Supreme Court regarded this concession as rightly made, and in no subsequent case has an attempt been made to establish the converse proposition. Thus compulsory purchase provisions like those in the Turf Development Act 1946 or the Housing Act 1966 (which of course provide for compensation) seem to be beyond constitutional challenge.[1]

In *Buckley* v. *Att. Gen.* [1950] I.R. 67 a dispute had arisen in regard to the ownership of the funds of the Sinn Féin organisation as established in 1905 and reconstituted in 1917. An action to determine the issue was ready for hearing in the High Court when the Oireachtas passed the Sinn Féin Funds Act 1947. This provided for the staying of all further proceedings in the pend-

---

[1] In *O'Brien* v. *Bord na Móna* [1983] I.R. 255 the plaintiff's challenge to a compulsory acquisition by the defendant Board, though based on constitutional grounds, did not involve the proposition that compulsory acquisition was *per se* prohibited. See Chap. 12, *supra*.

ing action and its dismissal by the High Court; for the payment of the funds to a Board (chaired by the Chief Justice) established thereunder, which was then to apply them in accordance with section 13. This empowered the Board to make payments to any person in needy circumstances "who, as a member of the Forces, gave service in the National Cause at any time during the critical period" (defined as April 1, 1916–July 11, 1921). The Supreme Court upheld the plaintiffs' constitutional challenge to the Act saying, *per* O'Byrne J., that its effect was to take away the trust funds from the plaintiffs and deprive them of all rights therein. But the Constitution did not permit this. The Court rejected the defendant's argument that Article 43.1.2° operated merely to prevent the total abolition of private property, and that the Oireachtas had power to take away the property rights of individual citizens. O'Byrne J. said (at 82):

> "We are unable to accept that proposition. It seems to us that the Article was intended to enshrine and protect the property rights of the individual citizen of the State and that the rights of the citizen *are* thereby protected, subject to the right of the State, as declared in (Article 43.2), to regulate the exercise of such rights. . . . "

Also rejected was the contention that what "the exigencies of the common good" required was peculiarly a matter for the legislature, whose decision was not capable of being reviewed by the courts. This "far-reaching proposition" was convincingly demolished by pointing out: (a) that the Oireachtas was forbidden to legislate in a way repugnant to the Constitution (Article 15.4); (b) that the courts had jurisdiction to determine whether it had done so (Articles 34.3.2° and 34.4.4°); (c) that whereas Article 45 declared its directive principles of social policy not cognisable by the courts, Article 43 contained no such statement. Finally the court said (at 83):

> "In the present case there is no suggestion that any conflict had arisen, or was likely to arise, between the exercise by the plaintiffs of their rights of property in the trust moneys and the exigencies of the common good, and, in our opinion, it is only the existence of such a conflict and an attempt by the Legislature to reconcile such conflicting claims that could justify the enactment of the statute under review."

While noting (at 81) that Article 40.3 covered property rights the Supreme Court said nothing about the relationship between that provision and Article 43. Later decisions, however, make it clear that they must be read together, and that something capable of justification under Article 43 cannot be an "unjust attack" for Article 40.3.2° purposes.[2] Another noticeable feature of the judgment is the search for a specific conflict between the plaintiffs' property rights and the common good. No such thing is found in the more recent cases; judicial attention has focussed instead on the interaction between the concepts of 'unjust attack" under Article 40.3.2° and social justice under Article 43.2. This may result from the fact that the term "conflict" (which does not appear in the Constitution) is misleading; the power of the Oireachtas is one to "regulate" the exercise of property rights.

If *Buckley's* case was thought to presage a strict approach towards interference with property rights any such idea would have required modification

---

[2] See the decisions in the *Dreher*, *O'Callaghan* and *Gormley* cases discussed *infra*.

after *Foley* v. *Irish Land Commission* [1952] I.R. 188.[3] This was an attack on the validity of section 2 of the Land Act 1946. The plaintiff had contracted with the Land Commission for the purchase of certain land, the Commission advancing the purchase price to him (to be repaid by an annuity). The land included a dwellinghouse and the Commission directed (as s.2 empowered it to do) that the plaintiff must reside therein. Subsequently the Commission concluded that the plaintiff had failed to do so and they moved to recover possession under section 2. The plaintiff argued that section 2 involved a forfeiture and violated the constitutional guarantees of his property rights. The Supreme Court rejected this contention. While again referring to both Article 40.3 and 43 the court did not discuss the relationship between them. It distinguished *Buckley's* case on two grounds:

(a) that the Act there took away from the plaintiffs the property in question and deprived them of all rights therein
(b) that in *Buckley's* case no question of a "conflict" arose.

The court went on to say (*per* O'Byrne J. at 153):

"(The appellant's argument) reduced to its logical conclusion, seems to involve the proposition that any limitation placed by the Oireachtas on private property, which may result in the loss of that property, by the owner, is repugnant to the Constitution and, accordingly, void. If this argument be sound, the Constitution has certainly placed serious fetters upon the Legislature in dealing with property rights and the Court is not prepared to accept such a far-reaching proposition."

The grounds on which *Buckley's* case was distinguished seem questionable. Ground (a) surely applied to section 2 of the Land Act 1946 as well. Despite the Supreme Court's implication that section 2 did not deprive Mr. Foley of his property and all rights therein, Dixon J. in the High Court had characterised it as working an expropriation without compensation (see [1952] I.R. 118 at 127). As to ground (b), the search for a conflict is misleading. Just as the Oireachtas thought the common good required section 2 of the Land Act 1946, so it obviously felt the Sinn Féin Funds Act 1947 a means to the same general end. That Act did not divert the trust money into the Central Fund; it established machinery designed to stop that money being frittered away in legal costs (as must have happened[4]) and to apply it instead for charitable purposes. The Act indeed may be regarded as building upon the judicially-created jurisdiction to apply charitable gifts *cy-près*—*i.e.* to an object as near as possible to that specified by the donor.[5]

Certain features of the Sinn Féin Funds Act 1947 made it vulnerable to challenge on separation of powers grounds, and the Supreme Court ruled to this effect also in *Buckley's* case (see Chap. 9 *supra*). If a similar measure which

---

[3] Perhaps the striking difference between the *Buckley* and *Foley* cases is due to a change in the composition of the court ($4\frac{1}{2}$ years separate the two judgments). The court in *Buckley* was Murnaghan, Geoghegan, O'Byrne, Black and Martin Maguire JJ.; that in *Foley* Maguire C.J., Murnaghan, O'Byrne, Lavery and Kingsmill Moore JJ. Thus only two members of the *Buckley* court sat in *Foley*.

[4] The ensuing case—*Buckley* v. *Att. Gen.* (*No. 2*) (1950) 84 I.L.T.R. 9—was at hearing in the High Court for 30 days. Nine counsel were involved.

[5] Modern Irish cases illustrative of this jurisdiction include *Governors of Erasmus Smith's Schools* v. *Att. Gen.* (1932) 66 I.L.T.R. 57: *Re Quinn* (1954) 88 I.L.T.R. 161: *Munster and Leinster Bank* v. *Att. Gen* (1957) 91 I.L.T.R. 34.

avoided those shoals were passed today it is not certain that it would be held to violate the Constitution's property guarantees.

The Supreme Court's next encounter with the property rights guarantees came in *Att. Gen.* v. *Southern Industrial Trust Ltd.* (1957) 94 I.L.T.R. 161. There a car owned by the defendant company and let on hire-purchase to one Simons was alleged to have been illegally exported from the jurisdiction by him without the defendants' knowledge. It was later seized by the Customs authorities and under the Customs (Temporary Provisions) Act 1945, s.5(1) the Attorney General asked that it be adjudged forfeit. The company argued that section 5(1) was unconstitutional insofar as it authorised the forfeiture of goods belonging to an innocent third party. In the High Court Davitt P. upheld the provision's validity. Obliged to follow *Buckley's* case,[6] he found a conflict between the defendant company's property rights and the common good, in that if a vehicle used for smuggling could not be forfeit because on H.P., such vehicles would be practically the only ones used. This would diminish the deterrent effect of forfeiture to the detriment of the common good. The 1945 Act was passed with a view to reconciling this conflict and, read in overall context, it struck a proper balance, for under other statutory provisions the Revenue Commissioners had power to deal with hardship cases.

On appeal the Supreme Court likewise upheld section 5(1), but in a judgment *per* Lavery J. which surely represents the court's least happy foray into the constitutional field.[7] While it did not (and could not) deny the jurisdiction of the courts to review the constitutionality of legislation infringing on property rights, the judgment conveyed the impression that claims were unlikely to succeed.[8] As to the *locus* of the guarantee, the court said that the property rights guaranteed were to be found in Article 43 and not elsewhere, and the rights guaranteed by Article 40 were those guaranteed by Article 43.[9] The judgment went on to refer to the many statutes providing for the forfeiture or seizure of goods (at 177). These showed that the State claimed the right to divest individuals of ownership of particular chattels. Legislation having this effect amounted to a "delimitation" under Article 43.2.2° and it was valid if in accordance with the common good and principles of social justice. These conditions were satisfied here.

---

[6] Had he not been constrained by authority Davitt P. would have construed Arts. 40.3 and 43 as follows: (a) Art. 40.3 protected an individual's right to the property he owned, but it was a qualified guarantee and the justice of the interference with the right had to be considered with reference to the common good; (b) Art. 43 guaranteed *the institution* of private property; (c) Art. 43.2 authorised legislation confining the limits of the *exercise* of property rights (*e.g.* restricting freedom of testation)—but it did not cover *deprivation* of an individual of his property; the power to do this was implicit, though conditioned by Art 40.3. As will appear subsequently this approach foreshadows that adopted by the Supreme Court in the *Blake* case; but it does not appear quite to represent the current position.

[7] In *Comparative Constitutional Law: Cases and Commentaries* (New York 1977) Professors Murphy and Tanenhaus state (at p. 306) that Lavery J. " . . . came to believe that the two sides, in their desire for a test case, had falsely stated the facts and refused to allow barristers to cite the case " This may be an additional reason for burying the judgment but it is not the only one.

[8] In an unfortunate passage (at 176) Lavery J. said that the Oireachtas had the function of legislating and determining social and economic policy. It was not the courts' function to determine such matters "or to criticise *or invalidate* the decisions of the Oireachtas" (emphasis supplied).

[9] This statement was explicitly disavowed by the Supreme Court in *Blake* v. *Att. Gen.* [1982] I.R. 117, 135.

In *Central Dublin Development Association* v. *Att. Gen.* (1975) 109 I.L.T.R. 69 Kenny J. discerned a conflict between the *Buckley* and *Southern Industrial Trust* cases and declined to follow the latter. The interpretation of the Constitution in that case would mean that the Oireachtas could, on a claim of promoting the common good, pass any legislation in relation to property and the courts would be powerless, even if they concluded that the Act was an unjust attack on property rights. Kenny J. expressed his agreement with Davitt P.'s approach to Articles 40.3 and 43 and gave his conclusions as set out earlier.

The measure questioned in the *Central Dublin Development Association* case was the 1963 Planning Act.[10] The grounds of challenge were many and various. It was argued that giving the planning authority power to acquire lands in an "obsolete area" (as defined in the Act) so that it could secure their development by making arrangements with a commercial corporation was an unjust attack on the property rights of those in the area. But Kenny J. observed that this might be the most efficient and economic way of developing such an area, and he did not see anything unjust in a planning authority taking advantage of a development company's skill in such work. It was then contended that prosperous businesses might be situated in an obsolete area; yet following compulsory acquisition the owners had no right to reinstatement. Kenny J. concluded that there was no unjust attack here. Stressing the problems a right of reinstatement might involve, he pointed out that an owner was entitled to compensation, not only for the value of the property, but for disturbance.[11] Next it was argued that when a planning authority fulfilled its obligation to make a development plan a necessary consequence would be a substantial reduction in the value of some private property in the affected area. Kenny J. rejected this argument, saying (at 90):

> "The making of a plan will necessarily decrease the value of some property but I do not think that the Constitution requires that compensation should be paid for this as it is not an unjust attack on property rights. If this argument were correct, many owners of houses would have been entitled to be paid compensation when the Rent Restriction Act, 1946, was passed."[12]

Finally the plaintiffs assailed the Act's compensation provisions.[13] Having

---

[10] Formally entitled the Local Government (Planning and Development) Act 1963.

[11] In *Berman* v. *Parker* (1954) 348 U.S. 26 the Supreme Court upheld broadly similar legislation, challenged on the above two grounds as violating the 5th Amendment ban on taking "private property . . . for public use, without just compensation."

[12] As *Blake's* case (*infra*) was later to show, Kenny J.'s assumption about the validity of the Rent Restrictions Acts was erroneous. But this does not necessarily affect the conclusion above.

[13] It is relevant to note that the Oireachtas Joint Committee on Building Land, which reported in June 1985, found that claims for compensation were threatening the achievement of zoning objectives in development plans. The size of some such claims had coerced local authorities into granting planning permission against their better judgment, or into compromise arrangements with developers. Thus up to March 1981, Dublin Corporation had paid only £135,000 in compensation to landowners since the coming into effect of the 1963 Act: *Report* (Pl. 3232), pp.77-77).

In *XJS Investments Ltd* v. *Dun Laoghaire Corpn.* [1987] I.L.R.M. 659 the claimants, who in 1981 had purchased 24.4 acres of land in Killiney, Co. Dublin for £40,000, applied for planning permission to construct houses. This was refused by the respondents, a refusal upheld on appeal by An Bord Pleanála. The claimants then invoked s.55 of the 1963 Act and sought compensation from the respondents in the sum of £2,375,000. When a special case stated by the property arbitrator on certain points of law came, on appeal, before the Supreme Court, McCarthy J., giving the judgment of the court, said (at 660-61):

laid down the general principle that compensation was payable when a decision refusing planning permission reduced the value of an interest in land, the Act developed a series of exceptions thereto. Thus section 56(1)(*a*) provided that compensation was not payable if permission to make a material change in the use of land or buildings (other than building on them) was refused. Kenny J. declined to see this as an acquisition of property without compensation. It was a provision that an interference with one of the rights that made up ownership was not to be the subject-matter of compensation. This was not a breach of Article 43 nor a failure to defend and vindicate the personal rights of property. The same applied to the provision that no compensation was payable when permission was refused because it was necessary to preserve any view or prospect,[14] or because the proposed development would endanger public safety by creating a traffic hazard.

Rents, rates and residence taxes

In the period 1981–1985 the courts decided eight cases on the property rights guarantees. Though the course charted was sometimes uncertain, these decisions clarified matters to a considerable extent. The key question appears to be—is the challenged provision an unjust attack on property rights? The answer to this question in any given situation will be difficult to predict. Important—though not necessarily decisive—factors will be the nature of the interference, and the presence or absence of compensation. A *physical* intrusion on property rights will be viewed less indulgently than a restraint upon user, and unless compensated for is likely to be ruled unconstitutional.[15] But compensation is not always required.

Blake v. *Att. Gen.* [1982] I.R. 117 was a challenge to the validity of the Rent Restrictions Acts 1960 and 1967. These measures—which were permanent in character—restricted the rents, and recovery of possession, of the "controlled premises" to which they applied—dwellings erected before May 7, 1941 and below a certain rateable valuation. (Between 45,000 and 50,000 dwellings were said to be covered.) Their effect was that the rents of controlled dwellings were essentially restricted by reference to the rents applicable on June 8, 1966; and the evidence showed a huge disproportion between the rents as thus restricted and the "market rent." The landlord was basically responsible for all repairs; he/she could recover possession only in special circumstances and that possession—with all associated statutory protection—could pass to different generations of the tenant's family or that of the tenant's

"Assuming that the amount of the claim . . . bears a real relationship to the award that may be made by the arbitrator, it will be seen that X.J.S. may anticipate a profit of over £2,000,000 on an investment of £40,000 in a period of 5 years. Such a profit will be at the expense of the ratepayers of Dun Laoghaire. I allude to this alarming circumstance, not because of any argument based thereon, but so as to direct attention to the question as to whether or not legislation which appears to authorise such a use of public funds is constitutionally proper. On that question, I express no view." The Local Government (Planning and Development) Act 1990 has now considerably restricted the right to claim compensation in respect of planning decisions.

[14] Legislation to the same effect was held by the U.S. Supreme Court not to constitute a "taking,"so as to require compensation, in *Penn Central Transportation Co.* v. *New York City* (1978) 438 U.S. 104.

[15] See *E.S.B.* v. *Gormley, infra.*

assignee. The Supreme Court held that Parts II and IV of the 1960 Act (these were the core of the legislation, dealing respectively with rent control and restriction on recovering possession) were invalid as an unjust attack on property rights, contrary to Article 40.3.2°. The court noted the Act's restricted coverage, observing that it did not apply to post-1941 dwellings or to local authority lettings. Part II, it was pointed out, took no account of tenants' needs or the financial resources of the landlord. Further, this legislation was not limited in duration nor associated with any emergency. The judgment, *per* O'Higgins C.J., continues (at 139–140):

> " . . . all owners whose rents are controlled are restricted in their income to the amount of the basic rent and to such lawful additions as may be related to increases in rates and to a percentage of actual expenditure on maintenance, repair or improvement. This absence of any power to review such rents, irrespective of changes in conditions, is in itself a circumstance of inherent injustice and cannot be ignored. When this is coupled with the absence of any provision for compensating the owners whose rental incomes are thus permanently frozen, regardless of the significant diminution in the value of money, the conclusion that injustice has been done is inevitable . . . the provisions of Part II . . . restrict the property rights of one group of citizens for the benefit of another group. This is done without compensation and without regard to the financial capacity or the financial needs of either group, in legislation which provides no limitation on the period of restriction, gives no opportunity for review and allows no modification of the operation of the restriction. It is, therefore, both unfair and arbitrary."

As regards Part IV the court held that such restrictions on recovery of possession were not necessarily invalid.[16] But Part IV was an integral part of an arbitrary and unfair scheme and it must also fall.

As a consequence of the *Blake* decision the Oireachtas passed temporary legislation[17] and then the Housing (Private Rented Dwellings) Bill 1981. This the President referred to the Supreme Court under Article 26: see [1983] I.R. 181. The Bill had the same coverage as the Rent Restrictions Act 1960, but the Supreme Court accepted the Attorney General's submission that the need for rectifying legislation following *Blake's* case supplied a valid reason for its limited scope. As regards recovery of possession the Bill's provisions were broadly similar to those of Part IV of the 1960 Act, but there was one major change. If the landlord recovered possession for occupation as a residence for himself or herself, or for a person in his or her whole-time employment, or in the interests of good estate management, he or she had to pay such sum as the District Court might determine in respect of the tenant's expenses in quitting the dwelling, together with up to two years rent of alternative accommodation. The court expressed no view on whether this

---

[16] Provided that the restriction was made on a basis that was not unconstitutionally unfair or oppressive, and had due regard both to the property rights of the landlord and the rights that should be accorded to tenants having regard to the common good. See [1982] I.R. 117 at 141.

[17] See the Rent Restrictions (Temporary Provisions) Act 1981—the long title of which is very interesting. This was expressed to last for six months from July 25, 1981 (less than a month after the *Blake* decision) but its duration was subsequently prolonged by the Rent Restrictions (Temporary Provisions) (Continuance) Acts 1981 and 1982, as a result of the decision in the *Housing Bill* case.

was valid, since the main criticism of the Bill related to the rent-fixing provisions and these were held unconstitutional. The Bill referred to the "gross rent," which was basically the market value; but the rent fixed by the District Court was to be the gross rent minus rebates on a five year sliding scale fixed by section 9. This, the court held, was an unjust attack on landlords' property rights. The gross rent must be regarded as the just and proper rent but under section 9 landlords were to receive less than this. The judgment, *per* O'Higgins C.J., continues (at 191):

> "In the absence of any constitutionally permitted justification, this clearly constitutes an unjust attack upon their property rights. The Bill offers no such justification for depriving the landlord of part of his or her just rent for the period specified in the Bill. This Court has already held that the pre-existing rent control constituted an unjust attack upon property rights. In such circumstances, to impose different but no less unjust deprivations upon landlords cannot but be unjust having regard to the provisions of the Constitution."

It is plain that what the Oireachtas did under the Rent Restrictions Act 1960 and the Housing Bill was virtually to conscript landlords of controlled premises into the social welfare system. That is, having determined as a matter of social policy that tenants of such premises should not be asked to pay the market rent, the Oireachtas implemented this by artifically and arbitrarily depressing the rents receivable by landlords. This was obviously easier on the exchequer but hardly fair to landlords—for some of whom, at least, the premises represented a source of outgoings rather than of income. In the *Housing Bill* case, however, the Supreme Court indicated that the tenants also had constitutional rights and that undue hardship to them might raise constitutional difficulties. Thus the Oireachtas was obliged to afford tenants *some* protection—yet this could not take the form of the 1960 Act or the 1981 Bill. Rarely has the legislature's range of policy options been so narrowed by judicial decisions. The (logical) solution eventually found was in the direction implicitly indicated by the judges—subsidising the tenant via the social welfare scheme.[18]

It should be noted that in the *Blake* and *Housing Bill* cases the Supreme Court was far from suggesting that rent control was *per se* invalid. The true position appears to be that controls (whether over rents, prices, mortgages, etc.) are valid provided that a reasonable balance between affected interests has been struck. And given that the relevant legislation will enjoy the presumption of constitutionality, it may be anticipated that a *perfect* balance is not required. But the decisions mentioned would seem fatal to the recommendations (dated March 1973) in the majority report of a committee chaired by Kenny J.[19] This body was established to make recommendations for controlling the price of building land and ensuring that the community reaped some profit from the increase in such prices. The difference between the price of agricultural land and building land was due to the provision of services (water, sewerage and drainage) by the local authority; hence the view that the community should share in the increased value. The committee canvassed a range of possible measures, the majority finally favouring a

---

[18] See the Housing (Private Rented Dwellings) Act 1982, particularly s.23.
[19] Committee on the Price of Building Land: *Report* (Prl. 3632).

scheme under which the High Court would be empowered to designate areas where lands were likely to be used for building houses or factories during the next ten years. Lands within any designated area could then be acquired by the local authority at existing use value plus 25 per cent. The majority (which included Kenny J.) thought that this would be compatible with the Constitution which, in their opinion, did not give each citizen the right to receive full market price for any property he decided to sell. If it were otherwise a landlord would have the right to the full market rent for his property so that the Rent Restrictions Acts would be repugnant to the Constitution. The minority disagreed with this view and also pointed out that a dual price system would probably result—one price for building land compulsorily acquired and another, higher price for building land sold in the open market. This discriminatory effect, they concluded, would raise grave constitutional difficulties. The subsequent decisions in the *Blake* and *Housing Bill* cases plainly provide strong support for that minority view. And though it is true that in *Dreher* v. *Irish Land Commission* (*infra*) the Supreme Court indicated that just compensation was not always equivalent to market value, the compulsory acquisition provisions upheld in that case did not involve a 75 per cent. gap between purchase price and market value.[20]

In *Brennan* v. *Att. Gen.* [1984] I.L.R.M. 355 the plaintiffs, a group of Wexford farmers, challenged the basis of the rating system on agricultural land. The rates payable depended on the value of the land but the valuations were wildly out of date. The evidence laid before Barrington J. in the High Court led him to the conclusion that the valuation system had failed to reflect changing patterns of agriculture, with the consequence that land which modern agriculturalists would regard as good often carried a low valuation while land which they would regard as inferior often carried a higher valuation. Barrington J. also found that the system did not produce uniformity throughout the State; indeed there was no consistency between county and county or within individual counties. And the whole system was "shot through with unnecessary anomalies and inconsistencies." The Supreme Court noted that the use of this valuation system for levying rates was required by section 11 of the Local Government Act 1946. Its consequence was that an unfair burden fell on the occupiers of poorer land. The continued use of such an outdated valuation system was an unjust attack on the property rights of persons like the plaintiffs. When this injustice became obvious the State had a duty to take action to protect those rights, but this it had failed to do. The judgment, *per* O'Higgins C.J., continues (at 365):

> "In continuing by means of s.11 of the Local Government Act 1946 the same system without revision or review the State again . . . failed to protect the property rights of those adversely affected by the system from further unjust attack. In the assessment of a tax such as a county rate reasonable uniformity of valuation appears essential to justice. If such reasonable uniformity is lacking the inevitable result will be that some ratepayer is required to pay more than his fair share ought to be. This necessarily involves an attack upon his property rights which by definition becomes unjust. The plaintiffs have established such injustice in this particular case."

[20] For a valuable discussion of this matter see Keane J.'s article "Land Use, Compensation and the Community" (1983) XVIII *Irish Jurist* (N.S.) 23.

The basic concern in *Brennan's* case—as in *Blake* v. *Att. Gen.*—is with reasonable fairness in the distribution of burdens. Thus a system of raising revenue which operates in an arbitrary way will be condemned. But a progressive taxation system is not *per se* arbitrary, nor is one which taxes certain items of property but not others. So much is clear from *Madigan* v. *Att. Gen.* [1986] I.L.R.M. 136. The plaintiffs here challenged the new residential property tax imposed by Part VI of the Finance Act 1983. This tax applied to houses with a market value over £65,000, provided that the family income was over £20,000. The principal arguments against Part VI were that the concept of market value therein was wholly artificial and an unjust attack on property rights because it assumed an unencumbered fee simple and made no allowance for mortgages, etc. Furthermore the aggregation of incomes provided for meant that the tax was imposed, not on the income of the person made liable, but on those of persons over whom he had no rights or control. This, too, constituted an unjust attack on property rights. The Supreme Court dismissed both contentions, laying heavy emphasis on the constitutionally assigned roles of the Government and Oireachtas in determining taxation policy. A tax measure necessarily interfered with the property rights of affected citizens but it was not an unjust attack if it was in accordance with social justice and inspired by the exigencies of the common good. As to the aggregation of incomes, this reflected social reality. There might be situations where the assessable person got no contribution from others who shared in the enjoyment of the residence, but these must be rare "and must depend for their continuance on a degree of tolerance by the assessable person which borders on foolishness" (at 163).

The combined effect of the *Brennan* and *Madigan* cases would appear to be that revenue-raising measures can be successfully challenged only where they are indisputably capricious in operation, having no relation to a person's ability to pay the levy imposed. While the burden of proof on a plaintiff asserting the invalidity of any such measure would plainly be very heavy, this is not to say that no such challenge could succeed.[21]

From Dreher to Gormley

Dreher v. *Irish Land Commission and Att. Gen.* [1984] I.L.R.M. 94 is significant for its statement of the link between Articles 40.3 and 43—a matter considered below. The case concerned a compulsory acquisition of the plaintiff's lands by the Commission, the purchase price being fixed at £30,000. The Lands Bonds Act 1934 required payment to be in Land Bonds equivalent in nominal value to the purchase price; so on the operative date in 1971 the plaintiff received £30,000 worth of $9\frac{3}{4}$ per cent. bonds. But on that date their sale value was £29,400. The plaintiff argued that he was entitled to just com-

---

[21] It is noticeable that the final paragraph of the *Madigan* judgment specifically states that the rejection of the plaintiffs' challenge there did not mean that another plaintiff might not successfully impeach Part VI.

In *Browne* v. *Att. Gen.* [1991] 2 I.R. 58 it was contended that s.4 of the Finance Act 1982—designed to tax as a benefit in kind a car provided by an employer—was unconstitutional as an unjust attack on property rights, by virtue of being ill-targeted, discriminatory and arbitrary. But Murphy J. held that s.4 was not, as alleged, full of inconsistencies and anomalies. Such anomalies as appeared to exist sprang from the special circumstances of the individual plaintiffs, or from the arrangements to which they and their employers were parties. The legislation could not be condemned as unconstitutional on this basis.

pensation for the acquisition; that the statutory provisions in question did not provide for this; and that they were therefore an unjust attack on his property rights. The Supreme Court rejected these contentions. Having analysed the relevant legislative provisions the court found that they required that the bonds be issued at a rate which kept them as near as could be to par value. When observed and carried out (as the court found they had been) those provisions went as far as reasonably possible to take into account the results of inflation and fluctuating interest rates so far as these were reasonably foreseeable. If beyond that there were inflationary trends or fluctuations in the rates of interest beyond the State's control, it could not be said that in failing to take account of these the statute was invalid. (The court noted that the rate of interest on Mr. Dreher's bonds in 1971 was "considerably better than that obtainable on bank deposits"—$9\frac{3}{4}$ per cent. as against five per cent. (later four per cent.))

P.M.P.S. Ltd. and Moore v. *Att. Gen.* [1983] I.R. 339 was an attack on the Industrial and Provident Societies (Amendment) Act 1978. The first plaintiff was a registered provident society in which the second plaintiff was a shareholder. The society lawfully conducted a banking business, but the 1978 Act stipulated that no such body should accept or hold deposits after November 15, 1983. This, it was argued, would make it impossible for the plaintiff society to carry on with its banking business. Legislation eliminating a branch of business without compensation was an unjust attack on property rights. The Supreme Court denied that the 1978 Act's prohibition was an expropriation of the society's business and thus of its shareholders' property rights. It was a regulation and control of the range of business the society could lawfully transact. In the High Court Carroll J. had concluded on the evidence that such regulation and control was reasonable, and was in accordance with the public interest and the requirements of the common good.[22] Thus it could not be regarded as an unjust attack on property rights.

In *O'Callaghan* v. *Commissioners of Public Works* [1985] I.L.R.M. 364 the plaintiff had in 1977 purchased lands in Co. Dublin on which was situated a promontory fort.[23] This, as the plaintiff must have known, was listed as a national monument under the National Monuments Acts 1930 and 1954; thus he was prohibited from interfering with it without due notice to, and the consent of, the defendant Commissioners. Nonetheless he embarked upon deep ploughing of the land, which was found on inspection to have caused damage to the archaeological potential of the fort. The defendant Commissioners consequently made a preservation order, under sections 8 and 14 of the 1930 Act, forbidding any further such activity. The plaintiff challenged these provisions as an unjust attack on his property rights, characterising this as an expropriation without compensation. The Supreme Court, however, found no constitutional flaw in them. The preservation order did not deprive

---

[22] Carroll J. found that when provident societies were exempted from supervision under the Central Bank Act 1971 this was because there were only two societies involved, in a small way, in banking business and there was no appreciable risk to the public at large. But the amount of business grew, as did the risk to the general public, for the societies did not observe the principles of sound banking practice insisted upon by the Central Bank. Hence the 1978 act.

[23] A promontory fort is a large defensive encampment, dating from 200 B.C.—100 A.D., situated on a headland where the neck of the promontory has been defended by the construction of banks and a ditch.

him of ownership or of his right to use the land in any way consistent with the monument's preservation. It *did* prohibit him from destroying the monument and to that extent might be said to constitute an attack on his property rights. But this was not an *unjust* attack. The common good required that national monuments be preserved and this legislation, directed to that end, was neither arbitrary nor selective; it applied to all monuments no matter who owned them. Nor was the absence of compensation unjust; it should be regarded as the common duty of all citizens to preserve such monuments.

The most recent property rights case to reach the Supreme Court is *E.S.B.* v. *Gormley* [1985] I.R. 129, which concerned the statutory powers of the plaintiff board to place electricity lines across land. The board was empowered to do this without the owner's consent under section 53 of the Electricity Supply Act 1927 (as amended in 1945); and it was also empowered to lop trees, shrubs or hedges which interfered with or obstructed the erection of lines—section 98 of the 1927 Act as amended in 1941.[24] The works intended to be placed on the defendant's lands were three masts, respectively 120, 85 and 80 feet high. Each would stand on four legs, making a rectangle the side of which was six and a half to nine metres long. Each leg would be set in a hole one metre square, filled with concrete rising to six inches above the ground. The defendant claimed that the relevant statutory provisions were invalid since they provided no right to compensation for the damage necessarily caused. Nor was this defect cured by the Board's practice of paying *ex gratia* compensation, since this did not involve assessment by an independent tribunal. The Supreme Court observed that section 53 (as amended) permitted permanent interference with the use of land affected and permanent damage to amenity. While the evidence established that the power to lay transmission lines compulsorily was a requirement of the common good, the absence of provision for compensation assessable by an independent person or body made this an unjust attack on property rights. And the existence of a scheme for *ex gratia* compensation showed that compensation was practicable.[25] With regard to section 98 (as amended) different considerations applied. The burden imposed was minor; the board was given no right to remove the lopped timber; and the landowner was entitled to carry out the lopping himself and to be indemnified by the board against the expense of so doing. The defendant had not succeeded in showing that this was invalid.

Doctrinal development

In *Blake* v. *Att. Gen.* the Supreme Court disavowed dicta in the *Southern Industrial Trust* case and, *per* O'Higgins C.J., stated the relationship between Articles 40.3 and 43 as follows ([1982] I.R. 117 at 135):

"(Article 43) prohibits the abolition of private property as an institution, but at the same time permits, in particular circumstances, the regulation of the exercise of that right and of the general right to

---

[24] s.53 was amended by s.46 of the Electricity (Supply) (Amendment) Act 1945; and s.98 by s.5 of the Electricity (Supply) (Amendment) Act 1941. The Supreme Court held that the nature of the amendments was such that the pre-Constitution Acts must be taken as having been effectively re-enacted. Thus the presumption of constitutionality—and the "one-opinion rule"—applied in this case.

[25] The Electricity (Supply) (Amendment) Act 1985 now provides for a *right* to compensation, assessable by an independent person, in such circumstances.

transfer, bequeath and inherit property. In short, it is an Article
directed to the State and to its attitude to those rights, which are
declared to be antecedent to positive law. It does not deal with a citizen's right to a particular item of property, such as controlled premises.
Such rights are dealt with in Article 40 under the heading 'personal
rights' and are specifically designated among the personal rights of citizens . . .

There exists, therefore, a double protection for the property rights of a
citizen. As far as he is concerned, the State cannot abolish or attempt to
abolish the right of private ownership as an institution or the general
right to transfer, bequeath or inherit property. In addition, he has the
further protection under Article 40 as to the exercise by him of his own
property rights in particular items of property."

But subsequent cases showed that Article 43 did more than institutionalise
private property. In *Dreher's* case [1984] I.L.R.M. 94 the Article moved back
to centre stage, for Walsh J., with whose judgment all agreed, said (at 96):

"The State in exercising its powers under Article 43 must act in accordance with the requirements of social justice but clearly what is social justice must depend on the circumstances of the case. In Article 40.3.2°
"the State undertakes by its laws to protect as best it may from unjust
attack, and in the case of injustice done, vindicate . . . (the) property
rights of every citizen.' I think it is clear that any State action that is
authorised by Article 43 of the Constitution and conforms to that Article
cannot by definition be unjust for the purpose of Article 40.3.2°. It may
well be that in some particular cases social justice may not require the
payment of any compensation upon a compulsory acquisition that can
be justified by the State as being required by the exigencies of the common good."

This passage was quoted in *O'Callaghan's* case [1985] I.L.R.M. 364 at 368,
where it was stated that in considering the question of unjust attack, Articles
40.3 and 43 must be read together to give effect, so far as possible, to both
provisions. And the National Monuments Acts there in issue were held to
have been enacted by the State in the discharge of its duty under Article 43.2.
In *P.M.P.S. Ltd. and Moore* v. *Att. Gen.* [1983] I.R. 339 also, the Supreme
Court implicitly reads Article 43 into Article 40.3.2°.

The position would therefore appear to be that legislation will not constitute an unjust attack on property rights if passed to reconcile the exercise
of those rights with the requirements of the common good, and if consonant with principles of social justice. It will rarely be difficult to establish
the "common good" basis of the impugned Act; the presumption of constitutionality obviously helps here. Consonance with principles of social justice may pose a greater problem. Prima facie those principles will require
compensation for the interference[26]—especially in the case of a physical
intrusion on land or a building equivalent to a permanent physical occupa-

[26] The principal statutory basis for compensation for compulsory acquisition of land is in the
Acquisition of Land (Assessment of Compensation) Act 1919, Rule 2 of which establishes the
principle of market value. The Joint Committee on Building Land (*Report* of June 5, 1985: Pl.
3232) sought counsel's opinion on whether it would be constitutionally possible to modify
this. Counsel (Mr. Peter Kelly, S.C.) answered that it would (see his opinion in Appendix 9 of
the *Report*).

tion: *E.S.B.* v. *Gormely* [1985] I.R. 129.[27] But compensation is not always required; the nature of the interference, as *O'Callaghan's* case shows, may be the decisive factor here. In the case of non-physical interferences—such as revenue-raising or price-controlling measures—the vital question seems to be whether they are fair in their coverage and may be regarded as striking a reasonable balance between the interests involved.

It will be clear that, because of the range of factors that may be involved, predicting the outcome of a constitutional challenge is far from easy. The same is true under the United States Constitution. In the *Penn Central* case (1978) 438 U.S. 104 Brennan J., speaking for the Supreme Court, said that what constituted a "taking" for 5th Amendment purposes had proved to be a problem of considerable difficulty. The court, he continued, had recognised that the 5th Amendment's guarantee was designed to prevent some people from being forced to bear alone public burdens which, in all fairness and justice, should be borne by the public as a whole. But the court had not been able to develop any set formula for determining when justice and fairness required that economic injuries caused by public action should be compensated by the government, rather than being disproportionately concentrated on a few persons. The court's decisions had identified several factors that had particular significance, but much depended on the particular circumstances of each case—indeed Brennan J. spoke of "these essentially ad hoc, factual enquiries . . . " These comments seem to apply equally to the position under Bunreacht na hÉireann, and the United States authorities surveyed in the *Penn Central* case may assist the Irish courts. It is not clear, however, that some of the United States cases would have been decided the same way in Ireland—*e.g. Miller* v. *Schoene* (1928) 276 U.S. 272, where legislation permitting the uncompensated destruction of ornamental cedar trees to prevent cedar rust from killing nearby apple orchards (the foundation of a significant industry) was upheld.

Though the Irish Supreme Court has recognised that compensation need not always follow a compulsory acquisition,[28] it has not indicated the cases in which this will hold true. But it seems likely that provisions for the confiscation of smuggled goods, animals, vehicles, etc. are beyond challenge—and that the same would hold in respect of the proceeds of crime, *e.g.* the seizure under judicial decree of money proved to have been earned by dealing in drugs.[29] Likewise, the freezing by court order of assets pending trial on relevant criminal charges would arguably be valid: the Judicial Committee repelled a challenge to such legislation in *Att. Gen. of the Gambia* v. *Jobe* [1984] 1 A.C. 689.[30] Indeed in *Clancy* v. *Ireland* [1988] I.R. 326 Barrington J. upheld the validity of the broadly analogous provisions of the Offences against the State (Amendment) Act 1985. Under this, the Minister for Justice could require a bank to pay into the High Court moneys held in an account, and

---

[27] In the U.S. physical intrusion equivalent to a permanent physical occupation constitutes a "taking" requiring compensation: *Loretto* v. *Teleprompter Manhatten C.A.T.V. Corporation* (1982) 458 U.S. 419.

[28] The *dictum* to this effect in *Dreher* has been subsequently approved in the *O'Callaghan* and *Gormley* cases.

[29] See the Law Reform Commission's report on *The Confiscation of the Proceeds of Crime* (LRC 35–1991).

[30] The Board noted (at 700) that "Freezing orders in the forms of what has now become known in England as a *Mareva* injunction, or in civil law countries as saisie conservatoire, are common practice in civil litigation . . . "

believed to be forfeit as the property of an unlawful organisation.[31] The bank
was also required to notify the persons in whose names the moneys were held
of the payment into the High Court. The Act made provision for the subsequent disposition of the moneys, but it also established a procedure under
which the High Court could decide any claim of ownership. If that court concluded that the plaintiff was the true owner of the moneys, it could direct
their payment to him/her, together with appropriate interest and compensation for any loss sustained. In the instant proceedings the plaintiffs claimed
to be the owners of moneys—amounting to over £1.75 million—in a Navan
bank account, which had been paid into the High Court under the Act's procedures. They sought the return of those moneys, but also claimed that they
had wrongly and unconstitutionally been deprived of their ownership of, and
disposing power over, these moneys, as a result of which they had suffered
loss and damage.

Barrington J. noted that the 1985 Act provided for the freezing of a bank
account and the payment of the funds therein into the High Court without
notice to the account-holder. But it did not confiscate the account-holder's
property or deprive him/her of a fair hearing. In the event of a mistake having been made, there was provision for the payment of compensation.
Barrington J. concluded that in all the circumstances the impugned Act
amounted to a permissible delimitation of property rights in the interests of
the common good.[32]

Property rights and family responsibilities

In *L.* v. *L.* [1992] I.L.R.M. 115 the Supreme Court, reversing a decision of
Barr J., declined to hold that Article 41 furnished a basis on which a separated wife and mother could be awarded a share in the matrimonial home
owned by her husband. Such an award could be made only where the relevant spouse had contributed directly or indirectly towards the acquisition of
the family home or the repayment of a mortgage upon it.[33]

The proceedings in *L.* v. *L.* were instituted before the coming into operation of the Judicial Separation and Family Law Reform Act 1989, which
consequently had no bearing upon them. But this Act confers very wide
powers on the courts to make property adjustment orders on granting a
decree of judicial separation (or thereafter). In particular, section 15(1)(*a*)
authorises the making of a property transfer order, by virtue of which one
spouse must transfer to the other any property to which the first spouse is
entitled either in possession or in reversion. Thus the court could order the
transfer of the title in the matrimonial home to the wife, even if the husband
was the legal owner and the wife had made no direct or indirect contribution
to its acquisition.[34]

---

[31] Under s.22 of the Offences against the State Act 1939 all property of an unlawful organisation
becomes forfeited to and vested in the Minister for Justice.

[32] Barrington J. referred to, and quoted from, the U.S. Supreme Court's decision in *Calero-Toledo*
v. *Pearson Yacht Leasing Co.* (1974) 416 U.S. 663. There a statute authorising the seizure of
property used for criminal purposes—without prior notice to, or provision for a hearing for,
the innocent owner—was upheld.

[33] See the Supreme Court's decisions in *McC.* v. *McC.* [1986] I.L.R.M. 1 and *N.* v. *N.* [1992]
127; also Paul O'Connor, *Key Issues in Irish Family Law* (Dublin 1988), p. 177 ff.

[34] See further William Duncan and Paula Scully, *Marriage Breakdown in Ireland: Law and Practice*
(Dublin 1990), Chap. 13.

These far-reaching provisions might appear vulnerable to constitutional challenge as authorising an expropriation of property without compensation. But the Oireachtas, in enacting them, was presumably motivated by those considerations of social justice and the common good to which Article 43 refers. And those concepts must surely be informed by the pro-family philosophy of Article 41. It seems likely, therefore, that the courts will reject any constitutional complaint against the 1989 Act, holding that it does not constitute an "unjust attack" on property rights. The Supreme Court's decision in *L.* v. *L.* [1992] I.L.R.M. 115 lends some support to this view, for despite their final conclusion the judges were sympathetic to the result achieved by the High Court. Thus Finlay C.J. (Hederman J. concurring) said in the penultimate paragraph of his judgment (at 122):

> "It is, of course, clear that if the legislature decides, as in fact it has done, by virtue of the provisions of the Judicial Separation and Family Law Reform Act 1989, to give to the court powers to declare a right in a spouse to a beneficial interest in the family home as part of the general jurisdiction of the court upon the granting of a separation, to make monetary provisions arising from it, the court may exercise that expressed statutory power in obedience to and furtherance of the provisions of this sub-article of the Constitution [Article 41.2.2°]."

Following *L.* v. *L.* there were calls for legislation to introduce the principle of joint ownership of the matrimonial home—an idea mooted, but not implemented, by Dr. FitzGerald's 1982–87 coalition Government. The Government responded sympathetically, and it seems likely that legislation to this effect *will* be introduced. Any fears that may have existed about possible constitutional difficulties seem to have been set at rest by the Supreme Court's attitude in *L.* v. *L.* [1982] I.L.R.M. 115, where Finlay C.J. (Hederman J. concurring) said (at 120):

> "I would have little difficulty in appreciating the very significant social and other values which are attached to what experience would indicate is a very common modern habit, whereby the parties to a marriage and the parents of a family, by agreement between them, become joint owners of the family home. It is difficult to deny the fact that anything that would help to encourage that basis of full sharing in property values as well as in every other way between the partners of a marriage, must directly contribute to the stability of the marriage, the institution of the family and the common good."

Reach of the property guarantees

The Irish courts have not attempted to list exhaustively what is embraced by "property" in the Constitution. But the cases show how wide is its scope. Land—and rights arising from ownership thereof—is covered[35]; but so, plainly, is movable property such as a vehicle. Intangible rights, such as

---

[35] It appears that a statutory right to a renewal of a tenancy may qualify as a constitutionally protected property right: see *Shanley* v. *Commissisoners of Public Works* (High Court, Carroll J., October 31, 1991).

Property Rights

those arising under a contract,[36] are also included, and this is likewise true of those arising under a franchise, such as a right to hold a market.[37]

The most difficult question has proved to be whether a common law right of action is a property right. The Oireachtas seems to take the view that it is; so when a cause of action is abolished it is usual to provide that this does not affect any action commenced before the passing of the Act. This is true of the Family Law Act 1981, ss.1 and 2, which abolish actions for *inter alia* criminal conversation and breach of promise.[38] But the position of the courts is unclear. In *O'Brien* v. *Keogh* [1972] I.R. 144 and *O'Brien* v. *Manufacturing Engineering Co. Ltd.* [1973] I.R. 334 the Supreme Court held that a right to litigate a particular claim *was* a property right, protected by Article 40.3.2° from unjust attack. But in *Moynihan* v. *Greensmyth* [1977] I.R. 55 this proposition was doubted, and it was noted that in neither *O'Brien* case had attention been directed to *Foley* v. *Irish Land Commission* [1952] I.R. 118 and *Att. Gen* v. *Southern Industrial Trust Ltd.* (1957) 94 I.L.T.R. 161. The judgment in *Moynihan's* case, *per* O'Higgins C.J., continues (at 70–71):

> "In these cases it was held in effect that the property rights guaranteed by Article 40, s.3, subs. 2, of the Constitution are not rights over particular items of property but are the property rights guaranteed by Article 43, namely, *the natural right to the private ownership of external goods and the general right to transfer, bequeath and inherit property*. To divest a citizen of the ownership of a particular item of property in certain circumstances was held to be permissible under Article 43, s.2 of the Constitution. If this opinion were to be adhered to, the reasoning underlying the decisions in the two *O'Brien* cases would seem to be incompatible with the Court's ruling in *Foley* v. *Irish Land Commission* and *Att. Gen.* v. *Southern Industrial Trust Ltd.* Accordingly, in order to give a comprehensive answer to the question posed by the present case, it would be necessary for the Court to give a considered ruling as to whether the right claimed by the plaintiff is a property right and, if so, whether it is one of the property rights guaranteed by Article 40, s.3, subs. 2, of the Constitution. For that purpose it would be necessary to review the Court's decisions in *O'Brien* v. *Keogh*; *O'Brien* v. *Manufacturing Engineering Co. Ltd.*; *Att. Gen.* v. *Southern Industrial Trust Ltd.*; and in earlier cases such as *Foley* v. *Irish Land Commission* and *Buckley and others (Sinn Fein)* v. *The Attorney General*—not all of which decisions are reconcilable with each other."

In the event, however, concessions by counsel obviated the need for a considered ruling; but the court emphasised that it did not necessarily accept that those concessions were well founded.[39]

---

[36] *Condon* v. *Minister for Labour* (High Court, McWilliam J., June 11, 1980). See Gerard McCormack, "Contractual Entitlements and the Constitution" (1982) XVII *Irish Jurist* (N.S) 340. See also the Supreme Court's decisions in *Hamilton* v. *Hamilton* [1982] I.R. 466, and *Cox* v. *Ireland* (July 11, 1991), where it was held that the property rights protected by the Constitution included " . . . the right to a pension, gratuity or other emolument already earned, [and] the right to the advantages of a subsisting contract of employment"; *per* Finlay C.J. at p. 20.

[37] The Supreme Court so held in *D.P.P. (Long)* v. *McDonald* [1983] I.L.R.M. 223.

[38] A similar reservation seems implicit in s.1 of the Family Law Act 1988, which provides: "After the passing of this Act, no person shall be entitled to institute proceedings for restitution of conjugal rights."

[39] The court specifically reserved the question whether *O'Brien* v. *Keogh* was correctly decided. In *Campbell* v. *Ward* [1981] I.L.R.M. 60 Carroll J. noted this but held that she was bound by the decision in *O'Brien's* case until it was actually overruled.

Since *Moynihan* v. *Greensmyth* the Supreme Court has, of course, decided eight cases on property rights, and clarified the relationship between Articles 40.3 and 43. Thus the problems of reconciling decisions have been exacerbated. Two possibilities seem open. Firstly, that a right of action *is* a property right protected by Article 40.3.2° against unjust attack; and that deciding whether restrictive legislation (such as limitation periods) constitutes such an attack involves those issues of the common good and social justice referred to previously. Alternatively, the right may be an unenumerated right qualifiedly guaranteed by Article 40.3.1°; and deciding what is "practicable" thereunder would seem to involve similar questions of balancing the common good, individual rights and social justice. That a constitutional right of some kind is involved here seems clear from the Supreme Court's decision in *Hamilton* v. *Hamilton and Dunne* [1982] I.R. 446. There the first defendant had agreed in writing to sell his house and lands to the second defendant in 1975. The sale was not completed by the due date and the second defendant sought and obtained an order for specific performance of the contract. Meanwhile the Family Home Protection Act 1976 had come into force, and the plaintiff (the first defendant's wife) sought a declaration that any purported conveyance without her consent—which would not be forthcoming—would be void. The High Court agreed and the purchaser appealed. Henchy J. (with whose judgment Griffin and Hederman JJ. agreed) said (at 481):

" . . . if the effect of the Act of 1976 was to extinguish or to stultify Frank Dunne's constitutional right to pursue his pending claim for specific performance . . . the Act of 1976 would be unconstitutional to that extent. . . . Neither at common law nor by the application of the relevant constitutional limitations could the Act of 1976 be held to be capable of trenching on Frank Dunne's right to carry through his pending specific performance action to a successful conclusion."

If litigation is carried through to a successful conclusion in the award of damages, may the plaintiff be deprived by the State of the fruits of victory? This happened in the United Kingdom, following the decision in *Burmah Oil* v. *Lord Advocate* [1965] A.C. 75, under the War Damage Act 1965. There the House of Lords had opened up the possibility of Crown liability in damages for the wartime destruction by Crown forces of the company's Burmese oil installations—destruction undertaken to deprive the Japanese of their use. The Act prevented the company from recovering any such damages. But that the Oireachtas may be barred from doing any such thing is suggested by the Supreme Court's decision in *Pine Valley Developments Ltd.* v. *Minister for the Environment* [1987] I.R. 23. In November 1978 the plaintiff company had purchased lands in Co. Dublin. These lands—originally agricultural—had the benefit of outline planning permission for industrial buildings granted by the defendant, on appeal from the planning authority's refusal, in March 1977. In February 1982 the Supreme Court held that the Minister's decision of March 1977 was *ultra vires* and a nullity; *State (Pine Valley Developments Ltd.)* v. *Dublin County Council* [1984] I.R. 407. Shortly thereafter the Oireachtas passed the Local Government (Planning and Development) Act 1982, section 6 of which gave retrospective validity to planning permissions such as this granted on appeal before March 15, 1977, save where such retrospective validation would conflict with a constitutional right of any person. It was accepted that the Pine Valley company was excluded from the benefit of sec-

tion 6 because it had exercised its constitutional right to litigate the validity
of the planning permission in the courts. Henchy J. (with whom Griffin J.
agreed) said (at 43) that this was not an unconstitutional discrimination
because the overriding purpose "was to avoid an unconstitutional invasion of
the judicial domain by attempting to give validity to any planning permission which the courts may have held to be lacking in validity." Lardner J.
observed (at 46):

> "No doubt it was apprehended that section 6(1) . . . might operate to
> reverse retrospectively this Court's decision and that this might consti-
> tute an unwarrantable interference by the legislature in a decision of the
> Courts. It seems probable that . . . section 6(2) was enacted with a view
> to avoiding such interference."[40]

Reid v. Limerick Corporation

The case of *Reid* v. *Limerick Corporation* concerned the level of compensation
for a compulsory purchase of houses owned by the plaintiff. The houses had
been subject to the Rent Restrictions Acts—which of course had been held
invalid in the *Blake* case. And it resulted from *Murphy* v. *Att. Gen.* [1982] I.R.
241 that those Acts were void *ab initio*. Under the relevant legislation the
compensation was assessable as of a date before the *Blake* decision; but the
plaintiff argued that since the Rent Acts were void *ab initio* the compensation
should be fixed on the basis that they did not apply to her houses. (This
would have made a difference of some £7000 in the figure.) But the High
Court ([1984 I.L.R.M. 366) and the Supreme Court ([1987] I.L.R.M. 83)
rejected this argument. Walsh J., for the Supreme Court, said that the arbitrator (who under the statute assessed the compensation) could concern himself only with the market forces operating at the relevant date. He could not
create a notional market in which one of the operative factors would be that
the relevant provisions of the Rent Restrictions Act 1960 did not apply on the
relevant date.

The *Reid* case came to the courts on a case stated by the property arbitrator. Thus the courts' function was simply to answer the questions posed
and there was no occasion to consider wider issues. Consequently nothing
was said about any liability the State might incur by maintaining the invalid
legislation in force. In the *Pine Valley* case mentioned earlier Finlay C.J. said
it was not necessary to decide—and he expressed no opinion on the question—whether an action lay for failure on the part of the Oireachtas to legislate in protection of personal rights, as distinct from an action to invalidate
legislation which failed adequately to protect or vindicate them. But that
such an action might lie is suggested by observations in the Supreme

---

[40] Subsequently the European Court of Human Rights held that the exclusion of the landowners
from the benefit of the retrospective validation of planning permissions violated their rights
under Art. 14 of the Convention, read with Art. 1 of its First Protocol: *Pine Valley Development
Ltd. and Ors.* v. *Ireland, The Times,* December 11, 1991. Art. 14 provides: "The enjoyment of the
rights and freedoms set forth in this convention shall be secured without discrimination on
any ground such as sex, race, colour, language, religion, political or other opinion, national or
social origin, association with a national minority, property, birth or other status." Art. 1 of
Protocol No. 1 states (so far as here relevant): "Every natural and legal person is entitled to
the peaceful enjoyment of his possessions. No one shall be deprived of his possessions except
in the public interest and subject to the conditions provided for by law and by the general
principles of international law."

Courts's judgment in the *Brennan* case. There the court said ([1984] I.L.R.M. 355, 365) that when the injustice of the farm rating system "had become obvious the State had a duty to take action in protection of the rights involved." The court went on to say that by continuing that system under the Local Government Act 1946 the State had perpetrated a further injustice.[41]

That the Rent Restrictions Acts constituted an unjust attack on property rights is established by the *Blake* decision; but the facts of *Reid's* case show that not every injustice caused by that unconstitutional legislation was cured by declaring it invalid. It would therefore seem that the State failed to fulfil its obligations under Article 40.3 in respect of such situations, and that an action for damages for breach of constitutional rights—under *Meskell* v. *C.I.E.* [1973] I.R. 121—would lie. It should be noted that the Article 40.3.2° duty extends to *vindicating* rights when an injustice has actually been done; and as Henchy J. pointed out in the *Pine Valley* case ([1987] I.R. 23, 41) the duty to vindicate rights—unlike that to protect them—is not qualified by the words "as best it may."

[41] See too *E.S.B.* v. *Gormley* [1985] I.R. 129 at 151.

19   Freedom of Religion

The whole of Article 44 is devoted to the topic of religion—indicating its importance in Irish society. Commenting on the results of a 1981 sociological survey of Irish values and attitudes, Professor Fogarty has written[1]:

> "The first impression . . . is that Ireland remains an outstandingly religious country . . . every indicator of belief, informal and formal practice, and attitudes to the Church or Churches shows Irish people, North and South, to be far more inclined to religion than those of other countries in Europe."

But he goes on to show that this general pattern conceals variations; many persons do not subscribe to orthodox religious views and this is particularly the case amongst younger people. Nonetheless this inclination to religion explains why Article 44 exists and takes the form it does. It may also help to explain why in Ireland Church/State issues rarely reach the courts, whereas in the United States they have generated a great deal of litigation.

Article 44 has several facets. It guarantees freedom of conscience and the free profession and practice of religion (s.2.1°). The State undertakes not to endow any religion (s.2.2°) and is prohibited from imposing disabilities or from discriminating on religious grounds (s.2.3°).[2] Legislation providing State aid for schools must be religiously neutral, and children have the right to attend State-aided schools without attending religious instruction there (s.2.4°). Finally, the autonomy of religious denominations is guaranteed (s.2.5°), and their property "shall not be diverted save for necessary works of public utility and on payment of compensation" (s.2.6°).

With this lengthy provision—redolent of Irish history[3]—may be contrasted the laconic terms of the 1st Amendment to the United States Constitution: "Congress shall make no law respecting an establishment of religion, or prohibiting the free exercise thereof." The terms of section 116 of the Australian Constitution of 1900 are also noteworthy:

---

[1] Michael Fogarty, Liam Ryan and Joseph Lee, *Irish Values and Attitudes* (Dublin 1984), p. 8. See too Professor Ryan's observations at p. 99.

[2] Art. 40.6.2° stipulates that: "Laws regulating the manner in which the right of forming associations and unions and the right of free assembly may be exercised shall contain no political, religious or class discrimination." Given Art. 44.2.3°, the reference to religious discrimination seems superfluous.

[3] Its framing caused more difficulties than that of any other provision of the Constitution: see Dermot Keogh, "The Irish Constitutional Revolution: An Analysis of the Making of the Constitution" in *The Constitution of Ireland 1937–1987* (Frank Litton, ed., Dublin 1988), pp. 19 ff.

"The Commonwealth shall not make any law for establishing any religion, or for imposing any religious observance, or for prohibiting the free
exercise of any religion, and no religious test shall be required as a qualification for any office or public trust under the Commonwealth."

Article 44 clearly covers some of the ground occupied by these other provisions. The specific Australian ban on religious tests for public office would
presumably be embraced by Article 44.2.3°.[4] The Australian and United
States prohibitions on impeding the free exercise of religion have their
counterpart in Article 44.2.1°. But unlike the Australian and United States
provisions, Article 44 does not plainly prohibit establishment of religion;
though, again unlike them, it forbids "endowment" of "any religion." Nonetheless, it can hardly be doubted that Article 44, read as a whole, militates
against any legal establishment, in the sense of setting up or recognising a
national church.[5]

The 1st Amendment of the United States Constitution has generated a
considerable amount of litigation over both its "establishment" and "free
exercise" clauses. These, of course, do not exist in water-tight compartments,
for an exemption from statutory provisions given in the name of free exercise
might be questioned as infringing the ban on establishment. Indeed the
United States Supreme Court has often referred to the tension between the
two clauses. Article 44 is capable of giving rise to similar problems of internal
conflict, as *Quinn's Supermarket Ltd.* v. *Att. Gen.* [1972] I.R. 1—discussed
infra—shows. That decision also indicates how useful United States precedents may be in resolving Article 44 issues; though it must be noted that
some Church/State controversies in the United States are not live issues in
Ireland. Thus, as noted in Chapter 17 *supra*, Irish education at primary and
secondary level is almost exclusively denominational, a situation approved
and ratified by the State via extensive funding of the relevant schools. This
was the position before independence and it seems legitimate to read public
acceptance of its continuance, and the absence of legal challenges[6] to the system, as a ratification of the established practice. Consequently the questions
raised before the United States Supreme Court in a continuing series of
cases[7] have so far failed to surface in Ireland, and it seems unlikely that they

---

[4] The Constitution itself imposes one religious test—the declaration to be made by the President and by judges clearly posits some kind of religious belief (see Art. 12.8 and 34.5.1°). If
statute required similar declarations from *all* holders of public office, thereby possibly excluding atheists and agnostics, would this be valid?
[5] Which is what the High Court of Australia understood "establishment" to mean: *Att. Gen.
(Vic.) ex rel. Black* v. *Commonwealth* (1981) 146 C.L.R. 559
[6] Since the establishment of the Campaign to Separate Church and State, such challenges are
now more likely, and some have been launched. But none have involved the *central* features of
the system.
[7] *e.g. Everson* v. *Board of Education* (1947) 330 U.S. 1 (New Jersey statute authorising expenditure
of public funds on transporting children to denominational schools); *Engel* v. *Vitale* (1962) 370
U.S. 421 (officially composed prayers in public schools): *Abington School District* v. *Schempp*
(1963) 374 U.S. 203 (Bible reading in public schools). The case law of the U.S. Supreme
Court is very *nuancé*. Regulations giving public school students time off to attend religious
instruction *outside* school have been upheld—*Zorach* v. *Clauson* (1952) 343 U.S. 306; but a similar arrangement involving such instruction in the school building was struck down—*McCol-
lum* v. *Board of Education* (1948) 333 U.S. 203. See too *Lemon* v. *Kurzman* (1971) 403 U.S. 602;
Committee for Public Education v. *Nyquist* (1973) 413 U.S. 756; *Wolman* v. *Walter* (1977) 433 U.S.
229: *Mueller* v. *Allen* (1983) 463 U.S. 388.

will do so in the foreseeable future. As in Canada and Australia these issues have been settled by political compromise rather than judicial fiat.

In Ireland the question of Church and State has been essentially a matter of politics rather than law. That is, it has surfaced only rarely in the courts and its central concern has been the influence of the majority Roman Catholic Church on certain issues of public policy—censorship of publications, education and, especially, family matters being among them. The degree of that influence is the subject of detailed examination in the late Professor John Whyte's magisterial *Church and State in Modern Ireland*.[8] In a more recent article he summarised his conclusions as follows[9]:

> "Down to the nineteen-seventies the position of the Catholic hierarchy in Irish public life seemed fairly clear. While it would be an exaggeration to call Ireland a theocratic state, the hierarchy had immense influence, receiving a deference that marked it out from other interest groups. In areas where it had a traditional interest, notably education and family law, Governments habitually consulted it before making policy changes and acted in accordance with its advice. Even where the bishops intervened in an area where they had not previously shown an interest, as happened with health legislation in the period 1947–53, their views received deference and could modify Government policy. The only known instance of advice from the hierarchy being rejected occurred over the Licensing Act 1960, which extended Sunday opening of pubs against the publicly expressed wishes of the bishops. All the indications are that this degree of deference existed with the support of the people. The reluctance of politicians, of whatever hue, to be seen as opposing the hierarchy suggests that there was no electoral dividend to be gained from appearing to stand up to the bishops."

But as is pointed out in the same article, the hierarchy's influence appears to be declining somewhat. Professor Whyte pointed to factors such as the passage of the family planning amendment Act in 1985 against the advice of the bishops and without consulting them, and the large vote against the anti-abortion constitutional amendment in 1983 despite repeated episcopal urgings in its favour. The Government decision of 1986 in favour of a referendum to introduce divorce legislation seems another instance, since although the bishops were consulted their advice was against divorce. However it would be wrong to suppose that episcopal influence is no longer significant; the bishops' opposition to the introduction of divorce obviously played a part in the defeat of the constitutional amendment for that purpose in 1986.[10] Another focus of controversy has been sterilisation, on which—together with other issues of human reproduction—there have been many episcopal pronouncements. Although sterilisation is not prohibited by law it is apparently

---

[8] 2nd ed., Dublin 1980. See also G. W. Hogan, "Law and Religion: Church-State Relations in Ireland from Independence to the present day" (1987) 35 *Am. Journ. Comp. Law* 47.

[9] "Recent Developments in Church-State Relations," *Seirbhís Phoiblí* (1985) Vol. 6, no. 3, pp. 4–10. The passage quoted is from p. 4.

[10] See further Brian Girvin, "Social Change and Moral Politics: The Irish Constitutional Referendum 1983" (1986) 34 *Pol. Studies* 61, and "The Divorce Referendum in the Republic; June 1986" (1987) 2 *Irish Political Studies* 93: John Coakley, "Moral Consensus in a Secularising Society: The Irish Divorce Referendum of 1986" (1987) 10 *West European Politics* 291: Tom Hesketh, *The Second Partitioning of Ireland?* (Dun Laoghaire, 1990), pp. 379–81: Basil Chubb, *The Politics of the Irish Constitution* (Dublin 1991) Chap. 5.

difficult to find public hospital facilities for the operation, which is not carried out in the publicly funded hospitals run by Catholic organisations. And
bishops have sought to have the church's anti-sterilisation policy applied by
doctors working in publicly-run hospitals; however, recent announcements
about revised ethical guidelines at the Coombe Maternity Hospital, for
example, suggest a lack of success in this regard.[11]

Article 44.1

Article 44.1 provides:

> "The State acknowledges that the homage of public worship is due to
> Almighty God. It shall hold His Name in reverence and shall respect
> and honour religion."

This echoes the terms of the preamble, which opens by invoking "the Name
of the Most Holy Trinity" and continues by "acknowledging all our obligations to our Divine Lord, Jesus Christ, who sustained our fathers through
centuries of trial. . . . " These provisions sound a distinctive religious note
unusual in constitutions and explicable essentially in historical and sociological terms.[12] Their precise legal significance, *i.e.* the nature and extent of the
obligation Article 44.1 places on the State—has not been explored and
remains unclear. In *Quinn's Supermarket Ltd.* v. *Att. Gen.* [1972] I.R. 1, 23
Walsh J. (with whose judgment Ó Dálaigh C.J., Budd and FitzGerald JJ.
agreed) said:

> "Our Constitution reflects a firm conviction that we are a religious
> people. The preamble to the Constitution acknowledges that we are a
> Christian people and Article 44, s.1, subs. 1, acknowledges that the
> homage of public worship is due to Almighty God but it does so in terms
> which do not confine the benefit of that acknowledgement to members of
> the Christian faith."

That these references to religion may sometimes shape judicial interpretation
of the Constitution is clear from *Norris* v. *Att. Gen.* [1984] I.R. 36 (discussed
in Chap. 12 *supra*). There O'Higgins C.J. (Finlay P. and Griffin J. concurring) said (at 64):

> "The preamble to the Constitution proudly asserts the existence of God
> in the Most Holy Trinity and recites that the people of Ireland humbly
> acknowledge their obligation to 'our Divine Lord Jesus Christ.' It can-
> not be doubted that the people, so asserting and acknowledging their
> obligations to our Divine Lord Jesus Christ, were proclaiming a deep
> religious conviction and faith and an intention to adopt a Constitution
> consistent with that conviction and faith and with Christian beliefs. Yet
> it is suggested that, in the very act of so doing, the people rendered
> inoperative laws which had existed for hundreds of years prohibiting
> unnatural sexual conduct which Christian teaching held to be gravely

[11] See *The Irish Times*, August 15 and 20, and October 10, 1985.
[12] See Whyte, *op. cit.*, pp. 53–56: Ronan Fanning, *Independent Ireland*, pp. 129–132: John Bowman,
De Valera and the Ulster Question (Oxford 1982), pp. 152–154.

sinful. It would require very clear and express provisions in the Constitution itself to convince me that such took place."

Until 1972 Article 44.1 contained other provisions. These declared that the State recognised various religious denominations (the Church of Ireland, the Presbyterian Church, the Methodist Church, the Society of Friends and the Jewish Congregations being named specifically). The State also recognised "the special position" of the Roman Catholic Church as the guardian of the faith professed by the great majority of citizens (Art. 44.1.2°). This latter provision caused some unease, though the Supreme Court ruled that it had no juridical significance.[13] These subsections were deleted by the Fifth Amendment of the Constitution Act 1972.

The overwhelming allegiance to religion in Ireland is mainly—though not exclusively—a matter of private practice. Unlike that of the United States, the coinage bears no message that could be regarded as religious. But there are many public manifestations of religion—such as ceremonies at defence establishments, the daily broadcasting of the Angelus on radio and television—and these many people find objectionable. Nonetheless, it is difficult to envisage litigation to bar such practices, on the lines of *Lynch* v. *Donnelly* (1984) 465 U.S. 668.[14] It seems probable that any such action would fail, with the courts invoking Article 44.1 to uphold the impugned practices.[15]

Article 44.2.1°

This guarantees freedom of conscience and the free profession and practice of religion, subject to public order and morality. Judicial attention has mainly been focussed on the profession and practice aspect of Article 44.2.1°, and the meaning of freedom of conscience has been little explored. In *McGee* v. *Att. Gen.* [1974] I.R. 284, however, Walsh J. gave his view on the matter (at 316–317):

> "It was submitted that social conscience, as distinct from religious conscience, falls within the ambit of Article 44. I do not think that is so. The whole context in which the question of conscience appears in Article 44 is one dealing with the exercise of religion and the free profession and practice of religion. Within that context, the meaning of s.2, subs. 1, of Article 44 is that no person shall directly or indirectly be coerced or compelled to act contrary to his conscience in so far as the practice of religion is concerned and . . . is free to profess and practise the religion

---

[13] *Quinn's Supermarket Ltd.* v. *Att. Gen.* [1972] I.R. 1, 23–24.

[14] This was a challenge, on 1st Amendment grounds, to a publicly financed annual Christmas display in Pawtucket, R.I. which included a nativity scene. By a 5–4 majority the Supreme Court rejected the challenge, holding that the purpose of the display was to celebrate the Christmas holiday and depict its origins, and these were secular purposes. The complexities of this branch of the law are amply demonstrated by the later decision in *County of Allegheny* v. *American Civil Liberties Union* (1989) 109 S.Ct. 3086.

[15] Different considerations would arise if the relevant public manifestation of religion could be said to involve a state endowment, contrary to Art. 44.2.2°. *The Irish Times* of July 18, 1987 refers to a High Court decision quashing a Southern Health Board resolution to erect a statue of Padre Pio in the grounds of Cork Regional Hospital, *semble* on the grounds that it was *ultra vires* and contrary to Art. 44.2.2°. But the application was reported as having been unopposed, and the precedent value of the case must be slight.

of his choice in accordance with his conscience. Correlatively, he is free to have no religious beliefs or to abstain from the practice of any religion. Because a person feels free, or even obliged, in conscience to pursue some particular activity which is not in itself a religious practice, it does not follow that such activity is guaranteed protection by Article 44. It is not correct to say . . . that the Article is a constitutional guarantee of a right to live in accordance with one's conscience subject to public order and morality. What the Article guarantees is the right not to be compelled or coerced into living in a way which is contrary to one's conscience and, in the context of the Article, that means contrary to one's conscience so far as the exercise, practice or profession of religion is concerned."

The other members of the Supreme Court did not pronounce on this matter but neither did they disavow Walsh J.'s conclusions. There is therefore no reason to suppose that those views would fail of general judicial acceptance.

Unlike the Constitution of India (Art. 25(1)), Bunreacht na hÉireann does not specifically guarantee freedom to propagate religion. It seems likely, however, that such freedom would be held to be implicit in Article 44.1. If so, legislative or administrative restrictions on proselytising activities—not clearly based on public order or morality—would be difficult to sustain. While it is unlikely that any such restrictions would be applied to the established denominations, it has sometimes been argued that they ought to be imposed on the activities of "fringe" religious groups. The activities of some such groups—the Church of Scientology is an example—have come under unfavourable review elsewhere.[16] Some minority cults, it is claimed, indulge in doubtful recruitment practices and unfairly exploit members so recruited, and people ought to be protected against this. But it is not clear whether laws purporting to offer such protection might offend against Article 44.2.1°. If the word "religion" in that Article has the meaning it bore in 1937 it would presumably cover only traditional theistic religion; but in modern Irish society there are small groups which do not cleave to this pattern. In the United States those who framed the Constitution 200 years ago presumably had traditional theistic religion in mind when the 1st Amendment was adopted, but the Supreme Court has held that its reach is not now so confined—*Torcaso* v. *Watkins* (1961) 367 U.S. 488. If so, what are the limits of religion? If it includes all matters of ultimate concern to an individual, then political creeds such as Fascism or Communism would seem to qualify.

So far such questions have not troubled the Irish courts; but they have given rise to much litigation and commentary in the United States.[17] There the Supreme Court has held that the courts cannot enter into questions of the *truth* of religious beliefs: *U.S.* v. *Ballard* (1944) 322 U.S. 78—nor may they decide between competing interpretations of a particular sect's religious beliefs: *Thomas* v. *Review Board of Indiana Employment Security Division* (1981)

---

[16] See, *e.g. Schmidt* v. *Secretary of State* [1969] 2 Ch. 149 (the Home Secretary's powers over immigration were used to prevent the entry of, and to refuse extended stays to, Scientologists. The Court of Appeal upheld this as valid.) See, too, *Van Duyn* v. *Home Office*, Case 41/74 [1974] E.C.R. 1346.

[17] To benefit under the Free Exercise clause, it is not necessary that an individual should belong to some particular sect; it suffices that his/her beliefs are sincere and religious in nature: *Frazee* v. *Illinois Dept. of Employment Security* (1989) 489 U.S. 829.

450 U.S. 707.[18] On the other hand the court has distinguished between a religious faith and a personal philosophical choice. In *Wisconsin* v. *Yoder* (1972) 406 U.S. 205 Burger C.J., speaking for himself, Blackmun and Marshall JJ., said (at 215–216):

> "A way of life, however virtuous and admirable, may not be interposed as a barrier to reasonable state regulation of education if it is based on purely secular considerations; to have the protection of the religious clauses, the claims must be rooted in religious beliefs. Although a determination of what is a 'religious' belief or practice entitled to constitutional protection may present a most delicate question, the very concept of ordered liberty precludes allowing every person to make his own standards on matters of conduct in which society as a whole has important interests. Thus, if the Amish asserted their claims because of their subjective evaluation and rejection of the contemporary secular values accepted by the majority, much as Thoreau rejected the social values of his time and isolated himself at Walden Pond, their claims would not rest on a religious basis. Thoreau's choice was philosophical and personal rather than religious, and such belief does not rise to the demands of the Religion Clauses."

These views have clear affinities with those expressed by Walsh J. in *McGee* v. *Att. Gen.*, and would probably win acceptance in the Irish courts. But they obviously do not provide a clear test for distinguishing between religious belief and philosophical and personal choice.

Article 44.2.1° was considered by the Supreme Court in *Quinn's Supermarket Ltd.* v. *Att. Gen.* [1972] I.R. 1. The case involved a Ministerial order of 1948, made under the Shops (Hours of Closing) Act 1938, which restricted the opening hours of butchers' shops. Kosher butchers' shops were, however, totally exempted from these restrictions. The plaintiff company, having defied this order, was facing prosecution, and therefore in these proceedings sought to have the order declared invalid because it discriminated on religious grounds contrary to Article 44.2.3°. The Supreme Court rejected this assertion. Walsh J. (Ó Dálaigh C.J., Budd and FitzGerald JJ. concurring) observed that the case showed a potential conflict between Article 44.2.1° and 44.2.3°. The latter provision meant that the State must make no distinction between persons on grounds of religious belief, profession or status—*i.e.* no discrimination, favourable or unfavourable. Since the order here did this it was prima facie unconstitutional. But on the other hand, if the order did not make some allowance for the special circumstances of Jews, their religious freedom would be interfered with and that would contravene Article 44.2.1°.

Walsh J. went on to say that this conflict must be resolved by referring to the overall purpose of Article 44.[19] That overall purpose was to guarantee the free practice of religion, and if a legislative distinction was necessary to

---

[18] See Laurence H. Tribe, *American Constitutional Law* (2nd ed., Mineola, N.Y. 1988), Chap. 14: Jerome Barron, C. Thomas Dienes *et al.*, *Constitutional Law: Principles and Policy—Cases and Materials* (3rd ed., Charlottesville, Va. 1987), Chap. 10. A valuable discussion of the terms "religion" and "religious" may also be found in the judgment of Latham C.J. in *Adelaide Company of Jehovah's Witnesses* v. *Commonwealth* (1943) 67 C.L.R. 116.

[19] In his separate judgment Kenny J. took a similar view, saying that a purposive rather than a literal construction of Article 44.2.3° must be adopted.

achieve this it would not be unconstitutional. It would be contrary to the spirit and intendment of Article 44.2.3° to make its provisions the means of restricting the free practice of religion.

The primary object of Article 44, is, then, to guarantee the free practice of religion—but since this is subject to public order and morality it is clear that not every claim made under this head will be upheld. As in the United States, it will hardly be an answer to a bigamy charge that one's religious beliefs imperatively require plural marriage: *Reynolds* v. *U.S.* (1878) 98 U.S. 145. As Waite C.J. there put it (at 166):

> "Laws are made for the government of actions, and while they cannot interfere with mere religious beliefs and opinions, they may with practices. Suppose one believed that human sacrifices were a necessary part of religious worship, would it be seriously contended that the civil government under which he lived could not interfere to prevent a sacrifice? Or if a wife religiously believed it was her duty to burn herself upon the funeral pile of her dead husband, would it be beyond the power of the civil government to prevent her carrying her belief into practice?"

It seems probable that in Ireland, as in the United States, religious groups may not claim exemption from statutes of general application restricting child labour; see *Prince* v. *Massachusetts* (1944) 321 U.S. 158.[20] Nor is it likely that an Irish court would accept religious motives as a defence to a manslaughter charge, as where a parent refuses to summon medical assistance which might save a child's life.[21] The range of situations where an asserted religious belief may conflict with legal provisions seems virtually limitless. May such beliefs justify a refusal, contrary to road traffic legislation, to supply a blood sample[22]; to serve on a jury; to testify in criminal proceedings; to have one's child vaccinated? Though cases involving all these issues (and others) have arisen in the United States,[23] Irish courts have not yet had to grapple with such problems and we have in consequence no guidance as to what the outcome would be. From other contexts, however, it seems safe to assume that in many such cases the presumption of constitutionality, combined with a marked deference to the legislature's judgment, would suffice to validate the impugned legislation.

Despite the volume of litigation on free exercise of religion matters in the United States, there are still many issues that await authoritative resolution by the Supreme Court. As in other areas of constitutional law, the ultimate issue appears to be one of balancing the individual's claims against those of society in general—"society" being understood to include those affected by the individual's actions who may not have an opportunity of speaking for themselves, such as the under-age Jehovah's Witnesses' children in *Prince* v. *Massachusetts* (1944) 321 U.S. 158, required by their parents to sell religious

---

[20] Or exemptions from other generally applicable criminal statutes: see *Employment Division, Oregon Dept. of Human Resources* v. *Smith* (1990) 110 S. Ct. 1595.

[21] The English Court for Crown Cases Reserved refused to accept this as a defence to a charge of manslaughter in *R.* v. *Senior* [1899] 1 Q.B. 283.

[22] Such a case arose in England in *R.* v. *John* [1974] 2 All E.R. 561, where the accused, unable to meet the alternative option of a urine sample, declined to give a blood sample on religious grounds. The Court of Appeal, Criminal Division, held that this was not a "reasonable excuse" in terms of the relevant legislation.

[23] See particularly the books by Tribe, and by Barron, Dienes *et al.*, cited in n. 18 *supra*.

material in the streets in defiance of state law. In Ireland such issues, which have not yet arisen, will be doubly difficult for the courts for not only do they involve Article 44 but the family, parental rights and educational guarantees of Articles 41 and 42 as well.

Should a case like *Wisconsin* v. *Yoder* (1972) 406 U.S. 205 arise in Ireland it seems probable that a similar conclusion would be reached. There parents who belonged to Amish communities had been convicted of violating Wisconsin's compulsory school attendance law, which required them to send their children to school until the age of 16. The parents had refused to send their 14 and 15 year old children to school because it was contrary to Amish beliefs to do so; high school education beyond the eighth grade, they held, placed their children in an environment hostile to Amish beliefs and took them away from their community during a crucial formative period of their lives. There was expert evidence that such compulsory attendance could be psychologically damaging to Amish children, and that such children were adequately prepared in the Amish community to be productive members of that community. The Supreme Court held that the Constitution prevented the statutory compulsion in issue here. The traditional Amish way of life was "not merely a matter of personal preference, but one of deep religious conviction, shared by an organised religious group, and intimately related to daily living. . . . " The law challenged here compelled Amish parents to act in a way inconsistent with their religious beliefs and threatened the very existence of their community. The justifications advanced by the state were rejected by the court, which laid heavy emphasis on the ability of the Amish people to function effectively in their daily lives and "to survive and prosper in contemporary society, as a separate, sharply identifiable and highly self-contained community for more than 200 years in this country."

As the judgments show, the Supreme Court here struck a balance between 1st Amendment rights and the legitimate interests of society, represented by the state. The case is not authority for a general exemption from compulsory school attendance laws in the name of free exercise of religion.[24] Nor does it decide what the position would be if the parents' religious views conflicted with the child's wishes, as Burger C.J. made clear. Finally, the decision relies heavily on the special and traditional characteristics of the Amish community. Burger C.J. stressed that the court was not dealing "with a way of life and mode of education by a group claiming to have recently discovered some 'progressive' or more enlightened process for rearing children for modern life."

The United States Supreme Court has also held that persons who leave their jobs because their work conflicts with their religious beliefs may not be denied unemployment benefit for voluntarily leaving employment: *Thomas* v. *Review Board of Indiana Employment Security Division* (1981) 450 U.S. 707. The court, *per* Burger C.J., emphasised that the fact that the individual's particular scruples might not be shared by all members of that faith was irrelevant. It was not within the judicial function to inquire whose perception of a creed's commands was correct, and the courts were not arbiters of scriptural interpretation. For legislation to condition receipt of an important benefit on

---

[24] A point particularly stressed by White J. (joined by Brennan and Stewart JJ.) in his concurring judgment. See also the decision of the Supreme Court of Canada in *Jones* v. *The Queen* (1986) 31 D.L.R. (4th) 569.

conduct proscribed by a religious faith, or to deny such a benefit because of conduct required by religious faith, was an infringement of free exercise of religion. Such an infringement could be justified only by state interests of the highest order, and the court concluded that none such had been shown to exist here. This again is an issue which has not so far arisen before the Irish courts. Should it do so, it seems likely that the *Thomas* case would be followed. The United States Supreme Court there followed its own earlier decision in the comparable case of *Sherbert* v. *Verner* (1963) 374 U.S. 398—an authority quoted from and founded upon by the Irish Supreme Court in *Quinn's Supermarket Ltd.* v. *Att. Gen.* [1972] I.R. 1. And that court's analysis of "free practice and profession of religion" in Article 44.2.1° closely follows the reasoning of *Sherbert* v. *Verner*.[25]

Another issue that has not yet arisen in Ireland—though it has in the United States and Canada—is the constitutionality of Sunday closing laws. In four cases decided on the same day a divided United States Supreme Court upheld such laws as infringing neither the non-establishment nor the free exercise clause of the 1st Amendment: see *McGowan* v. *Maryland* (1961) 366 U.S. 420; *Two Guys from Harrison—Allentown Inc.* v. *McGinley* (1961) 366 U.S. 582; *Braunfeld* v. *Brown* (1961) 366 U.S. 599; *Gallagher* v. *Crown Kosher Supermarket* (1961) 366 U.S. 617. The court's view was that although the original motivation behind such laws may have been religious, their current purpose was wholly secular—to provide a uniform day of rest for all citizens of a state. In contrast, the Supreme Court of Canada unanimously held the federal Lord's Day Observance Act inconsistent with the freedom of religion and conscience guaranteed by the Charter of Rights and Freedoms, s.2(*a*). Nor was it capable of being justified under section 1 as a reasonable limit demonstrably justified in a free and democratic society. On the Canadian authorities, said the court, the only conclusion open was that the Act had a religious purpose. Its effect might be secular but this was not sufficient to save it: *R.* v. *Big M. Drug Mart Ltd.* (1985) 18 D.L.R. (4th) 321.

In Ireland Sunday trading is regulated by Part IV of the Shops (Hours of Trading) Act 1938. Under section 36 it is an offence to open a shop for trading on Sundays—but this is subject to exceptions. Some are set out in the Third Schedule (pubs, for example, are subject to a different statutory regime); more generally, the relevant Minister is given very wide powers to make exemption orders. Thus he/she may exempt specific businesses (s.31(3)) or whole geographical areas (s.34). Were this subjected to constitutional challenge the courts would have to choose between the United States and Canadian approaches set out above. It is very difficult to predict what that choice might be. Ireland has been judicially declared a pluralist society (*per* Kenny J. in *Quinn's Supermarket Ltd.* v. *Att. Gen.* [1972] I.R. 1, 34)[26]—but perhaps it is not quite so pluralist as Canada. The Constitution's references to God, however, are hardly conclusive as to the 1938 Act's validity. The

---

[25] The Social Welfare (Consolidation) Act 1981, s.35(3) provides that a person may be disqualified from receiving unemployment benefit for a maximum six weeks if he/she " . . . has voluntarily left his employment without just cause. . . . " The presumption of constitutionality would obviously apply to the construction of this provision and would suggest a result similar to that in the *Thomas* case.

[26] *Cf.* also Henchy J.'s reference to "[t]he pluralism necessary for the preservation of constitutional requirements in the Christian, democratic state envisaged by the Constitution . . . ": *Norris* v. *Att. Gen.* [1984] I.R. 36, 78.

preamble to the Canadian Charter of Rights and Freedoms refers to the fact that "Canada is founded on principles that recognize the supremacy of God . . . " Yet this did not prevent the Canadian Supreme Court from reaching the conclusion indicated above.

Finally, it should be noted that Article 44.2.1°—unlike Article 44.2.3°—is not directed solely at the State, and it may therefore apply, in appropriate circumstances, to private actions. It could also provide a constitutional foundation for legislation restricting action by private citizens which might impinge on the free practice of religion.

Article 44.2.2°

This provision bluntly states: "The State guarantees not to endow any religion." But this apparent simplicity is deceptive and the subsection gives rise to several problems. The word "endow" presumably does not mean the same thing as "establish." (As noted above, nothing in Art. 44 explicitly forbids legislation to establish a church, in the sense of designating a particular creed as a national institution. Nonetheless, such a prohibition seems implicit in its terms.) A church could be established without being endowed—such is the position of the Church of England. Conversely, a state with no established church might be regarded as endowing religion if it paid the salaries of the clergy out of tax revenue—or if, as in West Germany, a certain proportion of a church member's income tax is handed over to the relevant denomination.[27]

Article 44.2.2° would seem to bar any discriminatory endowment of one church—as where money or other public property is given uniquely to a particular denomination. But this may well apply only where the aid is for exclusively religious purposes. Some of the largest hospitals in Ireland (such as St. Vincent's and the Mater in Dublin) are run by Catholic religious orders. In providing public funds for equipment and salaries in such hospitals—which are open to all—the State may not be acting contrary to this provision, even if only organisations belonging to a single church are engaged in this work.[28] Some authority for this proposition may be found in *Bradfield* v. *Roberts* (1899) 175 U.S. 291, where the plaintiff sought to enjoin implementation of an agreement, made under statutory authority, between the directors of Providence Hospital and the District of Columbia Commissioners. The agreement provided that the Commissioners would erect a building, paid for out of public funds, in the grounds of the hospital—this to be used for the treatment of such poor persons suffering from infectious diseases as the Commissioners should send there. The plaintiff claimed that the hospital, which was incorporated by Act of Congress, was run by Roman Catholic nuns and under church auspices, and that implementation of the agreement would violate the 1st Amendment. The Supreme Court unanimously rejected the claim, holding that the legal character of the corporatiom as non-sectarian and secular was paramount; its powers, duties and character depended solely on the incorporating statute. There was no allegation that the hospital's work was confined to church members or that the charter had

---

[27] For more details of this system, and of the Constitutional Court's approach to it, see Donald P. Kommers, *Judicial Politics in West Germany* (Beverley Hills/London 1976), pp. 218–220.

[28] On hospitals and their funding see further Brendan Hensey, *The Health Services of Ireland* (3rd ed., Dublin 1979), pp. 137–139.

been violated. However, there are factors in the Irish situation not present in *Bradfield's* case. The religious-run hospitals which benefit from State funds are usually not incorporated; and although these hospitals are open to all there are certain kinds of treatment—lawful but unacceptable to the church—which apparently will not be given in them. Under Article 44.2.5° (see *infra*) there can be no question of the Church's right to run such hospitals. But the constitutional validity of public subventions to them is another matter, and it is by no means clear that this is consonant with Article 44.2.2°.

As noted in Chapter 17 *supra* primary and secondary education in Ireland is mainly denominational in character—and the system is dependent upon very large State subventions. The constitutionality of this long-standing practice has never yet been challenged—though powerful philosophical objections to it, invoking Article 44, have been made by Professor Clarke.[29] He argues that it is inconsistent to say that religion shall not be endowed and simultaneously to channel almost all the funds available for primary education into religious schools which explicitly claim that the teaching of religion is their primary purpose.[30] Such financing, he contends, helps to determine causally the religious beliefs of citizens and thereby infringes on their constitutionally guaranteed freedom of religious belief. To the argument that this is what most parents want, Professor Clarke justly replies that parents are seldom consulted, and that in many instances they have no choice of schools. He concludes thus[31]:

> " . . . the only consistent principle, which is already clear in the Irish Constitution, is for the State to remain strictly neutral with respect to religious belief. This means that it should neither hinder nor encourage it; it should not discriminate in any way between citizens on the basis of their religious beliefs or their lack of such beliefs. If this principle is impartially applied to the early education of school-age children, it implies that the civil authorities should be strictly neutral with respect to religious teaching. It should not finance any religious indoctrination. Instead, it should actively defend the liberties of young citizens against all those who might, in good faith or otherwise, conspire to determine the religious beliefs of individuals in the hope of realising what, according to their own theological beliefs, is the salvation of individual 'souls'."

Despite the force of these arguments it is unlikely that if the status quo were challenged the courts would upset it.[32] Their analysis would probably run as follows. Article 44 must be construed not in isolation but as part of the whole Constitution (see *Tormey* v. *Ireland* [1985] I.R. 289). Article 42 stresses parental rights in educational matters, including religious education; and the

---

[29] Desmond Clarke, *Church and State: Essays in Political Philosophy* (Cork 1985), Chap. 8. See also his article "Freedom of Thought and Educational Rights in the European Convention" (1987) XXII *Irish Jurist* (N.S.) 28, arguing that current educational policy in Ireland is incompatible with the European Convention on Human Rights.

[30] Citing the 1965 Rules for National Schools which declare: "Religious instruction is . . . a fundamental part of the school course, and a religious spirit should inform and vivify the whole work of the school."

[31] P. 226.

[32] It would hardly be an objection that the framework is administrative rather than statutory (see Chap. 17 *supra*). The funds are granted by the annual Appropriation Act, which could be made the target for a declaration of invalidity. See *Att.-Gen. (Vic.) ex reln. Black* v. *Commonwealth* (1981) 146 C.L.R. 559, *per* Barwick C.J. at 576, Mason J. at 618 and Wilson J. at 651.

State's duty to provide "for" free primary education (Art. 42.4) is properly discharged via the existing system—*Crowley* v. *Ireland* [1980] I.R. 102. Article 42.4 additionally authorises the State "to supplement and give reasonable aid to private and corporate educational initiative," while Article 44.2.4° specifically contemplates State aid for denominational schools.[33]

Teacher training colleges pose a more difficult problem. The State recognises five colleges of education for national school teachers. All are denominational, mainly Roman Catholic (though one is run by the Church of Ireland), and all are heavily dependent on the State for capital and current costs.[34] The constitutional arguments which support denominational primary and secondary schools would not seem to apply here. Article 44.2.4° can hardly be prayed in aid, for these colleges are not "schools." And though Article 44.2.2°'s ban on endowment must doubtless be read in harmony with Article 42.4's permission to supplement private educational initiative, the latter can obviously be interpreted as having no religious overtones. Even if it is not, so that the State may aid denominational institutions of higher education, it cannot, consistently with Article 44.2.2°, aid some to the exclusion of others. That is, if the prohibition on endowment is not a bar to aiding *any religion whatsoever*, it must at least be a bar to favouring some over others. But the present system of funding teacher training would appear to do that.[35]

A similar problem arises with the case of St. Patrick's College, Maynooth. This multi-faceted institution—seminary, Pontifical University, recognised college of the National University—annually receives considerable sums from the exchequer via the Higher Education Authority. These funds, it appears, are applied only for secular education[36] though clerical students attend lectures and take examinations for National University degrees at Maynooth. Nonetheless, it is clear from the Supreme Court's decision in *McGrath and Ó Rúairc* v. *Trustees of the College of Maynooth* [1979] I.L.R.M. 166 that Maynooth's legal status is that of a seminary—an institution for training students for the priesthood. O'Higgins C.J. said that this followed from its founding statutes[37] and continued (at 173):

"The essence of Maynooth is that it is a religious seminary and only the

---

[33] In May 1991 it was reported that High Court proceedings were being instituted to test the constitutionality of paying salaries to chaplains in community (second-level) schools out of public funds: *The Irish Times*, May 8, 1991. By administrative arrangement these schools, it seems, are *required* to appoint such chaplains, who are in practice nominated by church authorities and are paid salaries equivalent to those of teachers. This, it is argued, contravenes Art. 44.2.2° as being an endowment of religion, and Art. 44.2.3° as a discrimination based on religious profession, belief or status.

[34] See Coolahan, *op. cit.*, p. 235. Since that book was published, Carysfort College in Blackrock, Co. Dublin, has been closed.

[35] Following the sale of Carysfort College by the Sisters of Mercy to private interests, the State was paid £1.75 million from the proceeds in return for capital grants paid to the college. In addition the sisters agreed to return all educational equipment and library stock purchased with State funds. The Minister for Education (Mrs. O'Rourke) so informed the Dáil on October 16, 1989: see 393 *Dáil Debs.*, c. 861. This may be not unconnected with the fact that in August 1989 High Court proceedings were brought against the State, in which it was claimed that Art. 40.2.2° had been infringed on the ground that funds had been contributed to Carysfort College without conditions, and without ensuring that the State's investment could be reclaimed: see *The Irish Times*, August 12, 1989.

[36] See the judgment of Kenny J. in the *McGrath and Ó Rúairc* case; [1979] I.L.R.M. 166, p. 211.

[37] Particularly the Act of the Irish Parliament of 1795, 35 Geo. III, c. 21.

Oireachtas acting within the Constitution can permit it to be otherwise."

Though the College had since acquired additional functions, no change in its
basic legal status had occurred.

The question of State funding for what is thus in law a Roman Catholic
seminary did not arise directly in the above case and the court expressed no
opinion on the matter. It is clear, however, that a constitutional question
mark must lie over the practice. Prima facie, the transfer of public funds to a
body with such a legal status would seem to infringe Article 44.2.2°. No
doubt the funds are devoted to secular education,[38] and the arrangement has
made additional university level places available without the capital costs
involved in establishing a wholly new college; but a benign motive seems
irrelevant to the question whether Article 44.2.2° has been infringed. And it
is difficult to see how it has *not* been infringed when public funds are given to
a seminary—even if for the university education of lay persons—especially
where no such funding is given to any similar body established to train ministers of religion for another church. Thus, if Article 44.2.2° forbids the State to
give money to any religion whatsoever, the funding of Maynooth seems constitutionally doubtful. The same is true if Article 44.2.2° merely requires the
State not to prefer some religions over others in the matter of endowment.[39]

In the *McGrath and Ó Rúairc* case Kenny J. observed that subventions to
Maynooth were authorised by the Higher Education Authority Act 1971,
which provided for such subventions to "a college of a university." These
words, said the judge, were wide enough to encompass a recognised college of
a university, a status Maynooth had had since 1910.[40] But this seems only to
establish that the H.E.A. was acting within its powers in aiding Maynooth.
It does not establish the constitutional validity of such aid. The provisions of
the Irish Universities Act 1908, under which the National University may
recognise colleges, can hardly be used to outflank Article 44.2.2°.

Article 44.2.3°

This provides as follows:

"The State shall not impose any disabilities or make any discrimination
on the ground of religious profession, belief or status."

Article 44.2.3° has generated more litigation than its companion provisions. In *Quinn's Supermarkets Ltd.* v. *Att. Gen.* [1972] I.R. 1 the Supreme
Court, *per* Walsh J., said (at 16) that the provision should be construed

" . . . as meaning that the State shall not make any 'distinction' on the
grounds of religious profession, belief or status. This is confirmed by the

---

[38] s.7 of the Irish Universities Act 1908 precludes the payment of State grants for *inter alia* "the
provision or maintenance of any theological or religious teaching or study." Thus H.E.A.
funds could not lawfully be used for such courses.

[39] The U.S. Supreme Court has upheld federal and state statutes providing funds for third level
institutions denominational in origin (though not in practice)—*Tilton* v. *Richardson* (1971) 403
U.S. 672: *Hunt* v. *McNair* (1973) 413 U.S. 734. But the statutes in question aided several institutions; and they were tested against the 1st Amendment, which does not specifically forbid
"endowment" of religion.

[40] Maynooth did, it seems, receive some State funding even before the trustees' decision of 1966
which opened the College to lay students. See J. B. O'Connell, *op. cit.*, pp. 48–49.

Irish text which says 'ná aon idirdhealú da dhéanamh . . .' To discriminate in that sense is to create a difference between persons or bodies or to distinguish between them on the ground of religious profession, belief or status."⁴¹

The court has therefore made it clear that benign as well as adverse discrimination is struck at by Article 44.2.3°. However, not every distinction is constitutionally invalid. In the *Quinn's Supermarket* case the Supreme Court, as noted, emphasised that free practice of religion was the dominant theme of Article 44, and thus a distinction necessary to achieve this overriding objective will be valid.⁴² The Supreme Court re-emphasised this in *Mulloy* v. *Minister for Education* [1975] I.R. 88. There, under regulations made by the Minister, Irish teachers who spent time teaching in certain developing countries could count that service for salary increment and pension purposes when they returned home. But this applied only to *lay* teachers. Father Mulloy, who was otherwise qualified under the scheme, claimed this exclusion violated Article 44.2.3°. Holding in his favour the Supreme Court said that the scheme made a distinction on the ground of religious status, by enabling a person who was not a religious to obtain greater financial reward for the same work than one who was. Such a distinction could not be regarded as necessary to implement the constitutional right to the full and free practice of religion.

Walsh J., speaking for the Supreme Court, said ([1975] I.R. 88, 96):

"There may be many instances where, in order to implement or permit of the full and free exercise of the freedom of religion guaranteed by the Constitution, the law may find it necessary to distinguish between ministers of religion or other persons occupying a particular status in religion and the ordinary lay members of that religion or the rest of the population. . . . "

The Supreme Court gave no guidance as to what kind of provision would fall within this principle. Presumably evidential privileges—such as freedom from compulsion to testify in certain instances—may be covered.⁴³ Likewise the Juries Act 1976, First Schedule, Part II provides that the following persons are excusable as of right from jury service—a person in holy orders, "a regular minister of any religious denomination or community" and "vowed members of any religious order living in a monastery, convent or other religious community." Such persons are thus *automatically* excusable, while

⁴¹ In his separate judgment Kenny J. adopted an identical construction of Art. 44.2.3°.
⁴² It was, presumably, Art. 44.2.3° that was invoked in the curious case of *Cochrane* v. *Govr., Wheatfield Prison* (*The Irish Times*, November 6, 1990). The applicant sought an order of mandamus, apparently directing the governor to allow him to travel weekly to a Free Presbyterian church in Monaghan to attend services. He claimed that he needed a congregation with him to participate in a service. Johnston J. refused the order sought, noting that on two occasions the State had paid for congregations to come to the prison to facilitate the applicant. One supposes that such benign discrimination would be justified under Art. 44.2.3°. On free exercise claims by prisoners in the United States, see *O'Lone* v. *Shabazz* (1987) 482 U.S. 342.
⁴³ Gavan Duffy J. recognised a sacerdotal privilege in *Cook* v. *Carroll* [1945] I.R. 515 (a civil action). His reasoning was based partly on the now repealed Art. 44.1.2°, referring to the special position of the Roman Catholic church. In *E.R.* v. *J.R.* [1981] I.L.R.M. 125 Carroll J. recognised a limited sacerdotal privilege in respect of marriage counselling; see Chap. 17 *supra*.

lay individuals must show cause to be excused—section 9(2). This is plainly a distinction but no doubt it is constitutionally justifiable.

Subject to this exception, then, Article 44.2.3° forbids the making of distinctions based on "religious profession, belief or status." The *Mulloy* case clarifies the meaning of this latter phrase. "Profession," the Supreme Court held, refers to the particular religious faith professed by an individual; "status" relates to a person's rank or position in a given religion, and "belief" includes non-belief. Thus the provision has a very wide sweep, forbidding distinctions based on belief or non-belief, or the particular faith professed by an individual or a person's rank or position in a given religion. It has therefore been suggested that it invalidates a corpus of ancient statutory provisions forbidding the election to parliament of certain kinds of clergymen.[44] Though the courts have not yet had to rule on this, it seems likely that they would accept this proposition. It is supported by United States authority, for in *McDaniel* v. *Paty* (1978) 435 U.S. 618 the Supreme Court held broadly similar Tennessee provisions incompatible with the free exercise clause of the 1st Amendment.

Since Article 44.2.3° opens with the words "The State," it arguably cannot be held to prevent discrimination by private individuals or bodies. But legislation to outlaw such private discrimination would surely be valid, for although it would make distinctions on the basis of religion it would do so to achieve Article 44's primary objective—the full and free practice of religion. Indeed it may be noted that dismissal on grounds of religious opinions is deemed to be unfair by the Unfair Dismissals Act 1977, s.6(2)(c).

The developments chronicled above make it highly unlikely that *Schlegel* v. *Corcoran and Gross* [1942] I.R. 19 would be followed nowadays. There the plaintiff let rooms in her house for use as a dental surgery by the first defendant's late father. The first defendant, who had succeeded to his father's interest in the tenancy, wished to assign that interest to the second defendant, a Jewish dentist. However, the plaintiff refused her consent, confessedly from anti-Semitic bias. Section 56(2) of the Landlord and Tenant Act 1931 stipulated that the landlord's consent in such a case should "not be unreasonably withheld." Gavan Duffy J. held that the plaintiff had *not* unreasonably withheld her consent, stressing that she continued to reside on the premises and refusing to accept that anti-Semitism was a caprice or "mere prejudice" or "a peculiar crotchet." He dismissed the suggestion that Article 44.2.3° had any bearing on the case. In the light of later decisions, however, it is arguable that this was wrong. While the State normally acts through the executive and the Oireachtas it also acts through the courts; and a court may not, therefore, ratify acts of religious discrimination by private parties. An instructive analogy is with the United States Supreme Court's decision in *Shelley* v. *Kramer* (1948) 334 U.S. 1, where it was held that a state court could not constitutionally lend its aid to the enforcement of a racially restrictive covenant attached to property. To do this would constitute action by the state in violation of the 14th Amendment's equal protection guarantee. Apart from this, the courts would now have to apply section 56(2) in conformity with the Constitution— see *Garvey* v. *Ireland* [1981] I.R. 75—and this would seem to preclude the view that religious discrimination is "reasonable."

[44] See further J. P. Casey, "The Development of Electoral Law in the Republic of Ireland" (1977) 28 *N.I.L.Q.* 357, 369.

The 1967 Committee on the Constitution pointed out that under the Marriage Acts[45] different conditions are prescribed for marriages performed in accordance with the rites of: (1) the Church of Ireland; (2) the Presbyterian Church; (3) other Protestant churches; (4) the Jewish faith. These conditions relate to prior residence, the district where the marriage is to be celebrated and the time and place of the marriage. No similar conditions are laid down for Roman Catholic marriages. The Committee noted that "the opinion has been expressed" (by whom it is not stated) that these provisions might fall foul of Article 44.2.3°. Such differentiation between marriage ceremonies, the Committee noted, had a practical object in that some of the smaller denominations were not sufficiently organised to ensure that persons presenting for marriage were in fact free to marry. The Committee therefore recommended adding to Article 44.2.3° a rider stating that the prohibition on religious discrimination should not prevent the enactment of different procedural rules relating to different kinds of marriage ceremonies with a view to ensuring that all legal rules were complied with by all the parties concerned.[46]

This recommendation has not been implemented, and although there has since then been a new Marriages Act (of 1970) it does no more than build upon the existing statutory structure. But subsequent judicial interpretation may avoid the problems feared by the Committee. The distinctions between denominations may conceivably be justified on free profession and practice grounds, especially if one of their goals is to ensure freedom to marry. In the light of Article 41 this is a matter no less important than the full and free consent to marry stressed by the Supreme Court in *N. (orse. K)* v. *K.* [1986] I.L.R.M. 75 (see Chap. 17 *supra*).

Article 44.2.4°

This provides as follows:

> "Legislation providing State aid for schools shall not discriminate between schools under the management of different religious denominations, nor be such as to affect prejudicially the right of any child to attend a school receiving public money without attending religious instruction at that school."

As already noted, there is a relative dearth of legislation on educational matters in Ireland and the system operates essentially on the basis of administrative arrangements. The *Rules for National Schools*, however, recognise the requirements of Article 44.2.4° by providing that periods of formal religious instruction must be indicated on timetables and that children of parents who disapprove of that instruction may withdraw.[47] However, the teachers' handbook for the curriculum taught in all national schools since 1971[48] calls for the integration of religious and secular instruction, with the consequence that periods of formal religious instruction disappear. It was reported in September 1991 that a High Court challenge to the constitutionality of this prac-

---

[45] For a detailed treatment of this very complex subject see Alan Shatter, *Family Law in the Republic of Ireland* (3rd ed., Dublin 1986), pp. 82 *et seq.*

[46] *Report*, op. cit., pp. 47–48.

[47] See Coolahan, *op. cit.*, pp. 158–159. A similar conscience clause applies in second-level schools: *ibid.*

[48] *Primary School Curriculum. Teacher's Handbook* (1971), Part I, p. 19.

tice was to be made by the parents of three children attending a Catholic-run national school in Dublin.[49]

Article 44.2.5°

This provides as follows:

"Every religious denomination shall have the right to manage its own affairs, own, acquire and administer property, movable or immovable, and maintain institutions for religious and charitable purposes."

Article 44.2.5° was successfully invoked by the defendants in *McGrath and Ó Rúairc* v. *Trustees of the College of Maynooth* [1979] I.L.R.M. 166. This case arose out of the dismissal of the plaintiffs from their teaching posts at Maynooth. Dr. McGrath had been dismissed for various infringements of the College statutes—in particular that as a priest (he had not then been laicised) he had failed to wear clerical dress in College and had, without the required permission, published writing prejudicial to ecclesiastical authority. Mr. Ó Rúairc's case was different. He had already been laicised before his dismissal, and the terms of the rescript (which came from Rome) forbade him to teach in a seminary. Both plaintiffs made the same constitutional argument—that their dismissals violated Article 44.2.3°. The contention was that Maynooth's original character had changed, and it was now effectively part of the university system. Like the N.U.I. colleges and Dublin University it was receiving funds from the State via the H.E.A. The statutes, which had not been revised appropriately, should not now be applied—especially since they discriminated between priests and lay persons on the College staff, imposing greater obligations on the former, and thus violated Article 44.2.3°. This bound the trustees because, receiving State funds as they did, they must be considered agents of the State.

The Supreme Court rejected this contention. All five judges held that whatever changes Maynooth might have undergone, its basic civil law character was as a seminary. Hence it was a religious institution and thus covered by Article 44.2.5°. In prescribing and enforcing standards of behaviour for clerical members of staff, and in deciding that a laicised priest could not teach in the College, the trustees were acting within their constitutional rights.

The plaintiffs' argument that a non-State body could, by receiving State funds, attract the provisions of Article 44.2.3° was specifically rejected by Kenny J. He said that the argument was not supported by the words of the subsection and was based on an unwarranted extension of their ordinary grammatical meaning. Since the other judges expressed no view on this matter it appears to be still open—and it is relevant to note that just such an expansive interpretation has been given by the United States Supreme Court to the 14th Amendment: *Burton* v. *Wilmington Parking Authority* (1961) 365 U.S. 715.

On the constitutional point raised by the plaintiffs Henchy J. said (at 187):

"(Article 44.2.3°) must be construed in terms of its purpose. In proscrib-

---

[49] See *The Irish Times*, September 17, 1991.

ing disabilities and discriminations at the hands of the State on the ground of religious profession, belief or status, the primary aim of the constitutional guarantee is to give vitality, independence and freedom to religion. To construe the provision literally, without due regard to its underlying objective, would lead to a sapping and debilitation of the freedom and independence given by the Constitution to the doctrinal and organisational requirements and proscriptions which are inherent in all organised religions. Far from eschewing the internal disabilities and discriminations which flow from the tenets of a particular religion, the State must on occasion recognise and buttress them. For such dis-abilities and discriminations do not derive from the State; it cannot be said that it is the State that imposed or made them; they are part of the texture and essence of the particular religion; so the State, in order to comply with the spirit and purpose inherent in this constitutional guar-antee, may justifiably lend its weight to what may be thought to be dis-abilities and discriminations deriving from within a particular religion."

The distinctions drawn in the College statutes were not prohibited by Article 44.2.3°; rather, they implemented the guarantee of Article 44.2.5°.

The Supreme Court's approach in the *McGrath and Ó Rúairc* case seems somewhat disingenuous. Maynooth's legal status as a seminary is the datum from which all else follows—it is a religious institution which necessarily benefits from Article 44.2.5°. The changes wrought in the College—particu-larly the large public subventions—are treated as separate issues not arising in these proceedings. It is reminiscent of cases where courts have refused to look behind a corporate veil to the realities of a company's composition,[50] and contrasts with other decisions where the Supreme Court has ventured beyond a legal facade.[51]

Article 44.2.5° presumably guarantees the right of religious denominations to run their own educational institutions—as they do. It plainly does *not* guarantee State funding for such institutions (nor does Art. 44.2.4°, which is purely permissive). Yet it has recently become clear that Roman Catholic national school boards—which receive such funds—have a policy of employ-ing only practising Catholics as teachers. But the case-law suggests that a constitutional challenge to this policy will be fruitless. A dismissed teacher who sued might well fail on the ground that he or she had accepted the post knowing that continuing religious profession was a term of the employment contract (see *Flynn* v. *Power and Sisters of the Holy Faith* [1985] I.L.R.M. 336). And a challenge to the system under which denominational national schools are funded seems unlikely to succeed given the Supreme Court's decision in *Crowley* v. *Ireland* [1980] I.R. 102. Yet this, if correct, leads to an odd result. The State may not, by statute or administrative action, make continuing religious allegiance a ground for dismissal from the public service or from private employment, since to do so would violate Article 44.2.3°. But if it

---

[50] See, *e.g. Roundabout Ltd.* v. *Beirne* [1959] I.R. 423.
[51] In *de Burca and Anderson* v. *Att. Gen.* [1976] I.R. 38 three members of the Supreme Court con-sidered in some detail the *actual operation* of the Juries Act 1927 (under which women were exempt from jury service unless they chose otherwise); see Walsh J. at 70, Henchy J. at 77 and Griffin J. at 80). In *McGee* v. *Att. Gen.* [1974] I.R. 284 the same three judges emphasised that the Criminal Law Amendment Act 1935, s.17, *effectively* made contraceptives unavailable save by infringing the law.

hands over to religious denominations money used for paying teachers' salaries, both it and they are free from constitutional constraints. There is surely something "Kafka-esque"[52] about such a situation.

Notwithstanding the wide terms of Article 44.2.5°, it is unlikely that the Irish courts will follow the United States Supreme Court in holding that civil courts may not embroil themselves in church disputes over doctrine, administration or organisation. The American court's view is that where decisions on such matters have been made by the proper church authorities their validity cannot be assailed in the courts as inconsistent with chuch rules—or even with secular due process: *Serbian Orthodox Diocese* v. *Milivojevich* (1976) 426 U.S. 696. In Ireland a denomination's right to manage its own affairs will shelter it from some forms of legal intrusion—it is not for the civil courts to determine whether the Roman Catholic church should ordain women. But the *McGrath and Ó Rúairc* case shows that decisions by church authorities, at least in matters of discipline, are not immune from judicial scrutiny and that the principles applicable are those which apply in regard to any domestic tribunal.[53]

Article 44.2.6°

This provides as follows:

"The property of any religious denomination or any educational institution shall not be diverted save for necessary works of public utility and on payment of compensation."

The antecedents of this provision are to be found in Article 8 of the 1922 Constitution, Article 16 of the Treaty and section 5 of the Government of Ireland Act 1920. It is a curious, and in some ways inapt, provision; witness its strange intrusion of a reference to "any educational institution," which might seem more appropriate in Article 42. Moreover, if "diverted" means "compulsorily acquired," then the provision for compensation is probably superfluous since it is a general rule that compensation must follow such acquisition: see *Dreher* v. *Irish Land Commission* [1984] I.L.R.M. 94.

Article 44.2.6° gives rise to several questions, none of which has as yet been elucidated by the courts:

(1) the meaning of "property of any religious denomination"
(2) the meaning of "diverted"
(3) the meaning of "necessary works of public utility"
(4) does "educational institution" receive a restricted interpretation?

(1) Clearly, the literal meaning of "the property of any religious denomination" is property which is owned by a religious denomination. But not all "religious property" is directly owned by denominations; much of it is held

---

[52] In *Melling* v. *Ó Mathghamhna* [1962] I.R. 1, 41 Ó Dálaigh J. referred to "some strange, unreal, Kafka-esque world . . . "
[53] It is noteworthy that the plaintiff Ó Rúairc argued that the trustees had misconstrued the terms of his rescript of laicisation; properly interpreted, he said, it did not prevent his teaching at Maynooth. The Supreme Court, though rejecting his argument, did not feel itself barred from interpreting the document or bound to accept episcopal views on its import.

by trustees in trust for a parish, a religious order or a diocese, or for educational or charitable purposes. It has been doubted whether property held by trustees for members of a religious order or for its purposes could be regarded as being the property of a religious denomination.[54] But this is only so if "property of any religious denomination" is given a literal construction; and as is shown in Chapter 11, literal construction is not the universal rule in interpreting the Constitution. What seems to be the purpose behind Article 44.2.6° would be frustrated by a literal interpretation; thus it seems more appropriate to read its opening words as meaning "property which, directly or indirectly, comes under the aegis of a religious denomination."

(2) The word "divert" is odd. It originally appeared in the Government of Ireland Act 1920, s.5 where it was used in respect of the property of religious denominations—the section also containing a much wider bar on "taking" *any* property without compensation. The distinction between "diverting" and "taking" is a puzzling one, but fortunately it seems to be of historical interest only. For the equivalent to "diverted" in the Irish text is "a bhaint díobh" and this clearly conveys the idea of taking or acquiring.

Is property "diverted" when rates are levied on land or buildings? Obviously the immovable property is not taken, but money is. Under current law churches or other buildings exclusively devoted to religious worship are exempt from rates, but other buildings of a religious character—Maynooth College is an example—are not. Nor are all educational institutions exempted.[55] But this is presumably valid, since in its context the word "property" seems to mean immovable property. One would hardly speak of diverting money for "necessary works of public utility."

(3) "Necessary works of public utility" is a phrase bristling with difficulties. "Works of public utility" would presumably cover roads, reservoirs, drainage schemes and so forth[56]; but what is the significance of "necessary?" It has been suggested that land acquired for public authority housing would not come under this rubric[57] but this seems questionable. A more tenable proposition from the same source is that the clause would prevent acquisition of property by a public authority for transfer to private builders for the construction of factories or houses. Finally the word "works" seems to preclude acquisition of property by the State for the purpose of enlarging small agricultural holdings.

(4) Given that the whole of Article 42 is devoted to education it is strange that the phrase "educational institution" should suddenly make an appearance here. On a literal construction this benefits any educational institution, no matter how secular it may be. Arguably, however, the phrase should be

---

[54] See the *Report of the Committee on the Price of Building Land* (Prl. 3632), p. 54. The committee was chaired by Kenny J. See, too, the extra-curial view of Walsh J.: " . . . the reference to 'religious denominations' is probably not susceptible of an interpretation that extends it to religious orders as such. A religious order is a group of individuals and it is free to change its religion as often as it likes or cease to be a religious order altogether. The property is always the property of the individuals who make up the order." (Brian Walsh, "The Constitution and Constitutional Rights" in Frank Litton (ed.), *The Constitution of Ireland 1937–1987* (Dublin 1988), p. 103.

[55] See further Ronan Keane, *The Law of Local Government in the Republic of Ireland* (Dublin 1982), pp. 289–299.

[56] Art. 8 of the 1922 Constitution referred to "roads, railways, lighting, water or drainage works or other works of public utility. . . . "

[57] *Loc. cit.*, n. 52 *supra*.

coloured by its context and read to mean "religious educational institution."
Thus Maynooth would obtain whatever protection Article 44.2.6° affords,
while University College Dublin would not. In the overall context of the
Constitution the latter would lose little thereby.

Index